T0398842

THE OXFORD HANDBOOK OF

THE
PHENOMENOLOGY
OF MUSIC
CULTURES

THE OXFORD HANDBOOK OF

THE

PHENOMENOLOGY

OF MUSIC

CULTURES

Edited by

HARRIS M. BERGER, FRIEDLIND RIEDEL,

and

DAVID VANDERHAMM

OXFORD
UNIVERSITY PRESS

Oxford University Press is a department of the University of Oxford. It furthers the University's objective of excellence in research, scholarship, and education by publishing worldwide. Oxford is a registered trade mark of Oxford University Press in the UK and certain other countries.

Published in the United States of America by Oxford University Press
198 Madison Avenue, New York, NY 10016, United States of America.

Library of Congress Cataloging-in-Publication Data
Names: Berger, Harris M., author. | Riedel, Friedlind, author. | VanderHamm, David, author.
Title: The Oxford handbook of the phenomenology of music cultures /
edited by Harris M. Berger, Friedlind Riedel, and David VanderHamm.
Description: [1.] | New York : Oxford University Press, 2024. |
Series: Oxford handbooks series | Includes index. |
Identifiers: LCCN 2023033888 (print) | LCCN 2023033889 (ebook) |
ISBN 9780190693879 (hardback) | ISBN 9780190693909 (epub) | ISBN 9780190693886
Subjects: LCSH: Music—Philosophy and aesthetics. | Music—Social aspects. | Phenomenology
Classification: LCC ML3800.O93 2024 (print) | LCC ML3800 (ebook) |
DDC 780.1—dc23/eng/20230801
LC record available at https://lccn.loc.gov/2023033888
LC ebook record available at https://lccn.loc.gov/2023033889

DOI: 10.1093/oxfordhb/9780190693879.001.0001

Printed by Sheridan Books, Inc., United States of America

Contents

SECTION 6. *RASA*, AFFECT, ATMOSPHERE

SECTION 7. ETHICS OF PERFORMANCE, ETHICS OF RESEARCH

PREFACE

FOUNDED at the turn of the twentieth century in the German academy, phenomenology is an intellectual movement with remarkable depth and vast influence. Within philosophy, thinkers operating within the phenomenological tradition have engaged every subfield of their discipline, from metaphysics and ontology to epistemology, politics, ethics, aesthetics, and beyond. But the phenomenological movement is by no means confined to philosophy. Ideas from its philosophical adherents have been picked up, carried forward, critiqued, and expanded by scholars from across the humanities and social sciences. Considering the scope of its impact, it would be difficult to disagree with Lester Embree's conclusion that "phenomenology is arguably the major philosophical movement of the twentieth century" (1997, 1). While subsequent approaches from Continental European philosophy have challenged phenomenology in a variety of ways, the tradition is far more than a relic of intellectual history. Actively pursued by a broad range of forward-looking philosophers and scholars from other disciplines, phenomenology today is vibrant with new ideas, intense internal debates, and bracing engagements with its intellectual competitors. It is a vital, living tradition.

From its inception, phenomenology has had a deep connection with music. An interest in this topic can be found in the early writings of phenomenology's philosophical tradition (e.g., Husserl [1929] 1964; Ingarden [1933] 1989),[1] and across the span of the twentieth century, scholars from the full range of music disciplines have taken up phenomenological approaches to forward their research and address questions central in their fields. In fact, the relationship between phenomenological philosophy and music has long been richly dialectical, with, on the one hand, philosophers developing phenomenologies of music and using musical examples and metaphors to think about philosophical issues, and, on the other hand, music scholars taking up philosophical ideas, not merely to apply them to music topics but to forge insights with implications far beyond their initial disciplinary contexts. While music is certainly not a universal, transhistorical category of expressive culture, there can be little doubt that the various things that people call music can have truly awesome power, both in terms of their ability to give rise to intense experiences in the performance event and in terms of their influence on other spheres of social life and culture. It is for this reason that scholars within and beyond philosophy have seen music as both a site for and a means of phenomenological research, and they have also drawn on phenomenological writings on music to speak to a broad range of scholarly concerns and research questions.

The themes that unite the chapters of this handbook are phenomenology, music, and culture, and its contributors are based in ethnomusicology and related disciplines, largely from the anglophone North American academy.[2] Each of its chapters offers a rich engagement with ideas from phenomenology's philosophical tradition and brings those ideas into dialogue with approaches and insights from the literature in ethnomusicology and disciplines allied to it. While some of the book's chapters are strictly theoretical, most are ethnographic or historical; here, voices from archives, stages, rituals, rehearsal spaces, memories, or interviews—and their cultural and intellectual milieux—are a third and co-equal party in the chapters' conversations. All of the ethnographic and historical chapters offer evocative interpretations of the cultural worlds and social experiences of their interlocutors. And whether its center of gravity is theoretical, ethnographic, or historical, each chapter offers fresh perspectives and insights that not only address the traditional concerns of ethnomusicology and allied disciplines but also speak to topics that are of wide interest across the humanities and humanistic social sciences today.

Whether they draw on classical writers from the phenomenological tradition like Maurice Merleau-Ponty, Frantz Fanon, or Hermann Schmitz or contemporary thinkers—within the tradition or beyond—like Edward Casey, Catherine Malabou, Toril Moi, Fred Moten, or Dan Zahavi, they also illustrate the capacity of ideas from phenomenology to change the way we ask our most important questions. In the past, scholars of music and culture have sought to understand the social nature of musical meaning, the relationship between music and identity, and the ways that human musical expression impacts other domains of social life. The contributors to this handbook reimagine the ways in which these long-standing topics are understood by using ideas from phenomenology to question foundational concepts that the traditional notions of music and culture entail, such as body, emotion, experience, sociality, sound, listening, and world. Revealing new possibilities of the person, tracing new cultural histories, and shedding light on new social dynamics, the contributors offer radical new ways of understanding the task of studying music and culture.

Theory's close counterpart is methodology, and for many years the study of ethnomusicology was commonly defined by its ethnographic methods. While fieldwork is no longer considered the *sine qua non* of ethnomusicological research, problems in the ethics and epistemology of ethnography remain an abiding concern for many scholars of music and culture. A variety of our contributors open up new opportunities here, calling into question the traditional imperative to know and master an other's experience, suggesting powerful new techniques of ethnographic research, and demonstrating the possibilities of sonic relations beyond the human. Time-honored topics and subdisciplines within philosophy are given provocative new treatments in the book as well, with chapters exploring topics like consciousness, embodiment, ethics, hermeneutics, metaphysics and ontology, musical aesthetics, and temporality. And it is not only traditional concerns that are viewed in new ways. The book's chapters explore a range of topics that are of vital interest to contemporary scholarship, including affect and atmosphere, alterity and relationality, Indigenous sovereignty, and musical virtuosity, and they engage richly with the literatures in ecomusicology, improvisation studies, new German media theory, music psychology, gender theory, anthropology's ontological turn, and voice studies. Ideas from sound studies—an interdisciplinary field that has in recent years coalesced into a highly influential, even dominant research area—are addressed throughout the collection.

This book has its origins in an international conference convened in 2018 at the Research Centre for the Study of Music, Media, and Place at Memorial University of Newfoundland titled "Phenomenology in Ethnomusicology: The St. John's Conference." The conversations that emerged during the meeting set the course for lively discussions that continued through a series of email exchanges, video calls, and progressively developed manuscripts. Thinking through the diverse topics that the contributors raise has, for us, been an extraordinarily stimulating and enjoyable experience. In an effort to share that pleasure with our readers, the editors and authors have sought to make these chapters as accessible as possible. Each chapter in the book provides a careful and detailed reading of the philosophical and theoretical sources that it draws upon. Although nothing can replace a deep and sustained engagement with original texts in philosophy or social theory, each chapter is intended to be comprehensible on its own terms, and we hope that the book will inspire readers to explore the literatures engaged here more fully. But the chapters in this book do far more than merely apply ideas from philosophy or theory to a fieldsite, historical period, or topic within music studies. Rather, the chapters offer unique insights and perspectives, ones that will not only interest scholars in ethnomusicology and allied disciplines but also, we hope, attract scholars throughout the humanistic social sciences and contribute to the wider phenomenological literature on culture and social life.

With four chapters, each of which is focused on historical or theorical issues, the book's first section places the project of the handbook in its intellectual context and suggests new directions for research. The first chapter, which is by the three editors of this volume, sets the stage for the investigations that follow. It begins with a brief sketch of key ideas and moments from phenomenology's philosophical tradition and then shifts the focus to provide a detailed history of phenomenological approaches to ethnomusicology developed by anglophone scholars working in the North American academy. Attention is also paid to work from allied disciplines and other national academies. After exploring a range of contemporary scholarship in these areas, the chapter closes by suggesting opportunities for future inquiry in the phenomenological study of music and culture. While no single chapter could serve as an introduction to the phenomenological movement, we hope that this work will serve as a useful point of entry into these literatures by discussing both canonical and contemporary writings from the tradition, indicating valuable secondary sources, and charting out some of the major historical currents. The second chapter in the section, which was written by Julia Kursell, examines Carl Stumpf's writings on music and sound. Stumpf had a significant influence on scholars in philosophy, psychology, and music in the late nineteenth and early twentieth centuries, and the two intellectual currents of phenomenology and ethnomusicology intersect in his biography: he served as habilitation supervisor for Edmund Husserl, the founder of phenomenology, and he was also a key figure in the development of comparative musicology, the discipline that preceded ethnomusicology.

Kursell explores Stumpf's productive theoretical work on the role of tacit assumptions and implicit standpoints in musical experience, thus revealing a need on the part of the researcher to postpone judgment (in a way resonant with but distinct from what Husserl later would call the epoché). To consider the ways in which any singular "musical utterance" is embedded in and shaped by a wider music culture, the chapter explores Stumpf's use of the notion of *Sachverhalt* (a state of affairs), a term that would become central to the phenomenological work of Husserl and Schmitz. Throughout the chapter, Kursell offers subtle readings of the relationship between Stumpf's ideas and those of his most famous pupil and suggests the relevance of this important and under-examined history for scholars of music and culture today.

The section's next chapter is by Roger Savage, who has for many years been developing a distinctive form of musical hermeneutics. With a breadth of historical reflection that extends from Martin Heidegger, Hans-Georg Gadamer, and Paul Ricoeur to John Blacking, Pierre Bourdieu, the "new musicology," Thomas Turino, and beyond, Savage rethinks that hallmark ethnomusicological concern, the relationship between music and culture. Exploring deep issues of temporality and the mimetic nature of meaning and existence, Savage argues that the powerful feelings that a community's musical forms evoke are nothing less than a means of establishing and renewing its way of being in the world, thus serving as a foundation for what he refers to as the "interface" between music and social life. The chapter's challenging and complex arguments are matched in scope by Jeff Todd Titon's contribution to the handbook, which closes out the section. Written by one of the founders of phenomenological ethnomusicology, Titon's chapter makes a bold case for the utility of phenomenological approaches for research on the sonic communication of non-human animals. Beginning with a personal reflection on the intellectual currents that steered him to phenomenology in the 1970s, Titon explores the development of ecomusicology, engages expansively with the contemporary phenomenology of Dan Zahavi and Sean Gallagher, and addresses ideas from ecology and anthropology's ontological turn. In so doing, Titon develops arguments about animal sound communication that provide a new theoretical foundation for ecomusicology. Going beyond even this ambitious goal, Titon develops his well-known ideas about *people making music* in powerful new directions, offering a vision of *eco-ethnomusicology* that seeks to do nothing less than fundamentally reimagine the disciplinary project of ethnomusicology.

In differing ways, the chapters of the next section explore three fundamental aspects of musical experience—memory, imagination, and consciousness. J. Martin Daughtry offers a phenomenology of auditory memory, with particular focus on the phenomenon of the "earworm." Drawing on a wide array of contemporary thinkers, Daughtry casts auditory memory as a fieldsite replete with all of the interpretive possibilities, struggles, and ambiguities of any physical ethnographic locale. Like other contributors to the handbook, Daughtry argues that our typical categories of sonic experience—sounds perceived in the physical world versus sounds in the "internal" world of memory and imagination—are porous and problematic. His careful analysis shows how perceived, imagined, and remembered sounds implicate and interpenetrate one another. The chapter examines the uncanny temporality of earworms and concludes with a powerful meditation on the role that auditory memory plays in grief and mourning. It is worth noting that in the chapter, Daughtry explicitly declines to label himself as a phenomenologist. Nevertheless, he richly engages with ideas from the tradition, as well as other sources, demonstrating that one need not be an adherent of the phenomenological movement to usefully employ its ideas. Where Daughtry's analysis centers on his own musical memories and auditory imaginings, the chapter by Ruth Herbert explores accounts of musical involvement gathered from others. Employing a method from the discipline of psychology known as *interpretive phenomenological analysis*, Herbert draws on in-depth interviews with adolescents in the United Kingdom to understand their everyday musical experiences and illuminate the varying, even contradictory, uses to which such experiences are put. In her adolescents' vivid accounts, music can be a tool to enhance one's focus on activities in the present, like playing video games, or a means for flights of fancy that take the listener away from mundane situations. For Herbert, musical experiences do not arise solely from internal, cognitive processes but depend on the complex interplay of person, music, and world. The chapter illuminates the wide variety of states of consciousness that arise in quotidian music listening, including dissociation and trance. Through a rich discussion of the relationships among phenomenological philosophy, music psychology, and ethnomusicology, the chapter further demonstrates the profound interdisciplinarity that an engagement with the phenomenological tradition encourages.

The chapters in the next section all address a common question: What are the possibilities of personhood and what role can music play in its transformation? Responding to the overemphasis on the discursive construction of gender in poststructuralism, Stephen Amico's chapter develops a notion of *polyphonic embodiment*. Detailing the affective dynamics at play in a concert in Estonia by the Russian pop superstar Valeriia, Amico shows that an attention to the materiality of the sexed body need not result in a new essentialism. His nuanced interpretations allow us to see a multitude of possibilities of performing and experiencing gender, ones that go far beyond the now-familiar critiques of the gender binary or currently taken-for-granted ideas like the gender spectrum. Along the way, Amico draws on a variety of classical and contemporary thinkers from Merleau-Ponty and Mikel Dufrenne to Casey and Moi. Exploring the bodily dimensions of memory, aesthetics, and interaction, Amico examines the ways in which music and sound may offer new possibilities in the experience of gender and evoke powerful transformations.

Andrew McGuiness continues the section by exploring the liberatory potential of funk music. Drawing on ideas from the phenomenology of race by Fanon, Moten, and Thomas Slaughter, as well as Husserl's work on perception and Pierre Bourdieu's notion of body hexis, McGuiness shows how a racialized subjectivity becomes embedded in body schemata. Detailed music analysis, narrative accounts of 1960s funk events, and careful argument illustrate how a dancer's engagement with funk's sophisticated rhythms may draw their attention to aspects of their body schema that otherwise escape notice, including the ways in which racist societies encroach upon Black embodiment.

For Black dancers, engaging with the music's complex, paradoxical temporalities creates an opportunity to challenge those schemata, offering the potential to experience raced subjectivity in new ways. Where Amico and McGuiness focus on the transformation of particular forms of identity in specific sociocultural or musical contexts (gender in Russian pop, race in funk), the chapter by Charles Sharp seeks to widen the field of view by arguing that the possibility of transformation is central to all musical experience, and ultimately, any art form. Drawing on ideas from phenomenological hermeneutics, especially those of Gadamer and Ricoeur, Sharp pursues the theme of musical improvisation to explore how the play of temporality and social interaction in performance necessarily involves the ongoing possibility of the revision of personal identity. In so doing, the chapter brings renewed attention to the active, dynamic nature of listening and offers a strong critique of traditional ideas about the relationship between music and culture, the nature of musical meaning and musical interpretation, and the means and ends of ethnographic fieldwork. All three chapters provide new insights into how, why, and to what extent music may accompany or drive transformations of the person.

While many chapters in this volume engage with issues of embodiment, the three that comprise the section titled "Intercorporeality, Perception, and Movement" maintain a distinct focus on this topic. In differing ways, each chapter argues against the widespread tendency to treat the body as a self-enclosed entity, one that is sharply separate from the world and that serves as a container for experience. David VanderHamm's chapter argues that individualist treatments of virtuosity—which generally focus on the impressive technique required for the execution of musical compositions or ideas, or the skill contained within a single, remarkable body—miss the central structures of the phenomenon: the fundamentally social, intersensorial, and intercorporeal nature of skilled performance. Developing this understanding of virtuosity in conversation with a range of thinkers, which includes Husserl, Merleau-Ponty, and Hannah Arendt, VanderHamm uses the Western reception of Ravi Shankar's music as a case study in the intercultural experience of virtuosity. Where many commentators—including Shankar himself—presume the universal appeal of virtuosity, VanderHamm demonstrates the varied ways that audiences failed to grasp Shankar's skill. But rather than disqualifying their experiences, the asymmetrical, imperfect sociality between Shankar and his audiences guaranteed the persistence of otherness in the phenomenon, which many judged as a key reason for its value. Ultimately, VanderHamm concludes, virtuosity is neither easy nor obvious; rather, it arises through prejudgments so central to people's experience of the world that they readily go unnoticed outside the confines of phenomenological reflection. The chapter by Monica Dalidowicz explores the acquisition of skill in another North Indian artistic practice—*kathak* dance. Taking intersensoriality as her main theme, Dalidowicz emphasizes the many ways that the kinesthetic and sonic aspects of kathak intertwine: dancers initially learn the dance not by imitating physical motions but through performing vocalized syllables that serve as representations of the rhythmic sounds that their movement will eventually produce. In this way, dancers experience movement and music not as fundamentally separate elements of an artistic practice but as different aspects of the same phenomenon. They emerge as a synesthetic whole. Through detailed ethnographic description, Dalidowicz's chapter puts flesh on the bones of abstract concepts from Hindustani music and dance aesthetics by showing how they are acquired and experienced as dancers grow ever deeper in the tradition.

The concluding chapter of the section, which is by Katharine Young, offers a unique approach to the phenomenology of sound. Beginning with a perceptual experiment that sought to isolate the experiences of vision and hearing, the chapter expands through ever-widening arcs to trace the complex and paradoxical relationships among the senses, from the phenomena of "single-sense epiphanies" (Kirshenblatt-Gimblett 1991, 58) to synesthesia and intersensoriality. Bringing the ideas of Merleau-Ponty into conversation with contemporary work in sound studies and a wide range of other sources, Young explores the nature of lived space, the complex relationships between sound and motion, and the differing forms of materiality that each sense discloses. The chapter's evocative language covers a wide range of examples, from descriptions of sound art installations and experimental music to accounts of perceptual experience by disabled writers, key works in historical acoustemology, and beyond. In so doing, she reveals the diverse ways that the senses place the person in the world, leading to broad insights into the social nature of embodiment. While the body is the central topic of the section, its chapters converge on other themes as well. Skill is a focus for both Dalidowicz and VanderHamm; VanderHamm and Young emphasize the intercorporeal nature of perception; and Young and Dalidowicz both take the perceptual experiences of disabled individuals as valuable guides. Exploring the diverse forms that embodiment may take, the chapters demonstrate that phenomenological accounts of perception continue to provide new perspectives into social life and culture.

The chapters of the book's next section, which is called "Ontologies," shift attention away from the older interest in structures of consciousness, which was important for one part of Husserl's phenomenology, in order to address modes of being and beings, as well as their transcendental (Simonett) or practical (Rahaim, Riedel) constitution. Matthew Rahaim's chapter challenges the presumption that voice is a unified phenomenon that universally projects immediacy and uniquely exemplifies the presence and unity of the subject. Rahaim shows that such figurations of voice not only animate Husserlian phenomenology but that they also persist in Derrida's influential critique of Husserl's notion of voice and the metaphysics of presence. With a careful reading of works from voice studies and an evocative ethnographic account of a Hindustani classical singer's struggles with a throat injury, Rahaim demonstrates the difficulties of these fundamentally nonsocial, irrelational, and unitary understandings of voice, and he illustrates the very different kinds of entities that are referenced by this word in varying settings and fields of endeavor (e.g., politics, art, and medicine). Working along the lines of Annemarie Mol's *practical ontology*, Rahaim shows that voice is disclosed in ontologically plural ways according to the situated and concrete relations in which it occurs. In his account, different kinds of voices do not necessarily share a common ground of being, and so an ontology of *the* voice will always be contradicted by the differing ways in which voices show up.

Where Rahaim multiplies the ontological possibilities of voice, Friedlind Riedel subjects the category of the human and the central phenomenological notion of the body (*Leib*) to a similar reckoning. Presenting a close analysis of a performance of a *pyazat* (musical drama) in Myanmar that stages the tragic transformation of a musician into a deity, she mobilizes philosophies of transformation from both Theravada Buddhism and contemporary French theory that stake out the limits of the phenomenological body, which, despite having been theorized as relational and malleable, can never account for radical change. Proposing to rethink the phenomena of transformation in terms of cultural techniques, Riedel takes a pragmatist turn by arguing that however sublime and metaphysical a transformation may be, it has to be brought about by concrete operations in order to show up. Her detailed analysis of the cultural techniques of transformation in contemporary performances of the nineteenth-century musical drama *U Shin Gyi, Lord of Brackish Waters* shows how a stage instrument, the Burmese harp (*saung gauk*), mediates transformation. Operations of plucking, sounding, and holding the harp, but also stage architecture and music, bring about the specific order of phenomena and process relations between thing and sign, the real and the imaginary, human and deity.

Unlike the chapters by Rahaim and Riedel, which explore ontological formations of voice, human, and body specific to particular settings or aesthetic milieux, Helena Simonett uses ideas from the anthropologist Philippe Descola to explore modes of being associated with entire societies. Charting a contrast between Western naturalism and the Indigenous analogism of the Yoreme of northwest Mexico, the chapter argues that the human-to-animal transformation found in the Yoreme deer dance ritual must be understood as a real, rather than symbolic, change. Drawing on ethnographic description, Heidegger's conceptual apparatus, and ideas from anthropology's ontological turn, Simonett shows that the ritual's sensory and musical density provides participants with tangible access to the enchanted world of the deer—one that is removed from the everyday world yet manifestly present to the dancers. The chapter concludes by drawing parallels between Heidegger's existential analytic of Dasein and the Yoreme's contemplation of the nature of being in the ritual. In this way, Simonett argues, deer dancing turns out to be a form of phenomenological inquiry itself.

The chapters in the book's next section center around a set of aesthetic concepts that all relate in one way or another to feeling: *rasa*, affect, and atmosphere. While these three terms come from three distinct philosophical traditions—rasa, an aesthetic concept theorized by the ancient Indian scholar Bharata Muni; affect, a central notion in the work of early modern Western philosopher Baruch Spinoza, which has enjoyed a revival in the past twenty-five years; and atmosphere, a term that German philosopher Hermann Schmitz developed as part of his "new phenomenology" in the 1960s—all three concepts avoid the idea that feelings are located within the autonomous subject and instead envision them as shared, spatially extended, emergent, preconscious, relational, and material. Here, feelings are understood as sites where sensory modes are synthetized (ras) or as states of affairs in the world that gravitate toward a kind of autonomy (affect) or a kind of objectivity (atmosphere).

The chapter by Inderjit N. Kaur is an ethnographic study of Sikh worship services in California, where food and music, poetry and people, and memories and aspirations come together to produce ethical, divine, and aesthetic "flavors" (*ras*) of great power. Listening for the resonances between ras philosophy (as articulated in Sikh songtexts and ethnographic accounts of Sikh worship practices) and Merleau-Ponty's notion of the *phenomenal field*, Kaur explores the ways in which *sabad kīrtan* (sung scriptural verse) performances become saturated with an ethical meaningfulness that spills over into everyday life. Since ras is fundamentally embodied, Sikh values such as humility, non-othering, and service become inscribed into the body's motor intentionalities and habits. Kaur shows how kīrtan sessions avoid dividing the world into the secular and the sacred, and instead weave together the spiritual, the aesthetic, and the political through the use of music and other expressive forms in religious practice.

Like Kaur, Deborah Kapchan presents us with sonorous scenes of collective worship. Using evocative ethnographic vignettes, she walks her reader through complex encounters and stirring memories of women's Sufi ritual events in Morocco and France. Rather than emphasizing dynamics of amalgamation and continuity, as Kaur does, Kapchan puts her finger on minor discontinuities and subtle discords, such as the micro-tonal divergences that emerge in the unison singing of women worshipers, which entail a logic of proximity. It is here, in deliberate and collectively performed sonic interferences, where affect intensifies and where a potential for empathy and auditory communality emerges. Rebutting polemical claims about the alleged incompatibility between affect theory and phenomenology, Kapchan mobilizes Merleau-Ponty's notions of the *flesh of the world* and *intercorporeity* to understand affect-laden situations, from religious worship to political protest and beyond. Throughout, Kapchan sees proximity as an ethical as well as an aesthetic concept, and she engages the writings of Judith Butler to explore the political implications of the sonic life of affect.

The final chapter in this section draws on Schmitz's so-called new phenomenology and, in particular, his notion of atmosphere. While this idea has often been invoked to understand decidedly positive processes, such as belonging, community, and ethical and spiritual integrity, the chapter by Daniel Fisher attends to atmospheric disturbances, focusing on moments of disintegration and displacement faced by marginalized Indigenous communities in northern Australia. Through rich ethnographic work, Fisher joins his interlocutors in asking how it is possible to (re-)gain Indigenous sovereignty in the face of colonialism and the experiences of grief, loss, and anger that come with it. Identifying media such as radio and recordings as an important resource for Indigenous politics and culture, Fisher's engaging account of the events that followed the death of a famous Indigenous singer meticulously charts the affective labor of individuals and collectives in their effort to assert sovereignty. In this context, Fisher shows how music mediated through radio allows Indigenous authority (*rom*) to gain objectivity as atmosphere, a process that is both widely dispersed and deeply felt.

The book's final section, "Ethics of Performance, Ethics of Research," offers a set of interlocking inquiries into two closely related topics: the ethical dimensions of research methods in the study of music and culture, and the ethical dimensions of social interaction in the performance event. The section begins with a chapter by three anthropologists with an international reputation for bringing phenomenological approaches into their discipline—Alessandro Duranti, C. Jason Throop, and Matthew McCoy. For many years, Duranti has worked closely on teaching and research projects with the renowned jazz guitarist Kenny Burrell. Based on extraordinarily close readings of video recordings of a musical performance by Burrell and his colleagues in a course on jazz aesthetics, the chapter brings Levinas's ideas about alterity and ethics into conversation with Erving Goffman's work on the presentation of self. Their subtle, eye-opening interpretations show how the tension between face-saving and vulnerability is at the heart of the jazz tradition. These reflections will certainly interest jazz scholars, but they will also inspire anyone interested in the social dynamics of the musical encounter. Of equal importance, the chapter makes a case for the utility of video analysis for understanding performance events.

A set of insights about ethics and ethnography related to but distinct from those that Duranti, Throop, and McCoy examine can be found in the chapter by Esther Clinton and Jeremy Wallach, which puts ideas from Levinas into conversation with those from the phenomenologist most frequently engaged by ethnomusicologists—Alfred Schutz. Clinton and Wallach's unique synthesis offers new perspectives on the crisis of ethnographic fieldwork and writing that have been a central concern in anthropology, ethnomusicology, and related disciplines since the 1980s. With a suggestive study of Indonesia's *dangdut* music, their perspectives on the musical encounter draw links among music, community, alterity, and performance that both resonate with those developed by Duranti, Throop, and McCoy and suggest new directions.

The next chapter in the section is Ritwik Banerji's exploration of the social world of free improvisation music, and, like the ones that precede it, the chapter offers a nuanced examination of the topics of interpersonal relationships in performance and techniques of ethnographic fieldwork. Across a range of disciplines, phenomenological research typically concerns itself with *structures* of lived experience, rather than the particular details of what an other experiences at a given moment. Working against the traditional approach, Banerji argues that those particulars should be a central concern for both philosophical and ethnographic work on music and culture, and he offers a unique methodology for uncovering them. Asking his research participants to engage in free improvisation with an artificial-intelligence program of his own design, Banerji is able to circumvent the reticence that free improvisers typically have in discussing their performances. Giving the feedback interview technique (e.g., Stone and Stone 1981) a radically new interpretation, the chapter makes a unique contribution to the literature on research methods in the study of music and culture and offers ideas about the nature of musical interaction that have wide implications. The relationship between the ethnographer and the research participant is also a central concern in the section's next chapter, which is by Dotan Nitzberg and Michael B. Bakan and draws deeply on the ideas of Levinas. While dialogue is often a central theoretical metaphor and even a guiding ethic for many authors in this volume, Nitzberg and Bakan engage in dialogue in a literal sense and seek its broadest implications. Their chapter is built around a series of conversations between Nitzberg, a concert pianist on the autism spectrum and PhD student, and Bakan, a long-standing collaborator with Nitzberg who is well known for his research on music and autism. Through a series of complex, ethically charged exchanges, the authors chart the transformation of their project from Bakan's quest to understand the nature of autistic musical subjectivity into a reflection on the fundamental place that alterity must hold in the study of music and disability, or, indeed, any ethnographic research. Along the way, they offer powerful insights into disability studies in music, the cultural politics of autism, and the ethics of ethnographic encounters with persons from marginalized groups.

No piece of mature scholarship is one-dimensional, and many of the chapters in the book could have been situated in other sections. For example, ethical concerns are central to the chapters by Kapchan and Titon, while those by Riedel and Simonett deal in differing ways with transformation and personhood. Likewise, a different set of topics could have been used to organize the chapters into sections. Approaches from hermeneutic phenomenology are pursued in the chapters by Savage, Sharp, and Simonett; politics is a central concern for Amico, McGuiness, and Nitzberg and Bakan; the interlaced nature of perception and imagination connects the chapters by Amico and Daughtry; the topic of death and mourning is discerningly explored by Daughtry and Fisher; and dance and movement are addressed in the chapters by Dalidowicz and McGuiness. The themes of embodiment and the negotiation of the performance event, ritual, temporality, and subjectivity run throughout the book. These topics in no way exhaust the links among the chapters, and we encourage readers to make their own paths through the book and discover connections of their own.

*   *   *

In the closing section of the introduction to *Theory for Ethnomusicology: Histories, Conversations, Insights* (2019, 14–15), Harris M. Berger and Ruth M. Stone argued against a tendency, common among North American humanities scholars, to distrust disciplinary formations. We find that in this academic culture there is a similar hesitancy about participating in an intellectual movement or espousing a commitment to a theoretical orientation.[3] Here, the most common attitude toward movements and orientations is something that we call *theoretical eclecticism*. Scholars who take this approach engage thinkers from a wide range of traditions and combine them in unique and even idiosyncratic ways. In its moderate forms, eclecticism does not entail an animus toward movements or orientations, but in its more strident versions, movements and orientations are seen as narrow, exclusionary formations that breed conformity, dogmatism, and closed-mindedness. By rejecting engagement with a tradition, eclecticists see themselves as forging distinctive insights and avoiding the herd mentality that traditions allegedly breed.

There can be no doubt that insightful and important work has been developed by scholars who subscribe to the eclecticist tendency, and we would in no way want to offer a blanket condemnation of this approach. We will observe, though, that in certain forms, eclecticism's distrust of movements, orientations, and traditions seems to originate from and reinscribe a worrisome individualism. Indeed, we have on occasion found it remarkable to encounter insightful scholars who, in other contexts, champion the fundamental sociality of human life—emphasizing dialogism, relationality, or the discursive formation of the subject—yet unthinkingly reproduce the worst tendencies of American rugged individualism and neoliberal subjectivity through their disdain for intellectual movements and traditions. There is no doubt that such formations *can* lead their adherents to cultish insularity and stagnation, but the dingiest dead end of the meanest street should never be allowed to serve as a synecdoche for the entire thoroughfare. We see intellectual movements as places in which the individual scholar can learn from the insights of past and present thinkers and work together with colleagues and comrades to contribute to an intellectual project, a thoroughly social effort to make an impact that is beyond the reach of the isolated individual.[4]

Movements and orientations offer theoretical rigor and depth, tools for thinking about and performing research, and the rewards of community, and they offer other advantages as well. Consider the topic of one's relationship to sources. In their writing and thinking, the eclecticist assembles a diverse cast of intellectual characters, and the singular nature of their theoretical constellations forces them to take responsibility for getting it all right, as there will exist few readers—at the stage of peer review or after publication—who can be expected to know whether their treatment of each idea or theoretical theme is idiosyncratic or broadly shared and well established. In this way, the eclecticist serves as the expert *tout court*. By contrast, one's mistakes are more likely to be identified and corrected when working within a theoretical tradition. Or take the topic of disciplinarity. While disciplinary formations can serve a variety of positive purposes, they can also lead to dogmatism and practices of boundary maintenance that are at the least unproductive and at the worst oppressive. Cutting across disciplinary boundaries, intellectual movements can work against these excesses, providing opportunities for creative approaches to interdisciplinary and transdisciplinary research.

Of course, none of this is to say that those working within a tradition should insulate themselves from the rest of contemporary intellectual life. Far from it. Participating in a movement, one may engage in sharp struggles with rivals and opponents, but one may also make common cause with fellow travelers, forge intellectual alliances, develop creative syntheses, and make other kinds of nuanced and creative connections with thinkers beyond one's home domain. Likewise, participation in an intellectual movement in no way requires a scholar to toe a party line or blunt their critical sensibilities. Across a history that spans over 120 years, those within the phenomenological movement have found much to dispute in phenomenology's past, and we would never want to equate participation in this movement with a worshipful reverence for either its canonical works or the writings of its contemporary luminaries. Neither does participation in an intellectual movement require assent to all of its prior tenets. Indeed, phenomenology has been famously characterized as a collection of "heresies" coming from creative, often disputatious engagements with the ideas of its founder, Husserl (Ricoeur [1954] 1967, 4). Understood in this way, phenomenology is a deep conglomerate of diverse intellectual formations that, at their best, have fostered a unique combination of pointed debates, incremental developments around core themes, and open-minded engagements with a wide range of interlocutors. Finally, we will note that intellectual movements may also serve the needs of those who consider themselves to be eclecticists, either by clearly articulating a position against which the eclecticist may react or simply by offering an ensemble of concepts from which the eclecticist may draw.

As we describe in the book's first chapter, phenomenologically oriented research in anglophone North American ethnomusicology and allied disciplines first emerged in the late 1970s and early 1980s, developed significantly in the 1990s and early 2000s, and saw an explosive growth in the last decade. We see this work as both a valuable intellectual formation in its own right and also as one part of the wider phenomenological movement. Not all of the contributors to this volume share our views about eclecticism and movement participation. For our part, though, we can say emphatically that we hope this book will help foster a critical engagement with the tradition of phenomenologically informed work on music and culture, and the wider world of phenomenological thought. Between the Scylla of an isolated dogmatism that unquestioningly adheres to a body of canonical works and the Charybdis of an individualistic eclecticism that rejects comradeship and community, we find not a narrow, treacherous passage but oceanic possibilities for scholarly practice. The great potential of such a wide middle way is to contribute to an ongoing intellectual endeavor while also engaging with the diverse currents of ideas alive in the contemporary world. It was in such a spirit that Merleau-Ponty closed the introduction to *Phenomenology of Perception* ([1945] 1962), and we have been animated by a similar desire in our work with the contributors to this book. We invite readers to join us in this project. Drawing on an intellectual heritage that we make our own and laboring together, we can develop ideas about music, culture, and the social world that can have a vital impact, both within the academy and beyond.

NOTES

1 A variety of authors have discussed the place of music in the history of phenomenology. In this volume, for example, see the chapters by Matthew Rahaim and Julia Kursell. A useful review of the history of work on the phenomenology of music from within philosophy can be found in Ferrara and Behnke (1997).

2 To be sure, phenomenological work on music happens far beyond these boundaries. We specify the disciplinary, linguistic, and regional scope of the book to signal its limitations and avoid implicitly equating North American, anglophone ethnomusicology and related fields with all phenomenological approaches to music and culture.

3 Here, we use the term *intellectual movement* to refer to a social formation constituted through intellectual practice, while *theoretical orientation* is used to indicate a discursive formation constituted by a body of ideas. We use the term *intellectual tradition* to refer to the emergent, historical dimension of movements and orientations, or, in a looser fashion, as a gloss for the ensemble formed by intellectual movements and the ideas that they foster.

4 Eclecticism, too, offers a kind of sociality, but in its most stridently individualist inflections, the kind of sociality that it allows is remarkably constrained. In assembling

an idiosyncratic cast of theoretical characters and offering only a personal, eclectic synthesis, this kind of intellectual practice treats one-to-one relationality as the ideal form of sociality, and combined with a disdain for movement participation, it suggests that larger collectivities are fundamentally compromised.

In critiquing strident theoretical eclecticism, we can learn much from the world of political action, where this tendency finds its counterpart in strident *horizontalism*. Both involve a vision of social life that juxtaposes a simple binary of (humane) one-to-one relationality and (dehumanizing) collectivity. Born in its contemporary manifestation from mid-twentieth-century fears of the "mass society" and the belief that the party form and vanguardism lead inevitably to the gulag, the ideology of strident horizontalism is associated with anarchism and left communism. Some Marxist critics, particularly Marxist-Leninists, argue that the ideology of horizontalism is ineffective in resisting the entrenched power of capital and unable to support sustained efforts to foster fundamental change. Of course, intellectual work is part of the wider political field, and we argue that the excesses of a strident horizontalist politics are reproduced in strident theoretical eclecticism. Such an approach offers the individual scholar great freedom, but it does so at the cost of isolating them from potential colleagues and comrades and the kind of wider intellectual impact that participation in a movement can provide. As in politics, so in the academy: we are stronger together, and we make our most lasting effects through organized action.

With both positive and negative inflections, the terms *horizontalism* and *vanguardism* come from the literature in left political theory and have a wide currency. While, as far as we are aware, Vladimir Lenin does not use the term horizontalism, his *Left-Wing Communism, an Infantile Disorder* ([1920] 2012) is a foundational articulation of the need for the party form and can be read as an early critique of what today would be called horizontalism. For an illuminating Leninist critique of horizontalism in the Occupy Movement, see Ibrahim and Roberts (2018). For a contemporary Marxist perspective on the need for multiple forms of revolutionary social organization, as well as the advantages and disadvantages of both horizontalism and vanguardism, see Harvey (2015).

Works Cited

Berger, Harris M., and Ruth M. Stone. 2019. "Introduction." In *Theory for Ethnomusicology: Histories, Conversations, Insights*, 2nd ed., edited by Harris M. Berger and Ruth M. Stone, 1–25. New York: Routledge.

Embree, Lester. 1997. "Introduction." In *Encyclopedia of Phenomenology*, edited by Lester Embree et al., 1–9. Dordrecht, Netherlands: Springer.

Ferrara, Lawrence, and Elizabeth Behnke. 1997. "Music." In *Encyclopedia of Phenomenology*, edited by Lester Embree et al., 467–473. Dordrecht, Netherlands Springer.

Harvey, David. 2015. "Listen, Anarchist." *Reading Marx's Capital with David Harvey* (blog). June 10, 2015. http://davidharvey.org/2015/06/listen-anarchist-by-david-harvey/.

Husserl, Edmund. (1929) 1964. *Phenomenology of Internal Time-Consciousness*. Edited by Martin Heidegger. Translated by James S. Churchill. Bloomington: Indiana University Press.

Ibrahim, Joseph, and John Michael Roberts. 2018. "Lenin's Lens: The Occupy Movement, an Infantile Disorder?" *Journal of Cultural Analysis and Social Change* 3 (1): 1–11.

Ingarden, Roman. (1933) 1989. "The Musical Work." In *The Ontology of the Work of Art*, translated by Raymond Meyer and John T. Goldthwait, 3–133. Athens: Ohio University Press.

Kirshenblatt-Gimblett, Barbara. 1991. "Objects of Ethnography." In *Exhibiting Cultures: The Poetics and Politics of Museum Display*, edited by Ivan Karp and Steven D. Levine, 386–443. Washington, DC: Smithsonian Institution Press.

Lenin, V. I. (1920) 2012. "'Left-Wing' Communism: An Infantile Disorder." In *V. I. Lenin: Collected Works*, vol. 31, translated by Julius Katzer, 17–118. Moscow: Progress Publishers. https://www.marxists.org/archive/lenin/works/cw/pdf/lenin-cw-vol-31.pdf.

Merleau-Ponty, Maurice. (1945) 1962. *Phenomenology of Perception*. Translated by Colin Smith. New York: Humanities Press.

Ricoeur, Paul. (1954) 1967. "Introduction: Husserl (1859–1938)." In *Husserl: An Analysis of his Phenomenology*, translated by Edward G. Ballard and Lester E. Embree, 3–12. Evanston, IL: Northwestern University Press.

Stone, Ruth M., and Verlon L. Stone. 1981. "Event, Feedback, and Analysis: Research Media in the Study of Music Events." *Ethnomusicology* 25 (2): 215–225.

ACKNOWLEDGMENTS

A book like this would not be possible without the contributions of many people. Since its initial inception, Anna-Lise Santella has offered the book's editors her constant support and insight, and we wish to express to her our deep appreciation. An early phase of this project was an international conference on phenomenology in ethnomusicology, which convened in June 2018 at the Research Centre for the Study of Music, Media, and Place (MMaP) at Memorial University. The editors gratefully acknowledge the Canada Research Chairs Program, the Office of the President at Memorial University, the Memorial University Conference Fund, and the Memorial University School of Music for their support of that conference. We also wish to thank Meghan Forsyth, then project coordinator at MMaP, and Spencer Crewe, MMaP's digital audio studio coordinator, for their work on the conference, and Dean Ian Sutherland and acting Dean Karen Bulmer, who have been steadfast in their support of all of MMaP's projects. Kati Szego contributed to an early stage in the book's development; the editors offer her our thanks. The editors also express our appreciation to Peter Verdin and Jacob Danson-Faraday, who served as research assistants at various phases of work on the book, and our excellent proofreader, Alison Jacques. David wishes to thank Chelsea, Celia, and Westley for their personal support throughout this project. Finally, we note with sadness the untimely death of our contributor and valued colleague and friend, Esther Clinton, who passed away during the final stages of work on this project. She will be missed.

Contributors

Stephen Amico, Associate Professor of Musicology, University of Bergen

Michael B. Bakan, Professor of Ethnomusicology, Florida State University

Ritwik Banerji, Assistant Professor of World Languages and Cultures, Iowa State University

Harris M. Berger, Canada Research Chair in Ethnomusicology, Director of the Research Centre for the Study of Music, Media, and Place, and Professor of Music and Folklore, Memorial University

Esther Clinton, Adjunct Professor of Popular Culture, Bowling Green State University

Monica Dalidowicz, Independent Scholar

J. Martin Daughtry, Associate Professor of Music, New York University

Alessandro Duranti, Distinguished Professor of Anthropology, University of California, Los Angeles

Daniel Fisher, Associate Professor of Anthropology, University of California, Berkeley

Ruth Herbert, Senior Lecturer and Director of Graduate Studies in the Department of Music & Audio Technology, University of Kent

Deborah Kapchan, Professor of Performance Studies, New York University

Inderjit N. Kaur, Assistant Professor of Musicology, University of Michigan, Ann Arbor

Julia Kursell, Professor of Musicology, University of Amsterdam

Matthew McCoy, Health Science Specialist in the Department of Veterans Affairs, Greater Los Angeles Healthcare System

Andrew McGuiness, Independent Scholar

Dotan Nitzberg, PhD Candidate, Faculty of Education, University of New Brunswick

Matthew Rahaim, Professor of Music, University of Minnesota

Friedlind Riedel, Department of Media Philosophy, Bauhaus-Universität Weimar

Roger W. H. Savage, Professor and Chair of the Department of Ethnomusicology, University of California, Los Angeles

Charles Sharp, Lecturer in the School of Music, California State University, Fullerton

Helena Simonett, Professor of Ethnomusicology, Lucerne University of Applied Sciences and Arts

Jason Throop, Professor and Chair of the Department of Anthropology, University of California, Los Angeles

Jeff Todd Titon, Professor of Music, Emeritus, Brown University

David VanderHamm, Assistant Professor of Humanities, Johnson County Community College

Jeremy Wallach, Professor of Popular Culture, Bowling Green State University

Katharine Young, Lecturer in Anthropology and Folklore, San Francisco State University

ABOUT THE COMPANION WEBSITE

www.oup.com/us/OHPMC

Oxford University Press has created a website to accompany *The Oxford Handbook of the Phenomenology of Music Cultures*. All audio and video examples referenced in-text with the symbol ⊙ are available there.

SECTION 1

HISTORICAL PERSPECTIVES AND DISCIPLINARY DIRECTIONS

CHAPTER 1

....

PHENOMENOLOGICAL APPROACHES IN THE HISTORY OF ETHNOMUSICOLOGY

....

HARRIS M. BERGER, DAVID VANDERHAMM,
AND FRIEDLIND RIEDEL

FOUNDED at the turn of the twentieth century, phenomenology is a tradition of Continental European philosophy that has had a profound impact on the humanities and social sciences. The movement has a deep historical relationship with the discipline of ethnomusicology; not only did the nineteenth-century German philosopher, musicologist, and psychologist Carl Stumpf serve as the habilitation supervisor for the founder of phenomenology, Edmund Husserl (Fisette and Martinelli 2015), but Stumpf and others in his milieu were also among the parents of comparative musicology, the precursor to today's field of ethnomusicology (Stone 2008, 169–170). Despite these related origins, it was only in the last two decades of the twentieth century that ideas from phenomenology were engaged by ethnomusicologists in a substantive way. The body of work that has emerged in this area is diverse. Ethnomusicologists have drawn on differing branches of the phenomenological tradition, interpreted ideas from that tradition in varying ways, and used them to investigate a wide range of topics—from the nature of the performance event to problems of meaning and being in music, and from issues of embodiment, flow states, trance, time, and politics to basic questions about research methods and the goals of the ethnomusicological project. While phenomenological ethnomusicology has developed significant insights into questions of concern to music scholars, and those in the humanities and humanistic social sciences more broadly, this literature is not as tightly synthesized as that of other intellectual orientations within ethnomusicology, in which a common body of founding works is universally cited and a highly coordinated scholarly dialogue tracks an unambiguous intellectual trajectory. Despite the diversity within this body of work and the occasionally loose weave of its discursive threads, we argue that a systematic analysis of this scholarship reveals significant advances on a variety of fundamental topics in ethnomusicology, music studies, and the study of expressive culture in general—advances that only become evident from looking at the literature as a whole. Weaving those threads together and illuminating those advances is the aim of this chapter. The potential range of scholarship here is vast. To make this body of work more manageable, our focus is on phenomenological ethnomusicology written in English by scholars based in North America and the United Kingdom, with some attention to German-language scholarship and English-language sources from other parts of the world.[1]

It is, of course, beyond the scope of the present work to provide an introduction to the phenomenological tradition in philosophy.[2] But to understand phenomenological ethnomusicology, one must have at least a general idea of the character and project of the philosophical tradition, and providing that context is the first topic this chapter addresses.

Although phenomenology has many branches and its major thinkers disagree on a variety of important issues, a concern for lived experience is at the heart of much of this tradition. In Husserl's thought, for example, phenomenology begins with a return to lived experience. As a first approximation—one that phenomenologists ultimately reject—one might think of lived experience as the contents of consciousness: the feelings felt, thoughts thought, objects seen, memories recalled, and so forth. Such a conception might suggest that phenomenology is the study of the realm of the subjective and the individual, and in the field of psychology, as well as in more casual usage in the humanities and social sciences, the term is often used in just that way. But such a perspective runs counter to the phenomenological project, and a careful examination of the nature of experience is the starting place for any work that is based in phenomenology.

In Husserl's view ([1913] 1962), centuries of philosophical discourse about the relationship between appearance and reality have made it difficult for us to see lived experience for what it is. To correct for these distortions, we must place an epoché (set of brackets) around the question of whether any given experience is subjective or objective and make rigorous descriptions of the phenomena before us, unprejudiced by prior metaphysical presumptions. When we do this, Husserl argues, we make surprising discoveries. For example, taken strictly as experience, perceptual phenomena retain their objective quality. As a result of this insight, we, like so many scholars in the past, start our discussion by considering the experience of our immediate physical setting—for us, the authors of this text, a computer keyboard sitting on a desk. (Since what we describe is true for each of us individually, we set the following phenomenological description in the first-person singular.) At this moment, I see only the top surface of this object, while its back and sides are hidden from me. But if I attend to the experience itself in an unprejudiced manner, I discover that I am aware that the keyboard has a back and sides, facets of the thing that may become focal in future viewings. Taken strictly as experience, the keyboard retains its objective character as a mind-independent reality, and doing a phenomenological description of my computer keyboard would mean exploring the modes through which the keyboard, strictly as experience, reveals itself to me as an objective reality. Based on this kind of descriptive work, Husserl insists that consciousness cannot be understood independently of things and phenomena but is always *about* something, directed *at* something, and he refers to this unavoidable directedness as the "intentionality" of consciousness. Expanding on this approach, we see that, from a Husserlian perspective, the phenomenological brackets are never to be removed. All experience is taken as experience per se: Husserlian phenomenology seeks to answer basic questions of philosophy and to provide a grounding for the sciences, social sciences, and humanities by basing all inquiry on rigorous descriptions of lived experience.

Seeing the subject as constitutive of the world, even in its objectivity, Husserl's project is known as "transcendental phenomenology," and it differs significantly from the existential phenomenologies of Martin Heidegger ([1927] 1996), Jean-Paul Sartre ([1943] 1948), Maurice Merleau-Ponty ([1945] 1962), and Simone de Beauvoir ([1947] 1975), who see the subject as thrust into a world beyond their making, both constituting and constituted by the world. The work of Heidegger, who was Husserl's student, differs even more sharply from Husserl's than that of Merleau-Ponty and Sartre, as Heidegger sees questions of experience as merely an entry point into more fundamental questions of being and the distinctive forms that human being-in-the-world takes. Heidegger also influenced Hans Georg Gadamer ([1960] 2004) and Paul Ricoeur ([1986] 1991, 2007), whose work brought new phenomenological approaches to hermeneutics (the centuries-old Western tradition of textual interpretation) to gain fresh perspectives on questions of meaning and culture, as well as metaphysics and ontology, ethics, and other traditional topics in philosophy. Despite the sharp differences among these thinkers, all of this work opposes a representationalist view, which sees lived experience as a mere subjective epiphenomenon of a deeper reality that is, in principle, inaccessible to the subject.[3]

The relationship between the phenomenological project and the motivations and presumptions that have animated ethnomusicology is complex. Seeking to avoid ethnocentric approaches to music cultures, many ethnomusicologists have seen their job as understanding the musical experiences of the people with whom they work, and evocative ethnographies of music and social life have been a staple of the field since at least the 1970s. Providing a rigorous philosophical grounding for the notion of experience, phenomenology would therefore seem to be well suited to the ethnomusicological project. But when some ethnomusicologists in anglophone North America first encountered phenomenologies of music by philosopher Roman Ingarden ([1933] 1989) or musicologist F. Joseph Smith (1979), storm clouds appeared in what initially seemed like a sunny relationship. Ingarden, for example, is certainly interested in the experience of music, but he spends a substantial amount of effort arguing that musical works should be understood as "intentional objects," and his phenomenological return to experience seems to depict musical meaning as inherent in the sound itself. Reifying compositions, projecting ideas from the Western conservatory about the autonomy of art into "the music itself," and giving short shrift to both performance and situated context, Ingarden's phenomenology seems to run counter to intuitions that are at the heart of so much ethnomusicological work.[4] There is no question that, from a contemporary ethnomusicological perspective, these are significant problems with Ingarden's analysis; however, there are also substantial insights here, and a deeper reading of his work will allow us to put the relationship between phenomenology and ethnomusicology on a proper footing.

Though Ingarden seeks a radical return to experience, he clearly universalizes what are only culturally specific intuitions, and his treatment of musical works as things akin to ideal objects runs counter to ethnomusicology's emphasis on music as a fundamentally social phenomenon. But if we read Ingarden's phenomenology as a musical autoethnography of listening in the Western conservatory tradition and listen more closely to his phenomenological descriptions, a very different situation emerges. At first blush, Ingarden seems to locate musical form and musical meaning in the sound itself, but a more careful attention to his method reveals that, for Ingarden, form and meaning depend not on the sound itself but on the person's engagement with that sound—the process by which the person confronts musical sound and constitutes it in their experience. While Ingarden fails to appreciate the profound ways in which our constitutive practices are shaped by cultural context, his work conceptualizes these practices and their embrace of music as his study object. This vision of study object—as both the music and the constitutive practices that bring it into experience—is at the heart of any richly phenomenological approach to our field. Without this kind of grounding, the scholar interested in understanding local perspectives on music may see musical form and musical meaning as constructs in the mind of the musician or listener. But listeners and musicians do not create meanings in their minds; they are not magicians on some psychological stage, making semiotic doves appear from puffs of smoke. On the contrary, musicians and listeners live in a public, social world of sounds and of other people, and we constitute our experience by engaging with the things of this world, bestowing sense but also opening ourselves to the contours and dimensions of the things we find here. While there are substantive differences among the interpretive approaches ethnomusicologists have taken to the phenomenological tradition, the thread that connects much of this work is an attention to constitutive processes; to forms of being in the world; to the social practices by which we as people engage with sounds, instruments, situations, and others, opening ourselves to the world that we find and making that world meaningful. As we explore the diverse ways in which ethnomusicologists have engaged phenomenology, this theme of constitutive processes will underlie our discussion.

FUNDAMENTAL ORIENTATIONS FOR RESEARCH: MEANING, EVENT, AND BEING IN PHENOMENOLOGICAL ETHNOMUSICOLOGY

The issue of meaning in music is an essential one for ethnomusicology, and it is here that phenomenological approaches to the field made their first contributions. For the phenomenological tradition, the word *meaning* does not merely point to the referential or denotative function of signs; on the contrary, in this context meaning is construed in a broad manner as a dimension of experience, and the interpretation of meaning is seen as a central component of the scholarly enterprise. Understood in this way, musical meaning includes the affective or stylistic valence that listeners or performers may find in music, processes of coordination and communication among participants in a performance event, the positioning of performances or works in terms of formal or generic systems, the negotiation of identity through music, and, in its widest sense, any ascription or discovery of significance in music or music making. The simple yet crucial phenomenological insight that links these varied modes of meaning making is the observation that meaning is relational and cannot be reduced to cognitive processes. Music is made meaningful in acts of composing, arranging, recording, performing, and listening, but also in discourses about music, from everyday talk to formal music criticism, and in every aspect of the music industry. The research on musical meaning in phenomenological ethnomusicology has developed from three starting places: Ruth Stone's ([1982] 2010, 1988) analyses of time, interaction, and performance, which are inspired by the writings of Husserl ([1929] 1964), Alfred Schutz (1962, 1964; Schutz and Luckmann [1973] 1975), and the symbolic interactionists (e.g., Blumer 1969); Jeff Todd Titon's (1988, 2008, 2009) and Tim Rice's (1994, 2001, 2003, 2008) approaches to issues of interpretation in music, which are grounded in the writings of the hermeneutic phenomenologists; and Stephen Friedson's (1996, 2009) Heideggerian inflection of the hermeneutic tradition, which is focused on questions of being in ritual and trance.

An ethnography of music making among the Kpelle of Liberia, Stone's *Let the Inside Be Sweet* ([1982] 2010) offers in its first few chapters nothing short of a thoroughgoing phenomenological reconstruction of the theoretical foundations of the discipline of ethnomusicology. Arguing against both musicological and anthropological visions of music research, Stone rejects the idea that either sound (as autonomous sonic form) or behavior (as the product of a cultural system) can account for the complex, lived reality of human music making. In contrast, she argues that ethnomusicologists must attend to the "dynamic, ongoing symbolic process in which participants—performer and audience—interpret the meaning of symbolic behavior" (8; original in italics). Understood in this way, ethnomusicologists can and should attend to sound and behavior, but these phenomena must be interpreted as the product of agents located in both situated and large-scale social contexts, ones who actively interpret the sonic, linguistic, and kinesic signs exchanged in performance. Stone takes the performance event as the indivisible unit of analysis, and her sensitive ethnography reveals how Kpelle performances are constituted by their participants through the interpretation and exchange of musical signs. More importantly, Stone shows how that exchange itself is the focus of aesthetic experience in the local culture,[5] and her analysis sketches out the first approach to a set of topics that have become central to phenomenological ethnomusicology: the nature of time in performance, the relationship of the situated event to larger social contexts, the interplay of musical and nonmusical expression in events, and the role of culture in performance. Articulated in a steady stream of books and articles (e.g.,

Stone and Stone 1981; Stone [1982] 2010, 1988, 2008; Stone-Macdonald and Stone 2013), Stone's Schutzian work has influenced generations of scholars in the anglophone North American academy, both those who self-consciously employ phenomenology (e.g., Berger 1999; Berger and Del Negro 2004; Berger 2010) and those who see the constitution of experience as their study object but do not use the formal theoretical apparatus of phenomenology in their research.

A second tradition in phenomenological ethnomusicology is grounded in the work of the hermeneutic phenomenologists, most prominently Gadamer and Ricoeur. The first development of this approach came in Steven Feld's often-cited article "Communication, Music, and Speech about Music" ([1984] 1994), which offers a systematic account of the various kinds of "interpretive moves" through which people make music meaningful. Though phenomenology is only one of the many streams of influence on Feld's ideas here, his focus on music making and listening as interpretive processes makes this article an important starting point for hermeneutic ethnomusicology, and in later studies (e.g., [1988] 1994, 1996) Feld went on to engage with ideas from phenomenology in highly productive ways.

The first hermeneutic ethnomusicological ethnographies came in rich and weighty monographs by Jeff Todd Titon and Timothy Rice. In differing ways, Titon's *Powerhouse for God* (1988) and Rice's *May It Fill Your Soul* (1994) explore how persons emerge from a preexisting discursive history; come together to confront particular musical works, repertoires, or traditions; develop pre-reflexive understandings of music; and re-emerge changed by those social, interpretive experiences. (This iterative, dialogic process of meaning making is sometimes referred to as the "hermeneutic circle," though that term has several differing uses in the field of philosophy.)[6] The relationship between, on the one hand, the pre-reflexive meanings that are constituted in the person's initial confrontation with a work or tradition and, on the other hand, any self-reflexive awareness that the person may later develop of her own interpretive processes, is taken up by Titon and Rice in differing ways. A study of music, verbal art, and exegetic discourse in an Appalachian Baptist community, *Powerhouse* offers sophisticated insights into the interplay among the meanings of various genres of expressive culture (e.g., hymn, prayer, sermon, and life story), exegesis about those genres, and the unmarked experiences of everyday life. In *May It Fill Your Soul*, an influential and multilayered ethnography of the politics and practice of Bulgarian music, Rice pays particular attention to the role of the body in hermeneutic processes, exploring how pre-reflexive embodied knowledge of music making resists incorporation into explicit pedagogy and examining the kinds of meanings that that know-how carries when a musician is able to assimilate it into their performance. Taking the ethnographies of Titon and Rice together highlights the fact that interpretive processes are not cognitive operations in the mind of an isolated subject but forms of social and embodied practice—actively achieved, shaped by both situated and large-scale social context, tied to the body, and dependent as much on social interaction as on the individual contemplation of works. Many of these insights emerge in the analysis of particular ethnographic moments, and broader theoretical constructions of these ideas can be found in Titon's and Rice's chapters in the edited volume *Shadows in the Field* (2008), which we discuss in more detail in the section on methodology below.

The ethnographies of Feld, Titon, and Rice form the first generation of hermeneutic phenomenology in ethnomusicology, and a series of articles emerged in the wake of these works that extend their approach to investigate a wide variety of topics. Whether they are exploring the role of technological mediation in musical interaction (Porcello 1998), the interpretive dynamics that play out across the life course of a single musician (Harnish 2001), the hermeneutics of memory (Conn 2012), or music's role in the production and contestation of social identities (Seeman 2019), the second-generation hermeneutic ethnomusicologists see meaning making as grounded in the person's cultural past, and they forward the broader ethnomusicological project of understanding what music means to the people who make it and listen to it (see also Catlin 1992; Simonett 2001; McIntosh 2006; Pieridou Skoutella 2015). A more radical recasting of the discipline's goals can be found in the hermeneutic approach of Michael Bakan's *Music of Death and New Creation*, a detailed study of Balinese gamelan *beleganjur* music (1999). While Bakan does not deny that interpretive practices are shaped by culture, he critiques ethnomusicology's traditional emphasis on cultural difference and highlights the common interpretive dynamics that all subjects share when confronting a musical work or tradition. Like many ethnomusicological ethnographies, Bakan's provides a detailed, first-person account of the author's attempts to learn an unfamiliar music, but Bakan rejects the typical ethnomusicological approach to music learning in the field, which had been to adhere strictly to the local style of musical pedagogy. Conceptualizing fieldwork as intercultural performance, Bakan collaborates with his teacher in forging a hybrid Western/Balinese gamelan pedagogy and treats his own unique learning experience as a legitimate object of study, rather than a means to reveal a reified "Balinese perspective." In so doing, Bakan takes seriously the Ricoeurian insight that what the fieldworker and the research participant share is a common interpretive predicament: placing ourselves before a culture's texts, confronting their complexities, internalizing their meanings, and allowing ourselves to be transformed by them. While Bakan's approach has not displaced the more traditional ethnographic aims in either phenomenological ethnomusicology or the field as a whole, his emphasis on the intercultural dynamics of interpretation has gained attention from a number of other scholars (e.g., Butler 2000; Noone 2013) and calls out for further inquiry.

While the problems of interpretation are important for the early Heidegger, his later work shifted away from hermeneutics (see Ramberg and Gjesdal 2013), and throughout his career Heidegger felt that the Husserlian emphasis on experience should be subordinated to what he believed were deeper questions of being. Taking Heidegger as a starting point, a third strand of phenomenological ethnomusicology sees the various forms that music making may take as culturally specific modes of being-in-the-world. Steven Friedson has consistently developed this perspective with rich ethnographic detail and penetrating insight. Drawing on hermeneutics and hermeneutic ethnomusicology to supplement his primarily Heideggerian approach, Friedson's *Dancing Prophets* (1996), a study of Tumbuka healing performance in Malawi, and *Remains of Ritual* (2009), which examines the Brekete/Gorovodu religion of the Ewe of southern Ghana, understand the ethnographic project as a process of participating in social interaction with one's research participants to uncover their particular modes of being-in-the-world. Friedson does not reject the utility of traditional methods of descriptive ethnography, and his books recount local cosmologies, the typical practices of their rituals, and the tropes and structures of the music performed there. But for Friedson, this information is merely preparatory, a first step that allows him to take part in and understand the forms of *Dasein* (literally, "there-being"; roughly, the human mode of being) at play in his fieldsite. Read through a Heideggerian lens, polyrhythm, which is a key feature of the music found in both of his fieldsites, is not merely a stylistic or aesthetic device but a way of being in time that opens up participants to trance states and the (perceived) medical efficacy of the music.

Since the turn of the 2010s, the work of Roger Savage and his colleagues has offered significant extensions of the Heideggerian and hermeneutic traditions. One part of Savage's tightly argued and insightful book *Hermeneutics and Music Criticism* (2010) brings ideas from phenomenology into conversation with those of John Blacking to suggest that what makes music distinctive is the ways in which its performance has the potential to carve stretches of time out of the mundane flow of everyday life and set them into an ontologically distinct realm. Savage contrasts ethnographic case studies by Friedson (1996) and Ali Jihad Racy (2003) to illustrate the culturally specific ways in which such time-out-of-time experiences are constituted. The articles in a special issue of the journal *The World of Music*, edited by Helena Simonett, extend Savage's approach with ethnographic examples from around the world and reveal a range of new dynamics (e.g., Ho 2009; Kapchan 2009; Simonett 2009; see also Simonett 2014). More recently, ethnomusicologists have used ideas from Ricoeur and other thinkers in the hermeneutic tradition to examine topics like the humane potentials of applied ethnomusicology projects (O'Connell 2015), the politics of cultural appropriation and memory (Gaulier and Martin 2017; see below), and musical creativity (Dessiatnitchenko 2019). Additionally, ethnomusicologists have built upon Tim Ingold's ([2000] 2022) development of the (Heideggerian-derived) concept of dwelling to produce another branch of inquiry concerned with the role that music and culture can play in the foundationally spatial and social nature of being-*in*-the-world. A special issue of the journal *The World of Music* edited by Barbara Titus presents insightful essays that explore the many ways that music shapes experiential space and the politics of belonging, with each author subtly deploying concepts of dwelling and orientation (Titus 2019). Dwelling has been a particularly fruitful theoretical tool for authors interested in environmental issues and dynamics, as these scholars leverage phenomenological insights to explore expansive topics like the ecological impacts of music and the personhood of non-human animals in northwest Mexico (Simonett 2016) or the use of music to maintain a sense of place in a South African borderland, where women navigate environmental and economic challenges amid ambiguous or absent national belonging (Impey 2018).

Differences of focus and intellectual apparatus separate Stone's event-oriented approach, the Titon- and Rice-inspired hermeneutic ethnomusicology, and the

Heideggerian inflection of hermeneutics found in the writings of Friedson and others. Nevertheless, all three strands of scholarship seek to deepen the ethnomusicological project by grounding research in the concrete realities of music making and music listening. Although we ethnomusicologists—and indeed all music makers and music listeners—are immersed in the experiential reality of our everyday lives, that familiar reality is also the site of our deepest ethnographic and philosophical conundrums. The situation involves subtle ironies, as finding ways to talk about that concrete reality leads us directly to problems of metaphysics and ontology that have historically been considered the domain of philosophy. What is the ontological status of the musical work?[7] What occurs when we encounter such works, and how does meaning emerge in those encounters? What is the nature of human being in musical performance? The theoretical traditions of the social sciences found in the ethnomusicology of the 1960s and 1970s—structural functionalism and structuralism—distracted scholars from these questions by treating practices of music making and music listening as secondary phenomena, the mere enactment of abstract sociocultural or cognitive systems. What phenomenology provides to the field of ethnomusicology is both a way of returning the focus of attention to the experiential reality of music and a set of intellectual tools for studying it (see Stone's remarks in Stone and Berger 2014, 1, 4). This return to the concrete is no escape from context. As all phenomenological ethnomusicologists recognize, acts of music making and music listening are necessarily informed by the participants' past interactions with others and oriented toward the possibility of future interactions. Understood in this way, "context" is not an abstract system (sociocultural, musico-cognitive, or otherwise) that produces experience; rather, context is the accumulation of past events sedimented in the person's way of being-in-the-world, a sedimentation that fundamentally informs, but does not determine, their present practice.[8] Developing these insights with theoretical work and ethnographic or historical case studies, phenomenological ethnomusicology provides a distinctive set of insights into ethnomusicology's traditional focus of research—music and culture.

THE BODY, SELF-REFLEXIVITY, AND MUSICAL INVOLVEMENT

Embodiment, Technology, and Disability

If phenomenology has offered ethnomusicology a new approach to foundational issues of theory, it has also provided tools for studying a wide range of more specific topics and research questions. Chief among these are a cluster of interrelated questions that revolve around the issue of embodiment in music: What is the relationship between musical structure and embodied practice? What significance does self-reflexive awareness (commonly referred to as "reflexivity") have in performance? How are we to under-stand moments of intense involvement in music, and what roles do "body" and "mind" play here? Writing against long-standing biases in the Western conservatory that view musical works as nothing more than abstract sonic structures in time, phenomenolog-ical ethnomusicologists have argued that music is necessarily, rather than contingently, embodied and have explored the complex, culturally specific ways in which embodied practice is essential to even the most seemingly disembodied, formal qualities of music. The starting point for most of this research is Merleau-Ponty's first major work, *Phenomenology of Perception* ([1945] 1962), which critiques empiricist and rationalist traditions in philosophy to show how all elements of lived experience arise from the body's primordial interactions with the world. Another phenomenological touchstone is *Ways of the Hand* (1978), a classic study by the sociologist and musician David Sudnow on the role of the body in jazz piano performance.

Published in the journal *Ethnomusicology*, Greg Downey's (2002) widely cited re-search on capoeira (a Brazilian martial art for which musical accompaniment is es-sential) illustrates some of the diverse ways that the body enters into music. Based on detailed ethnographic descriptions of performance events and subtle discussions of timbre and rhythm in capoeira's music, Downey shows how performers in the genre hear the parts played on the berimbau not as abstract structures of pitch and rhythm but as expressions of the musician's physical gestures, and his useful discussion illustrates the ways in which rhythms traffic freely between the musical phrases of the instrumentalists and the kicks and blocks of the fighters. Special attention is focused on the ways that those attending capoeira events mime the gestures of the berimbau player. Like the "air guitar" gestures so commonly performed by rock music fans, ca-poeira participants make sense of the music by articulating the physical gestures that create it; more importantly, their air berimbau gestures often play rhythms that com-plement the sounded part, rather than just identically copying the physical gestures that the berimbau player is currently performing. Where a structuralist might see abstract sets of musical forms coordinated through some generative, transformational grammar, Downey's discussion illustrates the fundamentally embodied nature of this music. Here, the body is not an output device for some underlying musical cognition; rather, it is the social and musical means by which musical structure itself is created.

Matthew Rahaim's research on the place of gesture in North Indian classical singing approaches related issues from a different angle (2012). Based on interviews, partici-pant observation, and video recordings of lessons and performances, Rahaim analyzes the wide variety of gestures that vocalists produce while singing. Though some gestures are straightforwardly iconic, as when a singer's hand motions trace the pitch contour of the melody, others operate in a very different way, such as the gripping gesture that accompanies a melodic phrase at the conclusion of a rhythmic cycle or the circular ges-ture that accompanies oscillations of pitch. Rahaim's point is that while Hindustani singers care deeply about sound, vocal melodies are more than a static ordering of pitches, as written transcriptions may imply. Singers also hear melody as motion through a pitch space, and for vocalists deeply involved in their work, that motion is experienced through multiple dimensions of embodiment—the unity of heard sound and the proprioceptive awareness of the vocal apparatus that is the seat of vocal experience, but also gestures of the hands, arms, shoulders, and upper body. For Rahaim, we understand melodic motion because we are bodies that move in space, and musical motion and corporeal motion cannot be separated.[9]

Downey and Rahaim represent only two of the ways that phenomenological ethnomusicologists have engaged issues of embodiment. As we noted previously, Rice (1994) has also explored how the musician's pre-reflexive bodily engagement with their instrument may resist articulation in verbal exegesis, and Bruno Deschênes and Yuko Eguchi (2018) elaborate the ways that the traditional literacy/orality binary fails to account for the body's role in conveying and acquiring knowledge in traditional Japanese music. Scholars like Louise Meintjes (2004), Jan Mrázek (2008), and Deborah Kapchan (2009, 2013) emphasize the role of embodiment in musical meaning, while studies by Judith Becker (2004), Martin Clayton (2008), and Clayton and Laura Leante (2013) combine ideas from phenomenology with contemporary work in cognitive science to get at issues of embodiment in music. Likewise drawing on cognitive science and phenomenology, Tomie Hahn and J. Scott Jordan (2017) use a movement and sound practice that Hahn developed called "banding" to explore the nature of "intercorporeality," the term Merleau-Ponty used to describe the fundamental sociality of our embodiment. The unity of the body is a theme that runs through much of this literature, and this unity is articulated along a number of dimensions. Forwarding ideas developed by Merleau-Ponty ([1945] 1962), Hermann Schmitz ([1969] 2005), and Don Ihde (1976), a wide array of studies by music scholars emphasize that, in most cases, the various sense modalities are not isolated from one another in sensory experience (Feld 1996; Downey 2002; Clayton 2008; Thacker 2012; Simonett 2014; Riedel 2015; Abels 2018; Kaur 2019; Turner 2020; Szego 2021). Rather, we draw on all of our sensory apparatus in a unified, systemic process, synthesizing sight, hearing, and tactile perception to bring the things of the world into lived experience. The same writers observe that the focus of our attention is less frequently on isolated sonic parameters (e.g., pitch, rhythm, or timbre) than it is on unified objects of perception. In capoeira, for example, event participants are less likely to hear the movement from one note to the next simply as a change in pitch than they are to experience that pitch change as the indication of some gestural process, such as the performer pressing a coin against the instrument's string; as Downey succinctly states, "The sound makes present the physical action that produces it" (2002, 496). But caution must also be exercised in the face of such enthusiastic adoptions of German and French phenomenologies. As Friedlind Riedel (2019, 88; 2020, 24–26) has pointed out, Schmitz's monumental phenomenology of the body takes a highly normalized human person as its point of departure and as a benchmark for his phenomenology of listening. Despite the utility of influential theories of the body from thinkers such as Schmitz and Merleau-Ponty, these ideas should not be treated as truths to be rehearsed nor as neutral frameworks describing a universal human body. Instead, phenomenological approaches should be seen as providing tools for undertaking inquiry, ones that may themselves be challenged, refashioned, or refuted in the process.[10]

As several sources already cited demonstrate, phenomenological attention to the body lends itself to a concurrent interest in the body's interaction with technological tools and apparatuses. Under the umbrella of "the tangible in music," Marko Aho (2016) illuminates the many ways that a supposedly ephemeral art form is firmly intertwined with tactility and embodiment, especially via the technological interface of musical instruments. Mats Johansson (2017) similarly focuses on the body's skillful manipulation of musical instruments, drawing on phenomenological theorizations of expertise to understand the development and deployment of improvisational skill in Irish traditional music. This interaction between body and instrument also takes center stage in David VanderHamm's (2020) retheorization of virtuosity through the case study of Tony Melendez, a guitarist born without arms who plays the instrument with his feet. Putting phenomenological insights into conversation with literature from disability studies, VanderHamm argues that any experience of virtuosity depends on tacit assumptions about the "limitations and possibilities of bodies, instruments, and repertoires" (292). But rather than relating virtuosity to some sort of external criterion that bodies must meet, VanderHamm suggests that the experience of virtuosity is primarily about the *relationship* between embodied subjects: audiences perceive virtuoso performers as exceptional in some ways but also in other ways like themselves. As the reception of Melendez's guitar playing makes clear, the body that interacts with technology is always a social body. The combined individual and social experience of impairment is the subject of Jonathan Sterne's *Diminished Faculties* (2021). Sterne considers himself an unlikely phenomenologist; his influential earlier work in the field of sound studies criticized universalizing approaches to experience, which he associates with several early proponents of the phenomenological tradition. Yet he draws on a nuanced understanding of political phenomenology—an approach tied to "feminist, queer, Black, Latinx, and disability traditions" (11) that he contrasts with the transcendental aspirations of Husserlian phenomenology—and his own vocal impairment to reflect on the "shifting sand" of embodied experience as a necessary but imperfect source for understanding the world and the range of facilities through which we (fail to) grasp it. Although their influences and arguments vary widely, both Sterne and VanderHamm emphasize the irreducible sociality of the body: Sterne describes impairment not as the "physical substrate" of disability but as "an orientation towards the world" defined by its relationality (2021, 194–195), while VanderHamm declares that disability and virtuosity are both "intensely personal but irreducibly social" (2020, 195). In these works, accessibility and accommodation—how tools and technologies may enable, influence, or constrain bodily action—emerge as a key aspect of all embodied experience, impaired or not, in music making or in daily life. The explicitly political nature of disability further highlights the fact that the body's status as the site of culture and agency also makes it the site of ethics and politics. This work connects with themes we have addressed earlier: in various ways, Berger (1999, 2010), Rahaim (2012), VanderHamm (2020), and the other sources cited above show how the embodied practices of the performance event are shaped by larger social forces and oriented toward other co-present participants, and thus entail ethical or political valences.

The theme of embodiment is taken in a different direction in Mrázek's *Wayang and Its Doubles* (2019), a book that draws on scholars from within phenomenology and a wide range of other traditions. Bringing Merleau-Pontian insights into conversation with ideas from Jacques Derrida and media theory, Mrázek explores the relationship between live and televised renditions of the *wayang kulit* (Javanese puppet theater). Critiquing any simple understanding of the live/mediated dyad, Mrázek views the body itself as a form of mediation, shows how live and televisual wayangs "haunt" one another, and emphasizes the complex ways that performance always depends on particular forms of cultural practice and technology. Ethnographic detail and lived experience are richly revealed in his subtle phenomenologies of taking in a wayang in the "midst" of others or watching it on a glowing television screen. Mrázek also brings Husserl's notion of the lifeworld and Heidegger's ideas about art and poetry into dialog with Javanese reflections on the meanings of liveness and mediatization. For many years, issues of technology and media have received significant attention in ethnomusicology (see, for example, Manuel [1993], Lysloff and Gay [2003], Miller [2012, 2017]), and Mrázek shows the value of phenomenology in exploring this vital topic.[11]

Considering the diverse forms of phenomenological work on embodiment, technology, and disability, it is worth emphasizing that the dynamics of embodiment theorized by Merleau-Ponty are profoundly dialectical. In *Phenomenology of Perception*, Merleau-Ponty neither romanticizes those phenomena traditionally denigrated as merely biological (our appetites and passions) nor erases those phenomena traditionally lauded as mental (thinking and rationality) but shows how all elements of experience depend on our physical engagement with the world. And far from romanticizing sensory immediacy, Merleau-Ponty sees this engagement as both technologically mediated and learned, as epitomized in his famous example of the blind man who uses a cane to sense the world around him (165). We emphasize the dialectical character of these insights to highlight the fact that all talk of embodiment implies a thing separate from the immediate concrete actuality of the body; in other words, talk of embodiment implies that some "thing" is being embodied. But as good dialecticians, we cannot see that thing as some immaterial essence, like a soul. On the contrary, the thing that is embodied is one possible deployment of our bodily and musical resources, which are framed by a penumbra of potentialities that were not brought into being. Thus, to articulate this gesture or play that phrase is also to have a structural awareness of other possible phrases in one's cultural repertoire—gestures or phrases that are no less corporeal for being absent from the concreteness of the current moment. We might think of this as a kind of material systematicity or structural corporeality, an intimacy between the abstract organization of parts and the material elements thus organized. This is only one of the many dialectics of embodiment. In describing the music-making body as a paradoxical unity of material flesh and "evanescent," dynamic form, Rahaim explores the temporal dimensions of this dialectic (2012, 87–90), and the topic is a deep one with significant implications for both ethnomusicology and philosophy. Understood in this way, the phenomenology of the body is not (or not merely) about repairing a Cartesian split or celebrating a corporeality defamed by Platonic philosophy. Rather, it is a way of recasting our ideas of body and mind, returning to lived experience, exploring issues like the body's technicity and the nature of ability and impairment, and seeing with fresh eyes how all of this operates.

Atmosphere

In attending to and theorizing through the body, phenomenologists have written at length about feelings and modes of affect. Among these, the contributions of German philosopher Hermann Schmitz ([2009] 2019)[12] have provided a pathway to new insights into a core ethnomusicological concern: the production, experience, and power of collective feelings and affective communities. Rather than taking feelings to be private states of a subject, Schmitz proposed to consider them as spatially extended atmospheres[13]—that is, as phenomena that can be observed, encountered, and sensed in the world. One important conceptual starting point for Schmitz, who writes extensively about musical listening and the hearing of sounds and noises ([1978] 2005), is the distinction between noticing a feeling (for instance, in an environment or in a performance space) and being affected by a feeling. Building on this idea, Anne Holzmüller (2020) interprets late eighteenth-century travelogues by German Protestant visitors to Rome to show how pilgrims remained ambivalent toward the clerical atmosphere they encountered when entering a Catholic church—a vast space flooded with music and light seeping through its stained glass windows. Maintaining a critical distance from the sacral staging, pilgrims were precisely *not* caught up in its grandeur, which ultimately struck them as profane. Schmitz's work allows Holzmüller to recognize the atmospheric feeling that palpably hangs in the air without immediately collapsing it into a subject's individual affective experience.

The musically amplified atmosphere of a religious site or event can also powerfully seize an individual who finds themself caught up in an environmental feeling and transformed in the encounter. Riedel (2015; 2020, 16) describes how, in the context of a small Christian congregation in rural Germany—which sets itself apart from the country's Christian mainstream—musical suggestions of movement, such as the transposition of a hymn into a higher key, channel collective feelings of devotion by quite literally moving the congregation to stand up. Furthermore, extended periods of silence heighten an atmosphere of authority, as even one's own silent and seemingly passive observation becomes implicated in the pious atmosphere of hush. Riedel's attention to the collective dynamics of spatially extended feelings allows her to critically reflect on the musical and affective dimensions of religious power and denominational alterity that otherwise remain difficult to pin down. Similarly, Tamara Turner's (2020) ethnography of Algerian Sufi ritual illustrates how environmental feelings can be steeped in norms. What is at stake in the performance of a ritual sequence is the musical cultivation of the *right* kind of atmosphere, one that corresponds with the character of a particular saint or spirit. Thus, Turner shows that atmosphere is of central and practical concern in ritual performance, where it is subject to the attentive affective labor of musicians and ritual specialists. In both Turner's and Riedel's accounts, atmospheres are carefully cultivated among communities of dissent across generations in order to articulate, render tangible, and heighten their dissociation from majority religious formations.

Ethnographic studies such as these have emphasized another central aspect of atmospheres: although described as feelings that show up in the world, Schmitz emphasizes that they do not simply exist *among things* but rather as holistic phenomena that pervade and envelop *everything* (Schmitz et al. 2011). Atmospheres can be noticed or experienced yet do not belong to anyone in particular. Paying attention to atmosphere thus means considering music and sound in their capacity to modulate and charge the totality of things (much as the weather that transforms an entire landscape) and to impact the individual only through this totality. Put another way, atmosphere emphasizes that the object of experience is not "music" or "sound" as such, but a situation, an environment, a scene, or a horizon of possibility that is musically modulated. Countering sensualist tropes that treat listening as a specific mode of experiencing a sequestered sonic world, German phenomenologists have spoken of "situation-listening" (Schmitz [1978] 2005, 44) or of "musical situations" (Anders [1930] 2017) to emphasize that what is appreciated in musical performance or in the hearing of noises and sounds is a total *Sachverhalt* (state of affairs). Comparing performances of a robotic gamelan and a gamelan played by human performers, Andrew McGraw (2016) notes "that our experience of music always occurs in a singular situational milieu rather than being a straightforward communication of information between author and recipient through an ether called 'society' or 'history'" (131). This observation—namely that "music" or "sound" does not show up as a distinct, perceptual phenomenon that would be given directly to perception but rather that musical performance transforms an environment or a situation as a whole—is central not only to much ethnomusicological scholarship on atmosphere (Torvinen 2019; Absaroka 2020) but is also echoed in adjacent scholarship on affect (Garcia 2020; McMurray 2020; Reisnour 2020). In contrast to this phenomenological emphasis on music's environmental mediation, Abels (2018, 2020) considers atmosphere in materialist terms, arguing for an unmediated, material unity of body and world in her study of atmosphere in Palauan vocal music and dance performance.

Given this logic of environmental mediation and collective transformation, the notion of music as atmosphere addresses a range of central ethnomusicological concerns. For example, invoking affective coherence and simulating participation by seemingly involving everyone and everything, atmospherically charged milieus often refract power. Indeed, the deliberate production and preservation of specific atmospheres can play a role in capitalist or totalitarian projects, as well as resistance to them. Attention to dynamics of "atmospheric sociality" (McGraw 2016) can thus illuminate the conflict-ridden relations that exist between an affectively charged environment and the bodies that may alternately resist or become involved in it. In order to address such dynamics of ambient power and to leave room for critique and resistance, Mikkel Bille and Kirsten Simonsen (2019) and Riedel (2020) have suggested that scholars shift attention away from the potentially ambiguous noun *atmosphere* in order to attend more fully to *atmospheric practices* and *atmospheric relations*. McGraw (2020), for instance, shows how residents in a North American jail actively resist and break out of an otherwise quite literally overpowering carceral atmosphere by claiming "music" as an absolute good. And instead of essentializing music as intrinsically atmospheric or moving, Dafni Tragaki (2020) details audile techniques in listening to postwar *rebetiko* love songs, which allow contemporary listeners to reckon with the traumas of mid-twentieth-century Greek society. Likewise, Andreas Melson Gregerson (2021) develops a notion of "atmosphering" to understand the practices by which pastors and volunteers of an Evangelical Lutheran Church in Copenhagen cultivate, stabilize, and unify a desired atmosphere to fashion an alternative spiritual space that would appeal to outsiders. With these developments, the evolving phenomenology of atmosphere offers powerful new opportunities for insight into the cultural life of music.

Reflexivity and Musical Involvement

Just as the world of perceptual objects and the atmosphere of particular locales have their dialectical partner in the lived body, perception itself has a dialectical partner in thinking, the series of reflective or self-reflexive thoughts in words or other abstract symbols that play such an important part in everyday experience. The place that thinking holds in musical performance has been explored by a number of scholars in phenomenological ethnomusicology. Building on ideas from Husserl and Merleau-Ponty, as well as the framework for phenomenological ethnomusicology forged by Stone, Berger's *Metal, Rock, and Jazz: Perception and the Phenomenology of Music Experience* (1999) investigates the organization of attention in music performance. Based on fieldwork in four music scenes in northeast Ohio, the book explores the complex foreground/background structure of lived experience and the ways that musicians shift the focus of attention among various kinds of phenomena (e.g., musical sound, their own bodies, other musicians, the audience, and reflexive thought in words) to constitute their experience of the performance event. Understanding the organization of attention as both actively achieved and necessarily informed by situated and large-scale social context, Berger argues that the constitution of lived experience is a kind of social practice, in the practice theory sense of the term (e.g., Giddens [1976] 1993, 1979, 1984; Bourdieu 1977). Further, his work shows that musicians from various music scenes have differing attitudes toward reflexivity in performance. None of the musicians that Berger interviewed wanted to be distracted from musical sound by anxious reflections or arduous musical analyses, and players from the commercial hard rock, death metal, and 1950s-style bebop scenes all said that an ideal performance was unencumbered with reflexive thought in words. However, musicians from the post-bop jazz scene said that, for them, an effortless flow of reflexive thought would often accompany the sound of the other musicians in performance. In the best situations, ideas for new harmonic approaches, melodic devices, or forms of interaction with the other players would arise on the stand, weaving in and out of the player's center of attention and informing their improvisation of musical lines without distracting from the sound of the other musicians or interrupting the act of performance. Comparing all of this with data on the organization of attention by participants in the Central Italian *passeggiata* (ritual promenade), Berger and Giovanna P. Del Negro ([2002] 2004) have argued that cultures of performance have what they call an "aesthetic of reflexivity"—a set of culturally specific ideals regarding the role of reflexive awareness in events.

The issue of reflexivity is most frequently taken up by phenomenological ethnomusicologists in the context of research on heightened states of involvement in music making. One well-known framework for exploring this topic comes from Mihaly Csikszentmihalyi (e.g., [1975] 2000, 1990), a widely influential psychologist who defined "flow" as a state of consciousness in which the person's cognitive and practical abilities are matched with the demands of the task that that person is performing. Situated in the informatic sweet spot "between boredom and anxiety," as the title of his classic 1975 monograph describes it, flow states involve pleasure; a tight focus on the immediate task at hand; and, in their deepest forms, the paradoxical sensation of both the loss of self and of being in total control of one's behavior. Perhaps most strikingly, these "deep flow" states are further characterized by a timeless quality, a kind of focused attention so intense that one's awareness of past and future drops away and one feels themself to be situated in an eternal present. Roger Savage's notion of "limit experiences" in music, which are typified by trance rituals or situations of musical ecstasy, approaches related phenomena from a very different perspective (2009, 2010). Where Csikszentmihalyi sees qualities like pleasure, the paradoxical loss and expansion of self, and timelessness as the result of the fortuitous confluence of cognitive abilities and the practical demands of the task at hand, Savage focuses on the temporal qualities of the limit experiences themselves. Following John Blacking in contrasting "music that is simply for having" with "music that is for being" (Blacking 1973, 50, cited in Savage 2009, 6), Savage argues that limit experiences carve a distinct temporal domain out of the linear passage of everyday time. Set apart from mundane temporality, limit experiences are "the other of time" (Savage 2017, 13), and Savage builds on Gadamer's ideas about play to argue that such experiences are "self-disclosing" (i.e., they exist only in their enactment). While Savage maintains that "music for being" is a universal phenomenon, the particular form that such limit experiences may take varies from culture to culture, and Savage explains that in these events, individuals experience the core mode of being of their society or historical epoch.

In many ways, the ethnographies of musical involvement carried out by phenomenological ethnomusicologists confirm the basic ideas of Csikszentmihalyi and Savage. For example, a number of scholars observe a two-stage process necessary for entering a heightened state. In *Let the Inside Be Sweet* ([1982] 2010, 111–133), Stone explains how Kpelle identify an initial phase of performance, called "making music one," in which the musicians focus on ensemble coordination, and a second, emotionally heightened phase of performance, called "making music many," in which the now-coordinated performers differentiate their parts from one another and engage in the aestheticized exchange of musical cues. A related view is reported by Sarah Weiss in her rich discussion of Javanese theories of performance (2003). Based on the analysis of religious texts and historical accounts of music making, Weiss explores the Javanese view that the invocation of *rasa* (feeling) can only arise in an event when an artist (a musician, but also a dancer or a shadow-puppet performer) has unified spirit and body through the deep internalization of the expressive resources of their genre. A similar perspective is shared by the UK indie rock musicians studied by Andy McGuiness (2013), who hold that the best performances take place when a musician has completely assimilated a song or musical passage. Standing apart from the music as it arises from their bodily performance, the rocker observes the song as it unfolds, each time in a unique way, and their musical identity is laid bare for the audience to observe. Drawing on the ideas of Sartre and others, McGuiness argues that, in such situations, the musician has a sense of ownership of their body (i.e., it is *my* body that is playing this instrument) but not a sense of agency (i.e., *I* am not directing the course of the action). Related themes play out in Dard Neuman's work on Hindustani music (2012). Throughout these studies, scholars show how a failure to master expressive resources or coordinate with other musicians inhibits intense musical experience, while facility with one's instrument, the technical demands of the piece one is performing, or the protocols of ensemble coordination enable heightened involvement and its striking experiential effects.[14]

Other scholars have emphasized the unique forms of temporality associated with deeply involving musical experiences and suggested the means by which such temporal experiences are achieved. Jonathan Shannon (2003) shows that in Syrian Arab music, entrance into *tarab* (a "state of emotional rapture or enchantment," 72) is associated with the use of repeated motifs and passages of rich melodic fluency that allow the listener to "detemporalize" experience—separating it from the linear flow of mundane time—while cadences and other transitional passages "retemporalize" experience, bringing the listener back to the everyday. In her later work on Kpelle music, Stone (1988) emphasizes how the "making music one" phase of Kpelle performance is associated with a focus on what Alfred Schutz (1951) referred to as "outer time" (the temporal progression of events in the public, intersubjective world), while the heightened experiences that occur when music is made many are accompanied by a focus on the "inner time" of affective experience. (We discuss Schutz's work further in the next section.) And in differing ways, Feld ([1988] 1994), Rice (1994), Bakan (1999), Shannon (2003), Titon (2008), Kapchan (2009), Simonett (2009), Turino (2014), McGraw (2016), and Turner (2020) concur with Csikszentmihalyi and Savage that musical involvement is often associated with a loss of self and intense affective experiences.

While heightened states of involvement can be deeply pleasurable and fulfilling, it is important to avoid romanticizing this phenomenon, and contemporary scholars have also employed phenomenology to understand very different forms of musical absorption. Steven Friedson (2019) examines both the positive and negative extremes by comparing practices of musical torture found in American prisons and practices of spirit possession found in the religious rituals of northern Ghana. This dialectical consideration of the musical erosion of agency—though they are different in many ways, one does not choose to be either tortured or possessed—highlights the all-encompassing nature of these experiences. Unlike possession, which allows for an escape from the self, sonic torture enacts what Friedson terms a total "being-there": disrupting the normal temporal structure of experience through sonic bombardment forces the prisoner to occupy an unrelenting musical "now." The thin temporality of the experience of unavoidable, undesired music serves to produce an inescapable, impoverished, and immiserated experience of the self, one that is locked in a claustrophobically narrow present. Exploring related topics, Martin Daughtry utilizes phenomenology and insights from sound studies to discuss issues of music, war, and violence more broadly, seeking to understand the structures of extreme sonic experience while also noting that some aspects of it are too terrible to be consciously lived through (2014, 2015). Although scholars of music and culture have often valorized their topic of study, Daughtry suggests that there is "a kernel of potential violence that exists within all sound," and that music may also be implicated in current ecological crises (2015, 165; 2020).

Romanticizing musical involvement is not the only pitfall to sidestep, here; we must also be careful to avoid smoothing over the various complexities of musical involvement that an overenthusiastic universalism may obscure. Consider the issue of the "loss of self" in performance. While many cultures equate heightened states with a quieting of the inner series of thoughts, this connection is by no means found everywhere. As we suggested previously, the post-bop jazz musicians that Berger interviewed in northeast Ohio do not find the inner thinking voice to be incompatible with flow states, and further reflection suggests other situations, such as the examples of chess players and surgeons that Csikszentmihalyi studied ([1975] 2000), in which thought in words or symbols may be an essential part of flow. Further, as Berger argues in other work (2004), the self is an extraordinarily complex phenomenon that emerges through a variety of experiential modalities, and the inner voice of thinking is only one form that the self may take. In the act of seeing, for example, the perspectival organization of visual phenomena constitutes a kind of perceptual self that is situated at the invisible "here" around which the things of the world are arrayed. Though some acoustic spaces envelop the listener in sound and diminish the sense of here, near, and far, other listening environments foster a perspectival and embodied sense of self that is similar to that found in vision. Merleau-Ponty's classic analyses of embodied subjectivity in tactile perception reveal other dimensions of the self that experiential involvement fails to annihilate (e.g., Merleau-Ponty [1945] 1962, 92; [1964] 1968, 147–148). Looking at the ways in which differing forms of the self might be fostered or diminished in heightened states points the way to more nuanced understandings of musical involvement.[15]

Phenomenological ethnomusicologists have done valuable work on the relationship between musical involvement and culture, but further research is needed in this area. Savage, for example, emphasizes that while the musical limit experience may be a universal category, it is always enacted in culturally specific ways. Further, he suggests that a culture's rituals of transcendent music are emblematic of its distinctive way of being-in-the-world—its way of "responding to the enigmas of existence" (Savage 2009, 17)—and a number of studies explore how such heightened experiences either enact religious ideologies (Humphreys 1991; Friedson 1996, 2009; Ho 2009; Simonett 2009; Riedel 2015; Turner 2020) or are freighted with social or political meanings (Berger 1999, 2004;

Shannon 2003; McGuiness 2013; Turino 2014).[16] While there is no question that both the form and the meaning of heightened states are culturally specific, most phenomenological research on this topic has focused on situations in which the ritual or musical genre from a more or less well-bounded social group is seen to align with a specific worldview and ontology. But for many years, theorists and ethnographers have focused attention on the diversity of experiences that emerge within a performance event, conflict and dissent within social groups, intercultural performance, and historical change. Studying musical involvement in contexts in which these sorts of dynamics are at play will enrich the phenomenological literature on this topic and open up new avenues of research.

TIME

One of the great achievements of the phenomenological movement has been to shed new light on the perennial problem of time in philosophy. Grounded in concrete descriptions of the phenomena of change and persistence in lived experience, Husserl and Schutz have provided scholars with a precise and comprehensible language for talking about the temporal dimensions of our lives, and two works from the tradition form the starting place for most of the phenomenological ethnomusicology of musical temporality.

The first of these is Husserl's *Phenomenology of Internal Time-Consciousness* ([1929] 1964), a groundbreaking study that shows that the present in which our experience is located is not, as our everyday talk might have it, an infinitely thin moment, like some monad-wide second hand, spinning endlessly on a metaphysical wristwatch. To have any kind of experience at all, our consciousness must embrace more than the temporal sliver of the "now-point"; rather, it must simultaneously embrace recently past events and anticipations of potential events in the immediate future (in the technical language, "retentions" and "protentions"). Husserl calls this dynamic arena of retention, now-point, and protention the "living present." All of our experiences exist in the thickness of this temporal space.

To get a firmer grasp on this idea, we need to be clear about the difference between retention and memory. In memory, Husserl showed, we draw past events that are currently absent from experience into the living present, as when we recall what we had for breakfast two days ago or the name of our third-grade teacher. Quite different from this, retention is not a recovery of absent phenomena into the present but a continuous survival of recent events in the conscious background of lived experience. As I read across a printed line of text, for example, my ability to retain the first words that I read is a necessary condition for my experience of sentence-level meaning. Reading "Jan eats fruit," I must hold "Jan" in the backgrounded retentional portion of the living present as I read "eats" and "fruit." If I do not, "eats" is simply an isolated word, and the sentence-level meaning does not emerge. Retaining the word "Jan" is not the same as remembering it. For the sentence to make sense, I must retain a backgrounded awareness of "Jan" as the temporal focus shifts to "eats." By contrast, to remember "Jan" is to bring that word, which is absent from experience, back from memory into the now-point of the living present, and I only need to do this if I failed to retain it in the first place. Just as retention is not memory, protention is not precognition. On the contrary, it is the dimly apprehended experience of *potential* phenomena—currently unrealized entities situated in the future portion of the living present. Retaining "Jan" and allowing "eats" to emerge into the now-point, an English speaker protends an open anticipation of things that can be eaten (e.g., bread, crackers, "humble pie"), which is in the next moment fulfilled by the word "fruit." Husserl's analysis of the retentional/protentional structure of the living present is foundational for all phenomenological work on time.[17] Within anglophone North American ethnomusicology, Ihde's *Listening and Voice* (1976), which draws on Husserl's ideas about time-consciousness along with the work of other thinkers, has been highly influential.

If Husserl's *Phenomenology of Internal Time-Consciousness* revealed the structure of the living present, Schutz's article "Making Music Together" (1951) offered new insights into the social dimensions of temporality. In this often-cited work, Schutz observes that musical experience is essentially "polythetic," occurring in a temporal, "step-by-step" fashion (90–91). To grasp the musical sense of a written score, for example, one must immerse oneself in the forward-moving flux of the series of notes that the composer specified; in doing so, one recapitulates the same temporal sequence that the composer, or other readers of the score, have formed. This social process aligns one's own experience with that of others in a way that partially transcends the space and time of the immediate situation. While Schutz sets up his discussion with a phenomenology of reading musical scores, the focus of his article is the sociality of time in face-to-face interaction. Here, he contrasts "outer time," our experience of the uniform, measurable flow of physical events, with "inner time," the qualitative feel of duration, such as the lived sense that a process is swift or plodding (88–89). Schutz argues that, in music making, we observe the physical gestures of the other to coordinate our sense of inner time with theirs. This "tuning-in" process constitutes a "We" relationship that is the foundation of live music making and communication in face-to-face interaction more generally. Schutz was a trained pianist and music scholar, and while "Making Music Together" is his best-known work on music, his extensive unpublished writings on the topic gained currency after his death when they were published under the title "Fragments on the Phenomenology of Music" (1976).

The ideas of Husserl and Schutz have been extended by phenomenological ethnomusicologists in a variety of ways. On a basic level, a number of authors have shown that, while the living present is a universal feature of experience, the ways in which events in time are made to cohere within that living present can vary enormously from culture to culture. Ruth Stone's work on Kpelle performance, begun in *Let the Inside Be Sweet* and developed further in *Dried Millet Breaking* (1988), is among the most fully worked-out analyses of the temporal structure of experience in a non-Western music culture, and the central concept in her discussion is the "expandable moment." Where the temporal experiences of Western conservatory music devotees are frequently parsed into units of measurable duration such as phrases or sections, the temporal unit of Kpelle performance is the "moment," which may be inflated to a greater or lesser degree, depending on the improvisatory interactions among the participants. Stone observes that Kpelle sometimes organize time in quantitative ways. However, their dominant manner of structuring the living present is qualitative, and her work shows how the shape of the living present in Kpelle performance is influenced by a wide range of musical devices and abstract organizing principles—from the tendency to fit many small musical motifs together to form coherent wholes, to tropes of exchange (such as call-and-response and interlocking rhythms) and interaction (such as the interplay between a lead vocal part and an underlying ostinato), and from narrative devices in an epic story that construct plot episodes around images of continuous motion to the broad principle of "action without direction" that shapes all dimensions of epic performance events. It is worth emphasizing that the tropes of musical texture that help the performer organize temporal experience are also tropes of social organization. To perform interlocking rhythms, for example, musicians must tightly coordinate their temporal experiences, hearing the flow of notes coming from one's own instrument and those of the other as forming a single unit as it processes through the living present, and Stone devotes substantial attention to the distinctive ways that Kpelle achieve the tuning-in necessary for the Schutzian "We-relationship."[18]

Across cultures, music may have varying forms of rhythmic organization, but it is the interplay among sound structures, the perceptual agency of listeners, their interactive social practices, and the mediating role of past experience (that is to say, culture) that determine the temporal form that any given musical experience will take. Consider the example of a listener hearing a musical passage with a repeating sequence of four drum strokes of equal duration, played at a moderate tempo with a strong dynamic accent on the first beat. Such a part may encourage the listener to hear the music in four-four time—that is, to conjoin together the four beats into a unit as the flow of sounds processes through the living present, with the accented beat protended or retained as the starting point. While listeners trained in the Western conservatory tradition are likely to experience the part in this manner, there are a variety of other ways of grasping the part—for example, actively protending and retaining the accented stroke that appears every two cycles to make a hypermetrical unit appear in the living present, or focusing on the timbral details of each individual stroke and pushing the protended and retained units into the deeper background to diminish in experience the appearance of the metrical block. Like all perception, listening is neither the result of personal whim nor a mechanical registering of objective reality in experience but rather is a social, interactive process by which the person engages with others and the world.

Attending to the interplay of music structure, perceptual agency, social interaction, and culture has been a focus for the phenomenological ethnomusicology of time. Following Ihde's well-known discussion of the phenomenology of multistable visual figures,[19] Friedson (1996), for example, argues that the rhythms of Tumbuka healing rituals have a kind of temporal multistability. Ritual participants can group the music's drum strokes in one of several different units and with varying starting places, and the participant's exercise of perceptual agency here is a central part of the meaning of these performances. Discussing time perception in heavy metal music, Berger (1997) shows how a heavy metal drummer shifts the focus of his attention from the level of eighth notes to that of quarter notes or to the second and fourth beats of the measure to achieve differing goals in performance. Focusing on the eighth notes as they progress through the living present, for example, allows the musician to play with a more smoothly flowing rhythmic feel, while attention to the quarter notes allows the drummer to synchronize his playing more tightly with the other musicians, an approach that may become useful when ensemble coordination is a problem.

The temporal organization of experience has implications for the perception of musical structure in sonic dimensions beyond rhythm, for broader issues of cultural meaning, and for a wide range of related topics. Exploring harmonic rhythm in a song from the death metal repertoire, Berger (1999) shows how both the tonal functions that death metal musicians hear in the music and the very different functions heard by listeners from the Western conservatory tradition depend on the listener's organization of sound in the living present. Finding patterns in metalheads' temporal experiences, Berger argues that their tendency to assemble moments in disjunct, fragmented patterns stems from the emphasis on rage and aggression in this music culture. McGuiness (2013) emphasizes that uncertainty is an essential quality of temporality and, drawing on the work of Sartre ([1943] 1948) and others, builds on this observation to illustrate how indie rockers' organization of musical experience in time connects to themes of shame and vulnerability. Thomas Porcello (1998) richly extends the Schutzian perspective to account for the complexities of media technology in the construction of the We-relationship, and his sophisticated discussion shows how participants who take up differing roles in the production of recorded music may engage with the temporality of recordings in differing ways. Stone (1988) argues that the forms of temporal experience constituted in Kpelle musical performance resonate with their temporal experiences in everyday life and a general cultural tendency toward qualitative time. Drawing on Merleau-Ponty, Rahaim (2012) shows that the phenomenon of melody cannot be reduced to static structures of pitch and reveals how both the static and dynamic dimensions of melodic experience are grounded in the lived body. Friedson (1996) reads Schutz through a Heideggerian lens to argue that the tuning-in process of the We-relationship enables the participants' shared co-presence, without which the ritual could not exist. As we have seen, Savage (2009) forwards this line of thinking when he argues that the significance of music as an ontological category depends on its ability to carve stretches of time out of the mundane flow of everyday temporality and create sharply framed domains of experience.

If Savage emphasizes music's ability to separate events from the flow of mundane temporality, other scholars have explored the ways that the present musical moment can be situated within larger scales of time-consciousness; in so doing, they also emphasize music's connection to worldviews and religious beliefs, a perspective that resonates with Savage's work. To have a sense of overall musical form, for example, one's foregrounded experience of the immediate phrase or section must appear in the living present against more deeply backgrounded protentions and retentions of the piece's other sections (see, e.g., Berger 1999, 237–241). Similar processes situate the present piece within our awareness of the overall music event, and these two examples do not in any way exhaust the range of time scales in which perception is nested. An example of such processes appears in a brief but remarkable article by Paul Humphreys (1991), which describes a monastic ritual in Rinzai Buddhism that is performed at sunrise and before bedtime each day. The ritual is always begun with the performance of a specific rhythmic passage on a heavy wooden board, and Humphreys convincingly argues that, as the day progresses, a deeply backgrounded retention of the morning performance and a deeply backgrounded protention of the evening performance frame the adherents' quotidian experiences. Humphreys provides a detailed analysis of the rhythmic design of the part and the ways in which it encourages the musician to shift from a distanced observation of the drum strokes to an immersion in the act of playing. Humphreys reads this in terms of ideas from Buddhist philosophy about the interdependence of duality and nonduality, and he argues that by framing the day's events with a visceral experience of the shift from duality to nonduality, the ritual helps practitioners deepen their Buddhist perspective. Turning to even larger time scales, Berger's book *Stance* discusses the variety of ways in which the situated moment may be framed by protentions and retentions on the level of calendrical cycles or the broader, open protentions of future phases in the course of a person's life (2010, 84–96). Two more recent publications use the notion of stance to situate temporal experience in the context of wider religious ideals. Shelley (2019) draws broadly on phenomenology and on Berger's work in particular to elaborate the "gospel stance," which he characterizes primarily as a form of musical protention that arises both in relation to the specific musical performance at hand and to the wider expectations that enculturated listener-participants have when experiencing the climactic vamp frequently found in gospel. Masterfully weaving together insights from phenomenology, his own ethnographic work, and music analysis, Shelley provides a dual emphasis on temporality and embodiment, illuminating the experience of the gospel vamp not just as a musical technique or formal category but "as a sonic resource used by many African American Christians to experience with their bodies what they believe in their hearts" (185). Inderjit Kaur (2016) takes up the concept of stance to gain insights into another religious tradition, exploring issues of embodiment and authenticity in the devotional tradition of Sikh *sabad kīrtan* (sung scriptural verse). Drawing on extensive fieldwork, Kaur demonstrates the inadequacy of conceptions of authenticity that treat it as a set of fixed criteria external to lived experience. Instead, Kaur shows how Sikh participants embody multiple forms of authenticity as aspects of their embodied stance, which are shaped in reference to both shared and individual experiences and "anticipated futures" (88).

If the phenomenological literature in philosophy has mapped the space of lived temporality, phenomenological ethnomusicology has illuminated dynamics within that space that could only be revealed by ethnographic methods. In this context, music— which is so often bound up with the temporal—is the ideal topic of such investigations. The studies of music cultures beyond the Western conservatory tradition by Stone,

Friedson, Porcello, Humphreys, Berger, Shelley, Kaur, and others suggest dynamics very different from those that Schutz illuminated, and there is no reason to assume that all of the possibilities of temporal organization have been exhausted. In the broadest sense, what Husserl and Schutz show is that experience is the result of a dynamic synthesis of elements in a temporal "space" that reaches across the now-point and beyond the individual. Like the material systematicity or structural corporeality that emerges in the analysis of embodiment, the temporal dimension of experience likewise involves an intimacy between structure and substance. Each sounding object, each musical form, each social dynamic appears to us within the living present and therefore—at a high level of abstraction—can be described in the phenomenological language that the philosophical tradition provides. But each one of these phenomena also involves a distinctive signature of emergence, persistence, and change, whose specificity eludes a priori explication. This is not because they transcend the living present that Husserl so ably sketched out but because our very understanding of time as an abstract category is always revealed through the particularities of changing and persisting things. Husserl's method of imaginative variation is one way of getting at the possibilities and limits of phenomena, but when we do fieldwork or engage richly with ethnographies, the new worlds that we confront force us to go beyond our past experience and learn new meanings for abstractions like "living present" or "polythetic experience." And because perception is both an openness to the things of the world and an agentive grappling with those things, experience has a plasticity that is unlikely to be exhausted by a library of phenomenological ethnographies, let alone the few shelves that we currently possess. Informed by philosophy and enlivened by ethnography, the phenomenological ethnomusicology of time offers vast new domains to explore.

RESEARCH METHODOLOGY AND THE ETHNOMUSICOLOGICAL PROJECT

For those new to phenomenologically oriented work, the issue of methodology is sometimes a stumbling block. I have my experiences, and you have yours, the newcomer states; there is, therefore, no way to bridge the gap between us, and phenomenological research is impossible. As Berger has argued elsewhere, such a perspective assumes that experience is strictly internal to the person, that each of us is an island of subjectivity separated by the frigid ocean of the physical world (Berger 1999, 230–231). At this point in the discussion, it should be clear why such a perspective is untenable. It is true, of course, that one can never see through the eyes of another person, precisely emulate the acculturation that has shaped their ways of hearing, or form an exact identity between their experience and one's own. But none of these things is necessary for phenomenological research. As Alessandro Duranti so eloquently argued in "Husserl, Intersubjectivity, and Anthropology" (2010), the phenomenological tradition shows us that we live in a shared and public world, that the dynamics of inter-pretation are a general feature of social life, and that our being as social and embodied subjects guarantees a sociability at its core; our intersubjectivity, common hermeneutic predicament, and intercorporeality make us fundamentally social and thus secure the grounding for social research.[20] Exploring that ground is a topic that has been ac-tively pursued by scholars in the phenomenological tradition. With its emphasis on the description of lived experience, the fundamentally methodological utility of the epoché, and the approaches of eidetic description and imaginative variation (Husserl [1913] 1962, section 70; [1931] 1960, section 34; see also Mohanty 1991), phenomenology has always been as much a way of doing philosophy as a body of positive claims and insights. No less than philosophers, the ethnomusicologists inspired by phenome-nology have taken up issues of research methodology; the insights into field research and the interpretation of data that they have developed address issues at the heart of the ethnomusicological project.

The first work on research methods in phenomenological ethnomusicology was Ruth and Verlon Stone's "Event, Feedback, and Analysis: Research Media in the Study of Music Events" (1981). Operationalizing the theoretical framework that Ruth Stone later discussed in *Let the Inside Be Sweet*, Stone and Stone argue for a deep common-ality between the activity of the fieldworker and the research participant that they study: both are engaged in the interpretation of music, and their interpretive practices underlie both music events and ethnographic interviews. In this context, the "feedback interview" is a research technique in which fieldworkers present research participants with mediated representations of past performance events and encourage them to engage in partially shared interpretive practices. Audio and video recordings are the most obvious source material for feedback interviews, but Stone and Stone construe the technique broadly to understand interviews based on field notes or memories as feedback-based research interactions. While Stone and Stone argue that feed-back interviews provide a powerful means for understanding both the meanings that participants find in music and the interpretive process by which those meanings are constituted, they avoid the simplistic view that feedback interviews provide direct or complete access to the world of the other's experience. In contrast, they argue that each kind of media introduces its own dynamics into the research process and shapes the data that emerge there. For example, audio and video recordings offer participants the opportunity to replay short segments of musical interaction and yield subtle, fine-grained interpretations, but that same replay capacity offers the participant a way of lis-tening that is absent from most live events. Using field notes and memories as the basis for feedback interviews does not allow the research participant to engage in the kinds of embodied, interpretive practices of sense perception that audio or video recordings do, but these materials open up other interpretive possibilities, allowing the participant to shift quickly from one event to the next, skip around in time, and organize infor-mation in locally salient ways. Understood in this manner, all interviews are feedback interviews, and Stone and Stone's analysis of this specific research technique ultimately yields general insights into the nature of musical interpretation itself. Thirty-two years after the publication of "Event, Feedback, and Analysis," Ruth Stone updated her work on feedback interviews in an article coauthored by Angela Stone-MacDonald (Stone-MacDonald and Stone 2013) that explores the new interpretive possibilities that digital video recording has enabled.

A recent book chapter by Kati Szego (2021) offers a distinctive new approach to these methods. Seeking to understand the meaning of *hula ku'i* songs for Indigenous youth in Hawai'i, Szego works to move beyond the kinds of interpretations that emerge in traditional interviews in order to shed light on meanings "that are so evanescent, incomplete, automatic or commonplace as to be unremarkable, so powerful or socially contrary as to be unutterable, or so complex as to defy easy expression" (20). To access these meanings, she asked her research participants to engage in an "auto-representational listening–writing exercise" (21). Listening to recordings by themselves, her participants would "reflexively observe their experiences . . . writing down the thoughts, images and sensations that manifested moment by moment[,] . . . jotting keywords and phrases," and drawing pictures (20). Later, they would elaborate on these notes, and all of this would serve as the basis for interview dialogs. In her book chapter, the interpretive work that Szego applies to these sources is highly sophisticated, revealing the diverse ways in which musical meanings are rooted in the body and showing how such embodied meanings are fundamentally social and political. Yielding nuanced readings, Szego's technique offers enormous possibilities for scholars seeking to understand the complexities of lived musical experience.

Perhaps the most frequently cited studies of methodology in phenomenological ethnomusicology are the chapters by Rice and Titon in *Shadows in the Field: New Perspectives for Fieldwork in Ethnomusicology* (Barz and Cooley 2008). Arguing that hermeneutics offers a way to overcome the insider/outsider dichotomy in ethnography, Rice provides an intimate account of his many years of fieldwork on Bulgarian music. The central moment in the narrative comes when Rice had surpassed a beginner's knowledge of the culture's bagpipe tradition but, despite many hours of lessons and interviews, was still unable to master its ornamental techniques, which are iconic of both the music culture and Bulgarian identity. Rice describes how he was finally able to acquire these techniques through a deep bodily immersion in the music, which revealed a set of corporeal practices central to the local experience but never thematized in traditional Bulgarian pedagogical discourse. In a nuanced discussion, Rice argues that having mastered the ornamental techniques, he found himself occupying a strangely liminal position between insider and outsider, musically "native" but not fully "inside" or "outside" the culture. Theorizing these experiences with ideas from Gadamer and Ricoeur, Rice argues that we should not take as our starting point the goal of seeing the world through our interlocutors' eyes but should instead begin from a recognition that both we and they are interpreters of culture. Read through the lens of the hermeneutic circle, our job as fieldworkers is to learn how to place ourselves before the works or traditions of the cultures that we study, allow ourselves to be transformed by this encounter, and enter the world that these works or traditions create. In his research, Rice's focus is still on understanding the experiences of his Bulgarian research participants;

however, the achievement of that task can only ever be partial, and it comes about as much through partially shared musical practices as it does through the elicitation of explicit exegesis in interviews.

Related themes are developed in Titon's chapter, which reviews the history of field methods in ethnomusicology and distinguishes "understanding" from "explanation" as modes of knowledge in social research (2008, 27). While Titon says that both fall within the purview of ethnomusicology, he argues that ethnomusicology should emphasize understanding, which is achieved through shared experiences of music making and the development of close emotional relationships with our research participants. The products of fieldwork—books, articles, recordings—are thus understood as narrativized representations of those relationships, and in a postscript to his chapter in the second edition of *Shadows in the Field*, Titon argues that the social relationships necessary for ethnomusicological understanding must be grounded in a kind of rapport that he defines as "friendship" (37–40).

While they differ in terminology, fieldwork technique, and engagement with the philosophical literature, Stone, Rice, and Titon all see ethnographic research as an interpretive project of partial sharing. These themes are carried forward in differing ways throughout the literature on methodology in phenomenological ethnomusicology. Articulating the hermeneutic approach through specifically Heideggerian language, Friedson takes as his study object the distinctive form of being-in-the-world that his research participants enact in music making. For him, fieldwork is grounded in a participation with the other, which allows the researcher to inhabit, and therefore later interpret, his interlocutor's mode of Dasein. Bakan likewise grounds his research on embodied social interaction with his interlocutors and, as we have seen, provides an alternative reading of the hermeneutic literature to develop new goals for ethnomusicological research. Drawing on ethnography and cognitive science, Tomie Hahn and J. Scott Jordan (2017, 268) argue that research strategies that place participants in novel situations can reveal features of experience that would otherwise remain hidden or abstract. Through a discussion of "banding"—which involves attaching participants together via large rubber bands and leading them in three rounds of activity—they show how the experience of being literally connected in such an unfamiliar way can "shed light on the nature of the prereflexive, ubiquitous intercorporeality" that characterizes our lives. In differing ways, Feld (1996), McIntosh (2006, 2009), Wolf (2006), Clayton (2008), Rice (2008), Titon (2008), Clayton and Leante (2013), McGuiness (2013), and Turino (2014) all argue that musical practice has a richness that is never fully captured by language, and these scholars therefore see interview techniques, exegetic discourse, and historical documents as less significant sources than participant observation (cf. Henderson 1996). McIntosh (2006, 2009) and Stone ([1982] 2010) emphasize the situated nature of fieldwork, while Stone and Stone (1981), Berger (1999), Rice (2008), and Titon (2008) all underline its dialogic qualities. These themes are also explored in an article by Deborah Justice and Fredara M. Hadley (2015), who use Berger's notion of stance to argue that new opportunities for ethnographic understandings emerge when fieldwork is pursued by teams of researchers.

Despite the common emphasis on partial sharing—of meaning, of the interpretive predicament, of modes of being-in-the-world—phenomenologically oriented ethnomusicologists approach field research in a variety of ways. Berger's work, for example, has argued that the emphasis on empathetic engagement with research participants that phenomenological ethnomusicologists so prize does not preclude the use of critical perspectives (1999, 251–297). Drawing on ideas from Sartre and the Marxist tradition of social thought, Berger observes that the power relations in which our everyday lives are situated shape both our experiences and the interpretations we make of them, often in ways that we do not fully understand. It is, of course, patronizing to assume that our research participants are little more than culture dopes, marionettes whose strings are pulled by the puppet masters of race, class, or gender. But it is also problematic, Berger argues, to assume that our research participants have a complete understanding of their experiences or that our research participants' interpretive processes are unaffected by the power relations in which they are situated. Every ethnographic encounter requires its own field techniques and styles of writing, and not all analysis must take politics or structures of inequality as its center of gravity. But in many situations, it is difficult to understand musical experience without exploring its connection to power, and the participants themselves do not always possess a clear or complete understanding of that connection. One technique for addressing such situations, Berger suggests (1999), is critical ethnographic dialogue. Here, multiple conflicting perspectives can come together; scholars and research participants explore the complex, often difficult politics of musical experience and social life; and interpretive closure is not always reached. This technique will not work in every field situation, but in many contexts it offers an opportunity for insights that approaches based solely on empathetic engagement might not uncover. (Silverstein [2019] and Cannon [2020], discussed further below, also examine the politics of ethnographic research.)

Methodology is theory operationalized, and the discussion in this section only begins to examine the complex issues of theory and method that phenomenological ethnomusicologists have taken up. As we suggested previously, a number of scholars (Becker 2004; Clayton 2008; Clayton and Leante 2013) have offered ways of bringing phenomenology into conversation with approaches from cognitive science and psychology, while work by Matthew Sansom (2005), Ruth Herbert (2011b, 2011a), and Robert Faulkner (2013) illustrates how interpretive phenomenological analysis (a research methodology from the discipline of psychology) may articulate with approaches from ethnomusicology. The debate among Becker (2009), Titon (2009), and Bakan (2009) in the journal *Ethnomusicology* illustrates the diversity of perspectives that exist regarding the relationship between approaches from the humanities and those from the social sciences, as well as the role of phenomenology in ethnomusicological research. While phenomenology is a body of thought that can be used to examine the full range of topics in ethnomusicology, many scholars in our field have combined ideas from this tradition with those from other movements in Western philosophy or social theory to develop new syntheses and craft new perspectives (e.g., Feld 1996; Rice 2001, 2003; Turino 2014; Novak and Sakakeeny 2015).[21] Turning to broader contexts, a number of researchers in our discipline have linked phenomenological approaches with ideas from non-Western philosophies to speak to problems of interpretation, theory, and method (e.g., Humphreys 1991; Slawek 1996; Weiss 2003; Ho 2009). As many scholars have observed, methodological discussions inevitably raise issues of ethics and politics—in the research encounter and beyond—and these are the topics to which we now turn.

MUSIC AND POWER

From Sartre's longstanding commitment to Marxism, to Simone de Beauvoir's ([1949] 2010) foundational work on gender and Frantz Fanon's ([1952] 2008) phenomenology of race, thinkers in the phenomenological movement have long made contributions to political philosophy, and a variety of ethnomusicologists have used these ideas to understand the politics of culture and the role that music plays in wider dynamics of power. In recent years, political concerns have come to the fore for a range of phenomenologically oriented ethnomusicologists, and two of the most significant inspirations for their work have been Fanon and Sara Ahmed.

Across the humanities, Fanon is most frequently understood as a postcolonial theorist; this characterization is certainly not wrong, but Fanon must also be understood as a nuanced phenomenological thinker. His landmark book *Black Skin, White Masks* ([1952] 2008) develops powerful insights into racialized subjectivity and the embodied experience of oppression it produces, and his work has led to a vital stream of phenomenological scholarship on the topic of race (e.g., Johnson [1976] 1993; Slaughter 1977; Alcoff 1999; Macey 1999; Trotter 1999; Salamon 2006; Mahendran 2007; Zeiler 2013). Fanon is discussed in detail in David Garcia's 2017 book *Listening for Africa*, a sophisticated study of the ways in which discourses of modernity and race have shaped key figures and historical moments in the music of Africa and its diaspora during the twentieth century. Set among a varied array of theoretical sources, Fanon's ideas not only serve as a crucial lens through which Garcia interprets cultural and political history; they also are an active force *within* that history, as Fanon had a wide influence on the politics and culture of the decolonizing world at mid-century and after. Drawing on Fanon's notion of disalienation and ideas from the philosopher Günther Anders ([1937] 2009), who studied with both Husserl and Heidegger, Garcia shows how a range of actors—musicians, dancers, researchers, and writers—sought to overcome the stultifying effect on musical and social experience of historical narratives that positioned music from Africa and its diaspora as an expression of the primitive. Arguing that "Fanon theorized the way for racialized black individuals . . . to take action not only in but *upon* the present" (175, italics in the original) and drawing on Veit Erlmann's (2010) readings of Anders, Garcia makes connections between the lived time of musical events and the long-scale temporality of colonialism's pernicious narratives about modernity. The book is filled with insights about race and music that deserve to be carried forward by ethnomusicologists interested in a wide range of historical periods and social contexts.[22]

(For an important discussion of Anders's phenomenology of musical listening and the pivotal role that it played in his philosophy of technology, as well as wider debates in mid-century Continental philosophy, see Babich [2021]; see also Erlmann [2010].)

Although Sara Ahmed has herself contributed to phenomenological work on race (2007), her 2006 book *Queer Phenomenology* has had the most significant impact on ethnomusicologists. While the book offers powerful ideas about gender and sexuality, Ahmed construes the notion of queerness broadly to develop wide ranging perspectives on the nature of power and social life. Starting from Husserl's observations about the body's necessarily oriented posture toward the things of the world, Ahmed shows how our situated conduct and social experience are shaped by power and the many ways that queer lives are lived against the grain of normative orientations. Ethnomusicologists who draw on her work have developed this viewpoint in important and provocative ways. For example, Alexander M. Cannon's (2020) chapter in the edited book *Queering the Field* (Barz and Cheng 2020) uses autoethnographic reflections on the author's experiences as a gay man to shed new light on ethnographic methods. Building on Ahmed's work, Cannon shows how the notions of queerness and queered orientations can sensitize the ethnographer to the way that the diverse practices and experiences found in their fieldsites may align with dominant orientations or work against them. The queered field methods that Cannon proposes thus help the fieldworker to resist the colonial impulse in ethnography to know and master the other, and the chapter develops a powerful theoretical apparatus around the ideas of "personhood, oppression, transgression, performance, and fieldwork" (125). Tes Slominski's contribution to the book (2020) draws on Ahmed's *Queer Phenomenology* and her writings on happiness (Ahmed 2010) to offer critical perspectives on ethnomusicology as a disciplinary formation. In an evocative ethnography of Syrian *dabke* that issues a powerful call for scholars in sound studies to attend to the fundamentally intersensorial nature of music, Shayna Silverstein (2019) uses Ahmed to highlight the opportunities for new insights that *dis*orientation affords fieldworkers. Less concerned with field methods than Cannon or Silverstein, Rachel Beckles Willson (2019) takes Ahmed's notion of orientation in a different direction, showing the complex ways in which representations of and musical practices with the *ʿūd* serve to establish orientations toward home for Palestinians living in Palestine or its diaspora, and her subtle analysis urges us to understand such orienting work as an ongoing, never completed process. Returning to the concern with sexuality, Stephen Amico engages ideas from Ahmed and Merleau-Ponty to illuminate the "corporeal connections between gay men and popular music in post-Soviet Russia" (2014, 28). Amico's dynamic combination of ethnography and theory—"a theoretically informed ethnography, or an ethnographically based theorization" (23)—similarly refuses to privilege either music or sexuality indeed, his study shows the many ways that each becomes imbricated with the other in and through the body.

Fanon and Ahmed are not the only sources for political work in phenomenological ethnomusicology. Armelle Gaulier and Denis-Constant Martin (2017) use Ricoeur's ideas on cultural appropriation and memory to understand the impact of the music of New Year's celebrations in Cape Town on South Africa's race politics. The primary frame for Michael Frishkopf's book chapter "Music for Global Human Development" (2021) comes from Jürgen Habermas ([1981] 1987), the second-generation Frankfurt school theorist who, drawing on Husserl and others, sought to understand how communicative action occurs within the horizon of a lifeworld and how such lifeworlds can be "colonized," as he put it, by an economic and political "system." In the context of Habermas's work, Alfred Schutz (e.g., [1932] 1967, 1951, 1964) and Martin Buber ([1937] 1958) provide Frishkopf with tools for understanding how musical practices and applied ethnomusicology projects can bolster a community's lifeworld and foster a humanizing politics.[23] Related themes can be found in Markus Verne's exploration of the existential projects of heavy metal musicians in Madagascar (2015) and Roberto Rizzo's study of the place of musical literacy in the performance traditions of Java and the experiences of students in an arts institute there (2020). In differing ways, these authors combine ideas from phenomenology's philosophical tradition with those from phenomenologically oriented work in anthropology to critique deterministic visions of culture and highlight the role that agency, situated conduct, and the constitution of lived experience play in the social dynamics of music. In a range of other studies (Gray 2007; White 2014; Fairfield 2019; Houston 2020; MacDonald 2020), phenomenological perspectives on musical meaning and musical practice are combined with ideas from other intellectual traditions to shed light on questions of power in a given social world. In all of this work, phenomenology offers ways of connecting larger social forces and their relations of power to lived experience and illustrates the important place that music can play there.

Another strand of politically oriented ethnomusicological work engages especially with the ideas of Emmanuel Levinas, who is famous for his emphasis on the primacy of the encounter with the other and the infinite ethical and political demands that such encounters produce. David McDonald (2013) draws on Levinas's concept of an "ethics of responsibility" to explore the possibilities for non-violent social relations entailed by Israeli-Palestinian hip-hop. He outlines an "ethics of a shared human vulnerability" based on Levinas's philosophy, arguing that the recognition of the other through music provides an opportunity to transcend discourses of exile and nationalism (2013, 78). Levinasian ethics go beyond simply creating imperatives for the self, for as McDonald points out, the self arises and develops in relation to its encounter with the other. Rahaim (2017, 2019) similarly takes up Levinas to think about the political necessity of openness to the other and the incomplete nature of our social encounters. Noting that critiques of discourses of otherness often focus on the role that this notion plays in justifying political oppression—the chapter cites Edward Said (1979) and Johannes Fabian (1983) as prominent voices in this regard—Rahaim argues that the attempt to collapse otherness into sameness is also politically dangerous. In place of the "metaphysics of unity" that presumes the joys (and ethical and political rightness) of musical participation, Rahaim proposes instead "a metaphysics of alterity [that] attends to what is lost when we dissolve separation into comprehensive, finite unity" (2017, 23). As Rahaim makes clear, the infinity attributed to the other by Levinas is not a mark of their superiority but of the inexhaustible nature of ethical encounter. Here, we enter into "the infinite play of [imperfect] rapport," never approaching "a perfected comprehension" (23). Rahaim's recent book on a diverse array of vocal practices in North India furthers these Levinasian insights, considering the degrees of distance and otherness that persist even in close (often formative) relationships, like those between students and their teachers or devotional singers and their patrons (2021, 176, 208). In a different vein, Jeff R. Warren (2021) builds on the work of Levinas and also that of Alphonso Lingis (1998) to explore the connections between ethical action and the sound of contemporary Christian worship music, focusing especially on the effect he calls "shimmer" in the music of the many ensembles connected to Hillsong Church (Hillsong Worship, Hillsong United, Hillsong Young and Free). Putting these phenomenological sources into conversation with voices from Object-Oriented Ontology (e.g., Harman 2005; Bogost 2012), Warren expands Levinas's ethical concern with relations between human beings to consider relations with the divine and with the non-human world.

While philosophers in the phenomenological tradition have certainly made important contributions to critical, emancipatory politics, we would be remiss if we did not acknowledge the regressive and painful elements of this history. For example, Edmund Husserl treated Edith Stein in a sexist manner (McDaniel 2016, 195); the racist elements of Sartre's thinking were critiqued by Fanon ([1952] 2008); and recent scholarship has examined how Levinas's philosophy—often celebrated by ethicists and postcolonial scholars—contains a troubling racism (McGettigan 2006; Moten 2018). Perhaps the most disturbing figure in phenomenology's history, however, is Heidegger.

The simple facts of the situation are concerning enough: it has long been known, for example, that Heidegger joined the Nazi party on May 1, 1933; served from April 1933 to April 1934 as rector of the University of Freiburg, where he implemented Berlin's program of Nazifying the university; and remained a member of the party in good standing until its dissolution at the end of World War II (Knowles 2020a). While scholarly opinion varies on the topic of Heidegger's relationship to Nazism (Wheeler 2020), the philosopher Adam Knowles convincingly shows that Heidegger eagerly promoted the Nazification of the German academy (2020a, see especially the prologue and epilogue) and that this work was an outgrowth of his larger philosophy of administration (Knowles 2020b). Further, as Hans Dieter Zimmermann demonstrates, Heidegger resigned from his position as rector and discontinued his ambitious project of developing a centralized, national academy for the philosophical training of all professors in Germany not, as he would later claim, to distance himself from Nazi ideology but because the university board was not ideological enough (Zimmermann 2005, 64–65). Since the second half of the twentieth century, scholars have argued about the role of fascism and antisemitism in Heidegger's thought; however, the defense of his work became more difficult in 2014, when some of Heidegger's *Black Notebooks*—a set of journals he began writing in the 1930s—first began to be published. (The notebooks have been released in a number of different volumes; see, for example, Heidegger 2015, 2016.) The *Black Notebooks* not only espouse an intense antisemitism but make clear that this hatred was deeply embedded in his philosophy. There, Heidegger elaborates the view that the manipulative, technological society of modern Europe came from a distinctly Jewish form of existence, and he characterizes the Holocaust as the ultimate outcome of this way of being. As a result, Heidegger depicted the Holocaust as the "self-annihilation of the Jews" (Heidegger 2015, 20).

Given Heidegger's vast influence on contemporary thought, working out the implications of these revelations remains a complex and important task, and in the years since the first publications of the *Black Notebooks*, scholars have continued to explore and debate this topic (e.g., Mitchell 2015; Farin and Malpas 2016). In recounting this history, we do not mean to suggest that Heidegger's ideas cannot be used in productive and valuable ways or to imply that anyone who cites Heidegger or draws upon his work is an antisemite. Indeed, Knowles himself has argued that the way forward for Continental theory is not to ignore Heidegger but to subject his work to a critical appraisal (Knowles 2020a). While no scholar in the tradition is as fundamentally compromised as Heidegger, it behooves us to read *all* theoretical writings with critical eyes, drawing on the insights of past scholars but also addressing their oversights and misdeeds, and the harms they may entail.

Conclusion

For many in our field, understanding the musical experiences of the people with whom we work is at the heart of the ethnomusicological project. Phenomenology offers a unique set of tools for pursuing that project. Attending to culture but sensitive to agency, deeply engaged with questions of ontology and metaphysics but alive to the most pragmatic and contingent elements of everyday life, phenomenology offers a way of making connections with our research participants, respecting and exploring our differences while still keeping sight of our common predicaments of interpretation, embodiment, and power. From its earliest roots in the philosophical phenomenologies of music, through the pathbreaking work of the 1980s-era ethnomusicological ethnographers, to contemporary developments in the field, those grounded in phenomenology have studied music as a unique and significant element in experience and also as a site for investigating the broader dynamics of social life.

In the last forty years, the range of study objects that ethnomusicologists in the tradition have explored has been broad. But this work has only begun to examine the variety of topics that are open to phenomenological investigation, and many areas of research remain unexamined. Husserl intended phenomenology to be a foundation for all forms of inquiry, and the scope of the tradition is and should be as broad as the scope of human experience. In that spirit, we want to suggest that the bounty of microsocial analyses in our field may have obscured the fact that the macrosocial world is equally amenable to phenomenological investigation. Here, we do not merely wish to indicate that situated conduct and lived experience entail a profound politics or are fundamentally shaped by larger social forces, though this is certainly true. Rather, we want to suggest that large-scale social phenomena *themselves* can be explored with the tools of phenomenology. That some may be surprised by such a claim is understandable. For example, Alfred

Schutz's *Phenomenology of the Social World* ([1932] 1967) in particular and phenomeno-logical social theory in general were given short shrift in the canonical early statements of practice theory by Anthony Giddens ([1976] 1993, 38) and Pierre Bourdieu (1977, 3–5). These writers dismiss phenomenology for reducing the social world to mere sub-jective impression, but as C. Jayson Throop and Keith M. Murphy have shown (2002), such criticisms conflate phenomenology with naïve subjectivism, which, as we have suggested throughout, is not tenable (see also Berger 2010; Rahaim 2012). As a result, phenomenology offers new possibilities to scholars interested in the macrosocial life of music. Taking a phenomenological approach to studying a sector of the music industry, for example, an ethnomusicologist would begin by investigating how people inhabit various institutional roles (musician, manager, promoter, etc.) and would continue by examining how their actions emerge within and respond to a horizon of other actors and institutions. The research would then work outward toward a phenomenology of those institutions, understanding them as the outcome of the intended and unin-tended practices of individual agents. Such work would seek to show how power rela-tions are both established and resisted by the constitutive practices of their participants. In so doing, it could advance the approach of practice theory by giving the theoretical building blocks of that tradition a firmer ontological foundation in lived experience.

Discussing Husserl's preface to the 1931 English translation of his foundational study *Ideas I*, Marianne Sawicki (n.d.) recounts the sense of breathtaking wonder that Husserl describes at having discovered the possibilities of phenomenological research. Husserl likens the new domain of philosophy that he had uncovered to a "new Atlantis," a "new continent," and ultimately a "promised land" (Husserl 1931, 15, 21, quoted in Sawicki n.d.). While many in contemporary scholarship do not share Husserl's view of phenom-enology as the investigation of transcendental subjectivity, the idea of a return to expe-rience has lost none of its power or awe-inspiring force. Returning to experience with eyes and ears vivified by the phenomenological project, we take the things most readily at hand as our object of study. Seen and heard in this new way, the things of the world retain their mundane reality, even as we go beyond that mundanity to wonder at their paradoxical nature. The world of experience is a world of things—as autonomous and independent from us as we know them to be, and yet always *present for us*, here and now, within the ambit of conscious life. The world of experience *is* a world of others—as separate from ourselves as our everyday intuition tells us they are and yet, through their very alterity, forming the foundation of sociality and thus the possibility of our own subjectivity.

If phenomenology opens us up to the paradoxical wonder of experience, then phe-nomenological ethnomusicology begins by drawing our attention to a subset of that experiential world, opening us up to new possibilities for insight even as it sharpens our focus. From the tedium of programmed music in retail environments to the most powerful experiences in a concert or between two earbuds, the things that are called music are vital study objects—both as elements of experience that contribute important threads to the texture of everyday life and as phenomena that stir our deepest passions. Of equal significance, the study of musical experience serves as an entry point to the rest of the social universe, a starting place for inquiry that draws the researcher beyond the music event to areas as diverse and significant as the affective life of capitalism, the neurobiology of trance, the nature of time, or the paradoxes of embodiment. As either an end or a starting place, music is therefore a vital object of study. In this context, phenomenological ethnomusicology continues to offer a profound potential for plumbing its depths and tracing out its connections.

Acknowledgments

We are grateful to Peter Verdin, who served as a research assistant during an early stage of this work, and Matthew Rahaim, who identified the useful source by Kris McDaniel.

Notes

1. Drawing boundaries of intellectual movements and academic disciplines is, of course, a complex and fraught task. Here, we focus our attention on works within the discipline of ethnomusicology that either draw directly on writings from phenomenology's philosophical tradition or ones that engage phenomenological ideas developed in fields adjacent to ethnomusicology, such as anthropology. Of course, many other intellectual traditions deal with phenomenology's hallmark concerns (e.g., embodiment, temporality, and experience). In general, we have avoided discussing such work, though not because we think that it is not valuable. (Clearly, the phenomenological tradition does not have a monopoly on philosophical insights!) However, citing such work without discussing the differences between phenomenological approaches and those from other traditions would run the risk of obscuring meaningful theoretical differences, and consistently analyzing the relationship between phenomenological and non-phenomenological approaches would be a massive undertaking and well beyond the scope of this chapter. That said, in notes 2 and 21 we briefly discuss the history and boundaries of phenomenology within philosophy.

   This chapter primarily addresses writing published before March of 2021. Although we have sought to discuss a variety of sources in phenomenological ethnomusicology, we do not claim to present a comprehensive review of this literature. For an overview of the contributions that the chapters in this volume make to contemporary phenomenological scholarship on music and culture, see the volume's preface. As we are completing this text, Jonathan De Souza, Benjamin Steege, and Jessica Wiskus are preparing *The Oxford Handbook of the Phenomenology of Music*, a project based in the disciplines of music theory, musicology, cognitive science, and philosophy, which complements our more ethnomusicological and ethnographic volume in important ways.

2. Like a visiting dignitary at a formal reception, phenomenology has been "introduced" many times, and the anglophone scholar interested in making a first approach to this literature often has difficulties selecting a starting point from among the many English-language works that seek to familiarize readers with this tradition. A highly readable introduction to phenomenology, which explains its basic concepts in plain language, is by Danish philosopher Dan Zahavi ([2003] 2018). Sophisticated and accessible, monographs by Don Ihde (1986) and Michael Hammond, Jane Howarth, and Russell Keat (1991) are two of the best introductions

to the tradition as a whole. The articles on phenomenology in the *Stanford Encyclopedia of Phenomenology* (Zalta 2022) and the *Encyclopedia of Phenomenology* (Embree et al. 1997) are useful reference works, while studies by Erazim Kohák (1978), James Schmidt (1985), and Hubert Dreyfus (1991) provide valuable English-language discussions of key works and thinkers. A helpful article by Lawrence Ferrara and Elizabeth A. Behnke in the *Encyclopedia of Phenomenology* (1997) offers a history of phenomenologies of music, primarily from the fields of philosophy and musicology. While Ferrara and Behnke do not write about the discipline of ethnomusicology, their discussion traces a history that develops in the direction of a rich understanding of the fundamentally social, cultural, and embodied nature of musical experience. Such a perspective is consonant with the approaches of the ethnomusicological tradition.

In a variety of works, ethnomusicologists have discussed the relationship between phenomenology and ethnomusicology or the history of their own engagement with the phenomenological tradition. For example, the first edition of Ruth Stone's *Theory for Ethnomusicology* (2008) includes a helpful discussion of the role of phenomenology in the founding of ethnomusicology's predecessor discipline, comparative musicology, as well as a broader exploration of the relationship between phenomenology and ethnomusicology. The link between phenomenology and comparative musicology, as well as the history of phenomenological thinking about musical temporality in ethnomusicology and other fields, is discussed with nuance in a book chapter by Stephen Blum (2016). A passage in the "Further Comments" that Charles Keil and Steven Feld provide after the "First Dialog" in their often-cited book *Music Grooves* (1994, 47) explains the role of phenomenology in the development of their thinking and offers a long list of citations to works in the tradition that they found especially useful. A similar aim animates the listing of sources in Bakan (1999, 336n11), while more recent works by Feld (2015, 2017) and Rice and Romero (2015) offer further reflections on their authors' engagements with the tradition. In differing ways, Stone ([1982] 2010, 165–176), Berger (1999, 19–25; 2010, vii–xix, 137–139nn6–7), Rice (2008), and Titon (2008) offer perspectives on the development of a phenomenological ethnomusicology. The many articles in the *Sage International Encyclopedia of Music and Culture* that discuss phenomenology (Berger 2019; Garlitz 2019; Pieridou Skoutella 2019a, 2019b; Savage 2019) attest to the importance that this intellectual tradition has had for the discipline.

3. For perspectives on the history of phenomenology, see Spiegelberg and Schuhmann ([1960] 1994), Hammond, Howarth, and Keat (1991), Embree and Mohanty (1997), and Smith (2013).

4. See Porcello (1998) for a sophisticated ethnomusicological critique of Ingarden's phenomenology of music.

5. For a more recent phenomenological discussion of the role of cuing in the constitution of music events, here in the context of American free jazz, see Steinbeck (2008).

6. For a brief summary of the varied meanings and uses of the hermeneutic circle, see Grondin (2016).

7. For a rich review of the literature on the ontology of music developed in analytic philosophy, a Western philosophical tradition that is usually seen as distinct from phenomenology, see Davies (2020).

8. This construction is influenced by ideas from the practice theory of the early Anthony Giddens ([1976] 1993, 1979, 1984) and Pierre Bourdieu (1977), a perspective that Berger has explored throughout his work (e.g., Berger 1999, 2010). It is worth emphasizing here that

the interplay of practice and context is not limited to culture or the micro-social realm. As the classical works of practice theory have shown, macro-social formations (e.g., music cultures, musical institutions like conservatories or corporations, and other large-scale social phenomena like states and societies) can be productively understood as the outcome of the intended and unintended consequences of situated practice. We return to these themes in the final section of this chapter.

9. On the problem of motion in musical time, see also Stone (1988). For alternative approaches to gesture in Indian classical music, see Clayton (2008) and Clayton and Leante (2013).

10. Grounded in rich ethnographic descriptions and deep analysis, Denise Gill's (2017) work on nostalgia in contemporary Turkish classical music and Kyra Gaunt's (2006) erudite and passionate study of Black girls' musical games powerfully recount the experiences and ideologies of the body in their fieldsites. These works avoid the danger of essentialism that could come from a normative reading of Merleau-Ponty or Schmitz, and they have much to offer ethnomusicologists who see themselves as grounded in the phenomenological tradition.

11. In the early twentieth century, scholars in the phenomenological tradition developed an interest in issues of technology (e.g., Heidegger [1927] 1996) and the relationship between philosophy and science (Husserl [1936] 1970). While the dominant voices of Science and Technology Studies (STS) are often understood as opposed to phenomenology (Latour and Woolgar [1979] 1986; Latour 1988; Haraway 1991), since the late 1970s Ihde (1979; 1990) has been a leading voice and creative (if often critical) phenomenological contributor to the burgeoning field of philosophy of technoscience and STS. Ihde's turn to "postphenomenology," which he defines primarily as a "non-essentialist" and "non-foundationalist" pairing of phenomenology with American neo-pragmatism (Ihde 2008), has brought aspects of phenomenological thought into ever closer conversation with areas of STS more aligned with sociology and Actor-Network Theory (see Latour 2005). This sociological strain of STS has often opposed phenomenology on the grounds of its perceived overemphasis on subjectivity (Selinger 2006), and, indeed, it was Ihde's own concerns about the potential privileging of subjectivity and phenomenology's tendency toward "foundationalism" that spurred his postphenomenological turn. For a brief overview of this disciplinary development and a critical assessment of Heidegger's treatment of technology, see Ihde (2010).

12. Schmitz's main oeuvre, his ten-volume *System of Philosophy*, was published between 1964 and 1980. For an introduction to his work, written by the philosopher himself in 2009 and translated into English ten years later, see Schmitz ([2009] 2019).

13. For an overview of the ethnomusicological scholarship on this topic, see the introduction to the edited volume *Music as Atmosphere: Collective Feelings and Affective Sounds* (Riedel and Torvinen 2020).

14. A unique and insightful contribution to the phenomenological scholarship on reflexivity and sound can be found in a 2021 article by Ryan McCormack on issues of aurality in the COVID-19 pandemic (2021). In section three of the essay (pp. 8–12), McCormack describes Husserl's notion of the inner voice and Derrida's famous critique of Husserl, and he sets this debate in the context of recent work by Alexandru Ovidiu Gacea on Plato's ideas about the "koinonic" nature of "internal dialog" (2019). McCormack argues that the conditions of self-isolation imposed by the pandemic have drawn new attention to role of the inner voice in social life, and popular conceptions of this phenomenon in Western culture have come to echo the perspectives of the philosophers whose ideas he rehearses.

Although the inner voice is no longer seen as a universal and stable foundation for individual subjectivity, it remains important. In popular discourse, the inner voice has come to be seen as contingent, relational, and paradoxical, and it affords the person complex relations with others and the larger world. McCormack sees this conception of the inner voice as leading to a new cultural emphasis on listening, which he connects especially to the Black Lives Matter movement and the wider racial politics of the contemporary moment.

15. Employing the metaphysics and semiotics of Charles Sanders Peirce, Thomas Turino (2014) explores related issues. See note 21 below.

16. Musical involvement is closely related to the topic of trance, and phenomenological ethnomusicologists have discussed this theme extensively. Friedson's discussion of trance as a form of Heideggerian "being away" (2009, 16–17, 35–37) is among the most sophisticated examinations of that issue in the scholarly literature, phenomenological or otherwise. For other studies of trance in phenomenological ethnomusicology, see Kapchan (2009, 2013), Sager (2009), and Simonett (2009, 2014). Phenomenology is combined with approaches from the social sciences in Judith Becker's celebrated *Deep Listeners: Music, Emotion, and Trancing* (2004), while a related configuration of methods underlies Ruth Herbert's important *Everyday Music Listening: Absorption, Dissociation, and Trancing* (2011a; see also Herbert 2011b). On music and disembodiment in situations other than trance, see Humphreys (1991), Henderson (1996), Berger (1999), Rahaim (2012), and McGuiness (2013). For phenomenological work on embodiment and place, see Feld (1996), Wolf (2006), and Conn (2012).

17. Ferrara and Behnke (1997) observe that in *The Phenomenology of Internal Time-Consciousness* ([1929] 1964), Husserl himself illustrated the structure of the living present with musical examples, and their article summarizes his discussions of protention and retention in the perception of melody, as well as his broader insights into the problem of the identity of works of music.

18. In "Making Music Together," Schutz frequently talks about the musical "We." The term "We-relationship" comes from the English translation of his *Phenomenology of the Social World* ([1932] 1967, 164). For other applications of Schutz's ideas in ethnomusicology, see Feld ([1988] 1994), Racy (1991), Friedson (1996), Porcello (1998), Shannon (2003), Rahaim (2012), Thacker (2012), and Clinton and Wallach (2016). See Wolf (2006) for a critique of Schutz's ideas of inner and outer time.

19. Multistable figures are illustrations that can be viewed in more than one way, such as Rubin's goblet (a drawing that is typically seen as either a vase or two silhouettes facing each other) and the Necker cube (a drawing that can be seen either as a cube viewed from below or a cube viewed from above).

20. The same conclusion can be reached by pressing the skeptical implications of the newcomer's objection to their logical conclusion. Thus, it is certainly true that we can never have a direct and perfectly repeatable access to the experience of the other in all of their particularity. However, we can never have that kind of direct and perfectly repeated access to our own experience either, since memory does not return our past experiences to us in exactly the same form that they originally appeared. If it can only be said that we know another's experience if we have direct and perfectly repeatable access to it, then our past selves are as unknowable to us as the other, and we are locked in a solipsistic now, truly knowing only our most immediate thoughts. This is, of course, an untenable position. If perfectly repeatable experience is a chimera, then we are forced to rethink the nature of experience itself and with it the metaphor of subjective islands adrift in an ocean of

objective reality, upon which the newcomer's objections to phenomenological methods are based.

21. Of particular note here is Thomas Turino's 2014 article, "Peircean Thought as Core Theory for a Phenomenological Ethnomusicology." In the piece, Turino reviews ideas from Charles Sanders Peirce's ontology and semiotics, discusses selected works of phenomenological ethnomusicology (most prominently, ones by Friedson and Titon), and makes a passionate argument for the utility of Peirce for research on music and culture. The piece is a wide-ranging and insightful work of theory and has drawn significant attention. In the article, Turino contrasts what he calls "Peircean" and "Continental" phenomenology, and given the way the text is framed, readers may come away from it with the impression that Peirce was a part of the phenomenological movement or that his work was, in a straightforward way, a branch of this tradition. The historical reality is different from this and much more complex.

As David Woodruff Smith (2013) has observed, the word "phenomenology" appeared in print as early as the 1730s and was used by a variety of writers in the eighteenth and nineteenth centuries. Husserl later adopted the term as the name of a new philosophy he was developing, which he intended as a decisive break from all forms of past thought. His *Logical Investigations*, published in two volumes in 1900 and 1901 (Husserl [1900–01] 2001), is widely understood as the founding document of the phenomenological movement. In our experience, the unmarked term "phenomenology" is generally used by contemporary philosophers in anglophone North America to refer to the intellectual tradition that flowed from this work. In contrast, Peirce was one of the founders of the philosophical school known as "pragmatism" (or, to use the term he later coined to distinguish his work from that of William James, "pragmaticism"; see Legg and Hookway [2021]). During a brief but significant period of his career, Peirce used the word "phenomenology" to refer to a form of research he was developing. After a few years, however, he rejected the word "phenomenology" and replaced it with a number of new terms, such as "phaneroscopy" and "phenoscopy" (Spiegelberg and Schuhmann [1960] 1994, 16; Short 2007, 61; Stjernfelt 2007, 143). Peirce scholars sometimes use the expression "Peircean phenomenology" to talk about this work, although in his influential *Pierce's Theory of Signs*, T. L. Short actively chose to use the term "phaneroscopy" to describe this research, so as to differentiate Peirce's thought from that of Husserl and his followers (2007, 61).

More important than the terminological issue is the historical relationship between Husserl and Peirce and the philosophical content of their work. A number of writers have shown that Husserl and Peirce had only a slight familiarity with each other's writings (see Spiegelberg 1956, 183; Spiegelberg and Schuhmann [1960] 1994, 16–18; Short 2007, 61; Stjernfelt 2007, 142, 144). Working in almost complete independence of each other, Husserl and Peirce developed distinct systems of thought with distinct intellectual apparatuses. While a number of writers have observed that the work of the two philosophers resonates together in interesting ways, scholars differ on the extent of the compatibility of their ideas. (See Berger's 2015 edition of this chapter for a more detailed exploration of this issue.) However one interprets the literature on the relationship between the two, it is clear that any scholar seeking to find similarities in the thought of Husserl and Peirce is only able to do so with substantial philosophical and historical effort—that is, by building bridges between their very different concepts, arguments, and systems. Framing its discussion in terms of an unproblematized contrast between "Peircean" and "Continental" phenomenologies, Turino's article might give some readers the impression that Peirce's work was, in a simple and direct manner, part of the phenomenological movement or one branch of this tradition. Our aim in this discussion is neither to suggest that Peirce's work isn't useful or that making connections between Peirce and the phenomenological movement is not productive but rather to clarify the intellectual history at play here. We hope that noting the distinctions between these two thinkers and their respective traditions might prove useful to both those seeking to find linkages between them and those who would cultivate productive points of debate.

22. David Garcia (2017) also gives a nuanced discussion of the mid-twentieth-century reception of mambo, which shows how Gabriel Garcia Marquez and the Venezuelan poet Juan Liscano drew on ideas from Sartre's existentialism to represent music as an avenue for those living in an alienated modernity to recover repressed aspects of the "primitive." Of course, Garcia does not endorse this view but reads it as yet another way in which music raced as Black was caught up in colonial narratives about modernity and culture.

23. Grounded in communication studies, Patrick Burkart's trenchant discussion of the colonization of the lifeworld by the global music industry (2010) offers another route to Habermasian insights about the social life of music.

Works Cited

Abels, Birgit. 2018. "Music, Affect and Atmospheres: Meaning and Meaningfulness in Palauan Omengeredakl." *International Journal of Traditional Arts* 2: 1–17.

Abels, Birgit. 2020. "Bodies in Motion: Music, Dance and Atmospheres in Palauan Ruk." In *Music as Atmosphere: Collective Feelings and Affective Sounds*, edited by Friedlind Riedel and Juha Torvinen, 165–183. New York: Routledge.

Absaroka, Ruard. 2020. "Timbre, Taste and Epistemic Tasks: A Cross-Cultural Perspective on Atmosphere and Vagueness." In *Music as Atmosphere: Collective Feelings and Affective Sounds*, edited by Friedlind Riedel and Juha Torvinen, 70–94. New York: Routledge.

Ahmed, Sara. 2006. *Queer Phenomenology: Orientations, Objects, Others*. Durham, NC: Duke University Press.

Ahmed, Sara. 2007. "A Phenomenology of Whiteness." *Feminist Theory* 8 (2): 149–168. https://doi.org/10.1177/1464700107078139.

Ahmed, Sara. 2010. *The Promise of Happiness*. Durham, NC: Duke University Press.

Aho, Marko. 2016. *The Tangible in Music: The Tactile Learning of a Musical Instrument*. Abingdon, UK: Routledge.

Alcoff, Linda Martín. 1999. "Towards a Phenomenology of Racial Embodiment." *Radical Philosophy* 95 (May/June): 15–26.

Amico, Stephen. 2014. *Roll Over, Tchaikovsky: Russian Popular Music and Post-Soviet Homosexuality*. Urbana: University of Illinois Press.

Anders, Günther. (1930) 2017. "Philosophische Untersuchungen über musikalische Situationen" [Philosophical investigations about musical situations]. In *Musikphilosophische Schriften: Texte und Dokumente* [Music-philosophical writings: Texts and documents], edited by Reinhard Ellensohn, 15–140. Munich: C.H. Beck.

Anders, Günther. (1937) 2009. "The Pathology of Freedom: An Essay on Non-identification." Translated by Katharine Wolfe. *Deleuze Studies* 3 (2): 278–310. https://doi.org/10.3366/E1750224109000658.

Babich, Babette. 2021. *Günther Anders' Philosophy of Technology: From Phenomenology to Critical Theory*. London: Bloomsbury.

Bakan, Michael B. 1999. *Music of Death and New Creation: Experiences in the World of Balinese Gamelan Beleganjur*. Chicago: University of Chicago Press.

Bakan, Michael B. 2009. "Measuring Happiness in the Twenty-First Century: Ethnomusicology, Evidence-Based Research, and the New Science of Autism." *Ethnomusicology* 53 (3): 510–518.

Barz, Gregory, and William Cheng, eds. 2020. *Queering the Field: Sounding out Ethnomusicology*. New York: Oxford University Press.

Barz, Gregory, and Timothy J. Cooley, eds. 2008. *Shadows in the Field: New Perspectives for Fieldwork in Ethnomusicology*. 2nd ed. New York: Oxford University Press.

Beauvoir, Simone de. (1947) 1975. *The Ethics of Ambiguity*. Translated by Bernard Frechtman. Secaucus, NJ: Citadel Press.

Beauvoir, Simone de. (1949) 2010. *The Second Sex*. Translated by Constance Borde and Sheila Malovany-Chevallier. New York: Alfred A. Knopf.

Becker, Judith. 2004. *Deep Listeners: Music, Emotion, and Trancing*. Bloomington: Indiana University Press.

Becker, Judith. 2009. "Ethnomusicology and Empiricism in the Twenty-First Century." *Ethnomusicology* 53 (3): 478–501.

Beckles Willson, Rachel. 2019. "Orientation through Instruments: The 'ūd, the Palestinian Home, and Kamīlyā Jubrān." *The World of Music* 8 (1): 23–48.

Berger, Harris M. 1997. "The Practice of Perception: Multi-Functionality and Time in the Musical Experiences of a Heavy Metal Drummer in Akron, Ohio." *Ethnomusicology* 41 (3): 464–489.

Berger, Harris M. 1999. *Metal, Rock, and Jazz: Perception and the Phenomenology of Musical Experience*. Music/Culture Book Series. Middletown, CT: Wesleyan University Press.

Berger, Harris M. 2004. "Horizons of Melody and the Problem of the Self." In *Identity and Everyday Life: Essays in the Study of Folklore, Music, and Popular Culture*, by Harris M. Berger and Giovanna P. Del Negro, 43–88. Music/Culture Book Series. Middletown, CT: Wesleyan University Press.

Berger, Harris M. 2010. *Stance: Ideas about Emotion, Style, and Meaning for the Study of Expressive Culture*. Music/Culture Book Series. Middletown, CT: Wesleyan University Press.

Berger, Harris M. 2015. "Phenomenological Approaches in the History of Ethnomusicology." *Oxford Handbook Topics in Music*, online edition. Oxford Academic. https://doi.org/10.1093/oxfordhb/9780199935321.013.30.

Berger, Harris M. 2019. "Phenomenology." In *Sage International Encyclopedia of Music and Culture*. Vol. 1, edited by Janet Sturman, 1688–1689. Thousand Oaks, CA: Sage. http://dx.doi.org/10.4135/9781483317731.n559.

Berger, Harris M., and Giovanna P. Del Negro. (2002) 2004. "The Role of Reflexivity in the Aesthetics of Performance: Verbal Art, Public Display, and Popular Music." In *Identity and Everyday Life: Essays in the Study of Folklore, Music, and Popular Culture*, by Harris M. Berger and Giovanna P. Del Negro, 89–123. Music/Culture Book Series. Middletown, CT: Wesleyan University Press.

Berger, Harris M., and Giovanna P. Del Negro. 2004. *Identity and Everyday Life: Essays in the Study of Folklore, Music, and Popular Culture*. Music/Culture Book Series. Middletown, CT: Wesleyan University Press.

Bille, Mikkel, and Kirsten Simonsen. 2019. "Atmospheric Practices: On Affecting and Being Affected." *Space and Culture* 24 (2): 1–15. https://doi.org/10.1177/1206331218819711.

Blacking, John. 1973. *How Musical Is Man?* Seattle: University of Washington Press.

Blum, Stephen. 2016. "Ethnomusicologists and Questions of Temporality." In *Music in Time: Phenomenology, Perception, Performance*, edited by Suzannah Clark and Alexander Rehding, 55–67. Isham Library Papers 9; Harvard Publications in Music 24. Cambridge, MA: Harvard University Press.

Blumer, Herbert. 1969. *Symbolic Interactionism: Perspective and Method*. Englewood Cliffs, NJ: Prentice-Hall.

Bogost, Ian. 2012. *Alien Phenomenology, or, What It's Like to Be a Thing*. Minneapolis: University of Minnesota Press.

Bourdieu, Pierre. 1977. *Outline of a Theory of Practice*. Translated by Richard Nice. Cambridge: Cambridge University Press.

Buber, Martin. (1937) 1958. *I and Thou*. Translated by Ronald Gregor Smith. 2nd ed. New York: Scribner.

Burkart, Patrick. 2010. *Music and Cyberliberties*. Music/Culture Book Series. Middletown, CT: Wesleyan University Press.

Butler, Melvin L. 2000. "Musical Style and Experience in a Brooklyn Pentecostal Church: An 'Insider's' Perspective." *Current Musicology* 70: 33–60.

Cannon, Alexander M. 2020. "Outing the Methodological No-No: Translating Queer Space to Field Space." In *Queering the Field: Sounding out Ethnomusicology*, edited by Gregory Barz and William Cheng, 120–138. New York: Oxford University Press.

Catlin, Amy. 1992. "On Interpreting Text, Context, and Performance in Cambodia, Laos, and Vietnam: A Hermeneutical Approach." In *Text, Context, and Performance in Cambodia, Laos, and Vietnam*, edited by Amy Catlin, vii–xvii. Vol. 9 of *Selected Reports in Ethnomusicology*. Los Angeles: Department of Ethnomusicology, University of California, Los Angeles.

Clayton, Martin. 2008. "Toward an Ethnomusicology of Sound Experience." In *The New (Ethno)musicologies*, edited by Henry Stobart, 135–169. Plymouth, UK: Scarecrow Press.

Clayton, Martin, and Laura Leante. 2013. "Embodiment in Music Performance." In *Experience and Meaning in Music Performance*, edited by Martin Clayton, Byron Dueck, and Laura Leante, 188–208. New York: Oxford University Press.

Clinton, Esther, and Jeremy Wallach. 2016. "Talking Metal: The Social Phenomenology of Hanging Out." In *Heavy Metal Music and the Communal Experience*, edited by Nelson Varas-Díaz and Niall Scott, 37–56. Lanham, MD: Lexington Books.

Conn, Stephanie. 2012. "Fitting between Present and Past: Memory and Social Interaction in Cape Breton Gaelic Singing." *Ethnomusicology Forum* 21 (3): 354–373.

Csikszentmihalyi, Mihaly. (1975) 2000. *Beyond Boredom and Anxiety: The Experience of Play in Work and Games*. San Francisco: Jossey-Bass.

Csikszentmihalyi, Mihaly. 1990. *Flow: The Psychology of Optimal Experience*. New York: HarperCollins.

Daughtry, J. Martin. 2014. "Thanatosonics: Ontologies of Acoustic Violence." *Social Text* 32 (2): 25–51.

Daughtry, J. Martin. 2015. *Listening to War: Sound, Music, Trauma, and Survival in Wartime Iraq*. New York: Oxford University Press.

Davies, Stephen. 2020. "Works of Music: Approaches to the Ontology of Music from Analytic Philosophy." *Music Research Annual* 1: 1–29.

Deschênes, Bruno, and Yuko Eguchi. 2018. "Embodied Orality: Transmission in Traditional Japanese Music." *Asian Music* 49 (1): 58–79.

Dessiatnitchenko, Polina. 2019. "Creativity at the Edges of the Mugham Model: Terms and Experiences." *Problems of Arts and Culture* 67 (1): 87–103.

Downey, Greg. 2002. "Listening to Capoeira: Phenomenology, Embodiment, and the Materiality of Music." *Ethnomusicology* 46 (3): 487–509.

Dreyfus, Hubert L. 1991. *Being-in-the-World: A Commentary on Heidegger's Being and Time, Division I.* Cambridge, MA: MIT Press.

Duranti, Alessandro. 2010. "Husserl, Intersubjectivity, and Anthropology." *Anthropological Theory* 10 (1–2): 16–35.

Embree, Lester, Elizabeth A. Behnke, David Carr, J. Claude Evans, José Huertas-Jourda, Joseph J. Kockelmans, William R. McKenna, Algis Mickunas, J. N. Mohanty, Thomas M. Seebohm, and Richard M. Zaner, eds. 1997. *Encyclopedia of Phenomenology.* Boston: Springer.

Embree, Lester, and J. N. Mohanty. 1997. Introduction to *Encyclopedia of Phenomenology*, edited by Lester Embree et al., 1–10. Boston: Springer.

Erlmann, Veit. 2010. *Reason and Resonance: A History of Modern Aurality.* New York: Zone Books.

Fabian, Johannes. 1983. *Time and the Other: How Anthropology Makes Its Object.* New York: Columbia University Press.

Fairfield, Benjamin. 2019. "Social Synchrony and Tuning Out: Karen Participation in Music, Tradition, and Ethnicity in Northern Thailand." *Ethnomusicology* 63 (3): 470–498. https://doi.org/10.5406/ethnomusicology.63.3.0470.

Fanon, Frantz. (1952) 2008. *Black Skin, White Masks.* Translated by Richard Philcox. New York: Grove Press.

Farin, Ingo, and Jeff Malpas, eds. 2016. *Reading Heidegger's Black Notebooks 1931–1941.* Cambridge, MA: MIT Press.

Faulkner, Robert. 2013. *Icelandic Men and Me: Sagas of Singing, Self, and Everyday Life.* Burlington, VT: Ashgate.

Feld, Steven. (1984) 1994. "Communication, Music, and Speech about Music." In *Music Grooves*, by Charles Keil and Steven Feld, 77–95. Chicago: University of Chicago Press.

Feld, Steven. (1988) 1994. "Aesthetics as Iconicity of Style (uptown title); or, (downtown title) 'Lift-up-over Sounding': Getting into the Kaluli Groove." In *Music Grooves*, by Charles Keil and Steven Feld, 109–150. Chicago: University of Chicago Press.

Feld, Steven. 1996. "Waterfalls of Song: An Acoustemology of Place Resounding in Bosavi, Papua New Guinea." In *Senses of Place*, edited by Keith H. Basso and Steven Feld, 91–135. Santa Fe, NM: School of American Research Press.

Feld, Steven. 2015. "Acoustemology." In *Keywords in Sound*, edited by David Novak and Matt Sakakeeny, 12–21. Durham, NC: Duke University Press.

Feld, Steven. 2017. "On Post-ethnomusicology Alternatives: Acoustemology." In *Perspectives on a 21st Century Comparative Musicology: Ethnomusicology or Transcultural Musicology?* edited by Francesco Giannattasio and Giovanni Giuriati, 82–100. Udine, Italy: Nota.

Ferrara, Lawrence, and Elizabeth A. Behnke. 1997. "Music." In *Encyclopedia of Phenomenology*, edited by Lester Embree et al., 467–473. Boston: Springer.

Fisette, Denis, and Riccardo Martinelli, eds. 2015. *Philosophy from an Empirical Standpoint: Essays on Carl Stumpf.* Leiden: Brill.

Friedson, Steven M. 1996. *Dancing Prophets: Musical Experience in Tumbuka Healing.* Chicago: University of Chicago Press.

Friedson, Steven M. 2009. *Remains of Ritual: Northern Gods in a Southern Land.* Chicago: University of Chicago Press.

Friedson, Steven M. 2019. "The Music Box: Songs of Futility in a Time of Torture." *Ethnomusicology* 63 (2): 222–246.

Frishkopf, Michael. 2021. "Music for Global Human Development." In *Transforming Ethnomusicology: Political, Social and Ecological Issues*, edited by Beverley Diamond and Salwa El-Shawan Castelo-Branco, 47–66. New York: Oxford University Press.

Gacea, Alexandru Ovidiu. 2019. "Plato and the 'Internal Dialogue': An Ancient Answer for a New Model of Self." In *Psychology and Ontology in Plato*, edited by Luca Pittelous and Evan Keeling, 33–54. New York: Springer.

Gadamer, Hans-Georg. (1960) 2004. *Truth and Method*. Translated by Joel Weinsheimer and Donald G. Marshall. 2nd ed. New York: Continuum.

Garcia, David F. 2017. *Listening for Africa: Freedom, Modernity, and the Logic of Black Music's African Origins*. Durham, NC: Duke University Press.

Garcia, Luis-Manuel. 2020. "Feeling the Vibe: Sound, Vibration, and Affective Attunement in Electronic Dance Music Scenes." *Ethnomusicology Forum* 1 (29): 21–39. https://doi.org/10.1080/17411912.2020.1733434.

Garlitz, Dustin. 2019. "Philosophy and Music." In *Sage International Encyclopedia of Music and Culture*, edited by Janet Sturman, 1696–1698. Thousand Oaks, CA: Sage. http://dx.doi.org/10.4135/9781483317731.n562.

Gaulier, Armelle, and Denis Constant Martin. 2017. *Cape Town Harmonies: Memory, Humour and Resilience*. Cape Town: African Minds. https://doi.org/10.5281/zenodo.824636.

Gaunt, Kyra Danielle. 2006. *The Games Black Girls Play: Learning the Ropes from Double-Dutch to Hip-Hop*. New York: New York University Press.

Giddens, Anthony. (1976) 1993. *New Rules of Sociological Method: A Positive Critique of Interpretive Sociologies*. 2nd ed. Stanford, CA: Stanford University Press.

Giddens, Anthony. 1979. *Central Problems in Social Theory: Action, Structure, and Contradiction in Social Analysis*. Berkeley: University of California Press.

Giddens, Anthony. 1984. *The Constitution of Society: Outline of a Theory of Structuration*. Berkeley: University of California Press.

Gill, Denise. 2017. *Melancholic Modalities: Affect, Islam, and Turkish Classical Musicians*. New York: Oxford University Press.

Gray, Lila Ellen. 2007. "Memories of Empire, Mythologies of the Soul: Fado Performance and the Shaping of Saudade." *Ethnomusicology* 51 (1): 106–130.

Gregersen, Andreas Melson. 2021. "Exploring the Atmosphere inside a Liturgical Laboratory." *Material Religion* 17 (5): 627–650. https://doi.org/10.1080/17432200.2021.1945990.

Grondin, Jean. 2016. "The Hermeneutical Circle." In *The Blackwell Companion to Hermeneutics*, edited by Niall Keane and Chris Lawn, 299–305. Chichester, UK: Wiley-Blackwell.

Habermas, Jürgen. (1981) 1987. *Lifeworld and System*. Vol. 2 of *The Theory of Communicative Action*. Translated by Thomas McCarthy. Boston: Beacon Press.

Hahn, Tomie, and J. Scott Jordan. 2017. "Sensible Objects: Intercorporeality and Enactive Knowing through Things." In *Intercorporeality: Emerging Socialities in Interaction*, edited by Christian Meyer, Jürgen Streeck, and J. Scott Jordan, 267–288. New York: Oxford University Press.

Hammond, Michael, Jane Howarth, and Russell Keat. 1991. *Understanding Phenomenology*. Cambridge, MA: Basil Blackwell.

Haraway, Donna Jeanne. 1991. *Simians, Cyborgs, and Women: The Reinvention of Nature*. New York: Routledge.

Harman, Graham. 2005. *Guerrilla Metaphysics: Phenomenology and the Carpentry of Things*. Chicago: Open Court Publishing.

Harnish, David. 2001. "A Hermeneutical Arc in the Life of Balinese Musician, I Made Lebah." *The World of Music* 43 (1): 21–41.

Heidegger, Martin. (1927) 1996. *Being and Time*. Translated by Joan Stambaugh. Albany: State University of New York Press.

Heidegger, Martin. 2015. *Anmerkungen I–V, GA 97*. Frankfurt: Klostermann Verlag.

Heidegger, Martin. 2016. *Ponderings II-IV: Black Notebooks 1931–1938*. Translated by Richard Rojcewicz. Bloomington: Indiana University Press.

Henderson, David. 1996. "Emotion and Devotion, Lingering and Longing in Some Nepali Songs." *Ethnomusicology* 40 (3): 440–468.

Herbert, Ruth. 2011a. *Everyday Music Listening: Absorption, Dissociation, and Trancing*. Burlington, VT: Ashgate.

Herbert, Ruth. 2011b. "Reconsidering Music and Trance: Cross-Cultural Differences and Cross-Disciplinary Perspectives." *Ethnomusicology Forum* 20 (2): 201–227.

Ho, Meilu. 2009. "A True Self Revealed: Song and Play in Pushti Marg Liturgical Service." *The World of Music* 52 (2): 21–42.

Holzmüller, Anne. 2020. "Between Things and Souls: Sacred Atmospheres and Immersive Listening in Late Eighteenth-Century Sentimentalism." In *Music as Atmosphere: Collective Feelings and Affective Sounds*, edited by Friedlind Riedel and Juha Torvinen, 218–237. New York: Routledge.

Houston, Christopher. 2020. *Istanbul, City of the Fearless: Urban Activism, Coup d'Etat, and Memory in Turkey*. Berkeley: University of California Press.

Humphreys, Paul. 1991. "Time, Rhythm, and Silence: A Phenomenology of the Buddhist Accelerating Roll." In *Tradition and Its Future in Music: Report of SIMS Osaka*, edited by Yosihiko Tokumaru, 287–293. Tokyo: Mita Press.

Husserl, Edmund. (1900–01) 2001. *Logical Investigations*. Edited by Dermot Moran. Translated by J. N. Findlay. New York: Routledge.

Husserl, Edmund. (1913) 1962. *Ideas: General Introduction to Pure Phenomenology*. Translated by William Ralph Boyce Gibson. New York: Collier Books.

Husserl, Edmund. (1929) 1964. *Phenomenology of Internal Time-Consciousness*. Edited by Martin Heidegger. Translated by James S. Churchill. Bloomington: Indiana University Press.

Husserl, Edmund. 1931. "Author's Preface to the English Edition." In *Ideas: General Introduction to Pure Phenomenology*, translated by William Ralph Boyce Gibson, 5–22. New York: Collier Books.

Husserl, Edmund. (1931) 1960. *Cartesian Meditations*. Translated by Dorian Cairns. The Hague: Martinus Nijhoff.

Husserl, Edmund. (1936) 1970. *The Crisis of European Sciences and Transcendental Phenomenology: An Introduction to Phenomenological Philosophy*. Translated by David Carr. Evanston, IL: Northwestern University Press.

Ihde, Don. 1976. *Listening and Voice*. Athens: Ohio University Press.

Ihde, Don. 1979. *Technics and Praxis*. Dordrecht, Netherlands: Springer.

Ihde, Don. 1986. *Experimental Phenomenology: An Introduction*. Albany: State University of New York Press.

Ihde, Don. 1990. *Technology and the Lifeworld: From Garden to Earth*. Bloomington: Indiana University Press.

Ihde, Don. 2008. "Introduction: Postphenomenological Research." *Human Studies* 31 (1): 1–9.

Ihde, Don. 2010. *Heidegger's Technologies: Postphenomenological Perspectives*. New York: Fordham University Press.

Impey, Angela. 2018. *Song Walking: Women, Music, and Environmental Justice in an African Borderland*. Chicago: University of Chicago Press.

Ingarden, Roman. (1933) 1989. "The Musical Work." In *The Ontology of the Work of Art*, translated by Raymond Meyer and John T. Goldthwait, 3–133. Athens: Ohio University Press.

Ingold, Tim. (2000) 2022. *The Perception of the Environment: Essays on Livelihood, Dwelling and Skill*. 3rd ed. London: Routledge.

Johansson, Mats. 2017. "Paraphrase This: A Note on Improvisation." *Ethnomusicology Forum* 26 (1): 26–45.

Johnson, Charles. (1976) 1993. "A Phenomenology of the Black Body." *Michigan Quarterly Review* 32 (4): 599–614.

Justice, Deborah, and Fredara M. Hadley. 2015. "Collaborative Fieldwork, 'Stance,' and Ethnography." *Yearbook for Traditional Music* 47: 64–81.

Kapchan, Deborah. 2009. "Learning to Listen: The Sound of Sufism in France." *The World of Music* 52 (2): 63–88.

Kapchan, Deborah. 2013. "The Aesthetics of the Invisible: Sacred Music in Secular (French) Places." *TDR: The Drama Review* 57 (3): 132–147.

Kaur, Inderjit N. 2016. "Multiple Authenticities in Motion: Styles and Stances in Sikh Sabad Kīrtan." *Yearbook for Traditional Music* 48: 71–93.

Kaur, Inderjit N. 2019. "A Multisensorial Affective Ecology of Sonic Worship: The Sikh Sacred Song Culture." *MUSICultures* 46 (2): 109–133.

Keil, Charles, and Steven Feld. 1994. "Further Comments (on 'Dialogue 1: Getting into the Dialogic Groove')." In *Music Grooves*, by Charles Keil and Steven Feld, 31–50. Chicago: University of Chicago Press.

Knowles, Adam. 2020a. *Heidegger's Fascist Affinities: A Politics of Silence*. Stanford, CA: Stanford University Press.

Knowles, Adam. 2020b. "Martin Heidegger: Force, Violence and the Administration of Thinking." *Zeitschrift Für Medien- Und Kulturforschung* 11: 125–138.

Kohák, Erazim V. 1978. *Idea and Experience: Edmund Husserl's Project of Phenomenology in Ideas I*. Chicago: University of Chicago Press.

Latour, Bruno. 1988. *Science in Action: How to Follow Scientists and Engineers through Society*. Cambridge, MA: Harvard University Press.

Latour, Bruno. 2005. *Reassembling the Social: An Introduction to Actor-Network-Theory*. New York: Oxford University Press.

Latour, Bruno, and Steve Woolgar. (1979) 1986. *Laboratory Life: The Construction of Scientific Facts*. Princeton, NJ: Princeton University Press.

Legg, Catherine, and Christopher Hookway. 2021. "Pragmatism." In *The Stanford Encyclopedia of Philosophy*, edited by Edward N. Zalta. Stanford University. https://plato.stanford.edu/archives/sum2021/entries/pragmatism/.

Lingis, Alphonso. 1998. *The Imperative*. Bloomington: Indiana University Press.

Lysloff, René T. A., and Leslie C. Gay, eds. 2003. *Music and Technoculture*. Middletown, CT: Wesleyan University Press.

MacDonald, Michael B. 2020. "Unspittable: Long-Form Ethnographic Music Video as Cine-Ethnomusicology Research-Creation." *Visual Ethnography* 9 (1): 115–137.

Macey, David. 1999. "Fanon, Phenomenology, and Race." *Radical Philosophy* 95 (May/June): 8–14.

Mahendran, Dilan. 2007. "The Facticity of Blackness: A Non-conceptual Approach to the Study of Race and Racism in Fanon's and Merleau-Ponty's Phenomenology." *Human Architecture* 5 (Summer): 191–203.

Manuel, Peter. 1993. *Cassette Culture: Popular Music and Technology in North India*. Chicago: University of Chicago Press.

McCormack, Ryan. 2021. "Aurality and COVID-19." *Music Research Annual* 2: 1–21.

McDaniel, Kris. 2016. "Edith Stein: On the Problem of Empathy." In *Ten Neglected Classics of Philosophy*, edited by Eric Schliesser, 195–222. New York: Oxford University Press.

McDonald, David A. 2013. "Imaginaries of Exile and Emergence in Israeli Jewish and Palestinian Hip Hop." *TDR: The Drama Review* 57 (3): 69–87.

McGettigan, Andrew. 2006. "The Philosopher's Fear of Alterity: Levinas, Europe and Humanities 'without Sacred History.'" *Radical Philosophy*, no. 140: 15–25.

McGraw, Andrew. 2016. "Atmosphere as a Concept for Ethnomusicology: Comparing the Gamelatron and Gamelan." *Ethnomusicology* 60 (1): 125–147. https://doi.org/10.5406/ethn omusicology.60.1.0125.

McGraw, Andy. 2020. "Feeling the Feels: Spinozist Ethics and Musical Feeling in an American Jail." *Culture, Theory and Critique* 61 (2–3): 267–282. https://doi.org/10.1080/14735784.2020.1858126.

McGuiness, Andy. 2013. "Self-Consciousness in Music Performance." In *Experience and Meaning in Music Performance*, edited by Martin Clayton, Byron Dueck, and Laura Leante, 108–134. New York: Oxford University Press.

McIntosh, Jonathan. 2006. "How Dancing, Singing, and Playing Shape the Ethnographer: Research with Children in a Balinese Dance Studio." *Anthropology Matters* 8 (2): 1–17.

McIntosh, Jonathan. 2009. "Indonesians and Australians Playing Javanese Gamelan in Perth, Western Australia: Community and the Negotiation of Musical Identities." *Asia Pacific Journal of Anthropology* 10 (2): 80–97.

McMurray, Peter. 2020. "What Is It Like to Be a Crane? Notes on Alevi Semah and the Sivas Massacre." *Culture, Theory and Critique* 61 (2–3): 151–168. https://doi.org/10.1080/14735784.2021.1886137.

Meintjes, Louise. 2004. "Shoot the Sergeant, Shatter the Mountain: The Production of Masculinity in Zulu Ngoma Song and Dance in Post-Apartheid South Africa." *Ethnomusicology Forum* 13 (2): 173–201.

Merleau-Ponty, Maurice. (1945) 1962. *Phenomenology of Perception*. Translated by Colin Smith. New York: Humanities Press.

Merleau-Ponty, Maurice. (1964) 1968. *The Visible and the Invisible*. Translated by Alphonso Lingis. Evanston, IL: Northwestern University Press.

Miller, Kiri. 2012. *Playing Along: Digital Games, YouTube, and Virtual Performance*. New York: Oxford University Press.

Miller, Kiri. 2017. *Playable Bodies: Dance Games and Intimate Media*. New York: Oxford University Press.

Mitchell, Andrew J., ed. 2015. "Heidegger's Black Notebooks." Special issue, *Gatherings: The Heidegger Circle Annual* 5.

Mohanty, J. N. 1991. "Method of Imaginative Variation in Phenomenology." In *Thought Experiments in Science and Philosophy*, edited by Tamara Horowitz and Gerald J. Massey, 261–272. Savage, MD: Rowman and Littlefield.

Moten, Fred. 2018. *The Universal Machine*. Volume 3 of consent not to be a single being. Durham, NC: Duke University Press.

Mrázek, Jan. 2008. "Xylophones in Thailand and Java: A Comparative Phenomenology of Musical Instruments." *Asian Music* 39 (2): 59–107.

Mrázek, Jan. 2019. *Wayang and Its Doubles: Javanese Puppet Theatre, Television, and the Internet*. Singapore: NUS Press.

Neuman, Dard. 2012. "Pedagogy, Practice, and Embodied Creativity in Hindustani Music." *Ethnomusicology* 56 (3): 426–449.

Noone, Matthew. 2013. "North Indian Classical Music and the Kolkata Experience: Alchemical Schismogenesis and Being-in-the-World in a Musical Way." *Ethnomusicology Ireland* 2–3 (July): 22–37.

Novak, David, and Matt Sakakeeny, eds. 2015. *Keywords in Sound*. Durham, NC: Duke University Press.

O'Connell, John Morgan. 2015. "Sounds Humane: Music and Humanism in the Aga Khan Humanities Project." In *The Oxford Handbook of Applied Ethnomusicology*, edited by Svanibor Pettan and Jeff Todd Titon, 602–638. New York: Oxford University Press.

Pieridou Skoutella, Avra. 2015. *Small Musical Worlds in the Mediterranean: Ethnicity, Globalization and Greek Cypriot Children's Musical Identities*. Burlington, VT: Ashgate.

Pieridou Skoutella, Avra. 2019a. "Issues in Ethnomusicology." In *Sage International Encyclopedia of Music and Culture*, edited by Janet Sturman, 868–870. Thousand Oaks, CA: Sage. http://dx.doi.org/10.4135/9781483317731.n269.

Pieridou Skoutella, Avra. 2019b. "Writing Ethnomusicology." In *Sage International Encyclopedia of Music and Culture*, edited by Janet Sturman, 2387–2389. Thousand Oaks, CA: Sage. http://dx.doi.org/10.4135/9781483317731.n794.

Porcello, Thomas. 1998. "'Tails Out': Social Phenomenology and the Ethnographic Representation of Technology in Music-Making." *Ethnomusicology* 42 (3): 485–510.

Racy, Ali Jihad. 1991. "Creativity and Ambience: An Ecstatic Feedback Model from Arab Music." *The World of Music* 33 (3): 7–28.

Racy, Ali Jihad. 2003. *Making Music in the Arab World: The Culture and Artistry of Tarab*. Cambridge: Cambridge University Press.

Rahaim, Matthew. 2012. *Musicking Bodies: Gesture and Voice in Hindustani Music*. Music/Culture Book Series. Middletown, CT: Wesleyan University Press.

Rahaim, Matthew. 2017. "Otherwise than Participation: Unity and Alterity in Musical Encounters." In *Music and Empathy*, edited by Elaine King and Caroline Waddington, 175–193. New York: Routledge.

Rahaim, Matthew. 2019. "Object, Person, Machine, or What: Practical Ontologies of Voice." In *The Oxford Handbook of Voice Studies*, edited by Nina Eidsheim and Katherine Meizel, 19–34. New York: Oxford University Press.

Rahaim, Matthew. 2021. *Ways of Voice: Vocal Striving and Moral Contestation in North India and Beyond*. Music/Culture Book Series. Middletown, CT: Wesleyan University Press.

Ramberg, Bjørn, and Kristin Gjesdal. 2013. "Hermeneutics." In *The Stanford Encyclopedia of Philosophy*, edited by Edward N. Zalta. Stanford University. http://plato.stanford.edu/archives/sum2013/entries/hermeneutics/.

Reisnour, Nicole. 2020. "If You Sing, You Will Surely Feel Happy: The Affect-Emotion Gap and the Efficacy of Devotional Song in Bali." *Culture, Theory and Critique* 61 (2–3): 133–150. https://doi.org/10.1080/14735784.2021.1884987.

Rice, Timothy. 1994. *May It Fill Your Soul: Experiencing Bulgarian Music*. Chicago: University of Chicago Press.

Rice, Timothy. 2001. "Reflections on Music and Meaning: Metaphor, Signification, and Control in the Bulgarian Case." *British Journal of Ethnomusicology* 10 (1): 19–38.

Rice, Timothy. 2003. "Time, Place, and Metaphor in Musical Experience and Ethnography." *Ethnomusicology* 47 (2): 151–179.

Rice, Timothy. 2008. "Toward a Mediation of Field Methods and Field Experience in Ethnomusicology." In *Shadows in the Field: New Perspectives for Fieldwork in Ethnomusicology*. 2nd ed., edited by Gregory Barz and Timothy J. Cooley, 42–62. New York: Oxford University Press.

Rice, Timothy, and Raúl R. Romero. 2015. "Timothy Rice: Human Musicality and the Future of Ethnomusicology; Musical Experience and the Perpetual Question of Objectivity." *El Oído Pensante* 3 (2). https://ppct.caicyt.gov.ar/index.php/oidopensante/article/view/7110.

Ricoeur, Paul. (1986) 1991. *From Text to Action: Essays in Hermeneutics II*. Translated by Kathleen Blamey and John B. Thompson. Evanston, IL: Northwestern University Press.

Ricoeur, Paul. 2007. *The Conflict of Interpretations: Essays in Hermeneutics*. Edited by Don Ihde. Evanston, IL: Northwestern University Press.

Riedel, Friedlind. 2015. "Music as Atmosphere: Lines of Becoming in Congregational Worship." *Lebenswelt* 6: 80–111. https://doi.org/10.13130/2240-9599/4913.

Riedel, Friedlind. 2019. "Atmosphere." In *Affective Societies: Key Concepts*, edited by Jan Slaby and Christian V. Scheve, 85–95. New York: Routledge.

Riedel, Friedlind. 2020. "Atmospheric Relations: Theorising Music and Sound as Atmosphere." In *Music as Atmosphere: Collective Feelings and Affective Sounds*, edited by Friedlind Riedel and Juha Torvinen, 1–42. New York: Routledge.

Riedel, Friedlind, and Juha Torvinen, eds. 2020. *Music as Atmosphere: Collective Feelings and Affective Sounds*. New York: Routledge.

Rizzo, Roberto. 2020. "Knowledge Transmission in Javanese Karawitan: Is It Time for an Ontological Turn?" *Asian Music* 51 (1): 94–117. http://dx.doi.org.qe2a-proxy.mun.ca/10.1353/amu.2020.0004.

Sager, Rebecca D. 2009. "My Song Is My Bond: Haitian Vodou Singing and the Transformation of Being." *The World of Music* 52 (2): 89–116.

Said, Edward W. 1979. *Orientalism*. New York: Vintage Books.

Sansom, Matthew J. 2005. "Understanding Musical Meaning: Interpretative Phenomenological Analysis and Improvisation." Paper presented at the 2005 Annual Conference of the British Forum for Ethnomusicology. http://www.matthewsansom.info/links/theory/mmipai.pdf.

Salamon, Gayle. 2006. " 'The Place Where Life Hides Away': Merleau-Ponty, Fanon, and the Location of Bodily Being." *Differences* 17 (2): 96–112.

Sartre, Jean-Paul. (1943) 1948. *Being and Nothingness*. Translated by Hazel E. Barnes. New York: Philosophical Library.

Savage, Roger W. H. 2009. "Being, Transcendence, and the Ontology of Music." *The World of Music* 52 (2): 5–20.

Savage, Roger W. H. 2010. *Hermeneutics and Music Criticism*. New York: Routledge.

Savage, Roger W. H. 2017. *Music, Time, and Its Other: Aesthetic Reflections on Finitude, Temporality, and Alterity*. New York: Routledge.

Savage, Roger W. H. 2019. "Hermeneutics and Music." In *Sage International Encyclopedia of Music and Culture*, edited by Janet Sturman, 1077–1079. Thousand Oaks, CA: Sage. http://dx.doi.org/10.4135/9781483317731.n341.

Sawicki, Marianne. n.d. "Edmund Husserl (1859–1938)." In *Internet Encyclopedia of Philosophy*. http://www.iep.utm.edu/husserl/#H1.

Schmidt, James. 1985. *Maurice Merleau-Ponty: Between Phenomenology and Structuralism*. New York: St. Martin's Press.

Schmitz, Hermann. (1969) 2005. *Der Gefühlsraum*. Bonn: Bouvier.

Schmitz, Hermann. (1978) 2005. *Die Wahrnehmung*. Bonn: Bouvier.

Schmitz, Hermann. (2009) 2019. *New Phenomenology: A Brief Introduction*. Translated by Rudolf Owen Müllan and Martin Bastert. Rome: Mimesis International.

Schmitz, Hermann, Rudolf Owen Müllan, and Jan Slaby. 2011. "Emotions outside the Box— The New Phenomenology of Feeling and Corporeality." *Phenomenology and the Cognitive Sciences* 10 (2): 241–259. https://doi.org/10.1007/s11097-011-9195-1.

Schutz, Alfred. (1932) 1967. *Phenomenology of the Social World*. Translated by George Walsh and Fredrick Lehnert. Evanston, IL: Northwestern University Press.

Schutz, Alfred. 1951. "Making Music Together: A Study in Social Relationship." *Social Research* 18 (1): 76–97.

Schutz, Alfred. 1962. *Collected Papers I: The Problem of Social Reality*. The Hague: Martinus Nijhoff.

Schutz, Alfred. 1964. *Collected Papers II: Studies in Social Theory*. The Hague: Martinus Nijhoff.

Schutz, Alfred. 1976. "Fragments on the Phenomenology of Music." *Music and Man* 2 (1–2): 5–72.

Schutz, Alfred, and Thomas Luckmann. (1973) 1975. *The Structures of the Life-World*. Vol. 1. Translated by Richard M. Zaner and H. Tristram Engelhardt. Evanston, IL: Northwestern University Press.

Seeman, Sonia Tamar. 2019. *Sounding Roman: Representation and Performing Identity in Western Turkey*. New York: Oxford University Press.

Selinger, Evan. 2006. *Postphenomenology: A Critical Companion to Ihde*. Ithaca: State University of New York Press.

Shannon, Jonathan H. 2003. "Emotion, Performance, and Temporality in Arab Music: Reflections on *Tarab*." *Cultural Anthropology* 18 (1): 72–98.

Shelley, Braxton D. 2019. "Analyzing Gospel." *Journal of the American Musicological Society* 72 (1): 181–243.

Short, T. L. 2007. *Peirce's Theory of Signs*. New York: Cambridge University Press.

Silverstein, Shayna. 2019. "Disorienting Sounds: A Sensory Ethnography of Syrian Dance." In *Remapping Sound Studies*, edited by Gavin Steingo and Jim Sykes, 241–260. Durham, NC: Duke University Press. http://www.degruyter.com/document/doi/10.1515/9781478002192-013/html.

Simonett, Helena. 2001. *Banda: Mexican Musical Life across Borders*. Music/Culture Book Series. Middletown, CT: Wesleyan University Press.

Simonett, Helena. 2009. "Narrativity and Selfhood in Mayo-Yoreme Mortuary Rituals." *The World of Music* 52 (2): 42–61.

Simonett, Helena. 2014. "Envisioned, Ensounded, Enacted: Sacred Ecology and Indigenous Musical Experience in Yoreme Ceremonies of Northwest Mexico." *Ethnomusicology* 58 (1): 110–132.

Simonett, Helena. 2016. "Of Human and Non-human Birds: Indigenous Music Making and Sentient Ecology in Northwestern Mexico." In *Current Directions in Ecomusicology: Music, Culture, Nature*, edited by Aaron S. Allen and Kevin Dawe, 99–108. New York: Routledge.

Slaughter, Thomas F. 1977. "Epidermalizing the World: A Basic Mode of Being-Black." *Man and World* 10: 303–308.

Slawek, Stephen. 1996. "Engrossed Minds, Embodied Moods, and Liberated Spirits in Two Musical Traditions of India." *Bansuri* 13: 31–41.

Slominski, Tes. 2020. "Fielding the Field: Belonging, Discplinarity, and Queer Scholarly Lives." In *Queering the Field: Sounding out Ethnomusicology*, edited by Gregory Barz and William Cheng, 217–234. New York: Oxford University Press.

Smith, David Woodruff. 2013. "Phenomenology." In *The Stanford Encyclopedia of Philosophy*, edited by Edward N. Zalta. Stanford University. http://plato.stanford.edu/archives/win2013/entries/phenomenology/.

Smith, F. Joseph. 1979. *Experiencing of Musical Sound: A Prelude to a Phenomenology of Music*. New York: Gordon and Breach.

Spiegelberg, Herbert. 1956. "Husserl's and Peirce's Phenomenologies: Coincidence or Interaction." *Philosophy and Phenomenological Research* 17 (2): 164–185.

Spiegelberg, Herbert, and Karl Schuhmann. (1960) 1994. *The Phenomenological Movement: A Historical Introduction*. 3rd ed. Norwell, MA: Kluwer Academic Publishers.

Steinbeck, Paul. 2008. "'Area by Area the Machine Unfolds': The Improvisational Performance Practice of the Art Ensemble of Chicago." *Journal of the Society for American Music* 2 (3): 397–427.

Sterne, Jonathan. 2021. *Diminished Faculties: A Political Phenomenology of Impairment*. Durham, NC: Duke University Press.

Stjernfelt, Frederik. 2007. *Diagrammatology: An Investigation on the Borderlines of Phenomenology, Ontology, and Semiotics*. Dordrecht, Netherlands: Springer.

Stone, Ruth M. (1982) 2010. *Let the Inside Be Sweet: The Interpretation of Music Event among the Kpelle of Liberia*. Bloomington, IN: Trickster Press.

Stone, Ruth M. 1988. *Dried Millet Breaking: Time, Words, and Song in the Woi Epic of the Kpelle*. Bloomington: Indiana University Press.

Stone, Ruth M. 2008. *Theory for Ethnomusicology*. 1st ed. Upper Saddle River, NJ: Pearson.

Stone, Ruth M., and Harris M. Berger. 2014. "Ethnomusicologists X Ethnomusicologists: Ruth Stone Interviewed by Harris M. Berger." *SEM Newsletter* 48 (3): 1, 4, 6.

Stone, Ruth M., and Verlon L. Stone. 1981. "Event, Feedback, and Analysis: Research Media in the Study of Music Events." *Ethnomusicology* 25 (2): 215–225.

Stone-MacDonald, Angela, and Ruth M. Stone. 2013. "The Feedback Interview and Video Recording in African Research Settings." *Africa Today* 59 (4): 2–22.

Sudnow, David. 1978. *Ways of the Hand: The Organization of Improvised Conduct*. Cambridge, MA: Harvard University Press.

Szego, Kati. 2021. "Kinetic Songscapes: Intersensorial Listening to Hula Kuʻi Songs." In *Perspectives in Motion: Engaging the Visual in Dance and Music*, edited by Kendra Stepputat and Brian Diettrich, 19–40. New York: Berghahn Books.

Thacker, Vanessa. 2012. "Experiencing the Moment in Song: An Analysis of the Irish Traditional Singing Session." *Ethnomusicology Review* 17. http://ethnomusicologyreview.ucla.edu/journal/volume/17/piece/601.

Throop, C. Jason, and Keith M. Murphy. 2002. "Bourdieu and Phenomenology: A Critical Assessment." *Anthropological Theory* 2 (2): 185–207.

Titon, Jeff Todd. 1988. *Powerhouse for God: Speech, Chant, and Song in an Appalachian Baptist Church*. Austin: University of Texas Press.

Titon, Jeff Todd. 2008. "Knowing Fieldwork." In *Shadows in the Field: New Perspectives for Fieldwork in Ethnomusicology*. 2nd ed., edited by Gregory Barz and Timothy J. Cooley, 25–41. New York: Oxford University Press.

Titon, Jeff Todd. 2009. "Ecology, Phenomenology, and Biocultural Thinking: A Response to Judith Becker." *Ethnomusicology* 53 (3): 502–509.

Titus, Barbara, ed. 2019. "Dwelling in Musical Movement: Making a Home in and through Music." Special issue, *The World of Music* 8 (1).

Torvinen, Juha. 2019. "Resounding: Feeling, Mytho-Ecological Framing, and the Sámi Conception of Nature in Outi Tarkiainen's *The Earth, Spring's Daughter.*" *MUSICultures* 45 (1–2): 167–189.

Tragaki, Dafni. 2020. "Acoustemologies of Rebetiko Love Songs." In *Music as Atmosphere: Collective Feelings and Affective Sounds*, edited by Friedlind Riedel and Juha Torvinen, 184–201. New York: Routledge.

Trotter, David. 1999. "Fanon's Nausea." *Parallax* 5 (2): 32–50.

Turino, Thomas. 2014. "Peircean Thought as Core Theory for a Phenomenological Ethnomusicology." *Ethnomusicology* 58 (2): 185–221.

Turner, Tamara. 2020. "The 'Right' Kind of Ḥāl: Feeling and Foregrounding Atmospheric Identity in an Algerian Music Ritual." In *Music as Atmosphere: Collective Feelings and Affective Sounds*, edited by Friedlind Riedel and Juha Torvinen, 113–130. New York: Routledge.

VanderHamm, David. 2020. "'I'm Just an Armless Guitarist': Tony Melendez, Disability, and the Social Construction of Virtuosity." *Journal of the Society for American Music* 14 (3): 280–307.

Verne, Markus. 2015. "Music, Transcendence, and the Need for (Existential) Anthropologies of the Individual." *Zeitschrift Für Ethnologie* 16: 75–89.

Warren, Jeff R. 2021. "'That Worship Sound': Ethics, Things, and Shimmer Reverberation." In *Ethics and Christian Musicking*, edited by Nathan Myrick and Mark Porter, 73–87. London: Routledge.

Weiss, Sarah. 2003. "'Kothong Nanging Kebak,' Empty Yet Full: Some Thoughts on Embodiment and Aesthetics in Javanese Performance." *Asian Music* 34 (2): 21–49.

Wheeler, Michael. 2020. "Martin Heidegger." In *The Stanford Encyclopedia of Philosophy*, edited by Edward N. Zalta. Stanford University. https://plato.stanford.edu/archives/fall2020/entries/heidegger/.

White, Bob W. 2014. "Listening Together, Thinking Out Loud: Popular Music and Political Consciousness in Congo-Zaire." *MUSICultures* 41 (2): 54–74.

Wolf, Richard K. 2006. *The Black Cow's Footprint: Time, Space, and Music in the Lives of the Kotas of South India.* Urbana: University of Illinois Press.

Zahavi, Dan. (2003) 2018. *Phenomenology: The Basics.* London: Routledge.

Zalta, Edward N., ed. 2022. *The Stanford Encyclopedia of Philosophy.* Stanford University. http://plato.stanford.edu/.

Zeiler, Kristin. 2013. "A Phenomenology of Excorporation, Bodily Alienation, and Resistance: Rethinking Sexed and Racialized Embodiment." *Hypatia* 28 (1): 69–84. https://doi.org/10.1111/j.1527-2001.2012.01305.x.

Zimmermann, Hans Dieter. 2005. *Martin und Fritz Heidegger: Philosophie und Fastnacht.* Munich: Beck.

CHAPTER 2

....

CARL STUMPF AND THE PHENOMENOLOGY OF MUSICAL UTTERANCES

....

JULIA KURSELL

"der sachverhalt ist ziemlich verwickelter art"

(The state of affairs is rather complicated.
Example sentence in Deutsches Wörterbuch von Jacob und
Wilhelm Grimm (1892), *for the term 'state of affairs')*[1]

THIS chapter looks at the contribution of the philosopher Carl Stumpf (1848–1936) to a phenomenology of music cultures. Stumpf counts both as a precursor of twentieth-century phenomenology and as one of the founding figures of what was first called "comparative musicology," namely the study of musics worldwide. He studied with Franz Brentano (1838–1917), one of phenomenology's forerunners, and he later became a mentor to Edmund Husserl (1859–1938). While Stumpf himself did not contribute to "phenomenology" in the sense that Husserl would coin the term, he did explore Brentano's notion of phenomenology as a "descriptive psychology." In so doing, he pushed the limits of that field toward philosophically grounded, experimental research on music. More specifically, he asked how the mental acts of music listening and musical understanding take shape, and he identified the importance of tacit assumptions and implicit standpoints along the way. Developing over the course of half a century, his terms and methods provide an interesting set of terminological suggestions that—so I propose—could become fruitful for phenomenological analyses of music cultures today.

It is important to note that Stumpf's focus lay on studying the mind. His quest for the "psychical functions" made him question what shapes perception and cognition during the moment when the mind makes sense of, for instance, tones. This included any mental activity during musicking, be it through listening, playing, or musically interacting, but it did not include the study of musical "products" or social interactions beyond the moment of musicking. My reading of his work therefore enters the topic of music cultures by a—rather extended—detour. During that detour, the main emphasis will be on how the research practice of this scholar of music and philosophy took shape *before* our current notion of phenomenology. As I will argue, Stumpf's methodological premises, on the one hand, tied his approach to music to the nascent phenomenological movement, while the object of study—namely the given mental setting of the musicking individual—on the other hand, revealed that individual's adherence to a particular musical culture. Thus, while we do not find any full-fledged study of such adherence in Stumpf, the traces of it may lead toward an enriched concept of the phenomenology of music cultures.

INTRODUCTION

In 1873, in his first position as professor of philosophy at Würzburg University and free to choose a new topic after the publication of a book on the mental representations of space (1873), Stumpf embarked on a project that was to occupy him for the next fifty years. He turned to music, making the perception and cognition of meaningful sound his main object of investigation. The two volumes of his *Tonpsychologie* (1883, translated as *Tone Psychology*, Volume 1, *The Sensation of Successive Single Tones* 2020; 1890), the first results of this endeavor, earned him recognition as a psychologist who integrated philosophy with the experimental study of the mind. After going on to hold positions as professor of philosophy at Prague, Halle, and Munich, he was eventually appointed to a prestigious chair of philosophy at Berlin University in 1894, where he also acted as founding director of the university's "Seminar of Psychology" and, after an upgrade in 1900, "Institute of Psychology." The institute not only brought forth the Berlin School of Gestalt Psychology but also hosted one of the earliest collections of ethnological sound recordings. Eventually growing to 30,000 phonographic cylinders, it became one of the largest of its kind.[2]

Stumpf has been credited with contributing to the beginnings of ethnomusicology as an academic discipline, especially in his role as the initiator of the archive (see, e.g., Christensen 1991; Koch 2013). To be sure, the archive was a thoroughly colonial project (see, e.g., Ames 2003). Stumpf's younger colleague—and, for a brief while, assistant—Erich Moritz von Hornbostel devised a set of instructions for colonial travelers to record the Indigenous populations (Ziegler 2006). Adding to that, a copying procedure for the fragile wax cylinders that Hornbostel had developed enabled researchers from all over the world to receive reliable copies of their acoustic treasures, while the Berlin archive always kept one exemplar for their own research purposes (see, e.g., Klotz 1998).

Aside from his role in the archive, Stumpf's 1911 book *Die Anfänge der Musik* (1911, translated as *The Origins of Music* 2012), as well as a handful of articles on music from specific regions, are seen as his main scholarly contribution to the field of ethnomusicology. His articles on collections of sound—written and recorded—were clearly guided by a concept of music that privileged tone relations. They provided a model for the emerging "comparative musicology" and its extensive comparisons among allegedly equal recorded items, just like the "pieces" in European composition, but that were in fact always already formatted by the device (see, e.g., Rehding 2005). Phonographic recording put its signature on the sound and its investigation: performers had to keep a certain maximal distance from the funnel, which in turn limited the range of sound. While this worked well for recording opera tenors, technical limitations meant that the intricacies of more complex settings were impossible to convey. When used to record ritual, for instance, thorough verbal description of the purpose and the setting of the recorded sound emerged as a necessary complement. These matters, however, would be tackled by later generations of researchers.

Stumpf's issues with recording were of a different nature. Beyond their failure to give access to the music's spatial and social settings, recordings precluded interacting with the recorded individuals. What this essay aims at highlighting, then, is that Stumpf would not have considered it acceptable for him to simply provide a description of the social setting without any methodology that allowed the experiencing individual to utter their perspective on what had happened in their mind while musicking. What I propose to call an "utterance" in the following is a single instance of musicking, whether undertaken passively or actively. The accompanying psychical functions and the "position" of such an utterance were at the center of Stumpf's quest into the human mind. (By position here, I don't mean to indicate the utterance's physical location but rather the subject's agential trajectory toward uttering something, whether musically or verbally.) To get access to such an utterance, Stumpf even shifted his research to speech sounds as his main object of investigation, a reorientation that took place after he had published the book on the origins of music in 1911. The new topic indeed took him back to the individual listener—not in the sense of the abstract subject discussed in philosophy but rather the sense of specific listeners who come to individual judgments. In parallel to Husserl's ([1913] 1982) concern with supplanting the "natural attitude" with a "phenomenological attitude," Stumpf questioned what appeared to be a not so "natural" attitude to begin with, finding instead that listener judgments were always shaped by individual and concrete experience.

In all its richness, Stumpf's work is difficult to place. He formulated no "principles" of psychology as did William James, with whom he kept a pen friendship until the latter's death, nor did he endeavor to speculate about nerve physiology as did Wilhelm Wundt, his adversary in a controversy over the usefulness of—or distortion by—expertise in experimental subjects.[3] To the readers of today, Stumpf's writing style, although rigorous in its logic, seems exuberant. Compared with twentieth-century phenomenologists, he did not strive for formalized expression. Perhaps the potential of Stumpf's writing lies in what makes it appear unfinished and meandering. What he offers to the phenomenology of musical cultures can be found in the strategy of postponing his own—that is, the researcher's—conclusive judgment.

Understood in this manner, Stumpf's work connects to the phenomenology of music cultures in two ways. First, Stumpf's earlier (but terminologically unsuccessful) attempt to conceive of a "phenomenology" needs to be distinguished from Husserl's later (and more widely adopted) terminology. And second, the central notion Stumpf provides and that I analyze throughout this chapter—*Sachverhalt*—is a defining feature of his peculiar way of writing, experimenting, and arguing. Compared with Husserl's later notion of ἐποχή (epoché), then, Stumpf's abstention from judgment relates to prejudice in a different way. While Husserl aimed to bracket the prejudice of the natural attitude, Stumpf made understanding the individual's mental setting a central objective of his research. How the subject judges can be seen not so much from the resulting judgments themselves but from how that setting is reflected in and can be reconstructed from the individual's judgments. The distinction is subtle: in the context of this chapter, it concerns mainly how the two notions involve historical context. Bracketing the natural attitude, Husserl also bracketed the historical setting in which that attitude is set to work. Stumpf, by contrast, gained a position of hindsight. The subject's "standpoint" or "settings of the mind," to use two of Stumpf's terms, by the same token could be historically, locally, and—most importantly—individually situated. It is this relation between the standpoint as it is inherent within a given judgment and the historical trajectory toward—and cultural embeddedness of—that standpoint that I will treat here as definitive of Stumpf's work.

The key notion for understanding the relationship between a musical utterance and the wider music culture in which it is embedded is Sachverhalt (state of affairs), and this concept can further unleash the potential of Stumpf's thought for contemporary scholars. Stumpf is credited with having contributed this term to philosophical discourse, and it is considered part and parcel of phenomenology's quest for logically formalizing the position from and within which phenomena appear to the subject. Although the notion he coined pertained specifically to logic, his research practice or *modus operandi* cannot be restricted to that discipline. Instead, Stumpf's actual research practices invite us to apply a broader notion of state of affairs to his work than he himself formulated.

The reading of Sachverhalt that I propose consists in intertwining the philosophical notion with its originally juridical background. In Stumpf's time, the constitution of a state of affairs in a lawsuit was a distinct step in the process toward a legal judgment. Not only did constituting a state of affairs precede the judgment, but the judgment also was meant to judge exclusively what was designated as part of the state of affairs. This richer notion of Sachverhalt sheds light on how the idea of a state of affairs is used in Stumpf's writings on logic, and its juridical background also permeates his research into music. My interpretation of the notion in Stumpf's work thus allows me to situate his practice as a researcher in the history of legal practice.

Even before Stumpf coined his logical notion of Sachverhalt, a significant juridical change had occurred during the first half of the nineteenth century: the elements that composed the Sachverhalt were no longer simply gathered in a written file. Instead, they had to be uttered and heard before court. That hearing takes on a double meaning in Stumpf's research, and I attempt to capture this duality through the notion of utterance. This opens a door to considering both the sonic and performative nature of musical utterances and their situatedness for the uttering subject. The legal origins of the notion can further assist in reading his work against the grain: Stumpf cleared a path for phenomenology in various ways while at the same time offering the potential to include music cultures as an object of study.

Several aspects in the transition from written files to public oral proceedings will be of interest in the present context, including the compilation of pertinent materials, the notion of musical utterance, and Stumpf's need for interaction with the experimental subjects. The file that provided the formulation of the state of affairs to be judged always comprised a multitude of items, from simple data to complex statements and narratives. It is in the process of composing such a file that Stumpf's activities as an experimental psychologist can be placed. To do so, this chapter proceeds in the following steps. Firstly, I will introduce the notion of Sachverhalt and, building upon research about the juridical origins of the term, contextualize Stumpf's use of it. As he sought to understand which mental functions are active when tones are judged, he assembled what I will call "musical utterances." I will, secondly, survey his strategies of assembling musical utterances over the stretch of three major projects, namely the psychology of tones as exemplified in the two volumes of *Tonpsychologie* (1883, 1890), the early phase of his research on non-European music, starting from his article "Lieder der Bellakula-Indianer" (1886, Songs of the Nuxalk) and the research on speech sounds, as exemplified in his late book *Die Sprachlaute* (1926, Speech sounds). These projects can also be seen as three stages in the development of Stumpf's method from formulating the Sachverhalt in a way that closely resembles the legal practice toward a fully experimental procedure. To the discussion of these stages, I will, thirdly, add a discussion of how Stumpf eventually did not insist on proposing his own notion of phenomenology. For this purpose, and in parallel to the reconstruction of the notion of Sachverhalt in relation to musical utterances, the phenomenology Stumpf developed will be summarized stepwise, so as to eventually specify Stumpf's approach in distinction to Husserl's phenomenological attitude. Thus, going back beyond the early history of ethnomusicology reveals the potential within the study of music to combine phenomenology and the individual's cultural embedding.

A TERM FOR A PROBLEM: STATE OF AFFAIRS

Stumpf's relation to phenomenology is ambiguous. Although his personal and institutional support for Husserl is undeniable, many aspects in Stumpf's work, including his critique of Husserl in the posthumous *Erkenntnislehre* (1939-40, Epistemology), distinguish his views from phenomenology.[4] A central figure in experimental psychology as it emerged in the last decades of the nineteenth century, Stumpf somewhat fell out of the scope of the history of philosophy and in particular phenomenology, due also to the latter's anti-psychologism.[5] Finally, a large share of his work, especially the part that concerned questions of auditory sensation and music cognition, has not been received as contributing to philosophy to begin with. Margret Kaiser-el-Safti (2011) explains in her foreword to a new edition of *Erkenntnislehre* that Stumpf pleaded for a "hands-on" approach to psychology. Stumpf thought such an approach would not exclude rigorous philosophizing, but that hands-on aspect has been considered incompatible with philosophy, and his contributions have instead been attributed to experimental psychology as well as various subdisciplines in systematic musicology (Kaiser-el-Safti 2011, 12).

Those who do position Stumpf within the history of philosophy generally do so by way of two of his papers, both of which were annotated and quoted by Husserl.[6] These are "Erscheinungen und psychische Funktionen" (1907b, translated as "Appearances and Psychic Functions" 2018)[7] and "Zur Einteilung der Wissenschaften" (On the classification of the sciences; 1907c),[8] written in 1905 and 1906 and both published in 1907. Central to both of these papers—and to attempts to relate them to phenomenology—is the term "state of affairs" or "Sachverhalt." This term situates the intersection that Stumpf saw in logic and psychology in yet another context, namely juridical terminology, which provided the background for Stumpf's work in both fields. In philosophy, Sachverhalt was first used around 1880 in the circles of Hermann Lotze.[9] The term became prominent in phenomenology in its Munich and Göttingen branches (Smith 1992; Salice 2020). Husserl singles out the term in the notes he took at the University of Halle, where he heard Stumpf's lectures on metaphysics, logic, and psychology (Rollinger 1999, 89f.; Fisette 2015a). For both lectures, Stumpf provided printed syllabi that have survived in Husserl's papers, including his annotations.

In the syllabus on logic, Stumpf defined the notion as part of the theory of judgment as follows: "From the matter of a judgment we distinguish its *content* or the *state of affairs* expressed in the judgment. E.g., 'God is' has God as its matter, the being of God as its content. 'There is no God' has the same matter, but the nonbeing of God as the content" (Rollinger 1999, 313; italics in the original). He came back to the term in "Phenomena and Psychical Functions," where he referred to Brentano and Bolzano as the source of the notion, specifying the linguistic structure of the judgment's content as "that-clauses" or "substantivized infinitives" such as the "being" or "non-being" of God (1907b, 29; translations after Rojszczak and Smith 2008, 165).

The use of the term "state of affairs" in juridical terminology widens the scope of the present discussion in important ways. Analyzing the legal connotations of the notion in the work of Ludwig Wittgenstein, philosopher Barry Smith has pointed to the training in law that provided a context for "German philosophical thinking and writing."[10] It has its roots in medieval political theory, where *status rerum* indicated a state of things (Smith 1978, 427), and the Latin term was translated as "state of affairs" and "Sachverhalt," respectively. The German word combines *Sache*, which distinguishes affairs as something that are dealt with from the notions of *Ding* (thing) and *Gegenstand* (object), with a substantivized form of the verb *verhalten*, which means the way in which something behaves (see Smith 1978, 1992).

It is important to note, though, that the concept of law behind the German term is that of a code of law, rather than the "concept of legal order derived from the common or case law of the Anglo-Saxon world." As opposed to the latter's "unwritten working rules, learned in application," Germanic law rests on codification and eventually "determines a logically definite legal space." In that space, "'ontological' principles express, for instance, the nature of 'property' or of a 'legal person.'" The principles must rest on some underlying theory of nature, man, society or, more specifically, guilt, innocence, and other relevant concepts, and the theory of those, in turn, "has been derived largely from theological notions" (Smith 1978, 425f.).

If we take case law to be a series of precedents set by the history of judicial rulings and interpretations, then the important distinction with the German situation lies in the role of sociality. Case law is activated in a process that includes social interaction. In contrast, a concept of law that derives from essentialist or even theological notions relates in very different ways to such interaction. The history of the juridical notion of Sachverhalt sheds light on this. Stumpf directly participated in the contexts explicated above. Not only did he share the cultural background of that German notion of law; he also studied law for a short while, be it only in the hope that the profession would leave him enough time for his main interest, namely music. In addition, he mentions in his 1924 autobiography that both his father and his mother's father were forensic physicians. His father was employed by the Bavarian state as *Landgerichtsarzt* (provincial court physician), a specific function in Bavaria of a forensic medical expert working for a court. While Stumpf himself mused that the many doctors in his family must have induced in him a sense for the empirical sciences (1924, 2), this family background may also have provided him with an intuitive understanding of the legal notions mentioned here. That Stumpf abandoned law when he heard the habilitation lecture of Franz Brentano does not derogate the importance of the juridical background for his mode of operating with philosophical terms. He decided to pursue philosophy with Brentano and even followed Brentano's example in taking up studies at the priests' seminary in Würzburg. Stumpf, however, did not become a Catholic priest. After taking his PhD, and later habilitation, with Lotze in Göttingen, he was appointed professor of philosophy at Würzburg University in 1873 with Brentano's and Lotze's support.

Stumpf's elaborations on the notion of state of affairs appeared at a peculiar historical moment. Phenomenology as well as another important strand of twentieth-century thinking, namely gestalt theory, were only about to take shape. Even more interesting is Stumpf's attempt to relate these two nascent fields in his philosophizing. The paper "Phenomena and Psychical Functions" introduced the term "Sachverhalt" in an "Excursion about the formations (*Gebilde*) of psychical functions." Among these Stumpf listed not only states of affairs but also concepts, collectives, and values.[11] The term "Gebilde," or formation, designated the correlate of a mental function. It indicated a separate level of description in Stumpf's analyses, to be situated between phenomena and the functions themselves. To substantiate that third level, he used an example from Christian von Ehrenfels's paper "Über Gestaltqualitäten" (On gestalt qualities, 1890). Ehrenfels, another student of Brentano, had argued that what makes a melody appear to us as such, rather than as an arbitrary sequence of sounds, was to be called gestalt qualities. Slightly shifting the terminology, Stumpf declared the mental function in the case of melody to consist in comprehending or epitomizing (*zusammenfassen*) the notes, thereby creating an *Inbegriff* (collective) or a "form." Even more fittingly, he added, referring positively to the second part of Husserl's *Logical Investigations*, the notion of formation could be seen here to correspond to Husserl's notion of "*Einheitsmomente*" (moments of unity).[12]

As with these two notions he drew from Ehrenfels and Husserl, Stumpf suggested his own notion of formation to refer neither to the mental function itself—"the bundle is not the bundling-up" (1907c, 30)—nor to the phenomenon (*Erscheinung*). Rather, it was "a third" (*ein Drittes*) that Stumpf sought for. What the emergence of a melody from tones that would otherwise be unrelated had in common with emergence of a concept and a state of affairs is that each was not just a phenomenon but something that involved a correlate of a mental function: something more comprehensive than just some unrelated multitude, something correlated to a mental function but not identical with it. Interpolated into this explanation of formation is the reiterated definition of state of affairs from the earlier one in the syllabus. The three levels appear most clearly in this case. In judgments, for example, about God's being or non-being, the matter is God, the content is in one case the being and in the other the non-being, and the judgment can in both cases be either negative or positive.

The interesting question for Stumpf in the context of the present argument is how both terms—formations and, more specifically, states of affairs—could be accessed in a concrete investigation. In both papers Stumpf specified that the conceptual work on the correlates of mental functions had to be done carefully in the absence of knowledge on brain physiology. Borrowing the nineteenth-century nerve physiologist Emil du Bois-Reymond's phrase for the scientist's structural ignorance about how mind and body relate, Stumpf emphasized that even at the time when brain physiology would have reached an "astronomical degree of knowledge" (1907b, 31) of the neural physiology behind mental functions there would still be matters (e.g., the specificity of the sensory modes) that neural physiology could not explain. Yet it was clear that the philosophers' concepts would eventually be related to questions such as those of localizing domains in the brain. For the moment, though, Stumpf was critical of how the research in this field was done. Cases of aphasia from lesions were discussed, for instance, in the journal *Zeitschrift für Psychologie und Physiologie der Sinnesorgane* (Journal for psychology and physiology of the sensory organs). Stumpf was one of the editors of this journal, but he criticized this research for failing to distinguish mental functions from their products.

The emphasis on carefully weighing descriptive terms in the absence of secure knowledge of facts brings us back to the juridical context of the term "state of affairs." According to the actual juridical process of German law, as Barry Smith explains, only that which has been heard in court is available for judgment. The judge, he writes,

> is confined to actually uttered sentences introduced into the locus of the court by the successive witnesses—or rather to the states of affairs which these represent and towards which, from the point of view of the court, their testimony is directed. And since he cannot reach through the reports in which these states of affairs are represented, through and onto independent events, it follows that legal space, the domain of depicted states of affairs, can never be transcended. The judge in passing

judgment does not attach the legal consequences to entities existing independently of the forms of representation with which he operates.

(Smith 1978, 430)

Thus, a state of affairs is that which results from the utterances available to the judge that provide a basis for the passing of judgment. This description unites the inaccessibility of facts with the need to gather utterances without as yet evaluating them. Referring to Arkadiusz Chrudzimski's reformulation of the state of affairs in Stumpf's logic, one could say that the term Sachverhalt steps between matter and judgment, enabling us to articulate the content of judgment in propositional form. As Stumpf writes in "Appearances and Psychic Functions,"

the state of affairs cannot be given on its own, independent of any immediately given function, and thereby also be real. It can only be real as the content of a judgment that actually takes place. Rather, any state of affairs, and also ones that are surely false or, indeed, absurd, would not only be true but indeed real. Functions (indeed, of course, only the conscious, distinct, and present functions) are thus immediately recognized facts; the configurations [i.e., formations], however, are facts in general only as contents of functions.

(Stumpf [1907] 2018, 105)

The state of affairs thus needs to be thought of as co-emerging with the function of judgment both in German legal practice and in Stumpf's logic.

States of Affairs in Law: Contextualizing the Collection of Utterances

Media theorist Cornelia Vismann has pointed out in her treatise on the media of legal practice that German law underwent an important shift after 1800. The German word for legal practice literally translates the Latin word *jurisdictio*:

That media technologies determine the technique of legal practice (*Rechtsprechung*) has not been a topic about which one can expect to get information from law. All that law says about it is contained in the word "Recht-Sprechen"—speaking the law. Speaking is the basic act of justice.

(Vismann 2011, 97)

Yet, as Vismann explains, spoken presence only became a *conditio sine qua non* in the nineteenth century. Before this, German law had developed a unique system of gathering written documents. Since the sixteenth century, local and lower-level courts had more and more regularly sought advice from university faculties of law. The dispatch of files, which in the beginning consisted of just one leaf explaining the state of affairs, grew into voluminous bundles by the eighteenth century that were sent back and forth between courts and law professors. Quoting historian Reinhart Kosselleck, Vismann explains: "Because much had to be written, more had to be written" (Kosselleck 1967, 666, quoted in Vismann 2011, 102). The decisive question became what entered the file and what did not: *quod non est in actis, non est in mundo* (what is not in the files, is not in the world). As the judgment had to be based on the file, anything not contained in it would not be considered.

The system of advice from law professors only found its official end with a law from 1879, which granted a monopoly of jurisdiction to courts (Vismann 2011, 110). By then, however, a new approach to jurisdiction was long established. The Napoleonic *Code de procédure civil et pénal* of 1806 prescribed that the proceedings before court had to happen orally and publicly. When in 1810 German judges in the French dominion became acquainted with the practice of the proceedings in the presence of the parties, they praised its advantages. It was cheaper and faster, and, as one author wrote, it did not even lead to an increase in criminality (Mittermaier 1845, 131). For German legal scholar Paul Johann Anselm Ritter von Feuerbach, who, in the early nineteenth century, was among the first to theorize the need for speech in the presence of the court, the new approach expressed the ideal of the autonomous subject. His student Carl Joseph Anton Mittermaier took the matter further, listening more closely to what speech did at court: the voice betrayed the speaker, their mental state, and also their sincerity. Mittermaier "took immediacy to refer to the immediate impression, which the speech of a person before court makes on the judges," whereas for Feuerbach, immediacy still had been "the principle, which installed the subject as the carrier of subjective rights" (Vismann 2011, 117).

With Mittermaier's 1845 treatise *Die Mündlichkeit, das Anklageprinzip, die Öffentlichkeit und das Geschworenengericht* (Orality, the principle of accusation, the public, and the jury), we reach the situation of legal practice in Stumpf's time. Mittermaier compared the various approaches in Europe, including the Kingdom of Bavaria. As elsewhere in the German lands, the principle of presence gained acceptance in Bavaria by the late 1820s, although even in 1845 the penal code was still based on inquisitorial, written, and closed proceedings. The debate about reform centered on the conditions on which the criminal act could be made accessible for the judgment, eventually replacing the written file with an oral and public hearing. If the standard account of the transition is rooted in the nineteenth-century concept of the autonomous subject, Vismann's account helps us scrutinize the means and media that enabled this concept to function. Both before and after the turn to orality, the state of affairs gained its full shape in specific constellations of records. The case to be judged—whether written or uttered—was prepared by gathering the pertinent records that included statements and materials for and against the question of culpability. In this context, "state of affairs" refers to the file that virtually created the "state" of the matter at hand that was meant to be judged.

This sheds light on how Stumpf used the term "Sachverhalt" in his philosophical writings. If a state of affairs depends on how its matter is phrased, whether in logic or when uttered before court—recall the different state of affairs depending on whether the content of the judgment was the being or the non-being of God—then the legal definition in addition introduces a temporal order. The state of affairs as that which is to be judged defines a demarcation line *after* gathering the relevant utterances and *before* judging them. In the logical definition of judgment, that order is concealed, or rather reduced to a logical dependence instead of a temporal sequence. Yet, before court, the temporality becomes apparent, and the transition from written to oral, public, and open proceedings profiled it even more sharply.

Collecting Utterances: The Development of Techniques and Strategies

This section explores Stumpf's practice of composing states of affairs. I will analyze what I take to be three steps in the development of his method over the roughly fifty years of his research into utterances musical and verbal. In all three steps I see a different approach to how an utterance is integrated into the state of affairs or—from his perspective as a researcher—into the matter to be investigated. Calling Stumpf's approach an investigation implicitly positions it between the domains of law and logic, and the three steps increasingly formalize the ways that Stumpf's methodology copes with the tensions between rigorous logic and a rich object of investigation. Pointing to this tension, Chrudzimski (2015, 185) remarks that the way in which Stumpf integrates both is one of the most surprising features of Stumpf's notion of Sachverhalt, and he relates it back to an "epistemization of the notion of truth" (178) no longer in need of transcendental objects as truth makers:

> The idea is that for the affirmative judgment "A is" only an object A is needed (and no strange "existential fact" that A exists) and that the negative judgment "A is not" is made true by the mere absence of A, rather than by an (even stranger) existential fact of A not existing. (178)

From the perspective of legal practice, this is perhaps not so surprising at all. Let us recall Stumpf's view on the Sachverhalt as a formation or third level between phenomena and functions. The logical notion of state of affairs referred not just to the matter to be judged but also to the judgment's content in the narrowest sense, thus phrasing the matter linguistically in such a way that it already includes a yes-or-no alternative without anticipating its affirmation or rejection in the judgment itself. This is in line with Brentano's translation of the four classic categorical propositions into a language that only operates with "is" and "is not." In Brentano, thus, "judging consists in accepting or rejecting a mentally presented object. This accepting or rejecting, furthermore does not consist in ascribing the object a strange property of exitance or non-existence. Rather it is a mental mode, which as such does not need any objective correlates" (179).[13]

The German legal notion of Sachverhalt, in turn, denotes a preparation of a judgment's content, without anticipating the judgment. The three steps I highlight here in the methodological development of Stumpf's work reach an ever more sharply defined setup for acting out exactly this procedure. While, in so doing, Stumpf gradually moved away from a practice that resembled the legal practice of composing a Sachverhalt, his own practice always insisted on bringing in the riches of unanalyzed actual utterance into his work.

Most important for the line of the present argument, however, is the fact that the legal practice of composing the Sachverhalt opens a gate that allows the cultural setting to flow into the process of judging. Even in the more mundane understanding of legal practice, composing the Sachverhalt required assembling pertinent information about the matter at hand. The file had to be rich, so as to lead to a judgment that—as holds for judgment in Brentano—could be passed "by someone who passes judgment based on evidence" (Chrudzimski 2015, 178). The impossibility of referring to anything that was not present in the files or at court provides, furthermore, a rather surprising commonality with Stumpf's approach to music, and this commonality places Stumpf's approach in opposition to the often-made assumption that music, as a rule-based endeavor, lends itself to comparisons with law or logic. Such an assumption most often does not allow one to take the musicking subject into account. Instead, it excludes anyone who, for whatever reason, does not follow one particular set of rules for music tout court. Stumpf's approach was remarkably different: he granted the right to speak up on music—musically or verbally—to anyone, because (and not although) his approach was rigorous in its logic and serious about the comparison with legal practice. He collected utterances of those performing, listening, sensing, and understanding music in various ways alongside, and on par with, the accessible records of musical utterances, such as sheet music and sound recordings.

This distinguished Stumpf from music theorists, such as Hugo Riemann (e.g., 1914–16), Ernst Kurth (1931), and Jacques Handschin (1948). To follow up on the metaphor of the court, they rather fit the position of the judge who took the rules of musical composition as their code of law. What the Swiss musicologist Handschin, for instance, called a "psychology of tone" was in fact a history of the power to internalize and follow rules evidenced in written records since Greek antiquity through the Middle Ages. He found Stumpf to be "strangely incredulous towards anything not palpable" (1948, 8) and, in explicit contrast to Stumpf, conceived of his own psychology as a speculative endeavor. Kurth's "powers" of listening and Riemann's mental "tone representations" resorted to the expert's mind. Riemann even provided a course manual for acquiring the appropriate tone representations in his treatise on *Tonvorstellungen* (Tonal representations).[14] In this way, others could join him by becoming music listening experts in the exact sense of his theory.

The exclusive reference to the utterances assembled to present a Sachverhalt for judgment, in contrast, would admit speculation or a training program such as Riemann's only under the condition that there was some subject who authored it. Thus, for Stumpf, the rules of harmony did not provide material, unless they were uttered by a subject providing testimony for their own listening. The testimony of such listening, however, brought individual interpretations of the rules into play. Not all listeners would connect rules and sensations in the same way; some clearly had no access to the alleged effects of the rules at all. Yet all these utterances could be equally relevant, depending on the question or, in other words, the state of affairs that would put them up for judgment. Additionally, the utterances Stumpf did collect were not necessarily preselected utterances in the sense of the current music discourse. They concerned tones, music, and speech sounds alike. Listening and playing could be dealt with on par. In sum, the practice of composing a Sachverhalt in preparation for but independently from judgment facilitated an understanding of music that we can subsume nowadays under a broad notion of musicking.

Opponent of an Accepted Theory

An early example of Stumpf's collection of utterances can be found in a case that is reminiscent of the previously described German legal practice. In the first volume of *Tonpsychologie* (1883), he presented a collection of listeners' reports concerning the question of whether and how they had any physical experience when thinking of concrete pitches or melodies. At the time, a specific theory on this matter was current: physiologists and philosophers claimed that muscle memory of the larynx helped in identifying pitch. Among prominent adherents to this theory was Stumpf's former mentor Lotze, whom he quoted saying, "No memory of tones and tonal series proceeds without being accompanied by a silent and intended speaking or singing" (Lotze 1852, 480, quoted in Stumpf 2020, 102). Indeed, a movement of the larynx was held to unconsciously accompany any imagination of melodies by many, such as experimental psychologist Georg Müller or the pathologist Salomon Stricker. Melodies would be thought of with the larynx moving into the appropriate position for singing along, just as the organs of articulation would move when reading written text.[15]

Some of Stumpf's informants, though, testified to the opposite. String players, especially, did not feel or imagine the throat movements of singing, which Lotze and others had described, nor did they imagine themselves playing their instruments.[16] Other reports stemmed from a composer and a conductor, and Stumpf also included his own introspective account. He found himself able to imagine timbres that he could not have produced through singing, as well as pitches without a particular timbral quality that he could transfer from one instrument to the other in his imagination. In other cases, he consciously activated his muscle memory, translating a tone he wished to memorize into muscle movements of his larynx.

A remarkable feature in this collection of utterances is that he obviously aimed at contradicting the theory of accompanying muscle movements. Among the sources were letters that his informants had written to him on his request, as well as statements from conversations. The introspection, here, acquires the status of a testimony alongside and on par with the other reports: "Self-observation shows me quite clearly that in many cases I do, but in thousands of other cases I do *not* use muscular sensations for imagination and for the formation of judgements" (2020, 104). The outcome was that musical practice and tonal representation related in inconsistent ways. "We may indeed assume," he summarized, "that laryngeal sensations as well as presentations of them are a concomitant phenomenon that habitually occurs mainly in the case of singers and lay 'music lovers' who indeed also usually 'do a little singing'" (2020, 106). In discussing the question of whether a muscle sensation accompanied imagined pitch, Stumpf thus opposed an established view. The testimonies from people with a specific musical education helped him to contest this view. Filing the letters and colloquial statements into his case, he could eventually dismiss the accepted theory.

Summarizing this strategy of compiling, we see that the compilation prepares the final judgment on the matter to deny a necessary role for muscle movement in cognition. This demonstrates the power of the two-step judgment: the compilation of the testimonies contained both those for and those against a compulsory movement of the throat. The evidence from the subjects, whether they would or would not experience muscle movements, was always embedded in a broader context. The subjects' trajectory of musical experience in a broader sense mattered: based on their individual standpoint, some subjects feel the sensation in question. The differences among standpoints do not relativize a judgment; instead, they provide the condition on which to judge.

What the Unmusical Have to Say: Devising a Method of Inquiry

In the same volume of *Tonpsychologie*, Stumpf also reported on another strategy, which challenged not simply one specific theory or view but the entire system of the rules of music. Soon after he arrived at his new position as professor of philosophy in Würzburg in 1873, he began soliciting "judgments on tones" from a specific group of listeners, namely people who declared to lack any talent for music. Stumpf invited them to his home and exposed them to a simple test: could they tell which of two notes was higher? They could not, as it turned out. Their answers were random. This convinced Stumpf that he was onto something, perhaps a promising new method. If judgments about tones could be unreliable to the point of not knowing one's way up and down the tone ladder, any statement about music from such an individual would be ungeneralizable or, in other words, not shaped by the rules of music. This raised the question of what remained of music when it was stripped of the rules. The "curious differences between musical and unmusical natures," Stumpf declared in the foreword to *Tonpsychologie*, give "the expert as many points of support in his investigation as they give the layperson obstacles" (2020, lxi). If previous philosophers had abstained from studying music, as Stumpf critically notes, now the comparison of statements through systematic collection, including "comparisons of peoples and ages, biographical information, etc." (2020, lxi–lxii), would disclose the most interesting features in the functions of the mind to the philosopher who was willing to engage with music.

This method must be sharply distinguished from Wilhelm Wundt's school of experimental psychology that developed in parallel to Stumpf's. As has been discussed, for instance, by Alexandra Hui in her book *The Psychophysical Ear* (2013, 237), Wundt produced data in the first instance.[17] Statistical methods in empirical psychology have one of their origins at the laboratory he founded at Leipzig University in 1879. Among the objects he and his collaborators studied was auditory perception. Wundt's idea of a physiological psychology that could determine as closely as possible the minimal physiological conditions for mental activity also involved psychophysics, that is to say, a systematic comparison between measurable stimuli and sensation. When applied to pitch, this went wrong, Stumpf thought. Their previous knowledge of music would guide the experimental subjects in judging the stimuli and thereby trigger mental functions that could not be properly grasped with the methods of psychophysics.

This led to a controversy between the two psychologists. While Wundt and his collaborators put as many individuals as possible to test without documenting the subjects' previous education, Stumpf denied the validity of such statistical tests for the case of pitch. Wundt hoped to find the physiological basis of psychology of, for instance, music listening; Stumpf was skeptical that such experiments would not simply reproduce the bias of the musically educated without gaining access to a reflection upon it. A question like "what is the middle value between two notes?" would be answered in a categorially different way by those for whom the notes were part of a system of rules to begin with.

Stumpf and Wundt seem to converge in that they considered empirical facts to provide insights into the human mind, but they differed in how they processed the material they collected from their subjects. Wundt strove for collecting data, whereas Stumpf collected utterances. Wundt's data needed statistical modeling, and in return promised a strong connection to facts. The utterances, in contrast, did not allow Stumpf to reach behind them toward a truth or fact. Beyond the state of affairs, the utterance did not yield data but dissolved in the biographical trajectory, cultural embedding, and historical and local situatedness of the uttering subject.

That "unmusical" subjects—or, as Stumpf also called them with a Greek-style euphemism, the "amusoi"—were granted a right to utter their hearing, that is to say, to describe their experience as listeners or musicking subjects more generally, was radically new. While early nineteenth-century music discourse highlighted talent (Gembris 1997), those without it fell out of the picture. Rare exceptions were to be understood against the background of Romantic notions such as genius. This changed with Stumpf. Parallel to his work and especially in the early twentieth century, cognitive distortions due to brain lesions were discovered as a source of physiological knowledge (Peretz et al. 2003; Peretz 2006; Kursell 2018). In contrast to this research, however, Stumpf's queries needed access to what the unmusical experienced. Accordingly, the descriptions of the subjects given in the two volumes of *Tonpsychologie* are extensive. The subjects are introduced with their musical preferences and distastes. Even among the unmusical, no homogenizing was applied.

Little by little, the way in which the two groups of musical and unmusical subjects differed molded into a new vocabulary. Stumpf spoke of a "standpoint" to designate the way that the musical subjects located notes in musical space. They would not just register a tone or note but would place it there in relation to "fixed signal staffs for the acoustic geodesy" (2020, 99).[18] This way of hearing musical notes within tonal space he eventually termed "analytical hearing," which also included providing interval names and degrees of dissonance or consonance for two simultaneous notes. The unmusical, in contrast, were left without orientation in tonal space. They remained in a state of sensation, as he would say, and they would not proceed further toward analyzing what they heard in the terms of tonal harmony.

What the unmusical heard and said, however, opened up a door to the conditions of the psychical functions of interest to Stumpf. As Stumpf realized when he was confronted with a performance of Nuxalk First Nation people in 1885, the musical subjects' standpoint, including his own, actually functioned like a firm attitude that, in practice, came down to prejudice or bias. In the performance of the Nuxalk, or "Nuchalkmch," as Stumpf notates their name, he suddenly found himself in the position of a listener without any signposts. Their singing seemed like "howling" to him, but he realized that he could not simply call it mistuned and grew eager to arrange a meeting with one of them. In fact, a meeting with the main singer, Nuskilusta, was granted by their impresario—the adventurer and founder of the zoo in Hamburg, Carl Hagenbeck, who "exhibited" the musicians (Ames 2003, 2008).

For several hours, Nuskilusta and one of the other members of the group patiently repeated the songs over and over again as Stumpf tried to jot down what he heard and regretted not having a "shorthand for music" (1886, 406).[19] The testimony of this different musical geodesy needed to be registered. Stumpf had learned the Gabelsberger shorthand system, which Franz Xaver Gabelsberger had developed to address the political exigencies of the Bavarian Parliament that had been constituted in 1818. The speech acts of legislation and jurisdiction required a written reference, and shorthand systems became the way to provide it. This system not only remained the main shorthand in southern Germany well into the twentieth century; it was also used by both Stumpf and Husserl for their personal notes. If in the legal context the exact wording of testimony mattered most, in other cases the use of shorthand prioritizes speed or privacy. Stumpf's preserved archival notes from his experiments are full of scribbles in Gabelsberger shorthand,[20] reflecting his thoughts and comments during experimentation. In this way, they offer a striking parallel to Husserl's practice of using shorthand (Moran 2000, 63). They document a train of thought, namely Stumpf's perspective on the experimental production of phenomena.

Notating the Nuxalk's singing as best he could in Western notation, Stumpf realized that staff notation already contained the European tonal listeners' standpoint. It proved difficult to fetch the important features of what he heard: Nuskilusta clearly did possess a standpoint, but it differed from Stumpf's own. Some of the features Stumpf implicitly expected from such a system would not be present in it, others seemed to be shared between the singer and his listener, yet others he could not make sense of from the spot.

Stumpf noted, for instance, that his informant transposed melodies, just as an individual raised under the same conditions as Stumpf himself would. Triumphantly, he remarked in the publication about the encounter that, in a later performance of the Nuxalk, he was able to follow their music and even identified deviations in their singing, commenting tongue in cheek, "There are certainly unmusical individuals among the savages, too" (1886, 408).

Stumpf's irony—clearly aimed at his contemporary German readers—short-circuited an allegedly superior ideal type of music with an equally alleged homogenous cultural adherence to that ideal type. This irony is echoed in the many detailed descriptions of the unmusical, such as a Professor G., a Dr. K., a Fräulein C., the students Be. and Bo. (i.e., colleagues, students, and staff at his various universities and across his own social stratum). Through Stumpf's description, feelings of superiority were reduced to the fact that any bearer of a standpoint—in this case a space of interval relationships—will not immediately accept a different standpoint, while assuming a homogeneity among peers with regards to their own standpoint. Though the encounter with Stumpf might have been one of the less unpleasant moments for the Nuxalk on their journey through Germany as an exhibit, the question remains how the whole encounter positions Stumpf and his research in the broader field of respecting knowledge that comes in different shapes. Within the given historical circumstances, however, the encounter demonstrates that the notion of music as an ideal type presupposes learning and abstracts it out from the concrete experiences during musical activity. Stumpf made no reference to his conviction of the superiority of Western musical composition as a complex elaboration, which he did in his speeches and his book *The Origins of Music*. The case at hand showed something different, and something important. The psychology of music was not about a single concept of music but about a single concept of the human mind. Its logical rigor did not produce universalist claims, but it enabled Stumpf to grasp difference and heterogeneity. While it exceeds the limits of the present chapter to test the approach presented here on the totality of Stumpf's research, it is important to note that, apparently, the postponement of judgment entailed by the concept of Sachverhalt contributed to the critical openness to the unfamiliar that Stumpf brought to this encounter.

What the Unmusical Have to Say When They Sing

The systematic comparison of standpoints and the trajectories that led to them proved cumbersome. As the encounter with Nuskilusta had shown to Stumpf, a study of the mind that took one way of musicking—and by the same token auditory cognition—for granted would miss its point. The idea of such comparison nevertheless seems to have lingered in Stumpf's mind, and it turned into an activity of collecting music when he had already become the founding director of Berlin University's Institute of Psychology. Erich Moritz von Hornbostel, who first had joined Stumpf as an assistant there and later became the director of the Berliner Phonogramm-Archiv, undertook a journey to Oklahoma in 1906 to carry out tests on subjects, especially schoolchildren, of various backgrounds, such as Pawnee, African American, and settler communities. He reported in a letter to Stumpf that he found a similar distribution of musical and unmusical children as one might expect back home. The features of both the musical and unmusical children's singing, however, differed from his expectations. He summarized that more measurements would be necessary—"perhaps Abraham will take care of this matter" (Kursell 2017a; on the journey more generally, see Koch 2013).

Otto Abraham, another assistant at the Institute of Psychology, indeed carried out a series of measurements. He did not measure the diverging systems of tonal space, nor did he inquire into the difference between correct or incorrect performance. Instead, he measured what performers thought to be correct intonation. Recording twenty-three wax rolls of singing, he found a surprising degree of divergence among what singers considered correct intonation. The comparison between subjective correctness and empirical measurements made the notion that a recording was a valid representation in the same sense as musical notation untenable. The Western notion of representation seemed to be surprisingly elastic and its alleged mathematical precision a delusion. If intoned values within the bandwidth of a third could match a performer's sense of correct intonation, then how reliable could measuring recordings or melodies from other cultures be? Abraham's article did not ask this question that nevertheless emerges from his work. In any case, measuring the pitch distances of recorded music had to be reconsidered as an undertaking of its own kind, rather than a search for the representable and represented tune.

Although Abraham's publication about the study came out only in 1923, the first recordings were made in 1907, after Hornbostel's journey and after Stumpf had written his two papers updating his philosophical terminology. What the recordings brought to the fore was rather unexpected also with regards to that terminology. The recordings of one unmusical subject are preserved at the archive, whose singing was not commented upon explicitly in the later publication. They demonstrate that the functional coherence that supposedly arose between the elements of a melody could not appropriately be described by Husserl's notion of "Einheitsmomente" or Ehrenfels's "Gestaltqualitäten" that Stumpf discussed in his 1907 paper on formations (1907b, 32). Or, to be more precise, whatever created that unity had to be detached from any notion of interval. This singer would reproduce contour without pitch, leaving the *Gestalt* without *Qualitäten*, and the *Einheit* without its *Momente*. Abraham elaborated: "We can thus state a rare case of an individual taking pleasure in music without (the historically grown) tone- or interval-quality sensations" (1923, 22). By the time Abraham had set to work on the matter, Stumpf's research already had established that the utterances of unmusical subjects could enter a state of affairs in judging musical matters. The same was true of the singing of the unmusical individual in this case: it was a fully valid utterance, provided that the state of affairs was carefully composed.

The new ways of collecting utterances gave a voice to unexpected utterance points.[21] These made the internal heterogeneity of the musical culture appear, which cut through the homogeneous notion of music. While the dominant discourse on music continued to privilege internalized tonal listening, the evidence from such experiments made things more complicated. The notion of music—or, rather, musicking—that emerges from them is dynamic. The practice of composing a state of affairs kept shifting the entire architecture of the disciplines busying themselves with music through the internal differentiations it evidenced. The practice of composing such a state of affairs can thus be seen to postpone the final evaluation of the utterances. The unmusical subjects demonstrated that neither the phenomena nor any functions could be deduced from a supposedly universal notion of music. Instead, the research that juggled with the correlates appearing in the musicking mind had to keep all these components in the air.

Producing Utterances Experimentally

The final stage of developing the strategies of collecting utterances can be found in the research Stumpf carried out after he turned from music and the comparison of standpoints to a new topic in the second decade of the twentieth century. In 1913, Stumpf initiated the construction of a device for the analysis and synthesis of sounds. The device, in its completed state, occupied six of the institute's eight rooms. Its main purpose was research into speech sounds, and its working principle was based on the interference of actual sound waves propagating through connected tubes. This so-called interference device was cutting-edge technology in its time. Interference was used for canceling out partial waves in sound by superposing them with their mirror images (Kursell 2017b, 2021). For the analysis of sounds, component frequencies could be canceled out one by one; for sound synthesis, it enabled the production of pure tones with one single frequency whose intensity could be modified. These pure tones, in turn, were used for producing synthetic frequency compounds. In short, the device brought many features into acoustic research that would soon—starting from the mid-1920s—be provided by electric circuitry with much less effort and using far less space.

One salient feature of the assemblage of tubes and devices was that a separate room allowed researchers to conceal the sources from the subjects. They could be presented with either synthetically or naturally produced sounds, and their judgments on the sounds—for instance, in reply to the quality of the vowel they heard—would happen without knowledge of the sounds' origins. Stumpf reported that he used such "uninformed trials" for checking the resemblance of synthetic to naturally produced vowel sounds. Not knowing what they would be confronted with, however, the experimental subjects produced an additional layer of information: they also conveyed their default assumptions. The default that stepped in when proper information did not guide their answers betrayed their previous assumptions on the matter at hand or, in other words, their bias. "In living speech," Stumpf wrote, "we constantly deal with directive settings [*richtungsweisende Einstellungen*]. Simply by setting our mind to the German, French, or Italian language, we exclude a great number of possibilities, and include others" (1926, 50).

The term that is used in the quote for the default is "*Einstellung.*" The occurrence of this term entertains a complicated relationship with Husserl's terminology. The original

German word is the same as the one Husserl used for distinguishing between the phenomenological and natural attitudes. In *Ideas Pertaining to a Pure Phenomenology and a Phenomenological Philosophy* ([1913] 1982), he coined his notion of "attitude" or Einstellung. The phenomenological attitude, he argued, had to temporarily switch off the "positing" (*Thesis*) that comes with unthinkingly adhering to an accepted conception of the world, in other words, the "natural attitude" (Husserl [1913] 1982, 51). Although the vocabulary Husserl ([1913] 1982, §§27–32) used to describe this shift in perspective bore technical overtones—most prominently in the word *Ausschaltung* ("switching off")—he did not pursue a comparison between technology and the mind.[22] Stumpf, in contrast, used "Einstellung" to refer to both the settings of his device and what one could call accordingly the settings of the mind.

This use of the newly coined term from phenomenology in an seemingly innocuous way nicely substantiates Kaiser-el-Safti's description of Stumpf's "hands-on" approach to psychology *and* philosophy. In the inauguration to his position as university rector of Berlin's Friedrich-Wilhelm University, Stumpf explained this as follows:

> I insist in that the philosopher should have learned and practiced some craft, that is to say, they should have been active in some concrete area be it of the humanities or the sciences. They should have experienced the sufferings and delights of research on their own, they should have acquired the right to participate in its discourse through fighting for their position, and they should master the language that prevails in that discourse.
>
> (Stumpf 1907a, 16)

Stumpf more than once escaped to other disciplines than philosophy—newly created ones, if need be—to allot his findings that did not match philosophical discourse. This time an established discipline became the host to his findings: phonetics. He published them in a book with the renowned science publisher Springer in 1926 under the title *Speech Sounds: An Experimental-Phonetic Investigation, with an Appendix on the Sounds of Musical Instruments*. In the foreword, Stumpf cautioned the reader: if ever a philosopher were to pick up the book by chance, they would "quickly put it away again, shaking their heads in disapproval" (vii). In fact, the research on vowel sounds aligned well with the standard research practices of phonetics, yielding valuable insights into vowel formants, that is, the resonance regions in vowel sounds.

Relativizing remarks—like the one above about the impact of native language on the possibilities available to perceiving sound—were not placed center stage in the book. Instead, they were smuggled in, while the main text reported on technical conditions of the trials and the data received from them. Two types of subjects are consistently involved in the workings of the apparatus. On the one hand, ignorant subjects were exposed to sounds in the chamber designed for this purpose. On the other hand, trained experts took on the role of observers of the sounds that resulted from the various settings of the apparatus. Stumpf emphasized that these two types of subjects also fulfilled very different roles. Next to the alleged main purpose of understanding the sound of vowels, however, a second strand of argument emerged: the ways in which the various subjects reacted to the sounds, the utterances of others they overheard, and the casual descriptions of their own expectations. If such observations would have provided food for a phenomenology of hearing as it seemed to correspond to Stumpf's own ideas of phenomenology, the term would have clashed with Husserl's. Phenomenology and Einstellung, or attitude, were already in use by that time.

More Trouble with Terms: Phenomenology and Gestalt Psychology

Going through the practice that resulted in the book on speech sound sheds new light on the debate between Stumpf and Husserl on what phenomenology does or should do, which has been reconstructed mainly from their direct interaction (e.g., Fisette 2015c). As authors such as Denis Fisette (2015c) have demonstrated, though, Stumpf did not always take positions directly; instead, he exerted considerable rhetorical effort to map his own conceptual constructions onto earlier figures in the history of philosophy. Although the book on speech sounds made no reference to phenomenology, which by the time of the publication would have been understood as a reference to Husserl's notion, it did substantiate Stumpf's own perspective on the tasks of phenomenology as he had formulated them earlier, in his two papers published in 1907.

In his paper "On the Classification of Sciences," Stumpf distinguished three "neutral scientific disciplines" from the two main branches of knowledge making, which he took to consist of the sciences and the humanities. Phenomenology was one of these three neutral disciplines, together with two more of his own invention, namely "eidology" (*Eidologie*) and "logology" (*Verhältnislehre*). Each of these dealt with one important condition for carrying out research in either the sciences or the humanities. Phenomenology, or the structural investigation of appearances, he declared to be a separate discipline, as would Husserl later. Logology, or the investigation of relations, dealt with the premises of any academic discipline, in that it concerned the relations between the entities of interest. Eidology took on the role to single out a third level between functions and phenomena that was discussed above; this dealt with formations in the sense used by Stumpf.

Stumpf's notion of phenomenology, which focused not on the genesis of phenomena but on the structural laws that were inherent in them, remained positioned between physiology and psychology. Phenomena in the sense of this subdiscipline (such as tones and colors) were different from phenomena in the sense of their physical causes (such as sound and light) and from the mental functions operating on them. Physics could never explain the different modalities of their appearance; therefore, some grounds had to be given for why seeing and hearing, for instance, are different for humans. Yet, phenomenology nevertheless depended on being fed by observation, but not because phenomenology could not do without the sciences. On the contrary, the physiological study of the brain, for the time being, could not do without observing the very same "phenomena" that phenomenology built upon: "In this give and take, the giving part resides still with phenomenology, while physiology is the taking part" (1907c, 31). That is to say: the mind would dictate to physiology what was there to be understood.

Stumpf came back to this take on phenomenology in the inauguration speech. There, he explicitly connected nineteenth-century sensory physiology to phenomenology:

> Another region has emerged in which psychologists and scientists collaborate, beginning with Helmholtz, in particular: phenomenology, i.e., an analysis of sensory phenomena as such into their last elements. The appearances of colors, tones, smells, formations in space and time, are not the physical world itself, as it appears to the mind of the scientist, nor are they the world of the psychologist. Yet they provide the material for the physicist and the point of departure and food for the inquiry into the life of the soul. Therefore, both the natural sciences and the humanities research, necessitate this [phenomenological] investigation, and even more so a philosophy, which sets itself the task to consider the laws of nature as well as the mind.
>
> (Stumpf 1907a, 21)

Even more clearly than a study of tones, a study of the speech sounds posited the object of investigation out of the reach of a mere empirical approach. What was there to be observed by scientists about language and communication would have to be sorted out by a study of the mind. A phenomenology of speech sounds was thus a production of observations, for which the science of phonetics depended on phenomena uttered by experimental subjects and observers.

The anti-psychologism of the next generation put that notion of phenomenology to a halt. Between 1900 and 1913, both Husserl and Stumpf changed their views on each other's work. Husserl dedicated his *Logical Investigations* to Stumpf in 1901, although by then he had already taken position against psychologism. Stumpf, in turn, promoted Husserl in his writing, while proposing his own understanding of phenomenology. Meanwhile, he delved into experimental phonetics up to the point of seemingly leaving philosophy for good. It is telling that Stumpf later dated the moment he turned to speech sounds back to 1913, the year in which Husserl published his *Ideas for a Pure Phenomenology*. In a paper to the congress of experimental psychologists of 1914, Stumpf boasted that his new device with ten systems of ninety-four extensible tubes could deal with frequency components in sounds starting from 75 Hz up to the upper threshold of hearing. Such an instrument, he recommended, should be owned by every institute carrying out acoustic experimentation in psychology. The very construction made a strong statement for empirical research within psychology.

The talk at the congress itself was devoted to "tone studies," a topic on which the organizing committee of the congress of experimental psychologists had asked Stumpf to speak. For the time being, there seemed to be no contradiction in subsuming the device under the field of tone studies. No mention was made yet of speech sounds as what would become the main object of investigation. The transition was seamless for Stumpf. In the talk, he discussed the work of his most promising doctoral student, Wolfgang Köhler, who had written his dissertation under Stumpf's tutelage on the pitch of vowel sounds. Köhler's findings included that there was a "vowel character" even in simple tones (see, e.g., Klotz 2019). These findings merited the greatest attention of psychologists, Stumpf emphasized, explaining the construction of the device with his intention to continue this research.

Three months later, war put the construction to a halt. For a while, the building materials became scarce, as they were used instead for producing weaponry, delaying the completed construction of the device until 1917. Stumpf himself was occupied with different tasks, as he got involved in military psychology as well as in the phonographic research at prisoner of war camps (see, e.g., Lange 2011). In 1918, Stumpf presented the device to the Prussian Academy of Science. The title of his report addressed vowel sounds: "Die Struktur der Vokale" (The Structure of Vowels). Meanwhile, Stumpf had extensively used the device for speech sounds, and he had combined this research with other methods known in experimental phonetics, such as using sets of finely differentiated tuning forks to find the resonant tones in articulated vowels and manipulating the playback speed of phonographic recordings (Pompino-Marschall 2003; Kursell 2011). The overarching term in this report was no longer "tone studies," nor did it become "phonetics." Instead, Stumpf now spoke of a "tone phenomenology." This comprised the "vowel quality" in simple tones that Köhler had researched. Stumpf referred to him again, when he wrote, "My investigations were prompted by these latter, most general questions of tone phenomenology. They began in 1913 and have been carried out in the order described here" (Stumpf 1918, 333).

The reference to phenomenology, however, disappeared from Stumpf's final publication on the subject, the book (1926). The shift could be summarized as follows. After 1900, Stumpf was still busying himself, as well as his doctoral students, with research topics in tone psychology in the broadest sense. For the talk at the congress of experimental psychologists, this research area could still be simply called "tone studies." No mention was made there of phenomenology, nor of Gestalt psychology. In the academy paper on vowels, he rebaptized it as "tone phenomenology." This report put Stumpf in a position to, indeed, give names to areas of study and identify terms to guide their practice. As an academy member reporting to peers, enunciating—in the sense of Michel Foucault's analysis of turning utterances into statements (1969, 89–91, translated as *The Archeology of Knowledge* 1989)—a redefinition of phenomenology might have seemed within reach.[23]

Yet, such a presumed empowerment would not persist in Stumpf's work. Little by little, Stumpf found his positions to be under attack from the anti-psychologism that gained momentum in philosophy in parallel with the rise of phenomenology. He mitigated the reference to phenomenology in the 1926 book, *Speech Sounds*. Also, it may have seemed unjust to subsume Köhler's work under the header of phenomenology by then.

Köhler had fully taken over the direction of the Institute of Psychology in 1923. More importantly, he had begun to establish Gestalt psychology as a new branch within the establishing discipline of psychology. Although Stumpf partly opposed the assumptions of his younger colleagues and did not embrace the term "Gestalt" for himself in the book or elsewhere, he apparently deemed it inaccurate to subsume his colleague's work under the header of phenomenology as well. Last but not least, the results of the research with the interference apparatus produced results that remained valid for quite a while within the linguistic subdiscipline of phonetics. They would only be superseded by the advent of acoustic spectrography in the 1940s.

CONCLUSION: SITUATING STUMPF IN RELATION TO THE PHENOMENOLOGY OF MUSIC CULTURES

In all its meandering ways, the research described here provides many potential links to the present volume. Rather than aligning with the next steps to come in the emergence of music ethnographies, Stumpf's respect for the subject's individual trajectories toward a given musical utterance brings him close to today's interest in positioning all parties in the research endeavor. Thus, the part of his research that may seem most relevant to the study of musical cultures writ large, namely the initiation of the Berliner Phonogramm-Archive and the book Stumpf wrote based on his own use of the archive's sources, received only brief mention. Yet, music culture is what his phenomenological practice was carving out by grounding itself on the notion of Sachverhalt. The music culture discussed here is that in which Stumpf dwelled and upon which he managed to propose a new perspective of the descriptive psychologist or phenomenologist in the sense of Brentano. Three aspects of this perspective can be summarized here. First, it dissociates the collection of evidence from judgment. Second and related to this, the notion of Sachverhalt allows for integrating diverging positions within the collected evidence. And third, the notion of utterance, which I introduced in order to better grasp the activity of preparing or composing the Sachverhalt, kept the threshold for entering the state of affairs low. In three steps I showed how Stumpf came to dissociate Sachverhalt from judgment, firstly through Brentanian logic and then through legal practice. Then I traced how he developed changing strategies for composing states of affairs and how this made him postpone judgment. And finally, I discussed how the strategies of collecting utterances eventually clashed with what by then had become phenomenology tout court. All three steps in my argument and in the corresponding stages in the development of Stumpf's method leave important questions open, which could provide additional substance to the argument. Stumpf's many narrative interpolations on the subjects who provided utterances for his research would deserve an account of its own. A phenomenology of music culture in this sense, as would come to the fore of such an account, takes time and space. Another open thread appeared in the last part of my argument, which introduced a distinction between utterance and enunciation. Further study could also expand on Stumpf's renunciation of a position of philosophical authority, tracing a line from his initial disjunction of Sachverhalt and judgment via Husserl's anti-psychologist formalization of the subject position toward its even stricter, discursive formalization in post-structuralism.[24]

Instead, I propose to follow the advice of my text processing program, which has been thinking of the notion of state of affairs all the way through this chapter as cumbersome: "More concise language would be clearer for your reader," it recommends, suggesting instead "situation." To avoid making a simple concession to automated reading, I turn instead to Donna Haraway's decidedly human suggestion to speak of "situated knowledge" (1988). Her term might indeed be the better proposal here, particularly when looking at the past. Yet, the very advantage of the historical notion of Sachverhalt, as this chapter has attempted to show, consisted in its capacity to serve as both a container for the complexity of the matter to be judged and a link to a rigorous logic of judgment. Calling to mind the background of German law for the work of the philosopher and music researcher Stumpf, the historically situated analysis of his notion of Sachverhalt shed light on an unused potential in the beginnings of phenomenology. His *modus operandi* shared the phenomenological reservations toward accepted parlance and conclusive judgment that fed into Husserl's notion of epoché, while at the same time allowing the richness of situated utterances to enter the state of affairs. It suggests both a rich and a rigorous understanding of the phenomenology of music cultures.

ACKNOWLEDGMENTS

The author would like to thank the editors of this volume for their tremendous support and inspiration as well as a generously supportive anonymous reviewer.

NOTES

1. Where not otherwise stated, translations are mine. This dictionary of the German language by brothers Jacob (1785–1863) and Wilhelm Grimm (1786–1859) was published in thirty-two volumes between 1852 and 1961. The brothers famously abandoned capitalization in their dictionary, and this was retained in the volumes that were finalized after their death. The volume quoted here originally appeared in 1892.
2. On the Institute of Psychology, see Stumpf (1910). For some standard literature items, see the following: on Stumpf's biography, see Sprung and Sprung (2006); on the Berliner Phonogramm-Archiv, including von Hornbostel's collaboration with Felix von Luschan for devising the travelers' instructions mentioned below, see Ziegler (2006); on the Berlin School of Gestalt Psychology, see Ash (1995).
3. On Stumpf and James, see Martinelli (2020); on Stumpf and Wundt, see Hui (2013) as well as Kursell (2021).
4. On this see Fisette (2015b).

5. On the notions of psychologism and anti-psychologism see, for instance, Textor (2020) and Kusch (2020). In his paper "Psychologie und Erkenntnistheorie" (1892, translated as *Psychology and Epistemology* 2020, 1182), Stumpf provides a short definition of psychologism as "reduction of all philosophical and especially all epistemological investigations to psychology" (2020, 1182), and he attributes it to Johann Eduard Erdmann's 1886 textbook on the history of philosophy. It was this type of psychologism, not Stumpf's work, which would be the main target of anti-psychologists from Husserl and Frege to Jean Cavaillès. In fact, Stumpf himself partly joined the critique (see, e.g., Fisette 2019).

6. During the past few years, an increase in the interest in Stumpf's work can be observed, accompanying efforts to disclose publications and source materials for the English-language reader, such as, e.g., Stumpf ([1911] 2012, [1907] 2018, [1883] 2020, [1892] 2020) and Martinelli (2020). See also Fitzner (2021) as an example of the German context.

7. When the 2018 translation is quoted, the page numbers of the original, which are included in this translation, are indicated.

8. My translation of "psychisch" as "psychical" and "Erscheinungen" as "phenomena" follows the English translation in Rollinger (1999) and in Fisette and Martinelli (2015), rather than translating these as "Appearances and Psychic Functions" as in Stumpf ([1907] 2018). The latter is occasionally consulted for quotes from this paper.

9. Smith (1989, 54) credits Julius Bergmann in his *Allgemeine Logik* of 1879 and Lotze in his *Logik* from 1880 with first bringing it up in philosophy. Milkov (2015) refers to uses in earlier versions of Lotze's *Logik* (2015, 116–117).

10. The *Oxford English Dictionary* traces the term "state of affairs" to two sources: the Latin term *status rerum* and Wittgenstein's use of state of affairs.

11. "Collectives" is my chosen translation for *Inbegriff*, following Rollinger (1999, 91). The word "Gebilde" comes from the verb "bilden" (forming) and associates the result of an activity of forming or building, most often with a connotation of its actual shape elapsing description. Fisette (2015c) uses "product" for Gebilde, Tracz (Stumpf 2018) chooses "configuration" for Gebilde and "set" for Inbegriff (Stumpf 2018).

12. For a discussion of Husserl's readings of Stumpf and Ehrenfels, see Rollinger (1999, 108).

13. Chrudzimski refers to Brentano's *Psychologie vom empirischen Standpunkte* of 1874. He claims that the epistemic notion of truth is not only to be found in the Brentano's late writing, but in all periods of his philosophy (Chrudzimski 2015, 178n4).

14. See Tan (2013) and Steege (2017) on Kurth; Kursell (forthcoming) on Handschin; Rehding (2000, 2003) and Kursell (2017c) on Riemann's Tonvorstellungen. It is perhaps not superfluous to say that endeavors such as Riemann's, who sometimes is called a phenomenologist, depend on having learned music's rules beforehand and therefore have little to do with, for instance, eidetic reduction as it is conceived by Husserl. For a cautious overview of such musical approaches, see Blum (2006).

15. See Kursell (2019a) on the role of experts in this study; on muscular sensation in speech perception and imagination within the history of theatre studies, see Tkaczyk (2018).

16. On the study of muscle and tone memory (and further literature on the matter), see (Kursell 2019a).

17. See also Kursell (2021).

18. The English language concept of "pitch" matches ideally in this respect. The complicated way in which Stumpf describes the effects of the standpoint for the musical individuals, by referring to the methods of cartography for understanding the earth's surface, could thus be summarized as follows: they cognize pitch.

19. Up until the turn of the century, Stumpf dismissed the use of the phonograph for scholarly purposes, as it only enabled recording but not the distribution of sound (1891). On Stumpf's early contributions to ethnomusicology see (Schwörer-Kohl 2017).

20. For some examples, see Kursell (2019b).

21. For this term, though in a more literal understanding, see Kursell and Schäfer (2009).

22. The translation in Husserl ([1913] 1982, 51–62) of Ausschaltung as "exclusion" is rendering the assumption of temporarily setting aside the natural attitude problematic, as it suggests that the exclusion is definitive. On the dilemma that results from bracketing the natural attitude for the claims of the phenomenological attitude's potential, see Beyer (2020). In Kursell 2021, I have argued that Husserl himself quickly proceeds from the technical metaphor of Ausschaltung to "Einklammerung," i.e., bracketing or "parenthesizing" (Husserl [1913] 1982, 57), which keeps the argument within the written, textual realm, to eventually reach his own term "epoché."

23. Foucault (1969, 105–107) starts off from the notion of *instances du discours.*

24. As is clear from all available biographical accounts, he did assume responsibility in the academic institutions of his own. By saying he renounced philosophical authority I do not mean to suggest that he avoided responsibility.

WORKS CITED

Abraham, Otto. 1923. "Tonometrische Untersuchungen an einem deutschen Volkslied." *Psychologische Forschung. Zeitschrift für Psychologie und ihre Grenzwissenschaften* 4: 1–22.

Ames, Eric. 2003. "The Sound of Evolution." *Modernism/Modernity* 10 (2): 297–325.

Ames, Eric. 2008. *Carl Hagenbeck's Empire of Entertainments.* Seattle: University of Washington Press.

Ash, Mitchell. 1995. *Gestalt Psychology in German Culture 1890-1967: Holism and the Quest for Objectivity.* Cambridge, New York: Cambridge University Press.

Beyer, Christian. 2020. "Edmund Husserl." In *The Stanford Encyclopedia of Philosophy*, edited by Edward N. Zalta. Stanford University. https://plato.stanford.edu/archives/win2020/entries/husserl/.

Blum, Arne. 2006. "Phänomenologie der Musik. Die Anfänge der musikalischen Phänomenologie im ersten Drittel des 20. Jahrhunderts." PhD diss., Universität Witten-Herdecke.

Christensen, Dieter. 1991. "Erich M. von Hornbostel, Carl Stumpf, and the Institutionalization of Comparative Musicology." In *Comparative Musicology and Anthropology of Music*, edited by Bruno Nettl and Philip Bohlman, 201–209. Chicago, London: University of Chicago Press.

Chrudzimski, Arkadiusz. 2015. "Carl Stumpf über Sachverhalte." In *Philosophy from an Empirical Standpoint: Essays on Carl Stumpf*, edited by Denis Fisette and Riccardo Martinelli, 173–202. Leiden, Boston: Brill Rodopi.

Fisette, Denis. 2015a. "Introduction to Stumpf's Lecture on Metaphysics." In *Philosophy from an Empirical Standpoint: Essays on Carl Stumpf*, edited by Denis Fisette and Riccardo Martinelli, 433–442. Leiden, Boston: Brill Rodopi.

Fisette, Denis. 2015b. "A Phenomenology without Phenomena? Carl Stumpf's Critical Remarks on Husserl's *Phenomenology.*" In *Philosophy from an Empirical Standpoint: Essays on Carl Stumpf*, edited by Denis Fisette and Riccardo Martinelli, 321–357. Leiden, Boston: Brill Rodopi.

Fisette, Denis. 2015c. "The Reception and Actuality of Carl Stumpf: An Introduction." In *Philosophy from an Empirical Standpoint: Essays on Carl Stumpf*, edited by Denis Fisette and Riccardo Martinelli, 11–53. Leiden, Boston: Brill Rodopi.

Fisette, Denis. 2019. "Carl Stumpf." In *The Stanford Encyclopedia of Philosophy*, edited by Edward N. Zalta. Stanford University. https://plato.stanford.edu/archives/spr2019/entries/stumpf/.

Fisette, Denis, and Riccardo Martinelli, eds. 2015. *Philosophy from an Empirical Standpoint: Essays on Carl Stumpf*. Leiden, Boston: Brill Rodopi.

Fitzner, Frauke. 2021. *Der hörende Mensch in der Moderne: Medialität des Musikhörens um 1900*. Göttingen: Wallstein.

Foucault, Michel. 1969. *L'archéologie du savoir*. Paris: Éditions Gallimard.

Foucault, Michel. (1969) 1989. *The Archeology of Knowledge*. Translated by A. M. Sheridan Smith. London, New York: Routledge.

Gembris, Heiner. 1997. "Historical Phases in the Definition of Musicality." *Psychomusicology* 16: 17–25.

Grimm, Jacob, and Wilhelm Grimm. 1892. *Deutsches Wörterbuch*, Vol. VIII. Digitized edition. Trier Center for Digital Humanities. https://www.dwds.de/d/wb-1dwb.

Handschin, Jacques. 1948. *Der Toncharakter: Eine Einführung in die Musikpsychologie*. Zürich: Atlantis.

Haraway, Donna. 1988. "Situated Knowledges: The Science Question in Feminism and the Privilege of Partial Perspective." *Feminist Studies* 14 (3): 575–599.

Hui, Alexandra. 2013. *The Psychophysical Ear: Musical Experiments, Experimental Sounds, 1840–1910*. Cambridge, MA: MIT Press.

Husserl, Edmund. (1913) 1982. *Ideas Pertaining to a Pure Phenomenology and to a Phenomenological Philosophy*. Translated by Frederik Kersten. The Hague, London: Nijhoff.

Kaiser-el-Safti, Margret. 2011. "Einleitung." In *Carl Stumpf: Erkenntnislehre*, edited by Carl Stumpf Gesellschaft, 5–45. Lengerich: Pabst Science Publisher.

Klotz, Sebastian, ed. 1998. *Vom tönenden Wirbel menschlichen Tuns. Erich M. von Hornbostel als Gestaltpsychologe, Archivar und Musikwissenschaftler*. Berlin, Milow: Schibri-Verlag.

Klotz, Sebastian. 2019. "Timbre, Komplexeindruck, and Modernity: Klangfarbe as a Catalyst of Psychological Research in Carl Stumpf, 1890–1926." In *The Oxford Handbook of Timbre*, edited by Emily Dolan and Alexander Rehding, 609–640. New York: Oxford University Press. https://www.oxfordhandbooks.com/view/10.1093/oxfordhb/9780190637224.001.0001/oxfordhb-9780190637224-e-2.

Koch, Lars-Christian. 2013. "Images of Sound: Erich M. von Hornbostel and the Berlin Phonogram Archive." In *The Cambridge History of World Music*, edited by Philip V. Bohlman, 475–497. Cambridge: Cambridge University Press.

Koselleck, Reinhart. 1967. *Preußen zwischen Reform und Revolution: Allgemeines Landrecht, Verwaltung und soziale Bewegung von 1791 bis 1948*. Schriftenreihe Industrielle Welt 7. Stuttgart: Klett.

Kursell, Julia. 2011. "A Gray Box: The Phonograph in Laboratory Experiments and Field Work, 1900–1920." In *The Oxford Handbook of Sound Studies*, edited by Karin Bijsterveld and Trevor Pinch, 176–197. New York: Oxford University Press.

Kursell, Julia. 2017a. "Experimental Cylinders: Experiments in Music Psychology around 1900." *Journal of Sonic Studies* 13. https://www.researchcatalogue.net/view/324247/324248.

Kursell, Julia. 2017b. "Musikwissenschaft am Berliner Institut für Psychologie: Carl Stumpf und der Interferenzapparat." In *Musikwissenschaft 1900–1930: Zur Institutionalisierung und*

Legitimierung einer jungen akademischen Disziplin, edited by Wolfgang Auhagen, Wolfgang Hirschmann, and Tomi Mäkelä, 73–90. Studien und Materialien zur Musikwissenschaft 98. Hildesheim: Georg Olms Verlag.

Kursell, Julia. 2017c. "Notenlesen." In *Medienphilologien: Konturen eines Paradigmas*, edited by Friedrich Balke and Rupert Gaderer, 172–195. Göttingen: Wallstein.

Kursell, Julia. 2018. "Carl Stumpf and the Beginnings of Research in Musicality." In *The Origins of Musicality*, edited by Henkjan Honing. Cambridge, MA: MIT Press.

Kursell, Julia. 2019a. "From Tone to Tune—Carl Stumpf and the Violin." *19th-Century Music* 43 (2): 121–139.

Kursell, Julia. 2019b. "Listening to More than Sounds: Carl Stumpf and the Experimental Recordings of the Berliner Phonogramm-Archiv." *Technology and Culture* 60 (2S): S39–S63.

Kursell, Julia. 2021. "Coming to Terms with Sound: Carl Stumpf's Discourse on Hearing Music and Language." *History of Humanities* 6: 35–59.

Kursell, Julia. Forthcoming. "1926. 'Jacques Handschin: Ueber Musikwissenschaft.' Kontext und Kommentar." In *Umfang, Methode und Ziel. Eine kommentierte Edition von Konzeptionen der Musikwissenschaft*, edited by Melanie Wald-Fuhrmann. Vol. 2 of *Spektrum Fachgeschichte Musikwissenschaft*. Kassel: Bärenreiter/Metzler.

Kursell, Julia, and Armin Schäfer. 2009. "Spaces beyond Tonality. I: The Long Nineteenth Century, II: John Cage, *Imaginary Landscape I*." *Immersed: Sound and Architecture* (OASE) 78: 82–102.

Kurth, Ernst. 1931. *Musikpsychologie*. Berlin: Max Hesse.

Kusch, Martin. 2020. "Psychologism." In *The Stanford Encyclopedia of Philosophy*, edited by Edward N. Zalta. Stanford University. https://plato.stanford.edu/archives/spr2020/entries/psychologism/.

Lange, Britta. 2011. "South Asian Soldiers and German Academics: Anthropological, Linguistic, and Musicological Studies in Prison Camps." In *South Asian Prisoners in World War I Germany*, edited by R. Ahuja, H. Liebau, and F. Roy, 149–186. New Delhi: Social Science Press.

Lotze, Rudolph Hermann. 1852. *Medicinische Psychologie oder Physiologie der Seele*. Leipzig: Weidmann.

Martinelli, Riccardo. 2020. "A Lifelong Friendship." In *William James, Carl Stumpf: Correspondence, 1882–1910*, edited by Riccardo Martinelli, 1–22. Berlin: De Gruyter.

Milkov, Nikolay. 2015. "Carl Stumpf's Debt to Hermann Lotze." In *Philosophy from an Empirical Standpoint: Essays on Carl Stumpf*, edited by Denis Fisette and Riccardo Martinelli, 101–122. Leiden, Boston: Brill Rodopi.

Mittermaier, Carl Joseph Anton. 1845. *Die Mündlichkeit, das Anklageprinzip, die Öffentlichkeit und das Geschworenengericht in ihrer Durchführung in den verschiedenen Gesetzgebungen*. Stuttgart: Cotta.

Moran, Dermot. 2000. *Introduction to Phenomenology*. New York: Routledge.

Peretz, Isabelle. 2006. "The Nature of Music from a Biological Perspective." *Cognition* 100: 1–32.

Peretz, Isabelle, Anne-Sophie Champod, and Krista Hyde. 2003. "Varieties of Musical Disorders: The Montreal Battery of Evaluation of Amusia." *Annals of the New York Academy of Sciences* 999: 58–75.

Pompino-Marschall, Bernd. 2003. "Carl Stumpf und die Phonetik." In *Musik und Sprache: Zur Phänomenologie von Carl Stumpf*, edited by Margret Kaiser-el-Safti and Matthias Ballod, 131–150. Würzburg: Königshausen und Neumann.

Rehding, Alexander. 2000. "The Quest for the Origins of Music in Germany ca. 1900." *Journal of the American Musicological Society* 53: 345–385.

Rehding, Alexander. 2003. *Hugo Riemann and the Birth of Modern Musical Thought*. Cambridge: Cambridge University Press.

Rehding, Alexander. 2005. "Wax Cylinder Revolutions." *Musical Quarterly* 88: 123–160.

Riemann, Hugo. 1914–16. "Ideen zu einer 'Lehre von den Tonvorstellungen.'" *Jahrbuch Musikbibliothek Peters* 21–22 (1914–15): 1–26; 23 (1916): 1–21.

Rollinger, Robin D. 1999. *Husserl's Position in the School of Brentano*. Dordrecht, Boston, London: Kluwer.

Rojszczak, Artur, and Barry Smith. 2008. "Theories of Judgement." In *The Cambridge History of Philosophy, 1870–1945*, edited by Thomas Baldwin, 157–173. Cambridge: Cambridge University Press.

Salice, Alessandro. 2020. "The Phenomenology of the Munich and Göttingen Circles." In *The Stanford Encyclopedia of Philosophy*, edited by Edward N. Zalta. Stanford University. https://plato.stanford.edu/archives/win2020/entries/phenomenology-mg/.

Schwörer-Kohl, Gretel. 2017. "Carl Stumpf und die Anfänge der Musikethnologie in Halle." In *Musikwissenschaft 1900–1930: Zur Institutionalisierung und Legitimierung einer jungen akademischen Disziplin*, edited by Wolfgang Auhagen, Wolfgang Hirschmann, and Tomi Mäkelä, 66–72. Hildesheim: Olms.

Smith, Barry. 1978. "Law and Eschatology in Wittgenstein's Early Thought." *Inquiry* 21: 425–441.

Smith, Barry. 1989. "Logic and the Sachverhalt." *The Monist* 72 (1): 52–69.

Smith, Barry. 1992. "Sachverhalt." In *Historisches Wörterbuch der Philosophie*, edited by Joachim Ritter, vol. 8, 1002–1113. Basel: Schwabe.

Sprung, Helga, and Lothar Sprung. 2006. *Carl Stumpf – Eine Biografie. Von der Philosophie zur Experimentellen Psychologie*. Munich: Profil.

Steege, Benjamin. 2017. "Antipsychologism in Interwar Musical Thought: Two Ways of Hearing Debussy." *Music & Letters* 98 (1): 74–103.

Stumpf, Carl. 1873. *Über den psychologischen Ursprung der Raumvorstellung*. Leipzig: Hirzel.

Stumpf, Carl. 1883. *Tonpsychologie*. Vol. 1. Leipzig: Hirzel.

Stumpf, Carl. (1883) 2020. *Tone Psychology*, Vol. 1, *The Sensation of Successive Single Tones*, translated by Robin D. Rollinger. London and New York: Routledge.

Stumpf, Carl. 1886. "Lieder der Bellakula-Indianer." *Vierteljahrsschrift für Musikwissenschaft* 2: 405–426.

Stumpf, Carl. 1890. *Tonpsychologie*. Vol. 2. Leipzig: Hirzel.

Stumpf, Carl. 1892. "Phonographierte Indianermelodien." *Vierteljahrsschrift für Musikwissenschaft* 8: 127–144.

Stumpf, Carl. (1892) 2020. "Psychology and Epistemology." Translated by Jessica Leech and Mark Textor. *British Journal for the History of Philosophy* 28 (6): 1181–1216.

Stumpf, Carl. 1907a. *Die Wiedergeburt der Philosophie: Rede zum Antritt des Rektorates der Königlichen Friedrich-Wilhelms-Universität in Berlin*. Berlin: Universitätsbuchdruckerei Gustav Schade (Otto Francke).

Stumpf, Carl. 1907b. "Erscheinungen und Psychische Funktionen." *Abhandlungen der Königlich Preußischen Akademie der Wissenschaften zu Berlin. Philosophisch-historische Abhandlungen* 4: 3–40.

Stumpf, Carl. 1907c. "Zur Einteilung der Wissenschaften." *Abhandlungen der Preußischen Akademie der Wissenschaften zu Berlin, Philosophisch-Historische Abhandlungen* 5: 1–94.

Stumpf, Carl. (1907) 2018. "Appearances and Psychic Functions." Translated by R. Brian Tracz. In *The Sources of Husserl's 'Ideas I,'* edited by Andrea Staiti and Evan Clarke, 81–113. Berlin, Boston: De Gruyter.

Stumpf, Carl. 1910. "Das psychologische Institut." In *Geschichte der Königlichen Friedrich-Wilhelms-Universität zu Berlin*, edited by Max Lenz, 202–207. Halle a. d. Saale: Verlag der Buchhandlung des Waisenhauses.

Stumpf, Carl. (1911) 2012. *The Origins of Music*. Edited and translated by David Trippett. Oxford: Oxford University Press.

Stumpf, Carl. 1914. "Ueber neuere Untersuchungen zur Tonlehre." In *Bericht über den VI. Kongreß für Experimentelle Psychologie in Göttingen vom 15. bis 18. April 1914*, edited by Friedrich Schumann, 305–348. Leipzig: Barth.

Stumpf, Carl. 1918. "Die Struktur der Vokale." *Sitzungsberichte der Königlich Preussischen Akademie der Wissenschaften* 1: 333–358.

Stumpf, Carl. 1924. "Selbstdarstellung." In *Philosophie der Gegenwart in Selbstdarstellungen*, edited by Raymund Schmidt, 205–265. Leipzig: Meiner.

Stumpf, Carl. 1926. *Die Sprachlaute: Experimentell-phonetische Untersuchungen nebst einem Anhang über Instrumentalklänge*. Berlin: Springer.

Stumpf, Carl. 1939–40. *Erkenntnislehre*, 2 vols. Leipzig: Barth.

Tan, Daphne. 2013. "Ernst Kurth and the Boundary of Music Theory and Psychology." PhD diss., University of Rochester, NY.

Textor, Mark. 2020. "Stumpf between Criticism and Psychologism: Introducing 'Psychologie und Erkenntnistheorie'." *British Journal for the History of Philosophy* 28 (6): 1172–1180.

Tkaczyk, Viktoria. 2018. "Whose Larynx Is It? Fields of Scholarly Competence around 1900." *History of Humanities* 3: 57–73.

Vismann, Cornelia. 2011. *Medien der Rechsprechung*. Edited by Alexandra Kemmerer and Markus Krajewski. Frankfurt/Main: S. Fischer.

Ziegler, Susanne, ed. 2006. *Die Wachszylinder des Berliner Phonogramm-Archivs*. Berlin: Ethnologisches Museum, Staatliche Museen zu Berlin – Preußischer Kulturbesitz.

CHAPTER 3

....

AESTHETIC EXPERIENCE, SOCIAL INTERFACES, AND THE PHENOMENOLOGY OF MUSIC

....

ROGER W. H. SAVAGE

THE idea that music's social significance is the locus of its value and worth is a widely accepted transdisciplinary precept. When, in the 1980s, self-identified postmodern musicologists denounced the metaphysical conceit of music's aesthetic autonomy, they ratified ethnomusicology's long-standing embrace of contextual accounts of music's role in cultural, social, and political life (McClary 1991, 1993, 1994; Kramer 1992, 1995, 2002). Explanations of the interfaces between music and the social worlds in which musical practices and performances figure abound. Such descriptions and explanations are as diverse as the theories invoked and the methodologies deployed. By taking aesthetic experience as my guide, I am not proposing to add to the repertory of "thick" descriptions that Clifford Geertz (1973) advocates as a way of interpreting the fundamentally symbolic character of cultural practices. Rather, through adopting a hermeneutical approach, I intend to explore how music occasions an experience that is the condition for the interfaces that subsequent fieldwork or textual investigations identify as central to music's social meaning.

By relating music's value and significance to the experiences that music affords, I intend to emphasize how music's expressive force is the spring of its worlding power, that is, its power to refashion dimensions of our experiences. This hermeneutically phenomenological understanding of music's affective force differs sharply from the interpretive strategies employed by cultural musicologists in deconstructing nineteenth-century ideals of music's aesthetic autonomy, its "metaphysical dignity" (Dahlhaus [1964] 1987, 173), and its alleged transcendence of material reality. Hermann Kretzschmar's proposal for a musical hermeneutics, which exploited the semantic features of narrative to identify a work's motivic and thematic features, for example, with specific affects, prefigures postmodern musicology's appropriation of musical hermeneutics as a means of decoding the social significance of musical texts in this regard (Kretzschmar [1902] 1990; [1905] 1990). Elsewhere (Savage 2010a), I have argued that privileging music's social values and uses at the expense of music's capacity to augment affective dimensions of our experiences preserves the schema to which deconstructive readings of music's social meaning are ostensibly opposed. In the course of this chapter, I will explain how hermeneutic phenomenology redresses this failure to account for music's power to express feelings and moods that are unique to it and that in turn open us to the world, and the world to us, in new ways. John Blacking will prove to be a worthy ally in this regard. While Blacking's orientation differs from my approach in some basic ways, the distinction that he implicitly draws between music's social utility and its ontological vehemence lends itself to a rigorously phenomenological investigation. The virtual worlds of time that, Blacking maintains, music creates owe their force to music's mimetic character. As I will explain, music's power to place our everyday experiences in suspense can only be confused with music's institution as an aesthetically autonomous entity at the cost of its expressive force.

The phenomenological orientation of my analyses and critiques is hermeneutically informed in this respect. Paul Ricoeur reminds us that hermeneutics and phenomenology belong to each other. Hermeneutics, he explains, has not ruined phenomenology but only Husserl's idealistic interpretation of it. If, on the one hand, "phenomenology remains the unsurpassable presupposition of hermeneutics" (Ricoeur [1986] 1991, 26), on the other hand, phenomenology can constitute itself only by reason of its hermeneutical presupposition. Since "every question concerning any sort of 'being' is a question about the meaning of that 'being'" (Ricoeur [1986] 1991, 38), hermeneutics cannot dispense with phenomenology's central concern. Conversely, to the degree that "phenomenology is an explication of evidence and an evidence of explication, . . . phenomenology can be realized only as hermeneutics" ([1986] 1991, 52).[1] Ricoeur remarks that the "ideal of scientificity, construed by Husserlian idealism as ultimate justification, encounters its fundamental limit in the ontological condition of understanding" ([1986] 1991, 29; see also Ricoeur 1967). Hermeneutic phenomenology accordingly joins descriptions of the structures of experience to a reflection on our manner of inhering in the world and our encounters with things and others in it. For such an analysis and such a reflection, music's expressive force is a crucial feature of its cultural value.

OUTLINE OF A HERMENEUTIC
PHENOMENOLOGY OF MUSIC

By drawing our attention to the difference between music's social utility and its power to create special worlds of time, Blacking invites us to address the question as to how music or, in his words, "humanly organized sound" (Blacking 1973, 32) occasions an experience that transcends the prosaic order of everyday life. This transcendence of the real, which places our ordinary sense of the passage of time in suspense, differs radically from the metaphysical conceit that in the nineteenth century privileged music, and especially instrumental music, as a language beyond language. When, as the "language of emotion" (F. A. Gelbcke, cited by le Huray and Day 1988, 355), music assumed pride of place as *the* romantic art, the distinction between the supposedly higher region to which music ostensibly provided special access and the material order of social life reached its apogee. Pierre Bourdieu argues that as "the most radical and most absolute form of the negation of the world, and especially the social world" (Bourdieu [1979] 1984, 19), music acquires its privileged status as a form of symbolic capital. Yet, as I will explain, sociologically informed critiques of claims regarding music's alleged aesthetic autonomy risk acceding to the effects of a history set in motion by Immanuel Kant's transcendental justification of judgments of taste. By suggesting that Blacking invites us to reconsider music's power to unfold special worlds of time that surpass our ordinary experiences, I propose to relate my hermeneutical account of music's mimetic character to his insight into the significance of the experience that music affords for the community in which, for which, and in some cases by which it is performed.

It may seem surprising that Blacking would identify "music that is for being" (Blacking 1973, 50), which he contrasts with music that fulfills an overt social purpose, with the Western concept of art. This reference at first seems strangely at odds with his insistence that music of different cultures should be regarded not as better or worse in terms of its complexity but as different. Blacking explains that for the Venda people of southern Africa, with whom he conducted fieldwork research, "not all music has the same value" (Blacking 1973, 49). According to him, all the music of the Venda "grows out of human experiences" (Blacking 1973, 49) and plays an overt role in social life. Yet only some of this music, Blacking adds, "is regarded as what John Dewey has called 'an instrument indispensable to the transformation of man and his world'" (Blacking 1973, 49; see Richter 1967).[2] Some music, he explains, is used to mark social occasions, such as songs of initiation that are important "markers of stages in ritual or as reinforcements of mnemonics of lessons" (Blacking 1973, 50). It is therefore tempting, Blacking writes, "to define the utilitarian functions of Venda music as those in which the effects of music are incidental to the impact of the social situation" (Blacking 1973, 50). Conversely, for him it is equally compelling to define those effects "in which the music *itself* is the crucial factor in the experience" (Blacking 1973, 50, italics added) as artistic, inasmuch as these effects are vital to enhancing human consciousness.

We can no doubt recognize how situating music in its social and cultural contexts leads to identifying music's value with the meaning and significance it has for the community in which it is created, circulates, and is performed. Why, then, would Blacking feel the need to supplement the notion that music has multiple social uses with the idea that music occasions an experience that augments the everyday world through enhancing the consciousness of participants? And how, we could ask, does music bring about an increase in being by creating a special world in which ordinary senses of time are placed in suspense?

However much Blacking's reference to the music *itself* evokes the specter of Western concepts of aesthetic autonomy, music's symbolic capital, and the institution of various forms of cultural privilege and social prestige, the emphasis he places on the way that music exercises its effects leads me to ask how, for him, the music *itself* gives rise to an experience that "sends" people. Identifying music that is *for* being with the creation of special worlds of time accordingly is indicative of music's expressive power. The "loss of self in being" (Blacking 1973, 52), to which Blacking credits the enhancement of human consciousness, is an effect of the way that music places ordinary senses of time in suspense. Once freed from the "restrictions of actual time," he tells us, we "often experience greater intensity in living" (Blacking 1973, 52) by virtue of the state of being achieved through music and dance. This "adventure into . . . the reality of the world of the spirit" (Blacking 1973, 28; see Savage 2009) countermands Bourdieu's assessment of how the belief in music's metaphysical dignity masks the way it circulates socially as a privileged form of cultural capital. For, far from providing a means of escape, the experience occasioned by *tshikona* (the Venda national dance) becomes a marker of Venda identity only through transcending its material social purposes. Through creating a "special world of time" (Blacking 1973, 48),[3] tshikona fulfills its ritual role through drawing the members of the community together. From this vantage point, the liminal experiences music affords through staking out the borderlines between time and eternity are proof, so to speak, of music's worlding power (Savage 2018; see also Dufrenne [1953] 1973; Heidegger [1927] 1962, 1971; Bowie 2007).[4]

By highlighting the connection between music's affective power and the creation of special worlds of time, I am clearly setting out the hermeneutical features of the distinction drawn by Blacking between music's social uses and its ontological vehemence, by which I mean the power it has to affect performers', participants', and listeners' manner of inhering in the world. However much Eurocentric allusions to the Western concept of art trade on the cultural heritage of widely discredited ideals of music's aesthetic autonomy, fidelity to the composer's intentions (*Werktreue*; see Savage 2010a; cf. Goehr 1992), and the belief and cultural investment in a "higher" realm where the human spirit was thought to be truly at home, the distinction Blacking implicitly makes between music's social uses and its affective power and force marks an important departure from the schema that sets the purported chimera of music's otherworldliness against the material conditions of ordinary life (cf. Kramer 1992). Opposing music's aesthetic autonomy to the social contexts and conditions of its creation, performance, and reception leads only to tearing music from its sustaining life contexts. Conversely, treating music's meaning and significance only as a function of these contexts and conditions comes at the price of placing music's affective power under erasure.

By setting the experiences occasioned by musical performances against the schema that institutes the opposition between music, now conceived as an aesthetically autonomous entity, and its social worldliness, I mean to draw out the hermeneutical and phenomenological implications of Blacking's reference to art. Within this schema, music's social worldliness paradoxically is stripped of its most critical feature. Elsewhere, I have argued that music's deleterious role in maintaining the status quo rests on music's power to renew our affective affinities with the world by occasioning experiences that are unique to it (Savage 2018). Similarly, the emancipatory potential that social theorists and literary critics, for example, credit to the aesthetic has its anchorages in literature, music, and art's power to break new paths into our ways of thinking, feeling, and acting. Music's subversive force takes hold in this power to renew reality from within by refashioning affective dimensions of our experiences in accordance with the worlds projected by individual works. Conversely, once assimilated to the schema bearing the stamp of the "subjectivization of aesthetics" (Gadamer [1960] 1989, 42), the notion that works perform cultural work by simulating or reproducing identifiable social structures and processes only obscures and marginalizes the potential for surpassing ideologically congealed systems and habits of thought.

Hans-Georg Gadamer's explication of the phenomenon of play provides a key insight that leads to a broader consideration of how music augments affective dimensions of our experiences in accordance with feelings and moods evoked by it. While his reference to the work of art might seem to privilege the concept of the work's canonic status within the Western art music tradition, his recourse to the phenomenon of play in fact combats the alienating effects of art and music's relegation to a separate, aesthetically insulated sphere. The history of the schema to which I alluded, which sets music against the material order of everyday life, is in part the result of German idealism's appropriation of Kant's claim that "Fine art is the art of genius" (Kant [1790] 1987, 175; cited in Gadamer [1960] 1989, 58). With the expansion of the concept of the symbol into a universal aesthetic principle in the nineteenth century, music came to be vested with metaphysical dignity. The nineteenth-century cult of *Bildung* (self-formation; see Koselleck 2002) consequently celebrated music for leading to a realm of freedom in which the human spirit was said to be truly at home. As music came to be revered as the object of aesthetic salvation, aesthetic consciousness severed itself from the experience that music occasions in the event of its performance.

Similar to Blacking, Gadamer is an ally when it comes to avoiding the trap prepared by the schema that opposes music's aesthetic autonomy to the material order of practical life. Gadamer's analysis of the phenomenon of play lays the ground for drawing out the connection between musical performances and the experiences occasioned by them. Play, Gadamer tells us, presents itself in the to-and-fro movement through which a game, for example, takes shape. The ordered movement through which the game unfolds manifests the dynamic character of the phenomenon of play. Gadamer emphasizes that, phenomenologically speaking, the ordered structuring of this movement brings the game as such to presentation. From this vantage point, play is "the occurrence of the movement as such" (Gadamer [1960] 1989, 103). This self-actualizing movement constitutes the mode of being of play. Hence, the "being of all play is always self-realization, sheer fulfillment, *energeia* which has its *telos* within itself" (Gadamer [1960] 1989, 113, italics added). Gadamer adds that each game has its own spirit, which takes shape through the manner in which the game unfolds. This spirit, we could therefore say, reveals itself in accordance with the way that a game, a work, or an extemporized performance structures spectators' or listeners' experiences of it.

Gadamer's ontological explanation of the mode of being of the work of art complements Blacking's notion of music *for* being and, at the same time, expressly thematizes how the movement through which the work achieves its expression also structures our experiences of the work through its performance. The idea that music's meaning and significance is related somehow to its power to transform our understanding of ourselves, the world, and our place in it, which I have suggested leads Blacking to place a particular emphasis on the music *itself*, takes on greater clarity in light of Gadamer's phenomenological account of the mode of being of play. If, in drawing out the implicitly phenomenological features of Blacking's notion of music *for* being, I have exceeded Blacking's intentions, I have also sought to account for his claim that we experience life in greater intensity in states of being evoked by music and dance. Earlier, I asked how music's creation of special worlds of time brings about an increase in being through placing our ordinary sense of time in suspense. In light of Gadamer's analysis, we could now say that the epoché of our everyday experiences, which in terms of Blacking's reference to music *for* being frees us from the restrictions of everyday time, stems from, and hence is attributable to, the worlding of the work.

As I have suggested, Gadamer's hermeneutical, phenomenological rejoinder to the alienating consequences of music and art's claim to its own autonomous standpoint provides a key insight into the way that the experience occasioned by music's performance rests on a critical feature of the phenomenon of play. Consequently, the second aspect of Gadamer's analysis to which I want to draw attention concerns the way that the closed world of play places in suspense those purposive relations that characterize our everyday social interactions with others and the world. This epoché of the real, which for phenomenology suspends the natural attitude toward things, is an effect of the way that play fulfills its aim through its self-presentation. That play closes itself off from the world of everyday affairs is the condition for the impact that music or any other cultural form of expression has with regard to its expressive power. We therefore must not confuse the closed world of play with the ideal of aesthetic autonomy, which founds the conscious differentiation between artistic entities as aesthetic objects and their sustaining life context on this ideal's methodological abstraction. On the contrary, music's worlding power places its stamp on a work's independent afterlife vis-à-vis its authors' intentions, the conditions and circumstances of its creation, and its original reception. This worlding power is the spring of music's hermeneutical autonomy. Consequently, the epoché of the practical order of everyday life is the negative condition for music's power to refashion affective dimensions of our experiences in accordance with feelings and moods to which tunes, airs, and the like give voice.

Mimesis, Expression, Affect

To offer an account of music's expressive features, I will briefly outline Ricoeur's theory of mimesis, which he sets out in the first volume of *Time and Narrative* ([1983] 1984).

Far from reduplicating reality, mimesis for Ricoeur is a creative imitation of it in which the power of imagination is at work. Following Aristotle, Ricoeur stresses that mimesis "produces what it imitates" (Ricoeur 1991, 138).[5] By setting the work's power to "penetrate the world of everyday experience in order to rework it from inside" (Ricoeur et al. [1995] 1998, 173) within the circle of mimesis, Ricoeur highlights how the world projected by a narrative, for example, restructures the evaluative field in which the reader (re)inscribes her or his life. This circle consists of three dynamically related moments: mimesis$_1$ (prefiguration), mimesis$_2$ (configuration), and mimesis$_3$ (refiguration). On Ricoeur's account, mimesis$_1$ refers to the narrative art's anchorages in the field of action with respect to our practical competence regarding interrelated terms such as agent, patient, helper, motives, circumstances, and the like (in sum, the semantics of action), action's symbolic mediation, and the temporal character of action. Mimesis$_2$ marks the entry into the kingdom of the *as if*. The epoché of the real that fiction, broadly conceived, brings about is the negative condition of the work's power to renew the real in accordance with the world projected by it. The movement from mimesis$_1$ to mimesis$_2$ accordingly bears out the fact that, in the case of the art of narrative, poetics never stops borrowing from ethics when it comes to revaluing, devaluing, or transvaluing action.

The third moment completes the arc of operations that joins mimesis$_2$ to mimesis$_1$ and mimesis$_3$ (refiguration). By defining the function of refiguration as mimetic, Ricoeur places the accent on the work's power to penetrate the world of our everyday experiences. From this vantage point, "if one can speak of truth in relation to the work of art, it is to the extent that this designates the capacity of the work of art to break a path in the real by renewing it *in accordance with the work itself*" (Ricoeur et al. [1995] 1998, 173–174, italics in the original). Ricoeur stresses that for hermeneutics, the distinction between the inside and outside of a work is a methodological artifact. Semioticians, he accordingly remarks, "believe they have given up the representative illusion by having constituted the text as an inside without an outside, or rather as an inside whose outside (be it author, audience, or socio-cultural circumstances) has become irrelevant" (Ricoeur 1991, 144). The work's power to refigure the real in accordance with the world projected by it calls into question the classical concept of truth in this regard. According to this concept, truth is defined as the unity of the alleged interiority of a private mental scene with the representation of something real. Mimesis explodes the univocity of this concept of truth along with the representative illusion. The work's ontological vehemence, which I identified earlier with the impact the work has on our ways of thinking, feeling, and acting, thus stands as proof, so to speak, of the mimetic force of its worlding power.

In view of Ricoeur's claim, following Aristotle, that narrative is an imitation of action, can we say that music goes even further than the narrative art in penetrating the real and reworking it from within by evoking feelings and moods that are unique to it? Ricoeur maintains that the full measure of mimesis could be taken only in the twentieth century when, for example, painting no longer aimed at representing identifiable objects. The function of mimesis, he accordingly explains, "is not to help us recognize objects but discover dimensions of experience that did not exist prior to the work" (Ricoeur et al.

[1995] 1998, 173). Music's expression of feelings and moods authorizes us to go even further in that the feelings and moods that music possesses, and which Ricoeur says it "establishes in us" (Ricoeur et al. [1995] 1998, 174), do not represent anything that corresponds to the real (see Savage 2010a, 2010b, 2020). Narrativizing interpretations deployed in the interest of deconstructing the chimera of absolute music's metaphysical transcendence of the material conditions of social life trade on references to "masculine" protagonists and the "feminine" Other, for example (see McClary 1991), at the expense of music's singular power. While he draws a distinction between, on the one hand, the narrative configuration of incidents and events that contribute to the structure of the plot and, on the other hand, music, Ricoeur also asks whether, "at the limit, could not one say that to each piece of art there corresponds a mood?" (1996; see Savage 2006, 2020). Feelings and moods that musical works establish in us are ones that these pieces possess. As such, these feelings and moods are properties exemplified by the tune, piece, extemporization, or work that expresses them.

We can therefore account for music's expression of feelings and moods in terms of the way that we draw a figure from the tones, the harmonic and timbral sonorities, and the like that follow one another in succession. When I said that for Gadamer, play consists in its self-presentation, I noted that, for him, a game reveals its spirit through the manner in which the game unfolds. The expression of the game's spirit, we could therefore say, is concomitant with the (self-)structuring movement that gives the game its shape and form. Similarly, a poem, Ricoeur remarks, "is like a work of music in that its mood is exactly coextensive with the internal order of symbols articulated by its language" (Ricoeur 1976, 59). Poetic language inverts the direction of reference of ordinary language (from thing to symbol, rather than from symbol to thing) by directing itself to a poem's interior makeup. Poetical discourse, we could therefore say, aims at communicating possible ways of inhering in the world through expressing moods and feelings that open us to the world and the world to us anew. For Martin Heidegger, in "poetical discourse, the communication of the existential possibilities of one's state-of-mind can become an aim in itself, and this amounts to a disclosing of existence" ([1927] 1962, 205). The mood exemplified by a poem or a musical work "introduces an extra-linguistic factor, which is the index of a manner of being" (Ricoeur [1975] 1977, 229). Like Heidegger, Ricoeur maintains that a "mood or 'state of soul' . . . is a way of finding or sensing oneself in the midst of reality" (Ricoeur [1975] 1977, 229; cf. Wallrup 2015).[6] The epoché of the real, consequently, is the "condition that allows poetry to develop a world on the basis of the mood" (Ricoeur [1975] 1977, 229) articulated by the poet. Hence, like music, the poem "opens up access to reality in the mode of fiction and feeling" (Ricoeur [1975] 1977, 229) in accordance with the mood that it possesses.

By maintaining that music's expression of feelings and moods owes its force to the schematizing operation involved in drawing a figure from a sequence of tones, for example, I am clearly crediting music's exemplification of these feelings and moods to the fit of the tones comprising a tune or a melody (see Savage 2010b, 2020). According to the *Oxford English Dictionary* (OED), one archaic meaning of the word "fit" is a "piece of music; [or] a strain." Furthermore, the OED defines a strain as a "musical sequence of sounds; a melody, a tune." From a hermeneutically phenomenological standpoint, the fit of a tune springs from the way that its constitutive components cohere. Just as the plot of a story "functions as the narrative *matrix*" (Ricoeur 1991, 105, italics in the original) by effecting the synthesis of the story's heterogeneous elements, the tune's melodic configuration gives a figure and a body to its affective character. Consequently, we could also liken the fit of the tune to the icon that, in the case of a metaphor, is the "schematization of [the] metaphorical attribution" (Ricoeur 1991, 126) drawn from the literal ruins of some initial semantic incongruency. In this case, the enigma of iconic presentation stems from the way that an emergent meaning arises from the predicative impertinence in a metaphorical statement such as "The peace process is on the ropes." Accordingly, we resolve this enigma each time we draw the intended meaning from the metaphorical statement's literal ruins by apprehending the image displayed in the thickness of the imagining scene.

Music differs from the narrative art and from the metaphorical attribution of nonliteral predicates in this regard. While every work has its affective tonality or tonalities, the pre- or hyperlinguistic expression of feelings and moods in music is singularly unique. In *Music, Time, and Its Other* (2018), I argued music is most profoundly human when it replies to the deficiency born from the difference between time and eternity through staking out the borderlines between them. Music's evocation of feelings of "being beyond" or "out of time" bear out its power to give voice to a variety of experiences in which time is surpassed by its other. Blacking's work on Venda ritual offers ethnographic evidence of how the creation of virtual worlds of time is vital to the musical practice of a cultural group. The experience that he describes as an adventure into the reality of the world of Venda spirits stands as a testament to how the creation or evocation of superreal worlds of time is a decidedly human, culturally significant, and even indispensably vital response to our human condition. Gilbert Rouget maintains that the material density given to time by music alters our consciousness of states of being, evoking states to which music alone can give us access. Similarly for him, the musical architecture of trance experiences and states of musical possession structures a superreal order that sanctifies ritual actions or possession states *hic et nunc* (Rouget [1980] 1985).[7]

AESTHETIC EXPERIENCE AND SOCIAL INTERFACES

In the last part of my chapter, I want to return to my claim that experiences occasioned by performances of music are the condition of the interfaces to which we often credit music's social value and worth. These social interfaces are themselves often the object of ethnomusicological analysis. Thomas Turino points out that scholars such as Manuel Peña (1985), Steven Feld (1988), Deborah Pacini Hernandez (1995), and Jane Sugarman (1997) "have succeeded in illustrating the intimate interfaces of sound structures, social structures, and identity" (Turino 1999, 221). Drawing on Charles Peirce's work, Turino proposes to account for the interface between music's emotional force and social identity to address what he identifies as a lacuna in ethnomusicological theory. Ethnography, he accordingly insists, is "crucial to social and musical semiotic analysis since it allows us to identify what the signs are, in relation to what object, for whom, and in which ways" (Turino 1999, 225).

Turino tells us that his account of the interface between music's emotional force and social identity is propaedeutic to a "theory of music in relation to what is usually called 'emotion'—our inadequate gloss for that mammoth realm of human experience that falls outside language-based thinking and communication" (1999, 221). Consequently, he attributes music's emotional force to semiotic processes that ostensibly operate below the level of linguistic expressions. Turino maintains that by "probing the instances in which semiotic chaining is halted before reaching the level of Thirdness (symbol, argument, linguistic-based interpretants)" (1999, 223),[8] he can account for music's distinctive potential for producing emotional effects. His theory of musical affectivity thus rests on the idea that a sign's affective potential is greater the further the sign is from linguistically mediated constructs of thought.

Turino's adaptation of Peirce's semiology clearly lends itself to ethnographic descriptions of emotive, musical behaviors. While I agree that music's pre- or hyperpredicative significance resists the kind of conceptual recuperation at which narrativizing interpretive strategies aim, I question whether the semiological processes that Turino identifies are themselves not dependent on, and hence derived from, the communicability of the experiences music affords. According to Turino, "*musical signs* are sonic events that create an effect in a perceiver" (1999, 234). However, these effects are in the first instance a function of the configurating operation through which music's exemplification of feelings and moods acquires its expressive force (see Savage 2018, 2020). Feeling's intentional structure, Ricoeur explains, is one in which feeling "designates qualities felt *on* things, *on* persons, *on the world* [at the same time that it] manifests and reveals the way in which the self is inwardly affected" (Ricoeur [1960] 1986, 84). Feeling is thus the privileged mode for revealing the "*élans* of our being and . . . its pre- and hyper-objective connections" (Ricoeur [1960] 1986, 86) with the world and with the things and others in it.

Music's power to touch us is thus far removed from any quasi-automatic reflex reaction. On the contrary, through internalizing moods to which music gives voice, we are not only touched by them but also moved to feel in like fashion inasmuch as we make feelings and moods exemplified by individual works our own. The sympathetic vibrations that resonate in the sounding body of a musical instrument are an imperfect analogy for this experience of being moved. This experience of being affected is even further removed from the metaphysics of inwardness. To be sure, emotive effects are indices of the body's visceral intensity orchestrating the "most subtle movement of the soul" (Ricoeur [1950] 1966, 264). Hermeneutically speaking, these viscerally powerful effects have their source in music's worlding power.

Are the "deeply felt, yet often unspoken, experiences of being *of* a group" (Turino 1999, 241) that Turino maintains depend upon the interruption—and even break—in the semiological process between emotional and energetic interpretants and linguistic-based ones[9] not then more radically rooted in the way that music renews our inherence in the world through redescribing our affective affinities with it? By attributing the communicability of experiences occasioned by musical performances to the capacity to apprehend various elements sounding in succession, I am clearly attributing music's affective power to the configurating operation through which each listener grasps a tune's, a melody's, or a work's expressive character. For each listener, the experience occasioned by a performance is singularly unique. How, then, we could ask, can music occasion an experience that brings the members of a group or community together? The distinction Blacking draws between music's social utility and its capacity to enhance our sense of belonging to a group, to a community, or to the world has its justification in the fact that these experiences precede, phenomenologically speaking, the social uses to which music is put. We could even ask if music would have any significance at all if it was not first able to move us and to affect us in ways that only it can. But then, should we not also ask how the communicability of an experience, which in each case involves an individual cultural practitioner, binds members of a group or community together through a shared feeling of belonging?

By indicating how a hermeneutically phenomenological account of music's worlding power uncovers the ground of sociologically oriented investigations into music's meaning and value, I am also opening the door to further inquiries into music's role in the formation of a group's or community's identity and its sense of itself. Feelings of belonging precede the objectification of agents' multiply intersecting social positions in this regard. These feelings attest to the priority of the experience of belonging to a history, culture, and tradition. The priority of this experience is borne out by the fact that we are affected by the histories, cultures, and traditions of which we are a part. Every methodological or critical stance adopted by the human sciences presupposes this experience, as Gadamer and Ricoeur have explained. Furthermore, Gadamer remarks how, within the humanistic tradition, the *sensus communis* refers to the sense in common that founds community (Gadamer [1960] 1989, 20ff.). This sense in common attests to the shared values, mores, convictions, and beliefs that give the will to live together its direction.

Like cultural nationalists and political propogandists who deploy music strategically in the interest of forging a sense of social cohesion, ethnomusicologists and cultural theorists have long recognized how music is a critical resource in promoting the feeling of being a member of, and hence of belonging to, a group. Yet, it is difficult to imagine that music could fulfill this strategic role apart from its power to refashion the real from within. Beyond deconstructions of the conceit of music's metaphysical dignity and the repudiation of the privileged status of Western art music, a phenomenological, hermeneutical reflection on experiences occasioned by musical performances leads to a broader consideration of music's affective power. Music's social, cultural, and even political relevance is inseparable from its capacity to refashion affective dimensions of our everyday experiences and to renew our manner of inhering in the world. As such, music's worlding power is the ground of the interfaces between music's expressive vehemence and social life.

NOTES

1. Ricoeur explains that the "necessity for phenomenology to conceive of its method as an *Auslegung*, an exegesis, an explication, an interpretation" (Ricoeur [1986] 1991, 43) lays bare its hermeneutical presupposition. Moreover, he adds that the "phenomenology that arose with the discovery of the universal character of intentionality has not remained faithful to its own discovery. The idealist theory of the constitution of meaning in consciousness has thus culminated in the hypostasis of subjectivity" (Ricoeur [1986] 1991, 36).

2. Blacking attributes this quote to John Dewey. However, the cited passage appears in Peyton Richter's introduction to a chapter on Dewey and Albert Camus entitled "Art, Experience, and Rebellion: Dewey and Camus" in Richter's edited anthology, *Perspectives in Aesthetics: Plato to Camus*, and refers more generally to views on art held by various authors, including Dewey and Camus (Richter 1967, 418).

3. By distinguishing between music's social utility and its aesthetic value, Blacking in effect identifies music's power to create superreal "worlds of time" with its ontological vehemence (see Savage 2009).

4. The notion of the worlding power of a work was initially proposed by Martin Heidegger in essays such as "The Origin of the Work of Art" and " . . . Poetically Man Dwells . . . " (Heidegger 1971).

5. Ricoeur emphasizes that mimesis (imitation) here "is no longer a reduplication of reality but a creative rendering of it" (1991, 133). Hence, mimesis "does not equate itself with something already given" (1991, 138).

6. Wallrup similarly acknowledges that for Heidegger, a mood disposes us toward the world. For Wallrup, "the act of musical listening opens up a world" (2015, 75). One might therefore ask whether, by placing the accent on the act of listening, Wallrup overlooks the significance of the work's worlding power vis-à-vis its expression of feelings and moods that open the world to us and us to the world anew.

7. According to Rouget, music "is an architecture in time. It gives time a density different from its everyday density. It lends it a materiality it does not ordinarily have and that is of another order. It indicates that something is happening in the here and now; that time is being occupied by an action being performed, or that a certain state rules over the beings present" ([1980] 1985, 121). Judith Becker likewise argues that trancing attests "to the divine presence in one's midst, legitimizing the religious beliefs and practices of the community" (2004, 1). For her, music "provides a link between alternate selves and alternate places and alternate times that become real places and real times in trance experiences. . . . One is moved from the mundane to the supra-normal: another realm, another time, with other kinds of knowing" (Becker 2004, 27).

8. According to Turino, "since musical signs usually operate at the levels of Firstness and Secondness[,] they will produce interpretants at these same levels in the chain where they occur. In contexts where these types of signs prevail and are the center of attention—for example in certain rituals, concerts, and dances—emotional and direct energetic effects can be prolonged, and movement to the level of Thirdness (language-mediated thought) postponed" (Turino 1999, 233; see Turino 2014).

9. Turino credits music's "emotional" force to semiotic processes that operate below the level of linguistic expressions. However much this strategy identifies music's affective significance with its pre-predicative or ante-predicative force, Turino offers no justification for why processes of semiotic chaining should be prolonged or halted in the manner in which

he indicates they are. He explains that "in order to understand music's special potential for creating emotional effects, I am interested in probing the instances in which semiotic chaining is halted before reaching the level of Thirdness (symbol, argument, linguistic-based interpretants)" (Turino 1999, 232).

Works Cited

Becker, Judith. 2004. *Deep Listeners: Music, Emotion, and Trancing*. Bloomington: Indiana University Press.

Blacking, John. 1973. *How Musical Is Man?* Seattle: University of Washington Press.

Bourdieu, Pierre. (1979) 1984. *Distinction: A Social Critique of the Judgment of Taste*. Translated by Richard Nice. Cambridge, MA: Harvard University Press.

Bowie, Andrew. 2007. *Music, Philosophy, and Modernity*. Cambridge: Cambridge University Press.

Dahlhaus, Carl. (1964) 1987. *Schoenberg and the New Music*. Translated by Derrick Puffett and Alfred Clayton. Cambridge: Cambridge University Press.

Dufrenne, Mikel. (1953) 1973. *The Phenomenology of Aesthetic Experience*. Translated by Edward S. Casey, Albert A. Anderson, Willis Domingo, and Leon Jacobson. Evanston, IL: Northwestern University Press.

Feld, Steven. 1988. "Aesthetics as Iconicity of Style, or 'Lift-up-over Sounding': Getting into the Kaluli Groove." *Yearbook for Traditional Music* 20: 74–113.

Gadamer, Hans-Georg. (1960) 1989. *Truth and Method*. 2nd rev. ed. Translated by Joel Weinsheimer and Donald G. Marshall. New York: Crossroad Publishing Company.

Geertz, Clifford. 1973. *The Interpretation of Cultures: Selected Essays*. New York: Basic Books.

Goehr, Lydia. 1992. *The Imaginary Museum of Musical Works: An Essay in the Philosophy of Music*. Oxford: Oxford University Press.

Heidegger, Martin. (1927) 1962. *Being and Time*. Translated by John Macquarrie and Edward Robinson. New York: Harper and Row.

Heidegger, Martin. 1971. *Poetry, Language, Thought*. Translated by Albert Hofstadter. New York: Harper and Row.

Kant, Immanuel. (1790) 1987. *Critique of Judgment*. Translated by Werner S. Pluhar. Indianapolis, IN: Hackett.

Koselleck, Reinhart. 2002. *The Practice of Conceptual History: Timing History, Spacing Concepts*. Translated by Todd Samuel Presner, Adelheis Baker, Kerstin Behnke, and Jobst Welge. Stanford, CA: Stanford University Press.

Kramer, Lawrence. 1992. "The Musicology of the Future." *Repercussions* 1 (1): 5–18.

Kramer, Lawrence. 1995. *Classical Music and Postmodern Knowledge*. Berkeley: University of California Press.

Kramer, Lawrence. 2002. *Musical Meaning: Toward a Critical Historiography*. Berkeley: University of California Press.

Kretzschmar, Hermann. (1902) 1990. "Anregung zur Förderung musikalischer Hermeneutik" [Suggestions for the furtherance of musical hermeneutics]. In *Musical Aesthetics: A Historical Reader*. Vol. 3 of *Aesthetics in Music No. 4: The Twentieth Century*, edited by Edward A. Lippman, 5–30. Stuyvesant, NY: Pendragon Press.

Kretzschmar, Hermann. (1905) 1990. "Neue Anregungen zur Förderung musikalischer Hermeneutik: Satzästhetik" [New suggestions for the furtherance of musical hermeneutics:

The aesthetics of musical compositions]. In *Musical Aesthetics: A Historical Reader*. Vol. 3 of *Aesthetics in Music No. 4: The Twentieth Century*, edited by Edward A. Lippman, 31–46. Stuyvesant, NY: Pendragon Press.

le Huray, Peter, and James Day, eds. 1988. *Music and Aesthetics in the Eighteenth and Early Nineteenth Centuries*. Cambridge: Cambridge University Press.

McClary, Susan. 1991. *Feminine Endings: Music, Gender, and Sexuality*. Minneapolis: University of Minnesota Press.

McClary, Susan. 1993. "Narrative Agendas in 'Absolute Music': Identity and Difference in Brahms's Third Symphony." In *Musicology and Difference: Gender and Sexuality in Musical Scholarship*, edited by Ruth A. Solie, 326–344. Berkeley: University of California Press.

McClary, Susan. 1994. "Paradigm Dissonances: Music Theory, Cultural Studies, Feminist Criticism." *Perspectives of New Music* 32 (1): 68–85.

Pacini Hernandez, Deborah. 1995. *Bachata: A Social History of a Dominican Popular Music*. Philadelphia: Temple University Press.

Peña, Manuel H. 1985. *The Texas-Mexican Conjunto: History of a Working-Class Music*. Austin: University of Texas Press.

Richter, Peyton. 1967. "Art, Experience, and Rebellion: Dewey and Camus." In *Perspectives in Aesthetics: Plato to Camus*, edited by Peyton Richter, 418–452. Indianapolis, IN: Odyssey Press.

Ricoeur, Paul. (1950) 1966. *Freedom and Nature: The Voluntary and the Involuntary*. Translated by Erazim V. Kohák. Evanston, IL: Northwestern University Press.

Ricoeur, Paul. (1960) 1986. *Fallible Man*. Translated by Charles A. Kelbley. New York: Fordham University Press.

Ricoeur, Paul. 1967. *Husserl: An Analysis of His Phenomenology*. Translated by Edward G. Ballard and Lester E. Embree. Evanston, IL: Northwestern University Press.

Ricoeur, Paul. (1975) 1977. *The Rule of Metaphor: Multi-disciplinary Studies of the Creation of Meaning in Language*. Translated by Robert Czerny with Kathleen McLaughlin and John Costello. Toronto: University of Toronto Press.

Ricoeur, Paul. 1976. *Interpretation Theory: Discourse and the Surplus of Meaning*. Fort Worth: Texas Christian University Press.

Ricoeur, Paul. (1983) 1984. *Time and Narrative*. Vol. 1. Translated by Kathleen McLaughlin and David Pellauer. Chicago: University of Chicago Press.

Ricoeur, Paul. (1986) 1991. *From Text to Action: Essays in Hermeneutics*. Vol 2. Translated by Kathleen Blamey and John B. Thompson. Evanston, IL: Northwestern University Press.

Ricoeur, Paul. 1991. *A Ricoeur Reader: Reflection and Imagination*. Edited by Mario J. Valdés. Toronto: University of Toronto Press.

Ricoeur, Paul. 1996. "Arts, Language and Hermeneutic Aesthetics." Interview by Jean-Marie Brohm and Magali Uhl. Translated by R. D. Sweeney. *Philo Recherche-Fac*, Philagora, September 20, 1996. http://www.philagora.net/philo-fac/ricoeur-e.php.

Ricoeur, Paul, François Azouvi, and Marc de Launay. (1995) 1998. *Critique and Conviction: Conversations with François Azouvi and Marc de Launay*. Translated by Kathleen Blamey. New York: Columbia University Press.

Rouget, Gilbert. (1980) 1985. *Music and Trance: A Theory of the Relation between Music and Possession*. Translated by Brunhilde Biebuyck. Chicago: University of Chicago Press.

Savage, Roger W. H. 2006. "Is Music Mimetic? Ricoeur and the Limits of Narrative." *Journal of French Philosophy* 16 (1–2): 121–133.

Savage, Roger W. H. 2009. "Being, Transcendence and the Ontology of Music." *World of Music* 51 (2): 7–22.

Savage, Roger W. H. 2010a. *Hermeneutics and Music Criticism*. New York: Routledge.

Savage, Roger W. H. 2010b. "Ricoeur and Musicology: Music, Hermeneutics and Aesthetic Experience." In *Ricoeur across the Disciplines*, edited by Scott Davidson, 211–228. New York: Continuum.

Savage, Roger W. H. 2018. *Music, Time, and Its Other: Aesthetic Reflections on Finitude, Temporality, and Alterity*. Abingdon, UK: Routledge.

Savage, Roger W. H. 2020. "Feeling, Interiority, and the Musical Body." In *Paul Ricoeur and the Lived Body*, edited by Roger W. H. Savage, 83–108. Lanham, MD: Lexington Books.

Sugarman, Jane C. 1997. *Engendering Song: Singing and Subjectivity at Prespa Albanian Weddings*. Chicago: University of Chicago.

Turino, Thomas. 1999. "Signs of Imagination, Identity, and Experience: A Peircean Semiotic Theory for Music." *Ethnomusicology* 43 (2): 221–255.

Turino, Thomas. 2014. "Peircean Thought as Core Theory for a Phenomenological Ethnomusicology." *Ethnomusicology* 58 (2): 185–221.

Wallrup, Erik. 2015. *Being Musically Attuned: The Act of Listening to Music*. Farnham, UK: Ashgate.

CHAPTER 4

....

THE EXPRESSIVE CULTURE OF SOUND COMMUNICATION AMONG HUMANS AND OTHER BEINGS

A Phenomenological and Ecological Approach

....

JEFF TODD TITON

SOUND is one of several ways in which beings communicate with one another, and like speech, music is a type of human sound communication with aesthetic and other performance dimensions. Music is not a given in the human world but rather is a cultural sonic domain with various assigned attributes, including musical structures, uses, sound-producing devices, and values. Music varies among different individuals and social groups over time and place. While ethnomusicologists accept these statements as axiomatic, in trying to understand music as culture, we diverge in methods and emphases. Lived experience is one such emphasis, and phenomenology is one such method.

I have divided this chapter into four sections. In the first section, I ask how phenomenological methods may inform field research and ethnographic studies of people making music.[1] This section will be personal because, in the opening chapter of this book, Berger, VanderHamm, and Riedel identify me as a pioneer in this area, and reminiscence may thus be of at least historical interest. In the second section, I ask how phenomenological methods may inform research on the various forms of expressive culture of same-species beings communicating with one another, with particular emphasis on sonic communication. I do so in the broader context of animal behavior, a subject normally reserved to biology, rather than in the narrower context of human (animal) behavior only.[2] By *expressive culture* I mean the processes, perceptions, cognitions, and emotions bound up in the production of cultural performances as experienced in everyday life.[3] The performance of culture in human life may have a strongly aesthetic dimension (as, for example, music-making, storytelling, and interior design often do), or its aesthetic dimension may be weak (as in ordinary conversation). The principal channel of ethnographic phenomenological inquiry—in which experience, as it is presented to consciousness, is interrogated—appears to be blocked in the study of nonhuman animals because such animals do not report to us on their experiences. My thesis in this second section is that phenomenology may nonetheless contribute to the study of expressive culture in animal sound communication, chiefly by means of direct ecological perception, direct perception empathy, and embodiment. In the last century, most scientists studying animal behavior found it both implausible and unnecessary to assume that animals had culture, consciousness, or experiences, while worldviews that ascribed intentionality, experience, reflective consciousness, thoughts, and beliefs to nonhuman beings were regarded as nonscientific, even if they appeared to operate more or less consistently, if tautologically, for the people that held them.[4] In this century, the "animal turn" that decenters humans and contemplates ecocentric values increasingly opens scientists and cultural anthropologists up to the possibility of these attributes,[5] at least to some degree, in nonhuman animals (Magliocco 2018, 3).[6] More specifically, in this second section I claim that the production and reception of sound is part of the lived experience of nonhuman as well as human beings. Moreover, I claim that their experiential, sonic communication moves beyond the instrumentality of stimulus-response toward an exchange of information that effectively serves as expressive culture, in nonhuman as well as human beings.

The third section of this chapter offers a preliminary inquiry into the ways phenomenology may contribute to our understanding of interspecific (i.e., across-species) sonic communication. The wider context for this work is diverse. For example, the animal rights movement relies on the assumption that the higher animals undergo experience, have emotions, and express moods, dispositions, and feelings. Here, animal expressive culture includes certain sounds, cries, and whimpers that humans—as well as conspecifics, presumably—interpret as signals of suffering. Scholarship on ritual and belief is filled with examples of expressive culture as interspecific sound communication, such as a Pentecostal speaking in tongues or a Native American of the Great Plains going on a vision quest. Such messages from the spirit world sometimes also involve an aesthetic dimension. The intellectual movement in anthropology known as *perspectivism* provides a phenomenological frame for understanding animal sound communication, one that differs significantly from behavioral ecology in proposing that both human and nonhuman animals are subjects or persons to themselves and their conspecifics, even as they apprehend reality from different viewpoints (Viveiros de Castro 1998). Finally, a sound ecology attempts to integrate insights from the ecological sciences with traditional and Indigenous ecological knowledges by means of an intersubjective ontology and epistemology anchored in the co-presence that arises from the sound connections—literal (physical) and metaphorical—that are made when animals communicate in sound.

The Anthropocene has encouraged the humanities and social sciences to reconsider their anthropocentric bias. Ecocriticism, ecomusicology, and the environmental humanities are thriving new fields that bring environmental studies from the periphery to the center of our concerns. Ethnomusicology and its predecessor, comparative musicology, always were interested in people's beliefs about music, other beings (physical and spiritual), and the environment, but they typically approached such topics from an anthropocentric perspective. Ecomusicology (the study of music, sound, nature, culture, and the environment in a time of environmental crisis) more explicitly opens our subject from people making music to beings making sound—that is, to the soundings of all beings. For that reason, the concluding section of this chapter, on the subject of interspecies communication, asks whether ethnomusicologists ought to rethink the orientation of our field and alter it to a more ecocentric concept, an eco-ethnomusicology of beings making sound, and here I discuss what might be gained and lost in so doing. Recognizing perspectives from Indigenous ecological knowledges as well as from contemporary Western science, I raise the curtain on a large and growing scholarly debate over the future of the field of ethnomusicology and revisit the issue of the place within it occupied by the study of sound.

People Making Music

Phenomenology in Ethnographic Fieldwork: A Personal and Historical Perspective

In the first chapter of this volume, Berger, VanderHamm, and Riedel date the beginnings of phenomenology in ethnomusicology to the 1970s and name me as one of three pioneers in this area; the others are Ruth Stone and Timothy Rice. To my knowledge, none of us was aware that the other two also were doing phenomenology until our work was well along. In her research with music of the Kpelle of West Africa, Stone ([1982] 2010) drew on performance theory and Edmund Husserl's philosophy of time and consciousness. Rice was especially concerned with hermeneutics and turned to the phenomenology of Hans-Georg Gadamer and Paul Ricoeur (Rice 1994). Although I too was interested in hermeneutic phenomenology and the work of those philosophers, my ethnographic research from 1973 to 1977 documenting sacred sound and music, shortly to be discussed further, was informed mainly by Ninian Smart's program for a phenomenology of religion (Smart 1969, 1970, 1973), which was influenced by Husserl. In the fall of 1977, I turned to Ricoeur's hermeneutic phenomenology for guidance in interpreting those research documents (Ricoeur 1974; see also Ihde 1971). Around 1981, I also began to rely on Clifford Geertz's anthropological hermeneutics, which likened culture to a densely intricate text (Geertz 1973a). The anthropologist's task is interpretive—creating "thick" (many-layered) descriptions and explanations of the cultural text found in the field (Geertz 1973b). The writings of James Spradley in ethnosemantics also were helpful, both in eliciting cultural texts and in decoding them (Spradley et al. [1972] 2004; Spradley 1979).[7]

In Smart's phenomenology of religion I found a methodology compatible with ethnomusicology's insistence on avoiding ethnocentrism and, instead, understanding the expressions of a social group on its own terms. Smart advocated that scholars of comparative religion adopt Husserl's phenomenological procedure of the epoché. For Smart, the observer should "bracket" (set aside) the truth-claims of the religion under study, suspending both belief and disbelief, and try to understand its worldview, doctrines, ideas, practices, and expressions as a whole, which operate in their own way and on their own terms (Smart 1969, 1970, 1973). It is possible that Smart had read Gerardus van der Leeuw's *Phänomenologie der Religion* ([1933] 1956). Van der Leeuw also suggested that the student adapt Husserl's epoché procedure, so as to suspend one's own beliefs about the sacred and describe a religion in a manner consistent and empathic with the way its adherents understood it. Whether these religious beliefs corresponded to reality or not, they corresponded to the believers' worldview and their sense of their place within it. I saw parallels with autobiographies, which I described as "fictions" in the sense that they are made (*facio*, the Latin root of fiction, means "making"), rather than merely discovered—even though for the autobiographer, as well as for the religious adherent, they are, so to speak, found revealed (Titon 1980).[8]

The implication of all of this for ethnographic fieldwork, as I saw it, was that regardless of whether or not the researcher was a member of the religious group under study, bracketing was called for so as to achieve the subject position best suited toward documenting the group's expressive culture and relying on members of that group to explain it. This, I felt, was best done by thinking of my subject position as that of a long-term visitor or guest. Smart believed that the sacred manifested itself in different ways in different human groups. One of those ways was in the dimension of lived experience, something that I knew resonated deeply in the singing, praying, musical preaching, and "affective presence" (Armstrong 1986) of the American Christian groups I was studying. As I learned more about Husserl's phenomenology, I understood that experience was at the center of its inquiry—how experience was presented to consciousness. I made this one of my chief areas of research inquiry during my fieldwork; that is, I asked the preachers and members of the congregations to tell me about their experiences of the sacred, to describe them in detail and speak about their affective and emotional dimensions, both in general and in response to preaching, singing, praying, and testimony (witnessing). In short, I was asking them to tell me about their expressive cultural experiences in the presence of performed sacred language.[9]

For these Protestant congregations, the sacred was made manifest in experiencing the felt presence of the Holy Spirit, which, they believe, comes to live inside the Christian disciple. Often, this presence was signaled by a change in sonic expression, as, for example, from speech to impassioned speech, chant ("whooping" in African American Baptist parlance), song, or (among holiness-Pentecostal believers) speaking in tongues (Titon 1978a). Smart had written that each religious tradition had an overarching narrative that explained its worldview and justified its practices. Among the people I was visiting, the Bible provided that overarching narrative, but narrative itself, as a speech mode, was not confined there. Rather, it was a habitual mode of thinking about, organizing, and expressing experience and its meaning. The church members' most important narrative genre was the conversion story, but, like the Puritans in the Massachusetts Bay Colony, they also thought of their daily experience as an ongoing story of how God was present in their lives. Their task, they believed, was to understand the meaning of that story by interpreting the pattern in the narrative as it went along (Caldwell 1985). In addition to their conversion narratives, each preacher also had at the ready the story of how they became preachers—not because *they* had planned to enter the ministry as a vocation but because they felt that God had planned it and was calling them to the ministry. Usually, they resisted for some time but ended up bending to God's will and giving up whatever else they might have intended to do in order to preach the gospel as a calling from God. These conversion and call-to-preach narratives were, foremost, spoken autobiographical accounts of personal experiences of the sacred, and they were the generative centerpieces of religious experience for these preachers and the members of their congregation.

As I considered the meanings and significances of these sonic narratives, songs, prayers, and sermons, I found hermeneutic phenomenology to be the approach that yielded the most satisfying interpretations: first, as a means of understanding the interpretative work done by the church members, and second, in understanding the entirety of the performed expressive culture as a text in Geertz's sense. Thus, I wrote *Powerhouse for God* (Titon [1988] 2018) from the standpoint of hermeneutic phenomenology. In the introduction to the book and elsewhere, I made explicit my debt to that philosophical tradition, giving special attention to Ricoeur. In sum, Husserlian phenomenology as adapted by Ninian Smart enabled me to do the initial work of documentation, whereas hermeneutic phenomenology and ethnosemantics enabled me to do the work of interpretation.

Heterophenomenology, Ethnography, and Autoethnography

It is important to distinguish the third-person phenomenology I did then from the first-person self-reflexivity that sometimes rises to the rigor of phenomenology and that ethnomusicologists have, at times, employed autoethnographically, when they themselves are members of the group whose music and culture they study. Third-person phenomenology asks not how experience is presented to one's own consciousness but rather seeks reports of how experience is presented to others' consciousness; these reports become the documentary raw data for ethnographers' phenomenological descriptions and their interpretation of others' experience. Possibly influenced by our conversations about my ethnographic fieldwork when we were friends and colleagues at Tufts University (1971–1985), the analytic philosopher Daniel Dennett has termed this third-person approach "heterophenomenology" and made it a part of his well-known work in philosophy of mind (Dennett 1991, 2003, 2007).[10] A strong critic of phenomenology, Dennett believes that his heterophenomenology can help to address the philosophical problem of other minds and that its third-person reports can provide objective, or at least neutral, evidence about the experiences of others. Working from within the phenomenological tradition, philosophers Shaun Gallagher and Dan Zahavi have expressed skepticism that Dennett's heterophenomenology obtains the objectivity that he claims for it. "Strictly speaking," Gallagher and Zahavi write, "heterophenomenology doesn't study conscious phenomena, since it is neutral about whether they exist; rather, it studies reports that purport to be about conscious phenomena" ([2008] 2012, 19). Further, they write that Dennett justifies this neutrality by comparing the activity to what "is required in an anthropological investigation" (19), while also allowing for the possibility that these reports might be in error (i.e., that the reported memories may themselves be false). Gallagher and Zahavi argue that "In attempting to say something about consciousness (or specifically about the experience of X [another person]), heterophenomenology fails to acknowledge that its interpretations of first-person reports must be based on either the scientist's own first-person experience (what he or she understands from his or her own experience to be the experience of X) or on pre-established (and seemingly objective) categories that ultimately derive from folk psychology" (20).

Nevertheless, whatever position one holds in this debate, heterophenomenology names an ethnographic interviewing method that various ethnographers, including myself, have employed to obtain other people's autobiographical reports of lived experience. Though they are not ethnographers, Gallagher and Zahavi have developed a critique of Dennett that is particularly interesting in this regard, as it identifies a key issue for phenomenological ethnography. As they observe, Dennett neglects the way that the observer's folk psychological categories may prejudice their reading of others' self-reports. For the ethnographer, though, the folk psychological categories implicit in the research participants' reports are of the first importance, because these categories contextualize and explain the subjects' experiences to themselves. Ethnographers who practice ethnosemantic analysis, as I did (Titon [1988] 2018), learn the words that represent these categories, and then, in dialogue with their subjects, they unlock the category relationships that articulate the structures and principles of the culture under study (Spradley 1979; Spradley et al. [1972] 2004). In this context, the object of my ethnographic work was not simply a study of conscious experience by means of obtaining reports based in a nonrigorous phenomenology of appearances. Rather, my object was to find out what those appearances are, how they are named, and how these names construct related categories of knowledge, in light of which the subjects interpret their lived experiences.

To make this concrete, imagine a preacher who is asked how she feels when her vocal delivery changes from ordinary speech to the heightened speech characteristic of oratory (which is louder and has a greater range of intonation) and then, for a period of time, to the musical speech of chant, in which a tonal center is established, syllables are lengthened, and a melody appears, maintained with repetitions. She may say that at those times when her preaching becomes musical, she feels as if the words she expresses are coming to her, not from her conscious mind as she would intend them, but rather from the outside; that she has no control over their content; and that at these times she has become a conduit for the Holy Spirit. For the ethnomusicologist taking an ethnosemantic approach to third-person reports of lived experience, the object is not to examine in a rigorous fashion the structures of the preacher's experience or how they appear in the preacher's consciousness to order her experience. Rather, the object is to determine the cultural categories that her experiential report both constructs and is based in. Observing behavior, participating in conversations, and conducting interviews, the ethnographer derives coherent cultural wholes. As noted, the insight gleaned is that a change of sonic mode from speech to heightened speech and then to musical chant signals sacred presence. Moving from ethnosemantics to a hermeneutic phenomenology informed by historical research, the ethnographer will come to realize that "whooping" carries African American cultural connections because of its African origins and its historical practice during slavery throughout the Americas, while also demonstrating the aesthetic and sonic power of its affecting presence.

As this book's editors show in their chapter in this volume, phenomenological approaches to ethnomusicology have developed considerably since the 1980s. Gradually, ethnomusicologists turned from musical phenomenologies of the other to phenomenologies of the self and others. I have used such approaches, for example, in autoethnographic research on old-time music, where I explored the ways that, as musicians playing along with others, we learn and execute a never-before-heard melody "on the fly," in the moment of our performing it (Titon 2012). I have also described moments of musical being-in-the-world when playing in a jam session; discussed peak experiences, which are often described as "flow states"; and suggested that a new epistemology based on the relational ontology of beings making music and sound—rather than on interpreting texts or experimenting with objects—may yield sound communities, sound economies, and a sound ecology (Titon 2001, [1997] 2008, 2015).

ANIMALS MAKING SOUND

Consciousness, Experience, and Sonic Communication

The ethnomusicologist questions people who make music and relies on their reports (as well as observation and other documentary evidence) to construct interpretative ethnographies of music. Because animals cannot talk to us, obtaining similar reports from nonhuman animals is, literally, out of the question. Claude Lévi-Strauss wrote, "No situation seems more tragic, more offensive to heart and mind, than that of a humanity coexisting and sharing the joys of a planet with other living species yet being unable to communicate with them. One understands why myths refuse to consider this an original flaw in the creation and see in its appearance the event that inaugurated the human condition and its weakness" (Lévi-Strauss and Eribon 1991, 138). However, animals do communicate with us, though they do so extralinguistically. By means of folk psychology (discussed below), humans familiar with their behavior infer attitudes, moods, feelings, desires, and experience from gestures, postures, sounds, movements, and actions from nonhuman animals, more or less as we do from humans. Phenomenologists have developed a rigorous examination of the conditions of embodied subjects (direct perception and empathy) that make such inferences possible for humans and nonhumans alike. To some extent, of course, animal experience is beyond human comprehension. We cannot fully know, as Thomas Nagel (1972) famously argued, what it is like to be a bat or other nonhuman animal. (I cannot fully know what it is to *be* you, either; however, by virtue of our both being human, I can know what it is *like* to be you.)

Moreover, whether animals undergo experience (in a recognizable human sense) and have consciousness is an unsettled subject of debate.[11] Whether they possess consciousness depends on how consciousness is defined. Until recently, its definition turned on whether it is simply a (conscious) state of being awake and aware, or if consciousness requires a self-reflexive awareness of oneself as an individual, with an identity and continuity of existence in the past, present, and future. Self-reflexive consciousness (self-consciousness), thought to be only a human attribute, is a prerequisite for phenomenological self-reflection; mere conscious awareness is not sufficient. However, neuroscience and evolutionary biology now indicate that consciousness is not an either/or proposition; it is *not* the case that one either has it or doesn't. Instead, it exists along an evolutionary continuum. For example, the *Cambridge Declaration on Consciousness* (Low 2012), a manifesto on behalf of animal consciousness, argued the matter on scientific grounds, claiming that humans are not unique in possessing the underlying neurological structures that generate consciousness, thereby implying that it is reasonable to suppose that the higher animals, at least, do have consciousness.[12] Upon its release, the *Declaration* received considerable attention in the press and from animal rights activists, who claimed that, at last, there was proof that animals were conscious beings who, in feeling pain, suffered. In other words, at a certain point or points on the evolutionary continuum, yet to be determined, consciousness begins to become self-reflexive, and then increasingly so. As Dennett put it, "Consciousness must then be a complex of talents and cognitive abilities realized in the medium of neural interactions . . . and these emerged gradually and spottily in evolution." Thus, Dennett concludes, human consciousness is far more open and versatile than animal consciousness; human consciousness is to animal consciousness roughly as human language is to birdsong (Dennett 2017a). Nevertheless, neuropsychologists, behavioral ecologists, and ornithologists have shown how the utterances of birds, whales, dolphins, and other creatures possess certain attributes of human language, such as recursiveness—as if, like consciousness, language is better understood in terms of an evolutionary continuum rather than as a binary (i.e., as something that humans have and other species do not; see Suzuki 2006; Boë et al. 2017; Meijer 2020; Dartnell 2001). Leaving the topic of language aside, it is unclear to what extent nonhuman animals undergo the range of experience that humans do. Animals closer to humans on the evolutionary spectrum—that is, some birds and mammals—do appear to share certain qualities of experience with humans. For example, they appear at least to have percepts of emotion, pleasure, and pain, and also to engage in play behavior (Earp and Maney 2013; Held and Špinka 2011). These qualities also suggest the possibility of an aesthetic dimension to their sonic communications—in other words, that some animal sounds are, for them, like music. I shall have more to say about these things shortly.

University textbooks treating animal communication within the context of animal behavior explain (i.e., predict) animal behavior without assuming that animals are self-conscious, undergo experience, or have intentions as humans do (e.g., Bradbury and Vehrencamp 2011; Alcock 2013). Therefore, on the principle of Occam's razor, they assume that animals are not self-conscious and do not undergo experience. These behavioral scientists discuss animal sound communication in terms of sound signals that are triggered by stimuli and transmitted by a sender to a receiver through a fluid medium, such as air or water, or through solids, such as trees or soil. From this perspective, sound signals convey information that influences the immediate behavior of the recipient. Following Richard Dawkins and John Krebs's landmark paper "Animal Signals: Information or Manipulation?," behavioral ecologists claim that to speak of "information" is misleading, because it implies intent on the part of the sender and a thought process in which the information is understood by the recipient—in other words, animal minds. Instead, they argue, it is better to think in terms of a stimulus that manipulates or influences the response behavior of the recipient, not information that is transmitted and decoded (Dawkins and Krebs 1978; see also Searcy and Nowicki 2005). Game theory is sometimes employed to predict these behaviors (Bradbury and Vehrencamp 2011). Animals are thus thought to have brains (cognition) but not minds (self-reflexive thought and consciousness). In Dennett's memorable phrase, they have "competence without comprehension" (Dennett 2017b).

Behavioral ecologists also assume that sound signals and responses are genetically programmed to maximize evolutionary "fitness." That is, they claim animals are programmed to thrive and survive so that they may mate, have offspring, and spread their genes as widely as possible to succeeding generations. Taking songbirds as a case in point, ornithologists distinguish alarm calls that warn of predators, songs by male birds that attract mates, territorial calls that maintain spaces for a mating pair to nest and raise offspring, contact or flight calls that keep the flock together, aggressive calls that maintain order within the community, and so on—all in service to fitness. Their sound signals may be "honest" (such as a flight call) or "deceptive" (such as the grouse's feigned broken wing flutter), but in both cases, they are manipulative. And whether these sound signals are honest or deceptive, mainstream thinking in behavioral ecology assumes no agency behind them (Stegmann 2013). Again, brains but not minds.[13] Nevertheless, a minority of animal behaviorists today question the idea that sound signals are triggers that produce automatic responses in animal brains and bodies, rather than transmitters of information to be processed in another animal's brain, the way human speech transmits information.[14] Like these animal behaviorists, field biologists such as Katy Payne and Jane Goodall, who have done what amounts to the equivalent of long-term ethnographic research with animal populations and their vocalizations, describe, from a human perspective, the personalities, activities, and interactions of individual animals they have known, suggesting that they have intentions, agency, emotions, and experiences (Payne 1998, 2003; Goodall 1986, 1990).

Direct Social Perception

If nonhuman animals have brains but not self-reflexive consciousness, first-person accounts of experience and heterophenomenology are blocked as means to study their
sonic experiences. However, recent developments in phenomenology that engage ecological psychology, specifically theories of direct social perception and empathy, do
not require the assumption that other beings have minds or self-reflexive consciousness in order for them to communicate with each other. These same theories also enable
humans, to a certain extent, to understand that communication among other beings on
the basis of our own behavior patterns. After reviewing these developments, I will assert, following the pioneering work of the Baltic naturalist Jakob von Uexküll ([1934]
2010), that nonhuman animals are subjects, have experiences, and express themselves
within their *Umwelt* (the affordances of their environments or perceptual fields).[15] This
is how animals perform their expressive culture. Contemporary theories of direct social
perception, empathy, and embodiment offer a promising basis for a phenomenological
study of animal sound communication as both visceral bodily connection and experiential intersubjectivity.

There are of course many explanatory theories for human behavior. In everyday life,
most people rely on what philosophers call "folk psychology," the idea that people behave as they do because of their needs, wants, beliefs, intentions, and desires. Two well-
known theories are behavioral determinism (the idea that all beings respond predictably
to stimuli and that they lack free will) and psychoanalytic explanations (which see behavior as based on unconscious motivations). Taking a different approach, in various
writings Zahavi and Gallagher summarize two mainstream psychological explanations
for humans' ability to understand the behavior of other people. Each assumes that understanding others requires that we apprehend their mental states. The first, called
"theory theory" (TT), assumes that people begin with third-person observation of the
other's behavior and then try to determine or theorize what mental beliefs, desires, and
intentions might logically have caused that behavior.[16] The second type of psychological explanation is simulation theory (ST). With simulation theory, instead of trying to
read *their* minds, we put ourselves in their place and read *our own* minds. Thus, we understand their behavior by reflecting on what we would do if we were them (Gallagher
2008, 535–536). Both TT and ST involve a kind of mind reading—using self-reflexive
thought to make an inference about the experience of the other. But Gallagher and
Zahavi offer a third explanation, which they call the phenomenological proposal (PP).
Notably, PP does not require any kind of mind reading. The phenomenological proposal depends on the claim that humans have a direct *perceptual* grasp of other humans'
feelings, intentions, and beliefs as embodied in their behavior. This intraspecies perceptual grasp comes prior to any reflection (Zahavi 2011).

This perception is more than mere observation of the other's behavior. As Gallagher
(2008) explains it, direct social perception involves awareness of the meaning of that
behavior, which is achieved through the perceptual act itself and not through the deduc-
tive reasoning involved in mind reading. Further, direct social perception is enactive;

it affords certain kinds of immediate actions on the part of the observer, ones that arise from the perceptual process itself and are not something that comes later upon reflection. Finally, direct social perception may be accompanied by an immediate emotional coloration—an immediate feeling about the observation and its relation to the observed and the observer. Gallagher claims that direct social perception is how most social behavior goes along in daily life, responding to the behavior of others without self-reflexive thought. Most people seldom have, or take, the time to puzzle over others' mental states while interacting with what others say and do. That comes later, if at all (Gallagher 2008). Gallagher writes, "In ordinary instances of interaction with others, I am not in the observer position; I am not off to the side thinking or trying to figure out what they are doing. Rather, I am responding to them in an embodied way. . . . What I perceive in these cases does not constitute something short of understanding. Rather my understanding of the other person is constituted within the perception-action loops that define the various things that I am doing with or in response to others" (2008, 540). Gallagher is of course assuming that both persons inhabit the same society and react pre-reflexively to each other's postures, gestures, and movements and proceed according to that society's cultural rules.

Psychologists Tom Froese and David Leavens have studied direct social perception among the higher animal vertebrates. Advancing the perspective of Gallagher and Zahavi, they note that comparative psychology of humans and other primates "continues to be premised on the doctrine that humans and nonhuman primates only perceive others' physical 'surface behavior,' while mental states are assumed to be perceptually inaccessible. However, a growing consensus in social cognition research accepts the direct perception hypothesis: primarily we *see* what others aim to do; we do not infer it from their motions" (Froese and Leavens 2009, under "Abstract," italics in original). Nevertheless, the accuracy of direct social perception depends to some extent on familiarity with the other person's cultural background and experience (Bernd Brabec de Mori, personal communication, January 21, 2020). In the presence of an alien being, direct social perception fails. Thus, culture enters into direct social perception by the back door. Zahavi appears to recognize this when he writes that "when making the claim that there is a fundamental form of social cognition which is direct, few, if any, phenomenologists would deny that the social understanding in question is influenced and enriched by background knowledge, contextual cues and past experiences"—in a word, by culture (Zahavi 2011, 547–548).

These ideas apply not just to human-to-human sound communication but also to the conspecific sound communication of other animals.[17] Vibrated by another animal's call, a listening animal hears what the signaling animal is likely to do; it does not infer it from the other's mental state but responds instead to its embodied sound signals. A chickadee responds to a flight call by direct social perception, vibrating in response to the other chickadee's sound. Thus, it becomes aware of the other bird's location and intention, even when it cannot see that bird. A young white-tailed deer embodies its immediate response to its mother's alarm snort by straightening up, head erect and unmoving, senses on the alert for danger. Neither the phenomenological proposal of direct social perception nor the behavioral ecologist's proposal of sound signal and response requires the assumption of minds, mental states, mind reading, or simulation. The responding deer need not reflect, make a conscious decision, wonder why its mother is sounding alarm, or imagine itself to be its mother sounding the alarm. The young deer reacts in an informed perception, colored, perhaps, by a percept of fear (if one grants that birds and mammals feel emotions).

Direct Perception Empathy

Dan Zahavi's phenomenological proposal of direct perception empathy offers a further opportunity to comprehend animal sound communication (Zahavi 2011). This is not empathy as we ordinarily think of it—reflective empathy, which arises from simulation (imaginatively taking the other's place). Rather, direct perception empathy is a first-stage empathy in humans that comes prior to mental understanding. Zahavi's ideas on empathy draw on the work of twentieth-century German psychologist Theodor Lipps. Prior to Lipps, the term "empathy" referred to a process of aesthetic appreciation, but as Zahavi explains, for Lipps it became the central means of recognizing others' mental states. According to Zahavi, Lipps "argued that when I see a foreign gesture or expression, I have a tendency to reproduce it, and that this tendency also evokes the feeling normally associated with this expression. It is this feeling which is then projected onto the other's perceived gesture" (Zahavi 2011, 542, paraphrasing Lipps 1907). For example, when you see someone smile at you, you involuntarily smile back prior to any reflection. Thus, an embodied action often produces an immediate imitation, which enables humans to perceive directly the actions, emotions, and sensations of others. Indeed, as Froese and Leavens write, "The mental lives of others are perceptually accessible because their minds are not hidden inside their brains but embodied and realized in their actions" (2009, 3).

Zahavi's concept of direct perception empathy has its critics, however (e.g., Fuchs 2019; Schear 2009). Thomas Fuchs calls attention to the phenomenon of "*bodily resonance* which . . . induces, on a pre-reflective level, a process of mutual modification of bodily and emotional states, thus enabling a primary form of empathy without requiring any representations" (Fuchs 2016, 195, italics in the original). He distinguishes this "intercorporeal empathy," or primary empathy, from reflective empathy, which would happen in an act of thinking. However, Fuchs later points out that if reflective empathy is withdrawn, as when a person recognizes that another person means them harm, primary empathy toward that person becomes blocked and direct perception empathy becomes impossible (Fuchs 2019).

Harris Berger and Kati Szego emphasize that direct social perception and direct perception empathy should not be confused with an unmediated understanding of the other and will go awry in cases of misunderstanding and deception (personal communication, December 7, 2019). Without an awareness of context, how could direct social perception or direct perception empathy accurately tell the difference between a blink and a wink, to take Clifford Geertz's famous example (1973b)? They could not. In the world of nonhuman animal expressive culture, misperception and deception also occur. A familiar example: A cat turns sideways, extends its tail, and puffs out its fur to make its enemy perceive it as larger than it really is and cause that enemy to retreat. Here, the enemy may indeed misperceive the cat. Yet, as Berger and Szego go on to point out, the fact that perceptual understandings of meaning may at times be mistaken does not invalidate the phenomenological proposal. Direct social perception and direct perception empathy do not guarantee accuracy. For the proposal to be true, direct social perception and direct perception empathy need not produce a perfect understanding of the other, which would amount to another kind of mind reading. The proposal only requires that the intent, mood, disposition, or affect of the other be grasped through perception, rather than through reflective thought.

Direct Perception Empathy and Expressive Culture in Birdsong

How might direct perception empathy function among nonhuman animals? The songbird that hears another's territorial song, for example, perceives it immediately as a warning to keep out, while simultaneously mimicking the song and assuming an aggressive posture. The two songbirds then duel with one another in song as they attempt to attract a mate. Animal behaviorists typically assume that the female bird always will choose the male with the loudest, longest-sustained song, as this indicates the fittest bird with the most energy and the best genes. But close observers report that the situation is more complicated. For example, the female sometimes accepts the weaker singer. Behavioral ecologists might postulate that in such a situation, the signal was deceptive, with the weaker singer successfully bluffing a strength he does not have, as a human might in a poker game. However, evolutionary biologist Joan Roughgarden (2012) hypothesizes that the female may be looking, as it were, not for the biggest, baddest bird but for qualities of companionship and nurturing necessary for success in pairing, nesting, and raising their brood.[18]

Birdsong may be understood as avian expressive culture in that, as a medium for meaningful interactive communication, it involves processes, perceptions, and cognitions. But does it also involve emotions, and might it have an aesthetic dimension? For centuries humans in many different societies have been charmed by birdsongs; composers have been inspired by them. Ethnomusicologist Marcello Sorce Keller (2012), who like other ethnomusicologists has long been curious about the sounds of whales, dolphins, and birds, has argued that ethnomusicology ought to embrace the relatively new field of zoömusicology. "Coined in 1983 by French composer François-Bernard Mâche," the composer Hollis Taylor writes, "zoömusicology studies the musical aspects of animal sounds" (Taylor n.d.). Among the qualities that distinguish music, apart from its sonic aspects such as pitch, duration, timbre, and rhythm, are melodic invention and an ability to provide aesthetic and affective experiences to the listener and performer.

Although most songbirds repeat relatively simple vocalizations, some have a repertoire of phrases that they insert in different sequences, giving the impression of variation and, possibly, improvisation (Titon 1978b; Marler 1981, 92; Boughey and Thompson 1976, 5). Of course, birdsong gives humans pleasure, but does it offer anything like an aesthetic experience to the birds themselves?

Behavioral ecologists deny that even the bird who "sings its heart out" is doing so for pleasure. Dawkins and Krebs write that either such a bird is bluffing (emitting a deceptive signal) to impress, and thus obtain, a more desirable mate or it is merely advertising its superior energy and strength for the same mating purpose (1978, 306–309). In either case, birdsong is merely a question of stimulus and response and does not involve meaningful experience. However, recent experiments in neuroscience not only confirm the operation of direct social perception and direct perception empathy in animal sound communication but also speak to this question of emotion and aesthetic pleasure. When a female songbird hears the song of her mate, she perceives and identifies it immediately as the cry of her companion. Upon examining the brains of female birds just after hearing the songs of their mates, neurobiologists Donna Maney and Sarah Earp discovered that they released dopamine, a chemical associated in human brains with pleasure and well-being. "All humans know what it feels like to hear their favorite song or a discordant racket. The results of the present study suggest that to songbirds, hearing conspecific song may result in similarly emotional experiences" (Earp and Maney 2013, 7–8). In an email exchange (February 10, 2013), I asked Maney to clarify what she meant by "emotional experiences" and whether or not she thought that birds experienced emotions. She replied that her experiments offer evidence that songbirds have "percepts of emotional experiences." She added her personal view: "I do believe that birds (and many other vertebrates) feel things we would recognize as emotion (fear, anxiety, longing, pleasure). And that the neural circuits controlling these are the same as in humans." These would, of course, be examples in birds of direct social perception colored by emotion. Beyond that, if birds have percepts of pleasure in hearing songs of their mates, we have a neurological basis for the argument that these songs offer them aesthetic experiences.[19] While the "bluffing" hypothesis fails to disprove direct social perception, direct perception empathy, and percepts of aesthetic experience, Maney and Earp's experiments suggest that birdsongs go beyond the narrowly instrumental universe of stimulus-response and enter the realm of nonreflective perceptual experiences.

Direct Perception Empathy and Mirror Neurons

Mirror neuron theory offers another avenue into direct perception empathy, animal expressive culture, and sound communication. In the early 1990s, Giacomo Rizzolatti and a group of Italian neuroscientists at the University of Parma discovered that when one monkey performed an action, thus activating a particular group of motor neurons in its brain, that same group of neurons would fire in the brain of a second monkey who either visually observed the action or heard that action from another room, the latter a metaphorical case of sonic resonance. The neurons firing in the brain of the onlooker or eavesdropper were named "mirror neurons" (Di Pellegrino et al. 1992). Writing about the history of this research for *Scientific American*, the science journalist Ben Thomas explained: "Over the next few decades, this 'action understanding' theory of mirror neurons blossomed into a wide range of promising speculations, . . . [among them] the distinct possibility that . . . mirror neurons might be involved in feelings of empathy" (2012). Summing up mirror neuron research two decades after their discovery, P. F. Ferrari and Rizzolatti wrote that by "showing that mirror neurons were basically motor neurons [the experiments demonstrated that] . . . the motor system is involved in understanding the actions and intentions of others." They continued, "The discovery of mirror neurons . . . demonstrated the validity of the phenomenological stance, at least in most everyday life conditions. It is important to stress that action understanding through the mirror mechanism is a *direct* activation of motor representation. It does not require a cognitive simulation of others' behavior as suggested by simulation theory of action understanding" (Ferrari and Rizzolatti 2014, 1, italics in the original). In other words, mirror neurons confirm the operation of direct perception empathy at the neurological level.

Birds are a rich source for research into mirror neurons. The songbird's brain, for example, has a high density of mirror neurons, and sound communication among most species of songbirds is learned behavior, with songbirds learning their songs and calls from their parents.[20] Experiments by neurobiologists Jonathan Prather and Richard Mooney have revealed that bird vocalizations depend on mirror neurons; that is, the fledgling learner bird's mirror neurons are activated when it hears the songs and calls of its parents (Prather et al. 2008; Prather and Mooney 2015), and they theorize that these mirror neurons enable the fledgling to imitate its parents' vocalizations. Prather and Mooney's research further confirms direct perception empathy in animal sound communication. Because these firings occur when animals make and hear sounds, their work also confirms the sound connection among beings, which, I believe, is the ontological foundation of a sound ecology (Titon 2020). Finally, if direct perception empathy and mirror neurons do not require cognitive simulation, then they do not require the kinds of self-consciousness that humans possess.

Phenomenology may also contribute to our understanding of animal sound communication by means of embodiment as a basis for animal subjectivity and expressive culture: that is, the body as the seat of being, perceiving, and knowing. Awareness begins in perceptual experience. And perceptual experience, arising from an animal's interactions with the environment, or perceptual field—what Jakob von Uexküll called its Umwelt—differs for each being according to its circumstances (von Uexküll [1934] 2010). In this insight, von Uexküll anticipated by forty years James J. Gibson's idea of affordances, which became the basis of ecological psychology. Von Uexküll believed, furthermore, that every being is a subject that lives in the center of its own world and interacts with it, in a sense cocreating it as it modifies it. He wrote that animals co-constitute meaning in their interactions with others. Embodiment, in other words, is always generating meaning, an idea that has direct parallels with the phenomenology of embodied consciousness developed by Maurice

Merleau-Ponty ([1945] 1962), who prioritized perception over cognition in his account of the subject. Following von Uexküll and Merleau-Ponty, then, animals are subjects by virtue of embodied perception, which generates meaning. (This body includes the brain and its cognitive processes.) Thus, if animals are subjects, and they have experiences, then they must have subjective experiences—which is another way of asserting that they have conscious experiences or consciousness, but in their own ways of being.

INTERSPECIES SOUND COMMUNICATION: HUMANS AND NONHUMANS

Phenomenology, Animal Rights, and Expressive Culture

Communication between humans and nonhumans offers a test case for exploring relations across species lines and for thinking about the nature of nature. As the anthropologist Philippe Descola has observed, "The relationship between humans and nature will, in all probability, be the most important question of the present century" (2013, 81). Interspecies communication is, of course, familiar to anyone who has had experience interacting with domesticated animals such as cats, dogs, horses, or farm animals. Across species, differences in culture, mental capacity, and abilities can be significant, and although such differences may cause interspecies miscommunication, continuities in the evolutionary spectrum ensure certain similarities in beings' body-to-world relations, body-to-body relations, and metabolism, which, taken together, offer some common ground for direct social perception.[21]

   Phenomenology has proven useful in comprehending the subjectivity of nonhuman beings. Consider animal suffering, for example. Pain is the physical perception of injury; suffering is the emotional response to it. Interspecific direct perception empathy encourages humans to interpret sonic signals of animal pain, such as cries and whimpers, as evidence that they are beings who have experiences of suffering. Based on the idea that because animals suffer, humans should not inflict pain upon them, laws against animal cruelty have existed for centuries. On this foundation, the moral philosopher Peter Singer has erected a modern animal rights argument derived from the nineteenth-century utilitarian Jeremy Bentham (Singer [1975] 2009). Singer's work reinvigorated the animal rights movement and, while he was not operating in the phenomenological tradition, his ideas encouraged some followers to attempt phenomenological approaches to animal experience and interspecies communication. According to philosopher Corinne Painter, their work derives from Husserl's claims in *Ideas II* about animals: that they share the "personalistic attitude" and possess consciousness, feelings, sensations, representations, psychic acts, and psychic states, such as love and anger. For Husserl, though, animals lack personhood, which is based in the "naturalistic attitude" and enables reflective self-consciousness (Painter 2007, 97–103).

Empathy, discussed earlier in connection with direct perception, offers possibilities for interspecies understanding. The account of empathy developed by Husserl's student Edith Stein ([1917] 1989) led Painter to assert that "empathy makes human access to the psychic life of the animal other possible, and that as such, it characterizes one of the most fundamental intersubjective relations[,] not only between humans but also between human and nonhuman animals" (2007, 95). Observing a bird losing its mate to a predator and then vocalizing incessantly, one risks anthropomorphizing in concluding that that vocalizing is the bird's cry of anguish, or even more so its "lament." Yet, interspecific empathy moves humans to oppose animal cruelty. The capture and subsequent torture of a pod of orca whales in 1970 in the Pacific Northwest, for example, resulted in a storm of outrage. "The sound of orca mothers screaming for their babies was so haunting," Lucy Atkins notes, "that some of the capturers broke down in tears," and finally in 1976 orca capture in North America became illegal (2018, 28). Summarizing environmental historian Jason Colby's descriptions in *Orca* (2018), Atkins writes that the whales "live in tight-knit matriarchal communities with social structures, traditions, habits, rituals and dialects" (2018, 29). A phenomenological approach to embodiment and animal subjectivity generates a defense of animal rights based on the understanding that animals have emotions, experiences, and social lives of their own. Zipporah Weisberg, writing from a phenomenological standpoint, moves beyond animal rights to argue that "focusing on the shared embodiment of human and nonhuman animals" enables phenomenology to "challenge human-animal dualism[,] not only by asserting animals' ethically relevant ontological similarity to humans, but also humans' long-repressed or repressively desublimated animality" (2015, 80). She views this as a step toward "an ethos of re-enchantment and a practice of epistemic humility towards other animals" (81) and identifies it with Martin Buber's concept of "the simple magic of life" (Buber [1923] 1996, 29, quoted in Weisberg 2015, 69)—that is, that being is common to every living creature.

It is not only empathic, phenomenological approaches that have led to the awareness of what we have in common with nonhuman animals. Some of the most widely known scientists and philosophers outside of the phenomenological tradition have also taken up the subject. Field biologists such as Katy Payne and Jane Goodall, and amateur natural historians such as Elizabeth Marshall Thomas, have written perceptively, from an empathic viewpoint, about the social behavior of elephants, chimpanzees, and dogs (Payne 1998; Goodall 1986; E. M. Thomas 1993). Payne, who pioneered the study of whale and elephant vocalizations, believes that whale song may have aesthetic qualities, while she told an interviewer that the elephants she worked with appeared to her to be highly emotional: they exhibited "fits of delight and fits of frustration." Anticipating the objection that she was anthropomorphizing their behavior, Payne replied, "I have to interpret it as a human [would because I am a human being]" (2007). Indeed, sometimes it is difficult to distinguish between an unavoidable human standpoint and an avoidable anthropocentric bias. Even when people understand nonhuman animals as subjects, their conceptualizations of animal subjectivity vary. For example, people sometimes talk to domestic animals in the pitch register that they use when speaking to little children, which suggests that they think of those animals as persons at an earlier state of development. Donna Haraway insists that dogs and cats should not be called pets but rather should be referred to as "companion species" (2003). Jacques Derrida famously writes that he is reminded of "the animal that I am" whenever, naked in his bathroom or bedroom, his pet cat (in an equally natural state) gazes at him (2002, 371). Philosopher Martha Nussbaum extends her "capabilities approach" to animal rights and welfare by arguing that animal well-being can be understood in terms of features like bodily integrity, health, and (echoing von Uexküll) the animal's ability to express itself within its environment (2011). The ecojustice movement advocates for environmental justice for vulnerable populations of animal and plant species, as well as humans, and it relies on Western Judeo-Christian intellectual traditions, as well as Indigenous ecological knowledges (Hessel n.d.; Titon 2019). The claim that nonhuman animals are enough like humans that they must be granted certain natural rights as well as justice rests in part on the observation that animals exhibit expressive culture, even though these philosophers and scientists do not use that term when they write about animal life.

Indigenous Ecological Knowledges and Perspectivism

Indigenous ecological knowledges theorize interspecific sound communication in an experiential epistemology wherein communication between humans and nonhumans takes on spiritual as well as practical dimensions. For much of the twentieth century, anthropologists and ethnomusicologists interpreted a belief in human communication with nonhuman beings as evidence of an animistic worldview or some other unrealistic substitute for science. In the past half-century or so, however, a broadly phenomenological approach to these matters has either bracketed their truth or falsehood while taking a pragmatic approach to their validity within their cultural contexts or held a more positive view of them as legitimately true systems of knowledge. Among those ethnomusicologists who acknowledge the influence of phenomenology on their studies of Indigenous worldviews is Steven Feld, who has described his project with the Kaluli of Papua New Guinea as a "social phenomenology and hermeneutics of senses of place" (1996, 91). In a recent essay on acoustemology (i.e., acoustic epistemology, a term he coined in the 1990s), Feld explains that, to the Kaluli he lived with in Papua New Guinea, birds are the embodiment of human souls who have died. They are thus referred to as "*ane mama*, meaning 'gone reflections' or 'gone reverberations'" of human lives. In this sense, "Birds are absences turned into presence, and a presence that always makes absence audible and visible" (Feld 2015, 16). The work of Brabec de Mori and Seeger explores related themes in the ethnomusicology of South American Indigenous groups. They point out that the Indigenous peoples of South America listen not only to sounds that would be audible to most other humans but also to ones that would not be considered audible: the inaudible sounds of so-called spirit-beings, which are present in entities such as plants, animals, landforms, and geophysical forces, like wind and water (2013, 271). Writing about the Kĩsêdjê (formerly called the Suyá) of the Amazon, Seeger affirms that "the cacophony I perceived in their sound-world was to them an interspecies communication with important implications and critical results" (Seeger [1987] 2004, 91). According to the Kĩsêdjê, animals "talk with one another, have families, and go hunting and gathering. And they perform ceremonies and sing" ([1987] 2004, 92).

Seeger understands the Kĩsêdjê ontology as an example of perspectivism, the anthropological term for an ontology shared widely among Indigenous societies of lowland South America that have played an important role in the contemporary study of Indigenous ecological knowledges of intraspècific communication (Seeger 2015, 92–93). Anthropologist Eduardo Viveiros de Castro, who was one of the first scholars to theorize this ontology, explains that, from a perspectivist standpoint, "the world is inhabited by different sorts of subjects or persons, human and nonhuman, which apprehend reality from distinct points of view" (1998, 469). That is, in their own worlds, animals view themselves and act in the same ways that humans see themselves and act in their worlds. Viveiros de Castro has written that he developed his theory of perspectivism "by means of a plausible phenomenological interpretation of Amerindian cosmological categories" (1998, 470). Indeed, according to many Amerindian myths, after the creation of the world, there existed a great number of subjective beings, all of whom possessed a unity of spirit and communicated with one another easily. After a catastrophic event, these beings retained their spiritual unity while taking on different bodies or natures. This transformation prevented intraspecific communication and produced the world that we find ourselves in today. On this view, entering the spirit world (as, for example, shamans do) enables present-day humans to communicate with nonhuman animals. Viveiros de Castro does not intend perspectivism to collapse the boundary between nature and culture, or between animals and humans, but rather to reconfigure it. He writes that where Western science is "founded on the mutual implication of the unity of nature and the plurality of cultures—the first guaranteed by the objective universality of body and substance, the second generated by the subjective particularity of spirit and meaning— the Amerindian conception would suppose a spiritual unity and a corporeal diversity." Viveiros de Castro calls this "multinaturalism" (1998, 470).

Developing a notion of "acoustic multinaturalism," the ethnomusicologist Ana María Ochoa Gautier claims that the relational ontologies of Amerindian perspectivism offer a possible alternative to capitalism and the Western scientific cosmology—an alternative that demands attention during the crisis of the Anthropocene. She criticizes ecomusicology for relying upon the Western scientific conception of nature and suggests that the acoustemology of the Kaluli, the Kĩsêdjê, and other Indigenous groups offers an opening toward a "radical transformation of the conditions for posing questions regarding what historically in the West have been considered the differential fields of nature and culture" (2016, 108). I offered an earlier, similar critique of ecomusicologists' conceptions of nature (Titon 2013). My argument was based not only on Indigenous relational ontologies and epistemologies but also on contemporary Western thought. There, I argued that ecomusicologists had uncritically accepted the ideas associated with scientific realism and the ecological "balance of nature" paradigm. Ecomusicologists did so, I noted, despite the critiques from feminist and postmodernist scholars of scientific objectivity and the nature/culture binary, and despite the fact that ecological science has largely abandoned the balance-of-nature paradigm in favor of a nonteleological view of a nature enmeshed in the flux of disturbance and change. In the essay, I suggested that ecomusicologists must learn to work with relational ontologies and epistemologies found in both traditional ecological knowledges and Western ecological science, as defined originally by Ernst Haeckel in 1866 as the study of organisms and their relations to one another and the environment (1866, 2:286).

Folklorist John McDowell and anthropologist Matthias Lewy have critiqued perspectivism in ways that are relevant to this discussion of phenomenology and interspecies sonic communication. In his ethnographic research with the Inga and Kamëntsá peoples in the Sibundoy Valley of Colombia, McDowell found that "Sibundoy cosmology offers ample evidence of core perspectivist and relativist postulates wherein humans and nonhuman animals are conjoined in a single experiential frame." However, Sibundoy narratives, "much like the worldviews of Western peoples, have the capacity to establish social hierarchies with species-centric and even ethnocentric attributes" (2018, 1–2). As a result, McDowell cautions those who, like Ochoa Gautier, would see in perspectivism an antidote to the species centrism (i.e., anthropocentrism) of Western thought concerning nature. Another critique can be found in Lewy's ethnographic field studies with the Pémon, an Indigenous group in Brazil's Amazon region. If perspectivism refers to the idea that each species apprehends reality from a unique viewpoint, then, according to Lewy, the Pémon believe that ritual singing can overcome such difference. Pémon ritual singing results in a cross-species interaction among the beings occupying the same world, but one in which the beings do not distinguish differences in species perspectives (2017, 9). In other words, "sound in its formalized mode of song defines the interaction between humans and nonhumans by transcending the mythical and non-mythical worlds" (2017, 1–2). Despite critiques and refinements like those from McDowell and Lewy, perspectivism offers experience-centered ways to understand the relationship between human and nonhuman worlds, offering phenomenological ethnomusicologists insights into the expressive culture of both intraspecific and interspecific sound communication, ones that, from its external and objective standpoint, Western behavioral ecology does not.

A Sound Ecology

A project that I have been calling a "sound ecology" takes intraspecies, as well as inter- and multispecies, sound communication as its starting point, broadening the discussion to the ecosphere to take into account geophonic as well as biophonic and anthropophonic sounds. Briefly, a sound ecology (Titon 2015, 2020) reorients contemporary Western ideas of human being and knowing from the subjective contemplation of external texts (as humanists are wont to do) or observation of external objects (as scientists chiefly do) to an intersubjective ontology and epistemology anchored in sound connections. Sound, of course, consists of vibrations transmitted between entities by means of longitudinal waves through a medium. Two or more entities, or beings, if thus connected in sound will vibrate together. This is a visceral, physical connection, although in some social groups, sounds also may be understood to open and maintain ritual connections with spiritual beings, whether incarnate or not.[22] Sound announces presences, while sonic connections establish co-presence that forms the basis for an epistemology of intersubjective relationships, with the important ethical corollary that the beings thus related are interdependent and thus responsible for one another's welfare. This recognition of interdependence and mutual responsibility leads away from economies and communities based in subject-object relations, such as those that are chiefly legal and contractual, and toward subject-subject relations that are personal and present. A sound ecology is an expression of this ethic, which has much in common with landscape ecologist Aldo Leopold's idea of Earth as a community: "We abuse land because we regard it as a commodity belonging to us. When we see land as a community to which we belong, we may begin to use it with love and respect. . . . That land is a community is a basic concept of ecology, but that land is to be loved and respected is an extension of ethics" (Leopold 1949, viii–ix).

If we grant that animals are subjects, not objects, we put phenomenology on an experiential path toward understanding animal sound communication as animal expressive culture. Such a view has two important implications. First, granting that animals are subjects enriches the possibilities for understanding how animal communication is situated on an evolutionary spectrum, from bean and corn plants whose root growth vibrates the soil, to the forest trees that emit sounds and communicate with one another through carbon exchanges, though stridulating insects, singing birds, dolphins, whales, and humans (Simard et al. 1997; Gagliano et al. 2017; Zweifel and Zeugin 2008; Rogers and Kaplan 2002). This perspective is in stark contrast with the poverty of the reductionist, neo-Darwinian model of animals as uncomprehending beings, emitting and responding to signals that manipulate behavior. Second, this view strongly reaffirms the ecological principle that beings are connected intersubjectively by means of sound. The sound connection is a vibrational link between and among the bodies of subjects. Sound experience thus becomes the basis for an ecological epistemology of connection and kinship, a community in which all beings are related, an economy in which exchanges are governed by intersubjective relations, and an ecology in which all beings are interdependent, related to one another, and responsible for one another and their environment.

In early October 2014, before the leaves had fallen off the deciduous trees and while the ground was wet from the September rains, a horrific early season wind, rain, and snowstorm at the edge of the ocean in East Penobscot Bay, Maine, broke off tree limbs, snapped living tree trunks in two, and uprooted white spruce, poplar, and apple trees. I took in the geophonic and biophonic sounds of this raging storm and the toppling trees from a safe spot on the porch of my house. Listening, I heard the breaking and crashing all around me. I worried that trees would smash into buildings. The lights went out; the familiar sounds of the refrigerator and well pump came to an abrupt halt. As the storm surged and the trees crashed to the ground, I grew convinced that I was experiencing the sounds of climate change. But soon I wondered if I was deceiving myself, captive to a poetic fancy, the pathetic fallacy. I considered the structures of my consciousness as I experienced those sounds. The first sound I heard was of a spruce trunk a hundred yards distant, at the edge of a field, snapping in two, falling over, and breaking further when tumbling to the ground. I heard the loud, high-pitched crack and knew what it signaled, even before my head turned—involuntarily, it seemed—in the direction of the sound. Then I saw the tree hit the ground as I heard the limbs scraping and cracking and breaking. Looking through the falling snow into the branches on the ground after they had settled, I perceived what might have been a bird's nest. After the storm, I looked more closely and found the remains of the nest of a hermit thrush. This tree itself was about fifty feet long and eighteen inches in diameter. I counted forty rings in the trunk when I bucked it up and dragged it off into the woods the following spring. A few weeks after the storm I wrote about my experience, convinced that I had been the recipient of an honest signal, akin to an interspecific communication. I had been eavesdropping on nature's alarm call, a warning in the storm of the approaching climate emergency (Titon 2016).

WHY SHOULD ETHNOMUSICOLOGISTS BE INTERESTED?

Why should a phenomenological and ecological approach to the expressive culture of sound communication in humans and other beings be of interest to ethnomusicologists today? In fact, an interest in the sonic productions of animals is not new for ethnomusicologists and those in related music disciplines. Comparative musicologist George Herzog took an empirical approach. He titled a 1941 essay for the *Bulletin of the American Musicological Society* "Do Animals Have Music?" and concluded that "From the purely formal point of view, there thus seems to be no reliable criterion that would establish a fundamental difference between animal and human expression in sound." Regarding sonic functioning, he wrote that "Sound patterning can have a great variety of functions and we do not as yet have an adequate understanding of these, whether for humans or animals. Until the problem of function becomes clarified, there seems to be no criterion for any theoretical separation of the vocal expression of animals from human music" (1941, 4). Carl Stumpf, one of the nineteenth-century founders of comparative musicology, studied animal as well as human *Tonpsychologie* (tone-psychology) and "the relation of music to language, and that of human speech to the utterances of animals" ([1924] 1930). The field of zoösemiotics (later biosemiotics), on the other hand, studies animal communication on universally applicable terms: yet semiosis, or the way something becomes a sign to an organism, is of course a humanly constructed subject, as is every product of human research.[23] We do not imagine that chimpanzees are constructing theories comparing their utterances with human speech. However, that doesn't mean that our models for understanding their experiences are worthless. As I affirmed earlier, there is a difference between an unavoidable human standpoint and an avoidable anthropocentric bias.

In the opening chapter of this volume, Berger, VanderHamm, and Riedel reveal the sometimes-hidden history of phenomenological ethnomusicology and its impact upon the experiential and humanistic turn in ethnomusicology, which began in the 1970s and which flourishes today, this volume being but one example. Phenomenological ethnomusicology has focused on the lived experiences of people making music. Most ethnomusicological writing about nonhuman beings is, understandably, anthropocentric insofar as it has concentrated on how those beings inflect human musical and ritual experience, rather than on the experiences of those other beings in their own social communities. A few, however, most notably Steven Feld, have explored the sonic cultures and experiences of those other beings (e.g., Feld [1982] 2012; Roseman 1993; Friedson 1996). This requires a double reframing: from music to the more inclusive category, sound, and from an anthropocentric perspective to an ecocentric one. Feld's 2015 formulation of acoustemology is one recent manifestation of an ecomusicological turn to "eco-ethnomusicology," a hybrid term that Margaret Guyette and Jennifer Post have used to emphasize the importance of place and environment in ecomusicology, as well as the ways in which humans interpret the sonic signals that occur there (Guyette and Post 2016, 42).[24]

The definition of ethnomusicology as the study of people making music will continue to serve those ethnomusicologists focused on both humans making the sounds they call music and music making as a cultural domain, insofar as "ethno" points both to "people" (without the undertones of race and nationality) and to "ethnographic" fieldwork, its typical methodology. Putting "eco" first emphasizes the ecocentric, ecological, eco-philosophical, eco-cultural, and eco-experiential aspects of this hybrid, eco-ethnomusicology, a field that seeks to have as its central aim not only people making music but also all beings making sound. Taking this approach, we come to realize that because humans are animals, the binary human/animal no longer obtains, and so we ask what Earth echosphere follows from that—what all living beings on a planet that is itself alive may share sonically with one another and what that commonality means for our collective futures.[25]

In this chapter I have suggested how one might extend phenomenological ethnomusicology from the study of people making music to the more inclusive eco-ethnomusicological study of beings communicating in sound. It would not be wise to leave the study of animal sonic worlds to biologists, ecologists, philosophers, and cultural anthropologists only. Rather, I suggest that we ethnomusicologists must engage in this research as well, pursuing our own methodologies and conclusions when advisable and collaborating with scholars from other disciplines when possible. As I have shown, the phenomenological notions of direct social perception and direct perception empathy, coupled with conceptions of embodiment and Umwelt, affordances, and ecological understandings, are congruent with important strains of neuroscientific research on birds, chimpanzees, and, it would appear, humans. Such approaches diverge from the behaviorist model of evolutionary biology in ways that are consistent with recent biological discoveries concerning the genome, the codependence of the genome with culture, and the coevolution of genes and culture (see, e.g., Richerson 2004, 2012; CARTA 2012; Comfort 2015). All of this offers important new avenues for research. I do not, of course, mean that ethnomusicology should abandon the study of people making music—far from it. Rather, I suggest that we should enlarge our understanding of our subject matter to include eco-ethnomusicology, expand our methods, and bring them to bear, in a way more appropriate to the times we live in, on the study of beings making sound. Using fieldwork observation, documentation, and interpretation, we can explore how all beings are implicated in a relational, multispecies sonic ecology that connects us with one another and with the environment as a whole, which includes the living Earth, the forces of nature, and the abiotic environment, as well as the built aspects of the environment, whether cathedrals and concert halls, HVAC systems and fire sirens, or birds' nests and beaver dams.

Acknowledgments

This chapter grew from my presentation of section one, "Phenomenology in Ethnographic Fieldwork," on the President's Roundtable at the 2013 meeting of the Society for Ethnomusicology. The subject of the Roundtable was "Phenomenological Approaches to the Study of Expressive Culture," as organized by Harris Berger, then president of the Society. Portions of sections two, three, and four were presented in papers delivered at the Phenomenology in Ethnomusicology conference in St. John's, Newfoundland, from June 4 to 7, 2018, and at the American Folklore Society conference in Buffalo, New York, on October 19, 2018. I am most grateful to Harris Berger, Kati Szego, Friedlind Riedel, and Bernd Brabec de Mori for their careful readings and helpful suggestions. Shortcomings are, of course, my own.

Notes

1. "The study of people making music" was how I defined ethnomusicology over thirty years ago (Titon 1992, xxi; [1989] 2015). By "making" I meant producing the sounds that people think of as music and also constructing the cultural domain of "music" or an equivalent. Different social groups throughout the world, of course, make different sounds and construct different domains. Because this definition is anthropocentric, and because my research since 2011 has focused more on beings making sound than on people making music, I've recently been asked whether I stand by that definition today. I answer that question in the last section of this chapter.
2. I write "human (animal)" to emphasize that humans are species of animals. In other words, I am seeking to expand the scope of inquiry not only from music to sound but also from humans to animals in general and beyond to all living beings.
3. This concept is elaborated in *Eight Words for the Study of Expressive Culture* (Feintuch 2003), where the contributors emphasize that expressive culture consists of creative expression within a cultural context. Some folklorists emphasize the play of tradition with innovation in the continuity of creative forms. Cultural anthropologists and performance studies scholars accentuate the aesthetic dimensions of embodiment in expressive culture. In the second and subsequent editions of *Worlds of Music*, I offered a music performance framework for understanding expressive culture that came to be known as the "four circles" model (Titon and Slobin 1992, 2–6).

4. Various writers have argued that animals have culture, understood in the traditional sense as learned behavior that is neither automatic nor innate. They have done so either because some animals have been observed to make and use simple tools or because certain animal behaviors, such as birdsong in certain species, have been shown experimentally to be learned and transmitted from one generation to the next (on birdsong as learned behavior, see, e.g., Marler 1981; Mooney 2009). As in the case of consciousness research, work in this area often assumes that culture is an either/or proposition: either a species has it or not. However, culture is better understood as existing on an evolutionary continuum, in which species possess its generative elements to varying degrees. Humans, with self-reflexive consciousness and other mental capabilities, are capable of using these elements to generate complex cultural systems.

5. "Ecocentric" means nature centered, in opposition to anthropocentric or human centered. Ecocentric values arise from a variety of sources, including Henry David Thoreau's conception of man as an inhabitant of nature ([1862] 2001); Aldo Leopold's notion of the "land ethic," which understands humans as citizens of nature and the environment (1949); and the "deep ecology" strain within environmentalist philosophy that, in placing an inherent value on all living beings and the environment, does not privilege the needs of humans or the human uses to which nature may be put (Naess and Rothenberg 1989). A recent manifesto on this topic proclaims that "Ecocentrism . . . is a worldview that recognizes intrinsic value in ecosystems and the biological and physical elements that they comprise, as well as in the ecological processes that spatially and temporally connect them. So when human wants clash with the health of the Earth as a whole or any of its ecosystems, the former should, practically and ethically speaking, give way to the latter: human needs, like the needs of other species, are secondary to those of the Earth as the sum of its ecosystems" (Gray et al. 2018, 130).

6. Discussing these ideas, the folklorist Sabina Magliocco writes, "Today some biologists and animal ethologists—among them the noted evolutionary biologist Mark Bekoff and primatologist and ethologist Frans de Waal—increasingly write about animal languages, cultures, emotions, and even morality" (2018, 3). To that group should be added Donald R. Griffin, an ethologist who in the last century argued persistently for the existence of animal minds, mental experience, and consciousness (e.g., Griffin 1976, 1984, 1992).

7. It is worth noting that ethnosemantics is not phenomenology. Sometimes called ethnoscience, it is the study of how the words spoken by members of a social or occupational group categorize, classify, and make sense of the world and their experiences in it. Ethnosemanticists key on specialized vernacular terms within such a social group. One of Spradley's frequent examples was to "make the bucket," as in this sentence from the vernacular among the tramps he studied: "I got pinched and made the bucket" (i.e., I was arrested and taken to the city jail).

8. When I began to read cultural anthropologists' descriptions of their studies of non-Western societies in the late 1960s, I noticed that the authors employed the literary conventions of plot, character, and setting that autobiographers and novelists used when writing in the first person and that first-person, anthropological accounts had much in common with the archetypal myth of the heroic quest for knowledge (and power). Although I was unaware of it at the time, my observations were similar to those of Susan Sontag in her 1963 review of Claude Lévi-Strauss's *Structural Anthropology*. My hypothesis for "Inventing Anthropology," a seminar I offered at Tufts in the mid-1970s, was that autobiographies, popular anthropological ethnographies, and novels were all literary

fictions, invented in the sense of being made, rather than discovered or found (Titon 1980). Geertz, I later learned, had come independently to the same conclusion (1973b, 15; see also Clifford and Marcus [1986] 2010).

9. I recorded the longer interviews with these preachers, singers, and congregation members from 1973 on. Most of these recordings are available to researchers at the American Folklife Center at the Library of Congress, and many are transcribed there. I am grateful to the center for lending me a Nagra tape recorder to make some of those recordings. Excerpts from some of these interviews may be seen in Dornfeld et al. (1989).

10. Dennett's idea of the "intentional stance" may also have been influenced by our discussions about ethnographic oral histories as fiction, which I wrote about in "The Life Story" (Titon 1980).

11. For an overview, see the entry "Animal Consciousness" in the *Stanford Encyclopedia of Philosophy* (Allen and Trestman 2016).

12. The *Cambridge Declaration* was written by three eminent neuroscientists. Its lead author was Philip Low of the Stanford University Medical School and inventor of the iBrain, a device that monitors brain activity at an unprecedented level of detail.

13. One wonders how the proverbial "scientist from Mars" might explain human behavior. Might this alien being, who could not know from experience what it is like to be human, conclude that human beings have brains but not minds? Might the scientist from Mars think that humans were zombies?

14. Stegmann 2013 contains eighteen essays on both sides of the debate, along with a convenient summary of the issues.

15. Tim Ingold (2000, 174–177, 243–249) is usually credited with introducing von Uexküll to the current generation of scholars in phenomenological anthropology and the anthropology of sound. Throughout his writing, von Uexküll metaphorically employed musical terms, especially harmony, to describe animal life (Gustafsson 2017, 7). Ingold's phenomenological anthropology has been deservedly influential in the twenty-first century. My path to von Uexküll, however, began earlier: first upon reading Henry David Thoreau's queries about why insects and animals behaved as they did, and then upon reading Maurice Merleau-Ponty, whose ideas about animals and embodiment in his *Nature* lectures (1956–60) were profoundly influenced by von Uexküll's writings (Merleau-Ponty 2003; see also Gustafsson 2017). Ingold was more attentive to sonic worlds than Merleau-Ponty but not as deeply enmeshed in them as Thoreau. My path to phenomenology and sound began with Don Ihde's *Listening and Voice* (1976) and F. J. Smith's *Experiencing of Musical Sound: A Prelude to a Phenomenology of Music* (1979).

16. In other words, a person does something; we ask ourselves why they did it; and by means of common sense and folk psychology, we "read their minds" (i.e., think about and interpret their behavior) to figure out the meaning of their actions.

17. Conspecifics would not represent alien beings to one another, and thus it is fair to assume that direct social perception operates in animal-to-animal communication as well. Cross-species animal sound communication also occurs when an animal of one species "eavesdrops" on communications of another, such as when an alarm call warns several species at once of a threat from a nearby predator.

18. Roughgarden (2012) has been a staunch proponent of what she calls "social selection" (sexual selection in animals on the basis of sociability, rather than physical strength), an idea that she developed as part of her opposition to the neo-Darwinian fitness theory, which was popularized by Dawkins as "selfish gene theory" ([1976] 2016). Other dissenting

scientists have revived the older theory of group selection (natural selection at the level of the social group rather than at the level of the individual) (see, e.g., Wilson 1975; Wilson and Wilson 2007).

19. In *The Survival of the Beautiful*, David Rothenberg contends that nonhuman animals have evolved to create art that is "far beyond what basic biological needs would seem to require" (2011, 3).

20. Ornithologists decades ago established that a bird of one species raised by foster parents of another species sings its foster parents' song, not its own species' song. For a summary of the ways birdsong offers neuroscientists an outstanding model for studying imitative learning processes in animals, see Williams (2004).

21. I am grateful to Harris Berger for showing how continuities in the evolutionary spectrum are expressed in these phenomenological categories.

22. In a December 7, 2019, email exchange, Bernd Brabec de Mori correctly pointed out to me that I have been developing this sound ecology project in terms of a naturalistic ontology, which is predominantly based upon materialist ideas, and that, in this view, social interaction among nonhuman animals relies primarily upon direct perception. A sound ecology erected primarily from the standpoint of Amerindian perspectivism or other Indigenous ecological knowledges would differ from this approach significantly.

23. Thomas Sebeok coined the term "zoösemiotics" to refer to the study of the semiotic aspects of animal communication (1972). After acquainting himself with von Uexküll's work in the 1970s, he sought the more fundamental biological principles underlying semiosis in all living beings. The term "biosemiotics" seems to have been in use in the early 1970s (see Stepanov 1971). Although Sebeok was reluctant at first to adapt the term, he too began using it in the latter half of the 1980s (Kull 2003, 12). Sebeok's earliest publication employing this term appeared in 1992. A summary of the development and influence of Sebeok's ideas may be found in Kull (2003).

24. I believe that Feld's research is deeply ecomusicological and that he began undertaking it several decades before ecomusicology became a named field.

25. By *echosphere* I mean the sonic environment of Earth. The pun on ecosphere is deliberate.

Works Cited

Alcock, John. 2013. *Animal Behavior: An Evolutionary Approach*. New York: Sinauer Associates.
Allen, Colin, and Michael Trestman. 2016. "Animal Consciousness." In *The Stanford Encyclopedia of Philosophy*, edited by Edward N. Zalta. Stanford University. https://plato.stanford.edu/archives/win2017/entries/consciousness-animal/.
Armstrong, Robert Plant. 1986. *The Affecting Presence: An Essay in Humanistic Anthropology*. Urbana: University of Illinois Press.
Atkins, Lucy. 2018. "Demons from Hell" (Review of *Orca* by James M. Colby). *Times Literary Supplement*, December 14, 2018, 6037.
Boë, Louis-Jean, Frédéric Berthommier, Thierry Legou, Guillaume Captier, Caralyn Kemp, Thomas R. Sawallis, Yannick Becker, Arnaud Rey, and Joël Fagot. 2017. "Evidence of a Vocalic Proto-System in the Baboon (*Papio papio*) Suggests Pre-hominin Speech Precursors." *PLoS ONE* 12 (1): e0169321. https://doi.org/10.1371/journal.pone.0169321.
Boughey, M. J., and N. S. Thompson. 1976. "Species Specificity and Individual Variation in the Songs of the Brown Thrasher and Catbird." *Behaviour* 57 (1–2): 64–90.

Brabec de Mori, Bernd, and Anthony Seeger. 2013. "Introduction: Considering Music, Humans, and Non-humans." *Ethnomusicology Forum* 22 (3): 269–286.

Bradbury, Jack W., and Sandra L. Vehrencamp. 2011. *Principles of Animal Communication.* 2nd ed. Sunderland, MA: Sinauer.

Buber, Martin. [1923] 1996. *I and Thou.* Translated by Walter Kaufmann. New York: Simon and Schuster.

Caldwell, Patricia. 1985. *The Puritan Conversion Narrative: The Beginnings of American Expression.* Cambridge: Cambridge University Press.

CARTA. 2012. "Culture-Gene Interactions in Human Origins." Center for Academic Research and Training in Anthropogeny, Salk Institute for Biological Studies, University of California, San Diego, April 13, 2012. Accessed May 31, 2020. https://carta.anthropogeny.org/events/culture-gene-interactions-human-origins. Media for each presentation is available on this website.

Clifford, James, and George E. Marcus, eds. (1986) 2010. *Writing Culture: The Poetics and Politics of Ethnography.* Berkeley: University of California Press.

Colby, Jason. 2018. *Orca.* Oxford: Oxford University Press.

Comfort, Nathaniel. 2015. "Dawkins, Redux." *Nature* 525: 184–185.

Dartnell, Lewis. 2001. "Is Humpback Whale Song a Language?" Unpublished manuscript. Accessed May 31, 2020. http://lewis.dsruptiv.net/en-gb/wp-content/uploads/2013/11/Is-Humpback-Whale-Song-a-Language.pdf.

Dawkins, Richard. (1976) 2016. *The Selfish Gene.* 40th Anniversary ed. Oxford: Oxford University Press.

Dawkins, Richard, and John R. Krebs. 1978. "Animal Signals: Information or Manipulation?" In *Behavioural Ecology: An Evolutionary Approach,* edited by John R. Krebs and N. B. Davies, 282–309. Oxford: Blackwell Scientific Publications.

Dennett, Daniel C. 1991. *Consciousness Explained.* Boston: Little, Brown.

Dennett, Daniel C. 2003. "Who's on First: Heterophenomenology Explained." *Journal of Consciousness Studies* 10 (9–10): 19–30.

Dennett, Daniel C. 2007. "Heterophenomenology Reconsidered." *Phenomenology and the Cognitive Sciences* 6: 247–270.

Dennett, Daniel C. 2017a. Remarks for a panel discussion. Animal Consciousness Conference, New York University, November 18, 2017. Accessed December 26, 2018. https://livestream.com/nyu-tv/AnimalConsciousness/videos/166146145.

Dennett, Daniel C. 2017b. *From Bacteria to Bach and Back: The Evolution of Minds.* New York: Norton.

Derrida, Jacques. 2002. "The Animal That Therefore I Am (More to Follow)." Translated by David Wills. *Critical Inquiry* 28 (2): 369–418.

Descola, Philippe. 2013. *The Ecology of Others.* Translated by Geneviève Godbout and Benjamin P. Luley. Chicago: Prickly Paradigm Press.

Di Pellegrino, G., L. Fadiga, L. Fogassi, V. Gallese, and G. Rizzolatti. 1992. "Understanding Motor Events: A Neurophysiological Study." *Experimental Brain Research* 91 (1): 176–180.

Dornfeld, Barry, Tom Rankin, and Jeff Todd Titon. 1989. *Powerhouse for God.* 58 min., 16mm, color documentary film. DVD distributed by Documentary Educational Resources, Watertown, MA. May also be streamed at https://www.folkstreams.net/search.php?q=powerhouse+for+God.

Earp, Sarah E., and Donna L. Maney. 2013. "Birdsong: Is It Music to Their Ears?" *Frontiers in Evolutionary Neuroscience* 4: 1–10.

Feintuch, Burt, ed. 2003. *Eight Words for the Study of Expressive Culture*. Urbana: University of Illinois Press.

Feld, Steven. (1982) 2012. *Sound and Sentiment: Birds, Weeping, Poetics and Song in Kaluli Expression*. 3rd ed. Durham, NC: Duke University Press.

Feld, Steven. 1996. "Waterfalls of Song: An Acoustemology of Place Resounding in Bosavi, Papua, New Guinea." In *Senses of Place*, edited by Steven Feld and Keith Basso, 91–135. Santa Fe, NM: School of American Research Press.

Feld, Steven. 2015. "Acoustemology." In *Keywords in Sound*, edited by David Novak and Matt Sakakeeny, 15–22. Durham, NC: Duke University Press.

Ferrari, P. F., and G. Rizzolatti. 2014. "Mirror Neuron Research: The Past and the Future." *Philosophical Transactions in Biological Sciences* 369 (1644): 1–4.

Friedson, Steven M. 1996. *Dancing Prophets: Musical Experience in Tumbuka Healing*. Chicago: University of Chicago Press.

Froese, Tom, and David Leavens. 2009. "The Direct Perception Hypothesis: Perceiving the Intention of Another's Action Hinders Its Imitation." *Frontiers in Psychology* 5 (February 18, 2009): article 65.

Fuchs, Thomas. 2016. "Intercorporeality and Interaffectivity." *Phenomenology and Mind* 11: 194–211.

Fuchs, Thomas. 2019. "Empathy, Group Identity, and Mechanisms of Exclusion: An Investigation into the Limits of Empathy." *Topoi* 38: 239–250.

Gagliano, Monica, Mavra Grimonprez, Martial Depczynski, and Michael Renton. 2017. "Tuned In: Plant Roots Use Sound to Locate Water." *Oecologia* 184: 151–160. doi:10.1007/s00442-017-3862-z.

Gallagher, Shaun. 2008. "Direct Perception in the Intersubjective Context." *Consciousness and Cognition* 17: 535–543.

Gallagher, Shaun, and Dan Zahavi. (2008) 2012. *The Phenomenological Mind*. 2nd ed. New York: Routledge.

Geertz, Clifford. 1973a. *The Interpretation of Cultures: Selected Essays*. New York: Basic Books.

Geertz, Clifford. 1973b. "Thick Description: Toward an Interpretive Theory of Culture." In *The Interpretation of Cultures: Selected Essays*, 3–30. New York: Basic Books.

Goodall, Jane. 1986. *The Chimpanzees of Gombe: Patterns of Behavior*. Cambridge, MA: Belknap Press of Harvard University Press.

Goodall, Jane. 1990. *Through a Window: My Thirty Years with the Chimpanzees of Gombe*. Boston: Houghton Mifflin.

Gray, Joe, Ian Whyte, and Patrick Curry. 2018. "Ecocentrism: What It Means and What It Implies." *The Ecological Citizen* 1 (2): 130–131.

Griffin, Donald R. 1976. *The Question of Animal Awareness: Evolutionary Continuity of Mental Experience*. New York: Rockefeller Foundation.

Griffin, Donald R. 1984. *Animal Thinking*. Cambridge, MA: Harvard University Press.

Griffin, Donald R. 1992. *Animal Minds*. Chicago: University of Chicago Press.

Gustafsson, Ryan S. 2017. "Depth, Nature, Participation." *Australian Feminist Law Journal* 43 (1): 89–105. https://doi.org/10.1080/13200968.2017.1327340.

Guyette, Margaret Q., and Jennifer C. Post. 2016. "Ecomusicology, Ethnomusicology, and Soundscape Ecology: Scientific and Musical Responses to Sound Study." In *Current Directions in Ecomusicology*, edited by Aaron S. Allen and Kevin Dawe, 40–56. New York: Routledge.

Haeckel, Ernst H. P. A. 1866. *Allgemeine Entwickelungsgeschichte der Organismen* [General history of the development of organisms]. Vol. 2 of *Generelle Morphologie der Organismen*.

Allgemeine Grundzüge der organischen Formen-Wissenschaft, mechanisch begründet durch die von Charles Darwin reformirte Descendenz-Theorie [General morphology of organisms: General principles of the science of organic form, mechanically founded on the theory of descent as revised by Charles Darwin]. Berlin: Georg Reimer.

Haraway, Donna. 2003. *The Companion Species Manifesto: Dogs, People, and Significant Otherness*. Chicago: University of Chicago.

Held, Suzanne D. E., and Marek Špinka. 2011. "Animal Play and Animal Welfare." *Animal Behaviour* 81 (5): 891–899.

Herzog, George. 1941. "Do Animals Have Music?" *Bulletin of the American Musicological Society* 5: 3–4.

Hessel, Dieter. n.d. "EcoJustice Now." Accessed May 28, 2020. http://www.ecojusticenow.org/page20/page20.html.

Ihde, Don. 1971. *Hermeneutic Phenomenology: The Philosophy of Paul Ricoeur*. Evanston, IL: Northwestern University Press.

Ihde, Don. 1976. *Listening and Voice*. Stony Brook: State University of New York Press.

Ingold, Tim. 2000. *The Perception of the Environment: Essays on Livelihood, Dwelling, and Skill*. New York: Routledge.

Kull, Kalevi. 2003. "Thomas A. Sebeok and Biology: Building Biosemiotics." *Cybernetics & Human Knowing* 10 (1): 47–60.

Leopold, Aldo. 1949. *A Sand County Almanac*. New York: Oxford University Press.

Lévi-Strauss, Claude, and Didier Eribon. 1991. *Conversations with Claude Lévi-Strauss*. Translated by Paula Wissington. Chicago: University of Chicago Press.

Lewy, Matthias. 2017. "About Indigenous Perspectivism, Indigenous Sonorism, and the Audible Stance. Approach to a Symmetrical Auditory Anthropology." *El oído pensante* 5 (2): 1–21.

Lipps, Theodor. 1907. "Das Wissen von fremden Ichen." *Psychologische Untersuchungen* 1: 694–722.

Low, Philip. 2012. *Cambridge Declaration on Consciousness*. Accessed December 16, 2018. http://www.fcmconference.org/img/CambridgeDeclarationOnConsciousness.pdf.

Magliocco, Sabina. 2018. "Folklore and the Animal Turn." *Journal of Folklore Research* 55 (2): 1–6.

Marler, Peter. 1981. "Birdsong: The Acquisition of a Learned Motor Skill." *Trends in Neurosciences* 4: 88–94.

McDowell, John Holmes. 2018. "Animal Agency in Sibundoy Ecospirituality." Paper presented at the annual conference of the American Folklore Society, Buffalo, NY, October 17–20, 2018.

Meijer, Eva. 2020. *Animal Languages*. Translated by Laura Watkinson. Cambridge, MA: MIT Press.

Merleau-Ponty, Maurice. (1945) 1962. *Phenomenology of Perception*. Translated by Colin Smith. New York: Humanities Press.

Merleau-Ponty, Maurice. 2003. *Nature: Course Notes from the College de France*. Compiled by Dominique Seglard. Translated by Robert Vallier. Evanston, IL: Northwestern University Press.

Mooney, Richard. 2009. "Neural Mechanisms for Learned Birdsong." *Learning and Memory* 16: 655–669. https://doi.org/10.1101/lm.1065209.

Naess, Arne, and David Rothenberg. 1989. *Ecology, Community and Lifestyle: Outline of an Ecosophy*. Cambridge: Cambridge University Press.

Nagel, Thomas. 1972. "What Is It Like to Be a Bat?" *Philosophical Review* 83 (4): 435–450.

Nussbaum, Martha. 2011. "The Capabilities Approach and Animal Entitlements." In *The Oxford Handbook of Animal Ethics*, edited by Tom L. Beauchamp and R. G. Frey, 228–252.

New York: Oxford University Press. http://www.oxfordhandbooks.com/view/10.1093/oxfor dhb/9780195371963.001.0001/oxfordhb-9780195371963-e-9.

Ochoa Gautier, Ana María. 2016. "Acoustic Multinaturalism, the Value of Nature, and the Nature of Music in Ecomusicology." *Boundary 2* 43 (1): 108–147.

Painter, Corinne M. 2007. "Appropriating the Philosophies of Edmund Husserl and Edith Stein: Animal Psyche, Empathy and Moral Subjectivity." In *Phenomenology and the Non-human Animal: At the Limits of Experience*, edited by Corinne Painter and Christian Lotz, 95–115. Heidelberg: Springer.

Payne, Katy. 1998. *Silent Thunder: In the Presence of Elephants*. New York: Simon and Schuster.

Payne, Katy. 2003. "Sources of Social Complexity in the Three Elephant Species." In *Animal Social Complexity: Intelligence, Culture, and Individualized Societies*, edited by Frans B. M. de Waal and Peter L. Tyack, 57–85. Cambridge, MA: Harvard University Press.

Payne, Katy. 2007. "In the Presence of Elephants and Whales." Interview by Krista Tippett. *On Being*, February 1. https://onbeing.org/programs/katy-payne-in-the-presence-of-elephants-and-whales/.

Prather, Jonathan F., and Richard Mooney. 2015. "Mirror Neurons in the Songbird Brain." In *New Frontiers in Mirror Neuron Research*, edited by P. F. Ferrari and G. Rizzolatti, 182–197. New York: Oxford University Press.

Prather, Jonathan F., S. Peters, S. Nowicki, and Richard Mooney. 2008. "Precise Auditory Vocal-Mirroring in Neurons for Learned Vocal Communication." *Nature* 451: 305–310.

Rice, Timothy. 1994. *May It Fill Your Soul: Experiencing Bulgarian Music*. Chicago: University of Chicago Press.

Ricoeur, Paul. 1974. *The Conflict of Interpretations: Essays in Hermeneutics*. Edited by Don Ihde. Translated by Willis Domingo et al. Evanston, IL: Northwestern University Press.

Richerson, Peter. 2004. *Not by Genes Alone: How Culture Transformed Human Evolution*. Chicago: University of Chicago Press.

Richerson, Peter. 2012. "Culture-Led Gene-Culture Coevolution." Conference on Culture-Gene Interactions in Human Origins, University of California, San Diego, February 14, 2013. Video, 19:00. https://www.youtube.com/watch?v=GonV1ER8Ubo.

Rogers, Lesley J., and Gisela T. Kaplan. 2002. *Songs, Roars, and Rituals: Communication in Birds, Mammals, and Other Animals*. Cambridge, MA: Harvard University Press.

Roseman, Marina. 1993. *Healing Sounds from the Malaysian Rainforest: Temiar Music and Medicine*. Berkeley: University of California Press.

Rothenberg, David. 2011. *The Survival of the Beautiful: Art, Science, and Evolution*. New York: Bloomsbury Press.

Roughgarden, Jane. 2012. "The Social Selection Alternative to Sexual Selection." *Philosophical Transactions of the Royal Society B* 367: 2294–2303.

Schear, Joseph K. 2009. "Experience and Self-Consciousness." *Philosophical Studies* 144: 95–105.

Searcy, William A., and Stephen Nowicki. 2005. *The Evolution of Animal Communication: Reliability and Deception in Signaling Systems*. Princeton, NJ: Princeton University Press.

Sebeok, Thomas. 1972. *Perspectives in Zoosemiotics*. The Hague: Mouton.

Sebeok, Thomas. 1992. "'Tell Me, Where Is Fancy Bred?': The Biosemiotic Self." In *Biosemiotics: The Semiotic Web 1991*, edited by T. A. Sebeok and J. Umiker-Sebeok, 333–343. Berlin: Mouton de Gruyter.

Seeger, Anthony. (1987) 2004. *Why Suyá Sing: A Musical Anthropology of an Amazonian People*. Urbana: University of Illinois Press.

Seeger, Anthony. 2015. "Natural Species, Sounds, and Humans in Lowland South America: The Kĩsêdjê/Suyá, Their World, and the Nature of Their Musical Experience." In *Current Directions in Ecomusicology*, edited by Aaron S. Allen and Kevin Dawe, 89–98. New York: Routledge.

Simard, Suzanne, David A. Perry, Melanie D. Jones, David D. Myrold, Daniel M. Durall, and Randy Molina. 1997. "Net Transfer of Carbon between Ectomycorrhizal Tree Species in the Field." *Nature* 388: 579–581.

Singer, Peter. (1975) 2009. *Animal Liberation*. New York: Harper Perennial.

Smart, Ninian. 1969. *The Religious Experience of Mankind*. Englewood Cliffs, NJ: Prentice-Hall.

Smart, Ninian. 1970. *Philosophy of Religion*. Oxford: Oxford University Press.

Smart, Ninian. 1973. *The Phenomenon of Religion*. New York: Seabury.

Smith, F. J. 1979. *The Experiencing of Musical Sound: A Prelude to a Phenomenology of Music*. London: Gordon and Breach.

Sontag, Susan. 1963. "A Hero of Our Time." *New York Review of Books*. November 28, 1963. An expanded version of this piece appeared in *Against Interpretation and Other Essays* (1970), titled "The Anthropologist as Hero," 69–81. New York: Picador.

Sorce Keller, Marcello. 2012. "Zoömusicology and Ethnomusicology: A Marriage to Celebrate in Heaven." *Yearbook for Traditional Music* 44: 166–183.

Spradley, James P. 1979. *The Ethnographic Interview*. Belmont, CA: Wadsworth.

Spradley, James P., David W. McCurdy, and Diana J. Shandy. (1972) 2004. *The Cultural Experience: Ethnography in Complex Society*. 2nd ed. Long Grove, IL: Waveland Press.

Stegmann, Ulrich, ed. 2013. *Animal Communication Theory: Information and Influence*. Cambridge: Cambridge University Press.

Stein, Edith. (1917) 1989. *On the Problem of Empathy*. 3rd rev. ed. Vol. 3 of *Collected Works of Edith Stein*. Washington, DC: ICS Publications.

Stepanov, Y. S. 1971. *Semiotika*. Moscow: Nauka.

Stone, Ruth. (1982) 2010. *Let the Inside Be Sweet: The Interpretation of Music Event among the Kpelle of Liberia*. Bloomington, IN: Trickster Press.

Stumpf, Carl. (1924) 1930. "Autobiography of Carl Stumpf." Classics in the History of Psychology. Accessed August 20, 2007. https://psychclassics.yorku.ca/Stumpf/murchison.htm.

Suzuki, Ryuji. 2006. "Information Entropy of Humpback Whale Songs." *Journal of the Acoustical Society of America* 119: 1849–1866. https://doi.org/10.1121/1.2161827.

Taylor, Hollis. n.d. "Introduction to Zoömusicology." Zoömusicology. http://www.zoomusicology.com/Zoomusicology/Introduction.html.

Thomas, Ben. 2012. "What's So Special about Mirror Neurons?" *Scientific American Blog Network*, November 6, 2012. Accessed December 15, 2018. https://blogs.scientificamerican.com/guest-blog/whats-so-special-about-mirror-neurons/.

Thomas, Elizabeth Marshall. 1993. *The Hidden Life of Dogs*. Boston: Houghton-Mifflin.

Thoreau, Henry David. (1862) 2001. "Walking." In *Thoreau, Collected Essays and Poems*, edited by Elizabeth Hall Witherell, 225–255. New York: Library of America.

Titon, Jeff Todd. 1978a. "Some Recent Pentecostal Revivals: A Report in Words and Photographs." *Georgia Review* 32 (3): 579–605.

Titon, Jeff Todd. 1978b. "Every Day I Have the Blues: Improvisation and Daily Life." *Southern Folklore Quarterly* 42 (1): 85–98.

Titon, Jeff Todd. 1980. "The Life Story." *Journal of American Folklore* 93 (369): 276–292.

Titon, Jeff Todd. (1988) 2018. *Powerhouse for God: Speech, Chant, and Song in an Appalachian Baptist Church*. 2nd ed. Knoxville: University of Tennessee Press.

Titon, Jeff Todd. (1989) 2015. "Ethnomusicology as the Study of People Making Music." *Muzikoloski Zbornik/Musicological Annual* (Slovenia) 51 (2): 175–185.

Titon, Jeff Todd, gen. ed. 1992. *Worlds of Music*. 2nd ed. New York: Schirmer Books.

Titon, Jeff Todd. (1997) 2008. "Knowing Fieldwork." In *Shadows in the Field: New Perspectives for Fieldwork in Ethnomusicology*, 2nd ed., edited by Gregory Barz and Timothy J. Cooley, 25–40. New York: Oxford University Press.

Titon, Jeff Todd. 2001. "Introduction." In *Old-Time Kentucky Fiddle Tunes*, edited by Jeff Todd Titon, 1–27. Lexington: University Press of Kentucky.

Titon, Jeff Todd. 2012. "Music, Mediation, Sustainability: A Case Study on the Banjo." *Folklore Forum* 28 (June). Accessed December 18, 2018. https://folkloreforum.net/2012/06/28/music-mediation-sustainability-a-case-study-on-the-banjo/#more-1147.

Titon, Jeff Todd. 2013. "The Nature of Ecomusicology." *Música e Cultura* 8: 8–18.

Titon, Jeff Todd. 2015. "Exhibiting Music in a Sound Community." *Ethnologies* 37 (1): 23–41.

Titon, Jeff Todd. 2016. "The Sound of Climate Change." *Whole Terrain* 22: 28–32.

Titon, Jeff Todd. 2019. "Ecojustice, Folklife, and a Sound Ecology." *Yale Journal of Music & Religion* 5 (2): 1–14.

Titon, Jeff Todd. 2020. "Sustainability and a Sound Ecology." In *Toward a Sound Ecology: New and Selected Essays by Jeff Todd Titon*, 254–275. Bloomington: Indiana University Press.

Titon, Jeff Todd, and Mark Slobin. 1992. "The Music Culture as a World of Music." In *Worlds of Music*, 2nd ed., edited by Jeff Todd Titon, 1–15. New York: Schirmer Books.

Van der Leeuw, Gerardus. (1933) 1956. *Phänomenologie der Religion*. 2nd ed. Tübingen: J. C. B. Mohr.

Viveiros de Castro, Eduardo. 1998. "Cosmological Deixis and Amerindian Perspectivism." *Journal of the Royal Anthropological Institute* 4 (3): 469–488.

von Uexküll, Jakob. (1934) 2010. *A Foray into the World of Animals and Humans, with a Theory of Meaning*. Translated by Joseph D. O'Neil. Minneapolis: University of Minnesota Press.

Weisberg, Zipporah. 2015. "'The Simple Magic of Life': Phenomenology, Ontology, and Animal Ethics." *Humanimalia* 7 (1): 79–108.

Williams, Heather. 2004. "Birdsong and Singing Behavior." *Annals of the New York Academy of Sciences* 1016 (1): 1–30.

Wilson, David S. 1975. "A General Theory of Group Selection." *Proceedings of the National Academy of Sciences* 72: 143–146.

Wilson, David S., and Edward O. Wilson. 2007. "Rethinking the Theoretical Foundation of Sociobiology." *Quarterly Review of Biology* 82: 327–348.

Zahavi, Dan. 2011. "Empathy and Direct Social Perception: A Phenomenological Proposal." *Review of Philosophy and Psychology* 2: 541–558.

Zweifel, R., and F. Zeugin. 2008. "Ultrasonic Acoustic Emissions in Drought-Stressed Trees—More than Signals from Cavitation?" *New Phytologist* 179: 1070–1079.

MEMORY, IMAGINATION, AND CONSCIOUSNESS

CHAPTER 5

∙∙

LISTENING BEYOND
SOUND AND LIFE
Reflections on Imagined Music

∙∙

J. MARTIN DAUGHTRY

In memoriam: Donald S. Daughtry

PART ONE: THE STRANGE BEHAVIORS
OF IMAGINED SOUNDS

∙∙

1.

I hear sounds in my head.

They are not "sounds" really, or at least not fully. To say that they are "sounds" is to invest them with a kind of vibrational materiality that these imagined entities lack. Nor, I suppose, do I actually "hear" them—at least not fully. To say that I "hear" them is either to say that I perceive them as audible events (this is the biological definition of hearing) or that I comprehend them (as in the English phrase, "I *hear* you," i.e., I get you, I understand you, I am no longer seeking your meaning but have found it).[1] Well, these are not vibrations in the air to be sensed, and I manifestly do not comprehend them. And they are not "in my head," really—or at least not fully. To say that they are "in my head" is to imply that they are *mine*, that they are private entities experienced by me alone, that they exist independently of the public, intersubjective sounds that envelop me and everyone else within earshot. None of these is strictly true.

While intermittent streams of these mind-dependent entities are present throughout my day, the most prominent and striking among them exhibit qualities I associate with music. Sometimes I attempt to conjure these sounds on purpose, but most of the time they appear unbidden. I have to admit that sometimes these instances of imaginary "music" are so insistently present, with their maniacal looping and their saturating affect, that I feel like I am being haunted by them. I feel like I am being hacked, as if a piece of malware has breached the firewall of my brain and installed a bug that uses up all of my available RAM. I feel like I am being so forcefully interpellated into the world of these imagined sounds that I forget, momentarily, to think the thoughts that make me *me*. In their presence I sometimes cease to be me.

At other times, imagined (or remembered, or anticipated) sounds blend so seamlessly with my perception of the external world that they withdraw from my consciousness altogether. The soft snippets of vague melodies that ebb and flow throughout my day just at or beneath the threshold of my attention; the echoic replay of recent sonorous events; the "inner voice" of me thinking, or remembering, or silently rehearsing the question I want to ask as soon as the colloquium speaker finishes her lecture—these are less sounds that I hear than they are facets of me. They are recursive thought-eddies within the smooth flow of my inner world worlding, of me being—of me *me-ing*.[2]

In light of the aforementioned, my opening sentence becomes very conditional:

"I"
"hear"
"sounds"
"in my head."

What is the relation between the mind-independent sounds we encounter in the world and the mind-dependent "sounds" of imagination, anticipation, and memory? Are they a pair of linked opposites, as public is to private, or presence is to absence? Or are they two fraternal members of a single class of phenomena, whose vibrational and non-vibrational aspects are of secondary significance? Are sounds in the mind faint facsimiles of sound in the world, copied onto neural pathways in the auditory cortex? Or does the fact that they aren't beholden to the laws of acoustics mean that imagined sounds are fundamentally *stranger* than vibrational sounds? Are these phenomena in a zero-sum bid for attention, where to focus on one causes the other to slip into the background? Or is their relation one of symbiosis, in which the perception of a vibrational sound both shapes and is shaped by its imagined doppelgänger? And what is the status of *my* imagined sounds vis-à-vis the multitude of human and nonhuman creatures who may also have mind-dependent auditory experiences? In other words, are imagined sounds idiosyncratic (i.e., unique to your individual experience), culturally conditioned (i.e., broadly shaped by communities), or universal (i.e., a uniform capacity of humans, or even of all hearing beings)? Put more directly: do the sounds I hear in my head resemble the sounds you hear in your head?

This essay proceeds from the understanding that the auditory imagination, rather than being a monolithic, abstract entity that we all tap into (like the Jungian collective unconscious) or a fundamentally private realm of insular thoughts, is best cast as an *ethnographic field site*: a palimpsestic ecosystem of interconnection and difference within which the discrete experiences of individuals and groups matter. In a sense, it is the ethnographic field site *par excellence*, where the challenge that all anthropologists (and, in a less-theorized but no less important fashion, all people) face—the challenge of knowing the other—is distilled down to its essence. *How to hear the imagined sounds of the other?* The seeming impossibility of this task engenders a healthy sense of humility: it is clear that we will never achieve perfect knowledge here. But of course we never can, even when attempting to understand something more concrete and public, like cultural institutions, or musical praxes, or warfare. All we can do is what we always do: think, and query, and listen, and share, and revise, and repeat.

Based on my preliminary work on this subject,[3] it appears that for some people the auditory imagination is a radically logocentric zone, a cloud of inner monologues and dialogues, of remembered and anticipated words. For others it is a relatively still space filled with long moments of rich silence; practitioners of meditation, for example, tend to work hard to still the jangly acoustic residue that seeps into consciousness from our often-cacophonous surroundings. For many musicians, by contrast, the auditory imagination is an engrossing and occasionally overwhelming swirl of rhythmic grooves and orchestral flourishes and low drones and muffled calliopes and unhinged yodels and glissando gurglings—it is the raucous, often joyous experimental zone where musical listening, improvisation, and composition take place. At the same time, for many survivors of armed combat or sexual violence, the auditory imagination can become, without warning, a fraught environment of unwanted traumatic memories, of "sounds" that are inextricably bound to the violent acts that produced or accompanied them. Imagined sound is, in this scenario, deeply entangled with the experience of post-traumatic stress.[4] Lastly, it is crucial to acknowledge that, for those whose epistemologies eschew a hard boundary between interiority and exteriority, between self and world, intracorporeal auditory experiences may be understood not as *imaginations* but as *visitations*, as social experiences of co-presence with a spectral human, animal, or spiritual interlocutor.[5] To study imagined sound or imagined music, then, is to explore not a singular phenomenon but an essential plurality of flickering, fluctuating events. These events can be banal or profound, life-affirming or deadening. But whatever they are, and whatever ontology one attributes to them, they make up the unsounded underside of the iceberg of musical experience and, even more fundamentally, much of the material from which consciousness is built.

2.

A quick word on terminology:

Neuroscientific and psychological literature tend to refer to the sounds you hear in your head as "auditory imagery"; this interestingly oculocentric term is often divided into subcategories such as "verbal imagery" (sometimes called "inner speech") and "musical imagery." "Auditory hallucination" is the pathologized term for imagined sounds that one cannot distinguish from sounds out in the world. Some scholars (e.g., Ihde

[1976] 2007) set up a contrast between "perceived sound" and "imagined sound." Others employ the "mind-dependent" and "mind-independent" binary that I mentioned earlier. "Involuntary musical imagery" (acronymized "INMI") is the scientific term for a song fragment that gets lodged in your consciousness, repeating itself independently of your desire. Regional idioms for this phenomenon abound, including the French *musique entêtante* (stubborn music) and Italian *canzone tormentone* (tormenting songs). The colloquial term "earworm" (borrowed from the German *Ohrwurm*) has become increasingly common in Anglophone academic literature.[6]

One recent treatise by Mark Grimshaw and Tom Garner joins audible vibrations and the auditory imagination together into a "sonic aggregate":

> The sonic aggregate comprises two sets of components: the *exosonus*, a set of material and sensuous components; and the *endosonus*, a set of immaterial and nonsensuous components. The endosonus is a requirement for the perception of sound to emerge. The exosonus is not. (2015, 4)

The exosonus, in other words, corresponds to vibration, and the endosonus to auditory imagery. While these two categories may appear at first glance to be mutually exclusive, they regularly cross-pollinate in practice. When produced by humans, at least, the exosonus—the thoroughly public, vibrational dimension of sound—is almost always the product of imaginative labor of one kind or another. Perhaps if you accidentally drop a plate, the sound the plate makes is not dependent upon your prior acts of imagination, anticipation, or memory; but whenever you make a sound intentionally—whenever you speak, sing, clap, walk, or even yelp in surprise at the plate you dropped—you draw upon a vast store of embodied memories and creative praxes that inform these sonorous (and, it must be said, always-more-than-sonorous) actions. Moreover, at the moment the plate crashes to the floor, it also crashes into your intellective world, enriching your memory of past events and your anticipation of future plates. In this way, the exosonus constantly invades the realm of the endosonus, while the endosonus ingests and digests the exosonus at every turn. To take another example: any trumpet fanfare that you could possibly conjure in your mind at this moment would be at least semi-dependent upon your past experiences of real-world trumpets.[7] Even if you were to attempt to imagine a radically new sound, one that has never existed before, your memory of real-world sounds would come into play, if only as the necessary foil or "other" against which your new sound is calibrated. All of this is to say that your imagination is not a pure, ethereal zone of immaterial chimeras, nor is the intersubjective world a realm devoid of your imaginative energies.

Take, for example, the activity known as "listening to music." Common sense holds (and the majority of music scholarship implies) that this activity involves—it seems too obvious to state—attending to a succession of audible, material, vibrational (i.e., exosonic) "sounds" that are unfolding within earshot of the listener. ("What are you listening to?" you ask. "Music," I respond, pointing my finger at the jazz band and not at my head.)[8] But Grimshaw and Garner contend that these vibrations alone are neither necessary nor sufficient conditions for "sound" or "music" to obtain. For them, the phenomenon known as "sound" refers not to these vibrations but to an "emergent perception" or "creative act within our mind" (2015, 3). In other words, vibrations only become "sound" when fused with the endosonus. By contrast, the endosonus in isolation *is* necessary and sufficient: according to their model, "imagined sound is sound."

The implication here is that at the very moment when you *think* you are listening to music out in the world, the focal point of your consciousness is actually oscillating rapidly and unpredictably between the musical exosonus and the endosonic activities that it triggers in your mind. In other words, when you think you are listening *out*, you are actually listening *in* as well. (I have tried to illustrate this oscillation of attention below in Figure 5.1, the first of several hand-drawn, back-of-the-napkin diagrams that accompany this essay.) This imaginative engagement is the hidden *sine qua non* of anything we might reasonably call "musical" or "aesthetic" or "hermeneutic" experience: we hear as "music" (or as "beautiful" or "meaningful") only that which triggers the creation of a parallel track of endosonic mimesis.[9] (Of course, we need not be aware of this imaginative track in order for it to be a force within our lives.)[10] This mixed environment is what phenomenologist Don Ihde ([1976] 2007) was referring to when he wrote about "that second modality of ongoing experience, the *imaginative mode*":

> With the introduction of a second modality of experience, in addition to what has been the predominantly perceptualist emphasis, listening becomes *polyphonic*. I hear not only the voices of the World, in some sense I "hear" myself or from myself. There is in polyphony a duet of voices in the doubled modalities of perceptual

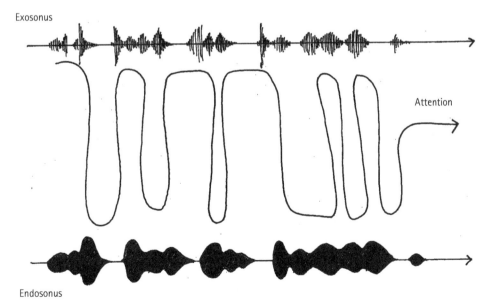

FIGURE 5.1: Oscillation of attention between exosonus and endosonus.

and imaginative modes. A new review of the field of possible auditory experience is called for in which attention would be focused on the copresence of the imaginative. (117, italics in the original)

Taking these propositions seriously means asserting the ubiquitous, active presence of the imagination, and of the endosonus in particular, within the terms "music" and "listening." It means understanding musical listening as a bicameral, "polyphonic" activity that always involves the creation of a parallel endosonic track to provide a subconscious or quasi-conscious point of calibration for the exosonic event, if indeed such an event is present.[11] To study music under these circumstances requires a lexicon like Grimshaw and Garner's, which acknowledges the fundamental entanglement of imagination and perception (i.e., in the "sonic aggregate") and the self-sufficiency of the endosonus as a mode of musical experience (i.e., "imagined sound is sound"). (Figure 5.2 presents these interrelationships in arithmetical terms.)

The other term of consequence for me here—phenomenology—is discussed in great detail in the first chapter of this volume. I should probably mention here that I do not consider myself a phenomenologist, nor would I be inclined to present my work, here or elsewhere, as being phenomenology in the strictest, most rigorous sense of the word. At the same time, like the other authors in this volume, I have been moved and inspired by a broad array of phenomenological writing.[12] Much of this writing, as I understand it, projects a playful, open, exploratory attitude toward the world, which I find attractive; it reminds me of the kind of pansensorial, let's-see-what-this-tastes-like inquisitiveness that my children had when they were young and that many of the artists I admire seem to have maintained well into adulthood. In particular, I like the spirit behind Edmund Husserl's ([1913] 1962) "phenomenological reduction," in which he asks you to bracket out all that you think you know about the thing in question (be that thing a physical object, a musical performance, a metaphysical framework, or whatever). In the relative quiet that results from placing all of your presuppositions toward this thing, or "phenomenon," out of play, he then asks you to approach the phenomenon anew, meticulously describe the way it unfolds before you, track the often subtle ways it changes you and you change it as you encounter one another, and try to discern the underlying structures shaping this encounter. One scholar recently wrote that the purpose of this exercise in radical description is to "sustain the awakening force of astonishment" (Cogan 2009) toward the phenomenon in question and toward the world more broadly.[13] If you ask me, that's not a bad way to do scholarship, engage with art, live life.

```
exosonus + endosonus = "sonic aggregate" = "sound"

sonic aggregate - exosonus = "sound"

sonic aggregate - endosonus < "sound"
```

FIGURE 5.2: Conditions for "sound" to obtain, according to Grimshaw and Garner.

Of course, the sense of radical openness that the phenomenological attitude engenders is not absolute. Maurice Merleau-Ponty ([1945] 2012, lxxvii) reminds us that the phenomenological reduction, valuable though it is, is always doomed to failure. In his words, "the most important lesson the reduction teaches us is the impossibility of a complete reduction." You can never forget all that you know; you can never create a pure state of *tabula rasa*. And yet, the Sisyphean struggle to actively explore, rather than presuppose, the nature of the phenomena that surround us can end up defamiliarizing the world in a way that allows astonishment to flood in—and with it, hopefully, a small measure of new understanding. In the second half of this essay I attempt a phenomenological description of a single endosonic experience in the hope that it will foster a sense of astonishment in you, reader, at the strange, Möbius-like curlings of your own auditory imagination. As an objective account of reality, my description is ultimately a failure, as you will soon see. But just as a fallen tree provides an ideal environment for a multitude of small creatures in the forest ecosystem, so too, I hope, will this quixotic attempt to describe a few fleeting scraps of auditory imagery serve as fecund ground for your own reflections.[14] This, as I see it, is how phenomenology articulates with ethnography: phenomenological investigation doesn't reveal atemporal, universal "structures of experience" so much as it provides a seed bed for asking grounded, ethnographic questions about the possible contours and variability of such structures. At the same time, the phenomenological project does suggest that there is some broadly shared experiential ground beneath the cultural variability that continues to be the primary object of fascination for ethnographers. When combined, then, phenomenological and ethnographic approaches form a robust system, one that can help us avoid the reductive pictures of the world that each may produce in isolation. The essays in this volume, along with a number of influential predecessors (e.g., Stone [1982] 2010; Rice 1994; Friedson 1996; Berger 1999) demonstrate the power of this fusion.

3.

Now, a quick word on intellectual history:

Western philosophical interest in the imagination dates back at least to Aristotle, who distinguished it from both perception and mind, and thought of it as primarily imagistic.[15] In the twentieth century, Husserl, Heidegger, Sartre, Merleau-Ponty, Casey, and others undertook phenomenological investigations of the imagination, although imagined sound was not the central concern for any of them.[16] Ihde's vivid account ([1976] 2007) of the auditory imagination focuses largely on "inner speech": the more-or-less constant state of being a person immersed in language.[17] Lydia Goehr (1992), Nicholas Cook (1990), and Harris Berger (1999) have undertaken detailed studies of the musical imagination within the context of classically trained composers (Goehr), performers (Cook), and popular music (Berger); and two generations of feminist musicologists, from Suzanne Cusick (1994) to Elisabeth Le Guin (2005) to Jenny Olivia Johnson (2015), have explored the nexus of listening, imagination, and embodied experience. Eldritch Priest (2018) and Fred Maus (2018) have published provocative essays on the auditory imagination that draw new insights from Continental philosophy (Priest) and psychoanalysis (Maus). The recent publication of the *Oxford Handbook of Sound and Imagination* (Grimshaw-Aagaard et al. 2019), comprising seventy essays spread over two volumes, attests to the emergence of auditory imagery as a robust area of study.[18] This work notwithstanding, the "massive lack of philosophical attention to the phenomena of auditory imagination" that Ihde ([1976] 2007, 134) first began to discuss in 1976 remains a problem at present, especially when compared to the rapidly growing body of empirical scholarship on imagined sound coming from the fields of experimental psychology and neuroscience.[19] At a moment when the neuroscientific understanding of auditory imagery is growing ever more detailed, it is up to scholars in the humanities, and in music studies specifically, to deepen our understanding of the ontological complexity, affective intensity, epistemological variability, and social permeability of the auditory imagination.

Before the subject of "purely" endosonic (i.e., "imagined," "remembered," "mind-dependent") music can be broached, we first need to reflect on the experience of listening to music within the regime of the sonic aggregate. As I mentioned earlier, it is a fundamental tenet of phenomenology that our experience of the world can only take place through a fusion of perception and imagination. Consider Husserl's classic discussions of "the living present," which he wrote between 1893 and 1917 ([1966] 1991, 21–75).[20] (NB: Matthew Rahaim analyzes Husserl's text in great depth elsewhere in this handbook.) Husserl observed that, in addition to the temporality of an event (e.g., the time it takes to perform a melody) or object (e.g., the relative stability of a piano between its formation and disintegration), consciousness *itself* has a temporality. In other words, we experience the world, its events and objects, not in a succession of "knife-edged moment[s]" (Kelly n.d.) or atemporal quanta, but rather within a *living present* that extends, dynamically and elastically, beyond any particular atomized *now*. To illustrate this principle, imagine you are listening to a recording of Judy Garland singing Harold Arlen's immortal song "Over the Rainbow" from *The Wizard of Oz*. Do you really perceive the first melodic gesture ("Some-where, o-ver the rain-bow . . . ") as a series of discrete notes? If so, this would mean that each time Garland finished singing a note, it would be instantly removed from your active experience. It would mean that, at the moment the "-bow" of "rainbow" is sounding, "some-" and "-where" and "o-" and "-ver" and "the" and "rain-" are fully absent, and so would need to be actively recalled, in their proper order, to make sense of the melodic gesture as a gesture and the phrase "somewhere over the rainbow" as intelligible language. Moreover, since each of her sung notes is extended in time, you would have to reassemble each note out of a long chain of atomized memories (e.g., not the sung syllable "-bow" in its totality but something more like "b.o.o.o.o.o.o.o.o.o.o.o.o.o.o.o.o.o.o.o.o.o.w"). If you didn't undertake this complex feat of memory, you wouldn't be able to perceive this song as a song at all—you could only experience a long string of unrelated vocal sounds.

Clearly, this is not how the human experience of the world works. Rather, your consciousness involuntarily holds on to a bit of an ongoing event that has just occurred and projects a sense of the immediate future of that ongoing event, without differentiating these phenomena from the present moment at hand. Husserl called the auratic presence of the near past of an ongoing event "retention" and likened it to a comet's tail. (Retention is the faint "-where" and even fainter "some-" that you hold in your experience while Garland is technically singing the "o-" of "over.")[21] Contrast this with the involuntary projection of the near future (the faint presence of "-bow" while Garland is singing "rain-") that he called "protention." This front edge of experience is necessarily more mercurial than the tapering tail of retention, as it involves a horizon of possibility that is by its nature plural. Protention takes on a more stable and elongated character, however, if you are experiencing something familiar or predictable and thus can draw on specific memories and/or patterns that project you just beyond the emergent edge of the phenomenon.[22] In any event, the retention and protention of sounds are not active feats of skill so much as they are structural aspects of your encounter with a world in time. Both of these emergent entities take place within your mind, and yet you generally perceive them *not* as internal, imagined phenomena but as hazy presences out in the world.[23] According to Husserl, these three elements—retention, protention, and the enigmatic "primal imprint" of the unfolding perceptual *now* that is nestled between them—form the thick living present of a smoothly flowing consciousness. Consciousness, it follows, is always a conglomeration of retained, protended, and actively perceived material elements, an "experiential aggregate," if you will (see Figure 5.3).[24]

While Husserl intended for this temporal model to apply to all conscious experience, it seems particularly suited to *musical* experience.[25] The structuring elements—repeating refrains, cyclical progressions, stable orchestrations, timbral envelopes, etc.—that are ubiquitous throughout most of the world's musical traditions allow listeners' retentions and protentions to stretch out luxuriantly; continued engagement with a particular tradition stretches them further. If I'm listening to a blues sung by Bessie Smith, say, my elastic musical "now" reaches out to encompass the entire twelve bars of the blues form that is familiar to me. I feel our (Smith and my conjoined) elastic position within that form, regardless of where the performance is at any given moment. I am not willfully *anticipating* the arrival of an absent subdominant chord sometime in the future so much as I am *experiencing* the protended subdominant chord that has not yet been struck into vibration, but that is already structurally (endosonically, phenomenologically) present.

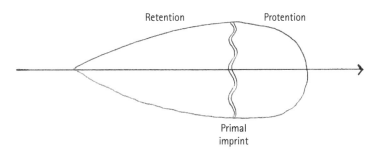

FIGURE 5.3: Protention, primal imprint, and retention, according to Husserl.

Smith sings "I hate to see / the evening sun go down," and Louis Armstrong's cornet responds to her plaintive call. But while he is doing so, he and Smith and their many listeners over the past hundred years and I, with overlapping consciousnesses that have been shaped by our individual histories with the blues, are already experiencing the repetition of her line over the future subdominant, whose gravitational, *protentional* pull we can actively feel. I urge you to stop your reading here and look up a recording of Bessie Smith's "St. Louis Blues." Listen to it once or twice, and then listen again, pausing the recording on the fourth beat of the fourth bar, as Armstrong's instrumental response to Smith's line "I hate to see/the evening sun go down" is concluding. As soon as you hit pause, direct your attention inwards. What do you notice? Do you find yourself awash in non-vibrational "sounds" and harmonic structures? Can you feel the ghostlike presence of the protended subdominant whose primal imprint lies one beat away in the future? If so, you have uncovered the ever-present endosonus, the silent mimetic byproduct of your listening, to which you have been, unbeknownst to yourself, sporadically attending all the while.[26]

Perhaps this delicious sensation of a radically elongated living present is one of the many reasons that music has remained so powerful throughout the world and throughout history, and why so much music across cultures remains tied to cyclic forms like repeating harmonic progressions and verse-chorus structures.[27] Such structures create an expansive, "audiotopic" (Kun 2005) environment that gives free range to the living present. The invigorating environments of free jazz, atonal art music, and many other forms of musical experimentalism, by contrast, draw upon the energy of surprise: here is music whose complex, cloaked structures refuse to allow your consciousness to stretch very far at all; this music calls out for listeners who enjoy the intensity of a living present that is compressed and therefore unpredictable—*unprotendable*. (Figure 5.4 is an attempt to visualize the difference between the elongated living present of predictable music [top] and the compressed living present of unpredictable music [bottom].)

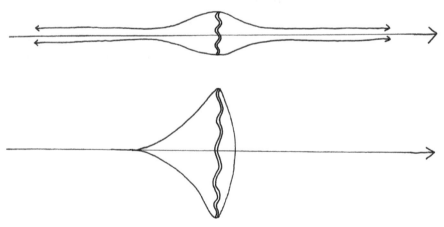

FIGURE 5.4: Elongated living present of predictable music, compressed living present of unpredictable music.

However, even at their most compact and contracted, the endosonic components of musical listening—the retained and protended sounds you unconsciously supply to the listening act—envelop, situate, and cathect the exosonus. This thick living present of retention, protention, and the primal imprint is the milieu within which music becomes meaningful.

4.

Whenever you are listening to music out in the world, you are experiencing a sonic aggregate in which your endosonic retentions and protentions are tethered to the exosonic vibrations of the primal imprint. Your consciousness of the living present is, in other words, yoked to the musical notes that are reverberating out in the world; it is moving unilinearly through time at the pace dictated by those unfolding tones.[28] But what happens when you experience music in the absence of the exosonus? What happens when the "music" that you are "listening to" is not "out in the world" but "in your head"? How does this fully endosonic, imagined music behave?

If you are able, go to a quiet place where you won't be disturbed and imagine a melody right now. Try to imagine a particular recording of a piece you know well. Make sure you don't tap your foot or bob your head along to whatever beat or rhythm may be there, as this would provide an exosonic, kinesthetic anchor to your imagining. Now, with the piece present in your mind, focus intently on the unfolding melody. Are you paying close attention to it? Now focus in even harder—try to really *hear* each musical gesture in all its timbral and harmonic richness. Do you notice anything strange? Whenever I attempt this exercise, the harder I concentrate, the more the endosonus undergoes a kind of temporal distortion; the melody begins to stall and loop and skip around, and multiple versions seem to appear and disappear without warning. My suspicion is that this strange looping and pausing and layering is the result of my inability to distinguish (1) an imagined melody that I am experiencing (i.e., the imagined correlate to the primal imprint) from my (2) retention and (3) protention of that imagined experience. In the absence of an audible vibration unfolding unilinearly through time, all three of these entities are made of the same material: the fungible, mind-dependent synaptic firings of memory-imagination-anticipation. Lacking an exosonic anchor, they provide no firm calibration point for my attention. In this situation, retention, protention, and the imagined imprint all serve as a plausible surrogates for one another—and so they begin to slide in and out of place, pile atop one another, circle back, and skip ahead. (Figures 5.5(a), (b), and (c) depict this situation. The imagined imprint [a] becomes indistinguishable from its retention and protention [b], thus creating a kind of phenomenological shell game [c] that is experienced as a looped melody.)

It is not just their temporal aspect that is strange. Attend to your endosonic melody once again, and ask yourself: *where* do these sounds appear to be coming from? Can you point to the location in space from which they appear to emanate? Are they in mono or stereo? Can you make the sounds appear as though they are coming from a point

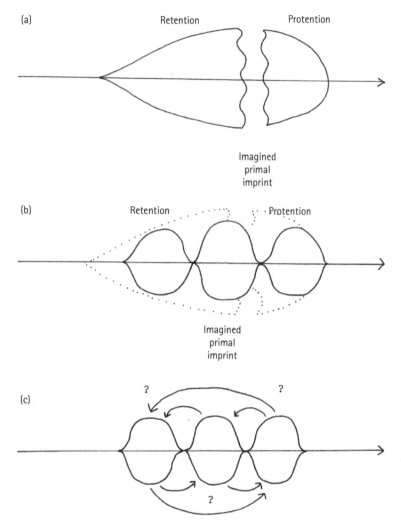

FIGURES 5.5: (a) Retention, imagined imprint, and protention of imagined music. (b) All three elements are made of the same substance: the endosonus. (c) Fungibility of retention, imagined imprint, and protention.

near your left ear? Or from ten feet above your head? Or as though they are echoing throughout a Gothic cathedral, or sounding dully in an anechoic chamber? And how "loud" are these sounds, really? Can you turn up the volume on them? Can you do so to the point that they drown out the ambient sounds that surround you? And are you sure that they are in the same key as the original? Can you shift them down a half-step? If so, are you sure that this new key isn't the key of the original recording? Now, consider the timbre of the imagined tune playing in your head. Is it really the same as that of the aggregate version with which you're familiar? Are you sure? Do you have the orchestration, such as it exists, accurately represented at all points? Over the past few years I have asked many people questions like this, and their answers reveal a wildly variegated terrain of capacities for imagining music.

The kind of intent endosonic listening that I just asked you to do is, of course, a profoundly unnatural exercise. I don't know about you, but normally I just enjoy—or perhaps more commonly endure—the presence of the music that pops into my head. If you encountered me humming under my breath and asked me what I was doing, I wouldn't pause, listen inward, and attempt to describe the intricacies of the experience I was having; I would say, simply, "I have Adele's 'Rolling in the Deep' stuck in my head." And at the moment I said this, I would believe it to be true. This isn't surprising; there is certainly *something* that is presenting itself to my consciousness, and that *something* shares enough of the attributes of "Rolling in the Deep" to allow me to identify it. But if I were to listen intently to it, to ask myself how these imaginary sounds are *actually* behaving, I would be unable to ignore the improvisatory wildness, structural weirdness, and radical contingency that characterize this ontologically slippery "Adele."

These slippery attributes pose a challenge to the phenomenological method, as it appears that the phenomenological attitude itself magnifies and multiplies the strange behaviors of the endosonus. Consider what Arlette Elkaïm-Sartre, in explaining Jean-Paul Sartre's approach to phenomenology, had to say about studying the imagination:

> [T]he mental image is almost inaccessible to [phenomenological] reflection; as long as 'I have an image', *I can say nothing of it without it vanishing*, since the intentionality becomes different; when it is not there I cannot give a detailed account of it; in addition, when I evoke an image, for example, of an absent friend or the tune of a song, I am guided by no present sensory impression—visual, auditory, or otherwise. This is why, for some psychologists, the mental image does not exist.
>
> (Elkaïm-Sartre 2010, x, my emphasis)

Sartre draws a distinction between "unreflective consciousness" (i.e., the general state of being absorbed in one's activities) and "reflective consciousness," or *consciousness of consciousness*. These terms help to clarify the paradoxical challenge faced by anyone attempting a phenomenological investigation of imagined sound: namely, the endosonus is a product of unreflective consciousness, but to describe its behavior requires an act of reflective consciousness. How can one *reflect* on an *unreflective* process without transforming or even annihilating it? Sartre calls such an activity an "impure reflection" and marks it as a futile enterprise, an instance of "bad faith." By this, he means that this kind of reflection necessarily transforms the previously unreflected-upon activity (here, the endosonus) into a "psychic object," a self-contradictory abstraction that, to the extent that it exists at all, operates according to a different mode of being than the original activity did.[29] (Sartre contrasts this with "pure reflection," an attentiveness to one's present state of mind that does not objectify it.) In his account, an emotion like "hatred" is a psychic object that is created through impure reflection upon the flux of one's own unreflective urges and repulsions. Like any virtual entity, once constituted, it appears to take on an agency of its own: now it's your abstract "hatred" of vermin, rather than the dynamics of a particular encounter, that causes you to squash the cockroach in the hallway. Similarly, my impure reflection on an evanescent experience of endosonic music constituted the psychic object called "earworm," which I then treated as if it were a faithful facsimile of Adele's "Rolling in the Deep."

Phenomenologist Edward Casey concurs with Sartre's characterization of this conundrum, arguing that "imagination is easy enough to enact or experience, but it is extremely difficult to capture in midair for purposes of scrutiny and examination" (2000a, 4). In a similar vein, Ihde has observed that "it is of the very essence of the imaginative noema to be easily changeable and variable. For no sooner do I 'think of it' than it is 'there.' Its dissolubility, its rapidity of transformation, its vivid but 'evanescent' presences make it difficult to 'fix' what is imagined" ([1976] 2007, 122). If the phenomenological project is precisely this, to "fix," through exhaustive description, the "noema" (i.e., the object-as-experienced), we may be sending ourselves down a rabbit hole with no discernable bottom. (This abyss is part of what Sartre was gesturing at with his discussion of "the illusion of immanence," the untenable notion that the imagination is made up of stable objects that we can observe.)[30] Under the intensity of the phenomenological attitude, the gossamer gestures of the endosonus writhe, multiply, withdraw, evaporate. If we are to engage with them, then, we need a sneaky, oblique phenomenology, one that won't disintegrate them with the directness of its gaze. We need a phenomenology of peripheral glances and eavesdropping, a poetic or speculative phenomenology that seeks less to *describe* a stable phenomenon than to *evoke* an evanescent one.

Katharine Young finds the possibility of just such a phenomenology in Sartre's concept of "intuition." "Despite these philosophical tangles," she writes, "there are in [Sartre's work] hints of a solution to the problem of catching a glimpse of my own consciousness." She continues:

> It is the moment reflection gets dirty but not yet impure or the moment impure reflection purges itself of its viscosity before it achieves the status of pure reflection. Just before impure reflection freezes my thoughts into objects, I get what Sartre calls an *intuition* of impure reflection (Sartre [1943] 1964: 136). I have not yet made my own psychic processes objects, but they are getting viscous; I have not settled into thinking and my consciousness is still, as [Iris] Murdoch puts it, *flickering* (1980: 42, 43, 66). Here, as I move from [unreflective consciousness] . . . to impure reflection, I might catch myself, in both the sense of getting an inkling of what I am like when I am not paying attention to myself and of stopping myself short of plunging from unreflective consciousness into either pure or impure reflection. At that moment, I am, however ephemerally, possessed by a sense of my own meaning as presence. (2011, 78)

Assuming, with Sartre and Young, that a brief, flickering "intuition" of the endosonus is possible, what would it reveal? More than anything, I think it would reveal that endosonic music is *surreal*—in the strict etymological sense of being above or beyond or unbeholden to perceptual reality, but also in the more historicized aesthetic sense that comes from the early twentieth-century artistic movement of the same name. This is an obvious point of reference for thinking about the endosonus, as the surrealist project that began in 1920s France was dedicated to uncovering the dynamics of "an absolute or 'super' reality" that blended rational thought and perception with "instinctual, subconscious, and dream experience."[31] Andre Breton's description, in the 1924 *Manifesto of Surrealism*, of the struggle to explore the mysterious realm that lay beyond rationalism and empirical reality will remind you of the scholars of the imagination I quoted above. "It requires," he wrote, "a great deal of fortitude to try to set up one's abode in these distant regions [of the imagination] where everything seems at first to be so awkward and difficult, all the more so if one wants to try to take someone there. *Besides, one is never sure of really being there*" ([1924] 2010, italics added). If one is never sure of really being in the realm of pure reflection, then an exhaustive description of the auditory imagination is not an option. One can only evoke, as the surrealists did, the hazy presence of strange entities and events that are both embedded in and not fully accessible to consciousness. Like a surrealist composition—or like many sacred performance practices around the world, or like much of the academic writing in the so-called "speculative turn," the list of fellow travelers goes on and on—our investigation of the auditory imagination must be attuned to uncertainty, amorphousness, opacity, and irrationality. For these are the salient attributes of an aggregate, intercorporeal world where internal and external realities are always already topographically conjoined and always already in a state of flux and overflow.[32] A description of the endosonus must be, for lack of a better word, *parodoxophilic*: comfortable with the contradictory nature of the "sounds" "we" "hear" "in our heads" and with the imperfection of our methods for examining and describing them.

My own imperfect, paradoxophilic method takes inspiration from the surrealist writing practice that was initiated in 1919 by Breton and his collaborator Philippe Soupault. That spring, the two young men, still reeling from their experiences as soldiers in the First World War, initiated an experiment in unselfconscious writing. Their goal was to break away from the rationalist discourse and mainstream morality that had led the world to war and a host of other "trials and tribulations" and instead create a "new morality" that drew upon the creative, irrational energies of the unconscious. Every day for a week they sat down and wrote as fast as possible, without ever pausing to revise or edit. The result was *Les Champs Magnetiques* (The magnetic fields) ([1920] 2020), the first major work of what came to be called "automatic writing."[33] In a similar vein, over the past several years, I have held dozens of half-hour sessions in which I sit in a quiet room, eyes closed, fingers on the computer keyboard, typing shorthand descriptions of the sounds I hear in my head. Initially, the act of writing severely disrupted my ability to "eavesdrop" on the sounds in my head; with time, however, the process became more fluid and less invasive. Like Breton and Soupault, I strove to detach myself from my inner censor, just letting the words flow without ever pausing to think about them. However, unlike them, my automatic writing experiments were designed not to unearth some kind of Freudian or collective unconscious but rather to capture an intuitive snippet of the "unreflective consciousness" that Sartre described in his writings. In another departure from the surrealists, I allowed myself to return to my "automatic" shorthand scribblings, flesh them out, and revise them extensively. The result is a careful elaboration of a kind of evanescent endosonic experience that lies at or just beyond the threshold of conscious reflection.

5.

I am of course far from the first person to attempt a description such as this. Ihde's work from the 1970s is replete with accounts of the auditory imagination. In his 1990 monograph *Music, Imagination, and Culture,* to take another well-known example, musicologist Nicholas Cook undertook a fine-grained description of a snippet of music he was imagining. I quote him at length to give you a sense of the depth of his insights:

> I am reading a novel when I realize that for some time I have been 'hearing' a passage from Allegri's *Miserere.* . . . But this 'hearing' is very different from what it would be like to hear the music in real life, for instance if someone suddenly switched on a radio in the next room. In particular *its temporal aspect is different, for there is a kind of static quality in the image that is quite alien to the world of real, audible music.* The music does not seem to progress from bar to bar in strict tempo: rather, it is focused on a single point in time, namely the high note sung by the boy soprano just before the melody falls to its melismatic cadence. . . . *[I]t is hard to describe this experience adequately in terms of our ordinary, perceptually oriented vocabulary for music.* It is not as if the phrase were repeating itself over and over again like a record player with a stuck needle, or as if the boy's high note were being sustained indefinitely like the sound of an organ with a jammed key: for though my image of the music is centred upon that note, *I grasp it as being already imbued with the melodic descent that follows it in the score.* That is to say, the temporal evolution of the phrase as a whole forms an essential part of my imaginative experience of the boy's high note, even though the experience itself does not seem to change from one moment to the next, or at least not in the same manner as the real, audible music does. (86–87, italics added)

Cook's description highlights some of the ontological differences between the endosonus and exosonus, differences more profound than the obvious one that one can be heard by other people and the other cannot. The "static quality" of some imagined sounds, the insistent presence of melodic gestures that have not yet properly occurred—a phenomenon we may call, following Stefan Helmreich (2015), *preverberation*—and the general aura of strangeness that he struggles to evoke are, I would argue, the inevitable result of a situation where protention, retention, and the imagined primal imprint all serve as surrogates for one another.

Cook presents imagined sound as having a set of affordances that overlap with but exceed those of sound in the physical world; he follows Sartre's contention that the "illusion of immanence" masks their differences, creating a false picture of fidelity between them. While it is possible to imagine the German tenor Dietrich Fischer-Dieskau singing in a naturalistic manner—moving from one note to the next, unilinearly through time—"it is equally possible (and perhaps more natural) to imagine simply Fischer-Dieskau's singing. . . . The image is at least in part a generic one" (Cook 1990, 90). You may think you are listening to a particular piece of "luxuriant orchestral" music with "graceful harmonies" that are being faithfully replicated by your imagination. But you are likely, Cook asserts, to be not "listening" at all but rather imagining the qualities of "harmonic gracefulness and orchestral luxuriance" that the original piece of music contained (92). To imagine sounds, in other words, may remove some of their fine-grained specificity, but it also may allow you to grasp them all at once, freed from the constraints of audible vibrations, which must unfold in time and space. (Figure 5.6 is an attempt to evoke the breadth of imagined sound's surreal affordances.)

Offering a more critical take on the endosonic dimension of contemporary life, media theorist Eldritch Priest has recently written about the involuntary, "sticky" presence of earworms, characterizing them as a kind of "parasite" feeding off our minds. He argues that the energy that drives this kind of parasitic imagined sound is linked to commerce, and specifically to

contemporary capitalism's aim to draw value from involuntary nervous activities. . . . From this perspective, earworms [are] . . . signs of a fatalistic tendency intrinsic to contemporary capitalism's nonstop expropriation of attention driven

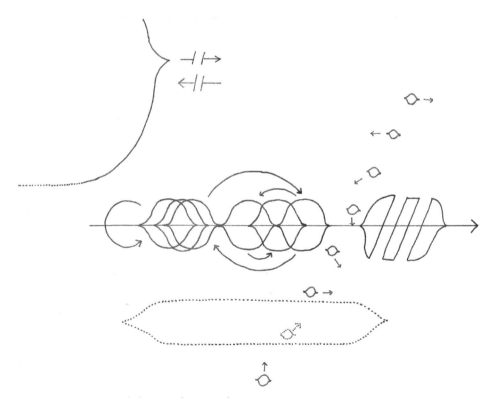

FIGURE 5.6: Strange behavior of imagined music.

by "the imposition of a machinic model of duration and efficiency onto the human body" (Crary, 2013: 3). This is to say that there is something strangely intelligent or logical about the appearance of earworms, and the correlative disappearance of musical sounds in them, that is proper to the accelerated functioning of capitalism.

(Priest 2018, 142)

According to this logic, advertising jingles, popular music in stores and on radios, film soundtracks, Mozart for babies, TV theme songs, Kenny G tracks played at the end of the Chinese workday, the most recent song you heard leaking through a pair of earbuds on the bus—these things are nothing less than the acoustic manifestation of global capitalism, and as such they are powerful colonizers of the auditory imagination. When we reproduce these commoditized sounds in our heads, we are thrust into a form of unwitting endosonic servitude. In this scenario, the earworm virally transports music throughout the global system, increasing the odds of a future purchase or stream, and also increasing the odds that the ideology or product with which a piece of music is entangled will be ingested and digested and recursively reproduced by the unwitting host.

Priest contends that, aside from generating this crude kind of value, earworms are strangely pointless:

Unlike daydreams, whose affair with counterfactuals and anticipated futures makes its streamy content rife with narrative coordinates and trajectories that can be continually exchanged for possibilities and alternatives, earworms *just twist and turn*. The earworm's loopy performance, in which its ending is at the same time its beginning, *cannot be exchanged for anything but itself*. . . . [E]arworms realize the entertainment apparatus's desire for sensation that "passes without obstacles." (2018, 156–157, italics added)

I wish Priest were wrong about the capitalist underpinning of the contemporary earworm, but I fear he is right. I know there are massive forces that have infiltrated the seemingly private realm of my imagination, and I imagine the same is true with yours. It is disquieting, in every sense of this term, to realize that your brain is unconsciously participating in a kind of silent labor that profits strangers at a distance. However, it would be a mistake to reduce the auditory imagination—or even the earworm, its most reprehensible inhabitant—to a simple, homogenous extension of the operations of capital. Earworms may be performing a kind of distributional labor by reproducing the obsessively looped soundtrack of neoliberalism and globalization, but this is not the only labor they are capable of performing. While they may appear to be the flat and mindless replication of commoditized sounds, earworms carry the potential to produce cathexis, solace, memory, communion, and other valuable forms of worlding. In what follows, I offer a detailed description of a single, exceedingly small endosonic incident that I experienced in the spring of 2018. In it, the earworm reveals itself to be more surreal and social and generous than you might expect. Here, reconstructed from my contemporaneous automatic sketches, is my story:

PART TWO: A HALF-REMEMBERED HYMN

I've got a song stuck in my head.

I can't remember its name, but it—or, rather, an enigmatic fragment of it—is *here*, inside me, insistently banging away. This is precisely the kind of mind-dependent object that the term "earworm" refers to: it is involuntary, partial, looped, unbanishable. If you asked me right now, however, I wouldn't call it an earworm. I would be compelled to call my private musical experience a "haunting," as that term foregrounds the uncannily fluid, ectoplasmic manner in which this specter of a song glided into my consciousness and the vaporous way it crowds in on me from all sides while simultaneously eluding the grip of my attention. However, if "haunting" is phenomenologically apt, the connotation of horror that accompanies it is all wrong: this song is a friendly ghost.[34]

While I can't recall its title, I can confidently say that the song in question is a hymn. I can tell because I recognize its hymn-like characteristics but also because I recognize the way it makes me feel. What does it mean, to feel? Here, at this moment, it means that, at the same time that I am aware of the presence of the fragment that haunts me, I am also aware of a vague pulling sensation, of a force pulling my attention toward an as-yet-undisclosed store of memories. I am not, to be clear, experiencing the memories themselves; they remain tantalizingly out of reach, in the future. But their affective agency, the humming energy of their potential, is present, like the radiated warmth of a sunbeam that lies around the next bend in a dark woodland path. Just as a lightening of the spaces between the leaves and a certain change in the damp coolness of the air presage the moment when you turn the corner and step into the full brightness and warmth of the sun, so do these small patches of affective intensity presage what it would be like to be immersed in the memory that lies in wait for me. This sensation of being pulled in the direction of an as-yet-unrecognized memory is somehow keyed to the church-like cadence of the fragment, the particular voicing of its chordal movement, and the knowledge that a plagal "Amen" is sure to follow. Increasing my attention to this unfolding moment, in which I find myself suspended somehow between a present and future cadence, intensifies the sensation of being pulled, of being coaxed or urged into a state of being different than this one. Nonetheless, the destination that is the memory of my own history with this hymn remains just out of reach. I am quiveringly adjacent to it. This, here and now, is what it means to feel.[35]

The fragment of the hymn that I hear in my head is instrumental, without words. It is cycling, never quite reaching the beginning of itself, failing to produce a conclusive end. The bulk of my attention is drawn to the fragment's "sound," but a portion of it is captured by a hazy, somewhat abstracted visual image of the keyboard that might plausibly be producing it (if the fragment and keyboard were real and not imagined). This image is accompanied by a subtle awareness of pressure on my fingertips, as if my fingers are currently playing this piece—though they aren't, and they couldn't even if I had a real keyboard in front of me, as I haven't yet quite figured out how this tune inside me goes. As I attend to the image of the keyboard, it appears to morph uneasily between a spinet (a low-slung upright piano) and a small organ. Its sound at this moment is that of both and neither; it is palpably present but weirdly indeterminate, like a lava lamp, or a wet lump of clay being shaped and reshaped on a potter's wheel. This spectral keyboard, whatever it is, is dreamily, gauzily producing a very familiar kind of four-part harmony, the kind that dates back to the Bach chorale, the kind that was ubiquitous in mainstream American Protestant churches in the homely, pre-megachurch 1970s. This last fact is unsurprising, because I'm sure I last heard this hymn when I was a boy, growing up the son of a Congregationalist pastor in that decade.

So yes, the hymn fragment is here, right now, inside me—but hazily so. The notes don't have a hard attack; it's as if they're swathed in cotton. They don't have the crispness or heft of vibrational sounds in the intersubjective world. That world, the world of sound and smell and sight and touch, is also present, of course; it attempts to pull me away from my introspection and into an engagement with it. I can see through squinted eyes my shorthand transcript of this experience haltingly marching across the screen of my laptop: my upper back and buttocks are pressing into a creaky wooden chair, the smell of spring vegetation and residual chimney smoke is in the air, and I can hear birds singing and a chorus of frogs croaking outside the window of the cabin I'm in. This expansive, empirical world vies for my attention but, at the moment, the secret inner performance is winning. I think of the spinet again, and independent of my desire the sound transforms into something closer to a piano's. Envisioning a pipe organ pulls the hymn into that instrument's lusher sound world, partially silencing the piano that preceded it. But soon the tune returns to its original, more neutral timbre, closer to the sound of the small, unremarkable organ in my dad's church four decades ago. But it's not fully that— it's not fully anything, really. It is the enigmatic timbre of an imagined sound, a sound that is experientially present and ontologically withdrawn.[36]

The hymn's strange, lava-like timbral shapeshifting is accompanied by an equally amorphous and unpredictable combination of temporal flows and stoppages. I can feel the hymn cadence, which means it is in motion, but at the same time it appears to be standing still, in a way that vibrational sound in the world cannot. The still version of the hymn, or rather of the fragment I possess, presents itself as an object, a fuzzy invisible structure—a sculpture, even: it is all there at once. How can this be? How can sound stand still? And how can a single piece of imagined music have one aspect or iteration that appears to move while another aspect or iteration remains in stasis? Things get stranger: when I give up my (naturalistic) search for the tune's identity and resume my (phenomenological) examination of "the thing itself" (Husserl), I notice an inverse relation between the intensity of my focus and the fragment's ability to move forward through time. When I attend closely to the fragment's ever-unfolding "now," it begins to retard, slowing down while maintaining its pitch. I increase my attention, and the three-note phrase I'm listening to slows further, and then begins a slippery, skipping motion, jumping back a few notes, slowly moving forward, holding in place, resuming its natural tempo, only to jump back again—without ever fully erasing its former position when it does so. It is as if the fragment is multiplying, efflorescing, calving off multiple versions of itself in response to the heat of my attention. But—and this is key—these different iterations are not clashing with each other, not creating a chaotic polyphony of static and moving lines.[37] Their co-presence is conceptual, not acoustic. Regardless of their behavior—stalled or sluggish, stuttering or fluid—they are all equal contenders for my attention. There is no obvious foreground or center to this multitude. All of these imaginary sounds are equally peripheral, equally remote, equally Other.

Returning to the quest for identity, the hymn's title is, as they say, on the tip of my tongue. As I frown and try harder to remember a single line of the text, I find myself in the presence of what appears to be human vocal timbre. My instrumental fragment just got choral: a group of invisible men and women are singing the hymn, but without the words. That's not exactly right: their singing has the generic qualities of words, but lacks the specific sounds of actual phonemes. It's as if they're singing the words but at a great distance. I can't quite make them out. This in itself is strange, as it also appears to me that these voices, if one can call them that, are nearby, close to my ear—no, *inside* my ears, *inside* my head, as if the choir is exciting my tympanic membranes from *within*. But not in the normal sense of "inside" or "within"—not in the sense that a headache is confined inside my head. Weirdly, when I attempt to locate the voices in space, it feels as if the sound is emanating from a single point inside my head that is roughly three feet to the right of my left ear, and an equal distance to the left of my right. Given that my head isn't six feet across, this point appears to exist in a strange, non-Euclidean space. This is a hard thing for me to wrap my mind around, but that is precisely where the voices appear to be located: inside a six-foot space that is inside my head, a surreal enclosure which, as I project my attention into it, expands to the size of a room, or, it occurs to me, of a small church.[38]

With an unexpected flash of intuition, I realize that I know how this tune got here! Just before it appeared, I was remembering a talk I gave in London last month. The talk was on music and the Anthropocene, and it discussed the possibility of a world after humans, a world after music. After my lecture, one of the audience members—I believe it was Roger Parker—and I were talking about the music on the deck of the *Titanic*, about how important the choice of music would be at a moment like that, when death was imminent.[39] This hymn is vaguely related to my memory of that conversation, I'm sure of it. I don't know why this should be, as the ensemble that played as the *Titanic* sank was a string quartet, not a piano/organ, and I think they played "Nearer, My God, to Thee" and not this hymn, which I still can't identify. But nonetheless the succession of thoughts is clear: *Titanic* → string quartet → mystery hymn. And now I hear, as if on cue, a string quartet doubling my organ-like instrument, and I am aware of the visual image of the dark deck of a ship at nighttime. I roll my eyes at the obviousness of this development. Luckily, before the actors Winslet and DiCaprio and the Irish flute appear (although of course they are already here, lurking somewhere deep in the wings) the string quartet and the deck image fade away. The fuzzy organ is back, alone, futilely gesturing toward the same two phrases.

I don't remember how this piece begins, and so *it can't begin*. It can only "middle," and end, although the end brings no sense of finality or resolution.[40] It is what in jazz they call a "turnaround," the melody's sinuous slide back to the beginning—only in my case it's back into the middle. (Figure 5.7 depicts this maddening situation.)

I concentrate harder. Where before I attended to location, I now focus on the specific sound the organ is producing. This mental intervention, this thinking about the organ, now ignites a flamboyant set of musical gestures from a Hammond B3 organ: double-handed glissando up, lots of vibrato, all stops out, Black gospel choir standing at the ready. But then that too dies away, replaced by the voices for a second, and then, because I'm thinking about its absence, by the presence of the piano. Everything is taking on an unruly and wild character, like a bronco bucking when the rider pulls the reins. My attention is the bit clamped between the imagined hymn's teeth, causing it to thrash and leap and attempt to throw the rider.

I'm losing control. I need another way to think about this.

It occurs to me that the attention I'm directing toward the hymn is somewhat analogous to the probing capacity of my fingertip, which at this moment is absent-mindedly tracing the pattern of the wood on the rough-hewn table at which I sit. If I close my eyes, I can almost see the wood's grain as my finger feels its way along the table's surface. The grain bends to accommodate a knot in the pine plank; I circle my finger around the unseen knot, and its shape comes into focus in my mind. As my finger twirls, my memory of the finger's approach to the knot fades away—the ridges I traced earlier are dark and quiet now. So too is this melody an object in the dark that I can coax to partial presence by rubbing my attention up against the section I can reach. From where I'm sitting, I cannot reach the far end of the table; likewise, the beginning of the hymn is outside my grasp.

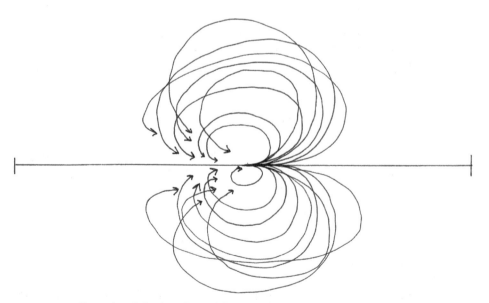

FIGURE 5.7: Eternal cycle back to the middle.

I am aware of my finger's sensation as it slides upon the table. At the same time, I am aware of the pliancy of the pine itself. If I applied pressure to the soft wood, I could scar it with my fingernail. If I replaced my finger with a saw, I could slice through it; I could burn a hole through it with a blowtorch. Similarly, I am aware both of the sensation of my mind brushing up against the surface of the hymn fragment and of the fragment's fragility, its vulnerability to the burning intensity of my attention. I remind myself that a light touch is what's required. I remind myself that the hymn in my mind is less like pine and more like Jell-O: soft, malleable, vulnerable, wobbly. A gentle, desultory sweep along the surface is what's needed, with no more pressure than a Braille reader would apply.

I relax my attention and try to float just above the music, allowing it to slip into the background and resume its previous pace. Now the fuzzy organ is back, doggedly trying to find the beginning that should precede this eternal middle. It occurs to me that the organ is not merely the instrument or medium of my straining-but-failing-to-remember; it *is* that act of labor and frustration. My attempt to recall a melody that is synaptically stored somewhere in the inaccessible recesses of my deep memory is manifest in the loop of that infernal organ. The effort and the instrument and I are, at this moment, inseparable. *We*—the quicksilver blob that is myself *and* the half-remembered melody *and* my struggle to recall the rest of it *and* the organ reverberating in the nonspace of my imagined skull, all of us together—*we* loop back to what *we* hope this time will be the beginning . . . but we fail. We fail to hook onto the opening notes of the submerged melody and drag it onto the banks of consciousness. We are like unlucky fly fishermen, making cast after cast into the river, never landing the trout.

Everything is tantalizingly close. I can even hear the soft felty thuds that fingers make when they release the keys of an organ, an inadvertent percussive accompaniment not unlike the quiet clacking of my fingers on the laptop keyboard now. With the arrival of this paradoxical sound of a phantasmagoric organist's nonexistent fingers, the melody withdraws ever further, retreating finally into the shadowy background hum of consciousness as smoothly as an octopus seeking shelter beneath a rock on the ocean floor.

Out of options, I phone my father, the retired pastor, who is now eighty-eight and living in Florida. I stopped attending church as a teenager, and he, for complex spiritual and logistical reasons, left the ministry in the 1980s and became a taxi driver. We seldom talk about religion, but the music runs deep in both of us. Before my mother died I would often catch him humming one hymn or another as he padded around the house. It occurs to me now that it's been years since he's done that. I wonder if he still hears those tunes in his head or if the sadness of widowerhood has extinguished them. A prolonged shuffling sound indicates that he's working to bring the receiver to his ear. After hearing his creaky-voiced "Hello?" I greet him with my habitual "Hiya, Pops!" and tell him I'm trying to remember a hymn that I imagine we used to sing in his church when I was a boy. I sing the two lines I know, without words, "la-la-la" to him over the phone. He is groggy—I think I woke him up—and he responds with a prolonged silence. Then, in his slow, melodious Charlestonian accent, he says he's sorry, but he can't recall the name of the hymn. I press him, asking if he remembers anything, anything at all, any snatch of melody or text. I sing the lines again. He is silent for an even longer stretch, and

I worry that the call has been disconnected or that he's dozed off. Then, just as I am about to call out, "Are you there?" I hear him vocalizing, softly. He isn't singing the melody; rather, he's producing an involuntary, prolonged drone, "*ahhhhhhhhh*," not unlike the famous groans that Glenn Gould and Keith Jarrett produced while performing.[41] It hits me that my father, separated from me by forty years and a thousand miles, is engaged in the same imaginary fishing expedition that I am, seeking to hook the very same fish. I wonder if his groan, and by implication Gould's and Jarrett's, is the sound of a person striving to hear a sound in his head—as if imagined sounds issued from a pump that needed to be primed. After what seems like a full minute, he softly utters three enigmatic words: "*mystic . . . sweet . . . communion.*" He says he thinks those words might have had something to do with it, and then abruptly hangs up to resume his nap.

A quick Google search of that phrase brings me to "The Church's One Foundation," composed by Samuel Sebastian Wesley (1810–1876) with a text by Samuel J. Stone (1839–1900) and published in the *Hymnal of the Methodist Episcopal Church* of 1878. In the space of one heartbeat's rush of blood through my veins I realize this is absolutely the source of my auditory imagery, which instantaneously attains the sharp lines and detailed shadings of a full portrait instead of the vague and incomplete surrealist sketch I had before. The sound of the hymn and its envoiced text comes flooding in, along with vivid memories of my long-dead mother, of me as a boy in a clip-on tie standing between her and my sister in a creaky wooden pew that smells of lacquer, propping a heavy, faded-blue hymnal on the back of the next pew, singing the words, oblivious of the theology but intoxicated by the goosebump-inducing sense of *communitas* created by voices lifted up together in song. This multisensory memorial swirl surges in with immediacy and then subsides, leaving the faint imagined melody—more or less intact now—in its wake. At this moment, satisfied, my mind smoothly shifts away from its introspective reverie and toward the external, outward-facing senses that had until now constituted the deep background of my secret hymn: I am once again conscious of my back on the chair, the frogs in the grass, my fingers on the keyboard. I take a deep breath and appreciate the smoky smell of the fireplace. The sound of my imagined melody, still present though attenuated, is entangled with my perception of my body and the world that surrounds me.[42]

Now, when I think of the hymn, it starts from the beginning. I can't easily access the looped, hyperstatic middle that had ensnared me before. My knowledge of "The Church's One Foundation" overwrites my now-hazy memory of not quite knowing it, forcing this memory of a partially withdrawn mental object itself to withdraw. I can remember experiencing the inchoate loop of the hymn's middle. I can remember more or less what it felt like to experience it. But I cannot for the life of me re-experience or rehear it as it was. This fragile, intimate musical event was site- and time-specific, the unique product of the particular discursive vectors, thought paths, sensory stimuli, social histories, musical logics, affective energies, and other contingencies that conjured it. Having happened, in all its ephemeral richness, it negates the possibility of faithful return. There was simply too much going on at once. The loping orbit around its own middle, the recursive skips and micro-wobblings as it moved and stayed still, the timbral and instrumental transmutations—all of these resist transcription. At the same time, the fragment's irregular orbit was rendered even more complicated by its smooth lateral movement across the domains of imagination and memory, inside and outside, will and submission, sound and silence, composition and reception, self and community, listening and seeing and thinking and feeling, blurring any boundaries we might want to draw between them. The particular trajectory of this musical specter—a trajectory so much more complex and cathected than the word "earworm" could ever convey—cannot be retraced, even with this text as a roadmap.

This is the submerged half of the iceberg of musical experience: the unsounded, unheard underside that silently cruises beneath the public sounds we compose and rehearse and record and enjoy and buy and sell and study. The drastic loops[43] and feverish images[44] of the auditory imagination precede, accompany, and perdure beyond the vibrational sounds with which they are intimately linked, from which they are ontologically withdrawn. When these imagined sounds are present, they provoke thoughts, distribute affect, inspire movement, trigger memories. They distract, disturb, delight, haunt. Their irreducible complexity and surreal intimacy combine to pull even the most banal experience (e.g., "I've got a song stuck in my head") in the direction of the sublime.

EPILOGUE: ON DEATH AND IMAGINED SOUND

I wrote this account of the elusive hymn fragment in the spring of 2018 for a conference that was to take place in Newfoundland that summer. On June 8th of that year, at Memorial University in St. John's, I read it aloud to the assembled audience. Later that evening, I called my father down in Florida, and we chuckled together at the fact that I started my career writing about Russian singer-songwriters, pivoted to study the sounds of warfare in Iraq, and have now, bizarrely, ended up writing about him and me talking on the telephone. Unbeknownst to us, this was to be our last conversation, as one day later, unexpectedly, he died. I will spare you a description of how it feels to lose a parent: if you haven't experienced this yourself, you probably will someday, and if you have, you don't need me to explain what it feels like. But I will tell you that, more than two years later, I can still hear the sound of his voice in my head, just as I could when he was alive. No . . . that's not quite right: it's not "just as I could." His voice in my head—the spectral product of memory and imagination and a now-useless, rudderless form of anticipation—is losing its capacity to serve as a vessel for any particular memory, any particular thing he once said to me. It is becoming *hypological*—a voice incapable of speech. At the same time, his endosonic voice fills me with the kind of tugging, throbbing gravity that I termed "feeling" earlier. It has become *hyperaffective*—capable of altering my mood, conjuring involuntary memories, moistening my eyes, placing a lump in my throat. When it is present, it gives my body extra weight and extra emotional burdens, and it does this whether I am reflecting upon it or not. Occasionally I willfully conjure it, but more often his voice simply visits me, floating up through layers of thought and feeling to act upon me before I have a chance even to recognize it. The unsummoned voice of my father is powerfully *performative*, in J. L. Austin's sense of that word; it is always doing something, even when it is saying nothing.

As Sartre once wrote:

> If the image of a dead loved one appears to me abruptly, there is no need for a [phe-nomenological] 'reduction' to feel the ache in my heart: it is part of the image, it is the direct consequence of the fact that the image gives its object as a nothingness of being. ([1940] 2010, 13)

It strikes me now, at the end of this essay, that the relationship between listening to music in the world and listening to music in your head is akin to the relationship be-tween experiencing the living and experiencing the dead. The entangled forces of im-agination, memory, and anticipation are present in all four types of encounter, but with music under the regime of the sonic aggregate—as with people under the regime of the living—these forces are tightly bound to empirical phenomena in the world; the twinned acts of retention and protention are shaped by, calibrated against, and beholden to the behavior of worldly sounds and animate bodies. With the dead—as with the endosonus in the absence of an exosonus—imagination, memory, and anticipation are released from the grip of vibrant, vibrating bodies and so begin to wander more freely, and act more strangely.

How robust are the similarities between the endosonus and the dead? Observe the ease with which I can recruit phrases from earlier in this essay to refer equally to both of these entities.[45] The ghostly presence of the dead, like the surreal behavior of imagined music, *is hard to describe . . . adequately in terms of our ordinary, perceptually oriented vocabulary.* When the memory of the dead, or of a piece of music, is alive within a sen-sate body embedded in the cacophonous world, *listening becomes polyphonic.* Both phenomena are non-linear and non-teleological: *they just twist and turn.* And both inhabit spatialities that resist rational description: despite initial appearances, nei-ther imagined music nor the specter of my dead father are *"in my head," really—or at least, not fully.* They are partly there, for sure, but their trajectories neither begin nor end within the confines of my mind. The imagined sound of a beloved song, like the haunting presence of a dead loved one, is inseparable from *the ache in my heart.* Both *are inseminated through and through with social energies that transcend the experiencing self.* And lest you think that with this mention of the transcendence of the dead I've allowed some kind of Christian or other eschatological vibe to sneak into this essay at the very end, let me state outright that one doesn't need to subscribe to any particular metaphysics to acknowledge the presence and profundity of this . . . *ahhhhhhhhh . . .* of this . . . *ahhhhhhhhh . . .* this . . . *mystic . . . sweet . . . communion*—the smooth process whereby perception, imagination, memory, anticipation, and our end-less entanglements (from the corporeal to the linguistic to the social, the ecological, the technocultural, and on and on) are transubstantiated into the unified thing we call "experience."

The freewheeling, surreal weirdness of the dead can be felt, faintly, as a latent energy humming within our cherished subjects (e.g., music, listening, sound, voice, history, society, etc.), troubling them, destabilizing them, creating resonant absences within them.[46] Likewise, the Möbius curlings of the auditory imagination haunt and enstrange our archives and our repertoires, our soundscapes and our social relations, our materialities and virtualities, our local neighborhoods and global networks, all of it.[47] One cannot fully understand the worlds into which we have been thrown without accounting for these ethereal entities.

But how to perform this accounting? As I mentioned at the beginning of this essay, I feel that I ultimately failed to coax the freedom-loving endosonus to full presence on the page. By "failed" I am referring not to the general inability of writing to capture life in all its complex richness but to the particular obstacles that imagined music presents to those who attempt to describe or understand it. I fear the most one can ever do with a fragile musical memory such as mine is to "fix" it, in the unyielding and mortal sense that a collector fixes a butterfly to a mounting board with a pin. The exoskeleton is there, neatly preserved, but the butterfly itself—that kinetic enigma, that airborne splash of color and consciousness, that vibrant knot in the planetary tangle—isn't. Turn your attention inward to eavesdrop on the endosonus and, like Euridice, the ghostly melody is pulled forever into the shadows. Try to reflect on unreflective consciousness, and impurities flood into it like formaldehyde. Paradox and opacity turn memory into caricature, expressivity into death mask—and unlike worldly music, the endosonus cannot be recorded, rewound, and heard again. In the end, it remains an open question as to whether this attempt at a phenomenological description of an earworm has any real utility, beyond its function as a personal work of mourning, or a textual exorcism, or a tremulous question cast into the darkness.

Hello?
Is anybody there?

I have a haunting song, and a dead man's voice, in my head.
. . .
Can you hear them?

ACKNOWLEDGMENTS

I have benefited greatly from conversations with friends and colleagues who are associated with this edited volume, especially Harry Berger, Matt Rahaim, Friedlind Riedel, Roger Savage, Charles Sharp, Kati Szego, David VanderHamm, and Katharine Young. Thanks to Deborah Kapchan for the deep insights into the auditory imagination that she shared with me and with our students during our team-taught seminars in the NYU Department of Performance Studies. I'm also grateful for incisive feedback from people who attended talks I gave at Columbia University (especially Casey O'Callaghan, Lydia Goehr, and Paul Boghossian); the Universidade Federal do Rio Grande do Sul (especially Pedro Silva Marra, who kindly translated my talk into Portuguese, as well as José Cláudio S. Castanheira, Marcelo Bergamin Conter, and Cassio de Borba Lucas); the University of Virginia (especially Michelle Kisliuk, Fred Maus, Nomi Dave, and Bonnie Gordon); and the Peabody Conservatory (especially Elizabeth Tolbert). Eldritch Priest's work on earworms, and the thoughtful comments of the anonymous reviewers, have improved my work considerably. Thanks as always go to my intrepid and generous colleagues and students at NYU; to the esoteric and jovial collective at the Analogue Humanities Archive and Symposium (a group that, by design, has no internet footprint); and especially to my family, who are my constant interlocutors on the auditory imagination and a host of other topics. This essay's errors, omissions, and infelicities are the only elements to which I claim sole ownership.

NOTES

1. Jean-Luc Nancy presents hearing as comprehension in his 2007 treatise *Listening*: "If 'to hear' is to understand the sense (either in the so-called figurative sense, or in the so-called proper sense: to hear a siren, a bird, or a drum is already each time to understand at least the rough outline of a situation, a context if not a text), to listen is to be straining toward a possible meaning, and consequently one that is not immediately accessible" (6). In Nancy's sense of these terms, then, I may not be fully "hearing" the sounds of the imagination, but I am certainly "listening" to them.

2. The concept of "worlding" comes to me from Heidegger via Donna Haraway, who, in a now-famous riff on Marilyn Strathern's contention that "it matters what ideas we use to think other ideas," wrote, "[i]t matters what thoughts think thoughts. It matters what knowledges know knowledges. It matters what worlds world worlds. It matters what stories tell stories" (Haraway 2016, 34–35). I might continue this wordplay here by saying, "it matters what I's me me," a locution that produces the interesting corollary, "it matters what you's me you." In other words, the stakes of investigating the auditory imagination are high (e.g., it is one of the tools we use to build our inner world and to occupy the world we share), but they are also radically contingent: my account of listening to myself becoming myself does not automatically tell you what you will hear if you listen to yourself becoming yourself.

3. I have conducted formal and informal interviews with a few dozen of my colleagues and friends outside academia, surveyed around one hundred students in various classes at New York University (NYU), and engaged in concerted introspective exercises as described in section four of this essay. A particularly fruitful stage of the research process involved two graduate seminars on listening that I co-taught with Deborah Kapchan, where the auditory imagination was a central object of our inquiry.

4. See Johnson (2015), Cusick (2008), and Daughtry (2014; 2015, 98–102) for discussions of sound, trauma, and the auditory imagination.

5. See Luhrmann (2012, 39–100) and Friedson (2009, 15–41) for ethnographic accounts of such visitations. See Viveiros de Castro (1998) and Juárez (2018) for grounded philosophical accounts of Indigenous epistemologies that avoid strict subject/object and self/world binaries.

6. See, for example, Priest (2018), Hubbard (2010), and Levitin (2006).

7. Thanks to Harry Berger for sharing this insight with me. See Berger (2010, 11–12).

8. While I have adopted Grimshaw and Garner's terminology in this essay, I remain interested in the vibrant conversation on the ontology of sound that has been taking place among analytic philosophers in the twenty-first century. Some of them consider sound to be an emergent perception, as Grimshaw and Garner do; some equate sound with acoustic waves moving through a medium; and some understand sound as a material vibrational event that is distinct from both waves and perceptions. See Nudds and O'Callaghan (2009) for an overview of this debate.

9. MRI studies of people listening to recordings that have had gaps of silence inserted in them suggest that this is the case. When the gap appears, subjects continue to listen to the endosonic trace that, unbeknownst to them, was running in parallel with the exosonic recording the whole time. See, for example, Kraemer et al (2005). For an early and influential empirical account of the relationship between internal and external sensory perceptions, see Llinás and Paré (1991).

10. If your consciousness fails to establish such a mental representation of a sonorous event, and so is unable to shuttle back and forth between them, then you will find yourself in a situation that I have elsewhere called the "audible inaudible"—a zone of bodily exposure to sounds that are within your range of hearing but that are beyond the reach of your consciousness. See Daughtry (2015, 77–80).

11. This position dovetails with, but adds some phenomenological granularity to, the widespread position within philosophical aesthetics that listening involves perception and imagination. Theodore Gracyk (2019, 467) asserts that, "[f]or over three centuries, major figures in philosophical aesthetics have argued that aesthetic engagement with art—and therefore music—includes pleasures of the imagination (Addison and Steele 1965). So listening is both perceptual and imaginative." In this important essay, Gracyk goes on to critique what he sees as an excessive emphasis, within discourse on aesthetics and musical meaning, on the role played by the imagination.

12. See, for example, Ahmed (2006), Casey (2000a, 2000b), Ihde ([1976] 2007), Merleau-Ponty ([1945] 2012), Neimanis (2017), and Sartre ([1940] 2010).

13. Cogan's "astonishment" can be fruitfully compared to the sense of "wonder" that Richard Rorty (cited in Ingold 2014) finds notable in philosophy and poetry and that Tim Ingold (2014, 388–389) locates in the anthropological project.

14. For a classic, albeit fictionalized, account of wondrous failure, see "Pierre Menard, Author of the *Quixote*," in Borges (1998).

15. See Aristotle, *De Anima* iii 3. The European and American cast of characters in what follows marks this intellectual history as a provincial one. While there are clearly intellectual traditions around the world that are concerned with the nature of the imagination, my aim here is to lay out a few notable works in the phenomenological tradition, which accounts for the lack of demographic diversity in this list.

16. See Merleau-Ponty ([1945] 2012, 183) for a discussion of "inner speech." See also Bullot and Égré (2010), O'Callaghan (2016), and Badcock (2010) for cogent discussions of imagined sound.

17. See in particular pp. 117–136, 137–144, and 203–215.

18. The *Oxford Handbook of Sound and Imagination* was published after this essay was first drafted, which accounts for its superficial treatment here.

19. See, for example, Liikkanen (2012), Kraemer et al. (2005), and Hubbard (2010). Margulis (2013) contains a large bibliography of empirical sources on auditory imagery. A 2006 article by Steven Brown provides a particularly interesting discussion that is based in the

psychological literature. In the article, Brown, who is a professor of psychology, offers a phenomenological account of his "perpetual [imagined] music track"—the near-constant stream of musical imagery that he experiences throughout the day.

20. Understanding the temporal dimension of consciousness was for Husserl the most "important and difficult of phenomenological problems" (Husserl [1966] 1991, Supplementary Texts IV, No. 39, quoted in Jacquette 2018, 284).

21. Retention is different from "recollection," which is the willful act of recalling something that is now absent. Retention is the perceived presence of the immediate past.

22. As Matthew Rahaim reminds us in his essay in this volume, protention is ubiquitous within the world of embodied action. Your flexing hand protends the ball-in-flight it is about to grasp; the singer's indrawn breath "protends the melody to come." (See also Merleau-Ponty [1945] 2012, 106.)

23. "Anticipation," for Husserl, is the imagination of a future that has not yet occurred. Two pairs result: recollection and anticipation, organized around absence, flank retention and protention, both of which are perceived as present.

24. In Grimshaw and Garner's terms, the primal imprint corresponds to the exosonus, and retention and protention to the endosonus.

25. Indeed, Husserl's preferred object for demonstrating the extended nature of the living present is a musical melody (see, for example, [1966] 1991, 235–237).

26. Ihde ([1976] 2007, 134) describes an instance of willed alternation between perceptual and imagined modalities. Here I mean to assert an unwilled, constant oscillation between these modalities whenever we think we are listening to music.

27. See Margulis (2013) and Fink (2005) for varying takes on the interlocked themes of music, repeatability, memory, and the aesthetics of the loop.

28. Of course, while I am arguing here that the endosonus is a crucial part of musical experience, this doesn't mean that it is always prominent enough to draw your attention; the long tails of retention and protention are generally so much fainter and more ethereal than the vibrational primal imprint that you could easily go your entire life without noticing their existence. (If you are like me, you only began to perceive them after you were exposed to Husserl's description of them.) These two qualities of the endosonus—its relative subtlety in the face of exosonic music, and its submission to the movement of the exosonus through time—appear to be relatively stable features within the experience of listening to music in the world. "Relatively stable" does not mean universal, however, as the burgeoning disability studies literature is teaching us. See Bakan et al. (2018) for a series of conversations on musical perception and imagination among people with autism.

29. Young describes "impure reflection" as "the attempt to turn my attention to what I am doing while I am doing it or to what I am thinking as I am thinking it. It arises as I try to make sense of myself. I try, as it were, to catch myself in my own act. Impure reflection is consciousness's paradoxical attempt to make itself its own object, as if it could break itself off and look back at itself or fold back over on itself and experience itself from both the inside and the outside" (2011, 76).

30. See Sartre ([1940] 2010). This inability to reflect directly on the imagination also fuels Derrida's critique of the "metaphysics of presence" that he claimed undergirded, and to a great extent invalidated, Husserl's phenomenology. See Derrida ([1967] 2010), especially chapters 4–6.

31. *OED Online*, s.v., "surreal, adj.," accessed October 4, 2019, https://www.oed.com/. Another illuminating definition comes from Breton's *Manifesto of Surrealism*: Surrealism is

"[p]sychic automatism in its pure state, by which one proposes to express—verbally, by means of the written word, or in any other manner—*the actual functioning of thought*. Dictated by thought, in the absence of any control exercised by reason, exempt from any aesthetic or moral concern" ([1924] 2010, italics added).

32. On the speculative turn, phenomenology, and philosophy as "weird realism," see Harman (2010). For a phenomenological investigation of the surreality of the audiovisual, see Richardson (2012). Of course, the Surrealists had a politics, metaphysics, and Freudian orientation that I do not mean to import into this discussion of the sonic aggregate at this time.

33. Here are Breton's instructions for automatic writing, which conclude with a phrase that is particularly evocative for scholars of the endosonus: "After you have settled yourself in a place as favorable as possible to the concentration of your mind upon itself, have writing materials brought to you. Put yourself in as passive, or receptive, a state of mind as you can. Forget about your genius, your talents, and the talents of everyone else. Keep reminding yourself that literature is one of the saddest roads that leads to everything. Write quickly, without any preconceived subject, fast enough so that you will not remember what you're writing and be tempted to reread what you have written. The first sentence will come spontaneously, so compelling is the truth that with every passing second there is a sentence unknown to our consciousness which is only crying out to be heard. It is somewhat of a problem to form an opinion about the next sentence; it doubtless partakes both of our conscious activity and of the other, if one agrees that the fact of having written the first involves the minimum of perception. This should be of no importance to you, however; to a large extent, this is what is most interesting and intriguing about the Surrealist game. The fact still remains that punctuation no doubt resists the absolute continuity of the flow with which we are concerned, although it may seem as necessary as the arrangement of knots in a vibrating cord. Go on as long as you like. *Put your trust in the inexhaustible nature of the murmur* . . . " ([1924] 2010, italics added).

34. The term "haunting" also conjures the specter of Jacques Derrida, whose discussion of "hauntology" has been applied to *musique concrete*, reel-to-reel bleedthrough, and other musical phenomena that involve layered temporalities or time disjunctures. More broadly, as Elisabeth Loevlie writes, "[t]he term has proven itself a fruitful critical topos because it permits the discussion of a repeated, ungraspable roaming that colours our lives. Hauntology questions (or haunts!) its homophone concept ontology as it attempts to indicate that which moves insistently in-between being and non-being, existence and death. Hauntology therefore performs and releases what I shall describe as an *ontological quivering*" (2013, 337). Note also that Oliver Sacks gave the title "Haunted by Music" to the first part of his popular study *Musicophilia: Tales of Music and the Brain* (2008, 2). For a compelling study of "haunting and the sociological imagination," see Gordon (2008). For a seminal text on the musical subculture that gathers under the label "hauntology," see Fisher (2014).

35. Fred Maus has recently proposed a model of understanding "musical imagery" that includes all that I mention above. "Calling up the music from within oneself," he writes, "will usually involve sonic imagery but need not be confined to sonic imagery. Typically it involves much more than that, *feelings beyond sound* such as emotional and kinesthetic images. I think we can call all these types of imagery 'musical images'" (2018, 445, italics added).

36. Philosophers working under the umbrella term "Object-Oriented Ontology" often draw from Heidegger the insight that all objects are partially withdrawn, in that they are never fully exhausted by their perception, theorization, or use. Something always remains in excess and is inaccessible. See Harman (2011) for a representative articulation of this position. As I understand it, phenomenologists working before the advent of Object-Oriented Ontology tended to have a narrower understanding of the withdrawn nature of objects, one that was more closely tied to the observer's positionality. For example, when you look at a coin, its obverse face is unavailable to your gaze.

37. In *The Imaginary*, Sartre makes a similar claim about images: "Two colours . . . which maintain a certain discordant relation in reality can coexist in imagery without having any kind of relation between them. The objects exist only in so far as they are thought" ([1940] 2010, 10).

38. Or perhaps, as Berger has suggested, "it's not that the space in one's head is non-Euclidean, but that the spatiality of memory and imagination aren't 'in' the head at all. . . . [T]he language of inner and outer are really just forms of metaphysical shorthand, and they do a poor job of accounting for the nature of lived experience. While memories are clearly mind-dependent . . . memory isn't *inside* my head at all, and what is needed is a much more complex phenomenology. To my mind, showing the limits of the spatial language of the natural attitude and its flawed metaphysics is the main work that the epoché does" (personal correspondence, June 26, 2018).

39. See Howells (2012) for a review of *Titanic*-themed films that portray the scene of "Nearer, My God, to Thee" being performed as the ship sinks.

40. See Beckerman (2011) for a groundbreaking discussion of musical middles.

41. See Moreno (1999) for a discussion of Jarrett's vocalization within the context of his pianism.

42. For me, this experience echoes Merleau-Ponty: "When I find again the actual world such as it is, under my hands, under my eyes, up against my body, I find much more than an object: a Being of which my vision is a part, a visibility older than my operation or my acts. But this does not mean that there was a fusion or coinciding of me with it: on the contrary, this occurs because a sort of *dehiscence* opens my body in two, and because between my body looked at and my body looking, my body touched and my body touching [equally *my body listened to and my body listening*—JMD], there is overlapping or encroachment, so that we must say that the things pass into us as well as we into the things" ([1964] 1968, 123).

43. Here I am using "drastic" in Carolyn Abbate's sense: "[D]rastic connotes physicality, but also desperation and peril, involving a category of knowledge that flows from drastic actions or experiences and not from verbally mediated reasoning. Gnostic as its antithesis implies not just knowledge per se but making the opaque transparent, knowledge based on semiosis and disclosed secrets, reserved for the elite and hidden from others" (2004, 510). With this as a reference point, we can say that imagined sounds are radically drastic.

44. Compare this with Peter Mendelsund's description of immersion in a text: "The story of reading is a remembered story. When we read, we are immersed. And the more we are immersed, the less we are able, in the moment, to bring our analytic minds to bear upon the experience in which we are absorbed. Thus, when we discuss the feeling of reading we are really talking about the memory of having read. And this memory of reading is a false memory" (2014, 9).

45. For the record, the italicized phrases in the sentences that follow are from Cook, Ihde, Priest, myself, Sartre, myself, and my father, in that order.

46. See Stanyek and Piekut (2010) for a provocative examination of the agency of the dead.

47. See Taylor (2003) on the archive and the repertoire, Peterson (2021) on soundscapes and social relations, Horton (2017) on materiality and virtuality, Steingo and Sykes (2019) on local and global sound entanglements.

WORKS CITED

Abbate, Carolyn. 2004. "Music—Drastic or Gnostic?" *Critical Inquiry* 30 (3): 505–536.

Addison, Joseph, and Sir Richard Steele. 1965. *The Spectator*. Vol. 3, edited by D. F. Bond. Oxford, UK: Clarendon Press.

Ahmed, Sara. 2006. *Queer Phenomenology: Orientations, Objects, Others*. Durham, NC: Duke University Press.

Badcock, Johanna C. 2010. "The Cognitive Neuropsychology of Auditory Hallucinations: A Parallel Auditory Pathways Framework." *Schizophrenia Bulletin* 36 (3): 576–584.

Bakan, Michael, et al. 2018. *Speaking for Ourselves: Conversations on Life, Music, and Autism*. New York: Oxford University Press.

Beckerman, Michael. 2011. "The Strange Landscape of Middles." In *The Oxford Handbook of the New Cultural History of Music*, edited by Jane F. Fulcher, 163–181. New York: Oxford University Press.

Berger, Harris M. 1999. *Metal, Rock, and Jazz: Perception and the Phenomenology of Musical Experience*. Music/Culture Book Series. Middletown, CT: Wesleyan University Press.

Berger, Harris M. 2010. *Stance: Ideas about Emotion, Style, and Meaning for the Study of Expressive Culture*. Music/Culture Book Series. Middletown, CT: Wesleyan University Press.

Borges, Jorge Luis. 1998. "Pierre Menard, Author of the *Quixote*." In *Collected Fictions*, translated by Andrew Hurley, 88–95. New York: Penguin.

Breton, André. (1924) 2010. *Manifesto of Surrealism*. Critical Legal Thinking (website). https://criticallegalthinking.com/2010/11/24/manifesto-of-surrealism/.

Breton, André, and Philippe Soupault. (1920) 2020. *The Magnetic Fields*. Translated by Charlotte Mandell. New York: NYRB Poets.

Brown, Steven. 2006. "The Perpetual Music Track: The Phenomenon of Constant Musical Imagery." *Journal of Consciousness Studies* 13 (6): 43–62.

Bullot, Nicolas J., and Paul Égré. 2010. "Editorial: Objects and Sound Perception." *Review of Philosophy and Psychology* 1 (1): 5–17.

Casey, Edward. 2000a. *Imagination: A Phenomenological Study*. 2nd ed. Bloomington: Indiana University Press.

Casey, Edward. 2000b. *Remembering: A Phenomenological Study*. 2nd ed. Bloomington: Indiana University Press.

Cogan, John. 2009. "The Phenomenological Reduction." In *The Internet Encyclopedia of Philosophy*. https://iep.utm.edu/phen-red/.

Cook, Nicholas. 1990. *Music, Imagination, and Culture*. Oxford: Oxford University Press.

Crary, Jonathan. 2013. *24/7: Late Capitalism and the Ends of Sleep*. London: Verso.

Cusick, Suzanne. 1994. "On a Lesbian Relationship with Music: A Serious Effort Not to Think Straight." In *Queering the Pitch: The New Gay and Lesbian Musicology*, edited by Philip Brett, Gary Thomas, and Elizabeth Wood, 67–83. New York: Routledge.

Cusick, Suzanne. 2008. "'You Are in a Place That Is Out of the World . . .': Music in the Detention Camps of the 'Global War on Terror.'" *Journal of the Society for American Music* 2 (1): 1–26.

Daughtry, J. Martin. 2014. "Thanatosonics: Ontologies of Acoustic Violence." *Social Text* 119 (2): 25–51.

Daughtry, J. Martin. 2015. *Listening to War: Sound, Music, Trauma, and Survival in Wartime Iraq*. New York: Oxford University Press.

Derrida, Jacques. (1967) 2010. *Voice and Phenomenon: Introduction to the Problem of the Sign in Husserl's Phenomenology*. Translated by Leonard Lawlor. Evanston, IL: Northwestern University Press.

Elkaïm-Sartre, Arlette. 2010. "Historical Introduction." In *The Imaginary: A Phenomenological Psychology of the Imagination*, by Jean-Paul Sartre, translated by Jonathan Weber, vii–xii. New York: Routledge.

Fink, Robert. 2005. *Repeating Ourselves: American Minimal Music as Cultural Practice*. Berkeley: University of California Press.

Fisher, Mark. 2014. *My Life: Writings on Depression, Hauntology, and Lost Futures*. Winchester: Zero Books.

Friedson, Steven M. 1996. *Dancing Prophets: Musical Experience in Tumbuka Healing*. Chicago: University of Chicago Press.

Friedson, Steven M. 2009. *Remains of Ritual: Northern Gods in a Southern Land*. Chicago: University of Chicago Press.

Goehr, Lydia. 1992. *The Imaginary Museum of Musical Works: An Essay in the Philosophy of Music*. New York: Oxford University Press.

Gordon, Avery. 2008. *Ghostly Matters: Haunting and the Sociological Imagination*. 2nd ed. Minneapolis: University of Minnesota Press.

Gracyk, Theodore. 2019. "Imaginative Listening to Music." In *The Oxford Handbook of Sound and Imagination*, vol. 2, edited by Mark Grimshaw-Aagaard, Mads Walther-Hansen, and Martin Knakkergaard, 467–488. New York: Oxford University Press.

Grimshaw, Mark, and Tom Garner. 2015. *Sonic Virtuality: Sound as Emergent Perception*. New York: Oxford University Press.

Grimshaw-Aagaard, Mads Walther-Hansen, and Martin Knakkergaard, eds. 2019. *The Oxford Handbook of Sound and Imagination*. 2 vols. New York: Oxford University Press.

Haraway, Donna J. 2016. *Staying with the Trouble: Making Kin in the Chthulucene*. Durham, NC: Duke University Press.

Harman, Graham. 2010. "On the Horror of Phenomenology: Lovecraft and Husserl," *Collapse: Philosophical Research and Development* 4: 333–365.

Harman, Graham. 2011. *The Quadruple Object*. Winchester, UK: Zero Books.

Helmreich, Stefan. 2015. *Sounding the Limits of Life: Essays in the Anthropology of Biology and Beyond*. Princeton: Princeton University Press.

Horton, Jessica L. 2017. *Art for an Undivided Earth*. Durham, NC: Duke University Press.

Howells, Richard. 2012. "One Hundred Years of the Titanic on Film." *Historical Journal of Film, Radio and Television* 32 (1): 73–93.

Hubbard, Timothy L. 2010. "Auditory Imagery: Empirical Findings." *Psychological Bulletin* 136 (2): 302–329.

Husserl, Edmund. (1913) 1962. *Ideas: General Introduction to Pure Phenomenology*. Translated by William Ralph Boyce Gibson. New York: Collier Books.

Husserl, Edmund. (1966) 1991. *On the Phenomenology of the Consciousness of Internal Time (1893–1917)*. Translated by John Barnett Brough. Dordrecht, Netherlands: Kluwer Academic Publishers.

Ihde, Don. (1976) 2007. *Listening and Voice: Phenomenologies of Sound*. 2nd ed. Albany: State University of New York Press.

Ingold, Tim. 2014. "That's Enough about Ethnography!" *HAU: Journal of Ethnographic Theory* 4 (1): 383–395.

Jacquette, Dale. 2018. "Cracking the Hard Problem of Consciousness." In *The Bloomsbury Companion to the Philosophy of Consciousness*, edited by Dale Jacquette, 258–285. New York: Bloomsbury.

Johnson, Jenny Olivia. 2015. "The Sounds That Know: Synaesthesia, Sexual Trauma, and a Musicological Confession." *Women and Music: A Journal of Gender and Culture* 19: 133–141.

Juárez, Nicolás. 2018. "Each of Us Is a Council House: Talking to Spirits, Psychoanalysis, and Language." *Critical Ethnic Studies* 4 (2): 141–163.

Kelly, Michael R. n.d. "Phenomenology and Time-Consciousness." In *The Internet Encyclopedia of Philosophy*. https://iep.utm.edu/phe-time/.

Kraemer, D. J. M., C. N. Macrae, A. E. Green, and W. M. Kelly. 2005. "Sound of Silence Activates Auditory Cortex." *Nature* 434: 158.

Kun, Josh. 2005. *Audiotopia: Music, Race, and America*. Berkeley: University of California Press.

Le Guin, Elisabeth. 2005. *Boccherini's Body: An Essay in Carnal Musicology*. Berkeley: University of California Press.

Levitin, Daniel. 2006. *This Is Your Brain on Music: The Science of a Human Obsession*. New York: Penguin.

Liikkanen, L. A. 2012. "Inducing Involuntary Musical Imagery: An Experimental Study." *Musicae Scientiae* 16: 217–234.

Llinás, R. R., and D. Paré. 1991. "Of Dreaming and Wakefulness." *Neuroscience* 44 (3): 521–536.

Loevlie, Elisabeth M. 2013. "Faith in the Ghosts of Literature: Poetic Hauntology in Derrida, Blanchot and Morrison's *Beloved*." *Religions* 4: 336–350.

Luhrmann, T. M. 2012. *When God Talks Back: Understanding the American Evangelical Relationship with God*. New York: Vintage Books.

Margulis, Elizabeth H. 2013. *On Repeat: How Music Plays the Mind*. New York: Oxford University Press.

Maus, Fred. 2018. "Listening and Possessing." In *The Oxford Handbook of Music Listening in the 19th and 20th Centuries*, edited by Christian Thorau and Hansjakob Ziemer, 441–461. New York: Oxford University Press. http://doi.org/10.1093/oxfordhb/9780190466961.013.21.

Mendelsund, Peter. 2014. *What We See When We Read*. New York: Vantage.

Merleau-Ponty, Maurice. (1945) 2012. *Phenomenology of Perception*. Translated by Donald A. Landes. London: Routledge.

Merleau-Ponty, Maurice. (1964) 1968. *The Visible and the Invisible*. Translated by Alphonso Lingis. Evanston, IL: Northwestern University Press.

Methodist Episcopal Church. 1878. *Hymnal of the Methodist Episcopal Church*. New York: Nelson and Phillips; Cincinnati: Hitchcock and Walden.

Moreno, Jairo. 1999. "Body'n'Soul? Voice and Movement in Keith Jarrett's Pianism." *Musical Quarterly* 83 (1): 75–92.

Murdoch, Iris. 1980. *Sartre: Romantic Realist*. New York: Barnes & Noble.

Nancy, Jean-Luc. 2007. *Listening*. Translated by Charlotte Mandel. New York: Fordham University Press.

Neimanis, Astrida. 2017. *Bodies of Water: Posthuman Feminist Phenomenology*. New York: Bloomsbury.

Nudds, Matthew, and Casey O'Callaghan, eds. 2009. *Sounds and Perception: New Philosophical Essays*. Oxford: Oxford University Press.

O'Callaghan, Casey. 2016. "Objects for Multisensory Perception." *Philosophical Studies* 173 (5): 1269–1289.

Peterson, Marina. 2021. *Atmospheric Noise: The Indefinite Urbanism of Los Angeles*. Durham, NC: Duke University Press.

Priest, Eldritch. 2018. "Earworms, Daydreams, and Cognitive Capitalism." *Theory, Culture & Society* 35 (1): 141–162.

Rahaim, Matthew. 2023 "Not Just One, Not Just Now: Relational Voices in Time." *The Oxford Handbook of the Phenomenology of Music Cultures*, edited by Harris M. Berger, Friedlind Riedel, and David VanderHamm. New York: Oxford University Press. https://doi.org/10.1093/oxfordhb/9780190693879.013.2

Rice, Timothy. 1994. *May It Fill Your Soul: Experiencing Bulgarian Music*. Chicago: University of Chicago Press.

Richardson, John. 2012. *An Eye for Music: Popular Music and the Audiovisual Surreal*. New York: Oxford University Press.

Sacks, Oliver. 2008. *Musicophilia: Tales of Music and the Brain*. New York: Vintage Books.

Sartre, Jean-Paul. (1940) 2010. *The Imaginary: A Phenomenological Psychology of the Imagination*. Translated by Jonathan Weber. New York: Routledge.

Sartre, Jean-Paul. (1943) 1964. *Being and Nothingness*. Translated by Hazel Barnes. New York: Citadel Press.

Stanyek, Jason, and Ben Piekut. 2010. "Deadness: Technologies of the Intermundane." *TDR: The Drama Review* 54 (1): 14–38.

Steingo, Gavin, and Jim Sykes, eds. 2019. *Remapping Sound Studies*. Durham, NC: Duke University Press.

Stone, Ruth M. (1982) 2010. *Let the Inside Be Sweet: The Interpretation of Music Event among the Kpelle of Liberia*. Bloomington, IN: Trickster Press.

Taylor, Diana. 2003. *The Archive and the Repertoire: Performing Cultural Memory in the Americas*. Durham, NC: Duke University Press.

Viveiros de Castro, Eduardo. 1998. "Cosmological Deixis and Amerindian Perspectivism." *Journal of the Royal Anthropological Institute* 4 (3): 469–488.

Young, Katharine. 2011. "Gestures, Intercorporeity, and the Fate of Phenomenology in Folklore." *Journal of American Folklore* 124 (492): 55–87.

CHAPTER 6

....

YOUNG PEOPLE'S LIVED EXPERIENCE OF MUSIC IN EVERYDAY LIFE

Psychological and Phenomenological Perspectives

....

RUTH HERBERT

UNDERSTANDINGS and applications of phenomenology within contemporary music psychology appear in some ways distinct from those in ethnomusicology. A prime example is the frequent conceptualization, within the field of psychology in general, of phenomenology as the study of subjective experience, understood as "the analysis of mental experience rather than behaviour" (Colman, 2015). This suggests an approach centered on the (internal) contents of consciousness—processes of cognition, perception, and affect—rather than an understanding of experience as necessarily *situated*, the sum of a systemic interaction between internal and external phenomena, self, and environment. In fact, a number of empirical methodologies grounded in approaches from phenomenology's philosophical tradition are available to researchers to use in order to tap qualities of individual lived experience. Potentially, however, psychologists (including music psychologists) may employ these tools regardless of the extent of their personal knowledge of philosophical literature (Wertz 2015, 96), which might suggest that the connection between these two disciplines is fairly superficial. This is far from the case, as this chapter will demonstrate.

Music psychology, ethnomusicology, and phenomenology were closely interlinked during the late nineteenth and early twentieth centuries (Clayton 2009, 75), a circumstance that is well known but is nevertheless intriguing. One preoccupation of comparative musicology (the forerunner of ethnomusicology) centered on psychological study of the perception of tone across cultures. This is evident in the work of pioneering figures in the field such as Charles Myers, author of a 1911 textbook on experimental psychology; Carl Stumpf, author of the 1883 *Tonpsychologie*; and Stumpf's student Erich von Hornbostel, who later served as Stumpf's coauthor and assistant at the Berlin Psychologisches Institut. Stumpf was a philosophy professor who had studied with Franz Brentano (frequently cited as a forerunner of the phenomenological movement; see Huerner [2017]) and acted (as Berger et al. note in the first chapter of this volume) as Edmund Husserl's habilitation supervisor.[1] An additional (and important) early link between phenomenology and psychology was a focus on qualities of individual experience, apparent in the work of Wilhelm Wundt and his pupil E. B. Titchener, who used what is now termed "classical introspection" to inaugurate in Germany and America the psychological study of experience as a scientific discipline (Pekala 1991, 14).

The developmental trajectories of both music psychology and ethnomusicology during the twentieth century meant that potential connections with topics and ideas from phenomenology's philosophical tradition significantly receded from scholarly view. In the case of music psychology, the study of processes of mind and—more broadly—consciousness was displaced and discredited during the early twentieth century by the rise of behaviorism, with its emphasis on scientific and objective investigative methods and observable stimulus-response behaviors. When a return to the notion of mentation as a legitimate area for psychological enquiry occurred, it was in the form of cognitive psychology, centering on the lab-based study of specific mental processes such as perception, attention, and memory. In terms of cognitive music psychology, this manifested in a preoccupation with the ways listeners and performers perceived and processed musical attributes such as pitch and timbre—that is, the relationship between musical structures and psychological processes, rather than a focus on musical experiences as multimodal totalities (Clarke 2005; Clarke et al. 2010).

While structuralist-cognitive approaches within psychology and music psychology were particularly dominant between the 1960s and mid-1990s, close connections between psychology and phenomenology endured. The growth of the field of phenomenological psychology was reflected in the founding of the *Journal of Phenomenological Psychology* by psychologist Amedeo Giorgi in 1970. The adoption of phenomenology to analyze the experience of qualities of musical works and sounds (characteristics such as motion and stability, temporality, foreground and background, focus, and fringe) was marked by a series of landmark publications by Don Ihde ([1976] 2007), Thomas Clifton (1983), and Lawrence Ferrara (1984, 1991).[2] Phenomenological approaches were increasingly adopted in music therapy research from the 1980s. (For an overview, see Ghetti 2016.)

The application of phenomenological approaches to the psychological study of musical experiences in so-called real-world (naturalistic) contexts is far more recent. One of the most extensive enquiries to date has been the pioneering research of Alf Gabrielsson (2011; Gabrielsson 2016) on the phenomenology of strong experiences of music (SEM), which has been the catalyst for much of my work. One reason for the sparsity of phenomenological studies of musical experiences in naturalistic contexts within the music psychology field is the domination of emotion models as explicatory frames for individual experience. The need to "focus on music experiences that do not clearly fall within the category of emotional responses" was highlighted by the *Oxford*

Handbook of Music and Emotion (Juslin and Sloboda 2010, 940), in which the editors identified the study of the phenomenology of music experiences as a key future direction for music psychology research.

In this chapter I explore the phenomenology of children's and adolescents' unfolding lived experiences of music. My primary focus here is on music listening (particularly listening to recorded music), as opposed to *all* kinds of musical practices (such as composition and performance). The transition from prepubescence through adolescence into early adulthood constitutes a period of intense development and flux, which is evident in internal (neuro-psycho-physiological) and external (sociocultural) changes that serve to mediate experience. Music is a pervasive presence in young people's daily lives, affording a popular means of self-orientation and self-regulation. Children and teenagers utilize music to negotiate daily routines, interact with micro- and macro-sociocultural environments, frame and modulate mood and emotion, and—via the process of enculturation—accumulate a range of subconsciously acquired meanings and ways of listening (Herbert and Dibben 2018; Schubert and McPherson 2016). I draw here on selected findings from a three-year inquiry into ten- to eighteen-year-olds' engagement with music, both as listeners and as performers, in the United Kingdom. The catalyst for this work was my previous study of the psychological processes involved in everyday music listening scenarios for a sample of individuals between ages fifteen and eighty-five. In a sense, both of these empirical studies lie at the intersection of music psychology and ethnomusicology. They explore processes of mind such as attention, awareness, memory, arousal, thought, and imagination, but—in accordance with ecological approaches to perception (Clarke 2005; Gibson 1979)—they acknowledge experience as necessarily *situated*, arising as the sum of a network of interacting variables. These variables include (1) the experiencer, including their habitual ways of responding, mood, intention, personality, age, and training; (2) the affordances of the music with which they engage; and (3) context (i.e., the particular environment, whether alone or with others). Additionally, both research projects draw on perspectives from consciousness studies, highlighting the presence of subtle shifts of consciousness in daily life interactions with music, particularly the processes of absorption (effortless involvement) and dissociation (detachment).[3] What distinguishes the young people and music study discussed here from my earlier work is the exploration of ways in which individual variables such as age and training may mediate experience.

I begin with a brief contextual backstory to the young people and music project, before outlining its aims and briefly explaining one of the methodologies employed (interpretative phenomenological analysis). I then discuss the phenomenology of young people's interactions with music, using firsthand reports of experiences, grouped under a sequence of emergent themes. Within this discussion, I relate the psychological characteristics of musical involvement for this age group to topics within phenomenology's philosophical tradition. I conclude with a reflection on the relationship between philosophical and psychological understandings of phenomenology, as well as potential relationships between phenomenological psychology and phenomenological ethnomusicology.

EXPERIENCING THE EVERYDAY

The last two decades have witnessed an upsurge of scholarly interest, within the music psychology field, in the role of music in the everyday lives of individuals in the industrialized West. (See Clarke et al. 2010 and Lamont et al. 2016 for overviews.) Notably, experience sampling methodologies (ESMs), which were originally developed by Mihaly Csikszentmihalyi and his colleagues (e.g., Csikszentmihalyi and Larson 1987) to probe the frequency and characteristics of what they called "flow" experiences, have been adopted to map real-world listening behaviors across large groups (Lamont et al. 2016, 711). However, the focal point of a significant number of everyday music listening studies has been on function—the "when, where, why" aspects of music adopted as a self-regulatory resource—as opposed to the assembly of detailed accounts of the psychological qualities of unfolding, lived experience.[4] Additionally, the musical experiences of children and young adolescents continue to be underrepresented, even though "for many young people, music is key to how they orient themselves in their lives" (Macdonald et al. 2012, 6).

The everyday musical practices of young people have most commonly been studied separately from those of adults, meaning that the literatures concerning these different age groups can appear relatively independent of each other. This is evident in their contrasting underlying concerns and the extant research they reference. Studies centering on young people's experiences of music have frequently been framed by research concerns regarding music education in school, including the issue of the disjunction between young people's experiences of music in and outside school in the United Kingdom (Boal-Palheiros and Hargreaves 2001; Lamont et al. 2003; North et al. 2000); the development of musical competencies and the impact of music upon social and emotional development and upon spatial, language, and reading skills (Hetland and Winner 2004); the pluralistic nature of young people's culture (e.g., Campbell 2010); the value of informal "enculturative" learning (North et al. 2000; North and Hargreaves 2008, 338); the primacy of music listening as an adolescent leisure activity (e.g., Boal-Palheiros and Hargreaves 2001; Lamont et al. 2003; North et al. 2000); age-related differences in music listening (Hargreaves 1982; LeBlanc et al. 1996); and the influence of digital technology on music education (Finney and Burnard 2008) and listening practices (Campbell 2010; Herbert 2011; Lury 2002).

The role of music in emotional regulation and mood management has been particularly emphasized (e.g., Chamorro-Premuzic and Furnham 2007; DeNora 2000; North et al. 2000; Saarikallio and Erkkilä 2007), including ways in which individuals (consciously or unconsciously) may adopt particular strategies that have adaptive or maladaptive potential for well-being (Saarikallio et al. 2015). Some evidence suggests that antecedent-focused strategies such as cognitive reappraisal of a situation or emotion via listening to music are associated with well-being, while reactive (response-focused) music listening strategies involving dissociation (variously termed detachment suppression, distraction, or avoidance) may be associated with depression or a negative mindset (e.g., Chin and Rickard 2014; Randall et al. 2014). Other evidence points toward a more nuanced picture of music listening employed to effect detachment from concerns of self, occupation, or situation. For example, Tia DeNora has provided an account of music as a means of positive asylum, offering "room and respite" from aspects of the environment (2013, 57).

As will be clear from this brief review, the music psychology literature has demonstrated an overtly nomothetic bias; that is, it seeks to establish common behavioral and personal tendencies across broad samples of young people. Idiographically based inquiries conveying a richer and more comprehensive view of the totality of experience are, to date, less common, but they nevertheless form a significant and expanding body of literature. Topics have included the role of music in adolescents' (aged fourteen to seventeen) mood regulation (Saarikallio and Erkkilä 2007), musical and nonmusical aesthetic experiences of fifteen- to sixteen-year-olds (Finnäs 2006), and retrospective descriptions of adolescent SEM (Gabrielsson 2011). In a landmark qualitative study of the musical lives of prepubescent children (from three to twelve years of age), Patricia Campbell (2010), influenced by Susan. D. Crafts, Daniel Cavicchi, and Charles Keil's landmark Music in Daily Life project (1993), tapped the lived experiences of children from varied sociocultural backgrounds via semistructured and open-ended interviews, nonparticipant observation, and ethnographic descriptions of children's informal musicking in varied real-world settings. She observed that "children's engagement in music frequently is paid minimal attention by teachers and parents" (Campbell 2010, 5). One explanation for the comparatively slim body of literature examining the phenomenology of children's and adolescents' musical experiences may well be that, within music psychology, the incentive to study young people's interactions with music is frequently aligned with the identification of practical applications of music for the promotion of well-being (for the use of educators, health professionals, and young people themselves), rather than with an exploration of the nature of experiences per se. Another reason for this is sampling convenience, as it is easier for researchers to recruit participants from within their immediate sample pool of undergraduates, awarding course credits as an attractor for taking part in empirical studies.

THE YOUNG PEOPLE AND MUSIC PROJECT

The young people and music project was a three-phase, mixed-method empirical inquiry designed to explore the psychological characteristics of children's and teenagers' experiences of listening to and making music in everyday scenarios in the United Kingdom. It involved 654 young people in total, ranging in age from ten to eighteen. All the young people who volunteered to take part regularly listened to music, but their levels of musical involvement and formal training differed, as did their sociodemographic backgrounds.[5] Each phase of the project addressed a particular

Table 6.1. *Young People and Music Project* Phases and Themes

Phase	Research Topic	Methodology	Participants	Theoretical Framework and Themes
1	Phenomenological characteristics of children's and adolescents' everyday musical experiences	Semistructured interviews 14-day diary study IPA	59	Social and applied psychology, developmental psychology, psychological phenomenology, ethnomusicology, ecological perspectives on listening, kinds of consciousness, trancing, ASC
2	Associations between musical involvement (listening to and making music) and personality, age, training, and gender	Online questionnaire study	511	Individual differences literature, including personality psychology and developmental psychology
3	Young people's holistic understanding of music	Online listening study—free responses to 20 experimenter-selected excerpts	84	Music aesthetics, social and applied psychology, intra- and extramusical meaning, heteronomous and autonomous listening modes

aspect of musical experience, informed by a primary theoretical vantage point or body of literature. The phases are summarized in Table 6.1.

The focus of this chapter is on phase one of the project—the phenomenological characteristics of children's and adolescents' experiences of music in everyday life.[6] In this phase, each individual initially completed a semistructured interview that was approximately one hour in length. The topics of function, context, and uses of music in daily life and lived experience were addressed by asking questions relating to "activation (extent of engagement with environment), attention span (wide or narrow), attentional focus (external/internal), alterations of sensory awareness, etc." (Herbert 2012, 425). In a later part of the project, the young people recorded their music listening experiences for a period of fourteen days in an unstructured diary (i.e., a diary employing free descriptions of recent experiential episodes).[7] Interviews and retrospective reports of experiences were analyzed using interpretative phenomenological analysis (IPA). Originally developed by UK psychologist Jonathan A. Smith, IPA is a qualitative methodology first adopted by researchers within the field of health psychology (Smith et al. 2009) but now utilized across a wide variety of fields, including the arts (Brooks 2015). Later in this chapter, I will discuss in detail the basis of IPA in phenomenology's philosophical tradition, but, in essence, IPA is an iterative methodology, involving multiple readings of interview or diary data from which emergent themes are inductively derived. It is idiographic in that analysis centers on individual cases before any comparison is attempted. IPA involves what has been termed a "double hermeneutic," as it "recognises both researcher and participant as intrinsically sense-making creatures" (Brooks 2015, 644). As Smith and Mike Osborn put it, in IPA "the researcher is trying to make sense of the participants trying to make sense of their world" (2004, 51).

Following analysis of individual interviews and diaries, cross-comparison highlighted four types of experiential episodes that appeared particularly prevalent from prepubescence to late adolescence. These featured the use of music (spontaneously or volitionally) to (1) create a sense of momentum, energy, excitement, and connection; (2) facilitate multimodal/multimedia involvement; (3) trigger daydreams or imaginative fantasies; and (4) dissociate or "zone out." It is to the phenomenology of these experiences that I now turn.[8]

Experiencing Music as a Teen or Tween

Momentum, Energy, Excitement, and Connection

Across the age range, young people described scenarios in which musical attributes (commonly a regularly marked pulse, rapid tempo, loud volume, and rhythmic and melodic repetition) served to enhance everyday experience, creating a sense of excitement, energy, momentum, and connection. This clearly aligns with a strategy Suvi Saarikallio and Jaakko Erkkilä termed "strong sensation," which they highlighted in their study of fourteen- to seventeen-year-olds' self-regulatory uses of music (2007, 98) and also with the psychological mechanisms of "rhythmic entrainment" and "emotional contagion" identified by Patrik Juslin and his collaborators (2010, 625). Episodes were solitary or social and inevitably involved movement (i.e., moving the body to music or heightened perception of movement in surroundings). Typical was an immersive, frequently multimodal interaction with music. This emerged as an evolved way of listening that was well established by prepubescence but then became more nuanced and multifaceted during adolescence, as illustrated by the examples to follow:

> This morning I listened to my new favorite song "212 (Clean Version)" by a rapper called Azealia Banks. It's like going on a rollercoaster. The music gets under my skin and into my body and I can't help but move. . . . It makes me feel ecstatic because the beat and the rhythm are addictive . . . the music flows through me, and I express it by dancing or working the chords out on the piano. I also rap along to her music. . . . I feel like I NEED to dance. I usually dance for about twenty minutes before school. I do the same when I come home. I have a drink and a piece of toast and then I listen to music, dance, rap, and play [piano]. . . . Dancing is my *best* way of concentrating on music. (Samuel, aged ten, diary entry)

This episode reveals an embodied, absorbed immersion in music, where attention is primarily present centered and distributed between different foci. Music is understood as an invitation to action on multiple levels—physical, cognitive, and emotional—and the processes of creating and receiving music blend together. The emphasis is on a high-energy entrainment to music; in a sense, Samuel "becomes" the music ("the music gets under my skin . . . flows through me"). Present-centered, nonreflective, active musical engagement (moving or wanting to move to music) appears particularly common for ten-to twelve-year-olds (Herbert and Dibben 2018). Scholars in both ethnomusicology and music psychology have framed experiences of music in terms of the various kinds of consciousness that it involves, and it is pertinent to do so here as well. Experiences centering on immediate perceptual engagement (rather than being informed by associations and memories) can be seen as privileging what has been termed *core* or *primary* consciousness (Damasio 1999; Edelman 1992).[9] By contrast, the next example can be seen as representative of more than one kind of consciousness. Fifteen-year-old Sarah listens to dubstep as she walks into town:

> Playing "Reptile" [by Skrillex]—the beat at the beginning immediately gets me moving, and the repetitiveness, buildup of noise and layers in the music slowly intensify the listening. . . . The drop is my favorite bit, where the buildup "drops" and even more sound and movement in the music appears. At the moment, my mind isn't wandering, but just following and eagerly wanting more sound. It [the music] . . . makes me high but also relaxed. . . . I think it's because the music is doing the noise and screaming and shouting so I don't have to. Walking down the street I feel so empowered and confident, striding to the beat, smiling and biting my lip—excited by the fact I'm listening to music I know so many people hate.

One of the most common scenarios for everyday music listening in the industrialized West is during what individuals may perceive to be a "routine period of empty time" (Bull 2003, 370), particularly travel. Music serves to configure the perceived tempo of experience, while mobile headphone listening (an extremely common practice for teenagers) also enables individuals to create customized, private spaces—so-called auditory bubbles (Bull 2007)—within public contexts. Sarah is visually connected with her surroundings, noticing the people she passes, but sonically disconnected from them, the music affording experimentation with a rebellious and powerful identity that remains (mainly) unobservable by those around her. The speed of the track (c. 110 bpm), slightly below the 120 bpm identified as the optimal walking tempo for synchronization with music (Styns et al. 2007), supports the "striding" walk and sense of confidence she describes. Music scaffolds the perceived temporal pace of experience in the manner of a soundtrack, enabling her to feel part of a vital environment.[10] The musical attributes of the track mediate her experience in two key ways: (1) repetition and regular buildups of texture and volume lead to a reduction of inner languaging and a raised level of arousal, and (2) the recording specifies a virtual space, in terms of depth (near and far sounds), movement (panning from left to right), and content (electronic sounds, interspersed with human shouts of "reptile," modified by high levels of reverb) that create the sense of a surreal, robotic sci-fi world. Sarah is both present in the real world and absent from it. Her absorption in qualities of sound appears present centered (representative of primary or core consciousness), but it is interspersed with reflections about the self and identity (representative of what Antonio Damasio [1999] and Gerald Edelman [1992] have respectively termed *extended* or *higher-order* consciousness).

Multimodal/Multimedia Involvement

Heteronomous listening, where attention is multiply directed toward a range of musical and extramusical sources, is recognized as the default mode of listening for the majority of children and teenagers in the industrialized West.[11] The majority of listening episodes reported by the young people and music study were multisensory (typically involving a perceptual blending of musical attributes with aspects of surroundings, altering or enhancing how they were seen) or multimodal (e.g., imagining being "inside" a video while listening to the audio on the move). The intentional use of music to blend together actual and virtual worlds—in effect to customize consensual reality—reflects the increasing ubiquity of digital technologies within daily life, and evidence suggests that this practice increases across adolescence. Some teenagers stated that, without music to "make sense" of the world around them, they felt disconnected from their daily lives, perceiving their surroundings as "static," "dead," "empty," "colorless," or "black and white."

Young people frequently reported multimodal experiences arising in conjunction with computer games, some of which featured media multitasking (a phenomenon that has shown a sharp upward trend due to the increasing range of social media apps, video-sharing websites, and music streaming services), as a comparison of the following two reports of computer gaming will illustrate:

> I look at music in a more abstract, visual, and frankly beautiful way when I play *AudioSurf*. . . . I found myself focusing on small details of songs or a hidden meaning within the lyrics while I steered my craft around the various blocks of the map . . . a split-brain thing. Definitely high-energy—sometimes I'm panicking about keeping my columns of blocks from overfilling, and sometimes I'm thinking about the music itself. . . . Sometimes I would imagine a fictional scene, triggered by a particular song section, and the gameplay became autonomous. *AudioSurf* took up my whole week. Every evening, for about four hours, with breaks to get drinks, food, etc. (Amelia, fifteen)

> On the Xbox playing *Halo Reach*, my attention is in several places. The music in the game comes in from the speakers on the front [of the monitor], my music comes in from the iPod dock, and I hear the people I'm talking to through the headset. I do hear the sounds from the game as well—they're louder than the music—if you fire your gun you'll hear it. . . . I'll be playing Xbox and might want to change the track I'm listening to, and then I'll go on Facebook for a minute and I might get a text, have to

reply to that and go back to Xbox again. They're all like going on at the same time—it doesn't feel like I'm leaving one [activity] . . . they're still sort of there. . . . I get really into it—an alternate world. . . . It's weird actually—I don't feel aggressive. Most of the time it's like kind of calming. (Jake, fourteen)

The different nature of these two computer games is one determinant of the differing experiences that the young people have in these games. Both provide virtual worlds in which the game player is the protagonist. However, *AudioSurf* is a "puzzle racer," played alone, where individuals steer virtual "crafts" through abstract landscapes to the accompaniment of self-chosen music (which determines the speed of the ride), clustering blocks of the same color together. The emphasis is on repetition of a small number of visual stimuli, which move, rhythmically and temporally, in a way that is congruent with the selected music. By contrast, *Halo Reach* is a "first-person shooter" game, where the player interacts with others (represented on screen by avatars), featuring weapon-based combat against a rapidly changing backdrop and a given soundtrack, including diegetic sounds (e.g., guns firing). Amelia and Jake both describe an experiential mode that is familiar, is regularly accessed, and incorporates a present-centered sense of immersion—a broad (equanimous) awareness of a number of visual and auditory phenomena together with a distributed attentional focus. Nevertheless, the two reports are distinct in a number of ways. Amelia's highlights a fluctuation between differing kinds of consciousness—from an "in the moment" (core consciousness) external focus on musical attributes or visual stimuli to internal reflection about the meaning of lyrics (extended consciousness), which at times make task completion automatic. The limited, repetitive stimuli create a hypnotic-like alteration of experience. Jake's report highlights a different type of involvement, marked by a restlessly distributed and shifting attentional focus and arising from a bombardment of sensory impacts, not all of which are congruent or perceived to interact.

Daydreams and Imaginative Fantasies

Daydreaming or mind wandering to music emerges as one of the most common forms of multimodal experience for children and teenagers, affording rejuvenation or temporary respite from everyday pressures and responsibilities. This type of imaginative involvement with music occurs spontaneously from infancy, evolving with the development of an extended conscious awareness as children engage in a process of musical meaning-making that arises from the repeated pairing of music with extramusical stimuli (evident in film, TV, computer games, and live contexts where music occurs; see Schubert and McPherson 2016). Cross-comparison of young people's reports of musical daydreams supports the notion of a change in the lived experience of music across this time span in terms of the contents of daydreams and the kind of meaning-making apparent, as illustrated to follow.[12]

Musical daydreaming in prepubescence and early adolescence (from age ten to around age thirteen) frequently displayed a strongly narrative quality, employing fictional settings and characters:

> I have a big habit of having daydreams, and when I'm listening to music I just seem to—all the daydreams seem to come out. . . . When I was listening to [a piece by] Astor Piazzolla ["Sex-tet" from the album *Luna*] in the car there was this rather creepy track, and I imagined there was someone being murdered—a small child actually, and there was this evil killer who we don't know of. No-one's ever seen their face as it's hidden under a black hood. . . . It sees a little poor baby. It's had some trouble with being a child in its previous life and it thinks that all children are horrible due to what's happened to it in its childhood. It looks at the child and it starts to feel sorry for the child. Then it forgets, throws it into the river, and starts murdering a whole load of other kids. . . . That's one of the stories. I can't really remember all of the stories I dream about. It's usually quite dramatic. (Lily, eleven)

Lily describes a process of what might be termed "storying" to music that is familiar to her and that she expects to occur. The episode features an inwardly directed attentional focus, marked by imaginative involvement. The contents of the daydream connect with musical attributes, indicating that she has absorbed a range of associative codes via the process of enculturation. The semiotician Philip Tagg has adopted the term "anaphone" from the word "analogy" to describe sound attributes perceived as similar to extramusical sounds, movements, or touch (2013). In the Piazzolla piece she hears, there are a number of anaphones that might mimic sinister actions (e.g., repeated, rapid, upward violin glissandi signifying the sharpening of a knife, and aggressive bass drum strokes signifying thumping or hitting). The visual imagery generated could have taken the form of a random succession of images but instead is spontaneously organized to form a complete, linear narrative.

By contrast, from mid-adolescence, musical daydreams featured an upturn in autobiographical references and were less likely to form linear narratives, instead of presenting as a dream-like succession of images that referenced ideal or alternate virtual realities. Episodes were often described as "daydreams," appeared highly absorbing, and were particularly common when traveling:

> ZAK: There's one piece of music ["Russian Privjet" by Bass Hunter] which is . . . it just makes you feel powerful, and I imagine myself with "powers." [giggles] This is embarrassing . . . like floating over the school controlling the weather, or making myself into two people—copies of myself, like illusions, holograms—very sci-fi and random. It's usually bits in the song where it cuts off from the heavy bass, goes quite soft and gets back in. At those points I imagine somebody dying and me resurrecting them or something else grand. It's really intense. Without the music my mind just goes on to useless, annoying things.
> INTERVIEWER: Is this a regular thing for you?
> ZAK: Daydreaming to music? Yes, every day. That one, two, or three times a week. Music allows me to deal with things in controlled amounts. . . . I know I can

control the music and therefore control my emotions. . . . Sometimes I don't
want to think, and that track creates my own little bubble where I don't have to
feel pressured. . . . It's like an alternate reality—one I'm completely in control of.
(Zak, seventeen)

Zak—like Lily—describes an established practice of daydreaming to music. However,
the musical interaction appears more practiced and intentional, demonstrating an
overt self-regulatory function. The "powers" fantasy is recurring, although containing
variants. Music facilitates a lessened awareness of surroundings and an increase of
imaginative involvement, which is highly absorbing. It also appears to mediate consciousness, constraining emotion and affording a means of escaping a state of "psychic
entropy" in which "the mind begins to wander . . . focus[ing] on unresolvable problems
that cause anxiety" (Csikszentmihalyi 1990, 36).[13]

Dissociation/Zoning Out

Zak's recurrent musical daydream clearly possesses dissociative qualities, evident
in his observations that music provides "my own little bubble/an alternate reality."
Dissociative experiences of music, involving the spontaneous or volitional use of music
to detach from self, surroundings, or activity, are extremely common during adolescence, with a marked increase observable from the age of fifteen (Herbert and Bagkeris
2015). Dissociation, as I noted toward the start of the chapter, is often conceptualized
as a maladaptive response, reflecting a historical focus in music psychology research
on pathological instances of it. In fact, the phenomenology of many everyday dissociative experiences accords with the view that dissociation may present as a normative response, understood as an adaptive defense mechanism (Cardeña 2004; Herbert [2011]
2016). For teenagers, the opportunity to "zone out" to music appears to be particularly
valued—an escape from emotional volatility and everyday preoccupations (including
experimentation with identity), as the following examples indicate:

If I'm really tired I put on what I call my "white noise" sort of music . . . non-diegetic
sound like Lemon Jelly, Flying Lotuses. . . . I have it in my ears to create a more
pleasant environment. . . . It's not real, it's definitely not the real world, just somewhere where I've got this absent-minded sort of blank non-state. (James, eighteen)

On the bus listening [to heavy metal music] I start looking out, and I do know I am
looking out and then eventually there is just a fade where I am just unaware that I am
unaware . . . kind of inside the music, disappearing. . . . It's not positive or negative,
just about an alternative space, somewhere else to go. . . . I am not aware of myself, I
am just aware of the track, like the track is my thoughts. (Jake, fifteen)

Both James and Jake reference an obviously well-practiced and familiar style of listening, in which the intention is to use music with specific attributes (e.g., very loud,

intense levels of sound or non-real-world, synthesized sounds) that they have come to associate with the facilitation of a gradual loss of perceived sense of self and dissociation from affect. Their experiences—marked by an absence of an extended, autobiographical conscious awareness—possess neither a positive nor negative valence.

BEING AWAY, BEING THERE AND AWAY, AND KINDS OF CONSCIOUSNESS

The young people's listening episodes discussed here show a prevalent use of music as a means of framing or scaffolding aspects of lived experience—for example, facilitating experimentation with identity or vicarious immersion in unfamiliar emotions. The theory of scaffolding derives from Lev Vygotsky's (1978) notion of a *zone of proximal development*—"the distance between what the child can do independently and what is possible with the help of more capable peers or adults" (St. John 2006, 1650). Music functions, in effect, as a virtual persona or agent of possibility—what DeNora (2000) describes as a "prosthetic technology" of consciousness, modulating the interaction between perceiver and everyday environment, facilitating subtle, often self-regulatory shifts of consciousness. The capacity of music to scaffold aspects of experience is likely a prime reason individuals appear to connect particularly closely with music from pubescence to late adolescence. And indeed, music has been identified as a key "developmental resource" during this transition (e.g., Miranda 2013; Miranda et al. 2015). As I noted at the start of this chapter, this is a time in an individual's development when marked neuro-psycho-physiological and sociocultural changes modulate subjectivity, including a peak of emotional reactivity in mid-adolescence together with a decline, from around age twelve, in hypnotic susceptibility, fantasy proneness, and a tendency to "be in the moment," as well as a reconstruction of the self-concept and concern with identity, which starts in early adolescence.[14]

What is it about music that makes it such an effective and widely adopted agent of consciousness change? A significant body of literature (notably the literature on *flow*, e.g., Csikszentmihalyi 1990; Hytönen-Ng 2013) indicates that interaction with a range of art forms (e.g., literature) and activities (e.g., different kinds of sports) may modulate experience, particularly in terms of creating a present-centered sense of immersion. Children's and teenagers' close connection with music is not explicable simply because, as "digital natives," it is "there"—available and omnipresent in daily life thanks to portable technologies, streaming services, and integration within multimedia formats (computer games, music videos, etc.). Neither is an acknowledgment of music's function as a badge of identity, its role in defining "in-groups" and "out-groups," sufficient (although this is a preoccupation of a substantial literature concerning young people's use of music). Rather, it is music's versatility and customizability (in other words, its wide range of affordances) that appear significant. Many of these affordances—some highlighted as themes in the previous discussion—have been the subject of study within phenomenological ethnomusicology. One is temporality, where, as we have seen, music may facilitate the disruption of temporal synchronicity, replacing one time frame with another, either increasing or decreasing perceived momentum or creating a sense of stasis. Another concerns the way music may provide a means of actual or virtual connection between the self and a variety of live and digital sociocultural worlds. A third centers around the multivalent nature of music, the wide range of attentional loci that music provides (e.g., sounds, mood, reminiscence, association), together with the way music may serve to blend together external sensory impressions (visual, olfactory, gustatory, tactile) with elements of internal awareness (thoughts, memories) to form a multimodal gestalt.

Crucially, as shown by the firsthand reports of musical experiences in this chapter, music affords particular modes of "being in the world" that help young people negotiate and enhance their everyday lives—from highly involved states of absorbed immersion with music to self-regulatory episodes of escape and detachment. As Berger, Riedel, and VanderHamm (this volume) observe, musical involvement, particularly when conceptualized as trance, is a topic that has been of considerable interest to phenomenological ethnomusicologists—notably represented in the ethnographic work of Steven Friedson (1996, 2009). As I have argued elsewhere (Herbert 2011), the subtle (or profound) transformations of consciousness that individuals experience in conjunction with music during the course of their everyday lives can be framed as instances of secular trancing.[15] Friedson's case studies (broadly, focused on sacred, communal, ritualistic contexts in Malawi and southern Ghana) appear to be very different from my own (secular, individual, informal musicking in the UK), as do our primary academic vantage points (the philosophical tradition of phenomenology versus phenomenological psychology). However, Friedson's concern to tap the *Dasein* ("there-being") of participating individuals aligns with my intention to understand UK ten- to eighteen-year-olds' modes of being in the world, and it is interesting to (briefly) consider his Heideggerian-influenced conceptualization of trance as "being away" with relation to young people's modes of musical experience.

In essence, Friedson distinguishes between different qualities of being, all coterminous with alterations of consciousness from what individuals (or observers) would perceive as a baseline "norm." "Being there and away" is perhaps the most familiar in terms of everyday scenarios, typically referring to situations in which attention is distributed and fluctuating—split between different activities, one of which may be subject to automatic processing, beneath conscious awareness. This would include "daydreaming while driving a car, attending a lecture, listening to music, or in countless other ways. During those moments, we somehow manage to withdraw our awareness of bodily emplacement even while we continue to do complex tasks" (Friedson 2009, 35).

By contrast, Friedson describes "being away" as attached to scenarios such as spontaneous daydreaming (while aware of nothing else) or dreamless (non-REM) sleep.[16] "Being away" and "being there" are not discrete experiential categories but may simultaneously overlap. For example, Friedson (2009, 37) contrasts scenarios where in-dividual trancers can be considered to be totally "away" (as in possession trance) with instances where an individual retains some control of trance, is simultaneously present and absent, and exhibits a split or double awareness of external and internal phenomena (as in shamanistic practices or lucid dreaming). How might these different qualities of being map on to the four main types of experience discussed in this chapter?

Friedson's definition of "being there and away" certainly appears to resonate with experiential episodes in which young people describe spontaneous or volitional interactions with music, where daydreams and/or imaginative fantasies are trig-gered. And indeed, Friedson includes the activity of listening to music in this category. However, music-listening episodes exhibiting an extreme sense of dissociation appear to more closely align with the notion of "being away." For example, Jake's experience of listening to heavy metal features an intentional escape from, or perhaps disappearance of, self (in terms of both awareness of mentation and bodily emplacement) and from ex-ternal surroundings, as he is spontaneously and informally "possessed" by music ("the track became my thoughts"). Reframing these two types of experience as about "being there and away" and "being away" appears to capture something profound and invalu-able about the essence of them. The same does not seem to be true for episodes featuring a present-centered immersion that is focused on energy, momentum, or connection, or for those featuring multimodal involvement and a distributed attention.

A complementary framework (as adopted in this chapter) is to accommodate phe-nomenological characteristics of lived experiences of music in terms of kinds of con-sciousness, following the work of Damasio (1999) and Edelman (1992), and as applied to trance by Judith Becker (2004).[17] Thus, episodes featuring a present-centered immer-sion appear to privilege a core or primary consciousness centered on a range of sensory qualia. In contrast, those featuring a multimodal and distributed attentional focus (in-ward and outward) demonstrate the working of a core/primary and autobiographical/extended awareness in tandem. Dissociative experiences may primarily implicate core consciousness or—when extreme—accord with the trance consciousness identified by Becker. Here, "core consciousness is unaffected, but . . . the autobiographical self, ex-tended consciousness, is temporarily replaced by a trance persona" (2004, 11, 141), and such experiences are marked by the cessation of inner languaging. Becker herself has noted that "there may be different kinds of consciousness coterminous with differing kinds of trancing" (2004, 165). For example, DeNora's hypotheses of "cool conscious-ness" (involving self-reflective awareness, thinking, and the verbalization of experience) and "warm consciousness" (an embodied, prereflective perceptual awareness; 2013, 102) overlap with but are not exactly equivalent to notions of core and extended conscious-ness. Any theoretical framework has the potential to illuminate but also to circumscribe the totality of lived experience. It is therefore important to preserve an inductive ap-proach to phenomenological inquiry—a tenet that has been central to phenomenolog-ical methodologies in psychology. The relationship between those methodologies and the philosophical tradition is the topic of the final section of this chapter.

Doing Phenomenology: Psychological Methodologies, the Philosophical Tradition, and Ethnomusicology

The impetus for my studies of music in the everyday lives of individuals in the industrialized West was a desire to gain understanding about the "feel" of lived experiences as gestalts or totalities. I sought to move away from a focus on function, mood, and emotion (prevalent within psychological studies of music listening in natural-istic contexts) and toward an approach that was inclusive of a wide variety of experiential phenomena. My starting point was not the phenomenological tradition in philosophy, nor indeed any specific discipline. Rather, it began with self-reflection upon my own mu-sical experiences, plus informal observation of the ways the people around me interacted with music.[18] Much of the research I drew upon in the early stages came from outside any music discipline (e.g., consciousness studies, scholarship on altered states of conscious-ness [ASC], hypnotherapy, and psychology). In addition to theorizations regarding kinds of consciousness (e.g., core [present-centered] consciousness and extended [au-tobiographical] consciousness), I explored literature relating to characteristics and dimensions of types of conscious experience (e.g., James 1890; Kokoszka 2007; Ludwig 1966; Tart 1972). One such work is psychologist Ron Pekala's (1991) Phenomenology of Consciousness Inventory (PCI), which is designed to map correlations between twelve dimensions of subjective experience: positive affect, negative affect, altered experience, imagery, attention, self-awareness, altered state of awareness, internal dialogue, ration-ality, volitional control, memory, and arousal. The PCI (essentially a retrospective self-report questionnaire) has been used in a variety of experiential scenarios, notably with relation to the phenomenon of absorption in music (e.g., Nagy and Szabó 2004; Vroegh 2018) and as applied to music therapy (e.g., Sandler et al. 2015).

Gabrielsson's (2011) groundbreaking development of a descriptive system to cap-ture the phenomenology of strong experiences of music (SEM-DS) was the first com-prehensive approach to address the holistic experience of music in real-world contexts. Gabrielsson developed the SEM-DS via content analysis of over 1,300 retrospective, free descriptions of strong experiences of music. Like the PCI, the SEM-DS categorizes ex-perience in terms of a series of overarching dimensions and subdimensions. The seven overarching dimensions are general characteristics (e.g., descriptions of experiences as special or possessing ineffable qualities), physical reactions and behaviors, perception, cognition, feelings/emotion, existential and transcendental aspects (including trance and ecstasy), and personal and social aspects. Both the PCI and the SEM-DS provided important frameworks for my study of the phenomenology of everyday experiences, and Gabrielsson has noted that a number of superordinate thematic categories I examine (e.g., reduction in thought, changed sensory awareness, imaginative involvement) have "direct correspondences in various SEM-DS categories" (Gabrielsson et al. 2016, 754).

Given that neither Gabrielsson's studies nor my own overtly reference the philosophical tradition of phenomenology, how far can our work be said to connect with it?

In an extensive discussion of phenomenological methods and their application in psychology, Frederick J. Wertz argues that phenomenological analyses may be carried out "regardless of whether one has been educated in phenomenology or calls one's approach phenomenological" (Wertz 2015, 95–96). This echoes the observation (Berger et al., this volume) that scholars may study the constitution of experience without necessarily adopting "the formal theoretical apparatus of phenomenology in their research." Both Gabrielsson's study of strong experiences of music and my study of everyday experiences of music would seem to accord with this approach. However, phenomenological methodologies adopted by music psychologists *do* demonstrate a clear connection to the philosophical tradition, and in the context of this chapter, it will be useful, in this final section, to make some of those connections explicit.

Phenomenological methodologies in psychology have burgeoned in the last few decades (Brooks 2015; Ghetti 2016), with multiple approaches apparent. Broadly speaking, these methodologies follow Husserl in regarding the world of lived experience (the *lifeworld*) as prereflective; that is, individuals focus on *what* they perceive, not *how* they perceive it (Brooks 2015, 642). Thus, psychological approaches demonstrate "an overall emphasis on describing and interpreting how people make sense of their experiences when such experiences are brought into consciousness" (Ghetti 2016, 770). Such methodologies detail a series of stages that enable researchers to suspend preconceptions and assumptions (i.e., engage in a process of bracketing) to facilitate an open attitude to the phenomenon under investigation. The theoretical perspective adopted by the researcher determines the kind of bracketing undertaken. In contemporary phenomenological psychology, methodologies are frequently described as coming from a descriptive or hermeneutic perspective. Descriptive methodologies, pioneered by Giorgi (e.g., Giorgi 1985; Giorgi and Giorgi 2008), demonstrate a Husserlian influence and require suspension of the majority of researcher suppositions (descriptive bracketing) to tap the true essence of a phenomenon, including "underlying structures or essences of that experience that might hold true for others" (Ghetti 2016, 775). Hermeneutic methodologies (e.g., Smith et al. 2009) draw on the work of philosophers in phenomenology's hermeneutic tradition (e.g., Martin Heidegger, Paul Ricoeur, or Hans-Georg Gadamer) and highlight a reflective-interpretative stance, as instanced by the concept of the *hermeneutic circle* (discussed later). Key is the assertion that it is impossible for researchers to suspend all assumptions (personal and cultural) during the research process. So-called *reflexive bracketing* (an alternation between the examination of researcher and participant perspectives) is utilized to make researcher assumptions explicit and to recognize that the "meanings that are derived during interpretative research [are] necessarily co-constitutional in nature" (Ghetti 2016, 777).

IPA, the method I have employed in all my analyses of everyday lived experiences of music, dates from the 1990s and is now one of the most widely used approaches in UK qualitative psychology (Eatough and Smith 2017, 193). In the last decade it has gained currency within music psychology, notably as applied to music therapy and amateur music-making contexts (Ghetti 2011; Pothoulaki et al. 2012; Taylor 2015).[19] IPA draws on a range of phenomenological thinking. It aims to go "back to the things themselves" (Husserl [1900–01] 2001, 168), free of existing assumptions, but it is influenced by hermeneutic phenomenology, particularly the writings of Heidegger. Experience is understood as inevitably situated and therefore an individual's interaction with the world is relational and interpretive. Toward the beginning of this chapter, I stated that IPA employs a "double hermeneutic" in that "the researcher is trying to make sense of the participants trying to make sense of their world" (Smith and Osbourn 2004, 51). IPA also employs the notion of the hermeneutic circle; researchers are encouraged to "work with their data in a dynamic, iterative and non-linear manner, examining the whole in light of its parts, the parts in light of the whole, and the contexts in which the whole and parts are embedded" (Eatough and Smith 2017, 198). In developing IPA, Smith sought to create a "rigorous and systematic" methodology whose theoretical vocabulary would enable "a dialogue with the cognitive paradigm of psychology" (Smith 2017, 304) and provide an idiographic focus that would complement quantitative psychological methods. The richness of any IPA analysis depends on the skills and insight of the researcher, but—as this summary indicates—it is clear that influences from phenomenological work in philosophy underpin this methodology (as they do with other phenomenological psychology methodologies), thus connecting psychological and philosophical perspectives.

In what ways might the phenomenological psychology of music inform phenomenological ethnomusicology? I would argue that ethnomusicologists have much to learn from the nuanced and sophisticated descriptions of consciousness and its processes offered by phenomenological psychologists of music. Their work is part of the broader field of consciousness studies, which uses theoretical and neurobiological perspectives to categorize and analyze the network of perceptual, cognitive, emotional, and physiological interactions that constitute the gestalt sum of subjective experience. The rich and detailed vocabulary employed by phenomenological psychologists to capture unfolding, lived experiences of music would certainly appear to have utility for ethnomusicologists, as do the rigorous methods and techniques used in this field. At the same time, phenomenological ethnomusicology has much to contribute to the phenomenological psychologists who study music. Crucially, this includes a sensitivity to the role of culture in the constitution of individual experience, illustrated by rich, ethnographic accounts of the situated context of music listening and the practices of social interaction that unfold there.

Phenomenological approaches to studying musical involvement accommodate experience as a holistic totality, avoiding unhelpful divisions between cognition and emotion. In psychology, the application of such approaches to the study of unfolding, lived experiences of music in everyday contexts in the industrialized West is still fairly new and relatively rare, perhaps, in part, simply because researchers are unfamiliar with available literature and methods. Ethnomusicology, to date, possesses a far more developed connection with the philosophical tradition. It is interesting to reflect upon differences in the ways phenomenology has been incorporated into the fields of ethnomusicology and music psychology. Most obviously, detailed methodologies and data collection techniques dominate in psychological studies of musical experience, whereas phenomenological ethnomusicology draws on theoretical models and overarching ideas (in tandem with data collection methods) to a far greater degree. This is explicable in terms of the intellectual histories of the two disciplines. In the case of music psychology, quantitative research (in controlled laboratory settings, with the aim of producing robust, replicable, and generalizable findings) has long been equated with scientific credibility, while qualitative research has had to become more methodologically developed to ensure widespread acceptance in the social sciences. However, there is increasing evidence of a move toward the adoption of pluralistic (mixed-method) approaches within quantitative psychology, in part to avoid "methodolatry" (Chamberlain 2012) and to recognize the complex and multidimensional nature of human experience. A small number of studies have crossed the boundaries between ethnomusicology, psychology, and philosophy. Cross-disciplinary exploration of lived experiences with and of music is an area ripe for future development.

ACKNOWLEDGMENTS

Portions of this chapter draw on a 2012 paper of mine that appeared in the *Proceedings of the Twelfth International Conference on Music Perception and Cognition and the Eighth Triennial Conference of the European Society for the Cognitive Sciences of Music*. Examples and extracts are reproduced with kind permission of the editors.

NOTES

1. The *Habilitation* is a qualification traditionally required for German academics wishing to proceed to a professorship.
2. For an extensive review of phenomenological work on music in a wide range of disciplines, see Christensen (2012).
3. The constructs of absorption and dissociation are subject to an extensive examination in my book *Everyday Music Listening: Absorption, Dissociation, and Trancing* (Herbert [2011] 2016).
4. Within music psychology, studies that examine the "function" of music focus on the uses to which music is put (e.g., to relax, pass the time, create an atmosphere) or so-called functional niches that music may occupy (e.g., travel, physical work, brain work, emotional work; see Sloboda et al. 2009). The emphasis here is on the *reasons* individuals choose to interact with music, rather than on the psychological *qualities* of experiences in which music is present. The use of this term in contemporary psychology is not related to the discredited functionalist school of anthropology, which understood function as the contribution that a social phenomenon made to social cohesion.
5. The young people were recruited from state primary and secondary schools in the United Kingdom, plus specialist private musical institutions such as cathedral schools and junior conservatoires.

6. Findings from this research study were extensive and necessarily disseminated across several publications. For a discussion of phase two findings, see Herbert and Bagkeris (2015). For a discussion of phase three findings, see Herbert and Dibben (2018).

7. Retrospective self-report is, of course, subject to the vagaries of memory, what an individual consciously chooses to report, and the constraints of verbal language. As Eric F. Clarke puts it, words "may lag behind a phenomenon whose corporeality, temporality, and multiplicity elude the rational, spatial, and linear character of the written word" (2011, 197–198). All data collection methods are necessarily limited in scope, however, and self-report (when complemented by an analytical method that minimizes ungrounded theorizing) remains richly insightful in phenomenological terms.

8. For a discussion of some of the experiences appearing in this chapter from a rather different perspective (personality psychology), see Herbert et al. (2019).

9. Antonio Damasio's and Gerald Edelman's theories of consciousness have informed a number of studies of musical experience, notably Becker's (2004) discussion of the neurobiological underpinnings of trance.

10. The use of music to inhabit or connect with two or more actual, virtual, and/or remote worlds simultaneously aligns with the increasing ubiquity of digital technologies. Reports indicated that some teenagers relied so much on music to mediate or focus everyday experiences and make sense of the world around them that, without it, they would feel disconnected from their daily lives. When describing situations in which music was absent, participants talked of perceiving the environment as "static," "dead," "empty," "colorless," or "black and white."

11. See Herbert and Dibben (2018) for a review of the literature on this topic and an experimental study of heteronomous listening practices during adolescence.

12. The online listening study (phase three of the project) provided further confirmation that musical meaning-making alters across adolescence and that both age and training mediate lived experience. The increased importance of self-chosen (rather than experimenter-selected) music to facilitate imaginative fantasies during mid- and late adolescence was clear. Only ten- to twelve-year-olds appeared equally prone to engage in "storying" to both self-chosen and experimenter-selected musical materials (Herbert and Dibben 2018).

13. Interestingly, Zak's recurrent "superpowers" daydream corresponded with one reported by John, his twin brother. An analysis of the data revealed that the twins had not discussed their musical daydreams with each other and were fiercely secretive about their musical tastes, both stating that music was an important means of defining their individual, independent identities. I discuss John's recurrent daydream elsewhere (Herbert 2012, 2019).

14. See Herbert and Dibben (2018) for an extended discussion of neuro-psycho-physiological and sociocultural changes across adolescence.

15. In the mid-twentieth century, the work of psychiatrist Milton Erickson (1901–1980), founder of the American Society for Clinical Hypnosis (1957) and the *American Journal of Clinical Hypnosis* (1958), transformed understanding of hypnosis and trance in the industrialized West, acting as the catalyst for an increase in the use of hypnosis in clinical contexts. Central to Erickson's approach was his recognition that subtle shifts of consciousness were a normal part of daily life, so familiar and evanescent in nature that individuals would not consciously apprehend them as altered states of consciousness (ASC). This was what Erickson termed "the common everyday trance": "The same situation [hypnotic trance in a clinical context] is in evidence in everyday life, however, whenever attention is fixated with a question or an experience of the amazing, the unusual, or

anything that *holds* a person's interest. At such moments people experience the common everyday trance" (Erickson and Rossi [1976] 1980, 450, italics in the original). The common everyday trance was subject to formal study in the early 1960s by psychologist Ronald Shor, pupil of the humanist psychologist Abraham Maslow (who had conducted extensive research into qualities of "Peak Experiences") and a pioneer of hypnosis research.

16. Friedson also uses the term "being in between" to refer to the out-of-time temporality often reported by possession trance participants (i.e., the sense that no time has passed since the trancer has been "away"; Friedson 2009, 38).

17. In a review essay on competing paradigms in the ethnomusicology of trance (centering on the work of Judith Becker, Richard C. Jankowsky, and Steven M. Friedson), Perman argues that Becker is the only one to "reconcile the contradictory methodologies and assumptions of contemporary neuroscience and phenomenological ethnomusicology" (2013, 330–331).

18. Clarke notes that "thinking in terms of 'subjects of study' rather than in terms of 'disciplines' highlights the continuity between psychological and other approaches" (2011, 12). The study of conscious (and preconscious or unconscious) experience is inevitably interdisciplinary. For example, contributors to the second volume of *Music and Consciousness* (Herbert et al. 2019) are drawn from a number of fields, including philosophy, neuroscience, ethnomusicology, anthropology, psychology, sociology, cultural theory, and performance studies.

19. Music psychologists are not always aware of IPA's connections to the tradition of phenomenology in philosophy, a factor that Smith has sought to rectify. Interestingly, Amedeo Giorgi has argued that IPA lacks a grounding in philosophical phenomenology (Giorgi 2010), a criticism that Smith (2010) has vigorously refuted.

Works Cited

Becker, Judith. 2004. *Deep Listeners: Music, Emotion, and Trancing*. Bloomington: Indiana University Press.

Berger, Harris M., David VanderHamm, and Friedlind Riedel. 2023. "Phenomenological Approaches in the History of Ethnomusicology." In *The Oxford Handbook of the Phenomenology of Music Cultures*, edited by Harris M. Berger, Friedlind Riedel, and David VanderHamm, 3–56. New York: Oxford University Press.

Boal-Palheiros, Graca M., and David J. Hargreaves. 2001. "Listening to Music at Home and at School." *British Journal of Music Education* 18 (2): 103–118.

Brooks, Joanna. 2015. "Learning from the Lifeworld: Introducing Alternative Approaches to Phenomenology in Psychology." *Psychologist* 28 (8): 642–643.

Bull, Michael. 2003. "Soundscapes of the Car: A Critical Study of Automobile Habitation." In *The Auditory Culture Reader*, edited by Michael Bull and Les Back, 357–374. Oxford: Berg.

Bull, Michael. 2007. *Sound Moves: iPod Culture and Urban Experience*. London: Routledge.

Campbell, Patricia Sheehan. 2010. *Songs in Their Heads: Music and Its Meaning in Children's Lives*. New York: Oxford University Press.

Cardeña, Etzel. 2004. "The Domain of Dissociation." In *Dissociation*, edited by Stephen J. Lynn and Judith W. Rhue, 1–31. Washington, DC: American Psychological Association Press.

Chamberlain, Kerry. 2012. "Do You Really Need a Methodology?" *Qualitative Methods in Psychology Bulletin* 13 (Spring): 59–63.

Chamorro-Premuzic, Thomas, and Adrian Furnham. 2007. "Personality and Music: Can Traits Explain How People Use Music in Everyday Life?" *British Journal of Psychology* 98 (2): 175–185.

Chin, Tan-Chyuan, and Nikki Rickard. 2014. "Emotion Regulation Strategy Mediates Both Positive and Negative Relationships between Music Uses and Well-Being." *Psychology of Music* 42 (5): 692–713.

Christensen, Erik. 2012. "Music Listening, Music Therapy, Phenomenology and Neuroscience." PhD diss., Aalborg University.

Clarke, Eric F. 2005. *Ways of Listening: An Ecological Approach to the Perception of Musical Meaning.* New York: Oxford University Press.

Clarke, Eric F. 2011. "Music Perception and Musical Consciousness." In *Music and Consciousness: Philosophical, Psychological, and Cultural Perspectives,* edited by David Clarke and Eric F. Clarke, 193–214. New York: Oxford University Press.

Clarke, Eric F., Nicola Dibben, and Stephanie Pitts. 2010. *Music and Mind in Everyday Life.* Oxford: Oxford University Press.

Clayton, Martin. 2009. "Crossing Boundaries and Bridging Gaps: Thoughts on Relationships between Ethnomusicology and Music Psychology." *Empirical Musicology Review* 4 (2): 75–77.

Clifton, Thomas. 1983. *Music as Heard: A Study in Applied Phenomenology.* New Haven, CT: Yale University Press.

Colman, Andrew M. 2015. "Phenomenology." In *A Dictionary of Psychology.* New York: Oxford University Press.

Crafts, Susan D., Daniel Cavicchi, and Charles Keil. 1993. *My Music: Explorations of Music in Daily Life.* Hanover, NH: Wesleyan University Press.

Csikszentmihalyi, Mihaly. 1990. *Flow: The Psychology of Optimal Experience.* New York: Harper Perennial.

Csikszentmihalyi, Mihaly, and Reed Larson. 1987. "Validity and Reliability of the Experience-Sampling Method." *Journal of Nervous and Mental Disease* 175 (9): 526–536.

Damasio, Antonio. 1999. *The Feeling of What Happens: Body and Emotion in the Making of Consciousness.* New York: Harcourt Brace and Company.

DeNora, Tia. 2000. *Music in Everyday Life.* Cambridge: Cambridge University Press.

DeNora, Tia. 2013. *Music Asylums: Wellbeing through Music in Everyday Life.* Farnham, UK: Ashgate.

Eatough, Virginia, and Jonathan A. Smith. 2017. "Interpretative Phenomenological Analysis." In *The Sage Handbook of Qualitative Research in Psychology,* 2nd ed., edited by Carla Willig and Wendy S. Rogers, 193–209. London: Sage.

Edelman, Gerald M. 1992. *Bright Air, Brilliant Fire: On the Matter of the Mind.* New York: Basic Books.

Erickson, Milton, and Ernest L. Rossi. (1976) 1980. "Two-Level Communication and the Microdynamics of Trance and Suggestion." In *The Collected Papers of Milton H. Erickson on Hypnosis.* Vol. 1, *The Nature of Hypnosis and Suggestion,* edited by Ernest L. Rossi, 430–451. New York: Irvington Publishers.

Ferrara, Lawrence. 1984. "Phenomenology as a Tool for Musical Analysis." *Musical Quarterly* 70 (3): 355–373.

Ferrara, Lawrence. 1991. *Philosophy and the Analysis of Music: Bridges to Musical Sound, Form, and Reference.* New York: Greenwood Press.

Finnäs, Leif. 2006. "Ninth-Grade Pupils' Significant Experiences in Aesthetic Areas: The Role of Music and of Different Basic Modes of Confronting Music." *British Journal of Music Education* 23 (3): 315–331.

Finney, John, and Pamela Burnard, eds. 2008. *Music Education with Digital Technology.* London: Continuum.

Friedson, Steven M. 1996. *Dancing Prophets: Musical Experience in Tumbuka Healing.* Chicago: University of Chicago Press.

Friedson, Steven M. 2009. *Remains of Ritual: Northern Gods in a Southern Land.* Chicago: University of Chicago Press.

Gabrielsson, Alf. 2011. *Strong Experiences with Music.* Translated by Rod Bradbury. Oxford: Oxford University Press.

Gabrielsson, Alf, John Whaley, and John Sloboda. 2016. "Peak Experiences in Music." In *The Oxford Handbook of Music Psychology*, 2nd ed., edited by Susan Hallam, Ian Cross, and Michael Thaut, 745–758. Oxford: Oxford University Press.

Ghetti, Claire M. 2011. "Clinical Practice of Dual-Certified Music Therapists/Child Life Specialists: A Phenomenological Study." *Journal of Music Therapy* 48 (3): 317–345.

Ghetti, Claire M. 2016. "Phenomenological Research in Music Therapy." In *The Oxford Handbook of Music Therapy*, edited by Jane Edwards, 768–797. Oxford: Oxford University Press.

Gibson, James J. 1979. *The Ecological Approach to Visual Perception.* Hillsdale, NJ: Lawrence Erlbaum.

Giorgi, Amedeo, ed. 1985. *Phenomenology and Psychological Research.* Pittsburgh, PA: Duquesne University Press.

Giorgi, Amedeo. 2010. "Phenomenology and the Practice of Science." *Existential Analysis* 21 (1): 3–22.

Giorgi, Amedeo, and Barbro Giorgi. 2008. "Phenomenology." In *Qualitative Psychology: A Practical Guide to Research Methods*, 2nd ed., edited by Jonathan A. Smith, 26–52. Los Angeles: Sage.

Hargreaves, David J. 1982. "The Development of Aesthetic Reactions to Music." *Psychology of Music* 98: 51–54.

Herbert, Ruth. 2011. "Reconsidering Trance: Cross-Cultural Differences and Cross-Disciplinary Perspectives." *Ethnomusicology Forum* 20 (2): 100–127.

Herbert, Ruth. (2011) 2016. *Everyday Music Listening: Absorption, Dissociation, and Trancing.* London: Routledge.

Herbert, Ruth. 2012. "Young People's Use and Subjective Experience of Music Outside School." In *Proceedings of the Twelfth International Conference on Music Perception and Cognition and the Eighth Triennial Conference of the European Society for the Cognitive Sciences of Music,* edited by Emilios Cambouropoulos, Konstantinos Tsougras, Panayiotis Mavromatis, and Konstantinos Pastiadis, 423–431. Thessaloniki, Greece: Aristotle University.

Herbert, Ruth. 2019. "Absorption and Openness to Experience: An Everyday Tale of Traits and States". In *Music and Consciousness 2: Worlds, Practices, Modalities*, edited by Ruth Herbert, David Clarke, and Eric Clarke, 233–253. New York: Oxford University Press.

Herbert, Ruth, and Emanoulis Bagkeris. 2015. "Tweens' and Teens' Engagement with Music in Daily Life: Individual Differences and Psychological Characteristics of Subjective Experience." In *Proceedings of the Ninth Triennial Conference of the European Society for the Cognitive Sciences of Music (ESCOM)*, edited by Jane Ginsborg, Alexandra Lamont, and Stephanie Bramley, 437–438. Manchester: Royal Northern College of Music.

Herbert, Ruth, David Clarke, and Eric Clarke, eds. 2019. *Music and Consciousness 2: Worlds, Practices, Modalities*. New York: Oxford University Press.

Herbert, Ruth, and Nicola Dibben. 2018. "Making Sense of Music: Meanings 10- to 18-Year-Olds Attach to Experimenter-Selected Materials." *Psychology of Music* 46 (3): 375–391.

Hetland, Lois, and Ellen Winner. 2004. "Cognitive Transfer from Arts Education to Non-arts Outcomes: Research Evidence and Policy Implications." In *Handbook of Research and Policy in Art Education*, edited by Elliot Eisner and Michael D. Day, 135–161. Mahwah, NJ: Lawrence Erlbaum.

Huerner, Wolfgang. 2017. "Franz Brentano." In *The Stanford Encyclopedia of Philosophy*, edited by Edward N. Zalta. Stanford University. https://plato.stanford.edu/archives/fall2017/entries/brentano/.

Husserl, Edmund. (1900–01) 2001. *Logical Investigations*. Edited by Dermot Moran. Translated by J. N. Findlay. New York: Routledge.

Hytönen-Ng, Elina. 2013. *Experiencing "Flow" in Jazz Performance*. Farnham, UK: Ashgate.

Ihde, Don. (1976) 2007. *Listening and Voice: Phenomenologies of Sound*. 2nd ed. Albany: State University of New York Press.

James, William. 1890. *The Principles of Psychology*. New York: Dover Publications.

Juslin, Patrik, Simon Liljeström, Daniel Västfjäll, and Lars-Olov Lundqvist. 2010. "How Does Music Evoke Emotions: Exploring Underlying Mechanisms." In *Handbook of Music and Emotion: Theory, Research, Applications*, edited by Patrik Juslin and John Sloboda, 605–642. Oxford: Oxford University Press.

Juslin, Patrik, and John Sloboda, eds. 2010. *Handbook of Music and Emotion: Theory, Research, Applications*. Oxford: Oxford University Press.

Kokoszka, Andrzej. 2007. *States of Consciousness: Models for Psychology and Psychotherapy*. New York: Springer.

Lamont, Alexandra, Alinka Greasley, and John Sloboda. 2016. "Choosing to Hear Music: Motivation, Process, and Effect." In *The Oxford Handbook of Music Psychology*, 2nd ed., edited by Susan Hallam, Ian Cross, and Michael Thaut, 711–720. Oxford: Oxford University Press.

Lamont, Alexandra, David J. Hargreaves, Nigel A. Marshall, and Mark Tarrant. 2003. "Young People's Music in and out of School." *British Journal of Music Education* 20 (3): 229–241.

LeBlanc, Albert, Wendy L. Sims, Carolyn Siivola, and Mary Obert. 1996. "Music Style Preferences of Different Age Listeners." *Journal of Research in Music Education* 44 (1): 49–59.

Ludwig, Arnold, M. 1966. "Altered States of Consciousness." *Archives of General Psychiatry* 15: 225–234.

Lury, Karen. 2002. "Chewing Gum for the Ears: Children's Television and Popular Music." *Popular Music* 21 (3): 291–305.

Macdonald, Raymond, Gunter Kreutz, and Laura Mitchell. 2012. "What Is 'Music, Health and Wellbeing' and Why Is It Important?" In *Music, Health, and Wellbeing*, edited by Raymond Macdonald, Gunter Kreutz, and Laura Mitchell, 3–11. Oxford: Oxford University Press.

Miranda, Dave. 2013. "The Role of Music in Adolescent Development: Much More Than the Same Old Song." *International Journal of Adolescence and Youth* 18 (1): 5–22.

Miranda, Dave, Camille Blais-Rochette, Karole Vaugon, Muna Osman, and Melisa Arias-Valenzuela. 2015. "Towards a Cultural Developmental Psychology of Music in Adolescence." *Psychology of Music* 43 (2): 197–218.

Myers, Charles S. (1911) 2010. *A Textbook of Experimental Psychology*. Whitefish, MT: Kessinger Publishing.

Nagy, Katalin, and Csaba Szabó. 2004. "Differences in Phenomenological Experiences of Music-Listening: The Influence of Intensity of Musical Involvement and Type of Music on Musical Experiences." In *Proceedings of the Eighth International Conference on Music Perception and Cognition,* edited by Scott Lipscomb, Richard Ashley, Robert Gjerdingen, and Peter Webster, 470–473. Sydney: Causal Productions.

North, Adrian, and Hargreaves, David. 2008. *The Social and Applied Psychology of Music.* Oxford: Oxford University Press.

North, Adrian C., David J. Hargreaves, and Susan A. O'Neill. 2000. "The Importance of Music to Adolescents." *British Journal of Music Educational Psychology* 70 (2): 255–272.

Pekala, Ronald J. 1991. *Quantifying Consciousness: An Empirical Approach.* New York: Plenum Press.

Perman, Tony. 2013. "Competing Paradigms in the Ethnomusicology of Trance." *Ethnomusicology* 57 (2): 330–338.

Pothoulaki, Maria, Raymond MacDonald, and Paul Flowers. 2012. "An Interpretative Phenomenological Analysis of an Improvisational Music Therapy Program for Cancer Patients." *Journal of Music Therapy* 49 (1): 45–67.

Randall, William M., Nikki S. Rickard, and Dianne A. Vella-Broderick. 2014. "Emotional Outcomes of Regulation Strategies Used during Personal Music Listening: A Mobile Experience Sampling Study." *Musicae Scientiae* 18 (3): 275–291.

Saarikallio, Suvi, and Jaakko Erkkilä. 2007. "The Role of Music in Adolescents' Mood Regulation." *Psychology of Music* 5 (1): 88–109.

Saarikallio, Suvi, Christian Gold, and Katrina McFerran. 2015. "Development and Validation of the Healthy-Unhealthy Music Scale." *Child and Adolescent Mental Health* 20 (4): 210–217.

Sandler, Hubertus, Uta Fendel, Eva Peters, Matthias Rose, Rainer Bösel, and Burghard F. Klapp. 2015. "Subjective Experience of Relaxation—Induced by Vibroacoustic Stimulation by a Body Monochord or CD Music—A Randomised, Controlled Study in Patients with Psychosomatic Disorders." *Nordic Journal of Music Therapy* 26 (1): 79–98.

Sloboda, John, Alexandra Lamont and Alinka Greasley. 2009. "Choosing to Hear Music: Motivation, Process and Effect." In *The Oxford Handbook of Music Psychology,* edited by Susan Hallam, Ian Cross, and Michael Thaut, 431–440. New York: Oxford University Press.

Schubert, Emery, and Gary McPherson. 2016. "The Perception of Emotion in Music." In *The Child as Musician: A Handbook of Musical Development,* 2nd ed., edited by Gary E. McPherson, 221–243. Oxford: Oxford University Press.

Smith, Jonathan A. 2010. "Interpretative Phenomenological Analysis: A Reply to Amedeo Giorgi." *Existential Analysis* 21 (2): 186–192.

Smith, Jonathan A. 2017. "Interpretative Phenomenological Analysis: Getting at Lived Experience." *Journal of Positive Psychology* 12 (3): 303–304.

Smith, Jonathan A., Paul Flowers, and Michael Larkin. 2009. *Interpretative Phenomenological Analysis: Theory, Methods, and Research.* London: Sage.

Smith, Jonathan A., and Mike Osborn. 2004. "Interpretative Phenomenological Analysis." In *Qualitative Psychology: A Practical Guide to Research Methods,* edited by Jonathan A. Smith, 51–80. London: Sage.

St. John, Patricia. 2006. "A Community of Learners: Young Music-Makers Scaffolding Flow Experience." In *Proceedings of the Ninth International Conference on Music Perception and Cognition,* edited by Mario Baroni, Anna R. Adessi, Roberto Caterina, and Marco Costa, 960–966. Bologna, Italy: University of Bologna.

Stumpf, Carl. 1883. *Tonpsychologie.* Leipzig: S. Hirzel.

Styns, Frederik, Leon van Noorden, Dirk Moelants, and Marc Leman. 2007. "Walking on Music." *Human Movement Science* 26 (5): 769–785.

Tagg, Philip. 2013. *Music's Meanings: A Modern Musicology for Non-musos*. New York: Mass Media Music Scholar's Press.

Tart, Charles. 1972. "Scientific Foundations for the Study of Altered States of Consciousness." *Journal of Transpersonal Psychology* 3 (2): 93–124.

Taylor, Angela. 2015. "Using Interpretative Phenomenological Analysis in a Mixed Methods Research Design to Explore Music in the Lives of Mature Age Amateur Keyboard Players." *Music Education Research* 17 (4): 437–452.

Vroegh, Thijs. 2018. "Absorbed in Music versus Hypnosis: Comparing Phenomenological Structures of Consciousness." Poster presented at the Twenty-Second Conference of the Association for the Scientific Study of Consciousness, Kraków, Poland, June 26–29, 2018.

Vygotsky, L. S. 1978. *Mind in Society: The Development of Higher Psychological Processes*, edited by Michael Cole, Vera John-Steiner, Sylvia Scribner, and Ellen Souberman. Cambridge, MA: Harvard University Press.

Wertz, Frederick J. 2015. "Phenomenology: Methods, Historical Development, and Applications in Psychology." In *The Wiley Handbook of Theoretical and Philosophical Psychology: Methods, Approaches, and New Directions for Social Sciences*, edited by Jack Martin, Jeff Sugarman, and Kathleen L. Slaney, 85–101. Chichester, UK: John Wiley and Sons.

TRANSFORMATIONS AND POSSIBILITIES OF THE PERSON

CHAPTER 7

SEXED BODIES/(IM)POSSIBLE BODIES/POLYPHONIC BODIES

STEPHEN AMICO

> . . . what we call "mind" and what we call "body" are not two things, but rather aspects of one organic process, so that all our meaning, thought, and language emerge from the aesthetic dimensions of this embodied activity.
>
> (Johnson 2007, 1)

I begin with a recounting of an experience, insofar as its multimodal plenitude served as the original impulse for my current inquiry. It was May 2017, at the tail end of an unusually fatiguing travel schedule, and I found myself standing on an overcrowded city bus heading back to my accommodation, where I would immediately begin packing for my flight early the next morning. I was surrounded by voices and bodies, almost all of them female; through the windows, huge Soviet-era apartment house behemoths were visible, as well as a no-less-imposing Orthodox cathedral silhouetted against the sky. Tuning in on the voices, the words—all of them Russian—I could discern discussions devoted to the concert which, it appeared, all of us had just attended, an audiovisual, affective space we had all shared: a performance by the Russian pop superstar Valeriia, a singer whose work I have followed for over a decade through videos, audio recordings, and written texts, various configurations of 0s and 1s, pixels, and pigments.[1] It was the second of Valeriia's concerts I had attended in the past two days (in two different cities), these being the only times I had seen her perform live. This propinquity to the singer, in this specific place—at times literally only a few meters from her, singing voice mixing with the rhythm tracks that vibrated architectural and corporeal walls—had impacted significantly upon and transformed my up-until-then "virtual" relationship with both personage and creative/expressive output.

To be clear, here I am referencing *an* experience, rather than experience in general—in John Dewey's sense, something with "its own particular rhythmic movement . . . its own unrepeated quality pervading it throughout" (1934, 35–36). A relationship to "environment" that exceeded the immediate present, this experience resonated corporeally, was more than (in its totality) "information processing": as the bus continued, the confluence of the recent past and processual present, as well as the projections into the future—song, sound, language, envoiced corporeality—reverberated with(in) me on a deeply somatic level. The pedal point of angst engendered by my seemingly endless peripatetics was momentarily muted as the language surrounding me provoked a corresponding change in my throat, mouth, and lips, even my posture, all adopting the shapes and attitudes necessary to respond (in Russian) to any possible interlocutor: in a very "real" sense, I felt myself to be in "my" "Russian" body and, via this remembering body (one that had lived in and continues to return to Russia on a somewhat regular basis), emplaced within a geocultural location I have often felt to be a home-like site of succor. Yet what is also called into question in this scenario is a conception of space/place defined via geography and/or materiality, an understanding of time as progressive and linear, and a conception of body conceived exclusively in terms of biology/genetics, insofar as this corporeal, experiential emplacement did not, in fact, occur in Russia, but in Estonia—in Lasnamäe, one of several districts in the city of Tallinn heavily populated by Russian speakers and/or ethnic Russians. Despite the supposed "facts" of my ethnic heritage (containing no Russian, so far as I know), my geopolitical placement, and the external visual data with which I was met, my experience occurred in large part via both audition and a corporeal memory that, to use the characterization of Maurice Merleau-Ponty, calls out "independently of any representation" ([1958] 2005, 161). My body's re-posturing could be understood as a taking up of "dispositions to respond to the solicitations of situations in the world" (Dreyfus 2002, 367), a reenactment of the past (rather than a representation), "not through images and words, but through immediate experience and action" (Fuchs 2012, 19).[2]

I offer this personal account not as the first step in what might be deemed (by the dictates of "social science") a misguided attempt to extrapolate subjective or solipsistic experience into a universal explanans—a move particularly problematic within the context of a phenomenological exploration of sex and gender, as I will attempt in this chapter—but to add some flesh to what is not, what can never be, a "purely theoretical" exploration of how the human subject lives in the (sonic, material) world. If, as Edward Casey suggests, the "absence of body memory would amount to the devastation of memory altogether" (2000, 179), any attempt to abstract experience—the mutually constituting interaction between subject and environment—away from the *lived embodied relations* that give rise to second-order conceptualizations is similarly liable to result in obfuscation (or obliteration), rather than elucidation. Moreover, understanding the complexities of perception and experience as suggested by even my short recounting (the ways in which time, space, sound, materiality, and imagination all defy neat compartmentalization or definition), I likewise want to exchange a privileging of "scientific data," certitude, and finality for an embrace of *possibilities* and *potentials*—horizonal liminalities that are, in fact, the essential stuff of experience. This implicit questioning of an "objective method" extends, moreover, to the very practice of phenomenology.

For example, understanding imagination to be an integral, indispensable component of the subject's relation to the world (and arguably a marker of human sentience), Don Ihde highlights the "variability and polymorphic capacity for refinement possible in imaginative modes of . . . experience," warning that "the dangers to a descriptive phenomenology are encountered . . . in the temptation to arrive too soon at a superficial, if apodictic, level of discovery" (2007, 119). Thus, this chapter will be marked not only by my decentering of data and my engagement with possibility but also by emphasizing the musical rather than the textual/linguistic; the aesthetic and the affective rather than the ideological; the (un)imaginable rather than the empirical; the auditory rather than the visual; the polyphonic rather than the univocal; and the sexed/corporeal rather than the gendered/discursive. In doing so, I hope to suggest alternative ways of approaching some of the dominant constructions encountered within academic theorizing, inviting us to understand these hierarchies to be just as malleable and open to alternative points of view (or points of *sense*) as the Necker cube, which Ihde invokes in order to highlight the "multistability" inherent in any "object" engaged by the human subject.[3]

Guided by these overarching principles, this chapter will explore the work of Valeriia, with reference not only to her live performances in Tallinn and Tartu at which I was present but also to her digitally mediated audiovisual output. I will argue that experience must be approached as a constant interplay—sometimes tense, but just as often not—between materiality (including corporeal, sexed materiality) and what are understood, phenomenologically, as the *horizons* (related to *possibilities*, in my reading) of any perception and experience. To conceive of the human subject as an organism guided primarily or solely by (mechanistic) responses to immediately available "data," or "objective assessments" of "concepts," would be to describe a subject as a result of, or soon to result in, psychological and physical pathology. Moreover, to ignore the very materiality of one's existence—the sensual materiality of the environment, and the sense-apprehending (and sensuality-*seeking*) capacities/tendencies of the human body—is to forestall the possibility of a holistic understanding of the ways that subjects and environments interact, including with and in musical, affective, and/or aesthetic sites, productions, and practices. Indeed, as I ultimately hope to show, it is in relation to just such sites as Valeriia's performances, as well as her musical/digital artifacts, that a sexed corporeality is implicated. However, this corporeality—via its meeting of and formation within the affective/sonic/aesthetic/imaginative—must not be conceived of as a foundational, essential (sexed) constraint but, much to the contrary, as a site of experiential multiplicity and opportunity, a material body with the innate capacity to exist as countless other (simultaneous) sensing/sensate (im)possible bodies. I note at the outset that "woman" or "female," as I use these terms, refers to complex interactions and matrices among and of cultural and material variables and must be understood in relation to perception and lived experience that, I argue, is fundamentally open, shifting, fecundating. As such, any definition that claims or attempts—with certainty and finality; via recourse to narrow understandings of body/biology—to delimit what woman/female "is" (universally, transhistorically, transculturally) must be rejected as entirely at odds with not only phenomenological theory but also the experience of corporeally being in the living world. What are currently understood, in specific contexts, as the embodied states of woman/female (or man/male; or trans*; or non-binary)—indeed, the question of which corporeal categories are considered foundational, foregrounded, (im)possible—can never be considered a closed question. As such, my goal is not to argue for an eradication of attention to cultural, discursive, or ideological variables but to highlight the necessary awareness of their interactions with material/corporeal aspects of lived experience—an awareness that does not limit but expands our understandings of being. Ultimately, I will suggest that attention to a sensually and materially lived multiplicity, conceived of sonically rather than visually—a type of *polyphonic embodiment*—allows us to grasp more fully the complexity of a capacious human-environment interaction that encompasses the arguably limitless components (material, geo-/socio-cultural, ideological, etc.) that contribute to the subject's formation and perpetual re-formations.

GENDERED SOCIOMUSICAL SPACES IN POST-SOVIET ESTONIA

Ihde's previously noted example of the Necker cube highlights the fallacy of understanding the object's perception as dependent upon an obliterating singularity of focus that effaces any of the possible facets and/or the myriad (re)interpretations of the ways the intersecting lines and points might be apprehended—an observation that extends to perception and experience more generally. And in this regard, as has been amply demonstrated by the literature on intersectionality, any exploration of gender, sex, and/ or sexuality must engage with the numerous co-constituting dynamics and variables in which they come to be lived. It is thus beneficial to understand the specificities of post-Soviet Estonia concerning questions of ethnicity, language, citizenship, and sociocultural space in relation to the Russian-speaking and ethnically Russian population there.[4] Following the dissolution of the Soviet Union, those who had previously been Estonian citizens (the majority of whom were ethnic Estonians) received their original citizenship from the reestablished state, while the large percentage of erstwhile Soviet citizens (approximately 30 percent of the population, the largest number of whom were Russian) were faced with a choice: apply for Estonian citizenship, accept citizenship from the Russian Federation, or refuse to choose and become a "stateless" person residing in the Baltic republic. While the majority of the Russian-speaking population chose Estonian citizenship, a significant number (up to 90,000, many of whom live in border cities such as Narva, where the population is more than 80 percent ethnically Russian or Russian-speaking) were classified as having "undefined citizenship" because of their refusals of both geopolitical choices and were thus issued "gray passports." Some have suggested that the rejection of the offer of Estonian citizenship stems, in part, from its complex application process, which includes a mandatory examination in the Estonian language—one that is considered extremely difficult for non-native speakers to learn and that a significant percentage of the ethnically Russian population neither use nor understand.[5] However, it is notable that even among those former Soviet citizens who have applied for Estonian citizenship and have fulfilled all of the application requirements—including a passing grade on the language exam—there remains for many a self-segregation on linguistic, cultural, and geographic levels,[6] a decades-long dynamic that has in many ways extended into the post-post-Soviet era.[7] In Tallinn, for example, both the districts of Lasnamäe and Põhja-Tallinn are home to majority-Russian populations, while other districts (including Nõmme, Pirita, and Keskinn) are overwhelmingly populated by ethnic Estonians; walking the streets of Kopli (a subdistrict of Põhja-Tallinn), the styles of architecture and dress; the language spoken on the streets, in the shops, or on public transport; the media and advertisements visible in kiosks, or plastered on walls in public spaces; and products in kiosks and grocery stores all contribute to the making of a distinctly Russian (and non-Estonian) space.

Another such Russian-made space was Valeriia's Tallinn concert on May 6, 2017. Held in the immense Tondiraba Ice Hall (Tondiraba jäähall / Тондираба ледовая арена) in the western part of the city, the program was nearly identical in terms of music, video images, performer banter, and sartorial accoutrements to that presented one night earlier in Tartu at the Vaneumise Concert Hall (Vanemuise kontserdimaja / Концертный зал Ванемуйне).[8] Both spaces were populated by what appeared to be almost exclusively Russian or Russian-speaking attendees; I did not hear Estonian spoken at either event, save for one or two of the facilities' staff members. But in addition to language and ethnic identity, both venues were sites in which gender—in relation to audience and performer, and the interactions between and among them—was highlighted. Here, the audience itself exhibited an asymmetry in relation to (binary constructions of) sex, with likely upward of 80 percent of the attendees being women. Valeriia herself—largely unknown to most in the non-Russian-speaking sphere, but a superstar among these populations worldwide—has, over the course of nearly three decades, produced a substantial body of work,[9] in consort with a deft self-fashioning, both of which offer rich territories for analysis of the discursive production of the feminine/female in contemporary Russia and its diaspora. In many ways, the superstar appears to be the epitome of what I would call the modern, successful—indeed, idealized and aspirational—"new post-post-Soviet" woman: awarded the title *Zasluzhennaia artistka Rossiiskoi Federatsii* (Honored artist of the Russian Federation) in 2005,[10] she has sold millions of albums in her home country and is a favorite of President Putin. And although she has, with only partial success, attempted to translate her native accomplishments to the international, anglophone market,[11] and lived in and continues to vacation in the West,[12] she is nonetheless perceived (and presents herself) as an upstanding Russian woman: supportive of her country (including Putin's annexation of Crimea and the anti-"gay propaganda" legislation),[13] a devoted wife and mother (albeit on her third marriage), and a self-professed devout Russian Orthodox Christian (although her current husband, Iosif Prigozhin, is Jewish). In addition, she has taken on roles and projects that represent her status as a model for women wishing to better their physical, economic, and interpersonal situations: beyond her singing career, she is a successful businesswoman whose interests have included a chain of fitness centers, as well as video, audio, and print versions of her own exercise regimes (including yoga). But perhaps the action and artifact that has been most resonant with large numbers of her fans was the publication of her 2006 autobiography, *I zhizn', i slezy, i liubov'* (И жизнь, и слёзы, и любовь; Life, tears, and love), which detailed the years of physical and emotional abuse from her former husband, manager, and songwriter Aleksandr Shul'gin, her escape from his control, her retreat from show business and the public eye, and her ultimate comeback: the once quirky, indie-type niche performer reemerging as a powerful, beautiful, designer-clothing-clad megastar, one who controls her creative output and has commanded (according to her current husband) upward of €100,000 per private performance before the Russian and ex-Soviet political and business elite (see *The Independent* 2008).

Both of Valeriia's 2017 Estonian concerts began identically: Lights dimmed, and the initial sounds of the first song were heard—a sequenced synthesizer ostinato, a rhythmic wah-guitar riff, and a sixteenth-note pattern on hi-hats articulating a quick quadruple meter—followed by the singer entering, attired in a black-sequined, hooded jumpsuit. Taking her place in the center of the stage, the microphone in her hand, she shouted "Dobryi vecher!" (Good evening!) and, as the audience cheered, began singing "Nichego lichnogo" (Nothing personal). Taken from what was at the time her most recent album, *Okeany* (Океаны; Oceans), the song and the video presented perhaps a quintessential distillation of Valeriia's artistic and public persona to that point.[14] The narrator of the song tells of a love that has slowly faded, though a residual affection for her one-time lover may still remain; but rather than mourn, pine, or suffer, she appears to reflect on the past with sanguinity and fondness. Occupied with the events of her own life ("Menia okruzhaiut drugie zaboty" [There are other things going on around me]), she tells her erstwhile paramour, "Zhizn'—takaia, kak est', i nichego lichnogo/Ia zhelaiu tebe, shtob bylo otlichno vse" (That's how life is, and [it's] nothing personal—I wish that everything will be great for you).

The video—which was not played at the concert but was almost certainly known by many in the audience[15]—fleshes out the scenario even more fully. In it, Valeriia straddles the line between "character" and "performer": the narrator/[Valeriia] wakes in her large, stylish (Moscow) apartment, displays her lithe figure while engaged in her morning yoga routine, puts on her jewels and designer clothing, makes an espresso, and heads outside for her waiting chauffeured Rolls Royce. The woman is eventually revealed as the editor of the Russian edition of *Marie Claire*, with the viewer/listener made aware of a romantic, most likely sexual relationship as well: cutting back and forth from present(s) to past(s), we see the narrator/[Valeriia] viewing the photograph of a handsome businessman profiled in a *Marie Claire* piece titled "Istoriia uspekha" (The history of success), a man with whom she will be seen sharing intimate, sensual moments.[16] However, following what appears to be the cessation of their relationship, she serendipitously eyes him across the room at a party, while singing the song's chorus to him—"that's how life is"—as part of what might be a karaoke performance. Ultimately, back in her apartment, she finds a photograph of the former couple while flipping through a glossy, coffee-table book on the Art Nouveau style. As the camera focuses on them, the man's picture slowly fades, only the narrator/[Valeriia] remains,[17] and the viewer is left to infer from the lyrics, the upbeat style of the song, and the rich, bright colors and sun-drenched lighting that mark the visuals of the video—as well as the woman's constant smiles and indications of sexual satisfaction—that the gentle dissipation of the man into nothingness is no cause for misery; "that's how life is," pleasurable and fulfilling, with or without a lover.[18]

Music, Experience, Phenomenology: Some Foundational Posits

The gendered aspects of the concert—comprising the composition of the audience, the contents of the song texts, the singer's sartorial style, and her banter with the audience— are not insignificant, and in the contexts of studies attempting to elucidate (asymmetric, discursively produced) power structures, the concept/construction of gender is arguably essential. However, I want to suggest that in order to explore the richness, complexity, and multimodality of lived subjectivity in and with the phenomenal world (indeed, to explore nothing less than being), attention to the physical, material, and sexed body offers possibilities for understanding both intersubjective and subject-environment relationships, as well as the opportunity to move away from sexual dimorphism and the limitations of gender and other ideological constructions. Although "discourse" and "ideology" are as "real" as the materiality they help to make legible, an obsession with either or both reduces the multifarious registers of existence to a sad, barren territory marked by inescapable subjective impotence. And if classical phenomenology might be critiqued for its belief in the possibility (or desirability) of bracketing off phenomena from their contexts (i.e., the Husserlian epoché), then a significant amount of cultural critique (emanating from myriad disciplines devoted to the exploration of expressive culture), via a near-obsessive focus on one register, must equally be viewed with suspicion and/or skepticism. The erasure of sex, smells, corporeal sensations, desires, affects, and aesthetics (inter alia) seems to be the necessary correlate to an unquestioned belief in the omnipotence of the discursive-ideological, which often appears as some sort of malevolent, exegetical deus ex machina.[19] What I want to suggest here is that it is exactly a phenomenological and theoretical engagement with such obliterated registers that offers the possibility of short-circuiting (the belief in the supremacy of) ideologically motivated discursive production of subject and environment. To begin and end an analysis of Valeriia's work with reference to gender (and/or political discourses)—eliding her own and her listeners' (sexed, geocultural, imaginative) materiality—is to render any such analysis incomplete.

As an initial step in attempting a more holistic analysis—referring back to my experiential introduction, and gesturing toward the forthcoming arguments and final conclusions—I suggest that, in order to fully understand the complexity of perceptual, embodied experience (and, consequently, to embrace the theoretical potentials of such understanding), we would do well to flip the script, and not only in relation to sex/gender differentiation; we must also approach the musical (in its corporeal, social, aesthetic, and auditory capacities) not as a special instance of the experiential added on to "a general theory of perception" but as the *necessary* locus for just such a holistic understanding, which cannot come into being via primary attention to the quotidian or "general." For with the musical, several dynamics essential to a comprehensive understanding of perceptual experience, which I will outline subsequently, are often intuitively (and, further, theoretically) understood as essential markers. In my estimation, it is not simply happenstance that so many phenomenologists, philosophers, and theorists of lived experience—from Edmund Husserl to Maurice Merleau-Ponty to René Descartes—have relied upon examples stressing musical practice and perception to elucidate key points in their works. This relation of the musical to the perceptual-experiential can be understood on several grounds.

First, it is essential to highlight that perception cannot be understood only as an engagement with the present, the literal, or with material "sense data"; on the contrary, engagement with the world relies as much upon the interrelated processes of memory and imagination, neither of which are cordoned off "in the mind" but rather marked by a "continuing close collusion with the lifeworld of its experience" (Casey 2000, x). Noting the insufficiency of theories of perception and reception based upon information theory or algorithmic models, Arnold H. Modell reminds us that "the construction of meaning is not the same as the processing of information" (2003, xii). Engendered by a wish for a neat and empirically verifiable certitude, such theories are impoverished insofar as they fail to take account of "human imaginative capacities," which "can bootstrap intentionality in the absence of immediate sensory inputs" (21)—capacities that are often spurred by auditory/aesthetic phenomena extending beyond the literal, and which can foster the experience of desire (an animating dynamic to which I will return later in this chapter).[20]

Second, due in part to the integral roles played by memory and imagination, experience cannot satisfactorily be conceived as a linear (and continually meliorative or teleological) process. Rather, it must be seen as one marked by and productive of a collapsing of strict delineations among supposedly discrete temporalities; such an understanding is clearly related to the musical. Merleau-Ponty shows that the "intentional arc" of our pre-reflexive motor behavior "projects round about us our past, our future, [and] our human setting" ([1958] 2005, 157), while Casey highlights the ways in which certain types of memory result in "an immanence rather than 'intersection' between past and present" (as well as a propulsion to the future) (2000, 168). And although Husserl's theory of the foundational role played by recollection in the construction of the apodictic certainty of the perceptual present (and the perceiving cogito) seems, on one level, to maintain temporal distinctions between past, present, and future (1985), it is arguable that his positing of experience and subjectivity as marked by "an endless stream from the past and an endless stream into the future" (i.e., retentions and protentions; 13) precludes the erection of impermeable barriers between one (temporal) state and another. Moreover, that the verification of ontological presence, in the present, is available only via recourse to a summoning of the past (in the present); that the present-existing subject (the ego) is marked by the ability (or necessity) of projecting a "transcendental future" before itself; and that retentions themselves will be continually and self-recursively modified, though each will "[carry] within [themselves] ... the heritage of the past in the form of a series of adumbrations" (Husserl [1928] 1991, 31), all point toward conceptions of time that are far more complex and layered than a simple linearity marked by unidirectional causality.

Third, I highlight the extent to which subjectivity, indissolubly linked to engagement with the world, has rightly become conceptualized as inextricable from embodied existence (in phenomenological inquiry as much as in, for example, neuroscience or psychology); similarly, any holistic understanding of musical practice (from performance to listening) cannot omit the somatic. While works by Merleau-Ponty, Simone de Beauvoir, and Jean-Paul Sartre (and those of later theorists such as Alphonso Lingis) may be seen as among the most important exponents of a corporeally focused phenomenological philosophy, the ineluctable pull of the somatic is apparent even in Husserl. In his discussion of memory and apodicticity, for example, he continuously makes his points by drawing attention to an acting body, the materiality of which often takes the form of vibration (i.e., music); the subject "[swims] together with ... [and] toward" a "phenomenologically reduced tone," or engages in "continuous grasping" "with open arms" when confronted with the self-illumined new (1985, 13). Moreover, his description of the meeting between subject and phenomenon takes, in one instance, an almost carnal, erotic tone, turning the perceived into a fleshly interlocutor (thus inherently questioning the unidirectionality of intentionality, as Merleau-Ponty would later do). Envoicing his compelling entity, Husserl writes,

> There is still more to see here, turn me so you can see all my sides, let your gaze run through me, draw closer to me, open me up, divide me up; keep on looking me over again and again, turning me to see all sides. You will get to know me like this, all that I am, all my surface qualities, all my inner sensible qualities, "etc."
>
> (Husserl 2001, 41; cited in Stoller 2013, 20–21).

As noted earlier, Casey and Thomas Fuchs both posit embodied memory as playing a formative, essential role in the production (and, one might infer, maintenance) of subjectivity, the former arguing that memory cannot be properly conceived of absent an understanding of the foundational, embodied nature of the person's relationship to the world.[21]

Finally, and of central importance to my approaching arguments, I underscore the importance of understanding that the various modalities of perception and experience, even subjectivity itself, are marked by dynamics of openness, undecidability, and, arguably, productivity. Such qualities may seem to be opposed to corporeality, but they are not. Merleau-Ponty's claims that "existence is indeterminate in itself" ([1958] 2005, 173) and that "a genius for ambiguity might serve to define man" (195),[22] as well as the emphasis that Mark Johnson (1987, 2007), George Lakoff and Johnson (1999), Modell, and Casey put on the centrality of metaphorization in human life—a process whereby an object's ontology is ambiguous (simultaneously is like / is not)[23]—all illustrate the extent to which twentieth-century philosophers have renounced claims about access to absolute knowledge, while highlighting the very flexibility of embodied existence. Indeed, rather than viewing Husserl's method of reduction as offering an inroad to irreducible essence, Merleau-Ponty portrays it as having the "function . . . to unveil a third dimension in which the distinction [between 'objective' and 'subjective'] becomes problematic" (1964, 264). And Husserl's own work also highlights the extent to which perception and experience are processual and multiple: by positing the ontology of the object as only graspable via a series of ever-productive adumbrations—via horizons which continually beget new horizons, new indeterminacies—he calls into question the very notion of closure,[24] by extension implicitly characterizing the perceiving subject as a "possibility-being" (Heinämaa 2012, 236). On a foundational level, that music's very ontology—its constant play of im↔materiality—is ambiguous highlights again the necessity of its centrality in analyses of perception and experience.

So, while both Husserl's and Merleau-Ponty's analyses often explore the ambiguity of perceptual experience "in general" (although certainly often via recourse to specific examples), I would argue that, insofar as I wish in my inquiry to highlight the importance of the somatic and the imaginary in relation to possibility, it is still the musical (or at least the auditory) that deserves pride of place. That the human nervous system may be conceived of as functioning in a parallel rather than serial manner suggests the utility of exploring our experiences with and in relation to sound rather than, for example, image (polyphonies rather than palimpsests, although both modes of experience may exist simultaneously).[25] Moreover, the vibrational character of sound—a vibration which is itself marked by multiplicity[26]—engenders a relationship between subject and environment that obtains, in significant measure, at the level of embodied materiality. Finally, Ihde explicitly asserts that what characterizes the imaginative mode lies closer not to the visual but to the auditory, that there is "a secret liaison between the 'flow' of imagination and the 'flow' of the auditory. Each begins with the same grammar" (2007, 122). As I will argue shortly, it is within and in relation to the musical that the corporeal, imaginative, and temporal combine in ways that offer extraordinary possibilities for understanding the complexity of lived experience. Musical experience(s), heightened not only by the simultaneity of registers that vibrate a lived understanding of openness but also—as I will discuss later in this chapter—by the intensities of the aesthetic and the affective, are thus those in and through which the human capacity and propensity for transformation may often occur.

Sexed Bodies

Валерия, Ваши песни- жизнь 😊 Слушая Ваши песни, я вижу ситуации, которые случались в моей жизни, жизни моей мамы 😊. Слушая Ваши песни, хочется жить, творить, развиваться, верить в лучшее, стремиться к своей цели 😔😔 Надеюсь, что когда-нибудь смогу лично познакомиться с Вами. It's my dream 💗💗 Спасибо Вам ❤❤❤♡♡♡♣

[Valeriia, your songs are life. Listening to your songs, I see the situations that occurred in my life, and the life of my mother. Listening to your songs, one wants to live, to create, to develop, to believe in the future, to aim for one's goals. I hope that sometime I will be able to meet you personally. *It's my dream.* Thank you.][27]

Помню её, когда она совсем молоденькой девочкой очаровала меня своим голосом, а сейчас она—высшее совершенство!

[I remember her when, as a young girl, she entirely enchanted me with her voice, and now she is beyond perfection!][28]

The foregoing outline of foundational posits may appear to give credence to criticisms that phenomenological analysis is deficient insofar as it takes recourse in decontextualized and transcendental universals; there is perhaps the unintended proposition that either (or both) geopolitical/geocultural location and/or gendered/sexed identity are insignificant "specificities" in exploring the workings of corporeal existence. In regard to this second variable, some feminist scholars have argued that phenomenology's reliance upon universalist and essentialist constructions—exploited in an attempt to hide a masculinist perspective "under the guise of neutrality and objectivity" (Fisher 2000b, 23)—precludes its use in any project animated by an ethical-political imperative to highlight the ways gendered and sexed bodies are differentially connected to and impacted upon by structures of (patriarchal) power.[29] Yet it is possible to suggest that, at least conceptually, such critiques may lead to theoretical impasses and untenable propositions. If we heed the calls to engage a specifically female corporeality, as a means to undoing a masculinist essentialism, there is arguably a risk of *re*-essentializing and othering the female body, of treating it as so radically different as to require a unique set of conceptual tools. Moreover, in cases where specific forms of embodiment that are exclusively female are taken as markers of the effaced category "woman"—for example, Iris M. Young's explorations of pregnancy (1984, 1985)—there is the danger that one bodily state becomes synecdochical for *all* women (thus essentializing, while simultaneously erasing those who have not borne children). But as Simone de Beauvoir's influential writings show, to accept the body's materiality, and its sexual morphology, is not to suggest a foundational relationship between sex and destiny. Moreover, as I will argue in the final sections of this chapter, to emphasize the sexed body—one that contributes to subjective and intersubjective relations to the world and others—is only essentializing so long as it is understood as that which obliterates (or, conceived of sonically, "drowns out") all other possible experiencing bodies that the subject may have/be.[30]

It is certainly the long and troubling history of biological essentialism—in relation to race, sex, class, and other variables—that has contributed to the poststructuralist project of reconceptualizing and questioning the human body's material facticity, looking instead for the possibilities of subversion (= liberation) via an understanding of the discursive and (in what has become the common, and unfortunately often superficial, parlance) "performative" production of an always already gendered sex. Yet it is arguable that the disembodied subjectivity that is often the unintended (or intended?) effect of poststructuralist theory is no less "transcendental" than that of idealist philosophy, the workings of "power" and "ideology" practically numinous in their inscrutability. In a trenchant and compelling essay critiquing the poststructuralist dismissal of the somatic and its valorization of the constructivist and the ideological as explanans, Toril Moi—contrasting the posits of theorists such as Judith Butler, Elizabeth Grosz, and Donna Haraway with those of Simone de Beauvoir and Gayle Rubin—notes that the split between the concepts of "sex" and "gender" is not found in all languages (Moi 1999). Considering Norwegian, Russian, or Dutch (to use examples from the languages with which I am familiar) as a verification, for example,[31] Moi's observation appears perspicacious and supports her argument that what has become sedimented as a social (or often seemingly transcendental) "fact" in anglophone scholarship (the sex/gender split) is but one culturally specific manner of exploring sexed materiality. In her estimation,

> While . . . structural theories of what a woman is enable feminists to produce quite remarkable critiques of sexist ideology and misogynist abuse of power, they have notorious difficulties in explaining what the sexually different body has to do with being a woman, or with women's oppression, and in providing a sufficiently nuanced account of individual subjectivity. Nor are they well placed to provide analyses of power relations more complex than that of domination and subordination. (25)

As Moi argues, much poststructuralist theory appears to be based upon an unyielding, intransigent belief in the power of a linguistic means of crafting a putatively compliant, inconsequential corporeal materiality into forms dictated by an omnipotent and omnipresent "power"—to, in fact, efface any trace of this apparently inert substance, to render it merely a carriage of discourse, an effect of the means itself. It is thus both ironic and apropos that she finds logical inconsistencies with this stance via recourse *to* linguistic structuring. Of course, to suggest that all poststructuralist thought uniformly vanquishes the body is to ignore the significant differences *among* poststructuralist theorists—feminist gender theory as opposed to sexual difference theory; the works of Butler, Eve Kosofsky Sedgwick, or Haraway contrasted with those of Julia Kristeva, Luce Irigaray, Rosi Braidotti, or Hélène Cixous, for example.[32] And it would be fallacious to infer that the sophisticated analyses of any or all of these theorists deny the material facticity of corporeality or preclude their utility in moving beyond a binary of body *or* (linguistically replicated) discourse. But taking Butler's analyses as in many ways exemplary,[33] I would argue that while a strictly digital differentiation between, for example, materiality and ideology has been foreclosed (for Butler, the terms cannot be understood as independent of one another), the very marker of binarity—namely, hierarchy (in relation to both qualitative and temporal aspects assumed to obtain in the relationship between discourse/ideology and materiality)—is, in a very un-poststructuralist fashion, maintained. Specifically, Butler states unequivocally that discourse *precedes* and *enables* any "I" "who utters or speaks[,] and thereby produces an effect in discourse." For Butler,

> there is no "I" who stands *behind* discourse and executes its volution or will *through* discourse. On the contrary, the "I" only comes into being through being called, named, interpellated, to use the Althusserian term, and this discursive constitution takes place **prior** to the "I"; it is the transitive invocation of the "I." (1993, 171; bold emphasis added; italics in the original)

By endeavoring to expose "subjectivity" as an effect rather than source of discourse, Butler troubles any attempts to claim the transcendental, originary status of any "I," but in so doing, they also reject any corporeal/biological "I" who might be posited as the material *source of* or *other to* (theories of) socially constructed gender. Yet one might argue that what has been accomplished here is not the eradication of the binary (exposing subject/discourse, sex/gender, or original/copy as unthinkable one without the other, in line with such Derridian formulations as supplementarity or *différance*) but rather its *inversion*. Arguing that the humanist subject can no longer be understood to precede those very things assumed to be of their making has not, in this formulation, led to an understanding of a mutually constitutive relationship but to the valorization of a triumvirate of discourse/ideology/power that holds an exclusive temporal, structural, and theoretical primacy, existing before and in superior relation to all other registers—including the somatic.

Indeed, although numerous theorists from varied fields of inquiry have argued for an understanding of the formative force of somaticity in relation not only to supposedly "universal" and "disembodied" theory but also to language itself, corporeality in Butler's work never appears to be unambiguously held to exist at the level of mutually constitutive simultaneity with discourse, let alone to take a causative role; for them, there is no body/nobody prior to discourse. Butler's work has been instrumental in contributing to the understanding of the complex relations between materiality and its discursive production. However, it is difficult to ignore that in the very analysis meant to address critics who claimed that bodies, for them, "don't [in multiple ways] matter," the reader is greeted from the very outset with a type of materiality that is, yet again, by its very nature incorporeal. "The materiality of the body," Butler argues in the introduction to *Bodies That Matter*, "will not be *thinkable* apart from the materialization of [the] regulatory norm," and materiality must be "*rethought* as the effect of power, as power's most productive effect" (1993, xii; italics added). It is not inconsequential that materiality is, from the outset, implicitly and "self-evidently" represented (and "*understood*") as unquestionably conjoined to the ideal (thought) rather than the experiential (thinking/doing) sphere, or that the latter seems to have no relation to the former. Moreover, one need go no further than the very preface to be greeted with the omnipotent, surreptitious puissance of the ideal over the somatic. Prior even to the introduction, Butler confesses that they "began writing [*Bodies That Matter*] by trying to consider the materiality of the body only to find that the *thought* of materiality *invariably moved me* into other domains" (viii; italics added).

I want to suggest that these few words, appearing where they do (their location in both this specific text and its wider intellectual context), are not inconsequential, that they highlight in distilled form dynamics, auras, tinges that animate and mark much poststructuralist thought, including Butler's. In their writing, references to the material body often seem to be made from a sense of grudging dutifulness, ensuing "howevers" always—to use their metaphors—hovering as specters that haunt the concessions, the conjunctive adverb seeking to whisk us away from the somatic as quickly as possible. Thus, the placement of the ineluctability of the ideational-discursive-linguistic-ideological (that "invariably" "moves"—compels—any and all subjects) in the opening moments of their text is notable. Might it be that this supposedly invincible matrix functions (subconsciously?) as a justification for the immediate retreat from embodiment that, although implicitly represented as either phantasmatic or a concatenation of benign, malleable, insensate stuffs, is quite to the contrary (subconsciously? experientially?) understood as extraordinarily dangerous? I am referring not to a danger one might find implicitly and explicitly hypothesized in myriad poststructuralist texts—the danger of unreflective, unwavering belief in biological essentialism—but to the peril of positing the material body as anything *other* than inert/malleable, the risk of sustained attention to corporeality and experience that strays from the very types of unreflective and unwavering stances assumed to be so deleterious. Moi, noting the extraordinary poststructuralist investment in the erasure of the physical body, has "the impression that poststructuralists believe that if there *were* biological facts, then they would indeed give rise to social norms. In this way, they paradoxically share the fundamental belief of biological determinists" (1999, 42). Such motivations lie, I believe, at the foundations of dogmatic poststructuralist thought, whereby mattering bodies are approached (to use a much more material, less ghostly metaphor) as a ring of fire impeding the journey into discursivity. Seeking to cover their bases, poststructuralist theorists might briefly note ideas of embodiment and experience, but they must be immediately traversed in order to reach the "real" (albeit incorporeal, practically supernatural) site of inquiry (norms, power, language, ideology); these blazing impediments are to be navigated with as much haste as possible, lest they make manifest (via their capacity to burn, to scorch the somatic subject) the profound capacity of the material to affect and be affected, to lie at the heart of what will ultimately be second-order theorization. The longer one stays with the body, the more difficult it becomes to ignore it in its sensing/sensate capacity, its power. While Butler and others highlight the formative (primary) role of language vis-à-vis "mattering bodies,"[34] they neglect (possibly owing to discomfiture) the significant ways our very linguistic structures and modes of cognition rely upon bodily metaphors borne of corporeal experience (Johnson 2007; Lakoff and Johnson 1999; Casey 2000; Modell 2003).

And so—in line with Moi's critique—I would maintain that to the extent a concept of gender obliterates the body as only ever (or primarily) an effect, a means of erasing somaticity as always already merely a construction, it may be of limited use in relation to a phenomenological exploration of lived corporeal subjectivity. This is not to suggest, of course, that there are existential states that are immune to or outside of the workings of ideology and discourse. For example, Fuchs notes a specifically "intercorporative" type of body memory (2012, 15ff) whereby—in line, I believe, with Bourdieu's ([1972] 1977) concept of habitus—one may consciously or unconsciously adopt (socially sanctioned) behaviors of others.[35] Yet lived, sentient beings in the world cannot be *reduced* to the effects of discourse-ideology, lest we lose, as Moi argues, "the concrete, historical body that loves, suffers, and dies" (1999, 49). These are exactly the types of bodies that animate the work of Alphonso Lingis, a scholar whose explorations engage the innumerable profundities of corporeality—from the human face to human lust, from bodybuilding to death, from the opacity of human flesh to the transparency of the box jellyfish (Lingis 1994, 2000, 2018). My goal here is not to diminish the importance or iron out the complexities of poststructuralist thought, to replace it with what might likely be dismissed as a return to simplistic, romantic, poetic, antediluvian figurations. Yet attending to the touch of one body against another body, skin against skin—experiencing (*not* conceptualizing) such contact as having been replaced by an indescribable void in the context of pandemic-mandated "social" distancing—the *limitations* of work such as Butler's become evident. Lingis's work, startlingly different yet no less complex, takes the body not as a grudging footnote, an illusory digression threatening deception, but as indeed pulsing with a poetry of which one need not be ashamed or afraid. Here, the body—no less discursively or ideologically defined and constructed but, concurrently, so much more than simply this—exceeds the limitations of the arid language and scopocentric theoretical logics that attempt to constrain it.

Finally, a hypertrophied reliance upon gender-as-discourse and ideology obliterates the embodied subject who—as Moi implies—is marked (indeed, is partly defined) by its affective capacities and capabilities. Extending Moi's analysis further, I want to suggest two ways that such an erasure, including the specific erasure of sexed bodies, is especially problematic in relation to explorations of the relationship of (inter)subjectivity to expressive culture—including the auditory, the musical (which, I am arguing, is central to an understanding of inter/subjectivity). First, to eliminate the corporeal is to entirely misrepresent one of the foundational ways the sonic and aesthetic are apprehended; and second, to speak of *an* embodied relationship to the auditory once again suggests a problematic corporeal—which is to say, a default masculine—universal. Pertaining to the first, and as I have discussed previously in relation to repetition (Amico 2014), the occlusion of affective modalities by a solitary focus on disembodied, putatively universal concepts (these inextricably bound to language)—repetition as compulsion, undergirded by dynamics of citationality and iterability, as opposed to the *experience* of repetition as a pleasurable and essential component of one's relationship to music and sex, for example—highlights the extent to which any "concept" removed from the living subject/environment engenders significant distortions. Understanding that innumerable forms of repetition mark existence and experience in intricate and foundational ways, I argue that the absence of attention to those instances where the affective, the expressive, the pleasurable are essential results in the degradation of something complex and rich to a one-dimensional, incorporeal shell. In one type of grim, poststructuralist universe of (discursively produced and gendered) bodies without (sexual) organs (phalluses, not penises; asperity, not bliss), near-automata are confined by apparently universal psychoanalytic structures. Yet what is absent is exactly that which appears, in fact, to be "universal," borne out by research in numerous disciplines: the human capacity, need, desire for organizing sound; for creating pictorial or three-dimensional representations; for adorning/modifying/beautifying the body; for creating / engaging in / sustaining (for centuries) rituals; all of this marked by a heightened, indispensable, and often overwhelming and ravishing affectivity. If the poststructuralist legacy has contributed to a mistrust of the foregrounding of corporeality in explorations of being and experience, I suggest that this is motived by nothing less than what appears to me a positively Victorian panic in the face of embodied desire and sexuality, a horror so complete as to obscure the liberatory possibilities of exploring our sentient, desiring, affectively and aesthetically engaged physicality, to which I will shortly turn.

AUDIOVISUALITY, THE CATALYTIC AIDE-MÉMOIRE, AND PROPRIOCEPTIVE AUTO-AFFECTION

Returning to the Estonian concerts, I begin this focus on the body by noting that in both Tallinn and Tartu, Valeriia preceded her performance of her then-recently-released song "Sil'nye zhenshchiny" (Strong women) by dedicating the piece to all of the women in the audience (mothers, wives, sisters, and daughters) for their fortitude in the face of life's many challenges.[36] The lyrics to the song present "woman" in what may be seen as a stereotypically Russian (indeed Soviet) manner, thus resonating with the concert's attendees: a combination of strength, sensitivity, and self-abnegation, with suggestions of moral superiority. Here "woman" is largely positioned in relation to family and the role of mother:

Счастливой, всецелой, каждая хочет быть	Every [woman] wants to be happy, whole
Высокую цену, за это судьбе платить	A high price is paid for this fate
Но сильной женщине и сильной маме	But for a strong woman and a strong mother
Тоже бывает больно, но никто не знает	Pain also occurs, but nobody knows
Сильные женщины тоже плачут	Strong women also cry
Если слёз не видно, это ничего не значит	If the tears aren't visible, this doesn't mean anything

Singing these words during the concert's second act, Valeriia—now dressed in a white, sleeveless, two-tiered print dress and crystal-studded stilettos, wrists and fingers

FIGURE 7.1: Screen grabs from the music video "Sil'nye zhenshchiny" (Verenchik 2015).

adorned with similarly glittering and light-catching jewelry—stood at the front of the stage, the images of the song's original music video projected behind her. These images reflected the hard/soft dichotomy that marks "woman" in the song, with a tiny Valeriia—dressed throughout the majority of the video in a flowing, smoke/sky-blue gown, long blond hair fluid and billowing like the chiffon of the gown's skirt—ultimately lifted and carried by three massive stone women, borne from the steep, jagged cliffs that mark the desolate landscape in which they all are found. This trio of Amazon-like figures ultimately transport Valeriia to a place, it appears, of hope and transcendence. Her blue gown momentarily turning to a vibrant (sexual) crimson (and ultimately shifting back to the almost angelic blue), she approaches a slit of gleaming radiance pouring through a crevasse in the cliff's face, a luminescence revealed by the labor of the three stone figures who have pulled one of the cliff's faces apart (see Figure 7.1).

The representation of the female genitalia here is arguably both symbolic and overt. And although this is one of the most conspicuous invocations of a specifically sexual, female corporeality in any of Valeriia's audiovisual output, it is notable that a significant number of her music videos feature presentations of embodied states that may likewise be read in both registers: from her expression of sexual/sensual desire, often surrounded by handsome, sexualized men, in the videos for "Telo khochet liubvi" (The body wants love) and "Kopel'kuiu" (Droplet), to expressions of physical, maternal tenderness in "Ty moia" (You are my [mine]; a duet with her daughter, Anna Shul'gina), to a portrayal of women who are met with physical and psychological violence in "Serdtse razorvano" (The heart is broken) or "Mikroinfrakty" (Heart attack). Moreover, in some videos, multiple versions of the female or the feminine are juxtaposed against each other, highlighting the multifarious ways of defining them in a specifically Russian context. In "Verni mne nadezhdu" (Give me back hope), for example, three archetypes are presented, the colors of each of Valeriia's outfits collectively mirroring those of the Russian flag: sexual desire (red sequin dress, the singer moving her body sinuously in a water-filled piano), strength and self-sufficiency (blue, two-piece pantsuit, the singer sitting in a "masculine" posture with legs apart and torso forward), and maternal nurturing (white robes, here worn by another woman who at one point appears to be nursing an infant). That Valeriia is known as a "fashionista" of sorts and that images of her in athletic clothing and swimwear have appeared frequently in the popular press (often with complimentary commentary that notes both her age and the fitness of her figure)[37] further highlights the extent to which body is an integral part of her self-presentation.

It would, however, be erroneous to assume that the relationship of singer to listener (and of listeners to singer, and to one another) can be fully explored if inquiry is left at the level of body-as-image (or at the level of disembodied gender as only/primarily a sociocultural/political construction). It is clear that, perhaps especially in the realm of popular music, the mediated image is inextricably linked to the sonic, the biographical, the spatial, and numerous other registers. Yet it is the auditory, the sonicity of embodied being that, I believe, offers fecund possibilities for understanding the ways in which a sexed (inter)subjectivity obtains. In this regard, I first suggest that we consider image as an intermediary or *facilitator* for the establishment of a deep connection of self and other, the formation of which comes about via something I will (perhaps inelegantly) term a *catalytic aide-mémoire* (and also via the proprioceptive capacities of the human body, which I discuss further later). Conceiving of the aide-mémoire in a specifically musical sense, we may envision the neumatic notation of Gregorian chant—a technology enlisted in order to provide a visual "reminder" for what was, in large part, an oral tradition (albeit one that existed in complex relation to the written).[38] Kenneth Levy contends that the producers of these manuscripts, who chose the "inexact" "staffless neumes" to transcribe the chants, "were content with incomplete representations of melodic substance because the full substance seemed safely logged in memory" (1987, 87). Yet conceiving such aides as residing solely or chiefly in "memory"—with suggestions of transcendent/immaterial consciousness—is problematic.

My appropriation and alteration of this term should be understood as follows. First, the additional qualifier ("catalytic") is meant to highlight the difference between the purposeful, goal-oriented taking up of a manuscript in one's hands in performance versus the way that images are encountered in concerts and videos, which serve as catalysts, potentiators. In emphasizing this difference, I do not mean to imply that viewers of music performances do not purposefully attend to the visual data; clearly, they do. Rather, I wish to draw attention to the fact that they do not do so to *intentionally* engender a new state of experience; rather, the catalytic aide-mémoire operates in a more subtle way, as an embodied experience preceding volition. Further to this, I wish to suggest that the aide-mémoire, as I conceive of it—including in relation to Gregorian manuscripts—cannot be thought of as (exclusively) transmitting "cognitive data" from image to (disembodied) "mind." Although they need not be explicitly representational in form, the images encountered in an aide-mémoire—whether in the service of goal-oriented action or not—almost certainly call forth an entire constellation of corporeal associations that may likewise be double-sided. That is, even in cases of intentional motility, the corresponding actions of the subject are not reliant exclusively on cognition, as Levy's conceptualization might seem to suggest, but depend on body memory. As Fuchs maintains, the phenomenon of body memory is an "impressive refutation of the dualism of pure consciousness and the physical body, for it cannot be attributed to either of them" (2012, 11).[39] And Casey's differentiation between recollection and body memory will assist in further highlighting the contrast between image and experience: positing the "depth" of the latter, which is related to the depth of the body itself, he suggests that a subject's recollection (here, his own) often results in

> a quasi-pictorial distance from myself as a voyeur of the remembered. No such voyeurism occurs in body memory, which takes me directly *into* what is being remembered. In such remembering, I leave the heights of contemplative recollection and enter the profundity of my own bodily being. (2000, 167)

Continuing to highlight the difference between the visual and the corporeal (and, as I will argue, a corporeality that may be conceived of in relation to the auditory), he also notes the ways in which the latter troubles temporal distinctions, suggesting that body memory is marked by "immanence rather than 'intersection' between past and present":

> Instead of taking up a perspective on the past—getting a clearer "view" of it as we so often attempt to do in recollection or reminiscence—in body memories we allow the past to enter actively into the very present in which our remembering is taking place. (168)

This perspicuity of the visual components of recollection—a "pictorial precision" which Casey implicitly relates to Alfred North Whitehead's conception of "presentational immediacy"—is contrasted with a body memory, "heavy in its dense implications for all subsequent re-membering" (178). And it is this "remembering" body—a body which is indeed not, as some feminist critics rightly maintain, "universal"; a body that is, as part of its proprioceptive comprehension, sexed—that is implicated in the deep relationship of Valeriia to her listener/viewer-fans, a relationship that is reflected, among other places, in their comments on various internet sites. When viewing the images of female sensual/sexual arousal, or the restraint of the female body by (male) force, or breast-feeding, or the enjoyment of self-presentations as scopic object of desire in the heat, water, and sunshine—all at the same time being (literally) vibrated by sound, affected by the chordal-melodic-timbral-rhythmic dimensions of her music—there may arise a resonance between listener and singer, and among listeners (in part potentiated but not *exhausted* by the visual), that far exceeds the limitations of language, image, or discursive production. A specific corresponding embodied knowledge of such states of a female body obtains, within and *as* one's own female body, immersive and not perspectival. Here, in the case of the erotic, it is not a question of sexual arousal in general, but *this* arousal, *those* sensations, based in part on one's anatomy (including the specific constellations and interactions of sensing, experiencing internal and external erogenous zones). There is a proprioception of femaleness that is not reduced to a de-sexed "general instrumentality" (i.e., allowing for the proper situation of one's self in relation to three-dimensional space) but that in its complex specificity is what I might call "auto-affective," feeling one's body *as* affected in relation to one's lived, experienced, felt internal and external morphology. We might note here Casey's analysis of body memory not as something general or generic but as exhibiting several distinct registers—traumatic body memory, for example, as opposed to erotic body memory. Following his work, I suggest that when Valeriia kinesthetically and sonically expresses the pains of an intimate relationship or the joys of erotic bliss—in the context of her own (known) biography; with sartorial, comportmental, and cultural attributes contributing to a sexed subject resonant with her specific (Russian) audience—it is more than possible that a sense of shared traumatic or erotic body memory may be implicated in the creation of a connection between audience and performer.

I am not, of course, arguing for an analysis based upon biological essentialism. I agree, for example, with Sara Heinämaa, who argues that sexed beings cannot be and are not exclusively "defined" by their genitalia (or, I would add, secondary sex characteristics) and that we may conceive of sexual difference "not as a difference between two substances but [as] a difference between two modes or modalities of relating," intersubjectively and with one's environment (2012, 236).[40] However, I am not quite convinced by her suggestion that "the sex/gender paradigm is preoccupied with organs and organic functions" (235); much to the contrary, when such paradigms occur in poststructuralist analyses, genitals, as I have suggested earlier, seem more a signifying absence than foundational sites. Penises and vaginas (and anuses, and nipples, and mouths, as well as other erogenous zones) are nowhere to be found, apparently (implicitly) constructed as objects of power and shame that must be eradicated. More often than not, sex/sexuality is treated as a discursive imposition. While Joan Scott maintains that the analysis of the discursive production of identity is not meant to suggest "a new form of linguistic determinism ... [but] to insist instead on the productive quality of discourse" (1991, 792–793), it is remarkable how often the attention to discursivity all but obliterates the sentient body. The move in such scholarship to understand human sexuality/sensuality as engaging more than genitalia is productive, inclusive, and essential; however, the (neo-Victorian) erasure of genitalia and specifically sexed body parts is an eradication that appears untenable when taking into account the sexual and sensual desires of embodied subjects in material circumstances.

Returning to Heinämaa's focus on inter-relations[41] and my posit of auto-affected proprioception engendered in relation to the catalytic aides-mémoire, we might thus conceive of an *intersubjective* proprioception.[42] That the experiencing of one's own body might seem to be inextricably linked to the bodies of others is given support by attending to the functioning of mirror neurons, early studies of which observed their firing in response to the intentional actions of others (not simply to objects). However, as Modell notes in a review of the literature in this area, more recent studies have found the operation of mirror neurons is even more extensive: "our brains resonate to the other's feelings in [a] manner similar to how we resonate with the other's intentional actions."[43] This suggests that one's body may be thought of as "a template that enables us to feel our way into the other's experience" (Modell 2003, 187) and that the roots of empathy lie in an unconscious corporeality. With this in mind, I finally want to suggest that, combined with attention to the visual extravagance of the concert sphere and the music video, we must not forget the auditory component of Valeriia's performances, must take into account her voice—noting, not insignificantly, that she is one of what has been until relatively recently very few Russian *èstrada/popsa* stars who sing live (something often remarked upon by her fans).[44]

Don Ihde conceives of voice as referring not only to the sound that emanates from the human subject but also to a wide array of other phenomena, a move that reminds us of the importance of the auditory natures of our environments and emphasizes that "a phenomenology of sound moves [us] . . . toward a listening to the voiced character of the sounds of the World" (2007, 147). While I am in agreement with such an approach, I want to focus here on that conception of voice as sounding human body, taking into consideration Ihde's additional observations, which serve to remind us of the complexity and multivalence of the auditory/vocal: specifically, voices can resound materially as well as imaginatively/internally (the one being no less, and no more, "real" than the other); they can constitute the subject at the level of the exterior/intersubjective as well as the interior/subjective (which respectively include, on the one hand, auditory or linguistic communities and, on the other, "inner speech"; 118); and the voice, as part of the sound field, can be that which enters, comes toward, and moves into us but is also that which we "follow" (and thus is both directional and surrounding; 82).[45] The observation that (the/a/one's) voice exists on numerous registers concurrently dovetails with the view that the subject is likewise multivalent, a corporeally experiencing entity that is *of* the self and the other, the interior and the exterior synchronously. In this regard, the voice of Valeriia—the making-present sounding of her corporeality—is perhaps the most "penetrative" potentiator of the intersubjective-proprioceptive relationship of body to body. In that sonicity/audibility that vibrates one's body and that transgresses the supposedly impermeable shell of self, vibrating the interior membranes of the ears; in those vibrations made by another's chest and lungs and throat that follow the contours of one's own chest, lungs, and throat, the embodied subject—corporeally remembering past instances of having produced such sounds and corporeally experiencing them in the act of singing along—is aware of their own capacities to produce such vibrations, understands (proprioceptively) what was/is needed, how it feels (how others feel) to sound this sexed body. Moreover, that this body is female, that this voice penetrates so deeply, highlights the extraordinary potentials of attention to the sonic: penetration—to penetrate / to be penetrated—is a rich experiential state available to all bodies, one that must not be narrowly aligned with sexed morphology or gendered ideologies; that may be potentiated/received by any body's various extremities and apertures; that exists in relation to flesh as much as sound; that both engenders and transgresses relationships among specifically sexed subjectivities.[46]

At both concerts I attended, late in the second act Valeriia descended from the stage and walked through the audience while singing her song "Po serpantinu" (By the winding road)—an upbeat number with a prominent dotted rhythm performed in a style approximating 1930s East European cabaret music (and not unlike the well-known song "Bei mir bist du schön").[47] As she sang, the audience became both visibly and audibly excited, people (myself included) standing and moving in order to get a better view of the superstar. I believe that—on a level that is not mediated by language, image, or "objective analysis"—the audience's aim here was not simply to view but to feel the vibration that occurs when one body, joined by an intersubjective/intercorporeal understanding of the other, moves closer to another. In his discussion of body memory, Fuchs uses this very term—"intercorporeal"—to define a specific "temporally organized, *musical* memory for the *rhythm, dynamics, and undertones* inaudibly present in interactions with others" (15; italics added).[48] This invocation of the musical in relation to the embodied subject (and the audible components of the production of [inter] subjectivity) is again significant, as attributes of music, musical sound, and musical interactions will be shown as instrumental in relation to a corporeality that has (a) sex / that has more than (a) sex.

AFFECTS, AESTHETICS, (IM)POSSIBILITIES

To understand some human beings as male or female, based in part upon their material morphology, is not to limit embodiment to *only* this differentiation; in fact, I want to argue, the concept of gender, owing to its very genealogy, is indeed limited to and dependent upon a limiting, binary masculine/feminine split and cannot avoid them as constitutive components (including subversions of one or the other, as well as various admixtures of the two). It is possible that the almost exclusive focus on the very construction of gender *as* construction (often assumed to offer the greatest possibility of "liberation," via "subversion") and the vilification or puritanical effacement of feeling, touching, dripping, pungent sex/sexuality/sensuality, in fact, forestalls the limitlessness that experiencing, material, sexual/sensual bodies inherently offer. And in order to explore the productive possibilities of the body—having argued at the beginning of this chapter for the necessity of attention to specifically musical phenomena in relation to explorations of experience—I wish to continue highlighting the expressive, the auditory, the corporeal, and the affective, and, to add one additional register, the aesthetic. Indeed, the musical concert spaces in both Tallinn and Tartu, the relationships between Valeriia and her audience, and the formation of subjectivity in relation to both sexual embodiment and geopolitical location cannot, I believe, be convincingly theorized without acknowledging the complexity of the aesthetic—a term that, I note from the outset, should not be taken to refer to "*the* beautiful" (as singular, universal, or transcendental) or "the/a work of art" but that encompasses the embodied subject, intersubjective relationships, the environment, and expressive production. Returning to the foregoing discussion of body awareness, I note Barbara Montero's suggestion that the proprioception of the lived body may be implicated in the formation of corporeal, intersubjective relationships that are based, in part, upon the aesthetic (2006); for example, dancers' movements may be proprioceived by viewers who, having judged the aesthetic qualities of such movements, then become aware of the aesthetic capacities and qualities of their own bodies. Also relevant here is Richard Shusterman's concept of "somaesthetics" (2008, 2012b), which he defines as "the critical study and meliorative cultivation of the soma as a site both of sensory appreciation [aesthesis] and creative self-fashioning" (2011, 14). Shusterman emphasizes the importance of heightened sensory perception and its relation to the aesthetic honing of the body, as well as the ways in which this refined corporeal knowledge of the self inevitably implicates a knowing of environment and other(s), a project with significant ethical implications.[49]

It is exactly in a space where musical communication is central and where the foundational dynamics of subjective experience discussed earlier—memory/imagination, elastic temporality, resistance to closure, and embodiment—operate at intensified affective levels that the role of the aesthetic in contributing to the possibility of escaping an essentialized sexual dimorphism without effacing the materiality of the sexed body may be productively studied. I begin with attention to Mikel Dufrenne's *Phenomenology of Aesthetic Experience* ([1953] 1973), although I note from the outset that I will be extrapolating his insights by applying them not only (or even primarily) to an "aesthetic *object*"—Dufrenne's "object" of study—but, rather, to aesthetic-affective *experience*, a process that comes about as an interaction between the subject and the expressive production they encounter. For Dufrenne, this aesthetic object is distinct from the work of art, insofar as the latter exists and endures independent of any separate, exterior subjectivity, but the former only manifests in relation to an experiencing subject. This aesthetic object is remarkable not only in its ability to engender a surmounting of the subject/object opposition or its creation of a unique spatiotemporal world not contingent upon objective/scientific fact but, rather, to offer nothing less than an experience of irreducible being. As Edward Casey explains in his 1973 translator's forward to the book, Dufrenne's aesthetic object appears as the "apotheosis of the sensuous," "amenable to the body," its very meaning dependent upon neither matter nor representation but immanent in its sensuousness, thus rendering it "akin to nature, the ultimate in-itself within human experience" (xxvii).

Central to Dufrenne's argument is his formulation of the concept of the "affective *a priori*," which is shared by both aesthetic object and subject, unmediated by any sort of external representation, and implicated in the creation of profound feeling and deep reciprocity (rather than division) between the two. But if the suggestion of the existence of a priori (transcendental?) states would seem yet again to confirm suspicions of phenomenology's dependence upon idealist and universalist constructions, it is essential to highlight that Dufrenne's formulation of subject and object suggests, in my estimation, not exclusively and/or unequivocally immutable essences but a possibility for revelatory co-constitutions wherein both difference and concordance obtain simultaneously; "the *a priori*," according to Dufrenne, "is the something in common that permits communication between subject and object, without abolishing their duality in a dialectical fashion" (Dufrenne 1955, 119, quoted in Casey 1966, xix). Moreover, having asserted that subjectivity can only be known to itself via acts, Dufrenne contends that "the *a priori* is known only through . . . the *a posteriori*. . . . [That is, it] is known only through the object which it constitutes . . . [and] only through our experience with the aesthetic object" (Casey 1966, 491).[50]

While it is possible to read this formulation as referencing an already existing affective state awaiting discovery (encountered via manifestation in the subject/object reciprocity of the experiential), I find Dufrenne's contentions suggestive not of essences but of the productive *potentials* engendered by aesthetic experience, a type of experience that can only ever be open-ended. It seems clear, for example, that any state or category that can *only* be known as it comes into being—its constitution indissoluble from subjective apprehension in myriad "presents"—owes part of its ontology to a specific present that cannot but trouble an eternal/immutable essence. Moreover, that the self/other divide is shown to be superable via aesthetic experience significantly troubles one of the foundational binaries undergirding epistemologies from philosophy to sociology to political theory, revealing being as a process of prolific co-creation rather than a succession of meetings among always-already-complete, essentially discrete entities.[51] But even if one accepts the possibility of transcendent and immanent states, this need not necessarily signal an incapacitating suzerainty of stricture. For example, Dufrenne offers nothing specific regarding the *quantity* of a priori affects, and it is possible—in my view, almost certain—that if affect itself is understood as resistant to (linguistic) reduction, the number of possible states that become manifest in aesthetic objects/experiences would be limitless, as they are contingent upon (likewise limitless) specific temporal and sociocultural contexts (with some, almost certainly, unnameable, inarticulable).[52] To this one must add the permutations occurring as innumerable a priori come to be experientially constituted in the mutual relations between countless individual, unique objects/experiences meeting with equally countless, individual, unique subjects (in countless cultural, material, discursive sites), resulting in an incalculable number of experiential possibilities. Moreover, Dufrenne's comments regarding the inexhaustibility of meaning, as well as the unforeseeability of artistic/aesthetic innovation,[53] signal a continuous open-endedness in line with Husserl's view that the perceptual object can only be known through a limitless series of fecundating adumbrations. That the object for Husserl comes to be known via "*an obscurely intended to* [sic] *horizon of indeterminate actuality*"[54] (Husserl [1913] 1983, 52; italics in the original)—an "empty horizon"—signals, according to Silvia Stoller, "not nothingness, but a kind of surplus" (2013, 20): "Every appearance," in Husserl's estimation, "implies a *plus ultra* in the empty horizon" (2001, 48; cited in Stoller 2013, 20).

What this suggests is not the perception of a closed/finite set of sense data, or the processing of information via visual, cognitive, discursive, and/or propositional means, but a perception—similar to Whitehead's formulation of "causal efficacy" ([1927] 1958)—of corporeally apprehended and affectively intensified *possibilities*. Far from being mere illusions (in contrast to the supposed "reality" of "presentational immediacy"—causal efficacy's other) these possibilities are, in relation to the phenomenological understanding of the (making) sense of self and/in environment, absolutely essential. They are the horizons of experience, not simply concepts; they entail adumbrations, protentions that signal the *human-defining necessity* of experience, the temporality and corporeality of which exceeds the present and the self. For, as I will now suggest, drawing upon an observation/experience at Valeriia's Tallinn concert—an occurrence among numerous subjects, three of whom I captured on my phone's video camera—attention to intersubjective aesthetic experience offers glimmers or glimpses of an embodiment that need neither eradicate nor take as foundational sexed corporeality, an embodiment that offers adumbrations of horizons.

It was the very end of the concert and, just as she had done in Tartu the previous evening, Valeriia preceded the final song of her performance by inviting all her fans in the front section of the parterre (where I was seated) to approach the stage, to be close to her, to be close to one another. The cavernous Tondiraba Ice Hall thus rendered more intimate via our shared proximity, she began to sing a pared-down version of one of her most well-known songs, "Ia tebia otpustila" (I let you go).[55] The intimacy heightened by the centrality of Valeriia's voice in the arrangement—here, accompanied only by a synthesized piano, instead of the lush orchestral texture featured on the song's recording—the narrator of the song describes to the listener the end of her relationship with the man who no longer loves her. And while a sense of melancholy is present, there is also a great sense of agency in the words, especially those of the chorus:

Не ищу, не грущу над свечою оплывшей	I'm not searching, I'm not sad about the burned-down candles
Я тебя отпущу, человек разлюбивший	I will let you go, person who has fallen out of love
На судьбу не ропщу, все забыла, простила	I won't complain to fate, I've forgotten, forgiven everything
Я тебя отпущу, я тебя отпустила	I will let you go, I have let you go

The text, of course, is not the sole bearer of meaning, and with the tessitura of the chorus high in Valeriia's chest voice, her belting of these words—allowing us to imagine/experience the stress of lungs pushing, throat tensing, chest expanding, breath making powerful sound—communicated something exceeding the lexical. It was during the chorus that I noticed a connection at the level of sound, body, affect, and aesthetic force (and surely more than these) that transcended (and/or paid no heed to, and/or existed alongside) sexual dimorphism. As Valeriia sang live on stage, a young man and a young woman, both apparently in their late twenties or early thirties, standing within a few meters of each other at the foot of the stage, sang along with her—in Russian, in Estonia—moving their throats, their lips, their tongues, and their palates in synchrony with hers and each other's, so that at that moment male and female appeared to have been superseded, denied as a site of insuperable difference, with the mouth, lungs, diaphragm, larynx, vocal folds signaling a site of intimate, affective, aesthetic, corporeal connection, in a specific linguistic/geographic space: an *us*.

Attending specifically to the mouth, I first want to highlight its ontological ambiguity: it is material yet serves as the last line of formation of that (voice) which is, in part, immaterial; it can receive but also expel (suck, swallow; blow, spit); it is the site of those constructions that have served as arguments for both our "civilized" and our "bestial" natures (language; sex); it is interior as well as exterior (throat, palate; lips, thrusted tongue). At the same time, I want to highlight the mouth's erotic qualities, which, as I will shortly show, are connected to these ontological ambiguities. Let me first recall the erotic beckoning of Husserl's example of perceptual experience, wherein the subject focuses on the "alluring" materiality of the perceptual object, an allure that engenders (produces, draws out) the attention it receives; here, the object impels/compels living subjectivity.[56] In this, we may see a reflection of what Merleau-Ponty posits as an enlivening, corporeally sited erotic perception, "not a *cogitatio* that intends as *cogitatum*" but a body aiming at another body, "accomplished in the world, not within consciousness" ([1958] 2005, 181). Furthermore, understanding perception itself as eternally propulsive, and by its very nature only ever partial, we may also highlight that which is linked to the erotic but which evades (supplements?) materiality: desire. Renaud Barbaras argues that it is exactly this—desire—that underlies the movement of life, "insofar as the world is only given to life as what continuously and indefinitely withdraws behind its own appearance" (2012, 100).[57] Moreover, the continuous movement toward that which always slips away pertains not only to the other but to the self. In his view,

> there is no appearance, including appearance of oneself to oneself, except in and through a distance that exceeds that distance manifested by a simple object. The subject can only make something appear insofar it is capable of relating to the transcendence of the world that hides itself, or better, slips away, in the appearance of the object. (100)

And thus I want to suggest that in the musical realm of heightened, affective/aesthetic sensory perception, a realm marked by an intensification of dynamics of undecidability, atemporality, and somaticity (all of which are dependent in myriad ways upon memory and imagination), this very fecundating undecidability with which subjects interact— not as concept or representation but as a process of being, and which may be experienced as a propulsion toward possibility—reveals an opportunity to conceive of (the possibility of experiencing) perhaps limitless types of bodies, far beyond simply two (male/female), far beyond "the body" we "have" or "are" or "see."

This leads us directly to the question of how a focus on bodily materiality may serve as a means of avoiding, rather than reproducing, an essentialized understanding of sexual dimorphism. Engaging Merleau-Ponty's concept of the anonymous body, Stoller suggests that a phenomenological optics would require us to "perceive [the gendered] other in its indeterminacy" (2013, 31),[58] while Heinämaa argues for an understanding of human interaction based not on the view of sexual difference as "substance" but, as noted previously, as "modes or modalities of relating . . . [which include] a multitude of variations and unlimited possibilities of diversification" (2012, 236). While I agree with both of these authors, my contention is that not only does the body itself (as inextricably linked to a modality) "matter," but also that we may do better, in fact, to simply dispense with the qualifier "gendered" and gender as a foundational concept. In this context, we need not fear substance once the variable of a coerced adherence to dimorphism is removed. For, as I observed previously, even if gender is understood as "flexible" or "fluid," it is difficult within current theoretical paradigms and commonplace understandings to extricate it from a genesis and history that has so fully marked it (constructed it, not "discovered" it) in terms of the masculine/feminine binary. Even conceiving of "variations" on the constituent parts, we still appear to conceive of these *in relation to* their supposedly superseded foundations: gender as a "spectrum" (comprising an infinitesimal number of points *between masculine and feminine*); gender as innumerable combinations, permutations, and admixtures (*of masculine and feminine*); gender as a subversion (*of masculine or feminine*). Even the sometimes superficial or decontextualized summoning of examples of "third genders" or "fluid genders" often require or *en*gender recourse back to the binary in order to render them legible to an audience so fully accustomed to thinking along lines of M(asc)/F(em). But what if the material, sensate body is understood as just as infinite, open, resistant to (linguistic/discursive) reduction as experience itself? Can that which has been so misrepresented as singular, suffocating, and straitjacketing finally be understood as offering a path leading ultimately past the current constricting binary of gender?

In this context, taking a cue from the relatively recent discipline of fat studies—one that places as central a form of corporeal existence different from those often presented as essential, foundational to the formation of subjectivity (for example, sex, race/ethnicity, disability, among others)—one might ask what other types of lived bodies might be implicated in the processual, (inter)subjective formation of the experiential self.[59] The answer could reveal multitudes: slow bodies, propulsive bodies, supple bodies, furious bodies, cold bodies, suffering bodies, fleshy bodies, bodies in fact unamenable to adjectival/linguistic definition. All are possible, and I contend that there are numerous instances of musical practice and audition wherein all have experienced a somaticity that is far more resonant than one based upon a choice of "genitals A" or "genitals B" (or C, D, or E . . .).[60] We accept and welcome the existence of countless genres and styles (and subgenres and sub-styles) of music, and we constantly witness—in disparate musical forms, products, and practices—the ways in which expressive/aesthetic work in the audiovisual serves as a site for exploring the limits of not (only) gendered but sexed bodies. Yet it appears that at this point in human history—perhaps owing to social structures erected upon the foundation of a supposed biological fact or imperative (viz., reproduction), the experience and understanding of which is, arguably, vastly different from what it was even a century ago—the question of "body" is often reduced to an either/or proposition and, moreover, a proposition that is understood as troublingly powerful in its ability to compel or utterly confound, to be beyond our physical or conceptual control.

With all this in mind, I return to my previous example of the intersubjective act of singing along, which I find to be profound on numerous levels. In doing so, and having already highlighted the erotics of the mouth, it is, of course, not my intent to obliterate the role of sex here. As only the most cursory attention to social structure, musical practice, and subjective experience confirms—and as I have discussed previously—sex and sexual desire are often intense motivations for the embodied subject who moves through / interacts with / co-constructs the environment in which s/t/he/y is/are situated. Yet it is likewise problematic to ignore the other, myriad ways in which the embodied co-production of sounding vibrations might serve as an equally important locus for the production of the intersubjectively understood self. Jacques Rancière suggests that the challenging of aesthetic boundaries via expressive cultural production can lead to "the formation of enunciative collectives that call into question the distribution of roles, territories, and languages" which can "contribute to the formation of political subjects that challenge the given distribution of the sensible" ([2000] 2004, 36). Yet it is the appearance of one word—politics— that, I believe, points toward our current limited capacity to conceive of our complex, rich embodied experience as offering countless sites for the production of selves. As I have noted earlier, it is, in part, an obsession with the textual and the linguistic—this often engendering an overly narrow conception of the political—that has been responsible for the processes that concurrently understand and allow for some bodies (defined along simplified and occluding understandings of race or sex, for example) to be indissolubly linked to the foundation of subjectivity, while others (more obscure, less amenable to expression in language, not "iterable"/"utterable") are tacitly constructed as unimaginable or *im*possible. "Identity" endures as a site of academic inquiry across numerous disciplines, yet the limits to the ways in which such inquiries continue to be framed may be found in the correspondence between the variables seen to construct the inquiry itself and those seen to undergird the continuing (now decades-long) frustration with the limitations and insufficiencies of "identity politics"—a frustration owing not to some supposed "political correctness" but to a visceral understanding of the ways human (embodied) experience, being, will never be fully accessible via concept-as-word.

As Linda Martín Alcoff has observed, to understand subjectivity as primarily, even exclusively, constructed by discourse, language, or politics is to "to erase all of those kinds of experiential knowledges unsusceptible to linguistic articulation" (2000, 47). And I contend vigorously that the non-articulable, encountered often via corporeal-sensual interaction with the affective-aesthetic, is not simply *another* mode of experience/existence—one of (m)any—but *essential* to the subject's being. Mika Elo and Miika Luoto (2014) suggest that the arts are marked by/as "something that essentially escapes both cognitive mastery and will of action"; we may think of the experience of the encounter with the aesthetic—with "art" (or expressive culture)—as occurring at the level(s) of touch, a touching which produces a "singular interruption of the significant order of the world ... [and] not [in service of] the production of meaning" (18). Thinking again of unison singing, of the ambiguities and erotics of the mouth, of the ambiguities and erotics of sound itself—that which comes from and goes into—might we not think of open or porous or conductive or vibrating or penetrated/penetrating bodies as sites of corporeally experienced subjectivities?[61] And if this seems unthinkable ("How could porosity, vibration, conductivity, penetration ever be as important as sex/ gender?!"), it is only because our conceptions of identity and subjectivity are so narrow, so tightly knitted to only those registers that allow for representation via concepts amenable to linguistic, or linguistic-juridical, representation. And such constraining (mis) understandings threaten to destroy everything we know corporeally to be crucial to being (healthy, sentient, moving, acting, desiring) in the world. To be *only* something that can be named is to be empty, moribund, practically dead.

Moi reminds us of Rubin's influential work (1975), wherein "gender" is seen as a tool of oppression and utopia is a space in which we might eliminate masculine and feminine. On this view, to understand any given behavior, "we would have to come up with more precise descriptions, to consider whether we think of the behaviour as wise, kind, selfish, expressive, or destructive *without* thinking of any of these terms as sex-specific" (Moi 1999, 28). To this compelling analysis, I encourage us to think not only of de-gendered behaviors but also of de-gendered (yet not de-sexed) bodies. And it is exactly a phenomenological exploration of the capacities of the body and its incalculable ways of sensing, living with, and experiencing the material (and more than material) world, in mutually constitutive relationships to the material (and more than material) body, that may have the potential to discover, highlight, or postulate any number of currently inconceivable, (im)possible bodies potentiated by the inscrutable auditory, the musical. The mania for erasing the body and erecting an omnipresent/omnipotent "ideology" is, I believe, at its most fundamental, a move made of terror: that is, the terror of losing one's agency is seen as somehow preferable to the horror of the completely (conceptually) unfathomable and ineffable, a physical existence that cannot be reduced to full elucidation via the meager tools we possess (language, propositional reasoning), the very tools that make "ideology" putatively legible (and thus, the devil we [erroneously believe we] "know").

Polyphonic Embodiment

Sound has no hidden face. . . . (Nancy [2005] 2007, 13)

. . . the work's meaning is not exhausted in what it represents. The work's meaning is not anything that can be defined, summed up, and explained as the objective meaning of an intelligible object can be, or as the meaning of prose language can be exhausted. What it represents is conveyed only through what it expresses; and expression, even when immediately grasped, is still elusive. (Dufrenne [1953] 1973, 65)

Это так же, как молчать, понимая все без слов

(It's just like being silent, understanding everything without words.)

("Космос" [Kosmos Cosmos], words and music by Arkadii Aleksandrov, recorded by Valeriia [2018])

Bodies meet and are formed via interaction with the world, a world of affects and aesthetics, and a component of this meeting/making occurs via a corporeality that is sexed and, concurrently, more/other than sexed. De Beauvoir has argued that while the facticity of the biological (female) body should not be ignored, it must likewise not be assumed to establish for women "a fixed and inevitable destiny" ([1949] 1953,

60); the body is, rather, understood as a "situation"—a "concrete" somaticity "experienced as meaningful, and socially and historically situated" (Moi 1999, 74). Discussing de Beauvoir's work, Moi highlights the fact that "there are innumerable different ways of living with one's specific bodily potential as a woman" (66) and that "the process of making and being made is open-ended," concluding only with death (72) (something that is similar, in my estimation, to perception/experience itself—including a "death" that is the result of an atrophy of desire). In this context, I do not want to suggest that the "fact" of a sexed corporeality is primary, singular, or the source of any sort of universal/inevitable experience, as is sometimes postulated in second-wave feminism. One may have the specificity of what is subjectively experienced and understood as a female body (which may not be limited to definitions based upon simplistic understandings of biological, genetic criteria), and in certain situations—such as in the flow of affective, aesthetic, musical phenomena in which one's lived female-ness/woman-ness appears reflected, reverberated, or highlighted—that body may be a site of intense intersubjective connection and auto-affection. Yet one may also concurrently experience the embodied self as heated or slow or agitated or open or fleshy or rhythmic or vibrated or injured, or any number of other possibilities—or present *im*possibilities that cannot yet be named. The sexed body, while not a disposable nothing, is likewise not omnipotent.

But if it appears that Russianness, or Estonianness, or Tallinnianness have receded to the background in my analysis, it has not been my intention to suggest that a proliferation of bodies trumps the complexity of locality. As Moi also notes, any woman's (any person's) encounter with the world—biology/environment in meeting/making relationships—is

> always inflected by [her] situation, and that means by her personal and idiosyncratic history as this is interwoven with other historical situations such as her age, race, class, and nationality, and the particular political conflicts in which she may be involved. (1999, 82)

Casey likewise posits the prominence of (embodied) place memory in relation to subjective experience, and as my opening anecdote suggests, emplacement was central to my feeling of relative succor in the midst of travel-induced anxiety—an emplacement via language as embodied action, a corporealization-spatialization of the textual likely experienced by those singing along with Valeriia, in Russian (whether audibly or not), in what is "objectively" "Estonian" space. Yet we may also be reminded of Butler's famous discussion of the "embarrassed 'etc,'"[62] encountered in much writing about (predicate-based) identity—a punctuation added to the end of a list of identity markers (race, class, gender, "etc.") which, it is always known in advance, can never be complete. If I attempt to elucidate "the" experience of Russian women—or Russian women in Estonia; or Russian women in the Estonian city of Tallinn; or Russian women in Tallinn who are over fifty ("etc.")—I am faced with a hopeless task. It would appear that any attempt to formulate a list of all possible combinations of the various components of subjectivity/identity/experience would lead to a list of millions of *Gestalten* in millions of combinations—a quantity so unfathomably large as to be utterly useless.

Stoller notes that Butler's "etc." signals that "the process of determination is in itself incomplete, and is, in fact, making room for *future* determinations" (2013, 27; italics added), once again gesturing toward a productive ambiguity that is an indissoluble, constituent part of phenomenal experience. Yet Butler's assessment itself is marked by incompleteness and insufficiency; here, the subject is figured not as existing prior to signification but rather as produced within it—a process intimately wedded to discourse and language in which "identity" is understood as a surface "effect" and interiority and "depth," as they might be conceived of in relation to the formation of the self, are dismissed as illusory. Butler's incisive theorizations of the subject, which move beyond biological imperatives and/or concepts of a transcendental free will, have righted several disturbing wrongs borne of the numerous dangerous recourses to essentialism. Yet perhaps unwittingly, such figurations (which foreground surface, discourse, language, representation, and which are often engaged in almost skeletal forms by other theorists) circumscribe our understanding of lived experience (thus, subjectivity) by obliquely yet ineluctably defaulting to and overvaluing the visual. Language, it appears, is something read and not heard, as are the "performative repetitions" of the subject; sound is effaced by the symbolic, the sign; the sensuous materiality of the mouth, palate, tongue, and lungs disappear as, apparently, "peripheral"; and the deep, penetrating vibrations found in sites of both sonic production and reception are effaced, stilled, silenced. Yet in understanding the complexity of lived subjectivity that encompasses an almost incalculable number of registers and variables, which are often shorthanded as "identities" or "contexts," a theoretical/critical, phenomenological approach—one that attempts "to articulate a generalized account of the structures of subjectivity from the perspective of individual subjectivity and ownness" (Fisher 2000b, 29) and that highlights sound and audibility—offers ways around the problematics of the "etc."

It is in this context that I would like to offer a preliminary sketch of a final theoretical construct that may be of use in understanding just such complexity as process and experience. Highlighting, again, the ways in which attention to music may offer a productive inroad to the understanding of the experiencing subject, I will provisionally offer the term *polyphonic embodiment*. Informed by Daniel Stern's concept of the layered self (1985), Mikhail Bakhtin's work on the polyphonic novel ([1929] 1984), and Edward Said's engagement of counterpoint/polyphony as a way of imagining social relations (1991, 1993; de Groot 2010),[63] with this concept I want to foreground not only the centrality of corporeality and the complexity of the self but also—via a specifically musical term—the ways lived experience constantly, implicitly questions time and space (and relies upon memory and adumbrations) and the extent to which aesthetic and affective variables impact upon our desiring relationship to the world. Moreover, by using a term that evokes the auditory, we avoid the snares of the omnipresent default to the visual—a literal optics that has undergirded Western theory for centuries (whether implicitly or explicitly) and has contributed to a distortion and impoverishment of understandings of self-world-other interactions. As Casey suggests, the difference between body memory and "recollection" may be attributed to the variable of "depth"; as I observed previously, the latter is often experienced with a "quasi-pictorial distance from myself as a voyeur of the remembered," while the former "takes me directly into what is being remembered" (2000, 167). Although Casey here does not specifically note a visual/auditory split, it is my contention that musical experience is indeed an experience of various depths (via both immersion and penetration; via the ontology of sound, as opposed to image). Understanding the extent to which embodied experiences of the materiality of (musical) sounds differ starkly from visual engagements—the former resonating/animating a proprioceptive knowledge of interior expanse and limit, of one's self *in* and *as* space— the sonic in many ways offers other possibilities, other alternatives for understanding human *being*, a lived being that gives the lie to a relegation of depth to a secondary "effect" of what is inscribed on the surface.

It is this attention to multiplicity and indeterminacy that underscores not only the impossibility of removing expressive culture from its specific cultural context but also the dangers of dismissing certain types of such production as "normative"—and, thus, unlikely or unable to offer any sort of illumination of the fluidity, flexibility, and ultimate (possible) freedom of the subject on anything but a level of negative reflection. Regarding the first issue, that of context: while I most certainly will not deny the importance of the melodic, rhythmic, harmonic, and timbral elements of Valeriia's music (including her vocal timbre, the sounding of her body), and while I likewise believe that questions of phrasing, intonation, dynamics, and other sonic variables are absolutely implicated in the aesthetic-affective power of the singer's musical communication, with respect to the specific concerns I have highlighted in this chapter, what is of equal importance to "the music itself" is this music (including this music as sound) *in relation to* this audience, this concert hall, this city, these sexed/other-than-sexed bodies, these languages, this historical moment—in short, in relation to the very complexity in which all subjects experience, and come into, being. Valeriia's audio-visual representations, invocations, and amplifications are certainly remarkable for their foregrounding of variables related to gender and sexed corporeality (including visual and sonic aides-mémoire); as such, her cultural productions, seen and heard by millions of subjects (the vast majority of them Russian-speaking, with a significant portion geographically dispersed outside the Federation's borders), are productive sites of inquiry into questions of gender, sex, and embodiment. Yet it is a holistic understanding of her work, and of any listener's apprehension in a specific sphere of geocultural, linguistic, and historical intersections, that can never be fully enumerated (Estonia[n] or Russia[n]; the post-Soviet, the "global," the Nordic, the Baltic, etc.) and that allows for a theoretical and grounded (generalized account→"ownness") exploration of embodied subjectivity.

Regarding the second issue—questions of change and normativity—I draw attention to another observation made at Valeriia's Tallinn concert, focusing on a woman sitting two seats to my left. In many ways, she appeared to be a "typical" representative of a certain segment of the Russian, post-Soviet citizenry: probably in her mid- to late fifties, she spoke Russian, had a short, simple (one might say "practical") haircut, and her clothing was modest, "proper," extremely neat. In many ways, she read as *kul'turnaia* (literally, cultured), a Soviet-era term with implications pertaining to both style and comportment. But in the course of the performance—in a context where the registers of the imaginative, the corporeal, the temporal, and the ontological are heightened via their collaborative co-presence, each serving as an experiential locus of the proof of openness and undecidability—there was a marked modification in her movements and interactions. When the concert first began and the four-on-the-floor kick drum sounded over the numerous massive speakers needed to fill the cavernous space (reverberating through the hall so loudly as to literally vibrate the attendees), I noted her obvious displeasure. She grimaced, turned toward her neighbor, knitted her brow, and shook her head disapprovingly. She closed her eyes, gave a brief mock shudder as she raised her shoulders a bit, and brought her hands up to the sides of her head, as if to symbolically cover her ears. Yet as the concert continued (at no lower a decibel level), both her countenance and comportment changed significantly. By the time the second act was in full swing—in this space marked by an intensification of the affective and the aesthetic—she was smiling, singing along in Russian (though, like Valeriia, physically situated in Estonia), clapping in time with the music in a manner typical for middle-aged, kul'turnye Russians (on the beat, both hands pointed upward—at chin/clavicle level—palms and fingers touching symmetrically), and moving in her seat, bouncing up and down on her thighs and buttocks. By the time Valeriia perambulated through the audience, the woman was on her feet, beaming with what appeared to be great happiness.

If this transformation seems positively banal (or not a transformation at all), I want to highlight that change, possibly via the tutelage of the instruments of hyperbole and hyper-amplification (e.g., the Hollywood blockbuster, or the many variations of "makeover" media—to say nothing of academic literature), is fetishized in capitalist culture, where it is often expected to be dramatic, stunning, jarring, to signal a decisive, violent break. As such, "genuine" change has often been assumed to occur in relation to "subversive," "radical," "alternative," or "underground" musics; conversely, it may appear counterproductive to explore the human-defining dynamic of the experience of possibility (in relation to perception, subjectivity, and the polyphony of the self) in musics assumed to be "normative," "commercial," or "capital-driven" (including those performed by singers such as Valeriia, whose political views might certainly be read as nationalistic and supportive of Putin's status quo). Might not change or possibility be more effectively explored in relation to the work of Russian artists such as Monetochka, Cream Soda, Ishome, Buttechno, Khashi, or Kedr Livansky (or Estonian artists such as Tommy Ca$h, Mart Avi, Kerli Kõiv, or Anni Nõps)—all of whose work (owing to symbolic and "political" content, musical "innovation," embrace of digital technology, and/or unconventional representations of "gender") appears to align more neatly with current understandings of sociocultural, meliorative, salubrious "change"? Yet such a narrow understanding of transformation comes about only insofar as it dovetails with a limited number of discourse-based "identities" (and "contexts") and focuses on noun rather than verb. A subject's transformations may often be barely perceptible, transient (to return again, or not); change may have the subtlety of a "changing same," a flux in an undulating cycle, an imperceptibly attenuated but often profound and unconsciously enacted alteration in direction, mode, sentience.

And it is, I believe, not only possible but probable that my neighbor's sensing, tactile, corporeal encounter with this audio/visual/affective/aesthetic (flowing) stream of stimuli—including stimuli at the level of the female body that is foregrounded in Valeriia's textual, visual, and sonic expressions, a body in some way at least partially shared with this listener/viewer, as well as her linguistic-geographical-historical "situations" (which are indissociable from her sex)—could not avoid being transformed in some way, her "comprehensible," "legible" registers of "identity" (Russian, Estonian, woman, middle-aged, etc.) mixing with those not (yet/ever) amenable to linguistic classification. The subject, in this case, no less than the "aesthetic object" theorized by Dufrenne, can never be fully explained (and certainly not experienced) within the confines of prose language or representation. In this context, it is not incidental that Valeriia's many sartorial and corporeal transformations over the course of her career may also be implicated, as types of implicit aides-mémoire, in the possibility of change(s) among her listeners (see Figure 7.2). Valeriia's more current style(s) may indeed be seen as resonating with a certain segment of Russian populations (marked by "traditional" values, but with "aspirations" toward "upward mobility"). Yet, as I have noted, it is dangerous to restrict an inherent ability to experience the phenomenal world as a site of ambiguity and transformation to a limited number of specific sites of human cultural production. It is not the sequestering/segregating/cloistering of "the possible" from "the quotidian"—a construction of change as somehow "other"—that underscores its power; rather, it is the propinquity of both, one to the other, cheek by jowl, that reveals possibilities to be always there, here, everywhere, touching upon the supposedly sedimented aspects of subjectivity, a foundational (rather than exceptional) dynamic in all human interaction with self, environment, and other.

Moreover, Valeriia's changes are not only experienced at the level of the visual: that her output has included material that is both quintessentially Russian (her albums of Russian *romansy* [sing. *romans*], for example, or her numerous songs employing chord progressions based upon the circle of fifths)[64] and is also marked by the influence of international trends[65] may suggest to her listeners and viewers the always available possibility of change, of transformation within the known, what we might call the auditory "home," a sonic reminder of the polyphony of the self whereby one "layer"—ontologically incapable of total opacity—cannot obscure another. Jean-Luc Nancy ([2002] 2007) eloquently argues for the necessity of attention to the audible in any exploration of the formation of the subject, enmeshed as it is in mutually constitutive relations to the environment and others (and, I would argue, the very materiality through which any self is a sense-making/experiencing self).[66] Suggesting a difference between hearing ("to understand the sense") and listening ("to be straining toward a possible meaning, and consequently one that is not immediately accessible"; 6), he highlights the extent to which meaning and the subject are both made in relation to referrals and returns— much like sound, which is always extending and echoing beyond itself, "spread[ing] in space where it resounds while still resounding 'in me' " (7). Suggesting that the listening

FIGURE 7.2: Screen grabs of Valeriia's "transformations." From top left to lower right, row by row, the source of each image is as follows. Personal photo circa 1987 of Alla Perfilova with her first husband, Leonid Iaroshevskii, from the documentary film *Valeriia: ne boisia bit' schastlivoi* (Valeriia: Don't be afraid to be happy; Treshchev 2018). Screen grab from a video of a performance by Valeriia (as Alla Perfilova) from *Konkurs molodykh ispolnitelei èstradnoi pesni "Iurmala"* (The Jurmala Young Estrada Singer Competition; *Iurmala-87* 1987). Screen grab from the music video "The Sky Belongs to Me" (Gavrilov 1992). Screen grab from the music video "Samolet" (Airplane; Petrosian 1995). Screen grab of video of a performance of "Malen'kii prints" (The little prince) from the December 31, 1996–January 1, 1997 New Year's Eve television program *Starye pesni o glavnom, 2* (Old songs about the important things, 2; Faiziev [1997?]). Personal photo of Valeriia circa 1997 with her second husband, Aleksandr Shul'gin, and daughter Anna Shul'gina, from the documentary film *Valeriia: ne boisia bit' schastlivoi* (Treshchev 2018). Screen grab from the music video "Mal'chiki ne plachut" (Boys don't cry; Maasik [2001] 2014).

self experientially breaks down the binarizations that have been used to define various registers of existence and experience, he notes,

> the "self" is precisely nothing available (substantial or subsistent) to which one can be "present," but precisely that resonance of a return [*renvoi*]. . . . For this reason, listening—the opening stretched toward the register of the sonorous, then to its musical amplification and composition—can and must appear to us not as a metaphor for access to self, but as the reality of this access, a reality consequently indissociably "mine" and "other," "singular" and "plural," as much as it is "material" and "spiritual" and "signifying" and "a-signifying." (12)

What Nancy offers, in my estimation, is a philosophy that depends upon or comes to full fruition in lived experience and is thus both theoretically and materially "available" to us. Attempting to conceive of the multiplicity of the self in visual terms, we might imagine a hall of mirrors—an image that evokes feelings of profound disorientation and distortion and suggests the schizophrenic, the pathological. Such an evocation perhaps sits well with the mania for offering exegetical pride of place to an omnipotent (and malevolent) ideology. However, the auditory, and specifically the polyphonic, suggests a subject giving and receiving (with others; with the materiality of their environment / their own flesh and blood)—a complexity not lacking tension but offering also a sensuous/sensate site of stability and harmony.[67] Indeed, in his book *Polyphonic Minds*, Peter Pesic, drawing upon research in neuroscience, highlights the fact that conflict or "dissonance" is an integral part of the learning, exploring mind; it is "not something superimposed on a presumably consonant structure, but so essential that one cannot imagine [its] removal . . . without the diminution or even extinction of mental function" (2017, 255). Understanding embodied experience, subjectivity, and consciousness as polyphonic doing (or relating) can thus accommodate an infinite number of "variables": one's geopolitical or imagined location, one's Russianness, one's Russian-in-Estonia-ness, one's ideological formation, one's material morphology, and one's ineffable, constitutional registers/voices—all experienced, in part, as a depth of feeling in/as the body.

FIGURE 7.2: Continued

Screen grab from music video "Bol'" (Pain; Badoev 2008), simultaneously released in an English-language version titled "Wild." Screen grab from the video of a live performance at *Gosudarstvennyi Kremlevskii dvorets* (State Kremlin Palace, Moscow) of the song "Ia tebia otpustila" (I have let you go; Shadrov 2011). Screen grab from a video of a live performance of "Nezhnost' moia" (My tenderness) at Crocus City Hall, Moscow (Valeriia and Prigozhin 2013). Screen grab from the music video "Moi liubimi" (My beloved; Adel'shin 2014). Screen grab from the music video "Telo khochet liubvi" (The body wants love; Golubev 2016). Backstage footage of Valeriia with her third husband, Iosif Prigozhin, from *Valeriia: Ne boisia byt' schastlivoi* (Valeriia: Don't be afraid to be happy; Treshchev 2018). Screen grab from the music video "Net shansa" (No chance; Rasskazova 2019). Screen grab from the music video "Do predela" (To the bitter end; Prigozhin and Visich 2020).

Casey notes that place memory serves two roles, "a role of containing" and a "role of synthesizing," that together constitute "a preserve, a virtual reservation, within which disparities can coexist" (2000, 203). Although I am not certain what to call it, I am still convinced of the existence of some sort of synthesizing center to which the various voices of the subject's polyphony are centripetally self-directed (a process that occurs simultaniously with their outward-directed engagement with the world). One may at the very same moment be in Estonia, but in Russia; be biologically male, but be resonating, reverberating with the sonically apprehended biological female; share and make social space and subjectivity, intersubjectively, with hundreds of strangers, via an aesthetic proprioception, "finding [others] within [one's own] experience" (Merleau-Ponty [1955] 1974, 166). Moreover, in present-day Estonia, where ethnic Russians very often inhabit geographic, cultural, and linguistic spheres separate from those of the ethnic majority, they nonetheless live within at least some of what one might call the "rhythms" of Estonian geography, culture, and language. In this context, it is worth noting the several initiatives (in the arts, as well as in social services) that aim to bring the Russian and Estonian spheres into closer contact, often at the level of language.[68] Yet none of this never-ending complexity should be assumed to be the bellwether for a future populated by centrifugally dissipated and destroyed subjectivity. Attending to Edward Said's published and unpublished writings, Wouter Capitain (2022) has shown how the author vacillated between the concepts of counterpoint and polyphony on the one hand and heterophony on the other. This latter term, according to Capitain, reflects the author's attempts to theorize the cultural dynamics of interaction via musical practices and structurings that avoid hierarchies (which are often related to ethnocentric narratives of musical evolution). This decentering of an imposed and obliterating center is certainly important in explorations of postcolonial, post-imperialist cultural contact and production, and perhaps a "heterophonic corporeality" might indeed prove to be a more apt term for what I am exploring. Yet the idea of subjectivity as inherently centered, in relation to both internal and external forces—a centering that is not universal, invariable, immutable—is something I find appealing and potentially productive, if conceived of and experienced as auditory/vibrational in nature.[69] A sonic center has the capacity to exert an organizing vibrational force among the countless components of any one subjectivity, yet at the same time is capacious and diffuse enough to allow for a potentially unlimited number of motile, kinetic "voices" to be constitutional parts of the whole. It is in relation to just such a conception that we may glimpse the phenomenology of transformative musical, aesthetic, embodied experience.

Notes

1. Valeriia (Валерия) is the stage name of singer Alla Perfilova. In this chapter, I use the Library of Congress Romanization system for the transliteration of her name (as well as all other Russian words). However, alternative transliterations might be encountered in English-language sources, among them "Valeria" or "Valeriya." Unless otherwise noted, all transliterations and translations are mine.

2. See also Arnold H. Modell's discussion of the literature on mirror neurons (2003). Modell highlights not only the fact that the "representation of the other's action by means of mirror neurons is direct and immediate and does not require any intervening symbolic code or mental language" (185) but also—with reference to the work of Vittorio Gallese (2001)—the importance of attention to the affective and somatic as implicated in the (unconscious) formation of empathy with others (187). On mirror neurons, see also Titon (2023).

3. Ihde's concept of multistability—central to several of his arguments in *Experimental Phenomenology* (1990)—highlights the extent to which ontology cannot be productively understood as essential or singular; rather, an object's meaning or utility can only ever come about via exploitation and relations, factors which are productive of perhaps limitless possibilities. Ihde's inquiries focus largely on the realm of media and technologies, with many of his key illustrations being visual in nature (e.g., "optical illusions" such as the Necker cube, which is a "single" image that can be perceived in multiple ways).

4. Following the occupation of the Estonian state by the Soviet Union, Russians became the largest "minority" (i.e., non-Estonian) ethnic group in the republic, comprising (according to the 1959 census) approximately 20 percent of the population. The percentage rose over the ensuing decades, and even after Estonian independence, ethnic Russians remain the largest minority group (approximately 25 percent of the population, according to the 2019 census). The percentage of native Russian speakers in the country is roughly similar, and it increases when taking into account the other ethnic minorities who also use Russian as their lingua franca (Ukrainians, Belarusians, Tatars, Armenians, and Azerbaijanis). On the (linguistic) Russification of ethnic minorities in post-1991 Estonia, see Aidarov and Dreschler (2013). Demographic figures for Estonia are available (in English) at the Statistics Estonia website, https://www.stat.ee/en. Statistics in the text come from both the Statistics Estonia website and Aidarov and Dreschler.

5. Gerli Nimmerfeldt, for example, suggests that "the strict requirements of the citizenship policy, mainly the Estonian language exam, hinder the naturalization process" for Russian and Russian-speaking populations (2011, 218). Nimmerfeldt's previous surveys of these populations revealed that "nine out of ten Estonian and Russian respondents considered the inability to learn Estonian one of the main reasons why there are still so many people without Estonian citizenship living in Estonia" (2011, 218; see also Nimmerfeldt 2008).

6. On the production of a distinctly Russian cultural-linguistic sphere in Estonia, see, for example, the work of Andres Jõesaar (2015), Maria Jufereva and Epp Lauk (2015), Raija Kemppainen et al. (2004), and Marju Lauristin et al. (2011).

7. Kadi Mägi's 2018 doctoral dissertation, which focuses on the Russian-speaking population in Estonia, highlights the extent to which citizens' locations within geographically-ethnically segregated spaces contribute to the formation of ethnic identity. Such self-identifications, moreover, impact significantly and materially upon individuals and groups, as well as the geography itself. Specifically, Russian-speaking citizens are often at the lower end of the socioeconomic spectrum—due, in part, to their geocultural segregation—and this concentration of lower-wage earners (with significantly higher rates of unemployment) in specific neighborhoods impacts upon the constitution of cities' cultural and material topographies.

8. Vanemuise has approximately 863 seats; Tondiraba has a capacity of 7,700, but only 4,000 to 5,000 people attended Valeriia's concert. The venue, often used for sporting events, is also a regular and popular destination for Russian superstar acts and has featured artists such as Basta, Loboda, Dima Bilan, and Timati.

9. From 1992 to 2017, the singer released eighteen albums and over seventy singles. A relatively comprehensive discography can be found at https://www.discogs.com/artist/907 332-Валерия.

10. In this context, *Zasluzhennaia* (заслуженная) may also be translated as *honored, meritorious,* or *distinguished.* The award is one level lower than the honorary title *Narodnyi artist Rossiiskoi Federatsii* (People's artist of the Russian Federation).

11. Valeriia's first album, *The Taiga Symphony* (1992), featured exclusively English-language texts. Her second album, *Pobud' so mnoi* (Побудь со мной; Stay with me), was released in 1992 and had packaging that featured the album title and the names of each song in both Russian and English; however, the tracks were sung exclusively in Russian. Her tenth studio album, *Nepodkontrol'no* (Неподконтрольно; Out of control), was released in 2008 in both Russian- and English-language versions. While the majority of her live appearances have taken place in Russia and various former-Soviet republics, she has also toured throughout the West—from New York to London, to recent (2019) appearances in Paris, Vienna, and Milan. Featuring often only Russian-language material, such performances have been aimed at Russian immigrant and expat communities. Following the release of *Out of Control*, however, her 2009 tour of the United Kingdom (with British band Simply Red) was clearly intended as an attempt to establish an international (i.e., English-language) career.

12. For example, the singer's Twitter account (https://twitter.com/valeriya_rus) features selfies in Switzerland, where her family previously owned a home and where her son Artemy currently resides.

13. I note that, owing to her various explicit and implied (or inferred) political stances, Valeriia is a problematic figure for some. For example, both she and her husband/producer, Iosif Prigozhin, were signatories to a document entitled *Deiateli kul'tury Rossii—v podderzhku pozitsii Prezidenta po Ukraine i Krymu* (Деятели культуры России — в поддержку позиции Президента по Украине и Крыму; Russian cultural figures in support of the President's position regarding Ukraine and Crimea), which was first published on March 11, 2014, on the website of the Russian Ministry of Culture (https://www.mkrf.ru/press/news/deyateli-kultury-rossii-v-podderzhku-pozitsii-prezidenta-po-ukraine-i-krymu20171009103201/?sphrase_id=2505361). In an interview with the Russian-language radio station *Radio Svoboda* (Radio Freedom, a partner with Radio Free Europe), however, Prigozhin later claimed that neither he nor Valeriia had intended their endorsement of this document to reflect support for the policies of annexation or aggression; rather, he said, they only meant to defend the "right" of the people and government of Ukraine to hold a referendum on the matter. Nevertheless, Valeriia was subsequently banned from entering Latvia due to her perceived support for the Russian government's actions (see *Forbes* 2014). Prigozhin's interview may be heard at https://www.facebook.com/watch/?v=10153656294127554 (see also *Bul'var Gordona* 2016).

Additionally, in a June 13, 2013, interview on BBC television, which took place in the wake of the Russian Duma's unanimous passage of the anti-"gay propaganda" legislation, the singer participated in a de facto debate with Anton Karsovskii, a television journalist who had been fired from his job for revealing his homosexuality during a live television broadcast about the law. In the interview, Valeriia explained her support of the legislation by claiming she had nothing against gay people but was only trying to protect her children from the "more aggressive propaganda of homosexuality," her remarks implicitly conflating homosexuality with the sexual exploitation of children. Noting that she had many gay friends who "[are] just normal people," "do not support . . . unisexual marriages," and "would never take part in gay parades," Valeriia also enlisted the now-common trope of Russia's immutable and foundational difference from "the West." There she stated, "What I know [is] that our society is based on Christian morality *still*, in spite of the enlightened Europe tendencies. . . . A lot of people try to . . . [make] us think the same way, but we are *different*." It is perhaps notable that the singer gesticulated in order to put mocking scare quotes around the term "enlightened Europe tendencies." The interview can be accessed at https://www.bbc.com/news/av/world-22891842/what-gay-pro paganda-vote-tells-us-about-russia-today.

14. The title of the album, *Okeany*, was also the title of the tour comprising the Estonian performances.

15. Although it is not possible to know how many people had seen the video in late 2017, as of September 21, 2019, it had nearly four million views on YouTube (https://www.youtube.com/watch?v=COiGJcOT1Xw). By November 2020, the total had increased to approximately 4,227,000.

16. Valeriia's love interest is played by Russian actor and television presenter Viktor Vasil'ev.

17. In the video, the disappearance of her lover from these old snapshots brings to mind the Soviet government's practice of erasing from official photographs people whom they constructed as "traitors," though it is not clear if this parallel was intended by Valeriia or her producers.

18. An article about the filming of the video on the website Woman.ru leads with the title "'Nichego lichnogo': Valeriia pokazala, kak stala schastlivoi i uspeshnoi zhenshchinoi odnovremenno" ("Nothing personal": Valeriia showed how she became a happy and successful woman at the same time) and is followed by the line "Valeriia uverena, chto sovremennaia zhenshchina mozhet uspeshno sovmeshchat' lichnuiu zhizn' i rabotu" (Valeriia is certain that a modern woman can successfully combine personal life and work) (Belaia 2018). As I have suggested, here also the line between the "character" in the video and the singer herself is blurred.

19. See also Hawkesworth (1997), who notes the problems associated with Butler's (and other poststructuralist theorists') privileging of the Symbolic (especially phallogocentrism) as an explanans for women's domination. According to Hawkesworth, such a move has the unfortunate consequence of contributing to the continued invisibilization of women, as well as tacitly suggesting that power is wielded via the "cunning of culture," "the ingenious means by which culture insures its own survival through the production of organizational practices and structures independent of the needs or intentions of individuals" (668). In Hawkesworth's reading, that such structures operate, according to Butler, to ensure reproductive heterosexuality, and that the mechanisms or roots of this "cunning" are left unexplored, leaves open the possibility—perhaps even the suggestion—that its origins in fact are related to biological imperatives, an obviously troublesome suggestion in relation to poststructuralist theory.

20. Modell's ideas are shared by Rodolfo Llinás, who argues that the brain is "primarily a self-activating system, one whose organization is geared toward the generation of intrinsic images" (2001, 57). Likewise, Modell argues that "the dream state, where we are cut off from sensory inputs, is a closer analogy to waking consciousness" (2003, 21).

21. Husserl's cognizance of the centrality of corporeality is evident in both his *Cartesian Meditations* ([1931] 1960) and *Analyses Concerning Passive and Active Synthesis* (2001).

22. I will engage Merleau-Ponty's figuration of the "anonymous body" later in this chapter.

23. The formulation is Paul Ricoeur's, who argues that "the 'place' of metaphor [is] . . . the copula of the verb *to be*. The metaphorical 'is' at once signifies both 'is not' and 'is like'. If this is really so, we are allowed to speak of metaphorical truth, but in an equally 'tensive' sense of the word 'truth'" ([1977] 2004, 6). Although Ricoeur is speaking specifically about meaning in language, Modell (drawing upon works by Johnson and by Lakoff and Johnson) highlights the fact that metaphorization is "an integral part of cognitive processing" and is also fundamentally rooted in somatic experience, a "centrifugal process arising in the body and spreading outwards into the world" (2003, 77–78). On the relationship between metaphor and somatic experience—including in relation to musical experience—see also Johnson (2007).

24. Husserl highlights the interplay between the determined and the undetermined, arguing that "proper to every appearing thing of each perceptual phase is a new empty horizon, a new system of determinable indeterminacy, a new system of progressing tendencies with corresponding possibilities of entering into determinately ordered systems of possible appearances, of possible ways that the aspects can run their course, together with horizons that are inseparably affiliate with these aspects" (2001, 43).

25. This line of thinking in relation to the nervous system has been pursued by a range of scholars. For example, the polymath John von Neumann held that "an efficiently organized large natural automaton (like the human nervous system) will tend to pick up as many logical (or informational) items as possible simultaneously, and process them simultaneously, while an efficiently organized large artificial automaton (like a large modem computing machine) will be more likely to do things successively—one thing at a time, or at any rate not so many things at a time. That is, large and efficient natural automata are likely to be highly *parallel*, while large and efficient artificial automata will tend to be less so, and rather to be *serial*" (von Neumann 1958, 50–51, quoted in Pesic 2017, 251). Similarly, in his classic work on musicking, Christopher Small contrasts the "one-thing-at-a-time" quality of visual processing—a linearity (or at least seriality) that is in fundamental ways related to our processing of text and language—with the "gestural" (or, one might say, gestalt-like) qualities of sound, as it is perceived by the subject (1998, "Interlude 2," 94–109).

26. In his discussion of the overtone series, Daniel J. Levitin reminds us that "it is a property of objects in the world that they generally vibrate at several different frequencies at once" (2006, 40). Levitin also notes that "[b]ecause most physical objects cause molecules to vibrate in several modes at once, and because for many, many objects the modes bear simple integer relations to one another, the overtone series is a fact-of-the world that we expect to find everywhere we look" (42).

27. The quoted passage is a comment left by "Елизавета Терновых" (Elizaveta Ternovykh) on the YouTube page for Valeriia's video "Nicehgo lichnogo" (https://www.youtube.com/watch?v=COiGJcOT1Xw). It is notable that Valeriia—or one of her staff, writing as the singer—often responds to her fans' YouTube posts. Also notable is the poster's form of address; while Ternovykh's language reveals a certain (desire for) intimacy with the singer, her post is also marked by its use of the formal address "Спасибо Вам" (*Spasibo vam*; thank you), instead of the informal "Спасибо тебе" (*Spasibo tebe*; thank you).

28. Comment left by user "Фатима Хасанова" (Fatima Khasanova) on the website Kino Galleriia in response to Valeriia's song/video "Telo khochet liubvi" (https://sitegallery.ru/video/A1tGCSYQLwA2JTg/valerija-telo-hochet-ljubvi-premera-klipa-2016.html).

29. As only one example, Fisher notes Iris M. Young's suggestion "that existential phenomenology had not previously addressed the topic of pregnancy [can be] taken as evidence of

its male bias" (Fisher 2000b, 24). For further discussions of feminism in phenomenology and the tensions and reciprocities between phenomenology and feminist theory in general, see Fisher (2000a, 2000b), Oksala (2006), and Stoller (2000, in response to Sullivan 1997), *inter alia*.

30. In what follows, it is not my intention to offer a definitive inventory of corporeal/material attributes that mark a body as inarguably female (or as woman) or to suggest that such an enterprise is even desirable or possible. Moreover, as noted, while I argue that attention to a body's sex is a productive of site of inquiry, I ultimately maintain that sexual dimorphism—however it is figured—should not be seen as an unbridgeable difference that separates one sexed body from any and all others in relation to subjective and intersubjective experience in and of the world. This notwithstanding, I take as valid possible critiques that my embodied status may make my theorizing of female embodiment problematic. While I hope that my explorations will not be seen as distorting or in any way deleterious, I accept that they may indeed be, at best, incomplete or partial.

31. The words in Norwegian, Russian, and Dutch are *kjønn*, пол (*pol*), and *geslacht*, respectively, each of which would most often be translated into English as "sex" but may also appear as "gender" in contemporary contexts. Where an author or speaker in these languages intends specifically and unambiguously to make reference to the concept of *gender*, they will generally employ the English word. In written Russian, a Cyrillic transliteration of the English word gender (i.e., гендер) is most often encountered. It is also notable that research on gender, sex, and sexuality from non-anglophone (and often non-Western and/or postcolonial) perspectives often problematizes the use of this concept; see, for example, the work of Maria Lugones (2008, 2010) and Howard Chiang (2012), the latter arguing that "the most radical approach to developing something that we might want to call Chinese transgender studies is perhaps by leaving behind Western-derived meanings of gender altogether—or at least problematizing them" (11).

32. For an extended exploration of the differences between, for example, feminist gender theorists and sexual difference theorists, see Foster (1999).

33. I do not, of course, take Butler's posits as exemplary of all poststructuralist gender theory. However, considering the influence that their writings have had on countless researchers from a vast number of disciplinary and geocultural locations ("tens of thousands" would be a gross underestimate), a focus on Butler's writings is both justified and warranted.

34. Butler notes, for example, that "performativity must be understood not as a singular or deliberate 'act,' but, rather, as the *reiterative* and *citational* practice by which discourse produces the effects that it names" (1993, xii). It is of course well known—and bears underscoring again—that their analyses are indebted to the theories of philosophers whose work has likewise highlighted the centrality of language in relation to the production of subjectivity, epistemology, and culture, including J. L. Austin (1962) and Jacques Derrida ([1972] 1988), from whose work, respectively, the concepts of the "performative" and "iterability/citationality" come. It is perhaps notable that neither of these works is cited in *Gender Trouble*, but both are cited in *Bodies That Matter*.

35. On the ways in which ideology—including ideologies of race/racism—impacts upon the subject's experience of their own body, see, for example, Lorde (1984) and Young (1984, 1985).

36. In early 2020, several media outlets reported on the singer's intention to create a social movement devoted to protecting women's rights and combatting domestic violence, operating under the same title as the song "Sil'nye zhenshchiny" (see BBC Russian

Service 2020 and *Fontanka* 2020). According to these reports—which uniformly quoted her husband, Prigozhin, and not Valeriia herself—the singer's ultimate goal was for the movement to grow into a bona fide political party. Within several months, however, Prigozhin announced to the press that neither the movement nor the party would be forthcoming and that the original impetus for both was his own political aspirations, rather than Valeriia's (who, he said, "is not interested in anything but music"; see Sutormina 2020). In another article—one of the few purporting to quote the singer herself—Valeriia states that Prigozhin's announcement was merely a hypothetical, a joke, offering: "I would not lead any party. This is not my story [история; *istoriia*] at all. Any kind of politics [политическая тема; *politicheskaia tema*]—this just isn't for me. A social [общественное; *obshchestvennoe*] movement, yes, some sort of assistance—yes, social work—that I can do" (MSN 2020). Valeriia did, however, increase both her media presence and her reputation as a supporter of victims of domestic violence with the 2020 creation of the YouTube channel *Mezhdu nami* (Between us; https://www.yout ube.com/c/mezdunami). Under the rubric *"Pochemu ia?"* (Why me?), the channel featured a series of videos in which the singer interviews various people who have endured hardships, including women who have been abused. Exhibiting Valeriia's usual talent for self-promotion in the age of social media, the channel's announcement was featured on Valeriia's Instagram account (https://www.instagram.com/p/CBKxfdUFrII/), as well as other sites.

37. For example, the singer has tweeted and posted to her Instagram account pictures in which she is wearing bikinis or exercising in form-fitting workout attire. The popular press has taken notice of these tweets and postings, disseminating the images to readers who may not make use of social media, often adding complimentary commentary in which the singer's figure is presented as remarkable for a woman of her age (see, for example, *Starhit* 2020; *Domashnii ochag* 2016; *Ren* 2018).

38. Leo Treitler has produced a highly influential body of work exploring the complex relationships among notation, singing, and reading in the production of early Western chant. For a representative collection of works, see Treitler (2003).

39. Fuchs notes that Merleau-Ponty conceives of body memory as a "third dimension between merely imagined movement and motor execution" (2012, 11).

40. Drawing upon Merleau-Ponty and Husserl, Heinämaa states, "Women and men, or feminine and masculine subjects, manifest two different forms of spontaneity and responsiveness. These dynamic forms cannot be characterized by the traditional concepts of substance or organism, but the phenomenological concepts of style, variation, and modification provide the basic framework for a description" (2012, 235). Moreover, "As stylistic characteristics of persons, 'manhood' and 'womanhood' are not anchored on any particular activities or objects, but are given as two different ways of relating to objectivity, acting on objects and being affected by them" (236). Although Heinämaa succeeds here in doing away with at least some sorts of essentialisms (biological and/or cultural), we are still left with a gendered/sexed binary: masculine/manhood vs. feminine/womanhood. The constraints of such a dualism, if they exist as a/the principal site of analysis, will be addressed later in this chapter.

41. Arguing against a "bio-scientific concept of organic sex" that elides questions of bodily relations, Heinämaa instead proposes that "human bodies are not just nodes in nexuses of causal-functional relations but are also expressive units tied to other expressive units by internal relations of sense, motivation, and communication" (2012, 232). In her estimation,

"the concept of sex is grounded on the idea of causal-functional connections and is ill-suited for the analysis of motivational and expressive relations" (233).

42. On proprioception, embodiment, and intersubjectivity, see, for example, Shaun Gallagher and Jonathan Cole (1995). On gender and subjectivity, see Heinämaa (2003, 2012, 2015).

43. See footnote 2, which also discusses Modell's work on mirror neurons.

44. On the YouTube page for her song "Mikroinfrakty," for example, one commenter states, "Valeriia is one of the few on our stages who has good vocals and knows how to sing. Her solo concerts are fantastic!" (https://www.youtube.com/watch?v=Ia8c7JCdGyc). Many similar assessments can be found on the Valeriia page of the Russian website Love/Hate. One commenter writes, "I adore Valeriia for her voice. For the fact that she sings really well live, and for her human quality. Because she doesn't suffer from the star disease." Another observes, "Valeriia is one of the few performers who have a good and strong voice! She's talented and excellent [превосходна; *prevoskhodna*]!" (http://www.lovehate.ru/Vale ria-singer/5). It is notable, however, that at both of the Estonian concerts, certain songs were sung "*pod fonogrammu*," or more colloquially, "*pod faneru*" (под фонограмму, под фанеру; lip-synched), with identical "choreographies" engaged in order to obscure this practice. For example, during the song "Nezhnost' moia" (My tenderness), apparently concerned that lip-synching the climactic, "belted" note—the song's tonic accent—would be telling, she turned to profile and obscured her face with the hood of her jumpsuit. In other songs, the recorded tracks included "mistakes" which were audible at both concerts, so as to appear imperfect and thus live.

45. Quoting Ihde at greater length will give a fuller account of his ideas on this topic. "Here, then, we reach the completion of a first survey of the field-shape of sound. It is an omnidirectional 'sphere' of sound that is variably full, rarified, or both in a ratio of relativity. This same ratio of relativity pertains to the co-presence of the 'shapes' of surroundability and directionality, manifestations of sound presences. The field of sound is also a penetrating presence that in certain instances unites and dissolves certain presumed 'individualities' by its penetration in and through interiors in a power of penetration. This power of sound is also a dynamic and animated or lively quality of sound. And while all these existential possibilities of the auditory field are present in sound, dramatic and selected variables reveal these qualities in more striking form" (2007, 83).

46. On the relationship between sound and penetration, see footnote 45.

47. It is interesting to note that the song's video, which was released in 2013, is similar in its visual style to the 2014 film *The Grand Budapest Hotel*.

48. As Fuchs notes, this conception has resonances with similar formulations by both Merleau-Ponty (1964), who speaks of an intercorporeal relationship that is a pre-reflective bodily understanding of the self-other relationship, and Daniel Stern (1985), who develops the notions of "schemes of being-with" and "implicit relational knowing." According to Fuchs, "each body forms an extract of its past history of experiences with others that are stored in intercorporeal memory" (2012, 15).

49. Shusterman argues against the modern (and modernist) tendency to limit aesthetics to questions of form (in works of "art"), focusing instead on its ethical-philosophical implications. Drawing on both Confucius and Xunzi, for example, he highlights the ways that the aesthetic may be understood in relation to balance (or harmony), musical sound and practice, and ethics and society. In his estimation, "Confucius insists upon the ethical importance of 'achieving harmony' rather than mere obedience to fixed moral codes or commandments, and he likewise stresses the important ways that aesthetic practices such

as music help establish and preserve such harmony" (2012a, 113). Likewise, Xunzi "insists on the aesthetical-ethical power of music and ritual for shaping the person's character and behavior into a more successfully harmonious form that contributes to the harmony of the wider social group" (2012a, 114).

50. To quote Dufrenne more fully: "Subjectivity never allows itself to be known completely, because it knows itself only through its acts. In other words, the *a priori* is known only through [*sur*] the *a posteriori*. Considered in its constitutive aspect, the *a priori* is known only through the object which it constitutes. Considered in its existential aspect, the *a priori* is known only in our concrete operations and in the actual use we make of it. Similarly, the table of affective categories, which we bear within ourselves as our essential ability to know the human and which we grasp only by means of a reflective and always provisional knowledge [*connaissance*], is known only through our experience with the aesthetic object" (1966, 491).

51. As Casey notes, "it is the dual aspect of the *a priori*—its subjective and objective sides— that convinces Dufrenne of its philosophical fecundity" (1966, xix). As I observed earlier, this roiling of the relationship between subject and object appears as at least somewhat reminiscent of Husserl's method of reduction, which achieves a similar result.

52. Dufrenne's highlighting of the affective a priori, and his suggestion that it exists prior to or independent of context, might be contrasted with Husserl's concept of *Reiz* (allure); see footnote 56.

53. Dufrenne notes, for example, that "the history of art reads like a history of unforeseeable innovations" (1966, 491). Later in the text, he likewise observes that "[t]he appearance of a new work which illustrates a category to which we have yet paid no attention may not be ordered by logical development. . . . Any logic in the movement of the aesthetic through history probably arises from a retrospective illusion" (492).

54. It is unclear if the translator sought to coin the construction "intended to" to capture what he saw as Husserl's meaning or if the translator meant to write "attended to" and the unusual construction is simply a typographical error.

55. Valeriia's recorded version of the song (with music by Igor' Krutoi and lyrics by Rimma Kazakova) is accompanied by a full orchestra. In her two Estonian performances, however, she was accompanied for the majority of the song only by a keyboard synthesizer that simulated the sound of an acoustic piano. The full band (bass, guitar, drums, and saxophone) joined only during the brief instrumental interlude that precedes the final chorus. This increase of musical forces was accompanied by an upward modulation, marking an audible move toward the climax of the piece.

56. Husserl uses the term *Reiz* (often translated as "allure") to identify the affective pull that objects in the world have on the subject. In this sense, Reiz might be seen as involving a "reversibility of intentionality" (Staehler 2017, 229) whereby the object "[awakens in the subject] an intention directed toward it" (Husserl 2001, 198). In a section from one of his lectures from the 1920s entitled "Laws of the Propagation of Affection," Husserl makes clear that this "allure" is neither mechanical in nature nor the result of any qualities inherent in any one object. Rather, an object's affective pull comes about via its relation to the entire perceptual field; as Victor Biceaga notes, "the force that turns an affective tendency into an actual affection depends on the shifting distribution of relative contrasts, intensities, and concrescences that make up the living present" (2010, 34). Casey's assessment of erotic body memory as that which propels the experiencing subject forward (to more experiences of pleasure) reveals similar aspects of perception, with

"allures," "intentions," and "affects" emanating from myriad sites and being animated in myriad ways.

57. In my estimation, Barbaras's highlighting of desire may be related to Silvan Tomkins's theory of affects, which he contrasts with biological drives. For Tomkins, the effect of "interest-enjoyment" is not the effect of a drive but rather "the major source of drive amplification" (1995, 76).

58. Stoller notes, "strictly speaking, one cannot simply *choose* not to be open toward the world or decide against indeterminacy, because the world itself is always ontologically characterized by indeterminacy or anonymity, as Husserl and Merleau-Ponty pointed out" (2013, 32). See also Megan Burke (2013) on what she terms "anonymous temporality."

59. Although fat studies scholars almost inevitably examine the discursive production of the meanings of fatness, many are also interested in pairing this discursive emphasis with an exploration of the embodied experiences of fat bodies. Katarina Kyrölä's monograph on fatness and media images (2014), for example, engages not only the visual but also the (corporeally) affective states engendered by representations. See also the edited volume by Esther Rothblum and Sondra Solovay (2009), the contributions to which explore fatness from myriad disciplinary and methodological standpoints.

60. As only one example, it is notable that traditional Chinese medicine suggests there are nine main body "types," which are not necessarily based on sex or gender. It is also perhaps notable that "personality types" (e.g., the "type A" personality) are likewise often conceptualized independent of gender. Finally, it is important to highlight that even the supposed materiality of a simple sexual dimorphism is a problematic oversimplification. See, for example, Fausto-Sterling (1993, 2000a, and 2000b).

61. Elsewhere, I have explored the relationships among the experiences of penetration, the formation of sexual subjectivity, and Russian popular music. See Amico (2014).

62. Butler notes, "The theories of feminist identity that elaborate predicates of color, sexuality, ethnicity, class, and able-bodiedness invariably close with an embarrassed 'etc' at the end of the list. Through this horizontal trajectory of adjectives, these positions strive to encompass a situated subject, but invariably fail to be complete" (1990, 196).

63. I also am informed by Peter Pesic's (2017) work on the concept of polyphony, which surveys and synthesizes research from the field of neuroscience.

64. Over the course of the past two centuries, songs from many genres and styles of Russian popular music have featured chord progressions based on the cycle of fifths. For a detailed discussion of this topic that includes the ways harmonic language may be related to embodied experience, see Amico (2014, chap. 2).

65. For example, the style of production found in Valeriia's 2004 hit "Otpusti menia" (Let me go) was influenced by euro/neo-disco, genres of commercial music enjoying international popularity at the time. The chord progression of the song's chorus was, moreover, based on the circle of fifths (see footnote 64).

66. Not incidentally, Nancy also highlights the relationship between, on the one hand, the auditory and, on the other, permeability and depth, reminding us that a listening self enters a sonic spatiality and is concurrently penetrated by it. On the concept of depth in relation to both color and (musical) tone, see Murata (2012).

67. Regarding imagination, Ihde contrasts the visual to the auditory mode; in his estimation, "this 'flux' of appearances, the apparent 'insubstantiality' of them, the 'flow' of them as events have shown themselves before. This characterization of imagination is 'like' the first characterization of the auditory dimension. Moreover, the 'flux' and 'flow' of these features

implicate again the sense of temporality that belonged dramatically to listening . . . there may also be a secret liaison between the 'flow' of imagination and the 'flow' of the auditory. Each begins in the same grammar" (2007, 122).

68. Some examples include the work of the Vaba Lava Theatres in Tallinn and Narva, as well as the music festival Station Narva, all of which display commitments to programming that reflects the linguistic and cultural diversity of the country; the Eesti LGBT Ühing (Estonian LGBT Association), which has sponsored bilingual events such as game nights held in Estonian and Russian (see https://www.facebook.com/events/385478945366377); and the online Estonian Feminist magazine *Feministeerium* (https://feministeerium. ee/), which has, through a combination of national and international funding sources, translated both Estonian- and English-language articles into Russian. It is of note that in some instances, rather than translating from Estonian to Russian (or vice versa), English is used as the linguistic meeting ground—a move related, in part, to the connection of younger Estonians (of all ethnicities) to a global, international sphere.

69. The concept of the vibrational as an organizing variable shares some conceptual space with Henri Lefebvre's call for a form of cultural analysis that is also, in certain aspects, related to the corporeal and the musical—a "rhythmanalysis" ([1992] 2004).

WORKS CITED

Adel'shin, Marat, dir. 2014. "Moi liubimi" [My beloved]. YouTube.com. https://www.youtube. com/watch?v=DtnHxTzSSeU.

Aidarov, Aleksandr, and Wolfgang Drechsler. 2013. "Estonian Russification of Non-Russian Ethnic Minorities in Estonia? A Policy Analysis." *Trames* 17 (2): 103–128.

Alcoff, Linda Martín. 2000. "Phenomenology, Post-structuralism, and Feminist Theory on the Concept of Experience." In *Feminist Phenomenology*, edited by Linda Fisher and Lester Embree, 39–56. Dordrecht: Springer.

Aleksandrov, Arkadii. 2018. "Космос." YouTube. https://www.youtube.com/watch?v=8fZA ZQCH7YI.

Amico, Stephen. 2014. *Roll Over, Tchaikovsky! Russian Popular Music and Post-Soviet Homosexuality*. Urbana: University of Illinois Press.

Austin, J. L. 1962. *How to Do Things with Words*. Cambridge, MA: Harvard University Press.

Badoev, Alan, dir. 2008. "Bol' " [Pain]. YouTube.com. https://www.youtube.com/watch?v= 8SOvFBMAGPM.

Bakhtin, Mikhail. (1929) 1984. *Problems of Dostoevsky's Poetics*. Edited and translated by Caryl Emerson. Minneapolis: University of Minnesota Press.

Barbaras, Renaud. 2012. "The Phenomenology of Life: Desire as the Being of the Subject." In *The Oxford Handbook of Contemporary Phenomenology*, edited by Dan Zahavi, 94–111. Oxford: Oxford University Press.

BBC Russian Service. 2020. "'Sil'nye zhenshchiny' i 'Za pravdu': Zachem v Rossii cozdaiut mnogo novykh partii?" ["Strong Women" and "To Truth": Why are so many new parties being created in Russia?]. February 25, 2020. https://www.bbc.com/russian/features-51625754.

Beauvoir, Simone de. (1949) 1953. *The Second Sex*. Translated by Howard M. Parshley. London: Jonathan Cape.

Belaia, Sasha. 2018. "'Nichego lichnogo': Valeriia pokazala, kak stala schastlivoi i uspeshnoi zhenshchinoi odnovremenno" ["Nothing personal": Valeriia showed how she became a happy and successful woman at the same time]. *Woman.ru*, February 19, 2018. http://www.woman.ru/stars/medley1/article/216738/.

Biceaga, Victor. 2010. *The Concept of Passivity in Husserl's Phenomenology*. Dordrecht, Netherlands: Springer.

Bourdieu, Pierre. (1972) 1977. *Outline of a Theory of Practice*. Translated by Richard Nice. Cambridge: Cambridge University Press.

Bul'var Gordona. 2016. "Prigozhin zaiavil, chto oni c Valeriei ne podderzhivali anneksiiu Kryma" [Prigozhin stated he and Valeriia did not support the annexation of Crimea]. August 19, 2016. https://gordonua.com/bulvar/news/prigozhin-zayavil-chto-oni-s-valeriey-ne-podderzhivali-anneksiyu-kryma-146221.html.

Burke, Megan. 2013. "Anonymous Temporality and Gender: Rereading Merleau-Ponty." *Philosophia* 3 (2): 138–157.

Butler, Judith. 1990. *Gender Trouble: Feminism and the Subversion of Identity*. New York: Routledge.

Butler, Judith. 1993. *Bodies That Matter: On the Discursive Limits of "Sex."* New York: Routledge.

Capitain, Wouter. 2022. "From Counterpoint to Heterophony and Back Again: Reading Edward Said's Drafts for *Culture and Imperialism*." *Journal of Musicological Research* 41 (1): 1–22. https://doi.org/10.1080/01411896.2020.178793.

Casey, Edward. 1966. "Translator's Introduction." In *The Notion of the A Priori*, by Mikel Dufrenne, xviii–xxviii. Evanston, IL: Northwestern University Press.

Casey, Edward. 1973. "Translator's Forward." In *The Phenomenology of Aesthetic Experience*, by Mikel Dufrenne, xv–xlii. Evanston, IL: Northwestern University Press.

Casey, Edward. 2000. *Remembering: A Phenomenological Study*. 2nd ed. Bloomington: Indiana University Press.

Chiang, Howard. 2012. "Imagining Transgender China." In *Transgender China*, edited by Howard Chiang, 3–19. New York: Palgrave.

Derrida, Jacques. (1972) 1988. "Signature Event Context." In *Limited Inc*, edited by Gerald Graff, 1–23. Evanston, IL: Northwestern University Press.

Dewey, John. 1934. *Art as Experience*. New York: Perigree.

Domashnii ochag [Hearth and home]. 2016. "48-letniaia Valeriia pokhvatalas' figuroi v bikini" [Forty-eight-year-old Valeriia showed off her figure in a bikini]. July 19, 2016. https://www.goodhouse.ru/stars/news/48-letnyaya-valeriya-pokazala-figuru-v-bikini/.

Dreyfus, Hubert. 2002. "Intelligence without Representation—Merleau-Ponty's Critique of Mental Representation: The Relevance of Phenomenology to Scientific Explanation." *Phenomenology and the Cognitive Sciences* 1 (4): 367–383.

Dufrenne, Mikel. (1953) 1973. *The Phenomenology of Aesthetic Experience*. Translated by Edward Casey. Evanston, IL: Northwestern University Press.

Dufrenne, Mikel. 1955. "Signification des 'a priori.'" *Bulletin de la société française de philosophie* 49 (3): 99–116.

Dufrenne, Mikel. 1966. *The Notion of the A Priori*. Translated by Edward Casey. Evanston, IL: Northwestern University Press.

Elo, Mika, and Miika Luoto. 2014. "Introduction: In Medias Res." In *Senses of Embodiment: Art, Technics, Media*, edited by Mika Elo and Miika Luoto, 7–19. Bern: Peter Lang AG.

Faiziev, Dzhanik, dir. [1997?] *Starye pesni o glavnom, 2* [Old songs about the main thing, 2]. YouTube.com. https://www.youtube.com/watch?v=ne30GQPx4Zo.

Fausto-Sterling, Anne. 1993. "The Five Sexes." *Sciences* 33 (2): 20–24.

Fausto-Sterling, Anne. 2000a. "The Five Sexes, Revisited." *Sciences* 40 (4): 18–23.

Fausto-Sterling, Anne. 2000b. *Sexing the Body: Gender Politics and the Construction of Sexuality*. New York: Basic Books.

Fisher, Linda. 2000a. "Introduction: Feminist Phenomenology." In *Feminist Phenomenology*, edited by Linda Fisher and Lester Embree, 1–15. Dordrecht, Netherlands: Springer.

Fisher, Linda. 2000b. "Phenomenology and Feminism: Perspectives on their Relation." In *Feminist Phenomenology*, edited by Linda Fisher and Lester Embree, 17–38. Dordrecht, Netherlands: Springer.

Forbes (Russian edition). 2014. "Latviia zapretila v"ezd v stranu Kobzonu i Valerii" [Latvia has banned Kobzon and Valeriia from entering country]. July 27, 2014. https://www.forbes.ru/news/263193-latviya-zapretila-vezd-v-stranu-kobzonu-i-valerii.

Fontanka. 2020. "'Sil'nye zhenshchiny': Pevitsa Valeriia gotova sozdat' svoiu partiiu i poiti v Gosdumu" ["Strong women": The singer Valeriia is ready to create her own party and go to the state duma]. February 20, 2020. https://www.fontanka.ru/2020/02/21/096/.

Foster, Johanna. 1999. "An Invitation to Dialogue: Clarifying the Position of Feminist Gender Theory in Relation to Sexual Difference Theory." *Gender and Society* 13 (4): 431–456.

Fuchs, Thomas. 2012. "The Phenomenology of Body Memory." In *Body Memory, Metaphor, and Movement*, edited by Sabine C. Koch, 9–22. Amsterdam: John Benjamins.

Gallagher, Shaun, and Jonathan Cole. 1995. "Body Schema and Body Image in a Deafferented Subject." *Journal of Mind & Behavior* 16 (4): 369–390.

Gallese, Vittorio. 2001. "The 'Shared Manifold' Hypothesis." *Journal of Consciousness Studies* 8 (5–7): 33–50.

Groot, Rokus de. 2010. "Said and Polyphony." In *Edward Said: A Legacy of Emancipation and Representation*, edited by Adel Iskandar and Hakem Rustom, 204–226. Berkeley: University of California Press.

Gavrilov, Georgii, dir. 1992. "The Sky Belongs to Me." YouTube.com. https://www.youtube.com/watch?v=UtCpfQrXbgY.

Golubev, Aleksei, dir. 2016. "Telo khochet liubvi" [The body wants love]. YouTube.com. https://www.youtube.com/watch?v=p22lAqClSWA.

Hawkesworth, Mary. 1997. "Confounding Gender." *Signs* 22 (3): 649–685.

Heinämaa, Sara. 2003. *Toward a Phenomenology of Sexual Difference: Husserl, Merleau-Ponty, Beauvoir*. Lanham, MD: Rowman and Littlefield.

Heinämaa, Sara. 2012. "Sex, Gender, and Embodiment." In *The Oxford Handbook of Contemporary Phenomenology*, edited by Dan Zahavi, 216–242. Oxford: Oxford University Press.

Heinämaa, Sara. 2015. "Anonymity and Personhood: Merleau-Ponty's Account of the Subject of Perception." *Continental Philosophy Review* 48 (2): 123–142.

Husserl, Edmund. (1913) 1983. *Ideas Pertaining to a Pure Phenomenology and to a Phenomenological Philosophy (First Book: General Introduction to a Pure Phenomenology)*. Translated by Fred Kersten. The Hague: Martinus Nijhoff.

Husserl, Edmund. (1928) 1991. *On the Phenomenology of the Consciousness of Internal Time (1893–1917)*. Translated by John Barnett Bough. Dordrecht, Netherlands: Kluwer.

Husserl, Edmund. (1931) 1960. *Cartesian Meditations: An Introduction to Phenomenology*. Translated by Dorion Cairns. The Hague: Martinus Nijhoff.

Husserl, Edmund. 1985. "The Apodicticity of Recollection." Translated by Deborah Chaffin. *Husserl Studies* 2: 3–32.

Husserl, Edmund. 2001. *Analyses concerning Passive and Active Synthesis: Lectures on Transcendental Logic*. Translated by Anthony J. Steinbock. Edited by Rudolf Bernet. Dordrecht: Kluwer.

Ihde, Don. 1990. *Technology and the Lifeworld: From Garden to Earth*. Bloomington: Indiana University Press.

Ihde, Don. 2007. *Listening and Voice: Phenomenologies of Sound*. 2nd ed. Albany: State University of New York Press.

The Independent. 2008. "Valeriya: Russia's Greatest Export (after Gas and Oil)." June 28, 2008. https://www.independent.co.uk/news/people/profiles/valeriya-russiarsquos-greatest-export-after-gas-and-oil-854990.html.

Iurmala-87 (Konkurs molodykh ispolnitelei èstradnoi pesni "Iurmala") [Jurmala-87 {The Jurmala young Estrada singer competition}]. 1987. Director unknown. YouTube.com. https://www.youtube.com/watch?v=nrLxTkwbolg.

Jõesaar, Andres. 2015. "One Country, Two Polarized Audiences: Estonia and the Deficiency of the Audiovisual Media Services Directive." *Media and Communication* 3 (4): 45–51.

Johnson, Mark. 1987. *The Body in the Mind*. Chicago: University of Chicago Press.

Johnson, Mark. 2007. *The Meaning of the Body: Aesthetics of Human Understanding*. Chicago: University of Chicago Press.

Jufereva, Maria, and Epp Lauk. 2015. "Minority Language Media and Journalists in the Context of Societal Integration in Estonia." *Medijske Studije* 6 (11): 51–65.

Kemppainen, Raija, Scott E. Ferrin, Carol J. Ward, and Julie M. Hite. 2004. "'One Should Not Forget One's Mother Tongue': Russian-Speaking Parents' Choice of Language of Instruction in Estonia." *Bilingual Research Journal* 28 (2): 207–229.

Kyrölä, Katariina. 2014. *The Weight of Images: Affect, Body Image, and Fat in the Media*. Farnham, UK: Ashgate.

Lakoff, George, and Mark Johnson. 1999. *Philosophy in the Flesh*. New York: Basic Books.

Lauristin, Marju, et al. 2011. *Estonian Integration Monitoring 2011*. Tallinn: Ministry of Culture/ Policy Center Praxis/TNS Emor.

Lefebvre, Henri. (1992) 2004. *Rhythmanalysis: Space, Time, and Everyday Life*. Translated by Stuart Elden and Gerald Moore. London: Continuum.

Levitin, Daniel J. 2006. *This Is Your Brain on Music: The Science of a Human Obsession*. New York: Dutton.

Levy, Kenneth. 1987. "On the Origin of Neumes." *Early Music History* 7: 59–90.

Lingis, Alphonso. 1994. *Foreign Bodies*. New York: Routledge.

Lingis, Alphonso. 2000. *Dangerous Emotions*. Berkeley: University of California Press.

Lingis, Alphonso. 2018. *Irrevocable: A Philosophy of Mortality*. Chicago: University of Chicago Press.

Llinás, Rodolfo. 2001. *I of the Vortex*. Cambridge, MA: MIT Press.

Lorde, Audre. 1984. "Eye to Eye: Black Women, Hatred, and Anger." In *Sister Outsider: Essays and Speeches by Audre Lorde*, 145–175. Berkeley, CA: Crossing Press.

Lugones, Maria. 2008. "The Coloniality of Gender." *Worlds & Knowledges Otherwise* 2 (2): 1–17.

Lugones, Maria. 2010. "Toward a Decolonial Feminism." *Hypatia* 25 (4): 742–759.

Maasik, Hindrek, dir. (2001) 2014. "Mal'chiki ne plachut" [Boys don't cry]. YouTube.com. https://www.youtube.com/watch?v=4Qhv7uYrZ_k.

Mägi, Kadi. 2018. "Ethnic Residential Segregation and Integration of the Russian-Speaking Population in Estonia." PhD diss., University of Tartu.

Merleau-Ponty, Maurice. (1955) 1974. *Adventures of the Dialectic*. Translated by Joseph Bien. Evanston, IL: Northwestern University Press.

Merleau-Ponty, Maurice. (1958) 2005. *Phenomenology of Perception*. Translated by Colin Smith. London: Routledge.

Merleau-Ponty, Maurice. 1964. *Signs*. Translated by Richard C. McCleary. Evanston, IL: Northwestern University Press.

Modell, Arnold H. 2003. *Imagination and the Meaningful Brain*. Cambridge, MA: MIT Press.

Moi, Toril. 1999. "What Is a Woman? Sex, Gender, and the Body in Feminist Theory." In *What Is a Woman and Other Essays*, 3–120. Oxford: Oxford University Press.

Montero, Barbara. 2006. "Proprioception as an Aesthetic Sense." *Journal of Aesthetics and Art Criticism* 64 (2): 231–242.

MSN (Russian edition). 2020. "Valeriia otkrestilas' ot partii 'Sil'nye zhenshchiny,' kotoruiu iakoby sozdala" [Valeriia has disowned the "strong women party," which she supposedly created]. July 30, 2020. Accessed September 1, 2020. https://www.msn.com/ru-ru/entert ainment/celebrity/валерия-открестилась-от-партии-сильные-женщины-короруюякобы-создала/ar-BB17mHH8.

Murata, Junichi. 2012. "Colours and Sounds: The Field of Visual and Auditory Consciousness." In *The Oxford Handbook of Contemporary Phenomenology*, edited by Dan Zahavi, 158–176. Oxford: Oxford University Press.

Nancy, Jean-Luc. (2002) 2007. *Listening*. Translated by Charlotte Mandell. New York: Fordham University Press.

Neumann, John von. 1958. *The Computer and the Brain*. New Haven, CT: Yale University Press.

Nimmerfeldt, Gerli. 2008. "Kodakondsus" [Citizenship]. In *Eesti ühiskonna integratsiooni monitooring 2008* [Monitoring the integration of Estonian society 2008], by Raivo Vetik, et al., 126–142. Tallinn: Integratsiooni Sihtasutus ja Rahvastikuministri Büroo. https://www. integratsioon.ee/sites/default/files/196_207.pdf.

Nimmerfeldt, Gerli. 2011. "Sense of Belonging in Estonia." In *The Russian Second Generation in Tallinn and Kohtla-Järve: The TIES Study in Estonia*, edited by Raivo Vetik and Jelena Helemäe, 203–228. IMISCOE Reports. Amsterdam: Amsterdam University Press.

Oksala, Johanna. 2006. "A Phenomenology of Gender." *Continental Philosophy Review* 39 (3): 229–244.

Pesic, Peter. 2017. *Polyphonic Minds: Music of the Hemispheres*. Cambridge, MA: MIT Press.

Petrosian, Armen, dir. 1995. "Samolet" [Airplane]. YouTube.com. https://www.youtube.com/watch?v=bv42u-8lXVA.

Prigozhin, Iosif, and Alesia Visich, dirs. 2020. "Do predella" [To the bitter end]. YouTube.com. https://www.youtube.com/watch?v=doB4li7Kn94.

Rancière, Jacques. (2000) 2004. *The Politics of Aesthetics*. Translated and edited by Gabriel Rockhill. London: Bloomsbury.

Rasskazova, Oksana, dir. 2019. "Net shansa" [No chance]. YouTube.com. https://www.youtube.com/watch?v=sVYCFoQ9Xjo.

Ren. 2018. "50-letniaia Valeriia vylozhila v Instagram foto v bikini" [Fifty-year-old Valeriia posted to Instagram a photo in a bikini]. June 30, 2018. http://ren.tv/novosti/2018-06-30/50-letnyaya-valeriya-vylozhila-v-instagram-foto-v-bikini.

Ricoeur, Paul. (1977) 2004. *The Rule of Metaphor: The Creation of Meaning in Language*. Translated by Robert Czerny, Kathleen McLaughlin, and John Costello. London: Routledge.

Rothblum, Esther, and Sondra Solovay, eds. 2009. *The Fat Studies Reader*. New York: New York University Press.

Rubin, Gayle. 1975. "The Traffic in Women: Notes on the Political Economy of Sex." In *Toward an Anthropology of Women*, edited by Rayna R. Reitner, 157–210. New York: Monthly Review Press.

Said, Edward. 1991. *Musical Elaborations: The Wellek Library Lectures at the University of California, Irvine*. New York: Columbia University Press.

Said, Edward. 1993. *Culture and Imperialism*. London: Chatto and Windus.

Scott, Joan W. 1991. "The Evidence of Experience." *Critical Inquiry* 17 (4): 773–797.

Shadrov, Artem, dir. 2011. *Iubileinyi kontsert, "Russkie romansy"* (Jubilee concert, "Russian romances"). YouTube.com. https://www.youtube.com/watch?v=uUz8-QmjaB8.

Shusterman, Richard. 2008. *Body Consciousness: A Philosophy of Mindfulness and Somaesthetics*. Oxford: Oxford University Press.

Shusterman, Richard. 2011. "Muscle Movement and the Somaesthetic Pathologies of Everyday Life." *Human Movement* 12 (1): 4–15.

Shusterman, Richard. 2012a. "Back to the Future: Aesthetics Today." *Nordic Journal of Aesthetics* 43: 104–124.

Shusterman, Richard. 2012b. *Thinking through the Body: Essays in Somaesthetics*. Cambridge: Cambridge University Press.

Small, Christopher. 1998. *Musicking: The Meanings of Performing and Listening*. Middletown, CT: Wesleyan University Press.

Staehler, Tanja. 2017. *Hegel, Husserl, and the Phenomenology of Historical Worlds*. London: Rowman and Littlefield.

Starhit. 2020. "Seksi blondinka! Foto 52-letnei Valerii v derzkom bikini" [Sexy blond! Photos of 52-year-old Valeriia in daring bikini]. October 20, 2020. https://www.starhit.ru/novosti/seksi-blondinka-foto-52-letney-valerii-v-derzkom-bikini-223835/.

Stern, Daniel N. 1985. *The Interpersonal World of the Infant*. New York: Basic Books.

Stoller, Silvia. 2000. "Reflections on Feminist Merleau-Ponty Skepticism." *Hypatia* 15 (1): 175–182.

Stoller, Silvia. 2013. "The Indeterminable Gender: Ethics in Feminist Phenomenology and Poststructuralist Feminism." *Janus Head* 1 (13): 17–34.

Sullivan, Shannon. 1997. "Domination and Dialogue in Merleau-Ponty's *Phenomenology of Perception*." *Hypatia* 12 (1): 1–19.

Sutormina, Anastasiia. 2020. "Prigozhin ob"iasnil, pochemu ne udalos' cozdat' partiiu Valerii 'Sil'nye zhenshchiny'" [Prigozhin explained why Valeriia's "strong women" party was never created]. *Radio Komsomol'skaia Pravda*, August 14. https://radiokp.ru/prigozhin-obyasnil-pochemu-ne-udalos-sozdat-partiyu-valerii-silnye-zhenschiny_nid33563_au67au.

Titon, Jeff Todd. 2023. "The Expressive Culture of Sound Communication among Humans and Other Beings: A Phenomenological and Ecological Approach." In *The Oxford Handbook of the Phenomenology of Music Cultures*, edited by Harris M. Berger, Friedlind Reidel, and David VanderHamm. New York: Oxford University Press.

Tomkins, Silvan. 1995. *Shame and Its Sisters: A Silvan Tomkins Reader*. Edited by Eve Kosofsky Sedgwick and Adam Frank. Durham, NC: Duke University Press.

Treitler, Leo. 2003. *With Voice and Pen: Coming to Know Medieval Song and How It Was Made*. Oxford: Oxford University Press.

Treshchev, Ruslan, dir. 2018. *Valeriia: Ne boisia byt' schastlivoi* [Valeriia: Don't be afraid to be happy]. YouTube.com. https://www.youtube.com/watch?v=DFUlisZRou4.

Valeriia [Alla Perfilova]. 2006. *I zhizn', i slezy, i liubov'* [Life, tears, and love]. Moscow: Azbuka.

Valeriia and Iosif Prigozhin, dir. 2013. *Iubileinyi kontsert, "Po serpantinu"* (Jubilee concert, "By the winding road"). YouTube.com. https://www.youtube.com/watch?v=2KWl3BtVIms.

Verenchik, Aleksei, dir. 2015. "Sil'nye zhenshchiny" (Strong women). YouTube.com. https://www.youtube.com/watch?v=eF9CzbfephI.

Whitehead, Alfred North. (1927) 1958. *Symbolism: Its Meaning and Effect*. New York: Fordham University Press.

Young, Iris M. 1984. "Pregnant Embodiment: Subjectivity and Alienation." *Journal of Medicine and Philosophy* 9 (1): 25–62.

Young, Iris M. 1985. "Pregnant Subjectivity and the Limits of Existential Phenomenology." In *Descriptions*, edited by Don Ihde and Hugh J. Silverman, 25–34. Albany: State University of New York Press.

CHAPTER 8

PHENOMENOLOGY AND HABITUS IN MUSIC LISTENING

ANDREW MCGUINESS

INTRODUCTION

Frantz Fanon, in his seminal *Black Skin, White Masks*, first published in 1952, identifies the body schema as productive of the self:

> I know that if I want to smoke, I shall have to reach out my right arm and take the pack of cigarettes lying at the other end of the table. The matches, however, are in the drawer on the left, and I shall have to lean back slightly. And all these movements are made not out of habit but out of implicit knowledge. A slow composition of my *self* as a body in the middle of a spatial and temporal world—such seems to be the schema. It does not impose itself on me; it is, rather, a definitive structuring of the self and of the world—definitive because it creates a real dialectic between my body and the world.
>
> (Fanon [1952] 1986, 111)

The body schema so described creates and expresses the individual as a subject with agency in the world: the desires and goals of the subject are conscious but the means by which the body achieves these are implicit. The racism experienced by Fanon stymies such unconscious ease: "In the white world the man of color encounters difficulties in the development of his bodily schema" (110). As a result, the body is experienced as an object:

> . . . the corporeal schema crumbled, its place taken by a racial epidermal schema . . .
> I was responsible at the same time for my body, for my race, for my ancestors . . .

> On that day, completely dislocated, unable to be abroad with the other, the white man, who unmercifully imprisoned me, I took myself far off from my own presence, far indeed, and made myself an object. (112)

It is easy to imagine how a person, who repeatedly and from birth experiences themself categorized in the way Fanon describes, will develop a habitual body schema that enacts their social position as subordinate, even abject (in the sense of not being permitted to be a full subject). This, too, Fanon describes:

> Sealed into that crushing objecthood, I turned beseechingly to others. Their attention was a liberation, running over my body suddenly abraded into nonbeing, endowing me once more with an agility that I had thought lost, and by taking me out of the world, restoring me to it. But just as I reached the other side, I stumbled, and the movements, the attitudes, the glances of the other fixed me there, in the sense in which a chemical solution is fixed by a dye. (109)

Reading *Black Skin, White Masks* offers a window into an experience which, as a White person, I cannot have. In doing so, it provides a means to reflect on how my own racial identity—implicitly experienced as "normal"—shapes my ways of being in the world. While I have to make an effort to gain awareness of my own racial identity, Fanon shows how racism forced upon him an urgent consciousness of a prescribed racial identity. However, in the third passage quoted above—where he notes a "liberation" of his body that turns out to be no liberation, since he becomes fixed in place by the gaze of "the other"—Fanon is describing an experience that might have gone unexamined. In this essay I will consider how implicit body schemata—inculcated in ways explored by Fanon—can be *revised* by funk music and dance.

Two caveats are important to note at the beginning. First, as a White man, I do not pretend to have firsthand experiences of being subjected to racism. This makes it all the more important for me, and for White scholars more generally, to engage with descriptions and articulations of that experience—in speech, writing, film, music, and visual arts—by those who have been on the receiving end of racism. By taking up the sense of the body so vividly described by Fanon, this chapter attempts to make detailed sense of how James Brown's funk became a driving force of Black nationalist consciousness in the United States in the 1960s. The tools with which I approach this project are Pierre Bourdieu's concept of *habitus* and the associated concept of *hexis* (which, I will argue, corresponds closely to the body schema as described by Fanon); analyses by Thomas Slaughter and Fred Moten of possible ontologies of subjectivity for the Black individual in a racist world; Gilles Deleuze's concepts of the transcendental field and "intensity"; Anne Danielsen's insightful analysis of the funk grooves of James Brown in her book *Presence and Pleasure* (2006); and Edmund Husserl's phenomenology of perception.

The second caveat is that a transformed body schema, which I argue may result from participation in a funk event, should not be thought of as "undoing race," as some kind of panacea for those subjected to racism. While music can have a powerful impact on a person's identity, the lived experience of race is shaped by a variety of factors, from everyday encounters with micro-aggression to implicit racist messages, explicit expressions of racist ideology, institutionalized racism, and the wider political economy of colonialism and White supremacy. How any liberatory potential of funk works within the tapestry of experience is a question I seek to ask, rather than to answer, in this essay.

My central argument is this: in participating as a dancer at a funk event, microtiming ambiguities in the music may lead to temporary confusion as to the period (or length) of the beat. This temporary confusion is corrected within the space of the groove cycle—only to be repeated again—leading to what I refer to as "perceptual revision," a moment of self-consciousness when the dancer becomes aware of two conflicting ways of perceiving the beat. Since movement in time with a beat is a skill of the body, perceptual revision or readjustment is a matter of body consciousness; it is this moment (repeated throughout a song, and in different ways in different songs) that I suggest may provide a particular self-reflective awareness of the body schema not otherwise available.

THE EXPERIENCE OF THE BODY

Habitus and Hexis

Of course, we are routinely aware of our bodies and movements, and yet, both the kinds of movements we make and the quality of those movements may be constrained in ways that escape our awareness. Pierre Bourdieu in *The Logic of Practice* describes habitus as "a spontaneity without consciousness or will" (Bourdieu [1980] 1990, 56). For Bourdieu, habitus is a system of "durable, transposable dispositions" that function as "principles which generate and organize practices and representations" (53). Habitus thus determines both the perceptions and actions available to an individual in any situation, as well as the representations of the world and the individual's place within it. (Bourdieu is largely concerned with social class.) The dispositions of habitus are "internalized as second nature"; they are "forgotten as history" and become a "state of the body" rather than of the mind (56). As such, they are not normally available to reflexive analysis by those who possess them (or, rather, are possessed by them). Habitus should not, however, be thought of as mechanical habit but rather as being adaptive to different situations while producing similar outcomes. Habitus might indeed be understood in terms of musical style where a musician's deep knowledge of a particular style operates as a disposition to make similar musical decisions. In contrast, the disposition that musicians refer to as "muscle memory" describes a *mechanical* habit that is not adaptive.

Bourdieu identifies homologies of physical movement between different activities (261). This notion of bodily hexis is a matter less of particular activities and the techniques by which these are accomplished than of a consistent comportment of the body that is exhibited across a range of practices as enacted by a particular social group: the similarity between the way members of a social category stand, walk, talk, or move the body from one position to another. Bourdieu defines hexis as "political mythology realized, em-bodied, turned into a permanent disposition, a durable manner of standing, speaking, *and thereby of feeling and thinking*" (Bourdieu [1972] 1977, 93–94; italics added).

A concrete example of the homology of hexis can be found in the public comportment of police officers that is inculcated in new recruits through a complex and ongoing process of socialization (Martin 1999, 113–114). For police officers in training, this may at first require conscious adjustment, to "learn new behavior regarding verbal, facial, and bodily displays that convey their authority to citizens. This includes learning not to smile (smiling may cool a situation but signals deference, so usually is inappropriate) and to avoid postures that indicate hesitation or unreadiness to act" (Martin 1999, 122). Over time, however, new recruits acquire a habitus and a hexis that are adjusted to the new environment that comes with their new role. Such inculcation of habitus (including hexis) is generally described by Bourdieu as occurring through a process of mimesis, implying "an overall relation of identification" ([1980] 1990, 73). But how are habitus and hexis related to racism and the suffocating experiences that Fanon so powerfully relates in *Black Skin White Mask*? It is true that being subjected to racism (as Fanon describes) is manifestly neither a matter of identification nor mimesis and cannot be contained within the notions of habitus and hexis; nevertheless, these two concepts offer a useful way of thinking about the experience. Bourdieu recognizes the original source of habitus in the exigencies of the social environment:

> the possibilities and impossibilities, freedoms and necessities, opportunities and prohibitions inscribed in the objective conditions . . . generate dispositions objectively compatible with these conditions and in a sense pre-adapted to their demands.
>
> (Bourdieu [1980] 1990, 54)

Writing that "the movements, the attitudes, the glances of the other fixed me there, in the sense in which a chemical solution is fixed by a dye" ([1952] 1986, 109), Fanon seems to recognize the violent imposition of a hexis of subordination. *Black Skin, White Masks* appears to me to be the product of a sustained effort not just to identify racist attitudes and behaviors to which the author was exposed but to explore how these imposed a "racial epidermal schema" on those at the receiving end of racism. Fanon knows he is racialized by the attitude of Whites; he can feel it. But he also feels that he has incorporated this racialized position as habitus in his own bodily movements and changing this, he realizes, lies outside of his control. No reflection, not even his clear analysis, is able to liberate his body from this habitus that is born of racial violence against him.

It should be noted that Bourdieu's theory has been criticized for its elimination of the agency of the conscious human subject. Throop and Murphy contend that Bourdieu is phenomenologically naïve in characterizing all nonrepresentational states as necessarily nonconscious, a naïvety born of lack of attention to his own phenomenology

(Throop and Murphy 2002, 198). They argue for a return of anthropological practice theory to the actual lived experience of agents, including the conscious experience of goals, ideals, and feelings (Throop and Murphy 2002, 198). Certainly, there are strong indications both that consciousness of social forces can exist and that habitus can be consciously practiced-in, as with the new police recruits described above. This is nevertheless consistent with the idea that *some* aspects of habitus and hexis operate transcendentally, beyond the reach of everyday awareness. This, in fact, is the account Fanon gives of his own phenomenology in *Black Skin, White Masks*: he can identify *that* his body performs a racialized subordination against his will, but he describes himself as trapped in that performance. The writing conveys a sense that he is unable to choose to do otherwise because the manner of his movement is determined transcendentally.

Epidermalizing the World

What effective response can there be to such a profound predicament? Thomas Slaughter (1977) finds possibility precisely in the ineluctable fact of his body. His starting point is the "double-consciousness" identified by W. E. B. Du Bois in his seminal text *The Souls of Black Folk*. Du Bois writes, "One ever feels his twoness,—an American, a Negro; two souls, two thoughts, two unreconciled strivings; two warring ideals in one dark body, whose dogged strength alone keeps it from being torn asunder" ([1903] 1969). As in Fanon's experience, racism, for Slaughter, is not merely "out there" in the society into which a Black individual is born but is produced *within* the body:

> Obviously, I exist by now both only through my particular body, but also, only in this peculiar society. And the case is both that my body-in-this-society induces double-consciousness, and that by now, double consciousness is my relation through this society to my own body, as this latter crucially is the public, first fact of my existence.
>
> (Slaughter 1977, 304)

It is probable, writes Slaughter, "that in my routine state, I carry White hatred of me within me as my own property" (304). The denigration of Blackness is inescapable; it is carried in the body itself. And yet, it is precisely in the "stubborn primacy" (304) of his lived body that Slaughter finds possibility: "the basic fact that I am me: however many 'warring ideals' there may be, I have but one life to live, and as long as I live, I live my body" (303).

This posture is nevertheless not an unproblematic reclaiming of his body. In Fanon's words, "every ontology is made unattainable in a colonized and civilized society" ([1952] 1986, 109). Slaughter finds that the "wretchedness of being colonized secretes 'guilt'"; as a result, "phenomenological access to the truth of my being is never merely descriptive" (1977, 306). Double-consciousness—recounted by Slaughter as the sociophysical gap between his own sense of self and the culturally imposed sense of ignominy—is still in force; that gap is spanned by "internalizing that contradiction and suffering it as an integral structure of my own character" (304). The externally imposed inferiorization and its internalization produces "a split of which by lopsided social contract, my body is the symbol" (304).

Nevertheless, the identification of the self with the necessarily single body that carries it distances Slaughter from the social system of credits for personal worth. He experiences a "throwness": he is beyond the pale, belonging to neither the time nor the place of his surroundings:

> I am an African person. I come from an ancient past; and I lean toward a cosmic future in which the principle of life will mangle the bind of race. The racialized will be the righteous. . . . Whereas before, my being to the world through my body was my condemnation, now, my body is my vindication. Blackness enshrines my innocence. I rehabilitate myself. (306)

Slaughter's skin "becomes the very seed" of his salvation: "Whereas Blackness was my condemnation; Blackness, subjectively revised, is my vindication" (307).

The Black man, writes Slaughter, is "a perennial cultural rebel, a cultural nationalist" (307). Certainly, James Brown filled both those roles. In 1969, writes Rickey Vincent (2008), James Brown was "at the forefront of a race conscious, collective emerging that was taking place in black America" (52); his music was perhaps the most unifying expression of Black popular culture at that time (51). Brown's style of explicit, articulate, and assertive delivery had never been heard in American popular music before, while the unique rhythmic contrast and tension of the performances "exuded confidence, strength, and pride for the participants" and captured the contemporary Black spirit of defiance, indignation, anticipation, and dignity (52). The music "reflected the harsh, unvarnished truths of black American life" (53). Brown himself described the funk music he developed as "a physically performed, roots-derived configuration of music that comes straight from the heart," designed to fill a need: "What was missing for me and my people was the rhythm of our own revolution—a soundtrack strong enough to bring us to the outside rather than keep us on the inside" (Brown 2005, 81). In all this, explicit political messages of Black pride were important, but the driving force came from the dancing body. Here is bassist Bootsy Collins's account of his first experience performing with James Brown:

> We hit every move. We knew all of his moves. If you noticed, it wasn't so much about his singing and screaming, it was all about his body. His moves. You had to pay attention! I ain't never paid attention that much! I mean every little move he made, if it was with his foot, you had to be on it.
>
> (Ellis 2008, 91)

Trombonist Fred Wesley offers a similar recollection of the recording of *Say It Loud, I'm Black and I'm Proud*:

> Mr. Brown was in control now. Pee Wee took his place in the reed section, and James counted it off. The groove was already strong, but when James counted it

off and began to dance and direct it, it took on a new power. The kids were doing their chant with a new energy. In fact the energy level in the whole studio was lifted. James went straight through the whole tune and that was it. After about four hours of preparation, "Say It Loud, I'm Black and I'm Proud" went down in one take.

(Wesley 2005, 107)

EXPERIENCE AND MEANING OF THE FUNK EVENT

If racism acts on the body, then can working directly with the body counter racism, at least to some extent, at least sometimes? The capacity for dancing to music to bring about a change of subjectivity through a change in the body is a recurring theme in music studies.[1] According to Susan McClary, "the musical power of the disenfranchised . . . more often resides in their ability to articulate different ways of construing the body, ways that bring along in their wake the potential for different experiential worlds" (McClary 1994). If this is so, it is of interest exactly *how* music offers the opportunity to articulate different ways of construing the body, how those different construals might themselves be described, and how they in turn offer the potential for different experiential worlds.

In what follows, I refer often to "funk" and the experience of funk. The term "funk" refers more generally to a musical style; however, in this chapter I have in mind events where a live band (as discussed here, the James Brown band) plays an extended set for an audience that shares a culture (the Black urban culture of the USA in the 1960s and 1970s) and the members of which attend closely to the music and dance to it. A video recording of a concert at the Boston Garden in 1968 is available[2] that gives some sense of the shared culture and musical focus, although little of the dance moves. Discussion of the experience of funk in this chapter refers to the experience of audience members actively participating in such a funk event. I should note, however, that I do not engage with the specifics of dance movement; this essay is concerned rather with how a particular rhythmic device ("counter-rhythm") found in James Brown's funk grooves prompts "perceptual revision," which in turn enables a consciousness of hexis.

James Brown (1933–2006), American soul singer and bandleader, was a leading force in the development of funk music in the 1960s and 1970s, playing a major role in foregrounding rhythm in popular music. By the late 1960s, Brown was a focus for the emerging Black arts and Black nationalist movements in the United States (Kennedy 2018; Lipsitz 2020). In that context, Danielsen (2006) notes that funk was regarded as both an expression and a means of spiritual upheaval. James Brown's lyrics promote pride ("Say It Loud, I'm Black and I'm Proud"), agency and involvement ("Get Up, Get

Into It, Get Involved"), and spiritual strength ("Soul Power") (204–209). Together with such verbal expressions, the *feeling* of funk is a "key aesthetic notion":

> It is about cultivating the right swaying motion; about accurate timing; about being in place, in time; about precision and relaxation at once . . . The only indication as to when it is right—whether one is dancing or playing—is a feeling, and not just any feeling: funk is about the "right" feeling.
>
> (Danielsen 2006, 198)

We can see in this a temporary antidote to the "crushing objecthood" of the body that Fanon describes, and perhaps to the imposed performance of subordination that succeeded it.

In the broad context of Black music as a site of negotiation and articulation of Black liberation politics in the United States of the late 1960s and early 1970s, Michael Hanson argues that what is significant about James Brown is musical—the non-lyrical elements of his music specifically—rather than any capacity to articulate a coherent political line or to be a spokesperson for the movement:

> Brown was not so much political as he was a primary emblem of black ingroup feeling—a funk ontology—which, when rubbed against the mainstream politics and culture of the day, became politicised for the black people who felt and identified his musical embodiment of blackness.
>
> (Hanson 2008, 358)

Hanson here crystallizes a dichotomy at the center of funk as a participatory practice for Black people at the time: is funk a matter of representation and after-the-fact meaning, or a matter of being? Funk was "felt" as the "musical embodiment" of Blackness; at the same time (or, perhaps, subsequently), it became an "emblem" of a particular political approach. As reflective meaning, funk can be said to have a force, of a kind, when it is no longer in being—that is, outside of an event where funk music is played and people dance to it. On the other hand, the articulation of a political position or the understanding of how marginalization is achieved on a day-to-day level do not in themselves provide an avenue of escape from the experience of subordination. Fanon describes discussing the issue of racism with friends, the recognition of the unjustness of the position of the Black man, and the intellectual understanding of equality: "And then . . . And then the occasion arose when I had to meet the white man's eyes" (Fanon [1952] 1986, 110). This is the point at which, as recounted at the beginning of this chapter, Fanon found his body first reduced to objecthood and then subsequently rehabilitated to subjectivity, but a subordinate subjectivity: the experience of the body is primary.

Hanson identifies feeling and embodiment as central to the political representational function of funk: the force of its symbolism in fact depends on the state of being that funk can engender and this state is therefore ontologically prior to the political representation it achieves, no matter how germane the symbolism is to the actual political situation of Blackness. The link between experience and meaning is not simple, and part of the complexity is in the experience itself.

The Case of Blackness

Underlying the triumphant chant of "Say It Loud, I'm Black and I'm Proud," the racist context that engenders the need to make an explicit statement of pride in Black skin is still evident. But there is also a sense that the environment of racism has become temporarily irrelevant. In order to explore more closely the "transcendent moments of triumph and celebration above all of the trials" (Vincent 2008, 53) of James Brown's music, it is necessary to return to the internalized contradiction, the split that Slaughter incorporated as integral to the structure of his own character. Fred Moten (2008) locates Blackness exactly in this gap between the social and the ontological selves, contained without resolution in a single body.

Moten's starting point is Fanon's apprehension that the Black man is positioned as Black in relation to the White. Fanon writes,

> Every ontology is made unattainable in a colonized and civilized society. . . . In the *Weltanschauung* of a colonized people there is an impurity, a flaw, that outlaws any ontological explanation.
>
> (Fanon [1952] 1986, 109–110)

If the Black individual cannot be an other for another Black person, if they can only be an other for a White person, then Black being cannot be for itself; there can be no ontology of the Black self in a racist society. It is this flaw, the gap between the fact of Blackness and the lived experience of the Black individual, that Moten embraces as productive (2008, 179). The problem is that "the world is never merely given. It is given always already as a racist world" (Slaughter 1977, 307). In this, the "given always already" is a problem on its own account. As Alia Al-Saji writes, "What is revealed, in addition to objectification, is a temporal projection or retrogression by which the racialized body (whether subject or viewer) is cast as perpetually past, coming 'too late' to intervene in the meaning of its own representation" (2019, 475). It is not just that the Black individual is forced into inferiorization, a false ontology; it is also the very fact that a fixed ontology is provided, that their self is always already represented. The Black individual is not permitted the luxury of being, of simply being and becoming, in an unformulated way. Moten is explicit: "already given ontologies" are inadequate to Blackness (2008, 187). But where Fanon mourns the loss of preconscious co-responding to the world, Moten consciously claims, in the name of Blackness, "an ontology of disorder, an ontology of dehiscence"; "some folks" he says, "relish being a problem" (187).

Fanon describes his involuntary response to the racist gaze: "I took myself far off from my own presence, far indeed, and made myself an object" ([1952] 1986, 112). Moten, rather than striving after a subjectivity precluded by the social position allocated according to the fact of Blackness, seeks "something obscured by the fall from prospective subject to object that Fanon recites—namely, a transition from thing(s) (*choses*) to object (*objet*)" (2008, 181). What emerges for Moten from Fanon's work is a sense of the dynamic by which things acquire meanings when subjects are engaged in the representation of objects, "an often unattended movement that accompanies largely unthought positions and appositions" (182). Put differently, we might say that Moten is concerned with how habitus, as defined by Bourdieu, comes to determine the perceptions and representations of the world available to an individual in any situation.

Moten, then, wants to put aside the opposition between subject and object—an opposition the axis of which is predetermined by a racist society—in order to investigate the "special ontic-ontological fugitivity of/in the slave," not accounted for in Fanon:

> So that in contradistinction to Fanon's protest, the problem of the inadequacy of any ontology to blackness, to that mode of being for which escape or apposition and not the objectifying encounter with otherness is the prime modality, must be understood in its relation to the inadequacy of calculation to being in general. (187)

It is as if Moten is saying, a racist world has made me an object: well then, what is the true nature of that object that I am? What if, he asks,

> the thing whose meaning or value has never been found finds things, founds things? . . . What if the thing sustains itself in that absence or eclipse of meaning that withholds from the thing the horrific honorific of "object"? . . . [What if] the non-attainment of meaning or ontology, of source or origin, is the only way to approach the thing in its informal (enformed/enforming, as opposed to formless), material totality? (181–182)

We have already a sense from this passage of how we should think about a "thing." Moten draws the term from Martin Heidegger's essay, "The Thing" ([1950] 1971), where it is discussed in relation to a pottery jug: "Its thingliness does not inhere in its having been made or produced or represented. For Heidegger, the thingliness of the thing, the jug, is precisely that which prompts its making" (Moten 2008, 183). There are two negatives here: thingliness is not a matter of having been made (although the jug was made), nor of now being represented (although it is represented). In Heidegger's words, the thing is "what stands forth . . . standing forth has the sense of stemming from somewhere, whether this be a process of self-making or of being made by another," and "no representation of what is present . . . ever reaches to the thing *qua* thing" ([1950] 1971, 166).

Moten takes Heidegger to have stepped away from the mode of thought that produces the kind of worldview "that accompanies, what, for lack of a better turn, might be called intersubjection"—by which Moten appears to mean the subordination of the authentic self to public perceptions. In contrast, Fanon's brief narration of the history of his own becoming-object, of "being-positioned in and by representational thinking," entails a fateful participation in that thinking (Moten 2008, 186). In simplified terms, Moten is proposing an approach to the transcendental by means of repeated refusal to accept any finished ontology. A racist society made Fanon "responsible at the same time for [his] body, for [his] race, for [his] ancestors" ([1952] 1986, 112). While Moten's method is a response to the situation experienced by Black people in a racist society, it is, even so, a strategy for reclaiming the becoming of—but not the arrival at—an individual, rather than an epidermalized ontology.

Thingliness is what *prompts* the making of an object; the thing, therefore, does not appear by means of human making. Nevertheless, things do not appear without the "vigilance of mortals" (Heidegger [1950] 1971, 179), vigilance for which the first condition is a step back from the thinking that merely represents or explains, to thinking that "responds and recalls" (179). This cannot be a simple shift of attitude, since all attitudes entail representation. Rather, the step back "takes up its residence in a co-responding which, appealed to in the world's being by the world's being, answers within itself to that appeal" (179). The necessary vigilance requires an active openness to the world, yet without falling into a representational attitude which makes objects of things. It is this kind of "co-responding" that Moten advocates as a means of refusing an ontology which is always-already given to the Black person, and that I argue below is made possible within a funk event.

The Transcendental Field

The means by which funk might engender the vigilance that calls forth thingliness can be approached through concepts found in the work of Gilles Deleuze, in particular the "transcendental field" and "intensity."

The concept of the transcendental field speaks directly to Heidegger's thingliness and to Moten's desire to move orthogonally to the subject-object axis. It was first introduced by Jean-Paul Sartre in *The Transcendance of the Ego*, where he argues that it is the synthetic unity of an individual's representations of the world that makes it possible to say "I think," rather than the "I" preceding and uniting the representations (Sartre [1937] 1957, 34–36). Sartre's argument turns on the incompatibility of the spontaneity of consciousness—which is "individuated through and through in duration" (50)—with the time-independence of transcendent objects:

> The unity of a thousand active consciousnesses by which I have added, do add, and shall add two and two to make four, is the transcendent object "two and two make four." Without the permanence of this eternal truth a real unity would be impossible to conceive, and there would be irreducible operations as often as there were operative consciousnesses. (38)

The transcendental field is a field of "pure spontaneities" that are not objects but that determine their own existence, whereas the "I" that we find when we reflect on consciousness is an object of consciousness, and not its owner (96–97).

Sartre accepts Husserl's dictum that consciousness is consciousness *of* an object "and composes no part of the object" (Sartre [1937] 1957, 13). Intentionality allows consciousness to transcend itself and so unify itself: the object is transcendent to the multiple successive consciousnesses that grasp it, "and it is in the object that the unity of the consciousness is found" (38). Nevertheless, the consciousness of each of us constitutes a synthetic and individual totality by reason of the incommunicability and inwardness of consciousness; it is this individuality that makes possible the unity and personality of the "I." There is no function for a transcendental "I"; the transcendental field is both individual and impersonal (or "pre-personal") (39–40).

Deleuze draws on Sartre's idea of the transcendental field in a late essay entitled "Immanence: A Life" ([1995] 1997):

> What is a transcendental field? It is distinct from experience in that it neither refers to an object nor belongs to a subject (empirical representation). It appears therefore as a pure a-subjective current of consciousness, an impersonal pre-reflexive consciousness, a qualitative duration of consciousness without self. (3)

In *Difference and Repetition* (Deleuze [1968] 1994), it is already clear that transcendence is not necessary for individuality:

> Beyond the self and the I we find not the impersonal but the individual and its factors, individuation and its fields, individuality and its pre-individual singularities. For the pre-individual is still singular, just as the ante-self and the ante-I are still individual— or, rather than simply "still," we should say "finally." (258–259)

We can see that for Moten to step back from any given ontology of self, in order to examine his being as a *thing* in all its individuality, would be to inhabit the transcendental field. "The transcendental field escapes every transcendence of the subject as well as of the object . . . Pure immanence is a LIFE, and nothing else" (Deleuze [1995] 1997, 3).

Intensity

Difference and Repetition (Deleuze [1968] 1994) is metaphysics rather than phenomenology, but Deleuze explicates a central concept of the work—"intensity"—in phenomenological terms. Intensity depends on difference at the most fundamental level of sensation, before it has been assimilated to an empirical category; it is "not phenomenon but the noumenon closest to the phenomenon" (222). The concept of intensity is notoriously difficult, and a full exploration of it is beyond the scope of this chapter. In what follows, I aim to lay out its salient features for the current project, without (I hope) doing too much violence to Deleuze.

First, intensities should be understood as traversing multiple human faculties, which communicate in non-commonsense ways. At this fundamental level, sensing is already an interplay between different channels, with higher-order intensities built on relations between lower-order intensities: "the peculiarity of intensities being to be constituted by

a difference which itself refers to other differences (E-E', where E refers to *e-e'* and *e* to
ε-ε' . . .)" (117). The relations between different faculties are not, however, organized in
terms either of some object or of a subjective unity (such as an "I think"); rather, they are
a "forced and broken connection which traverses the fragments of a dissolved self as it
does the borders of a fractured I" (145).

Intensities are quantitative but not measured. Mary Beth Mader (2014) notes the influence in Deleuze's work from the medieval philosophical conception of intensity in
terms of qualitative intensification. To the modern reader, the "more" and "less" of qualitative intensity appear to be adequately expressed by the quantitative sense of those
words. Thus, the qualitatively *felt* sense of heat is routinely substituted by the sense of
an increase or decrease of degrees of temperature measured by a thermometer. Mader
suggests that Deleuze would take a given temperature to be a different kind of thing
from a given measured temperature:

> The temperature would be an intensive ordinate; the measured temperature would
> be the co-ordination of such an intensive ordinate of temperature with the extended
> substance of, say, the mercury of a mercury thermometer. The extension of the mer-
> cury would be the extensive expression of the intensive ordinate of temperature, or
> its co-ordination with the extended mercury.
>
> (Mader 2014, 239)

Deleuze insists that "the expression 'difference of intensity' is a tautology . . . Every
intensity is differential, by itself a difference" ([1968] 1994, 222); Deleuze's frequent use
of that very expression "difference in intensity" should therefore be read as tautolog-
ical emphasis. Intensive quantity "includes the unequal in itself" (232), it is "already difference in itself and comprises inequality as such" (234). In the context of the present
project, I take this to mean that difference is part of intensity as a transcendental phenomenon, even without a concurrent dynamic change in itself (such as a change of temperature, in the example above).

Intensities define the "proper limits of sensibility" (230) and are the ground for the
perception of objectified qualities and extensities. Here is Deleuze discussing the relation between the extensity of distance and the intensity of depth:

> The ground [fond] as it appears in a homogenous extensity is notably a projection of
> something "deeper" [profond]: only the latter may be called *Ungrund* or groundless.
> The law of figure and ground would never hold for objects distinguished from a neu-
> tral background or a background of other objects unless the object itself entertained
> a relation to its own depth. (229)

Finally, both the restricted dimensionality of the examples provided (one-
dimensional for temperature and three-dimensional for space) and their reference to
transcendent objectivities should be understood as features of simplified analogies. In
applying the concept of intensity to the experience of funk, we should remember the

possibility of higher-order intensities, involving multiple human faculties, and in relations that are not pre-ordered.

The Phenomenology of Funk

We are now in a position to consider the concepts discussed above in relation to the experience of a funk event, specifically the mature funk of James Brown, as analyzed by Anne Danielsen in *Presence and Pleasure: The Funk Grooves of James Brown and Parliament* (2006).

Funk grooves are, of course, repetitive: yet to be "in" a funk groove is not to experience the repetition as repetitive; being continuously involved in the co-production of gestures, the participants are completely present in the groove without the distancing that would allow awareness of time and repetition. To be able to talk about this state of "being in funk" entails that one is no longer in it, that the experience can be related to other experiences, events, and places (Danielsen 2006, 193). Danielsen cites Paul Ricoeur's concept of distanciation, according to which understanding follows from awareness of our own state of mind "as the projection of our own-most possibilities in those situations where we find ourselves" (Ricoeur 1973, 140). Funk requires a total presence in the event, but an eventual shift to meaning is unavoidable; simply naming it is necessarily something that comes "always-already" after the fact of the event (Danielsen 2006, 196). As the shift to meaning occurs, in "the moment when one moves beyond the immediate situatedness within the body and tries to introduce funk in the universe of thought—that is, of reflection," the feeling that belongs to the experience of presence in the groove is objectified and becomes a memory (Danielsen 2006, 216). This is a problem of aesthetic interpretation in general, but Danielsen finds that in the case of funk "the question of meaning becomes particularly precarious" (2006, 214). The feeling of funk is immediacy, but to recognize this is to reduce it to meaning. In a sense, the meaning of funk stems from its very status as experience, rather than as expression or sign: "Funk may be an event whose meaning is to never be meaning"; but paradoxically, "this understanding may not be reached before the unavoidable shift to meaning actually has taken place" (Danielsen 2006, 202). And yet, "there is no state of being in funk before it is understood and labeled as such . . . distancing from the state of funk is constitutive of the state itself" (Danielsen 2006, 192–193).

We might ask why the experience of funk should be one that defers meaning, and conversely, why the state of funk can only be constituted through distanciation and meaning. The answers can be found by examining again Fanon's phenomenology of the racialized body. First, the body schema by means of which one performs one's subjectivity is negated by the experience of racism—the body becomes an object in consciousness. Second, Fanon's subsequent problem was that the subjectivity of the body is recovered but it is *fixed* by "the attitudes, the glances of the other" ([1952] 1986, 109). Fanon wanted "to be a man, nothing but a man," but such an easy relation to the world at large is now lost to him because "not only must the black man be black; he must be black in relation to the white man" (110). There is a meaning attached to his everyday competent motor actions that stems from his position as a Black man in a White world. In light of this, the immediacy and non-meaning of *being in funk* can be seen as a means of being simply a person, rather than a Black person—where "Black" is constituted in opposition to "White," and "White" is considered to be the paradigm of the human. The "right feeling" of funk, the being in place and in time, both precise and relaxed, is surely a momentary antidote to the sense of the body as alienated, a way of constituting the subjectivity of the body in direct relation to its environment. However, a state of bodily being that completely eschews self-reflection cannot become part of the consciousness that guarantees, through its continuity, the identity of a person. It is in this sense that distanciation from the state of funk can be said to be constitutive of the state itself—constitutive, that is, of the state of funk as part of the continuing subjectivity of the individual.

However, in the state of being in funk, the shift to meaning is deferred. There is a heightened experience of the event *as* event; we are absorbed in a delay of meaning. The style of funk with which we are concerned here is constructed mainly out of repeating cycles—the "groove unit." The cycle typically occupies one or two 4/4 bars, with bass, drums, and guitar repeating their figures almost exactly for each cycle. Individual instances of the cycle, or groups of instances, are sometimes decorated with a horn figure, which also serves to emphasize the boundary of the cycle. Over this ground occur James Brown's vocals, backing vocals in a call-and-response relation, and sometimes a horn or guitar solo. Now, if the fact of the groove unit's cyclic repetition is excluded from the participant's consciousness—that is, repetition as experienced from outside the process and that refers to the groove unit as a single concept with repeated instances—if this awareness of repetition is excluded from consciousness, then the participant is in a position to become conscious of their experience of being in the groove (rather than toward the groove as made up of its various elements).

According to Deleuze, true repetition "has no in-itself" ([1968] 1994, 70). What is important about repetition—especially for the present argument, regarding funk music and the body—is that it can be experienced without forming a concept of the repeated object of sense:

> *Re*-petition opposes *re*-presentation: the prefix changes its meaning, since in one case difference is only said in relation to the identical, which in the other it is the univocal which is said of the different. Repetition is the formless being of all differences, the formless power of the ground which carries every object to that extreme "form" in which its representation comes undone. (57)

It is this experience of repetition that Danielsen seems to claim for the state of being in the groove. For the participant in a funk groove, the groove cycle falls completely within the perceptual present (Danielsen 2006, 239n18). In Danielsen's analysis, the larger-scale time spans of pop music and the elements associated with these, such as melody and chord cycles, invite teleological listening (191). Although she does not make it explicit, it can be seen that teleological listening depends on a distanciation from the musical *now* in order to compare it with anticipated or contrasted sections of the form. In contrast, funk requires "absolute simultaneity" in processing musical experience; the processing of large-scale time spans is subordinated to presence in the perceptual now (214), The participant in groove has their attention focused within the time span of the groove's basic unit, with a heightened sensitivity towards tiny timbral nuances and timing inflections (189). However, a reflective consciousness of the experience of being in the groove is not guaranteed:

> If the state of being in the groove is that of a total absorption, and there is never any distance, one feels, pure and simple. There is no aesthetic reflection: one does not feel that one feels.
>
> (Danielsen 2006, 199)

Instead, we have what Lyotard (1991, [1991] 1994) calls the "tautegorical" reflection of aesthetic judgment, a consciousness of the state of being that nevertheless does not lead to knowledge of anything other than itself:

> Any act of thinking is thus accompanied by a feeling that signals to thought its "state." But this state is nothing other than the feeling that signals it. For thought, to be in-formed of its state is to feel this state—to be affected. The sensation (or the feeling) is both the state of thought and a warning to thought of its state by this state. Such is the first characteristic of reflection: a dazzling immediacy and a perfect coincidence of what feels and what is felt. . . . Pure reflection is first and foremost the ability of thought to be immediately informed of its state by this state . . .
>
> (Lyotard [1991] 1994, 11)

Tautegorical reflection is "without other means of measure than feeling itself" (Lyotard [1991] 1994, 11) and so cannot supply the distanciation required for the consciousness of meaning that will endure outside the event experience.

Danielsen addresses this problem through the notion (drawn from Deleuze) of "intensity." *Intensity* arrives—or can arrive—in response to some intervention: a musical device disrupts the participant's unreflective absorption in the groove. For example, the groove of James Brown's "The Payback" (1974) is interrupted during its progress from time to time by horn breaks; the breaks—cued by Brown in an apparently improvisatory way—are neither preceded by an increase in tension nor followed by a change in the rhythm: they are neither changes nor transitions, just interruptions to the continuity. They are positioned at unexpected points; they are "almost anti-prepared" (Danielsen 2006, 185) and are placed in such a way as not to imply a grouping of basic units of groove:

> The alteration has to be unprepared and also remain "unqualified": there is no sum-ming up of the musical events so far. The break implies no act of reflection upon the musical form, or upon repetition as such. There is no closure, no synthesis in time. Rather, the music has to ensure that the absorbed condition lasts right up to

the break, that the non-noticing of time continues all the way up to the "aesthetic now" and continues on the other side of it in a way which makes the now once again disappear.

(Danielsen 2006, 201)

It is important, however, that the participant experiences a shock that is enough to prompt a momentary consciousness of the feeling experienced in the groove:

> The minor alteration gives an instant of intensified feeling, as if we suddenly sense the state of being that we have moved away from, and now return to, in a new way. This "new" beginning underlines the qualities of that which was and now is: suddenly, there is a difference; for a moment, I feel that I feel.

(Danielsen 2006, 199–200)

That momentary consciousness occurs only during the break, although it is projected onto the rest of the experience; the "right feeling" of the groove is not intensity but "the transparency of reliability" (Danielsen 2006, 200); the brief distanciation produces not a reflective consciousness of the feeling of the groove in relation or in comparison to anything else but a heightened sense of the groove as intensive quantity. In this way, there can be a form of distanciation from the state of being in groove which constitutes that state for the subject, but without thereby objectifying it and reducing it to meaning.

If Deleuzian intensity arrives through being in the state of groove (as Danielsen has argued), then the participant has gone some way toward reconstituting the subjectivity of the body in direct relation to its environment. This experience is the key to the state of funk: the pre-reflective consciousness of a body schema not molded by a consciousness of race; and it is perhaps this that grounds funk's position as an emblem of Black nationalist consciousness. Experiencing Deleuzian intensity in the funk groove would be a way of subverting an inculcated racial hexis by absorption in the pure differences of the music and associated bodily expression in dancing. Fanon wrote, "not only must the black man be black; he must be black in relation to the white man" ([1952] 1986, 110). The Black man is set up as a category in opposition to the category of "White man"; in doing so, differences between individuals are submerged in favor of a racialized identity. To be in intensity in the groove provides an opportunity to be, once more, "just a man."

HUSSERL'S PHENOMENOLOGY OF PERCEPTION

So far, we have established that (1) the experience of racism can be carried in the body as the unconscious ground of the self; (2) being in the groove at James Brown funk events in the 1960s provided a means for a temporary recovery of the body, through a pre-representational immersion in the groove; and (3) musical devices of interruption encouraged consciousness of intensity within the groove unit without bringing about a conceptualization of the unit. I want now to introduce Edmund Husserl's phenomenology of perception, with a view to identifying the possibility of perceptual revision ("perceptual disappointment" in Husserl's terminology) within James Brown funk grooves.

Immanent Objects Are Temporal Objects

Walking around a table, turning the head, and directing the eyes are movements that produce different profiles or aspects, different *adumbrations* of the table:

> We find such concrete really immanental Data as components in more inclusive concrete mental processes which are intentive as wholes; and ... we find those sensuous moments overlaid by a stratum which, as it were, "animates," which bestows sense ... a stratum by which precisely the concrete intentive mental process arises from the sensuous ...
>
> (Husserl [1913] 1983, 203)

The sensuous moments are subsumed under the unifying intentionality toward the transcendent object (the table).

The perception of a physical object (something that occupies space and is wholly present while it endures) is a perceptual event (something that takes time and has different parts at different times). A passage of music, on the other hand, is not a physical object but an event in itself; it is phenomenologically constituted as an object not simply by unifying the immanent phases of perception (as we phenomenologically constitute an object such as a table from "sensuous moments" of "immanental data") but by constituting the objective temporality as phenomenological temporality. Thus, "By *temporal objects in the specific sense* we understand objects that are not only unities in time but that also contain temporal extension in themselves" (Husserl [1928] 1991, 24; italics in the original). It is surely no accident that Husserl used a melody as the paradigmatic example of perception in his lectures between 1893 and 1917, *On the Phenomenology of the Consciousness of Internal Time* ([1928] 1991). Music maps out the temporality of the perceptual event explicitly.

The temporal scale of perception with which I am concerned is the scale that Husserl occasionally refers to as "presence-time" (*Präsenzzeit*) (22) and in later writings as the "living present" (*lebendige Gegenwart*) (Husserl [1966] 2001, 184; 2006, Mat. XIII, 4); Danielsen's term for it is the "perceptual now" (Danielsen 2006, 214), which she identifies as "the psychological or perceptual present," encompassing a few seconds and which the basic groove unit never exceeds (239, n.18). According to Husserl, this is the interval of time in which sense-data are felt to be "present" in some sense of being vividly accessible, although some are already a little way into the past ([1928] 1991, 18–19). Our sense of the now, of present experience, seems to have a duration of some indeterminate extent: the sense-data both belong to a temporally ordered sequence of sensations and are in some sense simultaneously present during this duration (22).

Sense-data that are "not-now" but that nevertheless belong to the perceptual present, Husserl refers to as "retentions" (25). Retentions comprise neither persisting sense-contents (we don't hear a melody as an incrementally accumulating chord or cluster of notes), nor memory of sense-contents; they consist rather in an intentionality toward past sense-contents—an intentionality that contains the sense of the "pastness" of the sensation (33). Husserl describes intentionalities toward both the past (retentions) and the future (protentions) (89).

A Potential Problem

As with the perception of an object, with music there are current presentations of sense data, plus retentions and anticipations, and an intentional object that unifies all these. As with object perception, there is a continuous intention toward what Husserl calls the "apprehension-form," which is experienced as a unity (albeit potential and anticipated) from the start:

> That several successive tones yield a melody is possible only because the succession of psychic events is united "at once" into a total formation. They are in consciousness successively, but they fall within one and the same total act. ([1928] 1991, 22)

The phenomenological constitution of a temporal object, however, preserves the temporality of the objective event (the musical passage). In Husserl's words, the tones of a melody "form a successive unity with a common effect, the apprehension-form. Naturally, the latter is consummated only with the last tone" (22). Here is a problem for my argument: if the groove cycle is apprehended as a unity, there will be a tendency toward categorial perception of the cycle or, in Deleuze's terminology, perception of it under a concept; the participant in the funk event will no longer have their attention focused toward the details of events within the groove cycle and instead will become aware of the repetition of the cycle as repetitive. However, Husserl observes that unity of a temporal object need not progress to apprehension of its objectivity.

> For every sensuous object, static or in process, its being apprehended is nonessential . . . the processes of appearance passively combine into unities in just the same way whether or not the ego turns toward what appears in them in receptive apprehension. ([1939] 1973, 251)

Here, passive reception at the lowest level of sensing is at work:

> The objects of receptivity are pregiven in an original passivity with their structures of association, affection, etc. Their apprehension is a lower level of activity, the mere act of receiving the sense originally preconstituted in passivity. (250–251)

It seems plausible that the groove cycle might be seized on as a unit from time to time, and then—since there is no sense of either development or contrast evident at that level, so that there is little aesthetic profit to be had—returns awareness to processes taking place *within* the cycle. The reception of the groove unit as a whole will be passive, in Husserl's sense, but there will be a play of sensing over the elements contained within it. Passivity at the level of the unit potentially allows the sensing of Deleuzian intensities.

Perceptual Revision

For Husserl, as for Bourdieu, perception is structured by past experiences—in fact, by habits acquired in the past. We inhabit a world in which perceptual meaning is first constructed below the level of awareness, through the force of acquired habits. According to Husserl in the *Analyses Concerning Passive and Active Synthesis*,

> everything that consciousness undergoes through changes and transformations, even after the transformations, remains sedimented in it as its "history." ([1966] 2001, 77)

It is within the temporally extended event of perception that habit constructs perceptual meaning:

> The part "demands" the whole—something uniform awakens something else that is uniform, which is not yet at all constituted as a unity explicitly for itself; and it does not demand the whole by a pure and simple awakening, but rather by a co-connected "expectation," by the demand as coexisting as co-belonging to the unity. Even the force of this apperceptive expectation increases with the number of "instances"—or with habit, which amounts to the same thing. (240)

There is an "apperceptive expectation" whereby hyletic data prompt a perceptual recognition of the object as a whole, and thus the anticipation of subsequent hyletic data that will fulfil that expectation. There is a unification of current, previous, and expected future hyletic data in intentionality. Each moment of the perceptual event comprises retentions of previous adumbrations (that is, foreshadowings of expected hyletic data), the currently experienced *hýle*, and protentions or anticipations of future adumbrations. The retentions form a system that constrains the possibilities for what will come next in the perceptual event: "Every perceptual givenness is a constant mixture of familiarity and unfamiliarity, a givenness that points to new possible perceptions that would issue in familiarity" (48).

Husserl introduces the possibility of "disappointment" rather than fulfilment in the perceptual process. For example, if we see a "uniform, well-rounded red ball" but further adumbrations reveal that the back side of the ball is in fact green rather than red, and indented rather than being uniformly ball-shaped, then a conflict between the sense data and the "still living" intention occurs. "But," says Husserl,

> there is not only a conflict. By being presented in the flesh, the newly constituted sense throws its opponent from the saddle, as it were . . . The new sense "green" in its primordially impressional force of fulfillment is a certainty that has a primordial force which overpowers the certainty of the anticipation of "being red." We are now conscious of it *as* overpowered. (68)

We have not a smooth reorientation of consciousness to accommodate the unexpected sense-data but a continuing conflict of original and revised retentions and intentions. What is retained is not only the previous now-point with its retentions but also a retentional trajectory into which the previous now-point has been assimilated. This, which Husserl refers to as "perceptual disappointment," I call *perceptual revision*—simply to avoid the connotations of the word "disappointment." According to Husserl, a "retroactive crossing out in the retentional sphere" takes place, such that

> We would find in all the horizons of these retentional components not only the previous prefiguring in the previous structures of expectation and fulfillment, just as this prefiguring was originally motivated at that time, but we would find superimposed upon it the corresponding transformed prefiguring that now points continually to "green" and "indented." . . . For we are still conscious of the previous sense, but as "painted over," and where the corresponding moments are concerned, crossed out. (69)

Where such a retroactive crossing out of retentions occurs, the conflicting adumbrations have, as Husserl says, "the same mode of validity, 'questionable,' and each presentation that is questionable is precisely in dispute and contested by the other" (75).

It is important to clarify that the kind of perceptual revision under discussion is not mere perceptual surprise. An example of perceptual surprise in music is the *fortissimo* chord that ends the first, *pianissimo*, statement of the theme in Haydn's *Symphony No. 94 in G Major*. In this case there is no perceptual revision, since hearing the loud chord, unexpected as it is, nevertheless does not change our perception of the preceding phrase. What is required for perceptual revision is that we first have an apperception of a perceptual object—in the case of music, of a musical gesture or pattern—that sets up an expectation of the perception being completed in a certain way but without conscious awareness of the expectation: it is simply the taking of immediate perceptual input as part of a certain kind of whole. Then, as further perceptual input from the object (from the musical gesture or pattern) arrives we find that our original expectation was incorrect and must be revised. It is not only our expectation of the part of the pattern that leads to the necessary revision, but rather that our previous construal of the pattern leading up to that point becomes, in Husserl's words, "painted over" or "crossed out." That is, the original apperception persists but has attained a character of being incorrect and having been supplanted by the revised apperception. The key to perceptual revision is that the new apperception does not obliterate the original one but is rather superimposed over it: the two apperceptions exist simultaneously and throw doubt one on the other.

Perceptual revision is neither Lyotard's "tautegorical reflection"—just the consciousness of feeling, without "feeling that one feels"—nor "intensity," a consciousness of the feeling of being in the groove resulting from a momentary suspension of it. Perceptual revision is more akin to a recovered stumble, an occurrence that brings to sudden awareness the unconscious body schema of the walker. The central argument of this chapter is that (at least some) James Brown funk grooves engender perceptual revision of the beat by means of introducing counter-rhythms to the main beat, so leading to a consciousness of hexis. The next section explains the concept of counter-rhythms and how they engender perceptual revision.

MUSICOLOGY OF FUNK

In this section I want to explore Danielsen's (2006) musicological analysis of funk rhythm more closely.[3] First, however, I must clarify terminology. The beat of a piece of music is what we would normally tap our foot to; it is there whether the beats are marked by sound or not. We can usually find the beat quite reliably; this capacity is called "entrainment." Musical entrainment—like other kinds of entrainment in this tempo range, such as walking in step with someone—is often achieved physically, in the sense that we move (tap or dance) in order to find the beat. A beat, in this sense, is a series of implicit stresses that are equidistant in time, that is to say, they have the same period. Since there may be more than one beat that can be heard in a funk groove at various times, I will refer to the main beat—which generally comes in four to the bar—as the tactus. I will also adopt Danielsen's term of "density referent" for the smallest unit of pulsation to be found in a texture, faster than the beat. In general, the density referent is too fast (that is, its period is too small) to permit musical entrainment by humans. The perceptual attack time or P-center of an instrumental or vocal sound is that point in time that we perceive it as occurring. In general, for an instrumental sound there is a specific location that is heard as the point in time where that sound is located: this is the "P-center." All (or nearly all) P-centers in a funk texture nominally fall on a pulse of the density referent; however, a P-center may be placed slightly early or slightly late in reference to a pulse of the density referent.

Elements of the Black Atlantic Musical Tradition

At the core of Danielsen's detailed analysis of specific rhythmic devices in James Brown's music is a balanced tension between the main beat of the groove and one or more counter-rhythms; specific rhythmic devices and manners of playing lead to an ambivalence regarding where the beat falls and to which rhythmic gesture particular notes belong. It is this ambivalence between conflicting beats with slightly different periods that is the basis for the "perceptual revision" described above.

Funk is, of course, part of the "Black Atlantic" musical tradition of the African diaspora and shares features of the broader tradition, while transforming some of those in unique ways. An immediately apparent feature of much of the music is a layered complexity of rhythm. Simha Arom's (1991) analysis of *Aka* drumming in the Central African Republic in the 1960s identified the generative principle of rhythmic complexity in that music as the superimposition of short patterns, based on a division of time into cyclical units of equal duration. These patterns are organized to give rise to a recurring cycle that may be structured in various ways: a division of the cycle into two equal and symmetrical parts; even divisions of the cycle involving what can be called cross-meter (for instance, three beats against four); and categories where the cycle comprises rhythmic cells of unequal length (such as [7+7+2] or [7+5]). Musical entrainment occurs in response to periodicity (or at least, to quasi-periodicity, since small variations can be accommodated). The patterns of unequal groupings identified by Arom, as well as those found in West African music (such as 3+2+2+3+2, which occupies a repeated 12-pulse cycle) are not periodic (equi-distant) at the level of the grouping and so we cannot entrain directly to them; although, of course, we can recognize and reproduce them as metrical patterns.[4] The groupings are all organized in relation to "an invariable number of equidistant pulsations, manifest or implicit" that "constitute the temporal frame of the period" (Arom 1984, 54). These pulsations correspond to what Danielsen refers to as the "density referent" and are faster than the rate to which humans can entrain. Other basic features of the music include the absence of hierarchical meter and of regularly spaced strong beats; strict periodicity and a steady tempo "without accelerandos, rallentandos or rubatos" (Arom 1989, 91); some variation in the repetition of rhythmic cells; and including a principle of crossing and interweaving of individual rhythms rather than vertical organization.

Two related features in Arom's analysis are rhythmic tension and rhythmic ambiguity. Rhythmic tension arises as the result of the "antagonism" between rhythmic figures and the metrical structure and, at the same time, the conflict between different rhythmic figures (Arom 1984, 61–62). Further, the very regularity of a repeated rhythmic pattern, together with the absence of regular accentuation, creates ambiguity in the perception of how to subdivide the pattern:

> This feeling can be compared to what one might feel on a train if one thought one had caught the rhythm of the "clickety-clack" but suddenly noticed an offsetting of the periodic repetition: what one had taken as a "strong beat" marking the beginning of a new temporal cycle now sounds like a "weak beat" and vice versa.
>
> (Arom 1989, 91)

Olly Wilson, drawing on historical distinctions, differentiates simple syncopation in ragtime music (in which the accent is displaced from the beat) from what he calls "polyrhythm," in which a conflicting metrical framework is set up by a pattern that does

	3	+	3	+	2
Sax/Trumpet/Trombone	● ●		●		
Lead guitar	● ● ● ● ● ● ● ●		● ● ● ● ●		
Bass	● ● ● ● ● ● ●		● ● ● ● ● ● ●		
(16th note density referent) / (8th note pulses) / (¼ note tactus)	1	2 3 4	1 2	3 4	
Drums — Hi Hat	● ● ● ● ● ●		● ● ● ● ● ●		
Drums — Snare	● ● ●		● ● ●		
Drums - Kick	● ●		● ●		

FIGURE 8.1: Basic rhythm pattern for James Brown's "Super Bad." Snare drum and horns mark an eighth-note 3+3+2 pattern; guitar and bass mark the straight beat (with some sixteenth-note anticipations).

not map neatly onto the beat (Wilson 1974, 9–12). Wilson provides examples of West African Ewe dance rhythms with both equal groupings of four eighth notes against even groupings of three eighth notes, producing a cross-meter of three beats against four which coincide at the macro period boundary; and a 12-pulse pattern with unequal groupings of 3+2+2+3+2 against four equal groups of three. Thus far, Wilson's metrical categories are similar to Arom's: cross-meter and cycles comprising rhythmic cells of unequal length. However, Wilson goes on to relate the 3+2+2+3+2 cycle to the 3+3+2 pattern in James Brown's "Super Bad," clearly marked by horns and snare drum (and sometimes guitar), while the straight four-beat is marked by guitar, voice, and bass, with the bass pattern displaced by one beat (see Figure 8.1).

Danielsen finds the approach to rhythm in funk grooves similar to those outlined by Arom and Wilson, with some important differences. A funk groove is a hybrid of the kind of African rhythm described by Arom and traditional Western rhythm in which the basic beats are weighted (Danielsen 2006, 44). As in the music described by Arom, rhythmic figures are organized by reference to a series of pulses (not necessarily audible), but in funk—since the basic beats, generally four to a bar, are implicitly weighted—there are several levels of pulsation to deal with (quarter notes, eighth notes, and sixteenths). The rhythmic figures in a funk groove are organized as rhythmic dialogues. Each individual figure, Danielsen says, is played not in relation to all the other figures occurring in the texture but rather in dialogue with one other figure, usually complementary (52).

One of the elements involved is a density referent that is suggested by different components of the rhythmic texture without being explicitly expressed. The density of the rhythmic texture in West African drumming and in Afro-American music has been noted by many authors. A greater density here means a greater number of notes per beat and also (since funk beat speed tends toward the moderate rather than slow) a greater number of notes within a given number of milliseconds. In general, note timings are referenced to some subdivision of the beat, and the smallest beat subdivision is the "density referent." The continuous marking of the density referent is unnecessary (although sometimes present, either played by the guitar or the hi-hat, or distributed among different instruments or different parts of the drum kit). Some timing positions of the density referent coincide either with beats (the first of each group of four sixteenths), or with beat subdivisions (say, with the second eighth of a quarter-note beat); if these are articulated in isolation, they do not establish the density referent at the smaller subdivision. However, if a single note occurs on a density referent subdivision that cannot be assimilated to a slower pulse—for example, on the sixteenth immediately before a beat—then that contributes to establishing the density referent at the level of sixteenths.

Danielsen makes much of both the tension and ambiguity (or ambivalence) to be found within funk grooves but, importantly, identifies particular means by which these are produced, means that are compatible with the weighted beats of the hybrid African-Western rhythms of funk. Tension and ambivalence are mutually dependent, in her analysis, and are key to the production of perceptual revision in my argument; a detailed explication follows.

Suggestive Counter-Rhythms

Danielsen's analyses identify no instances of actual cross-meter in Arom's sense (for instance, of three evenly spaced beats occupying the whole bar, against the four of the tactus). However, she extrapolates from Wilson's analysis of the 3+3+2 pattern in James Brown's "Super Bad" to develop the concept of counter-rhythm—the suggestion of a cross-meter or cross-rhythm, which is not, however, carried through but which begins again with each new cycle. Thus, in the musical textures under discussion, there may be simultaneously present: (1) a tactus, or main beat; (2) a counter-rhythm that suggests or implies a beat to which it is possible to entrain and that is different from the tactus; and (3) the density referent, comprising smaller units of pulsation (typically sixteenth notes) that are too fast for entrainment but that form groups which fit to the tactus or cross-rhythm. The notion of "counter-rhythm" as conceptualized by Danielsen is different from the two main categories of meter identified by Arom: cross-meter (which has the same number of whole beats in every cycle), and cycles comprising rhythmic cells of unequal length. Counter-rhythm instead suggests an alternative beat—one that would not fit into a cycle with a whole number of beats but that is suggested anew with each recurring cycle.

Several such instances of "a counter-rhythm with a tendency to cross-rhythm" (Danielsen 2006, 62) can be found in James Brown's grooves. The term "counter-rhythm" is explicitly intended as a weak sense of "cross-rhythm" (or cross-meter); the weakness itself of the counter-rhythm is an essential feature of successful funk, according to Danielsen's analysis, and it is important to clarify exactly what she means by it. The first instance of counter-rhythm she finds in the chronological development of James Brown's style occurs in "Cold Sweat," where an asymmetrically grouped figure is marked through the interplay of snare drum and bass guitar and kick (see Figure 8.2). The figure is displaced so that it begins on beat two of bar one and marks two groupings of three eighth notes, ending on the first beat of bar two, "which comprises the third main beat of a virtual cross-rhythmic pulse" (63). It is clear that Danielsen makes a

	2:3 counter-rhythm	
Horns	● ●	● ●
Lead guitar ●	● ● ● ● ● ○ ●	● ● ● ● ● ●
Bass ●	● ● ● ● ● ●	● ● ● ● ● ● ● ●
(16th note density referent)(8th note pulses)(1/4 note tactus)	| | | | | | | | | | | | | | | | 1 2 3 4	| | | | | | | | | | | | | | | | 1 2 3 4
Drums – Hi Hat	● ● ● ● ● ● ● ●	● ● ● ● ● ● ● ●
Drums – Snare	● ○ ●	○ ● ○ ○ ●
Drums - Kick ●	● ● ○	● ● ● ●

FIGURE 8.2: Basic rhythmic pattern for James Brown's "Cold Sweat.: The counter-rhythm beat that falls between tactus beats three and four is strongly marked in the first bar of the cycle; the last eighth note of that bar is a pickup to the next beat, where counter-rhythm and tactus coincide. In the second bar, the bass and snare on the fourth tactus beat rather emphasize the tactus. Grey circles represent "ghost" notes.

distinction between a metrical framework of unequal groupings and an evenly spaced beat. Nor would the grouping of three eighth notes for the "Cold Sweat" cross-rhythm map onto two bars (sixteen eighth notes). The first sense in which "counter-rhythm" is a weak sense of "cross-rhythm" for Danielsen then, is that a beat is suggested but is not carried through because a whole number of beats does not fit into a bar. At least two other James Brown tracks exhibit more clearly marked counter-rhythms of this kind: "Stoned to the Bone" (1973) has an asymmetrical figure of 3+3+2, plainly marked by one of the guitars, while "The Payback" (1974) has a clear 4:3 counter-rhythm over the first three beats of the bar: "Both of these grooves, then, convey a play between a main rhythm and a counter-rhythm with competing basic pulses: they carry *a tendency towards cross-rhythm*" (Danielsen 2006, 63, italics in the original).

The other sense in which Danielsen hears the counter-rhythms of funk as weaker than those of traditional West African music is that the counter-rhythm is never equal to the tactus (the main beat) but is always subordinate to it. The pulse, or beat, of the counter-rhythm is, "as a rule, not sufficiently stated to make the music appear to be the product of two different pulse schemes. The groove *is* to sound like 'a single rhythm' . . . The counter-rhythm should destabilize the main meter without being so articulated as to threaten to take it over" (67). The influence of the counter-rhythm can be controlled through a limitation in time:

> If the counter-rhythm is clearly articulated, it has to be ended before the *pulse* of the counter-rhythm is established as such. Because the competing pulse might become too obvious compared to the pulse of the main beat, a regular pattern of syncopation cannot be allowed to continue too long. (67; italics in the original)

In "Stoned to the Bone," the pattern coincides with the first beat of the two-bar unit and starts over again on the second beat of the second bar of the two-bar unit; in between, the basic beat has sway. In "The Payback," the guitar marks the two straight eighth notes of the fourth beat of the first bar, in sharp contrast to the 4:3 cross-rhythm of the first three beats. The 3:2 figure of the guitar across the first two beats of the bar in "Doing It to Death" (1973) *would* fit evenly into the bar if continued, but the guitar's accent on the fourth beat disrupts the incipient cross-rhythm (Danielsen 2006, 67–68).

Other ways of subduing the influence of the beat suggested by the cross-rhythm can be utilized, either instead of or in addition to limitation in time. On James Brown's "Get Up, Get Into It, and Get Involved" (1970), the guitar's straight duple sixteenths are mixed toward the back of the sound-box, allowing the swung sixteenths of the congas and bass to predominate. The cross-rhythm marked by the horns in James Brown's "Soul Power" is limited in time and is articulated in the form of very light, short notes. "Make It Funky" has a 4:3 figure over the first three beats of the bar (four groups of three sixteenths each) but it is articulated as accents in a continuous stream of sixteenths, which make its relationship to the main beat clear. Similarly, "Hot Pants" articulates a pattern of 3+3+3+3+ 2+2 as accents on continuous sixteenths (Danielsen 2006, 66).

Of course, there are also other instruments in the texture that emphasize the main beat with various rhythmic figures, which also serves to balance the pull of the counter-rhythm. Danielsen finds the rhythmic ambivalence provided by this tension characteristic of funk grooves. The function of counter-rhythm as a "weak" cross-rhythm, as suggestive of a competing alternative beat without asserting it, is to animate the main beat from within by providing an element of tension. "The most interesting polyrhythmic relation in funk," she says, "is probably not where a clear-cut rhythm is combined with an equally clear-cut counter-rhythm" (71); rather, it appears when a layer of potential cross-rhythm is used to create small stretches of time that fall between a dominant basic pulse and hint at its virtual alternative. There is more to this than the simple creation of a subtle tension between tactus and counter-rhythm, however. Danielsen's startling insight is to show how subtle manipulations of timing can result in an ambivalent perception of the beat.

Part of how this works is that the small figures, which contribute to the basic rhythm, the counter-rhythm, or both, are woven into the overall fabric of the groove. Since counter-rhythmic figures are not permitted to blossom into fully articulated counter-rhythms, they often consist of a few notes—some of which coincide with main beat timings—with a single additional note that is timed to be ambivalent between two points of the density reference grid; a single note that could be thought of as an isolated syncopation but that also lightly marks the beat of a cross-rhythm. The term "ambivalence" carries a sense of contradictions contained but not resolved. Danielsen finds that the funk groove relies on this "borderland between syncopation and cross-rhythm" (70). The rhythmical ambivalence of notes that are timed so as to assimilate to two incompatible beats depends partly on the absence of a single instrumental part continuously and clearly articulating the density referent; such an unambiguous articulation would stabilize and make explicit each timing position of the density referent. In "Sex Machine," for instance, the sixteenths are instead distributed among snare, hi-hat, guitar, and bass, such that each instrument participates in marking some of the sixteenths for each beat (Figure 8.3). In Danielsen's words, "the groove is full of small, well-articulated gestures completing one another in a floating curtain of smoothly accented straight sixteenths"

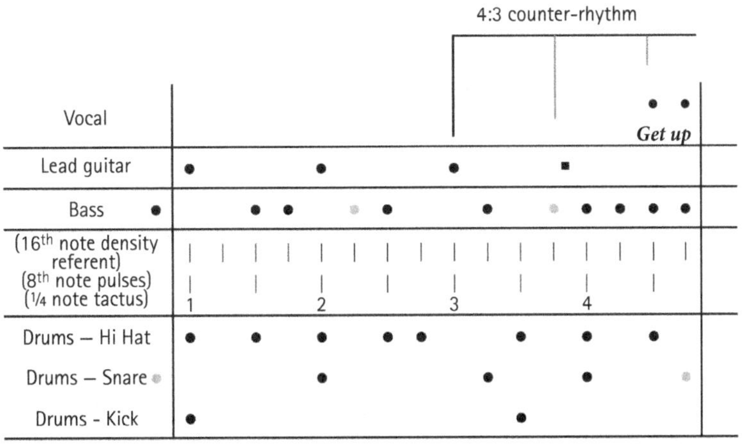

FIGURE 8.3: Basic groove pattern for James Brown's "Sex Machine." No instrument articulates the sixteenth note density referent throughout—rather, it is distributed between bass, drums, and the second beat of the guitar's 4:3 counter-rhythm (indicated thus: ■). This guitar note is timed ambiguously between the second beat of the 4:3 counter-rhythm and the fourth beat of the tactus; the tactus fourth beat is effectively destabilized. Grey circles represent "ghost" notes.

(77). The effect of this "floating curtain" is that there is a slight uncertainty of the density referent timing points due to slight timing differences between instruments and the ambiguity of timing produced as a result of the different attack times of different timbres.

Ambivalence of the Beat, Perceptual Revision, and Hexis

The counter-rhythm of the guitar in "Sex Machine" begins with a held guitar chord on beat three, followed by a short, chopped stroke on the last sixteenth before beat four. The actual scheduled time position of beat four is marked by the snare, but the early guitar stroke—accented and chopped short—catches the ear so that the dry snare hit is overshadowed (see Figure 8.3). The guitar stroke is slightly late relative to the sixteenth position to which it is referenced, and slightly early relative to beat four; it is "so ambivalent, so influenced by the main pulse and pulled towards its beat, that it could possibly be both on and off the one and the other" (Danielsen 2006, 78)—as such, this single stroke can be assimilated both to the main beat and the counter-rhythmic pattern.

This counter-rhythmic pattern in "Sex Machine" suggests an alternative beat at a 4:3 ratio with the main beat (that is, with an inter-beat period of three sixteenth notes). Danielsen argues that the ambiguous timing of the stroke destabilizes both the main beat and the alternative beat suggested by the counter-rhythm to which it belongs. The small duration of the fastest pulse facilitates such ambivalence, on the one hand, because the period of the pulses is small enough that assimilation to one or another timing point can be affected by small timing differences such as are found in stylistic performance; and on the other hand, because the much longer period of the main beat timings means that a timing adjustment of the beat at the level of the density reference is less obvious. It is in these spaces that small, "specifically funky" gestures can be performed almost on the beat and almost on another as well: "The point is not to combine a basic rhythm with the 'right' proportion of independent counter-rhythm but to 'deform' those figures so as to make them both one and the other, both rhythm and counter-rhythm at the same time" (71).

Perceptual revision occurs at the point where the participant in the funk event adjusts to the main beat, following the momentary confound between tactus and counter-rhythm. To make the whole process explicit in Husserlian terms: the repeated groove cycle sediments an expectation—specifically, the expectation that the beat will continue reliably and steadily. The intersection of the tactus and the counter-rhythm, achieved by "deforming" them both, fulfills the expectation of a reliable beat for both, but a moment later, is shown to be false. There occurs, in Husserl's terminology, "perceptual disappointment" (perceptual revision). This process can re-occur with each cycle of the groove unit due to the ambivalent timing of the relevant note: to continue steady entrainment to either beat entails experiencing the ambivalently timed note as belonging to it—only to be "disappointed" as the cycle begins again.

Perception of a musical beat, particularly when dancing, is expressed—even achieved—physically. Perceptual revision in this context can be expected to produce a momentary interruption to the transparency of hexis. I do not propose that Fanon, were he to participate in such a funk event, would at that moment gain a clear insight into the makeup of the "racial epidermal schema" imposed upon his body by the experience of being subjected to racism. What I propose is that a particular kind of consciousness of the body would occur, and that consciousness would go some way to restoring a sense of ownership and intimate agency to the body.

CONCLUSION

Bourdieu's concept of hexis refers to the underlying comportment of the body, which shapes expression and feeling and which, like other aspects of habitus, is beyond question because taken for granted. What is required to prompt a reflective awareness of hexis can be expected to be a point where a bodily action must be revised as a result of a perceptual revision. The introduction of ambivalent timing in the context of competing beat trains seems likely to trigger a reflective consciousness which momentarily brings about awareness of hexis.

I have argued that a component of habitus as defined by Bourdieu—bodily comportment or hexis—can be brought to awareness through perceptual crisis, as it occurs through dancing to funk. Perception, in Husserl's phenomenology, unfolds in time with a series of sense data that are unified in the intentionality toward the object of perception. Perceptual crisis occurs when an intention resulting from habitual perception is "disappointed" by a conflicting sense presentation. This results in a retrospective crossing-out of retentions and the continued presence in phenomenal experience of those retentions as canceled out. Music listening exhibits a similar temporal structure within the perceptual event, with the same possibility of perceptual crisis.

I do not claim all such changes in the experience of the self are engendered by the same mechanism for perceptual revision I have described above, or even that perceptual revision as described by Husserl is necessary at all. Conceivably, a variety of approaches can be found in different musical cultures by means of which the habitual patterns of bodily being in the world can be modified or escaped. For example, Walter Hughes argued that dancing to "four-on-the-floor" disco, with its unyielding beat, "represents, for certain gay men, a form of violence done to a conventional self in order to refashion it, much in the manner of military, religious or sadomasochistic discipline" (Hughes 1994, 150). This seems to be a way of altering the unthought comportment of the body—obliterating it, even—in favor of a different way of being, but without an underpinning process of perceptual revision. The notion of "perceptual revision" that I have put forward therefore prompts the tentative beginning of a taxonomy of how music can prompt "different ways of construing the body." To adapt George Clinton's dictum and the title of a P-Funk song: "Move your ass and your mind will follow."

NOTES

1. See, for instance, McRobbie (1993); Hughes (1994); Dimitriadis (1996); Mossière (2013); Inyabri (2014); and Espada-Brignoni and Ruiz-Alfaro (2021).
2. James Brown, 1968, live performance at the Boston Garden, filmed April 5, 1968, video, 2:11:21, https://www.youtube.com/watch?v=k59j0Z4fUvc.
3. Danielsen's analyses are necessarily of recorded performances, including studio recordings; I make the assumption that the relevant features of the recordings were also available to the participants in a live funk event.
4. It is necessary to distinguish between musical meter and musical entrainment (beat induction). Polak, London, and Jacoby (2016, 2) note that musicians, listeners, and dancers are typically at ease with both the isochronous and the non-isochronous meters found in musics in Europe, Asia, and Africa. Musical entrainment or beat induction is demonstrated by numerous brain imaging studies showing induction of a periodic brain rhythm in response to music; studies by Honing (2012, 88) suggest that isochronous beat induction—although not necessarily meter induction—is shared among adults and newborns, which supports a biological basis for the mechanism.

WORKS CITED

Al-Saji, A. 2019. "Glued to the Image: A Critical Phenomenology of Racialization through Works of Art." *Journal of Aesthetics and Art Criticism* 77 (4): 475–488.

Arom, Simha. 1984. "The Constituting Features of Central African Rhythmic Systems: A Tentative Typology." *The World of Music* 26 (1): 51–67.

Arom, Simha. 1989. "Time Structure in the Music of Central Africa: Periodicity, Meter, Rhythm and Polyrhythmics." *Leonardo* 22 (1): 91–99.

Arom, Simha. 1991. *African Polyphony and Polyrhythm: Musical Structure and Methodology.* Cambridge: Cambridge University Press.

Bourdieu, Pierre. (1972) 1977. *Outline of a Theory of Practice.* Translated by Richard Nice. Cambridge: Cambridge University Press.

Bourdieu, Pierre. (1980) 1990. *The Logic of Practice.* Translated by Richard Nice. Stanford, CA: Stanford University Press.

Brown, James. (2005). *I Feel Good: A Memoir of a Life of Soul.* London: New American Library.

Danielsen, Anne. 2006. *Presence and Pleasure: The Funk Grooves of James Brown and Parliament.* Middletown, CT: Wesleyan University Press.

Deleuze, Gilles. (1968) 1994. *Difference and Repetition.* Translated by Paul Patton. New York: Columbia University Press.

Deleuze, Gilles. (1995) 1997. "Immanence: A Life." Translated by Nick Millett. *Theory, Culture & Society* 14 (2): 3–7.

Dimitriadis, G. 1996. "Hip Hop: From Live Performance to Mediated Narrative." *Popular Music* 15 (2): 179–194.

Du Bois, W. E. B. (1903) 1969. *The Souls of Black Folk.* New York: New American Library.

Ellis, T. S. 2008. "From the Crib to the Coliseum: An Interview with Bootsy Collins." In *The Funk Era and Beyond*, edited by Tony Bolden, 89–103. New York: Palgrave Macmillan.

Espada-Brignoni, T., and Ruiz-Alfaro, F. 2021. "Culture, Subjectivity, and Music in Puerto Rico." *International Perspectives in Psychology* 10 (1): 3–12.

Fanon, Frantz. (1952) 1986. *Black Skin, White Masks.* Translated by Charles Lam Markmann. London: Pluto Press.

Hanson, Michael. 2008. "Suppose James Brown Read Fanon: The Black Arts Movement, Cultural Nationalism and the Failure of Popular Musical Praxis." *Popular Music* 27 (3): 341–365.

Heidegger, M. (1950) 1971. "The Thing." In *Poetry, Language, Thought*, 160–184. Translated by Martin Hofstadter. New York: Harper & Row.

Honing, H. 2012. "Without It No Music: Beat Induction as a Fundamental Musical Trait." *Annals of the New York Academy of Sciences* 1252:85–91.

Hughes, Walter. 1994. "In the Empire of the Beat: Discipline and Disco." In *Microphone Fiends: Youth Music and Youth Culture*, edited by Andrew Ross and Tricia Rose, 147–157. New York, NY: Routledge.

Husserl, Edmund. (1913) 1983. *Ideas Pertaining to a Pure Phenomenology and to a Phenomenological Philosophy: First Book: General Introduction to a Pure Phenomenology.* Translated by F. Kersten. Dordrecht, Netherlands: Martinus Nijhoff Publishers.

Husserl, Edmund. (1928) 1991. *On the Phenomenology of the Consciousness of Internal Time (1893–1917).* Vol. 4 of *Husserl Collected Works.* Translated by John Barnett Brough. Dordrecht, Netherlands: Kluwer Academic Publishers.

Husserl, Edmund. (1939) 1973. *Experience and Judgment: Investigations in a Genealogy of Logic.* Translated by James S. Churchill and Lothar Eley. Evanston, IL: Northwestern University Press.

Husserl, Edmund. (1966) 2001. *Analyses concerning Passive and Active Synthesis: Lectures on Transcendental Logic.* Translated by Anthony J. Steinbock. Dordrecht, Netherlands: Kluwer Academic Publishers.

Husserl, Edmund. 2006. *Späte Texte über Zeitkonstitution (1929–1934): Die C-Manuskripte.* Dordrecht, Netherlands: Springer.

Inyabri, I. T. 2014. "Youth and Postcolonial Subjectivity in Contemporary Nigerian Pop Music." *Postcolonial Text* 8 (3–4): 1–14.

Kennedy, Randall. 2018. "How James Brown Made Black Pride a Hit." *New York Times*, July 20, 2018. https://www.nytimes.com/2018/07/20/opinion/sunday/james-brown-say-it-loud-50-years.html.

Lipsitz, George. 2020. "James Brown." *Encyclopædia Britannica*. https://www.britannica.com/biography/James-Brown-American-singer.

Lyotard, Jean-Francois. 1991. *Leçons sur l'analytique du sublime*. Paris: Galilée.

Lyotard, Jean-Francois. (1991) 1994. *Lessons on the Analytic of the Sublime*. Translated by Elizabeth Rottenberg. Stanford, CA: Stanford University Press.

Mader, M. B. 2014. "Whence Intensity? Deleuze and the Revival of a Concept." In *Gilles Deleuze and Metaphysics*, edited by A. Beaulieu, E. Kazarian, and J. Sushytska, 225–248. Blue Ridge Summit, PA: Lexington Books.

Martin, Susan Ehrlich. 1999. "Police Force or Police Service? Gender and Emotional Labor." *The Annals of the American Academy of Political and Social Science* 561 (1): 111–126.

McClary, Susan. 1994. "Same as It Ever Was: Youth Culture and Music." In *Microphone Fiends: Youth Music and Youth Culture*, edited by Tricia Rose and Andrew Ross, 29–40. New York: Routledge.

McRobbie, A. 1993. "Shut Up and Dance: Youth Culture and Changing Modes of Femininity." *Young* 1 (2): 13–31.

Mossière, G. 2013. "Experience, Subjectivity and Performance: An Anthropological Approach to Pentecostal Rituals Based on the Body." In *Understanding Religious Ritual: Theoretical Approaches and Innovations*, edited by John P. Hoffmann, 54–72. New York: Routledge.

Moten, F. 2008. "The Case of Blackness." *Criticism* 50 (2): 177–218.

Polak, R., J. London, and N. Jacoby. 2016. "Both Isochronous and Non-isochronous Metrical Subdivision Afford Precise and Stable Ensemble Entrainment: A Corpus Study of Malian Jembe Drumming." *Frontiers in Neuroscience* 10 (Article 285): 1–11.

Ricoeur, Paul. 1973. "The Hermeneutical Function of Distanciation." *Philosophy Today* 17 (2): 129–141.

Sartre, Jean-Paul (1937) 1957. *The Transcendence of the Ego*. Translated by Forrest Williams and Robert Kirkpatrick. New York: Hill and Wang.

Slaughter, T. F. 1977. "Epidermalizing the World: A Basic Mode of Being-Black." *Man and World* 10 (3): 303–308.

Throop, C. Jason, and Keith M Murphy. 2002. "Bourdieu and Phenomenology: A Critical Assessment." *Anthropological Theory* 2 (2): 185–207.

Vincent, Rickey. 2008. "James Brown: Icon of Black Power." In *The Funk Era and Beyond*, edited by Tony Bolden, 51–72. New York: Palgrave Macmillan.

Wesley, Fred, Jr. 2005. *Hit Me, Fred: Recollections of a Sideman*. Durham: Duke University Press.

Wilson, Olly. 1974. "The Significance of the Relationship between Afro-American Music and West African Music." *The Black Perspective in Music* 2 (1): 3–22.

CHAPTER 9

....

PLAYING AND LISTENING
Phenomenological Hermeneutics and Improvisation

....

CHARLES SHARP

WHAT does improvisation tell us about the experience of music, and what does that tell us about the experience of being human? The academic discipline of ethnomusicology has generally assumed, and not without good reason, that these questions are best answered through ethnographic description of particular types of music, cultural locations, and historical situations. The tension between asking questions about the nature of music and being human and ethnographically observing musical practices that actualize those questions raises a third concern for this chapter, which is to make a case for the importance of philosophical reflection on aesthetics for ethnomusicologists. Here, I will use phenomenological hermeneutics to examine improvisation because that philosophical discipline suggests a rethinking of the traditional aspects of aesthetics and the connections between musical experience and human social life in a way that is attuned to temporality and thus has a powerful resonance with the experience of improvisation. Since human action itself can be thought of as improvised, nothing in the arts seems closer to everyday experience. It is tempting to blur that distinction between art and life, particularly for an ethnomusicology that is correctly suspicious of the claims of aesthetics. Phenomenological hermeneutics similarly questions the assumptions of a wholly subjective and transcendent aesthetics but allows us to maintain a useful interpretative autonomy for art, which, I argue, can encourage ethnomusicologists to further consider the transformative potential of musical experience.

My questions are ontological rather than epistemological; further, they are not directly concerned with a specific type of music, or a kind of improvisation, or even with people from particular cultural groups or places. This concern with ontology is extensively explored by the philosopher Hans-Georg Gadamer, whose hermeneutics is not merely about the interpretation of texts, as his work is sometimes characterized, but rather seeks to reflect on the nature of truth itself, separate from methodological questions about how we know particular facts or adequation.[1] Epistemology in the simplest terms refers specifically to the study of the nature of knowledge. Gadamer's conception of ontology and his critique of representationalist epistemologies are based in the notion of truth as *aletheia* (disclosure), a concept Gadamer inherits from Martin Heidegger.[2] It would be too much to suggest that ontology is a replacement for epistemology, though some have critiqued Gadamer for doing this (Hirsch 1967, 245–264; Rorty 1979, 358–361; see also Westphal 1999). Rather, in following Paul Ricoeur ([1986] 1991, 125–143), I suggest that epistemology attends to explanation while ontology is associated with understandings. Epistemological inquiry can contribute to new and different understandings, but all explanations presuppose an ontology. Rethinking the ontological conditions—the conditions for the possibility—opens different epistemologies. The detailed examination of Gadamer's ideas about ontology that follow are meant as a thorough rethinking of the condition for the possibility of music, improvisation, and their relationship to the world, with the goal of challenging how ethnomusicology addresses these issues in specific situations.

Gadamer's ideas about aesthetics are uniquely germane to discussions of improvisation, and a number of contemporary scholars have made his work central to their own projects. The philosophers Bruce Ellis Benson and Cynthia Nielsen, for example, both explore Gadamer's ideas in the context of jazz improvisation, defending his phenomenological hermeneutics against other philosophical approaches to aesthetics, ranging from postmodernism to post-humanism (Benson 2003; Nielsen 2016). Similarly, Nicholas Davey thoroughly examines Gadamer's aesthetic ideas, primarily in terms of visual art (2013). Benson, Nielsen, and Davey all emphasize the importance of considering ontology in aesthetics, and I extend their arguments in this chapter by drawing out their implications for ethnomusicology.[3] I believe that ethnomusicology, which encourages us to consider ontology in as broadly humanistic terms as possible through observable culture, has a useful role to play here, as its interest in transcultural understandings can help guard against mistaking a culturally specific aesthetic phenomenon for a universal condition of possibility for aesthetics.

It should be noted at the outset that Gadamer never developed a systematic aesthetic theory. Indeed, an approach to aesthetics where beauty is equated with a set of rules of objective criteria would be completely contrary to his thought. Gadamer's notion of aesthetics, first developed in *Truth and Method* ([1960] 2004), is rooted in phenomenology and centers on the experience of art. Such experience is for Gadamer exemplary of a kind of truth that stands in opposition to methodological deduction. Because experience is always situated between the work and the interpreter, it never becomes fully objective or subjective. This radically challenges any concept of aesthetics as wholly transcendent or escapist. Timothy Rice echoes this sentiment when he states, "ethnomusicologists have taught us that it demeans music to regard it only, or perhaps even primarily, as an art" ([2010] 2017, 173). Here, *art* refers to something wholly transcendent or decorative. Conversely, Gadamer freely uses *art* and other terms drawn from German aesthetics in his writings, yet this differing treatment of a central term should not obscure the fundamental agreement between these two authors: Gadamer too would reject aestheticism of any kind. Do Gadamer's ideas still work if they are separated from his own European, and even more specifically German, culture and traditions? Like Rice, I contend that they do (Rice [1996] 2017, 77–79). Moreover, I suggest that ethnomusicology, as well as any discipline in the humanities or social sciences that discusses what we can loosely term *expressive arts*, could benefit from a deeper engagement with phenomenological hermeneutics in order to help illuminate the interconnections between the imagination and ways of life.

Hermeneutics also reminds us that it is always necessary to speak from within a tradition, and the concept of art remains operative in many cultures. Rice notes, "While ethnomusicologists have been at pains to move beyond the shadow of the music-as-art metaphor to others, we need to recognize that it informs the experience of music for those raised not just in the traditions of European aesthetics but in most musical traditions we study" (Rice [2001] 2017, 92). Here, Rice is referring to the global influence of Western ideas about aesthetics, but his observation is of course no less true for Western musicians, who do not necessarily interrogate the philosophical presuppositions of their own cultural traditions. My own experiences as a performer and as an ethnographer are in the United States and with jazz and experimental music, where ideas of art as a vehicle for self-expression are so ubiquitous as to be almost completely taken for granted. Although ethnomusicologists may on occasion avoid the term, *art* is not an exhausted metaphor, especially if we divest *art* from aestheticism. Reinvestigating the way in which music is experiential, the awareness of which is raised by improvisation, emphasizes the interconnections between social life and the experience of art. Phenomenological hermeneutics' critiques of the radical subjectivization of aesthetics, which is very much a part of the Kantian concept of art, open a space for rethinking what we mean by this term. In emphasizing the temporary, improvisation already challenges one of the main concepts of Western art as comprised of historically lasting works. However, abandoning the concept of art entirely risks turning the experience of music into a mere reflection of the social world or community that makes it. How, in this sense, could music challenge the status quo? Ironically, this also suggests a kind of aestheticism in which the experience of art becomes indistinguishable from the experience of everyday life. Without refiguring the concept of art to include hermeneutic autonomy, neither completely escapist nor completely contingent, we are in danger of merely reversing a binary opposition that runs all the way down to subjective and objective, neither of which, if we follow Gadamer's thought, can be indicative of an appropriately human truth.

While Rice urges ethnomusicologists to take into consideration the way in which Western concepts are employed by musicians and listeners in non-Western places, I would like to push that further and urge ethnomusicologists to reflect on how those ideas shape their own observations and the discipline itself. My interest here is to rethink presumptions about art and aesthetics that we have inherited from within the tradition of the discipline, and to employ those ideas productively rather than attempting to replace one culturally based epistemology with another. These ideas about art, which are a part of our tradition of thought, inform any ethnographic observation we could make as well as our methodology. Interrogating the ontology of art opens up a space for different questions and different observations, or, to put it hermeneutically, it can refigure our reality. Gadamer's work encourages us to challenge the difference between theory and practice itself. He writes,

> Is theory ultimately a practice . . . or is practice, if it is truly human practice, always at the same time theory? Is it not, if it is human, a looking away from oneself and listening for the other? Life, then, is a unity of theory and practice that is the possibility and duty of everyone. Disregarding oneself, regarding what is: that is the behavior of a cultivated, I might almost say a divine, consciousness. It does not need to be a consciousness cultivated by and for science; it needs to be a humanly cultivated consciousness that has learned to think along with the viewpoint of the other and try to come to an understanding about what is meant and what is held in common. ([1983] 1998, 35)

"Listening for the other" is raised to a central concern in improvisation, and in emphasizing this, considering improvisation provides us with a new way of thinking about listening for our possible connections with others, which is ultimately a goal of ethnomusicology itself. Gadamer's refiguring of the ideas of theory and practice here also suggests a rethinking of the notion of culture itself and offers a way to see it not as a totalizing force but rather as our subtle engagement with others. This quote also raises one of the main difficulties that many scholars have with Gadamer's work: he seems to leave little room for the place of science within culture, perhaps placing scientific method outside of the experience of truth. It is here that the philosopher Paul Ricoeur is particularly useful in considering how methodological rigor might still be usefully employed in the explanation of culture, which also allows for the possibility of a humanistic social science, like the discipline of ethnomusicology, to work as a critique of culture and to affect cultural change itself. The work of ethnomusicologists can change the way people listen and, in doing so, change the way in which people are "listening for the other."[4]

This chapter, then, will try to locate the binary oppositions at work in our inherited concepts of art and aesthetics and then rethink them via Gadamer's ideas about the ontology of the work of art, which considers the conditions for the possibility of the oppositions themselves and attempts to root out any manifestation of aestheticism that would ultimately conceal the transformative power of music. As an ontological study, this chapter focuses on music's transformative power, rather than the epistemological instances in which music may fail to transform the listener. Since I don't want to entirely divorce ontological and epistemological concerns, I will emphasize that this transformative power is always just a potential, which needs to be realized in particular situations. The term *transformative* requires further explanation. While I don't want to discount the possibility of drastic change, which is so celebrated by Romantic philosophy, I emphasize that in any context, our understanding of a work or a situation itself always entails an ontological transformation of that situation.

In the chapter, I begin by analyzing the way in which improvisation is often thought of in binary opposition to composition and how that opposition is shaped by the way in which Western aesthetics has construed how art works can be meaningful. That opposition between subjective and objective ensnares any attempt to connect the social world and the experience of art. That ensnarement calls for a reassessment of ontology, which is my second main point. I will then review Gadamer's ideas about play as the ontology of the work of art and emphasize what this means in terms of musical improvisation. Play, in Gadamerian terms, is not merely a process of interaction with others that occurs in collective music making; rather, it is the condition for the possibility of any meaning that is occasioned by the experience of a work. Rather than reducing improvisation to the interactions among musicians, the notion of play as an ontology helps us see that the experience of music itself is always "in the moment," brought to presentation each time a work is experienced anew. Thirdly, I will examine how Gadamer's ontology highlights listening and thus provides a different way of connecting work and world, which is further extended via Ricoeur's thoughts on identity. It is here that I consider the transformative potential of the experience of art in the poetic transposition from work to world. Finally, I will return to the topic of ethnography to examine the questions raised by a hermeneutic ontology of improvisation.

Composition/Improvisation

Since the late nineteenth century, musicologists and music aestheticians have often treated improvisation as secondary to composition (if they consider it at all). This is despite the fact that prior to the late nineteenth century, improvisation in Western art music was a normal part of performance practice, not only as a means for stylistic embellishments but as a distinct art in and of itself (Goehr 1992; Moore 1992; Hamilton 2000; Sancho-Velazquez 2001). As musicology established itself as a discipline within the German-speaking academy in the early nineteenth century, scholars turned their attention toward scores as objectively "true" representations of the work. Here, scores were thought to be most fit for academic study, a perspective that fit with musicology's desire for a scientific, objective approach. Performers began to adhere slavishly to the score in an effort to remain true, in the epistemological sense of the word here, to the work. This *Werktreue* ideal relies solely on truth as an adequation: a work is the object created by the genius of a composer. A composition can be evaluated by its objective, structural, internal coherence, while a performance's authenticity can be measured by how closely it adheres to that object. Improvisation, if we follow this argument, then must be wholly subjective. Thus, it comes as no surprise that it was often ignored, as there was no way to establish its authenticity as anything other than a whim (see also Nettl 1998). Within the schema instituted by the Werktreue concept, there was no way, or reason, to critically evaluate improvisations: they had no truth status.

Despite the critiques raised against it from cultural musicology, Werktreue still haunts improvisation studies, particularly in jazz. Since virtuosity and individual talent play such important roles in improvisation, the concept of the genius continues to draw scholarly attention (Lewis and Piekut 2016, 6–7). The fact that there are uniquely talented individuals who improvise isn't so much the issue here. In improvisation studies, acknowledging that Black musicians can be geniuses created a space to appreciate their work as important within an academic musicology that systematically marginalized Black musicians, excluded improvisation, and downplayed the importance of performance over what was perceived as the intellectual work of a composer (see also Lewis [1996] 2004). The problem is that we are left with a predicament that is the target of the critique by cultural musicology: great improvisers can be conceptualized as isolated, self-positing individuals who, by the power of their genius, stand outside of culture and history to create works that ostensibly can be construed as also timeless and outside of the social sphere. Recordings of great improvisers replace the notion of the written score as the object, which are then left to be appreciated by individuals as abiding classics eclipsing any sense of the social world from which the works came.

The temptation then is to reverse the problem, rooting the experience of music solely in the social. This reflects something of the solution posed by cultural musicology, or what is still sometimes referred to as *new musicology*. While the history of the Werktreue concept is rarely addressed directly by ethnomusicology proper, the concept of seeking authenticity in the realm of a social sphere that is conceptualized in opposition to Western formalist musicology is very much a part of the history of the discipline.[5] Rather than music existing only in an aesthetic realm that can be measured via an objective score, its performance could be considered in terms of its social situations. Savage identifies this reversal as "social Werktreue" (2004). If the Werktreue concept focuses on authenticity in terms of adherence to the notated score, social Werktreue considers authenticity in terms of adherence to the social. Savage argues this ultimately conceals the ability of music to have any effect on the world:

> By eclipsing a work's independent afterlife, where the work speaks anew in different social and historical situations, such critiques limit the work's power by identifying its meaning with the context and circumstances of its original production. Critical strategies that map correspondences between music's internal features and its ideological contents succumb to the dogma that equates the truth of aesthetic representations with social and political agendas. (2004, 516).

Taking the notion of social Werktreue to its extremes and adhering only to the idea of truth as adequation, music then can be said to mirror, or at least directly correspond to, its social setting, social values, and historical moment, and thus cannot serve as a critique against those things. In this context, the older musicological notion of *genius* would be permanently embedded within a specific social group and historical moment. Rather than residing objectively in a score, the artistic authenticity of improvisations could be established through the subjective intentions of a composer/performer or as a reflection of a social group, scene, or historical moment. Beauty, which within this schema is synonymous with effectivity, would still be reduced to a determinative evaluation and governed by predetermined criteria. Any understanding of a beautiful improvisation would seem to be completely contingent on the performer/composer. This is not to say that music, and improvisations, do not or should not correspond to social situations. In fact, one of the main conceptual contributions of ethnomusicology is to remind anyone trying to study music that it always occurs socially. Such correspondences are not in and of themselves problematic, but they are secondary to the work of the imagination that occurs in the experience of the music, in the same way that a map shows only the end results of political boundary-making and real estate development. Identifying the quality of a musical performance in terms of correspondence to the social is part and parcel of the same Western aesthetic schema that denigrates improvisation against composition—it is merely a reversal of the schema. As a reversal, the concept of hermeneutic autonomy, the independent afterlife of works that Savage discusses, is lost. Without maintaining that autonomy, how can we consider the openness or adaptability of communities?

Gadamer identifies these problems as stemming from the radical subjectivization of aesthetics instituted by Kant, who reserved objective universality for the realms of science. Gadamer argues that the Kantian distinction between "free beauty" and "dependent beauty" is a "dangerous doctrine for the understanding of art" ([1960] 2004, 39). Free beauty, for Kant, is derived from a pure judgment of taste, distinct from any intellectual concept (Kant [1790] 2000, 114–116). He cites ornamental flowers, designs on carpets, and, perhaps most interesting for us, "musical fantasies" (114). These things have beauty as their ends, as opposed to dependent beauty in which the aim is not beauty itself but some other function or use outside of the aesthetic. Free beauty results in wholly autonomous art without purpose, while dependent beauty is bound up with the transmission or re-presentation of discrete ideas. In musicology, this division led to the nineteenth-century aesthetics of formalists like Eduard Hanslick ([1854] 1986), which saw beauty as necessarily free (in Kant's sense) and escapist (see Kivy 2009). It is tempting to reject formalist schemas by placing music under dependent beauty rather than free beauty, instrumentalizing music as a communication from the composer (usually via a performer) to the listener. If music is wholly autonomous on the side of free beauty, it is entirely contingent on the side of dependent beauty. Grondin asserts, "Gadamer battles on two fronts, those of historicism and the aesthetic, but against a common enemy. In both cases, it is a matter of the same reductionism of truth which has its source in the monopoly that the modern method claims over all issues of knowledge" ([1999] 2003, 30). Aestheticism, which culminates in the notion of "art for art's sake," celebrates art as wholly subjective and autonomous from social life, as opposed to thinking of it as merely decorative. However, this approach meant art could only be an escape from the real, rendering it ineffective in any sphere other than the wholly subjective art world. Historicism pulls in the opposite direction and makes art a contingent expression of its time, or ultimately its creator—the artist and their intentions. Improvisations seem caught between dependent and free beauty. Improvisations are still considered, particularly in relationship to Western concert music, as "musical fantasies," more the work of unrestrained imagination than the deliberative process of composition, and thus fitting with the concept of free beauty. Yet, with no intermediary between the composition and the performance, an improvisation also seems to be entirely dependent on the moment of its creation and its creators. Gadamer's argument is that the schema creates a false equivalence. Truth—especially when understood as disclosure (that is, the unfolding of the changing reality that characterizes human life)—cannot be neatly divided between subjective and objective judgments.

The experience of improvisation reveals the problems of Kant's schema because it is simultaneously free and dependent. (And, of course, Gadamer's point is that all that we identify as art is both.) Although we still want to be aware of the difference between improvisation and composition, treating them as opposites reiterates Kant's radically subjective schema, obscures the ontology that underlies all music, and thus occludes further inquiry into the idea of truths disclosed or revealed through the experience. It has proven exceedingly difficult to extricate that opposition in philosophical approaches to the aesthetics of improvisation, and this also reflects the tremendous influence that Kant has on thinking about art in general. Below, I will examine different approaches scholars have taken to the problem that improvisation poses to radically subjective aesthetics. I aim to show how Kant's schema is inscribed in these approaches and to preemptively illustrate the importance of rethinking the ontology of music in order to escape that schema.

The philosopher Andy Hamilton uses the methods of analytic philosophy to address the problems radical subjectivity raises for improvisation. He illustrates that the effective history of Western music since the 1800s has treated composition and improvisation as binary opposites (1990; 2000). The supposed timelessness of canonical compositions is set against improvisation's celebration of the moment in performance. The composer's deliberation over the formal components of their work is opposed to the spontaneity of improvisers co-creating. Formalist aesthetics served as the handmaiden for identifying the intention of the composer as objectively contained within the score. Improvisation studies reverses this and aims at identifying the subjective elements of performance. Without a score, performance—or what can be called the collective intentions of the performers, who now function as instantaneous composers—becomes the object of investigation. Hamilton suggests that the two conflicting views each have a distinct aesthetics: an aesthetics of perfection for composition, and a separate aesthetics of imperfection for improvisation (2000). Thus, the history of the eventual framing of improvisation as an opposite of composition could be explained by illustrating that two different systems of evaluation were being used but not always recognized. However, employing two different criteria for the evaluation of beauty only further leads to thinking of composition and improvisation not just separately but in opposition to each other.

It is on the surface a tempting solution: we might have one set of rules for appreciating composition and another for improvisation. An ethnomusicologist examining music that exists across borders or interculturally might be tempted to extend this argument further: each community or each genre of music has its own set of aesthetic rules, and to appreciate the music, one just needs to learn those rules. This is in danger of missing the power of music itself to effect change, of missing the way in which the imagination is needed in the very concept of identity, and it can be seen as reinforcing an essentialist and totalizing view of cultures and others. According to this view, we have music, now rendered as a set of objective rules, corresponding to either society or score.[6] In either case the rules are already after the fact, second order to the experience itself.

A similar but more nuanced approach to squaring aesthetics and improvisation is evident in the introduction to the edited volume *Improvisation and Social Aesthetics* by Georgina Born, Eric Lewis, and Will Straw (2017). What they term *social aesthetics* is used to remind us that aesthetic judgments of all kinds always involve and are influenced by the social world; they are best thought of not as objective lists of rules but rather as social discourse. Born, Lewis, and Straw mark two different aspects of improvisation that call for social aesthetics, but in both, improvisation is construed in binary opposition to composition. First, improvisation is often seen as a corrective to Western art music and the hierarchical relationships descending from the composer to the performers and then the audience (9); second, "group improvisation involves essentially dialogical engagement between the improvisers" as opposed to the solitary work of the Western art music composer (10). There is no argument that both propositions are correct, but if we follow their oppositional logic, we become ensnared in the oppositions of Kant's schema that Gadamer identified as radically subjective.

Born, Lewis, and Straw's first argument suggests that if composition represents the dominant culture, as a kind of hegemony of great art imposed from the top down, improvisation then can be construed as subversive and rebellious. This opposition suggests a kind of quick and ready alliance with political protest that is often the focus of studies of improvised music. But what happens if improvised music comes to represent the dominant culture? Jacques Attali's well known book *Noise* suggests precisely this—a utopic teleological end of music history in which the act of improvising, which he somewhat confusingly calls "composing," eventually liberates every person from the pitfalls of consumption ([1977] 1989, 133–148). That point has obviously not come yet, and since the publication of *Noise*, jazz has in fact become much more institutionally accepted, though not dominant. Jazz's institutionalization has come not with Marxist liberation but through an increased embrace of neoliberal corporate sponsorship and its own type of formalist methodologism (see Laver 2015 and Chapman 2018). Put in a global perspective, the historical importance of improvisation in the art of music of the ruling classes in the Middle East and India could hardly have been said to be politically rebellious, and its historical prominence did not exempt those countries from the problems of capitalism. This is not to say that improvisation has not been rebellious in specific situations or that it cannot be prophetic. Rather, the reasons we can understand improvisations as subversive cannot be rooted merely in their opposition to compositions.

Furthermore, if the power of improvisation is rooted simply in its difference from composition, then the experience of the music itself has less effect than the position of the music within the social field. Pierre Bourdieu's concept of *fields of cultural production* has been very influential in improvisation studies, yet mapping music onto social fields does little to explain how those fields came to be in the first place ([1979] 1987).

Construing music as only a symbolic reference to the social position of its listeners turns musical works into placeholders on a map, capable only of reflecting social groups oppositionally, a move that aligns with the concept of social Werktreue. Bourdieu's concepts help diagnose the power relations in social aesthetics in a world where consumption seems to overrun all aspects of human cultural activity, but if we are left only with oppositional tastes and cultures, the future would seem to be one of never-ending reversals and struggles for power (see also Savage 2010, 125–128).

Born, Lewis, and Straw's second argument suggests that collectively realized improvisations reveal aspects of social relations more directly than compositions that are the product of solitary composers. This concept calls for considering the social relations of the performing musician-composers as ethical relations. Leaving aside solo improvisations and collectively realized fixed compositions, it is quite correct that collectively realized spontaneous creativity does include the intentions of more than one individual and thus presents a real challenge to formalist aesthetics that are bound to the idea of the self-positing genius. However, emphasizing co-presence and collective action in only the production of music by musicians misses the importance and presence of listeners and their agency, thus confining meaning within the aesthetic. Even if it is now marked as "social" simply by the involvement of more than one author, meaning remains a separate entity, waiting to be decoded or read by an essentially passive listener or by the theorist, observing at a distance.

Extending the binary opposition a bit further, we can observe that if compositions require the intermediary interpretation of performers who bridge the gap between the composer and the audience, then improvisations accomplish a seemingly direct transmission of ideas. There are some simple objections to this binary, including composers who perform their own work and the degree to which improvisations might consist of musical patterns worked out in advance, but the deeper problem is that this opposition fails to credit any meaning to the activity of listening, where mediation occurs regardless of the intention. Listening to music, which entails giving sound (and silences) attention as meaningful, always involves the listener's mediation between the sensation of the physical sounds and their meanings, however we might construe them. Ethnomusicology's productive engagement with reception studies is helpful here in opening up this same critique from a different perspective than that of phenomenological hermeneutics: the social always implies listeners or an audience. I am in full agreement with Ellen Waterman when she states, "We need to do more work in critical studies in improvisation to account for difference in the experiences of listening subjects before we can really understand improvisation as a model for intersubjective communication" (2008).[7] To give primacy to the intentions of the musicians involved in spontaneous creation is to lock the meaning into a radical historicity of the now, cutting off the possibility of its afterlife (either in recording or in the thoughts and reflections of the participants after the event).

This raises the Cartesian problematic of the pairing of mind and body, which informed Kant's subject/object distinction. Composition in Western art music and formalistic aesthetics in general tend to be construed as placing the thinking mind over the acting body. The body then becomes the domain of improvisation and the locus of subjectivity there (see, for example, Sidall and Waterman 2016, 1–9). The idea of the body as distinct from the mind has been neglected or even entirely avoided in formalist aesthetics, and returning a focus to the subjective via the study of embodiment opens new realms of study and reveals structural imbalances.

Yet, we need to be cautious in inverting this schema and giving precedence to body over mind, as that cannot solve the problems raised by the opposition. If we take what is communicated through music as only the product of the agency of the performer/composer, regardless of whether it is the product of the thoughts or the bodies of a singular person or of many people, then we have reduced the musical experience to the transference of discrete knowledge or ideas. Meaning would thus be wholly in the realm of Kantian dependent beauty, and music would become a feeble language with no poetics. Furthermore, the lack of mediation of an interpreting performer and the impossibility of subsequent performances of un-fixed (e.g., improvised) works does not avoid the problem of the intentional fallacy. In such a situation, the only authentic meaning (or at least the most authentic one) is to be found in the mind of the composers, who, in the case of improvisation, also happen to be the performers. The problems of the mind/body opposition are reflected in the subjective/objective opposition as well. Our experience of music reveals that it occurs both subjectively and objectively. We, as listeners, *feel* it, and the sound acts on our bodies, but we also reflect on it and make judgments about it.

The final approach I'll examine in terms of these inherited binary oppositions that call for a turn to ontology is the way George Lewis's "Improvised Music after 1950: Afrological and Eurological Perspectives" draws out the real-world effects these oppositions created in a history that excluded Black music and people ([1996] 2004). His article, perhaps one of the most influential texts in contemporary improvisation studies, not only identifies the two different logics but also critiques the way in which each logic was received. He construes Afrological approaches to music as being connected to personal narrative and character, hence emphasizing the subjective, while Eurological approaches appeal to seemingly objective schema and formulas. The former is exemplified by jazz, while the latter is evidenced in contemporary concert music through composers like John Cage. Lewis notes that this distinction does not just apply to the racial identities of the composers/performers; rather, it also reflects a historical difference in conceptualizing how to create (and value) music. Improvised music drawing on Afrological approaches was not as readily accepted as "great art" compared with music drawing on Eurological approaches. Twentieth-century concert programmers, critics, musicologists, and music historians in North America and Europe gravitated toward improvised works that could be explained through the seemingly objective lens of the Werktreue concept. Drawing on the idea of indeterminacy, John Cage's music could be conceptualized as objectively realized, while John Coltrane's investigations into spirituality remain subjective, personal interpretations. Lewis's diagnosis could be said to reveal the structural imbalances in the field of cultural production, but, like Bourdieu's work, it does not say how that field might be altered or changed. In turning to a hermeneutically phenomenological account of improvisation, I want to illustrate that the subjective/objective pairing is not useful when considering the experience of music as meaningful. To do so requires shifting the focus from the acts of the composers/performers and focusing on interpretative acts of listening.

An ontology of improvised music will reveal the listening abilities that underlie and are implied by the logics that Lewis identifies, just as it can account for Hamilton's suggestion that we might have a different set of aesthetics for different types of musics. Examining the ontology that undergirds not only the two differing logics but also both improvised and pre-composed music helps construe how the experience of music connects to our being-in-the-world. However, this approach can only do that by matching an ontology of art with an ontology of self or identity that does not revolve around a mind/body dualism. The transformative power of music operates in relationship with the transformative capabilities of individuals.

UNRAVELING THE OPPOSITES: TURN TOWARD ONTOLOGY

Focusing on the ontology of music will help us out of this mire of oppositions, and the ease with which composition and improvisation can be confused is a clue to the force of the experience afforded by them. For example, when I have performed improvised music, naïve listeners have asked me how I memorized such long compositions, which were in fact spontaneously created. Similarly, I have performed intricate, through-composed pieces that some listeners assumed were nothing more than wholly improvised, aimless noodling. How can we make sense of these misinterpretations? Hamilton's notion of the contrasting aesthetics of perfection and imperfection, which I discussed earlier, imply not only different standards of beauty but also different ontologies for music (2000), and it is in this sense that Philip Bohlman's work on musical ontologies can be helpful (1999, 17–34). For Bohlman, different cultures, with different conceptions of individuality, art, and even function, construe music differently, and he uses the term *ontologies*, in the plural, to preserve and respect the plurality of cultural variety. Bohlman's work is useful in illustrating that the nature of musical experience is ultimately an ontological one. However, his work does not take a phenomenological approach to ontology or ask what all of the different types of music (and cultural groups) have in common or how they may be open to change.[8] While I agree that we might hold different works to different standards, we still must ask from whence these standards arise. The notion that different musics involve different ontologies suggests that our expectations of hearing pre-composed music might change based on our past experience with improvisation and vice versa. Hamilton and Bohlman see differing sets of cultural expectations giving rise to differing forms of musical ontology, but understanding ontology in this way prevents us from seeing how music can affect our actions in the world, a feature that is shared in all music cultures and all musical ontologies. Clarifying the force of the experiences proffered by composition and improvisation can help us establish the hermeneutic autonomy of each and shift the discussion from one that only revolves around subjective or objective interpretations of works.

In a famous, early article on improvisation, ethnomusicologist Bruno Nettl takes a globally comparative perspective, and his ideas can be a first step to help us see this underlying ontology (1974). Nettl suggests that the most important difference between composition and improvisation is how quickly each is accomplished. He suggests a continuum from quickly to slowly composed works as a useful way to think beyond the binary opposition of composition versus performance. Nettl's comparative perspective provides an interesting counterpoint to Hamilton, whose own focus is admittedly limited to music in the Western world. As an analytic philosopher, Hamilton's tendency to divide and separate runs up against the comparative goals of Nettl's ethnomusicology, which aims toward its own form of universalism, or at least its desire to translate music across cultural boundaries. (From his perspective, Hamilton might suggest distinct ontologies for Indian, Persian, and African musics, as Bohlman does.) Nettl offers the opportunity to consider a common point of departure for all music. Musical practices are construed very differently in cultures where improvisation is not considered in opposition to composition and where improvised works occupy a place in the tradition that is very different from that of Western concert music. Yet, we can recognize all these different types of music as meaningful cultural phenomena, which raises the question, "What do they have in common?"

The first step to answering this question lies in dismantling the work concept behind Werktreue. Christopher Small's influential concept of *musicking* reminds us that music is not a thing but an activity, and to music is to participate in any way—as composer, performer, or listener—in the musical event (1998). Without the fixity of a composition, improvisation then at the very least stands on the same ground as composition, united through the fact that they both necessitate and even call for participation. Small further suggests that since the activity always involves humans, every occasion of musicking is not just inherently social but is also *about* social relations, a claim that resonates strongly with the perspectives of many ethnomusicologists. Despite their utility, Small's ideas can easily slip into social Werktreue, particularly if we come to evaluate music in terms of the degree of social participation, seen not as a mental activity but as physical embodiment (Small 1998, 49). In inverting the subjective/objective schema, we open a space for music previously suppressed but only at the expense of the other music. The important lesson is that musical works, of all types, are a working.

The next step, then, is to turn to the experience itself to seek a different way to conceptualize authenticity. Drawing directly on Gadamer's writings, Bruce Benson offers a phenomenological examination of music that places improvisation at the center of the experience (2003). His work is focused solely on Western music, including jazz, but it turns the Western paradigm on its head by proposing that improvisation underlies the binary opposition between composition and performance.[9] Benson sees improvisation not just as spontaneous or extemporaneous composition but rather as the experiential phenomenon of coming to understand music: "the process by which a work comes into existence is best described as improvisatory at its very core, not merely in the act of composing but also the acts of performing and listening" (2). From a phenomenological standpoint, this recovers the centrality of improvisation in the Western tradition, which had been lost to formalist scholarship. Improvisation, for Benson, helps to reveal the ontology of music, but he suggests that the difference is found primarily in its reception. This risks repeating the binary oppositions between composition and improvisation, but now only the latter is authentic as determined by an audience, and it doesn't fully escape the opposition between subjective and objective.

Delving deeper into the phenomenon of music itself helps draw out that improvisation and composition are both meaningfully constituted in the temporal flow of lived experience. Before returning to Gadamer's concepts of ontology, it is worth examining the way this theme was developed by Alfred Schutz's 1951 article "Making Music Together: A Study of Social Relationships."[10] Schutz, in the process of suggesting ways in which the experience of music can be transposed to social relations, recognizes that such experiences are temporal, which we can identify as "listening." Listening in this sense is done both by performers and by an audience. Can one experience music without listening to it? Not in this sense: listening here refers to the fact that music requires participation in the experience. Thus, reading a score without hearing the performance, or even remembering a piece of music, can both be thought of as imaginative listening because they entail participation in the event. Conversely, as anyone who has played music professionally can tell you, one can perform music without really experiencing it as meaningful, but that does not change the potential experience.

While I agree with the importance and ineluctability of participation in the experience of music, which is especially evident in the performance of improvisations, this by itself doesn't resolve the problems of aesthetics' subjectivization. The problems of Werktreue are amplified in the case of music but still exist in other forms of art, wherever meaning is reduced to the simple transfer of the idea of a creator to perceiver. Thus, a reconsideration of the condition for the possibility of art allows us to rethink the problem from the ground up. In doing so, we come to understand the word "art" as not limited to Western ideas about "great art" or "master works" but as being about the temporal experience of the free play of the imagination. One might immediately object that this free play is all too Western, coming from Kant's idea of free beauty. It is true that I am working to recover and expand on useful ideas from within the Kantian tradition, and individuals' exercise of imagination in aesthetic experience is a universal assumption I am willing to stand for. I suggest that, phenomenologically speaking, we listen to improvisation and composition the same way. Both composition and improvisation are techniques for crafting works of art that are not meaningful until they are experienced through listening (meant in the inclusive sense outlined above). Schutz's argument that performance, as well as participation, in this sense arises not from the action of the musicians sounding notes but from the activity of listening, is apt. Pre-composed and improvised works of music confront us in the same manner. Following Gadamer, what music is "about" is apprehended only in the experience, which unless the only listener is the composer, can never be turned over completely to a subject's intention.[11] That composition and listening occur nearly simultaneously in improvisation is important, but I argue that stressing spontaneity reveals something inherent about the temporal and experiential aspects of all art, rather than being an invitation to emphasize the intention of an improviser.

PLAY AND IMPROVISATION

Musical experiences (of all kinds) present us with a very clear example of Gadamer's assertion that play is central to the work of art's mode of being. Gadamer defines play "as a process that takes place 'in between.' We have seen that play does not have its being in the player's consciousness or attitude, but on the contrary play draws him into its dominion and fills him with its spirit. The player experiences the game as a reality that surpasses him" ([1960] 2004, 109). Note that here, the word *play* does not refer to the act of sounding one's instrument. Gadamer uses the German word *Spiel*, which translates to English as *game* or *play*.[12] Play, then, is the medial and temporal quality of the experience of art, which was also identified by Schutz. For Gadamer, attending to the phenomenon of play gives us insight into the dire seriousness of art that has the potential to completely transform the player, even if the play happens to be fun or, even better, pleasurable ([1977] 1986, 1–53). To play is to lose oneself in the game, and the player's individual subjectivity is thus no longer in charge of what happens in the play experience. Rather, we surrender ourselves to the game. Playing the game also means respecting the game's rules and responding to the moves of others. Thus, the work of art is always and necessarily an unfolding conversation. Such a conversation always comes with a request, or at least the potential, to change one's position. Like a conversation, play is never one-sided and, if we are to experience it fully, it demands our response.

These ideas seem ready made to describe how we experience music and even more so improvisation. While performers are playing a piece of composed music, they are engaged in a game whose rules are created by the composer. The work unfolds in time as the notes sound; the structure is revealed through the course of the performance and exists finally only in the sounding out of it. This process is very similar to Schutz's description of the experience of inner time in music and is a clear enough example of a work being brought to presentation. If we now imagine performers freely improvising with no pre-composed themes, we can understand their actions as playing a game whose rules are dictated by each other. Each sound is an invitation to respond; that response can be anything (sound or silence; acknowledgment or indifference), and that *anything* then becomes the dictate for the game to proceed until the performers collectively devise the rule for ending the game. This bringing to presentation is perhaps more difficult to imagine when we shift our focus back to listeners, which I emphasize as the most important locus for the consideration of how art has a social impact. Play occurs between the work and the listener (or, in other media, the perceiver or reader). The listener needs to "play along" to follow the performance. In a sense, the listener asks, "Which aspects of sound are decisive or important in the unfolding of the performance? Which aspects are less important or even incidental?" A listener follows along with an improvisation by catching the calls and responses of the performers, which may or may not be evident to the performers themselves. Ultimately, the form of the piece is realized only in being played. This constant process of deliberation provides the rules of the game—the mediation of the piece as a meaningful experience. It is in this sense that I argue that improvisation and composition are identical. Both are brought to presentation through play as apprehended by the listener. The process of paying attention and following along with the sounds is the same, regardless of whether the music is composed in advance or spontaneously.

The fact that in improvisation, the composing occurs simultaneously with the work being brought to presentation reveals the fundamental temporality of play. All art, according to Gadamer, is contemporaneous with its play. In the case of fixed artistic forms, like a painting or a composed piece of music, every experience with the work is a renewal of its meaning, rather than a reliving of the moment of its now historical creation.[13] Even in situations in which we believe we are simply re-living an experience of art (as in the case of nostalgia, for example), we apprehend the work anew, because time has passed since our initial encounter, and we have since changed. Improvisation discloses that the moment of play is decisive. Gadamer himself uses an example of musical improvisation to emphasize that work is always a working, is always temporal:

> Let us take the case of an organ improvisation. This unique improvisation will never be heard again. The organist himself hardly knows afterwards just how he played, and no one transcribed it. Nevertheless, everyone says, "That was a brilliant interpretation or improvisation," or on another occasion, "That was rather dull today." What do we mean when we say such things? Obviously we are referring back to the improvisation. Something "stands" in front of us; it is like a work and not just an organist's finger exercise, otherwise we should never pass judgment on its quality or lack of it.
>
> (Gadamer [1977] 1986, 25)

The standing of the work arises through play, and even a single performance has such a standing, which allows us to evaluate it. Is it only a Western pretense that works must be evaluated? Can we enjoy a work without passing judgment on it? Gadamer would certainly say no, but only because he has a very different idea about what that judgment entails. For him, such a judgment is not the adequation between sounds and objective rules of aesthetics, though such correspondences could be made after the fact. Instead, play itself pulls us into the experience, and in recognizing that the work affects us, we are acknowledging this experience as art, which is the precondition for it to be evaluated, for it be to be worthy of our time and attention. The success or failure of the work's specifics, which arise from the ontologies identified by Bohlman, can and do vary. Gadamer's ideas about work as a working and about the "tarrying" of play thus present a view of the subject that is radically different from Kant's, where the subject takes disinterested pleasure in an aesthetic object. The point for Gadamer is that art reveals the human, not as a Kantian sovereign subject who designates their own internal rules but as a subject who is necessarily involved with the participation of others in the unfolding of time.

Gadamer's ideas about the ontology of the work of art allows us to rethink the separation of art from the everyday world in a way that does not rely on radical subjectivity. This separation, or distinction, is important if the work is capable of doing more than just reflecting the social. The experience of art, which Gadamer refers to as *Darstellung* (literally "presentation") or *Vollzug* ("realization" or "performance"), requires our willingness to participate in it. The notion of participation here is not the sociological category identified by Small but is closer to the Platonic concept of *methexis*, a kind of involvement with others that has both active and passive aspects as well as a sense of what Grondin identifies as "wonder," implying curiosity and awe ([1999] 2003, 43).[14] The separation of art from the world can never be complete, Gadamer argues, as the world is brought into the play only through its poetic transposition. The work pulls us in and demands a response. While that pull is rooted in the work, our response is rooted in ourselves. Gadamer terms this a "transformation into structure" (*Verwandlung ins Gebilde*). Using the term *Gebilde*, which is also translated as "creation," Gadamer shows that the work is a specific and discrete form that has arisen through the listener's participation with the world that the work creates. For Gadamer, this world is not simply pre-given for that listener to explore but rather is unfolded by the listener through their play. The world of the work in this sense is not a kind of fictive landscape created by a composer (or in other media, an author) but is a co-creation of the listener (or reader) and the material of the work itself. Discussing the pull that the work has on us and our response to it, Gadamer writes, "transformation into structure means that what existed previously exists no longer. But also that what now exists, what represents itself in the play of art, is the lasting and true" ([1960] 2004, 111). He is emphasizing a poetic aspect of "transformation" that is easy to miss if we expect to find the content of art only in its physical attributes rather than the experience we have with it. It is a bold and radical assertion to say that "what existed previously exists no longer," one that resonates with those aspects of transcendence that were so important to the aestheticians Gadamer critiques. But for Gadamer the transformation is not just in the consciousness of the person experiencing the art (nor with the physical material of the art) but in the experience, which is the structuring that occurs between the material of the art and the person experiencing it. Every experience is a restructuring. The "lasting and true" is not only the material of the work of art but the structure that arises from play and what the work reveals.[15] Again, the similarity with improvised music is clear. Returning to the organ improvisation Gadamer uses as an illustration, it is not the notes or the rhythm that are lasting but the newly unfolded world experienced and evaluated by those who were moved by the experience of play. The fact that a work of improvisation seems temporary and exists only in its performance does not make it any less lasting or true, since, from the perspective of phenomenological ontology, what is lasting and true about the work has to do with the work's being, not its status as a material object. For Gadamer, this is just as true for pre-composed music, poetry, painting, and other kinds of art. The objective physical stability of the material of the art, say the marble of a sculpture, is not the same as the truth of the experience: the sculpture is lasting and true not because it will not rot but because the experience of it continues to move us.

We can learn from fixed compositions that the ability to continually return to works reveals the inexhaustible surplus of meaning that works, both composed and improvised, hold. That is to say that we can return to the experience of that sculpture, and with each return, its meaning has changed ("what existed previously exists no longer"), not because its physical material has changed but because the experience we have with it is new every time. For music, both recorded and pre-composed, this is one of the reasons that we can listen to, and even be surprised by, works we have already heard. This surplus of meaning is still present in improvisation, but it is harder to locate because, at the limit, improvisational works may never be repeated, especially if they are not recorded. Perhaps, even in the case of completely spontaneously improvised music, we can find some degree of repeatability at the level of genre, thought of as a tradition at work within specific communities rather than as a marketing term.[16] In other words, every time I hear free improvisation, I am experiencing a repetition of a sort or a recurrence, as I am hearing it in relationship to all other free improvisations I have heard. We might also think of extending this repeatability into the works of specific individual improvisers. It is tempting then to understand meaning as the intention of individual improvisers, which would miss the fact that a listener still needs to construe that connection as a repetition and recognize this repetition is part of the play of understanding. The temporality of play reminds us that no work is ever really replicated, no matter how fixed (or improvised) it is. By embracing the impossibility of perfect replication, improvisation heightens our awareness of the uniqueness of every experience. Every work is made new in each experience of it. Neither the historicity of the work nor the subjectivity of the composer/performer or even the listener has the final say in the conversation.

Gadamer characterizes the understanding of a work as a "fusion of horizons." His use of *horizon* draws on the ideas of Edmund Husserl, who understood this term not only as a limitation (like the literal horizon, which is a point or line beyond which we cannot see) but also as that which extends meaning from what is immediately perceived to the entire context in which it is given (Gadamer [1960] 2004, 237–238; see also Vessey 2009). Thus, horizon is not just the backdrop for the perception of things but is also the orientation through which any movement must occur. Both the work and the listener are temporal and have a horizon. The horizon of the work indicates that all possible workings of work are informed both by the world it suggests and directed by the effective history of its workings. The horizon of the listener indicates their outlook, which is shaped by their history. The horizon of the work is everything that work brings into play, while the horizon of the listener is everything the player brings into play. The history of a work informs its horizon, just as the personal history of the listener will shape their experience of it. For Gadamer, any understanding of the experience represents a change, a transformation. That is to say that a horizon is there to move toward and is itself always on the move. If the experience is held as radically subjective, following Kant, transcendence from the real world would be complete and ultimately meaningful only as a kind of aestheticism. Gadamer suggests a hermeneutic autonomy for art as a transcendence within immanence.[17] This accounts for the ability of art to transform or change us, yet reminds us that this transformation is rooted both in our own experiences, as humans and as listeners, and in the historicity of the work itself, which, as I suggested above, may be found at the level of genre, rather than only at level of the work itself. The horizon can never be met, which is to say that the work of art is never completed; there are always new or better understandings.

Just as we cannot play or enjoy a game with unfamiliar rules, so too do our pre-understandings, or "prejudices," affect our experience of art (Gadamer [1960] 2004, 267–355). Prejudice in this case relates to our familiarity with the "rules of the game" of play. This includes the concept of the historicity of the work or its genre. We need to have some expectations of how the music is supposed to unfold for us to recognize it as music in the first place. However, those prejudices, on both the side of the work and the side of the listener, are never final, because the experience itself calls the prejudices into question and offers the potential for transformation. Gadamer proposes, "In fact, all artistic creation challenges each of us to listen to the language in which the work of art speaks and to make it our own" ([1960] 2004, 39). The language here is one that arises in the experience and, as art, it is an experience that is open to everyone. This might immediately recall the worn-out metaphor that music is a universal language; however, what Gadamer is suggesting here is that the language in which a work "speaks" arises only and uniquely through experience, contains a surfeit of meaning, exists only to transform its "listener," and is wholly symbolic and metaphoric. Note that when Gadamer is writing about aesthetics, as he is here, he is aiming toward identifying the human experience of truth; thus, we might also say "language is the universal music," reminding us that language is not merely nominalist but also poetic and expressive.[18]

LISTENING AND WORLD: TRANSFORMATIVE EVENTS

It is not just the prejudices that are transfigured but the worlds of both the listener and the work, a process Gadamer refers to as "the fusion of horizons" ([1960] 2004, 305). It is this transfiguration that marks the experience as art in the first place. Gadamer writes about the possibility for change in sweeping language. For example, while discussing how the symbolic in art brings forth a sense of unity implied in the ancient Greek sense of term, he states, "This [recognition of the symbol] means that in any encounter with art, it is not the particular, but rather the totality of the experienceable world, man's ontological place in it, and above all his finitude before that which transcends him, that is brought to experience" ([1977] 1986, 33). We might be tempted then to see Gadamer's ideas as aligned with a very romantic notion of complete and total change, but these encounters always take place within a horizon and are tempered by being grounded in pre-understandings. The differentiation between the world of the work, which arises through play, and the lived world, which is always embedded in a particular social context, is demarcated by the infinite nature of the work and the finitude faced by humans. Art then allows us to be confronted with some of the most human aspects of our life and also suggests that the play of art plays a role in shaping our practical reality. Gadamer is reminding us that deeply moving experiences should not be considered exceptions but rather that they are always possible and always rooted in tradition. Improvisation heightens our awareness of this because, as listeners, we transform the event of improvisation (which may be impossible to reduce to formal designs or individual will) into a composition that has the potential to move us.

Gadamer uses the word *Erfahrung* to refer to these kinds of transformative experiences, and he distinguishes them from *Erlebnis*, which is used to describe everyday experience. In English translations, both German words are usually glossed as "experience," but in German they carry an important distinction. Erlebnis implies being alive (*Leben*) while something is happening. It is the type of experience that can measured objectively, or we could say sociologically. Erfahrung, in contrast, implies a passing through (*Erfahren*) time, or a tradition in which accumulated experience guides an individual, which is what we mean in English when we say "I am an experienced musician." That does not mean that I have merely been present during the occasion of music, but rather that I have accumulated knowledge. Erfahrung designates those experiences that we might anthropologically refer to as "cultural," in that a cultural experience is not merely the occasion of an event but rather one in which heritage and tradition are at work. Gadamer particularly further emphasizes the fact that we are pulled into Erfahrung experiences and that we have a degree of responsibility to learn, grow, change, or renew our sense of self through them. Gadamer later refers to these experiences as related to the festive and ritual, which not only stresses the transformative power of the experience of art but notes its unique temporalities ([1967] 1986, 57–65).[19] Erfahrung could be said to refer to the momentous, while Erlebnis refers to the momentary and sensory. Erlebnis characterizes what we might call "everyday life" in its moment-to-moment lived reality, but the experience of art can suspend that. Improvisation certainly tempts us with the momentary and the sensuous, but if we leave it there, pleasurable only in the moment and in escape, we would be engaging in aestheticism—exactly the kind of radical subjectivization that emphasizes a self-positing, isolated individual. Gadamer uses Erfahrung to remind us that such pleasures, if they are to contribute to lasting, durable lifeways, are always engaged with others and premised on an interest in learning more about oneself with others (Davey 2013, 70–97). Improvisation heightens our awareness of the permanence of the temporary. Improvisation, like the festivals Gadamer discusses, celebrates the moment and thus challenges us as listeners to continue to engage with the work in a meaningful way, implying a sense of lasting or permanence. The confrontation with Erlebnis, which is ultimately not disconnected from Erfahrung, reminds us that the two—the sensuous, bodily, and immediate and the reflective, contemplative, and lasting—are never usefully separated.

Gadamer argues that distanciation marks the aesthetic experience, an idea that is opposed to Kantian disinterestedness. Disinterestedness suggests suspending one's biases to find subjective aesthetic pleasure, while distanciation involves the hermeneutic need to experience distance from the real in the experience of the world of the work—to put what we know about ourselves to the test, as it were.[20] This leads us away from indexical references within the work and toward the ontological concept of symbol itself. Indexical references, a concept from linguistics, implies that something in the music points to something outside the music: this sound points to a feeling or a place. Gadamer argues that symbols are a kind of unity, a world in and of themselves, thus that feeling or place is not just being referenced but is made real or whole by the experience of it in music. Gadamer writes, "The symbolic does not simply point toward a meaning, but rather allows that meaning to present itself" ([1977] 1986, 34). Moreover, he explains that "the work of art does not simply refer to something, because what it refers to is actually there. We could say that the work of art signifies an increase in being" ([1977] 1986, 35). He characterizes this increase in being as *mimesis*, by which he does not mean the servile imitation of something, but the symbolic action of the work itself in superabundance. In other words, the work exemplifies what the work is about.

Ricoeur also uses the term *mimesis* for the process of how works become meaningful ([1983] 1984). He construes this in three parts, depicting a movement from the prefigured world to configuration in which we confront the world of the work, and culminating in a refiguration of our world. The idea of the prefigured world loosely corresponds to Gadamer's notion of prejudice, by which he means the fact that we cannot simply enter into play without some anchorage in the practical world and that we ineluctably belong to history. This occurs in all forms of art; as we have seen, even in radically experimental improvised music, the expression of freedom is grounded in a pre-understanding of what is acceptable. Our familiarity with the rules of the game in what Ricoeur refers to as $mimesis_1$, or *prefiguration*, allows us to recognize the injunction issued from a work that draws us into the transformative event. Next, the configuration that occurs in what Ricoeur calls $mimesis_2$ suspends or brackets the practical order of everyday life. Here, entering the world of the work allows us to raise questions about the modality of our being-in-the-world. $Mimesis_3$ then is the return to a now refigured world.

Accounting for a phenomenological ontology of music, regardless of its historical traditions or the world from which the work arises, now opens the possibility for those different worlds to be transformed. Further, turning our attention toward the entire process of mimesis further guards against aestheticism. The experience of art is always transformative when carried through all three stages. Aestheticism relegates the experience to only the first stage. Art is trapped in the prefigured if it can only mirror already established rules, while we might see it as contained within $mimesis_2$ if the experience is thought to be wholly transcendent and thus escapist. The former seems possible, though dull, while the latter is only a fantasy masking the entire arc of a meaningful event. Ricoeur's tripartite concept of mimesis helps explain hermeneutic autonomy as characterized by transcendence within immanence, which I discussed above in relation to Gadamer's thoughts. It also notes that methodological examination of the experience of art can be bracketed out of the arc of experience itself. Analysis need not attempt to replicate the experience of the work itself, yet it may offer insight into new understandings of that experience.

Ricoeur develops his concept of mimesis specifically in terms of narrative art and its ability to configure time. As such, narrative is mimetic of action ([1983] 1984; [1985] 1988). Music is generally not a form of narrative, yet we can still consider its mimetic properties in its exemplification of mood.[21] Savage writes, "Set against the backdrop of metaphor's heuristic power, music's exemplification of feelings and moods modulates the modalities of our inherence in the world" (2010, 103–104). Mood may seem like a powerless romantic vestige, but at this ontological level it has real vehemence (Ricoeur [1986] 1991, 19–20; see also Savage 2010, 14, and Custer 2019). Heidegger relates mood to *Befindlichkeit* (affect), and as one of the basic parameters of human existence, mood gives *Dasein* (literally, "being-there," Heidegger's term for human existence as presence) an orientation toward the world ([1927] 1962, 176) both temporally and affectively. The experience of music, through play, works by refashioning our mood, our modality of being-in-the-world. In play, we encounter the real of the "as if." Removed from the practicalities of everyday life, we learn and become open to new possibilities, different ways of being toward the world. Mood is not social action but rather the springboard from which social action arises.

If the transformative and affective aspects of music are fundamentally temporal, we gain a greater understanding of music's temporality by setting the notion of time in its widest context. Moreover, the experience of art provides insight into the aporias of time itself. Savage, drawing on Ricoeur's identification of the aporias of time, suggests that music is unique in its refiguration of the disproportion between "time and the other of time" (2018, 13). The other of time refers to a sense of being out of time or that which is not time, for example, eternity. We can imagine a non-time, but there is no way to experience it directly. The experience of music is unique in providing a model of an experience outside of the constraints of cosmological time, thus allowing us to rethink time and its other (not time). By emphasizing instantaneousness, improvisation correctly reminds us that the experience of music is always about our confrontation with time. Music, like narrative, mediates between cosmological time, which is experienced as discrete units such as passing seconds, and phenomenological time, which is experienced as a present that has a past and a future (Ricoeur [1985] 1988, 244). It also gives us a clear demonstration of our ability to refigure time by losing ourselves to the experience, through the limit-experiences of trance, but also in that sense of inner time identified by Schutz. It is also worth noting that one of the distinct elements of free jazz is the suspension of a steady beat or identifiable swing, and attending to this further emphasizes how the temporality of all music requires what Schutz identified as a "tuning in together" (1951). In removing a simple connection to clock time (i.e., musical pulse measured in beats-per-minute), a greater emphasis is placed on the need to negotiate human time together and that time itself is characterized by flows of changing density and importance. Savage, via Ricoeur, reminds us that this experience of time is configured (in that it undergoes the three stages of mimesis I described above) rather than purely an escape from lived time (2018, 60–64). Even if music avoids a steady pulse, there is still a before and after; it cannot escape cosmological time, but it can refigure it. Understood in these terms, improvisation emphasizes that our imaginative refiguring of time is an ineluctable aspect of being-in-the-world.

The world, it follows, is not just an objective reality upon which the experience of art or the imagination is added but rather is comprised of imaginative acts. The experience of art gives us a world in which to live. The worlding effect of the work is occluded by treating art as an aesthetic object used for the purposes of escape from the world. The world that the experience of art gives us allows and even calls for change and transformation. It is not enough to just hermeneutically consider art; we must follow through with that consideration and see that the world itself is hermeneutic. Gadamer refigures Kantian aesthetics to account for a sense of human truth that is not merely a subjective truth that can stand against objective or scientific truth. The political philosopher Hannah Arendt follows this line of thought, refiguring the inherited Kantian concepts of the social and political, which are further examined by Ricoeur. Kant grounds taste in *sensus communis*, common sense or, even better, "sense-in-common," to explain the reason why aesthetic judgments are made as if they were universal (§40 of the third critique, [1790] 2000, 173–176; Gadamer [1960] 2004, 17–27). Arendt finds the "as if" to resound in political judgment as well, because it too involves a sense of communicability (Arendt [1954] 2006, 221; Ricoeur [1995] 2000). To find the echoes of aesthetic judgment in the political sphere is not to say that there is no difference between the experience of art and the experience of politics, but rather that the experience of art gives us insight into the kinds of judgments and imagination that are required for politics. Both aesthetics and politics require *phronesis* (prudential wisdom), reflective judgment in which the universal is sought in the individual case, as opposed to Kant's "determinative judgment" in which the specific is subsumed under the given universal.[22] Arendt and Ricoeur both suggest that concepts of exemplarity, which Kant finds central to aesthetic judgment, provide insight into the imagination required for political life. While art itself might not be necessary for society, imagination certainly is. The experience of art, when it is engaged, both reflects the social, through its pre-understanding, and informs it, through configuration.

Thus, the sense-in-common that arises through a transformative event can be thought of as a summoning of a community. Gadamer, responding specifically to the challenge of modern experimental art, writes, "The artist no longer speaks for the community, but forms his own community insofar as he expresses himself. Nevertheless, he does create a community, and in principle, this truly universal community (*oikumene*) extends to the whole world" ([1977] 1986, 39). Even works that challenge their own history issue a call to join their world. Radical or experimental art, including some improvised musics, is not the exception to this; rather, it heightens our awareness of the communicative power of the experience. A community is summoned as individuals heed the call of exemplary works. The community shares the refigured, enlarged reality and continues to learn from the experience of the work. That enlarged reality becomes transformed when the work is experienced again. The call is open to anyone prepared to hear it, and thus the oikumene is essentially capacious; to engage in it is to cultivate oneself to it, or to experience *Bildung*, the term Gadamer uses to refer to "culture." Understood as a process of cultivation, Bildung is always a "culturing" and the result of care, not only for ourselves but for and with others.[23] Specifically, improvisation stresses the importance of openness and adaptability because those aspects are given precedence in its experience. That these concepts are not just political but ethical reminds us of the ontological depth of the imagination signaled by the "as if." As Savage puts it, "Like the injunction that issues from the example of a singular moral act, the suitability of the world that is expressed by a work testifies to a possible modality of inhabiting the world" (2010, 115). The exemplarity of the moral act is the apprehension of the fit between the act and the situation to which it answers. The experience of art communicates potential ways of being in the world through the exemplarity of the work, that is to say, the work's "followability" (*Nachfolge*) (Ricoeur [1995] 1998, 183; see also Savage 2010, 115). To follow a work means to answer the call to community that the experience issues and to grasp the fit between work and world. Thus music sustains and supports a community in providing potential future ways of being together, just as a community might sustain and support music as "culture." Music is both cultural and culturing in this regard.

Listening to improvisation specifically emphasizes the aspect of passivity in the experience of art. Passivity is ontologically already part of every artistic encounter, corresponding to our willingness to submit fully to a transformative experience, but music draws this out further because of its unique capacity to refigure our sense of time. Savage writes, "Music's mimetic refiguration of time and the other of time avows the feeling of dependence [an avowal of passivity that occurs in the experience of music] that Ricoeur contrasts with the 'assertion of radical autonomy'" (Savage 2010, 224). It seems paradoxical to argue that music so often associated with radical freedom, as in the case of free jazz, is bound together with dependence or passivity, but I think that paradox is in fact productive in showing exactly what is exemplified as *free* in this music and how that affects our identity. Improvisation, in emphasizing listening both from the performers and from the audience, stresses the importance of passivity in freedom. Bobby Bradford, a senior figure in improvised music in Los Angeles, explained the difference between conventional jazz and the music played by him and his peers by observing that, in free jazz, "you are free to play anything—that is musically responsible" (Bradford quoted in Sharp 2008, 63). The em-dash here indicates a pregnant pause, but it doesn't do justice to the significance the pause conveys: freedom tempered by responsibility after the precisely perfect time span of contemplation. That responsibility is raised to the fore in improvised music because it becomes a demonstration of responsibility to and for others. In this sense, passivity may also entail activity, as listening in improvised music is not just responding or yielding but also knowing when to take the lead. This is exactly the same question posed by an audience member: what are the calls and what are the responses in this music?

When an improvising musical performer takes the lead or initiates a new musical motive, it is because the other musicians have recognized its authority and have chosen to yield. In responding to a motive initiated by another musician, the performers acknowledge the claim that a musical statement has made on them. Freely improvised music involves the constant making of decisions in the moment based on the (musical) situation in which you find yourself, with the acknowledgment that your decision may have an effect on the other performers and the structure and mood of the work as whole. These decisions require phronesis: the skilled improviser uses prudential wisdom in deciding which theme to take up, which to ignore, when to yield, and when to take the lead.[24] This is stressed even further when the conventions are determined in the moment of performance themselves, which is the case in freely improvised music. Within the context of the improvised composition, every single decision will have an effect—even non-action, resulting in silence. Listeners, with the musicians being something like the first or nearest witness to the performance, recognize that each and every performance of improvised music involves a series of decisions that must be made. The audience members are both witness to and participants in the processes of questioning, judging, and acting, and this presents a model of and for solicitude.

Gadamer notes that listening implies a kind of openness, which evokes a sense of freedom. Writing specifically about hermeneutical experience, of which aesthetics will demonstrate a kind of truth distinct from adequation, he argues,

> This openness does not exist only for the person who speaks; rather, anyone who listens is fundamentally open. Without such openness to one another there is no genuine human bond. Belonging together always also means being able to listen to one another. When two people understand each other, this does not mean that one person "understands" the other. Similarly, "to hear and obey someone" (*auf jemanden hören*) does not mean simply that we do blindly what the other desires. We call such a person slavish (*hörig*). Openness to the other, then, involves recognizing that I myself must accept some things that are against me, even though no one else forces me to do so.
>
> (Gadamer [1960] 2004, 355)

The conversational aspect of openness that Gadamer emphasizes here has clear resonances with his insistence that the real experience of art is conversational and transformative. We listen to music to learn more about the importance of listening. The freedom of being open to the other presents a different sense of freedom than free choice done by a self-positing individual. The philosopher James Marsh notes that for Ricoeur, "freedom is not only active upsurge and thrust. That is certainly an aspect of freedom . . . but freedom is also receptive listening and attentiveness to motives and values" (2008, 16). This characterization of freedom as drawing on both passivity and action also resonates with Ricoeur's work on identity, in which oneself is thought together with an other, attesting to our human condition of both acting and suffering ([1950] 1966; [1990] 1992).

Ricoeur proposes a hermeneutic concept of identity that counters the Cartesian notion of the *cogito*, the thinking self ([1990] 1992, 4–36). Just as Western aesthetics are trapped within a schema instituted by Kant, identity is trapped by Descartes's notion of the self-positing individual. The inverse of this would be a radically shattered cogito, an idea Ricoeur associates with Nietzsche, the ramifications of which are felt throughout postmodern ideas about the social construction of the self, which sees the subject as determined by discourse, power, or larger social forces.[25] The Cartesian concept of identity gives us the binary opposition of mind and body that is disastrous in attempting to understand the experience of art without rendering the experience as entirely sensuous (of the body) or entirely cognitive.

Ricoeur counters this problem by presenting identity not as sameness versus difference but as a dialectic of *idem* and selfhood, which he refers to as *ipseity* ([1990] 1992; [2004] 2005). Idem-identity operates only along the vectors of sameness and difference and refers to the objective, demonstrable difference between one person and another. It can answer the question of "What am I?" but it does not begin to answer the question "Who am I?," which is addressed by what Ricoeur calls ipse-identity. Ipseity responds to the linkages or imputability of an agent to an action. It is what projects the spatiotemporal idem-identity into the future and responds to our ability to keep our word, in which the "I" is not discoverable as or reducible to a biological entity but rather is found only through attestation. This sense of self-constancy entails a sense of permanence in time that is different from the one involved in idem-identity. Ricoeur suggests that "narrative identity" mediates between idem-identity and ipseity ([1990] 1992, 140–141). Our character, which is on the side of idem, is changed through the experience of our ipseity. It is not by coincidence that we use phrases like "character building" to describe onerous confrontations or that we might describe powerful works of art as "moving," even when they do not entail dance. Movement here refers to the fluidity of identity, which occurs largely through improvisations. Those moments of change or movement highlight our ability to narrate our lives and to become different people in the stories of our lives. We are characters in our own stories, as well as the stories of others. In this context, Ricoeur reminds us that who we are is always intertwined with the experience of other people.

Thus, the dialectic of identity is matched, in Ricoeur's treatment, with another dialectic, that of self and other. This is raised in relationship with the idea of conscience: we have a sense of conscience because our identity and our character are related to that of others. It is through a conscience (and not just consciousness or self-awareness) that we are indebted to a heritage or that we can attest to keeping our word. Ricoeur notes that "every action has its agents and its patients" ([1990] 1992:155), and thus all actions taken by myself have a potential effect on others, and vice versa. Further, passivity is the "phenomenological respondent to the meta-category of otherness" ([1990] 1992, 318). It is through the experience of passivity that we come to understand others, and this experience is fundamental not only to our identity, in terms of its ipseity, but also in terms of all our actions in the world, which can be said to be improvised as well. Our actions and reactions need to be undertaken in the moment; our history cannot be written in advance.

Thus, the sense of responsibility that Bobby Bradford highlights in the passage I quoted above is about the same imaginative acts needed in negotiating our identity with and even for others. All art allows for this exercise of imagination, but improvisation draws it to the fore and risks its very status as art, at least in relation to Western art music, because of its seeming impermanence. Rather than rushing directly to emphasize the musicians' responsibilities to each other or to the performance as a demonstration of ethics, which would cut off the autonomy of the music and reduce it to a communication of a particular, albeit very important, ethical lesson, understanding improvisation in terms of mimesis allows us to see that submitting to the experience of improvisation involves our productive imagination. The capacity to imagine offers us new understandings of our entire world. Our willingness to challenge our pre-understandings in order to fully participate in the experience of the art provides us with insight into what happens in conversations with other people, which always present us with a risk precisely because to converse genuinely means to transform our narrative identity.

That risk should also remind us of the potential danger involved in manipulating our identities. The fusion of horizons does not exempt aesthetic experiences from ideological distortions, and, given the importance Gadamer places on prejudices, his ideas help explain why propaganda is so effective. Yet, it is precisely the productive imagination that can allow us to wrest back personal interpretive power and imagine the world differently. It allows us to conceive of power not just as power over or against others but as the power of togetherness—the power of caring together. Both senses of power are occluded by only thinking of art as distracting from ideology or by only considering music as reducible to the social. In order for art to be transformative, in order for the experience to have power in terms of our identity, which is always a question of self and other, it needs to have critical distance. Instead of talking about *the* meaning of art, hermeneutics proposes possible meanings and potential interpretations. What new social worlds can be built on these possibilities?

Ethnography and the Transformative Event

That utopian bend toward the possible challenges conventional methods in ethnomusicology and the social sciences in general, particularly ethnography. If participant observation in ethnomusicology entails submitting oneself to the experience of music, the ethnographer should be transformed—not once, but every time a piece is heard. The transformation effected by the experience problematizes the insider/outsider distinction of ethnography (see also Rice 2017, 72–73). Ethnography, musical or otherwise, tends to freeze the dynamics of change and movement that characterize aesthetic experience, as well as the experience of life itself. The anthropologist Timothy Ingold reminds us of the sharp distinction between anthropology and ethnography. He writes, "Anthropology is studying with and learning from; it is carried forward in a process of life, and effects transformations within that process. Ethnography is a study of and learning about, its enduring products are recollective accounts which serve a documentary purpose" (2013, 3). Likewise, the anthropologist Paul Rabinow suggests that ethnography itself stands in the way of anthropology turning its focus toward *Bildung* (2008, 4–5). Ethnomusicology, because of its attention to listening (the hermeneutic making of music) and its inherent coevality, has a potential to inform the kind of anthropology Ingold and Rabinow are suggesting, but to do so it will need to reassess its tendency toward ethnographic documentation, which has its origins in colonial anthropology and the illusion of permanently different ethnographic others.

This means forgoing the idea of absolute knowledge about the meaning of works of music, which may prove difficult for many ethnomusicologists. Consider the following passage from Gadamer in light of common ethnomusicological methods: "So when it comes to art, it is meaningless to ask the artist what he or she meant. Likewise, it is meaningless to ask the perceiver what it is that the work really says to him or her. Both of these matters go far beyond the subjective awareness of one or the other" ([1997] 2007, 212). Following phenomenological hermeneutics, meaning is found neither in the intention of the musician nor the perception of the listener. Gadamer further explains:

> It simply goes beyond all thinking and knowing when we say, "That is good." In both cases this means that "it" has come forth. Thus the experience of the artwork is not only an emergence from hiddenness, but at the same time is something really there in its seclusion. It dwells in the work as if in security. The work of art is an assertion, but it is one that does not form an assertive sentence, although it is telling in the highest degree. . . . The assertion it makes will speak over and over again. ([1997] 2007, 212)

Meanings (which are inexhaustible or even ineffable) rather than meaning (understood as discrete and specific) are revealed to us through the experience of art. They are improvised in the moment of realization and within the horizons of the work and listener. That ineffable experience is foregrounded by its prefiguration, but that prefigured world is constantly in flux as well. Ethnomusicology can then be considered as a form of critique, even more so than anthropology since, presumably, ethnomusicology always engages the ethnographer in the direct experience of the music—an experience that is meaningful and infinite. The work we do as ethnomusicologists is always already a testament to the openness of work to new horizons, which is also to say that it is a testament to the human capacity for openness and understanding.

Paying closer attention to the way in which the experience of art provides testimony not just to being-in-the-world but to being caring and understanding in the world will sharpen ethnomusicology's critical approach. It refocuses on the poetic transposition that characterizes the transformation of decisions occurring in the experience of art and judgments made in the social world. If works give us a world, it is because anyone who experiences art, including ethnomusicologists and their interlocutors, is able to heed the call issued from the work and transpose the world of the work to the practical sphere.

Echoing his thoughts on the connection between theory and practice that I quoted at the start of this chapter, Gadamer notes,

> Understanding, like action, always involves risk and is never just the simple application of a general knowledge of rules to the statements or texts to be understood. Furthermore, where it is successful, understanding means a growth of inner awareness, as a new experience enters into the texture of our own mental experience. Understanding is an adventure and, like any adventure, is dangerous. Because it is not satisfied with simply wanting to register what is there or said there but goes back to our guiding interests and questions, one has to concede that the hermeneutical experience has a far lower degree of certainty than that attained by the methods of the natural sciences. But when one realises that understanding is an adventure, one realises that it affords unique opportunities as well. It is capable of contributing in a special way to the broadening of our human experiences, our self-knowledge and our horizon, for everything that understanding mediates is mediated through ourselves. ([1997] 2007, 245)

Understanding, in the sense Gadamer is referring to here, is always self-understanding. This is just as true of the musicians and listeners who are the subjects of ethnomusicological study as it is of ethnomusicologists themselves who are coming to an understanding of themselves and their place in the world. Such understanding cannot be replaced by explanation, which would always be epistemological.

Relying solely on ethnography, which treats its subject matter as sociologically observed behavior, overlooks the ontological understanding that prefigures any ethnographic experience and without which explanation would be pointless or just incorrect. If, as Timothy Rice has contended, ethnomusicology has failed to contribute to theoretical issues, this is, at least in part, the result of placing observable epistemological phenomenon over and above ontological understanding (2017). This is not to say that all ethnomusicology relies solely on ethnography, but rather that ethnomusicology as a discipline is often caught in a bind between the epistemological, which is observable and thus available for study, and the ontological, which is always at work in the experience of music and art. If we think of theory as disconnected from practice, we lose sight of the importance and necessity of what Ingold calls *making*—the human capacity for creativity (2013). Once the idea of creativity is divorced from Cartesian and Kantian ideas of discrete, self-positing individuals, that idea turns toward identity as an imaginative self-formation in relation to others in and through time, which is to say phenomenologically hermeneutic.

Thinking now of the work of ethnomusicologists, rather than the works they study, hermeneutics suggests that there are always better or more understandings to be accomplished and that this work of understanding, first and foremost, is a self-understanding. Gadamer states,

> Hermeneutic reflection merely uncovers the conditions under which understanding *always already* and in each case operates—as our "pre-understanding." . . . In no way

does this mean, either, that the human sciences and humanities now have to be left behind as "inexact" sciences to vegetate further in their regrettable defectiveness, insofar as they do not rise to the level of [presuppositionless] "science" and do not become a participating part of the wonderful *unity of science*. Rather, philosophical hermeneutics concludes that understanding is only possible when one brings one's own presuppositions into play!

(Gadamer [1997] 2007, 62, italics in original)

Ethnomusicology, through a critical evaluation of its own belonging to the Western tradition of social science and humanities, then has much to offer in that it focuses specifically on the question of the meanings of experience in art, or what Gadamer would term *Sache*.[26] This deepens the terms of what we usually consider the crisis of representation, which is not merely a matter of positioning ourselves within the text but about bringing our presuppositions into play as a productive part of the experience of any meaning. Gadamer continues:

> The productive contribution of the interpreter belongs in an indispensable [*unaufhebbare*] way to the meaning of understanding itself. Certainly philosophical hermeneutics does not legitimize private and arbitrary subjective biases and prejudices. Why? Because for it the sole measure which it allows is the "matter" [*Sache*] being considered at the time, or the text one is seeking to understand. Certainly the ineradicable [*unaufhebbare*] and necessary distance between time periods, cultures, classes, races, or even between persons, constitutes a more than subjective [*übersubjektives*] moment that imparts life and tension to each understanding. ([1997] 2007, 62)

The danger of entirely subjective meaning is particularly high for the study of improvisation because of the inclination to oppose it to the objective nature of composition, which is part of its effective history in the Western world. In revealing those implicit preunderstandings, I have illustrated that the experience of improvisation is about listening and hence reveals aspects of the experience of all music that are easily overlooked. The experience that improvisation heightens, which is an aspect of all music and other art forms as well, provides a model of and for hermeneutic understanding itself. In continuing that line of thought all the way through to where the experience of art would find application (hermeneutically speaking), I have outlined a phenomenological concept of identity that refigures our understanding of this topic. Rather than conceptualizing identity in terms of difference and sameness, we can see it as a play of self and other that is itself more than subjective and is intersubjective in a way that is more than just a multiplying of subjectivities.

What can ethnomusicology learn from improvisation? Resisting the temptation to reduce improvisation to practical and epistemological concerns, improvisation heightens our awareness of the temporality of listening together, which lies at the heart of ethical social action. Even before improvisation occurs in any specific community or in specific types of music, it problematizes Western conceptions of music, of art, and of culture and identity. Ricoeur argues, "In contrast to the tradition of the Cogito and the pretension of the subject to know itself by immediate intuition, it must be said that we understand ourselves only by the long detour of the signs of humanity deposited in cultural works" ([1986] 1991, 87). It is by rethinking the Western concept of identity and how that concept influences the way in which we think about the social, about art, and about the epistemological status of our own work as ethnomusicologists that we can strengthen the humanistic foundations of our discipline.

Notes

1. The philosopher Jean Grondin suggests that Gadamer's concern for truth is an engagement with the philosophical tradition of the metaphysics of being, which for Gadamer is linguistic in its nature (Grondin 2012, 239–240). Rather than taking language as separate from being and merely nominative (a means through which words describe things "out there" in the world), Gadamer thinks of being as fundamentally linguistic, and acknowledging this is the only way to describe being as understandable. This departs from a focus in earlier phenomenology on the ineluctability of interpretation in understanding (Laverty 2003). Gadamer's approach draws on the Heideggerian tradition but diverges from other post-Heideggerian philosophers, such as Jacques Derrida, who follow this same linguistic turn to argue for the impossibility of understanding.
2. Aletheia is a term used in Ancient Greek philosophy meaning "unconcealedness." In *Being and Time* ([1927] 1962), Heidegger revived the term to distinguish this notion of truth from the modern, Western notion of truth as the correspondence between ideas in the mind and things in the world. Gadamer elaborates on this idea throughout *Truth and Method* ([1960] 2004).
3. While ethnomusicology is a specific academic discipline, throughout this chapter I will use the term *ethnomusicology* to refer broadly to any attempt to study the ways in which music and sociocultural life are connected, noting that the scholars pursuing such work may not recognize themselves as belonging to a single, unified discipline. In the conclusion, I will directly address the problems of ethnographic methodology, which is commonly used in the discipline of ethnomusicology specifically, though it certainly is not the only methodology employed there. The aporias raised by the hermeneutics of improvisation suggest a rethinking of what we mean by participation in culture. Ethnomusicology, as a discipline rooted in participant observation, has much to offer other disciplines in light of this rethinking.
4. As a philosophical discipline, hermeneutics has been employed by ethnomusicologists for this purpose in a wide variety of settings (e.g., Conn 2012; Friedson 1996, 2009; Harnish 2001; Rice 1994; Simonett 2001; Titon 1988). Setting the hermeneutic approaches to ethnomusicology in a wider context, I would suggest that, ultimately, interpretation is at work in all forms of understanding; as a result, any ethnomusicological project (in the broad, multidisciplinary sense) involves hermeneutics and offers this potential for change.
5. Much of the critique that follows applies more to what could be termed *naïvely empirical ethnomusicology* than to any contemporary approach in ethnomusicology that seeks to distance itself from its roots in colonial anthropology. Here, I not only seek to criticize those colonial roots but also to invite a reflection on how much our own work relies on

the unexamined presuppositions of finding authenticity in the correlation of the social and music. I also note that this is especially prominent in improvisation studies, because its object of study is always occluded by its performativity. Shifting the object of study to a performance does not resolve the problems of naïve empiricism.

6. It is worth noting here that most contemporary ethnomusicology does not engage with analytic philosophy and certainly does not employ the notion of aesthetic rules in this literal and vulgar way. Here, I discuss the implications of the notion of aesthetic rules in these stark terms in order to illustrate the temptation that Hamilton's ideas would introduce when followed to their logical conclusion and placed in a cross-cultural context. Hamilton himself does not do this, nor is his article concerned with cross- or inter-cultural perspectives; however, by illustrating the implications of his approach, I suggest that the ideas of social Werktreue haunt his analytical account.

7. In their chapters in Gillian Siddall and Ellen Waterman's edited volume *Negotiated Moments* (2016), Andrea McCartney (2016) and Pauline Oliveros (2016) similarly draw attention to the importance of listening. Both chapters focus on the listening done by performers, rather than by audience members, but their important points about the creativity and imaginative resources of listening are apt for all listeners.

8. One might object that there is no use in asking what different types of music have in common, which is not the point Bohlman is trying to make at all (quite the opposite, really). What interests me in Bohlman's article (which does not directly deal with improvisation) is how rethinking musical ontology might help us better understand how the question of ontology is related to self-identity (1999, 34). I contend that without rethinking the ontology that underlies all types of music and all cultural or social groups, such relationships can only be rendered as after the fact, and, as such, the transformative power of music is obscured or mistaken as a social correspondence.

9. This is similar but not identical to the opposition between composition and improvisation posed by Hamilton. Benson uses the mediation of the performance as a model for listening, noting that every act of listening is a performance and thus is better understood as a kind of improvisation.

10. Schutz's relationship to Gadamer and hermeneutics is complicated. Much of Schutz's work was informed by the transcendental phenomenology of Edmund Husserl. Gadamer developed his hermeneutics as a way of overcoming the difficulties of transcendental phenomenology, and in reflections on the intellectual history of phenomenology, he observed that over the course of the twentieth century, Schutz and other followers of Husserl slowly stepped back (perhaps too slowly for Gadamer) from the transcendental approach ([1976] 2008, 163). Michael Staudigl (2014) speculated that had Schutz lived longer, his work might have taken hermeneutics into account. (Schutz died in 1959.) For Gadamer, Schutz's sociological work was particularly tied to the transcendental subject/object distinction, and to my reading, while Schutz's ideas about music are closer to hermeneutics than his purely sociological writings, they fall just short of hermeneutics, particularly in terms of the ideas about "play" that follow.

It is also worth noting that the only published work by Gadamer that is focused on music is the still untranslated 1988 essay "Musik und Zeit," which draws conclusions that are remarkably similar to those of Schutz (Gadamer [1988] 1993). There, Gadamer illustrates the connections between the temporality of music and the lifeworld, which he sees as the subject matter (*Sache*) of all musical experience.

11. This concept is also articulated by the philosopher Vladimir Jankélévitch in *Music and the Ineffable* ([1961] 2003). Discussing written literature, Paul Ricoeur develops a related idea, emphasizing that the author is the first reader of their own work ([1986] 1991, 109). The author's intention in composing the work is not the same thing as its interpretation, in which the reader must participate as a reader. This is uniquely emphasized in the cases of collectively improvised music, where multiple composers may simultaneously have distinctly different opinions about what the piece is about.

12. Gadamer's word choice is curious. He certainly was aware of the musical connotation of *Spiel* in German (as in *Glockenspiel,* for example), but he does not use it in that sense directly or in terms of technical skills we might associate with performing on a musical instrument, but rather in the sense of playing a game. The term *play* (and *Spiel* in this sense) often implies "fun" or "distraction," both of which are aspects of the subjectivization of aesthetics that he thoroughly critiques in the passage that immediately precedes his introduction of this concept. Here, one can't help but wonder if Gadamer knew of the English-language connotation of the word "spiel" as wordy, persuasive speech. I take his word choice as subversive and playful, in the best sense of the word, as it becomes clear that *play* lies at the very center of his conception of truth and nothing could be more serious.

13. In painting, the moment of the work's creation is not when the painter first puts brush to canvas but when the work is first experienced as a whole, presumably by the artist upon its completion. This is a subtle but important distinction, as all too often we assume that the most (or the only correct) interpretation of a work must be a recreation of the artist's interior psychological state. That may be an intersubjectively determined goal of understanding artworks, but if the work is to remain culturally meaningful, this conception can never exhaust the experience of the work. In this context, being "culturally meaningful" refers to the role that the work plays in the exercise of our imagination toward a shared understanding of the symbolically mediated world. That definition salvages the notion of canonical works as well as points out the problems that such work can sometimes entail: if we are not capable of continually reinterpreting ourselves through the experience of works, which may be forced upon us as culturally canonical, they are not working as art at all and instead are ideological tools.

14. Matthew Rahaim traces the ethnomusicological concept of participation back to *methexis* as well, following its treatment through the work of sociologist Emile Durkheim (Rahaim 2019, 220–221). Gadamer's reinterpretation of methexis is radically different than Durkheim's. Gadamer rethinks, and thus critiques, Plato in terms of the ontology at work in participation, while Durkheim construes it in strictly sociological terms as "individuals gathered together," a conception that emphasizes the active aspects of participation and eclipses the passive ones. Gadamer's critique of Plato notes that collectivity presupposes shared understandings (Gadamer [1997] 2007, 310–317).

15. The expanded world that arises from play—the transformed structure—then becomes what is restructured when art is experienced again. This is similar to the hermeneutic circle (in which one interpretation begets another). This circle can be thought of as more of a spiral in this case in that what was true in a prior experience is not negated by transformation. That would assume that truth is a constant, objective state or quality with no temporality. Gadamer is suggesting that this kind of truth is always in the process of being experienced or discovered.

16. Coined by guitarist Derek Bailey, the term "nonidiomatic improvisation" is often employed by musicians engaged in wholly improvised musical practices ([1980] 1993). The

term is useful in that it signals that the improvisers seek to find their own rules and sounds, often in the overlap of aesthetic preferences and ideas among the performers, and this is in opposition to music created by improvisers who employ schema specific to an individual genre, such as figured bass or chord changes. The term has been critiqued on the grounds that "nonidiomatic" is itself an idiom, with its own shared tastes and traditions (Borgo 2005, 13–35).

17. The term *transcendence within immanence* is most associated with Husserl (explicated in [1913] 2012, 78–80 and 111–115) and is a concept that inspired and was adapted by Heidegger in *Dasein* ([1927] 1962), which I discuss below. It is from this (Heideggerian) sense that Gadamer, who does not directly use the phrase, employs it in *Truth and Method* ([1960] 2004). Ricoeur further picks up and synthesizes the idea ([1985] 1988, 157–179). Though each philosopher follows this theme in a different way, they all share in a desire to rethink the notions of transcendence and immanence used by Kant. Dermot Moran examines the relationship between Dasein and Husserl (Moran 2014) and Davey discusses the notions of transcendence and transformation in Gadamer in relationship to Heidegger (Davey 2013, 76–80).

18. In a book chapter on semiotic approaches to musical meaning, Jayson Beaster-Jones has cited Katherine Meizel in suggesting that language is a universal music (2019, 45). In this context, it is worth noting that scholars in hermeneutics have offered critiques of semiotic approaches to meaning. Drawing on Gadamer, for example, Ricoeur has suggested that the conception of semiotics found in linguistics rests on the unacknowledged presupposition of a shared world of lived experience ([1975] 1977). See also my discussion of the way in which Gadamer describes the recognition of a symbol in art in the next section of this chapter.

19. This is very similar to Schutz's concept of inner time, though Schutz, particularly in his sociologically oriented work, grounds this in Erlebnis, thus putting less of an emphasis on transformation, transcendence, and the ability (or responsibility) of the subjects of the experience (Schutz [1957] 1975). See also Savage (2018, 29–30). For Gadamer, Erlebnis would remain only an interior psychological state, while Erfahrung was always between and among people discursively.

20. This theme is somewhat underexamined by Gadamer (see Davey 2013, 97–98; Arthos 2000). Gadamer de-emphasizes Erlebnis, or lived experience, without which it seems that there would be very little way to distance oneself from ideological distortions inherited from tradition. Ricoeur is very helpful in sorting out how lived experience and anthropological life are inter-related in terms of a threefold mimesis, which I discuss below.

21. Of course, music can be made into narrative: for example, characters can be inscribed onto the experience of musical sound, but this would be second order to the experience itself.

22. *Phronesis* is an ancient Greek word for wisdom. For Aristotle, it was the virtue of good judgment used in difficult ethical situations. It is this sense of the term examined by Gadamer to distinguish prudential wisdom from *technê*, or technical knowledge ([1960] 2004, 18–20, 311–319, 535–559).

23. *Bildung* literally means "education" or "formation." Gadamer recovers the term via a critique of German romanticism's embrace of Bildung as a kind of aestheticism in which self-cultivation was bound with subjective feelings (1960 [2004], 8–36).

24. Here I am implying that the choices made by improvisers are not best understood as random options or the result of strictly technical knowledge alone (regardless of the musicians' actual intentions), but rather that each choice contributes to the work as a

meaningful whole. As such they present a model for ethical decision-making, which also requires, according to both Aristotle and Gadamer, phronesis.

25. Rice argues that while ethnomusicologists frequently use the term "identity," the discipline lacks any unified concept of it (2017, 139–159). What I am suggesting here, via Ricoeur, is not meant to be taken as any such unified theory, which would be to read what I am proposing epistemologically. Rather, I am suggesting that phenomenological reflection on identity draws us toward very different questions about how imagination and creativity figure in self-understanding (as opposed to how they operate in epistemological identification). All of the uses of identity that Rice notes can be characterized as fitting within the schema that Ricoeur sees as having been instituted by Descartes—either self-transparent identity or radically "constructed identities" (i.e., ones created by social forces). There are very good reasons to assume that identity is always both self-constituted (though we are probably never entirely self-aware about this process) and socially constructed (though we are never without some ability for self-reflection, regardless of the culture through which this ontology is manifested). Based on this, I argue that neither ethnomusicology nor any social science should have a single, unified, epistemological concept of identity; rather, scholars should attend to the ways in which the ontology of identity is manifested through the specific culture in question. Or to put that in less philosophical terms, I agree with Rice's identification of the problem of identity in the discipline, but I don't think the solution to that problem will be found in any singular concept of identity.

26. While Gadamer, particularly in *Truth and Method*, is distrustful of any methodological explanation, Ricoeur makes a strong case that explanation may play an important role in the service of understanding (Ricoeur [1986] 1991, 142–143). For Ricoeur, explanation can never really be separated from understanding in that the former contributes to the later.

WORKS CITED

Arendt, Hannah. (1954) 2006. *Between Past and Future: Eight Exercises in Political Thought*. New York: Penguin Books.

Arthos, John. 2000. "'To Be Alive When Something Happens': Retrieving Dilthey's Erlebnis." *Janus Head* 3 (1). http://janushead.org/wp-content/uploads/2020/07/John-Arthos.pdf.

Attali, Jacques. (1977) 1989. *Noise: The Political Economy of Music*. Translated by Brian Massumi. Minneapolis: University of Minnesota Press.

Bailey, Derek. (1980) 1993. *Improvisation: Its Nature and Practice in Music*. New York: Da Capo Press.

Beaster-Jones, Jayson. 2019. "Linguistic and Semiotic Approaches to Ethnomusicology." In *Theory for Ethnomusicology: Histories, Conversations, Insights*, 2nd ed., edited by Harris M. Berger and Ruth M. Stone, 26–50. New York: Routledge.

Benson, Bruce Ellis. 2003 *The Improvisation of Musical Dialogue*. Cambridge: Cambridge University Press.

Bohlman, Philip. 1999. "Ontologies of Music." In *Rethinking Music*, edited by Nicholas Cook and Mark Everist, 17–34. Oxford: Oxford University Press.

Borgo, David. 2005. *Sync or Swarm: Improvising Music in a Complex Age*. New York: Continuum.

Born, Georgina, Eric Lewis, and Will Straw 2017. "Introduction: What Is Social Aesthetics?" In *Improvisation and Social Aesthetics*, edited by Georgina Born, Eric Lewis, and Will Straw, 1–31. Durham, NC: Duke University Press.

Bourdieu, Pierre. (1979) 1987. *Distinction: A Social Critique of the Judgement of Taste*. Translated by Richard Nice. Cambridge, MA: Harvard University Press.

Chapman, Dale. 2018. *The Jazz Bubble: Neoclassical Jazz in Neoliberal Culture*. Oakland: University of California Press.

Conn, Stephanie. 2012. "Fitting between Present and Past: Memory and Social Interaction in Cape Breton Gaelic Singing." *Ethnomusicology Forum* 21 (3): 354–373.

Custer, Paul Anthony. 2019. "Speaking, Vehemence, and the Desire-to-Be: Ricoeur's Erotics of Being." *Philosophy & Rhetoric* 52 (3): 232–346.

Davey, Nicholas. 2013. *Unfinished Worlds: Hermeneutics, Aesthetics and Gadamer*. Edinburgh: Edinburgh University Press.

Friedson, Steven M. 1996. *Dancing Prophets: Musical Experience in Tumbuka Healing*. Chicago: University of Chicago Press.

Friedson, Steven M. 2009. *Remains of Ritual: Northern Gods in a Southern Land*. Chicago: University of Chicago Press.

Gadamer, Hans-Georg. (1960) 2004. *Truth and Method*. Translated by Joel Weinsheimer and Donald G. Marshall. London: Continuum.

Gadamer, Hans-Georg. (1967) 1986. "The Festive Character of Theater." In *The Relevance of the Beautiful and Other Essays*, translated by Nicholas Walker, edited by Robert Bernasconi, 57–65. Cambridge: Cambridge University Press.

Gadamer, Hans-Georg. (1976) 2008. *Philosophical Hermeneutics*. Translated by David E. Linge. Berkeley: University of California Press.

Gadamer, Hans-Georg. (1977) 1986. "The Relevance of the Beautiful." In *The Relevance of the Beautiful and Other Essays*, translated by Nicholas Walker, edited by Robert Bernasconi, 1–53. Cambridge: Cambridge University Press.

Gadamer, Hans-Georg. (1983) 1998. *Praise of Theory: Speeches and Essays*. Translated by Chris Dawson. New Haven, CT: Yale University Press.

Gadamer, Hans-Georg. (1988) 1993. "Musik und Zeit." In *Gesammelte Werke*, vol. 8, *Ästhetik und Poetik I—Kunst als Aussage*, 362–365. Tübingen, Germany: J. C. B. Mohr.

Gadamer, Hans-Georg. (1997) 2007. *The Gadamer Reader: A Bouquet of the Later Writings*. Edited and translated by Richard E. Palmer. Evanston, IL: Northwestern University Press.

Goehr, Lydia. 1992. *The Imaginary Museum of Musical Works: An Essay in the Philosophy of Music*. Oxford, UK: Clarendon Press.

Grondin, Jean. (1999) 2003. *The Philosophy of Gadamer*. Translated by Kathryn Plant. Montreal: McGill-Queen's University Press.

Grondin, Jean. 2012. *Introduction to Metaphysics: From Parmenides to Levinas*. New York: Columbia University Press.

Hamilton, Andy. 1990. "The Aesthetics of Imperfection." *Philosophy* 65 (253): 323–340.

Hamilton, Andy. 2000. "The Art of Improvisation and the Aesthetics of Imperfection." *British Journal of Aesthetics* 40 (1): 168–185.

Hanslick, Eduard. (1854) 1986. *On the Musically Beautiful: A Contribution towards the Revision of the Aesthetics of Music*. Translated by Geoffrey Payzant. Indianapolis, IN: Hackett.

Harnish, David. 2001. "A Hermeneutical Arc in the Life of Balinese Musician, I Made Lebah." *The World of Music* 43 (1): 21–41.

Heidegger, Martin. (1927) 1962. *Being and Time*. Translated by John Macquarrie and Edward Robinson. Oxford, UK: Basil Blackwell.

Hirsch, E. D., Jr. 1967. *Validity in Interpretation*. New Haven and London: Yale University Press.

Husserl, Edmund. (1913) 2012. *Ideas: General Introduction to Pure Phenomenology*. Translated by W. R. Boyce Gibson. New York: Routledge.

Ingold, Timothy. 2013. *Making: Anthropology, Archaeology, Art and Architecture*. New York: Routledge.

Jankélévitch, Vladimir. (1961) 2003. *Music and the Ineffable*. Translated by Carolyn Abbate. Princeton, NJ: Princeton University Press.

Kant, Immanuel. (1790) 2000. *Critique of the Power of Judgment (The Cambridge Edition of the Works of Immanuel Kant)*. Edited by Paul Guyer. Translated by Paul Guyer and Eric Matthews. Cambridge: Cambridge University Press.

Kivy, Peter. 2009. *Antithetical Arts: On the Ancient Quarrel between Literature and Music*. Oxford: Oxford University Press.

Laver, Mark. 2015. *Jazz Sells: Music, Marketing, and Meaning*. New York: Routledge.

Laverty, Susann M. 2003. "Hermeneutic Phenomenology and Phenomenology: A Comparison of Historical and Methodological Considerations." *International Journal of Qualitative Methods* 2 (3): 21–35.

Lewis, George E. (1996) 2004. "Improvised Music after 1950: Afrological and Eurological Perspectives." In *The Other Side of Nowhere: Jazz, Improvisation, and Communities in Dialogue*, edited by Daniel Fischlin and Ajay Heble, 131–162. Middletown, CT: Wesleyan University Press.

Lewis, George, and Benjamin Piekut, eds. 2016. *The Oxford Handbook of Critical Improvisation Studies*. New York: Oxford University Press.

Marsh, James. 2008. "Ricoeur's Phenomenology of Freedom as an Answer to Sartre." In *Reading Ricoeur*, edited by David M. Kaplan, 13–29. Albany: State University of New York Press.

McCartney, Andra. 2016. "'How Am I to Listen to You?' Soundwalking, Intimacy, and Improvised Listening." In *Negotiated Moments: Improvisation, Sound, and Subjectivity*, edited by Gillian Siddall and Ellen Waterman, 37–54. Durham, NC: Duke University Press.

Moore, Robin. 1992. "The Decline of Improvisation in Western Art Music: An Interpretation of Change." *International Review of the Aesthetics and Sociology of Music* 23 (1): 61–84.

Moran, Dermot. 2014. "What Does Heidegger Mean by the Transcendence of Dasein?" *International Journal of Philosophical Studies* 22(4): 491–514.

Nettl, Bruno. 1974. "Thoughts on Improvisation: A Comparative Approach." *The Musical Quarterly* 60 (1): 1–19.

Nettl, Bruno. 1998. "Introduction: An Art Neglected in Scholarship." In *In the Course of Performance: Studies in the World of Musical Improvisation*, edited by Bruno Nettl and Melinda Russell, 1–24. Chicago: University of Chicago Press.

Nielsen, Cynthia R. 2016. "Gadamer on the Event of Art, the Other, and a Gesture toward a Gadamarian Approach to Free Jazz." *Journal of Applied Hermeneutics*, Article 6. https://doi.org/10.11575/jah.v0i0.53277.

Oliveros, Pauline. 2016. "Improvising Composition: How to Listen in the Time Between." In *Negotiated Moments: Improvisation, Sound, and Subjectivity*, edited by Gillian Siddall and Ellen Waterman, 75–90. Durham, NC: Duke University Press.

Rabinow, Paul. 2008. *Marking Time: On the Anthropology of the Contemporary*. Princeton, NJ: Princeton University Press.

Rahaim, Matthew. 2019. "Theories of Participation." In *Theory for Ethnomusicology: Histories, Conversations, Insights*, 2nd ed., edited by Harris M. Berger and Ruth M. Stone, 219–232. New York: Routledge.

Rice, Timothy. 1994. *May It Fill Your Soul: Experiencing Bulgarian Music*. Chicago: University of Chicago Press.

Rice, Timothy. (1996) 2017. "Toward a Mediation of Field Methods and Field Experience in Ethnomusicology." In *Modeling Ethnomusicology*, 63–85. Oxford: Oxford University Press.

Rice, Timothy. (2001) 2017. "Reflections on Music and Meaning: Metaphor, Signification, and Control in the Bulgarian Case." In *Modeling Ethnomusicology*, 87–108. Oxford: Oxford University Press.

Rice, Timothy. (2010) 2017. "Ethnomusicological Theory." In *Modeling Ethnomusicology*, 161–199. Oxford: Oxford University Press.

Rice, Timothy. 2017. *Modeling Ethnomusicology*. Oxford: Oxford University Press.

Ricoeur, Paul. (1950) 1966. *Freedom and Nature: The Voluntary and the Involuntary*. Translated by Erazim Kohak. Evanston, IL: Northwestern University Press.

Ricoeur, Paul. (1975) 1977. *The Rule of Metaphor: The Creation of Meaning in Language*. Translated by Robert Czerny with Kathleen McLaughlin and John Costello, SJ. London and New York: Routledge.

Ricoeur, Paul. (1983) 1984. *Time and Narrative*. Vol. 1. Translated by Kathleen McLaughlin and David Pellauer. Chicago: University of Chicago Press.

Ricoeur, Paul. (1985) 1988. *Time and Narrative*. Vol. 3. Translated by Kathleen McLaughlin and David Pellauer. Chicago: University of Chicago Press.

Ricoeur, Paul. (1986) 1991. *From Text to Action: Essays in Hermeneutics, II*. Translated by Kathleen Blamey and John B. Thompson. Evanston, IL: Northwestern University Press.

Ricoeur, Paul. (1990) 1992. *Oneself as Another*. Translated by Kathleen Blamey. Chicago: University of Chicago Press.

Ricoeur, Paul. (1995) 1998. *Critique and Conviction: Conversations with François Azouvi and Marc de Launay*. Translated by Kathleen Blamey. New York: Columbia University Press.

Ricoeur, Paul. (1995) 2000. *The Just*. Translated by David Pellauer. Chicago: University of Chicago Press.

Ricoeur, Paul. (2004) 2005. *The Course of Recognition*. Translated by David Pellauer. Cambridge, MA: Harvard University Press.

Rorty, Richard. 1979. *Philosophy and the Mirror of Nature*. Princeton, NJ: Princeton University Press.

Sancho-Velasquez, Angeles. 2001. "The Legacy of Genius: Improvisation, Romantic Imagination, and the Western Musical Canon." PhD diss., University of California, Los Angeles.

Savage, Roger W. H. 2004. "Social Werktreue and the Musical Work's Independent Afterlife." *The European Legacy: Toward New Paradigms* 9 (4): 515–524.

Savage, Roger W. H. 2010. *Hermeneutics and Music Criticism*. New York: Routledge.

Savage, Roger W. H. 2018. *Music, Time, and Its Other: Aesthetic Reflections on Finitude, Temporality, and Alterity*. London: Routledge.

Schutz, Alfred. 1951. "Making Music Together: A Study in Social Relationship." *Social Research* 18 (1): 76–97.

Schutz, Alfred. (1957) 1975. "The Problem of Transcendental Intersubjectivity in Husserl." In *Collected Papers III: Studies in Phenomenological Philosophy*, edited by Ilse Schutz, translated by Frederick Kersten, Aron Gurwitsch, and Thomas Luckmann, 51–83. The Hague: Martinus Nijhoff.

Sharp, Charles. 2008. "Improvisation, Identity and Tradition: Experimental Music Communities in Los Angeles." PhD diss., University of California, Los Angeles.

Siddall, Gillian, and Ellen Waterman, eds. 2016. *Negotiated Moments: Improvisation, Sound, and Subjectivity*. Durham, NC: Duke University Press.

Simonett, Helena. 2001. *Banda: Mexican Musical Life across Borders*. Music/Culture Book Series. Middletown, CT: Wesleyan University Press.

Small, Christopher. 1998. *Musicking: The Meanings of Performing and Listening*. Middletown, CT: Wesleyan University Press

Staudigl, Michael. 2014. "Reflections on the Relationship of 'Social Phenomenology' and Hermeneutics in Alfred Schutz: An Introduction." In *Schutzian Phenomenology and Hermeneutic Traditions*, edited by Michael Staudigl and George Berguno, 1–8. New York: Springer.

Titon, Jeff Todd. 1988. *Powerhouse for God: Speech, Chant, and Song in an Appalachian Baptist Church*. Austin: University of Texas Press.

Vessey, David. 2009. "Gadamer and the Fusion of Horizons." *International Journal of Philosophical Studies* 17 (4): 525–536.

Waterman, Ellen. 2008. "Naked Intimacy: Eroticism, Improvisation, and Gender." *Critical Studies in Improvisation/Études critiques en improvisation* 4 (2). http://www.criticalimprov.com/article/view/845/.

Westphal, Merold. 1999. "Hermeneutics as Epistemology." In *The Blackwell Guide to Epistemology*, edited by John Greco and Ernest Sosa, 415–435. Malden, MA: Blackwell.

SECTION 4

INTERCORPOREALITY, PERCEPTION, AND MOVEMENT

CHAPTER 10

···

VIRTUOSITY, OBVIOUSLY

Ravi Shankar, Historical Phenomenology, and the Valuation of Skill

···

DAVID VANDERHAMM

INTRODUCTION

···

In his coauthored 1964 booklet *Music Memory*, Pandit Ravi Shankar poses a simple question: "why is virtuosity or speed so admired by the lay listener?" Already equating virtuosity with speed and assuming its easy appeal, the internationally renowned sitarist goes on to explain that "the general public has not received an extensive education in Hindustani Classical Music and therefore cannot be expected to immediately understand all the nuances of the Classical performance." Until they could gain such expertise, "virtuosity or speed is something that can be appreciated by anyone" (Shankar and Estabrook 1964, 26–27). Shankar was probably thinking of novice listeners in India (based on the location of the book's printing and distribution), but it seems that the sentiment extended to his audiences elsewhere in the world. Organizers of Shankar's North American college tour of the same year certainly hoped that the book might "serve in the States too" (Estabrook 1964), and later commentators would affirm the intercultural intelligibility of virtuosity. David Reck (1985, 94), for example, argues that "the brilliant display of the fireworks of virtuosity," if not truly universal, is at least "a characteristic shared and highly valued in both [Western and Indian] musical cultures." Shankar's celebratory reception by Western audiences—with reviewers marveling at his "demonic virtuosity that virtually toppled the senses"—would seem to further confirm such widespread beliefs about virtuosity and its obviousness to all involved (Harrison 1956).

The supposed accessibility of virtuosity, especially across cultural lines, was not universally acknowledged or celebrated, however. In the wake of the "sitar explosion" of 1966–67 (Shankar 1968, 100), British organologist Jeremy Montagu (1968, 103) denied there was any real significance in the entire Western reception of Shankar: "what the untutored Indian thinks of Bach and the untutored Westerner of Ravi Shankar does not really mean anything." Although Montagu is not writing specifically about virtuosity (and setting aside his dismissive language), his basic assertion is quite relevant: cultural insiders are the ones with the requisite knowledge and perceptual awareness to appreciate and interpret the products of expressive culture. Put in these milder terms, Montagu's sentiment comes closer to an ethnomusicological and anthropological mainstream, which holds, as Clifford Geertz (1976, 1497) puts it, that "art and the equipment to grasp it are made in the same shop." At its best, this attitude serves to resist the appropriation or erasure of non-hegemonic systems of value, yet the fact that the "untutored Westerner" experiences music and virtuosity through their own cultural lens does not make it meaningless. It is precisely the "culturally specific ways in which people grapple with texts and cog them into structures of lived experience" that make those experiences meaningful, even if the recognition of skill by the untutored Westerner rests on a partial or incorrect understanding of the music and skill involved (Berger 2009, xiv).[1]

This chapter employs a phenomenological framework to argue that virtuosity is located—and lived—not in the isolated body of the performer nor the private judgments of the listener but in the intercorporeal social space of experience. Rather than mere speed or spectacle, virtuosity emerges as an intersubjective phenomenon that centers on skill made apparent and socially meaningful (VanderHamm 2020, 282). Within virtuosity, skill, understood as "capabilities of action and perception of the whole organic being (indissolubly mind and body) situated in a richly structured environment," comes to the foreground of perception as a locus of value (Ingold 2000, 5). Speed may draw attention to skill, and it may at times be the primary skill that audiences perceive, but it is not necessarily simple. Even when the "microperceptual focus" of direct sensory perception is on speed and dexterity, the "macroperceptual" experience of interpretation and valuation is always cultural, embodied, and therefore complex (Ihde 1990, 29).[2]

Especially in intercultural situations, phenomena like virtuosity present dangerous interpretive ground for ethnomusicologists. Scholars may easily fall into one of two opposing errors mentioned above, either affirming virtuosity as (nearly) universal or treating it as something so radically specific to a given culture that it cannot be understood by any outsider. The danger of the first error is that it can preclude fine-grained analysis of the musical and social phenomena we encounter; glossing virtuosity as speed and spectacle rarely offers much insight, even when these qualities seem to acceptably summarize a particular culture's approach to the display of musical skill. The danger of the second error is that it effectively negates the experience of all but the most knowledgeable of cultural insiders; what begins as a defense of cultural specificity readily becomes an elitist refusal of any non-expert interpretation. The historical-phenomenological approach I develop here proposes a middle way, attempting to "universalize our particulars" and "particularize our universals" (Wallerstein 2006, 49). That is, it takes the supposedly universal appeal of "charm and speed" (Howard 2008) as a particular fact of only some examples of virtuosity while taking the embodied sociality between particular performers and audience members as a universal (if also highly variant) structure of the phenomenon (Pincherle 1963, 10).

This chapter begins by elaborating two key ways that phenomenology clarifies the phenomenon of virtuosity before turning to the methodological problems and opportunities raised by phenomenology's application within historical contexts. I then elaborate the role of apperception and embodied intersubjectivity in encountering the skilled body of the performer and the importance of multiple forms of sociality within performance. I conclude by considering how intersubjectivity undergirds both evaluations of virtuosity that reflect back on the experience and prejudgments that make a particular interpretation of virtuosity possible. Pursuing these arguments in the context of Shankar's Western reception brings into focus an issue that seems to haunt virtuosity any time it escapes the social confines of the guild of experts and practitioners: how do we interpret people's claims to value what they don't seem to be capable of understanding or even fully experiencing? This chapter demonstrates that the intersubjectivity at the core of virtuosity is often partial, asymmetrical, or even flawed; however, rather than imperiling the experience or throwing its legitimacy into question, the persistence of some form of otherness within the encounter is a central structure and primary source of its value.

VIRTUOSITY AS SPECTACULAR AND MUNDANE

The tension between celebrations of virtuosity's widespread appeal and suspicions of it as shallow or even meaningless is hardly unique to Shankar's reception or to intercultural encounters more generally. It has long characterized discussions of virtuosity in European art music, where attempts to define "the imagined distinctions between transcendent and superficial virtuosity" became a standard feature of public musical discourse throughout Europe during the nineteenth century (Stefaniak 2016, 2–3). This conflict continued into the twentieth century, as critics noted with dismay how listeners' severe lack of musical knowledge did not stop them from following "their natural bent" in "worshipping" virtuoso violinists (Baughan 1902, 223). By mid-century, Marc Pincherle (1963, 15) declared that the concert culture of Western classical music was the site of a "quasi-permanent quarrel" about virtuosity. Writers, critics, and composers looked upon virtuosic display as a "debasement of taste," while the public "strongly favored" it (Pincherle 1963, 15). Thus, virtuosity may be associated with the exceptional and the spectacular, but disagreements about its value have long been quite mundane.

A phenomenological approach provides two key interventions that address this apparent impasse. First, phenomenology begins by instituting the epoché, a set of "brackets" by which we suspend our assumptions about the phenomenon, including our belief in the reality of the phenomenon and of the world in which it takes place.[3] We neither doubt nor presume the truth of these elements; we put them out of play, charting a middle way between the contrasting approaches of naïve empiricism and skeptical

idealism. If such broad intellectual contrasts between empiricism and idealism seem esoteric, disagreements about virtuosity's relative merits provide a very concrete example
of this philosophical conflict. One side (empiricism) declares that we must simply open
our eyes or ears to the amazing feats of skill before us, and the other (idealism) questions
skeptically whether the virtuosity we perceive is "real" or "false" (Kerman 1999, 63). Both
presume to know what the phenomenon is (or ought to be) and thus fail to ask fundamental questions about our experience of it.

Second, phenomenology posits the relationality of experience as its object of study.
As Maurice Merleau-Ponty demonstrates in the introduction to *Phenomenology of
Perception*, despite the differences between the seemingly opposed sides of empiricism and idealism, both spring from the assumptions of the natural attitude.[4] For although one searches for "absolute objectivity" and the other for "absolute subjectivity,"
both deal in separate, presumed "truths" rather than the actual contents of experience as
encountered by the embodied subject (Merleau-Ponty [1945] 2012, 41). Phenomenology,
by contrast, is "no more committed to subjectivity than to objectivity" (Young 2011, 56).
Neither side receives methodological preference; it is "the relationship that is primary"
(Welton 2000, 32). This relationship between subjects and the objects of their experience (including other subjects)—what the tradition refers to as "intentionality"—is
phenomenology's irreducible unit of study (Ihde 1990, 23).

This emphasis on the relation is in direct contrast to both celebrations and critiques
of virtuosity, which tend to focus on one side or the other of the phenomenon. Whether
celebrated for its power or derided as an easy trick, both sides locate virtuosity in the
more or less isolated entities of the performer's body or the musical performance itself,
and it is there that it is either easily recognized or unwittingly misinterpreted by the outside perceiver. We can observe this tendency to focus attention on either the objective
or subjective aspects of phenomena in an exchange about Indian music's accessibility to
novices at a 1964 conference in New Delhi. In the opening panel, Indian minister of fi-
nance T. T. Krishmanachari argued that Indian music was extremely challenging:

> It is not an easy thing to appreciate Indian music. If I can move from the sublime to
> the ridiculous I would say it is something like the taste a man acquires for certain
> types of liquor. I do not think that an average man who is not accustomed to whisky
> would like it. You cannot appreciate Indian music easily, more so South Indian music.
> I have often found my friends in North India wondering what it is that makes us sit
> for four hours listening to the performance of a South Indian musician of which they
> could make little sense.
>
> (Krishmanachari 1966, 4)

At the end of the same conference, the art historian Charles Fabri concluded that the one
point on which he disagreed with other attendees was that of difficulty:

> I never had the slightest difficulty in enjoying Indian music, not even on the first
> hearing. From the first moment I came here, I felt that this was my heritage. The

whole world is my heritage. *homo sum: humani nil a me alienum puto* [I am human, nothing human is alien to me]. Shakespeare is my heritage, Tolstoy is my heritage, Kalidas [a famous Sanskrit poet] is my heritage.

(Fabri 1966, 206)

Krishmanachari's whiskey analogy favors the object-pole of experience. If we could ask him to expand on his comments, he would likely focus on the object's qualities. He might explain that whiskey is strong and complex, its prominent flavors potentially overwhelming and its subtler aspects easy to miss. Fabri, on the other hand, is even more singularly focused on the subject-pole of experience. Indeed, in declaring his easy enjoyment of Indian music, he makes no comments whatsoever about that music, offering instead a string of statements about himself and his own cosmopolitan worldview. The opposing pole of the experience is certainly implied by both authors, but this is precisely the problem. Leaving one side implicit makes thematizing the relationship between them nearly impossible.

By bracketing the question of the truth or falseness of an experience—thereby walking a middle ground between skeptical doubt and naïve acceptance, all the while attending to the irreducible relationship between objects and subjects within experience—phenomenology brings the phenomenon into a field of inquiry. This restores the scholar's sense of "wonder" at the phenomenon, looking anew at the mundane conflicts over the spectacular (Merleau-Ponty [1945] 2012, lxxvii, 494n30; Fink 1970, 109). What is it we find within these brackets? At the outset of this chapter, I offered a definition of virtuosity as skill made apparent and socially meaningful. This definition is phenomenological in that it is derived from the process of reflecting on virtuosity within the brackets. But it is also phenomenological in the sense that its primary value is only apparent in the context of further phenomenological inquiry. For, taken on its own, the definition is remarkably (and intentionally) thin. Instead of enclosing cultural phenomena within a neat terminological box, it necessitates inquiry into the meanings of musical skill. This thinness precludes virtuosity from serving as a distorting category that allows us to interpret practices through its preordained criteria. For rather than answering key questions about virtuosity, it poses them anew: What counts as skill, and to whom? What practices of presentation, promotion, and perception bring it to the foreground? And as in the phenomenon itself, the agency at play within this definition evades clear-cut attribution. Who or what is making this skill apparent?

Two relatively simple observations can begin to answer these questions. First, virtuosity is a social phenomenon. This has been widely acknowledged in studies of virtuosity in the nineteenth century, as captured by Jankélévitch's (1979, 34) aphoristic declaration: "there are no unrecognized virtuosi." However, Jankélévitch's statement focuses on the virtuoso figure as a social identity, which does not directly challenge the tendency to think of virtuosity as a particular type or degree of skill that the virtuoso possesses and then publicly displays. My claim is slightly different: the social context—including practices of performance, mediation, and reception—is constitutive of the phenomenon, not a new setting in which an already existing phenomenon takes on additional meanings. In this account, listeners become a contributing, *structural feature* of the phenomenon rather than a secondary, complicating factor.

Second, virtuosity is characterized by an attention to musical process. Within the phenomenon of virtuosity, we may approach music as aesthetic object or as social practice, but we also attend to it as an action—as music *making*. Virtuosity thus occurs when the skilled labor involved in producing music comes to the foreground of experience. I mean labor here and throughout this chapter in the broad Marxist sense as productive action, but Hannah Arendt's ([1958] 1998) tripartite division of (and critical response to) this Marxist meaning can shed further light on the phenomenon. Arendt divides human activity into three spheres (labor, work, and action), which progress from the simplest and most private to the most complex and public. Labor relates to the "biological process of the human body" and the necessary maintenance of human life, whereas work involves the production of external objects through skill, thereby bestowing "a measure of permanence and durability upon the futility of mortal life and the fleeting character of human time" (Arendt [1958] 1998, 7–8). Action, the final sphere, refers to the conduct of a distinct individual that is still irreducibly social—"entirely dependent upon the constant presence of others" (Arendt [1958] 1998, 23). Action is the least clearly defined of these terms, although philosopher Anthony Skillen (1993, 345) suggests we think of action as "deeds," those "publicly esteemed actions of individuals living in or stepping into the 'arena' or 'stage' of decisions, enterprises, [or] struggles."

Musical labor could fall anywhere within this tripartite division, depending on its social role and the cultural attitudes toward it. It may be regarded as Arendtian labor, as when a parent sings a lullaby to a child to facilitate the biological necessity of sleep. The same parent might also engage in Arendtian work by recording lullabies or writing new songs that are culturally defined as more or less stable "compositions." Finally, virtuosity—the public display and valuation of skill—provides one case in which musical labor (in the broad, Marxist sense) can become action (in the Arendtian sense). Applying Arendt's formulation to musical activity demonstrates that the skill listeners attend to as virtuosic does not necessarily need to be better or more spectacular than other forms of skill. The musician in my imagined examples might even be the same person exercising the same skills, singing a jazz ballad to lull a child to sleep before leaving to impress attendees at a club with the very same song. The singer is unlikely to utilize the same exact musical strategies in these two very different settings and more likely to attempt to draw attention to their skill at the jazz club than by their child's bedside, but strategies that help initiate the phenomenon by drawing attention to skill should not be confused with the phenomenon itself. Virtuosity is skill that comes to matter to those that perceive it, skill thematized as an object of value rather than as the necessary and ubiquitous condition for music making.

A HISTORICAL PHENOMENOLOGY?

Before turning to the intersubjective structures of virtuosity, I must first address a simple question that opens onto more complex methodological concerns: if embodied sociality is central to virtuosity, why, one might ask, have I chosen to demonstrate these arguments through a historical case study in which corporeal co-presence is impossible? The first reason for doing so is relatively straightforward and has already been discussed above: the tendency to gloss virtuosity as mere speed or spectacle—as demonstrated in Shankar's opening quote—is a longstanding historical trend, and a historical example makes it easier to situate the specific case within that trend. Shankar's example is useful partially because it provides a broader historical view of his reception than strict ethnography might allow. Zooming out to examine Shankar's reception demonstrates that virtuosity was not always apparent or accessible to his Western audiences; early reviewers regularly found themselves perplexed rather than amazed (e.g., Shankar 1965). The second reason for applying phenomenology within a historical context is that the apparent frictions between methodology and study object provide an opportunity for elaborating central issues of presence and the role of language in phenomenological ethnomusicology and music studies more generally.

Phenomenology is no stranger to history, as classical and contemporary works by scholars such as Edmund Husserl ([1936] 1970), Hans-Georg Gadamer ([1960] 2013), Paul Ricoeur ([2000] 2004), and David Carr (2014) have all reflected extensively on the topic. Phenomenologists, however, are most often interested in historicity—what it means for human beings to *have* or *live* a history—rather than historical methods of inquiry. As Ricoeur (1976, 683) puts it, the primary implication of this philosophical work for historical scholarship lies in its demonstration of "the dependence of historical inquiry on the historical condition that characterizes human existence." We are able to undertake historical studies because we are historical beings. There has been "no radical moment of severance, in which a 'past' has given way overnight to an utterly separate 'present,'" and it is this degree of connection between past and present that underlies historical work (Thomas 1996, 61).

Despite phenomenology's own reflections on history and its application in fields like oral history (Kirby 2008), literature (Smith 2010), and archaeology (Thomas 1996), the tradition is still widely understood as essentially *presentist*. Indeed, Ihde's *Listening and Voice* ([1976] 2007, 25)—which provides an appealing entrée into phenomenology for scholars of music and sound—characterizes Husserlian "first phenomenology" precisely as a "philosophy of presence." If an understanding of phenomenology that revolves around *being (bodily) present* leads researchers to also prioritize the *present*, the results are often quite rewarding. Scholars in the fields of ethnomusicology (Stone 1982; Berger 1999; Rahaim 2012; Berger et al. 2023) and music theory (F. J. Smith 1979; Lochhead 1982; Clifton 1983) have effectively wielded phenomenology to elucidate the living present of the ethnographic field or musical structure, respectively.

Phenomenology's utility for historical scholarship, by contrast, may not be readily apparent to those who take its orientation toward the present for granted. Historians cannot enact the basic conditions under which most phenomenological accounts of music proceed: the researcher's living co-presence in the musicking moment. Furthermore, phenomenology's method of bracketing out theoretical explanation in order to focus on the description and analysis of lived experience may seem to preclude any historical approach. What does history have, we might ask, other than secondhand accounts? What does it lack more than "lived experience"? As Jonathan Sterne argues, "[h]istory deals in fragments, with traces, and whereas the fundamental condition for the ethnographer is some kind of co-presence, the fundamental condition for the historian is absence" (Sterne 2009, 65). Sterne makes these claims in the context of an important argument against the idealization of recorded media's potential to preserve the past whole cloth, but his comments should not lead us to overestimate the riches of the ethnographer nor the poverty of the historian.

Although the ethnographer's bodily co-presence certainly differs from the historian's engagement in the archive or the media room, neither can be construed in terms of pure presence or absence. Clifford Geertz (1973), whose oft-quoted essay on "thick description" might seem quite compatible with a presentist application of phenomenology, emphasized in the same famous essay that ethnographers are not simply present for events that are wholly transparent. The comparison he chooses is actually that of archival, even philological work: "doing ethnography is like trying to read (in the sense of 'construct a reading of') a manuscript—foreign, faded, full of ellipses, incoherencies, suspicious emendations, and tendentious commentaries, but written not in conventionalized graphs of sound but in transient examples of shaped behavior" (Geertz 1973, 10). As Geertz's comments make clear, ethnographers are never simply *there* in the field; they are constantly, painstakingly *learning to be there*, seeking to understand the ways in which presence itself is constructed and experienced in culturally and historically specific ways. This is not to say that there are no distinctions to be made between archival and fieldwork practices, only that historians and ethnographers are both chasing lived meaning, even if they do so in their own particular ways.

This understanding of presence—as partial and constructed, at once embodied and discursive, mediated through cultural frames—differs significantly from Husserl's early commitments, which Jacques Derrida characterized as a singular concern with the *"living present,* the self-presence of transcendental life" (Derrida [1967] 1973, 6; italics in the original; see also Rahaim, this volume). Yet rather than discrediting phenomenology as a whole, critiques of the role of such presumed presence in Husserl's project demonstrate alternate ways forward. When Derrida asserts that the phenomenological reduction as carried out through the epoché does not approach objects in their simple presence, but as if in *"a scene, a theater stage"* (86; italics in the original), such a critique strikes at the heart of Husserl's early characterization of phenomenology while also, according to Bruce Smith (2010), providing an opportunity:

> Derrida doesn't destroy Husserl's phenomenology; he pushes it to its logical conclusions. In doing so, he opens up the possibility for a specifically *historical* phenomenology. Metaphysical presence, absolute knowledge: that may have been Husserl's goal, but it does not have to be ours. We can accept that knowing-in-place-in-time is like a theatrical scene. We can accept the speeches and the props in that scene as artifacts, not natural givens. We can accept the fact that presence is an illusion made with those speeches and props. But we can still be interested in the illusion of presence and we can be interested in it in historical, culturally specific ways.
>
> (B. Smith 2010, 27–28; italics in the original)

Removing this commitment to presence maintains phenomenology's potential as methodology while allowing for a radical reconception of presence. According to Sara Ahmed (2006, 37), "the partiality of absence as well as presence" is one of the basic insights of phenomenological reflection. Attending to experience within the epoché does not reveal a phenomenon that is wholly present to consciousness but a presence shot through with absence and absence shot through with presence.

Taking Derrida's critique seriously thus provides an opportunity to undertake historical phenomenology while orienting that project toward the play of language and signification within experience. Put simply, the stories that historical subjects told themselves about the phenomena they experienced are not just all that is left to the researcher—they are as central to the phenomena as direct sensory perception (B. Smith 2010, 34). Taken phenomenologically, the question is not whether these stories are true or false but how they enter into and inflect experience. Attention to language is necessary even when dealing with recorded sound, which might raise hopes that scholars could do away with the confusing work of listening to words about music and instead get to some semblance of the sounds themselves. But the recorded artifact is not a perfectly preserved sonic moment; it is "less a memory and more a mnemonic" (Sterne 2003, 320). Texts about sound remain as important as recorded artifacts for understanding the meanings of these sounds in their particular time and place, because even sounds that have been preserved cannot be accessed in a direct and unmediated way (M. Smith 2015, 61).

This is not to say that experience can be reduced to its conceptual description in language but that the narratives conveyed by language help make sense of experiences and may even partially structure them from the outset. Carr (2014, 222) argues that experience itself evinces a narrative structure prior to any narrating acts that may reflect upon it, such that "narrative is at the root of human reality long before it gets explicitly told about." This motivates attention to those stories that people tell themselves about phenomena, while also justifying the narrative quality of scholarship itself: "the narrative explanation does not inhabit a different conceptual universe from the narrated and hence explained original scene." Instead, we revise our motives and reconsider our actions as we are in the midst of them, and in this sense, "the narrative account of the action, far from moving into a different universe of discourse from the events it depicts, is located on a continuum of repeatedly revised explanations, understandings, and interpretations that is part of life itself." Because it is "narratives all the way down," storytelling is an endless part of human experience. "That is, there is no definitive story" (Carr 2014, 223).

Narratives, then, can be understood as relational structures that orient subjects in and toward the world; language shapes, expresses, and positions subjects in relation to the objects of their experience. If we take the *relation* as primary and treat absence and presence as partial and connected to one another, historical distance in no way precludes phenomenology as a guiding methodology. Although the situated experience of a specific individual is often more accessible through ethnographic methods, scholars who work with texts, media, and material culture are not simply left with lifeless artifacts. From a phenomenological standpoint, any of these objects must be approached as what Husserl ([1913] 2014, 255–279) termed *noemata*: objects as encountered by an experiencing subject, of and within an experience.[5] If we do not allow these types of artifacts to be "abstracted from the lived experience by the natural standpoint and science," we can instead inquire into how they enter might enter into experience, asking how a person in a given time and place might constitute the artifacts as meaningful (Kohák 1978, 127). Because "cultural significance and the production of meaning are not encapsulated in any one sutured entity," the absence of one is not necessarily insurmountable so long as there is enough evidence to reconstruct the relationships between perceiving subjects and the objects of their experience (Thomas 1996, 30). Some methods of Husserlian phenomenology—first-person description and imaginative variation—may not be useful or even possible for the historian, but that does not reduce phenomenology's value as methodology (Husserl [1931] 1960, 70–72). It can provide the theoretical underpinning to guide archival, text-based, and media-based methods characteristic of many forms of historical inquiry, and it is equally robust as a platform from which to interpret the results of those methods.

APPROACHING VIRTUOSITY: APPERCEPTION AND INTERSUBJECTIVITY

Virtuosity as a phenomenon is widely understood to revolve around the virtuoso subject. Describing the recital context in which he displayed his skill so effectively, the nineteenth-century pianist Franz Liszt summarized his centrality succinctly: "[t]he concert is—myself" (Liszt 1894, 31). The singular importance of the virtuoso in Liszt's account might seem to leave little room for intersubjectivity; my purpose in foregrounding intersubjectivity is not to deny the centrality of the virtuoso subject asserted by Liszt, however, but to situate that subjectivity within an intersubjective world. As Dan Zahavi

(2001, 166) argues, "the three regions 'self', 'others', and 'world' belong together; they reciprocally illuminate one another, and can only be understood in their interconnection." For even as the virtuoso subject is differentiated from the "crowd" as a result of remarkable ability, virtuosity is not simply the accomplishments of a subject, nor is it *about* subjectivity. Rather, it is an intersubjective performance of subjectivity, agency, and the values that subtend these categories. Because virtuosity is already a saturated phenomenon—one full of gesture and sound—it may be tempting to treat these as the obvious center from which more abstract qualities must be interpreted. But virtuosity does not necessarily involve a logical extrapolation through which one considers the sonic and aesthetic qualities of a performance and concludes that it *must* be the result of another subject's skilled labor. Rather, drawing from the vocabulary of phenomenology, we can say that aspects of this skilled act of production and the laboring subject engaged in it are *apperceived*.

The term "apperception" (a concept with a long history in Western philosophy that took on a distinct meaning in Husserl's work) refers to the ways that perceptual experience always includes more than that which is directly presented. In Husserl's most straightforward example, it describes the ways that we experience multiple profiles of a physical object at once. When I look at a book, I directly perceive only a single side from my particular vantage point, but its other sides are also dimly present within my experience. Beyond "knowing" there are other sides, those sides are present to me despite their direct perceptual absence: they are apperceived. In this spatial example, I can directly perceive the other sides by adopting a different vantage point, but apperception does not necessarily depend upon this future reorientation (Dillon 1997, 116). Instead, Husserl argues that apperception "points back" to a prior moment "in which an object with a similar sense became constituted for the first time." I apperceive an object's other sides because I have previously encountered "things like this before, though not precisely this thing here." This is "not inference, not a thinking act," but a fundamental part of perceptual experience (Husserl [1931] 1960, 111).

In Husserl's more extended argument related to the term ([1931] 1960, 112–120), apperception provides the basis for an intersubjective "pairing," which Merleau-Ponty (1964, 118) adapts as a transfer of "corporeal schema" that forms the basis of an embodied intersubjectivity. On this view, I experience myself neither as "unextended thought" (an immaterial mind) nor "unthinking extension" (a brute material body) but as embodied consciousness (Dillon 1997, 128). Through apperception, I encounter the Other as a similarly embodied consciousness, and this grounds an intersubjectivity that is irreducibly intercorporeal. There is no need to overcome the "problem of other minds" because neither I nor others have ever been isolated minds. As fundamentally embodied in the world, virtuosity is intersubjective; I perceive the performing body as embodied subjectivity in the process of music making.

The concept of apperception further clarifies our experience of virtuosity by overcoming what Herbert Spiegelberg ([1960] 1982, 684) calls the "sense organ prejudice." Such a prejudice seems perfectly reasonable on its face: knowledge of the world comes from the senses, so any phenomenon that we experience must have been heard, seen, tasted, and so on. If one cannot clearly link a perceptual experience to a particular sense, so the argument goes, how legitimate can such an experience be? The desire for a "clear and distinct" sense thus leads to an "empiricist atomism" (Ihde [1976] 2007, 12–13) that distances us from the world and reveals very little about complex social phenomena like virtuosity. For although we regularly focus on the visual spectacle or sonic intensity of the skilled performance, virtuosity is not a matter of simply *hearing* or *seeing*. We experience it in a multisensorial, embodied context in which our direct perceptions are accompanied by complex acts of apperception that are just as embodied as sonic and visual experiences. We apperceive through the totality of our sedimented embodied subjectivity, which is at once social and cultural.

Because it depends on our ongoing embodied experience in the world, apperception might seem more useful for explaining experiences of virtuosity within shared cultural contexts, but it can also help explain how audiences might stand in awe of Shankar's ability despite their unfamiliarity with the music and its mode of production. It is their own body that serves as the medium through which an audience member grasps the laboring body of Shankar as skilled. In this way, Shankar's assumptions about speed's salience for novice audiences hold partially true. Although listeners may fail to grasp the actual challenges of playing the sitar and the skills needed to navigate the instrument, their tacit embodied knowledge suggests that any action is likely to be difficult when it demands both speed and precision. These qualities appear as intelligible markers of skill across many cultural frameworks precisely because of our experiences of our own bodies engaged in activities that require simultaneous accuracy and rapidity.

Lest it seem that this also affirms Shankar's claim about the universal immediacy of virtuosity, the concept of apperception can also help us seriously consider how the promotional materials that constantly touted Shankar's ability shaped the experience of novice listeners. As Husserl ([1931] 1960, 111) writes, "what is there perceptually motivates 'belief in' something else being there too." This invocation of belief indicates that apperception can be tied to discourse as well as previous experience. Such an interplay is particularly important for explaining the experience of listeners who encountered Shankar on an LP recording, where there was little else but sound to directly perceive. Although their unfamiliarity might make them unlikely to apperceive Shankar's skill via sound alone, the rhetoric of liner notes and of Shankar's celebrity advocates directed their attention, supplementing the multiple "other sides" of the phenomenon to which they did not have direct access.

Furthermore, much as promotional materials and newspapers articles often sought to make sense of Hindustani music through language, critics' descriptions can also be understood as attempts to safeguard its otherness. In other words, they invoked the existence of an "other side" to the music (especially its spiritual overtones) without necessarily attempting to provide access to it. Virtually every article on Shankar includes a brief discussion of ideas from Hindustani music theory, such as *raga* and *tala*. Most, however, do not go into much detail, opting instead to gesture toward the esoteric nature of such concepts for the Western listener. The play of explanatory language then could be understood as a way to "shut doors as well as open them" (Ruckert 2009, 108).

As ethnomusicologist and sarodist George Ruckert explains of his own experience, "[m]y students and even colleagues will say they 'don't understand the Indian music,' when it is really the language about it that befuddles them ('all those microtones—*srutis* I think they call them'). I tell them: 'just listen, there is nothing to understand'" (Ruckert 2009, 108–109).

Ruckert's point extends beyond Hindustani music, for many audiences listen to (and enjoy) music with which they are quite familiar—be it pop, jazz, or (European) "classical"—without an understanding of its philosophical underpinnings, internal procedures, or technical terminology. Put otherwise, program notes or reviews that emphasized a popular song's unusual hypermeter, a jazz musician's use of the super-locrian mode, or a Romantic composer's use of hemiola would likely mystify listeners just as much as talk of sruti, raga, or tala. Constantly rehearsing these terms and their definitions in program notes and other media could serve to overcome unfamiliarity, but it could also remind listeners who insisted on "just listening" to the music that such an act was happening in relation to music that was remarkably other. If such explanations were not actually desired, they gave listeners unfamiliar with Hindustani music the opportunity to intentionally put understanding aside.

SOCIALITY ON STAGE

The concept of intersubjectivity first entered philosophical discourse in the late nineteenth century, where it identified "something with universal validity" that remains "valid for everybody" despite the variations in each subject's particular perspective (Zahavi 2014, 97). In this formulation, intersubjectivity and objectivity are essentially synonymous. Husserl ([1973] 2006, 137) occasionally utilized the term in this sense to discuss the possibility of intersubjective knowledge (especially within the sciences), but already in his lectures of 1910–11 he also expanded the concept to mean "a plurality of subjects and the relation that exists between them" (Zahavi 2014, 97), which he came to see as "the most basic quality of human existence" (Duranti 2010, 16). In this sense of intersubjectivity, the fundamental "understanding" between two embodied subjects—necessary prior to any shared agreement about objects or the world—is their relation to each other precisely as fellow embodied subjects. As Jean-Paul Sartre put it: "my relation to the Other is first and fundamentally a relation of being to being, not of knowledge to knowledge" (Sartre [1943] 2003, 268).

This is not to say that "knowledge to knowledge" intersubjectivity (that is, agreement between two subjects about some aspect of the world or objects within it) is not real or important in certain contexts. Within the royal courts of feudal and colonial India where Hindustani musical practice flourished, a knowledge-based intersubjectivity between the performer and audience was central. In these performance spaces, as Bonnie Wade notes, audiences possessed at least some degree of musical understanding and they were expected to draw on this knowledge to judge and encourage the performer in real time (Wade 1984, 16). In this historical setting, which still serves as the performance ideal today, musicians sought "ongoing audience approval in the form of verbalizations of praise, bodily gestures, and facial expressions of rapture" from "an educated audience" (Slawek 1998, 337). The intersubjectivity at play in such a context foregrounds shared knowledge, especially an agreement on the quality and appropriateness of a particular treatment of a raga.

Other criteria used to judge the quality of a performance required very little knowledge but were nonetheless culturally specific. For many listeners, the sheer amount of time that a performer spent drawing out and elaborating upon the contours of a raga was widely understood as evidence of the musician's deep knowledge. Ravi Shankar (1966, 160) actually railed against this criterion of judgment: "How many times do we hear it said, 'Why, it wasn't much of a performance—he only played the *raag* [raga] for 45 minutes!' How is it that so many have come to rely on length as a test of a musician?" Yet even such a simple criterion failed to translate to audiences in Europe and North America, who generally possessed far less knowledge of Hindustani music than those in India. Rather than providing proof of the depth of a performer's knowledge, the length of performances posed a potential challenge to newcomers. Recognizing this, Shankar shortened the overall performance time to roughly two hours instead of the four or five that was common in India, and, as Wade has observed, he was also careful to begin his concerts in the United States and Europe with particularly short performances of a raga (Wade 1978, 32). Limits on audience attention were significant enough that Shankar left a reviewer for *Time* with the impression that he "consciously [held] himself in check while on tour," only occasionally playing as long as he would have personally preferred (*Time* 1964). Although audiences in this new context were often unable to react knowledgably to the performance, musicians like Shankar continued to read cues from their audience and adapt their performance accordingly. As Daniel Neuman has pointed out, "if the audience appeared to enjoy the *alap* [opening, unmetered exposition of a raga] it could be extended almost indefinitely. If they appeared restive or bored, the *alap* could be wrapped up on a moment's notice and an exciting *jor* [second, faster, and more melodically compact exposition of the raga] or *jhala* [fast, concluding section] could be initiated" (2015, 159). According to Shankar, this also extended to the devices employed in those contexts:

> "Playing to the gallery" is the expression used to say that the performer is playing to please the masses and not paying strict attention to orthodoxy in music. This is, however, not a new idea. It really came into vogue in the days of the Court musician with various competitions that were held. The musician did everything possible to please his benefactor and many different techniques evolved from this, such as the present Jawab-Sawal (the dialogue between two instruments). Now-a-days the musician has not only one person to please but a number of them and it is only natural that he should try in some instances to give them what appeals to them. This is perfectly alright as long as he does not allow it to go out of proportion, so that it becomes jarring.
>
> (Shankar and Estabrook 1964, 26–27)

Beyond the asymmetrical sociality between novice audiences and expert performers, many reviews of Shankar point to the social interactions of musicians on stage as key to the construction of virtuosity in an intercultural context. For example, a review of Shankar's 1956 New York performance, which was the first he gave there since the tours he conducted in the 1930s with his brother's dance troupe, began succinctly: "music is certainly not a universal language" (E. D. 1956). Writing in the *New York Times*, the reviewer (who was identified only as E. D.) describes feeling "like a very obtuse Westerner who could never hope to understand the subtleties of Hindu music" and recounts being at odds with "the seeming sameness of the music, a sort of mournful repetitiousness without apparent rhyme or reason."[6] Things began to change, however, during the second raga that Shankar performed, and E. D. wondered about this reason: "Perhaps it was the extraordinary virtuosity of Shankar, whose left hand flew across the frets with a dexterity to put some of our finest violinists to shame. Or was it the eloquence of the two little drums played by Chatur Lal?"

Faced with unfamiliar music that they found difficult to interpret, E. D. first resorted to what psychologist Gustav Jahoda calls "anchoring," a process whereby "foreign or disturbing elements are integrated into our own system of categories" (Jahoda 1999, 9–10; see also Blasco 2004, 28). Anchoring can be thought of as a form of the apperceptive transfer of sense that takes place in relation to the unfamiliar (Husserl [1931] 1960, 110). Here, the unfamiliar becomes intelligible because we interpret it in the context of—and against the background of—familiarity. In that sense, "*unfamiliarity* is at the same time always *a mode of familiarity*" (Husserl [1948] 1973, 37; italics in the original). But unlike apperception—which is present in some form in every perception, whether or not it is actively reflected upon—anchoring is often willfully adopted as a strategy for coping with the unfamiliar. E. D. does this first with a comparison of Shankar to a violinist, but the unfamiliarity of the music eventually led them to focus on the socio-musical exchange between Shankar and Chatur Lal:

> More than the virtuosity of either artist, it was the communicative understanding between the two and their growing musical excitement that communicated itself irresistibly to the audience. Since this music is half improvised on traditional rhythms and melodic formulas, it is perhaps natural that superb performance should impress itself first on the foreign listener.
>
> (E. D. 1956)

Absent the necessary background to interpret the sonic results of Shankar's actions with the critic's presumed authority, E. D. focused on the collaborative social context of improvisation in which they took place. Although E. D. didn't take the time to explain exactly how they observed the relationship between the two musicians, available signs of successful interaction are myriad, including sonic indications—like "question-and-answer" phrasing or the shared, perhaps surprising accented beat—and visual cues like head gestures, eye contact, and overall bodily comportment. Other critics employed similar anchoring strategies in their consistent comparisons between Hindustani music and jazz. Another *New York Times* reviewer, Howard Taubman (1955), wrote of Ali Akbar Khan's North American premiere that the musicians displayed "the flexibility and freedom of the best jazz improvisations. The players respond to each other with amazing sensitivity." Such comparisons were made throughout the 1960s, although Shankar and others consistently pointed out the problem with such an analogy (Quinn 1968, 17). Its persistence points not just to the lack of knowledge among American listeners but to the fact that all musical experience includes "some frame of reference," whether or not it is the "right" frame (Schutz 1974, 26).

Conclusion: Intersubjectivity, Evaluation, and Prejudgment

Thus far I have downplayed the role of judgment in virtuosity in order to focus on its intersubjective structures. Doing so has emphasized the *valual* aspect of experience, demonstrating that value (i.e., valence or significance) is part of the structure of the lived experience long before we evaluate it in reflection (Berger 2009, 137n2). In conclusion, I reincorporate the issue of judgment in order to consider the role of sociality within both evaluative judgments and prejudgments that make interpretation possible. This demonstrates that both value and sociality are ultimately on "all sides" of the experience: before, during, and after.

Although the term "judgment" often implies the individual weighing of a matter, intersubjectivity itself is widely utilized as a criterion for making evaluative judgments about virtuosity. A passage from philosopher V. A. Howard's analytic study of virtuosity, *Charm and Speed,* demonstrates this point. Considering some examples of non-musical virtuosity, Howard reflects on his experience of watching a cheetah chase a rabbit on television:

> "There!" I cried out at the screen. There is one of nature's great virtuoso performances. . . . But then, "Is it?" I asked myself in the next breath. Acceptable as a metaphoric description of the cheetah's behavior, what is missing here that disqualifies her behavior from literally being a virtuoso (or virtuosa) performance? Indeed, from being a performance of any kind? Reflection, I thought. . . . She lacks a discerning audience of peers as well as reflective self-criticism. Nor again literally, could she be said to express anything meaningful in or about her behavior, for that requires a symbolic medium to occur.
>
> (Howard 2008, 1)

It seems that Howard initially experiences the cheetah's acts in the television program as virtuosic, but he rejects this characterization upon subsequent reflection. This is partially because he conceives of virtuosity as an after-the-fact judgment of experts; it is a

"Seal of Approval bestowed by the critical community" (Howard 2008, 9). Such a characterization situates virtuosity not just within a community of cultural insiders but in
the legitimizing context of the informal guild; this is the "knowledge to knowledge" intersubjectivity discussed above (Sartre [1943] 2003, 268). Beyond this absence of discerning peers, Howard refuses to characterize the cheetah's act as virtuosic because of
the animal's presumed lack of reflection and language. Without these traits, which stand
as key markers of subjectivity and agency for Howard, he finds himself unable to affirm the degree of intercorporeal intersubjectivity he initially felt. This simple example
of everyday media consumption thereby inadvertently demonstrates the stakes of virtuosity. If the phenomenological approach to virtuosity as skill made apparent and socially meaningful initially provokes straightforward questions about what counts as skill
and how it comes to matter in a particular context, they may also form the background
of much more serious questions: Who counts as a subject? What counts as legitimate
labor? If the performer is somehow disqualified—whether classified as an animal body
without interiority or a mechanical automaton lacking vitality altogether—the affective
and valual force of the phenomenon dissipates.

And yet, positive assessments of intersubjectivity must not be too complete. For the
display of skill to be meaningful, a listener must find a degree of both commonality
and otherness, and this is what I refer to as the likeness-difference dynamic of virtuosity (VanderHamm 2020, 300). As performance studies scholar Judith Hamera argues
(2000, 149), the virtuosic body "rewrites plots of possibility for other bodies even while
demonstrating the inability of other bodies, including those of critics, to execute this
virtuous discipline themselves." Such "plots of possibility" are based on a presumed
intercorporeal likeness, while "the inability of other bodies" remains proof of the un-
absorbed difference.

This dynamic helps explain why Shankar's audiences in Europe and North America
did not always consider their lack of knowledge about Hindustani music to be a
problem. Asked if they "understood the music," many concertgoers rejected the terms of
the question outright, offering statements such as, "Well at first I didn't, but as I got with
it and sort of relaxed, I loved it," or "I didn't try to understand it, I just went with it, it was
beautiful" (Shankar 2010). Professional reviewers likewise found they could enjoy—and
be amazed by—this music without much understanding. A reviewer from the *New York
Herald Tribune* wrote of Ali Akbar Khan's New York premiere that, given the reputations
of the musicians, it was "not altogether a surprise to witness feats of solo and ensemble
virtuosity." However, "it was thoroughly astounding . . . to comprehend even a small
portion of the formative art which permitted two thirty-minute long compositions to
span so wide a range of moods" (L. T. 1955). In his *New York Times* review, Taubman similarly wrote,

> Even if one had no background in Indian music, one would have seen last night
> that these performers were masters of their art. One did not grasp it all, and yet
> one was repeatedly enchanted by rhythms, colors, sonorities and melodic bits. One

was especially impressed by the power of this modest ensemble speaking an exotic tongue to reach out and say something to another world.

(Taubman 1955)

Both reviewers agree that the most impressive thing about Khan's performance was that it managed to impress at all. The *Times* critic in particular shows how a lack of expertise can paradoxically serve to justify experiences of virtuosity rather than disqualify them. Put in colloquial terms, we might expect uninformed listeners to say, "It impressed me, but what do I know?" but in this situation the reviewers nearly exclaim, "I didn't even need any background to be impressed!"

The exoticism evinced in these reviews (and present in much of Shankar's Western reception) easily dovetailed with celebrations of virtuosity because both hinged on the meaning of otherness. The draw of Hindustani music for many American audiences—and the phenomenon of virtuosity that emerges within the experience of it—was that of an intersubjective encounter between radically different subjects. As such, those places where intersubjective *understanding* breaks down and the other emerges as fundamentally, perhaps irretrievably Other constitute a positive feature of virtuosity in many accounts, not a failure to connect. This recalls the meta-ethical philosophy of Emmanuel Levinas, who explicitly rejected the characterization of an encounter with the other as "fusion" of self and other. Instead, as Levinas ([1979] 1987) puts it, "the relationship with the Other is the absence of the other" (90). Obviously, audiences do not usually speak in such esoteric terms, but their comments reflect this emphasis on the persistence of otherness within intersubjectivity by pairing statements about Shankar's radical otherness with assertions of his general humanity. When asked by the interviewer to articulate the significance of Shankar's performance, one concertgoer declared, "It's not possible to produce music like that without being another kind of a human being," and another described him simply as an "unbelievable human being" (Shankar 2010). Placing intersubjectivity at the center of a phenomenological account of virtuosity begins to resolve the problem of the novice by demonstrating how the phenomenon becomes intelligible despite the imperfect "fit" between cultural knowledge and musical practice. For many audiences, the value of virtuosity lies precisely in the encounter with a laboring subject who provides both a site of empathy and an otherness that transcends their experience.

The tendency to find fault with novice experiences of virtuosity (where audiences seem to understand neither the musical sound nor the performer's actions that produced it) thus errs in two ways. First, as I have just suggested above, it fails to recognize that intersubjectivity itself is more primary than intersubjective agreement about some object of knowledge, such that a lack of the latter is not the disqualification that some would assume. Second, even those that accept the fundamentally social nature of virtuosity tend to assume that the phenomenon's significance arises from how audiences perceive musical sound or the performing musician. I would argue conversely that a great deal of virtuosity's significance lies in how audiences experience the relationship *between the two*: they apperceive a relationship between the laboring performer and the product of that labor. Occasionally, this apperceived relationship can carry more interpretive weight than the entities (of performer and performance) involved in it, and this is precisely what happens in Howard's earlier rejection of the cheetah's potential virtuosic display. There is nothing about the cheetah's act itself that disqualifies it; her skilled hunt impresses in both its execution and result. It is the animal's apperceived relation to her own action that Howard deems insufficient.

The apperceived relationships between the laboring process and the laboring subject were important to Shankar's reception as well. An audience member listening to a concluding jhala section, for example, would presumably note the increasing rhythmic intensity of the music and Shankar's quickening movements. But the experience likely also includes the apperception of the more or less hidden relationship between Shankar and the music. Many of the audience comments quoted throughout this chapter similarly suggest that what they encountered in Shankar's music was not simply the sound nor the labor that produced it but the relationship between Shankar's own laboring body and the product of his labor. It is this relationship—apperceived through the audience member's embodied relation to their own actions—that becomes central to how they value the display of skill, and audiences are prone to characterize it in various value-laden terms like mastery, ease, or hard work. Consider this audience member's description of her experience after a 1967 performance:

> There was one point in there, and you know, I can't really tell what he's doing from this distance. But he seemed to be, you know, moving with it. And he was just playing with one hand, and the other hand, he was, I don't know really getting into it. I don't know, it was sort of like watching a god, because he turns and he smiles at the tablaist, and it's like, it's their own little world. . . . He doesn't care if everyone out here is coughing, or looking at the names of the ragas, looking intellectually or something. Maybe if you started making noise maybe he'd mind, but it doesn't seem like an artist who's playing for the audience or is trying to evoke a certain emotion or something. It's just that he's doing it for himself and he's giving you the privilege of sitting in on it . . . for $4.95. [laughter]
>
> (unnamed audience member quoted in Shankar 2010)

Although we might anticipate that a description of Shankar as "godlike" will focus on seemingly superhuman technique or shows of power (the presumed hallmarks of virtuosity), what this listener experienced as a godlike display of agency was Shankar's sheer absorption in his musical labor and the meaningful social connection he enjoyed through it. Here, the audience member admits that she was too far away to even see Shankar's actions, yet the perceived relationships—between Shankar and his own labor and between the two musicians—made it a powerful experience for her.

The role of apperception and the valual judgments implied by listeners' descriptive vocabulary further suggest that some judgments *precede* the phenomenon. Because value is at the heart of individual identity, the valual structures through which virtuosity enters experience are often the very same structures through which people understand themselves and their relation to the world (Berger 2009, 27–30). Given their foundational function, the judgments that arise from these values are pre-given. They are "prejudices" in the positive rehabilitation of the term offered by Gadamer ([1960] 2013, 283–91): judgments that precede an experience and make meaningful interpretation of it possible. These prejudgments go a long way to explaining the vehemence of both celebrations and condemnations of virtuosity. If virtuosity is considered readily apparent, it is because it articulates deeply held beliefs about agency, bodily capacity, and the value of human labor. If it is considered obviously objectionable, it is because it violates these same beliefs. Thus the values and ideologies that constitute virtuosity and determine its positive or negative valence are there from the very beginning of our engagement with the world.

To be sure, such prejudices are not completely stable and self-determining; musical experience may indeed provide an avenue for the transformation of the structures of the self (McGuiness 2018). If, as Sherry Ortner argues, our actions and experiences put structures "at risk" of "revision or revaluation," they also provide an opportunity for the articulation and enactment of those structures in ways that may recursively affirm them (Ortner 2006, 10). Both change and entrenchment remain distinct possibilities, but there is no guarantee that any experience (musical or otherwise) will precipitate radical changes in one's aesthetics, ethics, or politics. This remains true of intercultural musical experiences, for, as Anthony Appiah (2006, 7–8) makes clear, exposure to or even affinity for other cultures does not by necessity produce a more inclusive or open-minded individual. Shankar's North American reception further demonstrates that exoticism and bias (prejudice in the decidedly negative, non-Gadamerian sense) can persist through sustained and seemingly successful intercultural encounters. To be sure, an encounter that fails to transform (or worse, entrenches) wrongheaded or discriminatory attitudes toward others is far from ideal; some might even insist that such an experience was somehow false or incomplete. Although it may be tempting to make normative claims about what virtuosity or intercultural exchange should be, phenomenology focuses our attention on the experience, daring us to encounter the phenomenon as it is actually lived.[7]

All of this makes virtuosity—supposedly an obvious phenomenon—almost too close to the valual structures of subjectivity to analyze, which is precisely why phenomenology is so necessary for explicating it. As Merleau-Ponty observed, applying the brackets loosens the "intentional threads that connect us to the world in order to make them appear." If dazzling displays of skill threaten to carry us away, "the only way for us to catch sight of ourselves is by suspending this movement, by refusing to be complicit with it" (Merleau-Ponty [1945] 2012, lxxvii). Completely separating ourselves from these experiences is impossible, but refusing our own participation—even for a moment—allows us to realize just how complicit we are in intersubjective phenomena like virtuosity.

Notes

1. Phenomenological discussions of the structure of experience often carry three interrelated connotations. First, structure is a relation, connecting parts of some larger entity. The basic object of study for the phenomenologist is the experience; by engaging the phenomenon, the phenomenologist seeks to identify and elaborate the structures that are immanent within in it. Second, describing experience in terms of structure posits an understanding of experience as something with recognizable contours, shaped by relations between the self and world that are in some way observable. This is against a conception of experience as an impenetrable, irretrievable subjective web. Third, the structures discussed by phenomenology vary widely in terms of their mutability. Some may be invariant and even transcendental (as is the case with intentionality), while others are highly contingent and entirely dependent on social and cultural practices.
2. Throughout this chapter, I use "valuation" to address the role of value within ongoing experience, and "evaluation" to describe reflective judgment upon that experience.
3. The epoché is central to Husserl's phenomenological methodology, although subsequent phenomenologists adopted a variety of stances with regards to its function, necessity, or possibility. More recently, Dan Zahavi (2021) has argued that bracketing is essential as a philosophical method but that anyone applying phenomenology in other fields of study (especially psychology) can draw on phenomenological insights without employing the epoché. Conversely, Harris Berger (2009) has long advocated for a phenomenological approach to music and expressive culture in which the epoché is central. In this chapter, I demonstrate the utility of the epoché for the study of music, especially when approaching phenomena like virtuosity that are so burdened by assumptions and judgments regarding their status as "real" or "false."
4. Husserl used the term "natural attitude" to describe the basic human presumption of a world that is "*simply there for me*," separate from myself and real ([1913] 2014, 48–55; italics in the original).
5. "Noemata" is the plural form; "noema" is the singular. Husserl emphasizes that noemata always arise through *noesis*, which is the term he gives to the act of consciousness that constitutes the objects of experience.
6. E.D., like many journalists in the US press of the time, regularly uses "Hindu" and "Indian" interchangeably, potentially reflecting a vague awareness of the religious logic behind the partition of the Indian subcontinent in 1947. This conflation of religion, nationality, and culture was especially misleading in the context of Hindustani music, where both Muslim and Hindu musicians were central to the development and continued practice of the art form.
7. It is worth noting that phenomenology does not entirely preclude normative theory, but a full phenomenological account must at least precede normative theorizing, lest we attempt to regulate what we have yet to truly grasp.

Works Cited

Ahmed, Sara. 2006. *Queer Phenomenology: Orientations, Objects, Others*. Durham, NC: Duke University Press.

Appiah, Anthony. 2006. *Cosmopolitanism: Ethics in a World of Strangers*. New York: W. W. Norton.

Arendt, Hannah. (1958) 1998. *The Human Condition.* 2nd ed. Chicago: University of Chicago Press.

Baughan, Edward. 1902. "In Defense of the Virtuoso." *Monthly Music Record* 32 (384): 222–223.

Berger, Harris M. 1999. *Metal, Rock, and Jazz: Perception and the Phenomenology of Musical Experience.* Middletown, CT: Wesleyan University Press.

Berger, Harris M. 2009. *Stance: Ideas about Emotion, Style, and Meaning for the Study of Expressive Culture.* Middletown, CT: Wesleyan University Press.

Berger, Harris M., David VanderHamm, and Friedlind Riedel. 2023. "Phenomenological Approaches in the History of Ethnomusicology." In *The Oxford Handbook of the Phenomenology of Music Cultures,* edited by Harris M. Berger, Friedlind Riedel, and David VanderHamm, 3–56. New York: Oxford University Press.

Blasco, Maribel. 2004. "Stranger to Us than the Birds in Our Garden? Reflections on Hermeneutics, Intercultural Understanding and the Management of Difference." In *Intercultural Alternatives: Critical Perspectives on Intercultural Encounters in Theory and Practice,* edited by Maribel Blasco and Jan Gustafsson, 19–48. Denmark: Copenhagen Business School Press.

Carr, David. 2014. *Experience and History: Phenomenological Perspectives on the Historical World.* New York: Oxford University Press.

Clifton, Thomas. 1983. *Music as Heard: A Study in Applied Phenomenology.* New Haven, CT: Yale University Press.

Dillon, M. C. 1997. *Merleau-Ponty's Ontology.* 2nd ed. Evanston, IL: Northwestern University Press.

Derrida, Jacques. (1967) 1973. *"Speech and Phenomena" and Other Essays on Husserl's Theory of Signs.* Translated by David B. Allison. Evanston, IL: Northwestern University Press.

Duranti, Alessandro. 2010. "Husserl, Intersubjectivity, and Anthropology." *Anthropological Theory* 10 (16): 16–34.

E. D. 1956. "Indian Sitar Recital Given by Rani [*sic*] Shankar." *New York Times,* December 7, 1956.

Estabrook, Penelope. 1964. Letter to Isadora Bennett, April 15, 1964. Isadora Bennett Collection, (S)* GMZMD 22. Jerome Robbins Dance Division, New York Public Library for the Performing Arts.

Fabri, Charles. 1966. "Concluding Session." In *Music East and West,* edited by Roger Ashton, 206–208. New Delhi: India Council for Cultural Relations.

Fink, Eugen. 1970. "The Phenomenological Philosophy of Edmund Husserl and Contemporary Criticism." In *The Phenomenology of Husserl: Selected Critical Readings,* edited and translated by R. O. Elveton, 73–147. Chicago: Quadrangle Books.

Gadamer, Hans-Georg. (1960) 2013. *Truth and Method.* Translation revised by Joel Weinsheimer and Donald G. Marshall. New York: Bloomsbury Academic.

Geertz, Clifford. 1973. *The Interpretation of Cultures.* New York: Basic Books.

Geertz, Clifford. 1976. "Art as Cultural System." *Modern Language Notes* 91 (6): 1473–1499.

Harrison, Jay S. 1956. "Shankar and Lal Perform on Sitar, Tabla at Y.M.H.A." *New York Herald Tribune,* December 7, 1956.

Hamera, Judith. 2000. "The Romance of Monsters: Theorizing the Virtuoso Body." *Theatre Topics* 10 (2): 144–153.

Howard, V. A. 2008. *Charm and Speed: Virtuosity in the Performing Arts.* New York: Peter Lang.

Husserl, Edmund. (1913) 2014. *Ideas I.* Translated by Daniel O. Dahlstrom. Indianapolis: Hackett Publishing.

Husserl, Edmund. (1931) 1960. *Cartesian Meditations: An Introduction to Phenomenology.* Translated by Dorion Cairns. The Hague: Martinus Nijhoff.

Husserl, Edmund. (1936) 1970. *The Crisis of European Sciences and Transcendental Phenomenology: An Introduction to Phenomenological Philosophy.* Translated by David Carr. Evanston, IL: Northwestern University Press.

Husserl, Edmund. (1948) 1973. *Experience and Judgment.* Translated by James Churchill and Karl Ameriks. Revised and edited by Ludwig Landgrebe. Evanston, IL: Northwestern University Press.

Husserl, Edmund. (1973) 2006. *The Basic Problems of Phenomenology: From the Lectures, Winter Semester, 1910–1911.* Translated by Ingo Farin and James G. Hart. Dordrecht: Springer.

Ihde, Don. (1976) 2007. *Listening and Voice: Phenomenologies of Sound.* 2nd ed. Albany: State University of New York Press.

Ihde, Don. 1990. *Technology and the Lifeworld: From Garden to Earth.* Bloomington: Indiana University Press.

Ingold, Tim. 2000. *The Perception of the Environment: Essays on Livelihood, Dwelling, and Skill.* New York: Routledge.

Jahoda, Gustav. 1999. *Images of Savages: Ancient Roots of Modern Prejudice in Western Culture.* London: Routledge.

Jankélévitch, Vladimir. 1979. *Liszt et la Rhapsodie: Essai sur la Virtuosité.* Paris: Plon.

Kerman, Joseph. 1999. "Virtuosity / Virtù." In *Concerto Conversations,* 61–82. Cambridge, MA: Harvard University Press.

Kirby, R. Kenneth. 2008. "Phenomenology and the Problems of Oral History." *Oral History Review* 35 (1): 22–38.

Kohák, Erazim V. 1978. *Idea and Experience: Edmund Husserl's Project of Phenomenology in Ideas I.* Chicago: University of Chicago Press.

Krishmanachari, T. T. 1966. "The Inaugural Session." In *Music East and West,* edited by Roger Ashton, 3–5. New Delhi: India Council for Cultural Relations.

L. T. "Concerts and Recitals." 1955. *New York Herald Tribune,* April 20, 1955.

Levinas, Emmanuel. (1979) 1987. *Time and the Other.* Translated by Richard A. Cohen. Pittsburgh, PA: Duquesne University Press.

Liszt, Franz. 1894. *Letters of Franz Liszt.* Vol. 1, edited by La Mara, translated by Constance Bache. London: H. Grevel & Co.

Lochhead, Judith. 1982. "The Temporal Structure of Recent Music: A Phenomenological Investigation." PhD diss., State University of New York at Stony Brook.

McGuiness, Andrew. 2018. "Music, Phenomenology, and Habitus." Paper presented at Phenomenology in Ethnomusicology: The St. John's Conference, Research Centre for the Study of Music, Media, and Place, Memorial University of Newfoundland, June 5, 2018. https://youtu.be/i2uvJ7sIgDc.

Merleau-Ponty, Maurice. (1945) 2012. *Phenomenology of Perception.* Translated by Donald A. Landes. New York: Routledge.

Merleau-Ponty, Maurice. 1964. *"The Primacy of Perception" and Other Essays on Phenomenological Psychology, the Philosophy of Art, History, and Politics.* Edited and translated by James M. Edie. Evanston, IL: Northwestern University Press.

Montagu, Jeremy. 1968. "Review of *Ethnomusicology.*" *Journal of the International Folk Music Council* 20: 101–104.

Neuman, Daniel. 2015. "The Ecology of Indian Music in North America." In *Studying India's Musicians: Four Decades of Selected Articles,* 152–163. New Delhi: Manohar Publishers.

Ortner, Sherry. 2006. *Anthropology and Social Theory: Culture, Power, and the Acting Subject.* Durham, NC: Duke University Press.

Pincherle, Marc. 1963. *The World of the Virtuoso*. Translated by Lucile H. Brockway. New York: Norton.

Quinn, Bill. 1968. "The Impact of Ravi Shankar." *DownBeat* 35 (5): 16–17, 38.

Rahaim, Matthew. 2012. *Musicking Bodies: Gesture and Voice in Hindustani Music*. Middletown, CT: Wesleyan University Press.

Reck, David R. 1985. "Beatles Orientalis: Influences from Asia in a Popular Song Tradition." *Asian Music* 16 (1): 83–149.

Ricoeur, Paul. 1976. "History and Hermeneutics." *Journal of Philosophy* 73 (19): 683–695.

Ricoeur, Paul. (2000) 2004. *Memory, History, Forgetting*. Chicago: University of Chicago Press.

Ruckert, George. 2009. "An Indo-European Music." *Journal of the Indian Musicological Society* (January): 103–109.

Sartre, Jean-Paul. (1943) 2003. *Being and Nothingness: An Essay on Phenomenological Ontology*. Routledge Classics Edition. New York: Routledge.

Schutz, Alfred. 1974. "Fragments toward a Phenomenology of Music." In *Collected Papers*, vol. 4, edited by Helmut Wagner, George Psathas, and Fred Kersten, 243–275. Dordrecht: Kluwer Academic Publishers.

Shankar, Ravi. 1965. "Talking about Music: East Comes West." Interview by Carl Wildman. October 31, 1965. BBC transcription disc, British Library.

Shankar, Ravi. 1966. "Hindustani Classical Music and the Demands of Today." In *Music East and West*, edited by Roger Ashton, 158–165. New Delhi: India Council for Cultural Relations.

Shankar, Ravi. 1968. *My Music, My Life*. New York: Simon and Schuster.

Shankar, Ravi. 2010. "West Meets East circa 1967: Responses to an Early US Appearance by Ravi Shankar Recorded in 1967." *Nine Decades, Vol. I: 1967–1968*, East Meets West Music EMW1000, compact disc.

Shankar, Ravi, and Penelope Estabrook. 1964. *Music Memory*. Bombay: Kinnara School of Music.

Skillen, Anthony. 1993. "Sport: An Historical Phenomenology." *Philosophy* 68 (265): 343–368.

Slawek, Stephen. 1998. "Keeping It Going: Terms, Practices, and Processes of Improvisation in Hindustani Instrumental Music." In *In the Course of Performance: Studies in the World of Musical Improvisation*, edited by Bruno Nettl and Melinda Russell, 335–368. Chicago: University of Chicago Press.

Smith, Bruce R. 2010. *Phenomenal Shakespeare*. Chichester, UK: Wiley-Blackwell.

Smith, F. Joseph. 1979. *The Experiencing of Musical Sound: Prelude to a Phenomenology of Music*. New York: Gordon and Breach.

Smith, Mark M. 2015. "Echo." In *Keywords in Sound*, edited by David Novak, 55–64. Durham, NC: Duke University Press.

Spiegelberg, Herbert. (1960) 1982. *The Phenomenological Movement: A Historical Introduction*, 3rd rev. ed. The Hague: Martinus Nijhoff.

Stefaniak, Alexander. 2016. *Schumann's Virtuosity: Criticism, Composition, and Performance in Nineteenth-Century Germany*. Bloomington: Indiana University Press.

Sterne, Jonathan. 2003. *The Audible Past: Cultural Origins of Sound Reproduction*. Durham, NC: Duke University Press.

Sterne, Jonathan. 2009. "The Preservation Paradox in Digital Audio." In *Sound Souvenirs: Audio Technologies, Memory, and Cultural Practices*, edited by Karin Bijsterveld and José Van Dijck, 55–68. Amsterdam: Amsterdam University Press.

Stone, Ruth M. 1982. *Let the Inside Be Sweet: The Interpretation of Music Event among the Kpelle of Liberia*. Bloomington: Indiana University Press.

Taubman, Howard. 1955. "Music of India Heard at Modern Museum: Performance Akin to Improvised Jazz." *New York Times*, April 20, 1955.

Thomas, Julian. 1996. *Time, Culture, and Identity: An Interpretative Archaeology*. London: Routledge.

Time. 1964. "Instrumentalists: And Now the Sitar." November 6, 1964, 84–86.

VanderHamm, David. 2020. "'I'm Just an Armless Guitarist': Tony Melendez, Disability, and the Social Construction of Virtuosity." *Journal of the Society for American Music* 14 (3): 280–307.

Wade, Bonnie. 1978. "Indian Classical Music in North America: Cultural Give and Take." *Contributions to Asian Studies* 12 (January): 29–39.

Wade, Bonnie. 1984. "Performance Practice in Indian Classical Music." In *Performance Practice: Ethnomusicological Perspectives*, edited by Gerard Béhague, 13–52. Westport, CT: Greenwood Press.

Wallerstein, Immanuel Maurice. 2006. *European Universalism: The Rhetoric of Power*. New York: New Press.

Welton, Donn. 2000. *The Other Husserl: The Horizons of Transcendental Phenomenology*. Bloomington: Indiana University Press.

Young, Katharine. 2011. "Gestures, Intercorporeity, and the Fate of Phenomenology in Folklore." *Journal of American Folklore* 124 (492): 55–87.

Zahavi, Dan. 2001. "Beyond Empathy: Phenomenological Approaches to Intersubjectivity." *Journal of Consciousness Studies* 8 (5–7): 151–167.

Zahavi, Dan. 2014. *Self and Other: Exploring Subjectivity, Empathy, and Shame*. New York: Oxford University Press.

Zahavi, Dan. 2021. "Applied Phenomenology: Why It Is Safe to Ignore the Epoché." *Continental Philosophy Review* 54: 259–273.

CHAPTER 11

....

THE SOUND OF MOVEMENT
Hearing Kathak Dance

....

MONICA DALIDOWICZ

THIS chapter originates out of an effort to comprehend how we perceive and experience our moving bodies through sound. As a dancer, the centrality of movement to the experience of the body is self-evident: we experience our bodies moving in place and between places, directed in and toward our material environment. Phenomenologist Maxine Sheets-Johnstone explains that the quintessential relationship between the body and the world "is through and through kinetic from infancy onward" (1999, 361). But one could similarly add that our relationship to the world is through and through a sonic one. How do bodies sound? How does sound orient our bodies to movement and the environment we inhabit? Sound guides our attention toward objects, surfaces, and aspects of the environment; we are prompted through auditory cues to move toward or away, to move slowly or quickly and with differing qualities of movement (forcefully, lightly, and so forth), and much of this happens without our explicit focus. Moving bodies themselves have an auditory dimension; sounds are created as the body interacts with the material world. Not only can we hear ourselves speak but we can tune into the way our bodies sound as we move (e.g., the sound of our feet as we walk). The nature of the North Indian dance form of kathak provides an important site for the exploration of these themes: dancers are in fact musicians producing complex rhythms through the sound of their feet. This is more than simply moving to the music but rather an experience of creating sound through the movements of the body.

The auditory dimension of experience has been a focal point for ethnomusicologists and a growing range of interdisciplinary academics, many of whom have explored the ways humans experience and interpret sound (see Ihde 1976; Feld 1996; Clayton 2008). But how does sound relate to our kinesthetic orientation to the world? For musicians, movement itself is primarily expressed in sonic form: the production of music is an embodied act in which an intimate tactile and kinetic relationship with the world brings forth sounds that can be taken as musically meaningful. Ethnomusicologist Matthew Rahaim (2012) has highlighted the way music is also a kind of motion through his study of the gestures of the hands and upper body that Hindustani classical singers make while performing. In dance, however, the auditory nature of corporeality often recedes to the background; in the Western academy, the study of dance movement has typically focused on its expression within the visual field. However, in the North Indian style of kathak, learning how to *hear* dance has primacy: the music-making body is a key focus. Movement intends to be expressed in both the visual and sonic fields. It is not only the quality of movement that defines kathak but also the quality of the rhythmic sound that the dancers produce as their feet rhythmically slap on the floor that becomes foremost in the dancers' orientation to their world. Further, bodily movements have a sonic equivalent and are first vocalized as mnemonic syllables, known as *bols*, which are then later expressed in movement. Kathak dance, like other Hindustani (North Indian) and Carnatic (South Indian) musical traditions, relies on a syllabic language of bols for its transmission. From the outset, kathak dance gesture involves an important sonic dimension: movement is first apprehended as sound, not as a visual representation to be mimicked. As I will explore, the deep association between the vocalized sound and the movement of the body means that sound and movement often emerge in the mind and body as the same phenomenon for the dancer. Kathak performance is grounded in forms of embodied motion, which are fundamentally intersensorial and which transcend the boundary between the sonic and the gestural. In this chapter, I undertake a phenomenological investigation of the musicking and moving body that examines how kathak dancers apprehend sound through movement and simultaneously perceive movement through sound. While our senses can be described empirically as discrete entities, phenomenologically speaking, this is not how we experience the world. It is this entangled and undifferentiated aspect of sensory experience that I explore here through an ethnographic description of the teaching and learning of North Indian kathak dance.

Central to this investigation is the phenomenological assumption that the moving body is foundational to our experience of the world. Following the work of Maurice Merleau-Ponty, I place the sensing, perceiving, and moving body at the center of my research and draw on his basic idea that the "lived body" is the means by which we have a world ([1945] 1962). As perceiving subjects, our focal attention moves in and toward certain aspects of the environment as we navigate the world from day to day. As dancers, we learn to home in on certain aspects of experience, to train and retrain the way we relate to the world, whether that is discovering how our foot feels and sounds as it slaps on the floor, finding our center of gravity and maintaining balance as we learn to take kathak pirouettes, known as *chakkars*, or developing a deep intuition for musical time as it frames the entire experience of the dance. We learn to tune in and are guided to focus on certain zones of perception that may typically remain beyond our explicit awareness; what I see or hear at any given moment is established in part because of the occlusion of other elements of the visual, auditory, and tactile fields.[1] Much as dancers can focus on one aspect of their training, my analysis follows in a similar fashion: I focus on the sonic dimension of experience in this chapter in order to illuminate the experiential, audible quality of the moving body that is often overlooked but nevertheless constitutes part of the holistic experience of being-in-the-world for a kathak dancer. Following the work of Don Ihde, "this deliberate change of emphasis from the visual to the auditory dimension at first symbolizes a hope to find material for a recovery of the richness of primary experience that is now forgotten or covered over in the too tightly interpreted visualist traditions" (1976, 13). While storytelling, elegance, beauty, the use of lines, diagonals, facial expression, gesture, and so forth, all exist as visible phenomena that are vital to kathak, I here direct focus to the audible aspects of dance experience. In this case, the phenomena of kathak might "yield more readily to an attention that is more concerned with listening" (Ihde 1976, 14). Kathak, as a rhythm-based dance form, presents the ideal opportunity for listening.

In this chapter, I also use sites of teaching and learning as the context for a phenomenological investigation of hearing kathak. While direct access to the individual experiences of anyone other than oneself remains elusive, close observations of teaching and learning, supported by supplementary conversations and interviews, provide one window into dancers' experience of sound and movement. Sites of teaching and learning cultural practices illuminate the ways in which culture is actively produced and worked on; this inevitably involves an active shaping of the perceptual and sensory modes through which we come to experience the world. This chapter is based on my own learning of kathak dance over the last twenty years, including training under the late Pandit Chitresh Das and his disciples, especially one of his senior disciples, Joanna de Souza. From 2004 to 2005 and again from 2007 to 2010, I undertook extensive anthropological fieldwork alongside Das in his schools in Kolkata, India, and San Francisco, United States. Since Das's passing in early 2015, my training resumed primarily with my first teacher, de Souza, who is based in Toronto, Canada. Kathak dance, like all Hindustani musical practices, is learned through closed lineages of artists, where disciplined training in one style and work with one guru ensures that a complete corpus of knowledge is handed down intact; this includes a "transmission" of stylistic preferences. While Das's style of kathak shares techniques, skills, and even repertoire with other lineages and gurus, his brand of kathak is well recognized. Das was well known for his rhythmic versatility, virtuosity, and the speed of his footwork, and he established what is now referred to as the "California gharana" (Chakravorty 2006; Morelli 2019). Das's own upbringing in Kolkata in the late 1940s in his parents' music and dance school, Nritya Bharati, influenced his relationships with well-known musicians, including Ali Akbar Khan and Swapan Chaudhuri, and was one of the contributing factors to his extraordinary penchant for rhythmic versatility. On stage, Das played masterfully with the most accomplished musicians. His depth of understanding of Hindustani music and his rhythmic playfulness certainly brought forward the rhythmic elements of kathak in new and exciting ways, which I discuss later in this chapter. De Souza, one of his earliest disciples, began training under Das in 1978 and brought her own musical background and rhythmic intuition to the dance. During my study with de Souza over the past five years, observation and firsthand experience of her sense of rhythmic playfulness, musicality, and pedagogic attention to sound quality inspired the questions about rhythm and sound that are at the root of this chapter.

KATHAK: AN APPRENTICESHIP IN HEARING

Up until now you have seen me dance, now hear me dance.

Pandit Chitresh Das

Kathak is a North Indian dance genre known for its rhythmic footwork, fast pirouettes, the elegance of its gestural vocabulary, and its storytelling component. Dance, music, and theater are all important elements in this classical form. It is commonly accepted that early kathakas descended from a hereditary class of male performers who traveled from village to village in order to narrate stories from the great Hindu epics, the *Mahabharata* and *Ramayana*.[2] Much of modern kathak, however, owes its developments and refinement to royal patronage "from Rajput kings throughout Rajasthan and in the Mughal courts of sixteenth through nineteenth century India" (Morelli 2019, 9). The Bhakti and Sufi devotional religious movements that swept through India during this period further shaped the kathak repertoire (Chakravorty 2008, 26). Many historical threads weave a complex and dynamic narrative; although multiple genealogies exist, it is widely accepted that from the sixteenth through to the nineteenth century, kathak flourished in the Mughal and Hindu courts of Jaipur, Lucknow, and Benares (see Chakravorty 2008).

Kathak today shares a deep connection with the Hindustani musical tradition of North India, both of which developed in the court environment (Morelli 2019, 9). The rhythms of the *pakhāwāj* and the *tablā* drums played an important role in kathak's development, and many of the rhythmic compositions use the language of these drums (Das et al. 2001, 11). Kathak is a percussive dance form, in which dancers share an intimate connection to the music, for they are not simply dancing to the music but creating it themselves through the sounds of their bare feet and *ghungrū*, the 150 or more brass bells wrapped around each of their ankles. Kathak dancers use sound in multiple ways: employing vocal rhythms, producing sound with the feet, and participating in the sonic environment that defines this cultural aesthetic. Learning to hear is thus an important part of the process of sensory enskillment that occurs in the learning of this art form, a process that psychologist James J. Gibson refers to as an "education of attention" (1966, 1979; see also Downey 2016, 14). Elaborating on this idea, the anthropologist Tim Ingold (2001) proposed Gibson's education of attention as a more ecologically valid way of understanding cultural learning: "In the passage of human generations, each one contributes to the knowledgeability of the next not by handing down a corpus of disembodied, context-free information, but by setting up, through their activities, the environmental contexts within which successors develop their own embodied skills of perception and action" (2001, 148; see also Ingold 2000). The more effectively individuals focus on sensory variables with crucial information, the more accurate and efficient they can be at extracting the information that they need (Downey 2016, 14). In the case of kathak, the perceptual skills required in the dance involve a deep training in learning to hear, in "discriminating and disciplining the attention of the senses" and learning to attend to one's environment (Grasseni 2004, 13). Skilled learning in almost any field illustrates the ways in which training in cultural practices hones our perceptual abilities and enskills the body (Downey 2002, 2016; Grasseni 2004, 2007). Certainly, any musical apprenticeship requires a perceptual training and developing of one's "ear." But the extent to which learning to hear is required in kathak dance requires a deliberate focus and attention not always afforded to those practices conceptually identified as "dance."

The Indian concept of *saṅgīt*, which refers to the combination of voice, instrument, and movement, provides a better framework to understand the multidimensionality of the arts in the Indian aesthetic system; discrete English terms such as "music" or "dance" fail to capture this interconnectedness (see Morelli 2019, 3). Dancers spend hundreds if not thousands of hours painstakingly refining the movements of their feet, arms, hands, wrists, neck, and eyes in line with the visual aesthetic ideal of kathak, but this is accompanied by an equivalent emphasis on musicality. Dancers must adhere to the structures of the Hindustani musical system. Kathak dancers are evaluated as much for their presentation of rhythm as for their beauty and grace. De Souza recounts that during her time living in Kolkata in the 1990s, it was still common to speak about going to "hear a dance concert" (personal communication, January 7, 2020). Today, lay audiences may need a prompt to tune into the sonic dimension of this dance form; Pandit Das, accustomed to newer audiences in diverse global locations, would often prompt his audiences to "listen" to the sound of his feet. Dancers too must train to cultivate this orientation to the sonic world and undertake an education of attention that habituates their bodies to the sonic world that supports the dance.

THE SONIC SPACE OF KATHAK: LISTENING AS A CULTURAL PRACTICE

In Hindustani music and dance, a distinction is often made between educated audiences and lay audiences, given that deep appreciation requires understanding of the complexities of its system. Ihde described this as a

> strange "grammar" of gliding, complex, and stylized pieces of Indian music which to the beginner first often appear as not even "music." The sounding of sympathetic strings and the use of twenty-two microtones, the whine of sitar and sarangi, present musical confusion. Yet once learned, Indian music proves to be one of the most highly classified, organized, and hardened musical traditions in musical history.
>
> (Ihde 1976, 157)

For patrons and artists alike, an education of attention teaches one to tune in to the sonic space in particular ways. The aesthetic background for kathak typically includes the percussive sound of the tablā or pakhāwāj; the melodic accompaniment given by the sitar, sarod, or sarangi; the drone of the tanpura; and the sound of the dancer. There is a range of other possible accompanists, including a harmonium player, a vocalist, and occasionally a *bansuri* (flute) player. This sonic world implicates listening as a cultural practice in which practitioners and aficionados must learn how to listen so as to understand the music's organization and its unique contours (Samuels et al. 2010, 330). Learning kathak requires a depth of understanding of Hindustani music that comes through acquaintance with the sound world that supports the dance. The key feature of that sound world is *tāl* (rhythmic cycle). Learning to hear this style of music, especially for the purposes of kathak, requires an understanding of its musical organization.

North Indian music and dance is structured by the framework of tāl; the most common is *tīntāl*, a sixteen-beat cycle akin to 4/4 time in Western music. Other common tāls in North Indian dance are *rupak* (a seven-beat cycle), *jhap* tāl (a ten-beat cycle), *dhamār* (a fourteen-beat cycle), and often more challenging half-beat tāls like 9½, referred to as *saade nau mātrā*. The chosen tāl provides a structure for the passage of time and establishes a relational frame in which musicians and dancers can effectively communicate, anticipate, and collaborate. Each tāl creates a different feeling; dancers and musicians speak of spending years dancing in one tāl to really get to know it. Learning to attend to the tāl is one of the most critical skills in dance. While there may be more variability in the way one gestures, turns, or moves through space, with the rhythmic cycle, you are either in tāl or *betāla* (without tāl).

The first and most important beat of any tāl is known as *sam*. Rhythmic compositions can start from anywhere within the designated cycle, lasting one or more cycles but typically concluding quite dramatically on the sam (pronounced "sum"). It is this resolution on sam that marks the successful completion of a rhythmic composition, providing one of the most aesthetically pleasurable moments of live performance. Dancing in tāl is, in fact, so crucial to successful performance that should a dancer land off sam, she must repeat the entire composition over again, even and especially on stage. Precision and accuracy of rhythmic expression within the musical meter is a defining feature of successful performance (see Dalidowicz 2015b, 2021). Fellow dancer and ethnomusicologist Ameera Nimjee reflected on her experience of getting acquainted with tāl after years of studying Western classical music: "You really are performing arrival, departure, and then back to arrival over and over and over again; this was a completely new way to relate to musical organization for me" (interview with author, August 4, 2020). Learning to attune to this temporal flow, whether it is marked melodically or percussively, is foundational in kathak.

Musicians relate to the tāl through commonly known drum stokes referred to as *thekā* (Ruckert 2004, 42). For example, the thekā for tīntāl in Das's lineage would be played and recited through the basic drum strokes represented in Figure 11.1.

The top line of Figure 11.1 marks the *vibhag* (sections of the tāl), the second line is the thekā, which represent varying strokes of the tablā, while the bottom line shows the numerical representation of the beats of the tāl.[3] Each vibhag is marked through claps or waves of the hand. Sam is indicated above with a plus sign, while beat nine, referred to as

VIBHAG (SECTIONS OF THE TĀL)	+				2				0				3			
THEKĀ FOR TĪNTĀL	DHĀ	DHIN	DHIN	DHĀ	DHĀ	DHIN	DHIN	DHĀ	NĀ	TIN	TIN	TĀ	TETE	DHIN	DHIN	DHĀ
NUMBERED BEATS OF TĪNTĀL	1	2	3	4	5	6	7	8	9	10	11	12	13	14	15	16

FIGURE 11.1: Thekā of tīntāl.

khālī (which means empty), is indicated by a zero and marked with a wave rather than a clap. This temporal flow is marked instrumentally through a repeating melody referred to as nagmā and is played by the accompanying stringed instruments of sitar, sarangi, sarod, or the hand-pumped harmonium. In kathak performance and practice, the key function of the instrumentalist is to play this repeating melody, which acts as an anchor that keeps the dancer oriented to the passage of tāl and one's place within it. Dancers must ensure tight coordination with the musical accompaniment, perfectly aligned with their rendering of the dance compositions, in order to stay on tāl and resolve successfully on sam.

Tāl is one of the more difficult aspects of kathak to master; it is similarly difficult to communicate how tāl sets up and creates the entire experience for the form. It is not a matter of simply dancing "to" the music; the dancer must be "inside" the music. In an interview with the author, de Souza described it this way: "We are dancing inside the frame . . . we are the painting inside the frame. The frame does not change, but the design inside the frame can change" (interview with author, May 5, 2020). Nimjee described dancing in tāl through the metaphor of being in a room: "The moment you turn on nagmā, it is like you opened a door into a room, that is contoured by this thing. And you cannot leave the room, so you have to be in the room and the way to be in the room is to be in tāl. . . . That is how I learned to explain because it is so hard to explain it to those who have no relationship to it. You open this door, and you are in it, and there is no point to do anything without the relationship with it, because then why are you in that room at all" (interview with author, August 4, 2020). What de Souza and Nimjee describe is the inseparability of tāl from both Hindustani music and dance: a dancer typically performs her art within the given structure of the tāl. Tāl contours the experience, and it is within the sonic space of tāl that dancers move and sound, and their dance becomes meaningful.

Learning to hear the nagmā and maintain nascent awareness of the passage of the tāl is a key skill in becoming a kathak dancer. I asked dancers, "When you are practicing, what is the focus of your listening?" All maintain the critical importance of attending to tāl or nagmā. As Nimjee put it in an interview, "I think there is a hierarchy of what I listen to, and the first is of course nagmā, and then listening for sam, and then my feet have a moral responsibility to uphold that" (interview with author, August 4, 2020). Fellow dancer and tablā player Anita Katakkar explained, "My ear will rotate through different sounds. If I am not solid, I will force myself to listen to the nagmā, listen to the melody, otherwise for me it is a little more subconscious. I may be listening to the bols in my head or my voice. If I am playing with multiple instruments, I usually focus on one at a time" (interview with author, August 12, 2020). Dancers and musicians communicate and keep the tāl by marking it with their hands, through claps, waves, and finger movements. Viscerally marking the tāl in this way helps internalize rhythm and pulse but also communicates the tāl visually to others. In learning a rhythmic composition, a student always learns to recite while marking the tāl with their hands. Knowing a rhythmic bol requires an embodied understanding of its relation to the tāl. This did not always come easily, and teachers intervened in a variety of ways, stressing gaps or the downbeat, or highlighting other markers that would help students become aware of the passage of tāl and one's relation to it.

Teachers encourage development not by transferring knowledge but, as Downey (2016, 14) would argue, by directing novices' attention to the most crucial sensory variables in the environment. Das and his disciples developed numerous strategies to build this awareness, including "kathak yoga," a pedagogic technique that did precisely this: directed learners' attention to the key variables of the sound world that supported kathak. Das's innovation of kathak yoga is a practice whereby dancers sing the repeating melody of the nagmā, thus replacing the role of the instrumentalist and creating the melodic frame of the tāl through their own voice. In this form of self-accompaniment, dancers sing the nagmā while executing dance compositions with their body and feet. In a more advanced version, students play *manjira* (hand cymbals), marking the main beat and the micro beats of the time cycle. Das played tablā while dancing; several of his disciples now play harmonium while dancing. Performing these tasks simultaneously—musical counting, singing, playing an instrument, and dancing—may be bewildering at first, but it ultimately serves as a pedagogical device that hones the dancer's attention to tāl and cultivates rhythmic versatility.[4] Doing so, the dancer "cannot avoid paying mind to this structure (the tāl) and the way in which a composition fits into the cycle, for there is nowhere to hide from the *thekā* when you are producing it yourself" (Morelli 2007, 173). Kathak yoga provides dancers with a deeper embodied understanding of the composition's relationship to the tāl, honing perception to the key elements of the sound world and ultimately preparing students for performing with live musicians by developing their "feel" for their place in the rhythmic cycle.

The ideal state to which dancers aspire is to internalize the tāl to such a point that it remains ongoing in their body, even without any external sound source. Among students of renowned artists like Das or the famed tablā player Swapan Chaudhuri, stories frequently circulate that illustrate their teacher's deep assimilation of tāl. Such narratives describe how the great dancer or musician is able to maintain ongoing awareness of the temporal passage of tāl without any external auditory cues. The artist will begin by marking the tāl and then engage in a normal conversation while they internally sense the passage of the cycle with metronomic precision. After several cycles of the tāl having passed, the teacher will bring the tāl back to explicit awareness and resolve exactly and emphatically on the moment of the sam.

THE SOUND OF FEET

Dancers create their own sound through the rhythmic use of their feet and the ghungrū wrapped around their ankles, both of which contribute to the acoustic environment of the dance. As students, we are taught to listen to the sound of the feet, although in early stages of training, a focus on the auditory quality of the movement invariably takes a secondary role as dancers attend to the coordination of their feet movements with those of their upper body, arms, wrists, hands, head, and neck. However, dancers do spend much of their time isolating the practice of footwork. During this focused training, they cultivate their stamina and speed and focus closely on getting the right sound. In Das's lineage, the basic eight-step footwork of *tatkār* is typically performed with the sound of the full foot striking the floor; this full-footed style is referred to as *aṭh śabd* tatkār. In audio sample 1, the dancer Seema Mehta recites the syllables associated with tatkār as she performs aṭh śabd tatkār (see ⏵ Audio Sample 1).

The basic eight-step tatkār pattern can also be performed by using different strokes of the feet to produce different sounds, for example, by using only the toes (*punje*) or by combining sounds of the heels and full foot (*eṛī*), as detailed in Figure 11.2 (see also Morelli 2019, 92).

Learning how to lift the foot and slap it on the ground to produce an audible sound is one of the more difficult elements for students to figure out, should they not be predisposed to a sonorous slap. Getting clarity of sound, with eight even sounds, is equally challenging. What Ingold says of sensory education in general is true of kathak dance; guided by teachers, "students learned how to make 'sensory correction(s)' by continually adjusting or 'tuning' the movement in response to an ongoing perceptual monitoring of the emergent task" (Ingold 2000, 353). If we consider the rather mechanistic task of slapping the foot upon the floor over and over, dancers need to learn how to hold their weight; how to initiate the movement while keeping relaxed in the hips, knees, and feet; and how to "tune" these movements in accordance with the sonorous production of a "slap" on the floor. The sensation of the foot on the floor and its

VOCALIZED BOL	TĀ	THEĪ	THEĪ	TAT	Ā	THEĪ	THEĪ	TAT
FOOTWORK PATTERN	RIGHT	LEFT	RIGHT	LEFT	LEFT	RIGHT	LEFT	RIGHT
AṬH ŚABD	FLAT	FLAT	FLAT	FLAT	FLAT	FLAT	FLAT	FLAT
EṚĪ	FLAT	HEEL	HEEL	BRUSH	FLAT	HEEL	HEEL	BRUSH
PUNJE	TOES	TOES	TOES	TOES	TOES	TOES	TOES	TOES

FIGURE 11.2: Sounds of the tatkār footwork pattern.

vibration is inseparable from the action's auditory expression, and dancers must continually monitor these varied sensorial inputs. Even the texture of the floor matters here; the acoustic property of the floor comes to life as dancers orient their movement toward their material environment. Teachers develop strategies to aid students in learning, and students adopt training techniques to help them develop the strength and dexterity to produce the idealized sound. De Souza frequently had students practice accenting different strokes of the eight-step pattern (e.g., 1 and 4, 2 and 5, 3 and 6, or 4 and 8). Each accent requires students to shift their weight in ways not usually anticipated in the basic pattern. The accent exercise teaches students to produce the full eight sounds for each cycle of tatkār, but in so doing, it also further develops dexterity and versatility (see Dalidowicz 2015b).

In performance, certain elements of a traditional solo are designed to highlight the rhythms of kathak. The *savāl-javāb* (question-answer) section of the kathak solo is an improvisatory exchange between the dancer and tablā player: the dancer produces unplanned rhythmic phrases with their feet, responding in a question-and-answer segment to the rhythmic phrases of the tablā.[5] *Ladi* (string or series) compositions used in tablā are also "good for listening," as de Souza explained; the dancer will play with a basic rhythmic phrase and variants through high-energy footwork. One of the most appreciated and controversial aspects of Das's repertoire was his performance of "Relgari" (rail car), often referred to as the "train," in which he sonically represented the journey of a steam train from one station to the next. He performed this without the support of musicians, using only his feet and ghungrū to represent what he has described as the "sound of a railway carriage leaving the station, changing tracks, gathering speed, crossing a bridge, passing open fields and trees, slowing down, changing tracks, gaining, and finally reaching its destination and coming to a halt on the platform" (Ghosh 1981, 5–6, cited in Morelli 2019, 61). Although Das's train was popular among audiences, staunch traditionalists criticized its overemphasis on sound (i.e., the dominance of the sounding rhythm over the visual), as well as its "rendering of an inanimate aspect of the modern world, as opposed to more common depictions of characters from India's ancient epics" (Morelli 2019, 62; see also Saxena 1991). In fact, other renowned dancers are known to have presented the sounds of the inanimate world, such as cannons, in dance (Morelli 2019, 61–62). Das also presented sounds of the natural world, such as galloping horses and peacocks. Das and his disciples, especially de Souza, were oriented to the sounding aspects of this form, and numerous productions were designed to highlight its rhythmic elements. For example, Das's ongoing collaboration with tap dancer Jason Samuels Smith, which was originally entitled "Fastest Feet in Rhythm" and later rebranded as "India Jazz Suites," highlighted the rhythmic play between these two artists.[6] De Souza's piece "HUM" was created for Toronto's Body Percussion festival in 2014 and required dancers to use only their bodies in the production of sound, providing de Souza an opportunity to highlight the ways kathak dancers use their feet, bodies, and voice to create rhythm.

Speaking Rhythm, Catching Rhythm

Learning kathak dance means first learning to "speak" the dance. As de Souza explained to a beginning group of kathak students, "everything we dance has a spoken language. Everything we dance, we can speak." Kathak dance, like most music and dance in India, is first learned through vocalized syllables known as bols. Bol comes from the word *bolna*, which literally means "to speak." Bols are often described simply as mnemonic syllables that aid the learning and remembering of what was, historically, an oral tradition. The use of what have been referred to as vocables to communicate musical ideas and represent musical sounds exists across Indian musical traditions and also in cultures beyond India, such as the *canntaireachd* used in Scottish bagpipe music (Fatone 2010) or the vocalized syllables of *Ipchangdan* in Korean drumming (Kwon 2015). Within the Hindustani musical system of North India, there is a shared language between kathak and the percussive instruments of tablā and pakhāwāj. While there are dance-specific bols for kathak, many of the bols kathak dancers use come from percussion. This rhythmic language provides units of sounds, phrasing, and a kind of grammar that allows dancers to express musical ideas.

Bols can be onomatopoeic in nature, imitating the sounds produced by the drum or the sounds of the foot and, in some instances, the sounds of nature. Certain bols may loosely replicate the sound of the foot striking the floor, such as "ta," which often indicates a flat-footed stroke. Bols may also reference myth. The sound of "ta" is said to have come from the sound of Krishna dancing on the head of the defeated demon snake Kaliya, with the sound of his bare foot slapping on Kaliya's hood expressed as "tā theī tat" (Das et al. 2001). Another narrative traces the language of the rhythmic art to the great Lord Shiva: "The little drum on which he played is called a *damaru* [waisted-shape drum]. And when he played at medium speed it sounded like 'diga diga diga.' When it went fast, it sounded like 'taka taka taka.' That is the first sound of all the drums, and also the basic sound of the footwork in the dance" (Zakir Hussain, quoted in Ruckert 2004, 50; phrase in square brackets in the original source). In general, the common footwork patterns are vocalized through bols that express the musicality of the pattern produced by the feet. For example, "ta re ki ta" indicates flat-heel-flat-heel, and "diga diga" indicates all heel sounds. ("Ta re ki ta" is illustrated in ⊙ Audio Sample 2.)

Other lesser used bols represent sounds of nature, such as "koo" for the call of the peacock. While bols may have originally shared an onomatopoeic relationship with the sounds that they are said to represent, multiple ways to execute the syllables have weakened this relationship over time (Ananthanarayana and Rao 2018, 1229). Bols are often interchangeable, and knowing how a bol should be expressed is contextual and relies on one-on-one training with a teacher who can explain how it should be played in a specific context. In most cases, the poetry of the bol composition takes precedence over maintaining a consistent matching to strokes. Figure 11.3 illustrates a basic

```
+                  |              |            |
tā – theī –    tat tat theī  –  a – theī –   tat tat theī  –

2                  |              |            |
theī – tā theī   – tā theī –   theī – theī –   tat – tat –

0                  |              |            |
theī – tā theī   – tā theī –   theī – theī –   tat – tat –

3                  |              |            |
tat – tat –    theī – tat –   tat – theī –   tat – tat –

+
(Dha)
```

FIGURE 11.3: Basic tatkār kī bandish composition in one cycle on tīntāl.

tatkār kī bandish composition using dance bols and lasting one cycle (see also Das et al. 2001, 27).

This basic composition contains common phrases used extensively in kathak, which can vary in speed, length, and complexity. All compositions are learned first through vocalized bols, to which movement is later attached. In initially learning a composition, a dancer attempts to grasp as much of the rhythm as possible in its vocalized form. The example above presents a beginner-level composition, but as one progresses, the compositions become increasingly complex. (⏵ Audio sample 3 illustrates a complex tatkār kī bandish composition.)

Most dancers with whom I spoke referred to a "catching of the rhythm" as a first step in learning the dance, where not all bols are intelligible and not all rhythmic phrases within the full composition are clear. In an interview, dancer Jane Morris described her experience of learning more complicated rhythmic phrases: "I first try to catch the rhythm. You can use nonsense syllables if you don't know them. It is the rhythm that you catch. Then I try to scat my way through the bols . . . . But it is the rhythm, first and foremost" (interview with author, July 28, 2020). Familiarity with phrasing allows dancers to catch rhythms quickly, and students can fill in the blanks and anticipate patterns based on experience. In an interview with the author, Kathak student and tablā musician Katakkar described this as follows:

> Everyone has a different approach, but in my experience, if you don't catch the recitation, then you are building stuff on a shaky foundation . . . . There will be patterns that start to repeat, so it starts to be like language, phrases that you have heard before, and they come up again. So the more you practice, the more you are able to catch on to familiar phrases. But typically when I'm learning . . . I will recite with tāl, and then I will know approximately where things fall, and then I try to fill it in, that's how I operate. . . . I'll just try and grab what it is I know I can hear and what I know is happening. And the rest, I try not to get too caught up on that; it is pointless. You can't always catch everything all at once. I catch what I can, and then I fill in the blanks.
>
> (interview with author, August 12, 2020)

The sound of the bols serves as an accessible introduction to the movement, whereby articulating the bols verbally (a visceral action in itself that involves gestures of the lungs, throat, tongue, and lips) allows the dancer to catch the rhythm; with this in place, the performers are then more easily able to express those motions in dance gestures of the arms, hands, feet, and so forth. In other words, vocalization of these patterns is already a fully embodied act. As I discuss further below, the way dancers speak about catching rhythm hints at the pre-reflexive bodily unity that allows perception to facilitate verbal gestures and verbal gestures to facilitate the dance.

Katakkar's quote highlights another important point: that the "grabbing" or "catching" of recitation only makes sense within the context of tāl. The cyclic nature of tāl gives the necessary temporal orientation, providing a structure for dancers to sit-uate the phrasing within. Discussing the Carnatic tradition, David P. Nelson describes the relationship between tāl and the specific rhythmic composition that a musician or dancer performs: "The tāḷa in its unwavering repetition exerts a centripetal force on the material, while the grouping into rhythmic phrases at times exerts a centrifugal pull with respect to the tāḷa. Rhythmic unity requires simultaneous attention to the structure of the tāḷa and the movement of the patterns" (1991, 2). In other words, the steadiness of tāl can create a "pull" on the rhythm, attracting the composition toward its unmistakable beat. This is a common mistake, where dancers inadvertently align the main stresses of the composition with the downbeat of the tāl. To produce the proper understanding of the relationship between the tāl and the composition, dancers and musicians will mark the beats of tāl with claps or waves of the hands (and fingers) while reciting the bols, informing their understanding of how the rhythm falls in relation to the basic frame. Marked with corresponding gestures, these downbeats provide way points along the temporal progression of the cycle, facilitating a tactile awareness of the progression of tāl and one's place in it. In initial stages of learning a new compo-sition, a teacher may provide vocal or gestural emphasis at certain points within the pattern to highlight the way the rhythm falls in relation to tāl, stressing certain syllables that land on the main beat or emphasizing the beginning of a new pattern to provide markers that students can easily catch. The teacher may slow down the laya (tempo of the tāl) to highlight gaps for the learner or count the microbeats to highlight exactly where the rhythm falls. Mark Johnson, interpreting the work of Suzanne Langer (1947), explains that

> When we are actively listening to music, we imaginatively enter into its "motion," experiencing all of the ways it moves, swells, hops, rushes, floats, trips along, drags, soars, and falls. This musical soaring, floating, or falling is experienced by us as our felt flow of experience. We feel it in our vital, tactile-kinaesthetic bodies. When the music builds up tension (for example, as it moves pitch-wise from the lower through the middle to a high range), we experience that tension in ourselves. If we didn't, music would never move us.
>
> (Johnson 2006,14)

This applies to the percussive rhythms of kathak. The relationship between the tāl and the composition is already a kind of motion in itself. Dancers initially feel the qualities of that motion (tensions, gaps, unity, and so forth) by listening, and they later engage the tāl and composition by vocalizing their rhythms. As a result of all of this, the motion of their rhythm flows into the dance.

HEARING WITH THE BODY

The vocalized form of the rhythm takes on a new and anticipated dimension in the kinesthetic, visual, and sonic fields, as rhythms are brought forth in movement and in the sound of the body in motion. In class with de Souza, a new composition will be introduced through vocalized syllables and, depending on the complexity of the piece and level of the students, may be repeated multiple times. Typically, the choreographed movements are learned soon thereafter, and from that point forward, the vocalized bol and the dance bol become inseparable. What enables all of this is the fundamentally intersensorial nature of motion and a unified consciousness from which discrete sensory modalities become mere abstractions, as I will show below. The rhythmic motion of the composition is manifest through learned techniques, such as footwork, gestures, or pirouettes. Included in a kathaka's vocabulary of movement are also the subtle gestures of the head, neck, hands, wrists, eyes, and eyebrows that bring forth the rhythm.[7] A rhythmic phrase could be performed in an endless variety of choreographed or improvised ways. Most compositions, however, are taught initially through basic or skeleton choreography, which draws on conventions within the lineage and makes use of accepted relationships between bols and dance vocabulary. Advanced students may be able to predict certain movement phrases, particularly dance bols that represent footwork or others that are commonly expressed in an accepted way and easily anticipated; for example, "kī ta taka tun" was often expressed using the lotus hand gesture, moving from above the head to chest level with a matched footwork pattern. Choreographed variations could go in many directions, even being performed purely through *gat bhāv* (storytelling), and as such, a student's ability to anticipate diminished quickly.

In his work on listening to the Brazilian dance and martial art form capoeira, Greg Downey writes, "Without the bodily predispositions incorporated from others through apprenticeship . . . the experience of hearing for most listeners . . . is bereft of its visceral dimensions. . . . For those who are trained in listening, however, movement and musical sound seem so closely linked that they can imagine music as a route to proficiency" (2002, 503). In kathak, dancers learn through long-term training to make this immediate link between sound and its visceral dimension. Movements are never learned in isolation from a vocalized equivalent, and in the bodies and minds of dancers, movements sound. Learning to dance involves embodying these learned associations between movement and their sonic counterparts. In hearing or reciting the bols, such as "tat tat theī tigga dha digga digga theī," a known movement phrase is called forth in the body of the dancer that involves a right-left-right footwork pattern with accompanying arm gestures, followed by a five-step turn. Part of skilled learning within kathak is thus cultivating the ability to understand the entrenched relationality between the vocalized rhythm and its kinetic counterpart. Although there is no exclusive relationship between bol and movement, the movement phrase itself is never independent of the vocalized bol. This enduring relationship of body movement with body sound marks one of the distinctive qualities of this dance form.

This relationship also allows the voice to be used instructively to provide cues as to how something should be danced. "You must recite to inform the body and to get the nuances of sound," de Souza explained (interview with author, August 1, 2020). Here, the voice can communicate how a rhythmic idea should be expressed in movement. The prosodic style of recitation employed by teachers like de Souza is used to indicate something about the quality of movement and how specific bols can be danced. Bols can be stretched, sharpened, or weighted heavily or lightly. Volume and pitch can be manipulated. De Souza uses melismatic vocalization of otherwise syllabic bols to inform movements. A change of pitch across one syllable could be indicative of movement being elongated and then released. Recitation, with pitch and intensity variation, is thus akin to the recitation of poetry (Ruckert 2004, 51). Here the voice informs the dancing, in as much as it sets the rhythmic structure. Rohit Ananthanarayana and Preeti Rao describe a similar pedagogic tool in tablā: "Despite the skeletal description embedded in the score, the bol recitation of the composition is highly expressive and packed with prosodic variations, and this information is passed on orally from teacher to pupil" (Ananthanarayana and Rao 2018, 1230). Much of what is transmitted in any oral tradition are the nuances and ornaments that give a bol its style and beauty; it is the "how to" of recitation rather than simply the structure of the composition itself. This is why direct study with a teacher has remained critical to the sharing of kathak as an oral tradition. Students learn to hear how the movement should be danced by first listening to the teacher and then reproducing it in their own recitation, which informs the body how to dance. Long-term study with one teacher also cultivates an adept ear, such that hearing the inflections and nuances of the teacher's voice brings a practical understanding of the teacher's style, preferences, and expectations for movement.

While bol compositions, which are passed on as part of a corpus of knowledge within a lineage, can be independently represented through transcription today, the transmission of knowledge remains an entirely embodied act. Even with something as directly representable as a bol, knowing comes through a process of guided discovery. As Seema Mehta, disciple of Das and director of the Chhandam Nritya Bharati Mumbai kathak dance school, explained, "You can give your book to someone but no one will be able to understand the bols you have written. It is still an oral tradition, even if you are writing [it] down. You have to physically be there" (personal communication, May 15, 2020). Written transcriptions of bols must ultimately be brought into the oral tradition if they are to serve kathak practitioners. Whether transcriptions are made in Roman or Devanagari script, these representational systems utilize arbitrary symbols that have no sensuous connection to the sounds they represent. In contrast, the vocalized bols are the sonic manifestation of motion. This goes directly to Merleau-Ponty's point that speech itself is an entirely embodied act, in which arbitrary symbols are given meaning through the body ([1945] 1962, 182). Johnson elaborates on Merleau-Ponty's ideas on the bodily basis for emergent meaning: "A composer does not frame conceptual meanings in her head, which she then somehow cleverly expresses in musical pitch contours. Rather, the meaning emerges only in and through the act of making music. Music is not an external sign system we use to express non-musical meanings or concepts. Rather, the meaning exists in the enactment" (2006, 10). Langer provides further insight: "A work of art does not point us to a meaning beyond its own presence. What is expressed cannot be grasped apart from the sensuous or poetic form that expresses it. In a work of art, we have the direct presentation of a feeling, not a sign that points to it" (1947, 133–134). Similarly, the musical or rhythmic meaning of the bol resides in its enactment by the living body. Contrary to representational systems that we find in written language, the sonic materiality of the vocalized bol is not arbitrary. The sound itself entails a form of motion. The perception of these sounds allows embodied subjects to assimilate forms of motion that can be manifested in dance gestures and other musical forms.

THE CONFLATION OF MOVEMENT AND SOUND

At first glance, it appears that learning a rhythmic bol follows a linear process whereby the vocalization precedes the movement and is a precursor to the next phase. In fact, recitation and movement work in tandem. Movements help dancers to make sense of parts of the bol that they may not have grasped only through vocalizing. As Nimjee explained, "Each informs the other; it is back and forth. There is something that happens when you recite the bol that triggers your body to remember things. But more so, when you are dancing in context, it helps you to make sense of a bol that you may not have rhythmically totally understood previously. You get the bol in its full integrity because you put movement into it. I really think one influences the other" (interview with author, August 4, 2020). In order to understand the experience of hearing musical sound, we should examine the processes through which it is apprehended, and these processes, as Downey argues, are often dance or movement (2002, 504).

Processes of recall and remembering similarly rely on the collaborative work of the voice and the movements of the body. Vocalized bols are described as mnemonic devices, but the bols are not always the precursor to remembering. I have witnessed dancers (myself included) who struggle to correctly recall elements of a particular vocalized bol composition add a motor dimension to the memory work and bring forth the correct verbal syllables by enacting the accompanying movements. Mehta reflects on her process: "It is a synchronized memory work because the movement helps to remember the bol and the bol helps to remember the movement. They go hand in hand. Especially for long compositions, if I don't have the recitation, I may start dancing, and then the movements definitely help me to remember the bols" (personal communication, May 15, 2020). In an interview, Katakkar similarly observes, "Dance is a real asset, because when you are using your body, you have your body memory. There are all these connections you can form with the movement and the bols that each feed each other. I wonder if it might be easier to remember compositions *because* you do dance them, and when you are dancing them, because you remember the movements, they remind you of the bols. It is a back-and-forth thing with dance that you don't have with tablā" (interview with author, August 12, 2020). Observing this process of learning, I saw clearly that the recitation was not simply the precursor to the movement.

What was striking about dancers' explanations of the relationship between recited bol and danced bol was their inseparability. Dancers think of movement through sonic equivalents and similarly think of sound through movement equivalents. Using the perspective of cognitive science, some learning theorists and psychologists have considered this "conflation phenomenon," which is often seen within traditions of oral music learning, as a kind of mapping of an ideal vocal image to an instrumental utterance (see Gordon 1989; Brinner 1995; Godoy 2003; McNeill 2005). In her study of Scottish bagpiping, Gina Fatone describes the "extraordinary adeptness of the mind to seemingly 'conflate' or translate images from and between various modalities of experience" (2010, 408). "In addition to instrumental demonstration, instructors used vocabelising, conducting gestures with the hands or the chanter, or verbally expressed, metaphoric images of object or body motion to convey musical information. The student then transferred these aural, visual, or imagined images into manual action made auditory through the pipe chanter" (Fatone 2010, 403). Following this line of thinking, the student's task involves transferring knowledge from one domain (the auditory) to another (the motor). Psychologists identify pedagogical tools such as these, which enable students to think of one thing in terms of another, as cross-domain or cross-modal cognitive processes—that is, mental operations involving the transfer or interaction of counterparts between different domains of experience (e.g., the visual, motor, auditory, vocal, or imagined domains; Fatone 2010, 397). Implicit in this approach is the assumption that with the transfer of cognitive processes there must also be a transfer between various modalities of experience. Yet, in listening to the kathak dancers describe their experiences and in analyzing my own, it became evident that the practice of recitation and dance was not a case of "thinking of one thing in terms of another." The vocalized and motor expressions of the bol were experienced as originating from the same place, and therefore as being one and the same. The experiences of the kathak dancer provide evidence of the synesthesia between informed hearing and corporeal activity, and the imbrication of the two as a perceptual system (Gibson 1966; Downey 2002, 503). To consider the multisensory way in which dancers learn to apprehend and recall rhythm, I turn to the phenomenology of Merleau-Ponty for another explanation of this conflation phenomena.

SYNESTHESIA AND THE SENSING BODY

> The senses translate themselves without the need for an interpreter: they understand each other without having to pass through an idea.
>
> (Merleau-Ponty [1945] 1962, 244)

The conflation of sound and movement in a kathak dancer's perception and experience highlights an important point. While empirically it may make sense to say that we have five discrete senses, phenomenologically speaking, this is not how we experience the world. As Merleau-Ponty suggests, perception of discrete sensory experiences is a learned attitude that blurs the basic, originary experience of knowing and being in the world:

> I say that my eyes see, and my hand touches, and that my foot hurts, but these naïve expressions do not convey my genuine experience. They already present me with an interpretation that detaches from its original subject. Because I know that light strikes my eyes, that contact is made by the skin, and that my shoe hurts my foot, I distribute the perceptions that belong to my soul into my body: I place perception within the perceived. But this is nothing but the spatial and temporal wake of conscious acts. If I consider them from within, I find a single knowledge that has no location, a soul that has no parts, and there is no difference between thinking and perceiving, or between seeing and hearing.
>
> (Merleau-Ponty [1945] 1962, 220)

Merleau-Ponty describes the synesthesia of senses as the basic form of lived experience, not an anomalous one. The dancer immersed in rhythms may be afforded a pre-objective sense of the body in its originary state of synesthesia. The lived experience of what has elsewhere been explained as cross-modal or inter-modal processes is better accounted for through a view of the whole body as the subject of perception: "The senses are distinct and yet indiscernible, like monocular images in binocular vision" (Merleau-Ponty [1945] 1962, 239). In this view, sensory registers mediate environmental input, but the single knowledge is embodied universally in a self that is undifferentiated.

Rhythm provides one of the more available opportunities for something akin to an experience of originary perception. Rhythms can be felt, heard, seen, and touched;

we find rhythm in sound, in visual images, in textures, in the flow of time, or in movements of the body. Restricting experience to a single sensory register is superficial and misrepresents the fundamental level of embodied experience. "Synesthetic perception is the rule and, if we do not notice it, this is because scientific knowledge displaces experience[,] and we have unlearned seeing, hearing, and sensing in general in order to deduce what we ought to see, hear, or sense from our bodily organisation and from the world as is conceived by the physicist" (Merleau-Ponty [1945] 1962, 238). The musicking and moving body provides an opportunity for synesthetic experience in which we can dispense with—if only momentarily—this logic that our bodies have internalized through participation in a rationalist world. If we look phenomenologically at the body, we can see that, at the originary layer of perception, senses are not indistinguishable, and these moments of intersensorial experience, or what has been referred to as cross-modality, are actually hinting at what is the basic, originary experience of knowing and being in the world. There is no requirement for representations to be transferred from one modality to another or for the requirement of sense experience to pass through an idea.

Disciplined training shapes the perceptual system, encouraging dancers to leverage the synesthetic possibilities of experience. If we consider Merleau-Ponty's view of synesthetic perception alongside a phenomenological view of skilled learning as a series of sensory corrections that requires continual adjusting or a tuning in response to an ongoing perceptual monitoring of the emergent task (Ingold 2000, 353), we can understand the conflation phenomena through a view of the body in its world, acting intelligently through ongoing interaction with the environment, rather than being the result of a purely mental activity. Learning and performing are not about the internal work of the mind accessing an accumulated store of representations; on the contrary, learning and bringing forth dance is a process that comes about through the agent's fine-tuned perception of the environment. For the kathak dancer, that fine-tuning of the body is directed to the sonic qualities of the material world. Through an ongoing education of attention, the very infrastructure of a dancer's perceptual system is shaped: this culturally generated mode of attention brings to the foreground of our experience the synesthetic possibilities of sensing our world.

PHENOMENOLOGY AND DANCE

What does it mean to hear dance? Dancers hear the vocalizations and rhythms of the dance through more than just their ears. The rhythms resonate through the body and can be felt from the feet to the fingers. In *Listening and Voice: Phenomenologies of Sound*, Ihde (1976) reminds us that hearing is never entirely an auditory experience: "Phenomenologically I do not merely hear with my ears, I hear with my whole body. My ears are at best the focal organs of hearing. This may be detected quite dramatically in listening to loud rock music. The bass notes reverberate in my stomach, and even my feet 'hear' the sound of the auditory orgy" (44). Tactile, kinetic, and even visual processes are central in creating our experience of sound. Scottish percussionist Evelyn Glennie, who is profoundly deaf, provides her take on hearing:

> Hearing is basically a specialized form of touch. Sound is simply vibrating air which the ear picks up and converts to electrical signals, which are then interpreted by the brain. The sense of hearing is not the only sense that can do this, touch can do this too. If you are standing by the road and a large truck goes by, do you hear or feel the vibration? The answer is both. . . . For some reason we tend to make a distinction between hearing a sound and feeling a vibration, in reality they are the same thing.
>
> (Glennie 2015)

Glennie further describes the role of vision in creating a sound experience: "We can also see items move and vibrate. If I see a drumhead or cymbal vibrate or even see the leaves of a tree moving in the wind, then subconsciously my brain creates a corresponding sound" (Glennie 2015). As a profoundly deaf musician, Glennie has tuned in to other sensory aspects of hearing that are, in fact, available to all of us. Although we have normalized the association between hearing and the function of the ears, sound experience draws on all sensory functions, in varying proportions and in ways unique to the person and their context. In learning to hear, kathak dancers similarly learn to tune in to other aspects of their world, to hear tactilely through the vibrations of their feet, to hear kinetically and visually through the gestures of body. Hearing *is* movement-based: sound and rhythm are apprehended, remembered, and expressed viscerally, through the whole body. From this perspective, all kinetic experience is irrevocably sonic, tactile, and visual. The fundamentally intersensorial nature of bodily being can be grasped more easily in an example like kathak, an art form in which embodied motion transcends boundaries between the sonic and the gestural.

The insights of phenomenology provide a perspective that uncovers to the kathak dancer's sonorous relationship with their world. Phenomenology, in this case, allows us to attend to aspects of dancers' perception and experience that may otherwise be missed through a conventional approach to the study of dance or music. Phenomenology can assist us to move past an empirical understanding of sense experience towards a richer description of the way things are lived and felt, challenging conventional rationalistic views of what it means and feels like to be human. For a dancer, the very infrastructure of perception is cultivated through systematic training, and this provides for a unique attunement to the world, one in which the sonic and kinetic fields intersect and interact in complementary ways, where sound and movement can be experienced as the same phenomena. I have here tried to evoke a sense of how the body is brought to life in new ways through training in a cultural aesthetic that ultimately shapes the way we perceive the world around us.

NOTES

1. Elsewhere, I have explored the ways that learning the dramatic art of storytelling within kathak required dancers to visually and kinesthetically attend to elements of the background world of India that typically escaped their conscious attention (Dalidowicz 2015a). During residency in India alongside their guru, Pandit Chitresh Das's American-trained students were directed to the tacit aspects of daily life in Kolkata, certain patterns of interaction, emotional relationships, or modes of deference that became critical to a total education in kathak. The passive pedagogies of being-in-place in Kolkata provided an invisible backdrop from which Das was able to foreground a particular historical horizon necessary to learning the affective dimension of the dance.

2. Although this view is commonly accepted, Margaret Walker's book *India's Kathak Dance in Historical Perspective* (2014) casts doubt on this familiar version of the genre's historical narrative.

3. In the transcription reproduced below, George Ruckert provides an example of a more commonly known thekā for tablā players. Ruckert explains how this thekā is played: "On the *tablā*, which is a combination of a left and a right hand drum . . . , the 't-' sounds [all of the sounds starting with the letter 't'] are produced with the right hand alone striking its right drum, while the 'dh-' sounds [all of the sounds starting with the letter 'd'] are produced by both drums striking simultaneously: a treble and a bass sound together" (Ruckert 2004, 43).

   dha dhin dhin dha | dha dhin dhin dha | dha tin tin ta | ta dhin dhin dha

4. For a YouTube video of Das, Antara Bhardwaj, and Rachna Nivas performing kathak yoga for an audience, see Asian Art Museum (2014).

5. For a YouTube video of Das performing this kind of call-and-response with a tablā player, see chhandam (2008).

6. For a YouTube video of Das and Smith performing this piece together, see chhandamfan (2007).

7. For a YouTube video of de Souza performing a series of compositions that highlight the vocalized bols and the accompanying movements, see personalladoos (2007).

WORKS CITED

Ananthanarayana, Rohit M., and Preeti Rao. 2018. "Acoustic-Prosodic Features of Tablā Bol Recitation and Correspondence with the Tablā Imitation." Paper presented at Interspeech 2018, Hyderabad, India, September 2018.

Asian Art Museum. 2014. "Kathak Yoga (Part 2 of 2)." YouTube. https://www.youtube.com/watch?v=R4g-GesBYvo.

Brinner, Benjamin. 1995. *Knowing Music, Making Music: Javanese Gamelan and the Theory of Musical Competence and Interaction.* Chicago: University of Chicago Press.

Chakravorty, Pallabi. 2006. "Dancing into Modernity: Multiple Narratives of India's Kathak Dance." *Dance Research Journal* 38 (1–2): 115–136.

Chakravorty, Pallabi. 2008. *Bells of Change.* Calcutta: Seagull Books.

chhandam. 2008. "Kathak—Lightning Speed Feet." YouTube. https://www.youtube.com/watch?v=3SxWyvli7es.

chhandamfan. 2007. "Fierce Kathak & Tap—Pt. Chitresh Das & Jason Samuels Smith." YouTube. https://www.youtube.com/watch?v=4sQn5bXbigo.

Clayton, Martin. 2008. "Toward an Ethnomusicology of Sound Experience." In *The New (Ethno)musicologies*, edited by Henry Stobart, 135–169. Lanham, MD: Scarecrow Press.

Dalidowicz, Monica. 2015a. "Being 'Sita': Physical Affects in the North Indian Dance of Kathak." In *Phenomenology and Anthropology: A Sense of Perspective*, edited by Kalpana Ram and Chris Houston, 90–113. Bloomington: Indiana University Press.

Dalidowicz, Monica. 2015b. "Crafting Fidelity: Pedagogical Creativity in Kathak Dance." *Journal of the Royal Anthropological Institute* 21 (4): 838–854.

Dalidowicz, Monica. 2021. "Upaj: Improvising within Tradition in Kathak Dance." In *Sound Changes: Improvisation and Transcultural Difference*, edited by Daniel Fischlin and Eric Porter, 175–199. Ann Arbor: University of Michigan Press.

Das, Chitresh, Gretchen Hayden Ruckert, George Ruckert, Joanna Das, Michelle Zonka, Sarah Morelli, and Seibi Lee. 2001. *Kathak Handbook*. San Rafael, CA: Chhandam School of Kathak Dance.

Downey, Greg. 2002. "Listening to Capoeira: Phenomenology, Embodiment, and the Materiality of Music." *Ethnomusicology* 46 (3): 487–509.

Downey, Greg. 2016. "Sensory Enculturation and Neuroanthropology: The Case of Human Echolocation." In *The Oxford Handbook of Cultural Neuroscience*, edited by Joan Y. Chiao, Shu-Chen Li, Rebecca Seligman, and Robert Turner, 41–56. Oxford Handbooks Online. New York: Oxford University Press. https://www.oxfordhandbooks.com/view/10.1093/oxfordhb/9780199357376.001.0001/oxfordhb-9780199357376-e-23.

Fatone, Gina. 2010. "'You'll Break Your Heart Trying to Play It like You Sing It': Intermodal Imagery and the Transmission of Scottish Classical Bagpiping." *Ethnomusicology* 54 (3): 395–424.

Feld, Steven. 1996. "Waterfalls of Song: An Acoustemology of Place Resounding in Bosavi, Papua New Guinea." In *Senses of Place*, edited by Steven Feld and Keith H. Basso, 90–135. Santa Fe, NM: School of American Research Press.

Ghosh, Anashua. 1981. "Taking Kathak Abroad: One of the Most Controversial Artistes Around Unwinds in an Informal Talk." *Telegraph* (India), September 22–28, 1981, 4–6.

Gibson, James J. 1966. *The Senses Considered as Perceptual Systems*. Boston: Houghton Mifflin.

Gibson, James J. 1979. *The Ecological Approach to Visual Perception*. Hillsdale, NJ: Lawrence Erlbaum.

Glennie, Evelyn. 2015. "Hearing Essay." Evelyn Glennie: Teach the World to Listen (website). https://www.evelyn.co.uk/hearing-essay/.

Godoy, Rolf I. 2003. "Motor-Mimetic Music Cognition." *Leonardo Music Journal* 36 (4): 317–319.

Gordon, Edwin E. 1989. "Tonal Syllables: A Comparison of Purposes and Systems." In *Readings in Music Learning Theory*, edited by Darrel. L. Walters and Cynthia C. Taggart, 66–73. Chicago: G.I.A. Publications.

Grasseni, Cristina. 2004. "Skilled Vision: An Apprenticeship in Breeding Aesthetics." *Social Anthropology* 12 (1): 41–55.

Grasseni, Cristina. 2007. "Good Looking: Learning to be a Cattle Breeder." In *Skilled Visions: Between Apprenticeship and Standards*, edited by Cristina Grasseni, 47–66. Oxford: Berghahn.

Ihde, Don. 1976. *Listening and Voice: A Phenomenology of Sound*. Athens: Ohio University Press.

Ingold, Tim. 2000. *The Perception of the Environment: Essays on Livelihood, Dwelling and Skill*. London: Routledge.

Ingold, Tim. 2001. "From the Transmission of Representations to the Education of Attention." In *The Debated Mind: Evolutionary Psychology versus Ethnography*, edited by Harvey Whitehouse, 113–153. Oxford: Berg.

Johnson, Mark. 2006. "Merleau-Ponty's Embodied Semantics: From Immanent Meaning, to Gesture, to Language." *EurAmerica* 36 (1): 1–27.

Kwon, Donna Lee. 2015. "'Becoming One': Embodying Korean P'ungmul Percussion Band Music and Dance through Site-Specific Intermodal Transmission." *Ethnomusicology* 59 (1): 31–60.

Langer, Susanne. 1947. *Problems of Art*. New York: Charles Scribner's Sons.

McNeill, David. 2005. *Gesture and Thought*. Chicago: University of Chicago Press.

Merleau-Ponty, Maurice. (1945) 1962. *Phenomenology of Perception*. Translated by Colin Smith. London: Routledge.

Morelli, Sarah. 2007. "From Calcutta to California: Negotiations of Movement and Meaning in Kathak Dance." PhD diss., Harvard University.

Morelli, Sarah. 2019. *A Guru's Journey: Pandit Chitresh Das and Indian Classical Dance in Diaspora*. Urbana: University of Illinois Press.

Nelson, David P. 1991. "Mṛdaṅgam Mind: The Tani Āvartanam in Karṇāṭak Music." PhD diss., Wesleyan University.

personalladoos. 2007. "Kathak Dance Solo Joanna de Souza." YouTube. https://www.youtube.com/watch?v=7IixNoEDJ14&list=PLmRBGhTsTNz7H1Nq6j_dr5ucuPIDYK3nE&index=94.

Rahaim, Matthew. 2012. *Musicking Bodies: Gesture and Voice in Hindustani Music*. Middletown, CT: Wesleyan University Press.

Ruckert, George. 2004. *Music in North India: Experiencing Music, Expressing Culture*. New York: Oxford University Press.

Samuels, David W., Louise Meintjes, Ana Maria Ochoa, and Thomas Porcello. 2010. "Soundscapes: Toward a Sounded Anthropology." *Annual Review of Anthropology* 39: 329–345.

Saxena, Sushil K. 1991. *Swinging Syllables: Aesthetics of Kathak Dance*. New Delhi: Sangeet Natak Akademi.

Sheets-Johnstone, Maxine. 1999. *The Primacy of Movement*. Amsterdam: John Benjamins.

Walker, Margaret. 2014. *India's Kathak Dance in Historical Perspective*. London: Routledge.

CHAPTER 12

SCRAPE, BRUSH, FLICK

The Phenomenology of Sound

KATHARINE YOUNG

AUDIBLE SPACE

Sound brings forth space. In contrast to visible space, audible space is kinetic and mutable, materializing and dematerializing. It is perhaps this motility that accounts for our feel for sounds as evanescent, hallucinatory, as if objects heard belong to a less dense reality than objects seen.

We who see suppose we perceive space visually; they who hear know space is audible. Theologian and professor of religious education John Hull, a hearer who cannot see, describes how rain makes space aurally perceptible.

> Rain has a way of bringing out the contours of everything; it throws a coloured blanket over previously invisible things; instead of an intermittent and thus fragmented world, the steadily falling rain creates continuity of acoustic experience.
> . . . I hear the rain sounding upon the fence which divides our property from that next door. In front, the contours of the path and the steps are marked out, right down to the garden gate. Here the rain is striking the concrete, here it is splashing into the shallow pools which have already formed. Here and there is a light cascade as it drips from step to step. The sound on the path is quite different from the sound of the rain drumming into the lawn on the right, and this is different again from the blanketed, heavy, sodden feel of the large bush on the left. . . . Over the whole thing, like light falling upon a landscape, is the gentle background patter gathered up into one continuous murmur of rain. (1990, 29–31)

We enter here into an audible architecture, a world that thickens around its perceiver as he hears. Sound does not suggest itself to Hull, as it does to the sighted, as bodiless, as diaphanous. On the contrary, a hitherto unencumbered emptiness condenses into materiality around Hull's ears. Rain makes present not just the great hollow of space

into which Hull's body is inserted but layers—serried ranks—of objects, one behind another, which open out around him. Hull hears depth, a property the sighted attribute to
vision. Both visual and auditory perceptions rely on the slight displacement of perceptual doubling—binaural hearing, binocular seeing—to round out the perceptual object.
For hearers who cannot see, audition encompasses a replete perceptual world; sighted
hearers experience hearing as adjunctive to visual perception. Audition oscillates between dematerializing materialities into sound and materializing materialities in sound.

   This essay investigates the experiences of extraordinary sound perceivers and sound
makers who bring forward auditory possibilities ordinary hearers and producers do not
notice. The descriptions are "radiant ignitions" for the act of imagination, which Elaine
Scarry calls "perceptual mimesis"—the way a reader is induced to perceive under "au-
thorial instruction," not by describing the sound to be imagined but by describing the
experience of hearing the sound (2001, 8, 6). The essay is designed to enter perceivers
into the imaginary space of sound events. Describing sensory experiences vivifies the
sounds they are experiences of. Perceptual mimesis is the secret of imagining. When we
do it well, the imagined begins to take on the sensuous vivacity of the real, to arouse our
senses as if to real experiences. The imaginary experience becomes perceptually available to us in subtle reverberation.

The Sensory Isolation Experiment

If I hear without seeing or see without hearing, I register the difference each makes to the
other. As a folklorist and phenomenologist, I co-taught a course on sound in film at San
Francisco State University with visual anthropologist Peter Biella. Film students tend
to regard film as a purely or predominantly visual genre. To reverse their valences, we
conducted a sense-isolation experiment with the class. Students put on either earplugs
or blindfolds and walked around campus in pairs, the sighted who could not hear leading
hearers who could not see, exchanging roles, and then writing up their impressions in
journals. By experiencing what it is like to see a silent world or to hear an invisible one,
students become sensitive to what sound can do in film. We called it the deaf/blind experiment, but that was an infelicitous choice of words. Nobody experienced what it was
like to be either deaf or blind. As disability theorist Tobin Siebers insists, to pretend to
the experience of the disabled is a shallow mockery (2010, 28). "Disability theorists have
attacked the use of simulations for a variety of reasons, the most important being that
they fail to give the student pretenders a sense of the embodied knowledge contained
in disability identities." The result is sentiment without insight. "Disability simulations
of this kind fail because they place students in a one-time position of disability, before
knowledge about disability is acquired, usually resulting in emotions of loss, shock, and
pity at how dreadful it is to be disabled" (Siebers 2010, 28). The sensory isolation experiment was not designed to mimic the experience of being deaf or blind but to eliminate
one sense in order to concentrate on the other: the audible in the absence of the visible;
the visible in the absence of the audible. Experiencing one sense without the assistance/

interference of the other deepens single-sense perceiving. Peter and I participated in the experiment. I quote from the journal entries each of us made at the time.

The First Pass: I Wear Earplugs; Peter Wears a Blindfold

Katharine/Ear-plugged
Interoception
I lead him down a long hall. My heel bone thunks against the hard floor and vibrates up through my skeleton to my ear bones. I hear/feel this sound inside me as an echo of movement but the echo of movement that usually sounds off the walls and the ceiling has gone out. My movement fails altogether to animate the world as I walk. I am no longer in tune with it, no longer welcome.

Peter/Blindfolded
The Small Death
My consciousness of being here and having physical and intellectual mastery of being here is determined by sight. When I put the goggles on, I was smiling but I also felt the noose tighten. It was a small death.

Katharine/Ear-plugged
Inside Out
There is no longer any audible difference between inside and outside. Inside, the flat surfaces of the walls press in on me visually; outside, the flat surfaces of the ground tip out and lie around me horizontally but the inside does not feel cozy or the outside spacious. It is more like they have no feel, only a look.

Peter/Blindfolded
Disappearances
After the experiment, in my office, others spoke of a relief at the disappearance of the walls, buildings, restrictions, artificial barriers to awareness of the world. That was beautiful and sorrowful. Soon after I began as blind, I felt too that the world had dropped its blinders, and that I was led to find some things truer and shapishly infinite.

Katharine/Ear-plugged
Pantomime
The flowing bodies of people walking eddy round standing pairs or groups of people gesturing. These are pantomime bodies. Their gestures, seamlessly integrated into talk when I hear, stand out as if they were conducting a performance. Gestures, unspeeched, look so improbable.

Peter/Blindfolded
This Emptiness of Where
She led us into the hell planet, my Virgil, through more waves of footfalls, skateboard scrapings, we descend voices rolling from white to black, happy annoyed triumphant oblivious.
 Each step in the volcano no directions except "down" and "other." Each location always already the same, voices sliding in and down of rumble chatter, nothing except further lost, each forward echo another endless footpath, space great blind plain, 15 pounds per square inch pressing me to this bottom, from out where.
 This emptiness of where aches me deeply, steals my oxygen.

Katharine/Ear-plugged
Bored
Suddenly, I am extremely bored. The visible world has no anticipations and no aftermaths. I realize how dependent I am on the sounds of things to announce their imminent appearance, to trail behind them after they pass. Coming before the objects they prognosticate, they create a little suspense, so that the actual appearance of the object provides a little satisfaction. Coming after it as it leaves, the sound of things gives them a sustained presence even though the things themselves have popped off.

Peter/Blindfolded
Hear World
Attentiveness, high focus, listen open ears far off faint follow sounds—as behind as here as those in front. This fat thick butter melt and n-dimension black unquitting hear world is cold comfort.

The Second Pass: I am Blindfolded and Peter is Ear-plugged

Peter/Ear-plugged
Guide
Maskoff Thatsbetter... My guide is now my charge, she buttons up her eyes, chipper, expectant. I am anxious, hearing in my head "nobody moves and nobody gets hurt." I confirm I must not lead her into danger—because she has said she will be afraid. Stairs, poles, slopes, holes, ignominious passersby. Do not let her fall do not let her bump.

I feel a sense of tender responsibility. And there is a new distance between us, being a guide is being a stranger.

Katharine/Blindfolded
Parking Lot
Blindfolded in the parking lot, space comes alive; I come alive. The rail I am leaning against vibrates to the sounds that leap into existence around me. Audition and vibration are deeply connected. We step out. I have a sensation of activated space, deep and shallow protrusions, looming presences overhead, moving forms to one side or another. An audible architecture experienced not so much as sound but as space. As we walk, the whole structure resonates overhead, underfoot. A cold breeze brushes my left cheek. There is no question about the difference between interior and exterior space. Outside, I feel vistas on my skin, uninterrupted distance falling away to the left. But it is not as if the inside is closed off. Auditorily, the parking lot has no perceptible structures, rather presences, thin substances, not walls, ceilings (floors are kinesthetic footholds, not auditory presences), but loomings, hauntings, pressures of air. What in the visual world was solid, opaque, in the audible world is vaporous, hallucinated, structures of air.

Peter/Ear-plugged
Yellow
I realize that I missed yellow most. The other colors only bring us to it.

Katharine/Blindfolded
Interior Theater
Peter leads me out of a large space into another space with different edges. It is an interior theater. Its sounds descend upon me from above, hanging at various altitudes, a low-pitched rhythmic rim of sound circles two stories up, a soft beat, not a drum, not a machine. What? It lasts through all the other episodic sounds punctuating the space of the theater. I feel as if I walk in among instruments, deep strings, trills of piano-like notes, hums, fragments of tune, coming from various sides. We exit this envelope of sound and move into yet another space. An aria, soprano, a single phrase, afloat above and from the side. Still the soft, almost pulse, almost train clack, rim of sound circling above. Instead of a building, I am inside an audible architecture which mounts above me in a façade of sound, textured, filigreed, some stories retracted, others thrust forward or angled in from the side. I am no longer interested in the insistent remote materiality of visible buildings but in this theater of the air that takes over interior space.

Peter/Ear-plugged
Who Needs So Much Sound?
I'm in my element of sight and keeping walls this side and that, even two of us plenty of room there not to bump . . . then bouncing up the temporary outdoor wheelchair graded ramp with nonslip surface, aluminum vibrations felt, each echo each step even in the evening light I note but do not care, I've gotten back to hear and sighted . . . who needs so much sound?

Katharine/Blindfolded
Felt Presence
This new space of air is empty of solid material structures. Instead, what I know to be walls, buildings, appear as attenuated material barriers that press themselves on my skin. I do not experience myself as hearing them but as feeling them. The world no longer consists of solid objects and empty spaces but of felt presences ensconcing me, except when I come up against a handrail, a doorframe. Then this thin materiality surrounding me auditorily condenses into a solid chunk of something specific that thins out beyond my grasp of it and that itself now retracts from me and closes off into an object set apart from my body. Even though I now touch it, it has become other.

Peter/Ear-plugged
Off
time untied, unhook lookout fresh faces so excited in the hall. It is a joy to see them in the flush—ears off, eyes' blinders off
    It was amazing, it was . . . everyone on this campus should do this
    wet eyed that hollow world, stuffed world

In bimodal perception for most perceivers, the visible absorbs the audible. My sense of space as spacious is for the most part an aural sense, but until I am deprived of it, I attribute spaciousness to sight. If I am blindfolded and walk toward a wall, I find myself stopping just before I run into it because my body recognizes the specific echo of the wall up close. It is not a faculty I am aware of having unless I take the risk of bumping into something I cannot see. If I have seen the wall, I pay no attention to this audible announcement; I already know it's there. For me in the sensory isolation experiment the audible world was a revelation; for Peter, it was not only a diminution but also a perturbation. His untethered fragments of language perhaps reflect this disturbance. The differential qualities of perceptual experience depend as much on the idiosyncrasies of any body as on the particularities of any sense. To foreground the audible here is not to romanticize it as somehow superior to the visible but to undo its absorption by the visible; doing so allows the perceiver to center on sense perceptions specific to hearing and, subsequently, to open hearing out toward other sense perceptions. Attending to the audibility of space acknowledges anthropologist Steven Feld's observation that "places are as potentially reverberant as they are reflective" (2005, 179), but the reverberations affect each body differently. Audible space has a different constitution from visible space. Its perceptible objects are highly elaborated and at the same time imprecise. I hear the shape of space, but I subsume my experience under visual perception.

Architectures of Air

Because the *soundscape*, to take up the term composer and musicologist R. Murray Schafer coined (1993), readily recedes behind the landscape, the audible can covertly colonize the visible. The social historian Alain Corbin describes the hold that bells had on the French countryside before the nineteenth century. "As an auditory synchronizer, the bell told its listeners when the market had opened, when the tax collector had arrived, when a flock had set off for the mountains, when the wine harvest was declared, when the community's bell was present, or when work on the roads had recommenced. . . . As a consequence, a subtle auditory rhetoric was developed. A bell had to have its own language, which varied from one commune to the next" ([1994] 1998, xi). By constructing their architecture in the air and descending upon their hearers, the bells issued their command of space and time as from on high. "Within aerial space, over which it still held a monopoly, this bronze voice, falling from above, hammered home the injunctions of authority" (Corbin [1994] 1998, x–xi). A disciplinary regime coalesces in thin air.

Before the French Revolution (1789–99), the Catholic Church held the authority the bells sounded. After the Revolution, the new regime undertook a "reduction in the sensual ascendancy of bells," razing bell towers, melting bells, destroying churches, and taking over the ringing of such bells as were left (Corbin [1994] 1998, 13). "The new policy was designed to bring about a disenchantment of the world, and it therefore has to do chiefly with the history of affectivity and with that of the culture of the senses" (Corbin [1994] 1998, 23). The destruction of the *ancien régime* was also the destruction of a sensory regime, for as Feld points out, "as place is sensed, senses are placed; as places make sense, senses make place" (2005, 179). With the death of the bells, sense has no place.

Soundscapes are instructions for perceiving. "If we are prepared to allow that a landscape is fundamentally a thing that is read, a way of directing one's gaze, or of being prepared to listen, the slow obliteration of the landscape that had been delineated by village bells preceded the bell towers' falling into silence and into rack and ruin" (Corbin [1994] 1998, 306). As Keiko Torigoe notes in her 2002 study of the Russian Orthodox Church bells in Kyoto, Japan, it is possible for the instructions to work even when there is nothing to hear. After the church stopped ringing the bells every day, some inhabitants of the city still reported hearing them (Torigoe 2002, 52). But once the affects a landscape expresses and the aesthetes who perceive them are gone, there is nobody left to read the instructions. This heralds what Corbin calls the "genesis of meaninglessness," the fate of sound regimes fallen into desuetude ([1994] 1998, xviii). Sounds are not innately moving, innately beautiful. They move hearers through sedimented topographies of sense and sensibility.

Ear Space

When audible space is conjoined with visible space, each sense coheres with the other. But when a soundscape the perceiver does not see is interpolated into a landscape the perceiver does not hear, the audible is no longer in thrall to the visible. The alienation of sound from its source precipitates the perceiver into the auditory configuration Schafer calls *schizophonia* (1977, 88). If I hear one space and see another, sound's capacity to conjure space is at once concentrated and diffused. The invention of the Sony Walkman in the 1970s inaugurated a schizophonic regime. The portable music player envelops the body in a cloud of music, imparting to the city through which its hearer walks an aesthetic it does not possess. Users perceive this re-sounding as an enhancement of their embodied experience. As a consequence, as sound theorist Michael Bull puts it, "Switching off becomes tantamount to killing off their private world and returning them to the diminished space and duration of the disenchanted and mundane outside world" (2002, 83). This sound envelope can be borne along undisturbed, despite the sonic variegations the body moves through but to which is it no longer tuned. With the invocation of a second sense-space, the body inhabits two realities simultaneously. By convention, the visuo-tactile space is dubbed the real and the audible space the virtual. In fact, neither reality necessarily holds sway over the other. Each takes hold of the body in a different sensory modality, which grants it—however fleetingly—primacy. If, listening, I trip over a curb, the tactile snatches me out of my auditory enclosure and thrusts me into my material surround. If something catches my eye, I return my attention to my visible surround. If, by contrast, I am absorbed in my music, it might infiltrate the material surround I feel or see. I walk to a rhythm, pulse to a beat, or dance to a tune nobody else hears, sustaining the persistence of audible alterity in my other reality. Jean-Paul Thibaud, sociologist and urban planner, calls the incongruous movements that my audible absorption inspires in my body as I walk a "micro-ecology of musical navigation" (2003, 329).

Portable music players permit this infiltration of one sensory reality by another in only one direction, from the audible into the visible and tactile. Mobile phones permit infiltration in both directions. I might issue commands to my remote interlocutor, or what my interlocutor says might stop me in my tracks. "The difference between the mobile phone and the Walkman inheres in this distinction: the mobile, unlike the Walkman, offers the possibility of remote intervention" (Bassett 2003, 344). We are engaged here not only in an oscillation between realities but also in their interlacing. And, as media theorist Caroline Bassett goes on to point out, the realities are multiple. "The spatial economy of mobile telephony is complex. To explore it demands consideration of the dynamics not only of virtual space (the bubble into which we speak when we make a connection), but also of physical space as it comes to be penetrated by virtual space. In this sense, whenever a mobile is used it connects not two spaces but four or more. Mobiles play a part in the production of contemporary space" (2003, 344). We eavesdrop on others' production of the virtual spaces they project into their imperceptible hearer's physical spaces. As historian of sound Jonathan Sterne argues, "Sound-reproduction technologies are artifacts of vast transformations in the fundamental nature of sound, the human ear, the faculty of hearing, and practices of listening that occurred over the long nineteenth century" and continue into the twenty-first (2003, 2). Simultaneous or sequential engagements with alternate realities are the nature of everyday life, but we transfer the sign of the real so seamlessly from one to another that we are rarely aware of this scabrous ontological topography.

The Horizons of Perception

A space can be both heard and seen, or it can be either heard or seen. If I hear what I cannot see or see what I cannot hear, each sense can capture what is beyond the other's perceptual limits. As Don Ihde ([1976] 2007), a phenomenologist of sound, points out, the horizon of the visible is the invisible; the horizon of the audible is the silent. Beyond its horizon, each sense is extinguished. The horizon of the visible closes down the spaces around me. A blindfold over my eyes occludes the visible world; the old clock on the mantelpiece conceals its insides, its back, and whatever is behind it; the punctured building I inhabit cuts away portions of the houses and trees outside as I look out the window; the hill hides the car disappearing over its brim; the earth conceals the sun every night, making its horizon the horizon of the visible at sunset (one of the few instances in which the horizon of the visible coincides with what we call the horizon line); cloud obscures sky; even the stars pepper the remotest visible space with tiny occlusions of sight. The horizon of the audible also closes down the spaces around me but in different places. Plugs in my ears silence the audible world; from my desk, I cannot hear the clock tick; out the window, the children playing in the park are animated mutes; the hum of the car's motor decrescendos to silence as it pulls away from me; the horizon of the audible never reaches the earth's horizon; remote space is utterly silent.

But it is possible for the two perceptual realities to overlap so that we *see* what is beyond the horizon of the audible or *hear* what is beyond the horizon of the visible. Each sense makes perceptible the other's imperceptible limit: "what may be taken as horizonal (or absent) for one 'region' is taken as presence for the other" (Ihde [1976] 2007, 52–53).

Blindfolded, I hear space; ear-plugged, I see space. The tick of the clock echoes inside it and off the wall behind it, making its invisible insides and back audible; the visible movement of its hands reveals the workings of the clock I cannot hear. The sound of the motor precedes and succeeds the sight of the car, sometimes even after it disappears over the brim of the hill. The horizon of the audible never coincides with earth's horizon but sometimes the sky grumbles or roars, cracking open the space behind the cloud. Each sense makes present the other's absence.

It is not just that I see what I cannot hear; the seeing evokes an echo of the hearing, just as hearing what I cannot see evokes a ghost of the sight. "I cannot see [the wind's] contorted writhing though it surrounds me with its invisible presence. . . . [T]he invisible is the horizon of sight. . . . Listening makes the invisible present in a way similar to the presence of the mute in vision" (Ihde [1976] 2007, 51, italics in original). Likewise, looking makes the inaudible present. Seeing a girl playing a violin through the glass window of the soundproofed music practice room, I feel the trace vibration of a certain plangent sound, as if my body were seeking the inaudible strain. Sensory reciprocity lends the imagined the vivacity of the real.

Hearing takes up time in a way that seeing does not. I cannot open my ears and hear as I can open my eyes and see, not because there is no sound to be heard but because I cannot hear the sound unless paradoxically I have heard it begin a moment *before* I hear it. Literary theorist Steven Connor writes, "To hear a sound, one must have already heard it start to decay, or come to an end: one must already have started finishing hearing it. One hears very largely analeptically, in memory, even with the most shockingly immediate of sound effects; they appear to punch a hole in auditory attention, which is then only slowly filled up with definition" (Connor 2013, 111). As Sterne puts it, "sounds exist only as they go out of existence" (2003, 18). Sounds pull the past into the present or push the present into the future, participating in the loop of time the German phenomenologist Martin Heidegger calls *temporal ecstasis* ([1927] 1962, 377). French phenomenologist Maurice Merleau-Ponty expatiates on Heidegger's concept.

> The present still holds on to the immediate past without positing it as an object, and since the immediate past similarly holds its immediate predecessor, past time is wholly collected up and grasped in the present. The same is true of the imminent future, which will also have its horizon of imminence. But with my immediate past I have also the horizon of futurity which surrounded it, and thus I have my actual present seen as the future of that past. With the imminent future, I have the horizon of past which will surround it, and therefore my actual present as the past of that future. ([1945] 1962, 69)

As Ray Birdwhistell used to say in the 1972 nonverbal communication class that I attended at the University of Pennsylvania, there is no such thing as the punctiform present. Hearing is not so much a matter of remembering the past of a sound as of experiencing the present sound gathering the past and future into itself. Suzanne Cusick writes about "the paradoxical temporality of sound: sound both endures in the infinitesimal traces of its waves' impact on the vibrating bodies that produce and repro-duce it and refuses to endure as what it was in any given moment" (2017, 41). Sight, by contrast, is proleptic. It anticipates encounters I do not yet have: the sturdy density of upcoming object and ground, the airy lightness of the space between. Bishop Berkeley conceived vision as tactile in the eighteenth century. He writes, "So swift and sudden and unperceived is the transition from visible to tangible ideas that we can scarce for-bear thinking them equally the immediate object of vision" ([1709] n.d., Section 145). Merleau-Ponty's conception of seeing as "a sort of touch effected by the eyes" draws on Berkeley's intimation of a tactile eye ([1945] 1962, 223). "The look . . . envelops, palpates, espouses the visible things . . . so that finally one cannot say if it is the look or if it is the things that command" ([1945] 1962, 133). Visible objects find their edge because they abut other visible objects; audible objects do not so much bump up against each other as infiltrate each other. Sounds are not set off against other sounds; they are separated by silence. They have nothing comparable to the edges of visible objects.

The visible world appears all at once, already replete with contiguous objects. It has no gaps or crevices, no empty spots where nothing is. The audible world, by contrast, announces itself episodically. I imagine space as filled with sound but I do not perceive this fullness as I perceive the fullness of visible space. To hear a sound, the perceiver must hear either the silence that precedes it and against which it announces itself or hear the sound that precedes it against which it contrasts or with which it is continuous. Hull writes, "The intermittent nature of the acoustic world is one of its most striking features. In contrast, the perceived world is stable and continuous. The seen world cannot es-cape from your eyes" (1990, 83). This intermittency of sounds gives auditory effects power. Hull writes, "I hear the distant tossing of trees across the park; it comes like a wave rolling across a beach. Now it breaks upon my body in a squall, a gust, like a fist. This is very exciting because of the anticipation and the wonderful feeling of having the knowledge in your body of what is going on" (1990, 108). Though Hull's hold on audible phenomena is prodigious, it brings forward the paucity of the sighted's senses of space. The materiality of the world can spring itself on the blind in ways that it cannot on the sighted. Blindness holds in abeyance presuppositions supported by sight, while seeing substantiates effects blindness calls into question. The strange presences that press in upon the sighted from all sides as the surfaces of things are for the blind intermittent materializations. Hull recalls his experience of being at a party. "When you are blind, a hand suddenly grabs you. A voice suddenly addresses you. . . . There is no lying low. I *am* grasped. I *am* greeted. I am passive in the presence of that which accosts me. I cannot escape it" (1990, 95, italics in original). For Hull, the wind's body, massive and muscular, conjures up out of thin air those enormous presences I see looming over me: trees. But my trees are earthbound, rooted and trunked. His are hitched to the upper airs by their tiny sound makers: leaves.

Moving Sounds

All sound is movement. Sounds mutate as we hear in a way that sights do not as we see. Even though blind hearers perceive objects by ear, the object heard is not stable, as the object seen appears to be. It vibrates. Suspended beside my ear, the sound shivers at its edges, shapeshifting as I listen. Sights do not scintillate as sounds vibrate. Even though it is made out of thin air, sound takes up space, but it is not contained in the space it takes up. The vibration impinges on its perceiver. It moves; I am moved. Connor considers this mutability.

> One apparent paradox of hearing is that it strikes us as at once intensely corporeal—sound literally moves, shakes, and touches us—and mysteriously immaterial. . . . Perhaps the tactility of sound depends in part on this immaterial corporeality, because of the fact that all sound is disembodied, a residue or production rather than a property of objects. When we see something, we do not think of what we see as a separable aspect of it, a ghostly skin shed for our vision. We feel that we see the thing itself, rather than any occasion or extrusion of the thing. But when we hear something, we do not have the same sensation of hearing the thing itself. This is because objects do not have a single, invariant sound, or voice. How something sounds is literally contingent, depending upon what touches or comes into contact with it to generate the sound. We hear, as it were, the event of the thing, not the thing itself. (2004, 157)

Sights stick to their objects; sounds split off from the objects that make them and move through space, so that sound and sound maker can be in two different places. Seeing and the seeable cannot. Because the sound reaches each ear at different times, at different volumes, and at different frequencies, binaural hearing permits the hearer to triangulate from the two audible sound streams to the object that made the sound. I can find an object by hearing it, but I cannot see an object I have not already found. Sight maker and sight made are always already sealed together; sound maker and sound made are at once separated and connected. The separation makes it possible for sound to be elsewhere; the connection makes it possible to follow the trajectory of the sound back to the object that made it.

Sounds animate and are animated by the space they move through. As the sound moves from maker to hearer, it accrues the specificities of the space it moves through. If the sound maker moves, the trajectory that connects maker to hearer moves, too. A hearer who moves, moves through a matrix of sound arcs. Even if the object making the sound stays in one place, the sound its hearer hears bounces off its surround from different angles, not only bringing out the contours of space but also changing the contours it brings out as the sounds that strike it change. This is akin to the way the visible aspect of an object changes as light moves over it, but for the eye, the object conveys its density—its object-ness—instantaneously; it solidifies for the ear only over time. Audible space is amove with the sounds of movement. For Hull, "it was a world of nothing but action. Every sound was a point of activity. Where nothing was happening, there was silence" (1990, 82). The sighted see movement, but the visible world persists even if nothing moves; the audible world switches off. For hearers who do not see, space is void—unless something moves. Nothing in Hull's auditory space holds still. If it did, he would not perceive it. As Sterne puts it, for Hull, "Sound is a little piece of the vibrating world" (2003, 133).

Having gone blind, Hull cultivates his audible recognition of once visible objects. In the early stage of his blindness, Hull sensed presences, large objects *looming*, as the sighted would say, up around him as he moved. When he first became aware of this sense of presence, he would wave his cane about and discover he was coming up to a large tree. At first lampposts were imperceptible. Too thin. But as he practiced his new auditory acuity, even thin presences became perceptible. Hull writes, "I gather from conversations that this experience is essentially acoustic and is based upon awareness of echoes. This certainly fits in with my experience, but at the same time it is important to emphasize that one is not aware of listening. One is simply aware of becoming aware. The sense of pressure is upon the skin of the face, rather than upon or within the ears. That must be why the older name for the experience was 'facial vision'" (1990, 27–28). For Hull, the tactile absorbs the visible: hearing is transmuted into a skin sense.

The term biological scientists gave to Hull's experience in the twentieth century is *echolocation*. Sounds vary as they bounce off or are absorbed by objects in the surround. Sophisticated hearers can perceive what the objects are as well as the shape of the space around them. Psychologist and educator Daniel Kish, himself blind, devised his own idiosyncratic version of this technique.

> I had to have both eyes removed by the age of one to save my life—I was born with an aggressive form of eye cancer called retinoblastoma. Ever since, I have made clicking noises with my tongue to understand my environment. I wasn't aware I was doing it, just as sighted people don't consciously teach themselves to see. It was only when I was 11 that a very bright friend realised that what I was doing was echolocation, the same technique that a bat flying in the dark relies on: I was navigating my surroundings by listening to the echoes as my clicks bounced off surfaces. (2012)

Ear navigation gets Kish around almost anywhere. Journalist Michael Finkel writes,

> Bats, of course, use echolocation. Beluga whales too. Dolphins. And Daniel Kish. He is so accomplished at echolocation that he's able to pedal his mountain bike through streets heavy with traffic and on precipitous dirt trails. He climbs trees. He camps out, by himself, deep in the wilderness. He's lived for weeks at a time in a tiny cabin a two-mile hike from the nearest road. He travels around the globe. He's a skilled cook, an avid swimmer, a fluid dance partner. Essentially, though in a way that is unfamiliar to nearly any other human being, Kish can see. (2012)

Echolocators inhabit a soundscape as the sighted do a landscape. As Kish remarks, "Every surface has its own acoustic signature—I can recognise a tree, for example, because the trunk produces a different echo from the leaves. The hard wood reflects the sound, whereas the leaves reflect and refract, too, scattering the sound waves. Everything around me becomes identifiable with a click. It provides me with a 3D image in my mind with depth, character and richness; it brings light into darkness" (2012).

Kish's body moves through movement. The soundscape is not laid out around him like a landscape, already all there any time anybody looks; it unfolds over time, animating space into being as the perceiver hears. He apprehends both variation in the sounds of objects as he moves through space and variation in the sound of sounds as they change over time. Feld writes, "The placing of auditory time is the sonic envelope created from the layered attack, sustain, decay, and resonance of sounds. The placing of auditory space is the dispersion of sonic height, depth, and directionality. Space-time inevitably sounds in and as figure and ground, as comingness and goingness. It's [*sic*] presence is forward, backward, side to side, heard in trajectories of ascent, descent, arch, level, or undulation" (2005, 185). The objects Kish hears mutate as he moves through their sound envelopes. He navigates among them even as they change around him, like a character in a cartoon kaleidoscope. Kish calls this effect *flash sonar*. "It's flashes. You do get a continuous sort of vision, the way you might if you used flashes to light up a darkened scene. It comes into clarity and focus with every flash, a kind of three-dimensional fuzzy geometry. It is in 3D, it has a 3D perspective, and it is a sense of space and spatial relationships. You have a depth of structure, and you have position and dimension. You also have a pretty strong sense of density and texture, that are sort of like the color, if you will, of flash sonar" (quoted in Hurst 2017). Despite the fuzziness of this geometry, Kish anchors himself in audible space as the sighted anchor themselves in visible space. "Those are flashes of sound that go out and reflect from surfaces all around me, just like a bat's sonar, and return to me with patterns, with pieces of information, much as light does for you. And my brain . . . has been activated to form images in my visual cortex, which we now call the imaging system, from those patterns, much as your brain does" (2015). The space that unfolds around him as he moves also unfolds into him as it he hears, attuning him wherever he is. Feld writes, "Sound both emanates from and penetrates bodies; this reciprocity of reflection and absorption is a creative means of orientation—one that tunes bodies to places and times through their sounding potential" (Feld 2003, 226). A moveable world materializes for Kish as he moves.

This reciprocal mobility of the audible world and the moveable body is available to the sighted as well as to the blind, but the sighted find both themselves and the world stopped by the stabilities of the visible surround (the things that hold still) and the durabilities of the material surround (the things that bump against them). It is as if the sighted have a predisposition for closure, for objects they cannot penetrate perceptually. They regard more attenuated perceptual objects with suspicion. Sound objects, taste objects, and smell objects threaten to dematerialize, to elude them or seep away, even as they perceive them. *What existential upheaval would ensue if perceivers shifted the sign of the real from solidities to fluidities or etherealities?*

SOUND ART

Audible art makes spaces present by ear just as visible art makes them present by eye. Audible representations are not projected on a surface that stands before me visually and that, by the same token, stands away from me visually; instead, they surround me. Journalist Curt Corrinth reports an auditory conjuring act for children in a library.

> And now the smiling librarian, a new record in her hand, goes up to the gramophone: the little room is filled with the deep breathing of a man, as loud as if a giant were snoring! . . . Then the narrow walls seem to fade away, a landscape appears, enlivened by the prattling and splashing of rushing streams. Then cars go racing through the tiny room, rumbling omnibuses and little rattling tin lizzies; a storm crackles and thunders by; noises of the stock-exchange emerge and turn into children's voices; we hear the wheezy organ on the merry-go-round and the subdued roar of the fair. . . . Again space dwindles to the size of the room, and suddenly invisible hands begin brushing clothes, crumpling paper, blowing noses, and then, in bewildering contrast, the walls extend into a factory with machines stamping and engines humming, harbor-noises surge up and mills creak. . . . The young lady smiles again, conscious of the astonishment in store for the listener: an entire zoo with its thousands of voices appears!
>
> (Corrinth quoted in Kahn 1999, 133).

The children listening to the record find themselves inhabitants of spaces other than the one their bodies are in. They embark upon imaginary journeys to other spaces and other times. Things that make sounds bring forth the spaces they make the sounds in, along with the sounds themselves.

Making things make sounds also brings forth objects. Sound artists Brandon LaBelle and Steve Roden materialize a sculpture by Harry Bertoia by coaxing sounds out of it: a single pong, metallic, resonant, deep, announces an object (LaBelle and Roden 1999). Dull thuds and tiny plinks in various pitches and intensities lay out a thin line of sound that threads along the object's surface. As the players move across the sculpture, its shape swells into a huge metallic hollow with reverberant echoes, a cascade of tings tintinnabulating along its great curved side. Sonorous vibrations thunk on my breastbone, lighten, thin, slip away. As the concert continues, the enormous shape of something sinuous thickens in the air. Most of Bertoia's sounding sculptures consist of tall metal rods of various heights and thicknesses soldered to a metal base. Some are variously curved metal disks like gongs. If struck, they create a spatial and textural environment Bertoia calls *sonambient*. His daughter "Celia recalls undersea explorer Jacques Cousteau hearing his gongs and exclaiming, 'Oh, my God, they sound just like whales!'" (cited in Masters 2015). It is possible that LaBelle and Roden took inspiration for the name of their concert from this recollection: they call it *The Blue Whale*. The hearer does not see the sculpture, but the sounds the artists draw out of it bring forth the huge undulating body of a whale as if it were there. Making sonambient sculpture present auditorily affords the hearer access to its material particularities in distinctive ways.

Bringing sculpture forth audibly raises the possibility of creating audible sculpture. Sound artist Michael Brewster makes sounds make things. The perceptible affordances of his sound sculptures have no analog in the material world. "You can't make sound become hard and solid; but you can make it seem to stand still, as if hovering in place, so that you can walk around inside its acoustic structures. Sustained sound in a room with good echo can appear to us as an archipelago of audio sensations of space. Standing still, sound is a dimensional substance you can move through without hitting your head on any thing. It's a real good material for sculpture" (1999, 101). The immateriality of these sculptures affords perceivers the untoward possibility of walking through sculpture. Brewster continues, "Walking through it in its resonant state provides an experience similar to perusing a landscape but from the inside, with all of your body instead of from the outside with just your eyes. It shows us the NEAR FIELD. Like a solid it has volumes, edges, planes, fullnesses, flatnesses, roundnesses, and hollows; the works. It comes FULLY EQUIPPED to elaborate our experience sculpturally" (Brewster 1999, 101). Sound art equips perceivers with uncanny powers and conducts them into uncanny spaces.

In Hildegard Westerkamp's sound work *Sensitive Chaos*, objects move in space (1999). Even if the speaker system is monaural, hearers perceive the direction things are going to or coming from, falling or rising. Listen: Click. Rustle. Clack. A metallic ball rolls across the floor from left to right, then back from right to left. Another roll from the right cuts across a dry tinkle from the left. Trails of varying sounds cut across each other through the space at various angles. A gurgle. A whoosh of water down a drain. A flood spreading over the ground and around at the perceiver's feet. Splashes, sprays, and squirts punctuate space at various locations. Hints of sounds suffused through water, a thundery roar in the distance, a faint watery hum in the ear. The composition moves the hearer down inclines, off steps, into enclosures, out onto vistas, through water, wind, and mud, into the paths of trains roaring into proximity and then sucking sound out of the air as they pull away. Evocative sounds fill the surround with audible movements. The movements encroach on the body of their hearer. I turn my head, duck, flinch, lift up my feet. Each sound is exquisitely clear at the same time that the space it invokes blurs, mutates, or shifts underfoot, juxtaposing discontinuous terrains in the auditory version of an M. C. Escher lithograph. The effect is not so much an audible soundscape as a musical composition. Westerkamp makes sounds make music.

The homely sound of crumpling paper can command perceptual imagination as vividly as the phantasmagoria of mutating worlds in the librarian's recording. Philip Corner provides instructions for an installation he calls "Ear Paper(s)." I quote the entire set of instructions:

> an environment set-up . . . with one, or more, suspended pieces of fine-sounding paper already crumpled, already listened to—ready to again, for any ear. (Disposable—Renewable).

[Written vertically in the margin] May be vari-colored. [On the facing page, there is a black and white photograph of a crumpled paper surface, a vertical dotted line along its inner edge, and an image of a scissors, cutting.] (1999, 27; ellipses and parentheses in the original; brackets added)

The crumpled paper could be re-sounded, but just the sight of it makes its perceiver hear its sound, even though there is nothing to hear. In this piece of audible art, the paper makes sound in a perceptual imaginary.

Sound is the result of moving two surfaces against each other. The crushed paper in Corner's installation bears the trace of what sound artist Loren Chasse calls *betweenity*.

> Betweenity is membranous. Immeasurable and momentous, so barely made from out of the minimal duration, the slightest sliver of space, a thing needs to be said to have had a life at all. (1999, 93)

> Often the paper that has been placed between things is left marked with faint trajectories and whirls, is patterned, perforated, wrinkled, stained, frayed or torn. When a rubbing results with the paper in relief, a dimension has been added to the betweenity, making it a place of its own. (1999, 95–96)

Sound is betweenity. There needn't be a paper, a membrane. Sound itself is crushed between surfaces.

A Phenomenology of Perception

No thing makes a sound; all sounds are made by two things. The sound we hear in Westerkamp's composition or LaBelle and Roden's metallic whale is not the sound of a thing. It is the sound of a thing moving up against another thing. The onomatopoeia of the words *scrape, brush, flick* retains the texture of this touch. As Ihde notes, "I hear not one voice, but at least two in a 'duet' of things" ([1976] 2007, 67). Steven Connor elaborates this philandering of things.

> When one hears a sound, one never hears just one thing. One hears the sound of contact, of echo, reverberation of one thing against each other; any sound is always at least two. One never even hears a particular commingled sound—a footstep, a punch, a shot, a shout—alone and uncommingled: one hears the sounding of the sound in a particular environment, the sound as it has been touched and retouched in the acoustic context through which it has spread, and which has imparted its own particular qualities to the sound, bleaching out certain frequencies, dampening or sharpening the attack or decay of the sound, desiccating or liquefying its timbre, emaciating it or doubling it in reverberation. There is no pure silence to be heard. (2013, 116)

The chairs, tables, vases, and sculptures that philosophers discuss inhabit what Ihde calls *the realm of mute objects*, as if all the philosophers who perceived them were deaf ([1976] 2007, 50). "The mute object does not reveal its own voice, it must be given a voice. . . . One thing is struck by another, one surface contacts another, and in the encounter a voice is given to the thing" (Ihde [1976] 2007, 67). If the philosophers had *listened* to their objects, the sureties of objectivity would have been confounded. In hearing, as in all the other senses except sight, perception impinges on the body. It is impossible to be entirely detached from objects that move me.

Sensory Worlds

See

Seeing opens up the space between the perceiving body and the perceptual object. Things hold themselves apart from me and seal themselves up in their own skins. The visible world presents itself as nothing but surfaces. Even my body presents itself to me visually as an object, a thing among things. I cannot see in. If I peel or cut into an object, including my body, I do not see an interior. What was once inside simply presents itself as more surface. I perceive a world without interiors. Vision preserves our illusion of the objecthood of objects, self-contained, freestanding things unaffected by my perception of them.

Touch

Touching, by contrast, closes up the space between the perceiving body and its perceptual object. The tactile world presses itself up against my skin so that sensations are at once sensations of the body and sensations of the world. I can no longer entirely distinguish myself from objects: they refuse to distance themselves. Objects jostle me. I configure my surface to their exteriors and feel what they are as my own skin. Tactility returns me to surfaces, but the surfaces of the body are intermingled with the surfaces of the objects they touch. Skin is no longer a seal but a conductor, extending tendrils of the world into the body and extending tendrils of the body out into the world. I feel my inside, not as an object whose contours I palpate but as an amorphous terrain enlivened by intermittent sensations. Tactility returns me to my material continuity with the world of objects, which now enter into my subjectivity and resist their objectification. Tactile perception requires skin-to-thing contact.

Taste

Tasting, too, requires skin-to-thing contact but this is no longer the surface contact of touch. I move the gustatory object into my body. In perceiving it, I engulf it. Its space is the inside of my mouth. The object I taste no longer has a surface and an interior. Its materiality mutates from thick to thin over the course of my gustatory perception of it, finally disappearing into my visceral depths in attenuated form. What taste appreciates about it are the more essentialized properties that the body's assault upon the object releases. Insofar as taste brings forth a space, it is the architecture of the inner tissues that it piques in the course of its dissolution. The body destroys its gustatory objects in the act of perceiving them. Things turn into me, obliterating subject/object distinctions.

Smell

Smelling, like touching and tasting, requires skin-to-thing contact, but the thing to be perceived has dematerialized into thin air. The body sucks this airy object into itself, titillating the interior of the nose as it passes. Their material continuity is so fragile that smells are barely objects. They transgress the boundary of the body but at the same time hover outside it, massing or clouding, and enveloping the body as much as the body envelops them. Though they take up space, olfactory objects have no surface. They condense and evaporate, coalesce and deliquesce, concentrate and disperse so that my perception of them is intermittent. The smellscape configures ethereal space. The olfactory object does not precisely disappear within. It enters into the continuous respiratory interchange I conduct with my immaterial surround.

Hear

Hearing, too, requires contact, not skin-to-thing contact but thing-to-thing contact. I hear the touch of objects. I participate in their tactile life. I am intimate by proxy with things I do not touch. Touch, taste, and smell require body and object to touch in order for perception to occur. Instead of separating the body from its object, as seeing does, hearing connects body to object, but remotely. The sound maker vibrates itself and me as one, despite the space between us. It is as if we are in telekinetic communication, I and things heard. To hear, something must move; to touch, taste, or smell, something must move me. All the senses perceive movement: either I move the perceptual object or it moves me. I taste, touch, or smell the movement up close but I hear movement at a distance: objects move each other. I see movement at a distance, too, but seeing is the only sense that permits me to perceive if nothing moves. Because objects that hold still stay visible, seeing sustains my sense of the world as stable. The other senses plunge me into the world's mutability: their perceptual objects are discontinuous, under transformation, and intermixed. Audible objects do not occlude one another as visible objects do. Multiple sounds blend, as do multiple tastes and smells; multiple sights stay discrete. Touching attests to the discreteness of visible objects, though not necessarily to their stability. Hearing insists on their invisible mutability.

The object I hear is not the thing that makes the sound. Hearing, like smelling, splits its perceptible object from its source. Though the source of the perception is material, its object—a sound, a smell—is immaterial. We receive intimations of remote materialities. Sounds and smells detach themselves from the things that make them and travel to us through the air. Sights stick to their objects but not to the body; tastes and touches stick to both. Sight extinguishes itself on the surface of the body—at the eye. Smells and tastes get extinguished just under the skin—in the mouth or nose. But sounds, like touches, travel through the body as well as originate inside it. Vibrating within, sounds and touches announce to me my own interior as well as the interiors of objects. I pick up a box: things rattle, something gurgles, a weight shifts inside (see Ihde [1976] 2007, 61–67). What is sealed off from sight, smell, and taste is perceptible to touch and hearing. Sight, by contrast, stops at the skin's surface at the same time that it fills up the world with surfaces. Only seeing offers a replete perceptual experience with no gaps or tears, and it offers it instantaneously: as soon as I look, it's there. The other senses are episodic, intermittent, unfolding over time. Any sound is set off by its own silence. But the replete visual world only opens up the space right before my eyes; behind me, the space is only audible. Hearing opens up parts of the world from which vision is closed off: I hear beyond the rim of sight.

Paradox

The senses are incommensurable. Each sense pulls me into a different reality, and yet I do not feel unmoored on my departure from one sense or cast astray on my arrival into another, nor do I feel split between them at any given moment. Despite the incommensurabilites among the senses, I inhabit a single sensible world.

This is the paradox of the senses:

- Each sense opens onto a different reality.
- All the senses open onto the same reality.

How do the senses conduct me to the real?

Although each sense opens onto the real, I cannot substitute one sense for another: the taste of a thing is not the *same thing* as the sound of the thing, presented in a different sensory modality; it is, in some sense, a different thing. Nor can I constitute an object by assembling my variegated sensory perceptions of it: the thing I see is not incomplete without the smell of it nor is the smell merely supplementary to the sight of it. The object is not a congeries of my variegated perceptions of it. I cannot fit the senses together like a jigsaw puzzle to make up a sensible world: there is no edge where sound notches into sight. Each sense pulls on, pushes against, distorts, intensifies, shrinks, or expands the others. This resonant incommensurability of the senses gives perception its depth, its richness, its inexhaustibility. Objects present themselves to the senses as *horizons of possibility*, as the phenomenologist Hubert Dreyfus put it in a 2005 lecture at the University of California, Berkeley, rather than completed things. The senses neither translate into each other, substitute for each other, nor complete each other. But they portend each other. This portentousness gives the perceptual world its "accent of reality," in Alfred Schutz's term: there is always more to it (1970, 254).

When I am engaged in ordinary acts, I do not dwell on my way of perceiving a thing. I move through perception into the world. What Merleau-Ponty calls the *arc of intentionality* runs through my body and its intentional objects. I am not thinking about things but acting through them. They are at once extensions of my intentionality and objects outside me. "This paradox is that of all being in the world: when I move toward a world I bury my perceptual and practical intentions in objects which ultimately appear prior to and external to those intentions, and which nevertheless exist for me only in so far as they arouse in me thoughts or volitions" (Merleau-Ponty [1945] 1962, 82). This is the unreflective perceptual modality Merleau-Ponty calls *motor intentionality* (110). In it, I do not think and then act; I act without having to think. My body is solicited by things. "I belong to objects and others before I belong to myself. I, objects, and others hang together in a matrix of meaningful acts in which we are, as Merleau-Ponty puts it, *intervolved* ([1945] 1962, 82)" (Young 2011, 80). My intentional investment in objects and their material continuity with me constitute an intersubjective, intercorporeal reality in which I am enmeshed. "It is this intentional arc which brings about the unity of the senses, of intelligence, of sensibility and motility" (Merleau-Ponty [1945] 1962, 136). In this mode, perception, as my colleague Dor Abrahamson puts it, is agnostic as to modality (personal communication, 2016). My senses come together in things.

Intersensoriality

The intentional locus of perception is not the body but the object. "The senses intercommunicate by opening on to the structure of the thing. One sees the hardness and brittleness of glass, and when, with a tinkling sound, it breaks, this sound is conveyed by the visible glass" (Merleau-Ponty [1945] 1962, 229). Because of the body's intersensorial unity, the look of a thing is already telling the perceiver what the thing feels like or what the thing sounds like. Any single sense perception portends what the whole thing is like. We encounter, as the anthropologist Michael Taussig writes, a "medley of the senses bleeding into each other's zone of expectations" (1993, 57).

> In the jerk of the twig from which a bird has just flown, we read its flexibility or elasticity, and it is thus that a branch of an apple-tree or a birch are immediately distinguishable. One sees the weight of a block of cast iron which sinks in the sand, the fluidity of water and the viscosity of syrup. In the same way, I hear the hardness and unevenness of cobbles in the rattle of a carriage, and we speak appropriately of a "soft," "dull" or "sharp" sound. Though one may doubt whether the sense of hearing brings us genuine "things," it is at least certain that it presents us, beyond the sounds in space, with something which "murmurs." and in this way communicates with the other senses.
>
> (Merleau-Ponty [1945] 1962, 230)

This murmurous something solicits the other senses, at least speculatively. Something somewhere moves. The movement has a certain style—soft, repetitive. I do not just hear a sound; I hear the sound of something palpable. Perception is intersensorial.

Deaf musicians put forward the explicitly intersensorial project of making music out of things that are not sounds. As Line Grenier and Veró Leduc remark, "Deaf artists have developed a wide range of musical forms, including corporal and vibro-tactile music." Such work challenges the assumption of our "audist societies" that "Deaf people cannot fully perform as artists, have access to, or appreciate" music, as if it were "solely audi-tory art" (Grenier and Leduc, n.d.). Making music out of sensations that are not sounds does not just transfer musical configurations from the ear to the skin. The world of Deaf music making is diverse, but in some cultures of Deaf music, these configurations may induce in perceivers a perceptual intimation of hearing, whether the listeners can now hear sounds, could once hear sounds, or perhaps even if they have never heard sounds. If vibro-tactile music does not undergo this transfiguration, it is not a musical art but a tactile art. The vibro-tactile suit designed by Not Impossible Labs promises this transfig-uration. As journalist Andy Herman reports, when he donned the suit, "Sure enough, a pulse timed to a kickdrum throbs into my ankles and up through my legs. Gradually, he brings in other elements: the tap of a woodblock in my wrists, a bass line massaging my lower back, a harp tickling a melody across my chest" (2018). Music is inscribed on the skin. If it works, the sound that the musical configuration brings about intersensorially is not imaginary but perceptually present, though unheard.

To make sound effects for film, some fabricated noises sound more like real sounds than the real sounds themselves. For instance, the sound of a solid object rubbing against baking soda sounds more like snow being crunched underfoot than crunching snow underfoot does. The coincidence in film of sound and image fuses them together in the process audio-visual theorist Michel Chion calls *synchresis*. "*Synchresis* (a word I have forged by combining *synchronism* and *synthesis*) is the spontaneous and irresistible weld produced between a particular auditory phenomenon and visual phenomenon when they occur at the same time" (1994, 63). Vibro-tactile music might be argued to substi-tute one sense for another instead of one sound for another, fabricating an intersensorial synchresis by which the perceiver feels music. Intersensorial sound art can evoke sounds it does not make in order to make music that hearers cannot hear but nonethe-less perceive. Musician and composer Andrew Hugill unmakes music by decomposing it into sound configurations that differential listenings re-compose into different musics. Hugill founded the Aural Diversity project in Britain in 2018 (Aural Diversity n.d.). It takes its name from the term John Levack Drever coined to describe a specific category of neurodiversity: "auraldiversity" (Drever 2019). The following year, seven musicians with disturbances of hearing, including Hugill, who has Ménière's disease, "a condition that causes severe hearing loss, tinnitus and vertigo," performed the first Aural Diversity concert in Bath, England (Bradshaw 2019b). As literary the-orist Melissa Bradshaw documents in the concert program (Bradshaw 2019a), instru-mentation ranged from sound-making objects like paper, metals, or bricks to classical instruments like bells, flutes, keyboard, banjo, and voice. The musicians performed and audience members engaged with the music through intersensorial connections that in-cluded "streaming to hearing aids or headphones, vibrations in the floor, sign language, surtitles and evocative videos" (Bradshaw 2019b). In the concert, sounds made evoke sounds not made, as if the concert were a sound map of sound, retaining certain audible properties of sound to allude to sounds not or no longer audible to perceivers. If a sound heard evokes a sound unheard, Hugill's music could be said to create an *intra*sensorial synchresis.

Making music make different sounds for different hearers has the curious result that everybody hears a different piece; nobody hears the whole piece. In a sense, there is no whole piece but an *acoustic palimpsest*, to take up Martin Daughtry's term. He writes, "I use this neologism to foreground the multiple acts of erasure, effacement, occupation, displacement, collaboration, and reinscription that are embedded in music composition, performance, and recording" (2017, 53). Hugill's composition consists of overlaid sonic elements, some of which are perceptible through others and some of which are not. Unlike a visible palimpsest, the layers of an audible palimpsest cannot be peeled back to arrive at the earliest inscription or the underlying composition. Rather, each hearer cuts into the audible assemblage from a different angle and slices out a different arrangement of elements. The question is no longer who hears but who hears what. If each hearer hears a different musical work, does the composition count as a single piece of music?

As sound becomes music, its link to space thins. Of course music, like any sound, reverberates off the contours of the space in which it is made and the instrument that makes it, but that reverberation is not the music. The music is held to be self-contained, detachable, and repeatable. Sound art extends beyond music's capacity to conduct its hearer elsewhere. But the elsewhere to which the hearer is conducted is not the *there* of a remote space or the *that* of sounding-making objects but an audible architecture of a different constitution. It is the affordances of this reconstitution that give sound art its aesthetic claim. Sound art is not the audible translation of visual or tactual perception but the fabrication of imaginary space. How sound art moves its perceiver into an auditory imaginary shifts across a spectrum from the audible overhearings of Corrinth's animal sounds to the audible inventions of Hugill's concert. All the auditory experiences under investigation here rely on the intersensorial unity of the body. In the sensory isolation experiment, sound brought forward space not seen; for Corbin and Torigoe, space brought forward sounds no longer heard. Hull and Kish heard tactile-kinesthetic space; Corrinth's sound-entranced children navigated unseen spaces by ear; LaBelle and Rosen heard the tactility of objects they did not touch; Brewster moved through tactile objects dematerialized into sounds; Westerkamp brought forward spaces sounds made up; and Corner made sights make sounds. Grenier' and Leduc's touches brought forward sounds not heard and Hugill's sounds brought forward sounds not made. Merleau-Ponty would argue that the intersensorial unity of the body that anchors all these sound experiences arises from a root synesthesia.

The Secret of the Senses

The secret of the senses is synesthesia, the capacity of one sensory experience to evoke the experience of another sense. "Synaesthetic perception is the rule, and we are unaware of it only because scientific knowledge shifts the centre of gravity of experience, so that we have unlearned how to see, hear, and generally speaking, feel, in order to deduce, from our bodily organization and the world as the physicist conceives it, what we are to see, hear and feel" (Merleau-Ponty [1945] 1962, 229). It is because of the trace of synesthesia in the body that, despite their perceptual disparities, all the senses open out onto the same world.

All infants are born synesthetic. Neurologists Daphne Maurer and Charles Maurer proposed in 1988 that " 'the newborn does not keep sensations separate from one another,' but rather 'mixes sights, sounds, feelings, and smells into a sensual bouillabaisse' in which 'sights have sounds, feelings have tastes,' and smells can make the body feel dizzy" (Maurer and Maurer 1988, 51, quoted in Maurer and Mondlach 2005, 193). This neurological work affirms Paul Schilder's mid-century psychoanalytic claim that "there does not exist any primary isolation between the different senses. The isolation is secondary. We perceive and we may with some difficulty decide that one part of the perception is based upon optic impressions. The synaesthesia is therefore a normal situation" ([1935] 1950, 38–39). In most humans this cross-modal perception disappears as they begin to explore their world corporeally and distinguish among sensations. The proliferation of neural connections among sensory systems gets pruned as the paths to each individual sense get strengthened experientially and the body loses its synesthetic faculty. The few people in whom this does not happen remain synesthetes. The separation of the senses is not a natural endowment but a learned faculty. What Daughtry calls the "palimpcestuous" quality of sound over sound also pertains to the synesthetic relationship between sound and sight, or sound and touch. Something vanishes—the visibility, the materiality of the perceived thing—but haunts the sound of it as a ghost of its effaced self (2017, 48, 53).

I can turn my attention to a particular sensory experience and *thematize* it in consciousness, to put it phenomenologically. When I do so, I switch from motor intentionality to the reflective modality Merleau-Ponty calls *representational intentionality*—intellection as opposed to perception. I no longer perceive a world but perceive my perception. In visual perception, "instead of yielding up my whole gaze to the world, I turn towards this gaze itself" ([1945] 1962, 226). In auditory perception, I listen and my world condenses into sound; other perceptual apprehensions fall away, fade out, drift off, lose savor. The intersubjectivity of my motor intentionality splits apart into subjectivity and objectivity. In this mode of attention, I distinguish among perceptual modalities. My world splinters into the visible, the tactual, the gustatory, the olfactory, and the audible. I think what I perceive. Doing so is one of our particular pleasures.

To bring forth an audible object in this way requires an intentional act. To facilitate this, in conventional Western classical music concerts not only are other sounds muted in the interest of thematizing the music but also lights are dimmed to mute vision, bodies are stilled to mute touch, and food and drink are prohibited to mute taste and smell. This is designed to produce what folklorist Barbara Kirshenblatt-Gimblett calls a *single-sense epiphany* (1991, 58). But the audible world that music brings forth is precarious. Other sensory modalities obtrude on my perceptual experience. Merleau-Ponty writes about the reality music opens up.

> When, in the concert hall, I open my eyes, visible space seems to me cramped compared to that other space through which, a moment ago, the music was being unfolded, and even if I keep my eyes open while the piece is being played, I have the impression that the music is not really contained within this circumscribed and unimpressive space. It brings a new dimension stealing through visible space, and in this it surges forward, just as, in victims of hallucinations, the clear space of things perceived is mysteriously duplicated by a "dark space" in which other presences are possible. ([1945] 1962, 222)

The musical architecture, by which I mean the space the sound carves out, exceeds the visible dimensions of the hall in which the music is played. It creates another space that paradoxically takes up the same space. "Music is not in visible space, but it besieges, undermines and displaces that space" (Merleau-Ponty [1945] 1962, 225). The sound space is at once more, less, and other than the seen space. Connor writes, "Sound, as Michel Chion has emphasised, has no frame. There is nothing to *hold* it in; so there is nothing to hold it *in*" (2013, 15). If it is provided a frame, sound announces the material properties of its holder without being altogether held in by it. Once launched, it proliferates outward, endlessly altering the audible surround. Visible space and audible space never coincide, never replicate each other, never extinguish each other. "The senses are distinct from each other and distinct from intellection in so far as each one of them brings with it a structure of being which can never be exactly transposed" (Merleau-Ponty [1945] 1962, 225). This tension among the senses is the perceptual insistence of the real, never reducing itself to its sensory constituents.

By contrast, in folk performances at festivals or in rituals, not only is the music accompanied by bursts of light and color, clouds of smell, tastes of foods, and crowds jostling bodies, but also the music itself bodies forth from a sea of sounds. Sensory suffusion and sensory confusion flood the body, in contrast to the pared down and purified sensory experience of conventional Western classical performance. Single-sense epiphanies contrast with multisensory ecstasies. Instead of pure sensation, I am subject to the dissolution of sensory categories. It is not in this instance that something exquisite and precise comes to the body as music but that the body comes to itself in music as a flood of sensations.

If sound brings forth space and the objects in it, the space is not necessarily the space the sound is made in, nor are the objects necessarily the objects that make the sounds. Sound makes its own space even as it makes co-present other spaces and objects. The sense of space is not unique to hearing and seeing. Smells make their own ephemeral spaces, even as they take up tactile and sometimes visible space. Tastes touch the tactile space of tongues, where they condense the ether of smells into the liquid of tastes. The touch of objects brings forth the invisible spaces inside and the visible spaces outside them, as much as it does the spatial density of the objects themselves. "Thus all senses are spatial if they are to give us access to some form or other of being, if, that is, they are senses at all. And, by the same necessity, they must all open on the same space, otherwise the sensory beings with which they bring us into communication would exist only for the relevant sense—like ghosts which appear only by night—they would lack fullness of being and we could not be truly conscious of them, that is to say, posit them as true beings" (Merleau-Ponty [1945] 1962, 217). The paradoxicality of the senses opening onto separate worlds and at the same time opening onto the same world dissolves in space.

Sound's Body

"But what hears?" writes folklorist and ethnomusicologist Deborah Kapchan. "Not just my ears. For sounds touch and resonate throughout my body. And why 'my' body, 'my' ears? Bone and liquid claim no ownership" (2017, 1). Sound is not suspended in the space between bodies, nor is it uniquely anchored in either the sensory apparatus of the body or the object that makes it. Sound gets under my skin. I perceive it as both a disturbance in the air and a disturbance of my tissues. As Bull contends, "Sound is essentially non-spatial in character, or rather engulfs the spatial; sound inhabits the subject just as the subject might be said to inhabit sound" (2002, 83). Because sound both pierces the body and escapes its container, "the enchantment of music . . . can also overwhelm inner self-presence. In its sometimes orgiastic auditory presence the body-auditory motion enticed in the midst of music may lead to a temporary sense of the 'dissolution' of self-presence. Music takes me 'out of myself' in such occurrences" (Ihde [1976] 2003, 62). As I am held by the music, my skin ceases to contain me. "Yet the site where sound touches flesh—the body—becomes a magnet for memories, an assembly of cells, of selves imagining themselves a unity, an author, a faithful student of sound knowledge" (Kapchan 2017, 1).

It is not just that I am in space; space is in me. Sound moves space through bodies, making their interior resonate with its exterior, puncturing skin with sound. Flesh moves with flesh, the flesh of the sound hearer with the flesh of the sound maker, entering the hearing body of the one into the sounding body of the other. Dance theorist Ana Pais describes this intercorporeal attunement as *co-motion* (2017, 238). This is not an enthrallment or captivation of one body by another. As affect theorist Anna Gibbs makes clear, "similarity is crucial, but so too is the difference produced in this sensory translation." Gibbs calls this intercorporeal effect "isomorphism without identity" (2010, 195). Here, the otherness of sound curls round the resistance of the body. The flesh folds back from it, nonetheless affecting and being affected in the course of the encounter, or the flesh yields, opening a path for otherness to seep in, to flow through, to flood the self. The co-motion of body and sound permeates the body of the other as well. As cultural theorist Jennifer Stoever-Ackerman puts it, "[S]ound is not merely a scientific phenomenon—vibrations passing through matter at particular frequencies—it is also a set of social relations" (Stoever-Ackerman 2010, 61). Hearing bodies attune to each other in audible space. Philosopher José Gil writes, "Bodily space is the product of the double investment of the body by space (the information coming from the physical world) and the investment of space by the body (as a certain kind of receiver-encoder of this information)" (1998, 130–131).

> Being in space means to establish diverse relationships with the things that sur-
> round our bodies. Each set of relations is determined by the action of the body
> that accompanies an investment of desire in a particular being or particular object.
> Between the body (and the organs in use) and the thing is established a connection
> that immediately affects the form and space of the body; between the one and the
> other a privileged spatial relation emerges that defines the space uniting them as
> "near" or "far," resistant, thick, wavy, vertiginous, smooth, prickly.
>
> (Gil 1998, 127)

If the sound maker is inside the body, it alters the space of the self. When I speak, my voice vibrates within me. It accrues body. "I hear through bone conduction as well as through the acoustical properties of the air, but the two 'media' of self-hearing are essentially separate. There is an essential sense in which *my hearing of myself is distinct from all other forms of hearing*" (Ihde [1976] 2003, 66; italics in the original). Thought, spoken, is fleshed and boned.

Music attunes bodies to themselves and each other in ways more precise, intricate, and ruthless than speaking, but these forms of attunement are not altogether different from each other. Speaking solicits co-motion in its rhythms but also interferes with it by, at the same time, soliciting the idiosyncratic processes of thinking, which were long since tuned up elsewhere, so that the processing of words for meanings might disrupt my absorption into the shared rhythms of speaking and listening bodies.

If the other speaks, voice loses body. Media scholar Douglas Kahn writes,

> While other people hear a person's voice carried through vibrations in the air, the
> person speaking also hears her or his own voice as it is conducted from the throat
> and mouth through bone to the inner regions of the ear. Thus, the voice in its pro-
> duction in various regions of the body is propelled through the body, its resonance is
> sensed intracranially. A fuller sense of presence is experienced as the body becomes
> attached to thought as much as the generation of speech is attached to thought. Yet
> at the same time that the speaker hears the voice full with the immediacy of the
> body, others will hear the speaker's voice infused with a lesser distribution of body
> because it will be a voice heard without bone conduction: a deboned voice. Where
> bones once stood, there will be only the air within which the voice's vibrations dis-
> sipate. (1999, 7)

Hearing materializes the speaking body. "This reflexivity [of hearing and speaking] is embodied doubly: one hears oneself in the act of voicing, and one resonates the physicality of voicing in acts of hearing. Listening and voicing are in a deep reciprocity, an embodied dialogue of inner and outer sounding and resounding built from the histor-
icization of experience. The ongoing dialogue of self and self, self and other, of their interplay in action and reaction, are thus constantly sited at the sense of sound" (Feld

2003, 225). I resonate to myself, the other, and the world. This is not passive perception, a body pelted by audible pings. I and the world are co-animated. As the religious historian Leigh Eric Schmidt points out, once assumptions about the passivity of hearing, in contrast to the activity of seeing, are "critically engaged rather than presumed, hearing's capacity for a similarly spirited exchange becomes recognizable—a dialogic movement between speaker and listener, a sympathetic vibration between sounding bodies" (2000, 34). It is possible, that is, for the voice of the other to vibrate within me as does my own. If it does, I am entered into such intimacy as to extinguish difference.

The poet Michael McClure, inventor of "meat language," converses with a leopard at the zoo.

> She puts her face within an inch of the wire and SPEAKS to me. The growl begins instantly and almost without musical attack. It begins gutturally. It grows in volume and it expands till I can feel the interior of her body from whence the energy of the growl extends itself as it gains full volume of fury. It extends itself, vibrating and looping. Then, still with the full capacity of untapped energy, the growl drops in volume and changes in pitch to a hiss. The flecks of her saliva spatter my face. I feel not smirched but cleansed. Her eyes are fixed on me. The growl without a freshly drawn breath, begins again. It is a language that I understand more clearly than any other. I hear rage, anger, anguish, warning, pain, even humor, fury—all bound into one statement.... I am surrounded by the physicality of her speech. It is a real thing in the air. It absorbs me and I can hear and feel and see nothing else. Her face and features disappear, becoming one entity with her speech. The speech is the purest, most perfect music I have ever heard, and I know that I am touched by the divine, on my cheeks, and on my brow, and on the tympanums of my ears, and the vibrations on my chest, and on the inner organs of perception.
>
> (McClure 1982, 155–156)

The ear has two ends. One end protrudes into the world; the other end intrudes into the body. From the outside in, auditory perceptions arouse, disturb, concentrate, intensify, or spread sensation at specific sites in the body. The body is, as it were, pricked into awareness from within. As these sensations open themselves up inside us, they present us with the outside on the inside. We acquire inner spaces to think and feel in. From the inside out, auditory perceptions extend the body out into the world to which they open us up. We acquire outer spaces to move in. Hearing makes events repeat themselves in us, changing their shape, changing our shape, making us into mimeses of what we hear. The body is suspended in an audible flow that runs right through it.

ACKNOWLEDGMENTS

In 2007, I gave a keynote address on sound at a graduate student conference at Indiana University, Bloomington, titled "Creative Bodies, Corporeal Knowledge: Extreme Folklore and Ethnomusicology." Since then I investigated sound in my 2010 "Film Body" course at the University of California, Berkeley, and my 2013, 2016, and 2019 "Anthropology of the Senses" course at San Francisco State University. This chapter is based on two presentations on the phenomenology of sound that I gave at Memorial University of Newfoundland, one an invited lecture in 2017 and the other a presentation at the Phenomenology in Ethnomusicology conference in 2018. My thinking about sound has benefited from discussions with students and colleagues on these occasions. The chapter itself was revamped in response to Harry Berger's and his coeditors' acute editorial suggestions and further complicated and deepened by the anonymous outside readers' incisive critiques.

Works Cited

Aural Diversity. n.d. "About." Accessed May 13, 2021. https://www.auraldiversity.org/about.html.

Bassett, Caroline. 2003. "How Many Movements?" In *The Auditory Culture Reader*, edited by Michael Bull and Les Back, 343–355. London: Berg.

Berkeley, George. [1709] n.d. "An Essay towards a New Theory of Vision." 4th ed. Classics in the History of Psychology (website), edited by Christopher D. Green. Accessed May 10, 2021. https://psychclassics.yorku.ca/Berkeley/vision.htm.

Bradshaw, Melissa. 2019a. "Aural Diversity: Concert 1." Aural Diversity (website). https://auraldiversity.org/concert1.html.

Bradshaw, Melissa. 2019b. "Aural Diversity Concert Series to Begin in July." *Rhinegold Publishing* (website). Accessed April 12, 2021. https://www.rhinegold.co.uk/classical_music/aural-diversity-concert-series-to-begin-in-july/.

Brewster, Michael. 1999. "Where, There or Here?" In *Site of Sound: Of Architecture and the Ear*, edited by Brandon LaBelle and Steve Roden, 101–107. Los Angeles: Errant Bodies Press; Smart Art Press.

Bull, Michael. 2002. "The Seduction of Sound in Consumer Culture: Investigating Walkman Desires." *Journal of Consumer Culture* 2 (1): 81–101.

Chasse, Loren. 1999. "Otic Diary." In *Site of Sound: Of Architecture and the Ear*, edited by Brandon LaBelle and Steve Roden, 93–99. Los Angeles: Errant Bodies Press; Smart Art Press.

Chion, Michel. 1994. *Audio-vision: Sound on Screen*. Translated by Claudia Gorbman. New York: Columbia University Press.

Connor, Steven. 2004. "Edison's Teeth: Touching Hearing." In *Hearing Cultures*, edited by Veit Erlmann, 153–172. Oxford: Berg.

Connor, Steven. 2013. "Sounding Out Film." In *The Oxford Handbook of New Audiovisual Aesthetics*, edited by John Richardson, Claudia Gorbman, and Carol Vernallis, 107–120. Oxford: Oxford University Press.

Corbin, Alain. (1994) 1998. *Village Bells: Sound and Meaning in the Nineteenth-Century French Countryside*. Translated by Martin Thom. London: Papermac.

Corner, Philip. 1999. "Ear Paper(s)." In *Site of Sound: Of Architecture and the Ear*, edited by Brandon LaBelle and Steve Roden, 26–29. Los Angeles: Errant Bodies Press; Smart Art Press.

Cusick, Suzanne G. 2017. "Musicology, Performativity, Acoustemology." In *Theorizing Sound Writing*, edited by Deborah Kapchan, 25–45. Middletown, CT: Wesleyan University Press.

Daughtry, J. Martin. 2017. "Acoustic Palimpsests." In *Theorizing Sound Writing*, edited by Deborah Kapchan, 46–85. Middletown, CT: Wesleyan University Press.

Drever, John L. 2019. "'Primacy of the Ear'– But Whose Ear? The Case for Auraldiversity in Sonic Arts Practice and Discourse." *Organised Sound* 24 (1): 85–95.

Feld, Steven. 2003. "A Rainforest Acoustemology." In *The Auditory Culture Reader*, edited by Michael Bull and Les Back, 223–239. Oxford: Berg.

Feld, Steven. 2005. "Places Sensed, Senses Placed: Toward a Sensuous Epistemology of Environments." In *The Empire of the Senses*, edited by David Howes, 179–191. Oxford: Berg.

Finkel, Michael. 2012. "The Blind Man Who Taught Himself to See." *Men's Journal*, May 4, 2012. https://www.mensjournal.com/features/the-blind-man-who-taught-himself-to-see-20120504/.

Gibbs, Anna. 2010. "After Affect: Sympathy, Synchrony, and Mimetic Communication." In *The Affect Theory Reader*, edited by Melissa Gregg and Gregory Seigworth, 186–205. Durham, NC: Duke University Press.

Gil, José. 1998. *Metamorphoses of the Body*. Minneapolis: University of Minnesota Press.

Grenier, Line, and Veró Leduc, Lead Researchers. n.d. "Musique au bout des doigts: Exploration des intersections musique et vieillissement au sein des communautés de sourd.es signeur.es á Montréal" / "Music at the Fingertips: Exploration of Intersections between Music and Ageing in Deaf Communities in Montréal." ACT (Aging + Communication + Technologies). Accessed July 18, 2019. https://actproject.ca/act/musique-au-bout-des-doigts/.

Heidegger, Martin. (1927) 1962. *Being and Time*. Translated by John Macquarrie and Edward Robinson. San Francisco: Harper Collins.

Herman, Andy. 2018. "Not Impossible Labs, Zappos Hope to Make Concerts More Accessible for the Deaf—and Cooler for Everyone." *Billboard*, September 25, 2018. https://www.billboard.com/articles/news/8476553/not-impossible-labs-live-music-deaf.

Hull, John. 1990. *Touching the Rock: An Experience of Blindness*. New York: Vantage.

Hurst, Nathan. 2017. "How Does Human Echolocation Work?" *Smithsonian Magazine*, October 2, 2017. https://www.smithsonianmag.com/innovation/how-does-human-echolocation-work-180965063/.

Ihde, Don. (1976) 2003. "Auditory Imagination." In *The Auditory Culture Reader*, edited by Michael Bull and Les Back, 61–76. London: Berg.

Ihde, Don. (1976) 2007. *Listening and Voice: Phenomenologies of Sound*. 2nd ed. New York: State University of New York Press.

Kahn, Douglas. 1999. *Noise, Water, Meat: A History of Sound in the Arts*. Cambridge, MA: MIT Press.

Kapchan, Deborah. 2017. "The Splash of Icarus: Theorizing Sound Writing/Writing Sound Theory." In *Theorizing Sound Writing*, edited by Deborah Kapchan, 1–22. Middletown, CT: Wesleyan University Press.

Kirshenblatt-Gimblett, Barbara. 1991. "Objects of Ethnography." In *Exhibiting Cultures: The Poetics and Politics of Museum Display*, edited by Ivan Karp and Steven D. Levine, 386–443. Washington, DC: Smithsonian Institution Press.

Kish, Daniel. 2012. "Experience: I Taught Myself to See." *The Guardian*, July 13, 2012. https://www.theguardian.com/lifeandstyle/2013/jul/13/experience-blindness-echolocation-daniel-kish.

Kish, Daniel. 2015. "How I Use Sonar to Navigate the World." TED (website). https://www.ted.com/talks/daniel_kish_how_i_use_sonar_to_navigate_the_world/transcript?language=en.

LaBelle, Brandon, and Steve Roden. 1999. "The Blue Whale." Track 8 on the compact disc that accompanies *Site of Sound: Of Architecture and the Ear*, edited by Brandon LaBelle and Steve Roden. Santa Monica, CA: Errant Bodies Press; Smart Art Press.

Masters, Marc. 2015. "Sculptures You Can Hear: Why Harry Bertoia's 'Sonambient' Art Still Resonates." *Washington Post*, March 27, 2015. https://www.washingtonpost.com/news/

arts-and-entertainment/wp/2015/03/27/sculptures-you-can-hear-why-harry-bertoias-son
ambient-art-still-resonates/.

Maurer, Daphne, and Charles Maurer. 1988. *The World of the Newborn*. New York: Basic Books.

Maurer, Daphne, and Catherine Mondlach. 2005. "Neonatal Synesthesia: A Reevaluation." In *Synesthesia: Perspectives from Cognitive Neuroscience*, edited by Lynn Robertson and Naom Sagiv, 193–213. Oxford: Oxford University Press.

McClure, Michael. 1982. "A Mammal Gallery." In *Scratching the Beat Surface: Essays on New Vision from Blake to Kerouac*, 149–160. New York: Penguin.

Merleau-Ponty, Maurice. (1945) 1962. *Phenomenology of Perception*. Translated by Colin Smith. New York: Routledge.

Pais, Ana. 2017. "Almost Imperceptible Rhythms and Stuff like That: The Power of Affect in Live Performance." In *Theorizing Sound Writing*, edited by Deborah Kapchan, 233–250. Middletown, CT: Wesleyan University Press.

Scarry, Elaine. 2001. *Dreaming by the Book*. Princeton, NJ: Princeton University Press.

Schafer, R. Murray. 1977. *The Tuning of the World*. Philadelphia: University of Pennsylvania Press.

Schafer, R. Murray. 1993. *The Soundscape: Our Sonic Environment and the Tuning of the World*. Rochester, VT: Destiny Books.

Schilder, Paul. (1935) 1950. *The Image and Appearance of the Human Body*. New York: International Universities Press.

Schmidt, Leigh Eric. 2000. *Hearing Things: Religion, Illusion, and the American Enlightenment*. Cambridge, MA: Harvard University Press.

Schutz, Alfred. 1970. *On Phenomenology and Social Relations*. Chicago: University of Chicago Press.

Siebers, Tobin. 2010. *Disability Theory*. Ann Arbor: University of Michigan Press.

Sterne, Jonathan. 2003. *The Audible Past: The Cultural Origins of Sound Reproduction*. Durham, NC: Duke University Press.

Stoever-Ackerman, Jennifer. 2010. "Splicing the Color-Line: Tony Schwartz Remixes Postwar Nueva York." *Social Text* 28 (1): 59–85.

Taussig, Michael. 1993. *Mimesis and Alterity: A Particular History of the Senses*. New York: Routledge.

Thibaud, Jean-Paul. 2003. "The Sonic Composition of the City." In *The Auditory Culture Reader*, edited by Michael Bull and Les Black, 329–341. Oxford: Berg.

Torigoe, Keiko. 2002. "A City Traced by Soundscape." In *Soundscape Studies and Methods*, edited by Helmi Jäviluoma and Gregg Wagstaff, 29–57. Helsinki: Finnish Society for Ethnomusicology.

Westerkamp, Hildegaard. 1999. "Sensitive Chaos." Track 2 on the compact disc that accompanies *Site of Sound: Of Architecture and the Ear*, edited by Brandon LaBelle and Steve Roden. Santa Monica, CA: Errant Bodies Press; Smart Art Press.

Young, Katharine. 2011. "Gestures, Intercorporeity, and the Fate of Phenomenology in Folklore." *Journal of American Folklore* 124 (492): 55–87.

ONTOLOGIES

CHAPTER 13

....

NOT JUST ONE,
NOT JUST NOW

Relational Voices in Time

....

MATTHEW RAHAIM

FEW philosophical themes evoke as much wonder as voice. There has been a long tradition of phenomenological reflection on vocal utterance: from Maurice Merleau-Ponty's evocative image of sonorous speech as "singing the world" (Merleau-Ponty [1945] 2012, 193) to Emmanuel Levinas's open-ended "traumatism of astonishment" that arises in face-to-face conversation (Levinas [1961] 1979, 73); from Don Ihde's living, breathing cosmic vocality, in which we are surrounded by the voices not only of people but also of sliding mugs, rolling dice, and popping firecrackers (Ihde [1976] 2007, 67), to Jean-Luc Nancy's rapturous reflections on "*Mmmmmmm*," the syllable that "resounds previous to the voice, inside the throat, scarcely grazing the lips from the back of the mouth, without any movement of the tongue, just a column of air pushed from the chest in the sonorous cavity, the cave of the mouth that does not speak" (Nancy [2002] 2007, 24–25).

But one particularly persuasive treatise on the phenomenology of voice seems to drown out all the others: Jacques Derrida's analysis of vocal presence in *Voice and Phenomenon* ([1967] 2011).[1] This work, and the critique of logocentrism that it inaugurated, is often construed as a damning rebuke, revealing both phenomenology and vocal philosophy to be "outmoded and backward," childishly attached to the voice's false metaphysical promises of presence, immediacy, and *logos* (Kane 2015, 672). At the very least, it shows Derrida to be a competent phenomenologist in his own right and an exceedingly subtle reader of Husserl in particular. *Voice and Phenomenon* focuses on one particular case of voicing that, Derrida argues, is fundamental to any descriptive phenomenology: a subject speaking to itself, cut off, in principle, from relations with others. Though this self-absorbed speech seems to offer an immediate, immaculate *expression* of inner meaning, Derrida demonstrates on phenomenological grounds that even the apparently pure voice of soliloquy has its own contingencies, unavoidably entangled in temporality, alterity, and interpretation. And if even speaking to ourselves is so messy, what of speech and song out there in the world—so often construed as originary, pure, and authentic in comparison to writing?

There is much for scholars of voice to learn from Derrida's critique. Husserl is not alone in figuring the inner voice as an unmediated source of evidence.[2] A surprising amount of discourse about "the voice" implicitly frames vocality as an expression of a sovereign individual or a monolithic collectivity, sounding out a pristine self-identity, insulated from the complex interplay of social relations. This expressivist figuration guides political discourse too. We speak casually—too casually, perhaps—of the unified "voice of the people," the unique "voice of a nation," of politicians who "give voice" to a putatively unanimous constituency, as though unblemished self-identical unison were the normative prior condition of any politics.

But we have much to teach as well. Public singing and speaking, chatting and harmonizing with others, vocal uproar, protest, and negotiation, so central to any ethnomusicological phenomenology of voice, appear in the Derridean critique only as exceptions to the Husserlian rule—or, as Derrida would have it, as manifestations of a single metaphysical "impurity": *absence* ([1967] 2011, 73). Ethnomusicologists, in contrast, have long afforded primacy to the social life of song, amplifying the life of voices bouncing relationally about, feeding back, plying their various trades among *others*: declaiming, seducing, transgressing, drawing together consociates. Michelle Kisliuk's classic work on Pygmy song focuses on vocal relationships rather than mere expressions of a pregiven social order, opening up a performative, temporally dynamic "micropolitics" (Kisliuk 2000, 26). Steven Feld's paradigmatic case of *groove* (by which sound structure *is* social structure) is a particular Kaluli practice of collective song (*dulugu ganalan*, or "lift-up-over sounding") that sounds out, negotiates, and cultivates (rather than merely reflects) a participatory, anarchic, egalitarian way of being (Feld 1984). The past few decades have seen an acceleration of focused ethnographic work on voice: on the ethical stakes of vocal comportment (e.g., Desai-Stevens 2017; Eidsheim 2015), the formation of vocal subjects (e.g., Weidman 2011; Harkness 2013), and the politics of public voicing (e.g., Kunreuther 2014; Schultz 2012). On the whole, this literature foregrounds the ongoing dynamism and plurality of vocal action, rather than construing the voice as an instrument of immediate expression.

This essay attempts to bring this ethnographic literature into conversation with Derrida's critique, suggesting ways in which an ethnographically grounded phenomenology of voice might highlight precisely the kinds of social relations that Husserlian soliloquy excludes. It also points to some of the politically consequential ways in which regnant social-theoretic construals of voicing presume a notionally atemporal, eternally present, perfectly expressive soliloquy. Our trajectory begins with the interwoven figurations of voice, temporality, and melody that underlie the Husserlian-Derridean thread and which seem to yield a figuration of voice that is utterly irrelational, cut off from social relations. We then turn to the temporality of vocal co-presence—the intersecting arcs of call, response, interruption, and affirmation. By the end, we will return to the temporality of relational voicing, its ontological possibilities, and its contingent forms of immediacy.

THE VOICE OF PHENOMENOLOGY

In what sense does a voice seem to offer immediate presence? Simon Frith suggests one way: since "we have bodies too, throats and stomachs and lungs . . . the voice seems so directly expressive [because] it doesn't take thought to know how that vocal noise was made" (1998, 192). In another obvious sense, the presence of a speaker can be a compelling illusion—for example, in the famously fraudulent vocal performances of Orson Welles's *War of the Worlds*, which was broadcast on CBS radio in 1938. The actor playing a news anchorman purports to offer an eyewitness report of a spaceship landing in New Jersey, narrating everything that he sees, at the very moment he is seeing it: "I can see peering out of that black hole two luminous disks. Are they eyes? It might be a face. . . . There, I can see the thing's body. It's large, large as a bear and it glistens like wet leather." So convincing was this first-person present narration of fictional *seeing* that some listeners seem to have taken it to be a real news broadcast. Even listening to this broadcast a century later, knowing full well that the report is fictional, we are still offered a vivid picture of an event unfolding *now*. Even a high-resolution photograph of a person—flat, silent, and still—lacks the absorbing sense of immediacy offered by a voice narrating in first-person present tense.

But there is a subtler sense in which a voice may seem to offer itself up as presence itself, and this is the theme that Derrida takes up in *Voice and Phenomenon*, a dense extended essay that provides the phenomenological grounding for Derrida's famous critique of the *metaphysics of presence*. Derrida is broadly concerned with the tendency to assign metaphysical priority to the living, sounding, immediate presence of speech rather than the spooky ambiguities, slippages, and silent absences of writing. Derrida's oft-cited historical claim that "Western" metaphysics has, since Plato, privileged the voice over writing turns out to be cherry-picked and incomplete at best (Cavarero 2005, 227–234; Dolar 2006, 43–52). The enduring value of Derrida's argument instead lies in his phenomenological analysis. As Kurt Gödel's *Formally Undecidable Propositions* did for Whitehead and Russell's mathematical logic, Derrida's *Voice and Phenomenon* probes the very fabric of Husserlian phenomenology using its own methods—and discovers a seam. In order to find it, as Derrida teaches us, we must listen (Derrida [1967] 2011, 74).

Derrida argues that phenomenology is founded upon a very particular kind of speech: *soliloquy*, or speaking to oneself. He begins from Husserl's early foray into semiotics in his *Logical Investigations*, which seems to grant soliloquy a kind of semiotic immediacy that colloquy (interpersonal speech) cannot have (Husserl [1900] 2001, 218–219). Husserl claims that while colloquy *indicates* a meaning through signs to someone else, soliloquy is radically different: it *expresses* a prior meaning that the speaker has already grasped in its totality. While we grasp the voice of an interlocutor partially and indirectly (following along the trail of the words, always a bit late), soliloquy seems to flash into being precisely at the same time as its meaning ("in the twinkling of an eye"). In Husserl's early semiotics, soliloquy is perfectly expressive: a meaning-to-say is expressed immediately in its entirety, without distortion, without stopping to work through what individual words indicate. Derrida argues that this figuration of apparently direct vocal expressiveness, which seems to promise immediacy, presence, and unmodified access to *logos*, is the characteristic condition of supposedly pure phenomenology. He highlights the peculiar lilt of phenomenological prose, which generally proceeds in the first person, in present tense, as, for example: "I see in pure reflection that this die is given continuously as an objective unity" (Husserl [1913] 1982, 39). Like the virtual journalistic reportage of *War of the Worlds*, the validity of this voice does not hinge on its being factually true but rather on its seemingly immediate access to its own experience. Of course, the phenomenological philosophy we encounter written on the page is inevitably indicative, rather than expressive, in Husserl's scheme: it re-presents the now-absent originary moment. Yet if it is to be a pure phenomenological account, its authority would seem to depend on an originary moment of soliloquy, in which the self speaks to itself in a field of unmediated self-presence, in which "the acts in question are themselves experienced by us at that very moment" (Husserl [1900] 2001, 191).

Temporality, then, is at the heart of this construal of phenomenological voice. As Derrida points out, though, we encounter a paradox. By Husserl's own later analysis of temporality, any lived present moment depends on retention of the just-past and protention of the just-about-to-come. In other words, even the presence of one's own voice requires the re-presentation of "absent" moments. To understand this temporal paradox, it turns out that once again, we must listen—in this case, to melody.

Two Melodic Temporalities

Melody has served as a model for many classic accounts of temporality, from Hume to Brentano, Bergson, Husserl, and beyond (Hume [1738] 1960, 36; Brentano [1874] 1995, 217; Bergson [1889] 2001, 100; Husserl [1928] 1991). Despite their vast mutual differences, nearly every such account tends to share a single model of melody: an evenly spaced sequence of discrete notes, plunked out on a piano, one by one.[3] Each tone has a clear beginning and end; each is the same length; none has any rhythmic or gestural priority over others. For philosophers, this paradigm is heuristically convenient, offering a comforting stability in an otherwise dynamic field of perception, providing (it seems) a simple set of building blocks for temporality to operate upon. For practicing musicians, however, such an account of melody can only appear naïve. Its peculiar temporal affordances (lacking in what is casually called "musical time") has led to a crucial paradox in the phenomenology of temporality. Call this model of melody (as a string of atemporal, notionally interchangeable objects) a *punctual* melodic paradigm; we will return to it and its implications for temporality later.

First, we turn to a rather different melodic paradigm—a *vocal-gestural* paradigm, in which any melodic utterance is actively performed over time. The voice projects rather different temporal possibilities than the ideal-typical piano assumed by most philosophers.[4] What is it to speak a word, to sing a word, to hear a word? It differs from the instantaneous *logos* of Husserlian soliloquy and from the digital plunking of discrete notes in at least one important way: it takes time. No one beeps out a note with the perfect acoustical precision of a tuning fork. Even the most tuneful singer overshoots minutely and corrects, or hovers around their destination with vibrato, or scoops or glides from tone to tone. Speech too is gestural. Consider the word "time"—or, better, say it. The plosive /t/ requires a buildup of air pressure for fifty milliseconds or so, and then releases it. After a barely discernible moment of hissing air, the vocal cords gradually engage on the vowel, a diphthong, moving from /a/ to /i:/. No sooner does the /a/ form than the back of the tongue begins pulling up to form /i:/; /m/ is enunciated by a gradual closing of the lips and a brief hum. Typically, at the end of a sentence, the word is finished off with a slight opening of the lips at the end, articulating a gentle, subtle "muh." We sing it too; it may rise ("Is it *time*?") or fall ("It's *time*.") (see Figure 13.1), or trace subtle trajectories of irony, taunting, or coaxing. In the figure, the successive phonemes are shown in noteheads for convenience, but the real action is shown in the spectrograph

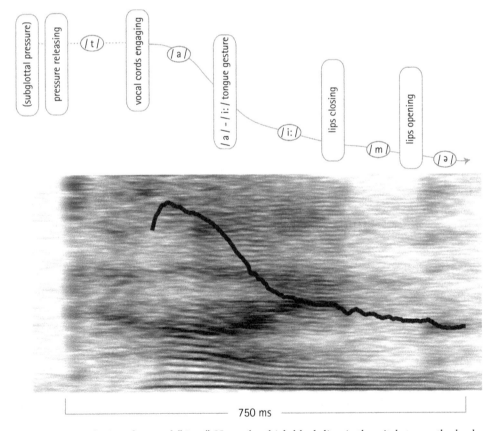

FIGURE 13.1: Saying the word "time." Here, the thick black line is the pitch trace; the background is a spectrogram showing the gradual shifts in overtones from vowel to vowel.

(the comblike striations that show timbre) and the pitch trace (the thick black curve): both are continuously shifting, articulating gestural motion rather than points.

The melodic shapes that allow us to distinguish a question from a solemn oath from a mocking impersonation unfold in expansive curves. These utterances become meaningful only through a temporal sense of where the utterance is going. These are constantly in motion and emerge with duration, not as instantaneous, discrete points. An infinitesimal moment could never suffice for this coordinated muscular action, nor could a millisecond, nor even ten. No solitary point on a horizontal axis can give even a single syllable; every real utterance has its own inherent temporal thickness.

Utterance furthermore maps out a temporal itinerary for itself. The thrill offered by minced oaths such as *shut the f . . . ront door* rests on the almost irresistible anticipation (*protention*) of the profanity heralded by /f/. The timing of a punchline relies on a magical play with an audience's expectations (Berger 2010, 48). Elaborate melodic action plays on just these expectations. When we hear a cohesive melody, we are already carrying out a remarkable act of temporal constitution: *retaining* the residual presence of the melodic arc and *protending* the arc to come. Thus, melodic apprehension—like any temporality—emerges in a presence that is inescapably "thick" (constituted by disciplined retentions and protentions), rather than "thin" (locked in a single, infinitesimally brief moment of perfect immediacy). These presences may come in various extents (ranging from a few hundred milliseconds to several seconds) and may carry various affective valences. We may feel curiosity, yearning, or dread for what is to come; we may delight in the elegant completion of a rhyming couplet, a modulation, or a *tihāi*. In any case, the attentional disciplines that lead to particular forms of protention and retention are not mechanically triggered by the sonic signal but require enculturation and training.

For example, Figure 13.2 shows a pair of phrases (A and B) sung by Amir Khansahab, one of the best-known Hindustani vocalists of the twentieth century, singing in Rāg Rāgeshrī. Phrases like this are *extemporaneously* generated—which is to say that Hindustani vocalists come up with them "at the moment." As should already be clear, this moment could never be infinitely thin; it already builds on the retained past and projects a protended future.

As with most extemporaneous utterances, spoken or sung, the hands are working alongside the voice (McNeill 1992; Kendon 2004; Streeck 2009). As in sentences, the hands trace breathing, neumatic arcs of rise and fall, antecedent and consequent, tension and release. In this case, they are playing with the temporal expectation of return to the tonic from an excursion. Phrase A in Figure 13.2 moves from tension to relaxation (see Figure 13.3). As Khansahab's right hand grips and gathers a virtual substance, the wrist and finger joints move from flexion (with muscle tension pulling toward the palm and little finger, with a loose grip) to neutral relaxation (wrist in line with the forearm, open handed).

Meanwhile, his voice moves along an oft-traveled path to the tonic, a modally specific cadence already burned into his listeners' sensibilities: *ga ma re sa*, {3 4 2 1}.[5] Or so we expect. Phrase A is different; he begins on the *ga ma re sa* path but slips *below sa* to touch *ni* {7♭} as his hand extends back the *other way*. He then overshoots again, this time above the tonic, flexing his wrist accordingly, before returning to *sa* {1} and relaxing his wrist.

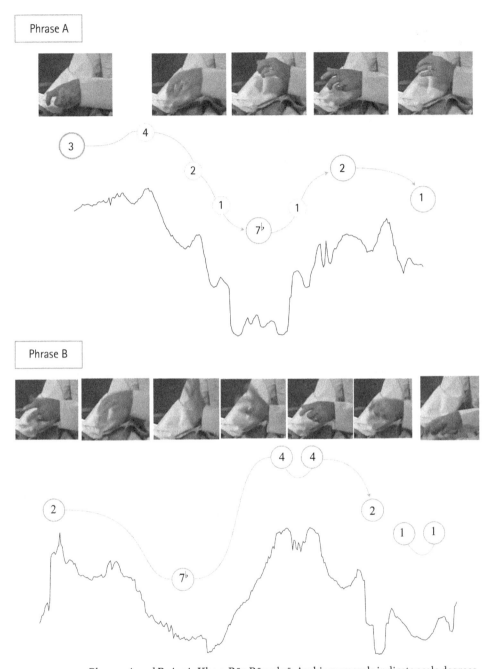

FIGURE 13.2: Phrases A and B. Amir Khan, Rāg Rāgeshrī. Arabic numerals indicate scale degrees.

But even here, his arm has not fully relaxed; his hand is raised, cupped, and ready for phrase B to complete it. Phrase B too delays the resolution to *sa* with a dramatic *re ni ma* {2 7♭ 4} swoop before coming to repose on the tonic.

To feel the melodic ebb and flow of these phrases, it is not enough to ride their pitch contours like a rollercoaster, locked utterly "in the moment," trapped in the flux of pure

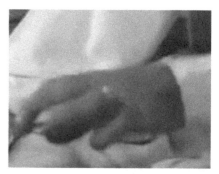

Flexion/Grip   Relaxation/Release

FIGURE 13.3: Flexion and relaxation. Amir Khan, Rāg Rāgeshrī.

awareness. As with the vocal-gestural utterance of a word, the melodic action in these phrases is all in playing with a listener's melodic expectation: their retention of the trajectory just past, and their protention of the resolution about to come.

Though often depicted as purely cognitive, protention is also a physical act. A gestural handshape forms protentively *before* it is deployed; as Merleau-Ponty observes, "from its very beginnings, the grasping movement is magically complete; it only gets under way by anticipating its goal" (Merleau-Ponty [1945] 2012, 106). Connoisseurs of raga music often mark culminations of metric cycles by raising and dropping their hand: the fulfilment of the cycle is felt in advance, and the hand is raised and prepared for the drop. As a goalie raises her hands before the instant of contact with the ball, protention often happens physically, publicly, even socially, as groups of connoisseurs "tune in" to the temporality of metric cycles, feeling the culmination together, moving as one. Breath too protends the melody to come. A singer opens her mouth and takes a breath in advance of singing a phrase. And once singing, she is always faced with a point on the temporal horizon when the next breath must come. This is no less true of instrumentalists. A guitarist playing in a "lyrical" style, a sarangi player evoking a wail or a sigh, and a sitarist playing in *gayaki ang* (a "singing way") all project an eminently gestural melodic logic. The hand of a pianist rises in preparation for a downbeat, falls, roots the thumb on D in preparation for an ascending tetrachord from E to A, and traces arcs across the face of the keyboard (Sudnow 1978). The temporality of the musicking body is the temporality of preparatory breaths, manual retention, dramatic satisfaction, or deferral of anticipations.

PARENTHESES: EMBODIMENT, STILLNESS, AND DISCLOSURE

To summarize this rich kinetic detail by saying that music is "embodied" is a decent provisional gloss, and a great deal of insightful literature has recently come under this rubric. However, the excessive polysemy of "embodiment" can lead to various misreadings, and it's worth pausing to comment on these.

A reliance on the term "embodiment" may suggest a pregiven anatomy shared by all singers—or worse, that each body begins and ends at the individual. But musicking bodies are plural, widely various, and socially enculturated (Rahaim 2012; Weidman 2012). And they are productive, in turn, of various vocal ontologies, according to their techniques (discussed later). "Embodiment" may also suggest a metaphysics in which some prior "disembodied" music is optionally and occasionally instantiated ("embodied") by some body. But having a body is a condition of possibility for the disclosure of a musical world in the first place: whether dancing, playing, singing, or listening, we are engaged in bodily acts. Perhaps most misleadingly, speaking of embodiment may suggest that some activities are embodied and some are not, as though sitting very still while singing is "disembodied" in contrast to singing while moving. But sitting still for an extended period of time is also a cultivated technique of the body, far more difficult to instill in children, for example, than clapping or dancing. The retrained stillness of Amália Rodrigues as she sings fado, for example, contrasts with the usual expressive gestures one would find in a spoken lament, complaint, or exclamation; this is an eminently disciplined musicking body, not its ghostly disappearance. Extended *padmasana* (i.e., yogic "lotus posture") affords meditative practices that disclose an inner landscape that is inaccessible while navigating a busy street; extended *sitzfleisch* (i.e., a still and quiet sitting posture) in the concert hall can disclose the forms and objects on which a distanced aesthetics can operate. Bodily techniques of stillness are world-disclosing practices no less than bodily techniques of overt motion.

Among the things that still contemplation can disclose is a world of melodic objects—sequences of notes, brightly salient against a background—that seem to outshine the kinetics of motion. The notes transcribed in Figure 13.2, like the phonemes in Figure 13.1, are actively discerned by an enculturated listener, not given in the sonic signal. Nowhere in the undulations of vocal pitch do we find a flat, steady line that simply corresponds objectively to a "note." The disclosure of notes requires repeated listening and study, sometimes with eyes closed, speeding up and slowing down a recording, testing my provisional notations against listening, until I am acceptably content with the result. A trained ear can discern them, to be sure, and this discernment requires considerable work. (This is why "ear training" requires years of disciplined practice even for skilled singers.) Not all—or even most—singers have this skill; few, if any, can achieve good melodic results by willfully piecing melodies together note by note.[6]

PUNCTUALITY, NOTATION, AND PRESENCE

Note-by-note is the logic of the punctual melodic paradigm outlined earlier. A punctual account of a melody does not work from a particular performance but from a sequence of notes, fixed and given like a string of beads. To be sure, these punctual accounts are directed toward uncovering the thickness of the retentional-protentional present (Husserl [1928] 1991, 11). To hear a melodic sequence, for example, {12323, 23434, 34545 . . . }, requires the retention of past phrases; harmonic tension derives its effect precisely from the protention of a resolution to come. And yet, oddly enough, the punctual paradigm can only offer flat, homogeneous sequences, without rhythmic impulse, speed, goal tones, energetic flow, or improvisational spontaneity. Even when Husserl's account stresses the fading away of tonal impressions over time, the fading is "incessant," each tone notionally equivalent and interchangeable in its linear decay, independent of phrasing, metric cycle, or breath, "until it disappears" ([1928] 1991, 32). In other words, such a temporality is grounded in tones that are, themselves, remarkably devoid of action, assuming, as Indian music theorist B. C. Deva puts it, "a spurious constancy of tones and tonal relations" (1959, 175). In such a conception, tones sit perfectly still, awaiting our perceptual uptake into a temporal schema. They occur in a definite, predictable order, without any need for a trained listener to make sense of them.[7] While conventional staff notation usually includes at least some indications of phrasing, the discrete tones that underlie the melodic accounts of well-intentioned philosophers typically do not. They have the same temporal ambiguity as a short series of photographs. As Hindustani musician and theorist Sakhawat Hussain Khan once vividly put it, sequential notation is a sort of vocal photography[8] that freezes the dynamic flux of singing frame by frame, so that a song can be learned instant by instant, note by note. Indeed, the usefulness of sequential notation is precisely that it may be studied and learned outside of the flow of melody. It does this by reconstituting the continuity of melodic motion as a series of successive snapshots of indeterminate spans of time. As photography obscures motion and generates an ambiguous sense of an infinitely still "instant" otherwise inaccessible to experience, so too does tone-based notation generate a punctual melodic paradigm.

We now begin to see the outlines of the paradox produced by the punctual melodic paradigm. Even if retention and protention are necessary to disclose a melody from a sequence of tones, for Husserl, "particular acts correspond to the individual tones" (Husserl [1928] 1991, 141). These acts (of attention, focus, and discernment) thus become tied to the curious entity that Husserl calls the *primal impression*—the "consciousness of the tone-now" that, along with retention and protention, completes his triadic model of temporal structure ([1928] 1991, 31). The primal impression poses extraordinarily difficult philosophical problems, as both Husserl and Derrida acknowledge; here, "words fail us" (Derrida [1967] 2011, 72n1). It is not clear from Husserl's text, for example, whether each primal impression is (1) a punctual, immediate experiential snapshot of the now-point that passes and instantaneously transforms into a retention, to be replaced in turn by another primal impression (and another, and another), or (2) a durative ("thick") moment, constituted temporally by a subject, always already bundled together with retention and protention (Zahavi 1999, 65). The term "primal impression" does read at times as though it occurs as a point (like a notional note-punctum), or as Derrida puts it with great self-assurance, "the identity of experience instantaneously present to itself" (Derrida [1967] 2011, 60).[9] When Husserl describes the constitution of motion (a far more intuitively musical situation than the tickertape "melody" described earlier), he has recourse to a "nucleus" in the midst of this continual flow, a "head attached to the comet's tail of retentions," and a "grasping-as-now that takes place moment by moment" ([1928] 1991, 32). As in the algebraic analysis of curves, we appear to have a play between the apprehension of a continuous span of motion ("during the time," "the comet's tail") and numerous discrete points by which the curve becomes knowable in primal impression after primal impression (i.e., a "grasping-as-now," "moment-by-moment"). There have been various readings of this ambiguity. On Derrida's reading, Husserl's primal impression is meant to be infinitely thin and nailed to the now-point, untouched by retention and protention. It is the temporal condition of soliloquy's self-presence: pure "auto-affection," which is "affected there by nothing other than by itself" (Derrida [1967] 2011, 73). And yet, were this actually the case, Derrida points out that the "itself" by which each primal impression is successively "affected" (i.e., replaced in turn), and by virtue of which it is a "now," is yet *another* successive primal impression. This supposedly pure self-presence, then, is shown to be always already founded on difference with something else. In these terms, Derrida is able to persuasively debunk the implication of immediate self-presence in Husserl's earlier account of inner speech: "the theme of a pure interiority of speech, or of 'hearing-oneself-speak,' is radically contradicted by 'time' itself [i.e., by temporality]" ([1967] 2011, 74).

But here is the paradox: in a punctual melodic paradigm, these two readings of the primal impression are indistinguishable, as tonal durations are indistinguishable from tonal instants. Since a sequence of internally homogeneous tones yields no difference, no change, over the span of each of its atomic tones, it could only offer a sequence of snapshots of pure "nows." Melody (which serves for all of these philosophers as a metonym for temporality in general) can only emerge sequentially, point by point. Each "tone" could, in principle, last for a minute or a millisecond; it could be sustained right up until the following tone or appear to be infinitesimally short. Within each point, temporality seems to disappear, deprived of any difference that would yield a sense of motion, progress, or change. It is indeed possible to approach this form of extraordinary temporality as a sort of psychedelic limit case—as, for example, in Steve Reich's "Pulse," Terry Riley's "Desert of Ice," or other forms of pointillistic minimalism that are remarkable, in part, for their uncanny distance from gestural utterance. As we have seen, though, this is not an accurate model of how song, speech, or even words actually unfold in performance. When the voice does come to rest on a tone (what is called a *nyāsa svara* in Hindustani music), it shows up as a distinctive noema, a special object, that stands out against a background of continuous motion (Rahaim 2012, 95). In a gestural melodic paradigm, by contrast, there could be no "thin" now-point, no primal impression independent of retention and protention.

It is hard to sustain Derrida's certainty about Husserl's intent, especially since Husserl himself was never satisfied with his solution (Zahavi 1999, 69–75). Indeed, his work starts from an explicit rejection of Brentano's theretofore regnant distinction between direct "perceptions" of the infinitesimal present and the indirect "presentiating acts" of retention and protention—a distinction he rejects precisely because it cannot account for the immediate perception of temporally unfolding events such as melody.

Indeed, the entirety of his work on temporality may be read as an insistence on a "thick" temporal presence. And yet, Husserl's famous term for the moment of the primary impression, "*im selben Augenblick*" ("in the glance of an eye"), seems to ride at the edge of "thick" and "thin" presences (durative yet almost imperceptibly brief).[10] Derrida conveniently renders *Augenblick* as "blink" (i.e., the closing of the eyelid, like the shutter of a camera) and then goes on to dedicate the fifth chapter of *Voice and Phenomenon* to the implications of this figment of his own creative mistranslation.[11] His aphoristic response comes in two phrases. The first phrase, "there is a duration to the blink," correctly emphasizes the temporal thickness of protention and retention. The second phrase, "the duration closes the eye," however, implies that protention and retention introduce an antagonistic *absence* ([1967] 2011, 56). Absence is Derrida's favored all-purpose metaphysical substance; it seems to encompass retention, memory, protention, anticipation, and, in the end, the thick present itself. Indeed, Derrida extends the metaphysical ambit of presence/absence so far that, in his later work, it seems perfectly natural for him to conflate, paradoxically, the always-incomplete gestural unfolding of neumes (vocal gestures) with Rousseau's fantasy of a "time reduced to presence" ([1967] 1997, 249).

The rhetorical force of *Voice and Phenomenon* largely rests on the imputation of a foundational, puritanical zeal to Husserl's work, as though phenomenology depended on sealing off the inner voice against what Derrida calls "contamination" by absence ([1967] 2011, 19). It is not clear that this was ever Husserl's position. More importantly, as Adriana Cavarero so compellingly demonstrates, Derrida's tightly focused analysis of soliloquy still "imprisons [voice] in the very metaphysical box that it was meant to disturb" (2005, 215). Even Derridean absence, after all, does not quite offer relationality.

THE POLITICS OF VOCAL IRRELATIONALITY

For ethnographers of voice, the resounding import of *Voice and Phenomenon* lies not so much in its successful indictment of phenomenology or of voice studies, but in its caution against a commonsense metaphysics that figures The Voice as solitary, immediate, and utterly free from relations. Such a "voice" is a ghostly caricature, not an ethnographic account of singing, arguing, or greeting. Indeed, it is inadequate even for the silent soliloquy of inner speech; it assumes that each subject has a single, eternally present, inner self who speaks and listens with absolute certainty. But numerous accounts of inner voice attest to polyvocality—plural inner voices that seem to interact, that take various stances, and that are often at odds with each other (Alderson-Day and Fernyhough 2015; Bakhtin 1981; Vygotsky [1934] 1987). One of the most striking empirical confirmations of polyvocality is found in Tanya Luhrmann's ethnographic work with evangelical Christians who train themselves to discern the voice of God from the voices of other various inner speaking selves (Luhrmann 2012). Luhrmann's work not only affirms the fact of polyvocal inner worlds but also emphasizes the need for *training* to discern a single voice among them. Husserlian soliloquy thus serves as a theoretical limit case, like a perfect vacuum or a tree falling alone in the forest. It forces us to confront the eeriness of a voice stripped of all forms of relation: solitary, purely expressive, atemporal—in other words, irrelational. As Cavarero points out, commitment to such a figuration comes at a very high ethical and political price: "the elimination of the other [and] of others" (2005, 46).

This ghostly, irrelational picture of voice still haunts us. It can be found, for example, in figurations in which "voice" is understood to be the direct expression of a sovereign subjectivity. The unambiguous ascription of voices to individual subjects dovetails conveniently with a liberal ethics in which it is morally incumbent upon each individual to find and express their unique voice. Indeed, as James Faubion has pointed out, this is one of the grand themitical demands of our age (2011, 258).

This solipsistic ethics of voice is far more serious, however, in the service of collectivist nationalisms, where the putative sovereignty of individual expression is projected onto large, notionally homogeneous groups of people, claiming a single voice for a sovereign nation-state, culture, or society. This "groupism" (Brubaker 2002) has been strangely persistent in ethnomusicology. It is common to encounter majoritarian nationalist ascriptions of voices to putatively homogenous nations, as with Umm Kulthum in Egypt or Lata Mangeshkar in India (Danielson 1998; Srivastava 2004; Lomax 2003, 267). Even more common are claims about the "voice of the people." Like invocations of putative "national conversations," these claims point vaguely toward thousands or millions of people. But a "voice of the people" does not have conversations. It may *refer* to an alien group, but it does not ordinarily *address* them, listen, or respond. In such an expressivist frame, any actual social relations that might obtain *between* voices is blotted out by a prior, encompassing, irrelational oneness. When a voicing group is construed as a single unanimous totality, it serves, social-theoretically, as a sovereign, self-identical individual in its own right, with perfect unmediated access to its own inner workings, and a single expressive voice. The result is structurally identical to Husserlian soliloquy: the self expresses the self to the self out of time, out of history, untouched by alterity, with no peer or interlocutor with which it can be in ensemble. At the turn of the twenty-first century, such vocal nationalisms might have seemed quaint, but the worldwide resurgence of ethnic nationalisms has lately infused them with new blood.

To construe the voice as immediately expressive of a nation-state, then, is to naturalize a collectivity that is, itself, peculiarly irrelational and devoid of sociality. "The voice of the people" isn't always congruent with the voice of the state; it has, at times, served to assert a contingent, tactical popular solidarity against oppression, domination, and colonial occupation. But this collectivist-expressivist vocal figuration is the quintessential "master's tool" (Lorde 2020, 102). In its increasingly common majoritarian statist figurations, insisting on timeless self-identity and the direct expressiveness of a collective voice is to deny the very possibility of dissent or diversity.

VOCAL RELATIONALITY

As ethnomusicologists, for better or for worse, we mostly work among chaotic reverberations, amid mediated feedback, and in dynamic relationship with other people: in town squares, in living rooms, at political demonstrations, in nightclubs. And these forms of sociality, as the essays in this volume attest again and again, are enriched, rather than undermined, by the situated practice of ethnographically oriented phenomenology, attuned to social relations rather than to soliloquy. This performed sociality is a rather different matter than the common casual recourse to "social" collectivities (discussed earlier in relation to national "voices"), which begin by assuming an a prior, univocal, fixed society,[12] one that often, suspiciously enough, turns out to be congruent with a nation-state. As a mediating force, "the social" tends to act as a fixed unity, like a lens; as a vocal force, as we've seen, it can do little more than to voice a putatively unanimous collectivity.

This is part of the reason so many ethnomusicologists have tended to prefer to approach voice as relational, even explicitly laying claim to what is sometimes called *relational ontology*. In brief, these approaches prioritize relations rather than sovereign entities or substances (Benjamin 2015). Anglophone and Francophone theorists of relationality tend to draw inspiration from Bakhtin (1981), Levinas ([1961] 1979), and Barad (2007); the tension between relational and substantialist ontologies also has a long tradition in Sanskritic metaphysics, often articulated as a tension between self-dependent being (*svabhāva*) and interdependent co-arising (*pratītyasamutpāda*; Dattreya [10th c.] 2018, 16; Nāgārjuna [3rd c.] 1987, 81).

Under the umbrella of "relationality" live a wide range of radically distinct analytic orientations. Some figurations, for example, stress the liminality of voice, which is seen to occur at the "boundaries" of discursive formations (Feldman 2015, 658). Others foreground vocal ensemble, demonstrating that certain kinds of vocality emerge only from joined voices (never from an individual voice), as, for example, in hocketing, counterpoint, or Kofi Agawu's general account of "an irreducible togetherness" in Ewe song (Agawu 1995, 32; 2016, 121). Historical and ethnographic accounts of voice cultivation often emphasize the inherent cultivatedness of voice, trained to be what it is by caretakers, teachers, and exemplars, so that it is "paramparic" rather than self-produced (Herbst 1997; Rahaim 2012). Approaches that emphasize communication figure voicing as inherently directed toward a listener, or even as intermaterial vibration between a vocalizer and a listener (Kreiman and Sidtis 2011, 7; Eidsheim 2015, 3). Analyses of vocal interaction emphasize the improvised temporal *attunement* among interlocutors (Schutz [1932] 1967; Stone 1981). A more ontologically explicit approach, which we will explore later, focuses on the situated disclosure of voices, by which voices are constituted by disciplined listeners (Rahaim 2019). Each of these approaches to "relationality" is distinct. For example, Agawu is able to claim without contradiction that the irreducibly communal ethos of African vocal ensemble practices also implies a diminished attunement to listeners (Agawu 2016, 120). Likewise, the sense in which a voice signifies a social totality or is found at discursive boundaries (as in Martha Feldman's figuration) begins from a sense of a voice with an inherent positionality, already stably located somewhere on a grid of signification, rather than unfolding in time or disclosed by situated practices of attunement.

Here, we will focus on just two of these (vocal interplay and the situated disclosure of voices), to return to our earlier theme of presence and temporality from another perspective.

THE TEMPORALITY OF VOCAL INTERPLAY

In Derrida's figuration of Husserlian voice, colloquy taints pure simultaneous self-presence with the inevitable, split-second absences of indication, retention, and interpretation. But in practice, colloquy relies far more richly on temporal play than just interpretive cognition. Vocal relations depend on rhythmic interaction on the scale of seconds. When I improvise a harmony over my friend's melody, I am anticipating where her voice is going based on what she has just sung; we are both mutually adapting (always imperfectly) to each other's rhythmic pulse, adjusting our volumes, finding our way into mutual tune, melding our vowels.

Though Derrida claims that Husserl's early account of vocal immediacy amounts to the "path down which . . . all of phenomenology has been pushed" (Derrida [1967] 2011, 3), this is certainly not obvious from the phenomenological literature. Most subsequent works in the tradition (e.g., Stein [1917] 1989; Schutz [1932] 1967; Merleau-Ponty [1945] 2012; de Beauvoir [1947] 1962; Levinas [1961] 1979) grapple with sociality, rapport, and contingent historical formations, rather than the absolute self-presence of a solitary, transcendental ego. Husserl himself seems to have intuited that an account of intersubjectivity was necessary to a well-rounded phenomenology ([1931] 1960, 89). The ambiguities that Derrida highlights may well be a result of the fact that Husserl's key work on temporality was gathered and edited from a series of orally delivered lectures in which he was working through problems that he never fully resolved. Husserl's reliance on a punctual melodic paradigm for his account of temporality may well have been a consequence of his rather tightly circumscribed musical education, which seems to have left him with a vision of music founded on finished, organically whole works, embodied in scores, rather than in performances (Ferrara and Behnke 1996, 468). Indeed, for an ethnomusicologist attuned to sociality, the most striking thing about the "music" of Husserl's temporality is that it is utterly asocial. It seems to simply *exist*, without any musicians, without purposive breath or gesture, without the disciplined practices of listening that disclose noemata in the first place, and without any sort of relationality. Jitendra Nath Mohanty, perhaps Husserl's foremost interpreter, considers this emphasis on soliloquy to be an incidental misstep on Husserl's part, pointing out

that phenomenology could not possibly proceed by reducing speech to private soliloquy; "on the contrary," he writes, "it would seem to need 'sharability' and 'communicability'" (Mohanty 1974, 243), as would, no less, an ethnomusicological phenomenology
that foregrounds relationality.

The classic phenomenological analysis of relational temporality was offered by Alfred
Schutz ([1932] 1967), whose account has been foundational for many ethnographers of
performance (e.g., Geertz 1973; Stone 1981; Berger 2010; Friedson 1996; Feld 1988).[13] In
Schutz's sociology, relationality is never simply a given fact like mass or electrical charge;
it is accomplished in time. I may well share citizenship or convictions with millions of
contemporaries that I've never met, but social intercourse with the *consociates* that I
meet face to face requires something decidedly more musical (Schutz [1932] 1967, 8).
Having a conversation, building a groove, taking a solo, singing in harmony, uttering
affirmative *uh huh*s and *yeah*s and *mmm*s, and the elaborate improvised choreography
of conversational turn-taking—all of these are acts that require the ongoing, virtuosic
negotiation of temporality with others: "mutual tuning-in" (Schutz 1976, 161). On this
basis, Schutz posits a sociological distinction between the causal linkage of mutually
anonymous contemporaries in a social system and the "mutually *interlocked*" actions
that intersubjectively link consociates in a "community of time." Schutz's term for the
latter (*aufeinander eingestellt*, "mutually adjusted" or "mutually attuned") emphasizes
the temporal dynamism of this kind of relationality (Schutz [1932] 1967, 180). For this
constantly shifting attunement, mere coexistence is not enough; nor is semiotic expression or indication. Instead, interlocutors "follow [each] others' action in its ongoing flux
as it unrolls phase by phase." Schutz specifies:

> When I look at my consociate's ongoing action, by protentions and anticipations I
> may expect its outcome even if I do not know his underlying project. . . . I partici-
> pate in the ongoing flux of his action as directed toward its terminus, the goal to be
> attained, the act to be accomplished, the problem to be solved, the state of affairs to
> be brought about. (1996, 63)

This distinction between those with whom we interact and those absent multitudes with
whom we merely coexist may seem to land us back in a Derridean metaphysics of presence. But the temporality that Schutz identifies in consocial interaction is radically different from the instantaneous self-presence of Husserlian-Derridean soliloquy. Social
relations, unlike the Derridean cartoon of "presence," could never happen in the one-
ness of solitude or the atemporal now-point marked by "the glance of an eye." Doubly to
the contrary, they unfold in a community of time. In such a community, retention and
protention, rather than heralding absence, are precisely what make face-to-face sociality
possible. Thus, attending to the temporality of voice is not an *alternative* to social analysis; temporality is a crucial *condition* of social relation.

Numerous ethnographic studies foreground the formation of contingent communities
of time in mutually tuned-in vocal interaction. Kpelle group song, which features extensive hocketing and interlocked ostinato, yields a distinctive "inside" and "outside"

of a performance, and a sense of "going down the same road" when everything fits to-gether properly (Stone 1981, 199–200). The interaction of Hindustani vocalists with their accompanists requires split-second reactions and fine mutual adjustment (Clayton 2007). The Kaluli practice of *dulugu ganalan*, in which voices overlap in exquisite cascades, brings singers into "non-hierarchical yet synchronous, layered, fluid group action" (Feld 1988, 83). Conversational interaction too relies on often-unconscious processes of rhythmic isochrony, whereby an elocutionary groove is reinforced by rhythmic interjections and turn-taking (Auer et al. 1999, 58–59). Each of these requires a finely disciplined temporal sense tuned for one particular form of ensemble.

Equally important are moments when ensembles break down, when voicely social actors "go down different roads" (Stone 1981, 200) or deliberately thwart established grooves. Kisliuk describes a particularly rich session of BaAka Pygmy song and dance performance where a separate men's group and women's group (each of which has members tuned in to each other but which, at the level of the two groups, are not coor-dinated) vie for control of which groove will come next (Kisliuk 2000, 30–37). In con-versation, an interlocutor may deliberately break from a pulse, placing a stressed syllable slightly earlier or later than expected, in order to assert a contrary position (Auer et al. 1999, 80). As Emmanuel Levinas reminds us, rupture in conversation is at least as ethi-cally productive as the "charm of rhythm" that pulls interlocutors toward participatory oneness ([1961] 1979, 203). These strategic temporal ruptures remind us that unity is just one part of social relations; alterity too is relational. But in all cases—in the cultivation of a participatory whole or in its contestation, in the formation of a temporal "bubble" or in its rupture—relationality depends on disciplines of retention and protention, rather than an instantaneous solipsistic immediacy.

VOCAL MULTIPLICITY

We have seen that attending to the temporality of vocal interaction may allow us to lib-erate the voice from the Husserlian-Derridean "metaphysical box." If this box seemed convincing in the first place—if Derrida's analysis of Husserlian soliloquy has seemed for the last fifty years to apply seamlessly to colloquy, song, political will, and public pronouncement—it surely is because "voice" is so often taken to be a coherent meta-physical category in the first place. The Voice (if there were such a universal, singular, transcendental entity) might appear to be paradoxical, everything and nothing at once: viscerally, materially *there*, yet invisible and intangible; at times distinctively individual ("she has finally found her voice") and at others inescapably collective ("the people have spoken"); at times an outward expression of an active subjectivity resisting oppression ("speak truth to power!"), at others the mark of a passive, malleable subject disciplined by forces beyond its control ("learn to speak properly!"). This wild multiplicity is some-times tamed under the sign of a single chimerical entity (The Voice) meant, in principle, to be all these things at once.

But the diverse entities that are placed under this category are as ontologically distinct as a handshake and a milkshake, despite the umbrella term "voice." The "voice" of a baby crying, the "voice" of reason, the "voice" of a televangelist, the "voice" of the French people—these are not just acoustically different, but ontologically distinct, which is to say that they *are* differently. These are not merely different perspectives on a single, prior vocal reality but tokens of various kinds of realness. They have no common ground of being: not acoustics, not physiology, not lexical meaning. The phenomenological task— using a method I have elsewhere called *practical ontologies of voice*[14]—is to reflect on the situated processes by which voices show up in the first place. The result is not a unitary theory of The Voice but something like what, following Annemarie Mol's brilliantly trod path (2002), we might call "The Voice Multiple." We begin not from the abstract category of "The Voice" or from a putative lowest common denominator (like soliloquy, vibrations, or personhood) but from the concrete, practical, situated actions by which voices become so palpably real in the first place. This is the task of vocal ethnographies and vocal histories, like the one I am about to hazard now.

We begin in a voice clinic in Bombay—the clinic of Dr. Sadhana Nayak, a well-known voice therapist. I'm sitting with one of her patients, Apoorva.[15] Apoorva is a versatile young singer of what in India is often called "light" music: romantic film songs, devotional bhajans, and the elaborate traditions of art song known as *ghazal* and *thumri*.[16] Her singing voice is bright and strong, every tone encased in a delicate, numinous nasal resonance.

I sought out Apoorva not only for her evident skill in singing but also to hear her story—a story about losing and regaining her voice. She's a compelling storyteller. Apoorva speaks in an even cadence; even when switching between Hindi and English midsentence, her syllables amble on without breaking stride. Once she gets into a groove, each sentence arcs downward in an attitude of a gentle resignation, without hedging, making its way to an inevitable tonic conclusion rather than soliciting approval or assent. Though she is speaking *to me*, answering my questions, there is no evident sense of feigning or fronting, of speaking for the sake of giving a certain impression. Following her from one point to another in her "talerealm" (Young 1987), I seem to simply hear *Apoorva* speaking, not *Apoorva's voice* as a discrete third entity between us. Her story has its own flow, and I get into it.

So here's her story. Four years previously, just as she had begun performing publicly, Apoorva was in a car accident that knocked her unconscious for a month and a half. When she woke up in the hospital, she had trouble coordinating the sides of her body; her right arm and leg in particular were sluggish and unresponsive. Walking, she said, became "harder than ballet." Her speaking voice sounded alien: low and hoarse and breathy. Worse, when she tried to sing, there was, as she put it, "no voice" at all—only a whisper.

That's when she went to see Dr. Nayak. Dr. Nayak numbed Apoorva's throat and inserted a tiny camera and strobe light to render visible the motion of her vocal folds. She soon saw the malfunction she was looking for. Apoorva's right vocal fold was hardly moving at all, apparently paralyzed from the neurological trauma. She turned off her instruments, sat Apoorva down, and gave her exercises to do, as a physical therapist might: repetitive, daily vocal exercises far removed from the luminous tone and subtle poetics of Apoorva's usual vocal life.

The drudgery paid off. After only a week of daily practice, Apoorva found some improvement. She said that she could hold a tone—for just a moment, less than a second. But it was only after several more weeks of practice that "the voice started coming out." Over the next few months, Apoorva's voice fully returned. It is now stronger than ever, and she's gone back to a successful career singing.

We now turn to reflection on the very different sorts of "voice" that we just encountered. First, consider the vocal capacity that Apoorva lost when she could speak but not sing. Here, the "voice" that is lost and later regained is not mere sound, nor mere vibrations. The whispery sound, though certainly vibratory and audible, is not it. Neither are the brief, tentative tones she made after a week (despite the fact that phonologists would call these utterances "voiced"). It is only the sustained, steady sound that came out after several weeks of practice that qualify as "*the voice coming out*."

The "voice" here, lost for a time and later recovered through practice, is not mere sound, nor mere vibrations, nor even the use of the vocal cords. It is the capacity for a clear, stable, tuneful tone, or what is often called *sur*. This tone, like all vocal utterances, is not characterized by an atemporal, perfectly unchanging frequency. It is not simply given in the acoustical signal (in which there is always a measurable fluctuation of several hertz) but discerned by a listener with a trained ear who recognizes sur when they hear it. This requires an attunement to steady, sustained notes: we don't sit there counting oscillations (nor could we, without the technological prosthesis to disclose the waveform visually). A spoken sentence does not ordinarily show up as in tune or out of tune; attunement to singing is co-constitutive with a *singing* voice. Further, recall that when Apoorva woke up from her coma, she could speak but not sing. This is a problem reported by other traumatized singers; speaking poses no problem, and yet sur will not come. This is, I think, a suggestion of just how radically different sur is from mere speaking, akin to the difference between grasping and pointing described by Merleau-Ponty ([1945] 2012, 106).

A rather different "voice" is the vocal mechanism that was damaged in the crash. Dr. Nayak's office maps out this mechanism in boldly drawn anatomical diagrams of the lungs, tongue, and larynx, a dizzying labyrinth of tissues depicted in black and white, red and blue. A computer screen offers close-up footage of a particular pair of vocal folds, glistening with mucus. The laryngoscope, the strobe light, the anatomical illustrations hanging on her wall—these all disclose a world of interwoven muscle, cartilage, fluid, and bone that otherwise would be hidden away behind the skin of the throat. When Dr. Nayak works with a client to fix damage done to their "voice," she is not referring to sur, or to a particular form of personhood, or to the voice that *is*, in some sense, Apoorva's story. The voice disclosed in the clinic is not sincere or insincere, true or false, in tune or out of tune. It is a complex organic mechanism made of flesh, which sustains damage, wears down, recovers, and—in this case, we hope—can be repaired.

Here, the guiding image of the laryngeal mechanism is the vivid, complex squirming of the living vocal folds. Seeing this is a rather different matter, practically, than counting the number of teeth in a patient's mouth. It's hard enough to see down there. But the squirming itself, unlike the teeth or tonsils, is not given to our senses at all. The slowest vocal vibrations—at dozens of cycles per second—are far too fast for the naked eye to resolve. Laryngeal stroboscopy uses a strobe light, in much the same way as a strobe-tuned phonograph reveals deviations from 33 1/3 RPM. A strobe light is tuned close to, but not precisely at, the frequency of the vibrations of the fold, offering a video image of the folds undulating like a stingray. The laryngoscope, the strobe light, the live feed on our computer screen, the careful tuning and focusing of each instrument until it looks the way we want it to—only with all of this in place is the living, moving mechanism of the voice disclosed visibly. (Still more sophisticated are the diagnostic techniques of laryngological seeing that disclose this squirming as symptomatic of health or disease.)

The third "voice" we encountered is that of Apoorva's story. Once we are with her in the flow of events, we are not faced with a sequence of words, nor a sequence of pitches. Indeed, as anyone who has transcribed an interview can attest, accessing these features after the fact requires real perceptual work. Nor even does her utterance show up as a set of historical *claims* to be challenged. Later, in reviewing the recording, I did indeed have to painstakingly reconstitute her utterances as a text, rewinding, slowing down parts where an individual word was lost, interpreting and transcribing pauses and inflections. I likewise constructed a timeline that I aligned with her doctor's account of the treatment. But in the moment of telling, the narrative texture of the talerealm is not marked for me as logically true as opposed to false. Nor is her sincerity a conclusion that I arrive at deductively from the words she says. Her story, her stance, and her person are bundled together in each utterance. I trustingly tune in. Don Ihde puts this beautifully:

> When I listen to an other I hear him speaking. It is not a series of phonemes or morphemes which I hear, because to "hear" these I must break up his speech, I must listen "away" from what he is saying. My experiential listening stands in the near distance of language that is at one and the same time *the other speaking* in his voice. *I hear what he is saying.* ([1976] 2007, 151)

Apoorva's sincerity, in other words, is relational, unfolding in the temporality of our interaction. It has been constituted in part by my own practices of listening: trusting, attentive, patiently following the arc of her story on the scale of minutes, tuned into the temporality of her phrases on the scale of seconds. Nor is this a silent perceptual matter. From the moment we are introduced, I find myself encouraging her telling with my own *mhm*s and *acchā*s,[17] offering not so much *logical* but *rhythmic* affirmation: mutual tuning in (see Figure 13.4).

By tuning in, by encouraging and affirming her telling, I become a participant in the story. While mutually engaged, it shows up to me as a more or less transparent report of what happened, not as a shrewd elicitation of sympathy or a set of claims to be challenged. The reliability of her sounding voice is not marked for me as logically true as

APOORVA: I learned it   for a-bout six months   but then my dad   got trans-fered from Hy-d'ra- bad   so...   I   had to   switch to Hin-du-stā-nī

MATT: hmmm   ac-chā   o-kay

FIGURE 13.4: Mutual tuning in.

opposed to false; nor is it a conclusion that I arrive at step by step, through deliberative reason. Such an appearance of sincerity may seem, in contrast to the suspiciously artificial persona of a poseur or a salesman, to be "im-mediate," that is, not mediated by an ulterior front between her and me. And yet sincerity itself is not an inherent feature of her voice to which I have gained direct access. Nor, even, is its status as a "voice" given in the acoustical signal. It is achieved in our mutual vocal performance. This improvised, provisional, unfinished intersubjective present that we share is by no means an unmediated metaphysical presence. We are mutually tuned in to the arc of each other's sentences, retaining what came before, protending their conclusions, timing our turn-taking in accordance with this empathy.

Each of these three "voices"—sur, mechanism, story—is disclosed through a particular stance, through a particular technique of listening, through a particular infrastructure. Tuning into sur, physiology fades into the background; getting into the flow of a story, sur fades into the background; attending to the details of physiology, narrative fades into the background. The referential span of these *voice*-s may well be a source of wonder, of curiosity, of humility. But The Voice as an abstract theoretical category has no *svabhāva*, no self-dependent being. Any of these phenomena called voice emerge only in *pratītyasamutpāda*: in a web of ongoing, interdependent interbeing.

VOCAL INTIMACIES AND IMMEDIA

All of this is not to say that laryngeal function, or in-tuneness, or sincerity, or any other vocal feature is not *real*. On the contrary, it is to affirm multiple (if not necessarily infinite) vocal realnesses. These are not mere personal subjective flights of fancy, whereby one hallucinates voices at will. That they are not arbitrary is evidenced by the very fact that each of these ontological formations affords surprise and rewards close investigation with more detail. (Indeed, even auditory vocal hallucinations, which are often dismissed as "all in the head," typically show up as being out there in the world.)[18] This is why it is possible for a group of properly enculturated and attuned vocalists to discern and correct an out-of-tune voice in a harmonic texture without any arithmetical calculations, for two laryngologists to collaboratively diagnose a vocal malfunction, or for a panel of judges to agree on which recitation of a sura from the Qur'an is the best. Even vocal impersonators succeed or fail on the evidence of how *real* their vocal "falsehood" is. Each of these ontological formations of voice has its own durable reality, internally consistent, even if mutually incommensurable with the others. Practical ontology foregrounds the skillful techniques that disclose each durable realness in its turn—or, at times, indeterminately, as two or more at once (Rahaim 2019, 30–31).

Various vocal immediacies are implied by these realnesses. For example, a live radio broadcast is (in a limited sense) "immediate" in comparison to one that is prerecorded; speech in person is "immediate" in comparison to a live radio broadcast; a spontaneous utterance is "immediate" in comparison to a memorized one; a song in its original language is "immediate" in comparison to a translation. None of these immedia, however, imply the immaculate metaphysical self-presence that Derrida diagnoses in Husserlian soliloquy. The inevitable "mediations" and "absences" of these contingent immedia—anonymity, temporal delays, durable habits, great distances—do not amount to a single metaphysical substance. Indeed, phenomenological reflection reveals that the "mediation" of, say, phonetic distinction has nothing essentially in common with the "mediation" of linguistic translation or the "mediation" of electronic transduction. Nor, indeed, does "immediacy" imply a lack of media (Kim 2016, 10). The palpable intimacy of Kishore Kumar's close-miked crooning, of Björk's audible intake of breath between phrases, of Zeki Müren's velvety tone, which reaches out to listeners in the privacy of a living room or a car, or even the "privatized auditory bubble" of headphones—all of these are made possible through sophisticated techniques of microphonic transduction, amplification, and reproduction (Stokes 2010, 61; Bull 2005, 344). Likewise, the palpable "immediacy" of face-to-face conversation or improvised polyphony could never happen *immediately*. Even the most intimate vocal presence unfolds in time, is disclosed through disciplined practices of listening and voicing, depends on spaces and infrastructures and technologies—and even what we conventionally call "media." Thus, simply invoking absence is not enough. The key phenomenological task for ethnographers is to account for the situated and widely varied conditions and practices that disclose a voice in the first place. This task is especially urgent when a voice seems to simply be there, self-sufficient, self-identical, self-expressive, in the blink of an eye.

Notes

1. The book's original title is *La voix et le phénomène*. The previous translation of the title as *Speech and Phenomenon* likely was to clarify the rather limited scope of "voice" at issue in the book; yet Derrida's extended critique of logocentrism nonetheless continued to thematize voice as such, as, for example, in his treatment of the neume in *Of Grammatology* ([1967] 1997, 249).
2. See, for example, Charles Taylor (1989, 362) and Mladen Dolar (2006, 87) on "inner voice" as a voice of truth, in contrast to the compromises and falsehoods of public voices.
3. In Hume's case ([1738] 1960, 36), the notes are tooted out on a flute.
4. An actual pianist playing a piano, of course, also is involved in gestural melody; their hands are always in motion, tracing arcs in space.

5. Hindustani vocalists refer to scale degrees in *sargam* syllables, akin to movable do solfege—*sā re ga ma pa dha ni*. In curly brackets, I have translated *sargam* into scale-degree numbers.

6. Most singers of raga music have a mastery of *svar-jnān* (the capacity to discern note names by ear), to be sure, but not all singers of kirtan, qawwali, film music, or pop music do. See Neuman (2004) and Rahaim (2012) for an account of raga singers who can sing fluidly without notation.

7. Elsewhere, in a discussion of the intuition of "incomplete" melodies, Husserl does seem to invite a conception of melody as motion ([1928] 1991, 141–155).

8. Sakhawat Hussain Khan's original Hindi phrase is *gāyan kaimara* ([1952] 1976). Max Katz's sensitive translation of this phrase (2012) correctly renders it as "singing camera," which for our present, nitpicking philosophical purposes may read ambiguously. To be precise, *gāyan* operates here as an adjectival noun, as in *gāyan samāj* (a connoisseur's society to support the art of singing, not a society that sings); notation is thus construed as a *camera for singing* (fixing song into punctual, frozen moments), not a *camera that sings*.

9. Zahavi explicitly points out that the primal impression is "Husserl's name for the consciousness of the now-phase of the [temporal] object, and not the name for this now-phase itself" (1999, 65).

10. Hubert Dreyfus (1995, x) points out that the term *Augenblick* has a specifically Lutheran heritage, translating the biblical "twinkling of an eye" in which "we shall be changed" (1 Corinthians 15:52).

11. To be precise, Derrida translates *Augenblick* as *clin d'oeil*, which ambiguously indicates both blinking and twinkling. He then exploits the pun by explicitly thematizing the closed eyelid of blinking, which is not implied by Husserl's original *Augenblick*.

12. See Latour (2005, 8–14) for a discussion of this distinction in sociology. There, he calls the collectivist approach the "sociology of the social" and the relational approach the "sociology of associations."

13. It's worth noting that in his application of Schutz's ideas, Clifford Geertz misreads the notion of a "community of time" to mean merely contemporaries on the scale of months or years and thus misses the rhythmic specificity of consocial interplay (1973, 364–365).

14. This term was coined by Gad et al. (2015; see also Rahaim 2019). Another common use of the term "ontology" simply refers to claims about what *is*. For example, we might say that a "materialist ontology" posits benches and bricks, but not fairies; we might say that a "relational ontology" sees a world in which relations are prior to discrete entities. I distinguish between these attempts to enumerate what exists from a *practical ontological* account, which reflects on the being of these entities, and *how* these worlds of entities are disclosed.

15. In this chapter, I have left out her last name to maintain her anonymity.

16. Though these genres are often characterized in the Hindustani tradition as types of "semi-classical" music (as compared with supposedly "classical" raga music forms such as *khyal* and *dhrupad*), ghazal and thumri are classical vocal forms in all of the usual senses of that term. Both ghazal and thumri draw on vast poetic, modal, and melodic canons; both have centuries of literate as well as oral tradition; and both are rooted in courtly milieu, aristocratic patronage, and aesthetic criticism.

17. *Acchā* is a Hindi expression meaning "good" or "I get it."

18. Describing the experiences of a patient with auditory hallucinations, psychologist Eugène Minkowski observed, "In the street, it is like a whispering that *envelops him entirely*; in the same way he feels deprived of his freedom as if *around him* people were always present; at the café, it is as if there is something nebulous *around him* and he senses a trembling; and

when the voices are particularly frequent and numerous, the atmosphere *around him* is saturated as if by fire" (Minkowski [1932] quoted in Merleau-Ponty [{1945} 2012, 545n77]; italics reproduced from Merleau-Ponty).

WORKS CITED

Agawu, Kofi. 1995. *African Rhythm: A Northern Ewe Perspective*. Cambridge: Cambridge University Press.

Agawu, Kofi. 2016. *The African Imagination in Music*. New York: Oxford University Press.

Alderson-Day, Ben, and Charles Fernyhough. 2015. "Inner Speech: Development, Cognitive Functions, Phenomenology, and Neurobiology." *Psychological Bulletin* 141 (5): 931–965.

Auer, Peter, Elizabeth Couper-Kuhlen, and Frank Muller. 1999. *Language in Time: The Rhythm and Tempo of Spoken Interaction*. New York: Oxford University Press.

Bakhtin, M. M. 1981. *The Dialogic Imagination: Four Essays*. Edited by Michael Holquist. Translated by Caryl Emerson and Michael Holquist. Austin: University of Texas Press.

Barad, Karen. 2007. *Meeting the Universe Halfway: Quantum Physics and the Entanglement of Matter and Meaning*. Durham, NC: Duke University Press.

Beauvoir, Simone de. (1947) 1962. *The Ethics of Ambiguity*. Translated by Bernard Frechtman. Secaucus, NJ: Citadel Press.

Benjamin, Andrew. 2015. *Towards a Relational Ontology: Philosophy's Other Possibility*. Albany: State University of New York Press.

Berger, Harris. 2010. *Stance: Ideas about Emotion, Style, and Meaning for the Study of Expressive Culture*. Middletown, CT: Wesleyan University Press.

Bergson, Henri. [1889] 2001. *Time and Free Will: An Essay on the Immediate Data of Consciousness*. London: Sonnenschein.

Brentano, Franz. [1874] 1995. *Psychology from an Empirical Standpoint*. London: Routledge.

Brubaker, Rogers. 2002. "Ethnicity without Groups." *European Journal of Sociology* 43 (2): 163–189.

Bull, Michael. 2005. "No Dead Air! The iPod and the Culture of Mobile Listening." *Leisure Studies* 24 (4): 343–355.

Cavarero, Adriana. 2005. *For More than One Voice: Toward a Philosophy of Vocal Expression*. Stanford, CA: Stanford University Press.

Clayton, Martin. 2007. "Time, Gesture and Attention in a 'Khyāl' Performance." *Asian Music* 38 (2): 71–96.

Danielson, Virginia. 1998. *"The Voice of Egypt": Umm Kulthūm, Arabic Song, and Egyptian Society in the Twentieth Century*. Chicago: University of Chicago Press.

Dattreya. (10th c.) 2018. *Avadhuta Gita: The Song of the Avadhuta*. Translated by Janki Parikh. Self-published. http://www.jankiparikh.com/.

Derrida, Jacques. (1967) 1997. *Of Grammatology*. Translated by Gayatri C. Spivak. Baltimore, MD: Johns Hopkins University Press.

Derrida, Jacques. (1967) 2011. *Voice and Phenomenon: Introduction to the Problem of the Sign in Husserl's Phenomenology*. Translated by Leonard Lawler. Evanston, IL: Northwestern University Press.

Desai-Stevens, Anaar. 2017. "Singing through the Screen: Indian Idol and the Cultural Politics of Aspiration in Post-liberalization India." PhD diss., Cornell University.

Deva, B. C. 1959. "The Vibrato in Indian Music: Studies in Indian Musical Scales II; Gamakas." *Acustica* 9: 175–180.

Dolar, Mladen. 2006. *A Voice and Nothing More*. Cambridge, MA: MIT Press.

Dreyfus, Hubert. 1995. *Being-in-the-World: A Commentary on Heidegger's "Being and Time, Division I."* Cambridge, MA: MIT Press.

Eidsheim, Nina. 2015. *Sensing Sound: Singing and Listening as Vibrational Practice*. Durham, NC: Duke University Press.

Faubion, James. 2011. *An Anthropology of Ethics*. Cambridge: Cambridge University Press.

Feld, Steven. 1984. "Sound Structure as Social Structure." *Ethnomusicology* 28 (3): 383–409.

Feld, Steven. 1988. "Aesthetics as Iconicity of Style or 'Lift-up-over Sounding': Getting into the Kaluli Groove." *Yearbook for Traditional Music* 20: 74–113.

Feldman, Martha. 2015. "Why Voice Now?" *Journal of the American Musicological Society* 68 (3): 653–685.

Ferrara, Lawrence, and Elizabeth Behnke. 1996. "Music." In *Encyclopedia of Phenomenology*, edited by Lester Embree et al., 467–473. Boston: Springer.

Friedson, Steven M. 1996. *Dancing Prophets: Musical Experience in Tumbuka Healing*. Chicago: University of Chicago Press.

Frith, Simon. 1998. *Performing Rites: On the Value of Popular Music*. Cambridge, MA: Harvard University Press.

Gad, Christopher, Casper Bruun Jensen, and Brit Ross Winthereik. 2015. "Practical Ontology: Worlds in STS and Anthropology." *NatureCulture*, no. 3, 67–86. https://www.natcult.net/wp -content/uploads/2018/12/PDF-natureculture-03-04-practical-ontology.pdf.

Geertz, Clifford. 1973. *The Interpretation of Cultures*. New York: Basic Books.

Harkness, Nicholas. 2013. *Songs of Seoul: An Ethnography of Voice and Voicing in Christian South Korea*. Berkeley: University of California Press.

Herbst, Edward. 1997. *Voices in Bali: Energies and Perceptions in Vocal Music and Dance Theater*. Middletown, CT: Wesleyan University Press.

Hume, David. (1738) 1960. *A Treatise of Human Nature*. Oxford: Oxford University Press.

Husserl, Edmund. (1900) 2001. *Logical Investigations*. Vol. 1. London: Routledge.

Husserl, Edmund. (1913) 1982. *Ideas Pertaining to a Pure Phenomenology and to a Phenomenological Philosophy*. Translated by F. Kersten. The Hague: Martinus Nijhoff.

Husserl, Edmund. (1928) 1991. *On the Phenomenology of the Consciousness of Internal Time*. Translated by John Barnett Brough. Dordrecht, Netherlands: Kluwer.

Husserl, Edmund. (1931) 1960. *Cartesian Meditations: An Introduction to Phenomenology*. Translated by Dorion Cairns. The Hague: Martinus Nijhoff.

Ihde, Don. (1976) 2007. *Listening and Voice: Phenomenologies of Sound*. 2nd ed. Albany: State University of New York Press.

Kane, Brian. 2015. "The Model Voice." In "Colloquy: Why Voice Now?" *Journal of the American Musicological Society* 68 (3): 671–676.

Katz, Max. 2012. "Institutional Communalism in North Indian Classical Music." *Ethnomusicology* 56 (2): 279–298.

Kendon, Adam. 2004. *Gesture: Visible Action as Utterance*. Cambridge: Cambridge University Press.

Khan, Sakhawat Hussain. (1952) 1976. "Gayan Camera: Notation." In *Swarna Jayanti Smarika* [Golden jubilee souvenir], edited by Puru Dadheech, 34–35. Lucknow: Bhatkhande Hindustani Sangeet Mahavidyalaya.

Kim, John. 2016. *Rupture of the Virtual*. DigitalCommons@Macalester College. https://digital commons.macalester.edu/books/1/.

Kisliuk, Michelle. 2000. "Performance and Modernity among BaAka Pygmies: A Closer Look at the Mystique of Egalitarian Foragers in the Rain Forest." In *Music and Gender*, edited by Pirkko Moisala and Beverley Diamond, 25–50. Urbana: University of Illinois Press.

Kreiman, Jody, and Diana Sidtis. 2011. *Foundations of Voice Studies: An Interdisciplinary Approach to Voice Production and Perception*. Chichester, UK: Wiley-Blackwell.

Kunreuther, Laura. 2014. *Voicing Subjects: Public Intimacy and Mediation in Kathmandu*. Berkeley: University of California Press.

Latour, Bruno. 2005. *Reassembling the Social: An Introduction to Actor-Network Theory*. New York: Oxford University Press.

Levinas, Emmanuel. (1961) 1979. *Totality and Infinity: An Essay in Exteriority*. Translated by Alfonso Lingis. Pittsburgh, PA: Duquesne University Press.

Lomax, Alan. 2003. *Selected Writings, 1934–1997*. Edited by Ronald D. Cohen. New York: Routledge.

Lorde, Audre. 2020. *Sister Outsider: Essays and Speeches*. New York: Penguin.

Luhrmann, Tanya. 2012. *When God Talks Back: Understanding the American Evangelical Relationship with God*. New York: Alfred A. Knopf.

McNeill, David. 1992. *Hand and Mind: What Gestures Reveal about Thought*. Chicago: University of Chicago Press.

Merleau-Ponty, Maurice. (1945) 2012. *The Phenomenology of Perception*. Translated by Donald A. Landes. New York: Routledge.

Minkowski, Eugène. 1932. "Le problème des hallucinations et le problème de l'espace." *Évolution psychiatrique* 2 (3): 57–76.

Mohanty, Jitendra Nath. 1974. "On Husserl's Theory of Meaning." *Southwestern Journal of Philosophy* 5 (3): 229–244.

Mol, Annemarie. 2002. *The Body Multiple: Ontology in Medical Practice*. Durham, NC: Duke University Press.

Nāgārjuna. (3rd c.) 1987. *Nagarjuna's Seventy Stanzas: A Buddhist Psychology of Emptiness*. Translated by Tenzin Dorjee and David Ross Komito. Ithaca, NY: Snow Lion Publications.

Nancy, Jean-Luc. (2002) 2007. *Listening: A History of Our Ears*. Translated by Charlotte Mandell. New York: Fordham University Press.

Neuman, Dard. 2004. "A House of Music: The Hindustani Musician and the Crafting of Traditions." PhD thesis, Columbia University.

Rahaim, Matthew. 2012. *Musicking Bodies: Gesture and Voice in Hindustani Music*. Middletown, CT: Wesleyan University Press.

Rahaim, Matthew. 2019. "Object, Person, Machine, or What: Practical Ontologies of Voice." In *The Oxford Handbook of Voice Studies*, edited by Nina Eidsheim and Katherine Meizel, 19–34. New York: Oxford University Press.

Schultz, Anna. 2012. *Singing a Hindu Nation: Marathi Devotional Performance and Nationalism*. Chicago: University of Chicago Press.

Schutz, Alfred. (1932) 1967. *The Phenomenology of the Social World*. Translated by George Walsh and Frederick Lehnert. Evanston, IL: Northwestern University Press.

Schutz, Alfred. 1976. *Collected Papers*. Vol. 2. The Hague: Martinus Nijhoff.

Schutz, Alfred. 1996. *Alfred Schutz: Collected Papers*. Vol. 4. Dordrecht, Netherlands: Springer Science & Business Media.

Srivastava, Sanjay. 2004. "Voice, Gender, and Space in the Time of Five-Year Plans: The Idea of Lata Mangeshkar." *Economic and Political Weekly* 39 (20): 2019–2028.

Stein, Edith. (1917) 1989. *On the Problem of Empathy*. 3rd rev. ed. Vol. 3 of *Collected Works of Edith Stein*. Washington, DC: ICS Publications.

Stokes, Martin. 2010. *The Republic of Love: Cultural Intimacy in Turkish Popular Music*. Chicago: University of Chicago Press.

Stone, Ruth. 1981. "Toward a Kpelle Conceptualization of Music Performance." *Journal of American Folklore* 94 (372): 188–206.

Streeck, Jürgen. 2009. *Gesturecraft: The Manu-facture of Meaning*. Philadelphia, PA: John Benjamins.

Sudnow, David. 1978. *Ways of the Hand*. Cambridge, MA: MIT Press.

Taylor, Charles. 1989. *Sources of the Self: The Making of the Modern Identity*. Cambridge, MA: Harvard University Press.

Vygotsky, L. S. (1934) 1987. *Thinking and Speech: The Collected Works of Lev Vygotsky*. Vol. 1. New York: Plenum Press.

Weidman, Amanda. 2011. "Anthropology and the Voice." *Anthropology News* 52 (1): 13.

Weidman, Amanda. 2012. "The Ethnographer as Apprentice: Embodying Sociomusical Knowledge in South India." *Anthropology and Humanism* 37 (2): 214–235.

Young, Katharine Galloway. 1987. *Taleworlds and Storyrealms*. Dordrecht, Netherlands: Martinus Nijhoff.

Zahavi, Dan. 1999. *Self-Awareness and Alterity: A Phenomenological Investigation*. Evanston, IL: Northwestern University Press.

CHAPTER 14

....

STAGING KARMA

*Cultural Techniques of Transformation in
Burmese Musical Drama*

....

FRIEDLIND RIEDEL

မတီးမမြည်

It does not sound if it's not played.[1]

—Burmese saying

ACCORDING to the Theravada Buddhist doctrine of *samsara*, when a being ceases to exist, another one will step into existence, each being giving rise to another. Death is not the end of life but an existential transformation. Upon death, a human may become an animal, an enlightened being, a kind of deity, or another human—rich or poor, gifted or incapable, depending on the karma acquired in previous existences—only to cease again and to shift into yet another different being. Ultimately, the "true transformation" is to overcome karma, to escape the cycle of living-dying (Abe 1987). Karmic cycles may also sometimes take tragic turns. And these tragic turns are the subject matter of several late nineteenth-century pieces of Burmese musical drama (*pyazat* ပြဇာတ်, literally "displayed-story"), also dubbed *nat hpyit pyazat* (နတ်ဖြစ်ပြဇာတ, "drama about a deity, a *nat*, coming into existence").[2] The plot of these plays—some of which are still performed today—always follows the same formula: as the result of a calamitous course of events, the human protagonist is savagely killed (often by their own family or companions), upon which they become a deity (*nat* နတ် or *deva* ဒေဝ).[3]

Performed on stage, however, these transformations are not mere fictional narratives; they unsettle the very difference between fiction and reality. As can be seen in performances by professional companies who still preserve the stage techniques of the late nineteenth century, the scene of transformation extends beyond the

FIGURE 14.1: Mobile stage set up for a night of performances, Dawei.

(Dramatic company: Thaethesa Zat Thabin တက်သစ်စဗောတ်ဇာတ်သဘင်, 2015)

imaginary world of the stage (Figure 14.1).[4] This can be observed in the well-known musical play about a skilled (human) harpist who foolishly played his harp (*saung gauk* ဇောင်းကောက်) in the wilderness and who fatefully transformed into the deity known by the name U Shin Gyi, a tutelary guardian who is venerated in littoral lands as the Lord of Brackish Waters. When the play reaches the scene of transformation, the performance changes in mode. It no longer simply recounts and represents the uncanny moment of transformation in which the deity came into existence in some mythical past. It repeats it. The transformation presented on stage is not diegetic. It is no longer fictional. Instead, it is the human actor (and not just the character he plays) who is said to become U Shin Gyi.[5] When the curtain rises to reveal the being into which the harpist has transformed, the amplified voice of a narrator reverberates into the dawning day, "ladies and gentlemen, here he comes, U Shin Gyi, Lord of Brackish Waters,"[6] as a mesmerized audience rises to pay obeisance to their guardian and to receive his blessing for another year to come.

This transformation is also enacted outside the dramatic context of the theater stage.[7] In cities and villages of coastal Myanmar where U Shin Gyi is venerated, an annual festival is held in his honor lasting several days and nights. Preceded by Buddhist sermons, the festival opens with an exuberant ritual (*natpwe* နတ်ပွဲ) held in the daytime in front of U Shin Gyi's shrine. Accompanied by professional musicians while also holding a harp himself, a lay person—always a man—will abandon himself and transform into the deity U Shin Gyi (Figure 14.2). This is followed by several nights (from nine in the evening to six in the morning) of *zatpwe*, a variety show on an elaborate makeshift stage which features the pyazat that tells and reenacts the story of the gifted harpist's transformation.[8]

FIGURE 14.2: Nat Pwe in Pandin-In village, Dawei, 2015.

Transformations are a basic axiom of Theravada Buddhist culture and philosophy. Thinkers in the Buddhist tradition hold that transformation is no harmless venture. Where transformation occurs, death seems inevitable. As Japanese philosopher Masao Abe points out, "transformation in Buddhism centers around the realization of death" (1987, 5). If anything, the moral of the musical play about the harpist is the realization— both in the sense of personal insight and of performance—that death may occur, and that music may play a part in it. And so, witnessing it, we too might be transformed. Reader, take heed, for I will recount for you the story of transformation in more detail in what follows.

Karma can be treated as an eschatological and ethical principle of Buddhist philosophies and their varied orthopraxy.[9] But if dramatic performances of death and transformation help us to realize that everything is impermanent, then karmic transformation is as much a matter of aesthetic operations and technical procedures of musical drama or ritual as it is of philosophical or religious reasoning. Karma is thus not a mere concept that imposes meaning on the world. Rather, much like a character, karma shows up on the pyazat stage. It not only informs the performance or situates the dramatic narrative within a "worldview" but also is itself processed by theatrical operations that render the discontinuity of existence observable.

Considering transformation as an aesthetic phenomenon that has to do with appearance and showing, however, does not rid it from religious meanings. Because transformations enact a threshold, they evade and constantly pollute any neat distinction between cultural spheres of art and religion, musical drama (pyazat) and musical ritual (natpwe), acting and becoming, body and sign, the imaginary and the real. Transformations therefore are semiotically convoluted and continuously yield confusion.

Instead of undoing ambiguity by way of mapping the relationship between performance and meaning according to a given register (namely, art or religion), this chapter attends to the "cultural techniques" (Siegert 2007) of staging and performing transformations, ones that precede any normative distinctions between ritual and drama. It starts from the observation that, in order to *show up*, even the most sublime and existential transformations require medial operations: techniques of disappearance and appearance, operations of framing and staging, musical procedures of presenting and meaning making, or dramatic techniques of narrating. This justifies and necessitates a rigorous analysis of the workings of Burmese musical drama in its historical and cultural specificity and of the dramatic and ritual operations that pertain to the figure of U Shin Gyi. As we will see, the opera about the harpist Maung Shin who became the deity U Shin Gyi features a specific device of transformation: a musical instrument, the saung gauk (harp, စောင်းကောက်), that the harpist carries with him in all scenes. What engenders transformation and rings in a new being is, however, not some kind of subversive potency of musical sound. Instead, the posture of playing and holding the instrument, techniques of tuning and plucking, material relations of signifying, and acousmatic modes of sounding operate the primordial difference that transformation in Burmese nat hpyit pyazat and natpwe is all about—that between human and deity. This chapter, then, is also a query into the mediations of stage instruments.

A PHENOMENOLOGY OF TRANSFORMATION

But what sort of phenomena are transformations of someone into someone else? Briefly put, transformations imbue an entity with discontinuity. They introduce a difference where we expect identity. Someone or something is no longer the same as they were before. Put another way, a transformation becomes evident from the *differences* that distinguish an entity from its previous appearance. In turn, transformations invoke an aesthetic of before-and-after that is highly affective. This is seen in the photographic technique, common in Burmese Buddhist households, where images of the same person are juxtaposed to show them before and after the change that comes with (an often temporary) monastic ordination: a shaved head and a saffron (male) or pink (female) robe. Differences spawned by transformation jump out at us; they intrigue us.

Transformations are, however, not mere shifts in appearance. They operate as periods in an ostensibly seamless continuity of an entity's existence. They defy any definition of "existing" as "permanence in being." But they do not simply amount to the individualist gospel that we are always able to *be* someone else, to transform into someone better. Conversions such as these are only a particular type of transformation, one premised on the fantasy of a blank slate. Instead, what transformations draw attention to is the relation between *appearing* and *being*. Watching their neighbor, father, or friend in transformation as U Shin Gyi, people ask: Does he only *sound* and *look* different? Is he only feigning, or has he truly become a deity? Is he possessed? Is the change permanent? Is he aware of his transformation? Am I still the same to him? "Hello, can you hear me?"—as if, if we only raised our voice, the person "inside" or "behind" the alien appearance would "come out." Transformations are, then, not so much about the continuities and discontinuities of a person before and after a change than about the ambiguity between *being* another person and *appearing* as another person.

Although transformations cannot be reduced to appearance, they not only frequently look like a show, but they are also shown and are given stages. Did you see that? Did you film that? She just changed into a deity. We point fingers and recording devices at them. The musical pomp and visual splendor of Burmese natpwes abundantly evince how procedures of transformation are escalated by dramatic techniques of showing (Nu Yi 2008; Tun 2013).

Furthermore, in contrast to the linear temporality of metamorphoses, transformations of a person into someone or something else seem to defy any temporalization. They occur in the proverbial blink of an eye, in a trice, and have been associated with the perceived instantaneousness of the sound of a trumpet.[10] Often they have no timescale at all and "happen all of a sudden, like a death" (Malabou 2012, 59). On the stages in Myanmar, they are indeed equivalent to death or are the last resort to escape from death. This also means that the very procedures by which a transformation is achieved tend to escape us since they take neither time nor place. The moment of transformation in the play about the harpist is staged as a blackout: not only is it unseen on stage but it occurs outside of seeing. In Kafka's *Metamorphosis* the transformation has already happened before the story even begins; it not only precedes the text but also lies outside narration. The actual event of transformation notoriously retreats from view and audition, however closely we zoom in. This is why some scholars relegate transformations to the realm of imagination (Hla Pe 1952, 10), while others align transformation with "the metaphysical," that is, with the agency of a being from another plane of existence (Maung Htin Aung 1962).

Transformations rarely (perhaps never) yield something unprecedented. Although an entirely new being may show up in place of the prior entity, one that feels and looks and is altogether different, their novelty is instituted qua similarity. No longer themselves, a transformed person appears *as* someone else. Techniques of transformation therefore often appear as mimicry. "I don't think the actor really becomes U Shin Gyi," Sein Pho Naing, the master musician of Thaethesa Theatre Company Dawei, insists. And then he laughs. "Most of the performers just pretend"; they just imitate U Shin Gyi. Apparently, what excites our attention and arouses contention is not so much *what* appears in transformation but *how* it appears. Are we fooled? Is the transformation real? How did he do this? What happened? Did you see that? In performance, transformations turn out to be sequences of medial operations that make someone, all of a sudden, appear as someone else. Transformation is then not so much a question of "techniques of acting" or "performance consciousness" (Schechner 1985, 4–14) as performance theory had argued, but of dramatic media—including stage architecture, curtains, prop, sound, music, light, posture, dress—all of which negotiate and ambiguate the relation between appearing and being.

In the first part of this chapter, I will summarize the dramatic events by which the harpist Maung Shin became the deity U Shin Gyi as told in the musical drama *U Shin*

Gyi, Lord of the Brackish Waters. The story reveals a particular logic of transformation, one that becomes distorted when grasped through a phenomenology of perception. The second part of this chapter dives into a detailed analysis of the transformation scene of this musical play as performed today by touring companies and lay theater associations in the Irrawaddy Delta and in the greater costal region of Dawei.

A Scene from the Libretto

The earliest documentation of the musical play about the harpist who became a deity, is a libretto written by prolific librettist Ko Maung Gyi and published in 1908 in two volumes of eighty pages each (Figure 14.3).[11] In the third act we encounter the transformation scene of the harpist by which the deity U Shin Gyi comes into existence.

> *Maung Shin, a destitute teenage boy from Bago, is known for his great skill on the harp (saung-gauk* စောင်းကောက်*). To earn money, he follows his cousin Ko Aung to sea, taking a job as a cook for a seafaring crew that heads for uninhabited islands in the Irrawaddy Delta to harvest timber and bamboo. Setting off into the wild forest, the crew leaves Maung Shin behind at the shore with the task of preparing food for them, warning him to refrain from playing his harp, as this would bring calamity upon him. Yet, "to cure his boredom," Maung Shin strings his instrument, then tunes and tests the strings by striking up a song. He sits in the boat, which has been anchored at the shore, and his mellow music pours out into the uncharted world between land and see. Alas, he is not alone. Two female deities (nat-thami* နတ်သမီး*) overhear his playing: "Among all the men who have come to the island for many years now, we have never seen anyone like Maung Shin Gyi, anyone who plays such delightful music on a harp," one enthuses. "It is so pleasant!" her sister concurs (Ko Maung Gyi 1908, 56). As they enter the scene, a string of the harp slips and the harpist has to repair the string and retune his instrument in anticipation of singing another song. But the nats intervene. "Now that he has finished repairing the string, awaken his feelings [mind] and inspire the sound of the harp to make him keep playing like that," said one of the nat-thami. The last song he will sing is a love song that expresses ardent longing for a princess, the intended, a bride he has not yet met and who lives in the "palace of the nat" and from whom he is separated by a vast mountainous landscape. Driven by the pleasure of listening, the two nat-thami hatch a plan to abduct the harpist, and with him the delightful sound of his harp.*
>
> *At last the rest of the crew returns, loads the harvested wood onto the boat, and weighs the anchor. But despite strong currents and every effort to row away, the boat will not move an inch. It is as if invisible hands are holding it back. The captain decrees that a member of the crew must be chosen by lot to be offered as a sacrifice in order to save his companions. Three times the lot falls on the harpist Maung Shin, who, in utter terror, sees the two nat-thami meddling with the lots, though his fellow boatmen cannot see them. The scene on the boat escalates. The roaring sounds of wind and water combine with shouting voices calling for the harpist and with the wailing of Ko Aung, who is so desperate to save his cousin that he begs the captain to be allowed to die in Maung Shin's stead. But there can be no surrogate death in karmic cycles of existence. "I accept this as the result of unwholesome actions in my past lives," Maung Shin mourns, "from an undefiled human I will become a nat and I will carry a harp." As the captain pushes him overboard, the two female nat take hold of him and carry him to the*

FIGURE 14.3: Title page of the libretto by Ko Maung Gyi, 1908, Part 2.

shore. In the stage directions, dramatist Ko Maung Gyi concludes: "He has become half-human, half-nat, standing upright at the shore." The harpist has escaped death but has transformed into another person. He has become "U Shin Gyi, Heavenly Deva, Owner of the Brown Island and Master of the Golden Harp, Lord of Brackish Waters ဒေဝသခင် ကျွန်းညိုရှင်ရွှေစောင်းတော်သခင် ရေငန်ပိုင် ဦးရှင်ကြီး."

Two Kinds of Transformation

Literary treatments of transformation abound. From Zhuangzi's *Butterfly Dream* through Ovid's *Metamorphoses* to Kafka's *Die Verwandlung*, transformations have been imagined as events replete with drama and distress. Often, however, as French philosopher Catherine Malabou observes in reference to Ovid's and Kafka's tales of change, it is "only the external form of being that changes, never its nature. Within change, being remains itself" (2012, 7). Although monstrously transformed, Kafka's Gregor Samsa essentially retains his identity when he finds himself one morning in a new and nonhuman body. And Ovid tells us that Daphne is in fact rescued and preserved when her body changes into a tree in a moment of flight.

But the transformation that the harpist faces seems to be of a different kind. Raising anchor to leave the enchanted island, the crew find themselves in a deadlock: they are unable to leave, as the boat is held back by invisible hands. But they are also unable to remain, for a storm is closing in. All that is left is violence: identifying the harpist as the "unlucky one" by lot, tying him up and pushing him overboard into a roaring sea. But his destiny is not death. The female deities, his hungry audience, catch him in the water and carry him to the shore. Alas, the person that emerges from the water is not the human boy anymore. Although described in the libretto as half-human, half-deity and although still holding a harp, the person that is seen "standing upright" on the beach is not the same as the one that had been pushed out of the boat. In place of the harpist Maung Shin, a new being has come to exist, with a new name, a new appearance, a new body, a new attire, a new duty, and a new abode. He is U Shin Gyi, guardian of the brackish waters. In contrast to Gregor Samsa, who "finds himself transformed," the harpist does not witness his change. Although he anticipates it in elongated sung laments, he does not himself go through the transformation, does not experience his own becoming-other. He neither shape-shifts into an other (form changes and being remains) nor is he possessed by an other (being changes and form remains). Instead, change overtakes his whole existence, a moment emphatically referred to in Burmese as *nat hpyit the* (a nat has come into existence).

Malabou has described transformations such as these as events of *destructive plasticity*: "a real and total deviation of being," the imposition of "a new form on their old form, without mediation" (2012, 6–7). But what strikes her as rare and obscure within conventional Western conceptions of change is a familiar conundrum within Theravada Buddhist philosophy. Theories of karma and rebirth regularly reckon with the difficulty of conceiving of transformation without assuming a continuity of identity across different lives. The *kan taya* (ကံ တရား), the karmic law, holds that no "consciousness or any other leftover component of the self" is reborn; "at death, beings are supposed to disappear completely to allow rebirth" (Brac de la Perrière 2015, 62). Following the Theravada doctrine of no-self (*anatta*), according to which the self is an illusion, neither form nor substance ever outlives change.[12] "There is no soul that spills over from incarnation to incarnation" (Obeyesekere 2002, 282). The transformation that occurs in death, or that indeed may supersede death, is instead driven by a karmic logic of ethical-material causation, moral "stuff" that autonomously issues forth from one moment to another, where it gives rise to something new that has no identity with any previous being or body (Obeyesekere 2002, 81).[13] Maung Shin, the harpist, relates this central doctrine of *samsara* (the cycle of existence) when he mourns, "I accept this [transformation into a deity] as the result of unwholesome actions in my past lives."

The change that befalls the harpist must thus be distinguished from those transformations that reinforce being and that are situated *within* the body. Librettist Ko Maung Gyi throws these two kinds of transformations into sharp relief. He depicts the harpist as someone who is on the verge of an ordinary becoming. The encounter with the female deities (*nat-thami* နတ်သမီး) instills in him the desire for love of a woman other than his mother. This sexual awakening marks an anthropogenic transition from child to adult, thus reinforcing his identity. But death comes prematurely; his fate is to die a virgin. "As a young man, yet to be married" (Ko Maung Gyi 1908, 61), he mourns as he faces the end of his human existence. In today's productions of the opera, the prospect of religious righteousness replaces the promise of romantic love. The deities pledge to provide for the boy's novitiation ceremony; earning money for his novitiation had been the very reason he had undertaken the boat journey in the first place. But the pledge was a con. Instead of becoming a novice, he becomes a deity. Instead of novitiation or sexual awakening, changes that would have each buttressed his (human) being, the harpist turns into a new being altogether.

In attempting to understand a transformation such as this, one might be tempted to turn to the performing body itself, the entity that undergoes a transformation. Phenomenologists have proposed to speak of the body as *Leib* to emphasize that anything that happens to the body is a matter of experience, of feeling, of affective involvement. Arguably one of the most central notions in both German and French phenomenology, Leib has been theorized as a site of flux and fragmentation, one that is always prone to change. In distinction to the objective materiality of the physical body (*Körper*) that ends at the limits of the skin, so Edmund Husserl had argued, the Leib—or what Merleau-Ponty adopted in French as *corps propre*—is imbued with an I, self, or person that *is* that body. When my body feels, resonates, perceives, then *I* feel, *I* sound, *I* hear. I *am* this body that feels. Although this incarnate body presumes a first-person perspective, it does not enclose the self in a box. On the contrary, for Merleau-Ponty, the body is unbounded and firmly entangled with others in an elemental "intercorporeity" (see Kapchan, this volume). Similarly, Hermann Schmitz situates the body (Leib) in collective feelings and atmospheric currents (see Fisher, this volume).

Such a view opens up important insights, but it has its own limitations when it comes to phenomena of transformation, since the concept of the felt body (Leib) implies a self in that experience. As Rahaim observes, the phenomenological bodies that have been fashioned in music and sound studies "are all dispositions of the self in various situations" (Rahaim 2012, 8). Even where scholars have studied transformations in the context of ritual performance, the embodied and ecstatic self they postulate is one that must necessarily persist throughout the process of transformation, since it is the very locus of experience and perception that phenomenologies of the body are all about (Kapchan 2009; Leistle 2014; Meneses 2016). Because it involves an inevitable first-person perspective, the Leib can only account for becomings and shifts of an original self, the very entity that *experiences* a transformation. As Catherine Malabou puts it, the incarnate body of phenomenology stays "anchored in an identity which can evolve but which nevertheless remains what it is" (Malabou 2015, 17). But it is precisely identity, being, the self that is interrupted and annihilated by transformation in the Burmese story. Karmic transformation thus compels us to shift our attention away from the body as the site of change toward the entire milieu in which transformations show up—or, as early phenomenology had put it, where something "shows itself." We thus have to turn to the relations and operations, the technical procedures, in short, to the manifold mediations that interconnect the beings that are respectively situated before and after a transformation.

Cultural Techniques of Transformation

Over the past thirty years, German media theory has adopted and advanced the nineteenth-century notion of *Kulturtechnik* (cultural technique) as a concept to study the logics and histories of procedures and practices that allow for the possibility of culture (Siegert 2007). "Culture" should not be understood here in the plural as referring to collectives of humans and/or things that "share" a culture.[14] *Kulturtechnik* might in fact better be translated as "cultivation technique" since it is concerned with the procedures and operations that bring something into existence, such as cultivating a field or cultivating a particular timbre on an instrument. But—and this is the important point—these techniques are not about the transformation of nature into culture nor about addressing how, for instance, performers meet culturally contingent ideals. Instead, basic operations, technical processes, or aesthetic procedures in their historical and cultural specificity are given "priority over both the specific order of phenomena they produce and the concepts that emerge from them," as Katrin Trüsted poignantly puts it (2020, 296). Lorenz Engell and Bernhard Siegert have usefully boiled this central claim of cultural techniques down to the single concept of *operative ontologies*. As they put it, cultural techniques are concerned precisely with those "operations that call something into being; that set up and maintain existence," and with the media "by which and in which these operations take place" (Engell and Siegert 2019, 6). This justifies and necessitates a rigorous analysis of practices and techniques that make up aesthetic milieus, and it avoids a line of reasoning that starts from universal claims about music, sound, or listening.

It seems necessary here—in particular given the context of an anglophone ethnomusicology (and anthropology) that globally dominates in the circulation of theory—to further distinguish a "cultural techniques" approach from the so-called ontological turn. Proponents of this theoretical current have insisted that ethnographic phenomena are to be read as ontological facts, that is, as evidence of distinct realities or diverse worlds which in turn cohere in communities of practice and thought. The theory of cultural techniques that I draw on here (which has its own distinct intellectual genealogy within German media theory) is, in contrast, concerned with the operations by which the real and the imaginary are distinguished in the first place. Instead of charting different ontological systems, research into cultural techniques asks *how* conceptual and ontological entities emerge from within material relations and aesthetic procedures. After all, even ontological presumptions rely on tools and means. Even the most sublime and existential transformations must be brought about by operations and technical procedures in order to *show up*. Grand ontological distinctions do not simply exist "in cultures." All distinctions are first *made*. And it is to this making and processing of karmic transformations, the procedures of reproducing an existential discontinuity in the mediatic milieu of Burmese musical drama, that I will attend to in the following.

INSTRUMENTS OF TRANSFORMATION

Let's turn to today's U Shin Gyi festivals that feature the musical drama about the boy who became a deity. It is almost 3 a.m. and the stage of Htei Tan Zat Thabin (a celebrated theatrical troupe based in Dawei but touring the greater region of Tanintharyi) is lit with ambient light. Having slept for a couple of hours while the pop band was playing, the musicians of the *hsaing waing* orchestra[15] awake again to take part in the last act: the *naubein zat* (နောက်ပိုင်းဇာတ်) (literally "last act"), the *opera*, as it is put in Burmese where the English loanword is used. Almost all scenes of the theater, whether sung or spoken, come with musical accompaniment that is provided by the orchestra from behind a curtain off to stage left.[16] The musicians deliver the expected musical phrases in line with the actions taking place on stage: they sound movements, gestures, and slapstick jokes by musically imitating them with the lag of a second; they provide the fast and energetic music for the dances; they accompany arias consisting of piteous and effusive laments; they demarcate the beginning and end of scenes and fill the transition between acts with interludes; and they shroud performers and the scenery in an affective atmosphere by endowing them with a musical presence. The sound is amplified and projected with massive loudspeakers from the corners of the stage into the wider surroundings. The audience sits, stands, squats, or lies a round on mats under starry skies, wrapped up in scarfs and blankets. Some are awake, some asleep, as the morning dew falls.

While the orchestra is loosely hidden behind a curtain and in the shadow of the stage, one instrument is visible on stage throughout the entire play: the harp that the lead character Maung Shin carries with him. Decorated with red and white cloth that clearly marks the instrument's affinity to the nats (deities), the harp is present throughout the entire performance. But most importantly, it persists throughout the transformation. When orchestra and curtain reveal the nat U Shin Gyi in the final scene, the harp is still there in his hands.

I argued before that the transformation of the harpist in the Irrawaddy Delta and the transformation of Franz Kafka's Gregor Samsa are different in kind. But is that true? Malabou notes that Gregor only changes in form. He does not fully become an other but retains his identity as an inner voice, a voice that appears to be the seat of his being. This voice-being stays astonishingly unaffected[17] by the radical change that his body undergoes as it turns, overnight, into a "monstrous vermin." Gregor's voice teams up with the reader in observing a transformation that only confirms his original identity rather than supersedes it. Similarly, something is retained in the transformation from the human harpist Maung Shin into the nat U Shin Gyi: not his voice, but his musical instrument, the saung gauk (the curved harp). In fact, U Shin Gyi is instantly recognizable as the former human boy Maung Shin because of the harp he holds. Ultimately, just as in his human existence, he is still a person with a musical instrument. And while a common subtitle of the opera is "nat hpyit pyazat," "a play about a nat coming-into-being," performers and audiences often dub it as "*saung zat tou*," "a harp story." In short, the harp seems to establish an identity between human boy and nat, as if it were the musical "self" that persists throughout the transformation.

But this argument already interprets the (*being* of the) musical instrument in its different occurrences as a sign. In fact, it posits the harp not as a musical instrument, a *tool* for sound production, at all, but as an idealized and representational object that signifies something, namely identity. To simply consider the harp as a "symbol" that references the harpist in both his human and nonhuman existence, however, misses an important point. It was the musical *sound* of the harp that brought calamity upon the harpist. To understand the transformation of the human harpist into the deity U Shin Gyi we must then ask, *how does the musical instrument transform from a device of sound production into a sign*?

Holding a Harp—or, How to Transform an Instrument into a Sign

As devices of sound production, musical instruments are poietic (Souza 2017, 24). Instruments are tool-beings; they are imbued with the function "in order to" (umzu) sound music (Harman 2002).[18] But nothing is a tool in and of itself; or, as organologist Laurence Libin puts it, *anything* could be a musical instrument (Libin 2018). The being of an instrument is instead defined by procedures. The harp is brought into being as a tool (of sound production) through operational chains of picking up and readying, tuning and testing, plucking, pressing, striking. Put another way, the ontological structure of the harp as a tool-being emerges from a whole variety of techniques.

In his 1908 libretto, Ko Maung Gyi puts particular emphasis on the tool character of the harp as we witness the protagonist of his opera setting up the instrument, adjusting the strings, and tuning and re-tuning throughout his playing. But this can also be observed on today's stages where the harpist sits down with his harp and first tests the strings before he launches into playing. Through operations of testing and tuning, culturally contingent differences are processed and established: between noise and music, sound and silence, (aural) pleasure and displeasure, tuned and untuned sound. But what are the techniques that transform the harp's mode of being from a poietic device into a sign?

We may turn to the countless shrines that honor the deity U Shin Gyi in the urban boroughs and rural villages of Myanmar's coastal regions. Almost all shrines feature the harp as a central iconic element, unambiguously identifying the wooden figurine as U Shin Gyi (Figure 14.4).[19] But is the harp held by the figurine still a tool-being ready to sound? Of course, stone and wood images cannot pluck strings. But the figurine in the shrine is unable to play the harp not due to its material condition but due to its *posture*. In order to play the saung gauk (harp), the player has to assume a specific position. The male player must sit "right down on one's seat with legs folded" and the female player sits "with feet tucked under, knees together" (U Khin Zaw 1981, 72). The harp then rests in the lap, with the rear of the harp's body under one arm. When playing, the player hugs the harp, proverbially "nursing" the instrument "like an infant" (Hla Pe 1985, 150). The right arm reaches around the strings to pluck them from the outside, while the thumb of the left hand stops the strings from the other side to raise the pitch of a string and thus obtain all notes of a scale. The left thumb plucks additional bass tones to the melody which is played with the right hand (Figure 14.5). In so doing, three tones may be plucked simultaneously, which, according to U Khin Zaw, endows the harp with "superiority over the technique of other percussion instruments" (U Khin Zaw 1981, 72) whose polyphonic potential is limited to a simultaneous striking of two tones with two hands. Since the fingers of both hands are used to pluck and stop the strings, the harp cannot be held up and played at the same time (just as it is impossible to stand, hold, and play a cello that has no endpin).

FIGURE 14.4: U Shin Gyi shrine in Hsinsei Jwa, Dawei, 2015.

FIGURE 14.5: A painting of the harpist Maung Shin playing his harp. Behind him is U Shin Gyi holding the harp with the nat-thami by his side.

(Picture taken in Hsin Hpyu Hpyin Village, 2016)

In order to play the saung gauk (harp), it must rest somewhere else, namely in the lap. In consequence, the technical structure of the instrument compels a specific posture of the player's body: a seated position on the floor. Because there is no neck-strap for the saung gauk nor any other accessory that might allow it to rest elsewhere, the player does not sit *as* she plays; she must sit *in order to* play.

Naturally, in those scenes of the opera where the boy Maung Shin plays the harp, he is always seated. On the theater stage, he sits when busking with his harp in front of a pagoda, and he sits in the anchored boat at the shore when playing his harp in solitude for his own pleasure. Although sitting upstage on the floor makes the performer and his harp invisible to the part of the audience crowded right in front of the stage, he never stands up. To avoid vanishing from sight, the performer may sometimes sit on a large wooden box in the middle of the stage—a remnant, I would suggest, from the nineteenth-century theatrical practices of *mye waing* (literally "ground circle"), performances that were held in the circle on the ground with a wooden box as a piece of stage scenery. On a stereoscope image from 1904 taken in colonial Rangoon, we see six men carrying a gigantic figure of the harpist (Figure 14.6). It is not only evident from his hairstyle—tied into a knot with no headband wrapped around his head—that the figure represents the human harpist and not the deity U Shin Gyi, but it is also clear from his seated posture with the harp resting in the lap that this is not the deity but the human boy Maung Shin.[20] And when you walk along a promenade path on the island Patet just off the shore of Myeik you will come upon a life-sized figurine that shows the harpist seated as a devout Buddhist, signified by the brown sash he wears, with his hands clearly plucking the harp in his lap (Figure 14.7).

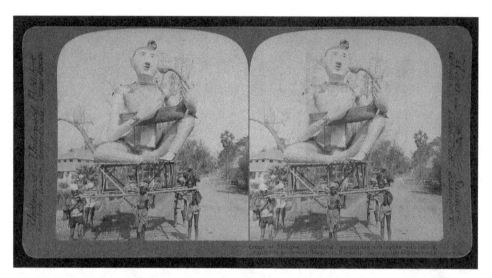

FIGURE 14.6: Stereoscope image of harpist, 1904.

FIGURE 14.7: Figure of the harpist Maung Shin, Island of Patet, Myeik.

FIGURE 14.8: *Tableau vivant* of U Shin Gyi in the final scene of the musical drama.
(Dramatic company: Theythan Zat Thabin ဆိပ်တန်နဲ့ဇာတ်ဇာတ်သဘင်, Dawei)

But the deity that succeeds the human boy no longer sits. Having sacrificed Maung Shin to the sea, the nat-being that reemerges at the shore is seen standing with his harp in his arm in Ko Maung Gyi's 1908 libretto.[21] And the curtain that is raised to reveal the nat after the transformation in the climactic final scene of today's performances invariably shows the nat U Shin Gyi standing upright on the wooden box on the stage with the harp in his hands (Figure 14.8). U Shin Gyi perpetually stands in countless shrines and has always been standing on depictions that date back to the turn of the century, always holding a harp in front of his chest or under his arm.

Ultimately, it is this erect posture that prevents the nat from playing the instrument, because it is impossible to simultaneously hold and play the harp.[22] Supporting the harp in his hands, the figure is unable to use his hands to play it. And even though a panchromatic film version of the U Shin Gyi pyazat from about 1950 by U Loun Phay underscores this scene with harp music, the nat U Shin Gyi whom we see in a special effect floating down from the heavens does not pluck the harp but holds it close to his chest.[23]

The change in posture has permanently upset the cultivated and organic synergy of hands, harp, and body. The ludic relationship between body and instrument, a relation on which Maung Shin's very human existence rested since he had economically depended on his musical performance, is extinguished. A new assemblage-being emerges that exists in a mode altogether different from that of a human musician. Despite holding a harp, the nat is no longer a musician. Despite being held by hands, the harp no longer emits musical sound.

But there is another inversion that occurs in the karmic transformation. The musical instrument compelled a particular posture of the human body while also enabling the boy to pursue an existence as a musician. But now it is the nat, in his upright posture, that transforms the harp from an instrument into a mere object. In the hands of the nat, the harp is no longer a tool-being with the essential phenomenal structure to *sound music*. The harp has shifted into a different ontological domain and has become an object-being that is merely present and literally *at hand* (*zuhanden*). The transformation from human to nat is an inversion of the technical hierarchy of body and harp.

The discontinuity of the human harpist and the deity in their relation to the musical instrument is not only visible on the opera stage and in the shrine but also made explicit in the 1908 libretto. Before Maung Shin is pushed into the water, the boy announces his own transformation by relating his destiny to his cousin and thus to the audience. "From an undefiled human I will become a nat. And I will carry a harp" (Ko Maung Gyi 1908, 66).[24] The choice of words in Ko Maung Gyi's libretto is significant here. As a nat he will no longer be the one who *plays* his harp—the one who indeed plays with such abandon that he has to be warned against playing everywhere, all the time. Instead, from now on, he is the one *holding* or *carrying* a harp "close to his bosom," as the word '*pai* ၀ိုက်' (carry) indicates. This shift from playing to holding, from sounding to signifying, is also explicit in the ritual (natpwe) that precedes the opera performance. U Tin Thein, a doyen of the cultural scene and master of the *naubein zat* (နောက်ပိုင်း, opera), explains that the deity U Shin Gyi is "invited [to the ritual] by *holding* the harp close to the bosom." The deity is not summoned by the sound of the harp but by a harp that has already transformed into a symbol for the deity. Pointing at the very instrument that is used in annual performances and that is exhibited on a shrine in his house, U Than Shwey from Phaung Gyi explains, "we can't play [this instrument]. This harp is just for holding. . . . When U Shin Gyi comes, he can hold it. He usually climbs onto the bamboo Nat shrine holding the harp in his arms."

But let's return to the 1908 libretto once again, for it features a scene that is not included in today's performances. The librettist Ko Maung Gyi foreshadows the transformation of the harp from a tool-being into an object-being. At the very moment that the nat-thami enter the scene to delight in the music that Maung Shin plays in solitude, a string of the harp snaps. Both an ill omen and even a punishable offence at the Burmese court, where a second instrument was always brought along when performing for the king so as to skip the act of re-tuning by substituting the entire instrument (Singer 1995, 21), the audible event of the snapping string ultimately causes the music to end and curtails the harp as an auditory presence. The instrument shifts into another mode of being and becomes present-at-hand. It is no longer a device ready to produce musical sound but a broken object. The accidental transformation of the harp, however, does not (yet) mark the end of the boy's human existence. Magically enticed by the listening women, Maung Shin is still able to reverse the change by repairing and re-tuning the instrument. By way of the technical operations of reinstating musical sound, of restoring the being of the harp as an instrument, he is also able to maintain his own existence as the adept musician that he is known to be. After all, being able to tune a harp is "a skill acquired only after much training" (U Khin Zaw 1981, 72). But when the boy ceases to exist and U Shin Gyi comes into being, the sound of the harp vanishes for good.

The cultural history of the saung gauk demonstrates that this transformation of the harp occurred beyond the stage as well. In 1993, Tekkatho Maung Thu Hlaing writes,

> today, harps are being used not merely as musical instruments: they are also used as artifacts to decorate the [entrance] room of dwellings. This is being done by way of honouring a musical instrument that has played an important role in [the] development of Myanma culture. More sophisticated musical gadgets will emerge as time passes but the harp will ever remain as a heritage of Myanma musical traditions.
>
> (Tekkatho Maung Thu Hlaing 1993, 8)

Just as the harp is placed in the arms of U Shin Gyi in ritual, shrine, or opera, so the harp is placed onto a shelf in the entrance room thus becoming a cultural signifier and an object of national pride. By divesting the harp of its ontological structure as tool-being and transforming it into a signifier, both nation-state and national history emerge as unified entities that can be signified.[25]

Sounding Instruments—or, How to Turn a Mock Harp into a Harp

In the previous section, we saw that the sonic potency of the harp rests not only in the organological technicity and materiality of the instrument but also in the relation of instrument and body. Holding the harp while standing, the instrument no longer shows up as a tool-being but as a symbol. But these are only visible cues of transformation. How did the harp *sound* in the hands of the human boy, and what do we *hear* when the deity no longer plays but holds the instrument? Is the vector of the annihilating transformation one that runs from music to non-music? Is the harp as symbol silent? Let's jump to the key scene where the boy Maung Shin plays his instrument in solitude, sitting in the boat anchored at the shore of the enchanted island. The female deities (nat-thami) enter the scene to relish the music by dancing to it (Figure 14.9).

Everyone has left the stage and the actor performing as the harpist sits elevated on the wooden box that is now hidden behind a piece of painted cloth stretched horizontally across the stage to represent the boat. But the harp that rests in his lap is not a playable instrument. It is usually a mock harp such as are sold to nostalgics and tourists, or a discarded harp with a broken body, or a harp long out of tune with loose strings and pegs that no longer hold. Furthermore, the harp is sometimes richly decorated with flowers tucked between the strings preventing any plucking and playing. In short, the harp that sits in his lap has no imminent capacity for musical sound. It cannot be played at all. Even though the entire plot revolves around the playing and sounding of the harp, the harp on stage does not emit any sound. Its purpose on stage is clearly not to *sound* like a harp but to *look* like a harp. But the harp on stage is not merely a symbol either. A

FIGURE 14.9: Maung Shin sitting on the boat and playing his harp. Two female deities come and dance.

(Dramatic company: Theythan Zat Thabin ထိပ်တန်ဇာတ်ဇာတ်သဘင်, Dawei)

careful observation of the theatrical procedures reveals how the mock harp in the hands of the actor transforms into an instrument of sound production through chains of musical operations.

First, the voiceless harp is imbued with a virtual sound. Instead of plucking its strings, the actor moves his hands and fingers through the air in order to simulate playing the idle instrument. In so doing, the unusable harp acquires technical potency, if only virtually, and appears as a tool-being on stage. The fundamental distinction that musical instruments process—namely, between sound and silence—is virtualized through gestures of playing. These gestures allow the mock instrument to transcend its material constraints and to show up as an instrument of (virtual) sound production. Furthermore, the harp is imbued with the capacity not merely to make sound but to make *musical sound*. When the deities enter the scene and gracefully dance, their movement transforms the virtual sound into music. The deities' diegetic listening manifests as dance movements, which virtualize another fundamental distinction—that between musical and unmusical sound. What the beautiful goddesses hear is not any sound but one that compels dance. As on-stage audience, they hear music.

Second, the virtual sound of the harp sonically actualizes the mock instrument; the voiceless harp becomes audible. This is achieved not by another harp but by another instrument altogether, one that engages in yet another medial operation: imitation. Ye Min Twei, a widely acclaimed twenty-six-year-old performer from Yangon who has repeatedly starred in the role of Maung Shin, explains: "I only provide the gestures [of plucking the strings of the harp], while the orchestra supports my gestures from behind the curtain." Seated below the level of the stage—either off to the side, where it is hidden by a curtain, or in front, where it is hidden in the shadow—the *pat waing* (diatonically tuned drum circle) plays a *kyo* song (ကြိုးသီချင်း; literally a "(harp-)string" song) as the actor on stage moves his hands along the loose strings of the mock instrument. The acoustic attack times of the tuned drums (the time it takes for the sound of a drum to go from silence to its loudest point) (Figure 14.10) and plucked strings (Figure 14.11) are equally short. Both harp strings and drum skins are dampened so as to articulate distinct and clearly pitched sounds, which drip like drops of water. Using only the high-pitched drums, the pat waing does not merely *represent* the sound of plucked strings; it uses the kyo song to invoke those strings, both musically and acoustically, employing a mimetic mode of playing that sounds the drums as strings. Thus, through techniques of acoustic mimicry, one instrument fashions the sound of another. According to Ye Min Twei, some ensembles also "use the piano to produce the sound of the harp" thus "singing (*so*) the sound of the harp on the piano." In turn, although the orchestra is hidden from stage, the music in the harp-playing scene is not simply acousmatic. The voiceless, mock harp shows up as a resonant body via the drum circle. But the inverse is

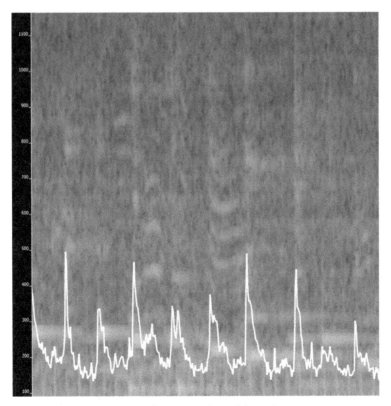

FIGURE 14.10: Acoustic attack time of pat waing (tuned drums).

FIGURE 14.11: Acoustic attack time of saung gauk (harp).

also the case. The sound of the pat waing shows up as harp sound via gestures of playing and dancing visible on stage.

These different procedures coalesce into a unified audio-visual event for two related perceptual reasons: one has to do with listening, and the other with the way that motion is experienced across sonic and visual domains. First, because listening is partly driven by source orientation—the urge to constantly identify the source of a sound (Clarke 2005, 126)—the audience is willing to engage in a self-deception: the acousmatic sound of the pat waing mingles with the imagined sounds of the visibly air-plucked mock instrument on stage until the latter is accepted as the source of the sound. It is a timbral mimesis that encourages this substitution of perceived source for physical source: the pat waing fashions drumbeats in a style that imitates the plucked tones of the harp strings. Ultimately the harp-sound thus created is "not so much an *illusion* as a *collusion* between audience, performer, and instrument" (Fales 2002, 81; italics added). Second, the movement of the harpist's hands, his manner of sitting and holding the instrument as if playing, but also the graceful dancing of the *nat-thami*, all bring about what Michel Chion terms "syncresis," an experience by which sound is soldered to that which is seen (2015, 116).[26] The movements of the air-plucking hands and of the dancing bodies synchronize with the music.

Plucking his harp, the performer on stage begins to sing. His mellow song "Kyune kyune bein tha kyo" (Island world song) speaks of the unfamiliar wilderness that surrounds him. Hsein Phone Naing, a senior master musician, explains:

> it is a tradition, already observed by our ancestors, to play gently and softly [for the harp-playing scene]. Kyo music is provided (*thi bei the*). Such has been the tradition since ancient times, and it has been passed on by musical masters from one generation to the next.

But what happens to the virtual-actual harp sound after Maung Shin has become U Shin Gyi, when change has taken place and the human musician transforms into the nat? The moment the harpist is sacrificed into the sea the stage turns black, the curtain falls. When it rises again, the curtain reveals U Shin Gyi standing upright, with a harp in his arms. But the deity no longer plucks the strings like the harpist before him. Being held by the deity, the harp has lost both its real and virtual capacity to sound. It has transformed from an instrument ready to sound into an image. At last, the difference between the actual unplayable harp-instrument on stage and the staged harp as a device of (virtual) sound production has collapsed. The imaginary harp now coincides with the real material harp. Both have become mere representations of playable instruments.

Stepping from the Imaginary into the Real

But music still sounds. It solemnly emanates from behind the curtain and is amplified by loudspeakers. Playing in the *yey kin* (water music) style that is also familiar from other operas, where it is employed for scenes involving the royal barge, the orchestra shrouds the new being that emerges on the stage in an enthralling majestic aura. The pauper's boy is no more. A royal personage has entered the stage: nat hpyit the. The musical event is now dominated by the *hne* (shawm), while the bright sound of crashing cymbals and the low and dull tone of the bass drum powerfully reverberate into the dawning day. All the mimesis between stage action and musical action, which had been so crucial for the illusion, is gone. Music is no longer diegetic but expressly atmospheric.

The nat that the final curtain reveals pushes into the real through a chain of operations that upset the entire theatrical arrangement. The rising curtain shows a *tableau vivant* in which the deity appears as a simulacrum of his own shrine image: elevated on the wooden box, he stands motionlessly glaring into the distance while cradling the harp in his arms (Figure 14.8). The four nat-thami (the female deities) by his side no longer dance but now stand in obeisance with palms folded together. All five appear from behind the low-hanging, painted cloth that had represented the boat. No longer a boat, the cloth now demarcates the bottom edge of this *tableau vivant*, cutting off the feet of the five figures and thus framing them as an image.

But the appearance of the nat as an image is only a temporary illusion. U Shin Gyi steps out of the image by crossing the portside-cum-forestage-cum-frame; this time, however, not to fall (from the boat) to his death into a watery abyss but to come alive, a *trompe-l'œil vivant*. In the preceding act the boat had served the harpist Maung Shin as a stage within the stage. Sitting on this stage within the stage, the human harpist had never really played for *us*, the real audience, but for another diegetic audience on stage. His listeners were the female deities, and we were mere witnesses to a scene of musical listening. When U Shin Gyi solemnly steps out of the frame-cum-boat he also steps off the stage-within-the-stage. At last, he appears for us as we become his audience.

But he does not halt there. In slow restrained steps, without moving his upper body, sometimes not moving at all but "riding" (*si*) upright on the back of (a person on all fours performing as) a tiger, he advances toward the front edge of the stage, crossing the proscenium frame, and steps, at last, into the nonrepresentative. The edge of the stage, which had, up to this point, stabilized the difference between play and reality, historical past and lived present, now collapses. U Shin Gyi enters the audience, an audience which has itself now arisen from the ground and from sleep, brimming with both pity and affection, to revere him as their guardian (Figure 14.12). The continuous acousmatic sound of the orchestra blazes his way, musically enforcing his presence as he steps onto a bamboo pole (*kyone sin* ကွန်းစင်) erected for him in the midst of the audience. The actor Ye Min Thwei describes this affectively charged moment in evocative terms: "The orchestra plays in the mode of *yey kin* in a very slow and gentle manner which gives rise to sublime feelings (ကြွ *kywa the*). If [the orchestra] plays in this way [the audience] will get goose bumps (*kye thi*)."

This transformation of a human boy into a nat, retold and repeated year after year in musical drama performance, is presented as the end of imagination. There is no more

FIGURE 14.12: U Shin Gyi in the midst of the audience just after sunrise.
(Dramatic company: Shwe Min Zat Thabin ရွှေမင်းဇာတ်ဇာတ်သဘင်, Dawei)

as if. Even though the harpist's cousin had offered himself, amid tears, as a surrogate to die in Maung Shin's stead, substitution was not a possible way out of the fix. The predicament, precipitated by the innocent harp playing, heralds the end of surrogacy, the end of acting, the end of staging. As the difference between real harp and represented harp dissipates, so the difference between role and actor collapses. Transformation has caught up with both form and being. Swept up in the karmic transformation of his stage persona, the actor shows up as the deity himself: motionless, voiceless, with frozen features on his strangely petrified face, and with a red band around his head as worn by all deities across Myanmar. Nat hpyit the, a nat has come into being. But what also "shows up" in the dawning day is musical drama as a machine of appearance capable of operating the relation between being and appearing and of processing the distinction between different realities—real and imaginary ones.

STAGING KARMA

Karmic transformations, according to Buddhist philosophy, annihilate both being and form. But if one entity simply ends and another begins, if there is no longer an "I" that remembers themselves, if one can no longer say *of* someone that "*he* has transformed" but a new person shows up in his stead, does it still make sense to speak of transformation at all? Buddhist philosophy has pondered this theoretical conundrum. But in performance, whether dramatic or ritual, it is also of practical concern. I suggested at the beginning that transformations become manifest in the differences that we can observe. We might now turn this around: karmic transformations presuppose an observer, a "we," a third party, an audience, a witness, a narrator, someone who distinguishes the differences, someone who *makes* the distinction. This entity is not expendable but a *sine qua non* for annihilating transformations to show up as such. Malabou's philosophy of destructive plasticity is so dazzled by the spectacle of extraordinary transformations that it fails to notice its own condition of possibility. For her, destructive plasticity eludes mediation (2012, 6). Yet, what reveals transformations as disjunctive events in the first place is her stance as observer—"I have witnessed these types of transformation" (13)—and her own narrative voice that holds the gaping halves of existential discontinuity together.[27] In this, mediation abounds. No matter how destructive, disruptive, or profound a transformation may be, it never simply "shows up," but it must be shown, staged, exhibited, or narrated since it requires techniques that "render observable the unity of the things distinguished" (Siegert 2015, 193). The mediatic milieu of musical, dramatic, and ritual procedures surrounding the tragic transformation of the harpist into the deity U Shin Gyi does precisely that: it assembles a whole set of fundamental techniques of showing and appearing capable of weaving together different beings and different realities—for us to witness. Narrating and staging are not ancillary to karmic theory but the very place of gaining insight and understanding, of doing philosophy.

Acknowledgments

I would like to explicitly highlight the staggering asymmetries and inequities of privilege between me and my colleagues in Myanmar and the impact this has upon knowledge production relating to the performing arts in Myanmar. Speaking Burmese only as a fourth language, I possess a knowledge of Burmese sources and an understanding of cultural layers of meaning that remain wanting, to say the least. Nevertheless, it is I who have had privileged access to education and funding in ways that many scholars in Myanmar can't even imagine, and it is I and not them who has the necessary scholarly and cultural agency to conduct research and now publish on this important Burmese performing arts tradition. Moreover, I am acutely aware that I do so in the very language of those who colonized the country (although English is a foreign language to me as well). My hope is that this work will highlight existing Burmese scholarship and inspire more global scholarship and equitable collaboration where possible.

I would like to thank Daw Htwe Htwe Mon for her support in conducting some of the ethnographic interviews referenced in this chapter and Daw Nu Nu Aung, Kyaw Thu, Henry Ashworth, and Ye Kyaw Swa for their patient work and assistance in translating materials used here. I am grateful to the anonymous reviewer for their insightful and encouraging remarks. I have benefited immensely from attentive comments on earlier drafts by Christiane Voss, Ruard Absaroka, Peter McMurray, Matt Rahaim, Anna Stirr, David VanderHamm, and Harris Berger.

Notes

1. This Burmese saying is used in situations where action must be taken in order to achieve something.
2. *Pyazat*—also referred to by the loanword *opera*—had initially flourished in the eighteenth and nineteenth centuries as an elite art form under the patronage of the Konbaung kings, a Burmese dynasty that ended violently in 1885 at the hands of the British Crown. But even outside the royal court, pyazat enjoyed wide popularity through the activities of touring companies (*zat thabin*) that employed professional dancers, actors, and musicians and that communities or individuals hired to present a variety of entertainments in nightlong performances. For an introduction see Maung Htin Aung (1937) and Hla Pe (1952).
3. Scholars, in particular those from the West, have insisted on the difference between *nat* and *deva*. In virtually all performance contexts that I have witnessed, however, deities are addressed by both terms interchangeably.
4. While scholars have analyzed "Burmese drama" as a historical and textual tradition (Maung Htin Aung 1937; Hla Pe 1952; Ye Dway 2014), to this day there exists no research into the performance practices of particular musical plays. Since any documentation of historical performances is rare and cursory, today's performances are also sources that contain important historical information.
5. To prepare himself for the final scene of the play, the lead actor will have fasted and meditated for several days in advance in order to purify himself for a transformation that ultimately will transcend him.
6. Unless otherwise noted, all translations from the Burmese are my own.
7. Scholarship on the nats in Myanmar has so far overlooked the important continuities between musical drama (pyazat) and ritual (natpwe) and has studied the latter exclusively as

a "religious cult" that centers upon the activities of "spirit mediums" who undertake "spirit possession rituals" (Brac de la Perrière 1989).

8. These shows include highly stylized dances, racy comedy, and popular songs. The *zatpwe* is staged by a company (*zat thabin*) of professional actors and musicians that has been hired for the duration of the annual festival. As the last part of the nightlong performances, a musical drama is presented. Often two dramas or two parts of one narrative are shown: one before midnight, the other in the early morning hours. That of U Shin Gyi, however, is always presented last.

9. On how "Burmese conceptualize souls" or if, and how, "they" believe in the law of karma and principles of rebirth see Brac de la Perrière (2015). My concern here is not with doctrines and belief but with performance.

10. "We shall all be changed, in a moment, in the twinkling of an eye, at the last trump" (1. Cor. 15, 51–52 KJB). See also Rahaim (this volume) on the fetishized and equally unmediated presence of the voice that occurs, according to Husserl (and Derrida), "in the blink of an eye."

11. The full pen name of the dramatist is Dabein Yein Hseya Ko Maung Gyi. Unfortunately, not much information about this writer exists, but about forty libretti published around the turn of the twentieth century were authored by him. This particular libretto went through at least two editions (1908 and 1910). I thank Ye Kyaw Zaw and Henry Ashworth for assisting in translating the libretto from the original Burmese (and Pali) into English.

12. Brac de la Pérrière has argued that in practice Buddhists in Myanmar diverge from the tenets of doctrinal Buddhism to instead hold an understanding of the self that is similar to conceptions found within monotheistic religions.

13. In contrast to the causational logic of karma, Malabou imagines a transformation that is itself bereft of logic. While the stories of transformations that Kafka or Ovid tell assume a being who witnesses and remembers their own change, Buddhists must cultivate meditation techniques and purify their minds over a long period of time to gain some faint knowledge of the beings that preceded them.

14. This differs slightly from Siegert, who maintained that "to speak of cultural techniques presupposes a notion of plural cultures" and who had aligned cultural techniques with Descola's "dispositives of being" (Siegert 2015, 11).

15. The orchestra consists of the pat waing (ပတ်ဝိုင်း), a tuned drum circle comprising a heptatonic series spanning four octaves, two similarly tuned gong circles, kyi waing (ကြေးဝိုင်း) and maung (မောင်း), a double reed aerophone hne (နှဲ), clappers and cymbals (ဝါး, စည်းတို, လင်းကွင်း), powerful bass drums (pat ma ပတ်မကြီး and chauk lon pat ခြောက်လုံးပတ်), and sometimes a flute belwe (ပဝဲ).

16. Traditionally, the orchestra was seated in front of the stage. This setup is still used in the Irrawaddy Delta. If seated offstage to the side (usually stage right), it faces the "pop" band also offstage across the other side (stage left).

17. Even the vermin that Gregor has become is, in contrast to vermin as we know them, still in possession of a voice, albeit a distorted one.

18. These conceptual ideas trace back to German philosopher Martin Heidegger. For an urgent critical assessment of Heidegger's antisemitism and white supremacist views see Knowles (2019). Heidegger claims that the being of a tool is defined by a totality of tools that "surround" it. Considered through the lens of cultural techniques, however, this may be revised. What turns a thing into a tool are operations.

19. Note that there are also other nat in Myanmar who are depicted with a harp, such as Minye Aungdin Nat or Mintha Maung Shin Nat.

20. Apparently ignorant of the story, the image is subtitled "image of 'harpist,' signifying 'propitiating evil spirits with music,' carried in procession."

21. Note that in an English-language version of the story by Maung Pye, U Shin Gyi is described as sitting and even playing his harp after having transformed into a nat (Maung Pye [1948] 1952, 98). This, however, I have never seen in any performance.

22. Even when one hand of the effigy still seems to reach the strings of the harp, as can be seen in some shrines, playing without the second hand to stop the strings (if possible at all) would significantly reduce the tonal material of the instrument and render any skillful manipulation of the strings impossible. The alleged "superiority" of the instrument would be lost. The artistic skill by which the human boy was known would at best become dull amateurism in the hands of the nat.

23. Maung Than Hswey maintains that U Shin Gyi is "playing his harp" in this very film scene, but he clearly only holds the instrument (Maung Than Hswey 2016, 114).

24. The original sentence reads: "လူစင်စင်ကယ်ကနတ်ဖြစ်မယ်ဆောင်းတော်ပိုက်ပါလို့."

25. For a detailed analysis of U Shin Gyi as an agent in the incremental burmanization of southern Myanmar, see Boutry and Brac de la Perrière (2013).

26. Syncresis is a neologism by Michel Chion made up of "synchronism" and "synthesis."

27. I am grateful to Christiane Voss for pointing this out to me.

Works Cited

Abe, Masao 阿部正雄. 1987. "Transformation in Buddhism." *Buddhist-Christian Studies* 7: 5–24.

Boutry, Maxime, and Bénédicte Brac de la Perrière. 2013. "Les représentations de naq en Birmanie comme vecteur d'intégration culturelle." In *Ethnocentrisme et création*, edited by Annie Dupuis, 323–348. Paris: Éditions de la Maison des sciences de l'homme.

Brac de la Perrière, Bénédicte. 1989. *Les rituels de possession en Birmanie: du culte d'Etat aux cérémonies privées*. Paris: Éditions Recherche sur les civilisations.

Brac de la Perrière, Bénédicte. 2015. "Possession and Rebirth in Burma (Myanmar)." *Contemporary Buddhism* 16 (1): 61–74.

Chion, Michel. 2015. *Sound: An Acoulogical Treatise*. Translated by James A. Steintrager. Durham, NC: Duke University Press.

Clarke, Eric F. 2005. *Ways of Listening: An Ecological Approach to the Perception of Musical Meaning*. Oxford: Oxford University Press.

Engell, Lorenz, and Bernhard Siegert. 2019. "Editorial." *Zeitschrift für Medien- und Kulturforschung* 10: 5–12.

Fales, Cornelia. 2002. "The Paradox of Timbre." *Ethnomusicology* 46 (1): 56–95.

Harman, Graham. 2002. *Tool-Being: Heidegger and the Metaphysics of Objects*. Chicago: Open Court.

Hla Pe. 1952. *Konmara Pya Zat: An Example of Popular Burmese Drama in the XIX Century*. London: Luzac.

Hla Pe. 1985. *Burma: Literature, Historiography, Scholarship, Language, Life, and Buddhism*. Pasir Panjang, Singapore: Institute of Southeast Asian Studies.

Kapchan, Deborah. 2009. "Learning to Listen: The Sound of Sufism in France." *The World of Music* 51 (2): 65–90.

Knowles, Adam. 2019. *Heidegger's Fascist Affinities: A Politics of Silence*. Stanford, CA: Stanford University Press.

Ko Maung Gyi စားဗိန်ကိုမောင်ကြီး. 1908. ရေးပိုင်ဦးရှင်ကြီးနတ်ဖြစ်ပြဇာတ်သစ် [U Shin Gyi, Lord of Brackish Waters. A play about becoming a deity, part 1]. Rangoon: Gae Nagumeira.

Leistle, Bernhard. 2014. "From the Alien to the Other: Steps toward a Phenomenological Theory of Spirit Possession." *Anthropology of Consciousness* 25 (1): 53–90. https://doi.org/10.1111/anoc.12019.

Libin, Laurence. 2018. "Musical Instrument." *Grove Music Online*. March 26, 2018.

Malabou, Catherine. 2012. *Ontology of the Accident: An Essay on Destructive Plasticity*. Translated by Carolyn Shread. Cambridge, UK: Polity Press.

Malabou, Catherine. 2015. Foreword to *Plastic Bodies: Rebuilding Sensation after Phenomenology*, by Tom Sparrow, 13–20. London: Open Humanities Press.

Maung Htin Aung. 1937. *Burmese Drama: A Study with Translations, of Burmese Plays*. London: Oxford University Press.

Maung Htin Aung. 1962. *Folk Elements in Burmese Buddhism*. London: Oxford University Press.

Maung Pye. (1948) 1952. *Tales of Burma*. Calcutta: Macmillan.

Maung Than Hswey မောင်သန်းဆွေ. 2016. မြန်မာရိုးရာနတ်ယုံကြည်မှုလေ့လာ [Myanmar tradition: believing in nats]. Vol. 1. Yangon: Kant Kaw Wut Yee Publishing.

Meneses, Juan Diego Diaz. 2016. "Listening with the Body: An Aesthetics of Spirit Possession outside the Terreiro." *Ethnomusicology* 60 (1): 89–124.

Nu Yi. 2008. *Smile as They Bow*. New York: Hyperion East.

Obeyesekere, Gananath. 2002. *Imagining Karma: Ethical Transformation in Amerindian, Buddhist, and Greek Rebirth*. Berkeley: University of California Press.

Rahaim, Matthew. 2012. *Musicking Bodies: Gesture and Voice in Hindustani Music*. Music/Culture Book Series. Middletown, CT: Wesleyan University Press.

Schechner, Richard. 1985. *Between Theater and Anthropology*. Philadelphia: University of Pennsylvania Press.

Siegert, Bernhard. 2007. "Cacography or Communication? Cultural Techniques in German Media Studies." *Grey Room* 29: 26–47. https://doi.org/10.1162/grey.2007.1.29.26.

Siegert, Bernhard. 2015. *Cultural Techniques: Grids, Filters, Doors, and Other Articulations of the Real*. New York: Fordham University Press.

Singer, Noel F. 1995. *Burmese Dance and Theatre*. Kuala Lumpur: Oxford University Press.

Souza, Jonathan de. 2017. *Music at Hand: Instruments, Bodies, and Cognition*. New York: Oxford University Press.

Tekkatho Maung Thu Hlaing. 1993. မြန်မာရိုးရာအနုပညာ ဆိုင်းဝိုင်းတူရိယာများ [Myanma traditional orchestra instruments]. Yangon: U Tin Ohn.

Trüstedt, Katrin. 2020. "The Fruit Fly, the Vermin, and the Prokurist: Operations of Appearing in Kafka's Metamorphosis." In *Cultural Techniques: Assembling Spaces, Texts, and Collectives*, edited by Jörg Dünne, Kathrin Fehringer, Kristina Kuhn, and Wolfgang Struck. 295–316. Boston, MA: De Gruyter.

Tun, Cathy. 2013. "The Relationship between Spirit Propitiation Ceremony and Drum Ensemble." *Dagon University Research Journal* 5: 73–80.

U Khin Zaw. 1981. *Burmese Culture: General and Particular*. Rangoon: Sarpay Beikman.

Ye Dway. 2014. *Myanmar Dance and Drama*. Yangon: Today Publishing House.

CHAPTER 15

···

INTUITIVE SENSORY PRESENTIATION AND RECOLLECTION

A Phenomenological Interpretation of the Deer Dance

···

HELENA SIMONETT

In memory of *maaso* Vicente Limón (1943–2021).

THE focus of this chapter is on the Yoreme deer dance, which forms part of a ceremony (*pájko* or *fiesta*) that includes two other types of dances (*pascola*), a range of performers, and a knowing audience (see Spicer 1962 and Griffith 1998 for the Yaqui; Ochoa Zazueta 1998, Olmos Aguilera 1998, and Simonett 2009 for the Yoreme).[1] From curing rituals to wakes, burials, folk-Catholic calendrical festivities, or the numerous patron saints' days, all Yoreme ceremonies involve pascola and deer dance music. Over the course of my fieldwork in northern Sinaloa, Mexico, from 2004 to 2014, I learned about the deer dance from observing, talking to, and living with the Yoreme people. In general, they tolerate the *yori* (non-Indigenous people) like me at their ceremonies, unlike the Yaqui (Yoeme), whose ceremonies are off limits for outsiders. My Yoreme interlocutors had been patient even when I, time and again, asked odd questions about things that were considered obvious or had no answers (or at least no answers in words). Despite repeated efforts over the centuries to convert Mexico's Indigenous people to Catholicism and "modernize" them, much of their worldviews and traditions perpetuate pre-Columbian cosmologies. What, I asked myself, could ideas from continental European thinkers possibly offer to understand Yoreme practices and concepts? After all, these erudite White men had never danced the deer or experienced *juiya annia* (the enchanted world of the deer). Nevertheless, I believe that concepts from phenomenology, as developed within Western philosophical history, coincide in many respects with Yoreme ideas and the lifeworlds that they inhabit. Ceremonial specialists, and everyday people as well, also ponder being and time and human finitude. The Yoreme do so not in writing but in singing and dancing. In that respect, phenomenology could well be seen as an intercultural philosophy, as I will argue in the following pages.

The preparation of a fiesta is a lengthy and highly complex process that adheres to traditional rules and involves a plethora of individuals who, committed either by *oficio* (ceremonial duty) or *promesa* (vow), dedicate much time, energy, and resources to its successful realization. While the ceremony proper, with its music and dance, is typically the domain of the men, the women are responsible for the physical well-being of all fiesta attendants (Simonett 2015). Makeshift cooking places are set up adjacent to the ceremonial center, which consists of an Indigenous "church" with an attached leaf-covered shelter under which the musicians and dancers perform. These "kitchens" are the meeting places where the performers fuel up to endure the strenuous nightly ritual. The musicians and dancers feast once before the ceremony, which typically starts around eleven o'clock at night, again after sunrise, and at the closing of the fiesta in the afternoon.

HISTORICAL ACCOUNTS OF THE DEER DANCE

The deer dance as practiced by Indigenous peoples in northwestern Mexico is a phenomenon that has attracted considerable attention from outsiders since it was first observed in the nineteenth century by foreigners who traveled to the region for research or to exploit the local resources (Hardy [1829] 1871; Zúñiga 1835; Escudero 1849; Velasco 1850; Hernández 1902).[2] For example, Lieutenant Robert Hardy was commissioned by the General Pearl and Coral Fishery Association of England to explore the Gulf of California. He reported with astonishment that "in their festivities the [Seri] Indians wear the head (with their horns on) of this animal [the deer], for ornamenting their own!" ([1829] 1871, 298). In the mid-nineteenth century, an officer of the commander-general of the province described the Yaqui's celebratory nature, playing into the stereotype of carefree natives: "They are always happy, bursting out in hollers [cries of joy]; from dusk to dawn, if not tired from working, they engage in dances called the Tesguin, the Pascola, the Deer, and the Coyote" (Velasco 1850, 74).[3] Fortunato Hernández, a medical doctor and ethnographer commissioned by the Mexican government to report on Sonora's tribes and their uprisings, ascribed a "mystic signification" to the deer dancer's attire: "The mask symbolizes strength and courage, the rattles of the rattlesnake mean nobility and extra-human power, and antelope hooves indicate agility and lightness" (1902, 55).[4] These firsthand accounts, of course, are grounded in nineteenth-century concepts about Indigenous people and their world. Despite lacking ethnographic detail, these early descriptions of the deer dance are nevertheless valuable for understanding its history.

William C. Holden, a Texan historian and archaeologist, circuitously described a Sonoran Yaqui fiesta, where a deer dancer, "naked to the waist," all of a sudden "broke into an orgy of dancing," and later "did an interpretative dance showing the movements and habit of the deer," concluding that "he was a splendid dancer" (1936, 48, 49, 50). For readers interested in a more detailed description of the deer dance, he referred to the eyewitness account of folklorist Frances Densmore (1932), who described the Holy Week celebrations in a Yaqui village near Phoenix, Arizona, in 1922.[5] Mexican ethnographer Carlos Basauri assumed that the deer dance imitated the hunt of the deer by a coyote: "After much dancing, the exhausted deer falls before the coyote who is represented by another dancer with corresponding mask" (1940, 275).[6]

By the middle of the twentieth century, ethnographies had become somewhat more edifying as scholars provided more detailed descriptions of the observed phenomena and strived for what they thought of as systematic objectivity (Herskovits 1948). Ralph L. Beals, a pioneer of modern Mexican ethnography, for example, described the deer dancer's behavior: "He dances solemnly, never smiling or laughing, and imitates the actions of the grazing deer" (1943, 68). In an expanded account, published a couple of years later, he wrote,

> The deer dancer dances at the same time the pascola dancers are dancing to the drum and flute, although not coinciding exactly. He does not costume himself until the music has started. His music is furnished by three or four singers singing the deer songs. One of the singers beats an inverted gourd floating in a wooden bowl of water set in the ground. The other two or three scrape notched rasping sticks, one end of which rests on a half gourd on the ground. The deer dancer wears a white kilt about the waist extending nearly to the knees. The upper part of the body is bare or covered with a flesh-colored jersey. The kilt, a small sheet, and two 'kerchiefs are furnished by the fiesteros [officials of the ceremony]. The deer dancer has cocoon rattles on his legs and a leather belt about his waist from which a hundred or more dew claws of deer dangle on strings. This is called gruhútisia. On his head is fastened a stuffed deer head (másokóbata), the horns adorned with paper flowers and streamers. He carries two large gourd rattles (aibósi) in his hands which are rattled continuously while he dances. He steps about slowly when dancing, imitating realistically the movements of a deer grazing and raising its head to look about. At intervals he rests a few moments. He never speaks and his mien is always serious. He does not smile. He ignores his audience. When the dance is over, he removes the deer head and sometimes his belt and usually leaves the dance place until it is time to dance again.
>
> (Beals 1945, 122–123)

No doubt Beals tried to convey a faithful representation of the deer dancer's attire and behavior, carefully attempting to avoid a subjective or speculative interpretation of the phenomenon (see also Spicer 1962; Kurath 1966). (In fact, his account largely corresponds with the practices of today's Yaqui and Yoreme communities.) But one wonders how much Beals's description was tainted by the deep-seated stereotype of the "stoic Indian," which photographer and ethnologist Edward S. Curtis so famously portrayed in his twenty-volume magnum opus, *The North American Indian* (1907–30).

Musicologist Leticia Varela (1986), likely influenced by Victor Turner's symbolic anthropology (1969), interpreted the deer dance as a symbol of the battle between the man-hunter (*hombre-cazador*) who hunts for sustenance and his victim, the deer who defends itself desperately but finally offers itself to man. Larry Evers and Felipe Molina hold that the deer dance is interpreted by the Yaqui "as gathering the wilderness world into a symbol of earthly sacrifice and of spiritual life after death" (1987, 129). Although Christian interpretations of the drama of resurrection are recurrent in the popular writings about the deer dance, Evers and Molina reject any parallels drawn between the deer and the "lamb of God" (1987, 129). Their interpretation is backed up by the fact that one of the authors, Felipe Molina, is a native deer singer who served as governor of Yoem Pueblo, Arizona, and as a member of the Pascua Tribal Council.

Contemporary ethnographer David Shorter holds that "[a]ll of the ethnographic literature, as well as the fieldwork that I carried out among Yoemem [Yaquis], suggest that deer dancing is associated with hunting—as a means of securing appropriate relations with the animal and plant world, especially the deer," and concludes that "[d]eer dancing, as a pre-hunting ritual, demonstrates Yoeme–deer reciprocity and an acknowledgment of their mutual sacrifice" (2007, 282, 300). It should be noted that Molina was one of Shorter's main interlocutors, which may explain why he has come to similar conclusions. In contrast, Mexican anthropologist Jesús Á. Ochoa Zazueta (1998), whose fieldwork was based in northern Sinaloa among the Yoreme, interprets the deer dance as a form of creation myth, not a mythification of the hunt.

Beyond historical and ethnographic accounts of the deer dance, another relevant body of literature is the writings on "animal impersonation songs" (Keeling 2012), which have interested scholars for many years, a majority of whom contend that performers simply *assume* or *act* the character of animals.[7] Notable exceptions are ethnomusicologist Lorraine Donoghue Koranda (1972) and anthropologist and filmmaker Barbara Myerhoff (1974). Describing the hunting songs she had recorded in Alaska, Koranda writes, "In many of the songs the animal speaks; often the animal takes human form. There are also instances of *man becoming animal*" (Koranda 1972, 1, quoted in Keeling 2012, 248; italics added). Myerhoff (who was deeply influenced by symbolic anthropology) wrote about the sacred journey of the Huichol, an Indigenous group from west-central Mexico who are linguistically related to the Yoreme. Striving to "consider Huichol religion and symbolism primarily in their own terms," Myerhoff emphatically insisted that the statements by the shaman Ramón "had to be taken as literal, not symbolic. The *peyoteros* were not 'acting like' the deities or impersonating them. There was no place for 'as if's' in the ritual; the participants had been transformed, and for them the experience was immediate and direct, not symbolic" (1974, 21). In the conclusion she adds that Wirikuta (the Huichol equivalent of juiya annia, the enchanted world) "is not an imaginary place" (263). Such insights are quite astonishing given the date of publication, as they resonate with current ideas about Indigenous ontologies and epistemologies, especially in the Amazon (Brabec de Mori et al. 2015; Lewy 2016; Brabec de Mori and Winter 2018).

BECOMING DEER

None of the literature about northwestern Mexican Indigenous people mentions transformations of dancers into animals. As for the Yoreme, neither the ethnomusicologist Miguel Olmos Aguilera (1998, 2013) nor Ochoa Zazueta (1998) talks about transformations. The fact that Yoreme refer to the deer dancer simply as *maaso* (deer; *venado* in Spanish), not dancer, and to the singer-musicians that perform during his dance as *maaso buicleerom* (deer singers) was not further scrutinized. (As I will explain in more detail below, in the ceremony, the deer dancer transforms into *seegua yoleme*, which can be translated as flower-deer-man or simply deer.) Ochoa Zazueta even reiterates a story he was told about the origin of Yoreme music making in which twin brothers become *venado-hombre* (1998, 202–206). In the story, one of the brothers transforms into a deer (venado) while the other is incapable of doing so and thus remains human (hombre). Ochoa Zazueta understands the narrative as a myth, symbolic at most, and does not further interpret its meaning. Yoreme must have told both Olmos Aguilera and Ochoa Zazueta—as they told me on various occasions—that there were still a few (pascola and deer) dancers that "became the animals they danced."

Although I had attended numerous ceremonies on various occasions, it was not until some years into my fieldwork that I finally grasped the meaning of these statements. In 2008, I went to a pájko in the *centro ceremonial* (Indigenous ceremonial center or "church") of an *ejido* (communal village holding) close to the city of Los Mochis in northern Sinaloa, where Vicente Limón, an accomplished deer dancer, had been invited to participate. The ceremony had started in the early morning with only a few onlookers. During evening rituals, it was often too dark to take pictures, so I took the opportunity to approach the dancer to take still photographs. Upon showing Limón the pictures some days later, he looked at me rather perplexed: he did not remember seeing me at the ceremony. As the only person present with a camera at the event, and having encroached upon the ritual space to take close-ups, his reaction puzzled me. When I related this story to other Yoreme, they pointed to the photograph (see Figure 15.1): "Look at his eyes," they told me. "He does not see with his own eyes; he sees through the eyes of the deer. He has become the animal."

Here, I couldn't help being reminded of Hannah Arendt's remarks in a letter to Martin Heidegger on March 20, 1971, from New York: "Wie seltsam, dass wir sehen müssen, um das *wahrzunehmen*, was wir nicht sehen können" (Arendt [1971] 2013, 363; italics added). The text was later translated into English as follows: "How strange that we have to see in order to *perceive* what we cannot see" (Arendt and Heidegger 2003, 174; italics added).[8] The original German verb "*wahrnehmen*," which may also be understood as "to take for real" (*wahr-nehmen*), points to the *veracity* of our perception. Hence, when

FIGURE 15.1: *Maaso* Vicente Limón, Centro Ceremonial, Ejido, 5 de Mayo, Los Mochis.

(Photo by Helena Simonett, 2008)

I finally noticed Limón's empty eyes on the photograph, it made me "real-ize" (understand clearly, make real in the mind) that a transformation had indeed occurred, that it was real, that, ensounded by the deer singers, Limón's sense of being had changed, and he truly saw the unfolding of the world through the eyes of the deer. Following Philippe Descola's ontological typology, this way of knowing the world is only possible from the vantage point of a type of analogism that is based on metonymical associations between man, deer, and flower, which I discuss in detail below.[9]

Unlike Yaqui deer dancers, who wear a white headscarf that covers their eyes and prevents them from seeing where they step, Yoreme do not cover their eyes. Beals noted that the deer dancer "does not costume himself until the music has started" (1945, 122). Indeed, after the three deer singers have sat down to "warm up" their instruments (a water drum and rasping sticks), the dancer mounts the stuffed deer head (*maaso cobba*), which is decorated with white silk paper flowers and ribbons. With a shattering shake of his handheld gourd rattles, he bends forward, his body tensed. The gesture of mounting the deer head is a sign that indicates to everyone at the ceremony the beginning of his transformation. The shattering sound of the rattles likewise serves as a sonic clue of his readiness to enter the deer world. Supported by the accelerating, pulsating beat of the water drum and the rasping sticks, singers and dancer enter juiya annia, fully entrained to one another and synchronized.

As Martin Clayton, Rebecca Sager, and Udo Will have observed (2004), entrainment in music is rooted in physical, social, and emotional aspects of the human experience. Entrainment is particularly vital for the performance of the deer songs, in which the words are sung in a more or less synchronized fashion by the three deer singers. It is important to emphasize that the words of these songs are not poetry, as some scholars have claimed (e.g., Evers and Molina 1987). Rather, they are created in the moment of ritual singing, using archaic expressions, formulae, and repetitions (see Simonett 2012). In order to create the songtexts, the three singers must not only entrain rhythmically to the "external auditory pulse" they are playing on their instruments; they must also "time-lock their behavior by integrating information across different sensory modalities" (Phillips-Silver et al. 2010, 3). The songtexts of the deer singers and the gestures of the deer dancer emerge from shared knowledge and experiences that result from inhabiting a common environment—the semi-desert of northwestern Mexico. Facilitated by the regular recurrence of rhythmic patterns that the deer singers produce on the water drum and rasping sticks, the sung world (*el mundo cantado*) completely absorbs the dancer. This being-together-in-time creates a special world of time, one that can only be experienced performatively. Moreover, the ritual environment is sensorially dense and thus conducive to trancing (Simonett 2014).

In *Becoming Animal* (2010), cultural ecologist and phenomenologist David Abram suggests that living beings are interrelated through their common sentient presence in the world, arguing that we can only become fully human by growing into our animality. Here, the phrase "becoming animal," which Abram adopts from Gilles Deleuze and Felix Guattari ([1980] 1987), is used metaphorically. I would argue, however, that if one is taking on what Abram calls a "participatory mode of perception" (1996, 27), the possibility of becoming animal in a real sense lies within humans' ability—particularly if we acknowledge non-Western ontologies. Although one might argue, along with Maurice Merleau-Ponty, that perception is always participatory and that it is through our bodies that we are able to perceive other (human as well as nonhuman) bodies and recognize them as other experiencing subjects, anthropologists had often not taken human-animal transformation at face value and instead had written it off as supernatural belief. From an Indigenous perspective, however, there is a substantial kinship between all sentient beings, and humans have a close affinity with other mammals and birds, particularly those that share their environment. "To be animal" is a distinctive way of understanding what it is to be a "human being." Because of, as philosopher Johanna Seibt writes, "the dynamic sense of being as becoming or occurrence, the conditions of spatio-temporal existence, the kinds of dynamic entities, the relationship between mind and world, and the realization of values in action" (2018), the phenomenon of human-animal transformation is indeed of philosophical concern.

FLOWER-DEER-MAN SUNG INTO "EK-SISTENZ"

Every human lives in a world of meanings, within which they imbue their existence with significance (Guignon 2012a, 2012b). As socially and culturally situated moral agents, individuals "are indebted to the historical traditions of a community, within and through which [their] self-interpreted life narrative makes possible a kind of freedom that enables meaningful choice" (Martin and Bickhard 2012, 11). If we wish to understand the deer dance phenomenon, we must take seriously the truth claim the Yoreme make. It requires setting aside our own commonsense views and prejudices, as Merleau-Ponty pointed out in the introduction to his magnum opus, *Phenomenology of Perception*: "[i]n order to see the world and to grasp it as paradoxical, we must break with our familiar acceptance of it" ([1945] 1962, xv).[10]

Following anthropologists of the ontological turn, I suggest that rather than trying to establish what is real or unreal to outsiders, we must suspend assumptions and implicit judgments about how things have to be. In order to do so, the modern Western way of thinking and knowing, and the ontological privilege that Western philosophy has granted to humanity, must be called into question. In his seminal book, *Beyond Nature and Culture* ([2005] 2013), the French anthropologist Phillippe Descola argues that the Western scientific way of differentiating between classes of beings is based on specific assumptions about their interiority (such as subjective or mental properties) and physicality (such as material properties)—assumptions that may not be shared by other societies.[11] Considering Descola's four fundamental generative principles can help us to understand the elementary components that form the relational systems that give meaning to the different possibilities of human existence ([2005] 2013, 124–125). Figure 15.2 shows the interplay of similarities and differences between the different entities (human or nonhuman) at the levels of interiority and physicality.

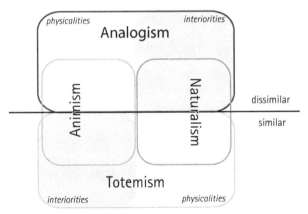

FIGURE 15.2: Philippe Descola's four major types of ontologies, adapted from Descola ([2005] 2013, 233). As the diagram shows, an animistic ontology is incompatible with a scientific (naturalistic) one. Animists hold that the physicalities of various classes of beings are discontinuous from one another, while their interiorities are continuous; in other words, from an animistic perspective, animals, for example, have bodies that are different from human bodies, but their souls, minds, or cultures are similar to those of humans. Animism and analogism overlap in that both maintain that bodies of different classes of beings differ from one another. In contrast, analogism is entirely opposed to totemism.

For Descola, the four cosmologies (animism, naturalism, totemism, and analogism) "define particular identities by the relations that institute them rather than by reference to reified substances or essences" (Descola [2005] 2013, 31). Animistic societies in the Amazon, for example, confer upon animals and plants attributes that are ascribed to humans and their social relations (e.g., intention, affect, speech, social structures, ritual activities, ethical codes), and they do this despite the fact that humans and nonhumans have different physical features (Viveiros de Castro 2015). Because of this, animistic cosmologies admit the possibility of communication and interaction between human and nonhuman beings, which Western science categorizes as sharply different (Descola [2005] 2013, 31). According to a naturalistic ontology, "nature" entails many different kinds of human and nonhuman, animate and inanimate entities, which are all united by the fact of their material being. Despite belonging to the same species, humans are thought to distinguish themselves from each other by their "cultures"; at the same time, humans differentiate themselves from nonhuman beings by way of "a reflective consciousness, subjectivity, an ability to signify, and mastery over symbols and the language by means of which we express those faculties" (Descola [2005] 2013, 173). According to Descola's scheme, analogist ontologies, such as that of the Yoreme, are partially compatible with naturalism (as well as with animism; see Figure 15.2) for they share some of the same characteristics. While naturalism holds that there is a dissimilarity of interiorities, analogism stipulates a difference of both interiorities and physicalities, although these differences are gradual and tend toward continuity (see Figure 15.3).

I would like to emphasize here that Indigenous viewpoints have often been written off by Westerners as "belief" or "superstition" instead of as ways of thinking and knowing based in a different ontology. Indeed, Yoreme do not naïvely assume that the deer dancer has transformed into a being with a deer heart, antlers, and hooves. In an analogical world, the whole collection of existing beings is divided up "into a multiplicity of essences, forms, and substances separated by small distinctions," which nevertheless can be recomposed "into a dense network of analogies that link together the intrinsic properties of the entities that are distinguished in it" (Descola [2005] 2013, 201). Thus,

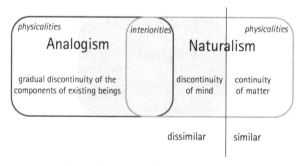

FIGURE 15.3: Comparison of naturalist and analogist ontologies in terms of the distribution of existing beings according to interiority and physicality (simplified scheme).

this ability to detect similarities between things, both animate and inanimate, and put them into a meaningful relation to one another is crucial for understanding human-animal transformation as practiced by the Yoreme.

Before going into more detail, I would like to direct attention to the philosophical understanding of "being" in Continental philosophy, which, like the analogist ontology, is concerned with the dynamic essence of human existence. According to Merleau-Ponty, phenomenology is "a philosophy which puts essences back into existence, and does not expect to arrive at an understanding of man and the world from any starting point other than that of their 'facticity'" ([1945] 1962, vii). Yet, existence does not simply mean the fact of being-in-the-world: it is *Dasein* in a Heideggerian sense of living out our possibilities (Heidegger [1946] 1996, 327; [1927] 1962, 33). As philosopher Tom Greaves explains, Heidegger invites us to "radically rethink the kind of beings that we are" (2010, 32). Greaves provides a useful commentary on Heidegger's concepts of thrownness and of facticity.

> What anchors or mobilizes the facts of any situation into which Dasein is thrown is thus the understanding of itself that it is working out as it lives. The facts of life are recalcitrant and immobile to the extent that we have, as we all have to one extent or another, a received understanding of ourselves that comes to us from our earlier selves and from others. Sometimes there is a tendency to think that it is our embodiment that presents us with the most recalcitrant and immobile facts. We may feel that while we can replace, alter or escape anything else in our situation, our bodies are always there and cannot be "escaped." It is always as embodied that I am thrown into a situation. However, this does not mean that the facticity that arises from being thrown into a situation as embodied is not open to question. . . . [L]iving out a situation . . . might involve very significant changes in our own embodiment. (2010, 29)

Dasein thus forms an understanding of its own openness, its ontological relation to what surrounds it. According to Heidegger, "life is a domain which possesses a wealth of openness with which the human world may have nothing to compare" ([1929–30] 1995, 255). Yet, life is always being-in-a-world with one another, one in which we are "never simply faced with other living beings, but . . . [are] transposed into their environment" (Greaves 2010, 34). Heidegger further developed this idea in his 1951 lecture "Bauen Wohnen Denken" (Building, dwelling, thinking; Heidegger 1971, 141–159),[12] where he used the term "dwelling" to capture the distinctive ontological manner in which we *belong in* the world as human beings with, and caring for, others. In this splendid address, Heidegger leads us through his specific way of historical and etymological thinking about the concept of "dwelling" (*wohnen, bleiben, verweilen*). In doing so, he reaches back to an earlier moment in the history of the German language to resuscitate the older sense of the notion of dwelling, showing how the phrase that today is used to assert one's existence—*ich bin* (I am)—is related to the Old High German word *buan*, which evolved into the modern German words *bauen* (to build) and *wohnen* (dwelling). The words *bleiben* (to remain) and *verweilen* (to linger), which are the other meanings of "dwelling," are linked to the idea of *zum Frieden gebracht* (being pacified). *Freien* is an older German word for *schonen* (to protect, to take care of) or *in seinem Wesen belassen* (literally "to leave in its being"; to allow something to be itself). Heidegger concludes his line of reasoning with the assertion that *wohnen ist Menschsein* ("dwelling is being-human"); being-with and caring-for are thus fundamentals of human existence. The anthropologist Tim Ingold has expanded on Heidegger's reflections on the essence of dwelling, arguing that humans "are brought into existence as organisms-persons within a world that is inhabited by beings of manifold kinds, both human *and non-human*" (2000, 5; italics added). "It is in dwelling upon the land—in the senses both of inhabiting it and of sustained focal attention towards its ancestral essence in acts of ceremony—that people forge their sense of being," Ingold observes (144).

These ideas of the thrownness of being and its mode of dwelling, in particular its horizon of possibility, shall serve as a starting point for exploring the Yoreme concept of juiya annia, where the flower-deer-man dwells. Both a physical space and a place that is perceived and remembered, juiya annia is evoked in the ceremonial fiesta that takes place under the *enramada*, a shelter with a cover made of interwoven twigs and leaves, which is traditionally attached to the Yoreme house to protect inhabitants from the burning sun. Branches from the *alamo* (cottonwood tree), which is considered sacred due to its healing powers, adorn the shelter. But the foliage is more than decoration: its scent contributes to the multisensorial setting of the fiesta, inviting participants to immerse themselves in the enchanted world of the surrounding *monte* (mountainous area). Here, the word "enchanted" does not mean imaginary or unreal: juiya annia is a concrete, sensorially perceivable (*wahrnehmbare*) world (Simonett 2012).

Sunk in the shining, shimmering, iridescent, always changing play of light, the landscape is described expressively in the *cantos de venado* (deer songs). It is the world as seen through the eyes of seegua yoleme, a Yoreme expression that translates as flower-deer-man. Uniting concepts that are separate in other languages, the term could be translated into Spanish literally as either *flor nativa/indígena* (native/indigenous flower) or *hombre-flor* (man-flower); used in this combination in the cantos, seegua yoleme refers to the maaso (deer) (see Figure 15.4). Based on Western conceptions of Indigenous utterances, such relations have often been inaccurately understood as metaphoric. Writing about the Nahua language, which like Yoreme (Mayo) belongs to the Uto-Aztecan language family, Miguel León-Portilla (1969), for example, argued that "flower and song" was the metaphorical name that the Aztecs gave to the word "poetry." More recently, however, this kind of textual interpretation has been criticized by the musicologist Gary Tomlinson, who holds that "the pervasive metaphoricity of modern Western culture might well appear a measure of our inability to perceive propinquities in the world more readily apparent—or simply more prized—in many other cultural settings" (2007, 27). Developing a different approach to meaning in Nahua language and culture, Tomlinson has proposed a Nahua "grammar of metonymies-collapsing-toward-identities," in other words, a form of meaning-making in language that posits continuity among the elements that relate. Put in a broader context, metonymies-collapsing-toward-identities could be seen as the linguistic expression of the emphasis

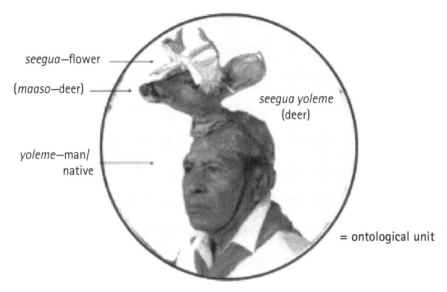

seegua–flower

(*maaso*–deer)

seegua yoleme
(deer)

yoleme–man/
native

= ontological unit

FIGURE 15.4: Continuity among beings collapsing into sameness: *seegua yoleme*, the ontological unit of the flower-deer-man.

on continuity in analogism, which exalts likeness into identity. Hence, "[i]t is not a question of songs being like flowers but simply of songs *being* flowers" (Tomlinson 2007, 75; italics in the original). From a Yoreme analogical perspective, then, the concept of seegua yoleme is not a human being that is *like* a deer but rather a "being man–being deer–being flower" (Simonett 2012). As Descola observes,

> Analogy is a flexible and polyvalent means of producing resemblances [between things] that is likely to make use not only of symmetry but of various forms of inversion, encompassment, and division. To this may be added links of attraction or sympathy, that is, action at a distance, which is also metonymic at least in the sense that it brings together in a sui generis relationship the previous separate relations that each thing had with its neighboring things. ([2005] 2013, 205–206)

Similarly, in *Thinking through the Body*, the archeologist Mark Pluciennik proposes to develop "ways of thinking, writing, doing . . . which do not necessarily privilege epistemologies and ontologies which tend to assume that things (words, images, parts of bodies and . . . artefacts) are in a metaphorical or representational relationship to the 'real'" (2002, 229). As I have noted elsewhere (Simonett 2012, 147), the relationship among the concepts of "flower," "deer," and "man" displays just this kind of metonymy and is not metaphoric. As Tomlinson observes, in Indigenous Mexican cultures, metonymy "is not a connection of part to whole but rather the contact of proximate aspects of the world, in contrast to the relations across distance struck up in metaphor" (2007, 73). In the context of the deer dance, this is a metonymy that—in the moment of ritual transformation—collapses into sameness. Describing the metonymic relations of flower, deer, and man, the ritual specialist Bernardo Esquer López explained to me, "The first humans originated from the flower, that's why the deer is called *seegua yoleme*: *flor indígena* or *hombre flor*" (personal communication, May 10, 2007; translated from Spanish). But this is not simply a word play: the deer *is* seegua yoleme. In the ritual, the deer dancer becomes the deer—the deer who comes into existence by eating the flowers of the "sacred tree." Figure 15.4 illustrates the flower-deer-man ontological unit, which emerges in the ritual. What to us appear as three different entities—a man, a deer head, and a flower—is for the Yoreme who partake in the ceremony simply one: seegua yoleme is the ontological manifestation of the transformation into sameness.

The flower and deer head that the dancer wears are, thus, not mere decorative objects or things that represent the deer. They belong to a complex set of relations that connect to other things or manifestations of the world, ones whose meaning is mostly hidden and, phenomenologically speaking, relies on the maaso (deer) to be brought into the clearing. The image of the deer stepping out of the dark forest into the bright clearing—a space in which the trees are thinned out, cleared out, or *lightened*—is not simply a metaphor or a play on words: the German *Lichtung* means both clearing (in the forest) and lighting. It is a place filled with sunlight, where things can be seen (i.e., *wahrgenommen*). In Heidegger's use of the term, the word *Lichtung* refers to an open space in which human existence can be newly conceived (1927, 133). Dasein's coming into the light (*Licht*) means its attainment of the understanding of truth in general. For the Yoreme, the clearing is opened up by a special human being (the dancer) with a unique way of being—that of seegua yoleme.

Holistic modes of perception, ones that make non-metaphoric connections such as these, are not unique to the Yoreme; rather, they are fundamental to Indigenous epistemologies around the world. Their underlying ontologies, the ways people find themselves in this world with others, however, may vary quite a bit (see, for example, Hallowell 1960; Scott 1989; Descola and Pálsson 1996; Anderson 2000; Ingold 2000; Brabec de Mori 2012; Viveiros de Castro 2015; Neurath 2015). As Colin Scott explains, "a society which concerns itself with analogies between phenomena in the world and itself will precipitate its own conventional context (e.g. communicative reciprocity [between Cree hunters and geese]) as the innate character of phenomena in general" (1989, 196). This is true not only of present Indigenous societies but of past ones as well. Esther Jacobson's analysis of ancient drawings and sculptures from shamanistic traditions in Siberia, in which the deer played a major role as cosmogonic source, lets her conclude that "[o]ne cannot help but find in the early images of the deer with tree-like antlers a prefiguration of the insistent shamanic conflation of deer, tree, and birds" (1993, 179). To perceive such apparently disparate concepts as a totality, as what Tomlinson would call "the interplay of adjoining parts of a whole" (2007, 41), seems to have been pervasive in past Indigenous ontologies, particularly those that understand the world in an analogical mode.

But what is the relation of these apparently different but linked objects? And why is it so difficult for those whose minds have been formatted in a naturalistic ontology to grasp the truthfulness of such different epistemologies and ontologies? To answer these questions, it must first be pointed out that in everyday life Yoreme, of course, do not always link the terms of flower, deer, and man. Further, it is not the terms that are similar but the relations between these entities. As we observed above, Descola maintains that "metonymic links include, in the first place, analogy in the strict sense, which applies to similarities among, not things themselves, but the relations that they maintain" ([2005] 2013, 205). These relations are unstable due to the multitude of components of each entity, but they can be momentarily stabilized in ritual actions such as dancing. Hence, it is through temporary relational engagements between persons and nonhuman persons—including what we used to call things (such as plants, crosses, statues, etc., which for Yoreme belong to the same cosmos as humans)—that, during the ceremonial fiesta, the deer dancer is able to become seegua yoleme (i.e., a deer) and can be perceived (*wahrgenommen*, "taken for real") as such by the attending Yoreme. "Relationality," religious studies scholar Amy Whitehead holds, "operates from the basic assumptions that all persons, human persons, statue persons, plant and animal persons, etc. are . . . equally capable of drawing one another into being in moments of active relating, and from the unique properties/ perspectives of their 'bodies,' whether deliberate, spontaneous or immanent" (2015, 105). I argue that, in the deer dance, it is the sensorially saturated ritual context, the scents, sights, and sounds, that allows for this "moment of active relating" to happen.

Thus, in accordance with the phenomenological method, we are not concerned with how we encounter things in the world but how our "directing ourselves towards things brings about their appearance" (Greaves 2010, 11). Seen in this way, it is not our everyday understanding of something objectively and self-evidently given—a man with a deer headdress—that is of interest, but the phenomenon as it "manifests itself, as opposed to merely appearing in or through some representational or referential intermediary" (Carman 2001, 563). Only in performativity, in ritual acts that bring things into the world, can the ordinarily hidden aspects of "what shows itself" (Heidegger [1927] 1962, 91) be disclosed and seized. The maaso, thus, must keep dancing.

To reiterate Whitehead's statement, relationality is not one-directional: it is as much the flower-deer that obligates the dancer to dance and, hence, into becoming the flower-deer-man, as Yoreme believe. Because individuals are "called" by other-than-human powers to serve in specific functions in the fiesta, they feel morally obligated to participate. Hence, not just anyone who wishes to be a dancer will be a successful one. Not just anyone who mounts a deer headdress becomes enchanted. On several occasions, I overheard Yoreme making scornful comments about uninitiated deer dancers that only imitate the movements and gestures of the deer but do not undergo the transformation: "bailan a rumbo" (they dance foolishly), veteran deer dancer Rosario Anguamea Valenzuela said to me (personal communication, May 12, 2010), or "baila cumbia" (he is dancing cumbia), a phrase used in a joking manner to describe the inappropriate hip shaking that an uninitiated dancer uses to make the deer hooves tangling from the belt rattle.[13] Even dancers who have been "called," such as Vicente Limón, must practice for many years in order to become a specialist.

The cantos do not describe a static landscape, as might be captured in a painting or a photograph, Esquer López told me in a conversation about the compositional process of the cantos. Rather, it is a *temporized* landscape—a landscape that is actively mediated through song and dance. From an external vantage point, the singers describe what the deer perceives as he is threading his own paths through the "meshwork." (Coined by Ingold [2011, 63] to explain how beings inhabit the world, the term "meshwork" is a fitting way to describe the landscape of impenetrable thorn bush found in this semi-desert region.) According to Esquer López, the cantos sketch momentary moving images, such as the sun and wind playing with the colors of the sky and the tree foliage. Deer singers thus say that it is neither the words nor the language but the *living images*—which at the same time are images of memory that the "performers" share in order to be able to enter the same world—that appear to them and that are important for creating a canto. Because the images emerge spontaneously at a specific moment in the ceremony, the cantos are not composed ahead of time with fixed words or melodies. They are neither poems nor songs in the common sense of those terms; they are based on an appearance of a figure, shape, or pattern (see Simonett 2012, 2014). It is that mythopoetic core, encapsulated in the cantos, that forms the roots of Yoreme humanity: through the cantos, the flower-deer-man is sung into existence. The following verse from a canto de venado, sung in the ceremonial Yoreme language and freely translated into Spanish by Esquer López (and rendered by me in English), shall serve as an example:

> *Tú hombre flor que te hiciste en la naturaleza, ¿dónde fuiste a caminar?*
> *En el otro mundo donde está una rama (árbol), que apenas está saliendo una flor, y el*
> *viento cuando la mece, te hace cantar.*

> (You man-flower born from nature, where did you walk?
> In the other world where there is a tree whose flower begins to blossom and when swayed by the wind, it makes you sing.)[14]

Ultimately, what the vivid images of the cantos describe is the flower-deer-man mode of existence, his way of being in the world of the deer. Existence here is understood in a Heideggerian sense as "*Ek-sistenz*" (ek-sistence), a term he developed from the Latin *exsistere*—*ex* (out) and *sistere* (to set, to place)—which may be translated as "to stand out," "appear," "emerge," "be present," "be visible," or "to show itself" (Heidegger [1946] 1996, 326). As the ritual specialist Ignacio Escalante Buitimea explained to me in 2010, the deer comes into existence by feeding on the flowers of the sacred tree, the white blossoms of the *palo santo* (tree morning glory, *Ipomoea arborescens*) that sprout after the rainy season.

In the context of the ritual, it may also be useful to understand the coming into existence of the deer in terms of the ancient Greek word *ekstasis* (ecstasy), which means "to be or stand outside oneself" or "to remove oneself to elsewhere." By casting himself out of his own given place and time, the maaso presentifies (brings into presence, makes visible) Dasein's way of being-in-the-world to the community present in the fiesta.[15] As Heidegger shows, *Da-sein* (there-being) always understands itself in terms of its existence, in terms of a possibility of itself: the essence of "Da" (there, here) consists in its disclosedness and openness. Thus, Ek-sistenz is not only defined by being-thrown-into-the-world but also by projecting oneself, by acting in the world, by seizing the possibilities it holds.[16] Dasein can only be understood within the horizon of its temporality, and lived time is always characterized by the finality of human existence. We therefore need to look more closely into the temporality of Dasein.

BEING AS PRESENCING

The deer dance may have once been a pre-hunting ritual, as the early writings of Shorter (and others) claim, but this cannot be the reason why it is still performed and why it keeps being meaningful in the contemporary lives of Yoreme as agricultural day laborers. In fact, the deer dance should not be understood as a celebration of past hunting practices or a demonstration of man-deer reciprocity "and an acknowledgment of their mutual sacrifice" (Shorter 2007, 300). Rather, it is more aligned with what Shorter later proposed in his book *We Will Dance Our Truth* (2009)—a historical consciousness embodied in performance, dances, and traditions. Indigenous historiographical thinking, Shorter argues, "lies within the embodied acts of ritual and ceremony" (2009, 180). But what exactly is this "historical consciousness"? What kind of historical concept underlies Indigenous Yoreme thinking?

In order to address these questions, I will again take recourse to Heidegger, particularly his reflections on the verb *sein* (to be), from which several other terms are derived (such as the present participle *seiend* and its noun *Seiendheit*, *Dasein*, and the past participle *gewesen* and its noun *Wesen*). I will also discuss his work on the temporality of being (understood in the sense of happening, occurring, or unfolding [*ereignen, Ereignis, Geschehnis*]) and his ideas of "being as presencing" (*Sichzeigen, Anwesenheit*) and presentation (*Vergegenwärtigung*).[17]

When the practical order of everyday life is put in suspense, as in ritual celebration, the "now" does not unfold within linear, chronological time: we may hear the music and see the dance as a temporal succession of sounds and movements, but these things do not tell us much about the existential structures of Dasein's existence, its way of being. *Da*-sein (being *here*) is in the world; this does not merely mean that we find ourselves in a physical location in the world but that we actively inhabit the world and are defined by the ways that we inhabit it. Hence, when the dancer puts on his headdress in order to become the animal, the everyday environment, the enramada or the monte, reveals what Heidegger ([1927] 1962, 91–148) would call "the worldhood of the world" (the reciprocal relationship between Dasein and the world in which Dasein dwells), that is, juiya annia—not just for the ritual specialists but for all the fiesta participants that share this ontological certainty. Entering the world of the deer does not merely entail entering a different place; it brings the participants into another time—the time of beginnings in which the flower-deer-man dwells.

The writings of John Blacking and Roger Savage can help shed light on this. Blacking holds that dancing and music can generate a state of being "in which people become keenly aware of the true nature of their being, of their 'other self' within themselves and other human [and, I would add, nonhuman] beings, and of their relationship with the world around them" (1969, 38). For "the essential quality of music is its power to create another world of *virtual time*," beyond the world of *actual time* in which ordinary daily experience takes place (1969, 37; italics in the original). Most importantly, Blacking argues that the virtual world of time found in music is very different from the experience of ordinary time, with its succession of occurrences perceived as continuous line.

Anthropologists have often described and analyzed the structure of a ritual in terms of chronological time (Blacking's "actual time") and, if music was considered at all, they preferred a structural-functionalist analysis of music's contribution to social cohesion. Indeed, in 2007 I observed an anthropologist from Mexico City sitting all night at a Yoreme ritual, absorbed by making a meticulous chronology of the ceremonial activities and not even noticing my presence in the event. My Yoreme interlocutors, who are very much aware of what is being written about their culture, silently shook their heads at his odd interest in discerning the clocked sequence of events. To them, the ceremonial acts happen within an organic timeframe that varies each time a ritual takes place.

In fact, the deeper meaning of ritual celebrations lies not in performing a series of prescribed actions, but rather concerns an experience of what Savage calls "the other of time" (2009, 7). As Savage explains, "ritual practices in which time is surpassed by eternity, by nonbeing, or by a return to a time *in illo tempore* [time of the beginnings], for instance, are nonspeculative, nonphilosophical modes of thinking that give voice to the moods that rule over them, and for which 'eternity transcends history from within history'" (2010, 118–119).[18] In other words, in ritual, ordinary existence is surpassed, transcended, and renewed. "Trance, ecstasy, and ritual practices," Savage writes, "in suspending the order of profane existence through the creation of special worlds of time, multiply the 'eternity' experiences that in their own ways reply to the enigma of time and its other" (2010, 119). Understood in this way, time's other is a "time beyond time," the absolute (eternal) present, the fleeting moment lifted out of its fleetingness, "over which time's corrosive effect has no power" (Savage 2018, 1–2).

Transcendent experiences (such as possession, ritual healing, or trancing induced by sound and movement) push practitioners beyond ordinary concepts of time with an ontological vehemence that challenges the enigma of time's inscrutability and, ultimately, refigures not just time's unrepresentability but also the meaning of our dwelling in the world (see Savage 2010, 118–123). Supported by the multisensorial nature of the fiesta, this special time envelops all those present. Ritual actions, thus, are capable of renewing people's inherence in the world. Rather than a historical past, the deer past is the mythic time of beginnings, and entering it sustains the life of the living. Or, in Ingold's words, "[t]o compose the world is not to represent life as if it existed beforehand, but to make life come out as it grows" (Descola and Ingold 2014, 37–38, quoted in Rivera Andía 2018, 6).

Cultural practices such as the deer dance allow their practitioners to come to terms with the temporally finite condition of Da-sein. As Savage observes, "[t]o the extent that human beings everywhere are subject to the constraints of mortal existence, limit experiences [such as trance, ecstasy, or ritual practices] are among the privileged way that different cultures respond to the human condition. In this respect, limit experiences are as different as they are striking in the replies they give to the enigma of time and the other of time" (2009, 7). The apparent stability that repetitive actions grant to ritual, however, is not "an inertial inheritance" (Torrance 1994, 70; see also Menezes Bastos 2013; Brabec de Mori and Seeger 2013). Rather than being simply an empty repetition of something that lies in the past, ritual actions re-trieve (*wieder-holen*, to gather, fetch, collect again) the past by making what Heidegger would call "a *reciprocative rejoinder* to the possibility of that existence which has-been-there [*gewesen*]" ([1927] 1962, 438). Discussing Heidegger's phenomenology of time measurement that also speaks to the nature of time in ritual, David Wood explains that "[t]he immediacy of the 'now' dissolves in an activity in which a bringing about of the present, making-present, presencing, presentifying . . . grasping/affirming something as present is itself 'performed' only in conjunction with an orientation that points forward and backward" (2001, 243; ellipses in the original).

Rituals can be understood as performative engagements with time—not as simple repetition but rather as a productive dramatization of the aporia between human and mythic (infinite) time. The deer dancer is obliged to presentify (*anwesend machen*), to bring into presence (Sichzeigen), to make visible what is hidden, invisible, or inconspicuous (*unscheinbar*)[19] to people trapped in the everyday now of the present (*Gegenwart*). Ultimately, the retrieval or recollection that takes place in ritual is less concerned with what has-been-there and is more interested in what will become, as it is always with regard to the future that we engage with anything. This is the obligation of the dancer, who is sung into existence by the deer singers, all of whom spend a lifetime practicing their special skills in order to keep the community alive (see Simonett 2009).

Concluding Thoughts

"Philosophy is not ultimately about learning doctrines or positions," as Greaves reminds us, "but about provoking and allowing oneself to be provoked into thinking" (2010, xiii). Taking this to heart, I have tried to approach from a phenomenological point of view some issues that emerged during my fieldwork among the Yoreme of northwestern Mexico. I am aware that such interpretations are ethnocentrically tainted; as Hans-Georg Gadamer (1960) reminds us, sensemaking is always based on preunderstandings that we inherit by belonging to particular cultural, historical, and interpretive traditions. In that sense, my approach to the deer dance phenomenon is intrinsically hermeneutic because phenomenology itself is hermeneutic. Indeed, as Taylor Carman observes, "phenomena in Heidegger's sense stand in constant need of interpretive rediscovery, evocation, and explication" (2001, 564).

The role of singing as a constitutive element in the making of the Indigenous world is fundamental. As Tomlinson points out, the power of singing lies in the telling of "stories about the self- and world-making practices of the societies that [deploy] them" (2007, 6). The deer dancer "uncovers" in gestures the world of juyia annia, as it is ensounded by the deer singers to the fiesta participants. Songs, music, and dance provide sensory clues that afford the participants access to a world of another time—a mythological time that does not simply lie in the past but is constitutive of the future (Simonett 2009). Serving a purpose that is similar to the one poetry serves in Western culture, the cantos, in conjunction with the dance, open up the realm of truth and persuade listeners to contemplate the elusiveness of the world and the nature of being-ness (*Seiendheit*; Heidegger 1971).[20]

It must be reiterated that, rather than pointing to a historical past or some particular origin in chronological time, the deer past sustains the life of the living. Ritual actions are a presentation, a re-enactive engagement with the past that makes it one's own and allows for the self-understanding of a community. The ritual does not belong to an inert past, reified by a series of prescribed actions; rather it is, in a Heideggerian sense, a beginning that is still, that stands before us. It is therefore not the return to some point of mythological origin but the event (*Ereignis*) of inauguration itself that is valuable (Wood 2007, 143).

Not only the ways in which humans live but also how they perceive their engagement with the world are manifold. If truth has "intra-ontological validity," as Bernd Brabec de Mori has shown (2012, 78), truth cannot be claimed as the "correct view of what is purely present, but as an uncovering that takes place in and through Dasein's way of being" (Greaves 2010, 91). According to Heidegger, what determines human existence is not a specific concrete world but the fact that the human dwells in a world. Thus, the essence of humanity is determined by the "truth of being," which depends on a kind of thinking that Heidegger calls *Denken des Seins* (thinking of being; Heidegger [1946] 1996, 316). The genitive in *Denken des Seins* contains a double meaning intended by Heidegger: on the one hand, thinking is dedicated to the "truth of being," and on the other, the genitive here (thinking *of* being) refers to the fact that thinking belongs to being because it occurs precisely from being. Humans cannot simply "think ahead" and thus promote truth but must, in accordance with this double relationship, keep themselves open—thinking—to what can be achieved from being.

Deer dancing is a way of disclosing possibilities, a way of truth, because it is through dancing, like all profound cultural activity, that Dasein discloses the world to itself (Heidegger 1927). "Truth is seen, not as an intrinsic or static property of a belief, as naïve symbolic analysis often assumes; rather, it is what happens to a belief when it is invoked, activated, put to work, and realized in the lifeworld" (Jackson 1996, 11). By opening himself up to juyia annia, the dancer re-enactively engages with the past for which presentation (*Vergegenwärtigen*) and remembrance (*Erinnern*) of the deer world is crucial. But again, it is the event of inauguration itself that is valuable. The stability advocated by the ritual should therefore not be understood as "an inertial inheritance but a continually renewed endeavor" (Torrance 1994, 70).

As Rudolf Bernet noted, it has always belonged to the phenomenologist's self-understanding that their work makes something visible that is mostly hidden from people trapped in worldly life (2009, 7). In that sense, we can regard the deer dancer as a true phenomenologist who, through his dancing, invites us not only to revise our prejudices about what we perceive as being true (e.g., that we see a dancing man with a deer headdress) but also to sense the inconspicuous, to intuitively grasp the essence of Dasein. Although it has its origins in Western philosophy, phenomenological thinking coincides in many respects with Indigenous ontologies and could therefore well be regarded as an intercultural philosophy.

NOTES

1. The Jesuit missionaries used the word "*Cáhita*" to refer to the native people in the area that today is northwest Mexico. This term was based on a misunderstanding, as *Cáhita* translates literally as "nothing." Historians assume that over the course of time, the numerous *naciones* (tribes) distinguished by the missionaries in the region either merged or disappeared. The authorities began to refer to the remaining native group in northern Sinaloa and southern Sonora as "Mayo," a term that is derived from the Indigenous word *mayóa* (shores of the river). However, the people refer to themselves as Yoreme or Yoleme (pl. Yoremem or Yolemem), which is derived from the verb *yore* and can be roughly translated as "the one to be born." This resonates with Heidegger's idea of the *Seinsverständnis des Menschen* (the self-understanding of Dasein; Heidegger [1927] 1962, 372–373). Similarly, the neighboring people to the north, known as the Yaqui, call themselves Yoeme (see Shorter 2009, 5–6).

2. In the nineteenth century, others wrote about the cultures of this region as well. Ramón Corral ([1884] 1959), a Sonoran politician who served as governor of Sonora and vice-president of Mexico, described the Yaqui and Mayo in his 1884 book, *Razas indígenas del estado de Sonora* (Indigenous races of the state of Sonora). Fortunato Hernández was commissioned by the state to report on the Yaqui and Mayos (1902). Hernández apparently observed the deer and pascola dances but credited Ignacio Zúñiga (1835) for his description of the dances (1902, 93–94). José Agustín de Escudero's description of the dance (1849) may not in fact be an eyewitness account, since his wording is almost identical to Zúñiga's.

3. Here and throughout, I will give the original text of non-English historical sources in notes. All of the translations are mine. "Siempre andan alegres, prorumpiendo en alaridos; de noche se ocupan cuando no están cansados del trabajo, en sus bailes llamados el Tesguin, el Pascola, el Venado y el Coyote, en los cuales amanecen." Note that no such dance as the "Tesguin" is known. *Tesgüino* is a corn beer made of sprouted maize customarily served during ceremonies. The other three dances are still performed today.

4. "La mascara de venado es emblema de fuerza y valentía, las sonajas de cascabel de serpiente significan nobleza y extra-humano poder, y las pezuñas de antílope indican agilidad y ligereza." Note that the leg rattles are not and have never been made of the rattles of the rattlesnake but rather of the cocoons of a giant month, the *mariposa cuatro espejos* (*Rothschildia cincta*). For an analysis of the leg rattles, see Simonett (2016) and Peigler and Maldonado (2005).

5. Earlier scholars tended to recycle knowledge, often without stating the original source. Gertrude Kurath (1966), however, acknowledged Ralph Beals (1945) and Frances Densmore (1932) as sources of information, and Leticia Varela (1986) cited Kurath.

6. "Este baile consiste en simular la cacería de dicho animal por un coyote. . . . Después de mucho bailar, el venado cae agotado a los pies del coyote, quien es representado por otro danzante con la máscara correspondiente."

7. The scholars mentioned by Keeling (e.g., Wissler 1912; Murie 1914; Herzog 1935; Halpern 1967; Philippi 1979; Tanimoto 2002) were undoubtedly distinguished ethnographers, but to describe specific sounds in animal impersonation songs as *imitations* and *representations* of animals' voices makes me wonder whether such terms truly capture the essence of the sounds emitted by the singers (see, for example, Brabec de Mori and Winter 2018).

8. While this is a translation of a simple exchange of letters between two philosophers, it points to the inherent problem of translation from one language into another. As the German philosopher Hans-Georg Gadamer noted with regard to translations: "If every language is a view of the world, it is not so primarily because it is a particular type of language (in the way that linguists view language) but because of what is said or handed down in this language" ([1960] 1994, 441). This will become even more significant when we venture into the translation of Heidegger's philosophical concepts, which are rooted in his particular "language-view" (442), in the structure and etymology of the German language.

9. On Indigenous auditive knowledge systems based on Descola's ontological typology, see Brabec de Mori and Winter (2018), Brabec de Mori (2016), and Lewy (2017).

10. In the original French, the passage reads "pour voir le monde et le saisir comme paradoxe, il faut rompre notre familiarité avec lui" (Merleau-Ponty 1945, viii).

11. Descola's concepts of interiority and physicality are more complex than the explanations in parentheses would suggest. I therefore quote him in full: "The vague term 'interiority' refers to a range of properties recognized by all human beings and partially covers what we generally call the mind, the soul, or consciousness: intentionality, subjectivity, reflexivity, feelings, and the ability to express oneself and to dream. It may also include immaterial principles that are assumed to cause things to be animate, such as breath and vital energy, and, at the same time, notions even more abstract, such as the idea that I share with others the same essence, the same principle of action, or the same origin: all these ideas may be objectified in a name or an epithet common to us all. In short, interiority consists in the universal belief that a being possesses characteristics that are internal to it or that take it as their source. Physicality, in contrast, concerns external form, substance, the physiological, perceptive and sensorimotor processes, even a being's constitution and way of acting in the world, insofar as these reflect the influence brought to bear on behavior patterns and a habitus by corporeal humors, diets, anatomical characteristics, and particular modes of reproduction. So physicality is not simply the material aspect of organic and abiotic bodies; it is the whole set of visible and tangible expressions of the dispositions peculiar to a particular entity when those dispositions are reputed to result from morphological and physiological characteristics that are intrinsic to it" ([2005] 2013, 116).

12. This lecture was given on August 5, 1951, in a symposium on the theme "Mensch und Raum" (Man and space), and was the second installment of the "Darmstädter Gespräche" (Darmstadt talks) series. It was published by Neue Darmstädter Verlagsanstalt in 1952. As of October 9, 2020, an audio recording of the lecture was available on YouTube (IkarusKK 2017). The omission of the commas between the nouns in the original title of the lecture, which is intended but grammatically incorrect, is another indicator of Heidegger's holistic concept of being-human.

13. Here, the speakers deliberately used the Spanish verb *bailar* instead of *danzar*. Both words mean "to dance," but the former is used in a secular context and the latter in a more formal or sacred one.

14. I would like to point out that both literal and free translations fail to do justice to the meaning of the original ceremonial texts.

15. In his "Brief über den 'Humanismus'" (Letter on humanism), Heidegger is concerned with human existence and Dasein's capacity for self-awareness. The dividing line between human beings and animals, as if they stood in opposition to each other (Heidegger [1946] 1996, 323; see also [1929–30] 2004, 263), can only be legitimized from a modern Western point of view that distinguishes sharply between "nature" and "culture." However, since the focus of this chapter is on the deer dancer's transformation into the deer as a possibility of human ek-sistence, disputing Heidegger's anthropocentric, naturalistic view here is not my intention.

16. In German, there is a linguistic relationship between the terms "thrownness" (*Geworfenheit*) and "projection" (*Entwurf*). Heidegger brings them together in the concept of *geworfener Entwurf* (1927, 148). As can be seen, both of these words are derived from the verb *werfen*, to throw, to cast (past participle: *geworfen*; noun: *Wurf*).

17. On the difficulty of translating Heidegger's terminology, philosopher David Wood noted, "For those who rely at all on the English translation of *Being and Time*, it becomes essential at this critical point for our understanding of the significance of a phenomenological reading to return to the German original. A number of translation choices that are justified independently come together to wreak confusion. Etymological connections are lost when they are important, and parallels appear which were never intended. In the sentence that ends 'an entity which is present-at-hand (vorhanden) for everyone in every "Now" (Jetzt), is made present (Gegenwärtigen) in its own presence (Anwesenheit),' the word 'present(-ce)' occurs three times, in various forms, in English, where three quite different words are employed in German" (2001, 241).

18. The quoted phrase at the end of this passage is from Paul Ricoeur ([1985] 1988, 266).

19. Jason Alvis states that "[a]lthough the German adjective *unscheinbar* (inconspicuous) could be translated directly as the privation of appearance, as 'non-shining,' or as in-sign-ificant, it perhaps more specifically characterizes what resists providing something meaningful through signification, yet still furnishes an intelligibility with which we more implicitly are 'involved'" (2018, 212). It is quite difficult to adequately capture Heidegger's concept of *das Unscheinbare* in the English language, but I would not entirely rule out translating it as "the invisible," like Alvis does (2018, 217). It is important to note that visibility (appearance) is by no means solely dependent on visuality; other sensory modes are involved as well. See Stenger (2009) on the generation and generativity of the visible.

20. For Heidegger, poetry is not a mere amusement or a form of culture but a force that opens up the realm of truth: it "admits man's dwelling into its very nature, its presencing being" (1971, 225).

Works Cited

Abram, David. 1996. *The Spell of the Sensuous: Perception and Language in a More-than-Human World*. New York: Vintage Books.

Abram, David. 2010. *Becoming Animal: An Earthly Cosmology*. New York: Pantheon Books.

Alvis, Jason W. 2018. "Making Sense of Heidegger's 'Phenomenology of the Inconspicuous' or Inapparent (*Phänomenologie des Unscheinbaren*)." *Continental Philosophy Review* 51: 211–238.

Anderson, David G. 2000. *Identity and Ecology in Arctic Siberia: The Number One Reindeer Brigade*. Oxford: Oxford University Press.

Arendt, Hannah. (1971) 2013. "Hannah Arendt an Martin Heidegger, 20. März 1971." In *Briefkultur: Texte und Interpretationen – von Martin Luther bis Thomas Bernhard*, edited by Jörg Schuster and Jochen Strobel, 363–366. Berlin: De Gruyter.

Arendt, Hannah, and Martin Heidegger. 2003. *Letters: 1925–1975.* Translated by Andrew Shields. Edited by Ursula Ludz. New York: Harcourt.

Basauri, Carlos. 1940. *La población indígena de México: Etnografía.* Vol. 1. Mexico City: Secretaría de Educación Pública.

Beals, Ralph L. 1943. *The Aboriginal Culture of the Cáhita Indians.* Berkeley: University of California Press.

Beals, Ralph L. 1945. *The Contemporary Culture of the Cáhita Indians.* Washington, DC: Smithsonian Institution, Bureau of American Ethnology.

Bernet, Rudolf. 2009. "Die Sichtbarkeit des Unsichtbaren." In *Die Sichtbarkeit des Unsichtbaren*, edited by Rudolf Bernet and Antje Kapust, 7–10. Munich: Wilhelm Fink.

Blacking, John. 1969. "The Value of Music in Human Experience." *Yearbook of the International Folk Music Council* 1: 33–71.

Brabec de Mori, Bernd. 2012. "About Magical Singing: Sonic Perspectives, Ambient Multinatures, and the Conscious Experience." *Indiana* 29: 73–101.

Brabec de Mori, Bernd. 2016. "What Makes Natives Unique? Overview of Knowledge Systems among the World's Indigenous People." In *Proceedings of "Past Future: 2016 Seminar on the Protection of Aboriginal Wisdom Creation*," 43–61. Hualien, Taiwan: National Dong Hwa University.

Brabec de Mori, Bernd, Matthias Lewy, and Miguel A. García, eds. 2015. *Mundos audibles de América. Cosmologías y prácticas sonoras de los pueblos indígenas.* Berlin: Iberoamerikanisches Institut; Berlin: Gebr. Mann Verlag.

Brabec de Mori, Bernd, and Anthony Seeger. 2013. "Introduction: Considering Music, Humans, and Non-humans." *Ethnomusicology Forum* 22 (3): 269–286.

Brabec de Mori, Bernd, and Martin Winter, eds. 2018. *Auditive Wissenskulturen: Das Wissen klanglicher Praxis.* Wiesbaden: Springer VS.

Carman, Taylor. 2001. "On Making Sense (and Nonsense) of Heidegger." *Philosophy and Phenomenological Research* 63 (3): 561–572.

Clayton, Martin, Rebecca Sager, and Udo Will. 2004. "In Time with the Music: The Concept of Entrainment and Its Significance for Ethnomusicology." *ESEM Counterpoint* 1: 1–45.

Corral, Ramón. (1884) 1959. *Razas indígenas del estado de Sonora.* Reprint, Hermosillo, Sonora: Biblioteca Sonorense de Geografía e Historia.

Curtis, Edward S. 1907–30. *The North American Indian.* 20 vols. Cambridge, MA: University Press. http://curtis.library.northwestern.edu/curtis/index.html.

Deleuze, Gilles, and Felix Guattari. (1980) 1987. *A Thousand Plateaus: Capitalism and Schizophrenia.* Translated by Brian Massumi. New York: Continuum.

Densmore, Frances. 1932. "Yuman and Yaqui Music." *Bureau of American Ethnology Bulletin*, no. 110, 1–216.

Descola, Philippe. (2005) 2013. *Beyond Nature and Culture.* Translated by Janet Lloyd. Chicago: University of Chicago Press.

Descola, Philippe, and Tim Ingold. 2014. *Être au monde. Quelle expérience commune?* Lyon: Presses Universitaires de Lyon.

Descola, Philippe, and Gísli Pálsson, eds. 1996. *Nature and Society: Anthropological Perspectives.* New York: Routledge.

Escudero, José Agustín de. 1849. *Noticias estadísticas de Sonora y Sinaloa*. Mexico City: Tipografía de R. Rafael.

Evers, Larry, and Felipe S. Molina. 1987. *Yaqui Deer Songs—Maso Bwikam: A Native American Poetry*. Tucson: Sun Tracks; Tucson: University of Arizona Press.

Gadamer, Hans-Georg. 1960. *Wahrheit und Methode*. Tübingen: J. C. B. Mohr.

Gadamer, Hans-Georg. (1960) 1994. *Truth and Method*. 2nd rev. ed. Translation revised by Joel Weinsheimer and Donald G. Marshall. New York: Continuum.

Guignon, Charles. 2012a. "Becoming a Person: Hermeneutic Phenomenology's Contribution." *New Ideas in Psychology* 30: 97–106.

Guignon, Charles. 2012b. "Achieving Personhood: The Perspective of Hermeneutic Phenomenology." In *The Psychology of Personhood: Philosophical, Historical, Social-Developmental and Narrative Perspectives*, edited by Jack Martin and Mark H. Bickhard, 40–56. Cambridge: Cambridge University Press.

Greaves, Tom. 2010. *Starting with Heidegger*. New York: Continuum.

Griffith, James S. 1998. "Yaqui and Mayo." In *South America, Mexico, Central America, and the Caribbean*. Vol. 2 of *The Garland Encyclopedia of World Music*, edited by Dale A. Olsen and Daniel E. Sheehy, 588–594. New York: Garland Publishing.

Hallowell, Alfred I. 1960. "Ojibwa Ontology, Behavior and World View." In *Culture in History: Essays in Honor of Paul Radin*, edited by Stanley Diamond, 19–52. New York: Columbia University Press.

Halpern, Ida. 1967. *Indian Music of the Pacific Northwest Coast*. Ethnic Folkways FE 4523. LP recording and liner notes.

Hardy, Robert W. H. (1829) 1871. *Travels in the Interior of Mexico, in 1825, 1826, 1827 and 1828*. Reprint, Glorieta, NM: Rio Grande Press.

Heidegger, Martin. 1927. "Sein und Zeit." *Jahrbuch für Philosophie und phänomenologische Forschung* 8: 1–438.

Heidegger, Martin. (1927) 1962. *Being and Time*. Translated by John Macquarrie and Edward Robinson. Oxford: Basil Blackwell.

Heidegger, Martin. (1929–30) 1995. *The Fundamental Concepts of Metaphysics: World, Finitude, Solitude*. Translated by William McNeill and Nicholas Walker. Bloomington: Indiana University Press.

Heidegger, Martin. (1929–30) 2004. *Die Grundbegriffe der Metaphysik. Welt – Endlichkeit – Einsamkeit*. Frankfurt am Main: Vittorio Klostermann.

Heidegger, Martin. (1946) 1996. "Brief über den 'Humanismus.'" In *Wegmarken*, 313–364. Frankfurt am Main: Vittorio Klostermann.

Heidegger, Martin. 1971. *Poetry, Language, Thought*. Translated and with an introduction by Albert Hofstadter. New York: Harper and Row.

Hernández, Fortunato. 1902. *Las razas indígenas de Sonora y la guerra del Yaqui*. Mexico City: Editorial J. de Elizalde.

Herskovits, Melville J. 1948. *Man and His Works: The Science of Cultural Anthropology*. New York: Alfred A. Knopf.

Herzog, George. 1935. "Special Song Types in North American Indian Music." *Zeitschrift für vergleichende Musikwissenschaft* 3: 23–33.

Holden, William C. 1936. *Studies of the Yaqui Indians of Sonora, Mexico*. Lubbock: Texas Technological College.

Ikarus KK. 2017. "Martin Heidegger—Vortrag 'Bauen Wohnen Denken' (1951)." YouTube. https://www.youtube.com/watch?v=mqSSzgg5eio.

Ingold, Tim. 2000. *The Perception of the Environment: Essays on Livelihood, Dwelling and Skill.* London: Routledge.

Ingold, Tim. 2011. *Being Alive: Essays on Movement, Knowledge and Description.* London: Routledge.

Jackson, Michael. 1996. "Introduction: Phenomenology, Radical Empiricism, and Anthropological Critique." In *Things as They Are: New Directions in Phenomenological Anthropology,* edited by Michael Jackson, 1–50. Bloomington: Indiana University Press.

Jacobson, Esther. 1993. *The Deer Goddess of Ancient Siberia: A Study in the Ecology of Belief.* Leiden: E. J. Brill.

Keeling, Richard. 2012. "Animal Impersonation Songs as an Ancient Musical System in North America, Northeast Asia, and Arctic Europe." *Ethnomusicology* 56 (2): 234–265.

Koranda, Lorraine D. 1972. *Alaskan Eskimo Songs and Stories.* University of Washington Press. LP recording with liner notes.

Kurath, Gertrude P. 1966. "The Kinetic Ecology of Yaqui Dance Instrumentation." *Ethnomusicology* 10 (1): 28–42.

León-Portilla, Miguel. 1969. *Pre-Columbian Literatures of Mexico.* Norman: University of Oklahoma Press.

Lewy, Matthias. 2016. "The Transformation of the 'Worlds' and the Becoming of 'Real Humans': Amerindian Sound Ontologies in Guiana's Songs and Myths." In *Music in an Intercultural Perspective,* edited by Antenor Ferreira Corrêa, 49–60. Brasilia: Strong Edições.

Lewy, Matthias. 2017. "About Indigenous Perspectivism, Indigenous Sonorism and the Audible Stance: Approach to a Symmetrical Auditory Anthropology." *El Oído Pensante* 5 (2): 1–22.

Martin, Jack, and Mark H. Bickhard. 2012. "Introducing Persons and the Psychology of Personhood." In *The Psychology of Personhood: Philosophical, Historical, Social-Developmental and Narrative Perspectives,* edited by Jack Martin and Mark H. Bickhard, 1–16. Cambridge: Cambridge University Press.

Menezes Bastos, Rafael José de. 2013. "Apùap World Hearing Revisited: Talking with 'Animals,' 'Spirits' and Other Beings, and Listening to the Apparently Inaudible." *Ethnomusicology Forum* 22 (3): 287–305.

Merleau-Ponty, Maurice. 1945. *Phénoménologie de la perception.* Paris: Librairie Gallimard.

Merleau-Ponty, Maurice. (1945) 1962. *Phenomenology of Perception.* Translated by Colin Smith. New York: Routledge.

Murie, James R. 1914. "Pawnee Indian Societies." *Anthropological Papers of the American Museum of Natural History* 11 (7): 543–644.

Myerhoff, Barbara. 1974. *Peyote Hunt: The Sacred Journey of the Huichol Indians.* Ithaca, NY: Cornell University Press.

Neurath, Johannes. 2015. "Shifting Ontologies in Huichol Ritual and Art." *Anthropology and Humanism* 40 (1): 58–71.

Ochoa Zazueta, Jesús A. 1998. *Los mayos: Alma y arraigo.* Mexicali, Baja California: Universidad de Occidente.

Olmos Aguilera, Miguel. 1998. *El sabio de la fiesta: Música y mitología en la región cahita-tarahumara.* Mexico City: Instituto Nacional de Antropología e Historia.

Olmos Aguilera, Miguel. 2013. "Etnografía musical del Noroeste de México." In *Los pueblos indígenas del noroeste: Atlas etnográfico,* edited by José Luis Moctezuma Zamarrón and Alejandro Aguilar Zeleny, 339–373. Mexico City: Instituto Nacional de Antropología e Historia; Hermosillo, Sonora: Instituto Sonorense de Cultura del Gobierno del Estado de Sonora.

Peigler, Richard S., and Merced Maldonado. 2005. "Uses of Cocoons of *Eupackardia calleta* and *Rothschildia cincta* (Lepidoptera: Saturniidae) by Yaqui Indians in Arizona and Mexico." *Nachrichten des entomologischen Vereins Apollo, N.F.* 26 (3): 111–119.

Philippi, Donald L. 1979. *Songs of Gods, Songs of Humans.* Tokyo: University of Tokyo Press.

Phillips-Silver, Jessica, Christina Athena Aktipis, and Gregory A. Bryant. 2010. "The Ecology of Entrainment: Foundations of Coordinated Rhythmic Movement." *Music Perception: An Interdisciplinary Journal* 28 (1): 3–14.

Pluciennik, Mark. 2002. "Art, Artefact, Metaphor." In *Thinking through the Body: Archaeologies of Corporeality*, edited by Yannis Hamilakis, Mark Pluciennik, and Sarah Tarlow, 217–232. New York: Kluwer Academic/Plenum Publisher.

Ricoeur, Paul. (1985) 1988. *Time and Narrative.* Vol. 3. Translated by Kathleen Blamey and David Pellauer. Chicago: University of Chicago Press.

Rivera Andía, Juan Javier. 2018. "Towards Engaged Ontographies of Animist Developments in Amerindian South America." In *Non-humans in Amerindian South America: Ethnographies of Indigenous Cosmologies, Rituals and Songs*, edited by Juan Javier Rivera Andía, 1–56. New York: Berghahn.

Savage, Roger W. H. 2009. "Being, Transcendence and the Ontology of Music." *The World of Music* 51 (2): 7–22.

Savage, Roger W. H. 2010. *Hermeneutics and Music Criticism.* New York: Routledge.

Savage, Roger W. H. 2018. *Music, Time, and Its Other: Aesthetic Reflections on Finitude, Temporality, and Alterity.* New York: Routledge.

Scott, Colin. 1989. "Knowledge Construction among the Cree Hunter: Metaphors and Literal Understanding." *Journal de la Société des Américanistes* 75: 193–208.

Seibt, Johanna. 2018. "Process Philosophy." In *The Stanford Encyclopedia of Philosophy*, edited by Edward N. Zalta. Stanford University. https://plato.stanford.edu/archives/spr2018/entries/process-philosophy.

Shorter, David D. 2007. "Hunting for History in Potam Pueblo: A Yoeme (Yaqui) Indian Deer Dancing Epistemology." *Folklore* 118 (December): 282–306.

Shorter, David D. 2009. *We Will Dance Our Truth: Yaqui History in Yoeme Performance.* Lincoln: University of Nebraska Press.

Simonett, Helena. 2009. "Narrativity and Selfhood in Mayo-Yoreme Mortuary Rituals." *The World of Music* 51 (2): 45–64.

Simonett, Helena. 2012. "*Cantos de venado*: New Insights into Mexican Indigenous Performance and Composition Practices." In *Flower World: Music Archaeology of the Americas / Mundo Florido: Arqueomusicología de las Américas*, edited by Matthias Stöckli and Arnd Adje Booth, 137–154. Berlin: Ekho Verlag.

Simonett, Helena. 2014. "Envisioned, Ensounded, Enacted: Sacred Ecology and Indigenous Musical Experience in Yoreme Ceremonies of Northwest Mexico." *Ethnomusicology* 58 (1): 110–132.

Simonett, Helena. 2015. "Sinaloa, Mexico." In *The Ethnomusicologists' Cookbook*, vol. 2., edited by Sean Williams, 107–111. New York: Routledge.

Simonett, Helena. 2016. "Yoreme Cocoon Leg Rattles: An Eco-organological Perspective." *Transcultural Music Review/Revista Transcultural de Música* 20. http://www.sibetrans.com/trans/article/526/yoreme-cocoon-leg-rattles-an-eco-organological-perspective.

Spicer, Edward H. 1962. *Cycles of Conquest: The Impact of Spain, Mexico, and the United States on the Indians of the Southwest, 1533–1960.* Tucson: University of Arizona Press.

Stenger, Georg. 2009. "Generativität des Sichtbaren: Phänomenologie und Kunst." In *Die Sichtbarkeit des Unsichtbaren*, edited by Rudolf Bernet and Antje Kapust, 169–190. Munich: Wilhelm Fink.

Tanimoto, Kazuyuki. 2002. "Music of the Ainu, Nivkhi, and Uilta." In *East Asia: China, Japan, and Korea*. Vol. 7 of *The Garland Encyclopedia of World Music*, edited by Robert C. Provine, Yosihiko Tokumaru, and J. Lawrence Witzleben, 783–788. New York: Routledge.

Tomlinson, Gary. 2007. *The Singing of the New World: Indigenous Voice in the Era of European Contact*. Cambridge: Cambridge University Press.

Torrance, Robert M. 1994. *The Spiritual Quest: Transcendence in Myth, Religion, and Science*. Berkeley: University of California Press.

Turner, Victor. 1969. *The Ritual Process: Structure and Anti-structure*. New York: Aldine.

Varela, Leticia. 1986. *La música en la vida de los yaquis*. Hermosillo, Sonora: Gobierno del Estado de Sonora, Secretaría de Fomento Educativo y Cultura.

Velasco, José Francisco. 1850. *Noticias estadísticas del estado de Sonora*. Mexico City: I. Cumplido.

Viveiros de Castro, Eduardo B. 2015. *The Relative Native: Essays on Indigenous Conceptual Worlds*. Chicago: Hau Press.

Whitehead, Amy. 2015. *Religious Statues and Personhood: Testing the Role of Materiality*. London: Bloomsbury.

Wissler, Clark. 1912. "Societies and Ceremonial Associations in the Oglala Division of the Teton Dakota." *Anthropological Papers of the American Museum of Natural History* 11 (1): 1–99.

Wood, David. 2001. *The Deconstruction of Time*. Evanston, IL: Northwestern University Press.

Wood, David. 2007. *Time After Time*. Bloomington: Indiana University Press.

Zúñiga, Ignacio. 1835. *Rápida ojeada al estado de Sonora, dirigida y dedicada al supremo gobierno de la nación*. Mexico City: Juan Ojeda.

SECTION 6

RASA, AFFECT, ATMOSPHERE

CHAPTER 16

....

TOWARDS A PHENOMENOLOGY OF *RASA*

Theorizing from Ras *in Sikh Sabad Kīrtan Practice*

....

INDERJIT N. KAUR

IN Indian theories of the aesthetics of performance, the notion of *ras(a)* (lit. juice; flavor, essence) holds a prominent place. Not only is a good performance one in which the audience savors some flavor, the very comprehension of the performance is considered to be truly possible only through the experience of ras(a). Notions of rasa (a Sanskrit term from the first millennium BCE) and ras (its vernacular counterpart) permeate the expressive culture of South Asia,[1] and, unsurprisingly, there is a vast literature on the subject. Most of this work pertains to rasa in classical Indian aesthetics, and much of it uses an exclusively conceptual approach. In this chapter, I take a methodological turn to ethnography and a focus on the process of ras generation and its workings in everyday life to elucidate ras as a phenomenon of experience in Sikh musical worship. Drawing from Sikh philosophy and practice, and engaging ideas from Western phenomenology on perception, consciousness, and subjectivity, I investigate the musical generation of ras among participants in worship sessions to reveal the embodied nature of this phenomenon and the intersensorial, intercorporeal, and situated processes at play here.

   A phenomenological approach to understanding ras is particularly productive. Arguing for the significance of phenomenology for ethnomusicology, this book's editors have observed that "a concern for lived experience is at the heart of much of . . . [the phenomenological] tradition" (4). It is precisely the lived experience of ras for my interlocutors that stood out for me and piqued my interest in exploring this subject. In my ethnographic work,[2] I learned that rather than having a discursive engagement with the concept of ras, my interlocutors were concerned with the embodied experience of ras and of the world lived through a ras-full body. ("Rasa-full" is a term that Sarah Weiss [2003] uses to describe Javanese musical performances that have rasa. Sikh communities do not use the term "rasa," and in this chapter I have adapted her usage to translate my interlocutors' references to bodies that have ras as "ras-full.")

In engaging the phenomenological tradition to explore ras, I am drawn particularly to the work of Maurice Merleau-Ponty. If ras is *essence*, phenomenology, according to Merleau-Ponty, "is the study of essences" ([1945] 2002, vii)—the essence of a phenomenon being the directly accessed somatic experience of it, unlaced by cognitive processes such as reflection and judgment (xvi–xix). If ras as a generalized feeling in the body points to a unity of experience, perceptual activity, according to Merleau-Ponty, is at once a unified, embodied experience of a whole phenomenon, not a process of synthesizing its constituent elements. If ras is an awareness fundamentally of the body, consciousness, according to Merleau-Ponty, is fundamentally embodied and not "in the universe of things said" (xvii).

In addition to an elaboration of the embodied and embedded nature of ras and the interrelationalities at play in its experience, my research reveals the relevance that Sikhs find it has for engaging with the lived world. In this chapter, I highlight in particular the critical ethical dimensions of this phenomenon, which are central to Sikh philosophy and practice in the quotidian. These pertain to the lived social and political aspects of existence, to how one inhabits this world.

In Sikh scriptural songs,[3] a number of ras flavors are specified. Most salient is divine-ras, which is termed *har-ras* and also *rām-ras*, both of which refer to the experience of a presence of the divine. The expressions of divine-ras include *prém-ras*, the experience of feelings of love for the divine; *amrit-ras*, the sweet experience of the eternal divine; and *ānand-ras*, the bliss of divine experience. In contrast to these valorized ras, scriptural songs caution against *an-ras* (lit. non-ras)—the taste for materialistic excess. Additionally, in the context of musical worship, Sikhs refer to *vīr-ras*,[4] that of courage and valor, and with a negative connotation, to *kan-ras* (lit. pleasure of the ear), which refers to the taste for mere musical sound devoid of the flavors of the divine. Ras is also used to describe the grocery offerings from the congregation that will become ingredients in the preparation of the sweet sacrament and the communal meal served in conjunction with worship. In this chapter, I focus on har-ras in terms particularly of its most salient attribute—the absence of *dooja-bhāv* (lit. Other-feeling) which, based on its elaborations in the scriptural songs, I term non-Othering (rejecting socially created differences, such as class, caste, race, or religion)—and on vīr-ras as it pertains to overcoming discriminatory social treatment.

RAS(A)

It has often been my experience that, over the course of a session of Sikh *sabad kīrtan* (sung scriptural verse), the participatory space feels increasingly intensified and saturated with affect. I remember in particular a regular Sunday session at the Sikh *gurdwāra* (public place of worship) in San Jose, California, in November 2014, when congregants all around me seemed deeply but quietly moved and feelingful. The "stage secretary" (emcee) thanked the musicians for their "*ras-bhinna*" (ras-drenched) kīrtan. Like many congregants, I proceeded backstage after the singing to personally thank the performers for the beautiful experience. There, I could hear others comment, "Bhai Sahib, aj té bahut hī ras āya" (Respected Brother, today there was so much ras) or "Bhai Sahib, bahut hī anand āya" (Respected Brother, there was so much bliss). Meanwhile the stage secretary had moved on to other matters. I could hear his voice over the microphone, thanking the congregants for the ras (grocery) offerings they had brought for the *langar* (free community kitchen and communal meal). As is the custom, I joined other congregants to enjoy the langar in the adjacent langar hall. There, the PA system was relaying the next kīrtan session. The lyrics of the sabad (scriptural song) caught my attention:

ਰਾਮ ਰਸੁ ਪੀਆ ਰੇ ॥ ਜਿਹ ਰਸ ਬਿਸਰਿ ਗਏ ਰਸ ਅਉਰ ॥ (Guru Granth Sahib, 337)[5]

Rām ras pīā ré. Jeh ras bisar gaé ras aor.

I drank rām-ras. With which other ras are forgotten.

These words seeped into my consciousness, as it seemed to do for other congregants around me, with varying degrees of attention. At this point, the kīrtan was more in the background, as I ate the delicious spicy vegetarian meal and sweet rice pudding, sipped the hot milky tea, and chatted with friends and acquaintances seated around me.

Driving home, other sabad on ras that I had heard in the past welled up in my consciousness. One emphasized the critical importance of ras and the embodied nature of knowledge:

ਰਸਿ ਰਸਿ ਗੁਣ ਗਾਵਉ ਠਾਕੁਰ ਕੇ ਮੇਰੈ ਹਿਰਦੈ ਬਸਹੁ ਗੋਪਾਲ ॥ (Guru Granth Sahib, 680)

Ras ras gūṇ gāvao ṭhākur ké morai hirdai basao gopāl.

Ras-fully (savoring) singing the virtues of the divine, the divine dwells in my heart.

Another underscored the crucial role of the congregation in the generation of ras and knowledge:

ਸਭਿ ਸੁਖ ਹਰਿ ਰਸ ਭੋਗਤੇ ਸੰਤ ਸਭਾ ਮਿਲਿ ਗਿਆਨੁ ॥ (Guru Granth Sahib, 21)

Sabh sūkh har ras bhogṇé sant sabhā mil giān.

Peace, har-ras, knowledge, all are experienced in pious congregation.

On another occasion in the langar hall, I became aware of a young woman (in her late twenties, I would guess) who was seated diagonally across from me and enjoying the kīrtan that was relayed on the PA system as she ate langar. The kīrtan was in the participatory-chant style known as AKJ (described further below), in which the singing proceeds through cycles of intensity that culminate in the chanting of the divine name, *wāheguru*. As the wāheguru chanting would begin, her eyelids would gently drop and her body slightly sway as she slowly finished chewing her food. It was as though the food she was tasting, ingesting, and savoring was part of the same experience as that of feeling the divine. Her connection to the sounding of wāheguru chants appeared to be automatic, of great ease. Her countenance was serene, deep in experience. Even the sounds of the hustle-bustle of the langar hall, where around two hundred people socialized as they ate, seemed to be literally transduced into an energy that was peaceful.[6] The ras in the sacred words, their musical sounding and audition, and the sacralized meal and communal dining, with its attendant sounds of sociality, seemed to come together seamlessly. It is such a phenomenon of ras that caught my interest, a lived experience, an experience that is embodied, embedded, and inter-relational—in and between people, things, and words, all intertwined in a participatory social field.

In the scholarship on both popular and elite Indian musics, the dominant understanding of Indian notions of aesthetics comes via the classical Sanskrit theory of rasa, particularly as expounded in two ancient treatises, the *Nātyashāsthra* and the *Abhinavabhāratī*.[7] It is curious that despite the widespread circulation of the term *rasa* in the ethnomusicological literature on Indian music, scholars have largely focused on explicating this theory, particularly in the context of art music,[8] rather than on presenting detailed ethnographic investigations of the phenomenon as a lived experience of participants. Even in the few ethnographic studies of rasa (e.g., Slawek 1996; Nuttall 2013; Krishnamurthy 2019), the starting point and much of the discussion is abstract rasa theory. Here, there is either an implicit assumption or a goal of the scholarship to show that this ancient theory of dramaturgy works in contemporary musical practice. Eminent Indian musicologist Prem Lata Sharma (1927–1998) has argued against such an approach. In an essay published in a collection of her works (Sharma 2000), she writes with reference to "*rāga*-music of the modern times" (98): "*Rasa* in its essential form of aesthetic delight is undoubtedly present in music, but its direct analysis in terms of traditional exposition is neither fully possible nor is it warranted" (108).[9]

Following ancient rasa theory, a common thread in ethnomusicological scholarship is that rasa is produced by the performer and evoked in the encultured audience, the *rasikā* (aesthete; lit. one who tastes). Here, the relationality of the rasa experience is predominantly described as one-sided—from an agentive performer to a recipient audience. As Slawek explains it, rasa is "something to be evoked from the culturally conditioned unconscious of the aesthete" (1996, 33).[10] In such accounts, then, rasa is conceptualized as a response in the spectator's body to an external stimulus emanating from an aesthetic object that is separate from their body, even if rasa is conceptualized as something that is evoked during moments of an experiential internalization of the aesthetic object. This notion of internalization has important implications, as it suggests the containment of rasa in *discrete* and *independent* entities, namely musical sound, performers, and audiences. Another feature of this scholarship is that there is little or no contribution mentioned of the context in which rasa is experienced. Here, it must be kept in mind that the ancient theory of rasa was written in the context of drama, and the contribution of musical sound to rasa was understood in terms of its role in plot development. In this context, music was considered as one of the many constituents for an effective theatrical performance. Needless to say, the context of contemporary concert-stage art music is vastly different.

Sikh practice and the philosophy that is expressed in scriptural songs point away from a decontextualized stimulus-response model toward a co-constitution of the human subject, objects, and ras, as well as toward a participatory-immersion model of ras co-generation. Here, agency is distributed across musicians and congregants, sacred texts and their musical rendition, sacred food and other sacred articles, as well as memories and aspirations. In an example that reflects this view, one of my interlocutors, who is a committed and accomplished musician, congregant, and organizer of AKJ kīrtan sessions, remarked to me, "Ras cannot be produced, it just happens." While musicians are appreciated for their virtuosity, congregants do not consider them the sole agents for evoking the experience of ras. Nor do musicians typically claim or accept agency, deflecting compliments to the scripture or congregation. This could be ascribed to culturally learned humility, but the requirement of humility itself can be said to speak to a recognition of distributed agency.

The notion of distributed agency that I will pursue here is intended to capture the social interrelationality of all participatory entities in a context, human and non-human. It builds on Alfred Gell's (1998) conceptualization of the agency of non-living objects and of "distributed personhood." Gell critiqued the "classificatory and context free" (23) approach to defining "human beings" (who are sentient and capable of intentional intelligence) and "things" (which are non-sentient and incapable of intentional intelligence) as missing the social nature of their relationship. In contrast, he emphasized that human beings are embedded in social relationships not just with other human beings but also with things. A soldier, for example, is not just a person but a person with a gun, each constituting and affecting the other. Both the ontology and the agency of the person is relational, and the same can be said of the thing as well. If the gun fails, it renders the soldier ineffective. It is in this sense that Gell argued that there exist social relationships between persons and things, rather than just among persons, and that he ascribed agency to things, in addition to living entities. Agency for him does not manifest as "permanent dispositional characteristics of particular entities" (21) but as "relationships in the fleeting contexts and predicaments of social life" (22). In this context, he conceptualized the intertwining of objects, people, cognition, and social action as "enchainment" (141) and agency as distributed across this chain. He thus developed an expanded understanding of personhood not as "internal" (contained within the individual body) but as distributed across people and things. Thus, he wrote,

> a person and a person's mind are not confined to particular spatio-temporal coordinates, but consist of a spread of biographical events and memories of events, and a dispersed category of material objects, traces, and leavings, which can be attributed to a person and which, in aggregate, testify to agency and patienthood during a biographical career which may, indeed, prolong itself long after biological death. (222)

Gell's ideas resonate strongly with Sikh philosophy and experience. In Sikh musical worship, the *rasiyā* (lit. one who savors ras) is not the rasikā, discussed above in the context of Hindustani music—a connoisseur of musical sound, a "knowledgeable listener" of its grammatical content responding just to aural stimuli. To the contrary, the Sikh rasiyā of har-ras is by definition one who savors ethical affects, not simply musical flavors,[11] and the subject here is one part of an enchainment, a domain of interactions that I will describe below as a phenomenal field in which ras "happens." The rasiyā in the Sikh kīrtan session partakes of the "[f]oundational reciprocity between the world and ourselves" (Berger 1999, 21) in the particular context of a congregation embedded in the sacred and ethical milieu of sabad kīrtan.

My explication of the Sikh context of musical worship, and its sociality, explores in detail how all constituent elements of sabad kīrtan events are intertwined in the co-generation and co-habitation of ras and how the constituent elements of the Sikh sacred ecosystem gain potentialities in their interdependent agency. Furthermore, a consideration of Sikh worship practice and philosophy moves me away from the analysis of ras as a form of aesthetics detached from the wider lived social and political life, to one in which ras is a mode of inhabiting this world. Ras thus reveals the very ontology of the self, community, and ethics[12] and an epistemology of the divine.

These perspectives lead me to pursue a "local phenomenology" (Halliburton 2002) of ras based on philosophy and practice in the Sikh tradition and engaging Western phenomenological ideas. As ethnomusicologists have long recognized, a culture's own views about its practices are of prime importance to the way they are carried out and therefore are centrally relevant to any discussion of that culture. Sikh kīrtan practice is based on the philosophy in the sabad, even if it sometimes falls short of its own ideals. With respect to ras, Sikh scriptural verses contain rich ideas about sensation, embodiment, intersubjectivity, and ethical comportment. I see the consonance of many of these ideas with elaborations in the Western phenomenological tradition, particularly Merleau-Ponty's thoughts on perception, consciousness, and embodiment and Edmund Husserl's views on the subject and subjectivity (discussed later). Drawing on all of this and my ethnographic findings, I theorize ras as a feeling that emerges in an experiential field co-constituted by people, objects, words, sounds, actions (including musicking), memories, and aspirations. I argue that ras's ontology can be found in the flow in and across interdependent, coexistent entities; that ras is in the very motility of the body, in its fundamental motor intentionality; and that ras is the flavor of the body's very inhabitation of the world.

Bodily Inhabitation of the Lived World

In *Phenomenology of Perception* ([1945] 2002), Merleau-Ponty rejects both empiricist and intellectualist approaches to perception and knowledge, as well as the implication of these things for the nature of the person and their relation to the world. Empiricist approaches privilege the empirical sciences to explain perception as a response of the sense organs to external stimuli, enlisting perception in a cause-and-effect process. Intellectualist approaches privilege conceptual and discursive processes in the construction of sensory knowledge. Seen from such an approach, the world is made up of independently existing, discrete sensations, which are synthesized via mental attention and judgment. Eschewing causal and interpretive analyses, Merleau-Ponty pursues a methodology of description, which he considers the essential phenomenological method, with a focus on process rather than internal representations of external objects.

For Merleau-Ponty, our perception of something is never the result of an isolated stimulus acting upon us. Rather, he advances the idea that there is no "pure sensation": every sensation is "already bound up with a larger whole" ([1945] 2002, 10). "The perceptual something is always in the middle of something else," he argues, "it always forms part of a 'field'" (4). Any perceptual experience comes into formation in relation to other sensations in the field and is experienced as part of that meaningful whole. Emphasizing the interdependence of sensations in the lived world, Merleau-Ponty shifts the focus away from the causal and mechanical relationships that are dominant in what he calls "objective thought" and that require the assumption of independently experienced sensory data.

To explain the interdependence of sensation, Merleau-Ponty uses the example of color perception.[13] Here he argues that rather than an objective, constant, and standard attribute of a visual phenomenon, the perception of the color of a thing is innately connected to other properties of that thing, and these connections are the conditions under which that perception takes place. These conditions make up a "phenomenal field," which can take many forms, such as a setting, a landscape, an atmosphere, or a horizon. So, for example, the perception of the red in a red carpet is sensed in relation to the many features of that carpet, such as other colors in it, the size and shapes in its pattern, and its texture and thickness. Relevant also are surrounding factors, such as, in this example, the color and reflective properties of the surface on which the carpet is placed and of the furniture surrounding it, as well as its lighting conditions. It is important to note here that the properties in this example are not only visual but also tactile and even sonic. In Merleau-Ponty's words,

> it is impossible completely to describe the colour of the carpet without saying that it *is* a carpet, made of wool, and without implying in this colour a certain tactile value, a certain weight and a certain resistance to sound. (376; italics in the original)

Describing the carpet's color simply as red, or as a shade of red, will be an incomplete description of the sensation of the redness of the carpet. It will not capture the woolly quality of the redness and a certain softness that would be different from the redness of, say, a piece of hard red plastic. Thus, a description of color that does not account for its embeddedness in a field of sensations will be an abstraction from the lived experience of that color and will mislead us from the actual nature of the perception of color, in which our senses work together to create an intersensorial gestalt of color perception. Further, we perceive texture in color—a roughness or smoothness—because what our eyes see, the varied reflection of light on the carpet's un-uniform surface, always emerges in conjunction with what our hands and fingers know as the tactile experience of that texture.

In another passage on color, Merleau-Ponty develops these ideas by discussing landscape painting:

> Cézanne declared that a picture contains within itself even the smell of the landscape. He meant that the arrangement of colour on the thing (and in the work of art, if it catches the thing in its entirety) signifies by itself all the responses which would be elicited through an examination by the remaining senses; that a thing would not have this colour had it not also this shape, these tactile properties, this resonance, this odour, and that the thing is the absolute fullness which my undivided existence projects before itself. (371)[14]

It is this "undivided existence" of the body, with its unified sensory and motor organs, that engages with the things of the world, such as the picture of the landscape or the carpet, as perceptually united phenomena. In the examples above, the visual sensations of the landscape are bound up with its olfactory sensations, while the redness of the carpet is bound up with its tactile sensations. Rather than a cognitive mechanism that receives compartmentalized stimuli and processes information into mental representations that translate into bodily responses, perception is an inseparable part of the very motility of the body, the pre-reflexive circuits of perception and action in everyday conduct that Merleau-Ponty refers to as our "motor intentionality." This sensory-motor unification of the body is anterior to any contents of experience. The body knows itself as a coherent functional unit, not as a collection of coordinated parts. As Merleau-Ponty writes, "my whole body is not for me an assemblage of organs juxtaposed in space. I am in undivided possession of it" (112). It is this unified body that is our access to the world. In Merleau-Ponty's words,

> what I call experience of the thing or of reality . . . is my full *co-existence* with the phenomenon, at the moment when it is in every way at its maximum articulation, and the "data of different senses" are directed towards this one pole. (371; italics added)

The pre-reflexive union of the body-subject and the sensed world stems from this bodily inhabitation of the world. That is, the body does not merely exist within the space and time of the world, but rather is enmeshed with them, defined by its relations with them, and can only be understood in terms of them. Space, time, world, and body, therefore, do not exist separately from one another but in conjunction with each other, and space and time come into being along with the lived body. When I perceive space and time, I have already been part of their constitution, and they have been part of mine. They are not given, objective entities, cognized or represented. The body, in its motor intentionality, has its own situated spatiality, which enacts its perceptual field. Within this bodily motility at any instance are enfolded previous and anticipated experiences. That is, the body's pre-reflexive grasp of the world at any moment includes already incorporated, undifferentiated elements from the past, what we refer to in everyday talk as "habits." For Merleau-Ponty, these are specifically "*motor* habits" ([1945] 2002, 177; italics added), and they form the bodily means by which we bring the past into the present. Further, our moving body is always geared toward and anticipates future states of affairs. Taken together, motor habits and the future orientation of our motility create the temporality of our embodied relation to the world. The past, present, and future are thereby integrated in the body's perceptual field. In this way, the body, space, and time are part of a totality; they are sensed together in relation to each other; they construct each other. As Merleau-Ponty says, "I am not in space and time, nor do I conceive space and time; I belong to them, my body combines with them and includes them" (162). In this sense, the world and the body-subject are co-constituted.

In the context of all of this, the body's motility—its meaningful, pre-reflexive engagement with the things of the world—forms the basis of Merleau-Ponty's notion of the embodied nature of consciousness. Building on Edmund Husserl's notion of intentionality, that, in Husserl's famous phrase, "[a]ll consciousness is consciousness of something" (Husserl quoted in Merleau-Ponty [1945] 2002, xix), Merleau-Ponty argues for a kind of intentionality that is operative in pre-reflexive bodily processes and conduct, rather than in deliberated judgment. "Consciousness is in the first place not a matter of 'I think that,'" Merleau-Ponty writes, "but of 'I can'" (159). In other words, consciousness emerges primarily not in the realm of words but in the realm of one's existence, one's bodily conduct in the world, and is directed toward the world as lived. Rather than an "intellectual" phenomenon (250) that observes a world from afar and cognizes about it, consciousness is "sensible" (250), sensing itself and the lived world together and in relation to each other. Body, consciousness, and world thus come into being and develop together. This "operative intentionality" of the body "establishes the natural and pre-predicative unity of the world and of our life" (xx). Merleau-Ponty's critique of empiricist and intellectualist approaches to philosophy is thus based on their neglect of the work of an embodied consciousness, "through which from the outset a world forms itself around me and begins to exist for me" (ix).

Just as perception and consciousness are "an intention of our whole being" (92) and a way of inhabiting the world, intersubjectivity too, for Merleau-Ponty, is primarily embodied and pre-reflexive. He gives an illuminating example:

A baby of fifteen months opens its mouth if I playfully take one of its fingers between my teeth and pretend to bite it. And yet it has scarcely looked at its face in the glass, and its teeth are not in any case like mine. The fact is that its own mouth and teeth, as it feels them from the inside, are immediately, for it, an apparatus to bite with, and my jaw, as the baby sees it from the outside, is immediately, for it, capable of the same intentions. "Biting" has immediately, for it, an intersubjective significance. It perceives its intentions in its body, and my body with its own, and thereby my intentions in its own body. (410)

Thus, as bodies, we are linked together in the lived world by our fundamental corporeality and preconscious intentionalities. Our common corporeality enables a pre-personal communication; one that is "anonymous." In other words, we constitute the perceptions and relations of each other's worlds by reference to a generalized person, and this generalized person is prior to the particularity of myself as myself and the other as an other, and is in this sense anonymous. Husserl ([1931] 1977) too, in advancing his idea of the subject, understood it to be fundamentally constituted by intersubjectivity, which he saw, at its core, as a process of empathy, of pre-reflexively apprehending sameness in others.

Merleau-Ponty's notion of "intercorporeality" is intensified by the phenomenon of language, since words have a motor presence. In a spoken word, there is a link between perceptual experience and the motor sensations of phonation. As Merleau-Ponty explains,

> The word "sleet," when it is known to me, is not an object which I recognize through my identificatory synthesis, but a certain use made of my phonatory equipment, a certain modulation of my body as being in the world . . . . One day I caught on to the word "sleet," much as one imitates a gesture, not, that is, by analysing it and performing an articulatory or phonetic action corresponding to each part of the word as heard, but by hearing it as a single modulation of the world of sound, and because this acoustic entity presents itself as "something to pronounce" in virtue of the all-embracing correspondence existing between my perceptual potentialities and my motor ones . . . . ([1945] 2002, 469)

Understood in this way, shared words, as for example in shared song, entail shared articulatory gestures of phonation involved in sounding them. These motor sensations reinforce the bodily experience of the shared meanings of the words. The word *ras*, for instance, is connected to the bodily sensations of ras as a feeling and the bodily sensation of sounding the word's phonemes. A common language thus deepens communication through embodied identification and reciprocity. It establishes a commonly inhabited world. We become "collaborators for each other in a consummate reciprocity" (413).

With this backdrop of Merleau-Ponty's description of our phenomenal inhabitation of the world as fundamentally embodied, and with the idea established that perception, intentionality, consciousness, and intersubjectivity are all first preconscious affairs of the body, I proceed now to describe the phenomenon of ras in Sikh musical worship. I start by providing a thick description of the Sikh phenomenal field and then move on to the analysis of a ras-drenched (*ras-bhinna*) kīrtan session. Finally, introducing the concept of "overlapping phenomenal fields," I reflect on the durational aspects of ras and its ontological and epistemological workings outside of worship sessions in everyday life. Here, I suggest that just as the body-subject is constituted by ras-full experiences, the ras-full body projects back into the lived world with preconscious intentionality.

The Phenomenal Field of Sabad Kīrtan

Along with sacred song and musicians, the main co-constituents of the phenomenal field of sabad kīrtan are the *Guru* (spiritual preceptor), *sādh sangat* (pious congregation), and langar (communal food). They co-constitute a sensorially rich phenomenal field that is much more than just oral and aural. It is one in which auditory, visual, haptic, olfactory, gustatory, and kinesthetic sensations are all enjoined, as are memories and aspirations. Importantly too, the host of kinesthetic ritual gestures that participants partake of are imbued with ethical meanings, such as non-Othering, humility, and service. Throughout this discussion, I foreground the ethical aspects of the phenomenal field, since har-ras is the term given to the somatic experience of the divine in all its ethical attributes. I show how the ethical flavor of har-ras is experienced through nondeliberative embodied practices rather than mentalist rationalizations.

Sacred Presence

Central to the phenomenal field of sabad kīrtan is the experience of the Guru (lit. spiritual preceptor). In the Sikh context, the Guru is a multidimensional entity with intertwined perceptual, textual, human, and affective dimensions. The Sikh faith was founded by Guru Nanak (1459–1539) and shaped by nine subsequent Gurus, who lived from 1504 to 1708. During their lifetimes, they canonized about five thousand of their songs into the Sikh scripture, and as an act of non-Othering, they also included a few hundred songs known to be from saint-singers of other faith traditions, duly ascribed. The first complete compilation was scribed in 1604 and known as the Adi Granth (First book). The finalized version was completed in 1704 by the tenth Guru, Gobind Singh, who in 1708 designated it the Guru Granth Sahib (lit. respected spiritual-preceptor book) and proclaimed that after his passing, the Guru Granth Sahib, and not a person, was to be accepted as the (eternal) Guru of the Sikhs. The Sikh idea of the divine is also that of a preceptor—the preeminent one, wāheguru (lit. awesome guru). For devout Sikhs, the unblemished divine spirit dwells in all forms of the Guru—the formless divine, the ten late human Gurus, and the sacred songtexts (sabad) that form the primary scripture, the Guru Granth Sahib. Sikhs experience all these dimensions of the Guru in closely connected ways, and often as a single entity. For many, the Guru Granth Sahib is the manifest body (*pragat déh*) of the human Gurus, and they refer to the scripture as a living Guru and to its pages as *ang*, that is, body part or limb. Significantly, following scriptural songtexts, as in the example below, Sikhs themselves aspire to embody divine attributes.

ਸਤਿਗੁਰ ਕੀ ਬਾਣੀ ਮਤਿ ਸਰੂਪੁ ਹੈ ਗੁਰਬਾਣੀ ਬਣੀਐ ॥ (Guru Granth Sahib, 304)

Satgur kī baṇī sat sarūp hai gurbāṇī baṇīai.

The true Guru's word is the embodiment of truth, become this embodiment.

In kīrtan sessions, the presence (*hazoori*) of the Guru Granth Sahib is deemed essential for the appropriate and best kīrtan experience, whether at a gurdwāra (public place of worship; lit. doorway to the Guru) or in private homes. Several interlocutors have expressed to me that they feel transformed in the presence of the Guru. This point was especially driven home to me in 2005 when I was curating an outreach program of historical compositions of Sikh sacred songs to be sung by the highly regarded tenth generation kīrtan singer, the late Bhai Avtar Singh Ragi.[15] Responding to my plan to host the program in a concert hall without the presence of the Guru Granth Sahib, he said in his gentle way, "Guru di hazoori vich hi behtar rehega" (It will be best in the presence of the Guru). What he indicated was that lacking the interrelational power of the Guru's presence in its affective, ethical, epistemological, and ontological dimensions, his singing would just not be the same. He knew from embodied experience that the musician and music are themselves co-constituted with other elements in a phenomenal field.

The Guru's presence is experienced by devotees through a variety of interactive and embodied engagements and thus manifests as a phenomenal field. The Guru Granth Sahib is the presiding entity in the worship hall, which is referred to as the Guru's darbār (lit. court); there, it is majestically enthroned, center stage, on a dais, endowing it with the same respect and authority due to royalty (see Figure 16.1). The enrobing and staging of the scripture is an elaborate process, including processional singing and ritual actions.[16] Entering a Guru's darbār to participate in a worship session entails a number of attendant gestural engagements, too. Before entering the sanctuary, devotees take their shoes off, wash their hands, and cover their heads as a sign of

FIGURE 16.1: Guru's darbār at Gurdwāra San Jose, San Jose, California.

(Used with permission.)

respect to the Guru. At the threshold, they bend over to touch the floor with their hands and then swipe their fingers on their heads. The belief is that this acceptance of the *charan dhoor* (foot-dust of a pious congregation) will help embody their ethical values. In the sanctuary, devotees walk up a central aisle and approach the dais on which the Guru Granth Sahib is staged with an attendant. They place any ras (groceries) they may have brought, or a small amount of cash, at the foot of the Guru and then gesticulate on all fours, touching their foreheads to the ground as a gesture of respect, humility, and willingness to imbibe the Guru's teachings. At this point, they may stand in silent prayer for several seconds, expressing supplication or gratitude. They then circumambulate around the Guru Granth Sahib, pausing behind the dais to bow and touch their forehead to it. On the way, they may stop to place a tip by the musicians. Finally, they proceed to the attendant with the *karāh parshād* (blessed pudding) and, receiving a handful in their cupped hands, sit down to enjoy the sweet sacrament and the melodious kīrtan (see Figure 16.2). All these ritual actions come together as an embodied, experiential engagement with the Guru.

Added to the various sensorial interactions with the Guru is the singing, which consists of the very songtexts that make up the scripture, linking sound and vision intimately. In fact, in the Sikh language for the scriptural songtext, no difference is made between oral utterance and written text (i.e., between their sonic and print forms). The sabad were first sung and later compiled into songbooks and ultimately into scripture. In all these forms, these songtexts are referred to as *sabad* (lit. word) or as *gurbāni* (lit. the Guru's word-utterance). This captures the fact that the experience of sabad does not admit a sensory/textual, or word/affect, divide.

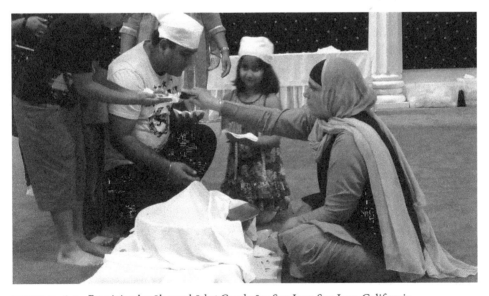

FIGURE 16.2: Receiving karāh parshād at Gurdwāra San Jose, San Jose, California.

Photo by Inderjit N. Kaur.

The engagement with the sacred text is visual, auditory, haptic, kinesthetic, psychological, cognitive, and affective all at once. The profound connection of devout Sikhs with the Guru Granth Sahib and all forms of the Guru, including the sabad, cannot be underestimated. A Sikh is definitionally a Sikh (lit. student) of the Guru. The Sikh and the Guru are thus ontologically co-constituted. The connection with the Guru is established young in life, through not only musical worship, festivals, and celebrations but also the everyday singing of sabad as lullabies and hagiographic stories of the late human Gurus. These hagiographies were traditionally oral and now are also transmitted through books, comics, and multimedia productions such as video, film, and theater.

Sabad quotes find their way into everyday speech too, in the form of phrases of inspiration, solace, gratitude, and joy. Key excerpts of the Guru Granth Sahib are also printed in smaller books—*gutkay* (which contain verse compositions), *pōthiāṅ* (which contain a section of the scripture), and *sainchiāṅ* (which contain sabad with exegesis)—and are used by Sikhs in worship sessions at the gurdwāra or at home to sing, chant, read (silently or aloud), and understand the meaning of sabad. All these book versions are kept in ornate cloth wraps and treated with great respect, the devotee often touching the book to the forehead before commencing engagement with it. Sikhs serving in the Second World War were known to have miniature versions of the Guru Granth Sahib tucked in their turbans for courage and resilience. The embodiment of courage has historically been a prominent ethic in Sikh culture, and below I will discuss how musical worship is a site for the inculcation of vīr-ras and how this ethically flavored, embodied ras might be retained for the phenomenal fields in everyday situations to affect lived conduct.

Congregation

The second significant co-constituent part of the phenomenal field of sabad kīrtan is the sādh sangat (pious congregation, lit. of similar pious ways). Members of the sādh sangat can be said to have shared constitutive experiences. In my framework, within the phenomenal field of musical worship various members co-constitute each other, and each does so in a way that is similar to, but not identical with, that of others. Congregants experience the intercorporeal field with a whole range of intensities and affects. For example, while sabad kīrtan is sung in a diverse array of musical styles and most gurdwāray (pl. of gurdwāra) have kīrtan sessions in these different styles, congregation members often have aesthetic preferences for certain kinds of sabad kīrtan rendition, and some even find certain styles unfavorable to a ras experience.[17] Many tend to go to those kīrtan sessions based on their musical style. In terms of the framework I am developing here, one could say that they find their ras-full co-constitution in their choice of a musical phenomenal field.

Congregating in formal and informal spaces for singing and chanting has long been a tradition among Sikhs, both at home and when on the move. In addition to assembling at gurdwāray, Sikhs have sought sangat for musical worship in a variety of settings—from circles of family and friends in homes to gatherings under trees when on army duty and at train depots when sent abroad as indentured laborers by a colonial government.

The scripture's ethic of the one-ness of humanity becomes embodied in the congregation through several practices. Gurdwāray and all their programs are held open house, free to people from all backgrounds. When possible, gurdwāra sanctuaries are constructed with doors on all four sides to symbolize this openness.[18] There is no required membership and no hierarchical seating arrangements or other preferential treatment for congregation members. All attendees (except those with special needs) sit on the floor together with people of all social backgrounds.[19] The inclusiveness in the congregation creates the conditions of possibility for transmission of a ras that has the flavor of non-Othering. The flow of this har-ras is a shared experience of that divine potential.

In Sikh musical worship, the practice of congregating takes on special form and significance for a community of Sikhs known as the AKJ (Akhand Kirtani Jattha, lit. uninterrupted kīrtan group). Their name derives from the fact that they congregate regularly for long kīrtan sessions that last from a few hours to all night (*raensabāē*, lit. night gathering). Importantly, the musical sounding of the sacred word is continuous and without interjection of any exegesis or announcement, not even the musicians' names. AKJ weekend gatherings, *samāgam* (lit. coming together similarly), consist of a series of kīrtan sessions at gurdwāray or homes of highly committed Sikhs. These events are open house, noncommercial, and completely mounted by volunteers. Local AKJ members get together in advance to organize and distribute responsibilities, from picking up arriving members and hosting them in their homes to arranging the sound and recording equipment to cooking, serving, and cleaning.

This emphasis on congregation is also reflected in their kīrtan ensemble structure. While the core ensemble is formed typically by only two members, the ensemble gets extended to the congregation, who sit next to and behind the lead performers (see Figure 16.3). This

FIGURE 16.3: AKJ ensemble in congregational form at Gurdwāra San Jose, San Jose, California.
(Used with permission.)

ensemble arrangement is known as *sangat roop* (lit. congregational form) and is explicitly recognized for dissolving the binarized roles of performer and audience. Below, I will further elaborate on the musical teamwork between what I call the "core ensemble" and the "extended ensemble." Here, it is important to note that it is the musicians from the seated congregation who take turns at sitting in front to assume the lead role in the ensemble and, after their turn is over, go back to their original role in the congregation. All participants thus bear the responsibility for the generation of a phenomenal field.

Communal Dining

The third major constituent of the phenomenal field of musical worship is communal dining. The pairing of worship and food has been a Sikh tradition since its founding in the early sixteenth century. Early gurdwāray functioned as rest houses for weary travelers, who stopped for free board and lodging, along with audiencing with the Guru.[20] In contemporary practice too, as mentioned above, it is typical for gurdwāray to have langar service that is open to all. Langar, the sharing of a simple vegetarian meal with all, irrespective of social, religious, and economic differences, is a cherished and proud component of Sikh worship activities (see Figure 16.4). It is an embodied practice of equality and non-Othering.[21] In the sacred setting, the ras in the langar, and in the parshād served in the sanctuary, becomes linked to the ras in the sacred word. Both

FIGURE 16.4: Langar at Gurdwāra San Jose, San Jose, California.

(Used with permission.)

need to be ingested and savored to gain knowledge of the divine, and both require an ethic of overcoming socially constructed differences.

In fact, the tongue, both as the sense organ of taste and as an organ for speech, is referred to as *rasna*. It is emphasized in the sabad that by chanting the sacred word, one develops a taste for it. This speaks to Merleau-Ponty's understanding of language, discussed above, which recognizes words as gestures of the body's organs of phonation. I have often heard in casual conversations among congregants, especially in the context of raising Sikh children, that it is most important to simply chant the sabad; this chanting, they feel, will lead to both a love for and an understanding of the sacred words, and this will teach one how to be a Sikh. I have also heard from San Francisco Bay Area Sikh parents how their children in general do not like to eat Indian food very much but love the langar in worship settings. In other words, participating in the phenomenal field of sacred word, pious congregation, and sacred food, their rasna becomes co-constituted differently.

Langar also combines with the ethic of *seva* (service) outside of the gurdwāra premises and worship context. A common Sikh practice is to offer free water and food from stands at events such as festivals and marathons, from food trucks on the street, and at places such as soup kitchens run by various communities. Some Sikh nonprofit organizations provide this service during disasters and other emergencies, such as serving food to the federal workers in the United States who were not paid their salaries due to the month-long government shutdown in 2019 and, as I write this chapter, to those in need, worldwide, due to the COVID-19 pandemic.[22]

Through these various activities (congregational musical worship, ras grocery offerings, and communal dining), the gurdwāra becomes a site of enactment of the Sikh tripartite motto for a good lived life—*Nām japō, kīrt karō, vand chhakō* (constantly remember the divine, earn an honest living, share your earnings). The phenomenal field of sabad kīrtan, and the ras experienced in it, draws, builds upon, participates in, and contributes to all of this. Through these embodied ethical connections, we begin to see the intertwining of the aesthetic, the social, the political, and the everyday. Here and below, I will continue to build upon the idea that ras is not just anchored in the aesthetic performance event and not just a response to aural-visual stimuli but is emergent and dynamic in and across the various realms, the overlapping phenomenal fields, of the Sikh lived world.

Bringing together these insights from Sikh philosophy and practice, and Merleau-Ponty's gestalt view of perception, I think of a phenomenal field as a dynamic, social realm of interrelational co-constitution of all participant elements. That the field is dynamic is highly significant, for there is always motion and change. Interrelationality is a critical aspect as well, as there is no independent construction of self and other, or of subject and object, and this co-constitution includes both musical sound and the experiential body. Significantly, also, historical memory and future aspirations are integrally at play here. As many ethnomusicologists have argued, the experience of musical sound is typically embedded in the social world, in historical memory, and future aspirations. In my framework of the phenomenal field, musical sound (and indeed each participatory element, including memory) is not an isolatable external stimulus but is itself constituted by the living body, just as the living body is constituted by the musical sound and all other constituent elements. It is with the co-constitution of, and immersion in, such a phenomenal field that congregants listen to and sing the sabad in a kīrtan session.

A "Ras-Drenching" Kīrtan Session

I turn now to the description of a particular kīrtan session to highlight some of the ways that the ras experience takes shape musically. This session is in the AKJ style; it is sung by the accomplished musician Bhai Jagpal Singh and accompanied on the *joṛi* (tabla drum pair) by the very talented Bhai Paramjit Singh. About an hour and a half long (see ⏵ Video 1), it was part of an all-night AKJ kīrtan program that began on the evening of February 25, 2018, at the Gurdwāra San Jose, in San Jose, California. The program itself was part of an all-weekend gathering.[23]

As I mentioned above, the AKJ style is highly participatory. While all styles of kīrtan operate within the phenomenal field that I have been discussing, a number of features of the AKJ kīrtan intensify the field and the emergence of ras within it. Among my various interlocutors, references to ras were usually emphasized in relation to AKJ kīrtan sessions. For example, a devout Sikh and fan of the AKJ style said to me, "Akhand kirtan vich bhij jaaidae" (In akhand kīrtan one gets drenched [in ras])." The notion of becoming drenched in divine rain, or dyed in divine color, is also found in various sabad.

The AKJ style uses a number of musical techniques to enhance the generation and circulation of ras. These include call and response, several repetitions of each line, and cycles of intensifications in rhythmic density, volume, and tempo. The singing begins at a slow tempo and gradually accelerates, passing through a number of cycles of ebbing and flowing intensification within each song. Cycles typically follow a pattern of phrase diminution, starting with complete lines of songtext and moving on to a repetition of key phrases. When the time seems ripe, cycles climax with the chanting of the divine name, wāheguru. (See ⏵ Video 2 for an example of this.) With successive cycles, the tempo increases steadily (i.e., each successive cycle begins at a slightly faster tempo than the previous one started at and ends at an even faster tempo). Typically, these cycles are also successively shorter. The overall effect is one of a whirling spiral that takes participants into ever deeper experiential states. Other intensification techniques that the lead singer(s) employ throughout include increases in the density of the songtexts and dynamics, changes in register, octave leaps, belting out melody lines and phrases, emphasis on key words, and elongation of the duration of vowels that occur at the end of phrases or lines.

The instruments play their part in intensification, too. The drummer shifts to playing in double-time as intensity cycles progress, uses more syncopated phrases and dynamics for emphasis, and employs strong, open-hand, resonant strokes on the joṛi bass drum for key moments of intensification. The *khartālaṅ* (shakers) player(s) typically follow the speed and dynamics of the joṛi. The *vājā* (harmonium) is used to play complementary melodic material with varying amounts of density, dynamics, and speed. During significant intensification moments, the playing becomes percussive, with the bellows pumped forcefully on the strong beats.

The AKJ session that I am describing here caught my attention in particular because it is centered on the theme of ras. In this session, not only do the congregants seem deeply immersed in ras-full experience but throughout the performance the lead singer can be seen leaning toward those around him (sometimes toward the joṛi player, at other times toward the congregants), thus seeking active inputs into the phenomenal field. The lead singer visibly wants a field of strong social interaction, and he gets it wholeheartedly. The "extended ensemble" (formed by congregation members seated around the "core ensemble," which includes only the lead singer and the drummer) participates actively and enthusiastically. In addition to the standard responsorial singing in repetition, congregants can be heard executing a variety of impromptu vocal enhancements—using tonal and dynamic emphasis on key words, melodic variations on key textual phrases, extended singing on line-ending vowels, and interjections of phrases from the sabad being sung. Emerging from the congregation's pre-reflexive engagement with the kīrtan and responding to the embodied presence of the singer, drummer, and other congregants, the inclusive and collaborative intercorporeality of their singing is an important contributor to the amplification of the phenomenal field and har-ras.

The first sabad of this session in fact states that the sabad-texts are themselves replete with flavors of the divine (*ras rasāl*), and singing them imbues the heart with divine color. The sabad emphasizes that har-ras must be drunk if one is to comprehend the divine.

ਹਰਿ ਕੈ ਰੰਗਿ ਰਤਾ ਮਨੁ ਗਾਵੈ ਰਸਿ ਰਸਾਲ ਰਸਿ ਸਬਦੁ ਰਵਈਆ ॥
ਨਿਜ ਘਰਿ ਧਾਰ ਚੁਐ ਅਤਿ ਨਿਰਮਲ ਜਿਨਿ ਪੀਆ ਤਿਨ ਹੀ ਸੁਖੁ ਲਹੀਆ ॥ (Guru Granth Sahib, 835)

Har kai rang ratā man gāvai, ras rasāl ras sabad ravaīā.
Nij ghar dhār chūai att nirmal jin pīā tin hī sukh lahīā.

The heart is imbued with divine color, singing the sabad, by nature replete with ras. Within the body the stream flows, so pure; it is they who drank [har-ras] who have obtained peace.

Couplets from other sabad are interpolated time and again to intertextually intensify affect. The successive sabad that are sung have themes that form a cyclical affective pattern (as is often the case in such sessions). They build up from tender sentiments of love and comfort to a noble theme of truthfulness, then ramp up to more vigorous feelings of courage and valor, circle back to sentiments of love and comfort, and finally center on peace and calm. These are all flavors of har-ras, the culminating feeling being one of serenity and ease with the embodiment of the ethical attributes. This overall cyclical pattern of intensification in the session envelops the smaller cycles of intensification in each sabad. The collaboratively engendered intensifications strengthen the transmission and circulation of ras among the participants, drawing them out of their everyday, isolated individuality into the deeper co-participation and co-presence of the event. The repeated and nested ras-full cycles aid somatic enculturation, so that har-ras may become a mode of inhabiting this world.

Here, the generation of ras is clearly intersubjective and generated not just by musicians but by all participants and components of this rich phenomenal field. Ras comes from the scripture, sacred words, music, food, and all congregants. Importantly, these elements are mutually constituted as a meaningful totality and experienced as a unified whole. The congregant does not engage in an intellectualist process of projecting meaning onto each component as an individual, external phenomenon. The aural, visual, tactile, and gustatory sensations are meaningful as a co-constituted gestalt, and this unified whole is sensed as a unified experience through the motility of the unified lived body, not separately by the ears, eyes, hands, and so forth. It is this unified, interrelational experience that is ras.

The singing begins with a gentle, unmetered introductory couplet (see ▶ Video 2) before moving on to the first sabad, which is accompanied by joṛi drums and shakers.

ਜਿਨਾ ਦਿਸੰਦੜਿਆ ਦੁਰਮਤਿ ਵੰਞੈ ਮਿਤੁ ਅਸਾਡੜੇ ਸੇਈ ॥
ਹਉ ਢੂਢੇਦੀ ਜਗੁ ਸਬਾਇਆ ਜਨ ਨਾਨਕ ਵਿਰਲੇ ਕੇਈ ॥ (Guru Granth Sahib, 520)

Jinā disandaṛiā durmat vañai mitar asāḍaṛé séī.
Hao ḍhūḍhédī jag sabāiā jan Nānak virlé kéī.

Seeing whom ill judgment leaves, true friends are they.
I search the whole world over, says devotee Nanak, rare are they.

As is standard in AKJ kīrtan, the lead singer, Bhai Jagpal Singh, accompanies himself on the vājā. An accomplished musician of this style, he engages the congregants in call-and-response on each line of the refrain multiple times, taking a good eight minutes to slowly move through a gradual warm-up and culminating in the chanting of the divine name wāheguru. (See ▶ Video 2.)[24] His pacing of the energy buildup and relaxation within each cycle and across successive cycles, as well as the increase in the overall tempo of the performance, is smooth and achieved collaboratively with the extended ensemble. This virtuosically shaped intensity of musical experience is a key factor in the intensification of ras in the AKJ style.

The call-and-response that is a constant feature throughout the kīrtan is also a significant means of the co-generation of ras and the co-constitution of the phenomenal field. Particularly notable here is that the call-and-response form does not only take place in a unidirectional manner from the ensemble to the audience, though that is its primary mode. These events also involve what I term here "call-and-response reversals" and "call-and-response shifts," which further distribute agency in the constitution of the phenomenal field. One way that call-and-response reversal often happens is in the initiation of the ecstatic wāheguru chant by someone in the extended ensemble who has reached a particularly ras-full stage, which the lead singer then follows. This can be seen in Video 3, which begins with a line initiated by the lead singer; immediately after, the congregation joins in and repeats the line responsorially (See ⏵ Video 3). Towards the end of the responsorial singing, which occurs around thirteen seconds into the video, the congregant who is wearing the orange scarf and seated right behind the lead singer initiates the wāheguru chant. The lead singer responds by joining in, and the congregation follows suit. This reciprocity in leading and following is a powerful element in the intercorporeal co-constitution of ras-full bodies in congregation.

The February 2018 kīrtan session was also rich in instances of call-and-response shifts, which I define as the transfer of the calling role from the lead singer to the drummer. In sabad kīrtan, the drummer is a key partner in the intensification process, offering up rhythmic patterns, dynamics, rhythmic densities, and tempi that complement the singer and shape the intensity of the event. This is especially so in the AKJ style, and in this context, it is natural that the drummer becomes moved to initiate calls sometimes. An instance of this occurs about half an hour into the February 2018 session, when the energy had built up quite a bit and the joṛi player had reached a stage of ras-fullness that yearns for the wāheguru chant. His intense affective state is expressed in his continuous playing of open-hand strokes on the bass drum, which occurs around twenty seconds into the video, and his interjection of "Pīā! Pīā!" (Drank! Drank [ras]!), which occurs at around forty-five seconds into the video, and these lead the congregation to launch into an ecstatic wāheguru chant (see ⏵ Video 4). The lead singer is moved by this increased energy and the diffusion of har-ras to introduce a couplet from another sabad that speaks more explicitly to har-ras's ethical realm, infusing the congregation with sensations of divine ethical attributes.

ਸੇ ਜਨ ਸਾਚੇ ਸਦਾ ਸਦਾ ਜਿਨੀ ਹਰਿ ਰਸੁ ਪੀਤਾ ॥
ਗੁਰਮੁਖਿ ਸਚਾ ਮਨਿ ਵਸੈ ਸਚੁ ਸਉਦਾ ਕੀਤਾ ॥ (Guru Granth Sahib, 955)

Se jan sāché sadā sadā jinī har ras pītā.
Gurmukh sachā man vasai sach saudā kītā.

They are forever truthful, who have drunk har-ras.
The Divine/Truth dwells in the heart of the Guru-oriented; they have struck the true bargain.

The kīrtan session proceeds in ebbs and flows of intensity, and the congregation seems to be, in the words of one of my interlocutors, drenched in ras. This ras, however, does not just come from the musical sound or from human musicking. All constituent elements in the event, human and non-human, are agentive. The sung sacred texts, for example, bring the Guru's revered message, along with a shared phonetic, corporeal force, especially during the wāheguru chant, deepening the intercorporeal reciprocity in the ras experience. The presiding Guru Granth Sahib brings into the event the phenomenal presence of the late human Gurus and the scriptural Guru, along with historical memory and aspirations, infusing sacred ethical flavors into the ras. The warm parshād, made with ras offerings from the congregants, gently releases its sweet aroma, reinforcing the har-ras experience with an olfactory presence of the sacred. At the end of the kīrtan, congregants will eat this parshād, savoring its taste, and through this gustatory action physically ingesting har-ras. After the worship session, congregants will share a langar also prepared with ras offerings and voluntary labor from the congregation—another act of corporeal ingestion of divine ethical flavors. What we see here is what Berger has called the "traffic and transformation" of meaning across different elements of an experiential field (2009, 43). Here, the presence of noema (entities in experience) with particular affective valences shapes the affective quality of the participant's noesis (the process of constituting experience). The various noema in the sabad kīrtan setting are rich in the affective valences of har-ras and reinforce each other in the constituted experience. Affective qualities, which are included in the category of meaning contents, can further expand into "disposition[s] ... a tendency to think, act, or feel in a certain way" (Berger 2009, 45). In the kīrtan context, the semantic meanings of the sacred text provide critical "affirmations" (45) of the ethical aptitude that Sikhs hope will become part of their everyday inhabitation of the lived social and political world outside of the worship setting. These differing but interrelated realms of life are what I am calling overlapping phenomenal fields.

RAS IN OVERLAPPING PHENOMENAL FIELDS

If my son has vīr-ras, school bullying will not crush him.
> Pritipal Singh (personal communication, San Jose,
> California, 2006)

The body is the vehicle of being in the world, and having a body is, for a living creature, to be intervolved in a definite environment, to identify oneself with certain projects and be continually committed to them.
> Merleau-Ponty ([1945] 2002, 94)

ਨਉ ਨਿਧਿ ਅੰਮ੍ਰਿਤੁ ਪ੍ਰਭ ਕਾ ਨਾਮੁ ॥ ਦੇਹੀ ਮਹਿ ਇਸ ਕਾ ਬਿਸ੍ਰਾਮੁ ॥
> Guru Granth Sahib ([1604] 1708, 293)

Nao nidh amrit prabh kā nām. Déhī meh is kā bisrām.

Full of [ethical] treasures, eternal, is the divine.
In the body is its place of dwelling.

More than just a concept for explaining the aesthetics of musical performance or the experience of worship services, ras has a direct role in daily life. I would suggest that, for the parent quoted above, if one's body, which is the vehicle of being in the world, is a ras-full one, one imbued with vīr-ras, its "intervolvement" with a challenging environment (i.e., its involvement in and coexistence with a particular social situation) becomes automatically committed to a project of resilience. Vīr-ras becomes an integral part of the unified body, through which the world is experienced and lived. In a body imbued with vīr-ras, ras is not engaged as a deliberated act but rather as automatic, operative intentionality—that is, the process by which one's pre-reflexive embodied consciousness engages directly with others and the world.

For Sikhs, vīr-ras is linked particularly to the memory of Guru Gobind Singh, who is remembered for his bravery in upholding freedom of faith at great cost to his family members' lives and his own at the hands of an oppressive political regime.[25] For most Sikhs, and particularly the AKJ members, embodying the articles of faith instituted by Guru Gobind Singh, and the ethic of being a saint-soldier (*sant-sipāhi*) modeled by him, are significant aspects of the phenomenal field in which a Sikh ras-full sensorium is nurtured. The embodiment of this ethic is enabled by the initiation ceremony known as *amrit sanchār* (lit. transmission of the nectar of immortality), which was begun by Guru Gobind Singh in 1699 in the month of Vaisakh (April/May) and subsequently celebrated as Vaisakhi. In the ceremony, *amrit* (sacralized sweetened water) is prepared by five deeply spiritual Sikhs, known as the "five beloved" (*panj pyāré*), and sprinkled on the initiate, as well as given to them to drink. The experience of imbibing amrit is also an experience of ras, as indicated by one of my interlocutors, a millennial raised in a devout Sikh family in California. During our conversation on the experience of ras in kīrtan participation, she related the following to me:

> The most powerful experience of simran [wāheguru chants] for me is on Vaisakhi occasions when those who have just taken amrit join the kīrtan. They come into the room led by the panj pyāré. Everyone stands up. If any among them can sing, they lead the kīrtan. In that simran, the amrit just comes into my mouth by itself. I can taste it. It is sweet.

Adherence to the articles of faith has not been easy for Sikhs, in either India or the diaspora. In post-9/11 America, the turban and beard have become for some outside the Sikh faith the image of terrorism in the name of religion. Sikh males with turbans and beards have continued to face acts of hate, from school bullying, hate speech, vandalism, and physical assaults, to fatal gun violence.[26] The quote above from my interlocutor on the importance of instilling his child with vīr-ras indicates how historical memory of courage against injustice links with future aspirations for a just lived world; how this link is maintained via ritual practices, including musical worship; and how the ras experienced in a rousing kīrtan session is not merely a detached aesthetic response but a way of developing a ras-full sensorium that carries over productively to another phenomenal field, that of the lived everyday social and political world. In Berger's theory of stance, the affective, aesthetic, or valual quality with which a person engages expressive practices is not only contained within the performance event itself; rather, "the meanings of [such] practice[s] often flow across the boundaries between domains" (2009, 99). The "stance-on-power" (111) that emerges in experiences of expressive culture, its ideology with respect to social power differentials, can therefore become embodied in one's bearing in the everyday, especially when that stance is the very spirit of one's culture.

In the kīrtan session I have been describing, vīr-ras is strongly foregrounded during the third quarter of the performance. By this point, the energy level among the participants has built up considerably. Using a series of excerpts from Guru Gobind Singh's sabad, along with historical references to valor and resilience, the musicking becomes more vigorous, loud, and emphatic. The drummer employs open-hand bass-drum strokes repeatedly. The participants reach a stage of peaked vīr-ras (see ⊕ Video 5) when the singer evokes a deeply poignant memory of the injustice of the killing of all of Guru Gobind Singh's four children and follows it with a roaring rendition of the call of the Sikh call-and-response battle cry—*Jo Bole So Nihal* (The one who speaks up is exalted). The congregation offers, with equal enthusiasm, the response part—*Sat Sri Akal* (Truth is eternal). This leads to an energetic and ecstatic wāheguru chant in a high vocal register matching that of the battle cry.

Participation and immersion in such an affectively rich, intersubjective phenomenal field transforms the participants' sensoria. As Husserl argued, the body is "a localization field for sensations and for stirrings of feelings, [a] complex of sense organs, and [a] phenomenal partner and counterpart of all perceptions of things" ([1952] 1989, 165). The immersive phenomenal field changes the participants' way of inhabiting the world, of perceiving and experiencing the world. In the case of vīr-ras, it creates conditions of possibilities for the body to experience emotionally and physically traumatic events with less emotional and psychological harm. It provides greater agency in shaping what Husserl ([1954] 1970) would call their "lifeworlds" (*Lebenswelten*); it opens up avenues of enaction.

The ras that is experienced in a phenomenal field is not merely a sum of individual responses to discrete stimuli from their constituent elements. Individual sensations are simultaneously in conversation with the whole. The interactive mutualities have an amplified affect that is presented as a comprehensive feeling in a unified body. One's experience of ras thus makes explicit one's awareness of the body as an integrated whole, not an aggregate of parts. The perception of ras is also the perception of the body in the world. Integrated in the body's motor intentionalities, ras is co-constitutive of the subject and of a particular kind of intersubjectivity, in both everyday life and musical worship. In this way, ras reveals ontological and ethical entanglements, which are involved in the making of the subject and its pre-reflexive ethical engagement in the lived world. Through these operative somatic intentionalities, ras reveals an ontology of the self and of ethics, and it reveals self-knowledge. In Merleau-Ponty's words, "remaking contact with the body and with the world, we shall also rediscover ourself, since, perceiving as we do with our body, the body is a natural self, and, as it were, the subject of perception" ([1945] 2002, 239). A lived life of constant rediscovery is what the sabad encourage. As one of the sabad states,

ਏ ਸਰੀਰਾ ਮੇਰਿਆ ਇਸੁ ਜਗ ਮਹਿ ਆਇ ਕੈ ਕਿਆ ਤੁਧੁ ਕਰਮ ਕਮਾਇਆ ॥

. . .

ਜਿਨਿ ਹਰਿ ਤੇਰਾ ਰਚਨੁ ਰਚਿਆ ਸੋ ਹਰਿ ਮਨਿ ਨ ਵਸਾਇਆ ॥ (Guru Granth Sahib, 922)

É sarīrā mériā is jag meh āé kai kiā tudh karam kamāiā.

. . .

Jin har térā rachan rachiā so har man na vasāiā.

O body mine, having come into this world, what [ethical] actions have you enacted?

. . .

The divine that constituted you, you have not enshrined in your heart.

If Sikh congregants believe that kīrtan is a means of experiencing the divine, perhaps it can be said that ras, as a coming together in a phenomenal field, is experienced as a union with something larger than all constituent elements—something that feels like divine essence (har-ras). Seen in this way, ras is central to both Sikh ontologies and epistemologies.

CONCLUDING REMARKS

Based on an investigation of ras in the Sikh musical worship context, I have theorized it in reference to Merleau-Ponty's phenomenology of perception as an interrelational experience that becomes emergent in a phenomenal field co-constituted by people, objects, sound, food, ideas, memory, and aspirations. Ras has epistemic value for gaining knowledge of self, community, and the divine. Ras also has a temporal dimension that accretes in the body and becomes productive in the overlapping phenomenal fields of everyday social and political life. Ras is thus ontologically informative, revealing our being in the world.

In their overview of phenomenological approaches in anthropology, Robert Desjarlais and Jason Throop ask, "What is the relation between the phenomenal and the discursive—between, that is, experience, being, and sensate perception, on the one hand, and language, aesthetic and rhetorical forms, and communicative practices more generally on the other hand?" (2011, 97). My ethnographic research on ras in Sikh philosophy and practice suggests deep connections between such categories.

Ras is in text and language, as much as in musical sound, food, and the experiencing human body, and it moves synergistically between such domains. As a flow in a phenomenal field, ras cuts through binaries such as mind/body, imaginary/material, word/affect, text/orality, ocular/aural, music/context, and theory/practice. The continuities of ras draw attention to the futility of hard analytical boundaries and caution us against those forms of analytical overcorrection that would, for example, privilege body over mind, sound over other sense modalities, or orality over text.

Ras also seeps from aesthetic and communicative practices into the concerns and contingencies that make up people's everyday lifeworlds—concerns and contingencies that have intertwined within them not only issues of aesthetics and emotions but also questions of ethics and morality, spirituality, and politics. This seepage is consciously supported in the Sikh context by the valorization of the ethic of *mīrī-pīrī* (lit. temporal-spiritual engagement), which urges us to attend to both the spiritual and the political in everyday life. Thus, the spiritual ras of har-ras and amrit-ras are experienced in relation to the ethical-political ras of vīr-ras. The spiritual ras of amrit-ras itself crosses these realms seamlessly, with its connotations of ethical purity and temporal longevity. Amrit literally means "that which does not die" (the prefix *a-* indicates negation and *mrit* means "dead") and indexes truth as eternal. Ras therefore links the sacred and the secular, and the past and the future, through the body's motor intentionalities and habits. In explicating the nature of ras in Sikh musical worship, I hope to have contributed fruitfully not only to ongoing conversations on rasa more broadly but also to work in phenomenological ethnomusicology and anthropology that seeks to understand how being-in-the-world is conditioned by musically engendered structures of experience, how knowledge is produced through this being-in-the-world as a lived reality, and how this knowledge is put back into world-making.

ACKNOWLEDGMENTS

I am grateful to the Akhand Kirtani Jatha organization for the use of their video recording on the *Oxford Handbooks* website. These recordings, which I have edited and subtitled, help considerably to drive home the points I have sought to make here. I am thankful to AKJ member Nirmaljot Singh, who kindly helped in a number of ways that were extremely valuable. I would also like to express my gratitude to the editors of this volume, especially Harris Berger and an anonymous reader, for their very helpful comments on this essay.

NOTES

1. In Southeast Asia too, rasa is an important aesthetic principle, with its own specificities, of course. See, for example, Becker (1993), Weiss (2003), and Benamou (2010).
2. My fieldwork was undertaken in India, the United States, and the United Kingdom and spanned the period from 2004 to 2018. In its most concentrated form, the fieldwork was undertaken in 2014 and 2015 in the greater San Francisco Bay Area.
3. Sikh scriptures are compilations of thousands of canonized songs and do not contain prose.
4. This is the dominant flavor of the non-scriptural heroic narrative songs (*ḍhāḍī vār*), which are most often sung on celebratory occasions to remember a history of oppression, resistance, and resilience and to infuse feelings of *jōsh* (zeal) and *chardi kalā* (optimism and high spiritedness) in the community. For a brief description of ḍhāḍī vār, see Kaur (2019a). Vīr rasa, along with *karūṇa* ("sad") rasa, is also an aesthetic in Hindu nationalistic kīrtan (Schultz 2013, 127–130).
5. All song quotes in this chapter are from the Sikh scripture, Guru Granth Sahib. All translations are my own interpretations. The English transliterations are adapted from the website Sri Granth: A Sri Guru Granth Sahib Search Engine and Resource (SriGranth.org).

6. On the transduction of sound into embodied energy, see Silverstein (2003), Henriques (2003), Helmreich (2015), Eidsheim (2015), Kapchan (2017), Eisenlohr (2018), and Kaur (2021). Here, I emphasize that serene experiences may also be highly intense ones. For a discussion of the coexistence of serenity and intensity in lived experience, see Mihaly Csikszentmihalyi's work on flow states (1990).

7. The *Nātyashāsthra* is a treatise on dramaturgy that was written roughly at the turn of the Common Era. Its author, Bharata, presented a classificatory scheme of eight rasa and the *bhāva* (emotions) that undergird it. The eight types of rasa are *shringāra* (erotic), *hāsya* (comic), *karuna* (pathetic), *raudra* (furious), *vīra* (heroic), *bhayanaka* (terrible), *bibhatsa* (disgusting), and *adbhūta* (wondrous). Around the tenth century CE, the aesthetician Abhinavagupta elaborated on this work in the *Abhinavabhāratī*, providing a detailed theoretical explanation and adding the ninth form of rasa, that of *shānta* (peaceful). For an English translation of the *Nātyashāsthra*, see Bharata Muni ([1950] 2016). For an English translation of the *Nātyashāsthra*, along with the commentary in the *Abhinavabhāratī*, see Ghosh (2006).

8. Some detailed theoretical discussions include those by van der Meer (1980), Rowell (1992), and Rao (2000).

9. In the context of Javanese musical performance, Judith Becker (1993) explicates that the Javanese aesthetics of rasa is related to the ancient Indian Tantric notions of rasa; Weiss (2003) argues that Javanese ideas of embodiment can explain how musicians make their performance rasa-full; and Mark Benamou (2010) offers a detailed ethnographic study, investigating the complex terminology and meanings related to rasa, their musical contexts, and what musicians feel about the relationship of rasa to performance.

10. Discussing Southeast Asian music, Weiss similarly explains, "In the course of this article, I will suggest that for a Javanese performance to be assessed as convincing, effective, or full of rasa, something from inside the performer(s)—some mixture of uninhibited emotion and deep knowledge (both terms associated with the word rasa)—must be felt by the performers and, *subsequently*, by the audience" (2003, 23; italics added).

11. An issue related to ethics should be mentioned here, though a detailed discussion of it is beyond the scope of this chapter. In Bharata's *Nātyashāsthra*, the ability to savor rasa is reserved for those of "high birth" (Higgins 2007, 46). Combined with the conceptualization of rasa as the experience of the universal spirit through the loss of ego due to unity with the aesthetic object, a view which is found in the *Abhinavabhāratī*, this stipulation of high birth reinforces the Brahminical caste system, which ontologically and epistemologically denies the experience of the divine to a large part of society. Like other vernacular faith traditions in India, Sikhī (Sikhism) arose as a protest against Brahminical systems of social hierarchy. Sikh philosophy explicitly accords to all the potential of ras and divine experience and emphasizes that feelings of social supremacy and hierarchy eliminate the possibility of experiencing har-ras and the divine.

12. The *Nātyashāsthra* does not comment on the relationship of ras to ethics. The *Abhinavabhāratī* adds the notion of the universalization of the spirit during the rasa experience, but this is seen as transcendence and is not related to everyday life. See also the ethical issues mentioned in footnote 11.

13. From his various examples, I chose to use the one relating to color, since the notion of imbuing the body with the color (*rang*) of the divine is significant in Sikh sacred songs, and Merleau-Ponty's arguments apply well to the experience of rang, as well as ras. In fact, rang is another widely used aesthetic principle in Indian expressive culture.

14. Merleau-Ponty's remarks assume, of course, that the subject has had previous experiences of landscapes in their visual, olfactory, and tactile dimensions. The same assumption goes for the perception of the woolly redness of the carpet (i.e., that one has had a tactile experience of its wooliness and the muted sound of, say, one's footsteps upon it).

15. For a DVD of this program, see Kaur (2005).

16. For a discussion of the multiple sensory modalities that come into play in experiences at Sikh gurdwāray, and their affordances, see Kaur (2019b).

17. For a discussion of the different musical styles of Sikh kīrtan and the congregants' stance toward them, see Kaur (2016).

18. The most revered Sikh gurdwāra, Harmandir Sahib in Amritsar, Punjab, which is commonly known as the "Golden Temple," is the model of this ethic. It has a daily estimated attendance of about 50,000 people from all social backgrounds.

19. Some gurdwāray divide the area where the congregants sit by gender, so that on crowded occasions women and men can avoid sitting knee-to-knee.

20. For a discussion of "audiencing" as aural-visual engagement, see Kaur (2019b).

21. Each weekday at the Golden Temple, for example, 40,000 to 80,000 people eat at the langar hall, which serves langar around the clock. The number doubles on weekends, and even more are present on holidays. For a video of the langar at the Golden Temple, see "Best Ever" (2018).

22. See, for example, *Tacoma Daily Index* (2019) and Roy (2020).

23. A nearly ten-hour recording of the all-night kīrtan can be viewed on YouTube (see AKG .Org 2018). The hour-and-a-half-long session I am describing here begins four hours, thirty-three minutes, and thirty-eight seconds into the video. ⓟ Video 1 on the *Oxford Handbooks* website presents the entire hour-and-a-half session from that video and is used by permission. ⓟ Videos 2–5 on the *Oxford Handbooks* website present short excerpts from this session. I have subtitled these clips with translations of the sabad, since the sacred texts are a critical part of the phenomenal field.

24. ⓟ Video 2 splices segments from the first eight-minute cycle into a two-and-a-half-minute clip.

25. In the Sikh tradition, the ḍhāḍī vār (non-scriptural songs of heroism and resistance) are a key musical mode of transmission of these historical narratives.

26. See, for example, SALDEF and Stanford University Peace and Innovation Lab (2013).

Works Cited

AKG.Org. 2018. "Live: (Rainsabaee) Bay Area CA Feb 2018 Annual Akhand Keertan Samaagam." YouTube. https://www.youtube.com/watch?v=s7NUnXuMaRE&t=16416s.

Becker, Judith. 1993. *Gamelan Stories: Tantrism, Islam, and Aesthetics in Central Java*. Monographs in Southeast Asian Studies. Tempe: Program for Southeast Asian Studies, Arizona State University.

Benamou, Marc. 2010. *Rasa: Affect and Intuition in Javanese Musical Aesthetics*. New York: Oxford University Press.

Berger, Harris M. 1999. *Metal, Rock, Jazz: Perception and Phenomenology of Musical Experience*. Middletown, CT: Wesleyan University Press.

Berger, Harris M. 2009. *Stance: Ideas about Emotion, Style, and Meaning for the Study of Expressive Culture*. Middletown, CT: Wesleyan University Press.

Berger, Harris M., David VanderHamm, and Friedlind Riedel. 2023. "Phenomenological Approaches in the History of Ethnomusicology." In *The Oxford Handbook of the*

Phenomenology of Music Cultures, edited by Harris M. Berger, Friedlind Riedel, and David VanderHamm, 3–56. New York: Oxford University Press.

Best Ever Food Review Show. 2018. "How India Cooks Lunch for 50,000 People for FREE! The MIRACLE in Punjab, India." YouTube. https://www.youtube.com/watch?v=qdoJ roKUwuo.

Bharata Muni. (1950) 2016. *Nāṭyaśāstram: A Treatise on Ancient Indian Dramaturgy and Histrionics*. Translated by Manmohan Ghosh. Chaukhamba Surbharati Studies 21. Varanasi, Uttar Pradesh: Chaukhamba Surbharati Prakashan.

Csikszentmihalyi, Mihaly. 1990. *Flow: The Psychology of Optimal Experience*. New York: Harper and Row.

Desjarlais, Robert, and C. Jason Throop. 2011. "Phenomenological Approaches in Anthropology." *Annual Review of Anthropology* 40: 87–102.

Eidsheim, Nina Sun. 2015. *Sensing Sound: Singing and Listening as Vibrational Practice*. Durham, NC: Duke University Press.

Eisenlohr, Patrick. 2018. *Sounding Islam: Voice, Media, and Sonic Atmospheres in an Indian Ocean World*. Oakland: University of California Press.

Gell, Alfred. 1998. *Art and Agency: An Anthropological Theory*. Oxford: Clarendon Press.

Ghosh, Manmohan, trans. 2006. *Nāṭyaśāstra of Bharatamuni: Text, Commentary of Abhinava Bhāratī by Abhinavaguptācārya, and English Translation*. Delhi: New Bharatiya Book Corporation.

Halliburton, Murphy. 2002. "Rethinking Anthropological Studies of the Body: Manas and Bōdham in Kerala." *American Anthropologist* 104 (4): 1123–1134.

Helmreich, Stefan. 2015. "Transduction." In *Keywords in Sound Studies*, edited by David Novak and Matt Sakakeeny, 222–231. Durham, NC: Duke University Press.

Henriques, Julian. 2003. "Sonic Dominance and the Reggae Sound System Session." In *The Auditory Culture Reader*, edited by Michael Bull and Les Back, 451–480. Oxford: Berg.

Higgins, Kathleen Marie. 2007. "An Alchemy of Emotion: Rasa and Aesthetic Breakthroughs." *Journal of Aesthetics and Art Criticism* 65 (1): 43–54.

Husserl, Edmund. (1931) 1977. *Cartesian Meditations: An Introduction to Phenomenology*. Translated by Dorion Cairns. The Hague: Martinus Nijhoff.

Husserl, Edmund. (1952) 1989. *Ideas Pertaining to a Pure Phenomenology and to a Phenomenological Philosophy: Second Book, Studies in the Phenomenology of Constitution*. Translated by Richard Rojcewicz and André Schuwer. Dordrecht, Netherlands: Kluwer Academic Publishers.

Husserl, Edmund. (1954) 1970. *The Crisis of European Sciences and Transcendental Phenomenology*. Translated by David Carr. Evanston, IL: Northwestern University Press.

Kapchan, Deborah. 2017. "The Splash of Icarus: Theorizing Sound Writing / Writing Sound Theory." In *Theorizing Sound Writing*, edited by Deborah Kapchan, 1–24. Middletown, CT: Wesleyan University Press.

Kaur, Inderjit N. 2005. *Puraatan Reetaan in Evening Raags: Compositions from the Sikh Music Tradition*. Sikh Music Heritage Institute. http://www.sikhmusicheritage.org/.

Kaur, Inderjit N. 2016. "Multiple Authenticities in Motion: Styles and Stances in Sikh *Sabad Kirtan*." *Yearbook of Traditional Music* 48: 71–93.

Kaur, Inderjit N. 2019a. "Sikhism." In *The SAGE International Encyclopedia of Music and Culture*, edited by Janet Sturman, 1952–1953. Thousand Oaks, CA: Sage.

Kaur, Inderjit N. 2019b. "Sonic Worship and Its Multisensorial Affective Ecology: The Sikh Sacred Song Tradition." *MUSICultures* 46 (2): 109–133.

Kaur, Inderjit N. 2021. "Theorizing the (Un)Sounded in Sikhī: Anhad, Sabad, and Kīrtan." *Religions* 12 (11): 1007.

Krishnamurthy, Thanmayee H. 2019. "Sing Rāga, Embody Bhāva: The Way of Being Rasa." MA thesis, University of North Texas.

Merleau-Ponty, Maurice. (1945) 2002. *Phenomenology of Perception.* Translated by Colin Smith. New York: Humanities Press.

Nuttall, Denise. 2013. "Rhythm Embodied: Training Rasa in Hindustani Tabla?" *Studies in South Asian Film & Media* 5 (1): 69–79.

Rao, Suvarṇalata. 2000. *Acoustical Perspective on Rāga-Rasa Theory.* New Delhi: Munshiram Manoharlal Publishers.

Rowell, Lewis. 1992. *Music and Musical Thought in Early India.* Chicago: University of Chicago Press.

Roy, Natasha. 2020. "Volunteers for Sikh Nonprofit Deliver Food and Supplies across L.A. amid Pandemic." *NBC News.* May 1, 2020. https://www.nbcnews.com/news/asian-america/volunteers-sikh-nonprofit-deliver-food-supplies-across-l-amid-pandemic-n1196556.

SALDEF (Sikh American Legal Defense and Education Fund) and Stanford University Peace and Innovation Lab. 2013. *Turban Myths: The Opportunities and Challenges for Reframing Sikh American Identity in Post-9/11 America.* https://issuu.com/saldefmedia/docs/turbanmyths_121113.

Schultz, Anna C. 2013. *Singing a Hindu Nation: Marathi Devotional Performance and Nationalism.* New York: Oxford University Press.

Sharma, Prem Lata. 2000. *Indian Aesthetics and Musicology: The Art and Science of Indian Music.* Edited by Urmila Sharma. Varanasi, Uttar Pradesh: Āmnāya-Prakāśana, Bharata-Nidhi.

Silverstein, Michael. 2003. "Translation, Transduction, Transformation: Skating 'Glossando' on Thin Semiotic Ice." In *Translating Cultures: Perspectives on Translation and Anthropology*, edited by Paula G. Rubel and Abraham Rosman, 75–105. Oxford: Berg.

Slawek, Stephen. 1996. "Engrossed Minds, Embodied Moods, and Liberated Spirits in Two Musical Traditions of India." *Bansuri* 13: 31–41.

Tacoma Daily Index. 2019. "Free Dinner Daily at Auburn Sikh Temple until Government Shutdown Ends." January 25, 2019. https://www.tacomadailyindex.com/blog/free-dinner-daily-at-auburn-sikh-temple-until-government-shutdown-ends/2444586/.

Weiss, Sarah. 2003. "'Kothong Nanging Kebak,' Empty Yet Full: Some Thoughts on Embodiment and Aesthetics in Javanese Performance." *Asian Music* 34 (2): 21–49.

van der Meer, Wim. 1980. *Hindustani Music in the Twentieth Century.* The Hague: Martinus Nijhoff.

CHAPTER 17

···

THE AESTHETICS OF PROXIMITY AND THE ETHICS OF EMPATHY

···

DEBORAH KAPCHAN

One's own body is in the world just as the heart is in the organism.

Merleau-Ponty ([1945] 2012, 209)

IN the *Visible and the Invisible*, Merleau-Ponty's last and uncompleted work, he defines the concept of flesh (*chair*) as an element:

> Flesh is not matter, it is not mind, is not substance. To designate it we should need the old term element in the sense it was used to speak of water, air, earth and fire; that is, in the sense of a *general thing*, mid-way between the spatio-temporal individual and the idea, a sort of incarnate principle that brings a style of being wherever there is a fragment of being. The flesh is in this sense an "element" of Being. . . . If we can show that the flesh is an ultimate notion, that it is not the union or compound of two substances but thinkable by itself, if there is a relation of the visible with itself that traverses me and constitutes me as a seer, this circle which I do not form, which forms me, this coiling over of the visible upon the visible can traverse, animate other bodies as well as my own. (1969, 139–140; italics in the original)

If, as Merleau-Ponty says, one's body exists in the world as the heart does in the body, where is the place of affect? Might we think of affect as the fascia, the connective tissue joining body and world, being and its milieu? In this chapter, I suggest that conjoining Merleau-Ponty's concept of flesh with theories of sound and affect can provide a way of understanding configurations of social aesthetics and ultimately their relation to ethics—that is, the political ramifications of styles of being and embodiment in the world.

Where does affect reside in a phenomenology of perception? And what is the relation of affect (and its translation into empathy) to aesthetics and ethics? Evoking Sufi sounds of worship as I have recorded and experienced them over the last two decades in Morocco and France, I illustrate what I call the "aesthetics of proximity," one based on the friction between sounds and bodies, and its implications for an embodied ethics of response. I begin, however, with what Merleau-Ponty says is the only means of approaching experience—phenomenological description.

Phenomenological Description I

> Phenomenology is accessible only through a phenomenological *method*. . . . It is a matter of describing, not of explaining or analyzing . . . [of returning] "to the things themselves."
>
> (Merleau-Ponty [1945] 2012 viii, italics added).

As soon as Sanae approaches the sanctuary, the rhythms of her metabolism change. I know this because she grasps my arm to steady herself and lets go a long sigh, "allah." We are not yet inside, but we are on the threshold. There is a long corridor to the women's entrance. We walk down a cement hallway in the semi-darkness and approach the door. We knock and hear someone shuffling in slippers on the other side.

Shkun? who is it? A woman's voice asks.

Qarib, a relative, Sanae answers. It is a rote question and a rote answer, meant only to determine the gender of the person seeking entry. Of course we are not blood relatives but we are "close"—which is what qarib actually means: proximate. And the proximity comes from being in the circle of the shaykh, a member of the Qadiriya Boutchichiyya Sufi Order.

The door opens and the young woman embraces us on both cheeks. I have seen her many times at Sufi gatherings but I don't know her name. She is Moroccan, but lives in Paris and comes regularly to the sanctuary, the zawiya.

Once inside, we follow the faqira to one of the closed sitting rooms that surround the open courtyard. There are women everywhere—sitting on banquettes, moving efficaciously in the kitchen, lifting large mukraj or kettles of boiling water off butagaz stoves and pouring the scalding liquid into several steel teapots (berred) filled with sugar, fresh mint, and green gunpowder tea from China. There are huge plates of minsimmin and baghrir, two variants of Moroccan pancakes, as well as cookies and some hard-wheat bread; there are several small plates of apricot jam and butter. These are brought past us as we stop at the threshold of the open door to remove our shoes. It is difficult to find a place to sit, but a hefty woman in a pink jellaba motions for us to approach. She encourages the seated women to scrunch together, pushing herself up and over against them, and making room for us. Before sitting, however, we both say "salam alay-kum" to the congregation and proceed to embrace each and every woman in the room on both cheeks. Luckily Sanae and I do not take up much room. We squeeze into the space allotted and are both handed a glass of steaming sweet tea by the pink-jellaba-ed woman, which we take from the rim so as not to burn our fingers.

Bismillah, *we both say, "In the name of God," and take a sip.*

Tafadl, *says another woman nearby, "Help yourself," and she motions to the tray of sweets. With another* bismillah, *we each tear off a piece of pancake from the larger portion and eat it slowly, savoring the soft buttery texture in our mouths.*

Al-baraka dyal sidi rabi, *the second woman says, "The blessing of our lord." It is a kind of communion, a ritual of hospitality that plays out every time a new guest arrives at the zawiya. And there are hundreds of women here in this house.*

After a while we are all escorted to a very large and carpeted hall. The older women are allowed to sit on the banquettes that line the walls, but most of us find a place on the floor.

bismi'llah er-rahman er-rahim . . . *The Yassine prayer from the Qur'an opens the liturgy. We intone a few other prayers and then,* allah, allah, allah, allah, allah, allah, allah, allah, *the chanting begins.*

*The women push the last unvoiced syllable of allah out of their diaphragms forcefully—*allah-ah allah-ah allah-ah allah-ah allah-ah allah-ah allah-ah allah-ah—*making this not just an invocation and intoning of the name of God but an exercise in rhythmic breathing. Indeed, most women chant each name using a major second, beginning on the note above (al—) and ending on the tonic (-llah), adding a third largely unvoiced syllable of exhaled breath—/h/—after the first two. This vocalization gets louder and more forceful as the repetitions increase. There is the buzz and tension caused by overlapping notes—like the sensations produced by half steps sung simultaneously, or the overtones caused by such friction. To me it sounds dissonant, but of course dissonance is a cultural interpretation. These are sound waves in close proximity, what Austrian ethnomusicologist Gerald Florian Messner (1990) calls the phenomenon of* Schwebungsdiaphonie, *beat diaphony.[1] They are the beats that are caused by the interaction of two sounds that are close in frequency.*

During the repetitions of these vocables—quick, forceful—the atmosphere changes. One becomes aware of the voices of others and how their synchronicity creates an energy that is palpable. No one is instructed on what note to begin, though it is generally understood that the invocations should be in tune and in sync. Because these are not songs but invocations, however, half-steps inevitably occur as voices ascend unevenly and pitches vary. It is a form of sensory stimulation. The repetition of these words is often accompanied by what in Sufism is called al-hal. Literally, a "state," the hal is a spiritual state of sublimity sonically signaled by the individual's departure from the same repetition with others and the inter-jection of new rhythms and sounds. Al-hal is the rapturous response to the sublime object. And the sublime object itself is the affect identified as muhabba, *divine love, circulating among those present.*

And then a woman breaks with the rest. She lets go a long al-llaaaaaah that sails over the ostinato of the repetitions like a wave. And she follows this with short staccato syllables that descend chromatically like a sigh: llah llah llah llah llah . . . The energy in the circle has changed for all of us. As if on cue, another woman breaks off in a cry, echoing the last syllables but in a syncopated rhythm. It is a conversation, an exchange of affect. She interjects allah! *I feel her body jump next to mine, which makes my body jump. We are all*

listening. And our listening is moving. We hear one woman crying, though we are not sup-
posed to look. After several hundred invocations the leader slows the rhythm down again.
We move on to another invocation.

My inquiries in this chapter arise from my experiences in the ethnographic field, in this case, twenty-five years of frequenting Sufi women's events in the Moroccan Qadiriyya Boutshishi order both in Morocco and in France. The "return . . . 'to the things themselves'" ([1945] 2012, viii) that Merleau-Ponty mentions—for him, a return to their materiality—comes from Edmund Husserl (2001), but there is no return without en-counter and description, and description is a *method*—a path toward, a quest, as well as a way of going. Insofar as my discussion relies on memories of things, people, words, and feelings, my methodology is necessarily a *return* to the things themselves. But it is also a *moving toward*, what Merleau-Ponty in his later work calls "intercorporeity," a place of intersubjectivity where affect resides in the flesh, as flesh resides in and indeed constitutes the world.

My experiences at these Sufi rituals, where a kind of deep listening is practiced, has alerted me to the power of listening to transform not just subjectivities but intersubjec-tive milieux (Becker 2004; Oliveros 2005). As Gilles Deleuze and Félix Guattari note,

> Bird songs: the bird sings to mark its territory. The Greek modes and Hindu rhythms are themselves territorial, provincial, regional. The refrain may assume other functions, amorous, professional or social, liturgical or cosmic: it always carries earth with it; it has a land (sometimes a spiritual land) as its concomitant; it has an essential relation to a Natal, a Native. A musical "nome" is a little tune, a melodic formula that seeks recognition and remains the bedrock or ground of polyphony (*cantus firmus*). The *nomos* as customary, unwritten law is inseparable from a distribution of space, a distribution in space. By that token, it is *ethos,* but the ethos is also the Abode.
>
> (Deleuze and Guattari 1987, 313)

This place-making through sound creates a sympathetic field of resonance. Deleuze and Guattari call it "abode-making"; all such homes are imbued with affect, whether home is the discrete body, or bodies and things in conjunction within a social field. Affect is the *place* of abiding, of feeling in common (con-sensus, notes Dorothy Noyes [2003, 132], is feeling together). Affect is a sanctuary in which humans may find refuge, and flesh is the substance that resonates with the sounds and presences of others, sen-tient and non-sentient. The body is a place, but it does not stop at the limits of the skin; rather, it joins and enjoins the flesh of the world.

Second- and third-generation French North Africans, as well as French converts to Islam, are initiated into the liturgy by "learning to listen" (Kapchan 2009). Despite the fact that many do not speak Arabic, they enunciate the liturgy beautifully by learning its component phonemes, attentive to where the voice rises and falls, where there is a breath, where there is a pause. After the liturgy, the women chant the names of God over and over: *allah, allah, allah, allah,* or *ya latif, ya latif, ya latif, ya latif* (oh subtle one, oh subtle one). It is at this point that the Sufi women go into states of rapture. Beginning together with monophonic and regular repetitions of the names of God, someone eventually breaks off, initiating a new rhythm on another proximate note. Others follow suit; cry breaks and syncopations ensue. This creates a rich a-harmonic fabric punctuated by polyrhythms. Unlike singing traditions where intervallic proximity is desirable and microtones are produced on purpose—to "ring like a bell" in the ears of appreciative listeners—the Sufi women in this tradition are instructed to chant *in unison* before they begin. The production of microtones is not deliberate. They nonetheless veer into chanting unwilled (if recognized) beat-producing seconds, and this modulation always *co-occurs* with a spiritual and affective departure into al-hal (Duranti 1986; cf. Schafer 1977; Turino 1993; Rice 2004).

Listening to these improvisations is also listening to the women listening to each other as they respond to changes in pitch, rhythm, and timbre. This has much in common with what ethnomusicologist Charles Keil has called "participatory discrepancies"—the way improvising musicians are intentionally slightly off the beat and out of tune as a way of communicating with each other (Keil 1987; cf. Keil and Feld 1994). A similar phenomenon is found in the Sufi *dhikr* ("remembrance") ceremonies, with the difference that no one would claim intentionality, at least not in the sense of conscious volition.[2] To the contrary, these changes of state are thought to be divinely inspired and unpredictable. But insofar as intentionality inheres in all actions (as an orientation toward the world), these sublime performances are in fact the axiological adhesive that binds subjects with the intersubjective and empirical world.[3]

Performances like the one above take us beyond the limits of the human to an affective experience that is no less material for being experienced as transcendent. For what is transcended is not materiality per se, which may be posited as the very immanent unit of being (energy, sound), but the enculturated and perceived limits of the human within materiality—what Sufis consider to be the veils that separate the human from the larger phenomenal environment. (This continuity, I would argue, is what Merleau-Ponty calls the flesh.) Immanence and transcendence are not opposites for the Sufis. Indeed, the divine is immanent, present in every molecule. What is transcended is the illusion of separateness. Audition and sound have a primary role in facilitating this movement.

THE AESTHETICS OF PROXIMITY

The polyphonic aspect of these invocations creates what I call an "aesthetics of proximity"—degrees of spatio-temporal as well as spatio-*tactile* closeness between sounds and bodies. Although the women are supposed to chant in unison, very soon after the chanting begins some women veer up or down in pitch, employing quarter-tones and other micro-tones.[4] These notes in close proximity create a sound mesh, a cacophony of beats and overtones, and it is this heterogeneous aesthetic that co-occurs with the emergence of sublimity in the Sufi ceremonies I have attended.[5] To a Western ear (my own), consonance disintegrates and is replaced with dissonance, and yet it is not the positive or negative charge that is important here but the intensity of the *affect* that is collectively generated.

Sound waves vibrate at a range of different frequencies.[6] When people sing in unison they are literally on the same wavelength; the frequency ratios are simple, the harmonics align, and although there are multiple voices, there is often a perception of consonances. In many cultures, this produces a sense of pleasure. And yet chanting, the voices unintentionally diverge; the frequency ratios are more complex (e.g., when the vocalists produce pitches that are within three semitones of each other), the notes share fewer harmonics (thus increasing the total number of the harmonics present), and subsequently more "beats" are produced. In many Western traditions, this is perceived as a dissonant or "rough" aesthetic.[7] Understanding the psychoacoustics of consonances and dissonance is beyond the scope of this chapter; however, it is important to note that the more complex the frequency ratio between tones—that is, the more proximate they are in the pitch space—the thicker the sound mesh. It is from within the mesh of sonic instability that sublimity arises in the ceremonies examined here.[8] Intervallic proximity amplifies the affect of bodies in proximity, a phenomenon that I call "body proxima." Indeed, it is this amplification in sonic and embodied proximity that accompanies the Sufis from one *hal* to another.

Extrapolating from this phenomenon, I assert that the "thicker" the sensorial interrelations (overtones, beats, but also sonic, visual, tactile, and gustatory cues), the more potential for empathy is generated, and this, because *proximity forces an intimate encounter with difference that displaces the boundaries of self-same.* Consonance is comfortable, as is community. But both ideals are rarely realized. Close affecting aesthetic encounters, however, disintegrate illusions of harmonic continuity, placing subjects firmly within the tension of difference, to linger in what may be a productive discomfort. Paradoxically, the fact of listening to many voices at once—voices that distinguish themselves rather than unify on the same note—creates a communality, not in sound but in the act of *listening*. There is an intimacy forged in the recognition of diversity. (This is beautifully exemplified in the songs of the BaAka, documented by Michelle Kisliuk [1998, 2017], but is also present, I would suggest, in the chants of Black Lives Matter protests).

This is not only relevant for the work that audition creates in the Sufi worlds examined here. More generally, it bears upon what Judith Butler calls the "obligations of proximity"—one's ethical relations to the stranger evoked in (mediated) connections that make the distant suffering of others (refugees, for example, or victims of structural racism) if not a present, up-close reality, then a social responsibility.

The Ethics of Proximity and Distance

Academic and theoretical emphases emerge from social contexts and political moments. With the current rise in social upheavals (the Arab Spring, wars in Syria and Yemen, refugees in Europe, the clash of secular and sacred worlds, global warming, economic and ecological crises in the rainforests of Latin America and elsewhere, to say nothing of the structural racism that has fueled the Black Lives Matter movement amid a global pandemic), it is not surprising that social theorists have turned to ethics as the pertinent philosophical landscape. For example, in their Neale Wheeler Watson Lecture at the Nobel Museum in Stockholm, Butler discusses the way "human suffering at a distance" implicates the witness in a non-consensual relationship, one they call an "unwilled ethical encounter" instigated by mediated images and discourses of human misfortune (Butler 2011). We can think of Susan Sontag's work here on the visual witnessing of the pain of others (Sontag 2003). Sontag finds that such images of suffering paralyze the viewer, eclipsing ethical action, but Butler questions this conclusion. Rather, they chart what they call the "obligations of proximity," an ethical relation to the stranger resulting from a "reversibility" of distance and closeness in human relations: the provocations for ethical action are distant, Butler asserts, but the actions inspired are proximate.

For Butler the contemporary moment is characterized by such changing relations to proximity and distance—that is, distant suffering inhabits the intimacy of our private spaces through mediated images and subsequently provokes a response. (The recorded murders of George Floyd and Ahmaud Arbery, for example, circulated and ignited protests across the globe.) What's more, Butler emphasizes that the circumstances of the contemporary moment render human life—all human life everywhere—precarious in a way it has not been before. Terrorism and violence have transformed civilians into soldiers and changed citizens of one nation into refugees in another, making the fragility and vulnerable relationality of all life apparent (Appadurai 2005). "If I am confounded by you, then you are already of me," Butler asserts, "and I am nowhere without you. I cannot muster the 'we' except by finding the way I am tied to 'you,' by trying to translate but finding that my own language must break up and yield if I am to know you. You are what I gain from this disorientation and loss. This is how the human comes into being, again and again, as that which we have yet to know" (Butler 2004, 49).

This beautiful passage delineates Butler's relational ontology: it is one of connection, often (they note later) through the experience of grieving. Knowing the other even in the imperfection of translation entails a loss of self, which nonetheless reconstitutes itself in the advance toward the not-yet-known. In Butler, beings only become human through a methodology reminiscent of Jacques Derrida's "promise of translation" (1985). While translation will always fail, the promise keeps the life-force alive, while always grieving for what is lost in the process—the self, the other. For Butler, some lives are deemed more grievable than others—resulting in disparate and often unethical responses to human suffering. (We see this in how the United States has allowed violence toward Black and Brown bodies to continue unpunished.)

While Butler clearly acknowledges the interdependence of humans, their starting point is different from that of Merleau-Ponty, for example, for whom intersubjectivity arises from a shared sensate and phenomenal field. For Butler, the relations forged through visually witnessing and identifying with the suffering of others *at a distance* in mediated images creates ethical relations of engagement that did *not* exist before electronic media.

While Butler does not engage phenomenology explicitly, their position assumes that technology informs if not determines our perceptions; by extension, such mediated images at a distance produce an embodied and ethical response. This is a post-phenomenological position, one that takes account of the role of technology in perception. And certainly insofar as "phenomenology investigates the conditions of what makes things appear as such," understanding the role of technology in perception is necessary (Ihde 1993, 133). The difficulty in such work lies in understanding the way mediation and technology are *translated* into ethical response. For Butler, "visual and linguistic translations" are what make ethical responses to distant suffering possible. But what becomes possible when the aesthetics of *sonic proximity* supersedes the visual and linguistic tropes of modernity?

Butler's meditations on the ethical response evoked by mediated images of suffering recall the debate about the value of "liveness" in the 1990s between performance studies scholars Peggy Phelan and Philip Auslander. Phelan (1993) argued that embodied live performances were different (newly emergent) every time, and thus not only ontologically different from mediatized performance but a priori (fundamentally prior to mediatized ones). Auslander (1999), on the other hand, found that position to be a romanticization. For him, live performance was not prior to or more essential than the mediated, nor did it create more community (or communitas); rather, it was only one of many forms of performance. At first sight, Butler would seem to fall in Auslander's camp; in fact, Butler's arguments advance this debate, as they assert that viewing mediated images of suffering actually *spurs the viewer into action* by virtue of being moved— affected—in the first place. For Butler, mediated images are a form of activism with issue in the world. Seeing is a form of knowing after all. And witnessing the suffering of others does implicate the viewer in an ethical relationship.[9] In light of what we know about the transmission of affect and sound, however, these ideas are due for review.

Music and sound more generally create not only place but a way of inhabiting it—what Merleau-Ponty might call a style of being that is necessarily intersubjective. What's more, the aesthetic expression has an "existence in itself"; it is not a translation of meaning into a medium but an actualization, an embodied performance. Merleau-Ponty notes that

> The musical signification of the sonata is inseparable from the sounds that carry it; prior to having heard it, no analysis allows us to anticipate it. Once the performance comes to an end, we cannot do anything in our intellectual analyses of the music but refer back to the moment of the experience. During the performance, the sounds are not merely the "signs" of the sonata; rather, the sonata is there through them and it descends into them. . . . Aesthetic expression confers an existence in itself upon what it expresses, installs it in nature as a perceived thing accessible to everyone, or inversely rips the signs themselves—the actor's person, the painter's colors and canvas—from their empirical existence and steals them away to another world. No one will object that here the expressive operation actualizes or accomplishes the signification and is not merely a matter of translating it. ([1945] 2012, 188)

It is not spurious that Merleau-Ponty draws upon the example of music to delineate the somatic power of aesthetic experience. When listening, one is "in" the experience, quite literally touched and moved by the sounds, and *inseparable from them* (Connor 2004). This is an "experience-near" phenomenon, to invoke Clifford Geertz (1976). Music is proximate. It entrains the body and the senses and may thus be said to create sympathy—resonances at similar wavelengths, literal and symbolic. It creates an affective abode. This is not necessarily what Butler means when they refer to an unwilled ethical encounter, but it is certainly *unwilled and empathic*. Does empathy always imply ethical engagement?

Aesthetics that are proximate are ultimately aesthetics that are transformative, on all scales of magnitude.[10] This is exemplified poignantly in the theater arts but is no less true off stage. No one would argue that seeing mediated images of violence is the same as being present to the violence. As theater director Joanna Settle noted in a recent conversation, "If we are in Gaza, we pick [the wounded] up and have blood on our hands. Watching the same moment on CNN leads me to 'consider' the 'conflict' or 'tragedy,' but it remains other than me. On location, whatever I do becomes *a part of me*. When watching the news, my observation is action-optional" (personal communication, May 2019).

Theater scholar Ana Pais echoes these sentiments in her analysis of affect in live performance, insisting as well upon the action of *listening*:

> the activity of the spectator involves an intensification and amplification of affect, enabling a moving together, a reciprocal movement between stage and audience. This movement, in turn, . . . [is] conceptualized as a co-motion that takes place through a specific kind of *listening—an affective resonance*. By influencing the quality of the event, that is, the charged, circulating, and fleeting affective quality of live performance, commotion produces the ontological difference of theater. (2017, 238; italics added)

Proximate bodies are bodies in commotion, bodies that are informed by an affect that is *not* "action-optional" because they are somatic and part of a larger fabric or milieu. While encounters are always mediated, the *form* of the mediation does affect the experience—phenomenologically at least. There is a qualitative intersensorial aspect of live performance that does not exist in the same way in mediation, if only because the density of sensory information is different. While an ethical response may be evoked at a distance, it is not necessarily translated into direct action. "There is a difference in time signature," notes Settle, and I would add that there is a difference in the sensorial thickness of the experience as well. There are ethics that are immediate and somatic, and others more cognitive—like those invoked by Butler—that take place in a longer durée. These are surely coiled together and it is precisely their intertwining that evokes empathic response. Had the images of George Floyd's murder been silent, for example, the protests may not have happened in the same way. But they were accompanied by his voice—"I can't breathe"—and this voice, I assert, made all the difference. We saw this in the way people turned up on the street in the midst of a pandemic, risking their health (and possibly their lives) to create an enfleshed abode, a "magnified" sound body insisting on justice (Kapchan 2015; Kisliuk 2017).

THE PHENOMENOLOGICAL BODY:
AFFECT IN PROXIMITY

The *Oxford English Dictionary* (OED) defines the body as "the complete physical form of a person or animal," and yet the body is never "complete" but is forever changing, sloughing off old cells, generating new ones. The OED says that the body is "an assemblage of parts, organs, and tissues that constitutes the *whole* material organism" (italics added). But what of the lived body, its hormones, chemicals, synapses, nerves; what of the plethora of molecules shedding and spreading beyond the skin, responding to the rhythms of the environment?

Anthropologist Thomas Csordas draws upon phenomenology to define what he calls "somatic ways of knowing"—that is, "culturally elaborated ways of attending to and with one's body in surroundings that include the embodied presence of others" (Csordas 1993, 138). In order to ground perception in its cultural life, Csordas adds Bourdieu's concept of "practice" to Merleau-Ponty's understanding of pre-objective perception (wherein subject/object relations are not fixed), as well as to the stances embedded therein.[11] This synthesis, he says, "suggests that embodiment need not be restricted to the personal or dyadic micro-analysis customarily associated with phenomenology, but is relevant as well to social collectivities" (137). This is an extremely important expansion of phenomenology in anthropology, but in fact, Merleau-Ponty's concept of flesh anticipates Csordas's delineation of embodiment as something that mediates the subjective and the intersubjective.

Building upon Csordas, I assert that another way to elaborate the notion of embodiment is to consider both sound and affect as actants in this phenomenal field. The body sounds, but it also resonates in the milieu it inhabits and creates, including the virtual. "When I think of my body and ask what it does to deserve that name," notes theorist Brian Massumi, "two things stand out. It *moves*. It *feels*" (Massumi 2002, 1; italics in the original). We can also say, it sounds. Every oscillation is in fact a vibration, and every vibration has a sound, however inaudible to the human ear. What we cannot hear, we can feel or intuit. Following Butler, this unwilled ethical encounter is qualitatively different than that produced by images at a distance, however. Audition and affect are both proximate experiences that do important work in the world. I assert that *for empathy to fully enter the realm of ethics, intersensorial proximity is required.*

PHENOMENOLOGICAL DESCRIPTION II

It is the summer of 2016 and I am driving through the fields and vineyards that line the potholed roads of southern France. I pass through small villages and hamlets, on narrow roads with speed bumps every few meters. I enter the outskirts of a larger town, one with rent-controlled apartments on the periphery. I find a space in the parking lot outside the building where I am going. I put a scarf on my head before getting out of the car, and look at the black socks on my sandaled feet as I get my bag out of the passenger seat and walk across the broken cement sidewalk to the lobby. The sun is strident.

I am not exactly sure which apartment is the right one. I consult my phone and send a text. I hear a door open on a landing above me and proceed up the stairs.

marhaba alalla,[12] *welcome sister, says the young woman by the door. I take my sandals off as soon as I enter.*

la toilette? *I inquire.*

It is understood that I will do my ablutions before joining the group in the ceremony.

When I have washed my face, my ears, my arms, my feet, I put my socks back on my feet and tiptoe into the room with the other women. The wooden slats of the blinds are lowered and a fan whirs. I sit on a quilted mat on the ground next to seven others. We are fewer today. It is summer and no doubt some women are traveling, or have obligations at home. The women are mostly silent. The only sound is that of their wooden prayer beads as they adeptly manipulate them, and their lips moving quickly in tandem, aspirating vocables under their breath. I tuck my legs under my djellaba and begin to do the same, silently intoning the first half of the testimony of faith: llah ilaha ila lllah, llah ilaha ila lllah, llah ilaha ila lllah, *there is no deity but God, there is no deity but God, there is no deity but God. It is like a mantra, and although we are each in our own inner sounds and rhythms, nonetheless our bodily rhythms align and concentration increases as soon as we are seated next to each other. Body proxima.*

Soon after I sit down the muqaddema, *the overseer or leader, intones* bismi'allah er-rahman er-rahim, *"in the name of God the merciful and compassionate," to initiate the* wadhifa *or ceremony. Like the word "liturgy" in English, the word* wadhifa *comes from the root "to work" (*wa dha fa *in Arabic). It is a labor for the community, an investment of time and intention (*niya*). We all open our chapbooks to the same page: Arabic on the left, its transliteration in the Latin alphabet on the right. We begin with the Yassine Sura from the Qur'an. It is long and I have not memorized it, so I turn to the correct page, though many of the others know it by heart.*

We then begin to intone aloud: the Fatiha prayer ten times, allah ilaha ila llah *100 times. And more. This is called* dhikr, *remembrance. It is an invocation of some of the 99 names of God, in order to both remember God (to invoke divinity) and to "re-member" the community. The atmosphere of the room changes. As we chant* allah, allah, allah, *the voices get stronger and louder. Although we begin on the same tone, one of the women has migrated a half-tone up. Someone else follows. We are ascending in pitch and amplitude. Then someone else migrates further. We do not follow, but the voices get more distinct. Between each* allah, *there is a conscious and quick exhale, which makes the uptake of the inhale more forceful as well. The weave of voices is now thicker, like a mesh of tones. One woman lets go a long wail:* allaaaaaaaaah *and follows it with* la ilaha ila llah, *even though we are not chanting that phrase. Another woman lets go a loud* al-lah! *And my nervous system starts.*

She is in al-hal, *a state of inspiration, of unity, of transformation. A state of grace. A state different than those we inhabit outside the "labor" of the group.*

Later, when I ask S about her experience of al-hal she says: "I used to have such dramatic states (pl. ahwal; sing. hal). As soon as I would approach the sanctuary, I would break down and cry. During the ceremonies, I would be seized, jump up and cry out over and over. But now things have quieted down. Now my states are silent."

A few months later, the shaykh of the order, Sidi Hamza, passes. He is ninety-five, a descendent of the prophet and has been the spiritual leader of the order since 1975. I learn that the new shaykh—his son Sidi Jamal—predicts that there will be fewer expressions of al-hal going forward. I wonder why this is so. Is the fervor of the order diminishing? Will it be replaced with another affect? No one has an explanation.

And yet, it is the affect of the sanctuary, and of the smaller sanctuaries abroad, that hold a palpable magnetism for adherents. They contain al-baraka dyal sidi rabbi-i, *the blessing of our lord, the Sufis say. Baraka (blessing, grace) in the North African Muslim context is thought to be contagious. Like the hal, it resides in a place, and creates an atmosphere, at the sight of the tomb of Sidi Hamza, for example, or in his body.*

"At the funeral of Sidi Hamza," said the husband of one of the sisters to me the following summer, "the wife of Sidi Jamal fainted. When she came to, she said that she had seen the baraka of Sidi Hamza rise up from the tomb of the shaykh and land on his son, Sidi Jamal."

What the baraka looked like, she didn't say. But it traveled, from death to life, from body to body, like a vibration, like an intensity. Like affect. And this intensity caused her to faint, to expire, to enter another state.

CAN THERE BE A PHENOMENOLOGY OF AFFECT?

What is circulated in the ceremonies evoked above? Is this the "transmission of affect" that Teresa Brennan (2004) talks about—a preconscious transmission of energy that subsequently changes the hormones and nervous system of the individual, the social collective and ultimately the milieu of performance?

The terms *emotion, affect, feeling,* and *sensation* have been debated and revised many times over the last centuries and with renewed vigor in the last several decades (Gil 2017). What's more, these definitions are, in part, a matter of disciplinary perspective. For example, philosophers have often pondered the "meaning" of emotions and their relation to rationality (Sartre 1970; Rorty 1980). Are emotions intentional? Are they judgments (Solomon 2004)? Do humans will them into being or do they happen to us (Schmitz et al. 2011)? What part of emotional experience is culturally determined and what part neurologically hard-wired? Are emotions human and cross-cultural or an interspecies phenomenon?

In 1980, Amélie Rorty noted that emotions are those parts of human experience that refuse to be categorized, and she asserted that a unified theory of emotions was far from being constructed. Indeed, various attempts have been made since 1980 to substantiate this theory, with debatable results. Constructing a theory from the emotions of anger or disgust will result in a very different perspective than if one begins with joy and contentment, for example. While all *affect* is in motion and thus changes the social field, negative *emotions* seem to be more involved in direct social political action, since dissensus arises from conscious discomfort.

Neurocognitive psychologists are more interested in what happens in the brain of an individual than in the feelings that sweep over large populations to create historical movements; however, these topics are related. What happens in the brain when an emotion is realized and experienced? What is the relation of that feeling to its object and to the subject experiencing it? Where is affect located? How does it move people and others into action? And is there value in understanding the agency of one particular emotion as it is evoked, experienced, and transmitted across bodies and spaces?[13]

For the purposes of this discussion, here I follow a particular trajectory in affect theory that builds upon the philosophy of Baruch Spinoza (1632–1677). For Spinoza, affect is the *experience* that always links the mind and the body, insisting upon the relation between the two. He defines "the affections of the body whereby the body's power of acting is increased or diminished . . . together with the ideas of these affections" (Spinoza 1959, part III, quoted in Schmitter 2010). Affect is a vital force that circulates unconsciously with sociopolitical ramifications. It has a power on the body and the mind. For scholars influenced by this line of thinking (including Deleuze and Guattari [1987], as well as Clough [2007] and Massumi [2002]) affect is a precognitive intensity that is *translated in context* as a particular emotion, such as fear, disgust, or rage. In this chapter, I espouse the definitions synthesized by Eric Shouse, who holds that "feelings are *personal* and *biographical*, emotions are *social*, and affects are *prepersonal*" (Shouse 2005). On this view, there is a material force to affect that is felt and only subsequently *translated* into individual and social realms.

This is congruent with Brennan's work on the "transmission of affect" (in her 2004 book of the same name). Brennan challenges the notion of the contained self, blaming this concept for skewed notions of the subject in psychology. She brings attention to how affect is transmitted both chemically and biophysically (through gestures as well as pheromones, for example). As a pre-personal intensity, *affect*, she asserts, creates an *atmosphere*. (Her opening gambit is the question "[i]s there anyone who has not, at least once, walked into a room and 'felt the atmosphere'?" [Brennan 2004, 1]).[14] Atmosphere is psychological, material, and profoundly social.[15] What's more, the transmission of affect circulates through bodies in ways that are experienced both positively and negatively.

Human enmeshment with affective worlds does not stop or start at the skin. Rather, affective intensities challenge the limits and agencies of things and bodies, including our relation to technology. Patricia Clough, in *The Affective Turn: Theorizing the Social*, puts it this way:

> [a]ffect constitutes a nonlinear complexity out of which the narration of conscious states such as emotion are subtracted, but always with "a never-to-be-conscious autonomic remainder." In this conceptualization, affect is not only theorized in terms of the human body. Affect is also theorized in relation to the technologies that are

allowing us both to "see" affect and to produce affective bodily capacities beyond the body's organic-physiological constraints. The technoscientific experimentation with affect not only traverses the opposition of the organic and the nonorganic; it also inserts the technical into felt vitality, the felt aliveness given in the preindividual bodily capacities to act, engage, and connect—to affect and be affected. The affective turn, therefore, expresses a new configuration of bodies, technology, and matter instigating a shift in thought in critical theory. (2007, 2)

What Clough does not say explicitly, but assumes, is that bodies no longer have the shape they did in the Enlightenment. Human experience does not begin and end at the visual parameters of the body but is intermeshed and continuous with other bodies, technologies, and environments. This idea is not anti-humanist but is post-humanist, and requires a post-phenomenology, one that expands the notion of the human to encompass both technology and the social-affective milieu of experience (Ihde 1993).

Would Brian Massumi agree? He argues that affect has a life that is separate from individual cognition. For example, he discusses an experiment conducted by Hertha Sturm and her colleagues wherein children's responses to film of a "melting snowman" were charted (Massumi 1995). The results showed that the children were often more "pleasantly" stimulated by the tragedy of the snowman's disappearance and death than they were by his continued existence. And yet their verbal explanations did not calibrate with their affective responses. From this data, Massumi deduces that affect has a life of its own. It is not a rational and logical response, nor is it limited to an individual; rather, it circulates and stimulates. It is "autonomous" to the extent that it does not arise from or depend upon one human subjectivity. It does, however, depend upon *transmission* from body to body, and these bodies are themselves vibrating with life (and resistance). These bodies are chiasms inhabiting the flesh of the world.

Affect is like a sound wave, circulating, touching, and transforming the bodies that it encounters. Indeed, affect, like sound, relies upon touch. It is thus always experienced as proximate—*even when it is virtual*. A phenomenology of affect must include an examination of what moves (humans, animals, even plants) through space. In such an understanding of affect, its potential to create new worlds (and subjects) is evident, since subjects are always *inter-subjects*, and subjectivity is, in the words of Anahid Kassabian (2013), always "distributed" across bodies with different cultural histories and intentions.[16] Bodies are enfolded in the flesh of the world.

Affect is always phenomenologically proximate, by which I mean it is felt at the level of the body by the senses, enfolding the subject into a larger environment. Sound is likewise proximate. (Even when below or above the threshold of human hearing, its vibrations are felt.) But if affect is pre-personal, if it is distributed not only across human bodies but across technology as well, then a phenomenology of affect is one that must begin *not* with the discrete body per se but with milieu, with place and abode. What Merleau-Ponty calls "chiasms"—places of condensation and conjoining (including subjectivity)—are always present. Styles of being are discrete at any given moment. And yet these experiences are always pieces of a larger sonic-affective milieu that disperse in time and to which consciousness only sometimes has access.[17]

If affect is not personal, how should we describe the feelings, sensations, and perceptions of the affective field? When we expand the limits of the body to the environment or to a larger set of bodies, are we reifying transcendence? Are we repeating, as Ruth Leys asserts, the mind/body split, favoring a mentalist world of imagination, and projecting ourselves within it? When we leave the five senses, and include intuition (the sixth sense according to Henri Bergson), what happens to phenomenological description? Are we in another realm (fantasy? science?) or is there a way of maintaining a sensate ground in the more-than-human realm of affect?

For some, a phenomenology of affect is a contradiction in terms. By this logic, affect is pre-experiential and pre-interpretive ("autonomous," in Massumi's words), and one cannot access and describe the feelings and sensations of the affective field, except through the mediation of subjective interpretation. But this conundrum rests on a misunderstanding, since most phenomenologists concur that humans are inter-subjects in direct contact with the world. Sentient beings (including humans) are part of the larger environment and "subject" to, even created by, its vagaries. All things arise from within the flesh of existence—interdependent, like plants whose photosynthesis creates the air that other species breathe. Both phenomenology and affect theory examine the fundamental entwinement of person and world. (This is why the epoché, the phenomenological reduction, is so important: it is the *method* by which the world is known.)

While it is impossible to address all of these subtleties here, we can observe that Merleau-Ponty points us in some productive directions on this topic, particularly in his later work. Merleau-Ponty's elaboration of the notion of the flesh allows us to join the ground of lived experience (the basis of phenomenological description) with a Spinozian-informed theory of affect through an examination of intersubjective and sonic experience at the level of milieu—the chiasm where bodies intertwine with other forms. Sound and affect create what Deleuze and Guattari would term territory (place, abode), and while such spaces are pre-experiential (fish are not aware of water), they can nonetheless be discerned. To understand affect, the task is not to engage in interpretation (though translation cannot be avoided) but to return to the milieux themselves, the intersubjective and phenomenological ground of experience.

PHENOMENOLOGICAL DESCRIPTION III

Before his death in 2017, I visited the abode of the shaykh Sidi Hamza. I took the train from Rabat north to Oujda, getting out at a small station before the train's terminus. It was the stop for the shaykh's summer residence. The terminal was small, the benches broken and there were posters in French dating from the colonial period on the wall. One of the shaykh's disciples was waiting for me, and we got in his car, traveling the potholed road through a small village and into the countryside. In thirty minutes we arrived, the driver beeped the horn and the guardian opened the gate. He parked and pointed me in the direction of the women's quarters.

Inside the walls was a large garden, with palm trees, a lawn, and wild roses on a pergola—a stark contrast to the sandy scrub of the region, with its aloe and prickly pear cactus. There was a large house in the center, and there were also buildings to the left for women and to the right for men.

It was around five in the afternoon, just after the 'asr prayer. When I entered the compound, some women were still doing their prostrations. Then I saw someone I knew, who greeted me and showed me around. There were several large rooms, all carpeted. I put my things down among other bundles—backpacks, small suitcases and clothes tied up in large scarves. These were the sleeping quarters, but in fact, not many would sleep that night. After washing off the dust of my journey in the bathroom, I put on my djellaba and scarf, and joined a group of women sitting in a circle. They had already begun the liturgy and most kept their heads down, but a few made eye contact with me and acknowledged my presence.

Hasbunallahu wa ni'mal wakil, Hasbunallahu wa ni'ma wakil, Hasbunallahu wa ni'mal wakil, they were chanting when I sat down, "God is sufficient and He is the best disposer of affairs." *I joined in. But then they began another chant:* huwa hu, huwa hu, huwa hu. "He is He, there is only Him."

The women pushed up the aspirated /h/ from deep within their bellies, our bodies were in sync. Like an orchestra we pulsed with a common breath. All at once, the woman next to me jumped up, lifting her bottom off the floor. Huwa! *she cried. She might as well have discovered a scorpion beneath her. But no, she was taken up in the hal. I jumped too. My heart raced. Another woman broke from the repetitions, crying "allah" loudly above the others. The affect of the group was changing, heating up.*

When the liturgy was over we got up and went together to the women's section of the main house. There were more than forty women, some sitting on brocade banquettes, some seated on the thick carpets. There were small tables within everyone's reach, and tea and sweets were set down. We helped ourselves.

Soon, someone began to sing.

Nadra nadra ah shaykh-i, anta sahibun al-hadra
Nadra nadra ah shaykh-i, anta sahibun al-hadra

The gaze, the gaze, oh sire, you are the friend of presence . . .
The song was addressed to the shaykh, from whom only one glance was enough to transform one's state. Indeed, the shaykh rarely spoke to the women, who filed past him when he gave them audience and often swooned from the effects of his regard.
We sang for most of the night, weaving the visible into the invisible, forming a new flesh.

In *The Visible and the Invisible*, Merleau-Ponty employs the metaphor of the specular to delineate the difference between what can be seen (thus known) and what always eludes the seer—what is hidden from sight:

> it is by looking, it is still with my eyes that I arrive at the true thing, with these same eyes that a moment ago gave me monocular images—now they simply function

together and as though for good. Thus the relation between the things and my body is decidedly singular: it is what makes me sometimes remain in appearances, and it is also what sometimes brings me to the things themselves; it is what produces the *buzzing* of appearances, it is also what silences them and casts me fully into the world. Everything comes to pass as though my power to reach the world and my power to entrench myself in phantasms only came one with the other; even more: as though the access to the world were but the other face of a withdrawal and this retreat to the margin of the world a servitude and another expression of my natural power to enter into it. The world is what I perceive, but as soon as we examine and express its absolute proximity, it also becomes, inexplicably, irremediable distance. (1979, 8; italics added).

For Merleau-Ponty, what is perceived by the closeness of the senses is also never completely graspable; there are always aspects that are withdrawn, distant. The experiences of the Sufi women exemplify this paradox: their performances create aesthetic proximity (discernable in sounded and embodied response) that nonetheless marks their ultimate separation from a non-human and thus unknowable God. This is a characteristic of the sublime. In the pre-Romantic era, for example, experiences of the sublime were characterized by distance: a magnitude that overwhelmed the human, like standing before a mountain range or a raging sea (Kant [1790] 2000). It was what made humans feel small. In the performances examined here, however, the sublime is found in proximity, in the friction between notes and bodies that produce rapture. As Butler correctly notes (2011), there is a reversal of notions of proximity and distance in modernity.

It is important to remember, however, that proximity and distance are always relative. Like the situations described in Zeno's paradoxes, the more we divide the line, the farther the distance to the destination seems. While Merleau-Ponty (1969) employs the visual world to understand intercorporeity, he also evokes sound and silence, as well as language and the unsayable. Indeed, the visible world "buzzes." But it is also without sound. His work brings out the enigmas of perception, as well as the way a figure arises from a ground that also creates it, since figure and ground are interconnected.

Proximity and distance are like the visible and the invisible—interdependent dualities. Like the senses, they rely on each other. Sound is touch and—as the song above attests—even the gaze can move its object, as well as be moved by it. There is "a relation of the visible with itself that traverses me and constitutes me as a seer, this circle *which I do not form, which forms me,* this coiling over of the visible upon the visible ... [that animates] other bodies as well as my own."

Think of proximity as a cipher, as an index of intersensorial thickness, of intertwining and density. Proximity is not just spatial; it is also temporal. As such, sound may be proximate even if it is acousmatic (i.e., even if the sound's origin is not visible). And images on a screen may trigger mirror neurons that activate body memory, so that the past inhabits the present as co-immanence (Casey 1987).

Sounding the Visible and the Invisible: Merleau-Ponty and a Phenomenology of Affect

For Merleau-Ponty, phenomenology is a philosophy based in the senses and particularly in the embodied *human* senses. One need only think of Merleau-Ponty's famous experiment of one's left hand touching one's right hand (and vice versa) to remember that subjectivity and objectivity are oscillating and contextual perceptions (Merleau-Ponty [1945] 2012, 95). This may seem obvious, but the assumption that the subject is bound by the skin, discrete, rational, and conscious continues to blind us to other possibilities. While scholars often assume individual perception to be the starting point of phenomenological investigation, in fact it has always recognized the intersubjectivity of experience. In affect theory the concept of the subject is likewise revised. Not only has the divide between the human and the technological blurred (pace Donna Haraway's notion of the cyborg [Haraway 1991]), but research on affect and its transmission demonstrates that we are not separate until we come together (in social groups, families, or the sexual act) and that humans share an affective environment that overdetermines them chemically, hormonally, and psychologically; we are, in fact, together until we create our separateness.

The Spinoza-inspired affect theory considered above might be deemed anti-humanist because it emphasizes the pre-experiential. However, if we broaden sensate feeling beyond the bounds of the human skin, what we might call the skin ego, and include what Merleau-Ponty calls the flesh of the world, then a phenomenology of affect may still be possible. Indeed, if we expand concepts of the body to include what I call the sound body—"a body able to transform by resonating at different frequencies" (Kapchan 2015)—then perception and intuition also expand to include a larger field of phenomena. Sound bodies are mutable bodies that *transduce* the sound affects of the environment. Thus "reading" the sound body is also reading its abode or milieu as the sound body transduces the effects of atmosphere. What's more, sound bodies defy the mind/body split cemented into discourses of modernity whose effects, it may be posited, are experienced at the level of feeling, understood as emotions, and circulated as intensities across a phenomenological field.

As observed above, for Merleau-Ponty flesh is an element of being like water, air, earth, and fire. It is a porous, reversible, and renewable substance. The human body is flesh, but it intertwines with the flesh of the world like a pulsing rhythm or a condensation of vibrations. Flesh is the continuity that links the perceiver's body with the world. In this work, Merleau-Ponty is reaching for a vocabulary of the interstitial. His writing is poetic, analogical. He is creating a philosophical concept from a material all humans (and mammals) share—flesh. But he extends it beyond the human, talking about the flesh of the world and of the encounter of self and other, world and Being. Flesh is an isthmus, a kind of fascia or connective tissue. It traverses at the same time that it forms. It is, we might say, always *trans*forming. Might we think of flesh as the affective intensity that links humans with other humans, with other bodies and environments?[18] And if so, might this be the entry point into a phenomenology of affect?

For Merleau-Ponty, flesh is the continuity that links the perceiver's body with the world, but "this continuity is marked by chiasms," intersections, and differentiations. A chiasm is based on the double helix of genetics; it is one strand made up of two coils. For Merleau-Ponty, there are nothing but chiasms, what he also refers to as the "thickness of flesh between the seer and the thing" (Merleau-Ponty 1969, 135). Taken into the realm of sound, flesh is vibratory. It is an arrangement of sine waves in particular formation. Taken into the realm of affect, flesh is that pre-personal intensity that, when contextualized and translated, forms the chiasms of psychosocial experience. Sounding out the possibilities of flesh in Merleau-Ponty's work, we might say the aesthetics of proximity are here in the flesh.

Empathy and Ethics—Sacred and Secular

The intertwining of person and world is brought home in both the ethics of Butler and the phenomenology of Merleau-Ponty. Following Butler (2011) human experience is not narrowly personal, individual, or subjective; rather, Butler emphasizes the interdependence of human lives and their (often socially uneven but nonetheless existentially generalizable) conditions of vulnerability. This is what makes us human, they assert, an incapacity to thrive without the thriving of others. Following Merleau-Ponty, the nullpoint of human perception is the self. Looking out from my eyes, I see you, but I need "you" to reflect myself back to me, in language, in gesture, in empathic response. And yet the boundaries of the self are not fixed. They do not stop at the skin but extend out like rays of affective and energetic feeling. The self is a node in an invisible but very present matrix of affective relations in which consciousness (and meta-consciousness) appears as a blinking lighthouse in an otherwise dark sea.

If the self is fundamentally relational, then proximity and distance are critical concepts for ethics; Butler shows that at this moment the relations between them are shifting. Can ethics be maintained solely in distal relations to the bodies of others?

Let me respond with a socio-political example from one of my field sites. In France, I would argue, Muslims are the sacred figure on the secular ground of society. Much of the time, this causes friction because sacred performances (whether sartorial or ceremonial) are either prohibited by the state or not tolerated by a majority of non-Muslims in public. Were these relations purely distant—mediated only by Facebook or Twitter and actual miles—the ethical call to answer the hatred and racism that arises in the encounter with the other would be qualitatively different, found in a response that is more comfortable because it is intellectual. However, the encounter is close: face to face, in schools and other public institutions, often resulting in violent reactions on both sides. (Think of the 2016 scandal, for example, of the French police making a Muslim woman disrobe on the beach in Marseille.) Visual distance resonates differently than embodied proximity. Indeed, ethics are easier to delineate at a distance and much harder to enact close-up, where prejudices are visceral.

Despite shifting relations of distance and proximity at this moment, I am not convinced that an "unwilled ethical encounter" necessarily produces empathic response. And such *affecting* empathy, I assert, is a requirement if ethical action is to have any long-term effect: it is not just ideas or even laws that need to change but the ways humans interact with each other and their quotidian environment. The revolution is affective. But what is an ethics of empathy at a time when physical proximity is dangerous to individuals, communities, and humanity?

CONCLUSION: PROXIMATE BODIES IN A TIME OF TECHNOLOGY

As I finish this chapter, the world has changed. A global pandemic has forced most people into their homes and apartments and out of the workplace. People are dying and suffering at racially disproportionate rates.

People are also communicating across time and space with an ease unimagined just a few months ago. But these interactions are virtual. Family, friends, and colleagues, artists, and audiences are now images and voices on a screen. As physical beings we are distant, but we are socially proximate as cyborgs: the flesh of the world extends to the flesh of technology like a second skin.

What happens to the body—its tastes and smells, its resonances and sensations—in this new reality? Where and what is affect when bodies are absent, one from another? If the aesthetics of proximity produces empathy and states of change, what happens in conditions of embodied distance?

With the quarantine, the Boutshishi Sufis began online liturgies every day, with prayers for the healing of the religious and global community. This allowed practitioners from all over the world to attend; time zones and space were transcended. There was a difference, of course. Not everyone could turn on their audio at once, as that would have caused pandemonium—hundreds of individual voices colliding over Zoom. So we listened to one small household praying and chanting, while others intoned to themselves in the privacy of their individual rooms. Many people left their cameras on so their praying could be observed if one scrolled through the faces, but the audio remained mute. Consequently, the dense mesh of voices, the aesthetic proximity, was absent. The difference was palpable. Listening practices changed; it was no longer possible to respond to the vibration of other bodies, the familiar ground of intersensorial experience that usually accompanies the ceremony. No one went into rapture. There was no hal. Rather, the liturgy did what liturgy does: it brought the community into being. And for this to happen, a co-presence in shared time was necessary, even if bodies were distant.

In moments of confinement, mediated sociality (when accessible) becomes more salient. Collectivities and audiences show up together "live" on screen. The actual presence of the other *in the same time* (and space of the platform) is important. It affords a different kind of imagined community—not one of nation per se (Anderson 1983) but of peer group, audience, and collectivity, whether based on religion or on the performances of taste. Watching a recording asynchronically is not the same, insofar as there is no imagined time-space continuity between participants. Showing up live in the coterminous virtual realm is a signal of belonging and commitment, a tattoo on the flesh of fluctuating existence. Presence, even in virtual performance, is a requirement for the threading of bodies into a shared affective weave.

But what is absent is also significant: the intersensorial thickness of flesh. In *The Absent Body*, phenomenologist Drew Leder asserts that the body appears to itself most poignantly when it is sick (1990). The body, he says, appears to itself in dysfunction—it "dys-appears." Much of the time, humans walk around incognizant of their embodiment and distant from their own sentience, but in sickness, the body is experienced as other than the mind, becoming an object of accusative awareness. While Leder talks about this in terms of the discrete individual, it also holds true for the collective. The global pandemic has made the social body aware of its ailing materiality—as institutions with insufficient hospital beds, as schools unable to respond to the needs of children. The social and political body appears to itself most poignantly when it no longer "works."

This is also true of democracy and all the more poignant in the examples of the Black Lives Matter movement. The murders of George Floyd, Ahmaud Arbery, Tamir Rice, and others were first seen and heard by the global public in online videos and, despite the risk of COVID-19 infection, people across the United States and around the world took to the streets. The sick social body appeared to itself in the extreme dysfunction of structural racism through videos that went viral and the response was, and had to be, an embodied co-presence.[19] Only such proximity forces an intimate encounter with difference that displaces the boundaries of self-same (in this case, the United States with its unmarked and misrecognized racism). What Butler calls the "obligation of proximity" is this: an immediate and corporeal response.

Why did the video of George Floyd's murder—so distant from the majority of its viewers—incite embodied resistance when those before it did not?

Perhaps it was the iteration of the death knell of Eric Garner's "I can't breathe." Perhaps it was Floyd's plea for the policeman to stop, the murderer's challenging stare into the camera, Floyd's calling for his mother, or the breathlessness of the pandemic as a backdrop. The combination of images, sounds, and his voice evoked an intersensorial density that triggered a collective trauma—a memory in the Black bodies of America (and throughout the world) that made the past a present and immanent reality, one that could no longer be ignored. Floyd's voice passed through mediated form and straight into the heart:

I can't breathe officer
don't kill me
they gon kill me man
come on man
I cannot breathe
I cannot breathe
they gon kill me
they gon kill me
I can't breathe
I can't breathe
please sir
please
please
please I can't breathe

(Floyd quoted in Lithwick 2020)

This voice, this plea, sent people to the streets raising their own voices: "no justice, no peace," a call and response, a wave of affect surging from behind closed doors and screens into the public sphere of history.

To be an ethnographic ear to sonic acts such as these, or to those of Sufi Muslim worship in secular Europe described above, it is necessary to resonate with the sound knowledge transmitted and to witness—indeed to empathically experience—the disintegration of the self-owning rational self of the Enlightenment (what I call the "juridical body") as it gives way to another, the sound body, a collective and affective sonic ontology (Kapchan 2015). Audition is a techné on this path, produced in part by the aesthetics of proximity—microtones, intersensorial thickness, social dissonance, and *lingering in the space of discomfort* long enough to resonate with the same.[20] It is not the human as such that is annihilated in this encounter but the conception of a consciousness limited to the body rather than extensive with the affecting flesh, the fleshly affect, of the world.

Acknowledgments

My thanks to Harris Berger, Michelle Kisliuk, Robert Rowe, Kati Szego, Katharine Young, and an anonymous reader for comments that helped improve this chapter.

Notes

1. Discussing this concept, Rytis Ambrazevicius (2017, 40) explains that *Schwebungsdiaphonie* refers to "the style of performance where dyads of parts form predominantly rough sonorities (or at least result in audible beats). The notion can be extended to music with

more than two parts. Examples of *Schwebungsdiaphonie* are found in the Balkans, Indonesia, and elsewhere."

2. I use the term "intentionality'" in the sense developed by the analytic philosopher John Searle, not in the sense that this term is given in the phenomenological tradition. Searle (1979) distinguishes between Intentionality (with a capital "I") and intentionality as a state of intending-to-do-something. The former is an orientation toward a propositional content with particular conditions of satisfaction, whereas intentional—that is, volitional—states are simply one example of the above. Given this micro-theory of the philosophy of mind, which assumes the existence of an empirical reality apart from my perception of it (i.e., naïve realism), the individual acts upon the world according to Intention, and that world also acts upon the individual, causing perceptions and responses to them. On the use of the term intentionality in phenomenology, see Kersten (1996).

3. For more on intentionality and performance, see Kapchan (2001).

4. Not only is *tawhid* (unity with God) one of the explicit goals of chanting the dhikr, but instructions are given for maintaining one pitch.

5. Similar aesthetics are found in nonsacred compositions as well, as in the works of William Basinski, Pauline Oliveros, or Arvo Pärt.

6. There is still much to be understood about why *perceptions* of consonance and dissonance differ. See, for example, Shapira Lots et al. (2008).

7. However, there is also some research that suggests that when two notes with more complex frequency ratios are sounded, they activate different neural pathways from those activated by two notes with simple frequency ratios. See Tramo et al. (2001).

8. I use the word "instability" because in many musical traditions—including those of the Arab world—intervals with complex frequency ratios are perceived to be unstable until they find resolution on the tonic.

9. Merleau-Ponty notes that in the observation of gesture, "everything happens as if the other person's intention inhabited my body, or as if my intentions inhabited his body" ([1945] 2012, 191), and surely intersubjectivities happen in all senses and through all senses, including the visual. We know as well that in observation, mirror neurons fire and replicate the experience in the somatic nervous system of the spectator.

10. In the analysis of media images, it is important to account for the positionality and perspective of the viewer. On a television, for example, the viewer is bigger than the story while at the movie theater the spectator is smaller. Videos create an archive that the spectator builds upon in deciding their next ethical (or unethical) response. While edited film directs the spectator's gaze to particular aspects of the performance (the close-up, the explosion), in live performance it is the personal history of the audience member that determines whether one attends to one detail of the story or another. What's more, the *affect* elicited by a character will inform how that character is encountered and perceived in subsequent scenes. As in life, there is an affective accumulation, as well as a feedback loop, between audience member and actor that is vital. (My thanks to my esteemed colleague Joanna Settle for her insights here.)

11. Developing related ideas, Harris Berger (2009, 5) defines *stance* as "the valual qualities of the relationship that a person has to a text, performance, practice, or item of expressive culture." For "traditions that understand the composition as an entity existing before the performance," he notes, "the musician will clearly have a relationship to that composition as she plays it—whatever its ontological status. This relationship is the most straightforward form of the notion of stance" (7).

12. *Lalla* literally means "Miss"; it is a nominative of respect used by all the women in the Sufi order. Sister (*khutti*) is also used.

13. Philosopher Martha Nussbaum (2001) has argued that emotions are not the opposite of rationality. As she observes, all rational decision-making is emotionally inflected and there is not a single decision taken that is not in some way informed by emotion. Likewise, the division between the thinking brain and the feeling body is patently false, as these functions of the person are inseparably linked. Embodiment is somatic, but the brain and the human capacities for language and reflection are also fundamentally embodied.

It is not only the case that feeling and thought are connected. Anthropologists studying emotion have elucidated the ways that culture determines subjective emotional experience. Paul Ekman, for example, delineated the human gestures portraying emotion. For Ekman (1972), there were genres of emotion, visual expressions—for disgust, surprise, anger, sadness, grief—that were pan-human. The apparent universality in the way these emotions are expressed in bodily gesture and visually interpreted, however, does not mean that emotions and their responses were not learned, nor does it imply that the same stimuli produce the same reactions across cultures. In the 1980s, Steven Feld brought attention to the inextricability of aesthetics and the feelings that differing forms of behavior bring forth in an individual or group. For Feld, ways of being are connected to styles of expression (cultural aesthetics and form), and emotion imbues all expressive culture (1980). For Catherine A. Lutz and Lila Abu-Lughod as well, emotions are not "natural" but emerge from socially prescribed discursive contexts (1990). In order to understand the cultural force and agency of emotion—its performativity—anthropologists developed studies of particular emotions in specific social contexts. Renato Rosaldo, for example, delineated how grief and rage came to define certain aspects of Ilongot culture (1989). Abu-Lughod (1986) demonstrated how emotions that were taboo in mixed-gender contexts—desire, love, disdain—found poetic expression among Bedouin women in Egypt, while Lutz brought attention to the way emotions are gendered and how that gendering creates stereotypes with social consequences (1990). Throughout this literature, emotion that is felt at the level of the individual body is also an integral factor in social life. What part of emotion, then, is shared? This is the question that theorists of affect ask.

14. Brennan also questions the current emphasis on genetic determinations for human behavior, noting that until the effects of "socially induced affect" are understood we cannot make genetic arguments.

15. Hermann Schmitz, who is credited with founding the "new phenomenology" (see, for example, Schmitz et al. 2011), begins his philosophy of emotion with a unique perspective on the phenomenological notion of the *Leib* (the lived body). For Schmitz, emotions are "spatial atmospheres" that are not limited to the individual but are nonetheless experienced at the level of the body. Indeed, these spatial atmospheres inhabit a realm of what he calls "surfaceless spaces," which include what might be called (following Brandon Labelle) "acoustic territories" or (following Schafer [1977]) "soundscapes" but which also may take in regions of the body or even forms of weather! While abstract, this concept is consistent with a Spinozian orientation, which understands affect as precognitive and agentive.

16. As Kassabian notes, "listening, and more generally the input of the senses . . . produces *affective* responses, bodily events that ultimately lead in part to what we call emotion. And it is through this listening and these responses that a nonindividual, not simply human, *distributed subjectivity* takes place across a network of music media" (2013, xi; italics in the

original). For Kassabian, it is through a (non-attentive) listening to sounds and music that affect is circulated. Indeed, Kassabian goes on to say that "[a]*ffect* is the circuit of bodily responses to stimuli that take place before conscious apprehension. Once apprehended, the responses pass into thoughts and feelings, though they always leave behind a residue. . . . This residue accretes in our bodies, becoming the stuff of future affective responses" (xiii; italics in the original).

17. This is exemplified in the work of the late performance studies scholar José Muñoz (2009), who builds upon philosopher Ernest Bloch's *The Principle of Hope* ([1959] 1986) to distinguish utopias that are ideal from those that are rooted in history. These "concrete utopias" are like material abodes brought into being by hope, an emotion with power to do things in the world.

18. There are resonances here with Karen Barad's notion of an "agential cut"—the way experience is intersected in any given time and place (Barad 2007). Building upon insights from quantum physics, Barad insists that independent objects, which she prefers to call *relata*, do not in fact exist independently of one another, but that all experience arises from a (performative) "cut" in the space-time continuum. World and human are not interrelated for Barad, but are coproduced in what she calls "intra-action." Phenomenological indeterminacy is itself the ground of being, punctuated by a myriad of possible intra-actions. While a full analysis of Barad's theory is beyond the scope of this chapter, it is clear that Merleau-Ponty's notion of the chiasm—forming a unique experience from the element of flesh—finds great resonance here.

19. Not all chiasms are equally affecting. Just as there are wounds that mend quickly and others that take a longer time to heal, there are affective valences that reverberate for shorter or longer periods of time and over shorter and longer distances.

20. As Jeremy Gilbert put it, "Music has *physical effects* which can be identified, described and discussed but which are not the same thing as it having *meanings*, and any attempt to understand how music works in culture must . . . be able to say something about those effects without trying to collapse them into meanings" (2004; emphasis in the original).

WORKS CITED

Abu-Lughod, Lila. 1986. *Veiled Sentiments: Honor and Poetry in a Bedouin Society*. Berkeley: University of California Press.

Ambrazevicius, Rytis. 2017. "Dissonance/Roughness and Tonality Perception in Lithuanian Traditional Schwebungsdiaphonie." *Journal of Interdisciplinary Music Studies* 8 (1–2): 39–53.

Anderson, Benedict. 1983. *Imagined Communities*. London: Verso.

Appadurai, Arjun. 2005. *Fear of Small Numbers*. Durham, NC: Duke University Press.

Auslander, Philip. 1999. *Liveness: Performance in a Mediatized Culture*. New York: Routledge.

Barad, Karen. 2007. *Meeting the Universe Halfway: Quantum Physics and the Entanglement of Matter and Meaning*. Durham, NC: Duke University Press.

Becker, Judith. 2004. *Deep Listeners: Music, Emotion, and Trancing*. Bloomington: Indiana University Press.

Berger, Harris. 2009. *Stance: Ideas about Emotion, Style, and Meaning for the Study of Expressive Culture*. Middletown, CT: Wesleyan University Press.

Bloch, Ernst. (1959) 1986. *The Principle of Hope*. Translated by Neville Plaice, Stephen Plaice, and Paul Knight. Cambridge, MA: MIT Press.

Brennan, Teresa. 2004. *The Transmission of Affect*. Ithaca, NY: Cornell University Press.

Butler, Judith. 2004. *Precarious Life: The Powers of Mourning and Violence*. London: Verso.

Butler, Judith. 2011. "Precarious Life: The Obligations of Proximity." The Neale Wheeler Watson Lecture, Nobel Museum, Svenska Akademiens Börssal, May 24, 2011. https://www.youtube.com/watch?v=KJT69AQtDtg.

Casey, Edward. 1987. *Remembering: A Phenomenological Study*. Bloomington: Indiana University Press.

Clough, Patricia Ticineto. 2007. "Introduction." In *The Affective Turn: Theorizing the Social*, edited by Patricia Ticineto Clough and Jean Halley, 1–33. Duke University Press.

Connor, Steven. 2004. "Edison's Teeth: Touching Hearing." In *Hearing Cultures: Essays on Sound, Listening, and Modernity*, edited by Veit Erlmann, 153–172. New York: Berg.

Csordas. Thomas. 1993. "Somatic Ways of Knowing." *Cultural Anthropology* 8 (2): 135–156.

Deleuze, Gilles, and Félix Guattari. 1987. *A Thousand Plateaus: Capitalism and Schizophrenia*. Minneapolis: University of Minnesota Press.

Derrida, Jacques. 1985. "Roundtable on Translation." In *The Ear of the Other: Otobiography, Transference, Translation*. Edited by Christie McDonald. Translated by Peggy Kamuf. New York: Schocken Books.

Duranti, A. 1986. "The Audience as Co-author: An Introduction." *Text & Talk* 6: 239–248.

Ekman, Paul. 1972. "Universal and Cultural Differences in Facial Expression of Emotion." *Nebraska Symposium on Motivation*, edited by J. R. Cole, 207–283. Lincoln: University of Nebraska Press.

Feld, Steven. 1980. *Sound and Sentiment*. Philadelphia: University of Pennsylvania Press.

Geertz, Clifford. 1976. "From the Native's Point of View: On the Nature of Anthropological Understanding." In *Meaning in Anthropology*, edited by Keith Basso and Henry A. Selby, 221–237. Albuquerque: University of New Mexico Press.

Gil, Denise. 2017. *Melancholic Modalities: Affect, Islam, and Turkish Classical Musicians*. Oxford: Oxford University Press.

Gilbert, Jeremy. 2004. "Signifying Nothing: 'Culture,' 'Discourse' and the Sociality of Affect." *Culture Machine* 6. https://culturemachine.net/deconstruction-is-in-cultural-studies/signifying-nothing/.

Haraway, Donna. 1991. *Simians, Cyborgs, and Women: The Reinvention of Nature*. New York: Routledge.

Husserl, Edmund. 2001. *Analyses Concerning Passive and Active Synthesis: Lectures on Transcendental Logic*. Translated by Anthony J. Steinbock. Dordrecht, Netherlands: Kluwer Academic Publishing.

Ihde, Don 1993. *Postphenomenology: Essays in the Postmodern Context*. Evanston, IL: Northwestern University Press.

Kant, Immanuel. (1790) 2000. *Critique of the Power of Judgment*. Edited by Paul Guyer. Translated by Paul Guyer and Eric Matthews. Cambridge: Cambridge University Press.

Kapchan, Deborah. 2001. "Exchanging Lies and Creating Truths: Intentionality in Moroccan Marketplace Performance." In *New Approaches to Theater Studies and Performance Analysis*, edited by Gunter Berghaus, 97–110. Tübingen: Max Niemeyer Verlag.

Kapchan, Deborah. 2009. "Learning to Listen: The Sound of Sufism in France." *The World of Music* 52 (2): 63–88.

Kapchan, Deborah. 2015. "Body." In *Keywords in Sound*, edited by David Novak and Matt Sakakeeney, 33–44. Durham, NC: Duke University Press.

Kassabian, Anahid. 2013. *Ubiquitous Listening: Affect, Attention, and Distributed Subjectivity.* Berkeley: University of California Press.

Keil, Charles. 1987. "Participatory Discrepancies and the Power of Music." *Cultural Anthropology* 2 (3): 275–283.

Keil, Charles, and Steven Feld. 1994. *Music Grooves.* Chicago: University of Chicago Press.

Kersten, Fred. 1996. "Intentionality." In *Encyclopedia of Phenomenology*, edited by Lester Embree et al., 350–355. Dordrecht, Netherlands: Springer-Science+Business Media, B.V. Option.

Kisliuk, Michelle. 1998. *Seize the Dance: BaAka Musical Life and the Ethnography of Performance.* New York: Oxford University Press.

Kisliuk Michelle. 2017. "Writing the Magnified Musicking Moment." In *Theorizing Sound Writing*, edited by Deborah Kapchan, 86–116. Middleton, CT: Wesleyan University Press.

Leder, Drew. 1990. *The Absent Body.* Chicago: University of Chicago Press.

Lithwick, Dahlia. 2020. "American Gasps for Air." *Slate*, May 30, 2020. https://slate.com/news -and-politics/2020/05/america-gasps-for-air.html.

Lutz, Catherine A. 1990. "Endangered Emotions: Gender, Power and Rhetoric of Emotional Control in American Discourse." In *Language and the Politics of Emotion: Studies in Emotion and Social Interaction*, edited by Catherine A. Lutz and Lila Abu-Lughod, 69–91. New York: Cambridge University Press.

Lutz, Catherine A., and Lila Abu-Lughod, eds. 1990. *Language and the Politics of Emotion: Studies in Emotion and Social Interaction.* New York: Cambridge University Press.

Massumi, Brian. 1995. "The Autonomy of Affect." *Cultural Critique* 31 (Autumn): 83–109.

Massumi, Brian. 2002. *Parables for the Virtual.* Durham, NC: Duke University Press.

Merleau-Ponty, Maurice. (1945) 2012. *Phenomenology of Perception.* Translated by Donald A. Landes. New York: Routledge.

Merleau-Ponty, Maurice. 1969. *The Visible and the Invisible.* Translated by Alphonso Lingus. Evanston, IL: Northwestern University Press.

Messner, G. Florian. 1990. *Schwebungsdiaphonie.* Cambridge: Cambridge University Press.

Muñoz, José. 2009. *Cruising Utopia: The Then and There of Queer Futurity.* New York: New York University Press.

Noyes, Dorothy. 2003. *Fire in the Plaça: Catalan Festival Politics after Franco.* Philadelphia: University of Pennsylvania Press.

Nussbaum, Martha C. 2001. *Upheavals of Thought: The Intelligence of Emotions.* Cambridge: Cambridge University Press.

Oliveros, Pauline. 2005. *Deep Listening: A Composer's Sound Practice.* New York: iUniverse, Inc.

Pais, Ana. 2017. "Almost Imperceptible Rhythms and Stuff like That: The Power of Affect in Live Performance." In *Theorizing Sound Writing*, edited by Deborah Kapchan, 233–250. Middletown, CT: Wesleyan University Press.

Phelan, Peggy. 1993. *Unmarked: The Politics of Performance.* New York: Routledge.

Rosaldo, Renato. 1989. "Introduction: Grief and a Headhunter's Rage." In *Culture and Truth: The Remaking of Social Analysis*, 1–24. Boston: Beacon Press.

Rice, Timothy. 2004. *Music in Bulgaria: Experiencing Music, Expressing Culture.* Oxford: Oxford University Press.

Rorty, Amélie Oksenberg, ed. 1980. *Explaining Emotions.* Berkeley: University of California Press.

Sartre, Jean-Paul. 1970. *The Emotions: Outline of a Theory.* Translated by Bernard Frechtman. New York: Humanities Press.

Schafer, R. Murray. 1977. *The Tuning of the World.* New York: Knopf.

Schmitter, Amy M. 2010. "Spinoza on the Emotions." In *The Stanford Encyclopedia of Philosophy*, edited by Edward N. Zalta. Stanford University. https://plato.stanford.edu/entr ies/emotions-17th18th/LD5Spinoza.html.

Schmitz, Hermann, Rudolf Owen Müllan, and Jan Slaby. 2011. "Emotions outside the Box— The New Phenomenology of Feeling and Corporeality." *Phenomenology and the Cognitive Sciences* 10: 241–259.

Searle, John. 1979. "Indirect Speech Acts." In *Expression and Meaning: Studies in the Theory of Speech Acts*, 30–57. Cambridge: Cambridge University Press.

Shapira Lots, Inbal, and Lewi Stone. 2008. "Perception of Musical Consonance and Dissonance: An Outcome of Neural Synchronization." *Journal of the Royal Society, Interface* 5 (29): 1429–1434. https://doi.org/10.1098/rsif.2008.0143.

Shouse, Eric. 2005. "Feeling, Emotion, Affect." *M/C Journal* 8 (6). http://journal.media-culture .org.au/0512/03-shouse.php.

Solomon, Robert. C. 2004. *Thinking about Feeling: Contemporary Philosophers on Emotions*. Oxford: Oxford University Press.

Sontag, Susan. 2003. *Regarding the Pain of Others*. New York: Farrar, Straus and Giroux.

Tramo, Mark Jude, Peter A. Cariani, Bertrand Delgutte, and Louis D. Braida. 2001. "Neurobiological Foundations for the Theory of Harmony in Western Tonal Music." *Annals of the New York Academy of Science* 930: 92–116.

Turino, Thomas. 1993. *Moving Away from Silence: Music of the Peruvian Altiplano and the Experience of Urban Migration*. Chicago Studies in Ethnomusicology. Chicago: University of Chicago Press.

CHAPTER 18

PHENOMENOLOGICAL DISPLACEMENTS

Voice, Atmospheric Disturbance, and Mediatized Grief

DANIEL FISHER

LAW AS SOUND: MUSICAL MEDIA AND ATMOSPHERIC ATTUNEMENT

This chapter introduces and examines recent theoretical engagements with the figure of atmospheres, putting phenomenological, new materialist, and affect-oriented scholarship into conversation with ethnographic research on Indigenous musical media in Australia's Northern Territory. What might be gained by approaching the mediatized politics of grief in northern Australia as a reflexive encounter with atmospheric disturbance? What critical ground emerges from attending to our interlocutors' and our own attunements to collective moods and modes of feeling that exceed any one body? What kinds of worlds and world-making might come into view when we attend to modes of attunement to affective climates?

I approach such questions ethnographically by attending to an atmospheric disturbance that followed the death of a celebrity singer in northern Australia. The unease, public questioning, and reflection that followed his passing were powerful and deeply unsettling—palpable and affecting even to myself, a relative outsider to the goings on. In telling this story, however, this chapter must also traverse a series of pointed, singular moments that highlight the relationship between death and disability, displacement, and musical media. My account pivots on the paradoxical materiality of an affective climate. Through ethnographic attention to musical media and sound in their relation to mourning, I will suggest that Indigenous authority is made and reaffirmed in moments of atmospheric attunement and co-composition. As such, the ground of its legislative force might be understood not solely in the ideals and overt targets of institutional power—nor in a largely unconscious "lawscape" (Philippopoulos-Mihalopoulos 2015) or milieu that directs and governs even (or especially) when we are unaware of its presence (Lea 2020; cf. Bille et al. 2015; Zhang 2018)—but also in collective surges of shared attention and action that at once build upon and also precede and exceed discursive elaboration, overt organization, or legal institution (Stewart 2011, 2016; cf. Bens 2018, Eisenlohr 2018).

This is close to what Timothy Choy and Jerry Zee call "a form of attention that is also a mode of relation, a way of being suspended"—a suspension they helpfully align with "agitation" (2015, 211–212). This chapter seeks to analyze a specific event of atmospheric agitation in relation to music, media, and grief, and also to critically reflect on the value of contemporary atmospheric thought in relation to music and sound. Authority is composed, I suggest, and to address that composition I underscore agitation as a vital facet of atmospheric scholarship. Provisionally, we might define *atmosphere* as a mood or affect taking spatial and material form, an extra-individual *Stimmung* constituted by bodies in relation (cf. Schmitz et al. 2011).[1] Atmospheres are not simply a "middle ground" or a form of inchoate feeling congealing as environment, quasi-object, or ontologized relation. But neither are atmospheres simply affective structures that transcend an individual consciousness. Instead, as Stewart (2011) suggests, they come to exist in and as modes of attunement themselves, and a phenomenology of atmospheric attunement is thus an effort both to follow form in motion—to see its shaping power in relationship to sets of persons and things—and to also ask why that motion might matter in a particular historical moment. Put plainly, in asking why this matters, why *this* affective climate was so very charged, I begin with the marked prevalence of displacement, illness, and death that summon the musical and atmospheric interventions of my interlocutors.

In a sense this chapter is about how sovereignty feels and how ideals of justice and forms of ethical sensibility are produced, made sensible, and also disturbed in and by sound. This formulation echoes Deborah A. Thomas, in her reckoning with modern sovereignty in relation to affect, violence, and witnessing (2019, 1). In dialogue with both Thomas and Audra Simpson (2020) I deploy the figure of sovereignty here cognizant of real tension between, on the one hand, post-Westphalian figures of sovereignty in relationship to jurisdiction—a sovereign's right to kill or let live, and the range of critical theory underpinning its entanglement with or displacement by biopolitics (Agamben 1995; Foucault [1976] 1978; cf. Barr 2013)—and, on the other, sovereignty's pragmatic refiguration by Indigenous peoples in claims that privilege the skein of relations and obligations to places, waters, and the beings and powers that comingle there—relations glossed in Australia as "country" (Moreton-Robinson 2007).[2] As I deploy the figure of sovereignty in this chapter, I mean to evoke both the compelling character of a living law, as well as its tense articulation with settler colonial jurisdiction and the ongoing impulse to ground Indigenous governance in Australia on a biopolitical logic (see also Simpson 2014; Stevenson 2014).

I explore these concerns by attending to the mediatization of *rom*, a Yolngu term most frequently translated as "law" that also encompasses notions of tradition, authority, and culture. Rom entails a binding, compelling force—a normative power that is no small part of its value for Yolngu people today.[3] While the analysis concerns events following the passing of an artist and international celebrity who was also a beloved friend of and family to many in Darwin, referred to in this chapter as "TC," I do not here detail the specific circumstances that led to his passing.[4] Although my research was drawn into the orbit of this singer and his family in the last days of his life, the account I develop instead focuses on the atmospheric effects that his passing entailed, building on the concerns and interpretations that others made clear in the weeks that followed. In writing about our shared apprehension of an atmosphere off kilter, I foreground the authority of this man's family and community and the law they ask others to acknowledge. I emphasize here at the outset that the substance and matter of such authority, its enduring and compelling character, and its negotiation of the mass mediated character of Australian musical culture are at the heart of this chapter's concerns.

Before unfolding an ethnographic narrative and directing attention to one moment of atmospheric attunement in relation to grief and rom's authority, I turn first to a film in order to make clear the everydayness of atmospheric attunement in its relationship to musical media and sound. I then canvass recent ethnomusicological and anthropological engagements with atmosphere as both concept-metaphor and worldly, empirical phenomena and relate this to the diffuse and law-like character of musical meaningfulness in northern Australia.

Radio's Lawlike Atmospheres

Samson and Delilah (2009), a film produced and directed by Indigenous Australian director and cinematographer Warwick Thornton, and winner of the Camera d'Or for best first feature at the 2009 Cannes film festival, pursues a narrative that is equal parts dystopian road movie and redemptive romance. The film is bookended by two scenes that make radio and country music central. The film opens with a radio, set beside a mattress, and the sounds of Charley Pride's "Sunshiny Day" coming across its small speakers. Its sounds are diegetic, initially, and they resound in the bedroom of the first character we meet, Samson. As the character wakes, he brings a tin can to his face and breathes deeply. As he inhales from the open tin the radio's music moves from diegetic to non-diegetic sound, and the sonic analog of this cinematic shift is the broad stage given to Charley Pride's voice and an accompanying pedal steel guitar as the soundtrack shifts from the small signal of that onscreen radio—accompanied by crackling static and whine—to a non-diegetic, clear and wide stereo platform.

The film strategically plays with this sonic boundary throughout, moving us back and forth between a diegetic and realist relational space and the non-diegetic, affect-laden environments of its characters and the narrative arc they traverse. The all-encompassing sonic environment of the film is a powerful force, lending access to the emotional lives of characters, but also making manifest the authoritative status of the polity they inhabit. These renderings of popular music and radio sound do narrative work; that is, they call attention to themselves throughout the film. By setting these filmic parameters in these first moments, Thornton hoped he would be able to do as he liked, in formal terms, in the film that follows—but he also wanted to prepare viewers for the tragedy to come (see Thornton 2017; cf. Buckmaster 2009). The basic elements of this scene are familiar to many Australian viewers: the wide reach and popularity of Aboriginal request and call-in radio programs, the even wider popularity of 1960s and 1970s country music across Indigenous Australia, and a generation of Aboriginal kids seemingly lost to petrol sniffing.

By the end of the film's narrative, Thornton's two protagonists have traversed the physical and mental torment induced by sniffing petrol, the violence of White Australia, and also the anger of their own community (incurred for not adequately externalizing grief on the death of Delilah's grandmother). The film leaves them resting outside of a tin shed, where Samson is being looked after by Delilah as he undergoes a kind of central desert rehab. He is listening to the radio and to one of the tracks that begins the film when a request comes over the radio: "That was going out to Samson from his father Jimmy. Only six months to go, son, and he'll be coming home." Samson laughs as the tune that follows takes prominence in the soundtrack, moving from the localized source of the onscreen radio to animate the screen itself with affecting, non-diegetic sound. It is another by Charley Pride, his 1969 recording of Dallas Frazier and Doodle Owens's song "All I Have to Offer You (Is Me)."[5]

The recurrence of radio sounds and radio requests throughout the film offers a form of realism, registering the results of activist work in media that has built an Indigenous radio network to which requests, remembrances, and exhortations from family members are central (Fisher 2016). From elder women scolding their grandchildren and underscoring the significance of making positive choices to the mass mediation of Indigenous languages, Aboriginal activists and advocates have built a radio-mediated sonic world that echoes the priorities, languages, and sensibilities of Indigenous audiences. In this sonic domain, claims to sovereignty are made not only in referential or declarative language but also performatively through sounds that link up dispersed communities, repairing relations sundered by displacement and dispersal, and fostering a distinctive feeling of sovereign belonging. This might be figured as the sonic unconscious of contemporary northern Australia, a media world built by and for Aboriginal people in which enveloping sounds attune listeners to the country on which they are standing.

The closing sequence thus offers an Indigenous perspective on what media ought to accomplish, in that radio lends a platform for the amplification of kin connection, while powerfully evoking the poles of a transformed relational space. The film's narrative and this radiophonic resolution can be seen as a condemnation of the conditions in which Aboriginal people are forced to live. But it is equally an exhortation, a critique leveled at these communities themselves: a "hard lesson for my mob," Thornton has said—that you should look after one another, that you should stick around to raise your kids, that you should stay off the drink and the drugs. *Samson and Delilah* remediates radio as cinema in order to scold as much as to celebrate—listen up, look after each other! Thornton's cinema reminds its audience how and to whom they ought to listen and suggests how it is that atmospheres can abet forms of comportment.

As with radio requests themselves, the film splits and rejoins speech and sound, playing with the speech-sound continuum such that its poles are stretched wide apart, their distinction exaggerated. For instance, vocalized speech does little narrative work and the primary characters do not for the most part talk in the film, though they do occasionally employ a central desert sign language. The character of Samson, for instance, does not speak, and one potential interpretation of this characteristic is that his efforts to vocalize are stymied by the ravages of petrol itself. Just as he lost the capacity to walk, so too has he lost the capacity to speak. Instead, vocalization happens primarily through the radios or cassette players that appear onscreen, almost as characters in themselves. The bodily voices of Thornton's characters, that is, are displaced and the voice itself problematized by recorded and mass-mediated popular song as the voices of radio DJs and recorded music at times act as their prosthesis or supplement.

What becomes apparent from Thornton's careful toggling between diegetic and non-diegetic sound, the marked separation of speech from sound throughout the film, and the displacement of voice and sound from bodies and onto a mediatized social or atmospheric surround is that sovereignty or law take shape as a feeling, an ambience, or mood. The all-encompassing sonic environments of the film lend access to the emotional lives of its characters but also make manifest the authoritative demands of kinship and the media artifacts of music and sound on which those relations now depend. Voices and music from a radio or sound recording shape inner space, realist space, and social space at once, and in the process also call attention to this shaping, cultivating viewers' attunement to atmospheric transformation, disturbance, and intervention. In the process, the film distills an Aboriginal atmospheric attunement to law that privileges musical and radio media on platforms that are controlled by Indigenous people. These are sounds that, in cultivating the affective substance of proper relations, offer a way to grasp a phenomenology of sovereignty, to see its vitality, its potency in social life, and its vulnerability to death.[6] It also begins to suggest something of the ways that sovereignty is always-already an unfinished project, a sensibility, and an atmosphere.

THEORIZING ATMOSPHERE

Though long of conceptual interest to phenomenology and aesthetic theory, "atmosphere" has attracted expanded interest in recent years as scholars with commitments to ethnomusicology, religion and ethics, environmental and ecological humanities, science and technology studies (STS), *inter alia*, have sought to bring affect theory and new materialism into a dialogue with environmental and ecological scholarship. Broadly influenced by Deleuzian modes of analysis and their echoes across the theorization of affect (Stewart 2007; Berlant 2011; Manning and Massumi 2014; Berlant and Stewart 2019), by phenomenology and its application to spatial and environmental questions (Casey 1993; Ingold 2000; cf. Feld 1996), and by a broader, post-human conceptual turn that has problematized environment, "ambience," and phenomenology itself across the humanities and social sciences (Harman 2005, 2011; Morton 2007; Thacker 2011; Grusin 2015), atmosphere has emerged as the analytical figure *par excellence* of our ecological moment.

A prominent thread in science and technology studies scholarship, for instance, addresses atmospheres in relating health, technoscience, and environment and in dealing with atmospheric substances, the harms they cause to human bodies, and the social, political, and intellectual entanglements that ensue (e.g. Mittman et al. 2004; Agard-Jones 2013; Shapiro and Kirksey 2017). This work deploys atmospheric concepts to attend to the distinctive materiality of air and environment, charting structural inequities and forms of subjectivity constituted along ever multiplying sociomaterial vectors of harm. This has offered powerful analytical language and conceptual affordances for traversing different scales of apprehension, motivated by the dispersed and unevenly distributed character of those threats pressing in across the globe.[7] Urgent questions of environmental justice, inequity, and catastrophe can thus overdetermine the turn to atmospheres: thought turns to atmospheres' ontology in our current moment, but it also turns on the tropes and conceptual figures given life and experiential validity amid atmospheric problems (Morton 2007; Choy and Zee 2015; cf. Sloterdijk [1998] 2011, [2002] 2009).[8]

This wide interest in atmospheres also partakes of a phenomenological investment in the modes of knowing, feeling, and acting disclosed by a range of shared attunements to atmospheric transformation and new kinds of ethnographic interlocutors (Stewart 2011; Choy and Zee 2015; cf. Berlant and Stewart 2019). Simply asking the questions "what kind of being do atmospheres have, how do they come to matter, and what methods might best suit their analysis?" has offered a generative problem space for rethinking relations among agency, affect, and environment and for multiplying the kinds of entities that come to matter as interlocutors in ethnographic praxis. As I will argue below, in dialogue with recent ethnographic engagements in ethnomusicology (McGraw 2016; Abels 2018; Riedel 2020), affect theory (Stewart 2011; Lepselter 2016; Luna 2018), diverse strains of media studies (Thacker 2011; Larkin 2014; Peters 2016; Eisenlohr 2018), and the thing theories of Object-Oriented Ontology (Bennett 2010; Harman 2011; Morton 2013), atmospheres may be understood to reflect on themselves in ways that productively complicate the humanist core of the phenomenological project itself even as they require its insights.[9] One gambit in these turns to atmospheres in social science and humanities writing, then, is that atmospherics afford space to think the place of the non- or more-than-human in thought and perception itself.

As an analytical figure in ethnographic scholarship on music and media, atmosphere has its most clear, programmatic ground in the neo-phenomenological work of Hermann Schmitz (Schmitz et al. 2011) and Gernot Böhme (2017) and a related interest in theorizing ambience (Thibaud 2011, 2015; Bille et al. 2015). These scholars direct attention to the situational locus of sensory experience, pointing to aspects of affect and mood that, they argue, should be located beyond the confines of any individual body. These atmospheric programs thus identify environmental entities that emerge from sets of bodies in relation but that exceed reduction to these relations. In such work atmospheres are distinguished from "environments" as consequential entities that inflect aspects of mood and tense; atmospheres, that is, may shape attention or canalize affect, but they resist easy categorization as either a subjective, social mood or an objective, material environment or ground. Atmospheres are entities that traverse both sides of this dichotomy as interstitial "quasi-objects."

For Schmitz, in some consonance with the broader interests of Continental phenomenology, the aim of exploring atmospheres conceptually is to identify and challenge historical, Western philosophical legacies that split an internal, mentalist conceptualizing from an external, material world. His own conceptual media for undoing this legacy is the felt body of the phenomenological tradition (*Leib*)—a culturally shaped apparatus that affords the ground of lived experience, a body that is not divorced from the world but rather suspended in and animated by a series of "significant situations." As Rudolf Owen Müllan and Jan Slaby write in their introduction to a translated article by Hermann Schmitz, such situations offer "rich modes of experience that cannot adequately be narrowed down to perception by means of the sense organs. Instead, sensing by means of the felt body is a holistic exchange of corporeal dynamics, a vibrant attunement to meaningful surroundings" (Schmitz et al. 2011, 244; cf. Abels 2018).[10] To translate this to the ground of northern Australia, when people grow concerned and start to probe a situation, they may have nothing to go on but the sense that "something isn't right." Only then, in turning their attention to that feeling, might they articulate that sensibility in the form of a question.

While putting forward the *Leib* as the first ground of any worldly involvement or knowing, Schmitz's contribution thus has been his phenomenological turn to bodies-in-relation to develop an anti-mentalist focus on the atmospheric densities of sociality. Schmitz's career-long efforts, which he designates a "new phenomenology," have drawn the interests of philosophers and ethnomusicologists, even as they have attracted critique for the normative, Euro-American, and human subject they presuppose (Riedel 2019; Slaby 2020).

Böhme's interests, on the other hand, are more closely aligned with aesthetics and more interested in a human capacity to generate or shape atmospheres through architecture and environmental design. But as with Schmitz, Böhme's writings ground aspects of experience that are often assigned to the individual body or consciousness instead in a multiplicity of bodies and things—to an arrangement, situation, or "constellation." As intersubjective phenomena, then, they reside "in between," mediating two sides (Böhme 2017, 1) as a domain of human experience, but also as objective facets of sound, light, architecture, and the environment writ large. From this spatial ground he thus suggests that atmospheres are "quasi-objective" in that they lie in between object and subject, and as such they are moods, affects, or feelings that exceed any individual body.[11] But if they are thing-like entities, "out there" in the world, they are such only in their capacity to affect subjects, and they are primarily characterizable in terms of such feelingful encounter (cf. McCormack 2018; Zhang 2018). Böhme's interests in the manipulation of atmospheres and the applied implications of his writing across design, architecture, and art worlds have meant that his work has found relevance in scholarship attuned to environmental design (Bille et al. 2015; cf. Zhang 2018), political geography (McCormack 2018), and legal philosophy (Philippopoulos-Mihalopoulos 2015).

Both Schmitz and Böhme work phenomenologically to make experience a primary ground of analysis. Yet both also can encourage what Friedlind Riedel (2020) calls a "mereological" approach—an analysis of part-to-whole and part-to-part relations that directs us beyond the abstracted, individualized body to constellations of entities in relation and to the atmospheres they compose as an encompassing situation.[12] Such entities offer an opening onto a variety of new materialist and ethnographic engagements with Alfred North Whitehead's ontology and Gabriel Tarde's sociology, decentering the relation of human subjects to objects and multiplying the kinds of entities we might consider a "subject" (Born 2018; Povinelli 2016; cf. Harman 2005, 2011).

The centrality of phenomenological approaches to atmosphere's conceptual reemergence has also brought qualification and critique. For Andreas Philippopoulos-Mihalopoulos, for instance, writing on atmospheres of law in their relationship to the city, phenomenological approaches to atmospheres are suspect insofar as they make atmospheric engineering difficult to apprehend and can make it all but impossible to make sensible the directives of atmospheric forces as they lure subjects into spatial orders of capital, law, government, *inter alia*: "However comfortable, an atmosphere is politically and legally suspicious because it numbs a body (via the body's own desire) into an affective embrace of stability and permanence" (2016, 151).[13] Instead, he argues, one must grasp atmospherics as themselves potent materializations of spatial power and consider ontological withdrawal from their appeal as a "strategic gesture" (161). In this analysis, a phenomenology without an ontology makes it too easy to misrecognize or uncritically encounter the character of a situation.[14] In part, this follows from the ways that atmospheres exceed experience; they compel attention or attunement, with the emphasis of this musical metaphorics of attunement on accord or resonance. For Philippopoulos-Mihalopoulos it is such accord that must be subverted.

On one level, this critique resonates with Jane Bennett's (2010) broader charge that phenomenology is so steeped in the human as to make it difficult to recognize the ontological alterity and vital autonomy of things (Goble 2017; cf. Ferro 2019).[15] Yet I underscore here that scholars of a new materialist bent such as Graham Harman and Bennett flag their interests in (and at times reliance upon) forms of experiential engagement and affective attunement but resist the a priori localization of either epistemological mastery or worldly agency in isolable human subjects. While I underscore the difference of new materialist scholarship from that on atmospheres, this also reads equally powerfully as an iteration of a problematic that Choy and Zee (2015) call "suspension," a term they use to explore the generative paradox of being at once caught up in—and constituent elements of—atmospheric phenomena. That is, the value of revisiting such interventions rests in making evident an aporia between phenomenological and materialist approaches to atmospheres, neither reserving subjectivity and "intentionality" solely for humans nor simply ascribing life to things that have long been imagined as non-life. Atmospheres, I suggest, like sound itself (cf. Born 2018), can offer a limit case with respect to the kinds of things that have been privileged in the thing theories of

Bennett, Harman, and others. Atmospheres do not easily resolve on either side of the subject/object, or human/more-than-human, boundary and thus require attending to their relational constitution and specificity.[16]

The strong attraction of atmospheric approaches to an anthropology of sounded worlds is the ways in which the felt body is at once primary and so often decentered, put in abeyance in lieu of attention to the constitution of atmospheres, to bodies in relation, and to the existence of entities, feelings, and other phenomena that escape the binary of matter and spirit. This approach also allows scholars to reflect on the work that affect performs in broader, mass-mediated worlds we navigate and negotiate. In ethnographically driven work by Birgit Abels, Patrick Eisenlohr, Andrew McGraw, Friedlind Riedel, and others, attending to atmospheres entails privileging the specificity of a situation and also reflexive modes of attunement and investment in that situation. This reflexivity need not be necessarily or even primarily discursive but may also occur in the regulation, production, or management of sound, performance, or musical media. To the extent to which people engage in musically keyed feedback loops, that is, they produce themselves and their environments, atmospheres, or, as Peter Sloterdijk ([1998] 2011) might have it more expansively, their spheres. This is to underscore the value for ethnographic work on atmospheres of what Harris Berger calls "stance"—"the affective, stylistic, or valual quality with which a person engages with elements of her experience" (2009, xiv). For Berger, drawing on Husserlian phenomenology, perception is itself compositional. As intentional, it involves not merely registering the world as it is but engaging pragmatically with its constitution and inherent meaningfulness (2009, 18–19).

In methodological terms, attending to attunement and relatedness means considering what people report but also how people engage in musical practice with one another (and one another's attunements) and with sounded atmospheres and sonic artefacts.[17] In Patrick Eisenlohr's work on the mediatization of na't (2018), for instance, atmosphere offers a perspicacious figure for understanding not simply the "sonic dimensions of religion" but also making clear the ways that ethical reflection takes shape in musical practice as a form of atmospheric engineering. Eisenlohr's interlocutors work with sound to shape affective intensities—acting with sound to foster pious comportment. Vocalization and engagements with audio media (and the forms of reflection they evoke) offer witnesses to a local theory of sonic atmospheres, a "sounded religiosity." In Eisenlohr's account, to grasp the significance of the mediatized voice to religious feeling requires attending to the constitution of an ambience, to the ways in which atmospheric effects depend upon but are not reducible to performance practices and media artefacts. In similar fashion, Andrew McGraw's (2016) argument for the relevance of atmospheric analysis to ethnomusicology asserts that music is fundamentally about atmospheres (cf. Riedel 2020). McGraw's methodological interest in bringing radical empiricism to musical process further brackets the ontological distinction between performance and mediation, beginning with a situation and deferring the ontological resonances of a specific sound's source. In both projects, audio media are constitutive instruments in atmospheric engineering and are compositional in this dual sense, animating a sonic environment while also shaping what Zhang (2018) terms in an adjacent, ecological humanities conversation, an "affective climate."

These scholars focus on what one might term a "meaningfulness" that relies upon music and sound but ultimately exceeds both the human and the sonic itself (cf. Abels 2018; Thibaud 2011).[18] Attention to atmospheres draws together in the one domain phenomenological and experiential, hermeneutic and interpretive, and material or "infrastructural" concerns—allowing space for a paradoxical phenomenology of audio media that might decenter the human to foreground an openness to the animals, artefacts, and those "affecting presences" (Armstrong 1971) traversing the worlds that anthropologists and ethnomusicologists engage. This is to include a range of non-human or more-than-human aspects of a "significant situation" (to use Schmitz's phrase), to which the presence of musical media or even non-human sound is an ingredient (as in Born 2018) but where the material presence of sound itself may be absent.

Atmospheres repay our attention, then, as phenomena that force us to question what makes a "thing" a thing or a relation a relation (McCormack 2018), asking that we be open to the singularity of a distinctive situation without erasing its diverse constituents or prefiguring its ontology or "meaning" (Abels 2018). And this brings me back to the science studies work I began with, which directs attention toward the co-implication of body and environment, and toward an undecidability in terms of bodies' boundaries and constitutive elements. Atmospheric analyses resonate with STS approaches to the transit of particulate matter (Shapiro and Kirksey 2017), as well as ethnographic ones to the transit of political affect across a room, a crowd, or an audience (Mazzarella 2018; cf. Born 2012; Daughtry 2015). Indeed, such analyses pursue both phenomenological and ontological accounts, decentering the privative first person, while embracing a radical empiricism that gives credence to the experience of things and their mereology alike (Riedel 2020; cf. Ferro 2019). It is a capacity to hold together such disparate positions, reckoning with the object of experience as well as beyond experience that I pursue in the following sections, asking how my interlocutors engage with the law-like and thing-like milieu that they find themselves suspended in, or better, for the events I recount below, troubled by.

Sounding the Voice: A Powerful Voice and Its Telephonic Prosthetic

The different worlds and normative imperatives given filmic coincidence in *Samson and Delilah* came crashing together in strikingly literal fashion in my own fieldwork amid the political upheaval that followed the death of an Indigenous musical celebrity. I spent July of 2017 in Darwin, capital of Australia's Northern Territory, working with the Larrakia Nation Aboriginal Corporation—the most visible institutional representative of Darwin's Indigenous traditional owners, the Larrakia. The Larrakia Nation has for many years sponsored a number of social outreach programs addressed to a growing concern with Aboriginal urban displacement with the many other Aboriginal peoples who occupy the city—many in government-run housing projects, many others in town and bush camps scattered around the edges of the city, in a coastal reserve stretching north form the city, for instance, or in the bush and scrub around the city's hospital. The latter are often termed "longgrassers" for the spear grass within which many of their camps are situated.

Broadly, this project seeks to minimize the risks that Aboriginal drinkers and those sleeping rough in town will harm themselves or others: if one can intervene and give people a lift to a home, a camp, or to a sobering-up shelter—locally called the spin dry— or even just move them along to somewhere else, perhaps then one can avoid a fight, keep an intoxicated person from wandering in front of a fast-moving car, or avoid a potentially violent encounter with police. I was helped in this research by Vince, a White Australian in his mid-fifties who had grown up in Darwin and who has over the past decade worked for the Larrakia Nation. He spent his formative years living and working with Aboriginal people across the Top End and in recent years has dedicated his days to the socially rich project of Aboriginal outreach.

One morning Vince called my mobile. He had been asked to assist in locating a person he knew well, a local and much revered celebrity singer who had missed several medical appointments and wasn't answering his phone. The hospital's Indigenous outreach staff, and his musical producers and partners, were worried and looking for him, and they had sought the Larrakia Nation's help.

The singer, TC, was a Yolngu man known for the singular timbre of his voice and his capacity to move listeners with traditionally themed songs sung in an emotive, popular gospel style. Stories of particular clan totems shared space in his catalogue with lamentation: "Bapa," for example, offers a spartan lyric expressing grief for a father, a grief that is redoubled in that it also refers to the singer's homesickness for his father's coastal, clan lands. This homesickness and loss are underscored further by reference in the song's lyric to the story of two Gumatj ancestors, "old boss ladies," sitting at this beach and crying.

Circling through Darwin, driving from housing projects at the end of Darwin's Cavenagh Street to a large coastal reserve just north of the city, Vince took his Toyota minivan off-road to small clearings and camps where he thought TC might be staying, the branches scratching and brushing loudly on the sides of the van as it jostled over deeply worn fire trails into the bush. At the end of the day Vince found him with his girlfriend, uncle, and several cousins and aunties in a beachside camp. TC was asleep, and his uncle convinced Vince to come back the following morning.

Vince returned early the next day with a small group that included a colleague from the Larrakia Nation's outreach program, Bernard, a man who also had long been close to TC and who had lived for years in his home community. TC was awake, and although he could joke with his visitors and found the energy to show himself alternately angry and affectionate with Bernard and Vince, he was very ill. As this conversation began, with Vince and his colleague squatting down beside the singer, his cousin hovered around the men, holding a smartphone that was replaying tracks from TC's first record and displaying the album's cover image on its small screen. "That's him! That's him here!" He held the phone to each of our faces in turn and gestured with his other hand toward TC.

The voice coming from the tiny soundstage of this smartphone at once miniaturized (as Adorno [(1941) 2002] might have it) and amplified TC's voice in its reproduction. Though its sound was almost drowned out by the ocean's waves and wind, the voice emerging from the phone still evoked the authority of a masterful singer in his musical prime, reminding us of his celebrity, success, and power, even if he now was weakened by illness. One of TC's aunties, herself worried about his condition, helped the Larrakia team convey him to the hospital, where the severity of his condition became more clear.

Several days later TC passed away from complications related to kidney disease. He was forty-six. This news traveled quickly, and families moved away from the beach where he had been staying, his death acknowledged by this collective withdrawal from the beachside camp. Then the press took hold of the story and TC was eulogized nationally by politicians, by Aboriginal leaders and celebrities, and mourned by almost every Australian I know.

When Vince called to share this news with me, he was grieving and angry. Vince had known TC when the latter was a child and had expressed familiarity and concern as we circled through the city looking for the singer. Vince soon met with a reporter and camera operator for the Australian Broadcasting Corporation. They met where the camp had been and sat down there to conduct his interview—a fact that would become important in the weeks to come. The reporters then recorded Vince's impassioned statement, including pointed questions about TC's care, the broader violence done to Aboriginal people by settler Australia, and Vince's own deep sense of loss. While his questions seemed to imply that family members and TC's friends in Darwin could have done more, they also evinced his shock and sadness in the immediate hours after learning of his friend's passing. Vince later told me that he had conferred with friends close to TC's family and felt he had been given the OK to speak publicly. In the press, however, Vince's grief and anger took shape as an accusation that, when reproduced on Facebook and the webpages of the Northern Territory press, quickly traveled through Darwin's Yolngu community.

Vince's grief was, I believe, amplified by his years of work in the long grass. He frequently remembered aloud to me experiences of being asked to identify Aboriginal men and women in the morgue, people who had been killed by speeding cars after trying to cross the dark roads of Darwin's suburbs, or others who had died from causes related to the drinking and sleeping rough so prominent across Darwin. His deep sadness and anger were palpable and seemed to come to a head in this interview.

My neighbor and TC's cousin, Charlene, herself in Darwin to undergo dialysis, told me that some in the family had learned of the death from the broadcast and social media circulation of Vince's interview. They were upset by this and felt that they should have learned about his passing in a less public fashion as a community. They were also angry, Charlene said, at the implication that TC had been neglected. Finally, they were disturbed by Vince's return with journalists to his final camp on the beach. "He should have known better than to take reporters there," she said. "Why did he do that?" TC's girlfriend and the others had left the camp, and it was empty now, she said—obliquely evoking Yolngu norms against visiting the last dwelling of the recently deceased (norms I discuss in more detail below).

Charlene and I spoke frequently in these days, and the events following TC's passing seemed all she wanted to talk about. She was certainly unsettled by his loss and told me stories of looking after him when they were children. But she was also upset by the on-going dispute around how to tell the story of his passing, around whose story would take prominence. She asked me and others about motivations, about what we understood to have impelled others' actions, and about what we thought might be happening.

Vince in turn sought to find some peace with his ongoing sense that TC's passing could have been avoided. And as he came to some accord with his grief, he also came to some accord with TC's family in the weeks and months that followed. Although Vince felt unfairly undermined by the reception of his interview, he sustained his rela-tionship with the family. In the short term, however, a sense of unease pervaded many conversations.

Between Charlene's questions and Vince's frequent phone calls and efforts to under-stand the particularities of this death, other conversations were taking shape in public media. TC's celebrity drew attention to the ongoing disparity in health care access and outcomes for Indigenous Australians, attracting renewed concern to a broader problem. The singular particulars of his death joined a broader attunement to aspects of the structural inequities and injustices that underpin health disparities across Indigenous Australia, amplifying the political implications of TC's passing. These were some of the very troubles that Vince's outreach work sought to ameliorate, now receiving renewed publicity. In the midst of these spiraling concerns, a subtle shift became perceptible as people became attuned to an atmosphere out of order, to multiple authoritative demands of grief, anger, and loss as atmospheric things.

SILENCING THE VOICE: MEDIATIZED GRIEF AND THE POLITICS OF SONIC ERASURE

Grieving over celebrity singers and musical icons has a recognizable and powerful place in public life the world over. Think of the streets of Cairo, thronged with people honoring the life and mourning the passage of Umm Kulthum in 1975—a musician whose fame rested on radio's reach across Egypt (Danielson 1997). Or, in our contem-porary worlds of social media, note the occasional transformation of a Facebook page into an ad hoc memorial with images of a deceased singer, as happened in April of 2020 when many Americans posted music videos and images to celebrate beloved singer-songwriter John Prine, killed by COVID-19. News of his passing was accompanied by a raft of lament voiced with the wry lyrics and often-recorded voice of Prine himself—the cocktails and cigarettes he'd have in heaven, the wish to be "cut up and passed around" rather than "buried in the cold, cold ground." The death of the singer causes old tunes to take new turns, to mourn their singer or author and sing powerfully to present grief—in the voice of the grieved. This can have a cathartic effect, the singer becoming or joining that audience's voice itself, with the lamentation drawing both emotion and atmosphere together around the media artifact itself (Danielson 1997; Fisher 2019; cf. Deger 2006).

In such instances, grief mediatized may become grief amplified, what Schmitz calls, using the spatial language of atmospheres, "an authority filling the space of the present" that does not simply instill grief in those confronted with its atmosphere but rather commands them to modulate their behavior, to pause, to take note of a change in tone and become attuned to a shift in the weather (Schmitz et al. 2011, 258). He compares in this text the poles of exuberance and languidness to those of joy and grief. In the former, the energetic person encountering a reserved group might take issue, might try to force them or "jolt" them from their languid state. In contrast, for Schmitz, a joyful person encountering collective grief is compelled to measure their own comportment. Schmitz underscores here that an encounter with grief need not mean that an individual person grieves but rather that one is compelled to note a shift in mood, or *Stimmung*, and to be affected by its gravity—to modulate and attune oneself to the dense pull of a compelling situation.

The virtue of such an account of grieving for northern Australia is the resolutely public, spatial, and authoritative form it suggests—something that exceeds the person by leaving the privative boundary of the body, emphasizing the relational, spatial, and extra-human form it may take as a milieu, the twining of affect and law as atmosphere (cf. Philippopoulos-Mihalopoulos 2015). Here death often solicits an attunement to atmosphere that evokes a phenomenological interest in reaching beyond the surface of things' immediate perceptual rendering, a constitutional engagement with and reckoning of diverse, experiential, and atmospheric imperatives (cf. Ferro 2019; Harman 2005).[19]

In northern Australia, however, such circuits of mass-mediated grief and their atmospheric effects also can seem short-circuited by protocols and practices that forbid sharing images or playing recordings of the celebrity singer's voice (Fisher 2019). The desires of some that a singer mourn their own passing are mediated by norms of circumspection and erasure, by proscriptions that carry the force of law in their performative efficacy and the possibility of violence in their breach, as Vince was reminded in the days following his public comments. When a person dies, people move away from the camp (or house) where the deceased has been living. Some will burn the smaller belongings of the deceased. As is widely reported, families and communities tend to display great care and circumspection with proper names and photographic likenesses of the deceased. They stop using the deceased person's proper name, and any images or recordings, filmic and audio, are proscribed from circulation, at least in the short term. Not only might these different tokens of historical persons act as weights on the dead, distracting them from "moving on," they also can cause enormous grief and even illness, and many people will assert that it is simply inconsiderate and disrespectful to contravene a normative emphasis on erasure.[20] In the case of TC, all these dangers were amplified by the celebrity character of his voice, the prominent place of lamentation in his repertoire, and the great desire by so many to hear TC's voice lament its own passing.

I hasten to add that these practices are not uniform across northern Australia, nor across generations; they are subject to negotiation and transformation (Fisher 2019). But the default, often, is to err on the side of caution; the use of kin terms or indirection predominates in discussing those who have passed. Linguistic anthropologist Murray Garde (2013) has observed for central Arnhem Land that when people pass away others certainly do not stop speaking of them, but that speech is pushed into areas of great circumspection and circumlocution, to a range of kin terms and sociocentric markers that might draw people together (or pull them apart) through their mutual relation to the deceased. The disturbance created by the sudden absence of a voice, a face, a particular relation, is met by the amplification of other kinds of relationality, by attention to grief's distribution, a kind of sociocentric regulation of grief in the interests of the relations between living others.

Michael Jackson thus writes of a Warlpiri need to exteriorize grief, riffing on Durkheim to characterize the societal need for an outward display of interior pain that "satisfies the demands of social reality":

> As Warlpiri see it, it is imperative that a person exteriorize his or her emotions and not keep grief or grievances bottled up inside. Cutting or gashing oneself, sitting in sorry camp, abstaining from speech, covered with dust, unable to fend for yourself, are all powerful metaphors for mourning. The sorrow felt within is shown without, and if it is not then people of your moiety (your *makurntuwangu*) will abuse and wound you until appearance satisfies the demands of social reality. The question of whether or not such emotions are by our standards genuine does not arise.
>
> (1995, 129–130; cf. Musharbash 2008, 30–31)

This "social reality" is precisely what was at stake in the first days and weeks following TC's passing; sentiments of grief found powerful, outward expression on the news and in the publicly broadcast comments of one owner of TC's record label, whose public tears and deference to the family's own grief lent his remarks deep resonance for many.

As the news of TC's passing began to circulate, many felt as though Vince had transgressed these norms and struck out on his own. In contravening the ways that Yolngu people grieve, he had, as Charlene suggested later, seemed to act in his own interests. Frances Morphy (2008) analyzes the kinship-based metaphorics that animate Indigenous evaluations of such acts, observing that to behave as such is to act like a White person: *gurrutu-miriw*, literally, "without kin."[21] While the record label owners offered emotive and authoritative testimony to their grief, referring their speech to the authority of others—and Vince himself was attuned to such relations—the broadcast version of Vince's interview had taken another, though still recognizably grief-stricken, path. In foregrounding angry declamation, the edited and televised interview might be said to have confronted Yolngu sensibilities by unifying author, animator, and owner in the one gesture of a privatized relation to the deceased. Reframed as an individual action, the interview was understood initially as a kind of transgression, challenging Yolngu expectations of what grief ought to look like.

In the immediate days following TC's passing it was unclear how to proceed. This was a highly visible celebrity of international acclaim: his music was everywhere, his image was everywhere, though most frequently that circulated now with his face obscured. A documentary film about his life and career was in the final stages of post-production, but the status of the film now seemed unclear. Would it be released? When? Under what terms? And could another story begin to circulate that would displace the scandal that attended Vince's interview? Perhaps his Yolngu family should conduct their own interview? In my frequent conversations with Vince and with Charlene in this period, their grieving was accompanied by a pointed sense that something was awry and by efforts to imagine a path forward, a set of possible actions or events that might put things back in accord.

For their part, TC's record label reassured his family and a broader court of public opinion that they had been looking after him. The family too asserted its kinship in their own mass-mediated interviews, while his clansmen and women began to plan his funeral, a massive undertaking reaching across and beyond northeast Arnhem Land to include leading Aboriginal activists, and likely the prime minister and other Australian political leaders as well.

In part, the interpretive contests between these different agencies and relations took on an overtly biopolitical register around the meaning of TC's care itself. Was the intervention on the beach a caring act by Vince (and by extension the Larrakia) that came too late? Or did it instead instantiate something of the "violence of making live" (cf. Stevenson 2014)? In the first days several people asserted that Vince and Bernard, and by extension the Larrakia Nation, had gone against TC's wishes by forcing him into the hospital. Perhaps he wanted to stop receiving medical treatment, they said, and to spend his last days on the beach. Others, however, sought and succeeded in finding a less conflict-ridden path forward. What I wish to underscore in this is that the significance of bringing TC into hospital was as yet undecided, as were the participant roles and participation structures that might push that significance in one direction or another.

CONCLUSION: LAW'S SOUND RESOUNDING

Initially I tried to think about these events and the biopolitical conflict they indexed through such linguistic anthropological analytics of participation structures (Goffman 1981; cf. Irvine 1996), concerned with the role of media technologies as agentive participants in broader structures of participation and representation.[22] Who is authorized to speak, to sing, and to speak for? In what terms and with what consequences did a contest over how to distribute such roles proceed? And what kinds of things became alive in this negotiation? What dangers and potentialities become affixed to what kinds of sounds, to what voices or modes of address? And what constituency or assemblage (of persons and things) was required to bring a recorded voice like TC's back to life? The concern over participation structures should be understood as concern with the authority to let this voice resound, one tangled up with multiple relations, radical differences, and incommensurable levels of affinity and collectivity both within this northern city and beyond it. But this attention to participant roles and representation might paper over a collective, at times conflict-ridden attunement to an atmosphere out of joint and the ways this corralled outreach workers and elders, my neighbor included, into the management of atmospheric affects as symptomatic of a broader struggle around sovereign power.

Michel Foucault's distinction between sovereignty and biopolitics offers an alternate, political hermeneutic for what was at stake in this moment of atmospheric attunement in its relationship to sovereign power. For Foucault, sovereignty names the control over the ritualization of death, and is famously about the rights of the sovereign to kill ([1976] 1978, 138). He poses this figure against his notion of biopolitics, the management and administration of life and the "disqualification" of death itself. Both might be said to be at stake here amid a conflict waged through atmospheric disturbance and re-composition. That there was an effort to refigure the Larrakia's intervention as itself a violent act throws into relief the ways that efforts to right an atmosphere off kilter might also be seen as a reassertion of a kind of sovereign power. This might be identified in the ways these efforts made rom evident and also in the ways they implied a critique of death's very "disqualification" in the biopolitics of securing life at any cost, the tension between what Foucault figured as "letting live" and "making live" (Foucault [1976] 1978, 137–140).

But these conceptual coordinates also risk relegating analysis to the negotiation of a representational space and set of transactional concerns that, while generative and important on one axis, nonetheless make it possible to leave unexamined the affective apprehension of absence, ancestral presence, and law as well as vast domains of experience that are crucial for opening up the subtle ironies alive in such attunements. This is to say that it was not only the biopolitical debate that took prominence in this period nor an adjudication of who would take on what role in the reanimation of TC's voice. It was also an attunement to grief's authority that consumed my Yolngu friends as a form of atmospheric imperative. It is this affecting power of law that I want to return to through this phenomenology of sovereignty—asking what law (as one aspect of rom) and sovereignty feel like, how they take shape amid atmospheric disturbances, and how they give rise to, or emerge from, forms of sensibility and attunement—and offer avenues for rethinking how we reckon law and sovereignty as sound.

As TC's voice diminished in these events, a mediatized public grieving gave it new prominence in both metaphorical and material fashion. It is the affective density and apprehension of something awry that accompanied TC's death that I think requires phenomenological attention to the atmospherics animated by the voice's mediation, including all these conversations, negotiations, public interviews, and associated contests and questions that blossomed across the city and northeast Arnhem Land after TC's passing. It is important to stress here the understanding of my interlocutors and friends in northern Australia that the management of grief and human relations with the deceased is something ordered by rom, or law.

What Yolngu call rom is itself affect-laden ground, and that sovereignty might, like this iteration of "law," also be apprehended as a kind of atmospheric density or imperative—a distinctive atmospheric attunement. Rom is law, as I have been told again and again by Yolngu friends in northern Australia. It is not simply a term for the sacred or for custom, nor is it a set of discursive rules for acting around some separable more-than-human force or figure, and neither does it simply describe the relation of a fixed series of objects. Instead, it acquires the halo of juridical obligation and force that widespread figures of "two laws" (one settler, the other Indigenous) only begin to comprehend (Williams 1987; cf. Povinelli 2002). When confronted by the sensibilities of institutions concerned with the management and prolongation of life itself, sovereignty can seem here aligned with death's ritualization. But, although a useful hermeneutic, it does not allow one to grasp law as atmospheric density, as something "poured out into space" in the ways that accord with the sensibilities and practices so pronounced in northern Australia.

Not long after these events I visited with my neighbor, TC's elder cousin. Charlene was a senior woman in the North East community from which TC also hailed, and she had quizzed me several times in efforts to get a clearer picture of his last hours on the beach. In part she sought to understand the motivation for Vince's interview. "Why would he do that?" she asked. But she seemed concerned for me as well, it appeared, concerned that I might be entangled in the events due to my proximity to Vince's emotive transgression. I learned later that she was a central figure in pursuing the questions and untangling the local confusion that TC's death, and Vince's interview, had occasioned.

Charlene came to the chain link fence and gate, the latter always padlocked shut in order to keep drinkers and hangers-on away. As she shuffled forward, hands on her wheeled walker, the sounds of gospel music floated down the drive with her, drawing me into an encompassing envelope of soft musical sound. This was not new; she often spent the afternoon on the front porch of her housing commission bungalow, smoking cigarettes, talking on the phone, and listening to MP3s and a streaming radio service from northeast Arnhem Land.

As Charlene undid the padlock, I asked her about the music: what was she listening to today? In response she laughed and lifted the seat of her wheeled chair to pull out a small Bluetooth speaker. "Do you like it? This is Evie Tornquist." Her response led us to a conversation about Tornquist and about the radio stations and sounds she would listen to on the porch. As she described it, Charlene understood this practice as a way not simply to stay connected to her community or be reminded of family and friends, but rather as a way to stay connected to "Law" or at times "culture," by listening to the clan songs and dances recorded by radio producers at major cultural festivals and then rebroadcast throughout the year across this Arnhem Land radio service. She would listen for particular relatives as they traversed key ancestral country in song—country to which she could no longer travel but through which she could move with them in song. She would also listen as a means to "remind" herself of her community of fellow

Christians in Darwin and Arnhem Land—humming with Tornquist and traveling, after a fashion.

The figure she employed, "to be reminded," suggests that sounds tune her as much as she tunes them. The mobile and its radiophonic capacities offered a means of transforming space and a nexus within which Yolngu Law and Christian faith might acquire a shared life. I too was transported by these sounds, made to think in that moment about the ways that TC's voice might register for some Yolngu listeners an unsettling sense of things coming apart, as when heard unbidden in an unauthorized transmission, but also might afford a feelingful law-*restoring* attunement—allowing its authority a second life—both in the cross-regional "common sense" response to a transgression and in the ways it encouraged, perhaps, an attunement that could put a dispersed set of relations in accord. I too was made to compose a situation, bringing its specificity into being by tying together different moments of music playback, three moments of voiced sound resounding from the transducers and tympanic energies of radios and mobile phones.

Recall the small radio that I began with, played from Samson's wheelchair in the closing of *Samson and Delilah*, and made by Warwick Thornton to filmically stage the value of kinship and the efficacious atmospherics of radio sound. Recall that other cell phone, waved in our faces on the beach as a restorative supplement to an ill body and a reminder of the authority it still carried—not as though it could simply revitalize his ailing body but in order to revitalize his relation to us, and our relation to him and to one another around his authority and renown. The singer's voice resonated powerfully from that little speaker, even if he himself was barely able to speak in the moment. Finally, recall Charlene's own small phone and the voices of her distant family, amplifying the power of law to lend her home an atmospherics of tradition's continued resonance (cf. Tacchi 1998). Weaving these moments of atmospheric engineering together in my own ethnographic description now feels akin to what Stewart (2016), drawing on Deleuze, calls "points of precision"—singularities in the composing of worlds. In these moments, the telephonic transducer brings a sonic body to bear on injury—not healing an individual, corporeal subject alone but instead working to right an assemblage of materials and bodies to recuperate an atmosphere out of joint and reassert the authority and salient force of rom.

So, how do we get from sound, affect, and atmospheres back to law and sovereignty? How might we think about the quasi-objective, diffuse meaningfulness of the former alongside the qualities of institutional durability and legislative, prescriptive force of the latter? Many scholars and activists have sought to analyze the relation between the common law and Aboriginal law, stressing the former's initial blindness to, and subsequent difficulties in reckoning with, the systematic, legislative character of the latter. In Australia, such work has often redeployed the vernacular figure of "two laws," a widespread assertion of equivalence between settler government and an Indigenous domain. But while the figure of two laws resonates deeply for people in northern Australia, it also may mask the character by which Indigenous law is apprehended, arrested even, in its relation to Australian common law. Between the Native Title Act of 1993 and the Yorta decision of 2006, for instance, Australian courts have over many decades now decisively limited the scope and reach of Native Title—positing not its vitality but rather its vulnerability to history, its capacity only to diminish, being enclosed by Australian Common Law and surviving solely by virtue of a demonstrable continuity with a pre-contact Indigenous sovereignty.

It is just such a vitality that the musical and mediatic atmospherics of law in northern Australia evince. These direct us to consider law's multiplicity, to consider the worlds coming to life as law in an expressive voice, a music recording, or the tympanic cone of a cellular phone's transducer. As Vince, Charlene, and TC's family negotiate ways of relating, and ways of reckoning their disparate ways of relating in their relation (Merlan 2018), they adjudicate a common sense, buttressing the affective character of law's force. In the weeks following TC's passing, that force rose to our attention as a thing both of and beyond ourselves, in part via the opacities and demands of mediatic things, and in part as shared preoccupations, modes of apprehension, and mood. Atmospheric analytics offer a means if not to resolve, then to note and engage with an aporia between new materialist and phenomenological approaches to the powers of musical sociality. They also offer accounts that make law's force and sound's materiality inseparable, as interanimating conditions of possibility.

NOTES

1. A Heideggerian figure, translating to English as "mood," *Stimmung* offers a key conceptual aspect of his counter and complication to Cartesian purifications of human cognition contra an objective world. This is so because for Heidegger mood is itself not simply ascribed to or laid over an objective world by an agentive, prior subject. Instead Stimmung is a condition of being itself. In Heidegger, that is, Stimmung is a way of talking about situatedness, thrownness, or attunement in the language of mood: "A mood assails us. It comes neither from 'outside' nor from 'inside,' but arises out of Being-in-the-world, as a way of such Being" (Heidegger [1962] 2008, 176; cf. Slaby 2017).
2. Simpson draws out the difference as between a sovereignty figured as "western exceptionalism and dominance" and "sovereignty as belonging, dignity, and justice" (2020, 686).
3. To write here of mediatization, as opposed to mediation, is to point to a means of reckoning the significance of modern media institutions, artifacts, and technologies beyond any specific moment of transmission, to ask how the objects of mediation are always already taking shape in relationship to the possibility of their mediation (see discussion in Fisher 2016, 12).
4. I employ pseudonyms throughout this chapter in order to protect the anonymity of my interlocutors and respect widespread Indigenous Australian norms proscribing the use of a person's name following their death (see also Fisher 2019). Furthermore, I do not seek to write in detail about the celebrity whose death led to the events I describe. Although his image and name now circulate in Australian media with the blessing of this singer's family, I use "TC" in this chapter in order to maintain respectful distance from his proper name and also in an effort to keep the focus on the impact of his passing, on the wake that this left behind.

5. This track is notable for many reasons as one of only a handful of recordings by African American artists to achieve the number one spot on Billboard's country music chart. It was Pride's first number one single, but he would go on to release a further twenty-eight. His success in the US music market is easily matched by his popularity across Aboriginal Australia and his prominence in Indigenous radio and media platforms across the country (see Fisher 2016; Walker 2000).

6. It is not an accident, then, that Thornton is perhaps the best-known Australian representative of a generation of Indigenous filmmakers invested in producing "sovereign screens" (cf. Dowell 2013).

7. For example, atmospheric language seems wholly appropriate to talk of the ash and smoke suffusing Australia in the catastrophic fire events of 2019–20, tying it to the bodies and lungs of individual persons. Likewise, the aerosolization of the COVID-19 virus draws our attention to our immediate oxygenized atmosphere and also to the uneven harm that atmospheric events inflict on populations. Some (nurses, doctors, transit workers, grocery clerks) are at greater risk of exposure while others (Black and Brown communities, spaces of durable pollution) are at greater risk of a wide array of harm from such exposure.

8. Choy and Zee make the twinned movement evident in noting how the problematization of environmental phenomena becomes also an affordance to thought, a productive attentiveness: "The wrong air of the Anthropocene trains our attention to the mechanics of suspension, to how things lift and settle in mediums, to how things exist in atmospheres" (2015, 211).

9. Timothy Morton (2007) draws attention to "ambience" as a conceptually slippery space where ideas of nature, the unconscious, and the environment can easily shade into one another—and cease to be an environmental ground once they attract our attention as figure. Thacker (2011), more abstractly, distinguishes between the world for us and the world in itself and notes the paradoxical character of the latter so far as the instant we think it, it ceases to be in itself and becomes for us. As will be evident below, these are an instructive contrast to atmospheres, which differ insofar as they are understood to be entities in our world but also entities that exceed our intentions or proclivities. A crucial facet of atmospheres is that they may draw attention to themselves; they are at once "for us" and "in themselves" in this sense (see also McGraw 2016).

10. The language here resonates with Merleau-Ponty's own, but note the emphasis on a body among and with other bodies.

11. This has powerful resonance with, but is not quite the same "thing" as, Michel Serres's influential figure of the quasi-object, something that is at once "contract" and "thing." For Serres, objects can be apprehended through a social lens, not unlike Alfred Hitchcock's "MacGuffin," an alibi for the relations and situations they afford. But their thingness does not then disappear; rather, it remains ingredient and consequential (see Serres [1980] 2007; cf. Schiermer 2011). The quasi-object as it emerges from neo-phenomenological writings is neither "social" nor "material." It is instead an entity whose status is undecidable.

12. *Mereology* is a philosophical term for the study of parthood and part-whole relations. Its contemporary form took shape in the late nineteenth and early twentieth centuries in the works of Brentano and Husserl, but it has its origins in presocratic philosophy. For an extended discussion of the term and its relation to Husserl and Whitehead, see Varzi (2019).

13. My thinking in this chapter has also been assisted by Philippopoulos-Mihalopoulos's figure of the "lawscape" (2015) and his articulation of the ways that law's force and the city require one another. As I read his work, he takes "city" in both the modern sense as urban

space and in an Aristotelian sense as political community, and both as the infrastructure of law's materialization as atmosphere (for further analyses of law in relation to atmospheres, see Kahn 2017 and Wall 2019).

14. There is a powerful resonance here with Tess Lea's (2020) proposition that we understand policy as itself a milieu and that we think about the resonance of governmental interventions less as transparent directives and more as contributions to the growing and consequential detritus of prior intervention.

15. Some have noted that Schmitz's own emphasis on the felt body limits his phenomenology, risking a humanist, even Eurocentric, solipsism (e.g. Eisenlohr 2018; Riedel 2019).

16. It is in this sense that considerations of atmospheric effects and the constitutive work of "worlding" occupy Stewart's literary and auto-ethnographic attention to compositional aspects of atmospheric attunement (2016; cf. Heidegger [1950] 1971). For Stewart, the act of description is "a peering, accidental glimpse of what matters—what *comes into matter* in the cocomposition of objects in contact, what shifts its matter in a moment of recognizable, though unnamed and partial, significance" (2016, 31; italics added). Stewart draws on the new materialist scholarship of Harman (2011) and Morton (2013) to grasp forms of emergence immanent to constellations of entities, but also to foreground the inexhaustibility of entities to such relations. Objects relate to one another and to humans with an allure, depth, and unfathomability for these scholars in ways that incite not just attention or reflection but rather agitation and composition (see also Coren and Brinitzer 2019 on the figure of composition in relation to milieu).

17. In these terms, Steven Feld's *acoustemology* (1996) is a mode of atmospheric attunement, a listening that is also a making or musicking. As Feld argues throughout his work in both Papua New Guinea and Ghana, histories of sounding are also histories of listening.

18. Abels (2018) provides an ethnographic discussion of meaningfulness in relationship to atmosphere, building specifically on the former term's deployment by Schmitz and developing those facets of musical experience that exceed both reduction to language and "the clear-cut boundaries of the physical body" (13) while complicating the mind-body dualism that (she argues) has reemerged in some theorizations of affect in relationship to meaning. As Abels suggests, "interpretively qualified emotion" and affective intensity are unhelpfully opposed by such thinking: "In situations characterized by musical atmospheres, very disparate layers of meaning and meaningfulness coalesce in the experience of sound" (2018, 3).

19. For Merleau-Ponty ([1964] 1968) and Alphonso Lingis (1998), the style of things is not an account of their surfaces, nor of similarities across a series of surfaces or things, but an animating element emerging as depth, horizon, and a kind of summoning or imperative (cf. Harman 2005). Together with Lingis's account of a space or medium that is neither object nor perceptual quality but something in experience as yet undefined, this offers a powerful iteration of the problem that atmospheres has begun to address and an analog perhaps for the conceptual figure of atmosphere itself.

20. See Rosaldo (1984) for an analogous account that captures something of the density of associations and the intensity of anger and emotion that can accompany such recordings (and, Rosaldo suggests, grief itself).

21. "[A]ny action that shows that a person is 'working just for themselves' is a sign of that person being *gurrutumiriw*, and this is unambiguously undesirable. People will say of such a person: 'he's not a Yolngu anymore—he's acting like a Ngäpaki [White person]'" (Morphy 2008).

22. Drawing on Erving Goffman's (1981) disaggregation of communicative events, structures of participation offer powerful means to address the disaggregation and distribution of voice, audience, authority, and authorship. Whose account will be authoritative? Who has the authority to represent the events and their significance? Who is being cited and produced as an authority and who an audience in the reproduction and remediation of that account (see Goffman 1981; cf. Irvine 1996)? An analysis foregrounding such participation structures would underscore that this contest was not just about the meaning of what happened but also about who had the authority to decide on and to represent that truth.

WORKS CITED

Abels, Birgit. 2018. "Music, Affect and Atmospheres: Meaning and Meaningfulness in Palauan omengeredakl." *International Journal of Traditional Arts* 2. https://tradartsjournal.ncl.ac.uk /index.php/ijta/article/view/16/11.

Adorno, Theodor. (1941) 2002. "The Radio Symphony." In *Essays on Music*, edited by Richard Leppert, translated by Susan H. Gillespie, 251–270. Berkeley: University of California Press.

Agamben, Giorgio. 1995. *Homo Sacer: Sovereign Power and Bare Life*. Translated by Daniel Heller-Roazen. Stanford, CA: Stanford University Press.

Agard-Jones, Vanessa. 2013. "Bodies in the System." *Small Axe* 17 (3): 182–192.

Armstrong, Robert Plant. 1971. *The Affecting Presence: An Essay in Humanistic Anthropology*. Urbana: University of Illinois Press.

Barr, Olivia. 2013. "Walking with Empire." *Australian Feminist Law Journal* 38 (1): 59–74.

Bens, Jonas. 2018. "The Courtroom as an Affective Arrangement: Analysing Atmospheres in Courtroom Ethnography." *Journal of Legal Pluralism and Unofficial Law* 50 (3): 336–355.

Bennett, Jane. 2010. *Vibrant Matter: A Political Ecology of Things*. Durham, NC: Duke University Press.

Berger, Harris M. 2009. *Stance: Ideas about Emotion, Style, and Meaning for the Study of Expressive Culture*. Middletown, CT: Wesleyan University Press.

Berlant, Lauren. 2011. *Cruel Optimism*. Durham, NC: Duke University Press.

Berlant, Lauren, and Kathleen Stewart. 2019. *The Hundreds*. Durham, NC: Duke University Press.

Bille, Mikkel, Peter Bjerregaard, and Tim Flohr Sørensen. 2015. "Staging Atmospheres: Materiality, Culture, and the Texture of the In-Between." *Emotion, Space and Society* 15: 31–38.

Böhme, Gernot. 2017. *The Aesthetics of Atmospheres*. Translated by Jean-Paul Thibaud. London: Routledge.

Born, Georgina. 2012. "On Tardean Relations: Temporality and Ethnography." In *The Social after Gabriel Tarde: Debates and Assessments*, edited by Matei Candea, 230–245. London and New York: Routledge.

Born, Georgina. 2018. "On Nonhuman Sound—Sound as Relation." In *Sound Objects*, edited by James A. Steintrager and Rey Chow, 185–207. Durham, NC: Duke University Press.

Buckmaster, Luke. 2009. "Interview with Warwick Thornton, writer/director of Samson & Delilah." *Crikey*. May 12, 2009. Accessed December 22, 2020. https://blogs.crikey.com .au/cinetology/2009/05/12/interview-with-warwick-thornton-writerdirector-of-sam son-delilah/.

Casey, Edward. 1993. *Getting Back into Place toward a Renewed Understanding of the Place-world*. Bloomington: Indiana University Press.

Choy, Timothy, and Jerry Zee. 2015. "Condition—Suspension." *Cultural Anthropology* 30 (2): 210–223.

Coren, Gabriel, and Cameron Brinitzer. 2019. "Editors' Introduction: As Adventurous as Life." *History of Anthropology Newsletter* 43. Accessed August 24, 2020. http://histanthro.org /notes/adventurous-as-life/.

Danielson, Virginia. 1997. *"The Voice of Egypt": Umm Kulthum, Arabic Song, and Egyptian Society in the Twentieth Century*. Chicago: University of Chicago Press.

Daughtry, J. Martin. 2015. *Listening to War: Sound, Music, Trauma and Survival in Wartime Iraq*. Oxford: Oxford University Press.

Deger, Jennifer. 2006. *Shimmering Screens: Making Media in an Aboriginal Community*. Minneapolis: University of Minnesota Press.

Dowell, Kristin. 2013. *Sovereign Screens: Aboriginal Media on the Canadian West Coast*. Lincoln: University of Nebraska Press.

Eisenlohr, Patrick. 2018. *Sounding Islam: Music, Media, and Sonic Atmospheres in an Indian Ocean World*. Berkeley: University of California Press.

Feld, Steven. 1996. "Waterfalls of Song." In *Senses of Place*, edited by Steven Feld and Keith Basso, 91–135. Santa Fe, NM: School of American Research Press.

Ferro, Floriana. 2019. "Object-Oriented Ontology's View of Relations: A Phenomenological Critique." *Open Philosophy* 2: 566–581.

Fisher, Daniel. 2016. *The Voice and Its Doubles: Music and Media in Northern Australia*. Durham, NC: Duke University Press.

Fisher, Daniel. 2019. "To Sing with Another's Voice: Animation, Circumspection, and the Negotiation of Indigeneity in Northern Australian New Media." *American Ethnologist* 46 (1): 34–46.

Foucault, Michel. (1976) 1978. *The History of Sexuality*. Vol. 1. Translated by Robert Hurley. New York: Pantheon.

Garde, Murray. 2013. *Culture, Interaction and Person Reference in an Australian Language*. Amsterdam: John Benjamins.

Goble, Erika. 2017. "Beyond Human Subjectivity and Back to the Things Themselves: Jane Bennett's Vibrant Matter." *Phenomenology & Practice* 11 (2): 70–78.

Goffman, Erving. 1981. *Forms of Talk*. Philadelphia: University of Pennsylvania Press.

Grusin, Richard, ed. 2015. *The Nonhuman Turn*. Minneapolis: University of Minnesota Press.

Harman, Graham. 2005. *Guerrilla Metaphysics: Phenomenology and the Carpentry of Things*. Chicago: Open Court.

Harman, Graham. 2011. "Realism without Materialism." *SubStance* 40 (2): 52–72.

Heidegger, Martin. (1950) 1971. "The Thing." In *Poetry, Language, Thought*, translated by A. Hofstadter, 163–180. New York: Harper Colophon Books.

Heidegger, Martin. (1962) 2008. *Being and Time*. Translated by John Macquarrie and Edward Robinson. New York: Harper Perrenial.

Ingold, Timothy. 2000. *The Perception of the Environment: Essays in Livelihood, Dwelling and Skill*. London: Routledge

Irvine, Judith T. 1996. "Shadow Conversations: The Indeterminacy of Participant Roles." In *Natural Histories of Discourse*, edited by Michael Silverstein and Greg Urban, 131–159. Chicago: University of Chicago Press.

Jackson, Michael. 1995. *At Home in the World*. Durham, NC: Duke University Press.

Kahn, Jeffrey S. 2017. "Geographies of Discretion and the Jurisdictional Imagination." *Political and Legal Anthropology Review* 40 (1): 5–27.

Larkin, Brian. 2014. "Techniques of Inattention: The Mediality of Loudspeakers in Nigeria." *Anthropological Quarterly* 87 (4): 989–1015.

Lea, Tess. 2020. *Wild Policy: Indigeneity and the Unruly Logics of Intervention*. Stanford, CA: Stanford University Press.

Lepselter, Susan. 2016. *The Resonance of Unseen Things: Poetics, Power, Captivity, and UFOs in the American Uncanny*. Ann Arbor: University of Michigan Press.

Lingis, Alphonso. 1998. *The Imperative*. Bloomington: Indiana University Press.

Luna, Sarah. 2018. "Affective Atmospheres of Terror on the Mexico–U.S. Border: Rumors of Violence in Reynosa's Prostitution Zone." *Cultural Anthropology* 33 (1): 58–84.

Manning, Erin, and Brian Massumi. 2014. *Thought in the Act. Passages in the Ecology of Experience*. Minneapolis and London: University of Minnesota Press.

Merlan, Francesca. 2018. *Dynamics of Difference in Australia: Indigenous Past and Present in a Settler Society*. Philadelphia: University of Pennsylvania Press.

Merleau-Ponty, Maurice. (1964) 1968. *The Visible and the Invisible*. Edited by Claude Lefort. Translated by Alphonso Lingis. Evanston, IL: Northwestern University Press.

Morton, Timothy. 2007. *Ecology without Nature: Rethinking Environmental Aesthetics*. Cambridge, MA: Harvard University Press.

Morton, Timothy. 2013. *Hyperobjects: Philosophy and Ecology after the End of the World*. Minneapolis: University of Minnesota Press.

Mazzarella, William. 2018. "Sense Out of Sense: Notes on the Affect/Ethics Impasse." *Cultural Anthropology* 32 (2): 199–208.

McCormack, Derek. 2018. *Atmospheric Things: On the Allure of Elemental Envelopment*. Durham, NC: Duke University Press.

McGraw, Andrew. 2016. "Atmosphere as a Concept for Ethnomusicology: Comparing the Gamelatron and Gamelan." *Ethnomusicology* 60 (1): 125–147.

Mittman, Greg, Michelle Murphy, and Christopher Sellers. 2004. "Introduction: A Cloud over History." *Osiris* 19: 1–17.

Moreton-Robinson, Aileen. 2007. "Introduction." In *Sovereign Subjects: Indigenous Sovereignty Matters*, edited by Aileen Moreton-Robinson, 1–15. St. Leonard's, NSW: Allen and Unwin.

Morphy, Frances. 2008. "Invisible to the State: Kinship and the Yolngu Moral Order." Paper presented at the conference Negotiating the Sacred V: Governing the Family, Monash University, August 14–15, 2008. Accessed August 23, 2020. https://www.academia.edu/20726361/Invisible_to_the_state_kinship_and_the_Yolngu_moral_order.

Musharbash, Yasmine. 2008. "Mortality, Mourning and Mortuary Practices in Indigenous Australia." In *Mortality, Mourning and Mortuary Practices in Indigenous Australia*, edited by Katie Glaskin, Myrna Tonkinson, Yasmine Musharbash, and Victoria Burbank, 21–36. London: Ashgate.

Peters, John Durham. 2016. *The Marvelous Clouds: Toward a Philosophy of Elemental Media*. Chicago: University of Chicago Press.

Philippopoulos-Mihalopoulos, Andreas. 2015. *Spatial Justice: Body, Lawscape, Atmosphere*. New York: Routledge.

Philippopoulos-Mihalopoulos, Andreas. 2016. "Withdrawing from Atmosphere: An Ontology of Air Partitioning and Affective Engineering." *Environment and Planning D: Society and Space* 34 (1): 150–167.

Povinelli, Elizabeth. 2002. *The Cunning of Recognition*. Durham, NC: Duke University Press.

Povinelli, Elizabeth. 2016. *Geontologies: A Requiem to Late Liberalism*. Durham, NC: Duke University Press.

Riedel, Friedlind. 2019. "Atmosphere." In *Affective Societies: Key Concepts*, edited by Jan Slaby and Christian v. Scheve, 85–95. New York: Routledge.

Riedel, Friedlind. 2020. "Atmospheric Relations: Theorising Music and Sound as Atmosphere." In *Music as Atmosphere: Collective Feelings and Affective Sounds*, edited by Friedlind Riedel and Juha Torvinen, 1–42. London: Routledge.

Rosaldo, Renato. 1984. "Grief and a Headhunter's Rage: On the Cultural Force of Emotions." In *Text, Play, and Story: The Construction and Reconstruction of Self and Society*, edited by Edward M. Bruner, 178–195. Washington, DC: American Ethnological Society.

Shapiro, Nicholas, and Eben Kirksey. 2017. "Chemo-Ethnography: An Introduction." *Cultural Anthropology* 32 (4): 481–493.

Schiermer, Bjørn. 2011. "Quasi-objects, Cult Objects and Fashion Objects: On Two Kinds of Fetishism on Display in Modern Culture." *Theory, Culture and Society* 28 (1): 81–102.

Schmitz, Hermann, Rudolf Owen Müllan, and Jan Slaby. 2011. "Emotions outside the Box—The New Phenomenology of Feeling and Corporeality." *Phenomenology and the Cognitive Sciences* 10: 241–259.

Serres, Michel. (1980) 2007. *The Parasite*. Translated by Lawrence R. Schehr. Minneapolis: University of Minnesota Press.

Simpson, Audra. 2014. *Mohawk Interruptus: Political Life across the Borders of Settler States*. Durham and London: Duke University Press.

Simpson, Audra. 2020. "The Sovereignty of Critique." *South Atlantic Quarterly* 119 (4): 685–699.

Slaby, Jan. 2017. "More than a Feeling: Affect as Radical Situatedness." *Midwest Studies in Philosophy* 41 (1): 7–26.

Slaby, Jan. 2020. "Atmospheres—Schmitz, Massumi and Beyond." In *Music as Atmosphere: Collective Feelings and Affective Sounds*, edited by Friedlind Riedel and Juha Torvinen, 274–285. London: Routledge.

Sloterdijk, Peter. (1998) 2011. *Spheres*. Vol. 1, *Bubbles*. Translated by Wieland Hoban. Cambridge, MA: MIT Press.

Sloterdijk, Peter. (2002) 2009. *Terror from the Air*. Translated by Amy Patton and Steve Corcoran. Cambridge, MA: MIT Press.

Stevenson, Lisa. 2014. *Life beside Itself*. Berkeley: University of California Press.

Stewart, Kathleen. 2007. *Ordinary Affects*. Durham and London: Duke University Press.

Stewart, Kathleen. 2011. "Atmospheric Attunements." *Environment and Planning D: Society and Space* 29: 445–453.

Stewart, Kathleen. 2016. "The Point of Precision." *Representations* 135: 31–44.

Tacchi, Jo. 1998. "Radio Texture: Between Self and Others." In *Material Cultures: Why Some Things Matter*, edited by Daniel Miller, 25–45. Chicago: University of Chicago Press.

Thacker, Eugene. 2011. *In the Dust of This Planet*. New York: Zero Books.

Thibaud, Jean-Paul. 2011. "A Sonic Paradigm of Urban Ambience." *Journal of Sonic Studies* 1 (1). http://journal.sonicstudies.org/vol01/nr01/a02.

Thibaud, Jean-Paul. 2015. "The Backstage of Urban Ambiances: When Atmospheres Pervade Everyday Experience." *Emotion, Space and Society* 15: 39–46.

Thomas, Deborah A. 2019. *Political Life in the Wake of the Plantation: Sovereignty, Witnessing, Repair*. Durham, NC: Duke University Press.

Thornton, Warwick. 2017. "Not in Kansas Anymore: Warwick Thornton on Samson & Delilah." YouTube Interview with Warwick Thornton for *Sight and Sound*. Accessed December 22, 2020. https://www.youtube.com/watch?v=Vj_l4sdjfZc.

Varzi, Achille. 2019. "Mereology." In *The Stanford Encyclopedia of Philosophy*, edited by Edward N. Zalta. Stanford University. Accessed May 8, 2020. https://plato.stanford.edu/archives/spr2019/entries/mereology/.

Walker, Clinton. 2000. *Buried Country: The Story of Aboriginal Country Music*. Crows Nest, NSW: Pluto Press.

Wall, Illan Rua. 2019. "Policing Atmospheres: Crowds, Protest and 'Atmotechnics.'" *Theory, Culture and Society* 36 (4): 143–162.

Williams, Nancy. 1987. *Two Laws: Managing Disputes in a Contemporary Aboriginal Community*. Canberra: Australian Institute of Aboriginal Studies.

Zhang, Dora. 2018. "Notes on Atmosphere." *Qui Parle* 27 (1): 121–155.

ETHICS OF PERFORMANCE, ETHICS OF RESEARCH

CHAPTER 19

....

JAZZ ETIQUETTE

Between Aesthetics and Ethics

....

ALESSANDRO DURANTI, JASON THROOP,
AND MATTHEW MCCOY

THIS chapter draws on ideas from phenomenology and interactional approaches to human experience to examine the ways in which the practice of improvisation in the jazz tradition is guided by aesthetic and ethical principles. Contrary to recent claims that "there is no categorical distinction between improvisation and performance" and that, in any genre of music, there is a process of "continuous accommodation" (Cook 2017, 64), we show that jazz musicians execute, conceptualize, and evaluate improvisation in distinct aesthetic and ethical terms, which draw from and reconstitute genre-specific attitudes toward creativity and cooperation.

Dominant among the aesthetic and ethical requirements of jazz as a cultural tradition is the practitioners' acceptance and celebration of the risk-taking entailed by any live jazz performance, where not only the order and length of individual solos but also even some of the harmonic, rhythmic, and melodic choices made by the players emerge live in performance and are not fully predictable in advance. Much like Aristotle's virtues, which necessarily require a particular context for their specific mode of actualization, the aesthetic and ethical dimensions of virtuosic musical performances in jazz are made possible through the ongoing and often explicitly foregrounded potential for challenge and exposure.[1] As Aristotle argued, virtues are embodied dispositions that are responsive to the particularities of circumstance. From this perspective, the virtue of courage, for example, arises when an individual confronts a risk to their well-being without self-serving motivations in a difficult situation in an effort to pursue some perceived good. As a form of practical discernment, courage is a mean between rashness and cowardice, two responses that, Aristotle argues, either under- or overestimate the risks associated with a given course of action in a particular social context. In opening themselves up to the risk of exposure, jazz performers simultaneously cultivate and enact embodied dispositional capacities for a courage-like discernment to navigate musical challenges in ways that will push them to improvise in a virtuosic manner. Virtuosity, like virtue, is thus conditioned by its specific context of collaboratively contingent actualization.

Following the phenomenological philosopher Emmanuel Levinas ([1961] 1969), whose ethics is founded upon the responsibility that the naked "face" (*visage*) of the other imposes on us before any conceptualization or rationalization, we argue that it is precisely in the existential dynamics of face-to-face encounters that we become exposed to excessive and unthematizable dimensions of alterity, dimensions that, in the end, may resist established conventions or shared stocks of knowledge. According to Levinas, one's primary obligation to others, what he terms our "infinite" responsibility to them, becomes disclosed through this vulnerable experience of exposure. Drawing from both Aristotle's virtue ethics and Levinas's ethics of alterity, which we see as distinctive but complementary perspectives on moral experience, we will show how, in the context of jazz players' interactions *qua* musicians, leaving oneself open to exposure can itself become a cultivated virtue, one in which breaking out of the structure of the song becomes both an aesthetic and ethical imperative.

While all forms of musical performance likely entail such contextualized risks, jazz performance stands out as a special case because the potentiality for exposure is a foregrounded aspect of the genre's aesthetic ethos. Indeed, jazz musicians often challenge one another by playing novel and surprising variations in the context of an otherwise familiar musical piece or make unexpected decisions that are meant to break the routine quality of a performance and produce what Whitney Balliett (1959) aptly called "the sound of surprise." To catch another musician off guard, to see if they are able to catch up and keep up while also being prepared to step in to repair any emerging breakdown that may follow from their missing a beat, cue, or transition, these are actions usually associated with bigger-than-life personalities like Miles Davis (Davis and Troupe 1989; Carr 1998; C. Smith 1998). In this chapter, we argue that, in fact, such actions are a defining feature of jazz aesthetics and ethics.

The complexity of jazz performance is realized in such moments when differing sonic layers of the unfolding musical composition and various embodied and interactional elements of the performance become salient and individual players respond to one another's efforts to create surprising and novel phrasings, rhythms, and harmonic substitutions. As Harris Berger notes in his now-classic phenomenological study of jazz, performance in this tradition thus entails "a complex juggling act in which different flows of experience are arranged in a delicate and dynamic structure" that arise through the organization of the players' attention (1999, 145; see also Throop 2003). With various sonic textures, rhythmic configurations, and embodied actions shifting between the foreground and background of a given musician's moment-to-moment awareness, attention actively organizes, and is organized within, the flow of performance; further, attention can also be passively arrayed (Husserl 2001) in response to novel or surprising occurrences. For instance, one's attention may be "pulled" by an unexpected note or beat, a glance from a fellow musician, or a missing musical element in the expected unfolding of the song. Such forms of *attentional pull* (Throop and Duranti 2015) disclose not only the virtuosic improvisational responsiveness of jazz musicians but also their vulnerability. When understood in this light, jazz performance is both virtuosic and virtuous, the latter being a quality of music that Jane O'Dea (1993, 52) traces to Aristotle's discussion of music in his *Politics*, where he asks "whether we ought . . . to think that music tends in some degree to virtue (*pros aretén*)" and concludes that "music has the power of producing a certain effect on the moral character of the soul." It is for these reasons that Aristotle held that music should be taught to the young (1944, 661).

To understand the ethical implications of improvisational responsiveness and vulnerability to exposure, we seek to put Aristotelian virtue ethics into conversation not only with Levinas but also with the work of sociologist Erving Goffman (1959, 1967). In so doing, we are not using jazz improvisation to further test whether Goffman was a phenomenologist (Parsons 1968; Lanigan 1988; Raffel 2002; G. W. H. Smith 2005). Rather, we suggest that the ideas about self and other that these thinkers develop are complementary, and drawing them together can help us illuminate the relation between the vulnerable side of performance and the sense of responsibility band members feel toward each other and the jazz tradition. It is therefore in the midst of intersubjectively arrayed experiences of vulnerability and responsibility that possibilities for the cultivation and enactment of virtue arise.

With regard to responsibility, we take from Goffman the view of everyday encounters as rituals where participants create a shared sense of reality and a public image that protects their inner and true self from being exposed to the judgment of others. Central in Goffman's work is the notion of "face," which he uses to explain public behavior as a kind of performance. Here, social actors engage in "impression management," a process by which they "work" (hence his term "face-work") at making a positive impression and avoiding embarrassment (1967, 97–112). In this respect, the work that people do to establish and maintain a particular face is by definition strategic and covers both information that they "give" and information that they "give off" (1959, 2). In other words, for Goffman, the individual performs in order to control how he or she is being evaluated by others. On the stage of social life, a person avoids feeling "shame, leading him to minimize the chances he takes of exposure" (1959, 253). A jazz ensemble in performance can thus be understood as sharing a "collective face," which each member has some responsibility to protect.

Goffman's ideas about face-work shed light on the social life of music, and his ideas are important context for our work. We argue, though, that the imperative to impression management that Goffman describes accounts for only some of what goes on in musical performance and that the aesthetic and ethical dispositions of individual music cultures introduce other dynamics. In jazz, for example, a distinction must be made between the collective face of established bands, whose members must conform to their fans' expectations or risk disapproval, and a "pickup group" like the one we will be discussing in this chapter. In the latter case, the musicians *themselves* may constitute the primary audience for their performance, especially when the audience is not familiar with the kind of music a band is playing (Bogen 1987). In this respect, we cannot take for granted that "what musicians perform first and foremost is not music, but their own identities as musicians, their musical personae," as Philip Auslander has argued in a well-known article that treats musical performance as the Goffmanian presentation of self (2006, 102).

When jazz musicians encounter moments of vulnerable exposure—for instance, as we shall see, in experiencing a sonic "vacuum" in the midst of a performance—the preoccupation with one's own public face in Goffman's sense may be superseded or augmented by an emergent ethical sense of responsibility toward others and toward something more consequential than the immediate context, such as the revered musical tradition being reproduced. This is an experience that is closer to what Levinas saw as the ethical response to a "risky uncovering of oneself, in sincerity," which may give rise to "the abandon of all shelter, exposure to traumas, [and] vulnerability" (Levinas [1974] 1998, 48).

In this sense, we find a key tension between Levinas's and Goffman's accounts of face-to-face encounters. The same moments that can be characterized in terms of openness and shared vulnerability can also underlie and institute an individual's face-work, as players project the concern for their own "sacredness" (Goffman 1967, 47) onto the respectability of the other players and the music they are playing. For these reasons, the insights of both scholars are needed to illuminate the risky moments of improvisational collaboration among jazz musicians and their pragmatic implications. Significantly, these emergent moments are *not* (or not only, as Goffman might have framed it) ways of getting back on track after a violation of a routine. Rather, risky moments of improvisational collaboration are ruptures of routine activities that make apparent the responsibility of the self toward the other. Exposure, for Levinas, is "radically different from thematization. The one [person] is exposed to the other as a skin is exposed to what wounds it" ([1974] 1998, 49). In the midst of Goffman-like routine exchanges filled with memorized melodies, trusted licks, and rehearsed chord progressions—that is, in the midst of coherent musical and social thematizations—jazz musicians, we argue, invite the possibility of a Levinasian wounding and, in doing so, cultivate a kind of virtuous courage in the Aristotelian sense. In addition to (or beyond) a remedial response of the kind described by Goffman in moments of embarrassment, a violation of expectations by one player can elicit a *reaffirmation* of the ethical fabric of playing music with and for others. This is made possible by jazz as an improvisational genre. In this way, jazz performance is an emergent moral experience in which musicians are attuned and mutually responsive to each other.

The moral implications of musical performances, practices, and interactions can thus inform current debates within the so-called ethical turn in anthropology (Mattingly and Throop 2018). Through their interactions, jazz musicians show how ethics is not just about cultivating fixed ethical responses to situations but about responding to a surplus of potentiality, which includes letting improvised interactional modes of exposure and surprise break the frame of routine predictability. Jazz musicians, as we will show, actively risk the coherence of the musical performance through their vulnerability to the other and thus court what Jarrett Zigon calls a "moral breakdown," a moment when the taken-for-granted and un-self-conscious way of performing suddenly halts and gives rise to "dynamic moments of openness, creativity, and becoming" (2014, 20). Given Zigon's interest in mapping out how the human is fundamentally a "relational-being" engaged in a dynamic "nexus of potentiality," the moral import of maintaining fidelity to the unfolding interactions, even if part of this fidelity is pursuing interactional breakdowns, is shown by the jazz ethic of vulnerability.

In the discussion to follow, we start with a brief description of the setting from which most of our data on jazz improvisation are taken—the musical and verbal interactions of guest jazz musicians in a college-level course on the aesthetics of jazz. In this research, multiple cameras were used to record the musical performances, the exchanges with and among the musicians before they began to play, and the question-and-answer (Q&A) sessions that followed each song or tune.[2] As we shall show, these recordings provided us with a very rich source of information about the musicians and their interactions. As a case study in the decisions and responses of jazz artists in the music-making event, this chapter focuses on the performance of the song "Softly, as in a Morning Sunrise," a well-known jazz standard that is often referred to as "Softly." We examine the interactional assumptions and consequences of particular choices made by band members during the performance.[3]

Despite the song's canonical structure (or "form") and the genre-specific musical knowledge that the musicians share, even the selection of the tune to be performed contains an initial moment of exposure for the musicians. During such an experience of exposure, the performers feel pressure to quickly find a song that everyone knows, even though each player's knowledge of the jazz repertoire varies. Analyzing this performance of "Softly"— and in particular, the temporal unfolding of the embodied and interactive qualities of signaling and recognition—we highlight how musicians position themselves to be responsive to one another as the song progresses. This temporal unfolding includes those moments when the musicians are pulled to attend to unexpected features of the performance. The attentional pull of surprising features is particularly important in the constitution of *emergent improvised arrangements*. Such arrangements often occur during the introduction to songs (Reinholdsson 1998, 219–223), but they also can appear throughout a performance, as when, for example, musicians alternate between playing the main melody and playing a counter melody, or from playing to not playing. The aesthetic demands of jazz require that these arrangements be improvised but also that they sound rehearsed. The form and the sequential arrangement of "Softly" establishes a *sonic ground*, which makes possible variation on the song's structure and the ways in which that structure is performed by specific players. To illustrate this point, we examine a particular moment in this performance when one of the musicians becomes cognizant of a palpable vacuum, an interactional breakdown that demands a responsive effort at repair. The vacuum evinces a strong attentional pull that compels a response by the pianist, who feels morally responsible to fill the role of soloist left open by the sax player, who did not initiate his solo as expected.

Performing Music in the Jazz Classroom: Documenting the Black Aesthetic

Four times between 2002 and 2011, legendary jazz guitarist Kenny Burrell and linguistic anthropologist Alessandro Duranti, who are both faculty members at the University of

California, Los Angeles (UCLA), taught a course for juniors and seniors entitled The Culture of Jazz Aesthetics (CJA).[4] During the first half of most class sessions, a small group of jazz musicians invited by Burrell would play for the students, and after their performance, the guests would engage in an unstructured Q&A session. The questions addressed the topic of the day (e.g., the great soloists, the role of the rhythm section, arranging, records that became influential, the future of jazz) and whatever else emerged in the interaction or seemed relevant to the theme of jazz aesthetics as a cultural tradition. The classroom, located on the first floor of Schoenberg Hall, was equipped with a grand piano, a record player, and music stands, which the students often used as desks. The classroom was spacious enough to include an entire drum set, which allowed for a jazz combo of four to six musicians to play together.

Even though a classroom might at first seem to be a far cry from the settings where jazz performances usually occur, what ended up happening each week closely resembled other settings where jazz is played, either privately or in front of a paying audience. In most weeks, the topic of the class was defined broadly, and the guest musicians were familiar with each other, making the musical interactions in the course similar to those of a jam session. Spontaneous and unrehearsed, the musicians' performances were typical of jazz practice, which celebrates the creativity that emerges out of the partly unpredictable circumstances of improvised music. The high level of musicianship of the artists invited by Burrell ensured that each performance was an example of the kind of interactional imagination that the instructors wanted the students to experience.

Over the four times that the course was offered, more than forty musicians participated as experts and guest artists, and some of them appeared more than once. Excluding guests who were students in the UCLA Jazz Program, a total of twenty-five musicians performed in the class.[5] Most of these musicians were instructors in the UCLA Jazz Program or had taught there in the past. With the exception of one musician, all of the guests performed, including a singer and a dancer.[6] The guests were ethnically diverse and ranged in age from their twenties (Miles Mosley) to their eighties (Gerald Wiggins, Gerald Wilson). Fifteen of the professional guest musicians were African American, six were white, and three were Hispanic. There was less gender diversity, with only three women out of twenty-four guests: a vocalist (Barbara Morrison), a violinist (Lesa Terry), and an arranger, pianist, and vocalist (Michele Weir). The guests were highly talented musicians and, by and large, had played or recorded with Burrell. All had local or international reputations. The group of students in the Jazz Program, who were all college age, showed a different demographic, with fewer African Americans, some Asian Americans, and more whites. The gender disparity, however, remained. There were very few women in the Jazz Studies Program between 2002 and 2011.

Throughout the life of the course, Burrell treated jazz as a very broad category and emphasized its connection to a wider "black aesthetic," out of which came a great variety of styles. In this view, jazz is a lasting, hybrid, and ever-evolving musical tradition that includes not only forms typically seen as jazz subgenres (e.g., bebop, hard bop, and modal jazz) but also many other forms of American popular music. Viewing jazz in this way had significant aesthetic and political implications, and this perspective was made explicit early in the course's history. For example, when the anthropologist of music Maureen Mahon spoke in the CJA course in October of 2002, she mentioned that before the commercial success of the band Living Colour, the musicians in that group, who were African American, had been told by music producers that they should stick to jazz or to rhythm and blues (see Mahon 2004). To illustrate Living Colour's music, Mahon showed two video clips: one of B. B. King playing "Why I Sing the Blues" and the other of Living Colour playing the same song. In the discussion that followed, Burrell used the two renditions of the same song to lay out his vision of the relationship between jazz and popular music:

> What [the members of Living Colour] were doing is something that has developed with them as African-Americans through their life, through their community, through their neighborhood, through their friends, through their family; which is something some of us loosely call "the black aesthetic," which is part of a subculture which exists in this society, which fosters . . . most of the new genres of music which you hear—the latest being hip-hop, rap, etcetera, but [also] jazz and all of its forms, and rock. . . . That is part of the thing that grows out from the community. It grows out naturally. . . . There are many reasons for it. Part of it is survival . . . , but it's really a means of expression of a certain group of people from the United States that has helped them survive and has helped them communicate with each other. . . . Jazz is a part of it. Jazz . . . has been at the forefront of this, not only of this cultural phenomenon . . . this black aesthetic, this music from the African-American [community] but of the American music; therefore since we're the most influential in the world, of the world music, jazz is still in the forefront.[7]

Burrell's vision of the Black aesthetic and ideas about the nature of musical genre shaped his understanding of jazz, and this perspective was an essential part of the course. For example, Burrell was highly critical of the use of narrow genre labels in the music industry, which he felt artificially separated musicians who were influenced by each other or who drew inspiration from the same musical sources and which diminish the role that African Americans have played in music the world over. In his own practice, Burrell generally avoided such labels, with the exception of the word "bebop," which he occasionally used in commercial clubs to describe one or more tunes he had just played with his band. In the first decade of the twentieth century and in light of Burrell's own vast discography,[8] his use of the term "bebop" must be understood as covering a much broader spectrum of tunes, harmonies, rhythms, and arrangements than those associated with the original bebop style created by Dizzy Gillespie and Charlie Parker in the 1940s.[9] As a cohost and often a coperformer in the CJA, Burrell's musical choices and style certainly played a role in the kind of music that was played in the course, but there was also considerable variation among the performances of the individual players and from one group to the next. In most cases, the choices of tunes and the styles in which they were performed were dictated by the theme of the week. Some tunes were played in a style that was meant to honor the musicians who made them famous through their recordings and live concerts (Day 2000, 101).

A PERFORMANCE OF "SOFTLY"

On April 25, 2006, five musicians served as guest artists in the CJA class. Four of them were professionals with long and successful careers: Michael Melvoin (piano), George Bohanon (trombone), Jeff Clayton (alto sax), and Clayton Cameron (drums). The fifth musician was Noah Garabedian (standup bass), a student in the Jazz Program who was taking the course for credit. He had been asked at the last moment by Burrell to substitute for a professional musician and instructor who was not available (Roberto Miranda). In combination with other musicians, all five players had been guests in the course once or twice before. As usual, Burrell brought his guitar to class, which signaled his willingness to play and take on the roles of co-instructor and guest artist. On the day in question, the guest musicians and Burrell played three well-known standards—"Softly"; an untitled, improvised blues song started by Burrell; and Dizzy Gillespie's "A Night in Tunisia." Each performance was followed by an extensive Q&A.

Selecting the Song to Play and Agreeing on Its Key

Before they can start to perform, jazz musicians who do not have a list of songs or repertory that they regularly play together must collectively decide which song they will play. As Robert Faulkner and Howard Becker (2009) have pointed out, this is a socially complicated affair because knowledge of the vast jazz repertoire is unequally distributed among jazz players. Further, when an audience is present, there is pressure on the musicians to quickly come to an agreement about which song to play next. When a song is chosen, some of the players may not remember all of the song's parts, or they may be unfamiliar with the recorded version of the piece or the standard arrangements that others know, perform, or merely hint at. The fact that some musicians may be willing to play a tune that they do not know well and the fact that others might see no problem in imposing their song choice on everyone else in the ensemble illustrate how chance, risk, and unequal decision-making authority are constitutive of jazz as a joint activity—even before a single note is played. Given the ever-present risk that something could go wrong and the song could fall apart before the musicians even get started, calling out and initiating a potentially unfamiliar song involves a particular kind of Aristotelian-like courage, a willingness to put oneself at risk in an effort to pursue a great good—the enactment of a virtuosic improvised piece.

Like other performances in CJA, the choice of "Softly" on April 25, 2006, was made on the spot and with minimal negotiation. While the audience was waiting to hear the musicians play, Burrell asked, almost in a whisper, "What should we do?" Trombone player Bohanon answered, "Softly." Burrell immediately played the first few notes of the

VIDEO FRAME 1. Pianist Mike Melvoin cups his hand around his ear to gesture for clarification about the title and key of the first song.

(UCLA Office of Instructional Development, April 25, 2006)

tune on his guitar, while student bass player Garabedian repeated the title of the song with a smile and a nod, thereby showing his satisfaction with the choice. Burrell's next question was "What key is that in?" Garabedian answered right away: "C minor." The volume of the exchange was so low that Bohanon had to repeat "C minor" and Burrell had, in turn, to repeat the title and key for pianist Melvoin, who had signaled the need to be informed by placing a cupped hand behind his right ear (see Video Frame 1).[10]

These quick exchanges, which were not intended to be heard by the audience, are typical of the cultural tradition of jazz and illustrate the informal ways in which jazz musicians establish a common ground before playing as an ensemble. It was especially important in this case for the two players of the chordal instruments (guitar and piano) to know not only the title of the song but also the key in which to play it. While Burrell and Bohanon seemed concerned with finding a tune that was known by the student bassist (Garabedian), they did not turn to consult the alto sax player (Clayton) or the drummer (Cameron), who merely overheard the exchange. We interpret this apparent exclusion as an implicit vote of confidence toward two professional musicians who could be expected either to be familiar with "Softly" or to have the musical competence required to participate in its performance even if they didn't know it.

The Business of Starting and Establishing the Tempo

In the absence of a conductor, the members of a jazz combo need a way to coordinate when and how to start the tune and to agree about the tempo at which to play it. In most cases, both goals can be achieved by having someone "count in time" according to the time signature of the song. In the case of "Softly," which is in 4/4 time, one performer would count, "One. Two. One-two-three-four" (with the first "one" and "two" counted on the first and third beats, respectively). Another way of starting a group performance is for one musician to play a few measures of music that are harmonically related to the song or melodically similar to its tune. These measures not only establish the tempo of the performance but also suggest a particular rhythmic feel for the song. They are also a practical device to let the other members of the band get ready and enter the song "on time" and "in time." This is what happened during the April 25 performance: pianist Melvoin played some ad lib chords and melodic lines that morphed into an in-tempo and harmonically appropriate introduction to "Softly." During the Q&A that followed the performance, Bohanon, who was at the time an instructor in the Jazz Program, spelled out for the students the implications of Melvoin's decision:

Excerpt 1 (CJA April 25, 2006)

> BOHANON; Michael [Melvoin] started on a wonderful, you know, solo piano intro
> which we didn't know how <u>he</u> was going to get into this tune. But then we heard
> a ((*imitating with the voice the rhythm and timbre of the piano*)) "humpf bum
> bu:m. bu:m bum" that was a pulse that made us- that introduced the <u>tempo</u>
> of the tune. you know, we didn't have to say "how fast are we going to play?
> Let's play- . . ." it was automatic. <u>he</u> set the tempo not the drummer. ((*pointing
> and looking at drummer behind him*)) because here again is another rhythm
> instrument ((*pointing to the piano*)) that's able to set the pulse and the mood for
> what we were going to play.

In praising Melvoin's playing, Bohanon's phrase "it was automatic" proudly expresses the ease with which he and the other players could hear and immediately adapt to the rhythm and tempo established by the piano player. The phrase also makes it known that there is a cultural category—and, with it, a cultural convention—of "a solo piano intro" (i.e., an introduction played and improvised on the piano), which has a particular cultural function. If we "bracket" and momentarily "suspend" (Husserl [1913] 1931, §§31–32) our natural acceptance of Bohanon's claim that "it was automatic" for him and the other players to hear and immediately adapt to the rhythm and tempo established by the piano player, we can then ask what makes possible the recognition of what Melvoin is playing as an introduction to "Softly." In so doing, we can come to recognize this practice as an invitation to coordinate around a particular tempo and rhythm. One answer to the question of what makes this recognition possible is found in Pierre Bourdieu's notion of the *habitus*, a concept most notably applied to music by sociologist François Dortier.

Explaining in musical terms Bourdieu's famous definition of habitus as "structured structures predisposed to function as structuring structures" (Bourdieu [1972] 1977), Dortier writes that "it is only after having internalized musical codes and constraints (the '*structured structures*') that a pianist can then compose, create, invent, and transmit her music (the '*structuring structures*')" (2012, 5). As we show later, there is plenty of evidence of a musical habitus being involved in this act of signaling by the pianist and of its recognition by the other players.

Our multicamera audio-visual recording of the performance of "Softly" allows us to further refine Dortier's Bourdieusian account by identifying the embodied and interactive quality of the musicians' habitus. In addition to the internalized musical competence that the musicians utilize (what Alfred Schutz [1945, 87] would call the "stock of knowledge at hand with all its hidden social references"), the video recordings also show that the players are making selective use of both aural and visual communication to coordinate their actions. As Melvoin begins playing, we see him looking down at his fingers and the keyboard. During this phase, most of the other musicians can be seen looking at him and displaying a "waiting" posture (Video Frame 2).

VIDEO FRAME 2. Musicians looking at pianist Mike Melvoin while he plays a solo introduction to "Softly, as in a Morning Sunrise."

(UCLA Office of Instructional Development, April 25, 2006)

VIDEO FRAME 3. Pianist Mike Melvoin looks up at trombonist George Bohanon.

(UCLA Office of Instructional Development, April 25, 2006)

After a few seconds, we can see Melvoin lift his head and look at Bohanon, who is right in front of him (Video Frame 3).

Bohanon then lowers his head in a subtle nod, looks away, lifts up his trombone, and then brings the mouthpiece close to his lips (Video Frame 4). At the same time, Burrell moves to the front of the stage, while Garabedian shifts from embracing the neck of the standup bass with his arms and stretching his fingers (visible in Video Frame 3) to a ready-to-play posture, with fingers spread above the upper portion of his bass's neck in the anticipation of a C-minor chord (Video Frame 4). At this point, drummer Clayton Cameron is also ready to start.

The visual documentation of Bohanon, Burrell, Garabedian, and Cameron watching Melvoin and getting in a "ready" posture demonstrates that what Melvoin is doing on the piano—his choice of notes, chords, phrasing, and rhythm—has a high attentional pull for the other players, and their actions can be read as reactions to what they hear him do musically. A key difference between Video Frame 2 and Video Frame 3 is that the latter shows Melvoin while he is shifting from playing ad lib to playing an in-tempo comping part in C minor, which had a rhythmic pattern spread over two measures. Parts such as this are typically recognized by the other musicians as a vamp (i.e., a musical phrase that loops), which gives them time to adjust to the tempo before joining in (see Bohanon's discussion in "Excerpt 1," earlier). In other words, the vamp is used by the

VIDEO FRAME 4. Trombone player, bass player, and drummer stand ready to play.
(UCLA Office of Instructional Development, April 25, 2006)

other musicians as a guide to enter into the musical flow established by the pianist. The exact time at which each of the players does enter, however, is not fixed or predictable. This is shown in the schematic representation offered in Table 19.1, which indicates the entry points of the various instruments along the same timeline. The vamp created by Melvoin on the piano is shown here to be made of two sets of four beats, with each beat represented in the table by an "x." The beginning and ending of each vamp unit (4+4 beats) are marked by a double oblique (//xxxx/xxxx//).

Table 19.1. Schematic Representation of Entry Points by the Different Instruments in the Improvised Introduction to "Softly"

	vamp 1	vamp 2	vamp 3	vamp 4	melody
Timeline					
piano	//xxxx/xxxx//	xxxx/xxxx//	xxxx/xxxx//	xxxx/xxxx//	plays chords of song
bass		xxxx//	xxxx/xxxx//	xxxx/xxxx//	plays bass line of song
drums			//xxxx/xxxx//	xxxx/xxxx//	keeps playing same beat
guitar				xx//	plays melody
alto sax				//	plays melody
trombone				//	plays countermelody

As the timeline reproduced for each instrument shows, the other players took Melvoin's introductory vamp as an invitation to come in at their discretion, within certain conventional boundaries. The bass player is the first who joins Melvoin. Starting to play at the beginning of the fourth measure, he shows that he does not need a full repetition of the vamp to know that it will be repeated. The drummer starts two beats later, exactly at the beginning of the third repetition of the vamp. The other three musicians (the two horn players and the guitarist) join in after the fourth repetition of the two-bar vamp and start to play the melody. As they do, the pianist and the bass player shift to the chords of the song, the alto sax and the guitar play the melody in quasi-unison, and the trombone plays a countermelody. When they get to the B section of the song, Bohanon and Clayton shift roles, with Bohanon playing the melody and Clayton playing a countermelody.

The Introduction as an Emergent Improvised Arrangement

When one listens to this rendition of "Softly," it sounds as if the musician's parts had been written and memorized, or at least rehearsed. In fact, the various ways that the six instruments enter the harmonic and melodic space defined by the piano player is an emergent improvised arrangement. Using this term, we do not mean to suggest that the organization and content of this de facto introduction was a *complete* invention, a combination of musical choices and ideas never before heard or played by these or other musicians. On the contrary, several aspects of this type of "setting up," "getting ready," and "getting into" a song are familiar to jazz musicians and their fans, starting from the total number of times the vamp was repeated (four) and the number of measures (also four) that were played between the moment when the drummer joined in and the beginning of the song, which his drum roll had anticipated and suggested. A four-bar introduction is quite common in jazz recordings from the 1940s and 1950s, but its routine character does not guarantee that it will be executed to the satisfaction of the band members and the audience. Like the everyday encounters examined by Goffman (1959, 1967) or the openings of telephone calls studied by Emmanuel Schegloff (1986), the successful performance of song introductions in jazz should not be taken for granted. They are, each time, an achievement. Such achievements are the result of a successful coordinated effort to collectively produce something that could sound, count, and work as an introduction to this particular song for this particular combination of instruments on this particular occasion. Without the right musical experience, a musician might not catch the cue that both establishes the tempo and demarcates a possible starting point for the band's entrances.

The importance of this kind of shared knowledge was made explicit on other occasions by other guest musicians. Before beginning a song in his April 18, 2006, performance in the class, pianist Tamir Hendelman announced, "I'm going to start with a little introduction and then they [bassist Roberto Miranda and drummer Clayton

Cameron] are going to come in." After all three had finished playing the song, Duranti asked Miranda and Cameron, "How do you know when you come in [i.e., when it's time for you to start playing], when the introduction is over?" Miranda responded first, pointing out that he and Cameron had identified what Hendelman was playing as the second part of a song they knew. He said that they also heard Hendelman "pedal on the fifth [note] of the scale," a convention based on the "five/one [dominant/tonic] relationship in Western music." By emphasizing the fifth note of the key in which the song is set, this device sets up the expectation of a harmonic resolution, usually to the tonic. In Cameron's words, this device will "lead you back to the beginning of the tune."

The experienced jazz musician's ability to pull off such spontaneous and coordinated arrangements defines their art, and with a high rate of success, the performers make such coordinations look easy. In reality, the musicians are playing something that is unrehearsed and in a wide range of ways is not fully predictable. These unpredictable features include how the piece will start, how it will end (Black 2008, 286–289), and, as we discuss later, who will solo, the order of the solos, and how long each solo will last. Jazz musicians, especially those of Burrell's generation, show considerable pride in being able to coordinate their performance in a way that sounds rehearsed, even though it is not. Such musicians seem eager to underscore the smooth execution of improvised arrangements by making tongue-in-cheek comments. After this performance of "Softly," for example, Burrell said ironically, "Just like we rehearsed it," and after the performance by Hendelman, Miranda, and Cameron, he similarly asked, "Just like you rehearsed it, right?" to which Hendelman replied, "Just like we rehearsed it." On both occasions Burrell waited for the applause to end before making these comments, which suggests that he wanted them to be heard. Such comments suggest a form of aesthetic perfectionism that is different from, but is at least as challenging as, the perfectionism found in music traditions where performance is based on a flawless execution of a score, like Western art music.

In fact, jazz musicians often display a critical stance on written music. This can be attributed to the difficulty of using the Western notational system to capture how jazz music is played (Duranti 2009) and the consequent primacy in the jazz canon of recordings over written scores (Williams 2001; Brackett 2017, 118); however, there are also historical and political dimensions of their defiant attitude toward the musical conventions of the dominant European aesthetic culture. This attitude is supported by the desire among jazz musicians to be treated as equal to those who play music— as beautiful and as complex as it can be—that was written by the celebrated European composers of the past. For jazz musicians, authenticity is not understood as the exact reproduction of an original combination of content and form. Rather, it is the ability to create something that was not imagined ahead of time and yet, once completed, appears to have been planned.

Making something appear "rehearsed" relies on the kind of shared knowledge illustrated earlier, which we refer to as the sonic ground. In each case, there was enough common background in the group to make the musicians comfortable in their respective roles and allow them to enter the sonic space of the song at different moments but still arrive at a common point of convergence. Not limited to the introduction of songs, this type of creative coordination is pervasive in jazz performance. In the next section, we focus on two additional aspects of the sonic ground—the song's "form" and expectations about the sequential organization of the various parts of the song, including turn-taking by the soloists.

The "Form"

Conventions are necessary in all collaborative art forms (Becker 2008). One convention shared by all jazz musicians is the classification of tunes in terms of their harmonic structure, which is organized around the number of different sections, number of measures in each section, and sequence of its chords. In jazz, all of this information is referred to as the song's "form." Once memorized, the form helps musicians improvise and accompany a singer or a soloist.

There are many possible forms in the jazz repertoire (see Berliner 1994, chap. 3). Two of the most common are the twelve-bar blues and a set of song forms organized around a sequence of eight-bar sections, each of which is referred to by letter (an "A" section, a "B" section, and, when needed, a "C" section). In the 1950s and 1960s, free jazz and jazz fusion did away with these conventions, but they continue to be relevant for many contemporary jazz groups, including those that performed in CJA. Organized in a series of eight-bar sections, "Softly, as in a Morning Sunrise" was written by Sigmund Romberg (music) and Oscar Hammerstein (lyrics) for a 1928 operetta entitled *The New Moon*. Like other songs of that period, "Softly" has what jazz musicians refer to as a "thirty-two-bar AABA" form (see Faulkner and Becker 2009, 22–24). In this form, the three A sections are melodically and harmonically similar to one another, and the B section (or bridge) has its own melody and chords.

As an organizing principle of both composition and performance, the form of a song provides the sonic ground to simultaneously link and differentiate the musician's performance and serve the jazz aesthetic. Either developed live in performance or established in advance through a written score or a rehearsal, variations on the form are interpreted as ways to make the song more interesting to an audience and to the other players. In the April 25 performance of "Softly," the shared understanding of the song's AABA form allowed the musicians to make sense of the decisions that were individually and collectively executed, including the sequential organization and duration of the solos.

Sequential Organization of a Jazz Tune: Head, Solos, and Trading Eights

When jazz musicians have not had time to rehearse or agree on an arrangement, the collective performance of a song can usually be expected to be organized in terms of three major sequentially ordered parts. First, the band plays the melody (or "head"),

Table 19.2. Order of Solos in April 25, 2006,
Performance of "Softly"

1. Trombone (George Bohanon)
2. Piano (Mike Melvoin)
3. Alto sax (Jeff Clayton)
4. Guitar (Kenny Burrell)
5. Bass (Noah Garabedian)

with varying degrees of conformity to the way it was originally written or recorded. (If the tune is a blues song, the melody is repeated twice.) Next come the solos. One after the other, each of the musicians plays an improvised part over the chord changes of the original tune or a modified version of those chords. Sometimes, one or more musicians may choose not to take a solo, and the duration of each solo is measured in terms of how many times the soloist plays through the entire form of the song, which is referred to as a "chorus." Finally, all of the musicians play the head melody and end the song.

The April 25 performance of "Softly" began as usual with the head, followed by all of the musicians except the drummer taking solos, each of which was two choruses (sixty-four measures) long.

After the sequence of soloists shown in Table 19.2, the trombonist started to improvise again, but this time he only played for eight measures, instead of the song's full thirty-two measures. When he stopped, drummer Cameron soloed for eight measures while the other members of the band rested. Next, the bass and piano joined in, with the pianist Melvoin improvising some melodic lines for the next set of eight measures. This new round of solos was still built on the AABA form but with each player only improvising for an eight-measure section, a routine called "trading." Trading typically features the drummer alternating solos with each of the other players. If there is no drummer, then the turn-taking goes from one player to the next, always in the sequence established in the first round. The length of the solos that musicians may trade vary from song to song, with four- or eight-bar solos being the most common. These conventions illustrate the importance of musical structure, which is usually represented numerically, for coordinating the jazz ensemble's performance. Jazz musicians are very aware of this. During the Q&A after the performance of "Softly," for example, Cameron stated that "all tunes have structure."

Excerpt 2 (CJA April 25, 2006)

CAMERON; I might take a solo on a [twelve-bar] blues. [The other musicians] may give me twelve bars [to improvise on] or we may do it- break it up in fours but we probably wouldn't do eights. if we did eights then, you know, someone's going to be playing fours you know, because of the number of bars. [. . .] So just depending on the structure of the tune, it all usually works out mathematically.

Table 19.3. Sequential Order of Solos during the
"Trading Eights" Portion of "Softly"

1. Trombone (Bohanon) – 8 bars	(A1)
Drums (Cameron) 8 bars	(A2)
2. Piano (Melvoin) – 8 bars	(B)
Drums (Cameron) 8 bars	(A3)
3. Alto sax (Clayton) – 8 bars	(A1)
Drums (Cameron) 8 bars	(A2)
4. Guitar (Burrell) – 8 bars	(B)
Drums (Cameron) 8 bars	(A3)

In Cameron's explanation, the number of bars that are "traded" depends upon the total number of bars in the song. "Softly" is thirty-two bars long, with each eight-bar sequence corresponding to one of the four sections of the AABA form. The sequence of solos in the trading section is provided in Table 19.3, where we have also noted the correspondence between each eight-bar solo and its place in the AABA form.

The "mathematics" of the musical structure is highly symmetrical, which allows for predictable coordination between the musicians and fair distribution of solo time (though drummers and bass players typically take fewer solos than the other musicians). The total number of "eights" that are played adds up to sixty-four measures, which corresponds to twice the thirty-two-bar AABA form (i.e., two choruses). This means that the trading-eights portion of the performance is as long as each of the individual solos. While the two-choruses pattern was not prearranged, the pattern's duration is not accidental. The thirty-two-bar AABA form reproduced itself, or rather, the musicians kept relying on it, individually and collectively. The mathematical, symmetrical recurrence of this structure helps to give the impression of a prearranged and smoothly achieved performance. Another advantage of following the AABA form is that it allows the musicians to know when to start (at the beginning of A1) and when to stop their solo (at the end of A3). In trading, the form remains relevant to each segment. Starting his solo after the second set of eight bars (A2), for example, the pianist is expected to improvise on the chords of the B section, which are different from those of the prior two A sections. Keeping track of the form during this kind of exchange is a basic requirement for jazz improvisation and an important skill for students to quickly master (Berliner 1994, 176–180).

The exploitation of the mathematical side of the form is only one of the ready-made properties of songs that can be used to allow for tight coordination. Just as actors in improv theater build upon the elements of setting and plot established by others earlier in the scene—the well-known "Yes and . . . " rule (Sawyer 2001)—jazz players may also use an element that was just performed as a model for what to do next. This was revealed by Bohanon when Duranti asked him about how he and the others figured out the order of the solos in the "trading eights" section of the performance.

Excerpt 3 (CJA April 25, 2006)

DURANTI; How did you know what to do- when- when you would go [to start trading eights]?
BOHANON; well we- we did it the same order as we did our solos. I started my solo [first] so I started the eights [first]. ((*moves forward, gestures with right hand toward the drums*))
And then drummer played eights.
((*Points with right arm and hand back to pianist without looking at him*))
Michael [Melvoin] played second [during the earlier solos] so he'll play eight ((*use hands to mimic playing the piano*))
((*turns to gesture with open right hand to drummer*)) the drummer played eight.
So we just followed ((*makes a rolling gestures with two hands*)) the same sequence.

This logic is schematically represented in Table 19.4 and constitutes what we might call the *build-on-history model*, which suggests that once something is done during a performance, it can be used as a model for what is done later. In this case, the order of the individual solos becomes a model for the turn-taking in the trading-eights portion of the performance.

Table 19.4 reveals something else that was not mentioned in the Q&A—that the bass player did not participate in trading eights. In terms of the social organization of the performance, this is an example of exclusion, and the fact that it seems to be taken for granted by the musicians is a good reason for trying to explain it. There are at least three possible criteria that can be invoked. The first criterion is historical and specific to the instruments involved, with bass players being the band members

Table 19.4. Order of Solos during the Full-Chorus Solo Section Compared with Order of Solos during "Trading Eights" Section

Solos (2 sets of 32 bars each player)	Trading (8 bars each player)
1. Trombone (Bohanon)	Trombone (Bohanon)
	Drums (Cameron)
2. Piano (Melvoin)	Piano (Melvoin)
	Drums (Cameron)
3. Alto sax (Clayton)	Alto sax (Clayton)
	Drums (Cameron)
4. Guitar (Burrell)	Guitar (Burrell)
	Drums (Cameron)
5. Bass (Garabedian)	

who tend to take fewer solos than other instruments in a band (unless the bassist is the band leader, such as Ray Brown or Christian McBride). A second is seniority, with the bass player in the April 25 performance being the youngest and least experienced player in the group. The third is structural and involves, again, the form of the song. To let Garabedian solo for eight bars right after Burrell would have caused the band to end up with an extra A section after having completed the AABA form, producing a sequence that would have been "ungrammatical." One effect of this would be that the musicians wouldn't know when to return to the head melody, which is necessary to complete the performance. Further, including Garabedian in the eights would not have resulted in an equal distribution of the traded solos, because after the bass player's first A, there would have been only three more sets of eights left—A2, the bridge, and the final A (A3). This would have meant that another player would have been left out of their second chorus.

Borrowing a term from conversation analysis (Sacks et al. 1974), we could say that the adoption of the AABA form as the reference point for trading eights entails that the end of the last A (A3) is always a possible *transition-relevance place*; here, they could either start another round of trading or go back to playing the melody. Like Sacks et al., we use the word "relevance" to emphasize that after any A3 section, the end of trading is *possible* but not necessary. The question then arises how a decision is made and communicated among the band members. Based on the empirical evidence available in our video recordings, we can say that visual access to the body and face of the other band members plays a key role in allowing the musicians to coordinate their actions. Camera 3 shows that after his eight bars of soloing—and as soon as the drum solo starts—Burrell lifts his head to look and nod in the direction of both Bohanon and Clayton, who is seen (on Camera 2) to nod back. At first, this suggests that the decision to stop trading eights and return to the head was made by Burrell and accepted by the others. As the host and most senior (and famous) player in the group, one could say that Burrell has the positional authority and personal prestige to make such a decision. But if we take into consideration Goffman's idea that any predictable social arrangement must be reenacted, we should be cautious in assuming the relevance of the status relations among the players and return to what actually transpired in the video recording.

When we repeatedly watched in slow motion the recording made by Camera 3, we saw that before Burrell looked up from his guitar to signal the return to "the head," Bohanon had *already* slightly lifted his head and turned to look at Burrell. The way he performed these head gestures suggests that he was making known his expectation that a change was likely to occur next, with a return to the head as the most likely option at that point. Thus, what had at first seemed to be Burrell's embodied directive could be reinterpreted as Burrell's *response* to something that had been suggested by Bohanon's look.

Whether one accepts this interpretation or not, it is clear that the musicians achieve their tight coordination by paying close attention to one another and by making their intentions or preference known (and thus relevant) to each other by means of visible gestures or changes of posture. Using Goffman's dramaturgic metaphor of human interaction, we could say that players are performers not only in the traditional sense of that term (people who act in front of and for an audience) but also in the sense that they are socially enacting a set of interactional principles, which thereby become relevant to the ongoing activity. By providing embodied visual cues to each other about what could or should come next, players make the historically sedimented expectations about solo turn-taking—for example, "this is the right duration for trading" or "we are sounding good, let's keep going"—relevant for their coordination with the rest of the band. Under these circumstances, a priori hierarchies based on prestige or seniority may or may not be relevant to the actions of other band members, as projected by subtle gestures and changes of posture. In rapid and nuanced exchanges, the force of the other's "face" may not rise to the level of the ethical imperative posited by Levinas; nevertheless, such glances are often informationally rich enough to suggest one course of action over another.

The Ethics of Jazz "Etiquette"

In this section, we show how an inquiry into a matter of sequential order of the solos turned into a discussion of etiquette in performance. An important concern in the jazz tradition, the phenomenon of etiquette can be used as a testing ground for the notion of face, in both the Goffmanian and Levinasian senses of the term. In evoking the need to show respect, jazz musicians practice a unique sense of etiquette while making choices during performances.

In CJA class, Burrell and Duranti encouraged the students to be curious observers of the performances and actively participate in the Q&A that followed each song. Responding to the students' questions, the musicians told stories about themselves or other jazz performers and gave accounts of the musical choices they had made in the song they had just played. After Bohanon's remarks about the order for trading eights, which we quoted in Excerpt 2 earlier, a student asked a question about visual communication in the performance.

Excerpt 4 (CJA April 25, 2006)

STUDENT; So you traded . . . eights in the same order that you did solos.
BOHANON; yes.
STUDENT; so did you- I was trying to see if you guys were <u>eyeing</u> each other.
BOHANON; ((*shakes his head*)) no.
      [
STUDENT;   Is that how you decided who was going to do a solo?
CLAYTON; ((*nods*)) We <u>were</u> . . . eyeing each other.
STUDENT; okay. ((*laughing*)) ha-ha.
OTHERS; ((*join laughter while Clayton confirms*))
CLAYTON; ((*overlapping with laughter*)) yes. yes. yes.

This transcript captures a rare moment of disagreement in the interactions among the guest musicians: Bohanon says that they were not eyeing each other, but Clayton immediately and emphatically contradicts him. The difference between their answers went unnoticed in the Q&A, partly because Bohanon quickly adjusted his stance, first by nodding slightly after Clayton's remarks and then by smiling at what has now been taken by the audience as a humorous confession. It turns out that Clayton had a bigger point to make, namely, that "there is an etiquette" to playing jazz.

Excerpt 5 (CJA April 25, 2006)

CLAYTON; people think it's intuitive but- but there is a: :- . . . a:- . . . uhm there is an
etiquette. about it. and- and you can step on other people's . . . jazz feet. . . .
STUDENTS; ((*laugh*))
CLAYTON; if you don't- if you don't follow the rules and pay attention to the etiquette.
and then of course you are also allowed to- do whatever you want. so. . . usually you
are very respectful of your musicians=These are great musicians ((*pointing toward
the rest of the band*)). so you don't want to just jump out there and say "this is The
Jeff Clayton Show." ((*while saying this, he walks forward, mimicking someone who
tries to grab all the attention of the audience*))
STUDENTS; ((*laugh*))
CLAYTON; that's- that's not what it's about. It's about us playing together so uhm . . . so
I like to play together I like to be a team player. I like to be a part of what's going on
around- all around. uh in the band. so: I- I like to follow the rules and . . . do those
things ((*nods*))

Once introduced, the term "etiquette" becomes the overall conceptual umbrella for other musicians to talk about the choices that they made during the performance. After Clayton said that one should be respectful of the other musicians and not make the performance into one's own individual show, it is not surprising that Bohanon took the floor again, this time to explain—if not justify—why he played the first solo.

Excerpt 6 (CJA April 25, 2006)

BOHANON; Another thing to- to- to piggy back on what you asked . . you know . . . Jeff
[Clayton] played the melody actually first so . . . just it would seem . . feasible that if
he had the melody I might play the first solo. If I had the melody, he would probably
play the first solo. that's just the way . . . we think. you know I didn't want to come
play the melody then play all the solo, you know, this way we had a variety going on.
Everybody would kind of be going around . . . and we didn't- we didn't speak about
it. we didn't even have to talk about it=but it sort of- it felt right to do it that way. that's
usually the case . . . you know, it's about how does the music feel. Michael [Melvoin]
started on a wonderful you know, solo piano intro. . . .

Bohanon's remarks speak to the student's implicit question about whether the musicians needed to look at each other to coordinate their actions while soloing.

Bohanon points out that they "didn't speak about" who was going to solo first, and immediately after this passage, he goes on explaining that the musicians also do not need to discuss the tune's tempo. (See the remarks quoted in Excerpt 1, which immediately followed those of Excerpt 6.) The criterion for the decision about the order of solos is said to be available from the immediately prior interaction: "Jeff [Clayton] played the melody actually first," and therefore, "it would seem . . . feasible" for Bohanon to solo first. The solo was "feasible" in this context, but it was by no means obvious or certain. In a large number of jazz recordings, the band member who plays the melody also takes the first solo. Further, the statement that "Jeff played the melody" is only partly accurate, as Clayton had only played the melody of the A sections, while Bohanon had played the B section. In addition to suggesting that jazz etiquette expresses the culture's democratic ethos—a debatable claim (Hagberg 2006, 472; Duranti 2009, 21)—Bohanon here is explicit about another criterion for selecting who should solo next: "variety." Both the egalitarian ethos and the variety principle are echoed in Clayton's subsequent account of his decision not to play his solo after Bohanon.

Excerpt 7 (CJA April 25, 2006)

CLAYTON; that's very interesting because after George's [Bohanon's] solo, . . and after I had already played the melody I felt that I shouldn't play the melody [i.e., not start a solo]. That I should stand down. So Mike Melvoin took the solo after . . . George. was that true?
MELVOIN; ((*nods*)) hum-hum
CLAYTON; yeah.
MELVOIN; and I waited (all those) bars to be<u>gin</u>=
                      [
CLAYTON;   because I thought there was too much horn (going on)

In Excerpt 7, Clayton confirms the relevance of jazz etiquette by saying that he felt that he should not be the next one to improvise because he had just played the original melody. He also provides support for Bohanon's call for "variety" by claiming that he decided to let someone else go next to avoid "too much horn," which also shows concern for an aesthetics of timbre.

What Clayton leaves unsaid is that his choice *not* to play next created a problem for everyone else. This is made explicit in Melvoin's subsequent comments, starting with his implicitly apologetic remark, "and I waited (all those) bars to begin." As shown in Excerpt 8 (which follows the last two turns of Excerpt 7), Melvoin does not expect to solo next and initially looks to Burrell as a possible candidate for the second solo. Once he realizes, however, that Burrell is not starting to solo, Melvoin feels the weight of responsibility upon himself. Here, the musician's etiquette takes an ethical turn. Courage is needed to keep going in the face of the pending unraveling of the song. This unfolding of courage begins with the recognition of "a vacuum" created by Clayton's unexpected decision and continues with the invocation of a collective responsibility toward the music that is being played.

Excerpt 8 (CJA April 25, 2006)

MELVOIN; and I waited (all those) bars to be<u>gin</u>=
                    [
CLAYTON;   because I thought there was too much horn (going on)
MELVOIN; =because like I thought perhaps. <u>Kenny</u> would play the next solo
                    [
BOHANON;   ((*points toward Clayton, then corrects gesture to Burrell*))
((*Bohanon, Clayton, and Cameron all laugh*))
MELVOIN; and I didn't hear (it/him). and like . . . part of the etiquette is that if- . . . if a
    vacuum exists longer than ((*turns to look at Burrell*)) <u>two</u> beats ((*laughs*)) ha-ha.
MELVOIN; ((*to audience*)) you know, we are very very aware . . .
                    [
CLAYTON;   (you) jump into it.
MELVOIN; we are all just- we're just playing <u>one</u> music . . .. all of us together. This is just
    one music not ((*gestures with hand toward others in the band*)) an individual music
    for each one of us=we are <u>all</u> in this com<u>ple</u>tely together. and- a solo- <u>a</u> solo starts
    <u>now</u>! and it hasn't started yet and that's two beats in. and so that was my cue that it
    was my solo . . .
BOHANNON; mh-mh.
CLAYTON; mh.

We could speculate about why Melvoin would expect Burrell to go next by once
again evoking seniority, fame, previous experiences playing together, or other reasons.
We could also speculate about why Burrell did *not* go next. We have chosen, instead, to
focus on the implications of Melvoin's mention of "a vacuum."

The Vacuum

During a music performance, everyone present—players as well as members of the
audience—listens to the same sounds, but not everyone hears them in the same way.
What Melvoin, a studio musician with a long list of credits in both jazz and pop music
(including participation in the recording of the Beach Boys' famous "Good Vibrations"),
hears as a vacuum may have gone unnoticed to the audience, especially because the
musicians in the rhythm section continued to play. Melvoin's comments reveal not only
this individual player's musical sensibility but also his assumption of responsibility for
how the music is being played and how the band performs as a collective enterprise,
where the choices of each member reflect on the whole, and vice versa.

   In Goffmanian terms, the vacuum that Melvoin hears is potentially face-threatening
for him as an individual and for the band as a group. Melvoin's report about having waited
to start his solo ("I waited all those bars . . . ") can be read as a confession of his embarrassment at not having been an attentive band member, while his evocation of etiquette
is a way of emphasizing the need to come to the rescue and fill the vacuum with something as quickly as possible. These statements suggest that music performance requires
the same kind of impression management that Goffman found in other kinds of public

behaviors, where social actors seek to give "an impression of infallibility" (Goffman 1967, 43). But drawing on Levinas's vision of ethics as an exposure to vulnerability, we think that something else is also going on here. Rather than trying to appear infallible, what jazz musicians want to project is the ability to overcome errors by transforming them into challenges to be met. This attitude finds expression in Burrell's comment "Just like we rehearsed it," though this is not meant to be taken literally. The specific ethical virtuosity implicit in this comment lies in the tension between jazz musicians' desire to sound "as if" they rehearsed and their simultaneous introduction of all kinds of variations, impromptu arrangements, and unexpected choices. This means that rather than merely playing something they had rehearsed or memorized, jazz musicians also want to be seen as embracing the risk and fallibility of improvisation (Monson 1996, 154–171; Feurzeig 1997; Klemp et al. 2008). Of course, in performance most audience members do not notice errors and jazz musicians do not draw attention to them. However, this issue is sometimes addressed when musicians are directly questioned.

This was the case, for example, in a 2002 Q&A session that followed guest pianist Gerald Wiggins's masterful performance of the jazz standard "Body and Soul." In the course, Wiggins introduced to the students the concept of "clam," by which he meant "a mistake that you would like to cover up." Asked by Duranti to give an example, Wiggins again began to play the beginning of "Body and Soul," this time inserting altered chords that sounded increasingly distant from the original chords of the song and increasingly discordant. As discussed in Duranti and Burrell (2004), the exercise turned into a test for the other musicians, who were asked to identify exactly at what point a "mistake" could be said to have occurred. After others had identified one clam or another, alto saxophonist Jeff Clayton, who was another guest on that day, rejected the premise of the exercise. Rather than making mistakes, Clayton claimed that Wiggins had done what jazz musicians routinely do:

> We [jazz musicians] play and we play and we play and we paint ourselves . . . in and out of corners all the time, and so what I just heard from what Gerald [Wiggins] was playing, was . . . I heard him paint himself into a harmonic corner and manage to get out because there was - there was tension, and there was release, so I just thought it was just something else beautiful, he meant to go there.
>
> (Wiggins quoted in Duranti and Burrell 2004, 85)

This experience of hearing "something else beautiful" and of hearing that Wiggins "meant to go there" is precisely what arises in the midst of painting oneself "in and out of corners." It is an existential condition that is virtuous in its acceptance of the risk of exposure and, for that very reason, calls for a virtuosic solution.

CONCLUSION: UNCHARTED FUTURES

In this chapter, we have applied an interactionally informed phenomenological approach to jazz performance to argue that what makes jazz distinct from other kinds of musical traditions is not simply the ubiquity of improvisation but the interactional implications of the uncertainty that improvisation produces. The unplanned arrangements that emerge in the course of the performance are virtuosic solutions to routine problems such as starting a song, establishing a tempo, and providing room for soloists to be creative. At the same time, the inability to know ahead of time exactly who will do what makes players vulnerable to the choices made by others. A case study in the unfolding dynamics of musical collaboration, our analysis of this performance shows how one musician's desire to create sonic and timbral variation created a problem for another musician, who felt responsible for filling what he perceived as an emerging vacuum. Though the problem of the vacuum was overcome almost as soon as it arose, it threatened the collective quality of the performance as a coordinated group effort around a well-known song. Problems like the vacuum occur because jazz musicians subscribe to an aesthetics that is built on being open to risks. Rather than giving off the impression of infallibility—to each other or to the audience—jazz musicians thrive when masterfully coping with contingency of their own making, including what might be heard as an error.

The interactions that occur in jazz are complex, and taken alone, no single theoretical orientation can do justice to them. In this performance of "Softly," the musicians' performance could be interpreted as an example of Goffmanian impression management or the players' Levinasian desire to respect the infinite responsibility toward an individual or collective other. Indeed, both theorists must be evoked because, for jazz musicians, there is a continuous tension between the need for impression management and the ethical imperative to respond to the challenge initiated by others. This tension arises out of, and in turn reinscribes, the open-ended, sedimented, virtuous dispositions such as courage that defined Aristotle's ethics. Because virtuous conduct is fundamentally situated and emergent, the details of social interaction matter, and an awareness of this situation has shaped our research methods. In our discussion, we have been guided by an empirical commitment to documenting what actually happens during a live performance. The simultaneous multicamera view of the various participants allowed us to analyze the interactional articulation of the musicians' embodied dispositions and their reactions to each other's musical production. Mutual aural and visual access constitutes the ground on which both routine and innovative solutions must be found and interpreted. "Jazz etiquette" is, thus, a name for what may appear as subtle moves. We would argue, however, that no matter how small, such moves are always consequential because they are open to aesthetic and ethical evaluation.

Levinas's philosophy can also help us interpret the weight of the educational context where the performance of "Softly" took place. In the classroom setting, the microsociality of the face-to-face interactions proceed to a more encompassing and richer sense of musicians' intersubjective attunement. Attuning and adjusting to one another occurs within a thick temporal space that encompasses the jazz musicians' past performances, risky present, and virtuosic, if uncharted, future amidst jazz audiences to come. In a classroom with expert performers, student musicians, and other students who were not musically educated, what transpired was not simply an ethics of responding to other musicians but one of teaching nonexperts. This is the kind of teaching that, for Levinas, "comes from the exterior and brings me more than I contain" ([1961] 1969, 51). Indeed, to be taught in a Levinasian sense is to allow oneself to overflow with more than one can contain from the other. To be sure, such situations involve risk. In the context of jazz performance, moments such as the vacuum or the clam are precisely a desirous site to respond to an ethical call and thus to extend and exceed oneself through learning. The jazz musicians experience what Levinas calls the "Desire" to go beyond the routinized stocks of knowledge and open oneself to the other. This Desire continually opens up the excessive dimensions of exposure. As Levinas writes, "in Desire there is no sinking one's teeth into being, no satiety, but an uncharted future before me" ([1961] 1969, 117). In jazz, such uncharted futures include the teaching of others. In the pedagogical context, the ethical potential to respond to the other by exposing oneself to failure serves to instill in learners such ethical virtues, which let the alterity of past jazz performances and current performing overflow unto uncharted futures. This is the nature of the dynamic and intergenerational conversation characterized by an ethics of vulnerability that seeks to rupture the historical precedents, routines, and stocks of knowledge through exposing oneself to the face of the other.

Rather than being limited to the moment when a musician takes a solo, improvisation pervades all corners of the performance. It starts from the first few beats of a pianist's introduction and continues throughout the piece in emergent arrangements and unexpected decisions that, at any moment, may narrow or broaden the possibilities of subsequent actions, reproducing a previous order or shifting to a less predictable soundscape. The combination of an interactional approach with a phenomenologically inspired ethics of alterity reveals how jazz musicians' continuous and mutual auditory and visual monitoring is not just a practical solution for cooperation. Rather, it cultivates virtues and an ethical responsiveness to the temporal unfolding of collective performance before an audience. If, as Arnold Davidson (2016) has argued, improvisation is the form that freedom takes, jazz can be understood as a music that is both designed and realized so that all participants, players and audience alike, can experience freedom, each on their own terms. And with freedom comes responsibility, which starts with the question of how to respond (Lewis 2019, 441). In the interaction we analyzed, Clayton's choice *not* to play at one transition was heard by Melvoin as a call to fill a vacuum. In trying to quickly figure out who might solo next, Melvoin took upon himself the responsibility of the band as a whole and of the jazz tradition as collectively reproduced. In his words, "we are just playing one music . . . all of us together. This is just one music not an individual music." In this moment, like others we analyzed in this chapter, the term "jazz etiquette" refers to the ways that the musician simultaneously attends to the aesthetic, ethical, and practical dimensions of the performance. Using ideas from phenomenology to guide an empirical investigation of the players' actions before, during, and after the performance of one song, our analysis uncovers the complex moments where the individual and the collective face mutually inform, support, and give meaning to each other.

Appendix: Transcription Conventions

The excerpts provided in this chapter are based on videotaped interactions of musicians, students, and other participants in the Culture of Jazz Aesthetics (CJA) course. Following standard conventions in discourse and conversation analysis, we have not edited the interviews for content or form. Our goal has been to reproduce as accurately as possible the verbal part of the original interactions, with the understanding that any correction or editing of the original exchanges is likely to alter our ability to assess how, at the time of recording, participants themselves were constructing their utterances and making sense of what was being said or done. To help readers understand the transcripts, we provide here a list of the conventions used in the excerpts.

(1)	the number on the top left corner of the excerpt refers to the sequential place of each example in this chapter
Burrell;	name of speaker is separated from the transcription of talk by a semicolon (;) and one or more spaces
We <u>were</u>	underlining represents emphasis or contrastive stress
last time,	a comma indicates that the phrase ends with a slight rising intonation (e.g., the intonation used when speakers are projecting further talk or more items in a list)
I do.	a period indicates falling intonation, which often suggests the potential for the end of a turn
[	left bracket between two turns indicates the point of overlap between two turns
(him/it)	talk between parentheses indicates the transcriber's uncertainty about what was said
(?)	question marks between parentheses indicate that a portion of talk could not be heard accurately and no guess was possible
((*laugh*))	information about nonverbal action is surrounded by double parentheses and set in italics
...	three dots indicate an untimed pause
Jeff [Clayton]	text surrounded by square brackets is information that is likely to be understood by participants
[...]	three dots between square brackets mean that a portion of the transcript was left out

Acknowledgments

We express our appreciation to Kenny Burrell and all of the other musicians who, between 2002 and 2011, participated in the Culture of Jazz Aesthetics course and gave permission to be video-recorded during class time or in other contexts. (See note 4 for the names of the guest artists.) Sincere thanks also go the staff of the UCLA Office of Instructional Development and its then director Larry Loher, who generously supported video recording with multiple cameras in the classroom and in concert halls. A number of people collaborated with Duranti to make these video recordings; among them, special thanks go to John Bishop, Steven Black, Paul Connor,

Devin Hahn, Jeremy Konner, Heather Loyd, and Dario Mangano. We are also grateful to the many people over the years who helped copy, transcribe, and organize the large corpus of video material from which the examples discussed here are taken. Earlier drafts of this chapter benefited from detailed comments by Harry Berger, Kati Szego, and an anonymous reviewer. Any errors or misinterpretations of the interactions analyzed in this chapter are solely ours.

NOTES

1. In a famous passage from the *Nicomachean Ethics*, Aristotle describes the situated nature of the virtues: "I refer to moral virtue, for this is concerned with emotions and actions, in which one can have excess or deficiency or a due mean. For example, one can be frightened or bold, feel desire or anger or pity, and experience pleasure and pain in general, either too much or too little, and in both cases wrongly; whereas to feel these feelings at the right time, on the right occasion, towards the right people, for the right purpose and in the right manner, is to feel the best amount of them, which is the mean amount—and the best amount is of course the mark of virtue" (1999, 93).
2. Jazz musicians typically refer to a musical work as a "song" or "tune," even if there is no singer present in a performance. Throughout this chapter, we will use the terms interchangeably.
3. This work is part of a larger project by Duranti on jazz socialization. In this research, performances and interactions among jazz musicians were recorded in a wide range of contexts, including auditions, student concerts, and other courses in the UCLA Jazz Program; club dates featuring Burrell as band leader in Los Angeles; and once, a celebration of Burrell's seventy-fifth birthday at Yoshi's restaurant and nightclub in Oakland, California. Some of the songs performed at Yoshi's were included in the 2007 CD *Kenny Burrell. 75th Birthday Bash Live!*
4. Burrell holds a joint appointment in the Department of Ethnomusicology and the Department of Music. During the period of this research, Burrell was the director of the UCLA Jazz Studies Program, which he founded. Now housed in the UCLA Herb Alpert School of Music, the program has recently been renamed "Global Jazz Studies."
5. Between 2002 and 2011 the following professional musicians were guests in the CJA course: Justo Almario, Louie Bellson, George Bohanon, Clayton Cameron, Frank Capp, Billy Childs, Jeff Clayton, Sherman Ferguson, Charlie Harrison, Tamir Hendelman, Hubert Laws, Bennie Maupin, Mike Melvoin, Roberto Miranda, Barbara Morrison, Miles Mosley, Charles Owens, Tom Ranier, Bobby Rodriguez, Lesa Terry, Trevor Ware, Michele Weir, Chester Whitmore, Gerald Wiggins, and Gerald Wilson. Some of these musicians appeared more than once.
6. One of the guests, Bennie Maupin, narrated to the students his development as a jazz musician, including the experience of being hired by Miles Davis to play bass clarinet on *Bitches Brew*, portions of which he commented on while the record played in the background.
7. A French translation of this quote appeared in Duranti (2018, 227–228).
8. See AllMusic (n.d.) and Discogs (n.d.) for listings of Burrell's recordings.
9. The term "post-bop" was suggested by Harris Berger (personal communication) as a way of capturing something of the style or genre in which Burrell and his guests performed "Softly." We recognize that this label might help some readers get some sense of how the song was played. Given the sensitivity of the issue of music genre categorization, we are, however, reluctant to use it in our description without having had a chance to discuss it with the musicians themselves.
10. On the role of the cupped hand gesture in social interaction, see Mortensen (2016).

WORKS CITED

AllMusic. n.d. "Kenny Burrell | AllMusic Discography." Accessed August 5, 2020. https://www
.allmusic.com/artist/kenny-burrell-mn0000006878o/discography.

Aristotle. 1944. *Politics*. Translated by H. Rackham. Cambridge, MA Harvard University Press.

Aristotle. 1999. *Nicomachean Ethics*. 2nd ed. Translated by Terence Irwin. Indianapolis:
Hackett Publishing Company.

Auslander, Philip. 2006. "Musical Personae." *Drama Review* 50 (1): 100–119.

Balliett, Whitney. 1959. *The Sound of Surprise: 46 Pieces on Jazz*. 1st ed. New York: E. P. Dutton.

Becker, Howard S. 2008. *Art Worlds*. 25th Anniversary ed., updated and expanded. Berkeley:
University of California Press.

Berger, Harris M. 1999. *Metal, Rock, and Jazz: Perception and the Phenomenology of Musical
Experience*. Hanover, NH: University Press of New England.

Berliner, Paul. 1994. *Thinking in Jazz: The Infinite Art of Improvisation*. Chicago: University of
Chicago Press.

Black, Steven P. 2008. "Creativity and Learning Jazz: The Practice of 'Listening.'" *Mind, Culture,
and Activity* 15 (4): 1–17.

Bogen, James. 1987. "Finding an Audience." *Papers in Pragmatics* 1 (2): 35–65.

Bourdieu, Pierre. (1972) 1977. *Outline of a Theory of Practice*. Translated by Richard Nice.
Cambridge: Cambridge University Press.

Brackett, David. 2017. "The Social Aesthetics of Swing in the 1940s Or the Distribution of the
Non-sensible." In *Improvisation and Social Aesthetics*, edited by Georgina Born, Eric Lewis,
and Will Straw, 113–134. Durham, NC: Duke University Press.

Carr, Ian. 1998. *Miles Davis: The Definitive Biography*. London: HarperCollins.

Cook, Nicholas. 2017. "Scripting Social Interaction." In *Improvisation and Social Aesthetics*,
edited by Georgina Born, Eric Lewis, and Will Straw, 59–77. Durham, NC: Duke
University Press.

Day, William. 2000. "Knowing as Instancing: Jazz Improvisation and Moral Perfectionism."
Journal of Aesthetics and Art Criticism 58 (2): 99–111.

Davidson, Arnold I. 2016. "Spiritual Exercises, Improvisation, and Moral Perfectionism: With
Special Reference to Sonny Rollins." In *The Oxford Handbook of Critical Improvisation
Studies*, vol. 1, edited by George E. Lewis and Benjamin Piekut, 523–538. New York: Oxford
University Press.

Davis, Miles, and Quincy Troupe. 1989. *Miles: The Autobiography*. New York: Simon and
Schuster.

Discogs. n.d. "Kenny Burrell | Discography | Discogs." Accessed August 5, 2020. https://www
.discogs.com/artist/30184-Kenny-Burrell.

Dortier, Jean-François. 2012. "Les idées pures n'existent pas." *Sciences Humaines* 15 (February–
March): 3–8.

Duranti, Alessandro. 2009. "L'oralité avec impertinence: Ambivalence par rapport à l'écrit chez
les orateurs samoans et les musiciens de jazz américaines." *L'Homme* 189: 23–47.

Duranti, Alessandro. 2018. "Jazz pris pour cible et la politique de la reconnaissance artistique."
In *Politique et music*, edited by Mariella Pandolfi and Laurence McFalls, 211–234. Montreal:
Boreal.

Duranti, Alessandro, and Kenny Burrell. 2004. "Jazz Improvisation: A Search for Hidden
Harmonies and a Unique Self." *Ricerche di Psicologia* 27 (3): 71–101.

Faulkner, Robert R., and Howard S. Becker. 2009. *Do You Know . . . ? The Jazz Repertoire in Action*. Chicago: University of Chicago Press.

Feurzeig, David Kahn. 1997. "Making the Right Mistakes: James P. Johnson, Thelonious Monk, and the Trickster Aesthetic." PhD diss., Cornell University.

Goffman, Erving. 1959. *The Presentation of Self in Everyday Life*. Garden City, NY: Doubleday.

Goffman, Erving. 1967. *Interaction Ritual: Essays in Face-to-Face Behavior*. Garden City, NY: Doubleday.

Hagberg, Garry L. 2006. "Jazz Improvisation: A Mimetic Art?" *Revue internationale de philosophie* 60 (238): 469–485.

Husserl, Edmund. (1913) 1931. *Ideas: General Introduction to Pure Phenomenology*. Translated by W. R. Boyce Gibson. New York: Collier.

Husserl, Edmund 2001. *Analyses Concerning Passive and Active Synthesis: Lectures on Transcendental Logic*. Translated by Anthony J. Steinbock. Dordrecht: Kluwer.

Klemp, Nathaniel, Ray McDermott, Jason Duque, Matthew Thibeault, Kimberly Powellet, and Daniel J. Levitin. 2008. "Plans, Takes, and *Mis-Takes*." *Critical Social Studies* 1: 4–21.

Lanigan, Richard L. 1988. "Is Erving Goffman a Phenomenologist?" *Critical Studies in Media Communication* 5 (4): 335–345.

Levinas, Emmanuel. (1961) 1969. *Totality and Infinity: An Essay on Exteriority*. Translated by Alphonso Lingis. Pittsburgh, PA: Duquesne University Press.

Levinas, Emmanuel. (1974) 1998. *Otherwise than Being, or, Beyond Essence*. Pittsburgh, PA: Duquesne University Press.

Lewis, George E. 2019. "Listening for Freedom with Arnold Davidson." *Critical Inquiry* 45 (Winter): 434–447.

Mahon, Maureen. 2004. *Right to Rock: The Black Rock Coalition and the Cultural Politics of Race*. Durham, NC: Duke University Press.

Mattingly, Cheryl, and C. Jason Throop. 2018. "Anthropology of Ethics." *Annual Review of Anthropology* 47: 475–492.

Monson, Ingrid. 1996. *Saying Something: Jazz Improvisation and Interaction*. Chicago: Chicago University Press.

Mortensen, Kristian. 2016. "The Body as a Resource for Other-Initiation of Repair: Cupping the Hand behind the Ear." *Research on Language and Social Interaction* 49 (1): 34–57.

O'Dea, Jane. 1993. "Phronesis in Musical Performance." *Journal of Philosophy of Education* 27 (2): 233–243.

Parsons, Talcott. 1968. "Interaction." In *International Encyclopedia of the Social Sciences*, edited by D. L. Sills. New York: Macmillan.

Raffel, Stanley H. 2002. "If Goffman Had Read Levinas." *Journal of Classical Sociology* 2 (2): 179–202.

Reinholdsson, Peter. 1998. *Making Music Together: An Interactionist Perspective on Small-Group Performance in Jazz*. Studia Musicologica Upsaliensia. Nova Series 14. Uppsala: Uppsala University.

Sacks, Harvey, Emanuel A. Schegloff, and Gail Jefferson. 1974. "A Simplest Systematics for the Organization of Turn-Taking for Conversation." *Language* 50: 696–735.

Sawyer, R. Keith. 2001. *Creating Conversations: Improvisation in Everyday Discourse*. Cresskill, NJ: Hampton Press.

Schegloff, Emmanuel A. 1986. "The Routine as Achievement." *Human Studies* 9 (2–3): 111–151.

Schutz, Alfred 1945. "Some Leading Concepts of Phenomenology." *Social Research* 12 (1): 77–97.

Smith, Chris 1998. "A Sense of the Possible: Miles Davis and the Semiotics of Improvised Performance." In *In the Course of Performance: Studies in the World of Musical Improvisation*, edited by Bruno Nettl and Melinda Russell, 261–289. Chicago: University of Chicago Press.

Smith, Gregory W. H. 2005. "Enacted Others: Specifying Goffman's Phenomenological Omissions and Sociological Accomplishments." *Human Studies* 28: 397–415.

Throop, C. Jason. 2003. "Articulating Experience," *Anthropological Theory* 3 (2): 219–241.

Throop, C. Jason, and Alessandro Duranti. 2015. "Attention, Ritual Glitches, and Attentional Pull: The President and the Queen." *Phenomenology and the Cognitive Sciences* 14 (4): 1055–1082.

Williams, Patrick 2001. "De La Discographie et de son usage. L'œuvre ou la vie?" *L'Homme* 158–159 (April–September): 179–199.

Zigon, Jarrett. 2014. "Attunement and Fidelity: Two Ontological Conditions for Morally Being-in-the-World." *Journal of the Society for Psychological Anthropology* 42 (1): 16–30.

....

CHAPTER 20

FACING THE MUSICAL OTHER

Alfred Schutz, Emmanuel Levinas, and the
Ethnography of Musical Experience

....

ESTHER CLINTON AND JEREMY WALLACH

THIS essay argues that ethnographic inquiry into musical experience entails both an ethical practice of encounter and an ethical practice of writing, and we draw on the phenomenological thought of Alfred Schutz and Emmanuel Levinas to ground these arguments. To our reading, one of phenomenology's primary strengths is its emphasis on and foundation in the experiences of the social individual. Here, the bracketing of theoretical assumptions and judgments outside experience allows us to return to the phenomena anew.[1] This bracketing can be an important way for the ethnographer to understand their research participants; however, there is a danger that such an approach can reinforce a kind of narrow individualism, and the threat of solipsism was a concern from the very beginning of phenomenology. Edmund Husserl's original formulation of phenomenology was focused on individual consciousness (and, to a lesser extent, cognition), and although Husserl acknowledged the social nature of human experience, Schutz and others have argued that he underplayed the significance of that sociality.[2] (For a discussion of Schutz's criticisms of Husserl, see Carrington 1979.) When handled poorly, the interest in lived experience can certainly lead one to treat consciousness as something possessed by an isolated person, but phenomenology doesn't have to lead to such an approach. It can instead be used in ways that affirm the view—held widely by folklorists, anthropologists, and ethnomusicologists—that consciousness is fundamentally shaped by culture and social relations.

In this chapter, we seek to combine the ideas of Schutz, whom the anthropologist Alessandro Duranti described as "one of Husserl's most informed and creative interpreters within the social sciences" (Duranti 2010, 18), and Levinas to extend Harris Berger's phenomenological ethnomusicology and address the problem of ethics. This is not an idle intellectual exercise, for our goal is to account for the social dimensions of musicking in a way that acknowledges the ethical ramifications of ethnographic research. Schutz (1932, English trans. 1967; see also Carr 1994) sought to unite the socio-logical insights of Max Weber with Husserl's phenomenology, while Levinas theorized the ethics of encounter with another consciousness. Though similar in background and age, these thinkers represent different traditions within phenomenology and are seldom discussed together. (An exception to this is Duranti et al. 2023, which is based on the ideas of Levinas and Goffman but also engages the work of Schutz.) Yet we have found that their writings on ethics,[3] if drawn upon purposefully and strategically, can illumi-nate the ethnographic investigation of musical experience.

Both Schutz and Levinas offer ways of seeing individual experience as inherently tied to social life. Of course, there are a number of significant differences between the two thinkers; Levinas was born in Lithuania in 1906 and wrote in French, while Schutz, who was born in 1899, was Austrian and wrote in German (and sometimes English). Levinas lived much longer, passing away in 1995, while, sadly, Schutz died at the rel-atively young age of sixty (Jonas 1959). We would argue that due to his profound in-fluence on Clifford Geertz, Schutz's ideas have been more consequential than many American anthropologists, ethnomusicologists, and folklorists realize. (See Duranti 2010 and Atkinson 2010 for discussions of the value of Schutz for anthropological in-quiry.) For his part, Levinas has in the last fifteen years become somewhat more familiar to anthropologists (see, for example, Bernasconi 2005, 2018; O'Neill 2020; Rapport 2015, 2019; Duranti et al. 2023).[4]

While Levinas and Schutz differ in many respects, they also share important similarities. Both were European Jewish thinkers whose lives were profoundly disrupted by the trauma of World War II. We suspect that this helps explain why they both focus on morality (albeit in quite different ways), as well as on social relationships. Schutz and his family left Austria after the Nazi annexation, ultimately ending up in the United States in 1939. Levinas's experience was more difficult: after joining the French armed forces as a translator, he spent most of the war in Fallingbostel concentration camp as a POW, returning to scholarship in France almost immediately after the war ended (Bergo 2019). Both men also referred to music and sound in their phenomenological writings: Schutz was an accomplished pianist (Wagner 1970, 36) and wrote about music in reference to temporality, collective music making, and the relationship in Western art music between composer, musician, and audience (Schutz [1951] 2004; Schutz 1976; see also Clinton and Wallach 2016). Levinas's investment in music and sound was less obvious than Schutz's, but he did write about sound, with some scholars arguing that sound was more important to Levinas than vision (see Wu 2015, who refers to Derrida's [(1967) 1978, 123–124] remarks on Levinas's prioritizing of sound over sight).

Bringing the work of these thinkers together, the present chapter is divided into six sections. First, we briefly introduce Schutz and Levinas and explain how their work can contribute to ethnographic inquiry and cultural theory. In the next section, we describe what we see as the classic anthropological impasse, which has for the last forty years kept too many scholars trapped, and suggest how phenomenology can help overcome it. In the third section, we narrow our focus to examine the ethnographic study of musicking and explore the phenomenon of the musical "we." The fourth section discusses how power imbalances, which, of course, can never be ignored, should be considered in ethnographic research and writing that is guided by Schutzian and Levinasian insights. The fifth section argues that musical genres can entail ethical stances and offers a case study of the Indonesian music genre known as *dangdut*. In the sixth and final section, we once again address the issue of morality and ethnography in academic writing practice. Throughout, our focus will be on the ethnographic encounter as an ethical and epistemological challenge.

To set the tone of the work that follows, we quote here from Levinas. Though he is writing about interpersonal experience in general, not about ethnography, the quote is a particularly apt way to commence our analysis, as it describes so effectively the ethical stakes of the ethnographic encounter.

> [T]he judgements of true knowledge and thematic thought are summoned—or invented—starting from or apropos of certain exigencies that depend on the ethical significance of the Other, inscribed in his face—imperatives in the face of the other who is incomparable to me and is unique, certain exigencies that make justice concrete. . . . [R]esponsibility for the Other signifies an original and concrete temporality, and . . . the universalization of presence presupposes it. ([1947] 1987, 104)[5]

Thus for Levinas, the facticity of the face of the Other in one's experience *necessitates* ethics. We develop the implications of this insight for ethnographic research in later sections of the chapter.

PHENOMENOLOGY AND ETHNOGRAPHY: SYMPATHETIC APPROACHES

The contemporary ethnographic enterprise that grounds much American ethnomusicological research is based not in a romantic rejection of scientific reason, as is sometimes supposed, but in a different project altogether: that of social phenomenology, a philosophical effort that seeks to ground rationality (i.e., a logic that traverses different subjectivities without losing its integrity) in everyday experience. Clifford Geertz's project of thick ethnographic description (1973), which was essential to Steven Feld's ethnoaesthetics (Feld 1982; see Wallach 2019) and much ethnomusicological work since the 1970s, should therefore not be seen as the fanciful application of a humanist's literary flair to the cold science of anthropology but, we argue, as a cross-cultural application of Alfred Schutz's social phenomenology. This project, we suggest, does not demand a surrender to irrationalism but should rather be seen as expanding rationality (for only totalitarians thrive in irrational soil). As Berger (2009, xviii) and Schutz himself ([1944] 1962, 99) point out, phenomenology is a rational pursuit, despite its undeserved reputation for mysticism. Rather than seeing an opposition between rationality and emotion, we argue that *both* can be considered responses to a perceived environment; moreover, both are mediated by worldview, a term we discuss in more detail below, which can only be illuminated through careful ethnographic inquiry (Clinton and Wallach 2016).

Due to the formative influence of Max Weber's thought ([1905] 1930),[6] Schutz's philosophical investigations do not elide the social matrix within which lives and selves are made coherent. Indeed, as sociologist Wing-Chung Ho (2008a) observes, "Husserl starts his analysis of the natural world with 'I' and Schutz starts with a given 'we'" (236). The anthropologist and philosopher Nigel Rapport (2019, 72) finds a similar impulse in Levinas: "There are depths of insight in Levinas that address what I would take to be anthropology's core issues: how best to know the human condition, how best to represent the human condition, and how best morally to secure the human condition." Like Levinas, Schutz was made sensitive to culture by life circumstances. As a refugee in France and, later, the United States, he found himself a "stranger" (see Schutz [1944] 1964, 87–91), a situation that clearly influenced his ideas about culture and the process of enculturation. Reflecting on this predicament, he noted that "the stranger . . . becomes essentially the man who has to place in question nearly everything that seems to be unquestionable to the members of the approached group" (87). Schutz writes with great empathy about the experience of being a stranger and of having to learn what he calls the "recipe" of a new culture,[7] observing that "the cultural pattern [of the new culture] and its recipes represent only for the members of the in-group a unit of coinciding schemes of interpretation as well as of expression" (90). For the outsider, however, they represent a set of unfamiliar ideas and practices, and their internal logic must be discovered with great effort.

Though Schutz was writing about a person becoming a member of what is for them a new culture, his insights can also be applied to ethnographers seeking patterns in the culture that they study, which to them are often unfamiliar. We thus begin our discussion of phenomenology's value to ethnography with a deceptively simple question: What is the purpose of ethnography? What do anthropologists, folklorists, ethnomusicologists, and others who use Geertzian ethnography try to learn through this method? Obviously, the answers to this question vary depending on the scholar and their project. Yet we would argue that one thing good ethnographies share is the desire to understand how people in another cultural context think about the world and how they fit into it. We term this whole *worldview* and see it as central to Geertz's project, the phenomenological tradition to which his work is tied, and to the ideas of non-phenomenological theorists, such as Mikhail Bakhtin (1986) and Michel de Certeau ([1980] 1984), who struggled for a term to refer to the system of meanings, mostly taken for granted, that structures experience.

In his introductory essay to *The Interpretation of Cultures* (1973), Geertz, we would argue, derives much of the cultural theory he outlines from Schutz, though he shifts the emphasis from how meanings mediate human relationships to the meanings themselves. The systematically related inventory of publicly available sign vehicles that Geertz identifies constitutes his semiotic-interpretivist conception of the cultural system.[8] As he famously proclaims,

> The concept of culture I espouse, and whose utility the essays below attempt to demonstrate, is essentially a semiotic one. Believing, with Max Weber, that man is

an animal suspended in webs of significance he himself has spun, I take culture to be those webs, and the analysis of it to be therefore not an experimental science in search of law but an interpretive one in search of meaning. (1973, 5)

Schutz and Weber were equally central to Geertz's intellectual development, though he is likely paraphrasing the former, not the latter, in the above passage. Compare it to Schutz's 1955 English characterization of the lifeworld (*Lebenswelt*):

> Thus, the social world into which man is born and within which he has to find his bearings is experienced by him as a tight knit web of social relationships, of systems of signs and symbols with their particular meaning structure, of institutionalized forms of social organization, of systems of status and prestige, etc.
>
> ([1955] 1964, 230; see also Schutz [1957] 1970)

Given how close the two statements are, particularly the importance of the web analogy, we believe that Schutz's influence on Geertz's well-known passage is clear.

In an earlier essay, Schutz explains that institutionalized forms of social organization arise to provide ready-made solutions to common social problems in everyday life, thereby allowing them to "replace truth hard to attain by offering comfortable truisms, and to substitute the self-explanatory for the questionable" (Schutz [1944] 1964, 95). This is reminiscent of de Certeau's concept of "making do" ([1980] 1984), which he uses to explain how, except during times of trauma or desperate need, humans get through life without stopping to consider the logic and ethics of seemingly ordinary decisions. After all, humans have many responsibilities—to other people (particularly friends and family), to our occupations, and potentially to great callings such as art or religion. Anyone who too frequently stops to consider the logic and ethics of ordinary decisions not only impedes the flow of daily life and mundane activity but also risks significant emotional turmoil.

It should be apparent how important it is for people to accept the elements of the socially given worldview that allow them to make do. In order for this to work, however, such beliefs cannot be questioned. Schutz writes:

> The system of knowledge thus acquired—incoherent, inconsistent, and only partially clear, as it is—takes on for the members of the in-group the appearance of a sufficient coherence, clarity, and consistency to give anybody a reasonable chance of understanding and of being understood. Any member born or reared within the group accepts the ready-made standardized scheme of the cultural pattern handed down to him by ancestors, teachers, and authorities as an unquestioned and unquestionable guide in all the situations which normally occur within the social world. The knowledge correlated to the cultural pattern carries its evidence in itself—or, rather, it is taken for granted.
>
> (Schutz [1944] 1964, 95; see also Schutz [1957] 1970, 119–121).

We suggest that one important purpose of ethnographic research is to identify the cultural assumptions taken for granted in specific social worlds. Though this is not easily accomplished, it has the potential to allow the scholar to perceive and interpret the web of symbols in which a specific group of people is enmeshed. Of course, no individual person accepts all aspects of their culture's taken-for-granted schema, and even when specific schemata are accepted, they are often interpreted differently. Nevertheless, one cannot deny that such schemata are important.

Schutz also discusses the challenges of understanding such taken-for-granted systems. First written in 1932,[9] decades before the period of Schutz's flight from Europe, the remarks quoted below show a remarkable sensitivity to the problems of cross-cultural understanding. Here, Schutz distinguishes between, on the one hand, situations in which the scholar is an observer and the person being observed is unaware of their presence and, on the other, when the scholar is a "participant" (Schutz 1970, 196), which is what most anthropologists, ethnomusicologists, and folklorists would consider ethnography to be. He writes,

> But in any direct social observation carried on outside a social relationship, my interpretation of another's behavior cannot be checked against his own self-interpretation, unless of course I exchange my role as an observer for that of a participant. *When I start asking questions of the person observed, I am no longer a mere observer.*
>
> (Schutz 1970, 196; italics in the original)

Indeed, as ethnographers know well, it is often through asking the right questions that ethnography leads to understanding (Briggs 1986).

Contemporary scholars recognize that the forms of participation Schutz discusses here are unavoidable in ethnographic research. As Sherry Ortner noted in a landmark essay, ethnography is a research modality in which "the self—as much of it as possible—[is] the instrument of knowing" (1995, 173). Thus, ethnographic research is by definition idiosyncratic, since every researcher is unique. Moreover, the ethnographic research encounter is by necessity ethically fraught. Engaging in this kind of work, the researcher cannot hide behind the impersonal role of the scientific data-gatherer. If the whole self is not invested in the research encounter, the research suffers. This is why ethnography is so difficult, particularly for Americans who are socialized to jealously guard their selves from external "contaminants" and close themselves off from others, especially strangers.

Sociocultural matrices form selves, a process humanistic social scientists often refer to as identity formation. Yet commonsense understandings of self and society in contemporary North America tend more toward an "essentialist" way of looking at things. Individual subjectivities, including certain fundamental characteristics that scholars generally identify as socially constructed, are viewed as existing prior to the webs of significance and networks of human relationships that constitute social existence. The elision of the kinds of sociality that we have been discussing in this section—the emergence of identity from the lifeworld and the forms of participatory ethnography that Schutz and Ortner discuss—have become a stumbling block in the politics of representation in contemporary ethnography. Successive waves of critics have justly attacked anthropology, ethnomusicology, folklore, and other ethnographic disciplines for their roots in colonialism, a desire for a mastery of the other stemming from a Nietzschean will to power, or a Foucauldian exercise of power/knowledge that serves the needs of discipline and hierarchy through the imposition of totalizing frameworks.[10] We would suggest that a phenomenological ethics can provide a counternarrative to the dismal, and by now quite familiar, litany of epistemological crimes pinned on the ethnographer, because it suggests a moral, prosocial purpose for research disconnected from the science of domination.

GETTING BEYOND THE ANTHROPOLOGICAL IMPASSE

The contemporary critique of ethnographic writing began with landmark works by George E. Marcus and Michael M. J. Fischer (1986),[11] James Clifford and Marcus (1986), Clifford (1988), and Ruth Behar and Deborah A. Gordon (1996). The legacy of these thinkers remains contested. While their critical insights regarding the politics of representation were groundbreaking for their time, the inability of subsequent generations of scholars to rebuild credibly the ethnographic enterprise in the wake of their intervention plagues research to this day.

In a trenchant critique of these developments, anthropologist Bruce Knauft observed that (already in the mid-1990s!) "strategies that were once considered experimental in cultural anthropology now risk their own hegemonic baggage in the fastest-growing branches of the field" (1994, 118). Indeed, he argues, anthropologists influenced by what he terms "postmodernist and existentialist" thought (broadly, approaches derived from Nietzsche and Heidegger via Foucault and Derrida) "risk falling into inescapable ethical and epistemological traps" (118). For Knauft, the problem with those approaches is their foundations in a philosophy wary of fully and accurately acknowledging the social nature of human existence. Critiquing the Heideggerian legacy, he writes that

> Heidegger's view of the social is fundamentally negative. This view fuels his drive to isolate existence and Being as an atomized self-conscious state prior to practical life in the social world (cf. Sartre's "Being-for-itself"). The larger goal is to allow the wholeness of human Being to be self-conscious and then, secondarily, to be outwardly actualized. But this is an inverted pyramid balanced on an asocial base.
>
> (Knauft 1994, 138)

If the Heidegger of *Being and Time* elided the social through the opposition that he erects between personal authenticity and social conformity, the early work of Michel Foucault represented the inverse elision. By treating the subject as a product of discourse, the anthropology inspired by Foucault leaves no room for the kind of sociality that Schutz identifies and Ortner sees as central to ethnographic fieldwork. Twenty-six years after the publication of Knauft's article, Kevin Lewis O'Neill (2020) writes about anthropology's continued frustration with Foucault and Foucauldian theorists (182–183). In this context, there is still a need for Knauft's ethnographic strategy premised on a "critical humanism that cross-cuts reflexive representations with bracketed moments of assumed objectivity" (1994, 121). We suggest such a strategy would be enhanced by the phenomenological concepts discussed in this essay. Otherwise, we fear researchers will remain trapped in the impasse originating with our forebears.[12]

Phenomenological approaches to expressive culture appeal to us because they constitute a way out of the perennial impasse between an anthropology that sees subjects constructed by discourse and a focus on subjective experience that fails to account for the role of power in social life. We maintain that only a focus on the *inter*subjective elements of experience can ground an ethnography of musical meaning. Moreover, the phenomenological approach offers the additional advantage of being based in critical reason. (Husserl was, after all, a mathematician.) Ethnomusicology is often characterized as a romantic enterprise that, in valorizing musical experience and non-Western epistemologies, challenges (to use Veit Erlmann's phrase) "the arrogance of reason" (2010, 339). Faced with the ineffability and overwhelming intersubjective emotional power of music, the temptation is great to reject reason as uptight, unfeeling, even ethnocentric. The conceit of nonrational approaches to music and culture is that they will empower voices "on the margins." Yet existentialist, Nietzschean-derived perspectives empower those who can wield the most rhetorical force, usually the already-empowered (see Knauft 1994, 135). A related critique can be made of Heidegger. In his evisceration of German existentialism's "jargon of authenticity," Theodor Adorno warns of the dangers of the "disdainful pride of inwardness" ([1964] 1973, 56) rooted in an asocial, nondialectical intellectual framework that valorizes the will to power and denounces ethical conduct.

We agree with Adorno's critique of Heideggerian philosophy as nondialectical and solipsistic ([1964] 1973) but reject his dismissal of nonmaterial factors in historical change and, of course, his elitist denunciations of popular music. In essence, Adorno criticizes German existentialism (which he loosely defines as ideas originating with Heidegger and Karl Jaspers, and their subsequent popularization in German society) for its refusal to grant a relational dimension to Being, thereby rendering all social life, including class struggle, secondary to the individual's quest for self-actualization.[13] It is precisely this form of relationality that we see as central to Schutz's vision of selves and lifeworlds and which, we will show, is also central to musical experience.

The Musical "We"

Music and other forms of expressive culture often both depend and reflect upon aspects of the social. The meanings that emerge in expressive culture are key to tacit worldviews and participating in what Schutz called the "we-relationship" (Schutz [1932] 1967, 164), the distinctive form of relational intersubjectivity that emerges from situated interaction and allows us to gain access to the lived experiences of cultural others. In "Making Music Together," the essay by Schutz that is perhaps best known to ethnomusicologists, he describes how music is essentially about *durée*—subjective time experienced by the individual, in this case the time of a musical composition, which is distinguished from the objective time measured by clocks. Discussing the temporality of musical experience, he writes,

> We have therefore the following situation: two series of events in inner time, one belonging to the stream of consciousness of the composer, the other to the stream of consciousness of the beholder, are lived through in simultaneity, which simultaneity is created by the ongoing flux of the musical process. It is the thesis of the present paper that this sharing of the other's flux of experiences in inner time, this living through a vivid present in common, constitutes . . . the mutual tuning-in relationship, the experience of the "We," which is at the foundation of all possible communication. The peculiarity of the musical process of communication consists in the essentially polythetic character of the communicated content, that is to say, in the fact that both the flux of the musical events and the activities by which they are communicated, belong to the dimension of inner time. ([1951] 2004, 207)

Schutz's notion of shared temporality has wide implications. As we read his work, the we-relation entails both the traditionally construed subjectivity of personal experience (it is a flux of phenomena grasped by an individual person) and a direct form of sharedness that transcends the individual. Generalizing the we-relation in music to the broadest possible context, we argue that the full experience of being human both escapes that which is representable by society yet still *contains shareable elements*.[14] Selves are therefore not completely unknowable to each other because persons are predisposed to encounter other humans as humans, as social beings. While there are things that cannot be shared with others—many of the excruciating sensations one of us experienced suffering from severe brain damage defy normal description, for example—it is also common to find cultural forms that "speak to you," that, in other words, unlock one's own experiences and hold them up for conscious examination in a new light. In "Making Music Together," Schutz describes the musical we-relation in terms of the social roles of composer, performer, and audience, all construed in terms of the dominant Western art music culture of his day. In its details, his account does not, of course, apply to all forms of musicking, but one can readily see wider implications in his conception. Schutz continues:

> It is the eminent social function of the performer—the singer or player of an instrument—to be the intermediary between composer and listener. By his recreation of the musical process the performer partakes in the stream of consciousness of the composer as well as of the listener. He thereby enables the latter to become immersed in the particular articulation of the flux of inner time which

is the specific meaning of the piece of music in question. It is of no great importance whether performer and listener share together a vivid present in face-to-
face relation or whether through the interposition of mechanical devices, such
as records, only a quasi simultaneity between the stream of consciousness of the
mediator and the listener has been established. The latter case always refers to
the former. The difference between the two shows merely that the relationship
between performer and audience is subject to all variations of intensity, intimacy, and anonymity.

(Schutz [1951] 2004, 207–208)[15]

What we take from this passage is not just that music involves shared temporality but
that the "we-relationship" created in making music together is inherently communal
and therefore alluring. In developing these ideas, Schutz offers a vision of music that
allows "variations of intensity, intimacy, and anonymity" without neglecting the fundamental role of sociality in musical experience.

Schutz's ideas not only address the social nature of musical experience in general;
they also speak to contemporary issues in popular music studies. For the sociologist
Pierre Bourdieu ([1979] 1984, [1982] 1991), forms of artistic behavior like music always
emerge in fields of cultural production, and the social life of these expressive forms
is best understood as a struggle to acquire cultural capital.[16] Though Bourdieu initially developed his ideas about fields and capital to apply to so-called high culture,
they have been highly influential in popular music studies, where scholars interpret
the practices of musicians and fans as a competition for status within their scenes.
While the processes that Bourdieu describes sometimes play out in popular music, we
see Bourdieu's vision as reductionist and ethnocentric. In many societies, individual
status-seeking is frowned upon as selfish and threatening to group solidarity, and, as
we have argued in a 2016 article that takes the global metal scene as a case study, similar sentiments can be found in many popular music genre cultures as well. Moreover,
the Bourdieusian emphasis on status and capital stems from an economistic view of
humans as self-interested, autonomous agents in perpetual competition. Following
Knauft (1994, 133), we would argue that such a perspective, which fits Americans
and western Europeans best, derives from the antisocial, nihilistic thinking of poststructuralist theorists in the tradition of Nietzsche and Heidegger. An emphasis on
cultural capital accumulation at the expense of other kinds of social processes has
the potential to misrepresent the motivations that musicians and fans have for involvement in music-based subcultures, particularly if one takes seriously (as one
should) what subculture members actually tell researchers. If Schutz's ideas offer a
rigorous means of understanding the cultural dynamics of music without resorting to
Bourdieusian economism, a distinct but related set of insights about music and ethnography can be gained by exploring Levinas's insights into the ethical dimensions of
social interaction.

ETHNOGRAPHY AND ETHICS: FROM OBJECTIVITY TO RESPONSIBILITY

"Science" has been a controversial rhetorical figure in American public debate for more than a century, yet its claims to objectivity remain compelling to many (Jewett 2020). When Geertz first published his spirited defense of interpretivism over positivism (1973), there was little room to contemplate the ethical ramifications of ethnographic research, as the most pressing task of the time was to challenge American anthropology's reigning positivism (e.g., Harris 1968), which erroneously considered itself to be value-neutral. Such a claim would be seen as naïve today, but along with the realization that even quantitative research cannot unproblematically claim valual neutrality came the understanding that the intense intersubjective encounters necessary for successful ethnographic research are especially fraught from an ethical point of view and necessarily involve issues of power, representation, and responsibility.[17] Furthermore, the ethical entanglements of ethnography do not end when the research encounter concludes. During the write-up phase, the prejudices that the reader may bring to the material must be anticipated. Failing to do this risks misrepresenting the experience of fieldwork and one's research consultants.

Considering all of this, we argue that ethnography needs not only social phenomenology's theory of intersubjectivity (see Duranti 2010) but also phenomenological ethics.[18] Although we agree with philosopher Michael Barber (1991) that Schutz's ideas are inherently motivated by a deep moral concern for the outsider, the subject of ethics is only implicit in Schutz's work. To address the ethical dimensions of ethnography, we turn to Levinas, who spent his career examining the responsibilities that acting subjects have to one another.[19] In *Totality and Infinity* ([1961] 1969), Levinas wrote powerfully about how encountering the Other forces one to consider one's own precariousness, leading to a sense of profound ethical responsibility. "It is not the insufficiency of the I that prevents totalization," Levinas argued, "but the Infinity of the Other" ([1961] 1969, 80). This is a key statement, for a central insight of the study is that the Other cannot be assimilated (totalized, mastered through knowledge) by the self; at the level of the ontology of social relations, total knowledge of another consciousness is impossible. The implications of this for ethnographic research are obvious, and they call for a posture of deep humility in the face of the Other. Moral responsibility depends on recognizing the Other's humanity as well as acknowledging their fundamental alterity, an ethical relation that in no way seeks to collapse the difference between self and other (which would be impossible).

One can also extrapolate from this the importance of the *lack* of required reciprocity in the Levinasian encounter. If the Other is a mystery then its response to encounter is not guaranteed in advance, yet the ethical challenge the Other presents is no less urgent.

For the Levinas of *Totality and Infinity*, the "face to face encounter" is the crucial context for experiencing another subjectivity. This encounter "involves a calling into question of oneself, a critical attitude which is itself produced in face of the other and under his authority. . . . The face to face remains an ultimate situation" ([1961] 1969, 81). In other words, face-to-face encounters must involve a *surrender* of authority in order for one to truly encounter an Other. In Rapport's words,

> One might have been misled by culture into thinking one knew [about the world]. . . but coming face-to-face with the Other, facing the Other's absolute difference, is to discover the relativity of one's habitual concepts and categories. For the Other cannot be comprehended, cannot be expressed—cannot even be thought. The Other is an enigma, opaque to understanding; there is infinity to be found looking into another's eyes. (2019, 73)

The impossibility of totalization can be—but doesn't have to be—a cause for despair, and it doesn't mean that all forms of understanding are out of the question. As Knauft observes, "Absolute impossibilities should not blind us to pragmatic possibilities for comprehension, translation, and representation across the intersubjective divide" (1994, 122). To successfully access even these partial achievements, the ethnographer must surrender certainty, security, and autonomy in the face of the Other. This certainly can be difficult. Yet in his critique of Descartes's *cogito*, which is often cited as the origin of the Western idea of the autonomous, thinking subject, Levinas suggests that only in the encounter with the Other can the self affirm its existence:

> The I in the negativity manifested by [Cartesian] doubt breaks with participation [with the other], but does not find in the *cogito* itself a stopping place. It is not I, it is the other that can say *yes*. From him comes affirmation; he is at the commencement of experience. Descartes seeks a certitude, and stops at the first change of level in this vertiginous descent; in fact he possesses the idea of infinity, and can gauge in advance the return of affirmation behind the negation. But to possess the idea of infinity is to have already welcomed the Other. ([1961] 1969, 93)

In other words, Descartes didn't go far enough in his analysis: the self doesn't affirm its existence on its own through the cogito's negation; it requires congress with another. This is why the ethnographic project, however fraught and partial, is *necessary*: no form of knowledge is possible without coming face to face with the infinite possibilities of the Other.

Levinas is considered an extremely difficult thinker. Indeed Colin Davis (1996, 122, quoted in Rapport 2020, 185) has written about what he calls the "Levinas effect," by which the obscurity of Levinas's ideas allows anthropologists to interpret him in ways that are most useful to whatever argument they happen to be making. In that context, we will admit that our discussion here is partial, directed as it is toward a specific application of Levinas's concept of alterity for problems in ethnography and the interpretation of musical activity. Despite the difficulty of his writing, there are great opportunities for insight in his work. In seeking to apply accurately Levinasian ethics to cultural research, we join scholars such as David A. McDonald (2013a) and Matthew Rahaim (2017), who have interpreted various kinds of musical performance and reception through a Levinasian lens.

In an evocative passage, for example, McDonald argues that

> In realizing the face of the Other we are ruptured, interrupted, held hostage to the obligation to respond. This obligation is the foundation of what Levinas termed an "ethics of responsibility." To fully respond to the Other is to recognize the Other, to seek justice, to be responsible for the Other's life above and beyond one's own. In order to fully meet this obligation, one must be cognizant of the vulnerability of the Other and the fragility of life itself. (2013a, 78)

McDonald applies this understanding of Levinasian ethics to an investigation of hip hop artists in Israel, Palestine, and the diaspora over the tumultuous period from 2000 to 2010. In an appraisal of "People Not Places," a music video by the Israeli-American rapper Invincible, he shows how the song

> explicitly recounts the Israeli nationalist narrative from the perspective of its Others, its victims, revealing in vivid detail the ways in which Israeli lives are profoundly implicated in the lives of others. And perhaps most importantly, Invincible begins the story of the experience of violence not with actions committed against the communal "we," but rather attends to the violence and vulnerability of the Other, in symmetrical dialogue with the vulnerability of the self: "You'll never be a peaceful state with legal displacement." (2013a, 84)[20]

Without a Levinasian understanding of alterity, the ethical relations that the song entails would be impossible to understand.

Matthew Rahaim (2017) is also interested in the ethical dimensions of musical performance and the ethical imbrication of the ethnographer in a fieldsite. Ethnomusicologists often interpret musical participation as a desirable merging of self and other, and Rahaim uses Levinas to offer a profound challenge to such an approach. He offers radical alterity, the persistence of unassimilable difference, as an antidote to overidealized notions of communal homogeneity that still find their way into contemporary music research. Rahaim applies his metaphysics of alterity to specific musical contexts, including improvisation, teaching world music, and the master-disciple relationship, arguing that while musical empathy seeks to "subsume" self and other, an ethical music scholarship cannot demand totalizing knowledge of either music or the experiences of others.

As these studies demonstrate, Levinasian ideas can be fruitfully applied to ethnomusicological topics in multiple ways. In this essay, we are interested in how they can help us clarify the ethics of the ethnographic encounter, and we see his ideas as closely related to those of Schutz. Teasing out the ethics implicit in Schutz's social phenomenology, Barber (1991) argues that Schutz's work recognizes the responsibility that each of us has to accept the other as every bit as human as ourselves. While Levinas often emphasized the asymmetry between self and other, we see a resonance between Schutz and Levinas here, as recognizing the other's humanity means granting the other the right to their own thoughts and experiences, joys and sorrows, sense of a finite existence, and aesthetic preferences. Accepting the other's humanity reminds us of our own finite and imperfect humanity and therefore provokes empathy and the realization that, as we hope others feel an ethical responsibility to us and our humanity, we must feel a responsibility to them and their humanity.[21]

For Levinas, the miracle of mutual recognition is evidence of the divine ([1982] 1987, 116–117).[22] In this context, the philosopher Sarah Allen writes that, for Levinas, "the face of the human other always carries the trace of God" (2011, 35). We believe that this is an important reason that Schutz and Levinas are rarely thought of together: The only suggestion of a divine presence in Schutz occurs implicitly in his discussion of the potential of art to connect humans across time and space. Even there, Schutz is careful to base this solely on the fact that another consciousness created the art being experienced and to argue that a relationship to the divine in such a situation can only be inferred. Levinas, in contrast, sees divinity not only in art but in the very possibility of our acknowledgment of another's humanity. Regardless of these specific orientations to the divine, their writings call attention to the miraculous nature of intersubjective signification, and in the next section we focus on the characteristic forms such expressions can take.

THE "STANCE" OF GENRE

Harris M. Berger is perhaps phenomenology's most passionate advocate in American ethnomusicology. He has described the approach as "a key that opens endless doors" (2009, xii), and, among other scholars, he has helped establish phenomenology as a major theoretical approach in the field. Throughout his work, Berger argues that experience is a necessary consideration in any assessment of aesthetic meaning, and his project is built on the fundamental insight that "the meaning [that] scholars seek to study is *not* the product of texts; it is the product of *texts in experience*" (2009, ix; italics in the original).

In a 2009 monograph, Berger developed a theory of stance, a term that he glosses as "the affective, stylistic, or valual quality with which a person engages with an element of her experience" (xiv). Stance encompasses much more than genre, but in the context of music, the orientations that genre provides for both performers and listeners are crucial to developing stances, which in turn are paramount to judgments of meaning and value. Berger writes,

> In genres dense with information, where multifaceted bodies work on sensitive and continuous media such as light and sound, the scholar can endlessly enumerate [musical] features [i.e., techniques of performance or other elements of sound that convey meaning]. The interpretation of features is certainly not a futile task, but

such work is most fruitful when we understand that the meaning of those features is framed by stance and that such features are often intended and interpreted as traces of stances. (65)

Stated another way, if stance is the valual quality with which a person constitutes their experience, "genres operate as the encapsulation of stances. When a body of musical works is taken as a genre, their common features operate for their adherents as a kind of guiding principle for our ways of engaging with texts, others, and the world" (Berger, personal communication, 2021).

Some musicians and fans dismiss genres as little more than convenient labels imposed by the music industry to facilitate commerce. But, as Bakhtin argued in his work on speech genres (1986) and more recent scholars have shown in studies of popular music in the US (Holt 2007) and Indonesia (Wallach and Clinton 2013), genres are much more than that. Like genres in other forms of expressive culture described by Berger and Giovanna P. Del Negro (2004) and Berger (2009), popular music genres are self-contained moral universes, encapsulating worldviews and possessing their own "horizons of significance," to borrow a term from Charles Taylor (1991).

A large part of the music ethnographer's mission is to determine the *stakes of genre skirmishes*. If genres are ethical constructs, then gatekeeping actions do not merely preserve the exclusivity of the subcultural in-group. To the adherents of a genre culture, such actions defend the moral integrity (or the general valual qualities) of the genre formation and the community it represents. This is why debates over genre boundaries are charged with affective significance, for they are also debates about community boundaries, about inclusion, exclusion, and the importance of shared values.

The ethnomusicological literature is teeming with genre cultures. In exploring the affect-laden links between music genre and place (Gray 2013), class (Berger 1999; Fox 2004), ethnicity (Meintjes 2003; Byl 2014), or nation (Yano 2003; Wallach 2008; McDonald 2013b), ethnomusicologists have sometimes made use of phenomenological methods and theories (whether or not they explicitly acknowledge the origins of their ideas). In the next section, one of us (Wallach) reflects on his fieldwork to demonstrate how an approach that combines the insights of Schutz and Levinas can interpret the significance of genre in Indonesian popular music.

The Dangdut Stance

When I began my ethnographic work in Indonesia in the late 1990s, I learned that dancing to dangdut music was considered to be inherently pleasurable. Dangdut took one's mind off one's problems, and dancing to it put one in a sort of blissful trance. It seemed like everyone in the Jakarta neighborhoods I visited—young and old, male and female—knew the words to the latest hit songs. Some would perform them nightly on battered guitars and water cooler bottles, which they played like *gendang* drums. I was told dangdut songs "represented" the hard lives of the people who listened to them. I was also told that the music touched something deep in the "Malay" soul, such that even middle-class Indonesians who insisted emphatically they didn't like dangdut would find fingers or some other unmonitored body part wiggling to the music when it was played.

Cognizant of dangdut's status as an authentic yet abjected genre in Indonesia, one that was both celebrated and disavowed, I attempted in my ethnographic writings to present the music as its fans, performers, and mediators told me they experienced it. (Even now, hearing the dangdut rhythm makes me sway to and fro, at least in my mind.) While the cultural politics of dangdut is important in Indonesian society and has been the focus of scholarly writings on the topic (Weintraub 2010), to fans it was more important that I convey the experience of hearing, playing, and dancing.

For them, dangdut was a music culture like no other. Circulated on cassettes, it was performed by local bands on makeshift stages in amusement parks, nightclubs, wedding celebrations, and night markets. The music's fans and performers (amateurs, semi-professionals, and recording stars) were all aware of dangdut's low reputation in Indonesian polite society. "Katanya kampungan" (They say it's low-class) was a frequent lament, but they refused to deny the intense pleasure they derived from the music, which appeared to rival that of recreational drugs. And they were proud of the growing recognition (abetted by the writings of foreign observers) that dangdut was *the* music of their country. The timbral distinctiveness of bamboo flutes and the gendang drum announced dangdut's difference from globally circulating pop music, its melismatic vocals signifying instead an affinity with Indian filmsong and "Eastern" values. Buttressed by distorted guitars, swirling synthesized strings, and propulsive hand percussion, dangdut's eroticized, affect-laden lyrics were sung in the national language of Indonesian, granting the country an internal life it lacked in the newspapers and political pronouncements that also employed that language. Thus the dangdut stance was both intimately embodied and deeply nationalist (Weintraub 2010; Wallach 2014). The dancing audience its rhythms conjured forth was said to be the nation itself, united in Andersonian comradeship across age, region, ethnicity, and class.

A great deal of the work done on popular musics in the non-Western world is exciting because it reveals how musical performances imaginatively summon a participatory, egalitarian national community, even where none currently exists in actuality. That is what happened with dangdut in mid-twentieth-century Indonesia. When the country began its transition to democracy in 1998, the political sphere aligned itself more closely with the musical one (Wallach 2008).

But there is more to dangdut than that. For me, learning to make sense of dangdut's "recipe" entailed setting aside previously acquired understandings of what constituted "legitimate" Indonesian music and culture. And it was only through non-superficial encounters with dangdut performers and audience members—Donny the Betawi hotel security guard and gendang player; Ridwan the Javanese cigarette stall vendor and avid dangdut fan; Pak Cecep, the Sundanese recording engineer; the Betawi relatives who made up OMEGA Group, a local, part-time performance ensemble; Anita and Oppie, two semi-professional Betawi singers; Edy Singh, a Chinese-Indonesian cassette producer—that I could jettison pre-existing perceptions of the music as derivative, mass-produced, and bathetic. Such judgments were commonly held by middle-class Indonesians, as well as Westerners living in the country. (In conversation, intellectual members of both groups occasionally cited Adorno's critique of popular music to reinforce their disdain.) What those attitudes lacked was a proper *dangdut stance*. This stance, informed by class-inflected cultural experiences that I could never fully access, is an example of the "incoherent, inconsistent, and only partially clear . . . taken for granted" that Schutz describes in the passage quoted above (Schutz 1970, 80–81).

In the dangdut context, Schutz's we-relation can be understood as the organization of experience that creates a space in which musicians and fans may come into contact with the Other. Put another way, the we-relation allows for Levinasian openness (Berger, personal correspondence, August 21, 2021). Above all, dangdut music demands a *surrender* of authority, a willingness to be "carried away" by its intoxicating rhythm, which allows for that openness to the Other in a shared communal ecstasy—a surrender that Westerners tend to find troubling (Rahaim 2017, 189). In Indonesia, I learned that dangdut was an abject form, subjected to vociferous disavowal by Indonesian middle-class people precisely because of the threat it constituted to the integrity of "modern" autonomous selves. Opening the door, as it were, to Levinasian encounters with a co-present Other (or, we might suggest, Others), dangdut allows for what Rahaim calls "musical empathy . . . [that] subsumes the I and the Other" (2017, 188). The *anti-dangdut* stance, then, refuses empathy with (nonaffluent) others unlike oneself and instead desires the "modern," which comes at the cost of repressing musical pleasure and collective solidarity.

For me, gaining a partial understanding of the dangdut stance meant coming face to face with a musical Other and refusing to tremble at the awareness that full knowledge of its infinite difference was impossible. I still struggle to convey this, but I have not stopped trying. Indeed, I believe continuing to attempt to share what I have learned is an ethical imperative, because only then can I convey the depth of human investment in this artistic form and its connection to an other way of being.

CONCLUSION: ETHICS AND SCHOLARSHIP

The relationship between self and other occupies a central place in the thinking of both Schutz and Levinas; it is precisely this relationship around which all ethnography revolves. Ethnographic texts evoke encounters between acting subjects (readers, writers, ethnographers, and consultants) who, by virtue of their encounters and the facticity of their co-presence, bear ethical responsibility to one another. Dangdut musicians and fans above all want respect from the wider society; rather than shrinking from the obligation that demands like this entail, scholars should welcome them as opportunities to live up to our ethical responsibilities. When Wallach's ethnographic monograph was translated into Indonesian (Wallach [2008] 2017), a new audience from the country's middle class was able to read about how meaningful dangdut was to its working-class fans and view this much-maligned genre in a new, more respectful light.

Above, we discussed the attempts by anthropologists in the 1980s and 1990s to de-construct and decenter ethnographic authority. Here, we suggest that those projects are no more likely to succeed than the well-meaning (but doomed) efforts that some have made to deny the privileges that they experience based on their race, gender, or nationality. (Moreover, it is worth noting that the "authority" of the ethnographer in the academy has never been that high to begin with, despite the fact that this research method has proven its effectiveness countless times.) But just as privilege can be weaponized for positive purposes, ethnographic authority can be harnessed, instead of disavowed. For this to be a viable strategy, ethnographic inquiry must be taken se-riously as an *ethical practice of encounter* between perceiving subjects, and the *stance of the reader* of the eventual ethnographic text must be anticipated as a component of that ethical sensibility.

While we acknowledge the challenges of putting these ideas into practice, we are continually surprised by how few studies in anglophone ethnomusicology operate at a level of abstraction between the stratospheric heights of phenomenologists like Schutz and Levinas and the detail-oriented research of fieldworkers. This is one reason that the work of Feld and Berger, and of non-ethnomusicologists such as Benedict Anderson (1983) and Arjun Appadurai (1990), is so valuable: it occupies the intermediary stratum of "middle range theory"[23]—that is, a set of conceptual tools that can be readily ap-plied to and facilitate empirical work. Our modest hope is to contribute to this corpus by bringing the relation between self and other—a fundamental and intimate aspect of lived experience often theorized at lofty heights—into a middle ground that can both serve and challenge ethnomusicological research practices.

ACKNOWLEDGMENTS

This chapter was researched and written while Esther Clinton's father was dying of pancreatic cancer. The authors would like to thank the editors for their support and understanding during this time. We would also like to thank Matt Rahaim for his helpful comments. Any errors that remain are our own. Finally, we dedicate this chapter to Dr. Nye Clinton Sr., a man who deeply cared for the Other, a smart scientist who appreciated and defended the humanities, and an ex-cellent father who always read and supported our work. We wish you were here to read this one.

In July 2022, as this essay was in production, Esther herself passed away suddenly at the age of fifty. Sadly, she did not live to see the final version.

NOTES

1. For some scholars, the method of phenomenological bracketing is a means for setting aside questions of truth and addressing phenomena on their own terms, which can be par-ticularly important when studying, for example, personal experiences with the supernat-ural (see Hufford 1982) or illness (Diedrich 2001; Cheyne 2009; Ratcliffe 2009).
2. Though see Bernasconi (2005) for a brief history of the influence of anthropology, partic-ularly the work of Lucien Lévy-Bruhl, on Husserl's thought, including a 1932 letter Husserl

wrote to Lévy-Bruhl thanking him for sending an advance copy of *Primitive Mythology* ([1935] 1983). It is well known that Lévy-Bruhl's ideas about non-Western others were often condescending and depended for their sources too much on the accounts of colonial European observers (as did Husserl; see Bernasconi 2005, 235). Nonetheless, we feel it is significant to note that anthropology and phenomenology have mutually influenced one another since phenomenology's inception.

3. Schutz doesn't explicitly address ethics in his writing. However, we agree with Michael Barber (1991), who argues that ethics is implicit in Schutz's theories, a point we address later in this chapter.

4. See O'Neill (2020, 184) for a helpful overview of Levinas's growing influence on anthropology. Rapport (who is quoted numerous times in our essay) applies his reading of Levinas to a larger project of arguing for an ethics of cosmopolitan love rooted in a culture-transcending humanism (2020). This view of a perfect, non-objectifying love relationship that is unencumbered by the detritus of human things and categories, we would argue, can be found in the early work of Hegel ([1799] 1971). We would suggest that the Levinasian notion of the infinity of the Other refuses the Hegelian totalizing move of relationality and that alterity is unknowable and, by definition, eludes even the bonds of affection. Thus, we concur with Richard Cohen's elegant summation: "Unlike the Hegelian phenomenology . . . [Levinas's] stages [of being] mark a progression toward alterity rather than toward totality; they are driven by a desire to break out of the circuits of sameness rather than a yearning for complete comprehension" (1987, 1).

5. Unfortunately, the English translations of works by both Levinas and Schutz use the gender-specific term "man" and the pronoun "he" in passages like the one we have quoted here. Given that their works were translated in the mid- to late twentieth century, we assume that "man" refers to all humans. We hope that readers new to their excellent writings will not be put off by this sexist language.

6. Weber's response to the totalizing theoretical projects of his time, chiefly Marxism, was a rigorous exploration of empirical historical evidence. The result can be seen in his book *The Protestant Ethic and the Spirit of Capitalism* ([1905] 1930), a painstaking demonstration of how innovation in the cultural "superstructure" could precede changes in the economic mode of production. Weber's cautious sociological empiricism, which influenced Schutz, failed to persuade Marx's most ardent disciples, including the anti-empiricist Theodor Adorno and the structuralist Louis Althusser (not to mention Althusser's rebellious pupil Michel Foucault). As a consequence, even now some non-phenomenological thinkers see culture as nothing more than "false consciousness." Schutz's philosophical work, by contrast, is not characterized by implacable hostility to capitalism, which is somewhat unsurprising, given that he maintained a career in business for much of his life (Psathas 2004, 5–6).

7. We like the "recipe" metaphor, as it implies flexibility not simply with regard to the "ingredients" of culture but also in terms of how those ingredients are "combined" and "cooked." We feel that this metaphor shows that what matters in culture is not just the ideas that are found there but how those ideas are presented, justified, and enforced.

8. Another phenomenological influence on Geertz's thought was Paul Ricoeur, whose time at the University of Chicago briefly overlapped with that of Geertz. See Ricoeur ([1983] 1984).

9. Duranti (2010) discusses how the posthumous publication of Schutz's work in English influenced anthropology's growing interest in intersubjectivity, which is detectable in Geertz's writings as well.

10. For a thorough recent survey of these developments, see the various contributions to Berger and Stone (2019).

11. The sociologist Wing-Chung Ho (2008b) has argued that the mid-twentieth-century debate about methodology between Schutz and Talcott Parsons, which centered on the ontological status of scientific and lay knowledges, prefigured many of the issues that Marcus and Fisher (1986) address. "The focus of contention in the Schutz-Parsons debate is that Schutz acknowledges an ontological break between the commonsense and the scientific world, but Parsons only considers it 'a matter of refinement'" (Grathoff 1978, 69; quoted in Ho 2008b, 384).

12. Wallach will never forget the senior anthropologist who mordantly told him in graduate school, "I'm afraid we've left you with an inheritance of ashes!"

13. We sympathize with this criticism of Heidegger, which is why we don't discuss his phenomenology here. For trenchant recent examinations of the fascist proclivities of Heidegger's philosophical project, see Bax (2017), Gaston (2019), Rapport (2019), and especially Knowles (2019). For a consideration of Heidegger's influence on Levinas, see Allen (2011).

14. An example of such shareable elements comes from the global heavy metal scene. Alex Skolnick, lead guitarist of the thrash metal band Testament, writes of the band's Japanese admirers, "These fans seemed to really notice the emotion expressed in my guitar solos, as though they related my pain to their own lives. This was incredibly interesting to me—here was this culture that was largely based on keeping expression and emotions in private. Yet they were actually hearing what I'd been trying to express through all the double kick drums, crunchy riffing, and growling vocals" (Skolnick 2013, 254). The remarkable ability of heavy metal music to convey meaning across cultural boundaries is of paramount importance to the genre's global purchase (see Wallach et al. 2011).

15. Note that in the quoted passage, "it is of no great importance" to Schutz whether the music in question is performed live or recorded. The question thus arises, are listeners' parasocial encounters with recordings a type of musical experience? Whatever Schutz's views on this subject, it is certainly the case that ideas from phenomenology have been used to illuminate the role of recording technology in musical experience (e.g., Porcello 1998; Wallach, forthcoming), and it is striking to us that technological mediation does not seem to sap music of its emotional potency, or at least does not sufficiently diminish it so as to render it unpleasurable. See Wallach (2003) for a discussion of the ways in which recording techniques are exploited to enhance the affective power of recorded music and compensate for the absence of live, co-present performers.

16. See Atkinson (2010) for a discussion of how Schutz's ideas can address shortcomings in Bourdieu's theories.

17. We address the fraught issue of power differentials in the ethnographic encounter in the final section of this chapter. For a lengthier consideration of power asymmetries in ethnomusicological fieldwork, see Wallach and Clinton (2019).

18. Indeed, Levinas ([1984] 1989) famously insists that ethics is the true "first philosophy" and must precede ontology and epistemology.

19. Rapport (2020, 77) asserts that Levinas's phenomenology implicitly argues against reducing any person to identity categories like race, class, gender, or sexuality. Some scholars have therefore argued that Levinas's concept of alterity fails to account for collective sources of difference (e.g., Ahmed 2007; Drabinski 2016; Bottos 2019). We understand this concern but follow Bernasconi (2018, 92) in thinking it misplaced, particularly since

Levinas's ideas were so clearly shaped by his Jewish identity, which is not racialized in contemporary America but certainly was throughout much of European history. See Levinas ([1979] 1989, 279) for a discussion of his views on anti-Semitism.

20. This article was written, amidst myriad other tragedies, during a period of renewed hostilities in the region, lending these words even greater poignancy.

21. Broadly speaking, there have been two divergent interpretations of Levinas's philosophy. On the one hand, writers such as Knauft, Rapport, and Rahaim see Levinas as extending the classic nineteenth-century humanist project. On the other hand, scholars such as Judith Butler (2004) and Jacques Derrida ([1967] 1978; [1993] 1995) see Levinas as offering an anti-humanist rejoinder to that tradition. In emphasizing the role of a common humanity in our reading of Levinas, we follow the former interpretation.

22. Levinas pursued two lines of thinking in his long career—a relatively secular phenomenology and an explicitly Jewish hermeneutics. Despite keeping them separate, he occasionally used theological language in his phenomenological writings. Bettina Bergo (2019) argues that this crosstalk between Levinas's religious and secular writings is key to his originality as a thinker.

23. "Middle-range theory" has a long history in the social sciences. The term originated with the sociologist Robert Merton (1949) and became influential in numerous related disciplines. It is akin to the "humble theory" in folkloristics advocated by Dorothy Noyes (2007).

WORKS CITED

Adorno, Theodor. (1964) 1973. *The Jargon of Authenticity*. Translated by Knut Tarnowski and Frederic Will. Evanston, IL: Northwestern University Press.

Ahmed, Sara. 2007. "A Phenomenology of Whiteness." *Feminist Theory* 8 (2): 149–168.

Allen, Sarah. 2011. "Reflections on the Metaphysical God after His Demise: Heidegger and Levinas in Dialogue." *Levinas Studies* 6: 29–51.

Anderson, Benedict. 1983. *Imagined Communities: Reflections on the Origin and Spread of Nationalism*. London: Verso.

Appadurai, Arjun. 1990. "Disjuncture and Difference in the Global Cultural Economy." *Theory, Culture and Society* 7 (2–3): 295–310.

Atkinson, Will. 2010. "Phenomenological Additions to the Bourdieusian Toolbox: Two Problems for Bourdieu, Two Solutions from Schutz." *Sociological Theory* 28 (1): 1–19.

Bakhtin, Mikhail M. 1986. *Speech Genres and Other Late Essays*. Edited by Caryl Emerson and Michael Holmquist. Translated by Vern W. McGee. Austin: University of Texas Press.

Barber, Michael. 1991. "The Ethics behind the Absence of Ethics in Alfred Schutz's Thought." *Human Studies* 14 (2–3): 129–140.

Bax, Chantal. 2017. "Otherwise than Being-with: Levinas on Heidegger and Community." *Human Studies* 40 (3): 381–400.

Behar, Ruth, and Deborah A. Gordon, eds. 1996. *Women Writing Culture*. Berkeley: University of California Press.

Berger, Harris M. 1999. *Metal, Rock, and Jazz: Perception and the Phenomenology of Musical Experience*. Middletown, CT: Wesleyan University Press.

Berger, Harris M. 2009. *Stance: Ideas about Emotion, Style, and Meaning for the Study of Expressive Culture*. Middletown, CT: Wesleyan University Press.

Berger, Harris M., and Giovanna P. Del Negro. 2004. *Identity and Everyday Life: Essays in the Study of Folklore, Music, and Popular Culture*. Middletown, CT: Wesleyan University Press.

Berger, Harris M., and Ruth M. Stone, eds. 2019. *Theory for Ethnomusicology: Histories, Conversations, Insights*. 2nd ed. New York: Routledge.

Bergo, Bettina. 2019. "Emmanuel Levinas." *The Stanford Encyclopedia of Philosophy*, edited by Edward N. Zalta. Stanford University. https://plato.stanford.edu/archives/fall2019/entries /levinas.

Bernasconi, Robert. 2005. "Lévy-Bruhl among the Phenomenologists: Exoticisation and the Logic of 'The Primitive.'" *Social Identity* 11 (3): 229–245.

Bernasconi, Robert. 2018. "Levinas, Social Vulnerability, and the Logic of South African Racism." *Suomen Anthropologi* 43 (3): 91–101.

Bottos, Lorenzo Cañás. 2019. "Comment [on 'Anthropology through Levinas' by Nigel Rapport]." *Current Anthropology* 60 (1): 80.

Bourdieu, Pierre. (1979) 1984. *Distinction: A Social Critique of the Judgement of Taste*. Translated by Richard Nice. Cambridge, MA: Harvard University Press.

Bourdieu, Pierre. (1982) 1991. *Language and Symbolic Power*. Translated by Gino Raymond and Matthew Adamson. Cambridge, MA: Harvard University Press.

Briggs, Charles L. 1986. *Learning How to Ask: A Sociolinguistic Appraisal of the Role of the Interview in Social Science Research*. Cambridge: Cambridge University Press.

Butler, Judith. 2004. *Precarious Life: The Powers of Mourning and Violence*. London: Verso.

Byl, Julia. 2014. *Antiphonal Histories: Resonant Pasts in the Toba Batak Musical Present*. Middletown, CT: Wesleyan University Press.

Carr, David. 1994. "Alfred Schutz and the Project of Phenomenological Social Theory." In *Phenomenology of the Cultural Disciplines*, edited by Mano Daniel and Lester Embree, 319–332. Boston: Kluwer Academic Publishers.

Carrington, Peter J. 1979. "Schutz on Transcendental Intersubjectivity in Husserl." *Human Studies* 2 (2): 95–110.

Cheyne, Ria. 2009. "Theorising Culture and Disability: Interdisciplinary Dialogues." *Journal of Literary & Cultural Disability Studies* 3 (1): 101–104.

Clifford, James. 1988. *The Predicament of Culture: Twentieth-Century Ethnography, Literature, and Art*. Cambridge, MA: Harvard University Press.

Clifford, James, and George E. Marcus, eds. 1986. *Writing Culture: The Poetics and Politics of Ethnography*. Berkeley: University of California Press.

Clinton, Esther, and Jeremy Wallach. 2016. "Talking Metal: A Social Phenomenology of Hanging Out in Metal Culture." In *Heavy Metal Music and the Communal Experience*, edited by Nelson Varas-Díaz and Niall W. R. Scott, 37–55. Lanham, MD: Lexington Books.

Cohen, Richard A. 1987. "Translator's Introduction." In *Time and the Other*, by Emmanuel Levinas, 1–27. Pittsburgh, PA: Duquesne University Press.

Davis, Colin. 1996. *Levinas: An Introduction*. Cambridge, UK: Polity Press.

De Certeau, Michel. (1980) 1984. *The Practice of Everyday Life*. Translated by Steven Rendall. Berkeley: University of California Press.

Derrida, Jacques. (1967) 1978. "Violence and Metaphysics: An Essay on the Thought of Emmanuel Levinas." In *Writing and Difference*, translated by Alan Bass, 79–153. Chicago: University of Chicago Press.

Derrida, Jacques. (1993) 1995. *The Gift of Death*. Translated by David Wills. Chicago: University of Chicago Press.

Diedrich, Lisa. 2001. "Breaking Down: A Phenomenology of Disability." *Literature and Medicine* 20 (2): 209–230.

Drabinski, John E. 2016. "Introduction: Levinas, Race and Racism." *Levinas Studies* 7: vii–xx.

Duranti, Alessandro. 2010. "Husserl, Intersubjectivity and Anthropology." *Anthropological Theory* 10 (1–2): 16–35.

Duranti, Alessandro, Jason Throop, and Matthew McCoy. 2023. "Jazz Etiquette: Between Aesthetics and Ethics." In *The Oxford Handbook of the Phenomenology of Music Cultures*, edited by Harris M. Berger, Friedlind Riedel, and David VanderHamm. New York: Oxford University Press. https://doi.org/10.1093/oxfordhb/9780190693879.013.3.

Erlmann, Veit. 2010. *Reason and Resonance: A History of Modern Aurality*. New York: Zed Books.

Feld, Steven. 1982. *Sound and Sentiment: Birds, Weeping, Poetics, and Song in Kaluli Expression*. Philadelphia: University of Pennsylvania Press.

Fox, Aaron. 2004. *Real Country: Music and Language in Working-Class Culture*. Durham, NC: Duke University Press.

Gaston, Sean. 2019. "Comments [on 'Anthropology through Levinas' by Nigel Rapport]." *Current Anthropology* 60 (1): 81–82.

Geertz, Clifford. 1973. *The Interpretation of Cultures*. New York: Basic Books.

Grathoff, Richard, ed. 1978. *The Theory of Social Action: The Correspondence of Alfred Schutz and Talcott Parsons*. Bloomington: Indian University Press.

Gray, Lila Ellen. 2013. *Fado Resounding: Affective Politics and Urban Life*. Durham, NC: Duke University Press.

Harris, Marvin. 1968. *The Rise of Anthropological Theory: A History of Theories of Culture*. New York: Crowell.

Hegel, G. W. F. (1799) 1971. "Love." In *Early Theological Writings*, translated by T. M. Knox, 302–308. Philadelphia: University of Pennsylvania Press.

Ho, Wing-Chung. 2008a. "The Transcendence and Non-discursivity of the Lifeworld." *Human Studies* 31 (3): 323–342.

Ho, Wing-Chung. 2008b. "Understanding the Subjective Point of View: Methodological Interpretations of the Schutz-Parsons Debate." *Human Studies* 31 (4): 383–397.

Holt, Fabian. 2007. *Genre in Popular Music*. Chicago: University of Chicago Press.

Hufford, David. 1982. *The Terror That Comes in the Night: An Experience-Centered Study of Supernatural Assault Traditions*. Philadelphia: University of Pennsylvania Press.

Jewett, Andrew. 2020. *Science under Fire: Challenges to Scientific Authority in Modern America*. Cambridge, MA: Harvard University Press.

Jonas, Hans. 1959. "Alfred Schutz, 1899–1959." *Social Research* 26 (4): 471–474.

Knauft, Bruce M. 1994. "Pushing Anthropology past the Posts: Critical Notes on Cultural Anthropology and Cultural Studies as Influenced by Postmodernism and Existentialism." *Critique of Anthropology* 14 (2): 117–152.

Knowles, Adam. 2019. *Heidegger's Fascist Affinities: A Politics of Silence*. Stanford, CA: Stanford University Press.

Levinas, Emmanuel. (1947) 1987. *Time and the Other*. Translated by Richard A. Cohen. Pittsburgh, PA: Duquesne University Press.

Levinas, Emmanuel. (1961) 1969. *Totality and Infinity: An Essay on Exteriority*. Translated by Alphonso Lingis. Pittsburgh, PA: Duquesne University Press.

Levinas, Emmanuel. (1979) 1989. "Politics After!" In *The Levinas Reader*, edited by Seán Hand, translated by Roland Lack, 277–283. Oxford: Basil Blackwell.

Levinas, Emmanuel. (1982) 1987. "Diachrony and Representation." In *Time and the Other*, translated by Richard A. Cohen, 97–120. Pittsburgh, PA: Duquesne University Press.

Levinas, Emmanuel. (1984) 1989. "Ethics as First Philosophy." In *The Levinas Reader*, edited by Seán Hand, translated by Seán Hand and Michael Temple, 75–87. Oxford: Basil Blackwell.

Lévy-Bruhl, Lucien. (1935) 1983. *Primitive Mythology: The Mythic World of the Australian and Papuan Natives*. Translated by Brian Elliott. St. Lucia: University of Queensland Press.

Marcus, George E., and Michael M. J. Fischer. 1986. *Anthropology as Cultural Critique: An Experimental Moment in the Human Sciences*. Chicago: University of Chicago Press.

McDonald, David A. 2013a. "Imaginaries of Exile and Emergence in Israeli Jewish and Palestinian Hip Hop." *TDR: The Drama Review* 57 (3): 69–87.

McDonald, David A. 2013b. *My Voice Is My Weapon: Music, Nationalism and the Poetics of Palestinian Resistance*. Durham, NC: Duke University Press.

Meintjes, Louise. 2003. *Sound of Africa! Making Music Zulu in a South African Studio*. Durham, NC: Duke University Press.

Merton, Robert K. 1949. *Social Theory and Social Structure*. New York: Free Press.

Noyes, Dorothy. 2007. "Humble Theory." *Journal of Folklore Research* 45 (1): 37–43.

O'Neill, Kevin Lewis. 2020. "Some Reflections on Levinas and Ethics: A Response to Alvi." *Anthropological Theory* 20 (2): 180–189.

Ortner, Sherry. 1995. "Resistance and the Problem of Ethnographic Refusal." *Comparative Studies in Society and History* 37 (1): 173–193.

Porcello, Thomas. 1998. "'Tails Out': Social Phenomenology and the Ethnographic Representation of Technology in Music-Making." *Ethnomusicology* 42 (3): 485–510.

Psathas, George. 2004. "Alfred Schutz's Influence on American Sociologists and Sociology." *Human Studies* 27 (1): 1–35.

Rahaim, Matthew. 2017. "Otherwise than Participation: Unity and Alterity in Musical Encounters." In *Music and Empathy*, edited by Elaine King and Caroline Waddington, 175–193. New York: Routledge.

Rapport, Nigel. 2015. "Anthropology through Levinas: Knowing the Uniqueness of Ego and the Mystery of Otherness." *Current Anthropology* 56 (2): 256–276.

Rapport, Nigel. 2019. "Anthropology through Levinas (Further Reflections): On Humanity, Being, Culture, Violation, Sociality, and Morality." *Current Anthropology* 60 (1): 70–79.

Rapport, Nigel. 2020. *Cosmopolitan Love and Individuality: Ethical Engagements beyond Culture*. Lanham, MD: Lexington Books.

Ratcliffe, Matthew. 2009. "Belonging to the World through the Feeling Body." *Philosophy, Psychology and Psychiatry* 16 (2): 205–211.

Ricoeur, Paul. (1983) 1984. *Time and Narrative*. Vol. 1. Translated by Kathleen McLaughlin and David Pellauer. Chicago: University of Chicago Press.

Schutz, Alfred. (1932) 1967. *The Phenomenology of the Social World*. Translated by George Walsh and Frederick Lehnert. Evanston, IL: Northwestern University Press.

Schutz, Alfred. (1944) 1962. "Some Leading Concepts of Phenomenology." In *Collected Papers I: The Problem of Social Reality*, edited by Maurice Natanson, 99–117. The Hague: Martinus Nijhoff.

Schutz, Alfred. (1944) 1964. "The Stranger: An Essay in Social Psychology." In *Collected Papers II: Studies in Social Theory*, edited by Arvid Brodersen, 91–105. The Hague: Martinus Nijhoff.

Schutz, Alfred. (1951) 2004. "Making Music Together." In *Popular Music: Critical Concepts in Media and Cultural Studies*. Vol. 1, *Music and Society*, edited by Simon Frith, 197–212. New York: Routledge.

Schutz, Alfred. (1955) 1964. "Equality and the Meaning Structure of the Social World." Paper presented at the Fifteenth Symposium of the Conference on Science, Philosophy and

Religion, Columbia University. In *Collected Papers II: Studies in Social Theory*, edited by Arvid Brodersen, 91–105. The Hague: Martinus Nijhoff.

Schutz, Alfred. (1957) 1970. "Some Structures of the Life-World." In *Collected Papers III: Studies in Phenomenological Philosophy*, edited by Ilse Schutz and translated by Aron Gurwitsch, 116–132. The Hague: Martinus Nijhoff.

Schutz, Alfred. 1970. *Alfred Schutz on Phenomenology and Social Relations*. Edited by Helmut Wagner. Chicago: University of Chicago Press.

Schutz, Alfred. 1976. "Fragments on the Phenomenology of Music." Edited by Fred Kersten. *Music and Man* 2 (1–2): 5–72.

Skolnick, Alex. 2013. *From Geek to Guitar Hero*. New York: Louder Education.

Taylor, Charles. 1991. *The Ethics of Authenticity*. Cambridge, MA: Harvard University Press.

Wagner, Helmut. 1970. Introduction to *Alfred Schutz on Phenomenology and Social Relations*, edited by Helmut Wagner, 1–50. Chicago: University of Chicago Press.

Wallach, Jeremy. 2003. "The Poetics of Electrosonic Presence: Recorded Music and the Materiality of Sound." *Journal of Popular Music Studies* 15 (1): 34–64.

Wallach, Jeremy. 2008. *Modern Noise, Fluid Genres: Popular Music in Indonesia, 1997–2001*. Madison: University of Wisconsin Press.

Wallach, Jeremy. (2008) 2017. *Musik Popular Indonesia 1997–2001: Kebisingan dan Keberagaman Aliran Lagu* [Indonesian-language edition of *Modern Noise, Fluid Genres*], edited by Rahmat Edi Sutanto, translated by the Kobam Collective. Depok, Indonesia: Komunitas Bambu.

Wallach, Jeremy. 2014. "Notes on Dangdut Music, Popular Nationalism and Indonesian Islam." In *Sonic Modernities in the Malay World: A History of Popular Music, Social Distinction and Novel Lifestyles (1930s–2000s)*, edited by Bart Barendregt, 271–289. Leiden: Brill.

Wallach, Jeremy. 2019. "Rainforest to Raves: Ethnomusicological Forays into Popular Music." *Journal of World Popular Music* 6 (2): 223–227.

Wallach, Jeremy. Forthcoming. "The Entextualization of Performative Sociality: Ethnomusicological Approaches to Sonic Encoding and Decoding." *The Ethnography of Recording Studios*, edited by Serena Facci and Giovanni Giuriati. Venice: Fondazione Giorgio Cini Intercultural Institute of Comparative Music Studies.

Wallach, Jeremy, Harris M. Berger, and Paul D. Greene. 2011. "Affective Overdrive, Scene Dynamics, and Identity in the Global Metal Scene." In *Metal Rules the Globe: Heavy Metal Music around the World*, edited by Jeremy Wallach, Harris M. Berger, and Paul D. Greene, 3–33. Durham, NC: Duke University Press.

Wallach, Jeremy, and Esther Clinton. 2013. "History, Modernity, and Music Genre in Indonesia: Introduction to the Special Issue." *Asian Music* 44 (2): 3–23.

Wallach, Jeremy, and Esther Clinton. 2019. "Theories of the Post-Colonial and Globalization: Ethnomusicologists Grapple with Power, History, Media, and Mobility." In *Theory for Ethnomusicology: Histories, Conversations, Insights*, 2nd ed., edited by Harris M. Berger and Ruth M. Stone, 114–139. New York: Routledge.

Weber, Max. (1905) 1930. *The Protestant Ethic and the Spirit of Capitalism*. Translated by Talcott Parsons. New York: Routledge.

Weintraub, Andrew N. 2010. *Dangdut Stories: A Social and Musical History of Indonesia's Most Popular Music*. New York: Oxford University Press.

Wu, Roberto. 2015. "The Recurrence of Acoustics in Levinas." *Levinas Studies* 10: 115–136.

Yano, Christine. 2003. *Tears of Longing: Nostalgia and the Nation in Japanese Popular Song*. Cambridge, MA: Harvard University Press.

CHAPTER 21

....

ARTIFICIAL INTELLIGENCE AND PHENOMENOLOGICAL ETHNOGRAPHY

....

RITWIK BANERJI

How closely can an ethnographer understand their research subject's lived experience as it unfolds? What might allow an ethnographer to apprehend that lived experience in the same manner as their research subject and at the same time as this subject?

Various phenomenological approaches to ethnographic fieldwork have established the importance of striving to understand a given sociocultural sphere or phenomenon from a subject's first-person standpoint (Jackson 1996b; Maso 2001; Desjarlais and Throop 2011). By focusing on how the world appears, sounds, and feels for subjects, such approaches challenge the tendency toward generalization and abstraction of much scholarship on sociocultural phenomena (Jackson 1996a). This work repeatedly reveals how multiple subjects can experience the putatively "same" action or social formation in divergent ways and invites explanations of diverse characterizations of apparently similar experiences. Phenomenological ethnography has also illustrated how a subject's reality often differs from a so-called "objective" account of the same sociocultural sphere and raises the question of why such differences emerge.

As vital as these approaches have been, there are major limits to what a researcher can fathom about the way that being in a certain sociocultural environment appears, sounds, or feels for its participants. No matter how sensitively or empathetically ethnographers pursue their fieldwork, distance remains. While they may be able to observe the outer traces of a subject's internal consciousness as manifested in speech and bodily comportment, ethnographers will neither be able to experience the same environment in the same way that another subject does, nor will they be able to fully grasp what a subject reports about their experience. Whether for phenomenologists in philosophy (Husserl [1931] 1960, 1989; Levinas [1991] 1998), anthropology (Desjarlais 2003; Linger 2010; Desjarlais and Throop 2011), or ethnomusicology (Berger 1999) or for philosophers of mind in the analytic tradition (Nagel 1974; Dennett 1991), the possibility of knowing another's experience as they do and at the time that they have that experience is limited. For ethnography, this means that, at best, researchers and their interlocutors can only achieve a "partial sharing" of their experiences (Berger 1999, 16). An ethnographer's account can be very "near" their interlocutor's experience (Geertz 1983, 57) but is not that experience itself.

This basic problem in the ethnographic study of first-person experience has prompted a variety of experiments with field research techniques, including the use of electronic and digital media as a means of eliciting a subject's commentary on what they undergo in everyday social events. These fieldwork practices benefit not only those interested in an experiential account of subjects' encounters with the world but the practice of ethnographic fieldwork more widely. By no means, however, have possibilities for new field techniques been exhausted. In particular, experiments with media as a tool for elicitation are yet to fully explore the use of artificial intelligence (AI), a media form uniquely suited to reproduce the experience of human sociality itself, even if only partially. This is rather striking given that Hubert Dreyfus used a series of critiques of AI research and development (1972, 1992, 2007) as empirical examples for illustrating the validity of several claims about the constitution of human experience developed in the twentieth-century phenomenological tradition in philosophy.

The efficacy of AI as a means of doing phenomenological ethnography is most evident in a field technique I have practiced over several years, in which I have staged encounters between humanlike, AI-driven virtual social interactants and human beings. Such encounters radically expand the possibility of accessing participants' lived experiences. As I illustrate in what follows, a meeting between AI and social actors elicits a human participant's commentary on their experience of being with others in a given sociocultural sphere in the course of face-to-face, real-time interaction. This mode of fieldwork enables a far closer account of a subjects' lived experience of a given moment than has been possible through previous phenomenologically oriented ethnographic experiments by allowing subjects to comment on their experience more or less as it takes place.

While this method enables a researcher to gain a more intimate understanding of the subject's experience as it unfolds, key elements of the subject's conscious encounter with the world will, of course, still remain inaccessible. All the same, these encounters greatly augment the possibility of understanding what an ethnographic subject experiences, and yet this method has hardly been put to work. As more and more cultural practices are re-embodied in artificial life and other algorithmic, interactive modes of representation and performance, the development of such methods for ethnographic fieldwork will have all the more purchase and utility. To illustrate this point, this chapter describes my use of AI as a tool for the ethnographic examination of a subject's first-person experience. In what follows, I describe an experimental ethnographic methodology in which I have designed several humanlike AI performers of free improvisation and subjected these to the critique of human improvisers in Berlin, Chicago, and San Francisco. As I illustrate below, such encounters enable musical practitioners to comment on their experiences of this form of music as a social practice nearly as they happen and do so with a level of directness and candor that is not possible through other forms of ethnographic fieldwork.

THE SIGNIFICANCE OF THE PRESENT CONTENTS OF AN INDIVIDUAL'S LIVED EXPERIENCE

A subject's account of a particular moment of their lived experience is neither the sole focus of phenomenological ethnography, nor is phenomenological ethnography necessarily impossible if a researcher cannot completely understand every detail of what their research participants experience.[1] Phenomenology deals with *structures* of experience, such as subject-object relations, the body-world relation, or the relations among the phases of lived time. Hence a first-person account is just one point in a constellation of empirical and theoretical considerations in phenomenology.[2] Sometimes referred to as "internalism" (see Zahavi 2004), a focus on the internal flow of thoughts, feelings, and physical sensations in a subject's mind and body often gives short shrift to the pivotal role of embodied action in the makeup of lived experiences. Though the body is typically a constituting element of how a subject apprehends the world, a subject's consciousness often barely registers the state of the body (Merleau-Ponty [1945] 2002; Polanyi [1966] 2009). Much like the body, a subject may also be similarly unaware of the discourses and ideologies that shape their first-person experience of the world (see Berger 1999, 251–297). Thus, focusing on first-person perspectives may lead the researcher to greatly overlook what gives rise to what a subject experiences.

Naturally, a subject's experience of a given phenomenon (such as improvisation) typically takes shape over the course of numerous moments rather than just one instant. More often than not, no single moment really constitutes the essence of what a subject experiences of various cultural formations or routine social activities. Indeed, it is a basic tenet of Husserlian phenomenology that a subject experiences a single instant of objective time as a fusion of various past and future moments (see Husserl [1928] 1966). Nevertheless, a subject's experience of a particular moment of action remains an important element of phenomenological ethnography. For a more thorough account of the structures of experience, researchers must strive to improve their ability to access the *contents* of these experiences, even if it is difficult or ultimately infeasible. Among many possible applications, a better understanding of their subjects' experience at a specific moment will enable a researcher to have a more holistic consideration of how the events of that moment motivate subsequent behaviors. Moreover, if a particular object for an ethnographic subject is composed of an aggregate of their experience during a series of present nows, then understanding what the subject undergoes at those moments is useful for giving an account of the structures of experience, as well as how those structures vary from one point in time to another.

ETHNOGRAPHIC APPROACHES TO ACCESSING LIVED EXPERIENCE

The Sisyphean task of grasping a subject's lived experience at a given moment has prompted ethnographers of music to explore several methodological solutions.[3] Given the relatively basic problems of using interviews as a means of understanding specific moments of a subject's experience (see H. S. Becker and Geer 1957),[4] these have mostly taken the form of incremental elaborations upon the general framework of participant observation. For example, experiments with "feedback methods" (Stone and Stone 1981; Stone-MacDonald and Stone 2013) as well as the interface between phenomenology and cognitive science (J. Becker 2009) also offer small but significant solutions to the basic issue of accessing the subject's experience in the course of fieldwork. Overall, however, none of the methods succeed in enabling researchers to know and feel a sociocultural environment or phenomenon in the same way as their ethnographic subjects, nor do researchers pretend that they do. Broadly speaking, two axes of distance frustrate an ethnographer's ability to fathom a subject's lived experience: person (*"I am not you"*) and time (*"this now is not the previous one"*).

Participant Observation and Its Limits

Participant observation in its various forms offers a means of achieving greater proximity to the subject's experience. By taking part in the same actions as their subjects, researchers are able to partially reconstruct what those subjects might experience in the course of similar moments, actions, or situations. For example, Friedson's (1996) study of music and dance in the healing rituals of the Tumbuka of Malawi examines the conditions of bodily action and sensory attunement that afford his interlocutors a culturally specific form of altered consciousness—trance—integral to local practices of medico-therapeutic care. Without asserting that his own participation in music and dance produces the same states of being as his interlocutors, Friedson details how the intensity of bodily movement within a forceful sonic environment of percussion enables his interlocutors to experience the physiological healing effects they describe.

His participation as an apprentice dancer and musician reveals several of the central paradoxes of participant observation as a means of conducting phenomenological ethnography. Even as his participation is driven by his desire to understand his Tumbuka interlocutors' reported experiences of healing and altered consciousness, it highlights the fact that it preserves the gulf between his experience and theirs, as Friedson readily notes. The stakes and goals of his participation are rather distinct from his interlocutors' since his participation serves primarily as a means of data collection for the purpose of writing about his experiences later on as a researcher of cultural practice. Friedson's Tumbuka interlocutors, on the other hand, participate in these events for fundamentally different purposes. Similarly, his participation is largely temporary while the Tumbuka engage in these practices for a duration closer to a lifetime. This means he—or any other ethnographer who is not themselves a lifelong participant of the community they study—is largely liberated from the consequences and realities of a life in the social realm he studies. No matter how well integrated an ethnographer is in a community, they always occupy a position which is socially separated from that of their subjects (Bourdieu 1977, 1).[5] The divergence between what an ethnographer and their subjects experience also stems from any basic differences in their personal and social identities. Experience is rooted not just in a general fact of embodiment but rather in having a particular body of one's own as well as all the social worlds within which that body and being have traveled (Merleau-Ponty [1945] 2002, 475). Hence each individual's way of parsing phenomena that are objectively "the same" is at least minimally distinct from any other individual's.

Whatever form of participation one assumes in ethnographic work (i.e., as performer, dancer, listener, recording engineer, etc.), it can often allow one to understand what subjects experience far more readily than what one would learn from merely talking with them. Nevertheless, a researcher and subject experience the "same" moments within the habitual actions of a given social milieu rather differently. On this point, Rice's (1995) reflections on learning the *gaida*, a traditional Bulgarian bagpipe, are illustrative. As Rice notes, the instrument is less "taught" in a formal student-teacher sense, but rather learned through a combination of gradually more complicated practical use and self study. Rice himself went beyond these traditional methods by recording gaida performances and playing them back at slow speeds. In this sense, self study enables researchers to acquaint themselves with the many moments that are integral to the experience of their ethnographic interlocutors. All the same, a researcher's passage through these moments is incommensurate with that of their subjects.[6]

Feedback Techniques

Not all phenomenological approaches to ethnography involve experiments in field methodology; rather, they typically constitute shifts in how one understands the nature and experience of fieldwork. What the ethnographer does in the field often remains more or less the same, while phenomenological thinking informs their conceptualization of research objectives and their analysis of ethnographic data. Feedback techniques (Stone and Stone 1981; Stone-MacDonald and Stone 2013), however, are a distinct mode of engagement and offer a salient approach to understanding what subjects experience. Here, the researcher reviews one or more fixed-media representations (e.g., field notes, photographs, recordings) in conversation with participants in order to elicit their commentary on various moments of action.[7] For example, Harris Berger's ethnography of popular music in northeastern Ohio uses this method as a way of understanding the subject's experience of certain moments of performance by listening to field recordings with the subject (Berger 1999, 174–241). This method is an effective means of allowing the researcher to gain a better understanding of what a social actor undergoes from their first-person standpoint. As the ethnographer and the research participant review specific moments of the fixed media object collected in fieldwork, the subject is often able to give a detailed description of elements of their experience that might not have been so easy to elicit: Where was their attention directed? What went through their mind? What were they doing with their body? How did it feel? Indeed, Berger's dialogs with musicians in the context of feedback interviews readily reveal their purchase.[8]

Alongside its virtues, Berger recognizes the shortcomings of this method. He notes that feedback interviews can be "tedious" and "exhausting" for participants (Berger 1999, 174). As suggested by other theorists of practice (Bourdieu 1977; Rice 1995; Polanyi [1966] 2009), fluent, highly skilled practitioners are often quite unaware of precisely what they are doing or attending to at various points in a performance.[9] While this might seem to suggest a simple lack of skill or proficiency, it is often the result of an exceptional degree of expertise (S. E. Dreyfus and Dreyfus 1980; Brinner 1995). As soon as they acquire basic fluency in various elements of practice, these recede in a subject's conscious awareness of action. This liberation of cognitive resources enables them to focus on more complex elements of practice, but even so, much of what takes place may still not be a point of conscious awareness for the practitioner.

Rather than simply recovering a past moment of lived experience, the feedback interview actually creates new experiences for both fieldworker and ethnographic subject, even if these experiences concern the past (Stone and Stone 1981; Berger 1999, 186). While the feedback interview certainly allows a researcher to understand more clearly what a subject experiences during moments of practice, it becomes difficult to know which moment of experience is really being examined in the process of the interview: Is it a moment in the past being reflected upon or a moment in the present feedback interview?

Post-hoc analysis of an experience at a specific moment in the recorded past has the power to break the flow of time, allowing a subject to share their moment-to-moment experience with the researcher. But does this moment of analytical reflection after the fact yield an accurate understanding of what the subject experienced at the moment in question? Quite understandably, Berger's description of his use of the feedback interview is imbued with an anxiety about the ways in which it risks distorting the subject's understanding of their own experience and, therefore, the researcher's ability to accurately comprehend what the subject really saw, heard, felt, or even did at certain moments.

Given these various problems, methodological and analytical experiments are well warranted in phenomenological ethnography, and they underscore the importance of continuing to find ways of accessing what an individual experiences at specific points in time. All the same, the incompleteness of this access is continually confirmed, and two basic gulfs of experiential understanding between researcher and subject endure: time and person. Participant observation brings a researcher closer to understanding specific moments of action, but the basic existential differences between ethnographer and subject perdure. Likewise, feedback interviews may allow a researcher to understand an individual's highly personal, subjective experiential flux, but given that the feedback interview takes place after the fact, the gap of time, memory, and reflection all contribute to preserving an essential distance between a subject's experience and what a researcher will really ever understand of that experience.

Encountering Technological Re-embodiments of Human Musical Experience

If another individual's experience is never fully accessible, are there field techniques that would enable the researcher to gain a slightly clearer understanding of what another individual undergoes?

A possible, partial solution to this problem is found in the encounter between artificially intelligent virtual social agents and the human beings whose practices these systems are built to re-embody.[10] It is widely recognized (see H. L. Dreyfus 1972, among many others) that such technologies are constructed with the goal of duplicating the *cognitive capabilities* of human beings. By contrast, it is far less widely recognized how the design of these systems is fundamentally oriented towards creating the *experience* of interacting with one or more members of the human species.[11] Crucially, while AI practitioners often present their work as if it embodies supposedly universal human traits, many scholars have criticized the heavily biased, partial, and particular nature of how humanness is algorithmically reproduced in these systems (Edwards 1997; Lewis 2000; Forsythe 2001; Suchman 2006). When a designer creates a system that might behave like "a" human being, that designer always has a very particular conception of what that "human" is, how that human behaves, and ultimately what the experience of interacting with another human being should feel like. Hence these human like technologies must always be understood as depictions of culturally specific experiences of human social practice, not the "universal" human being that designers typically imagine they are copying.

As such, human encounters with artificial social agents offer numerous possibilities for examining the structure of distinct forms of human sociality and how these structures vary across cultural milieux. Though this mode of research is virtually unexplored in the humanities and social sciences, it has become an essential research practice in the field of human-computer interaction. In order to improve the design of such systems, researchers subject them to the critique of the people who are most likely to interact with those systems, often by collecting feedback on how the system's actions fit with the goals and habits of the target population. But beyond the purpose of refining design, a small contingent of theorists has noted that the encounter between a human being and a human like technology can and should be applied to the study of human sociocultural practice more generally (Dourish 2006; MacDorman and Ishiguro 2006). One such purpose would be the pursuit of a greater understanding of what the ethnographic subject experiences during various moments of their participation in a given cultural practice in order to expand the methodological possibilities of phenomenological ethnography.[12]

In some ways, the encounter between an artificial social interactant and a human being resembles the basic structure of a feedback interview. In both, the conversation between ethnographer and subject focuses on a mediated artifact in order to elicit an experiential account of the event rendered by the medium. This broad resemblance aside, feedback interviews and AI-human interactions differ significantly; while the former rely on fixed media, the latter involve a media artifact which actively responds to the human subject that critiques it. Like fixed media, the design of an artificial social interactant is a method of depicting the nature of a given social practice. Unlike fixed media, however, an artificial social interactant does far more than simply depict a practice. By engaging with such media, a research subject is not merely a viewer or listener but, rather, a partner in interaction. Further, the medium is not a static object; it actively performs the role of a human actor in the course of social interaction.

Here, a research subject does not simply comment on their experience of a past event but instead engages in an interaction. In an encounter with another human, a subject would likely refrain from halting the progress of an event to share the minutiae of their experiential state. In contrast, the encounter with an artificial social interactant enables the human subject to comment on what they experience almost as soon as they experience it.[13] Of course, their commentary on this experience is not to be equated with the experience itself; nevertheless, their utterances and expressions in this context may be the closest that one can come to accessing and understanding the flow of their first-person orientation to the world in the event that just occurred.

MAXINE AND THE ROUTINE SOCIALITY OF IMPROVISERS

Designing humanlike virtual social agents and staging encounters between them and their human counterparts has been an integral element of my work as both an artist and an ethnographer. This element of my methodological repertoire has continually illustrated its distinct efficacy as a means of examining a subject's experience of human sociality. Similar in concept to George Lewis's Voyager system (1993, 1999), but distinct in design, Maxine (Banerji 2012, 2014, 2016)[14] is a virtual performer of free improvisation and the primary system I have used to experiment with this approach to ethnographic fieldwork.[15] Drawing on my experiences as an improvising saxophonist, an observer of performers in concert, and a keen listener of recordings of this practice, and numerous conversations with performers over several years, I designed Maxine to be a virtual improviser that spontaneously composes and performs music while adjusting its performative trajectory in response to the sonic actions of fellow players in its midst. Through a concatenation of microphones, cables, audio interface, algorithms of my own design, and a loudspeaker, Maxine is built to perform the culturally specific form of sociomusical interactivity characteristic of free improvisation.

As is the case for any artificial social interactant (or any other cultural representation, for that matter), there is no reason to assume that human practitioners will find that these systems amount to an adequate portrayal of their social or musical practices of real-time human interaction. That is, it is usually a given that people depicted by a scholar will dispute their depiction or that practitioners of a certain activity will take issue with how an engineer has rendered these actions in a system's construction. The human tendency to dispute such representations or portrayals revealed itself in my fieldwork only shortly after a first complete version of Maxine was developed in 2009, when I began arranging a variety of occasions for fellow participants in Chicago's free improvisation scene to "meet" and play with the system.

Initially, the purpose of private meetings was to allow improvisers time to get to know the system as a player—just as they would with a human musician—but also to collect their feedback on how the system compared to a human improviser.[16] As soon as I began conducting these meetings, it quickly became obvious that they could serve a far broader purpose than the merely utilitarian goal of gathering critical assessments of the system in order to develop new objectives and strategies for subsequent design. Critiquing the system became an occasion for improvisers to talk about their experience of sonic interaction with other players and to do so with a degree of frankness that was uncommon in their face-to-face interactions with other players. Commenting on the system's resemblance to or difference from human musicians enabled improvisers to narrate their experience of co-presence and interaction with other performers with a level of detail that is rarely afforded by their typical modes of sociality.

In our discussions, a great deal of what improvisers had to say about their experience of playing with Maxine was negative. This is a significant departure from the polite social veneer that improvisers typically presented to me in other modes of ethnographic engagement. The performers I have worked with over the course of my ethnographic fieldwork in various scenes showed a marked, consistent tendency to mask their distaste for other performers or particular approaches to free improvisation with a variety of platitudes or deferrals of opinion. Clearly, improvisers have a lot more to say about each other's playing than they tend to openly enunciate in routine social situations.

When the musicians did make negative commentary about Maxine, including the occasional vulgar or incendiary remark, it was largely unsolicited. When asking improvisers to talk about their experience of playing with the system, I made an effort to avoid any verbal or affective display of my own aesthetic appraisal of what I was hearing.

Like many designers, I want to offer participants an opportunity to express their evaluation of Maxine without feeling pressure to agree with my own assessment. As an improviser who has spent a great deal of time working with the system, both as its developer and as its principal collaborator in public performance, I am, of course, biased in my opinion of the system as a "musician." I have been frustrated by working with this system, but I have also been delighted; both sentiments similarly apply to what I have heard in improvised interactions between human performers and Maxine. While others are playing with Maxine, I often hide my face as I listen, usually by turning my head away from the other performer, just as a judge might hide their reaction to a disturbing (or underwhelming) image from a crime scene, so as to not bias the jury. After playing a piece with the system, I try not to let performers know what I really think by keeping a "straight" face as we talk. I will break that expression, however, after they have had sufficient time to express their view, and I typically do this if I agree with their assessment.

Though an ethnographer's expression of aesthetic judgments is not completely avoidable, displaying such judgments complicates the fieldwork encounter, regardless of whether those judgments are positive or negative. If a performer were to see that I am delighted by what I am hearing—which I often am—it would make it harder for them to express a negative sentiment, if this was truly what they felt. The same is true for the opposite case. To preserve a performer's opportunity to offer honest assessments of their playing partner—a rare thing that is created by Maxine's simultaneously nonhuman and yet still humanlike social presence—I attempt to control the more unruly artifacts of the ethnographic apparatus, such as my face and body language.

How Improvisers Get Along

In the three scenes where I conducted fieldwork over several years, I found that in their routine social interactions with one another, improvisers rather consistently refrain from instructing or criticizing other players or specific approaches to this musical practice.[17] No directions are given before a piece begins. No composition is used. No player serves as a leader.[18] Whether or not players expect their peers to conform to specific stylistic norms, such conventions are never explicitly specified.[19] The piece proceeds for as long as the players decide it should. Endings take place when all players have stopped playing; the desire to end is usually confirmed by the fact that all players have stopped intentionally producing sounds and are either engaged in a mutual gaze in the midst of this silence or looking at some point in the distance.

It is largely unheard of for players to stop in the middle of a free improvisation during a private playing session. Instead, a piece "ends" when the players have all come to a mutual silence. This is in sharp contrast to the performance of pre-set compositions. In a wide range of music scenes and genres, musicians will often stop a rehearsal or private performance if they feel that a mistake has been made or that some element of music (e.g., expressive intentions or style) requires further discussion. Since they neither use compositions nor explicitly acknowledge notions of aesthetic normativity (i.e., what constitutes "correct" execution), it would defy the interpersonal communicative logic specific to the culture of free improvisation for a player to stop prior to the mutual silence that typically occurs at the end of the piece.[20] If there is no composition, it is difficult for an individual to ground a potential claim that a given action in the course of the performance constitutes a "mistake" or could be executed more "correctly." Making such a claim would imply that this individual believes they have a clearer idea of how others ought to exercise the freedom afforded to them through this practice. If there is no *explicit* stylistic tendency, then there is nothing that another player can say is "wrong" about a particular performative moment, since the community of practice itself has largely refused the notion of "right" or "wrong."

Likewise, outside of moments of making music, players largely refrain from instructive or evaluative commentary indicating their feeling that the piece should proceed in a particular manner. After a piece, expressions of obligatory praise—"That was great!" "Nice!" "Glad we could get together!"—are quite common, even if they do not reflect what a player really felt. In the Chicago, Berlin, and San Francisco scenes where I conducted fieldwork, players commonly expended a significant amount of effort in avoiding direct enunciations of negative commentary. As I often observed, if one player found themselves disinterested in the stylistic tendencies of their peer, they would seek to maintain a cordial social relationship while politely declining requests to participate in any further collaborative musical activities.

Similar tendencies have been observed in ethnographic work on other free improvisation scenes, such as the Southern California scene that David Borgo has studied (2002, 17). Borgo observed that his interlocutors were reluctant to explicitly articulate their disagreements with a group member's approach to collective playing. Free improvisation has become more common in university music instruction, and one might reasonably expect a greater tolerance for evaluative commentary there. However, Maud Hickey's qualitative study of such settings clearly suggests otherwise (2015). Even in a context where participants were able to express their views anonymously, improvisers show a strong proclivity towards self-censorship, actively avoiding the open expression of negative aesthetic judgments about their peers (Pras et al. 2017). My fieldwork among improvisers confirms what others have observed. At a 2008 concert in Chicago, for example, I openly expressed my curiosity to one white improvising cellist, whom I will call "Carl,"[21] about whether there were certain ways of playing, listening, and interacting that he preferred in his collaborators. "What makes a 'good' improviser, in your opinion?" Brusquely disabusing me of my apparent ignorance, he refused the very idea that any sort of normative framework was at all relevant for free improvisation: "there's no such thing as a 'good' improviser."

This denial of a notion of "correct" practice has deep roots in the ideologies of freedom and egalitarianism in discourses on free improvisation (Smith 1973; Bailey [1980] 1993; Borgo 2005; Steinbeck 2010; Corbett 2016). While disciplining or correction by peers is tolerated as an acceptable interpretation of egalitarianism in numerous other social spheres (Boehm 1993), improvisers subscribe to a widely held conception of equality, in which the very utterance of instruction or critique by peers is regarded as antithetical to the egalitarian ideal (Freeman 1972; Béteille 1977). Critical commentary from one player directed to another functions as what language and social interaction scholars refer to as a "speech act" (Austin 1962) that places the speaker in a position of authority over the addressee. Without stating this explicitly, improvisers appear to deem critical commentary as a kind of infringement of the creative liberty that the practice of free improvisation is supposed to offer each participant.

Collaborative Ethnographic Phenomenology with Maxine

Improvisers habitually refrain from instructing or criticizing their peers, but this hardly means that they do not experience a desire to express such sentiments. An encounter with Maxine readily reveals that improvisers not only experience a desire to tell other musicians what they really think of their playing, but that experiencing such desires is a near constant feature of being with other improvisers. For one player, a white Swedish double-bassist whom I will call "Torsten," the opportunity to critically comment on how another improviser, whether human or machine, conducts themselves was both singularly unprecedented and extremely welcome. In the midst of his litany of criticisms of Maxine, Torsten interrupted himself with a broader remark about how the interaction reminded him of the remarks he held back from other players: as he put it, "I *wish* I could tell other people things like this!"

In addition to allowing players to be more forthright about their experiences, an encounter with a virtual improviser like Maxine allows musicians to feel far more comfortable stopping in the middle of a piece to make a comment. Compared to the feedback interview, or really any other approach to fieldwork currently used in the ethnography of music or social practice, stopping Maxine at the moment that one wishes to share an experiential narrative with a researcher allows a far more vivid and direct understanding of what a subject experiences in the midst of real-time human sociality. The fact that improvisers are so at ease in stopping Maxine in order to share details of their experience emerged from the beginning of the system's encounters with human improvisers in 2009.[22] Once I observed that players were comfortable stopping Maxine on their own, I explicitly offered them the option of either ending the piece as they normally would with another improviser or calling a halt in order to comment on what they were experiencing. Stopping a piece in the middle can provide better understanding of what the improviser might be experiencing at a given moment, especially compared to what they might be able to recall after the piece is concluded.

In part, the fact that improvisers are so remarkably reticent about offering critical commentary after a performance may stem from their rapid interplay with one another and the quick decision-making that occurs during the course of performance. Free improvisation may leave many players with the feeling that their memories of precise events of the piece are blurred. As saxophonist Evan Parker puts it, the interactional nature of the practice produces a sense of confusion about the nature of cause and effect in this form of music-making, even for experienced improvisers. For example, Parker describes this experience as an ongoing question: "did you do that because I did that? Or did I do that because you did that" (Parker, quoted in Corbett 1994, 203)?

Feelings of confusion about the path of cause and effect in these interactions likely stems from the fact that an improviser's attention is split between several distinct targets at any given moment during a piece.[23] Players are simultaneously listening, composing, and performing. Listening takes place in several directions as players listen to themselves as well as the rest of the ensemble. Self-directed listening focuses on the relationship between what they intend to play and what comes out of their instruments.[24] Partner-directed listening analyzes how players are interacting with one another.[25] In addition to listening, players are also conceptualizing new musical material as the piece proceeds, a task with demands similar to the act of composing notated music, but with the added complexity of a real-time constraint (Nettl 1974; Pressing 1988). To make matters more complicated, many improvisers choose to make music with tools that are either physically unstable and cumbersome (i.e., objects stacked up precariously and thus prone to toppling) or using sound-production techniques with unpredictable results (i.e., extended techniques for which sonic results are often uncertain).

An improviser handles all these tasks at every moment. Indeed, the complexity and mutual interference of music-making tasks contribute to what improvisers find exciting about this practice. For the ethnographer, though, the clutter in the attentional field means that even sober, experienced improvisers may have a foggy recollection of what took place in a performance. As a result, it is not surprising that they may have little to say about a performance immediately after its conclusion, other than a handful of hackneyed expressions of perfunctory praise.

Maxine and Morten

By stark contrast, offering players the opportunity to abruptly halt a performance's progress allows the experience of social interaction through musical improvisation to come into focus. That is, it enables researchers and performers to highlight a particular musical phenomenon and understand how that phenomenon may structure social experience for its participants, as well as the values inscribed in these practices of interaction (see Banerji 2018). It facilitates an investigation of how "cultures" are at least partly defined by experiences of face-to-face interaction for their participants.

As was the case for many other improvisers, the encounter between Maxine and "Morten," a white Norwegian double-bassist, illustrated the many ways that this methodology greatly enables subjects to articulate specific moments of experience in social interaction. In a sparsely populated, quiet, industrial neighborhood on the southern side of Berlin, I met with Morten at my studio one morning in December of 2015 so he could play with Maxine and offer his feedback on how the system compared to a human improviser. As I have typically done since 2009, I invited Morten to play with Maxine as long as he liked for each piece, making it clear that he was welcome to stop in the middle of the piece to comment on whatever he wanted to. Like many others, Morten simply let the first two pieces, each lasting around six minutes, come to their typical conclusion—a mutual silence between him and Maxine, and a shift in the focus of his bespectacled eyes toward me and away from the bridge of his bass, which was the usual target of his gaze when playing.

Generally speaking, Morten found the system's reaction to his playing in these first two pieces to be a bit strange, but it was not necessarily stranger than what he might find playing with a human musician for the first time. Nevertheless, Morten felt that the system had an inability to commit to particular ideas. It would introduce new material, which would often prompt Morten to respond by producing similar sonic textures and structures. Rather than staying on the same idea, as Morten might have preferred, Maxine kept shifting to something new.

These comments helped to shed light on the expectations that improvisers had for one another in the course of musical interaction, especially given their nearly pious commitment to acting as if such preferences do not exist. Still, it was difficult to pinpoint precisely which moments in the piece Morten had in mind when he criticized Maxine's performance. For example, regarding the second piece, Morten referred to a moment when the system introduced a new idea, onomatopoeically describing it as a "ding" or "long" tone ((▶) Audio Example 1).[26] In listening to the piece, it is difficult to precisely locate when this new idea occurred, if it did at all.[27] However, the experiential truth Morten reported at the end of the piece still holds; how he framed his experience is surely how it "was" for him in his consciousness and memory. Be that as it may, the question remained: What moment was he referring to?[28]

Morten's experience of such moments became far clearer in the third take, when he finally elected to stop mid-performance to make a comment. In this piece, Maxine was played using a timbral setup closely resembling an electric guitar with numerous electronic effects pedals. Just prior to the stop, both Morten and Maxine had been focused on a sonic terrain of relatively inharmonic sounds.[29] In the midst of this, Maxine played a handful of clear, resonant notes in a sequence. To Morten, this suggested an intention of moving to a new sonic arena, one in which melodic material and pitch movement would be foregrounded. After a few moments in which Morten and Maxine shifted to this more melodic approach, Maxine turned back to the more abstract texture, frantically winding around its virtual fretboard and playing mangled tones ((▶) Audio Example 2).

A few seconds after Maxine's turn back to the previous texture, Morten signaled for me to stop the piece:

M: Yeah, actually that—that's a place where . . .
R: Yeah, please.
M: where, where it introduces an idea, that's super clear, and then I kind of went along with it and then it kind of *grah!* just went off in a, a completely different direction!

I have had many similar experiences playing with Maxine. Often, when Maxine suggests a new direction within the overall evolution of the piece, I follow this suggestion.

Nevertheless, Maxine frequently makes yet another abrupt change like a player who is suddenly disinterested in pursuing what they have just suggested. After I briefly shared these experiences, Morten continued:

> M: A minute before that I was thinking "Ah, it would be great if it would just like, you know, kind of just break off what it does and then . . . maybe throw in a completely different idea" . . . I find [that] super stimulating as an improviser. If you're playing with somebody who just stops, you know, in the middle of [an idea] . . . where *you* wanted to continue, but then the other guy just . . . breaks off, and then suddenly like throws in something else that forces you to like refocus your whole . . .
>
> R: Yeah
>
> M: . . . idea, and then it kind of in a way did that . . . but then it didn't follow up on it, which . . .
>
> R: Right
>
> M: . . . would have been great . . . I think.

Breakdown

Morten described a very specific dimension of experience in this situation. He did more than just describe the way the situation appeared, sounded, and felt as a whole, though these elements are surely present in the narrative he offers. He also described the experience of a *variance* between how events proceed and his expectations for how they should be. This variance is a thoroughgoing feature of the experience as a whole.

Inasmuch as Morten's engagement with Maxine elicited commentary on what free improvisation is, not as practice but as experience, it also created an opportunity to understand structures of experience more generally. In post-Heideggerian thought, the form of experience Morten described falls into the broad category of "breakdown" (Heidegger [1926] 1967, §16; H. L. Dreyfus 1991, 70–83).[30] In such moments, the givenness and routine quality of everyday action is interrupted for some reason; in turn, the interruption leads a subject to become more aware of a variety of taken-for-granted features of their existence, experience, and embodiment than they would be in the course of smooth, undisturbed, habitual action. Whereas one might have never reflected on or questioned the nature of certain actions because they are utterly regular and basic to one's typical way of dealing with the world, breakdown prompts a kind of reflection about what those actions are, why one is engaged in them, and why they tend to take place the way that they do.[31] In Morten's case, Maxine's behavior and its deviance from his expectations prompted him to reflect on what it means to make music of this kind with another human being. While Morten would not likely reflect on what defines a person as a performative, interactive, co-present being in the world, Maxine's nonhuman status enables him to reflect on his assumptions about how the humanness of another being's presence signifies itself to him in a typical encounter.

Though it is often glossed as a single concept, breakdown refers to three different kinds of disturbance and three different ways that human beings deal with such disturbances. Each of these three is relevant not only to Morten's meeting with Maxine but also to any and all practices where improvisatory modes of action take place. In the situation of "conspicuousness" (*die Auffälligkeit*),[32] action is interrupted or takes place in a way other than expected, such that it prompts no reflection on the nature of the action itself; the problem emerges but is immediately solved. For example, a rock drummer's unaccompanied solo break drags or rushes, but the rest of the band comes back in precisely as expected because the drummer clearly indicates where the downbeat or other anchoring temporal location should be. In the situation of "obstinacy" (*die Aufdringlichkeit*), a more significant interruption takes place. Coping requires thought and effort. This thought and effort prompts a momentary reflection on the way action routinely takes place, so that the problem can be addressed. For example, consider the situation in which the drummer's solo break does more than just drag or rush; a whole beat is added or inserted, thereby requiring the group to think fast and decide how to deal with the gaffe to keep a smooth flow to the performance.

In the situation of obtrusiveness (*die Aufsässigkeit*), action comes to a halt. This situation prompts a more pronounced reflection on the nature of the action, its necessity, and why the routine manner of executing it is so easily accepted. In our second example, the inaccuracy of the drummer's break may result in one of two things: it either sends the band into a (hopefully) short period of emergency regrouping procedures, so that the form of the song is preserved or at least reinstated; this would be an example of obstinacy. If the band stops entirely, unable to make sense of how to proceed in the moment, the situation could be characterized as obtrusive. As a consequence, the drummer may also be relieved of their duties indefinitely, or the band may discuss whether giving the drummer a solo is worth the risk.

Morten's interruption of his third piece with Maxine exemplifies obtrusiveness. Events proceeded in a manner that displeased him or upset his expectations. He called action to a halt. Together, we reflected on why Maxine is a frustrating player to work with, a conversation that also led us to discuss what makes a good playing partner. Without Maxine's obtrusiveness, we might not have reflected on a routine and taken-for-granted aspect of improvisatory musical interaction and tacit expectations about how these interactions should occur—specifically, the expectation that the player who introduces new material should commit to the ideas they have just introduced, especially when other players implicitly assent to this shift in direction through their sonic choices after the initiating player's suggestion. With Maxine, this expectation was not met because the system did not continue in the direction it suggested, even as Morten accepted the musical suggestion himself. The fact that Maxine declined to do what we both might have expected led us to consider what we desire from the conduct of another improvising musician in this context.

But beyond the obtrusive way that Maxine played tricks on its human collaborators, Morten's commentary on the system's behavior also suggests that the less drastic forms of breakdown—conspicuousness and obstinacy—are also common elements of playing with other improvisers. In fact, these two forms of breakdown may be intrinsic to improvisation. In cases of conspicuous breakdown, one player's actions require others to quickly move on to a different musical idea. In such cases, an individual's intended or achieved course of action is one that they come to feel is inappropriate or undesired by others; they shift course, but the shift requires little or no active cognitive labor. These moments do not prompt improvisers to reconsider the basic grounding principles of the practice of free improvisation. In Morten's case, conspicuousness takes place in the moments where Maxine changes the direction of the piece; here, Morten is prompted to move on to new material, but this shift hardly requires reflective thinking on his part. It simply happens.

Likewise, obstinacy takes place when an improviser notes that things have gone awry, whether with Maxine or another human being, and momentarily thinks about how to proceed. A brief reflection on the way things have been taking place passes through the improviser's conscious awareness, and a new course of action is chosen. It is often the case in an improvisatory practice that it is not clear how one should respond to the situation, especially if another player engages in actions one is not expecting; this lack of clarity prompts a brief moment of active reflection about how to proceed.

Ultimately, the encounter with Maxine invites an elaboration of the post-Heideggerian concept of breakdown. The three subcategories of breakdown retain their utility as a means of distinguishing between various moments when routine action is interrupted. However, Morten's commentary on Maxine suggests the three-fold distinction is rather precarious. In other words, a moment of obtrusiveness could easily have been one of mere obstinacy or conspicuousness. The instability of the distinction stems from the fact that the category of obtrusiveness refers to moments when action cannot be continued and in which neither quick coping nor brief, deliberative course correction is possible, as is the case in moments of conspicuousness or obstinacy, respectively. The obvious question raised by this distinction is whether in a given situation it is permissible or even possible for an actor to discontinue their action. For example, in many performance practices before an audience, it is rather exceptional for performers to stop before the conclusion of the piece, however "piece" is defined. Similarly, it may not be possible for an actor to engage in even a brief moment of self-reflective coping in order to handle what Heidegger describes as an instance of obstinacy.

Whether a moment of breakdown turns out to be obtrusive, obstinate, or conspicuous depends on whether the structure of the actor's present activities allows them to stop action entirely or pause to think about how to proceed. When cessation of action is possible, obtrusiveness is possible. When deliberation is possible, obstinacy is possible. When neither are allowed, conspicuousness is the only form of breakdown that takes place. Going back to Morten's experience, the encounter with Maxine and the fact that it uniquely enabled him to feel comfortable stopping the action allowed for breakdown to take the form of obtrusiveness, rather than mere conspicuousness or obstinacy. Likewise, because obtrusiveness brings action to a halt, it further invites the subject to speak more directly about what they experienced or at least attempt to verbally assemble an account of that experiential moment.

In Search of Obtrusiveness

In terms of field methodologies, the privileging of obtrusiveness afforded by the encounter between an artificial social agent and its human counterparts enables an ethnographer to more closely examine a subject's moment-to-moment experiential, first-person engagement with the world. While Heidegger's writings have enabled his posthumous interpreters to further theorize breakdown, that work still leaves open the question of how a social scientist might empirically examine such experiences. In the way that Heidegger describes them, the various forms of breakdown sound almost as if they would be readily apparent and perceptible; that is, an ethnographer would hardly struggle to identify them in the course of fieldwork.

Indeed, breakdown takes place all the time. Insofar as improvisation is a ubiquitous dimension of everyday action (see Lewis and Piekut 2016), it gives rise to the ubiquity of breakdown. Aside from the cataclysmic disruption of obtrusiveness, however, moments of breakdown are hardly perceptible because of the fluent coping that is integral to routine human functioning in the world. Though they do not draw on the Heideggerian notion of breakdown, a variety of theories and empirical observations of social action, within and beyond music, sustain this thinking (Goffman 1967; Schegloff et al. 1977; Brinner 1995). That breakdown takes place cannot be equated with the notion that breakdown is easily recalled or observed.

On the one hand, the fact that an encounter with Maxine elicits an improviser's account of their experience of social interaction is a product of the specific ideological legacies cooked into the history and practice of free improvisation. Improvisers in this scene deeply value freedom and egalitarianism. This leads to their abstention from commentary on what they experience as they improvise. On the other hand, it is not at all uncommon for individuals to undergo a broad range of forms of breakdown in the midst of daily goings-on with others. Because people are primed to create smooth social interactions, they rarely comment upon those moments of breakdown, or even recall them. This is hardly unique to forms of musicking which are self-consciously understood as "improvisatory"; rather, it is an essential feature of the improvisatory nature of everyday life, within music or beyond.

As is the case with the feedback interview or participant observation, the encounter with an artificial social interactant provides no means of directly accessing what a subject experiences and how the world manifests itself to that individual's consciousness. Several forms of distance remain. The subject articulates their experience in words; while these words give a sense of the experience they describe, they are at best just a close approximation. Even though encounters with Maxine allow one to stop mid-performance and immediately comment on any element of what one experiences, there is always at least a slight delay between the onset of that experiential now and the moment that the experiential contents of one's state of being are then related to a researcher verbally. While Morten explicitly discusses a kind of irksome experience in improvisation he might not talk about otherwise, his description of his experience still leaves out a lot of the detail that would be helpful in gaining a better understanding of what certain moments might have been like for him.

Such limitations aside, these encounters enable a proximity to the subject's experience that has not been possible through other methods currently practiced within the arena of phenomenological ethnography. It is nonetheless quite easy to understand why most ethnographers of music and social practice have not pursued this approach. Given the centrality of computational skills in creating a system like Maxine and the fact that ethnographers are rarely, if ever, trained to do such work, it would appear that this method is a novelty that can be pursued by the handful of polymaths possessing the rare combination of capacities it requires.

As daunting as this may seem, there are many options for ethnographers interested in integrating such methods into their fieldwork. Aside from designing such systems themselves, music researchers might collaborate with scholars who possess the requisite skills, or they might focus on virtual re-embodiments of musical practice as research objects in and of themselves. For example, ethnomusicologist James Kippen and computer scientist Bernard Bel's "Bol Processor" project is similar to my fieldwork with Maxine (Kippen and Bel 1989). Built to create improvisatory rhythmic patterns according to the stylistic framework of North Indian tabla performance, Kippen and Bel used the Bol Processor to elicit commentary from expert musicians on the validity of the system's output with respect to their understanding of the norms of this practice.[33]

Besides participating in collaborations such as this, the opportunity to pursue such fieldwork is available to any scholar interested in the ever increasing population of non-human musicians, which re-embody a variety of longstanding musical practices. The purchase of this method for phenomenological work on music has already been recently established (McGraw 2016). Other ethnographers have also illustrated how the study of AI performers provides insights into the "human" qualities of human music-making (Eidsheim 2009; Kenmochi 2010; Wilf 2013). Nevertheless, there remains much to be explored in this area.

Despite "Impossibility"

Subjecting virtual musicians like Maxine to the critique of their human counterparts presents numerous possibilities for gaining a better understanding of what musicians experience in the course of music as a social practice. Nevertheless, a basic distance remains between a subject's lived experience and what a researcher understands of that subject's encounter with the world. There is certainly far more to phenomenological ethnography than simply seeking a vivid sense of what another subject experiences. As Dan Zahavi (2019) has recently emphasized, an examination of "what things are like" is only one means in the broader phenomenological project of uncovering the variety of ways that experiences are assembled, the conditions that enable their possibility, and how the experiential revealing of the world comes to differ from a rationalist, scientific account of things as they are.

Be that as it may, there can be no question that any and all efforts that researchers make to improve their ability to understand precisely what a subject experiences in the moment will help to produce more holistic accounts of structures of conscious experience. The fact that it is impossible for a researcher to experience precisely what the other subject does should not be taken to mean that scholars must give up the pursuit of field methods that might enable this kind of understanding. If anything, the difficulties of knowing what others experience should prompt ethnographically trained phenomenologists to experiment with approaches that may allow for a more intimate, vivid conception of how a social environment is revealed in the experience of a particular individual (Desjarlais 2005; Desjarlais and Throop 2011).

As Morten's encounter with Maxine demonstrates, the critique of artificial reembodiments of human presence serves as a vital, yet almost completely unexplored, means of doing ethnographic phenomenology. Though the methodology put to work here actively foregrounds such encounters, it builds on a longer arc of criticism begun by Hubert Dreyfus (1972, 1992, 2007), which uses the failure of AI research in order to illustrate the validity of the thinking of a variety of phenomenological considerations of human existence and consciousness. There is a fascinating irony here. While almost constantly pointing out how the project of artificial intelligence research was a colossal and astronomically expensive failure, Dreyfus's critique of AI inadvertently demonstrated how incredibly useful these failures were as case studies for corroborating phenomenological ideas about the structures of human experience.

In his work, Dreyfus noted the starkly disembodied conception of human consciousness that drove "symbolic" AI, which largely assumed that human knowledge took the exclusive form of explicit, propositional statements. While the AI community of the early 1990s gradually accepted the fundamental flaws of the symbolic paradigm, Dreyfus pointed out that Merleau-Ponty ([1945] 2002) and Polanyi ([1966] 2009) had already offered a number of reasons why such a conception of knowledge was flawed (H. L. Dreyfus 1972, 147–167). Human knowledge only partially takes an explicit, declarative form. A great deal of what human beings "know" manifests itself in the form of what Merleau-Ponty understood as embodied knowledge (or what Polanyi called "tacit knowledge")—implicit, bodily understandings that are part of a person's experience but that exist on the edge of their attention and are often difficult to articulate and describe. Rather ironically, the failure of the disembodied approach of symbolic AI served as a rather vivid illustration of Merleau-Ponty's ideas about embodied consciousness, which he theorized decades earlier.

Another irony manifests itself in the disembodied quality of Dreyfus's commentary on AI itself. Despite his emphasis on the problems of a disembodied approach to understanding consciousness, his critique of AI was not based in an embodied encounter with thinking machines themselves. Rather it was based in his close readings of the design rationale of AI researchers who built these systems.[34]

It is one thing to critique AI as a failure to comprehend the nature of human consciousness or particular human practices; that any and all such representations or performative re-presencings of human practice will fail is inevitable, be it an ethnographer's attempt to faithfully render their subjects' experiences in words (Feld 1987; Brettell 1993; Fassin 2015; Abu-Lughod 2016), a filmmaker's attempt to depict them artistically in moving images (Madison 2005), or a programmer's attempt to model them in computer code. It is quite another, however, to carefully examine how and why such representations— textual, filmic, sonic, performative, or algorithmic—fail when they come into contact with the human beings they purport to represent. For all the richness and creativity of Dreyfus's critiques of AI, they only begin to suggest the potential that lies in a critique of artificial social interactants from the perspective of their interlocutors; they are only a small step in the broader project of exploiting the failures of such technologies as a means of ethnographically examining the structures of experience.

In addition to revealing details of the person's moment-to-moment experiences, the research methodology described in this chapter illustrates how local notions of social prestige challenge the efficacy of phenomenological ethnography. Return to the case of the double-bassist Torsten. Like many other improvisers over the past half century, Torsten values freedom and egalitarianism as basic ethical principles of his coexistence with other players. This constrains how and when he feels free to be honest about what he experiences when working with other musicians, especially when those experiences are undesired. To openly discuss or give an unambiguous indication of his thoughts and feelings (e.g., scowling angrily, rather than having a neutral gaze) would be to indicate to others that he does not respect the individualistic notions of freedom that ground this domain of artistic practice. Spurning this value risks a loss of social prestige among other improvisers.

In the scenes of free improvisation where I have conducted fieldwork, the values of freedom and egalitarianism create a barrier to frank discussions of how individuals experience social interaction with other performers in the course of music-making. Beyond the case of Torsten, this means that ethnographers must be attentive to the types of reported experiences that are deemed socially valuable in a given cultural world. For example, in many social spheres, the claim of a connection to the divine is highly prized. Those who can make such a claim are often the beneficiaries of greater social status and privilege. While not denying that some sincerely believe in the truth of their experiences with the divine, a measure of skepticism about such reports is warranted, as it is at least minimally plausible that the experiences a person may describe are informed by their desire to acquire or maintain prestige. Local social values shape what kinds of experiences an ethnographer's interlocutors will likely report. If an ethnographer is interested in what people experience, then they may want to find ways for their interlocutors to be frank about their experiences without the pressure to assert that their experiences accord with local social values.

The use of the methodology described in this essay does more than enable ethnographers to examine experience in novel ways; it pushes them to ask the question "what is a human being?" This methodology pushes the question beyond the issue of biological classification into the domain of performance: "What is 'humanness' as a dimension of performance?" Returning to Heidegger's maxim, "ontology is only possible through phenomenology" (Heidegger [1927] 1996, 31); an encounter with a quasi-being like Maxine is not about what human beings "are" from a scientific viewpoint. Rather, it is about what makes one human being feel as though they are in the presence of another, even if the "other" is not a human being at all. Given that free improvisation, like any musical practice, is a specific cultural form, the specificity of the encounters that occur there highlights the ways in which the performative definition of "humanness" is always culturally specific. What might be regarded as a more "human" performance in one cultural context may be regarded as less so in another. The use of AI in ethnographic fieldwork as described in this essay presents a novel method of enabling humanists and social scientists to examine how "humanness" is conceptualized in terms of specific features of social performance in real time. A method that allows the ethnographer to examine how participants of a specific social world conceptualize "humanness" can only further enable them to understand the phenomenology of music and social life as culture.

Notes

1. This does not mean that an analysis of the structures of a subject's experience is the sole focus of phenomenology, either. As an experience in and of itself, an ethnographer's encounter with persons, situations, and environments in fieldwork is also a body of sensations, actions, and feelings that are also an important object of analysis, especially since these experiences are the basis for the ethnographer's claims about social life in their field site. It is just as important for the ethnographer to analyze the structure of their own experiences of fieldwork as it is for them to examine these structures in the everyday lived experience of their ethnographic subjects (for further reflection on these issues, see Rice 2008; Titon 2008).

2. Where many qualitative researchers assume that first-person experience is the primary goal of phenomenology, philosopher Dan Zahavi (2019) has recently pointed out that this is a misreading of why first-person accounts really matter for a consideration of structures of experience. They are of crucial importance, but primarily as a waypoint in a broader

endeavor to understand the relationship between *how* the world seems to the subject and *why* the world seems so.

3. Harris Berger, David VanderHamm, and Friedlind Riedel (2023) review many of these in their overview of phenomenological approaches to the ethnography of music.

4. This is not to say that language completely fails to transmit what someone experiences, but rather that the problems of self-reported accounts tend to raise more questions than answers. The questions they raise are ones that the researcher might not have encountered otherwise, and so interviews and other verbal descriptions of individual experience remain quite valuable alongside other phenomenological techniques in ethnographic fieldwork (see Good 1994; Mattingly 1998). A subject's narrativization of experience may not be objectively verifiable, but it is often a fruitful path to a researcher's understanding of an individual's encounter with the world.

5. Reflecting on the relationship between participant-observation and phenomenological ethnography of music cultures, Rice (2008) and Titon (2008) make similar claims.

6. In a rather provocative way, Bakan's approach to phenomenological ethnography (1999) embraces the divergence between what a subject and a researcher experience as they participate in the same sociocultural practice in order to suggest that the ethnographer is ultimately only qualified to speak on their own experiences rather than the experiences of their ethnographic subjects.

7. This technique is identical to elicitation methods used in visual anthropology (De Maaker 2000; Harper 2002). Without explicitly referring to their fieldwork technique by either of these terms, a number of scholars have used similar approaches (Feld 1987; Widdess 1994). In many ways, the feedback interview functions as a critique of the epistemological validity of ethnographic participant observation. One can see and hear the bodily behavior of one's interlocutors while participating in actions with them, but this does not mean that one can accurately infer what those individuals experienced in those moments (see Stone 1982).

8. Berger's work with his interlocutors raises dozens of new questions for a phenomenological perspective on the concept of tonality, and it invites music theorists to move away from the objectivist stance that tonality is determinate once pitch values and durations have been established. Taking a pragmatic view, his work suggests that the tonal center of gravity of a given musical passage is a product of a player's embodied encounter with sound in real time.

9. In another moment, Berger notes that a player became "exasperated" (Berger 1999, 151) when he was asked to comment on what he was paying attention to at various moments in a performance. As a skilled and experienced performer working night after night, he did not reflect on what he was doing in this manner.

10. Though AI systems are built with this pretension, it is never to be assumed that they are perfectly successful in evincing a human presence through their interactive or sensory qualities.

11. This point applies mainly to virtual social agents, which are referred by a variety of names, such as "androids," "embodied conversational agents," or "social robots." While these kinds of systems differ in various ways, they are all designed to engage in social interaction with human beings as they would with one another. While the development of such agents comprises a large swath of research in AI and the related field of artificial life (AL), both fields are far wider than this. For example, some AI researchers seek to create technologies that do humanlike thinking but do not engage in humanlike interaction. That said, even

these AI agents can be understood as modeling social interaction, as the productive tasks that they execute are meant to supplant forms of human action that would take place as a collaboration between individual humans.

12. Bernard Bel and James Kippen's "Bol Processor" algorithmically models the Hindustani classical practice of using vocables as a framework for generating and describing rhythmic sequences; it is an important predecessor for the methodologies I describe in this chapter (see Kippen and Bel 1989, and several other publications from these two in the same time period). Their project was less concerned with modeling musical interaction or understanding musical experience than it was with understanding the principles by which improvisers compose rhythmic sequences as they perform.

13. Superficially, this method resembles the ubiquitous social practice of teacher-student interaction. In a music lesson, the teacher typically reserves the right to stop musical action in order to offer feedback and commentary. The crucial difference, however, is that the commentary a teacher gives is rarely concerned with describing their own consciousness; rather, the commentary is intended to instruct the student in how to improve their acquisition of the practice. Nevertheless, a teacher-student encounter could well serve as a productive means of pursuing forms of ethnographic research practice with a view to eliciting first-person experience. Aside from a handful of examples (Rice 1995; Downey 2008), ethnographers have yet to fully explore this possibility.

14. While the name of the system is gendered, I did not intentionally design Maxine to perform a particular gender in social interaction. As I explain elsewhere, I spent several months referring to the system as "Max" before renaming it "Maxine" after a literary inspiration (Banerji 2010). While improvisers encountering the system know it by a gendered name, not all accepted this gendering. Some refer to Maxine in their commentary as "it," while others (particularly Francophones, who often hear the system's name as "Maxime") refer to it with the gendered pronoun "he." The pronouns that a player uses to refer to Maxine may reflect how they experience Maxine's gender, but this complex issue is beyond the scope of this essay.

15. Since Lewis's pioneering work, many other designers have created AI systems that function as fellow performers of free improvisation in collaboration with human performers (Blackwell and Bentley 2002; Assayag and Dubnov 2004; Hsu 2005; Casal and Morelli 2007; Collins 2008; Young 2008; Bown 2011; Yee-King 2011; Carey 2012; Linson et al. 2015). Design of these systems differs drastically. Overall, however, the systems are all built to function as fellow performers in collaboration with a human performer of musical free improvisation.

16. Naturally, I had my own thoughts on this matter, having developed the system as a duo partner with myself on saxophone. Given the obvious bias that I have in evaluating the system, I thought it wise to seek the feedback of other players, particularly those with no interest in music computation. Regrettably, it is all too rare that the evaluation of such systems includes the feedback of musicians other than the designer.

17. These observations are based on my ethnographic work as a performer (saxophonist) and participant in scenes of free improvisation in Chicago, Berlin, and San Francisco over the past decade, and I assert that they hold for this performance genre more generally. I conducted fieldwork in Chicago from mid-2007 to fall 2010, in the Bay Area from fall 2010 to summer 2014, and in Berlin during May 2010, summer 2012, and from fall 2014 to fall 2016. Of these three scenes, Berlin's was the by far the most active in terms of concerts taking place per evening and the number of players residing in the city (see Arthurs 2015);

the Chicago and Bay Area scenes were also quite active, but less so compared to Berlin. The choice of these field sites was a mixture of convenience and intention. Since I was already a performer in the Chicago scene, I used this as an opportunity to conduct ethnographic fieldwork. When I relocated to the Bay Area to pursue a doctoral degree at the University of California, Berkeley, I began conducting fieldwork there as well. By contrast, Berlin was a field site I chose far more deliberately and largely due to its historic importance as a hub of free improvisation from the 1970s onward and the fact that it currently boasts what is arguably the largest concentration of performers of free improvisation in the world, thereby making it far easier for me to find research participants.

18. One or two players may be responsible for arranging the gathering or ensemble. Even so, players tend to deny that this puts them in a position of leadership. Whether or not implicit leadership or hierarchy emerges is a different matter entirely.

19. Despite claims that free improvisation is unconstrained by musical style, a half century of recordings and performances, mostly in western Europe, North America, and Japan, reveal a few basic trends in the stylistic contours of free improvisation: the avoidance of functional harmony and pulse-based organizational structures in rhythm, and the privileging of the exploration of the timbral possibilities of one's instrument, voice, or sound-making apparatus (see Backstrom 2013). Of the scenes in which I conducted fieldwork, approaches varied considerably. Some focused on historically common performance techniques and timbres for their instrument; others attempted to redefine the sound of their instrumental apparatus by using extended techniques, "preparation" (i.e., making mechanical modifications to their instruments, as in the practice of prepared piano), and other physical or electronic manipulations of the sound. In terms of stylistic range, few players were solely active in free improvisation, with jazz, rock, and Euro-American elite music being the main genres that these players regularly performed.

20. This is not to say that no performer of free improvisation performs notated or otherwise composed music. Indeed, this kind of work is common among many proponents of free improvisation. Nor is it to deny that improvisers occasionally use notated compositions in their improvisatory work. These exceptions aside, the practice of free improvisation is characterized by the kind of abeyance of composition described here.

21. Throughout, I refer to all of my interlocutors with pseudonyms. This essay focuses on only a handful of the more than two hundred improvisers with whom I have conducted fieldwork, nearly one hundred of whom have played with Maxine. Rather than try to address the breadth of their remarks, I focus on a few improvisers, an approach that offers a sense of depth that would be lost in a broader review. Their commentary is largely representative of the many players I have worked with in the course of my fieldwork.

22. Not all improvisers chose to stop playing in the middle of a piece and comment on their experience. In many cases, the player would end their improvisation with Maxine in the same way that they would with human players—by arriving at a prolonged mutual silence and making gestural and gaze-directional cues that signal the piece's end. There is nothing about Maxine as a system that gives improvisers a unique ability to stop in the middle of a performance. A similar approach could be taken in private playing situations among human improvisers, wherein players would be invited to stop when they have something to say. However, to speak up, the players would need to be comfortable with openly disclosing their sentiments about the interaction, a type of disclosure that improvisers are typically unwilling to make.

23. This is quite similar to the cognitive demands of listening in real time while burdened by other tasks, as described by ethnographers who have studied other practices of improvisation (see Berliner 1994; Berger 1999; Duranti 2009) and other types of ensemble performance (Bregman 1994; Keller 2001).

24. This is not unlike the self-directed listening that is integral to everyday speech (see Levelt 1983).

25. For further commentary on the analytical nature of listening as an element of musical interaction in free improvisation, see commentary from George E. Lewis (quoted in Chadabe 1997, 300).

26. It is not uncommon for seasoned performers of free improvisation to refer to various timbral types onomatopoeically. This differs from the practice that Thomas Porcello documented in his work on professional recording studios, where musicians and engineers tended to avoid onomatopoeic descriptions of timbre (Porcello 2004). The use of such descriptive strategies is quite common among improvisers, a factor which lends further difficulty to the understanding of which moment in a piece they might be referring to.

27. For example, there was a moment in the piece when it was difficult, even from a third-party perspective, to tell whether it was Maxine or Morton who had introduced a "new idea." Such moments resonate with Evan Parker's claim (referenced previously) that there is a sense of ambiguity inherent in highly improvisatory musical interactions.

28. This question remains especially open given that there are several candidates for the kind of shift or exchange he described.

29. An inharmonic sound is one that has a number of components with relatively constant frequencies, but those frequencies do not aggregate into the production of a clearly audible pitch (see Smalley 1997).

30. The term "breakdown" is often attributed to Heidegger (Koschmann et al. 1998), even though no such term appears in the two widely read English translations of *Being and Time*. Further, the passages commonly referenced for this concept do not use any German term that closely corresponds to the English word "breakdown." This term is therefore best understood as a handy refashioning of Heidegger's thinking, which was developed most prominently in Hubert Dreyfus's commentary on *Being and Time* (H. L. Dreyfus 1991); it is for this reason that I use the term "post-Heideggerian" to describe this concept. "Breakdown" is often discussed as if it were a unified concept in Heidegger's work (see Zigon 2007, for example), but a more careful reading of Heidegger reveals that it is collection of sub-concepts, each of which describes more specific ways that human beings respond to disturbance.

31. The kind of reflection prompted by breakdown is not unlike the kind of sudden awareness of the taken-for-granted nature of the social world precipitated by Harold Garfinkel's "breaching experiments" (1967, 35–75), in which a rupture of everyday social norms is used as a way of examining the constitution and performance of norms themselves.

32. The two translations of *Sein und Zeit* in English (Heidegger [1927] 1962, [1927] 1996) concur on the English rendering of the German terms for the three forms of breakdown.

33. The "virtual gamelan" project at the Künstuniversität Graz also centered upon the design of an artificial ensemble of performers (Grupe 2008), though it is not clear if a similar elicitation method was used there.

34. Of course, this is not Dreyfus' fault. Given the disembodied nature of the early work in AI, opportunities for an embodied encounter with an AI were few and far between.

WORKS CITED

Abu-Lughod, Lila. 2016. "The Cross-Publics of Ethnography: The Case of 'the Muslimwoman.'" *American Ethnologist* 43 (4): 595–608.

Arthurs, Tom. 2015. "Improvised Music in Berlin 2012–13: A Brief Ethnographic Portrait." *Critical Studies in Improvisation/Études Critiques en Improvisation* 10 (2).

Assayag, Gérard, and Shlomo Dubnov. 2004. "Using Factor Oracles for Machine Improvisation." *Soft Computing* 8 (9): 604–610.

Austin, John Langshaw. 1962. *How to Do Things with Words*. London: Oxford University Press.

Backstrom, Melvin James. 2013. "The Field of Cultural Production and the Limits of Freedom in Improvisation." *Critical Studies in Improvisation/Études Critiques en Improvisation* 9 (1). https://doi.org/10.21083/csieci.v9i1.2147.

Bailey, Derek. (1980) 1993. *Improvisation: Its Nature and Practice in Music*. New York: Da Capo Press.

Bakan, Michael B. 1999. *Music of Death and New Creation: Experiences in the World of Balinese Gamelan Beleganjur*. Chicago: University of Chicago Press.

Banerji, Ritwik. 2010. "Maxine Banerji: The Mutually Beneficial Practices of Youth Development and Interactive Systems Development." *eContact! Journal of the Canadian Electroacoustic Community* 12 (3).

Banerji, Ritwik. 2012. "Maxine's Turing Test: A Player-Program as Co-ethnographer of Socio-aesthetic Interaction in Improvised Music." In *Proceedings of the 1st International Workshop on Musical Metacreation (MUME 2012)*, edited by Philippe Pasquier, Arne Eigenfeldt, and Oliver Bown, 2–7. Palo Alto, CA: AAAI Press.

Banerji, Ritwik. 2014. *Maxine and the Astromusicologist: Palmer Square*. Compact disc. San Diego: pfMentum.

Banerji, Ritwik. 2016. "Balancing Defiance and Cooperation: The Design and Human Critique of a Virtual Free Improviser." In *Proceedings of the International Computer Music Conference*, edited by Hans Timmermans, 48–53. Utrecht, Netherlands: HKU University of the Arts Utrecht.

Banerji, Ritwik. 2018. "De-instrumentalizing HCI: Social Psychology, Rapport Formation, and Interactions with Artificial Social Agents." In *New Directions in Third Wave Human-Computer Interaction*, edited by Michael Filimowicz and Veronika Tzankova, 43–66. Heidelberg, Germany: Springer Nature.

Becker, Howard S., and Blanche Geer. 1957. "Participant Observation and Interviewing: A Comparison." *Human Organization* 16 (3): 28–32.

Becker, Judith. 2009. "Ethnomusicology and Empiricism in the Twenty-First Century." *Ethnomusicology* 53 (3): 478–501.

Berger, Harris M. 1999. *Metal, Rock, and Jazz: Perception and the Phenomenology of Musical Experience*. Middletown, CT: Wesleyan University Press.

Berger, Harris M., David VanderHamm, and Friedlind Riedel. 2023. "Phenomenological Approaches in the History of Ethnomusicology." In *The Oxford Handbook of the Phenomenology of Music Cultures*, edited by Harris M. Berger, Friedlind Riedel, and David VanderHamm, 3–56. New York: Oxford University Press.

Berliner, Paul F. 1994. *Thinking in Jazz: The Infinite Art of Improvisation*. Chicago: University of Chicago Press.

Béteille, André. 1977. *Inequality among Men*. Oxford: Basil Blackwell.

Blackwell, Tim, and Peter Bentley. 2002. "Improvised Music with Swarms." In *Proceedings of the World Conference on Computational Intelligence*, 1462–1467. Piscataway, NJ: Institute of Electrical and Electronics Engineers (IEEE).

Boehm, Christopher. 1993. "Egalitarian Behavior and Reverse Dominance Hierarchy." *Current Anthropology* 34 (3): 227–254.

Borgo, David. 2002. "Synergy and Surrealestate: The Orderly Disorder of Free Improvisation." *Pacific Review of Ethnomusicology* 10 (1): 1–24.

Borgo, David. 2005. *Sync or Swarm: Improvising Music in a Complex Age*. New York: Continuum.

Bourdieu, Pierre. 1977. *Outline of a Theory of Practice*. Translated by Richard Nice. New York: Cambridge University Press.

Bown, Oliver. 2011. "Experiments in Modular Design for the Creative Composition of Live Algorithms." *Computer Music Journal* 35 (3): 73–85.

Bregman, Albert S. 1994. *Auditory Scene Analysis: The Perceptual Organization of Sound*. Cambridge, MA: MIT Press.

Brettell, Caroline, ed. 1993. *When They Read What We Write: The Politics of Ethnography*. Westport, CT: Bergin & Garvey.

Brinner, Benjamin. 1995. *Knowing Music, Making Music: Javanese Gamelan and the Theory of Musical Competence and Interaction*. Chicago: University of Chicago Press.

Carey, Benjamin. 2012. "Designing for Cumulative Interactivity: The _derivations System." In *Proceedings of the International Conference on New Interfaces for Musical Expression (NIME 2012)*, edited by Georg Essl, 1–4. Ann Arbor: University of Michigan.

Casal, David Plans, and Davide Morelli. 2007. "Remembering the Future: Applications of Genetic Co-evolution in Music Improvisation." In *Advances in Artificial Life: Proceedings of European Conference on Artificial Life 2007*, edited by Fernando Almeida e Costa, Luis Mateus Rocha, Ernesto Costa, Inman Harvey, and Antonio Coutinho, 1–6. Berlin and Heidelberg, Germany: Springer-Verlag.

Chadabe, Joel. 1997. *Electric Sound: The Past and Promise of Electronic Music*. Upper Saddle River, NJ: Prentice-Hall.

Collins, Nick. 2008. "Reinforcement Learning for Live Musical Agents." In *Proceedings of the International Computer Music Conference (ICMC)*, 1–8. Ann Arbor: Michigan Publishing.

Corbett, John. 1994. *Extended Play: Sounding Off from John Cage to Dr. Funkenstein*. Durham, NC: Duke University Press.

Corbett, John. 2016. *A Listener's Guide to Free Improvisation*. Chicago: University of Chicago Press.

De Maaker, Erik. 2000. "Integrating Ethnographic Research and Filmmaking: Video Elicitation for a Performance-Oriented Analysis of the Teyyam Ritual." *Visual Anthropology* 13 (2): 185–197.

Dennett, Daniel Clement. 1991. *Consciousness Explained*. Boston, MA: Little, Brown and Company.

Desjarlais, Robert. 2003. *Sensory Biographies: Lives and Deaths among Nepal's Yolmo Buddhists*. Berkeley: University of California Press.

Desjarlais, Robert. 2005. "Movement, Stillness: On the Sensory World of a Shelter for the Homeless Mentally Ill." In *Empire of the Senses: The Sensual Cultural Reader*, edited by David Howes, 369–379. Oxford: Berg.

Desjarlais, Robert, and C. Jason Throop. 2011. "Phenomenological Approaches in Anthropology." *Annual Review of Anthropology* 40: 87–102.

Dourish, Paul. 2006. "Implications for Design." In *Proceedings of the SIGCHI Conference on Human Factors in Computing Systems*, edited by Rebecca Grinter, Thomas Rodden, Paul Aoki, Ed Cutrell, Robin Jeffries, and Gary Olson, 541–550. New York: Association for Computing Machinery (ACM).

Downey, Greg. 2008. "Scaffolding Imitation in Capoeira: Physical Education and Enculturation in an Afro-Brazilian Art." *American Anthropologist* 110 (2): 204–213.

Dreyfus, Hubert L. 1972. *What Computers Can't Do: A Critique of Artificial Reason*. New York: Harper & Row.

Dreyfus, Hubert L. 1991. *Being-in-the-World: A Commentary on Heidegger's Being and Time, Division I*. Cambridge, MA: MIT Press.

Dreyfus, Hubert L. 1992. *What Computers Still Can't Do: A Critique of Artificial Reason*. Cambridge, MA: MIT Press.

Dreyfus, Hubert L. 2007. "Why Heideggerian AI Failed and How Fixing It Would Require Making It More Heideggerian." *Philosophical Psychology* 20 (2): 247–268.

Dreyfus, Stuart E., and Hubert L. Dreyfus. 1980. *A Five-Stage Model of the Mental Activities Involved in Directed Skill Acquisition*. Berkeley: Operations Research Center, University of California, Berkeley.

Duranti, Alessandro. 2009. "The Relevance of Husserl's Theory to Language Socialization." *Journal of Linguistic Anthropology* 19 (2): 205–226.

Edwards, Paul N. 1997. *The Closed World: Computers and the Politics of Discourse in Cold War America*. Cambridge, MA: MIT Press.

Eidsheim, Nina. 2009. "Synthesizing Race: Towards an Analysis of the Performativity of Vocal Timbre." *TRANS-Revista Transcultural de Música* 13: 1–9.

Fassin, Didier. 2015. "The Public Afterlife of Ethnography." *American Ethnologist* 42 (4): 592–609.

Feld, Steven. 1987. "Dialogic Editing: Interpreting How Kaluli Read Sound and Sentiment." *Cultural Anthropology* 2 (2): 190–210.

Forsythe, Diana. 2001. *Studying Those Who Study Us: An Anthropologist in the World of Artificial Intelligence*. Edited by David J. Hess. Stanford, CA: Stanford University Press.

Freeman, Jo. 1972. "The Tyranny of Structurelessness." *Berkeley Journal of Sociology* 17: 151–164.

Friedson, Steven M. 1996. *Dancing Prophets: Musical Experience in Tumbuka Healing*. Chicago: University of Chicago Press.

Garfinkel, Harold. 1967. *Studies in Ethnomethodology*. Englewood Cliffs, NJ: Prentice-Hall.

Geertz, Clifford. 1983. *Local Knowledge: Further Essays in Interpretive Anthropology*. New York: Basic Books.

Goffman, Erving. 1967. *Interaction Ritual: Essays on Face-to-Face Behavior*. Garden City, NY: Anchor Books.

Good, Byron J. 1994. *Medicine, Rationality and Experience: An Anthropological Perspective*. Cambridge: Cambridge University Press.

Grupe, Gerd, ed. 2008. *Virtual Gamelan Graz: Rules, Grammars, Modeling*. Aachen, Germany: Shaker Verlag.

Harper, Douglas. 2002. "Talking about Pictures: A Case for Photo Elicitation." *Visual Studies* 17 (1): 13–26.

Heidegger, Martin. (1926) 1967. *Sein und Zeit*. 11th ed. Tübingen, Germany: Max Niemeyer Verlag.

Heidegger, Martin. (1927) 1962. *Being and Time*. Translated by John Macquarrie and Edward Robinson. Oxford: Blackwell Publishers.

Heidegger, Martin. (1927) 1996. *Being and Time: A Translation of Sein und Zeit*. Translated by Joan Stambaugh. Albany: State University of New York Press.

Hickey, Maud. 2015. "Learning from the Experts: A Study of Free-Improvisation Pedagogues in University Settings." *Journal of Research in Music Education* 62 (4): 425–445.

Hsu, William. 2005. "Using Timbre in a Computer-Based Improvisation System." In *Proceedings of the International Computer Music Conference (ICMC)*. Ann Arbor: Michigan Publishing.

Husserl, Edmund. (1928) 1966. *The Phenomenology of Internal Time-Consciousness*. Translated by James S. Churchill. Bloomington: Indiana University Press.

Husserl, Edmund. (1931) 1960. *Cartesian Meditations*. Translated by Dorion Cairns. The Hague: Martinus Nijhoff.

Husserl, Edmund. 1989. *Ideas Pertaining to a Pure Phenomenology and Phenomenological Philosophy. Second Book: Studies in the Phenomenology of Constitution*. Translated by Richard Rojcewicz and André Schuwer. Dordrecht, Netherlands: Kluwer Academic Publishers.

Jackson, Michael D. 1996a. "Introduction: Phenomenology, Radical Empiricism, and Anthropological Critique." In *Things as They Are: New Directions in Phenomenological Anthropology*, edited by Michael D. Jackson, 1–50. Bloomington: Indiana University Press.

Jackson, Michael D, ed. 1996b. *Things as They Are: New Directions in Phenomenological Anthropology*. Bloomington: Indiana University Press.

Keller, Peter E. 2001. "Attentional Resource Allocation in Musical Ensemble Performance." *Psychology of Music* 29 (1): 20–38.

Kenmochi, Hideki. 2010. "VOCALOID and Hatsune Miku Phenomenon in Japan." In *Proceedings of the Interdisciplinary Workshop on Singing Voice of the International Speech Communication Association*, edited by Keikichi Hirose. Rundle Mall, Australia: Causal Productions.

Kippen, James, and Bernard Bel. 1989. "Can a Computer Help Resolve the Problem of Ethnographic Description?" *Anthropological Quarterly* 62 (3): 131–144.

Koschmann, Timothy, Kari Kuutti, and Larry Hickman. 1998. "The Concept of Breakdown in Heidegger, Leont'ev, and Dewey and Its Implications for Education." *Mind, Culture, and Activity* 5 (1): 25–41.

Levelt, Willem J. M. 1983. "Monitoring and Self-Repair in Speech." *Cognition* 14 (1): 41–104.

Levinas, Emmanuel. (1991) 1998. *Entre Nous: On Thinking-of-the-Other*. Translated by Michael B. Smith. Edited by Barbara Harshav. New York: Columbia University Press.

Lewis, George E. 1993. *Voyager*. Compact disc. Tokyo, Japan: Avant Records. Avan 014.

Lewis, George E. 1999. "Interacting with Latter-Day Musical Automata." *Contemporary Music Review* 18 (3): 99–112.

Lewis, George E. 2000. "Too Many Notes: Computers, Complexity and Culture in *Voyager*." *Leonardo Music Journal* 10: 33–39.

Lewis, George E., and Benjamin Piekut, eds. 2016. *The Oxford Handbook of Critical Improvisation Studies*. 2 vols. Oxford: Oxford University Press.

Linger, Daniel T. 2010. "What Is It Like to Be Someone Else?" *Ethos* 38 (2): 205–229.

Linson, Adam, Chris Dobbyn, George E. Lewis, and Robin Laney. 2015. "A Subsumption Agent for Collaborative Free Improvisation." *Computer Music Journal* 39 (4): 96–115.

MacDorman, Karl F., and Hiroshi Ishiguro. 2006. "The Uncanny Advantage of Using Androids in Cognitive and Social Science Research." *Interaction Studies* 7 (3): 297–337.

Madison, D. Soyini. 2005. *Critical Ethnography: Method, Ethics, and Performance*. Thousand Oaks, CA: Sage.

Maso, Ilja. 2001. "Phenomenology and Ethnography." In *Handbook of Ethnography*, edited by Paul Atkinson, Amanda Coffey, Sara Delamont, John Lofland, and Lyn Lofland, 136–144. London: Sage.

Mattingly, Cheryl. 1998. *Healing Dramas and Clinical Plots: The Narrative Structure of Experience*. Cambridge: Cambridge University Press.

McGraw, Andrew. 2016. "Atmosphere as a Concept for Ethnomusicology: Comparing the Gamelatron and Gamelan." *Ethnomusicology* 60 (1): 125–147.

Merleau-Ponty, Maurice. (1945) 2002. *Phenomenology of Perception*. Translated by Colin Smith. London: Routledge.

Nagel, Thomas. 1974. "What Is It Like to Be a Bat?" *Philosophical Review* 83 (4): 435–450.

Nettl, Bruno. 1974. "Thoughts on Improvisation: A Comparative Approach." *Musical Quarterly* 60 (1): 1–19.

Polanyi, Michael. (1966) 2009. *The Tacit Dimension*. Chicago: University of Chicago Press.

Porcello, Thomas. 2004. "Speaking of Sound: Language and the Professionalization of Sound-Recording Engineers." *Social Studies of Science* 34 (5): 733–758.

Pras, Amandine, Michael F. Schober, and Neta Spiro. 2017. "What about Their Performance Do Free Jazz Improvisers Agree Upon? A Case Study." *Frontiers in Psychology* 8: Article 966.

Pressing, Jeff. 1988. "Improvisation: Methods and Models." In *Generative Processes in Music*, edited by John Sloboda, 129–178. New York: Oxford University Press.

Rice, Timothy. 1995. "Understanding and Producing the Variability of Oral Tradition: Learning from a Bulgarian Bagpiper." *The Journal of American Folklore* 108 (429): 266–276.

Rice, Timothy. 2008. "Toward a Mediation of Field Methods and Field Experience in Ethnomusicology." In *Shadows in the Field: New Perspectives for Fieldwork in Ethnomusicology*, edited by Gregory Barz and Timothy J. Cooley, 42–61. New York: Oxford University Press.

Schegloff, Emanuel A., Gail Jefferson, and Harvey Sacks. 1977. "The Preference for Self-Correction in the Organization of Repair in Conversation." *Language* 53 (2): 361–382.

Smalley, Denis. 1997. "Spectromorphology: Explaining Sound-Shapes." *Organised Sound* 2 (2): 107–126.

Smith, Leo. 1973. *Notes: 8 Pieces. A New World Music—Creative Music*. New Haven, CT: Kiom.

Steinbeck, Paul. 2010. " 'Patience, Sincerity, and Consistency': Fred Anderson's Musical and Social Practices." *Critical Studies in Improvisation/Études Critiques en Improvisation* 6 (2).

Stone, Ruth M. 1982. *Let the Inside Be Sweet: The Interpretation of Music Event among the Kpelle of Liberia*. Bloomington: Indiana University Press.

Stone, Ruth M., and Verlon L. Stone. 1981. "Event, Feedback, and Analysis: Research Media in the Study of Music Events." *Ethnomusicology* 25 (2): 215–225.

Stone-MacDonald, Angela, and Ruth M. Stone. 2013. "The Feedback Interview and Video Recording in African Research Settings." *Africa Today* 59 (4): 3–22.

Suchman, Lucy A. 2006. *Human-Machine Reconfigurations: Plans and Situated Actions*. New York: Cambridge University Press.

Titon, Jeff Todd. 2008. "Knowing Fieldwork." In *Shadows in the Field: New Perspectives for Fieldwork in Ethnomusicology*, edited by Gregory Barz and Timothy J. Cooley, 25–41. New York: Oxford University Press.

Widdess, Richard. 1994. "Involving the Performers in Transcription and Analysis: A Collaborative Approach to Dhrupad." *Ethnomusicology* 38 (1): 59–79.

Wilf, Eitan Y. 2013. "Sociable Robots, Jazz Music, and Divination: Contingency as a Cultural Resource for Negotiating Problems of Intentionality." *American Ethnologist* 40 (4): 605–618.

Yee-King, Matthew John. 2011. "An Autonomous Timbre Matching Improviser." In *Proceedings of the International Computer Music Conference*, 122–125. Ann Arbor: Michigan Publishing.

Young, Michael. 2008. "NN Music: Improvising with a 'Living' Computer." In *Computer Music Modeling and Retrieval: Sense of Sounds*, edited by Richard Kronland-Martinet, Sølvi Ystad, and Kristoffer Jensen, 337–350. Berlin and Heidelberg, Germany: Springer.

Zahavi, Dan. 2004. "Husserl's Noema and the Internalism-Externalism Debate." *Inquiry* 47 (1): 42–66.

Zahavi, Dan. 2019. "Getting It Quite Wrong: Van Manen and Smith on Phenomenology." *Qualitative Health Research* 29 (6): 900–907.

Zigon, Jarrett. 2007. "Moral Breakdown and the Ethical Demand: A Theoretical Framework for an Anthropology of Moralities." *Anthropological Theory* 7 (2): 131–150.

CHAPTER 22

WAYS OF THE MIND

Toward a Phenomenological Ethnomusicology of Autistic Musical Experience

DOTAN NITZBERG AND MICHAEL B. BAKAN

In scholarly, clinical, and popular discourses alike, the objectification of autistic people is commonplace, and this is as true in the world of music as it is in other domains of social life.[1] The goal of this chapter is to challenge such forms of objectification by presenting a case study of the musical experiences of the chapter's first author, the pianist Dotan Nitzberg. Drawing on a wide array of theories and methods, we propose and model a progressive approach to research at the intersection of autism studies and music studies, one through which scientific frames of objectivity-aspiring, anonymizing representation are replaced by ethnographic and phenomenological frames of personhood-aspiring, individual re-presentation.

On one level, this chapter continues an ongoing project in the ethnomusicology of autism that we as coauthors—Nitzberg, an Israeli concert pianist with an autism spectrum condition (ASC) diagnosis of high-functioning autism (HFA), and Bakan, a US-based ethnomusicologist who has conducted extensive research on the musical lives of autistic individuals—have pursued together as collaborators for several years.[2] On another level, it forges an entirely new direction for that project through its explicit engagement with the phenomenological tradition.

Key to this transformation have been Bakan's readings of Emmanuel Levinas's *Totality and Infinity* ([1961] 1969) and, to a lesser extent, Hans-Georg Gadamer's *Truth and Method* ([1960] 1989). The arc of this transformation might be characterized as a journey away from an initial desire for a Gadamerian fusion of horizons toward a Levinasian emphasis on alterity. We also draw on more recent approaches to phenomenological research, including those of the medical anthropologist and occupational therapy researcher Cheryl Mattingly (2017) and the ethnomusicologist Matthew Rahaim. His 2017 book chapter "Otherwise than Participation: Unity and Alterity in Musical Encounters" shows how Levinas's insights may be applied productively to virtually any ethnographic—and thus, any ethnomusicological—situation, as Levinas's ethics of respecting alterity, which is consistent with ethnographic priorities, stand in direct opposition to a general human desire to know and master the Other, which defies contemporary ethnographic values. Rahaim further shows that such insights hold particularly great significance in any ethnography focused on stigmatized groups. The ethnography of autism is thus a strong candidate for Levinasian modes of inquiry.

In short, we posit that phenomenological approaches, and those informed by a Levinasian philosophy of alterity in particular, have the capacity to affirm the agency and humanity of people on the autism spectrum, foster an appreciation for their difference, and contribute to a larger activist agenda of reducing the stigma and marginalization to which they have historically been subjected. Through this chapter, we endeavor to advance that position and to offer an example of its realization within an ethnomusicological context.[3]

OBJECTIFYING VERSUS HUMANIZING DISCOURSES ON AUTISM AND AUTISTIC PERSONHOOD

Historically, autism has been conceptualized as a medical disorder, a psychiatric disorder, and a reason for institutionalization. It has been positioned as a condition to be diagnosed and treated, rather than an expression of human diversity to be culturally understood. As Joseph N. Straus explains, "The medical model of autism provides a point of departure for a discussion of autistic culture, but in that model, the autistic style and creative imagination are stigmatized as symptoms of a defective body and mind" (Straus 2013, 467).

This alleged defectiveness becomes inextricable from a "triad of impairments" that defines autism diagnostically: (1) qualitative impairment in social interaction, (2) qualitative impairments in communication, and (3) restrictive, repetitive, and stereotyped patterns of behavior, interests, and activities (Straus 2013, 467). Subsumed within this triadic formulation of lack and deficiency exists a litany of more specific so-called symptoms, among them "deficits in executive function, lack of theory of mind, inadequate drive toward central coherence, impairments in social and communication skills, [and] abnormal functioning in imagination" (Straus 2013, 467). This is a profoundly deficit-focused lens through which to view autistic people and the lives they lead, with the result that, within the epistemological logic of the Western medical model, *autism* becomes "a medical term with a strongly stigmatizing impact" (Straus 2013, 467). This perspective has dominated mainstream thinking since at least the advent of autism as a diagnostic category in the 1940s (Kanner 1943; Molnar-Szakacs and Heaton 2012).

Two examples will serve to illustrate this point. The first is from the "Autism Spectrum Disorder Fact Sheet" of the National Institute of Neurological Disorders and Stroke (NINDS), which is part of the US government's National Institutes of Health. The fact sheet states,

> Autism spectrum disorder (ASD) refers to a group of complex neurodevelopment disorders characterized by repetitive and characteristic patterns of behavior and difficulties with social communication and interaction. The symptoms are present from early childhood and affect daily functioning. . . .
> A diagnosis of ASD includes an assessment of intellectual disability and language impairment. . . .
> ASD occurs in every racial and ethnic group, and across all socioeconomic levels. However, boys are significantly more likely to develop ASD than girls. The latest analysis from the Centers for Disease Control and Prevention estimates that 1 in 68 children has ASD.
>
> (National Institute of Neurological Disorders and Stroke 2019)

The second example is excerpted from a 2012 article published on the website of the American Music Therapy Association: "Music Therapy as a Treatment Modality for Autism Spectrum Disorders." Here, music is primarily seen to be of value for autistic people not as a medium of creative expression or meaningful social engagement but rather as a treatment modality with the capacity to reduce symptoms, foster acceptable behavior, and improve functionality:

> Music therapy can stimulate individuals [with ASD] to reduce negative and/or self-stimulatory responses and increase participation in more appropriate and socially acceptable ways. . . . Because music is processed in both hemispheres of the brain, it can stimulate cognitive functioning and may be used for remediation of some speech/language skills [in persons with ASD].
>
> (American Music Therapy Association 2012)

The ostensible objectivity and neutrality of the third-person (or no-person) accounts of autism and autistic people highlighted in the previous examples is deceptive, and, from a phenomenological perspective, it is inherently problematic. Autistic personhood is negated in both instances, and the second quotation in particular suggests that the value of music to autistic people is effectively limited to its functionality as a clinical tool. Moreover, such characterizations seem to imply that autistic people are not truly "of value" to music either.

These are fallacious and damaging constructs. There are far better means of conceptualizing autism, the ways in which autistic people make and experience music, and the reasons that it matters to them (Bakan 2015b). As Straus proclaims, there is need for a different point of departure, one premised on "a belief that autism is not a defect or pathology, but rather an aspect of naturally occurring and inherently desirable human variability." In such an approach, so-called symptoms of "autistic disorder" may be productively "reinterpreted and recast as differences rather than deficits." Understood in this way, autism is not seen as "a defect but a distinctive and valuable style of thinking and imagining—a vibrant and interesting way of being in the world" (Straus 2013, 467). Phenomenology lends itself well to such positionality.

Phenomenological Turns

As our work developed, the collaborative enterprise shared by this chapter's coauthors came to reflect Levinas's conception of the term *creation*, a dynamic relationship through which "the kinship of beings among themselves is affirmed, but at the same time their radical heterogeneity [is] also" (Levinas [1961] 1969, 293). Arriving at such a Levinasian approach was not easy. Bakan, at least, had entered into the chapter's formative dialogues with Nitzberg motivated by aspirations—even expectations—that over the course of the chapter's process of becoming, the two of us would together move toward a provisional, Gadamerian *Horizontverschmelzung* ("fusion of horizons"; Gadamer [1960] 1989, 302–306; see also Malpas 2018). Discussing this concept in *Truth and Method*, Gadamer writes that if we "put ourselves into someone else's shoes," then "we will understand him—i.e., become aware of the otherness, the indissoluble individuality of the other person—by putting *ourselves* in his position" (Gadamer [1960] 1989, 304–305). Here, Gadamer is not claiming that the process of understanding involves one person overcoming their own subjective position and grasping another's internal subjective state; as Jeff Malpas explains in his entry on Gadamer in *The Stanford Encyclopedia of Philosophy*, Gadamer's hermeneutics "rejects the idea of understanding as achieved through gaining access to some inner realm of subjective meaning" (Malpas 2018). Yet Gadamer does view understanding "as a matter of negotiation between oneself and one's partner in the hermeneutical dialogue[,] such that the process of understanding can be seen as a matter of coming to an 'agreement' about the matter at issue. Coming to such an agreement means establishing a common framework or 'horizon' and Gadamer thus takes understanding to be a process of the 'fusion of horizons' " (Malpas 2018).

Such "agreement" did not materialize in our work on this chapter, at least not on anything like a holistic level. What did materialize was of a rather different order, one far more reflective of Levinas's conception of "the impossibility of conciliation of beings" (Levinas [1961] 1969, 294) than Gadamer's fusion of horizons. For Levinas, the inevitability of nonconciliation between actors, of an inescapable condition of separation and separateness, occurs not as a consequence but rather *by virtue of* the inevitability of radical heterogeneity. It is radical heterogeneity itself that sets in motion the core relational processes that define individual personhood and which in turn defines all of the self/other relations into which we enter as well.

That is what we experienced in the cocreation of this chapter. Why? Because our situation—a term we understand in Gadamer's sense to mean "a standpoint that limits the possibility of vision" (Gadamer [1960] 1989, 302)—is one in which, for all our similarities and shared goals and aspirations, basic neurocognitive differences between us accentuated alterity. Indeed, this alterity effectively kept us out of each other's proverbial shoes, compelling us to remain resolutely in our own as we walked different yet intertwined routes along alternately parallel, intersecting, and divergent paths.

In place of a fusion of horizons, then, our relational dynamic has foregrounded "a separation resistant to synthesis" (Levinas [1961] 1969, 263), and the yield of that separation—the presence of multiplicity and disjuncture in place of unity of voice or view—is evident throughout this work. We find ourselves in concert in this respect with what Rahaim, drawing also from Levinas, characterizes as "an always-deferred, infinite striving" over the "totalizing achievement of comprehension" in realms of social-musical encounter (Rahaim 2017, 187). Initially, and indeed throughout the process of our work on this chapter, such lack of synthesis, unification, and mutual comprehension proved frustrating. Yet seen in retrospect, through the lens of Levinas's phenomenological project, we suggest that these qualities may have turned out to be the source of this work's most significant contribution.

Levinas's writing on the nature of the encounter between self and other is inspiring. "There is an anarchy essential to multiplicity," he asserts. "In the absence of a plane common to the totality (which one persists in seeking, so as to relate the multiplicity to it) one will never know which will, in the free play of the wills, pulls the strings of the game; one will not know who is playing with whom. But a principle breaks through all this trembling and vertigo when the face [of the other] presents itself, and demands justice" (Levinas [1961] 1969, 294). In the realm of autism, the nature of what that principle is and the kind of justice it demands has been explored by Cheryl Mattingly. She argues that the ethical encounter between the autistic person and the neurotypical person requires us to place the highest priority on listening to and representing autistic voices and views, without pretense or ambition toward the kinds of diagnostic, rehabilitative, reductionist, or resolution-oriented outcomes that have been systemically normalized in most autism-related literature and discourse. As Mattingly asserts, phenomenology offers powerful tools for such redress:

> The phenomenological tradition within philosophy involves the strong claim that objectivity itself is but one attitude within the range of necessarily engaged and first-person ways in which we are enmeshed with the world. That is, objective or third-person descriptions merely offer one way to represent the world—and ourselves. They suggest one interpretive possibility, a possibility that may have its uses but can also be misleading. From this, it follows that traditions of knowledge that depend upon a third-person perspective are not "objective" and therefore "truer" than first-person accounts; rather they are derivative. Reality may be apprehended and named by us in the manner of the objective, external world, a world of facts and impersonal objects, but this interpretive move always rests on a more primary intersubjective relationship we have with the world. We are not merely neutral observers of our lives but participants in them. We are called to respond to life, to the world. The world, or reality, is constituted for us through this responsive interconnection.

> (Mattingly 2017, 251)

Within this world of responsive interconnection, myriad possibilities exist to challenge, rethink, and reconstitute the category-generating mechanisms that have historically defined autism. Efforts in this direction can begin to reverse the pervasive historical tendency to turn autistic individuals into nameless, faceless representatives of one *non*ideal type or another.

Mattingly's article uses phenomenology to do just that. Identifying the harm that the medical model inflicts on autistic persons, she examines the lived experience that comes from being subjected to the third-person category of ASD. Mattingly argues that, from "a phenomenological perspective, social categories like 'autism' are called into being as they are lived—as they call to us in a first-person way." This calling, she insists, "can be treated dialogically . . . [,] directing attention to the complexity and ambiguity of our responsiveness to disability categories and their normative implications" (Mattingly 2017, 251, 256; cf. Sterponi and Fasulo 2010).

The present chapter seeks to apply this kind of phenomenological approach. Set in the context of a five-year relationship encompassing diverse activities of social, musical, intellectual, and professional life (see Bakan 2021, 94–118; Nitzberg and Bakan 2019), we embarked on a series of conversations about autism and musical experience. In our dialogues and the subsequent processes of dialogic editing, expansion, and critique, we adopted a Levinasian, phenomenological understanding of the Other's rights (Davidson 2012, 183). As glossed by Levinas scholar Scott Davidson, this concept insists on "the absolute *standing* of the other," on a conviction "that the other has the unqualified or unconditional right to be heard and to make claims for a specific type of treatment, regardless of any consideration of his or her social status, citizenship, or group membership" (Davidson 2012, 183–184). To this listing, we would add status within the broad human spectrum of neurodiversity, including but not limited to identification on the autism spectrum.

CONVERSATIONAL GOALS, PRIORITIES, AND APORIAS

Our conversations over the years have been motivated by a joint effort to explore the musical lifeworld of one musician with an autism spectrum diagnosis (Dotan) and to do so within a methodological context that we describe as dialogical, re-presentational ethnography.[4] At the outset of our work on this chapter, it appeared that phenomenology would be a supplement to our long-standing methods, and Michael described the aim of the project in an August 20, 2018, text to Dotan:

> A useful brief definition of phenomenology is this one, Dotan: "Phenomenology insists that phenomena be presented as they present themselves to consciousness."[5] So basically, what I'm interested in exploring in this conversation is how,

from a phenomenological perspective, you approach being a pianist—how your experiences of learning to play the piano and as a performer present themselves to your consciousness, that is, to the way you know and understand yourself as a pianist. It's sort of like having you get inside your own mind to examine your learning and performing processes, and then bringing them "outward" to explain them.[6]

The basic premise that Michael outlined here seemed straightforward enough, but as the two of us pursued this project, we experienced pervasive tension that was borne out of our very different viewpoints and priorities. On the one hand, these differences may be attributed to the fact that we are simply two rather different individuals; on the other hand, they can be seen as stemming from an alternate (albeit not unrelated) source identified earlier in the chapter—our fundamentally different neurocognitive make-ups. We are "wired" differently—Dotan in an autistic way, Michael in a nonautistic way—and that ontological distinction yields a fundamental incommensurability between us, at least on certain levels. The resulting disparities of experience and worldview essentially preclude the possibility of our finding "common ground" in at least some domains, which leads to frustration for both of us.

Yet we came to regard this aporia less as a problem to be solved than a problematic to be made explicit through our actual, re-presented dialogues. As Levinas notes, the truth of being has to do not with a clarity of shared vision between interlocutors but rather in "being situated in a subjective field which *deforms* vision" in the intersubjective encounter (Levinas [1961] 1969, 291). This leads to a "curvature of the intersubjective space [that] inflects distance into elevation; it does not falsify being, but makes its first truth possible" (Levinas [1961] 1969, 291). In other words, through the grapplings of dialogue, what begins as remoteness may be transformed into a mode of intersubjective revelation that is increased, rather than diminished, by heightened degrees of difference between the interlocutors.

Our dialogues, especially the most recent ones of 2018, show two determined individuals diving headlong into a rather Ricoeur-esque "conflict of interpretations[,] within which we perceive the being we seek to understand" (Thompson 1981, 19; cf. Ricoeur 1981, 193). We regard the ensuing relational complexity, ambiguity, and discontinuity as cause for the Levinasian turn of the latter part of the chapter, as well as for the prioritizing of a Mattingly-inspired "first person" engagement in our considerations of autism and autistic personhood, to which we now direct our focus.

Autism and Intersectionality

A rich ethnography of a family with an autistic child, Mattingly's "Autism and the Ethics of Care" presents a convincing case that the same autism spectrum diagnosis may yield very different outcomes for different "kinds" of individuals, and that such disparities tend to be intimately tied to *other* identity categories. The article explores the intersection of autism and race and shows how the social experience of autism for African American children in the United States is profoundly different from that of "Anglo American" children, a difference that is exacerbated by socioeconomic factors.[7] As she explains,

> In the United States, especially for African Americans, autism reveals the subtleties and local inffections of very dramatic health disparities along race and class lines in terms of delayed or nondiagnosis and lack of services. The comparatively lower rates of autism among African Americans, especially those living in poor areas, suggests a health disparity that shows up as diminished prevalence. . . . Children from an ethnic or racial minority group are more likely to experience delayed diagnosis. . . . This does not mean that these children are "escaping" a mental health diagnosis. Rather, they are being diagnosed differently. African American children are 2.6 times less likely than Anglo-American children to receive an autism diagnosis on their first clinical visit and three times more likely to be given conduct or adjustment disorder diagnoses[,] which are more stigmatizing and have less services attached . . . .
>
> (Mattingly 2017, 253)

The disparities that Mattingly identifies mean that European American children have a greater chance of receiving critically important opportunities, accommodations, services, and forms of social acceptance than their non- or late-diagnosed African American peers. Stigmatization and marginalization intensify when autistic behaviors are misconstrued as symptomatic of other conditions, and the insidious effects of such processes are magnified exponentially through their systemic pairing with exclusionary markers of race and class.

To be autistic in a neurotypical-dominated society is challenging under the best of circumstances, but to be autistic without being recognized as such—while at the same time having to contend with the societal burdens and barriers of systemic racial discrimination—is to be placed in an ontological condition of chronic precarity. Such precarity makes one easy prey for dismissal by "mainstream society," with incarceration, institutionalization, and other forms of exclusion and expulsion serving as both mechanisms and justifications for myriad socially sanctioned strategies of dehumanization. In the terms of a certain ableist (il)logic, to be "disadvantaged" and "dysfunctional" across so many intersecting planes makes one hardly human at all, and this same logic enables social and institutional practices that endorse the treatment of some human beings as less fully human than others, whether through explicit, implicit, or subliminal means.

A variation on this same theme may be found in a customary tendency to deny the very possibility of "true musicality" among autistic musicians. We must emphasize, however, that we do not regard the consequence of oppression stemming from musical identity as being commensurate with that of racial identity: no autistic musician has been beaten or killed by the police simply for being a musician.[8]

The consequence is real nonetheless. A strong affinity for music has been part of the autistic profile virtually from the time of the invention of autism as a diagnostic category in the 1940s. While the exceptional musical skill sets of autistic individuals in certain areas—especially regarding absolute pitch, extraordinary feats of memorization, and technical performance abilities (especially on piano)—have long been subjects of public awe and fascination (see Molnar-Szakacs and Heaton 2012), even the most gifted autistic musicians have not received recognition as bona fide musical *artists*. Rather, the very musical attributes that tend to inspire public admiration and wonder are turned *against* the autistic musicians who exhibit them.

In this context, the standard narrative acknowledges that there are autistic musicians who can play with great speed and accuracy, memorize immense repertoires of music, and distinguish discrete notes within clusters of multiple pitches in uncanny ways, but the "machine-like" quality of their musicianship, its inherently "unemotional" quality, is seen to preclude even the possibility of real musical artistry *ipso facto*.[9] The underlying, ableist trope implies that because autistic people are not fully human—on account of their so-called deficits in the experience and expression of empathy, emotion, and social reciprocity—they cannot possibly be fully musical either.[10]

The quintessential example of this pattern is the designation *savant* (autistic savant, musical savant) to highly accomplished autistic musicians (see Straus 2014), which effectively eliminates any possibility for *a*rtistic acceptance of *au*tistic musicianship, and in turn drastically limits prospects for their professional success beyond a limited "enfreakment" market (Garland-Thomson 1996).[11] But with or without the ultimately damning savant designation, autistic musicians suffer at the hands of their nonautistic critics, whose bigotry renders the already prohibitive challenges of living as autistic people in a neurotypical-dominated world even more daunting. This conundrum has impacted Dotan profoundly, as we detail below.

Dotan's Story

My passion for music is absolute and harks back to my very earliest childhood memories. I grew up in Israel in the southern coastal town of Ashkelon, and by the age of one I could speak Hebrew fluently. My first complete sentence was "That's what I want ... Music! Music!" Before I was a year old, I came down with a sickness of unknown cause and was rushed to the hospital. I was gravely ill, but my condition improved dramatically when my father placed a toy keyboard next to my pillow. I was fascinated to discover that when I pressed a row of keys it produced a very pleasant sound.[12]

By the age of three, I was fluent not only in Hebrew but also in English. I had a voracious appetite for knowledge of all different kinds, combined with an excellent memory. I was able to memorize large numbers of stories, fairy tales, songs, trademarks, even the license plaques of different cars. I was always keenly interested in music, in history, and in different cultures and languages, and I would usually become so fascinated by one subject that I would refuse to move on to any other until I had finished my "research" on the previous one. This seemed normal to me, but other people said it was a peculiarity of mine, even an obsession.

I think I was always "idiosyncratic" socially. I often preferred not to connect socially with other people, especially other children. Childhood games did not interest me, and I preferred spending time with adults or listening to music alone in a quiet corner to spending time with children my own age.

These preferences, combined with my not being good at athletics or math, made me an easy target for bullies and teasing. Things got a bit better in junior high school. I was generally treated better there, by both the other students and the teachers, but it was still difficult.

Music was my refuge. I had a superb piano teacher, Yanina Kudlik, with whom I studied for twelve years. She taught me all the rudiments. I built a large repertoire of pieces and made quick progress. But at some point, my progress slowed down a bit because of panic attacks, which originated because of rough experiences I'd had, fears I kept within myself, and constant feelings of low self-esteem.

Because of these problems, my parents and I sought professional help. This eventually led me to Dr. Roni Hegesh, who originally diagnosed me with Asperger's syndrome (an autism spectrum disorder; see note 2). As soon as I received the diagnosis, I felt relieved, since it answered many unsolved questions I had been carrying within myself for a long time.

With the help of both Dr. Hegesh and Ms. Kudlik, I was able to really thrive. I won several competitions and scholarships and got to study abroad in the United States. I received an artistic certificate under Enrique Graf at the College of Charleston, a master's degree with Roberta Rust at Lynn University in Florida, and a second master's degree in piano performance and pedagogy at Florida State University (FSU), where my main teachers were Dr. Read Gainsford and Dr. Diana Dumlavwalla. I also got to study with other members of the piano faculty, including the famous concert pianist Ian Hobson.

By the time I arrived at FSU in 2015, which followed a brief period at the University of North Texas, I had been collaborating with Michael Bakan on the study of music and autism for a couple of years; our main focus was a chapter that was eventually published in one of his books (Bakan 2021, 94–118). I ended up having him serve on my master's supervisory committee, and I played in his Balinese gamelan for a semester as well (see Bakan 2021, 111–112). After graduating from FSU, I moved to Canada to attend the University of New Brunswick, where I am pursuing a PhD in Education.

I have accomplished a lot in my life, and I'm proud of who I am and what I've achieved. But there has been much frustration and trauma along the way, and I carry a lot of painful memories. Some of my challenges come from being autistic and living in a world that isn't set up very well for people like me. But others come from the fact that lots of people who are not autistic seem either unwilling or unable to accept me the way I am, including the way I am musically. So even though I am comfortable *being* autistic, it is still sometimes painful when other people *call* me autistic. It can be rough to hear, mainly due to negative past experiences with that term that are lodged in my memory. I talked about this to Michael in 2014 in one of our conversations for the book I mentioned before (Bakan 2021). Here's what I said then, which is still accurate in terms of how I think about it now:

> Many musicians [have] offended me by saying [that I was] "emotionally hand-icapped," "playing like an autist," and other derogatory comments as such. People who claim that are ignorant and should be ignored. They do not comprehend that at the moment [autistic pianists] tackle a piece they recognize the character and "emo-tion" right away. It's instilled there. Their intensity, concentration, and involvement [are] so high that it seems as if they are [just] "doing their own thing," [but that's a wrong impression]. . . . Only people with [a] sixth sense—that is, endowed with sen-sitivity beyond the average—can catch it.
>
> (Nitzberg quoted in Bakan 2021, 116)[13]

I will mention something that may strike some readers as amusing, though it is in fact accurate. In 2018, several years after the 2014 conversation with Michael that produced the previous quotation, he brought up my "sixth sense" comments in another conversa-tion we were having via text messaging.

Michael wrote, "Regarding what you have described as the 'sixth sense' that you and others on the spectrum possess, which enables you to capture the deep emotion in-herent in a piece of music, can you verbalize for me what that sixth sense is, how you use it, how you know whether someone has it?" I wrote back: "DANGER! ON THE DAY I'LL BE ABLE TO DO THAT I CEASE TO BECOME AN AUTIST!"[14]

Discussed later in more detail, this example illustrates how the kinds of things that nonautistic people ask autistic people to do sometimes do not make sense from an au-tistic perspective. Actually, there have been many moments like that between Michael and me in trying to write this chapter, probably because doing phenomenology requires ways of thinking that don't line up well with the way an autistic mind works, at least mine.

As for what it is like generally to live with my condition, it certainly has its challenges. In the end, though, I am at peace with it, and it enables me to do many positive things. I believe in my musical ability and my musicianship. As for what other people think and say about me or any other musician on the spectrum, they can agree or disagree with our grasp of the music, but they have no right to condemn us just because we are autistic and act or think differently. They may believe that I can't be a true musical artist *because* I am autistic, but that is not correct. Just because my body language or my facial expressions may be different from what they are expecting, or because I look different when I bow on stage or sound different when I speak to the audience, or even because I can take a different approach to things like tempo changes or dynamics, none of these factors disqualify me from being a musical artist. My playing is full of expression and emo-tion and feeling; it *is* musical, and anyone who really listens to me, rather than making assumptions about what they are hearing, will know that. People can criticize me if they want to, but I know the truth about myself.

Here is another quote of mine from the book I worked on with Michael. It accurately accounts for what I still believe:

> Those who claimed I am unable of accomplishing a task due to my "DISABILITY" deserve my mercy because they are so full of prejudices. And those who said "I AM NOT SUFFICIENTLY MATURE," woe to them as well, since I grow up and develop, and I do it my way, with my own pace, and I do it with so much fun, pleasure, and grace. Every instant!
>
> (Nitzberg quoted in Bakan 2021, 117)

ALTERNATE ONTOLOGIES AND DIFFERENT OPERATING SYSTEMS

So if, as Dotan suggests, autistic musicians "act or think differently" than their nonautistic peers, and if such differences extend outward from the personal lifeworld of the autistic individual to myriad social domains—for example, the challenges Dotan and Michael faced in "doing phenomenology" together in writing this chapter, as well as the forms of prejudice that lead nonautistic people to assumptions like the one that casts "autism" and "musical artistry" as an oxymoronic pairing—then this all begs a basic question: What is autism? And that fundamental question inspires at least one other: What characterizes autistic subjectivity and cognitive experience and distinguishes it from its ostensibly neurotypical (nonautistic) counterpart? To address these questions, we turn to the work of the autistic critical theorist and social activist Nick Walker.

According to Walker, "Autism is a genetically-based human neurological variant. The complex set of interrelated characteristics that distinguish autistic neurology from non-autistic neurology is not yet fully understood, but current evidence indicates that the central distinction is that autistic brains are characterized by particularly high levels of synaptic connectivity and responsiveness," making the subjective experience of autistic people—and thus their subjective processes of consciousness as well—"more intense and chaotic than that of non-autistic individuals" (Walker 2014). The autistic mind, Walker suggests, tends "to register more information" than its nonautistic counterpart, and "the impact of each bit of information tends to be both stronger and less predictable." Drawing a computer analogy, he explains that autistic individuals have a "different neurological operating system" than their nonautistic peers: not a better or worse system, just a different one. Dotan's self-assessment of "two different types" of persons he embodies, related to Michael during a 2014 conversation, offers a poignant example:

> Within my brain, . . . zillions of thoughts are traveling at the speed of light[,] and sometimes it causes confusion, procrastination, stress, etc. . . . [If] I am trying to

absorb and classify [all this] information at once, it's not going to work. The brain I possess can record a huge amount of knowledge; the absorption is quick but the classification process is slower, [and] this gap is hampering. . . . The pianist in me and the person in me are two different types. The pianist in me is someone that does [things] almost immediately and instinctively (and quickly); the person is not always as nimble as at the keyboard. That's the main difference.

(Nitzberg quoted in Bakan 2021, 104)

The cognitive differences between autistic and nonautistic people need not, and indeed should not, be a problem in most instances. However, they almost invariably end up that way. Offering an autism-specific gloss on the broader line of critique that has been foundational to "the social model of disability" in disability studies and related discourses (see Shakespeare 2013), Walker contends that the vast majority of human societies are "designed around the sensory, cognitive, developmental, and social needs of non-autistic individuals," with the result that "autistic individuals are almost always disabled to some degree—sometimes quite obviously, and sometimes more subtly" (Walker 2014).

Thus, the wide range of "distinctive, atypical ways of thinking, moving, interaction, and sensory and cognitive processing" that characterize autistic personhood across the vast heterogeneity of the autism spectrum translate into pervasive conditions of marginalization and disenfranchisement affecting autistic people (Walker 2014). That same atypicality may also become manifest in the expression of distinctive abilities, perspectives, and insights that are productive and advantageous, however. It is a proverbial double-edged sword, and one that brings us back again to Straus's contention that autism is best conceptualized as difference rather than deficit, as a manifestation of neurodiversity rather than a pathology rooted in disorder (Straus 2011, 2013). As Walker explains, "Autism is widely disregarded as a 'disorder,' but this view has been challenged in recent years by proponents of the neurodiversity model, which holds that autism and other neurocognitive variants are simply part of the natural spectrum of human biodiversity, like variations in ethnicity or sexual orientation (which have also been pathologized in the past). Ultimately, to describe autism as a disorder represents a value judgment rather than a scientific fact" (Walker 2014).

Neither we nor Walker would deny the very real and often profound challenges that living with autism entails, but this does not justify the myriad scripts and narratives on autism—scholarly and popular alike—that trade in currencies of lack, inability, and loss while ignoring, muting, or at best marginally accounting for the actual voices and views of autistic people. A phenomenological perspective on autism must begin and end with attempts to describe the ways in which phenomena appear *to particular autistic individuals*, and it must relate these modes of appearance to the specific processes of consciousness that these individuals experience and articulate, and upon which they critically and eloquently reflect.

A Lecture-Demonstration by Dotan

"How to Teach Piano to People with Asperger," a lecture-recital that Dotan presented at the World Piano Teachers Association (WPTA) conference in Novi Sad, Serbia, in 2012, shows the practical value that such reflective thinking and articulation can yield. In this section, we will quote from the lecture at length.[15]

In the introductory section of his talk, Dotan explains that "The most important thing I want you to know is that Asperger's syndrome [and by extension ASC generally] is something rather fragile and complicated, sometimes even beyond our own grasp, since it's very individual in its ways of expression and it has several ranks of functioning within it; briefly, it's like a theme with endless variations, the theme remains consistent but the variations always evolve" (see also Nitzberg 2012; cf. Bakan 2021, 103).

"Asperger's syndrome is something very dual," Dotan tells the audience at another point. "It has its luminous points and it has its dark points: people with Asperger are usually very unusual; hence, those points can be referred to as 'Idiosyncrasies.' "

"Before going on," Dotan continues, "let me put something in brackets. Although the subject [of this presentation] is how to teach piano to people with Asperger, I can [really only] talk about my own experience; hence I ask you to see the generalization, because I have no other way to talk about it but through my own eyes. In my particular case, those idiosyncrasies can be subdivided in three sectors: Musical, Social, and Intellectual."

Dotan goes on to classify, list, and describe some of his self-identified, ASC-rooted "idiosyncrasies":

Musical Idiosyncrasies:

- An ability to play by ear (including classical pieces).
- An ability to improvise.
- A keen interest in "musical peculiarities." For example, "when I was about twelve or thirteen years old I was a groupie of Percy Grainger's music."

Social Idiosyncrasies:

- Body language that "can be considered awkward and make people wonder what I'm all about." Illustrating the point, Dotan explains that "I bow on stage in a very unique way, somewhat old-fashioned. It seems out of context but that's my body language. I mean something and the others get something else. It's very common among all Aspergers."
- Unusual modes of social interaction: "I like nearness, yet, sometimes I am too personal. . . . I don't always know how to balance formality and informality."

Intellectual Idiosyncrasies:

- An ability to learn foreign languages quickly (he speaks nine).
- An ability to "memorize texts and musical pieces in excessive amounts." Dotan explains that "back when I was a child, this capacity helped me [in] memorizing not only pieces of music, but also entire children's books and poems by foreign authors."
- A tendency to "express emotions in a very unique way (either too economic[al] or too extroverted), to such extent that it seems to others as an 'emotional shortage,' 'lack of expression' etc." This, however, is a misunderstanding. "Throughout my life I had opportunities to play for fellow musicians, and whenever they were asked to give me their [assessments], many of them didn't manage to absorb my distinct way of expression and said I have an emotional shortage. To tell you frankly, it left me confused since Aspergers have [an] overdose of feelings, not a shortage!" (Nitzberg 2012; cf. Bakan 2021, 97–98)

In reviewing this list, nonautistic readers will surely see in it elements of themselves and of other nonautistic people they know. Autistic people by no means have a monopoly on improvisational prowess, awkward body language, or Percy Grainger fixations. Yet in its holistic totality, Dotan's self-reflexive portrait of his autistic "idiosyncrasies" forms a gestalt that aligns more closely overall with autistic than nonautistic personhood. In this regard, there is a notable similarity between Dotan's lecture and the essay by Nick Walker (2014) that we quoted earlier. Just as Walker is able to use his "cultural insider" expertise to help nonautistic people better comprehend and interact with their autistic peers, Dotan prescribes a set of pedagogical methods and priorities for piano instruction that, while not limited in relevance to teaching autistic piano students, are especially well attuned to their needs (see Nitzberg and Bakan 2019).

Autistic people are not alone in exhibiting what Walker calls "distinctive, atypical ways of thinking, moving, interaction, and sensory and cognitive processing" (Walker 2014). Indeed, it would be no exaggeration to state that there is probably no human being on the planet who does not fit that description at some level or another. Yet Walker (2014) and Nitzberg (2012) alike capture an essential sense of autistic-ness in their descriptions, exhibiting a grasp on what Straus (2011) has referred to as a recognizable "autistic cognitive style," one that is inextricable from an array of observable, behavioral, and experiential correlates and manifestations.

Watching the YouTube video of Dotan's WPTA lecture helps clarify this point (Nitzberg 2012). The adage that "Once you've met one autistic person, you've met one autistic person" is true; there is no stock "type" of autistic individual. Yet at the same time, autistic people from across the spectrum do share a basic ontology, a common, neurocognitively defined way of constituting experience that might be understood as a "stance" in Berger's sense of the term (2010). The essential quality of that ontology is as fundamental to how autistic people recognize and identify *with* one another as it is to how nonautistic people recognize and identify autistic people *as* Other. Even a brief encounter with Dotan's lecture video will quickly clarify to which of those "camps" you belong.

In the lecture, Dotan defines this way of being in terms of a set of idiosyncrasies, a kind of autistic mode of personhood and engagement with the world. Perhaps a better gloss would be to frame it in cultural terms, as Joseph Straus does in his essay "Autism as Culture" (2013). Either way, Dotan's reflexivity generates a typology of autistic being that serves productive ends in prescribing effective pedagogical methods for teaching piano to people on the spectrum. His published work on this subject (Nitzberg 2012; Nitzberg and Bakan 2019) benefits greatly from his "emic perspective."[16]

Inspired by this lecture-demonstration, Michael approached Dotan in the summer of 2018 with the idea of using phenomenological methods to continue this work. Michael hoped that gaining access to Dotan's insider perspective on autism as a mode of lived experience—as a culture rather than a compendium of idiosyncrasies; a difference, not a deficit; an alternate operating system, not an inferior one—would shed light on not just Dotan's unique lifeworld but the autistic cognitive style and its effects on musical praxis and conceptualization, broadly conceived. It was in this spirit that we began our dialogues.

WAYS OF THE MIND: RE-PRESENTATIONAL DIALOGUES ON PERFORMANCE AND INSPIRATION

Dialogue 1: August 20, 2018

It's a Monday evening just after 8:00 PM and we are just getting started with our first typing- and texting-based Google Hangouts online dialogue for this chapter. Within minutes, it is clear that Dotan is not at all convinced of the need to have it.

"I don't have a different approach now than I did before [with the earlier publications]," Dotan texts to Michael. "All the materials accumulated [up to now have] defined those points well, I think."

"Yes, but we need to move in a new direction," Michael insists. ". . . Perhaps if I generate a line of 'phenomenological questioning,' it will lead to new perspectives and insights regarding your process."

"Let's give it a shot," Dotan offers gamely, though still skeptical.

"OK!" Michael exclaims, diving in. "We have established well from our earlier dialogues that there is no such thing as 'autistic piano playing,' yet we have also established that your approach to piano learning and performing—and your particular skills, proclivities, etc.—are marked by features that relate to your, to quote Joseph Straus [2011, 163–165], 'autistic cognitive style.' Would you still agree that this is true?"

"Well, I am an all-included package," Dotan quips. "Hahaha."

"And the 'package' contains [being on the spectrum], which is integral to how you learn and play, yes? Even if one does not 'hear' that in the playing itself."

"Even when I am walking down the street or doing the chores," Dotan affirms. "One cannot eject his brain when going outside, and it is true for all human beings on Earth."

"True!" Michael agrees. "So your autism is just integral to who you are. There is no separation of it from anything you think, learn, or do. Is this correct?"

"Absolutely," Dotan fires back. "But that applies not only to me. Can a person with diabetes leave his diabetes at home and lock it up? No!"

"Good analogy. Let's follow up on it for a moment, shall we?"

"Shoot!"

"OK. So, let's say I have diabetes and I play the piano. That does not mean that you can hear diabetes in my piano playing. However, it does mean that my approach to learning, practicing, and performing as a pianist are influenced by the fact of my diabetes. So, compared to another pianist of similar ability and training, I might not practice for as long in one sitting, I might have a different kind of stool to accommodate neuropathy in my feet, I might have a different pre-concert ritual that involves eating different foods, or performing certain kinds of stretching or breathing exercises to ensure optimal performance. If you were then to ask me how diabetes influences my experiences as a pianist, I would engage in a certain kind of introspection to see how all those practices, etc., impact my process."

"Clearly, diabetes causes issues of blood circulation," Dotan acknowledges, "so definitely you might have a different set of habits. (For example—and this may interest you, Michael, since you were a violinist in your youth—one of my favorite violinists, Eugène Ysaÿe [1858–1931], struggled with diabetes and had his distinct set of habits.) In other words, a condition influences all sorts of daily functions; for instance, my mother's glaucoma afflicts her substantially."

"Yes, though I think it may be different with autism," Michael suggests, "because it's not physiological in the same sense that glaucoma or diabetes is. Yet still one could say, to paraphrase you, that autism is 'a condition [that] influences all sorts of daily functions,' and, of particular relevance here, that it influences all sorts of practices, values, and ideals that you bring to your art as a concert pianist. Thought of in such a framework, how do you regard autism as being influential to your practices, values, and ideals as a pianist?"

"I never *gave* it a thought," contends Dotan. "Maybe other people who hear and watch me playing can convey their observations. But generally, a human being is made of genetics, environment, learning, and personality. But still, point of view is based upon personal observations of reality."

"What about when you observe yourself playing, say, on a video?" Michael asks. "Is there anything that you see, hear, or perceive that you regard as distinguishing you from other pianists you have listened to and watched, regardless of whether or not that distinction has anything to do with being autistic?"

"Not really. I do not compare myself to them. There was an eminent pianist and peda-gogue in Tel Aviv named Ilona Vincze (1902–1998), and I would like to paraphrase her as saying I'd rather be better than myself only."

"And what would make you better than yourself then?"

"I cannot really verbalize it. It is an inner feeling of mine. (It is more of a sensory than a verbal issue.)"

"Which reminds me of something you've mentioned before but that I'd like to dig into more deeply now," Michael writes. "That is what you described as the 'sixth sense' that you and others on the spectrum possess, which enables you to capture the deep emotion inherent in a piece of music. Can you verbalize what that sixth sense is, how you use it, how you know whether someone has it?"

"DANGER! ON THE DAY I'LL BE ABLE TO DO THAT I CEASE TO BECOME AN AUTIST!" Dotan shouts back in all caps. "Again, it is a brute inner feeling that cannot be translated to words. It is simply existent."

"LOL!" Michael volleys back. But he is not yet ready to yield on the larger question of this sixth sense or leave unexamined Dotan's remark that his experiences "can't be translated into words."

"But you *have* [addressed those kinds of issues] in some of our earlier dialogues," Michael challenges Dotan, "like when you talked about the zillions of thoughts running through your head, . . . [which you related] metaphorically to the dancing gnomes in the Liszt *Gnomenreigen* piece you told me about [Bakan 2021, 97, 103–105]. All that kind of stuff. Quite frankly, I think you are eminently capable of such introspection. Just give it a whirl, damned be the consequences! ☺ What does it feel like for you when you are on stage playing for an audience? What thoughts run through your mind? What do you hope to capture in your performance and convey to those listening to you?"

"Aha! That's another story," says Dotan. "It has nothing to do with the 'sixth sense.' "

"Fine. Then let's go with that story!"

"Well," Dotan begins, "the main thoughts running through my head are the expecta-tion for a 'perfect performance' versus the surprises emerging in real time. It's not really about the applause," he adds, setting up for a joke. "The audience applauds even when [Israeli prime minister] Benjamin Netanyahu is delivering a speech."

"Haha," Michael laughs. "Let me follow up first on your 'perfect performance' vs. 'surprises emerging in real time' comment. Do you look forward to such surprises?"

"No, I just want to surprise myself."

"Huh? In what ways?"

"In having this sensation of rendering an outstanding performance, even better than what I thought [it would be]."

"I see," says Michael. "And beyond technical perfection, what factors make it outstanding?"

"Gee, it reminds me of the questions of my grandmother Yona Nitzberg."

"Well, I'm just a bubbe [grandmother] in disguise ☺," Michael jokes.

"Alright. If you are in the mood, I'll answer!"

"Of course I am. Go ahead!"

"You cannot separate autism from a person," Dotan proclaims, "[and you] cannot literally differentiate all details (or components) of a musical performance one from the other either."

In the dialogue to this point, the basic terms of the debate have been set: where Michael will seek introspection, differentiation, and interpretation from Dotan, Dotan will insist on a holistic presentation of his selfness and musicality—one that defies pat associations between things autistic and things musical, let alone between ways of being autistic and of being musical. Indeed, Dotan's presentation of self will consistently be one that might be described as consistent with Levinas's ideas about persons. "The idea of the individual does not consist . . . in letting itself be identified *from the outside* by the finger that points to it," writes Levinas. Rather, it consists "in being oneself, in identifying oneself from within" (1961 [1969], 289).

"Agreed," Michael replies to Dotan's comments about the inextricability of person and autism, and about the inextricability of the individual components of a musical performance as well. "But don't concern yourself with autism. I'm interested now in your experience, in what factors (again, not including technical perfection) you regard as having the potential to make a performance of yours outstanding."

Dotan comes back with a quick list of factors: "The quality of the piano, the comfort of the stool, the socks or shoes that are not too rough, the suit that is not too itchy, and also not having a loud sneeze while playing a soft passage. It is not fixed in every recital. I guess one can summarize it in two words: Inspiration and Incident."

"Ah, I love that," Michael types, "inspiration and incident. But the list that you just gave—stool, socks, suit, etc.—most of those are *sensory* things. So when you are talking about factors involved in the quality of the performance, many of them seem to have to do with the way things *feel* for you, physically, when you're on the stage. Is this correct?"

"True!" Dotan confirms. "And it's also about the vibes I have from within."

"Do you have words to describe those 'vibes,' even if they don't capture the essence fully?"

"Well, excitement!" Dotan offers up. "I have no other explanation."

"OK," Michael writes, implying clear comprehension of Dotan's last few remarks but actually feeling pretty confused. He tries to figure out a way to ask Dotan a question that will help him to explain the connections between excitement, itchy suits, vibes from within, and the rest.

"Now let me ask you something," Michael ventures. "If the suit is itchy, or the socks or shoes are rough, or the stool isn't very comfortable, is this likely to affect the quality of your performance? Will these kinds of things lead to technical mistakes, or interfere with the excitement and vibes coming from within, affect you in some other way, or not affect you at all?"

Dotan's reply sheds at least a dim light on the issue. "It was a humorous-picturesque way to say that it is a matter of the integration of many components, all of which depend on a situation or an instant, and that every attempt to define it is surely a 'miss.'"

"Fair enough," Michael responds. "Let's go back to something you said a while back then, namely, that [one of] the keys to an outstanding performance [is] inspiration. What are some of the sources of inspiration that tend to elevate your playing to, quoting you, its 'utmost heights'?"

"Special types of people," Dotan writes back almost instantly.

"People in the audience?" Michael inquires.

"Audience is never a function," Dotan shoots back, catching Michael off guard. "For example," he continues, "back in 2007, I played with a symphony orchestra in Assisi, Italy, at the Cathedral. I felt like [I was] soaring there. All the components worked so well that evening: Atmosphere, People, Conductor, Piano, Setting, etc."

Michael is again confused. "So if the audience is never a function, then the 'People' to whom you referred (other than the conductor), who were they?" He ventures a guess. "Were they the other musicians, the players in the orchestra?"

"Yes," Dotan confirms.

"OK. So about the audience, I remember you telling me once before that it doesn't matter to you whether the audience applauds when you play, and now you're telling me that the audience is 'never a function.' Does this mean that you don't really care what the audience thinks of your performance or how they respond to it?"

"Well, the audience is important for its function of applauding and/or giving feedback," Dotan clarifies, "but first and foremost I play for myself because playing is an integral part of who I am. In other words, I do care for the public but only to a certain degree."

The dialogue continues for a while, and at its close, Michael is not at all convinced that he has a clear sense of Dotan's experience.

Dialogue 2: August 23, 2018

"I want to return to one of the subjects of our last conversation, about the audience," Michael types after he and Dotan have exchanged greetings to start their second dialogue of the series. "Do you get nervous, or experience 'stage fright,' when you perform in front of an audience? I wonder, since lots of people do, yet if you have little concern about audience reaction, it seems possible that you would not have 'stage nerves' either."

"No, I don't," Dotan replies matter-of-factly. "I have other personal fears in my pantry but they have nothing to do with the public. It is all between me and myself."

"So that's interesting," Michael notes. "Do your personal fears affect you equally whether on the concert stage in front of an audience or in the practice room? In other words, does the setting of the performance matter, or is it more strictly an internal matter of the expectations you set for yourself?"

"Without penetrating too much into it, those are fears that escort me wherever I go and whatever I do. They have nothing to do with music."

"Ah, I understand," Michael responds. "In that case, nervousness—or stage fright, performance anxiety, or whatever we want to call it—which is such a major issue for so many performing musicians, is really not an issue for you. Is this correct?"

"That is true," Dotan confirms.

"So we have talked a great deal in our earlier sessions [from past years] about the advantages vs. disadvantages of your autism. This would seem to be a huge advantage for you, i.e., being not so concerned about what the audience thinks of your playing (or of you), so that the burden of stage fright, which is one of the greatest challenges for most musicians, does not weigh on you at all! If that's accurate, it's a huge asset for one who is a concert artist like yourself!"

"Since I am thinking of music very often," Dotan explains, "everything related to music is thrilling me. Therefore, neither audience nor performance platform are obstacles. On the contrary, they are very positive stimulations."

"That's great," Michael affirms. "I think I've mainly reached a stage like that in my own development as a performer, but I'm still sometimes prone to getting nervous on stage even today, and that's after some forty years of performing professionally. To be honest, I envy your 'immunity' from that kind of challenge!"

"I see," Dotan replies, leaving it at that. Michael had been hoping for a bit more engagement. When it doesn't materialize, he resumes his line of questioning.

"Next I want to ask you a question or two about the 'very positive stimulations' you get from the audience and from the public performance experience itself. Give me a moment to compose the first of those questions."

"Alright, take your time."

"In our last session," Michael types, "you said that [one of] the keys to achieving outstanding performance for you was inspiration. You then said that a great source of inspiration for you was 'special people.' So the first thing I'm wondering is whether it matters to you, say, when you're doing a recital, whether there are any of these special people in the audience."

"Oh, sure," Dotan types back without hesitation. "It is a great pleasure having a special person in the audience."

"Who are some of the special people that have attended your recitals in recent years?"

Dotan's list pops onto the screen almost immediately: "Ian Hobson at my final recital at FSU. Dr. Adi Rosenkranz, Mr. Yoram Ever-Hadani, and Dr. Roni Hegesh at my final recital in Tel Aviv. Dr. Roberta Rust from Lynn University. Father Armando Pierucci, Maestro Volodymyr Vynnytsky, and the list is endless. And even my maternal grandmother, Bobe [Bubbe] Raquel Graupen."

"It seems like you have pretty much instant recall of the special people who've attended your recitals going back many years. Is that correct?"

"Oh, yes! Definitely!" Dotan affirms. "They will accompany me forever. They are unusual people, one by one."

"I know some of those names of course," says Michael. "The well-known pianists, like Ian Hobson and Roberta Rust—and your grandmother—but many of the others I don't know. Are they all musicians? (I'm guessing Father Pierucci might not be.)"

"Some of them are, and Father Pierucci is a musician," Dotan corrects. "He is the elderly Franciscan priest who sat next to me while I was playing in Jerusalem. He is a composer, organist, and educator."

"I see," says Michael. "So this may be a difficult question for you to answer, but let's try it! Is there any basic quality—a 'lowest common denominator'—that qualifies someone as a special person in your estimation, as the kind of person that inspires you?"

"It has something to do with personality," Dotan advances.

"Okay. So it is not necessarily that they have to be, say, outstanding musicians?"

"Not necessarily. For instance, Dr. Hegesh is not a musician and neither is my grandmother, but still, there is something about their presence that makes the whole difference."

"What do you think that is?"

"Their personality conveys an air of simplicity to my brain. Like Dr. Hegesh. She is the one who first diagnosed me and took care of my [autism spectrum–related] issues. She kept doing that until a month ago when she retired."

"And what is it about Dr. Hegesh that conveys that 'air of simplicity' you find appealing?"

"Her humor," Dotan states plainly, "and it is also a function of my capacity for 'smelling' the inner qualities of people, especially the good ones. It is true of Dr. Hegesh and all the people I listed above."

"Aha. So these are people we might describe as individuals of excellent character?"

"I don't know about that," Dotan cautions, "yet there is something unique about their integrity that is very compelling and inviting. I am always delighted to have their company."

"It is interesting that you use the word 'company' in this context," Michael observes. "It's almost as though, for you, giving a recital is like throwing a party, hosting a social gathering, like it's an opportunity to get together with friends—people you care about and who care about you. Does this ring true in any way?"

"No, it wasn't my intention," Dotan states. "By saying company I mean presence."

Michael is stumped. Where to go from here? "OK," he ventures. "But a key to what you find special about all these special people is, in your words, 'their integrity,' which makes them 'very compelling and inviting.' Am I accurate on that count at least?"

"It is very difficult to find precise words," Dotan counters. "It is a matter of inner feeling. Any attempt to define or verbalize it misses the target."

Michael is again unwilling to yield; he wants the words, the verbalization of ideas. Such compulsions would appear to be symptomatic of neurotypical people. "Yes, that is reasonable, Dotan, but I am going to challenge you now. You are a doctoral student. One of the main expectations of students at that highest level is to attempt to articulate in words these very things that seem to defy words! It is what the musicologist Charles Seeger called 'the linguocentric predicament,' i.e., the predicament that we, as humans, create forms of expression—music being a primary example—for the very reason that they enable us to communicate things that words alone cannot [Seeger 1977, 33]. And yet, as musicologists, for example, our job is mainly to find words to account for those elusive things. (That's the predicament.) Seeger also came up with another term to describe the 'location' of a more specific type of predicament: the musicological juncture [Seeger 1977, 19]. The musicological juncture is a place where the words we have at our disposal as musicologists run up against the reality that they are insufficient to capture many of the most important things about music that we wish to describe (whether having to do with music sound itself or broader cultural domains connected with music—morality, faith, love, etc.). So, with all that said, [do you have] anything more to add on what constitutes 'integrity' among the special people who have inspired you?"

Dotan stands his ground. "First, I am not a musicologist (in the narrow sense of the word)," he argues, "and second, there are things related to autism that, no matter how hard one tries, are impossible to dissect, especially when it comes to inner feelings."

Michael stands down.

"However," Dotan continues, almost in a conciliatory vein, "there are people [whose] character and personality I can attribute to a pet or a cartoon character."

Michael gladly picks up on this new thread, though in doing so he stubbornly refuses to fully let go of the last one. "So is there a cartoon or TV or movie character who we could use as a symbol of the compelling, inviting type of person of integrity that you appreciate as a special person?" he asks Dotan, awkwardly.

"My mother is the Road Runner, for instance," Dotan replies, politely skipping over Michael's tortuous question and, in the process, getting things back on track by continuing his own more interesting train of thought.

"Ah, excellent, especially since I know her," Michael writes back, "so this will be easier for me to relate to! What personality traits or aspects of character do your mother and the Road Runner share in common?"

Dotan lists them: "Swiftness, Kindness, and Cleverness."

"Yes, that does capture her very accurately," Michael agrees, adding, "I like this game!"

"Who is Ian Hobson?" Michael asks next, referring to the well-known concert pianist and FSU faculty member.

"Ian Hobson reminds me of Pope Francis," Dotan answers, "and Dr. Dumlavwalla is Smurfette," he adds in a humorous nod to his piano pedagogy mentor at FSU.

"Haha. Wow! Those are good ones!" Michael exclaims—and they are! "We'll go quick here, since I know you have to leave in a couple of minutes. How about you yourself?!"

"Well, I am a mixture of Charlie Brown, Schroeder, Wallace (from Wallace and Gromit), three-quarters Snoopy (because he is silent but well heard), and many more."

"That sounds about right!" Michael types in closing. "I've enjoyed this chat. Bye for now!"

"Lehitraot [Goodbye]!" Dotan signs off.

Dialogue 3: August 30, 2018

"Shalom!" Michael signs on for this, the third and final dialogue of the series. "Ready when you are, Dotan."

"I am ready!" Dotan replies.

"Excellent. Let's continue with our 'cartoon characters' conversation, okay?"

"Fine with me."

"You described yourself last time as a combination of Charlie Brown, Wallace, three-quarters Snoopy, and many more," Michael recaps. "First, remind me, please: in Wallace and Gromit, is Wallace the dog?"

"No, Wallace is the owner. An inventor by training," Dotan corrects.

"Ah, thank you."

"Gromit is the dog."

"Right. And what qualities of Wallace do you share?"

"He is very likable and creative."

"Yes, as are you, so that makes sense!"

"Aha. Thanks!"

"Talk to me a bit about your creativity," Michael requests. "Do you think about that applying mainly to your activities in music?"

"Not only music."

"What other areas?"

"Puns, humor, word games, jokes, etc.," Dotan lists. ". . . There are social situations that seem very humorous and it stimulates my natural ability to invent puns and jokes. That is something I cannot pre-construct. It just happens."

"I see. Now, what about in terms of piano playing? What qualities and attributes of your playing do you attribute to your creativity?"

"Well, I make 'Tzimmes' out of pre-existent musical pieces, à la Liberace," Dotan replies. "I used to do that at Lynn University, and my lecturers were rolling on the floor laughing."

"Forgive me, what are 'Tzimmes'?" Michael inquires, adding parenthetically, "(My Yiddish is poor.)"

"They're like mashups.[17] I make mashups of classic and popular [music] at the same time, as Liberace used to do."

"Ah, now I understand. Do you do that right on the spot or have you worked them out ahead of time?"

"I have the general concept preset, but it is spontaneous in most cases," Dotan clarifies.

"So there is a large element of improvisation, yes?" Michael asks.

"Sure."

"Give me an example of one of these mashups. What pieces were combined?"

"In one," says Dotan, "I took Liszt's *Liebestraum No. 3*, fused it with 'Jingle Bells,' and presented it as 'Jinglestraum.'"

"Haha. That sounds great! Do you have recordings or videos of that one, or of any of these?"

"Sadly not. Maybe someday I'll post it."

"That would be great!"

"Liberace is among the artists that influenced me greatly," Dotan continues.

"I see. In what ways?"

"Well, I took the template [from him] of combining classical with popular and making mashups. . . . Moreover, I do not know many people who know how to combine showmanship with good taste [like Liberace did]. Back in the past it was more apparent, but today it is quite rare."

"So I'd like to know more about the creative process that went into 'Jinglestraum,'" Michael resumes. "May I ask you some questions about that?"

"Sure."

"How did the idea first come into your mind to put the two pieces together: *Liebestraum* and 'Jingle Bells'?"

"Well, I had the *Liebestraum* in my fingers," Dotan recounts, "and as far as I can remember, I was about to present my tribute to Liberace slightly before Christmas, so I thought of something that correlates with the season. So I came up with two numbers, 'Jinglestraum' and the 'Russian Christmas Carol,' which is a mashup of the second movement of Tchaikovsky's Piano Concerto No.1 and 'Silent Night.' Moreover, those popular Christmas songs sound very convincing to me when played in the same keys as [those] classical pieces."

"And then how did you figure out how to make the mashups work?" Michael asks. "Did you have to arrange them ahead of time and practice them before the performance?"

"I practiced them a little bit in my free time just to form the concept, but most features were invented on [the] spot," Dotan answers.

"That's impressive, Dotan. What is going on in your mind in the moment of performance when doing something like that? Do you just play the classical piece and then segue directly into the popular tune, or are you combining the two pieces together at the same time?"

"Well, back when I was doing that I was 24 or 25," Dotan relates to Michael, "so naturally, some of the details have faded out of my memory, but as far as I can remember it all happened in parallel (or in tandem, as many academicians like to write in papers). Thinking of keys, time signatures, stark differences of character and melodic inflections, similarities of different kinds, etc., were my guidelines (most likely). You see, the whole magic is doing the right things without even blinking."

"Is the magic also in doing the right things without even *thinking*," Michael posits, "or are you, rather, quite conscious of what you're constructing—re: key signatures, inflections, and the rest—as you're creating in the moment of performance?"

"Well," Dotan remembers, "the whole idea was to take pieces I was playing back then and make an appropriate popular match for them. I knew exactly what the pieces were, and while planning the layout, more concrete ideas popped out all of a sudden. It was a synthesis of planning and improvisation, as is usually the case at jazz concerts and in jam sessions (*NB*: I know you are part of the jazz scene, so I think this example is an appropriate one)."

"Yes, thanks. So I have to go teach in a few minutes," writes Michael, "but I'd like to get in one more question before we sign off. This will take a minute to compose."

"Alright," Dotan replies.

"OK. It's long. Please bear with me. Here it is: This series of interviews has been rather interesting, almost like a chess match in which I keep attempting to get you to critically reflect on your creative process, strategies as a performer, etc., and you keep finding clever ways to in a sense dodge my advances, returning time and again—almost like in a rondo—to the idea that these things you do as a musician, a performing artist, an improviser, are essentially beyond words, beyond explanation—that they just happen.

"This is interesting to me," Michael continues, "because it is so different from my own process relative to such things. Granted, a great deal certainly happens 'in the moment' for me too, and as a response to some kind of direct inspiration as well. After the fact, though, I'm usually inclined to reflect back and say to myself, 'Ah yes, when I created that arrangement of "When the Saints Go Marching In" for jazz band and Balinese gamelan, I was thinking about various things: how to combine the different tonal systems of the jazz and gamelan instruments, how to bring an element of surprise to the audience (including humorous surprise), how to juxtapose the fully composed nature of the gamelan parts [that I wrote] with the improvised solos of the jazz musicians, how this "collision" of two very different musical worlds can yield music that is moving, or powerful, or aesthetically pleasing.'

"When I've heard you perform—for example, your amazing FSU recital performance of Mussorgsky's *Pictures at an Exhibition* in 2017[18]—I've inferred that a lot of that kind of thinking was going on in your head as well: how to evoke the Catacombs and the castle in musical sound, how to capture that elusive balance between the music's seriousness and its humor, how to bring the figure of Mussorgsky himself 'into the room,' loping gait and all. And I maintain that all of that is there, but from what you tell me it all happens at a rather subconscious level, and one that you are not inclined to reduce to mere words. I respect that, but I'm also going to take one more crack at asking you to try, in words, to tell me what it is that makes you 'tick' as a performer, as a creative artist? In reflecting upon your musical life and experiences, what can you share—beyond your music itself—that may offer insights into the subjective processes underlying your musical artistry, the modus operandi that makes you the unique musician you are? And finally, to bring Straus [2011, 163–165] back into the mix one last time, does any of this have anything to do with your 'autistic cognitive process'? Forgive me for this long and rambling question. I'll leave the chat box open and look forward to reading your response after I return from class in a couple of hours. Goodbye for now, and thank you!"

"Let's see if I can extract my 'modus operandi,'" Dotan begins. "My Autistic Cognitive Process is not manifested in the way you describe, because I take a new piece of music, observing it, checking fingerings, articulations, and sound qualities; it is as if I am sitting in front of a mixing console at the recording studio. I have nothing preset. In your case, you can anticipate how you want the piece to sound and how to make it effective. In my case, it just happens. In my case, I can play a certain passage that can evoke a certain image or character that will influence the way I shape and/or play it, and sometimes it is a matter of 'just doing it.' That is the only autistic link that makes me so idiosyncratic. And if my interpretation of *Pictures at an Exhibition* seems or sounds to you the way you perceive it (as highly evocative and expressive), then perhaps it has something to do with a site or a place (even something untitled), and with what brings out the effect of the scary Catacombs, for instance. (To put it briefly, it has something to do with associative thinking.) That is a sheer autistic feature that is woven into all of my thoughts and actions."

MICHAEL'S STORY

I'll be honest. In my real-time experience participating in the previous dialogues with Dotan—and in the subsequent process of working toward converting those dialogues into the basis of this chapter—I was frequently frustrated, sometimes disheartened. Try as I might, it seemed that I was incapable of finding the right groove with Dotan. I wanted us to be in sync but felt that we too often weren't. I wanted our conversations to flow organically out of our "transposed selves" (Gadamer [1960] 1989) into the illuminating vistas of a fused horizon, but that didn't seem to happen much either. I resorted to various tactics of persuasion in hopes of a "better" outcome. In so doing, I asked questions in ways intended to elicit "useful" responses from Dotan and even appealed to him to indulge me in the interest of generating a specific kind of phenomenological discourse—to play nice with me in the Gadamerian sandbox, as it were—for the sake of ultimately yielding a manuscript suitable for publication in an edited volume on phenomenological ethnomusicology.

Sometimes the effort bore fruit, like in the section where we did find a shared groove via dialogue around cartoon characters like the Road Runner and famous musicians like Liberace. And while Dotan is critical of nonautistic performers who fail to recognize the artistry that autistic musicians possess, he probably shares a lot in common with them, at least in disposition. (Ethno)musicologists are perpetually confronted in their research by musicians who resist being pinned down, who don't want to be cast as examples of a "type" (racial, ethnic, gendered, etc.), or who are either unfamiliar with or resistant to describing the processes that constitute their lived experiences, musical or otherwise.

So yes, Dotan and I did find our groove on some occasions, and yes, Dotan's mode of self-presentation is perhaps no less limited or evasive than that of a great many musicians who aren't autistic. Yet none of that changes the reality that through much of our conversational exchange, Dotan kept me at arm's length, defying my "urge-to-merge" with him, to invoke what Charles Keil so famously said of the participatory unity that comes from musical grooves specifically (Keil 1987, 276). The separateness troubled me, but him not so much, I think. Time and again, he refused to take the bait, standing firm in his positions despite my many efforts to get him to bend, compromise, or deviate from them—even just a bit—for the sake of expediency or a good story. Was such "stubbornness" the product of an unwillingness, an inability, or just a disinterest on Dotan's part to accommodate the needs and wants of the Other? Was it a manifestation of his distinctive "autistic cognitive style" (Straus 2011, 2013), or did autism have nothing do with it at all? Did any of this really even matter?

During our dialogues and in the days that followed, such questions began to consume me, and it all started to swirl in my mind. The perceived disjunction between anticipated and experienced outcome in this project was so vast that I came to seriously doubt that the work could ever be completed. And this, I thought, was a real shame, for I saw significant potential for Dotan and me to create a phenomenological bridge between autistic and nonautistic ways of understanding how music is made and experienced, and how it matters to the people who care about it. Levinas provided a different perspective, and indeed one that enabled me—and in the end, the two of us together—to move toward a realization of such aspirations.

CONCLUSION: LEVINAS AND THE ALTERITY OF THE ETHNOGRAPHIC OTHER

In "Otherwise than Participation," Matthew Rahaim invokes Levinas in highlighting encounters with "an ungraspable Other who is never quite what we think, with whom we never quite join" in moments of musical, social, or intellectual encounter (Rahaim 2017, 188). In a sense, we, Dotan and Michael, experienced each other largely in such ungraspable terms in the creation of this chapter. That seemed problematic to us (mainly to Michael) until quite recently. It doesn't now, however, because our engagement with Levinas has provided us with a phenomenological solution to the problem of our ostensible discursive disjointedness.

The central idea in Levinas's *Totality and Infinity*, discussed earlier in the chapter, is that the essential separation of self and other that characterizes one-to-one relationality is not some failure of intersubjectivity that needs to be overcome. On the contrary, it is the very foundation of social life. The other, and most especially the human other, is not part of our totality. For Levinas, totality emerges from the human desire to develop schemes of categorization, in what ultimately constitutes a form of mastery. Science masters the physical world with its typological schemes, even to the point of taming and domesticating that which is unknown *as* unknown, rather than as merely un-named. This is the "totality" of *Totality and Infinity*, and it is generally regarded as relatively unproblematic with respect to elements of the physical world, since "rocks or stars in the sky are none the worse for being categorized."[19]

Such is not the case for the other, however, and it is most especially not the case for the human other. To categorize another person within one's own totality is to risk the doing of great harm, for the human other is and must be an infinity, not merely in the narrow sense of a depth of interiority to which we do not have access but also in the wider sense of an agency and power that does not conform to our typological schemes and that has a capacity for an infinite range of unpredictable responses.

Rahaim quotes from *Totality and Infinity* to emphasize the infinite quality of the human other in relational contexts, stressing that the goal of the interpersonal encounter "is not a disappearance of distance, not a bringing together [*rapprochement*] . . . but a relationship [*rapport*] whose positivity comes from remoteness, from separation, for it nourishes itself, one might say, with its hunger" (Levinas [1961] 1969, 34, quoted in Rahaim 2017, 189). For Dotan, that nourishing sense of separation from his interlocutor,

Michael, was relatively easy to accommodate; for Michael, there was resistance to it, but he was able to move ever closer to accepting it through the course of this work.

The problem, it turns out, has a lot less to do with autistic ways of being than with the refusal of nonautistic people to engage with and accept autistic people on their own terms. Neurotypical people may want autistic people to think, act, and be in ways that make their autistic modes of being-in-the-world readily digestible: If they could only be more "normal," wouldn't that be for the best? Failing that, neurotypical people often wonder, couldn't autistic people just submit to their perpetual infantilization within the standard narrative of autism as a "childhood disease"? At the very least, why don't autistic persons just accept the categories (delayed, disordered, disabled, dysfunctional) that "we"—with the best of intentions and for their own good—assign to them, so that they can get the accommodations and services they need?

Many nonautistics desire such things of autistic people, and even those who don't, like Michael, can still get caught up in the same trap when they try (with the best of intentions) to get people like Dotan to "open up" for the sake of, say, a better phenomenology of autistic musical experience. But when someone like Dotan remains true to their autistic sensibilities and ontologies in the face of appeals from someone like Michael, they teach those people lessons that need to be learned.

Cheryl Mattingly's first-person mode of engagement with—and re-presentation of— the experiences of an African American child and his family teaches lessons about the realities, rather than the reified neurotypical fantasies, of the identity politics of autistic-racial intersectionality. In a related vein, our first-person way of adherence to the realities of remoteness and separation between an autistic musician and his nonautistic ethnomusicologist interlocutor teaches lessons about the realities of alterity that animate autistic and nonautistic ontologies and intersectionalities—musically, dialogically, and otherwise. They show that disjuncture and lack of resolution across neurocognitive lines are not there to be resolved, but are rather just there because they are there (so deal with it). When Dotan speaks in these pages in his own words, and when the child at the center of Mattingly's case study is presented to the reader as a flesh-and-blood human being defined principally by individuality, family membership, and community belonging (rather than diagnostic and racial labeling), one has the opportunity to shift away from perceiving the individual person as a type "identified *from the outside* by the finger that points to it" and toward accepting that person as a unique individual, identified in "being oneself, in identifying oneself from within" (Levinas [1961] 1969, 289). That shift is of paramount importance.

As Scott Davidson has observed, Levinas persistently reminds us that "we have a responsibility to allow the voices of all [O]thers to be heard" (2012, 184), a prescription with which Dotan and Michael align. This may seem like a small ask to make, but that is deceptive. To commit to the project of really hearing, and truly listening to, those others with whom we share our world—to fellow individuals who can so often seem out of reach, unfamiliar, separate, or remote, whether on account of their autistic ways of being or their neurotypicality, depending on one's particular positionality and stance— is a major undertaking. This was well understood by Levinas, who, as Bettino Bergo has observed, advanced the notion that "no event is as affectively disruptive for a consciousness holding sway in its world than the encounter with another person" (Bergo 2017). And if that other person is an individual whose alterity, whether neurocognitively grounded or otherwise, makes them unable, unwilling, or just uninterested in letting you be the one who "in the free play of the wills, pulls the strings of the game" (Levinas [1961] 1969, 294), then the disruption—and concomitantly the temptation to resist, ignore, negate, or otherwise marginalize its source—will be all the greater.

But that temptation needs to be resisted. Autistic and nonautistic people alike can no longer afford the luxury of indulging tradition-sanctioned forms of ignorance when faced with the discomfiting separateness of otherness, and the greatest burden of responsibility for resisting such temptation rests with the nonautistic majority, who have for far too long marginalized, ignored, and silenced the autistic minority. It is imperative that this majority not just hear autistic voices but truly listen to them, not just tolerate feelings of remoteness in their interpersonal encounters with their autistic counterparts but celebrate them, not just be aware of autism but accept autistic people. It is our hope that this initial foray into a phenomenologically oriented ethnomusicology of autism will prove useful in providing both direction and inspiration for pursuing such epistemologies and ethics of alterity.

NOTES

1. In autistic communities, the phrase "autistic people" is often preferred to "people with autism." As the anthropologist of autism Elizabeth Fein has explained, "In many disability contexts and communities, using 'person-first language' (i.e., *Steve is a person with autism*) is considered to be more respectful than using language that characterizes that person according to their condition (i.e., *Steve is autistic* or *Steve is an autistic*). However, in the autism world, this formulation of the relationship between person and condition is not so straightforward. Many in the autistic self-advocacy community have voiced a strong preference against person-first language, arguing that autism is not, in fact, separate from themselves in the way such language implies" (Fein 2012). See also Sinclair (2012) and Grace (2012).

2. Our reference to "autism spectrum condition" (ASC) rather than the more common designation "autism spectrum disorder" (ASD) aligns with a general movement across the current autistic self-advocacy, neurodiversity, and disability studies communities today. See Fein and Rios (2018).

   Regarding Dotan specifically, as a young child in Israel he was originally diagnosed with Asperger's syndrome, an autism spectrum disorder. The diagnosing physician was Dr. Roni Hegesh. Many years later, Dr. Hegesh would change the diagnosis to high-functioning autism (HFA). Bakan suspects that this change of diagnosis may be attributable to a combination of two factors: (1) the elimination of Asperger's syndrome (a.k.a. Asperger disorder) from the fifth edition of the *Diagnostic and Statistical Manual of Mental Disorders* (American Psychiatric Association, 2013; for historical and critical perspectives on this development, see Silberman 2015), and (2) the establishment of conclusive evidence in support of the formerly debated claim that the Austrian pediatrician Hans Asperger had significant involvement with the Nazis' child euthanasia programs during World War II (Czech 2018). Nitzberg sees this change as stemming from the first of these factors. As he explained to Bakan during an August 20, 2018, Google Hangouts exchange, "I've heard of Hans Asperger and his collaboration with the Nazis . . ., but it really doesn't matter. Autism is still autism. . . . It has nothing to do with Hans Asperger. The terminology has changed. . . . Since the DSM has been updated and revised [in 2013], we all became autists. I prefer to identify myself as having high functioning autism."

Like many on the spectrum, Dotan now prefers the HFA label to Asperger's as a term of self-identification; nevertheless, the "high functioning" vs. "low functioning" distinction is regarded by many autistic self-advocates, including Elizabeth Grace, as both controversial and deeply problematic (see Grace 2012). In certain sectors, alternate terms, such as "lower support needs autism" vs. "higher support needs autism," are preferred for distinguishing between different manifestations of ASC across the vast range of the autism spectrum.

Regarding Bakan's work in this area, see Bakan (2009, 2014a, 2014b, 2014c, 2015a, 2015b, 2016a, 2016b, 2018a, 2018b, 2021) and Bakan et al. ("Saying Something," 2008; "Following Frank," 2008). Nitzberg and Bakan's collaborative publications include Nitzberg and Bakan (2019) and the sixth chapters of Bakan (2018b) and (2021).

3. Berger's essay 2015 "Phenomenological Approaches in the History of Ethnomusicology" was helpful in our initial conceptualization of what a phenomenological ethnomusicology of autism might be. A revised version of that essay, coauthored by him, David VanderHamm, and Friedlind Riedel, is the first chapter of this volume.

4. In re-presentational ethnography, by way of contrast with the more established medium of representational ethnography, the dialogues between ethnographer and interlocutor themselves do not serve as a point of departure for the types of description, analysis, and interpretation that usually foster the creation of ethnographic texts. Rather, these dialogues *are* the text, with the direct contributions of the researcher being limited, first, to what they contributed *to* the conversation in the role of dialogue partner, and second, to the making of a layer of narration—and as light a layer as possible—provided to ensure that the core dialogue text comes through with sufficient clarity and cohesiveness to make it engaging and readily understandable. See Bakan (2018a, 2018b, 2021) and Nitzberg and Bakan (2019).

5. Bakan's gloss on phenomenology here borrows from Stewart and Mickunas (1990, 91) and was originally inspired by his readings of Jeff Todd Titon's work on the phenomenology of music (2008, 93).

6. Bakan's perspective here was influenced by his reading of David Sudnow's work (2001).

7. In the article, Mattingly uses the term "Anglo-American," rather than "European American" or "white."

8. Race is one of the primary axes of power in American life. By using Mattingly's ideas about the intersection of autism and racial identity to discuss the relationship between autism and music, we do *not* mean to suggest that the marginalization that autistic musicians experience *as musicians* is comparable in its severity to the experiences of oppression that African American autistic people experience by virtue of being Black. Rather, our point is to show how the disadvantages that autistic people experience inflect their musical lives as well, and Mattingly's discussion of intersectionality helps to make this point clear.

9. The "machine-like" and "unemotional" stereotypes habitually applied to autistic musicians are depressingly similar to the essentialisms directed at Asian and Asian American musicians, particularly in the world of Western art (classical) music. "Under the watchful eyes of their immigrant parents," writes musicologist Mina Yang, "a disproportionate

number of Asian Americans have achieved some measure of success in classical music. The success of 'Asian upstarts,' however, is seldom looked upon favorably by the American mainstream. The Confucian work ethic, for instance, is often construed as a substitute for real artistry or intellectual substance" (Yang 2007, 13; cf. Yoshihara 2007; Wong 2004). Drawing from survey data she collected from students at the San Francisco Conservatory, Yang quotes a Korean American flutist who stated that "Asians are expected to have incredibly perfect technique and typically considered to not have musicality of their own." She additionally quotes an Asian American singer from Minnesota who asserted that "Asians are expected in some degree, to be extremely meticulous and technically proficient, and in some degree to be more mechanical than musical" (Yang 2007, 14). Such examples serve as a reminder that in Western cultures, concepts of disability and race—including the pervasive forms of stigmatization to which they are tied—were conceived together and remain intertwined.

10. In his chapter in *Music and Empathy* (King and Waddington 2018), Adam Ockelford offers an alternate perspective on this issue (Ockelford 2018).

11. The artist/autist wordplay employed here invokes a trope of autistic culture. See note 14 for a fuller discussion of this topic.

12. For a related account of Dotan's life story, see *Music and Autism: Speaking for Ourselves* (Bakan 2021, chap. 6).

13. The interview transcripts published in Bakan (2021) also appear in Bakan (2018b).

14. The word "autist" is frequently used by individuals on the autism spectrum as a term of self-identification, sometimes with a deliberate, playful sense of its similarly to the word "artist." "Autist" usually has positive connotations, at least when used by autistic people themselves and by their allies. There are instances, however, in which it can be perceived as offensive. One example of this is in the quotation from Dotan cited earlier, in which he recounted being insulted by other musicians who said he was " 'emotionally handicapped' [or] 'playing like an autist' " (Bakan 2021, 116).

15. A video recording of the complete lecture may be accessed on YouTube (Nitzberg 2012).

16. Works with a related orientation include Shore (2003) and Ockelford (2018).

17. The language here is metaphorical, as *tzimmes* is in actuality a sweet stew found in Ashkenazic Jewish cuisine.

18. A video of Dotan's performance is available on YouTube (see Nitzberg 2017). *Pictures at an Exhibition* begins twenty minutes and forty seconds into the recording.

19. The quotation is from a November 25, 2019, email from volume coeditor Harris Berger to chapter coauthor Michael Bakan. Other ideas articulated by Berger in that same email inform the next two paragraphs in the body of this chapter.

WORKS CITED

American Music Therapy Association. 2012. "Music Therapy as a Treatment Modality for Autism Spectrum Disorders." http://www.musictherapy.org/assets/1/7/MT_Autism_2012.pdf.

American Psychiatric Association. 2013. *Diagnostic and Statistical Manual of Mental Disorders.* 5th ed. Washington, DC: American Psychiatric Association.

Bakan, Michael B. 2009. "Measuring Happiness in the 21st Century: Ethnomusicology, Evidence-Based Research, and the New Science of Autism." *Ethnomusicology* 53 (3): 510–518.

Bakan, Michael B. 2014a. "Ethnomusicological Perspectives on Autism, Neurodiversity, and Music Therapy." *Voices: A World Forum for Music Therapy* 14 (3). https://voices.no/index .php/voices/article/view/799.

Bakan, Michael B. 2014b. "The Musicality of Stimming: Promoting Neurodiversity in the Ethnomusicology of Autism." *MUSICultures* 41 (2): 133–161.

Bakan, Michael B. 2014c. "Neurodiversity and the Ethnomusicology of Autism." *College Music Symposium* 54. http://symposium.music.org/index.php?option=com_k2&view=item&id=10673:neurodiversity-and-the-ethnomusicology-of-autism&Itemid=128.

Bakan, Michael B. 2015a. "Being Applied in the Ethnomusicology of Autism." In *The Oxford Handbook of Applied Ethnomusicology*, edited by Svanibor Pettan and Jeff Todd Titon, 278–316. New York: Oxford University Press.

Bakan, Michael B. 2015b. "'Don't Go Changing to Try and Please Me': Combating Essentialism through Ethnography in the Ethnomusicology of Autism." *Ethnomusicology* 59 (1): 116–144.

Bakan, Michael B. 2016a. "Music, Autism, and Disability Aesthetics." In "Colloquy: On the Disability Aesthetics of Music," edited by Blake Howe and Stephanie Jensen-Moulton. *Journal of the American Musicological Society* 69 (2): 548–553.

Bakan, Michael B. 2016b. "Toward an Ethnographic Model of Disability in the Ethnomusicology of Autism." In *The Oxford Handbook of Music and Disability Studies*, edited by Blake Howe, Stephanie Jensen-Moulton, Neil Lerner, and Joseph N. Straus, 15–36. New York: Oxford University Press.

Bakan, Michael B. 2018a. "Music and Autism, Representation and Re-presentation: An Ethnomusicological Perspective." In *Autism in Translation: An Intercultural Conversation on Autism Spectrum Conditions*, edited by Elizabeth Fein and Clarice Rios, 109–128. Culture, Mind, and Society Series. Cham, Switzerland: Palgrave Macmillan.

Bakan, Michael B. 2018b. *Speaking for Ourselves: Conversations on Life, Music, and Autism*. New York: Oxford University Press.

Bakan, Michael B. 2021. *Music and Autism: Speaking for Ourselves*. New York: Oxford University Press.

Bakan, Michael B., Benjamin D. Koen, Megan Bakan, Fred Kobylarz, Lindee Morgan, Rachel Goff, and Sally Kahn. 2008. "Saying Something Else: Improvisation and Facilitative Music-Play in a Medical Ethnomusicology Program for Children on the Autism Spectrum." *College Music Symposium* 48: 1–30.

Bakan, Michael B., Benjamin Koen, Fred Kobylarz, Lindee Morgan, Rachel Goff, Sally Kahn, and Megan Bakan. 2008. "Following Frank: Response-Ability and the Co-creation of Culture in a Medical Ethnomusicology Program for Children on the Autism Spectrum." *Ethnomusicology* 52 (2): 163–202.

Berger, Harris M. 2010. *Stance: Ideas about Emotion, Style, and Meaning for the Study of Expressive Culture*. Middletown, CT: Wesleyan University Press.

Berger, Harris M. 2015. "Phenomenological Approaches in the History of Ethnomusicology." In *Oxford Handbooks Online*. New York: Oxford University Press.

Bergo, Bettina. 2017. "Emmanuel Levinas." In *The Stanford Encyclopedia of Philosophy*, edited by Edward N. Zalta. Stanford University. https://plato.stanford.edu/archives/fall2017/entries/levinas/.

Czech, Herwig. 2018. "Hans Asperger, National Socialism, and 'Race Hygiene' in Nazi-Era Vienna." *Molecular Autism* 9: 29. doi.org/10.1186/s13229-018-0208-6.

Davidson, Scott. 2012. "The Rights of the Other: Levinas and Human Rights." In *Totality and Infinity at 50*, edited by Scott Davidson and Diane Perpich, 171–187. Pittsburgh, PA: Duquesne University Press.

Fein, Elizabeth. 2012. "The Machine Within: An Ethnography of Asperger's Syndrome, Biomedicine, and the Paradoxes of Identity and Technology in the Late Modern United States." PhD diss., University of Chicago.

Fein, Elizabeth, and Clarice Rios, eds. 2018. *Autism in Translation: An Intercultural Conversation on Autism Spectrum Conditions*. Culture, Mind, and Society Series. Cham, Switzerland: Palgrave Macmillan.

Gadamer, Hans-Georg. (1960) 1989. *Truth and Method*. 2nd rev. ed. Translation revised by Joel Weinsheimer and Donald G. Marshall. New York: Continuum.

Garland-Thomson, Rosemarie. 1996. *Freakery: Cultural Spectacles of the Extraordinary Body*. New York: New York University Press.

Grace, Elizabeth J. 2012. "Labels; Also, Intense Teaching Is Realer than 'Cure.' " *Tiny Grace Notes (Ask an Autistic)*. October 23, 2012. http://tinygracenotes.blogspot.com/2012/10/labels-also-intense-teaching-is-realer.html.

Kanner, Leo. 1943. "Autistic Disturbances of Affective Contact." *Nervous Child* 2: 217–250.

Keil, Charles. 1987. "Participatory Discrepancies and the Power of Music." *Cultural Anthropology* 2 (3): 275–283.

King, Elaine, and Carole Waddington, eds. 2018. *Music and Empathy*. SEMPRE Studies in the Psychology of Music. London: Routledge.

Levinas, Emmanuel. (1961) 1969. *Totality and Infinity: An Essay on Exteriority*. Translated by Alphonso Lingis. Pittsburgh, PA: Duquesne University Press.

Malpas, Jeff. 2018. "Hans-Georg Gadamer." In *The Stanford Encyclopedia of Philosophy*, edited by Edward N. Zalta. Stanford University. https://plato.stanford.edu/archives/fall2018/entries/gadamer/.

Mattingly, Cheryl. 2017. "Autism and the Ethics of Care: A Phenomenological Investigation into the Contagion of Nothing." *Ethos* 45 (2): 250–270.

Molnar-Szakacs, Istvan, and Pamela Heaton. 2012. "Music: A Unique Window into the World of Autism." *Annals of the New York Academy of Sciences* 1252 (1): 318–324. doi:10.1111/j.1749-6632.2012.06465.x.

National Institute of Neurological Disorders and Stroke. 2019. "Autism Fact Sheet." https://www.ninds.nih.gov/Disorders/Patient-Caregiver-Education/Fact-Sheets/Autism-Spectrum-Disorder-Fact-Sheet.

Nitzberg, Dotan. 2012. "How to Teach Piano to People with Asperger." Lecture-recital presented at the World Piano Teachers Association, Novi Sad, Serbia, June 28, 2012. https://www.youtube.com/watch?v=g7LTFboZAqk.

Nitzberg, Dotan. 2017. Dotan Nitzberg Live at FSU (March 2017). YouTube video. https://www.youtube.com/watch?v=UlMIgTmZbXg.

Nitzberg, Dotan, and Michael B. Bakan. 2019. "Resilience and Adaptive Management in Piano Pedagogy for Students with Autism Spectrum Conditions." In *Cultural Sustainabilities: Music, Media, Language, Advocacy*, edited by Timothy J. Cooley, 249–261. Urbana: University of Illinois Press.

Ockelford, Adam. 2018. "Towards a Developmental Model of Musical Empathy Using Insights from Children Who Are on the Autism Spectrum or Who Have Learning Difficulties." In *Music and Empathy*, edited by Elaine King and Carole Waddington, 39–88. SEMPRE Studies in the Psychology of Music. New York: Routledge.

Rahaim, Matthew. 2017. "Otherwise than Participation: Unity and Alterity in Musical Encounters." In *Music and Empathy*, edited by Elaine King and Carole Waddington, 175–193. SEMPRE Studies in the Psychology of Music. New York: Routledge.

Ricoeur, Paul. 1981. *Hermeneutics and the Human Sciences*. Edited, translated, and with an introduction by John B. Thompson. New York: Cambridge University Press.

Seeger, Charles. 1977. *Studies in Musicology, 1935–1975*. Berkeley: University of California Press.

Shakespeare, Tom. 2013. "The Social Model of Disability." In *The Disability Studies Reader*, 4th ed., edited by Lennard J. Davis, 214–221. New York: Routledge.

Shore, Daniel. 2003. *Beyond the Wall: Personal Experiences with Autism and Asperger Syndrome*. 2nd ed. Shawnee Mission, KS: Autism Asperger Publishing.

Silberman, Steve. 2015. *NeuroTribes: The Legacy of Autism and the Future of Neurodiversity*. Foreword by Oliver Sacks. New York: Avery.

Sinclair, Jim. 2012. "Why I Dislike 'Person First' Language." In *Loud Hands: Autistic People, Speaking*, edited by Julia Bascom, 223–224. Washington, DC: Autistic Press.

Sterponi, Laura, and Allesandra Fasulo. 2010. "'How to Go On: Intersubjectivity and Progressivity in the Communication of a Child with Autism." *Ethos* 38 (1): 116–142.

Stewart, David, and Algis Mickunas. 1990. *Exploring Phenomenology: A Guide to the Field and Its Literature*. 2nd ed. Athens: Ohio University Press.

Straus, Joseph N. 2011. *Extraordinary Measures: Disability in Music*. New York: Oxford University Press.

Straus, Joseph N. 2013. "Autism as Culture." In *The Disability Studies Reader*, 4th ed., edited by Lennard J. Davis, 460–484. New York: Routledge.

Straus, Joseph N. 2014. "Idiots Savants, Retarded Savants, Talented Aments, Mono-Savants, Autistic Savants, Just Plain Savants, People with Savant Syndrome, and Autistic People Who Are Good at Things: A View from Disability Studies." *Disability Studies Quarterly* 34 (3). http://dsq-sds.org/article/view/3407/3640.

Sudnow, David. 2001. *Ways of the Hand: A Rewritten Account*. Foreword by Hubert L. Dreyfus. Cambridge, MA: MIT Press.

Thompson, John B. 1981. "Editor's Introduction." In *Hermeneutics and the Human Sciences*, by Paul Ricoeur. Edited, translated, and with an introduction by John B. Thompson. New York: Cambridge University Press.

Titon, Jeff Todd. 2008. "Knowing Fieldwork." In *Shadows in the Field: New Perspectives for Fieldwork in Ethnomusicology*. 2nd ed. New York: Oxford University Press.

Walker, Nick. 2014. "What Is Autism?" *Neurocosmopolitanism: Nick Walker's Notes on Neurodiversity, Autism, and Cognitive Liberty*. March 1, 2014. http://neurocosmopolitanism.com/what-is-autism/z.

Wong, Deborah. 2004. *Speak It Louder: Asian Americans Making Music*. New York: Routledge.

Yang, Mina. 2007. "East Meets West in the Concert Hall: Asians and Classical Music in the Century of Imperialism, Post-colonialism, and Multiculturalism." *Asian Music* 38 (1): 1–30. http:www.jstor.org/stable/4497039.

Yoshihara, Mari. 2007. *Musicians from a Different Shore: Asians and Asian Americans in Classical Music*. Philadelphia: Temple University Press.

INDEX

Tables and figures are indicated by *t* and *f* following the page number